Berlin Transit

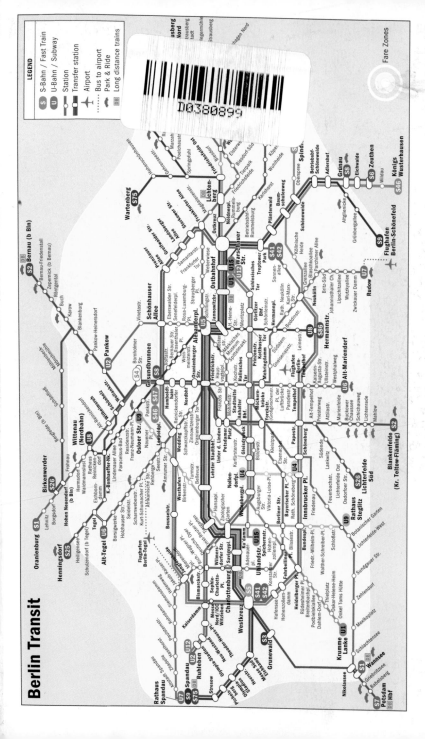

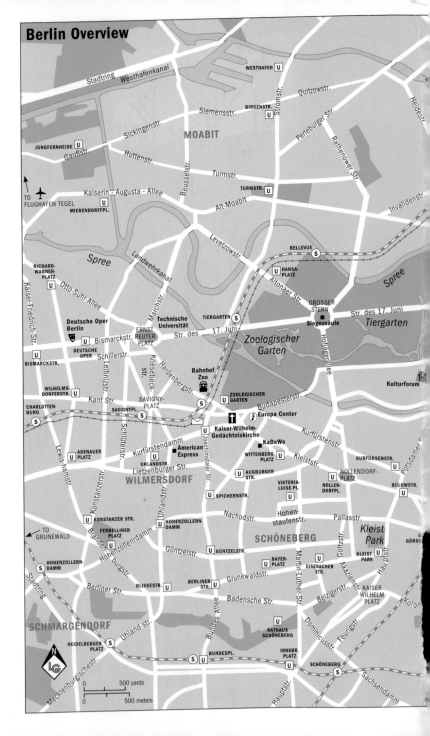

Berlin Overview

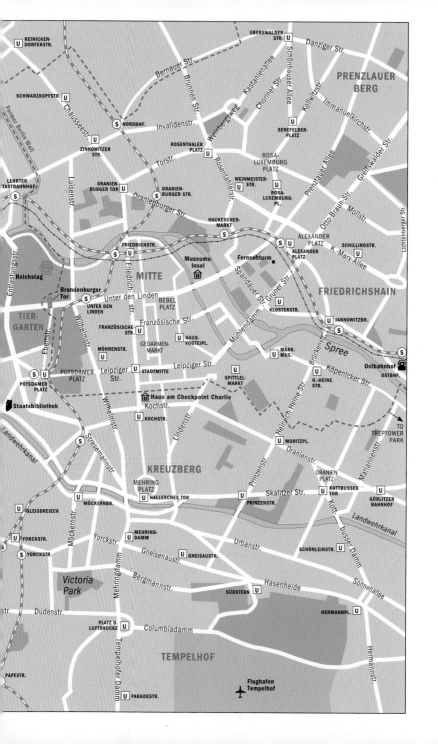

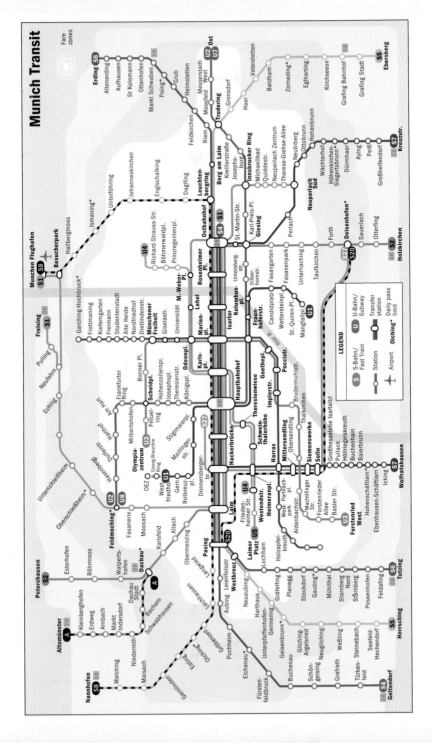

LET'S GO

■ PAGES PACKED WITH ESSENTIAL INFORMATION

"Value-packed, unbeatable, accurate, and comprehensive."

—The Los Angeles Times

"The guides are aimed not only at young budget travelers but at the independent traveler; a sort of streetwise cookbook for traveling alone."

—The New York Times

"Unbeatable; good sight-seeing advice; up-to-date info on restaurants, hotels, and inns; a commitment to money-saving travel; and a wry style that brightens nearly every page."

—The Washington Post

■ THE BEST TRAVEL BARGAINS IN YOUR BUDGET

"All the dirt, dirt cheap."

—People

"Let's Go follows the creed that you don't have to toss your life's savings to the wind to travel—unless you want to."

—The Salt Lake Tribune

■ REAL ADVICE FOR REAL EXPERIENCES

"The writers seem to have experienced every rooster-packed bus and lunar-surfaced mattress about which they write."

—The New York Times

"[Let's Go's] devoted updaters really walk the walk (and thumb the ride, and trek the trail). Learn how to fish, haggle, find work—anywhere."

—Food & Wine

"A world-wise traveling companion—always ready with friendly advice and helpful hints, all sprinkled with a bit of wit."

—The Philadelphia Inquirer

■ A GUIDE WITH A SPIRIT AND A SOCIAL CONSCIENCE

"Lighthearted and sophisticated, informative and fun to read. [Let's Go] helps the novice traveler navigate like a knowledgeable old hand."

—Atlanta Journal-Constitution

"The serious mission at the book's core reveals itself in exhortations to respect the culture and the environment—and, if possible, to visit as a volunteer, a student, or a teacher rather than a tourist."

—San Francisco Chronicle

LET'S GO PUBLICATIONS

TRAVEL GUIDES

Australia 9th edition
Austria & Switzerland 12th edition
Brazil 1st edition
Britain 2007
California 10th edition
Central America 9th edition
Chile 2nd edition
China 5th edition
Costa Rica 3rd edition
Eastern Europe 12th edition
Ecuador 1st edition
Egypt 2nd edition
Europe 2007
France 2007
Germany 13th edition
Greece 8th edition
Hawaii 4th edition
India & Nepal 8th edition
Ireland 12th edition
Israel 4th edition
Italy 2007
Japan 1st edition
Mexico 21st edition
Middle East 4th edition
New Zealand 7th edition
Peru 1st edition
Puerto Rico 2nd edition
South Africa 5th edition
Southeast Asia 9th edition
Spain & Portugal 2007
Thailand 3rd edition
Turkey 5th edition
USA 23rd edition
Vietnam 2nd edition
Western Europe 2007

ROADTRIP GUIDE

Roadtripping USA 2nd edition

ADVENTURE GUIDES

Alaska 1st edition
Pacific Northwest 1st edition
Southwest USA 3rd edition

CITY GUIDES

Amsterdam 4th edition
Barcelona 3rd edition
Boston 4th edition
London 15th edition
New York City 16th edition
Paris 14th edition
Rome 12th edition
San Francisco 4th edition
Washington, D.C. 13th edition

POCKET CITY GUIDES

Amsterdam
Berlin
Boston
Chicago
London
New York City
Paris
San Francisco
Venice
Washington, D.C.

LET'S GO

GERMANY

STEPHANIE O'ROURKE EDITOR
PAUL KATZ ASSOCIATE EDITOR

RESEARCHER-WRITERS
AMELIA ATLAS
SAMUEL BJORK
NICHOLAS COMMINS
MARION GUILLAUME
CATHERINE JAMPEL
LISA SHU

SHIYANG CAO MAP EDITOR
SAMANTHA GELFAND MANAGING EDITOR

ST. MARTIN'S PRESS ✹ NEW YORK

HELPING LET'S GO. If you want to share your discoveries, suggestions, or corrections, please drop us a line. We read every piece of correspondence, whether a postcard, a 10-page email, or a coconut. **Address mail to:**

Let's Go: Germany
67 Mount Auburn St.
Cambridge, MA 02138
USA

Visit Let's Go at **http://www.letsgo.com,** or send email to:

feedback@letsgo.com
Subject: "Let's Go: Germany"

In addition to the invaluable travel advice our readers share with us, many are kind enough to offer their services as researchers or editors. Unfortunately, our charter enables us to employ only currently enrolled Harvard students.

HOW TO USE THIS BOOK

COVERAGE. In *Let's Go: Germany*, each *Land* (province) is presented in its own chapter, starting with Berlin and moving clockwise around the map. The major city or transportation hub within each *Land* introduces its chapter, followed by other significant **cities, towns,** and **villages.** Because not every one of Germany's ancient castles or quirky museums is the sort of place you'd want to spend the night, we've also included tons of **daytrips,** single-day excursions from nearby towns. The book also features extensive coverage of **outdoor areas,** including national parks and adventure sites. For each area, we recommend gateway towns—nearby villages that offer easy access to the parks, lakes, and mountains where you'll really want to spend your time.

WHY PRAGUE? At the end of the book, we list everything you'll need to know to visit the mother of all gateway cities, ❚**Prague.** We've included this essential coverage to enable you to sample one of Europe's sweetest destinations, readily accessible from Dresden, Munich, Berlin—or wherever, really.

PLANNING YOUR TRIP. Our **Discover** section is the best place to begin your trip preparations. Brimming with advice on when to go, where to go, and what to do, the chapter's tools include **suggested itineraries**—themed routes across the country—and ❚**Let's Go Thumbpicks**—highlights carefully selected from an entire country's worth of castles, beaches, hostels, and clubs—to bring you to Germany's must-see destinations on and off the beaten path. The **Life and Times** chapter is a primer in German history and culture. Read it and you'll be able to order a *Märzen* from Rilke's favorite *Jugendstil* beer hall on *Allerheiligen*—and know what all of it means! To help you actually get yourself to Germany, the **Essentials** section will tell you more than you've ever wanted to know about passports, customs, airline tickets, railpasses, health, and safety.

LISTINGS. We list establishments in order from best to worst value, and assign food and accommodations a price diversity ranking from ❶ (cheapest) to ❺ (most extravagant). We've detailed the prices for each rank and the corresponding services you can expect on our **price diversity** page (p. xvi).

ABBREVIATIONS. In order to pack the book with as much information as possible, we have used a few **standard abbreviations.** Please note that "Pl." is short for "Platz," "Str." for "Straße," and "G." for "Gasse."

LANGUAGE. Because gesticulating wildly doesn't always cut it, we've included **essential phrases** on the inside back cover, as well as a **glossary** in the Appendix. Whenever relevant, we translate sights and phrases as such: *German* (English).

PHONE CODES AND TELEPHONE NUMBERS. Area codes for each region appear opposite the name of the region and are denoted by the ☎ icon. Phone numbers in text are also preceded by the ☎ icon.

A NOTE TO OUR READERS. The information for this book was gathered by *Let's Go* researchers from May through August of 2006. Each listing is based on one researcher's opinion, formed during his or her visit at a particular time. Those traveling at other times may have different experiences since prices, dates, hours, and conditions are always subject to change. You are urged to check the facts presented in this book beforehand to avoid inconvenience and surprises.

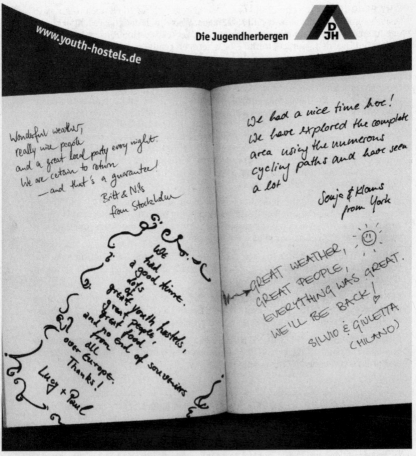

CONTENTS

RESEARCHER-WRITERS

Amelia Atlas   *Berlin and Brandenburg*

A *Let's Go* vet, Molly applied her hard-earned savvy to a new destination. Her witty flair and eye for detail were more than up to the challenge of behemoth Berlin. Researching in Hungary prepared Molly to look eastward, and in doing so she revamped our coverage of Berlin's up-and-coming neighborhoods. Braving World-Cup mayhem and churning out some of the best copy the series has seen, Molly still had time to regale us with her stories.

Samuel Bjork   *Baden-Württemberg, Rheinland-Pfalz, Hessen*

Off-the-cuff and ready for adventure, Sam left a flurry of pensive and energetic copy in his wake. Though no one was really sure where he was at any given point, we were too entranced by his highly evocative and original work to worry. With a penchant for veering off the beaten path, Sam used his sense for subtlety to refine our coverage of a route beset with challenges.

Nicholas Commins *Niedersachsen, Sachsen, Sachsen-Anhalt, Thüringia*

Denizens of eastern Germany may have been surprised to find a 6'4" playwright and mathematician from San Francisco in their midst, but to his editors at *Let's Go*, there was nothing unexpected about the energy and skill with which Nick took on the former DDR. Deft and zany, he probed the eastern psyche as he weathered erratic train schedules and freak hail storms, penning mounds of creative copy (and the occasional *Sound of Music* parody) along the way.

Marion Guillaume   *Hamburg, Mecklenburg-Vorpommern, Schleswig*

A seasoned sailor, Marion was perfectly suited to tame Germany's nautical north. This quadrilingual history major certainly amazed her editors with her broad communication skills, but it was in her English prose that her true linguistic talent shone. Ready to take on massive projects at a moment's notice, Marion's sociability and adaptiveness saw her through Hamburg's sweatiest nightclubs, Amrum's most remote beaches, and Mecklenburg's tiniest towns.

Catherine Jampel   *Bayern*

Declaring war on shoddy prose and kid-gloved reportage, veteran researcher Catherine took Bavaria by storm, hiking and biking across every hectare of Germany's largest *Land*. Together with *Münchener Kindl*—her trusty bike—Catherine left Bavarians and her editors alike impressed by her no-holds-barred attitude and her unfailing dedication to honest reviewing, producing rich national park coverage and fantastic nightlife overhauls.

Lisa Shu   *Nordrhein-Westfalen, Rheinland-Pfalz, Niedersachsen*

This spirited New Yorker tackled our most diverse route with unprecedented vigor. Lisa effortlessly integrated with all walks of life. With quite a travel record behind her, this psychology and economics student spiced up her coverage with unflinching honesty and an uncanny eye for hidden gems. Lisa brought unpracticed suavity and zippy humor to her prose while visiting quite possibly every café with wireless Internet in northwestern Germany.

CONTRIBUTING WRITERS

Sameer ud Dowla Khan is a graduate student in Linguistics at the University of California, Los Angeles, with a focus in phonology and phonetics.

Will B. Payne studies German history and literature at Harvard University. Will was also associate editor of *Let's Go: Germany* in 2005.

Barbara Richter was a Researcher-Writer for *Let's Go: Austria & Switzerland*. A native Austrian, Barbara received a Gates Scholarship to study chemistry and physics at Cambridge University in England.

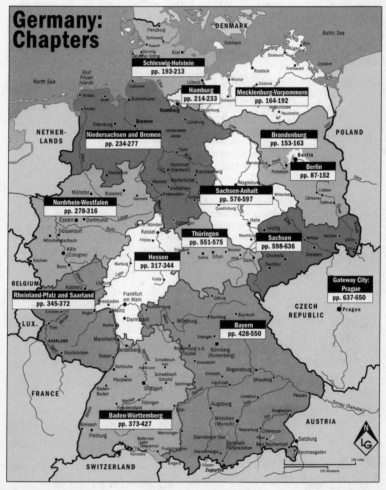

ACKNOWLEDGMENTS

TEAM GERMANY THANKS: Our RWs, who are fearless, witty, and dapper. Sam, for inimitable guidance and trust. Team Britain, for a memorable war zone. Shiyang, for his tireless efforts. The Office, for food and friendship. Ken, for fabulous crunching and RW notes.

STEPHANIE THANKS: Paul, for knowing better than me. And—of course—for being nice about it, for the baby voice, for hilarity and understanding, and for sub-par sandwiches. Sam, for many many things. Matthew and Melinda, for childish antics and moral support. My family, for love and for sending me out there in the first place. Gilly, for Saturday mornings and being my friend. Rachel, Kim, and Avis, for giving me something to look forward to. Molly, for unknowingly talking me into this. CF, for introducing me to Germany.

PAUL THANKS: Stephanie—notice the admission of vulnerability here—I'm truly indebted to you for your flexibility, your dedication, your trust in me, and your propensity to say outrageous things with so little provocation. Matthew and Melinda—for being so much more efficient but not making me feel bad about it. Sam—for the cow, *sans* dung. Isaac, Natalie, Polina—for not setting the chain lock. Maddie, Melissa, Robin—for seeing me through the summer. Hart—for showing me *Deutschland*. Mom, Dad, and Jonathan—for being some of the most wonderful people I'm lucky enough to be shackled to forever.

SHIYANG THANKS: Steph and Paul for the edits, Cliff for bearing with him, Mapland for the laughs, the RWs for lots of numbers and colors, his roommate Howard for doing the dishes, his girlfriend Yiying for support and his family for everything.

Editor
Stephanie O'Rourke
Associate Editor
Paul Katz
Map Editor
Shiyang Cao
Managing Editor
Samantha Gelfand
Typesetter
Ankur Ghosh

LET'S GO

Publishing Director
Alexandra C. Stanek
Editor-in-Chief
Laura E. Martin
Production Manager
Richard Chohaney Lonsdorf
Cartography Manager
Clifford S. Emmanuel
Editorial Managers
August Dietrich, Samantha Gelfand,
Silvia Gonzalez Killingsworth
Financial Manager
Jenny Qiu Wong
Publicity Manager
Anna A. Mattson-DiCecca
Personnel Manager
Sergio Ibarra
Production Associate
Chase Mohney
IT Director
Patrick Carroll
Director of E-Commerce
Jana Lepon
Office Coordinators
Adrienne Taylor Gerken, Sarah Goodin

Director of Advertising Sales
Mohammed J. Herzallah
Senior Advertising Associates
Kedamai Fisseha, Roumiana Ivanova

President
Brian Feinstein
General Manager
Robert B. Rombauer

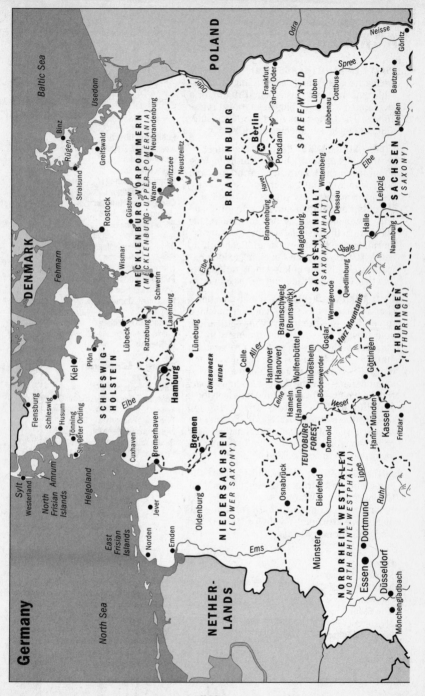

Germany

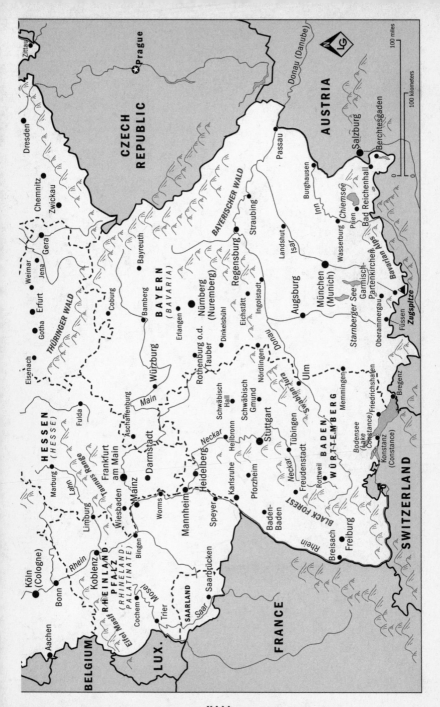

XIII

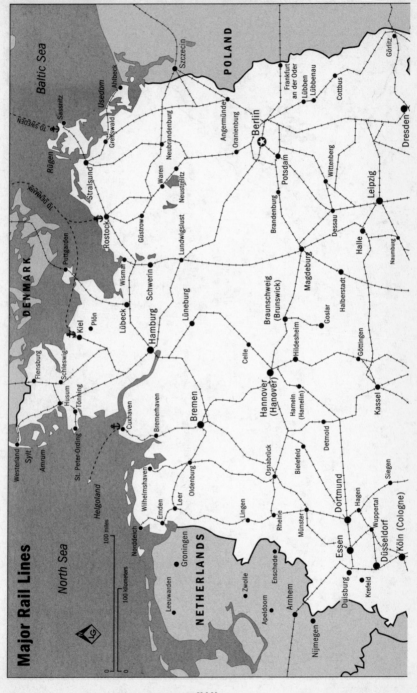

Major Rail Lines

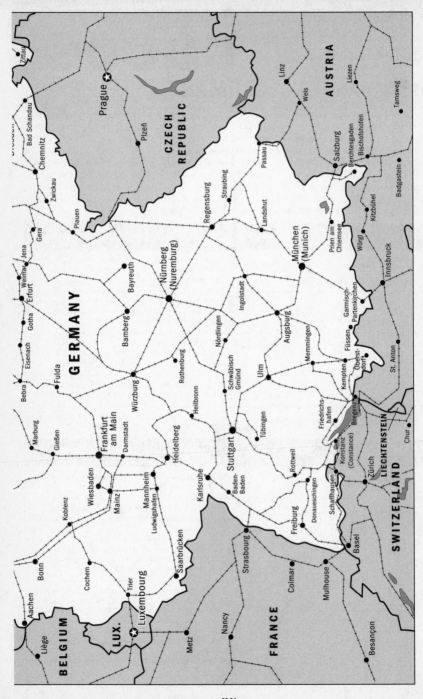

PRICE RANGES>>GERMANY

Establishments in our coverage are listed in order of value from best to worst; our favorites are denoted by the Let's Go thumbs-up (🖑). Since the best value is not always the cheapest price, however, we have also incorporated a system of price ranges, based on a rough expectation of what you'll spend. For **accommodations,** we base our range on the cheapest price for which a single traveler can stay for one night in high season. For **restaurants** and other dining establishments, we estimate the average amount a traveler will spend in high season. The table tells you what you'll *typically* find in Germany at the corresponding price range; keep in mind that no system can allow for every individual establishment's quirks, and you'll typically get more for your money in larger cities.

ACCOMMODATIONS	RANGE	WHAT YOU'RE *LIKELY* TO FIND
❶	under €15	Campgrounds, dorm rooms, or dorm-style rooms. Expect bunk beds and a communal bath; you may have to provide or rent towels and sheets.
❷	€15-25	Upper-end hostels or lower-end pensions. You may have a private bathroom, or there may be a sink in your room and a communal shower in the hall.
❸	€26-35	A small room with a private bath, probably in a budget hotel or pension. Should have decent amenities, such as phone and TV. Breakfast may be included in the price of the room.
❹	€36-50	Similar to 3, but may have more amenities or be in a more highly touristed or conveniently located area.
❺	above €50	Large hotels or upscale chains. If it's a 5 and it doesn't have the perks you want, you've paid too much.
FOOD	RANGE	WHAT YOU'RE *LIKELY* TO FIND
❶	under €4	Probably a fast-food stand, *Imbiß*, university cafeteria, or bakery. Rarely ever a sit-down meal.
❷	€4-8	Some sandwich shops, pizzerias, and take-out options, but also quite a few ethnic restaurants. May be take-out or sit-down.
❸	€9-12	Entrées are more expensive, but chances are, you're paying for decor and ambience. You'll probably have a waiter or waitress, so the tip will bump you up a few euros.
❹	€13-20	As in 3, higher prices are probably related to better service, but in these restaurants, the food will tend to be fancier or more elaborate, or the location will be especially convenient or historical.
❺	above €20	Your meal might cost more than your room, but there's a reason—it's something fabulous or famous, or both, and you'll probably need to wear something other than sandals and a t-shirt.

DISCOVER GERMANY

While there is no shortage of images that characterize Germany—*Lederhosen* and busty barmaids, ultra-modern skyscrapers, unconscionable heaps of meat and potatoes—perhaps the most accurate explanation of this compelling country lies not in a preconception but in a word: *Gestalt*. This German term, literally meaning "shape," characterizes something that is distinctly more than the sum of its parts. *Gestalt's* evocative brand of holism speaks both to Germany's geographical diversity, sweeping from the jagged snowy peaks of the Bavarian Alps to the sprawling sandy beaches of the north, and to its historical legacy and ever-evolving sense of national identity. A country equally split between Protestantism and Catholicism forged from dozens of squabbling principalities, Germany has never been homogeneous. Yet a new influx of non-German immigrants and the challenge of collective guilt has forced an entire nation—once confident in its own shared ethnic heritage, if nothing else—to question what it means to be German in an ever-shrinking world and a rapidly diversifying *Land*. Poised at the juncture of common tradition and forward-looking cosmopolitanism, and facing tremendous uncertainty coupled with the uplifting potential of change, Germany is uniquely positioned to offer travelers culture, adventure, and the opportunity to discover—along with the German people themselves—the phantasmic *Gestalt* of contemporary Germany.

FACTS AND FIGURES

Jan. 18, 1871: The date of German unification, 95 years after the birth of the US.

27: The number of times Germany could fit inside the borders of the US.

82.5 million: Germany's total population.

105,000: The size of Germany's current Jewish community, the third largest in Western Europe.

3.2 million: The number of Muslims living in Germany.

4: The number of Muslim deputies in Germany's *Reichstag*, out of 614.

99.9: The percentage of German adults who are literate, the highest in the world.

€500: The maximum cost, per semester, of University education in Germany.

120: The number of liters of beer consumed per German per year.

1/10: The fraction of the world's beer produced by German breweries.

56: The percentage of German men who are overweight, a casualty of *wurst*, potatoes, and beer calories.

Infinity: The speed limit on the *Autobahn*. (Its recommended speed is 130km/hr.).

12.5: The percentage of the world's cars that are made in Germany.

3: Germany's rank on a list of the world's largest economies, after the US and Japan.

14: The percentage of Germany's electricity made from renewable energy sources.

WHEN TO GO

Airfares and tourists increase with the temperature in July and August. May, June, and September have fewer vacationers and cooler, rainier days. Cold and wet weather should never be unexpected in Germany: between one-third and one-half of the days each year bring some amount of precipitation, and even in July hailstorms can blow in to blue skies with little warning. In June and July, school groups overrun state-run HI hostels, bringing noise, confusion, and hallway-soccer in their wake—don't say we didn't warn you. Larger cities typically sport better non-HI offerings. In the winter months, some German hostels close and museum hours may be shortened. Winter sports gear up in November and continue through April; peak season for skiing is mid-December to March. For charts listing average temperatures and national holidays, see **Appendix**, p. 651.

WHAT TO DO

Germany's alpine wonderlands, seaside resorts, medieval relics, and cosmopolitan metropolises cohese to form one of Europe's most diverse destinations. The trademark of any German effort is its intensity: lively modern cities are hyper-active, droll storybook villages are fiercely provincial, and scenic wilderness preserves are thoroughly natural. Within each of the country's historically distinct cities and regions, travelers will find outdoor activities, intellectual wonders, aesthetic thrills, and drunken adventures. For regional attractions, see the **Highlights of the Region** section at the beginning of each chapter.

UNDISCOVERED NATIONAL PARKS

Germany's national parks are gorgeous, fantastically varied, and surprisingly lightly touristed. Our **National Parks** itinerary (p. 7) will give you an idea of what's available; refer to the National Parks section of the **Index** (p. 659) to find thorough coverage of individual parks.

NAVES AND KNAVES

Early examples of fine German engineering can be seen in the resplendent castles and cathedrals scattered across the country. Two hundred years after rural fortresses went out of style, Mad King Ludwig II commissioned **Neuschwanstein,** the unfinished gem of the **Bavarian Royal Castles** (p. 464) and one of Germany's most-recognizable landmarks. Set in a meticulously contrived (but still stunning) park in Potsdam, **Schloß Sanssouci** (p. 156) sports a frilly French Rococo style. In the cliffs over the Rhein River, the romantic half-ruins of **Burg Rheinfels** (p. 351) have underground passages that you can tour by candlelight. Check out our **Sloshed and Schloß-ed** itinerary (p. 5) for a tour of Germany's grandest residences (and a few beers along the way). The architectural heights achieved by German secular rulers are answered literally and figuratively in the churches and cathedrals that have been erected across Germany. The epitome of Catholic extravagance, Cologne's unforgettable **Dom** (p. 278), is the largest High Gothic cathedral in the world, built between 1288 and 1880. Other important cathedrals include the imposing **Münster** (p. 310) in Freiburg, which rings the oldest bells in Germany; the **Frauenkirche** (p. 443) in Munich, whose two distinctive towers dominate the city skyline; and the **Münster** (p. 310) in Ulm, where the largest spire in the world peaks at 161m. Protestant houses of worship stake a claim to German skylines as well. Wittenberg is home to the **Schloßkirche** (p. 579), upon which Martin Luther nailed his *95 Theses* in 1517, sparking the Protestant Revolution. Hamburg's **Große Michaeliskirche** (p. 223) has a famous copper tower which is the city's symbol. The **Nikolaikirche** in Leipzig (p. 633) is doubly famous as the church in which Bach composed his *St. John's Passion* and as the rallying point for the demonstrations in early October 1989 that hastened the fall of communist East Germany.

FESTIVALS AND HOLIDAYS

If Germany works hard, it plays even harder—time your trip right, and you can hit a festival in every town you visit. Themes range from the humble (local produce) to the lofty (high culture) to the downright gratuitous (sex, drugs, techno, and pancakes). A few even claim international renown: Munich's **Okto-berfest** (Sept. 22-Oct. 7, 2007) began as a wedding celebration centuries ago and continues to fill the city with reveling beer drinkers every year. Berlin's **Love Parade,** held annually in mid-July, reverberates all weekend without sleeping. Famous DJs are imported, bodies are bared, and general hullaballoo ensues. In the early spring, Cologne hosts the yearly **Karneval** celebration (Feb. 16-21, 2007), where extravagantly costumed fools traipse in parades and generate revelry for the week before Ash Wednesday. During Advent, traditional **Christmas Markets** spring up all over Germany, serving *Glühwein* and other holiday spirits. Nuremberg's *Christkindlmarkt* with its glorious *Lebkuchen* (gingerbread) is the most famous. Finally, for film fanatics, Berlin hosts the young but prestigious **Berlinale Film Festival** (Feb. 8-18, 2007) every year.

DISCOVER

◤ LET'S GO PICKS

BEST ART-IS-LIFE EXPERIENCE: Subordinate form and function to a full night's sleep in Dessau's famous **Bauhaus** architectural school (p. 580).

BEST PLACE TO SLEEP IN YOUR CAR: Go nowhere fast in a VW Beetle-turned-bed in Berlin's Bax Pax hostel (p. 142).

BEST DELUSION OF ROYALTY: Spend the night in a 12th-century castle among the vineyards of Bacharach at the **Jugendherberge Stahleck** (p. 352).

BEST BATHROOMS: Check out the bathroom "art" at the **Schwarzes Café** (p. 109) in Berlin's Charlottenburg—it's like peeing in a Prince video. And the **Old Commercial Room** (p. 223) in Hamburg has a throne that's actually...a throne.

BEST TAKE ON "WORSHIP": The monks at the **Andechs monastery** (p. 456) serve the holiest—and at 12%, most potent—brew in Bavaria.

BEST USE OF A METER STICK: The **Hansens Brauerei** (p. 212) in Flensburg sells its suds 100 centimeters at a time.

BEST PLACE TO *WEIN*: Nothing to complain about in **Neustadt** (p. 371), where a 2hr. sampling of *Reisinger* runs €6.

BEST DANCING: Try Berlin's electronica-drenched **Week-End** (p. 132), Hamburg's industrial **Fabrik** (p. 233), or Leipzig's subterranean **Moritzbastei** (p. 636).

BEST PLACE TO LIVE A FAIRY TALE: Mad King Lugwig's fantastical Bavarian Königsschlößer (p. 464) inspired Disney's Cinderella Castle.

BEST *KULTUR:* It doesn't get more grandiose than the **Markgräfliches Opernhaus** at Bayreuth (p. 542), nexus of all things Richard Wagner, including the elaborate annual **Wagner Festspiele.**

BEST TOTALITARIAN SLOGAN: The Orwellian edifices lining **Straße der Nationen** (p. 623) in Chemnitz (formerly Karl-Marx-Stadt) remind passers-by that "the party has a thousand eyes."

BEST BEACHES: Sunbathe with the stars on **Sylt** (p. 206), avoid the crowds on nearby **Amrum** (p. 208), or dip into the Baltic Sea along **Rügen Island** (p. 188). The **Bodensee** (p. 419) on the Swiss border is a tropical respite from Germany's wet, gray climate.

BEST PLACE TO SNIFF AWAY YOUR TROUBLES: The **Kleingradierwerk Ramsau** (p. 480), an "outdoor brine inhalatorium," promises to cure what's ailing you with its potent saline air.

BEST ESCAPE FROM REALITY: Hike your way through Bavaria's dramatic **Berchtesgaden National Park** (p. 470) and overnight in one of the park's secluded *Alpenhütte.*

BEST DIRTY FUN (CLEAN VERSION): Run across the quicksand-dotted **Wattenmeer mudflats** (p. 202) between the islands of Sylt and Amrum at low tide.

BEST DIRTY FUN (RED-LIGHT VERSION): Soak up the grime along Hamburg's Reeperbahn (p. 214); nearby Hebertstr. almost makes Amsterdam's red-light district look benign.

DISCOVER

GERMANY'S GREATEST (1 MONTH)

Lübeck (1 day)
Soak up the culture of Germany's nautical North (p. 193).

Berlin (5 days)
World-class museums, chaotic nightlife, and cutting-edge culture spread over a city eight times the size of Paris (p. 87).

Hamburg (3 days)
The burliness of a port, the feckless abandon of a party town (p. 214).

END

Potsdam (1 day)
The splendor of Neoclassical palaces and manicured gardens (p. 154).

Bremen (1 day)
A cosmopolitan city with a distinctively medieval ambiance (p. 259).

Hanover (1day)
Broad avenues, lush parks, and high culture (p. 234).

START

Cologne (2 days)
Home to Germany's largest cathedral and driving nightlife (p. 278).

Leipzig (1 day)
The soul of a college town, the heart of a cosmopolitan city (p. 629).

Weimar (1day)
Goethe and the Bauhaus saturate this capital city in history (p. 551).

Koblenz (1 day)
Gateway to the Rhein and wine (p. 345).

Frankfurt (2 days)
Ultra-modern skyscrapers, swanky nightlife, and flights to everywhere (p. 317).

Dresden (2 days)
A city rebuilt and a nexus of alternative culture (p. 598).

Rothenburg (1 day)
Germany's best-preserved medieval city (p. 524).

Regensburg(1 day)
More cafés and bars than you can shake a cappuccino at (p. 513).

Heidelberg (1 day)
Germany's oldest University sits among romantic ruins (p. 381).

Munich (4 days)
Biergarten on every corner and plenty of Bavarian Gemütlichkeit (p. 428).

Berchtesgaden National Park (1 day)
Hiking, biking, and skiing amid breathtaking mountains (p. 476).

Freiburg (1 day)
Cathedrals, nature, and a relaxed pace of life (p. 404).

Castle Road (1 day)
Live Ludwig II's fairy tale at the mad king's Royal Castles (p. 520).

SLOSHED AND SCHLOß-ED (3 WEEKS)

Hamburg (2 days)
The notorious Reeperbahn never slows down; escape the pervasive red light at peaceful Schloß Bergedorf (p. 214).

Düsseldorf (1 day)
500 pubs have earned this city the title of "longest bar in the world"; stumble over to Schloß Benrath when you've conquered them (p. 299).

END

Berlin (4 days)
A nightlife nexus, from Mitte's techno clubs to Prenzlauer Berg's hardcore scene (p. 87).

Potsdam (1 day)
A quick jaunt from Berlin, and a Rococo recovery from the chaos of the capital's club scene (p. 154).

START

Cologne (2 days)
No famous castles here, but plenty of bump-and-grind nightlife and endless Kölsch (p. 278).

Dresden (2 days)
Sample East Germany's resurgent nightlife and tour the Baroque Schloß Moritzburg (p. 598).

Bonn (1 day)
Intimate local pubs and the ruins of Drachenfels, a castle immortalized in the poetry of Lord Byron (p. 288).

Koblenz (1 day)
At the foot of an eleventh-century fortress and within easy reach of breathtaking Schloß Stolzenfels (p. 345).

Nuremberg (1 day)
Packed with bars and clubs, Nürnberg is best seen from atop Kaiserburg's massive castle walls (p. 534).

Cochem (1 day)
Eleventh-century Burg Eltz and neo-Gothic Reichsburg overlook this traditional German wine-making village (p. 357).

Heidelberg (1 day)
A lively student scene thrives here, but the romantic, crumbling Schloß is Heidelberg's real draw (p. 381)

Munich (4 days)
Guardian of German *Bier* culture and home to the resplendent Schloß Nymphenburg (p. 428).

Castle Road (1 day)
These crazy castles belong in another (fairy-tale) universe (p. 520).

DISCOVER

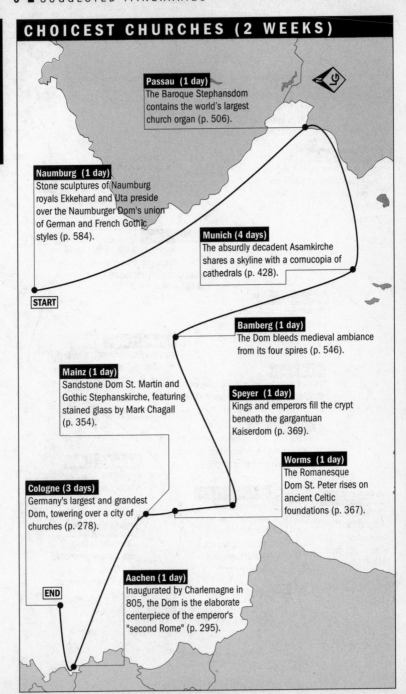

CHOICEST CHURCHES (2 WEEKS)

Passau (1 day)
The Baroque Stephansdom contains the world's largest church organ (p. 506).

Naumburg (1 day)
Stone sculptures of Naumburg royals Ekkehard and Uta preside over the Naumburger Dom's union of German and French Gothic styles (p. 584).

Munich (4 days)
The absurdly decadent Asamkirche shares a skyline with a cornucopia of cathedrals (p. 428).

START

Bamberg (1 day)
The Dom bleeds medieval ambiance from its four spires (p. 546).

Mainz (1 day)
Sandstone Dom St. Martin and Gothic Stephanskirche, featuring stained glass by Mark Chagall (p. 354).

Speyer (1 day)
Kings and emperors fill the crypt beneath the gargantuan Kaiserdom (p. 369).

Worms (1 day)
The Romanesque Dom St. Peter rises on ancient Celtic foundations (p. 367).

Cologne (3 days)
Germany's largest and grandest Dom, towering over a city of churches (p. 278).

END

Aachen (1 day)
Inaugurated by Charlemagne in 805, the Dom is the elaborate centerpiece of the emperor's "second Rome" (p. 295).

MOUNTAINS AND MUDFLATS (2 WEEKS)

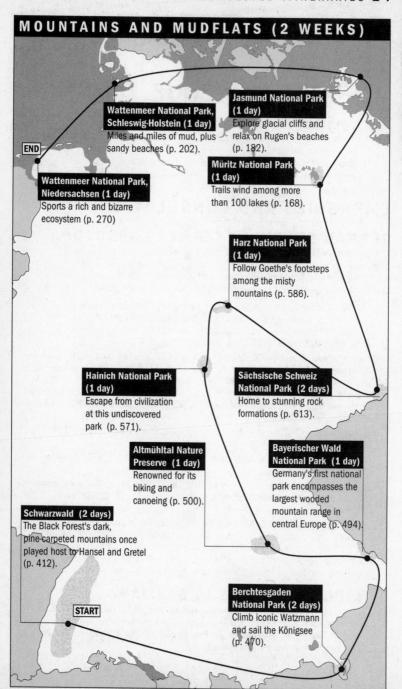

Wattenmeer National Park, Schleswig-Holstein (1 day)
Miles and miles of mud, plus sandy beaches (p. 202).

Jasmund National Park (1 day)
Explore glacial cliffs and relax on Rugen's beaches (p. 182).

END

Wattenmeer National Park, Niedersachsen (1 day)
Sports a rich and bizarre ecosystem (p. 270)

Müritz National Park (1 day)
Trails wind among more than 100 lakes (p. 168).

Harz National Park (1 day)
Follow Goethe's footsteps among the misty mountains (p. 586).

Hainich National Park (1 day)
Escape from civilization at this undiscovered park (p. 571).

Sächsische Schweiz National Park (2 days)
Home to stunning rock formations (p. 613).

Altmühltal Nature Preserve (1 day)
Renowned for its biking and canoeing (p. 500).

Bayerischer Wald National Park (1 day)
Germany's first national park encompasses the largest wooded mountain range in central Europe (p. 494).

Schwarzwald (2 days)
The Black Forest's dark, pine-carpeted mountains once played host to Hansel and Gretel (p. 412).

START

Berchtesgaden National Park (2 days)
Climb iconic Watzmann and sail the Königsee (p. 470).

ESSENTIALS

PLANNING YOUR TRIP

ENTRANCE REQUIREMENTS
Passport (p. 9). Required of citizens of Australia, Canada, Ireland, New Zealand, the UK, and the US.
Visa (p. 11). May be required of citizens of other countries.
Work Permit (p. 11). Required of all foreigners planning to work in Germany.

EMBASSIES AND CONSULATES

GERMAN CONSULAR SERVICES ABROAD

The German embassy or consulate in your home country can supply legal information concerning your trip, arrange for visas, and direct you to a wealth of other information about tourism, education, and employment in Germany. For a listing of German embassies and consulates worldwide, visit www.auswaertiges-amt.de.

Australia: Canberra, 119 Empire Circuit, Yarralumla, ACT 2600 (☎02 6270 1911; www.germanembassy.org.au). **Consulates:** Melbourne, 480 Punt Rd., South Yarra, VIC 3141 (☎03 9864 6888; meldiplo@bigpond.net.au); Sydney, 13 Trelawney St., Woollahra, NSW 2025 (☎02 9328 7733; info@sydney.diplo.de).

Canada: Ottawa, 1 Waverly St., ON, K2P 0T8 (☎613-232-1101; www.ottawa.diplo.de). **Consulates:** Montréal, Edifice Marathon Ste. 4315, 1250 Blvd. René-Lévesque Ouest, Québec, H3B 4W8 (☎514-931-2277; www.montreal.diplo.de); Toronto, 77 Bloor St. West Ste. 1702, ON, M5S 2T1 (☎416 925 2813; www.toronto.diplo.de); Vancouver, World Trade Centre Ste. 704, 999 Canada Pl., BC, V6C 3E1 (☎604-684-8377; german-consulatevancouver@telus.net).

Ireland: Dublin, 31 Trimleston Ave., Booterstown, Blackrock/Co (☎01 269 3011; www.germanembassy.ie).

New Zealand: Wellington, 90-92 Hobson St., Thorndon (☎04 473 6063; www.wellington.diplo.de/en/Startseite.html).

UK: London, 23 Belgrave Sq. SW1X 8PZ (☎020 7824 1300; www.german-embassy.org.uk). **Consulate:** Edinburgh, 16 Eglinton Cresc., EH 12 5DG (☎0131 337 2323).

US: Washington, D.C., 4645 Reservoir Rd., N.W. 20007 (☎202-298-4000; www.germany-info.org). **Consulates:** New York, 871 U.N. Plaza, NY 10017 (☎212-610-9700; fax 610-9702); Los Angeles, 6222 Wilshire Blvd., Ste. 500, CA 90048 (☎323-930-2703; losangeles@germany.info); other consulates in Atlanta, Boston, Chicago, Houston, Miami, and San Francisco (see embassy website for contact information).

CONSULAR SERVICES IN GERMANY

For the latest information, contact the **Auswärtiges Amt,** Wederscher Markt 1, 11017 Berlin (Federal Foreign Office ☎030 50 00; www.auswaertiges-amt.de). Foreign embassies in Berlin are listed on p. 97. For a complete list of foreign missions in Germany, see www.auswaertiges-amt.de/.

Australia: Frankfurt, Neue Mainzer Str. 52-58, 60311 (☎069 90 55 80; fax 90 55 81 19).

Canada: Düsseldorf, Bernratherstr. 8, 40213 (☎0211 172 170; ddorf@international.gc.ca). **Hamburg,** Ballindamm 35, 20095 (☎040 460 02 70; hmbrg@international.gc.ca). **Munich,** Tal 29, 80331 (☎089 219 95 70; munic@international.gc.ca). All are listed at www.dfait-maeci.gc.ca/canada-europa/germany/menu-en.asp.

Ireland: Cologne, Frankenforsterstr. 77, 51427 (☎022 04 609 860; fax 04 609 861). **Frankfurt,** Graefstr. 99, 60487 (☎069 977 883 883; fax 977 883 880). **Hamburg,** Feldbrunnenstr. 43, 20148 (☎040 44 18 61 13; fax 44 18 85 51). **Munich,** Denninger Str. 15, 81679 (☎089 20 80 59 90; fax 20 80 59 89).

New Zealand: Hamburg, Domstr. 19, 20095 (☎040 44 25 550; fax 44 25 5549).

UK: Düsseldorf, Yorckstr. 19, 40476 (☎0211 944 80; info@britischebotschaft.de). **Hamburg,** Harvestehuder Weg 8a, 20148 (☎040 448 03 20). **Munich,** Bürkleinstr. 10, 80538 (☎089 21 10 90; info@munich.mail.fco.gov.uk). All listed at www.britischebotschaft.de.

US: Düsseldorf, Willi-Becker-Allee 10, 40227 (☎0211 78 88 09 27; fax 788 89 38). **Frankfurt,** Gießener Str. 30, 60435 (☎069 753 50; fax 753 52 277). **Hamburg,** Alsterufer 27/28, 20354 (☎040 411 71 10; fax 41 32 79 33). **Leipzig,** Wilhelm-Seyfferth-Str. 4, 04107 (☎0341 213 840). **Munich,** Königinstr. 5, 80539 (☎089 288 80; fax 280 99 98).

TOURIST OFFICES

The **German National Tourist Board** is based at Beethovenstr. 69, 60325 Frankfurt (www.germany-tourism.de). This umbrella organization supervises Germany's international tourist infrastructure and provides trip-planning information.

Australia: Sydney, G.P.O. Box A980, N.S.W. 1236 (☎02 9267 8148; gnto@germany.org.au).

Canada: Toronto, 480 University Ave. Ste. 1410, ON M5G 1V2 (☎416 968 1685; info@gnto.ca).

UK: London, P.O. Box 2695, W1A 3TN (☎09001 600100; www.germany-tourism.co.uk).

US: New York, 122 E. 42nd St., New York, NY 10168 (☎212-661-7200; www.cometogermany.com). **Los Angeles,** 8484 Wilshire Blvd. Ste. 440, Beverly Hills, CA 90211 (☎323-655-6085; gntolax@aol.com). **Chicago,** P.O. Box 59594, Chicago, IL 60659 (☎773-539-6303; gntoch@aol.com).

DOCUMENTS AND FORMALITIES

PASSPORTS

REQUIREMENTS
Citizens of Australia, Canada, Ireland, New Zealand, the UK, and the US need valid passports to enter Germany and to re-enter their home countries. Germany does not allow entrance if the holder's passport expires in under six months; returning home with an expired passport is illegal and may result in a fine.

NEW PASSPORTS
Citizens of Australia, Canada, Ireland, New Zealand, the UK, and the US can apply for a passport at any passport office or at selected post offices and courts of law in their home countries. Any new passport or renewal applications must be filed well in advance of the departure date, though most passport offices offer rush services for a steep fee. Note that "rushed" passports still take up to two weeks to arrive.

ONE EUROPE. European unity has come a long way since 1958, when the European Economic Community (EEC) was created to promote European solidarity and cooperation. Since then, the EEC has become the European Union (EU), a mighty political, legal, and economic institution. On May 1, 2004, 10 South, Central, and Eastern European countries—Cyprus, the Czech Republic, Estonia, Hungary, Latvia, Lithuania, Malta, Poland, Slovakia, and Slovenia—were admitted to the EU, joining the 15 existing member states: Austria, Belgium, Denmark, Finland, France, Germany, Greece, Ireland, Italy, Luxembourg, the Netherlands, Portugal, Spain, Sweden, and the UK.

What does this have to do with the average non-EU tourist? The EU's policy of **freedom of movement** means that border controls between the first 15 member states (minus Ireland and the UK, plus Norway and Iceland) have been abolished, and visa policies harmonized. Under this policy, formally known as the **Schengen Agreement,** you're still required to carry a passport (or government-issued ID card for EU citizens) when crossing an internal border, but once you've been admitted into one country, you're free to travel to other participating states. On June 5, 2005, Switzerland ratified the treaty but has yet to implement it. The 8 newest member states of the EU are anticipated to implement the policy in October of 2007. Britain and Ireland have also formed a **common travel area,** abolishing passport controls between the UK and the Republic of Ireland.

For more important consequences of the EU for travelers, see **The Euro** (p. 14) and **European Customs** and **EU customs regulations** (p. 11).

PASSPORT MAINTENANCE

Photocopy the page of your passport with your photo, as well as your visas, traveler's check serial numbers, and any other important documents. Carry one set of copies in a safe place, apart from the originals, and leave another set with a friend or relative at home. Consulates also recommend that you carry an expired passport or an official copy of your birth certificate separate from other documents.

If you lose your passport, notify the local police and the embassy or consulate of your home government. *Let's Go* lists consulate services in the **Practical Information** section of each city. To expedite its replacement, you must show ID and proof of citizenship. A replacement may take weeks, and it may be valid for a limited time. Any visas in your old passport will be irretrievably lost. In an emergency, ask for temporary traveling papers that will permit you to re-enter your home country.

VISAS, INVITATIONS, AND WORK PERMITS

VISAS

As of June 2006, citizens of Australia, Canada, Ireland, New Zealand, the UK, and the US do not need visas for stays of under 90 days, though this three-month period begins upon entry into any of the countries that belong to the EU's **freedom of movement** zone. For more information, see **One Europe** (p. 10). All non-EU citizens need a **residence permit** for visits exceeding 90 days, which include variations for **work permits** or **student permits.** Whereas general residence permits simply grant the right to live or travel in Germany or for longer than 90 days, student permits allow travelers to register at a German university. Citizens of the following countries can obtain any form of residence permit after arriving in Germany: the EU, Australia, Canada, Israel, New Zealand, and the US. These take roughly 25 days to process, and require a US$40 application fee, two passport photos, a valid passport, and evidence of sufficient funds (in most cases, a bank statement). Those applying for a study permit must also provide a letter of acceptance from a German institution. Individuals not from the aforementioned countries must acquire a residence permit before leaving for Germany, which usually takes six to eight weeks to process and costs US$40. For opportunities, see **Beyond Tourism** (p. 78).

WORK PERMITS

Those planning to work in Germany must apply for a work permit (see **residence permit,** above). In addition to the materials required for the general residence permit, applicants must provide a contract or letter of intent from their future employers and a police certificate of good conduct. The same restrictions for general residence permits apply, and only those from countries specifically mentioned above may apply after having arrived in Germany. For work opportunities in Germany, see **Beyond Tourism** (p. 78).

IDENTIFICATION

When you travel, always carry at least two forms of identification on your person, including a photo ID; a passport and a driver's license or birth certificate is usually an adequate combination. Never carry all of your IDs together; split them up in case of theft or loss, and keep photocopies of all of them in your luggage and at home.

STUDENT, TEACHER, AND YOUTH IDENTIFICATION

The **International Student Identity Card (ISIC),** the most widely accepted form of student ID, provides discounts on some sights, accommodations, food, and transportation; access to a 24hr. emergency helpline; and insurance benefits for US cardholders (see **Insurance,** p. 21). Discounts within Germany range from bike and car rentals to tattoo parlors. Applicants must be full-time secondary or post-secondary school students at least 12 years of age. Because of the proliferation of fake ISICs, some services (particularly airlines) require additional student ID.

The **International Teacher Identity Card (ITIC)** offers teachers the same insurance coverage as the ISIC and similar but limited discounts. For travelers who are under 26 years old but are not students, the **International Youth Travel Card (IYTC)** also offers many of the same benefits as the ISIC.

Each of these identity cards costs US$22. ISICs, ITICS, and IYTCs are valid for one year from the date of issue. To learn more about ISICs, ITICs, and IYTCs, try www.myisic.com. Many student travel agencies (p. 24) issue the cards; for a list of issuing agencies or more information, see the **International Student Travel Confederation (ISTC)** website (www.istc.org).

The **International Student Exchange Card (ISE Card)** is a similar identification card available to students, faculty, and youths aged 12 to 26. The card provides discounts, medical benefits, access to a 24hr. emergency helpline, and the ability to purchase student airfares. An ISE Card costs US$25; call ☎800-255-8000 for more info, or visit www.isecard.com.

CUSTOMS

Upon entering Germany, you must declare certain items from abroad and pay a duty on the value of those articles if they exceed the allowance established by Germany's customs service. Note that goods and gifts purchased abroad at **duty-free** shops are not exempt from duty; "duty-free" merely means that you need not pay a tax in the country of purchase. Duty-free allowances were abolished for travel between EU member states on June 30, 1999, but still exist for those arriving from outside the EU. In order to expedite your return, make a list of any valuables brought from home and register them with customs before traveling abroad, and be sure to keep receipts for all goods acquired abroad.

> **CUSTOMS IN THE EU.** As well as freedom of movement of people within the EU (see p. 10), travelers in the 15 original EU member countries (Austria, Belgium, Denmark, Finland, France, Germany, Greece, Ireland, Italy, Luxembourg, the Netherlands, Portugal, Spain, Sweden, and the UK) can also take advantage of the freedom of movement of goods. This means that there are no customs controls at internal EU borders (i.e., you can take the blue customs channel at the airport), and travelers are free to transport whatever legal substances they like as long as it is for their personal use—up to 800 cigarettes, 10L of spirits, 90L of wine, and 110L of beer. Duty-free allowances (in which you need not pay tax for an item purchased abroad upon arriving in your home country) were abolished on June 30, 1999 for travel between the original 15 EU member states; this now also applies to Cyprus and Malta. However, travelers between the EU and the rest of the world still get a duty-free allowance when passing through customs.

Non-EU citizens may "import" gifts and items for personal use into Germany according to the following limits: 200 cigarettes (or tobacco equivalent); 1L of spirits stronger than 44 proof, or 2L of weaker spirits, sparkling wines, or liqueur; 2L of table wine; 50g of perfume; and 500g of coffee. To prevent problems with transporting **prescription drugs,** bring their original bottles and a copy of your prescription. The total value of all other personal use goods cannot exceed €175. Upon **returning home,** you must declare all articles acquired abroad and pay a duty on the value of articles that exceed the allowance established by your country's customs service. Germany also levies a Value-Added Tax on all consumer purchases, but non-EU tourists can usually get these taxes refunded on large items (p. 17).

MONEY

CURRENCY AND EXCHANGE

The currency chart below is based on August 2006 exchange rates between local currency and Australian dollars (AUS$), Canadian dollars (CDN$), European Union euro (EUR€), New Zealand dollars (NZ$), British pounds (UK£), and US dollars (US$). Check the currency converter on websites like www.xe.com or www.bloomberg.com, or check a major newspaper for the latest exchange rates.

As a general rule, it's cheaper to convert money in Germany than at home. While currency exchange will probably be available in your arrival airport, it's wise to bring enough foreign currency to last for the first 24 to 72 hours of your trip.

When changing money abroad, try to go only to banks or *bureaux de change* that have at most a 5% margin between their buy and sell prices. Since you lose money with every transaction, **convert large sums** (unless the currency is depreciating rapidly) but **not more than you'll need.**

If you use traveler's checks or bills, carry some in small denominations (the equivalent of US$50 or less) for times when you are forced to exchange money at disadvantageous rates, but bring a range of denominations. Store your money in a variety of forms; ideally, at any given time you will be carrying some cash, some traveler's checks, and an ATM and/or credit card.

EURO (€)		
AUS$ = €0.597	€1 = AUS$1.675	
CDN$ = €0.695	€1 = CDN$1.438	
NZ$ = €0.499	€1 = NZ$2.003	
UK£ = €1.476	€1 = UK£0.677	
US$ = €0.78	€1 = US$1.285	

THE EURO. The official currency of 12 members of the European Union—Austria, Belgium, Finland, France, Germany, Greece, Ireland, Italy, Luxembourg, the Netherlands, Portugal, and Spain—is now the euro.

The currency has some important and positive consequences for travelers hitting more than one euro-zone country. For one thing, money-changers across the euro-zone are obliged to exchange money at the official, fixed rate (see below), and at no commission (though they may still charge a small service fee). Second, euro-denominated traveler's checks allow you to pay for goods and services across the euro-zone, again at the official rate and commission-free.

At the time of printing, €1=US$1.285=CDN$1.44=NZ$1.79=UK£.69. For more info, check a currency converter (www.xe.com) or www.europa.eu.int.

TRAVELER'S CHECKS

Traveler's checks are one of the safest and least troublesome means of carrying funds. American Express and Visa are the most-recognized brands, but Travelex/Thomas Cook checks are also accepted by many German banks. Check issuers offer refunds if the checks are lost or stolen, and many provide additional services, such as toll-free refund hotlines abroad, emergency message services, and assistance with stolen credit cards or passports. Traveler's checks are accepted in heavily touristed areas; however, debit cards and ATMs are very common and generally provide better rates. To avoid excessive fees, try to cash traveler's checks at banks or at American Express offices.

American Express: Checks available with commission at select banks, at all AmEx offices, and online (www.americanexpress.com; US residents only). American Express cardholders can also purchase checks by phone (☎800-528-4800). Checks available in Australian, British, Canadian, European, Japanese, and US currencies, among others. American Express also offers the Travelers Cheque Card, a prepaid reloadable card. Cheques for Two can be signed by either of 2 people traveling together. AmEx service centers: Australia ☎800 688 022, New Zealand 050 855 5358, UK 0800 587 6023, US and Canada 800-221-7282; elsewhere, call the US collect at 801-964-6665. In Germany, contact the Frankfurt customer service office (☎069 21 93 88 60).

Travelex: Thomas Cook MasterCard and Interpayment Visa traveler's checks available. For information about Thomas Cook MasterCard in Canada and the US call ☎800-223-7373, in the UK 0800 622 101; elsewhere call the UK collect at +44 1733 318 950. For information about Interpayment Visa in the US and Canada call ☎800-732-1322, in the UK 0800 515 884; elsewhere call the UK collect at +44 1733 318 949. For more information, visit www.travelex.com.

Visa: Checks available (generally with commission) at banks worldwide. For the location of the nearest office, call the Visa Travelers Cheque Global Refund and Assistance Center: in the UK ☎0800 895 078, in the US 800-227-6811; elsewhere, call the UK collect at +44 2079 378 091. Checks available in British, Canadian, European, Japanese, and US currencies, among others. Visa also offers TravelMoney, a prepaid debit card that can be reloaded online or by phone. For more information on Visa travel services, see http://usa.visa.com/personal/using_visa/travel_with_visa.html.

CREDIT, DEBIT, AND ATM CARDS

Credit cards are usually accepted by large establishments in Germany, and more rarely by private pensions or small restaurants. Where they are accepted, credit cards often offer superior exchange rates—up to 5% better than the retail rate used by banks and other currency exchange establishments. **MasterCard** (a.k.a.

EuroCard in Europe) and **Visa** are the most frequently accepted; **American Express** cards work at some ATMs and at AmEx offices and major airports.

The use of **ATM cards** is widespread in Germany. Depending on the system that your home bank uses, you can most likely access your personal bank account from abroad. ATMs get the same wholesale exchange rate as credit cards, but there is often a limit on the amount of money you can withdraw per day (usually around US$500). There is typically also a surcharge of US$1-5 per withdrawal and a transaction fee that is paid to the bank that owns the ATM. Check with your bank in advance to see if they have established partnerships with German banks whose ATMs you can use without an additional fee.

Debit cards are as convenient as credit cards but have a more immediate impact on your funds. A debit card can be used wherever its associated credit card company (usually MasterCard or Visa) is accepted; the money is withdrawn directly from the holder's checking account. Debit cards often also function as ATM cards and can be used to withdraw cash from associated banks and ATMs throughout Germany. While credit cards can procure cash advances from ATMs in the place of debit cards, be wary of their noticably higher interest rates.

The two major international money networks are **MasterCard/Maestro/Cirrus** (for ATM locations ☎ 800-424-7787 or www.mastercard.com) and **Visa/PLUS** (for ATM locations ☎ 800-847-2911 or www.visa.com). **American Express** and **Diners Club** cards are not as prevalent in Germany as elsewhere, but may be accepted in more upscale restaurants and accommodations, or in heavily touristed areas.

PINS AND ATMS. To use a cash or credit card to withdraw money from a cash machine (ATM) in Europe, you must have a four-digit **Personal Identification Number (PIN).** If your PIN is longer than four digits, ask your bank whether you can just use the first four, or whether you'll need a new one. **Credit cards** don't usually come with PINs. If you intend to use your credit cards at ATMs to get cash, request a pin from your credit card company before leaving.

Travelers with alphabetic, rather than numerical, PINs may also be thrown off by the lack of letters on European cash machines. The following are the corresponding numbers to use: 1=QZ; 2=ABC; 3=DEF; 4=GHI; 5=JKL; 6=MNO; 7=PRS; 8=TUV; and 9=WXY. Note that if you mistakenly punch the wrong code into the machine three times, it will swallow your card for good.

GETTING MONEY FROM HOME

If you run out of money while traveling, the easiest and cheapest solution is to have someone back home make a deposit directly into your bank account. Failing that, consider one of the following options.

WIRING MONEY

It is possible to arrange a **bank money transfer,** which means asking a bank back home to wire money to a bank in Germany. Note that some banks may only release your funds in local currency, potentially sticking you with a poor exchange rate. German banks do not issue personal checks to their customers, and therefore won't cash a traveler's personal check unless that individual has an account with the bank. Other options include online banking and PayPal. Money transfer services like **Western Union** are faster and more convenient than bank transfers—but also much pricier. To find a Western Union, visit www.westernunion.com, or call in Australia ☎ 1800 173 833, in Canada and the US 800-325-6000, in the UK 0800 833 833, or in Germany 0180 18 18 123. Money transfer services are available to **American Express** cardholders and at some **Thomas Cook** offices.

10

TOP TEN LIST

TOP 10 WAYS TO SAVE IN GERMANY

Traveling in Germany can be expensive, but the savvy traveler will find a wealth of free sights and activities. Here are a few of our favorites:

10. Healing Waters. Take the waters at Baden-Baden (p. 402), or breathe some soothing brine in Ramsau (p. 480).

9. Relaxing Beaches. Expose yourself (literally, if you wish) to the sun and sand on Sylt (p. 206) or Rugen (p. 182).

8. Sacred Churches. Rid yourself of guilt, but not of *gelt*, at some of Germany's greatest cultural landmarks, including Cologne's imposing Dom (p. 283).

7. Händel's Organ, Halle. Enjoy free concerts on the organ where Händel honed his harmonies (p. 582).

6. Rothenburg Town Wall. Traipse where medieval city guards once stood watch (p. 524).

5. Outdoor Concerts, Munich. Join the crowds in Olympiapark to tune in to famous bands (p. 449).

4. National Parks. Hike, bike, ski, or swim among glacial lakes and dense forests (p. 7).

3. Museums. Enjoy complimentary culture at Berlin's East Side Gallery (p. 138), Frankfurt's Struwwelpeter Museum (p. 326), or any of Germany's free collections.

2. Reichstag, Berlin. Climb Germany's house of parliament for an unmatched panorama of the capital (p. 126).

1. Love Parade, Berlin. Dance 'til you drop at the world's largest public party, one of the country's many wild festivals (p. 107).

US STATE DEPARTMENT (US CITIZENS ONLY)

In serious emergencies, the US State Department will forward money within hours to the nearest consular office for a US$30 fee. Contact the Overseas Citizens Service division of the US State Department (☎202-647-5225, toll-free 888-877-8339).

COSTS FEATURE

The cost of your trip will vary considerably, depending on where you go, how you travel, and where you stay. The most significant expenses will probably be your round-trip **airfare** to Germany (see **Getting to Germany: By Plane,** p. 24) and a **railpass** or bus pass (see **Getting To Germany: By Train,** p. 28; **By Bus,** p. 30). Before you go, spend some time calculating a reasonable daily **budget.**

STAYING ON A BUDGET

To give you a general idea, a bare-bones day in Germany (camping or sleeping in hostels/guesthouses, buying food at supermarkets) would cost about US$32 (€25); a slightly more comfortable day (sleeping in hostels/guesthouses and the occasional budget hotel, eating one meal per day at a restaurant, going out at night) would cost US$55 (€43); and for a luxurious day, the sky's the limit. Don't forget to factor in emergency reserve funds (at least US$200) when planning exactly how much money you'll need.

TIPS FOR SAVING MONEY

Some simple tactics include searching out opportunities for free entertainment, splitting accommodation and food costs with trustworthy fellow travelers, and buying food in supermarkets rather than eating out. Bring a **sleepsack** (p. 17) to save on sheet charges in hostels, and do your **laundry** in the sink (unless you're explicitly prohibited from doing so). Museums often have days when admission is free; plan accordingly. If you are eligible, consider getting an ISIC or an IYTC; many sights and museums offer discounts to students and youths. For getting around, bikes are the most economical option (see **Getting Around Germany: By Bicycle,** p. 35). Drinking at bars and clubs quickly becomes expensive. It's cheaper to buy alcohol at a supermarket and drink before going out.

TIPPING AND BARGAINING

Tipping is not practiced as liberally in Germany as it is elsewhere. Most Germans only round up a euro or two in restaurants and bars as tip, no matter the bill, and may give a small tip when getting a service, like a taxi ride. Tips in Germany are not left on the table, but handed directly to the server during payment. If you don't want any change, say *"Das steht so"* (dahs SHTAYT zo) or *"Das stimmt so"* (dahs SHTIMT zo). Germans rarely bargain except at flea markets.

TAXES

Most goods and services bought in Germany include a **Value-Added Tax** of 16% (7% for books, food, and agricultural products) called the *Mehrwertsteuer* (MwSt). Non-EU citizens can usually get MwSt refunded for large purchases (not services). Ask for a **Tax-Free Shopping Form** at points of purchase, and present it at customs upon leaving the country, along with your receipts and the goods (which must remain unused until you leave the country). Refunds can be claimed at **Tax Free Shopping Offices,** found at most airports, road borders, and ferry stations, or by mail (Tax-Free Shopping Processing Center, Trubelg. 19, 1030 Vienna, Austria). For more information, contact the German VAT refund hotline (in English, ☎0228 406 2880; vathotline@bff.bund.de).

PACKING

Pack lightly: Lay out only what you absolutely need, then take half the clothes and twice the money. The Travelite FAQ (www.travelite.org) is a good resource for tips on traveling light. The online **Universal Packing List** (http://upl.codeq.info) will generate a customized list of suggested items based on trip length, expected climate, planned activities, and other factors. If you plan to do a lot of hiking, also consult **The Great Outdoors,** p. 43.

Luggage: If you plan to cover most of your itinerary by foot, a sturdy **frame backpack** is unbeatable. (For the basics on buying a pack, see p. 44.) Toting a **suitcase** or **trunk** is fine if you plan to live in one or two cities and explore from there, but not a great idea if you plan to move around frequently. In addition to your main piece of luggage, a daypack (a small backpack or courier bag) is useful.

Clothing: No matter when you're traveling, it's a good idea to bring a warm jacket, a wool sweater, a rain jacket (Gore-Tex® is both waterproof and breathable), sturdy shoes or hiking boots, and thick socks. Flip-flops or waterproof sandals are must-haves for grubby hostel showers, and extra socks are always a good idea. You may also want one outfit for going out, a nicer pair of shoes, and modest dress for religious sites.

Sleepsack: Some hostels require that you either provide your own linen or rent sheets from them. Save cash by making your own sleepsack: fold a full-size sheet in half the long way, then sew it closed along the long side and one of the short sides.

Converters and Adapters: In Germany, electricity is 230 volts AC, enough to fry any 120V North American appliance. 220/240V electrical appliances won't work with a 120V current, either. Americans and Canadians should buy an adapter (which changes the shape of the plug; US$5) and a converter (which changes the voltage; US$10-30). Don't make the mistake of using only an adapter (unless appliance instructions explicitly state otherwise). [Australians and New Zealanders (who use 230V at home) won't need a converter, but will need a set of adapters to use anything electrical.]

Toiletries: Condoms, deodorant, razors, tampons, and toothbrushes are often available, but it may be difficult to find your preferred brand. Contact lenses are likely to be expensive and difficult to find, so bring enough extra pairs and solution for your entire trip. Also bring your glasses and a copy of your prescription.

First-Aid Kit: For a basic first-aid kit, pack bandages, a pain reliever, antibiotic cream, a thermometer, a multifunction pocketknife, tweezers, moleskin, decongestant, motion-sickness remedy, diarrhea or upset-stomach medication (Pepto Bismol® or Imodium®), an antihistamine, sunscreen, insect repellent, and burn ointment.

ESSENTIALS

Film: Film and developing in Germany is expensive, so consider bringing along enough film for your entire trip and developing it at home. If you don't want to bother with film, consider using a digital camera. Just be sure to bring along a large enough memory card and extra (or rechargeable) batteries. Less serious photographers may want to bring a disposable camera. Despite disclaimers, airport security X-rays can fog film, so buy a lead-lined pouch at a camera store or ask security to hand-inspect it. Pack film in your carry-on luggage, since high-intensity X-rays are used on checked luggage.

Other Useful Items: For safety purposes, you should bring a **money belt** and a small **padlock.** Basic **outdoors equipment** (plastic water bottle, compass, pocketknife, sunglasses, sunscreen, hat) may also prove useful. **Quick repairs** of garments can be done with a needle and thread; consider bringing electrical tape for patching tears. If you want to do laundry by hand, bring detergent, a small rubber ball to stop up the sink, and string for a makeshift clothes line. Other things you're liable to forget include: an umbrella, sealable **plastic bags** (for damp clothes, food, and spillables), an **alarm clock,** safety pins, a flashlight, and garbage bags. A **cell phone** can be a lifesaver (literally) on the road; see p. 38 for information on acquiring one that will work in Germany.

Important Documents: Don't forget your passport, traveler's checks, ATM and/or credit cards, adequate ID, and photocopies of all of the aforementioned in case these documents are lost or stolen (p. 9). Also check that you have any of the following that might apply to you: a hosteling membership card (p. 41); driver's license (p. 11); travel insurance forms (p. 21); ISIC (p. 11), and/or rail or bus pass (p. 31).

SAFETY AND HEALTH

GENERAL ADVICE

In any type of crisis situation, the most important thing to do is **stay calm.** Your country's embassy abroad (p. 8) is usually your best resource when things go wrong. The government offices are listed in the **Travel Advisories** box (p. 19).

LOCAL LAWS AND POLICE

While in Germany, you must abide by the local laws, including those which may seem harsh or unusual to you; most English-speaking countries will not be able to bypass the local judicial system to get you out of jail. Always carry a valid passport, as German police have the right to ask for identification.

DRUGS AND ALCOHOL

A meek "I didn't know it was illegal" will not fly in Germany; it is your responsibility to familiarize yourself with local laws. If you carry insulin, syringes, or any prescription drugs, you must have a copy of the prescriptions and a doctor's note. Avoid public drunkenness; it can jeopardize your safety and earn the disdain of locals. The (not strongly enforced) drinking age in Germany is 16 for beer and wine and 18 for spirits. The maximum blood alcohol level for drivers is 0.08%.

Needless to say, **illegal drugs** are best avoided; the average sentence for possession in Germany is seven years. In 1994, the German High Court ruled that while **possession of marijuana or hashish is still illegal,** possession of "small quantities for personal consumption" is not prosecutable. Each *Land* has interpreted "small quantities" differently (anywhere from 6 to 30 grams). More liberal areas like Berlin and Hamburg tend toward the higher end of this range, while East Germany and more conservative provinces like Bavaria are less lenient. The worst offense is carrying drugs across an international border; not only could you end up in prison, you could be stained with a "Drug Trafficker" stamp on your passport for life. Embassies may not be willing to help those arrested on drug charges.

SPECIFIC CONCERNS

XENOPHOBIC SENTIMENT

Anti-Americanism is almost non-existent in Germany. Even Germans who are vocally opposed to the policies of the US government tend to be welcoming of American tourists. Skinhead gangs in Germany are relatively rare despite their resurgence in the last 10 years. Violence against non-ethnic Germans ranges from unfocused demonstrations to brutal, and sometimes deadly, hate crimes. The government has made a concerted effort to ban neo-Nazi groups, and these bans have coincided with a depreciation of skinhead activity. Though these groups are unequivocally condemned by mainstream German thought, even some politically moderate Germans remain suspicious of the Turkish population in Germany (see **Minority Travelers,** p. 49), and political diplomacy has been lukewarm. Neo-Nazism is more prevalent in eastern Germany. Harassment of any type is not tolerated in public places in Germany, so if you do experience it, head for the closest public area immediately.

TERRORISM

Although former East Germans are now fairly used to travelers' presence, neo-Nazi skinheads maintain a potentially uncomfortable presence in disadvantaged areas of Germany. Many neo-Nazis sport the traditional uniform of flight jackets worn over white short-sleeved shirts and tight jeans rolled to reveal high-cut combat boots. Often, white supremacists and neo-Nazis will distinguish themselves with white laces, while anti-gay skinheads wear pink laces. Left-wing, anti-Nazi "S.H.A.R.P.s" (Skinheads Against Racial Prejudice) favor red laces.

International relations remain volatile in the wake of recent terrorist activities and wars. Security, beefed up after September 11th, remains tight, so be sure to always carry identification, and don't joke about bombs, illegal substances, or terrorists in public places, as officials have been instructed to arrest anyone who might pose a threat.

PERSONAL SAFETY

EXPLORING AND TRAVELING

To avoid unwanted attention, try to blend in as much as possible. Respecting local customs (in many cases, by dressing more conservatively than you would at home) may placate would-be hecklers. Familiarize yourself with your surroundings before setting out, and carry yourself with confidence. Check maps in shops

TRAVEL ADVISORIES. The following provide an updated list of your home country's advisories about travel.

Australian Department of Foreign Affairs and Trade: ☎612 6261 1111; www.dfat.gov.au.

Canadian Department of Foreign Affairs and International Trade (DFAIT): Call ☎800-267-8376; www.dfait-maeci.gc.ca. Call for their free booklet, *Bon Voyage...But.*

New Zealand Ministry of Foreign Affairs: ☎044 398 000; www.mfat.govt.nz.

United Kingdom Foreign and Commonwealth Office: ☎020 7008 1500; www.fco.gov.uk.

US Department of State: ☎888-407-4747; http://travel.state.gov. Visit the website for the booklet *A Safe Trip Abroad.*

and restaurants rather than on the street. If you are traveling alone, be sure someone at home knows your itinerary, and never tell anyone you meet that you're by yourself. When walking at night, stick to busy, well-lit streets and avoid alleyways.

There is no sure-fire way to avoid all the threatening situations you might encounter while traveling, but a good **self-defense course** will give you concrete ways to react to unwanted advances. **Impact, Prepare,** and **Model Mugging** can refer you to local self-defense courses in Australia, Canada, Switzerland and the US. Visit the website at www.modelmugging.org for a list of nearby chapters. Workshops (2-4hr.) start at US$50; full courses (20hr.) run US$350-500.

If using a **car,** learn local driving signals and wear a seatbelt. For drives in desolate areas, invest in a cellular phone and a roadside assistance program (see p. 33). Park your vehicle in a garage or well-traveled area, and use a steering wheel locking device in larger cities. **Sleeping in your car** is the most dangerous way to get your rest, and is illegal in many countries. For info on the perils of **hitchhiking,** see p. 36.

POSSESSIONS AND VALUABLES

Never leave your belongings unattended; crime occurs in even the most safe-looking hostel or hotel. Bring your own padlock for hostel lockers, and don't ever store valuables in a locker. Be particularly careful on **buses** and **trains;** horror stories abound about determined thieves who wait for travelers to fall asleep. Carry your bag or purse in front of you where you can see it. When traveling with others, sleep in alternate shifts. When alone, use good judgment in selecting a train compartment: never stay in an empty one, and use a lock to secure your pack to the luggage rack. Use extra caution when traveling at night or on overnight trains.

There are a few steps you can take to minimize the financial risk associated with traveling. First, **bring as little with you as possible.** Second, buy a few combination **padlocks** to secure your belongings either in your pack or in a hostel or train station locker. Third, **carry as little cash as possible.** Keep your traveler's checks and ATM/credit cards in a **money belt**—not a "fanny pack"—along with your passport and ID cards. Fourth, **keep a small cash reserve separate from your primary stash.** This should be about US$50 (US$ or Euros are best) sewn into or stored in the depths of your pack, along with your traveler's check numbers and photocopies of your passport, your birth certificate, and other important documents.

In large cities **con artists** often work in groups and may involve children. Beware of certain classics: sob stories that require money, rolls of bills "found" on the street, mustard spilled (or saliva spit) onto your shoulder to distract you while they snatch your bag. **Never let your passport and your bags out of your sight.** Hostel workers will sometimes stand at bus and train station arrival points to try to recruit tired and disoriented travelers to their hostel; never believe strangers who tell you that theirs is the only hostel open. Beware of **pickpockets** in city crowds, especially on public transportation.

PRE-DEPARTURE HEALTH

In your **passport,** write the names of any people you wish to be contacted in case of a medical emergency, and list any allergies or medical conditions. Matching a prescription to a foreign equivalent is not always safe or possible, so if you take prescription drugs, consider carrying up-to-date prescriptions. For tips on packing a **first-aid kit** and other health essentials, see p. 17.

IMMUNIZATIONS AND PRECAUTIONS

Travelers over two years old should make sure that the following vaccines are up to date: MMR (for measles, mumps, and rubella); DTaP or Td (for diphtheria, tetanus, and pertussis); IPV (for polio); Hib (for *haemophilus* influenza B); and HepB (for Hepatitis B). For recommendations on immunizations and prophylaxis, consult the Centers for Disease Control and Prevention (CDC; see p. 21) in the US or the equivalent in your home country, and check with a doctor for guidance.

INSURANCE

Travel insurance covers four basic areas: medical/health problems, property loss, trip cancellation/interruption, and emergency evacuation. Though regular insurance policies may well extend to travel-related accidents, you may consider purchasing separate travel insurance if the cost of potential trip cancellation, interruption, or emergency medical evacuation is greater than you can absorb. Prices for travel insurance purchased separately generally run about US$50 per week for full coverage, while trip cancellation/interruption may be purchased separately at a rate of US$3-5 per day depending on length of stay.

Medical insurance (especially university policies) often covers costs incurred when traveling abroad; check with your provider. **US Medicare** does not cover foreign travel. **Canadian** provincial health insurance increasingly does not cover foreign travel; check with your provincial Ministry of Health or Health Plan Headquarters for details. **Homeowners' insurance** (or your family's coverage) often covers theft during travel and loss of travel documents (passport, plane ticket, railpass, etc.) up to US$500.

ISIC and **ITIC** (see p. 11) provide basic insurance benefits to US cardholders, including US$100 per day of in-hospital sickness for up to 100 days and US$10,000 of accident-related medical reimbursement (see www.isicus.com for details). Cardholders have access to a toll-free 24hr. helpline for medical, legal, and financial emergencies overseas. **American Express** (☎800-338-1670) grants most cardholders collision and theft car rental insurance on rentals made with the card.

USEFUL ORGANIZATIONS AND PUBLICATIONS

The American **Centers for Disease Control and Prevention** (**CDC;** ☎877-FYI-TRIP; www.cdc.gov/travel) maintains an international travelers' hotline and an informative website. Consult the appropriate government agency for consular information on health, entry requirements, and other issues (see the listings in the box on **Travel Advisories,** p. 19). For quick information on health and travel warnings, call the **Overseas Citizens Services** (M-F 8am-8pm from US ☎888-407-4747, from overseas 202-501-4444), or contact a passport agency, embassy, or consulate abroad. For information on medical evacuation services and travel insurance firms, see the US government's website at http://travel.state.gov/travel/abroad_health.html or the **British Foreign and Commonwealth Office** (www.fco.gov.uk). For general health info, contact the **American Red Cross** (☎202-303-4498; www.redcross.org).

STAYING HEALTHY

ONCE IN GERMANY

ENVIRONMENTAL HAZARDS

Heat exhaustion and dehydration: Heat exhaustion leads to nausea, excessive thirst, headaches, and dizziness. Avoid it by drinking plenty of fluids, eating salty foods (e.g., crackers), abstaining from dehydrating beverages (e.g., alcohol and caffeinated beverages), and wearing sunscreen. Continuous heat stress can eventually lead to heatstroke, characterized by a rising temperature, severe headache, delirium, and cessation of sweating. Victims should be cooled off with wet towels and taken to a doctor.

Sunburn: If you get sunburned, drink more fluids than usual and apply an aloe-based lotion. Severe sunburns can lead to sun poisoning, a condition that can cause fever, chills, nausea, and vomiting. Sun poisoning should always be treated by a doctor.

Hypothermia and frostbite: A rapid drop in body temperature is the clearest sign of overexposure to cold. Victims may also shiver, feel exhausted, have poor coordination or slurred speech, hallucinate, or suffer amnesia. *Do not let hypothermia victims fall asleep.* To avoid hypothermia, keep dry, wear layers, and stay out of the wind. When the temperature is below freezing, watch out for frostbite. If skin turns white or blue, waxy, and cold, do not rub the area. Drink warm beverages, stay dry, and slowly warm the area with dry fabric or steady body contact until a doctor can be found.

High Altitude: Allow your body a couple of days to adjust to less oxygen before exerting yourself. This is particularly relevant in the mountainous regions of Germany.

INSECT-BORNE DISEASES

Many diseases are transmitted by insects—mainly mosquitoes, fleas, ticks, and lice. Be aware of insects in wet or forested areas, especially while hiking and camping; wear long pants and long sleeves, tuck your pants into your socks, and use a mosquito net. Use insect repellents such as DEET and soak or spray your gear with permethrin (licensed in the US only for use on clothing). **Mosquitoes**—responsible for malaria, dengue fever, and yellow fever—can be particularly abundant in wet, swampy, or wooded areas, but are not very common. **Ticks**—which can carry Lyme and other diseases—can be particularly dangerous in rural and forested regions, and are most menacing in southern Germany.

Tick-borne encephalitis: A viral infection of the central nervous system transmitted during the summer by tick bites (primarily in wooded areas) or by consumption of unpasteurized dairy products. The risk of contracting the disease is relatively low, especially if precautions are taken against tick bites. See **Lyme disease.**

Lyme disease: A bacterial infection carried by ticks and marked by a circular bull's-eye rash of 2 in. or more. Advanced symptoms include fever, headache, fatigue, and aches and pains. Antibiotics are effective if administered early. Left untreated, Lyme can cause problems in joints, the heart, and the nervous system. If you find a tick attached to your skin, grasp the head with tweezers as close to your skin as possible and apply slow, steady traction. Removing a tick within 24hr. greatly reduces the risk of infection. Do not try to remove ticks with petroleum jelly, nail polish remover, or a hot match. Ticks usually inhabit moist, shaded environments and heavily wooded areas.

Other insect-borne diseases: Lymphatic filariasis is a roundworm infestation transmitted by mosquitoes. Infection causes enlargement of extremities and has no vaccine. **Leishmaniasis,** a parasite transmitted by sand flies, can occur in Central and South America, Europe, Africa and the Middle East, and the Indian subcontinent, usually in rural rather than urban areas. Common symptoms are fever, weakness, and swelling of the spleen, as well as skin sores. There is a treatment, but no vaccine.

FOOD- AND WATER-BORNE DISEASES

Prevention is the best cure: be sure that your food is properly cooked and the water you drink is clean. German tap water is generally safe to drink except in the most polluted areas of the former DDR, though most Germans drink bottled mineral water. Peel and wash fruits and vegetables from street markets. Use your own judgment when it comes to *Imbiß* (snack bar) fare and food from street vendors—some places are cleaner than others. While there has been recent concern about vCJD (the human variant of BSE, or "Mad Cow Disease") throughout Europe, cases are extremely rare. Other culprits are raw shellfish, unpasteurized milk, and sauces containing raw eggs.

Traveler's diarrhea: Results from drinking fecally-contaminated water or eating uncooked and contaminated foods. Symptoms include nausea, bloating, and urgency. Try quick-energy, non-sugary foods with protein and carbohydrates to keep your strength up. Over-the-counter anti-diarrheals (e.g., Imodium) may counteract the problem. The most dangerous side effect is dehydration; drink 8 oz. of water with ½ tsp. of sugar or honey and a pinch of salt, try uncaffeinated soft drinks, or eat salted crackers. If you develop a fever or your symptoms don't go away after 4-5 days, consult a doctor. Do so immediately for treatment of diarrhea in children.

Giardiasis: Transmitted through parasites and acquired by drinking untreated water from streams or lakes. Symptoms include diarrhea, cramps, bloating, fatigue, weight loss, and nausea. If untreated it can lead to severe dehydration. Giardiasis occurs worldwide.

Leptospirosis: A bacterial disease caused by exposure to contaminated water or soil. It is most common in tropical climates but has been found in large German cities. Symptoms include a high fever, chills, nausea, and vomiting. If not treated it can lead to liver failure and meningitis. There is no vaccine; consult a doctor for treatment.

OTHER INFECTIOUS DISEASES

The following diseases exist in every part of the world. Travelers should know how to recognize them and what to do if they suspect they have been infected.

AIDS and HIV: For detailed information on Acquired Immune Deficiency Syndrome (AIDS) in Germany, call the US Centers for Disease Control's 24hr. hotline at ☎800-342-2437. Note that Germany screens incoming travelers for AIDS, primarily those planning extended visits for work or study, and may deny entrance to those who test HIV-positive. Contact the German consulate for information.

Sexually transmitted diseases (STDs): Gonorrhea, chlamydia, genital warts, syphilis, herpes, and other STDs are easier to catch than HIV and can be just as serious. Though condoms may protect you from some STDs, oral or even tactile contact can lead to transmission. If you think you may have contracted an STD, see a doctor immediately.

OTHER HEALTH CONCERNS

MEDICAL CARE ON THE ROAD

Germany has good medical care readily accessible to travelers. EU citizens in possession of an E11 form can get free first aid and emergency services. Travelers from outside the EU may visit private practitioners and pay on a per-visit basis (US$40 for a non-specialist visit is reasonable) for non-emergency situations.

If you are concerned about obtaining medical assistance while traveling, you may wish to employ special support services. The *MedPass* from **GlobalCare, Inc.,** 6875 Shiloh Rd. East, Alpharetta, GA 30005, USA (☎800-860-1111; www.global-care.net), provides 24hr. international medical assistance, support, and medical evacuation resources. The **International Association for Medical Assistance to Travelers (IAMAT;** US ☎716-754-4883, Canada 519 836 0102; www.iamat.org) has free membership, lists English-speaking doctors worldwide, and offers detailed info on immunization requirements and sanitation. If your regular **insurance** policy does not cover travel abroad, you may wish to purchase additional coverage (see p. 21).

Those with medical conditions (such as diabetes, allergies to antibiotics, epilepsy, or heart conditions) may want to obtain a **MedicAlert** membership (first-year US$35, US$20 annually thereafter), which includes among other things a stainless steel ID tag and a 24hr. collect-call number. Contact the MedicAlert Foundation, 2323 Colorado Ave., Turlock, CA 95382, USA (☎888-633-4298, outside US 209-668-3333; www.medicalert.org).

WOMEN'S HEALTH

Women traveling in unsanitary conditions are vulnerable to **urinary tract (including bladder and kidney) infections.** Over-the-counter medicines can sometimes alleviate symptoms, but if they persist, see a doctor. **Vaginal yeast infections** may flare up in hot and humid climates. Wearing loosely fitting trousers or a skirt and cotton underwear will help, as will over-the-counter remedies like Monistat or Gyne-Lotrimin. Bring supplies from home if you are prone to infection, as they may be difficult to find on the road. **Tampons, pads,** and **contraceptive devices** are widely available, though your favorite brand may not be stocked. First-trimester **abortion** is legal in Germany, but a three-day wait and counseling are required; contact **PRO FAMILIA Bundesverband** (a family parenthood group; www.profamilia.de).

GETTING TO GERMANY

BY PLANE

AIRFARES

Airfares to Germany peak between June and September; holidays are also expensive. Airfares are lowest in the winter. Midweek (M-Th morning) round-trip flights run US$40-50 cheaper than weekend flights, but they are generally more crowded and less likely to permit frequent-flier upgrades. Not fixing a return date ("open return") or arriving in and departing from different cities ("open-jaw") can be pricier than round-trip flights. Patching one-way flights together is the most expensive way to travel. Flights between Germany's capitals or regional hubs—Berlin, Frankfurt, Munich, Hamburg, and even Stuttgart—will tend to be cheaper.

If Germany is only one stop on a more extensive globe-hop, consider a round-the-world (RTW) ticket. Tickets usually include at least five stops and are valid for about a year; prices range US$1200-5000. Try **Northwest Airlines/KLM** (☎800-225-2525; www.nwa.com) or **Star Alliance,** a consortium of 16 airlines including United Airlines (www.staralliance.com).

Fares for roundtrip flights to German hubs from the US or Canadian east coast cost US$600-950, in winter US$350-550; from the US or Canadian west coast US$900-1400/750-1200; from the UK, UK₤20-100/10-75; from Australia AUS$1490-2000/1900-2600; from New Zealand NZ$2500-3500/2400-3000.

BUDGET AND STUDENT TRAVEL AGENCIES

While knowledgeable agents specializing in flights to Germany can make your life easy and help you save, they may not find you the lowest possible fare—they get paid on commission. Travelers holding **ISICs** and **IYTCs** (p. 11) qualify for discounts from travel agencies.

CTS Travel, 30 Rathbone Pl., London W1T 1GQ, UK (☎020 7447 5000; www.ctstravel.co.uk). A British student travel agent with offices in 39 countries including the US, Empire State Building, 350 Fifth Ave., Ste. 7813, New York, NY 10118 (☎877-287-6665; www.ctstravelusa.com).

STA Travel, 5900 Wilshire Blvd., Ste. 900, Los Angeles, CA 90036, USA (24hr. reservations and info ☎800-781-4040; www.statravel.com). A student and youth travel organization with over 150 offices worldwide (check their website for a listing of all their offices), including US offices in Boston, Chicago, L.A., New York, Seattle, San Francisco, and Washington, D.C. Ticket booking, travel insurance, railpasses, and more. Walk-in

FLIGHT PLANNING ON THE INTERNET. The Internet may be the budget traveler's dream when it comes to finding and booking bargain fares, but the array of options can be overwhelming.

Many airline sites offer special last-minute deals on the Web.**STA** (www.statravel.com) and **StudentUniverse** (www.studentuniverse.com) provide quotes on student tickets, while **Orbitz** (www.orbitz.com), **Expedia** (www.expedia.com), **Opodo** (www.opodo.com), and **Travelocity** (www.travelocity.com) offer full travel services. **Priceline** (www.priceline.com) lets you specify a price, and obligates you to buy any ticket that meets or beats it; **Hotwire** (www.hotwire.com) offers bargain fares, but won't reveal the airline or flight times until you buy. Other sites that compile travel deals include www.bestfares.com, www.flights.com, www.lowestfare.com, www.onetravel.com, and also www.travelzoo.com.

Increasingly, there are online tools available to help sift through multiple offers; **SideStep** (www.sidestep.com) and **Booking Buddy** (www.bookingbuddy.com) let you enter your trip information once and search multiple sites.

An indispensable resource on the Internet is the **Air Traveler's Handbook** (www.faqs.org/faqs/travel/air/handbook), a comprehensive listing of links to everything you need to know before you board a plane.

offices are located throughout Australia (☎03 9207 5900), New Zealand (☎09 309 9723), and the UK (☎08701 630 026).

Travel CUTS (Canadian Universities Travel Services Limited), 187 College St., Toronto, ON M5T 1P7, Canada (☎866-246-9762; www.travelcuts.com). Offices across Canada and the US including Los Angeles, New York, Seattle, and San Francisco.

USIT, 19-21 Aston Quay, Dublin 2, Ireland (☎01 602 1904; www.usit.ie), Ireland's leading student/budget travel agency has 20 offices throughout Northern Ireland and the Republic of Ireland. Offers programs to work, study, and volunteer worldwide.

Wasteels, Skoubogade 6, 1158 Copenhagen K., Denmark (☎3314 4633; www.wasteels.com). A huge chain with 180 locations across Europe. Sells Wasteels BIJ tickets discounted 30-45% off regular fare, 2nd-class international point-to-point train tickets with unlimited stopovers for those under 26 (sold only in Europe).

COMMERCIAL AIRLINES

The commercial airlines' lowest regular offer is the **APEX** (Advance Purchase Excursion) fare, which provides confirmed reservations and allows "open-jaw" tickets. Generally, reservations must be made seven to 21 days ahead of departure, with seven- to 14-day minimum-stay and up to 90-day maximum-stay restrictions. These fares carry hefty cancellation and change penalties. Book peak-season APEX fares early. Use **Expedia** (www.expedia.com) or **Travelocity** (www.travelocity.com) to get an idea of the lowest published fares, then use the resources outlined here to try and beat those fares. Low-season fares should be appreciably cheaper than the **high-season** (mid-June to Aug.) ones listed here.

TRAVELING FROM NORTH AMERICA

Basic round-trip fares to Germany range from roughly US$350-950: to Berlin, US$600-800; Munich, US$450-800; Frankfurt, US$350-750; Hamburg, US$550-900. Standard commercial carriers like American and United will probably offer the most convenient flights, but they may not be the cheapest, unless you manage to grab a special promotion.

AirIndia: (www.airindia.com). Flies primarily to Frankfurt.

Alitalia: (www.alitalia.com). Good timing, gets you to Frankfurt for rock-bottom prices.

IcelandAir: (www.icelandair.com). Offers promotional deals as well as low seasonal prices. Be wary of layovers lasting more than 12hr.

If direct flights to Germany from North America (or Australia or New Zealand) are prohibitively expensive, consider buying a seat on a cheaper flight to another European destination and using a discount carrier to complete your trip. In addition, a number of airlines—including those listed below—offer coupon packets for further travel within Europe available as tack-ons for transatlantic passengers.

Europe by Air: (US ☎888-321-4737; www.europebyair.com). *FlightPass* allows you to country-hop to over 150 European cities. US$99 per flight.

Iberia: (US ☎800-772-442; www.iberia.com). *Europass* allows passengers flying from the US to Spain to add 2 or more additional destinations in Europe. US$133 each.

TRAVELING FROM THE UK AND IRELAND

Because of the many carriers flying from the British Isles to the continent, we include only discount airlines or those with cheap specials here. The **Air Travel Advisory Bureau** in London (☎020 7306 3000; www.atab.co.uk) provides referrals to travel agencies and consolidators that offer discounted airfares out of the UK. Also consult the list of discount airlines in **Getting to Germany: By Plane** (p. 31).

Aer Lingus: Ireland ☎0818 365 000; www.aerlingus.ie. Return tickets as low as €40 from Cork, Dublin, Galway, Kerry, and Shannon to Düsseldorf, Frankfurt, and Munich.

British Midland Airways: UK ☎0870 607 05 55; www.flybmi.com. Departures from throughout the UK. London to Frankfurt UK£112 in the low season.

easyJet: UK ☎0871 244 2366; www.easyjet.com. Serves 72 destinations in Belgium, the Czech Republic, Denmark, Estonia, France, Germany, Greece, Hungary, Italy, Latvia, the Netherlands, Poland, Portugal, the Slovak Republic, Slovenia, Spain, Switzerland, and the UK.

KLM: UK ☎0870 507 40 74; www.klmuk.com. Cheap return tickets from London and elsewhere to Frankfurt and Düsseldorf.

Ryanair: Ireland ☎0818 303 030, UK 0871 246 0000 (UK£0.10 per min.); www.ryanair.com. From Dublin, London, and Glasgow to Berlin, Erfurt, Hahn (near Frankfurt), and Friedrichshafen. Deals from as low as UK£6 for flights on weekdays.

TRAVELING FROM AUSTRALIA AND NEW ZEALAND

Airfares Flights: www.airfaresflights.com.au/flights. Great promotional fares from Australia. Also operates sites for customers in the UK and US.

Quantas: Australia ☎02 9691 3636; www.quantas.com.au. Special deals from New Zealand to Europe.

Singapore Air: Australia ☎13 10 11, New Zealand 0800 808 909; www.singaporeair.com. Flies from Auckland, Sydney, Melbourne, and Perth to Western Europe and offers occasional special fares.

Thai Airways: Australia ☎1300 65 19 60, New Zealand 09 377 02 68; www.thaiair.com. Occasionally offers competitive deals to destinations worldwide.

AIR COURIER FLIGHTS

Those who travel light should consider courier flights. Couriers help transport cargo on international flights by using their checked luggage space for freight. Generally, couriers must travel with carry-ons only and deal with complex flight restrictions. Most flights are round-trip only, with short fixed-length stays (usually one week) and a limit of a one ticket per issue. The majority of flights also operate only out of major gateway cities, largely in North America, although some organizations offer courier fares from the UK, Australia, and New Zealand. Couriers are almost always required to be over 18, and in some cases over 21. In summer, the most popular destinations usually require an advance reservation of about two weeks; you can usually book up to two months ahead. Super-discounted fares are common for "last-minute" flights, and are usually available three to 14 days before departure.

FROM NORTH AMERICA

Round-trip courier fares from North America to Germany run about US$150-500. Most flights leave from Los Angeles, Miami, New York, or San Francisco in the US; and from Montreal, Toronto, or Vancouver in Canada. For an annual fee, the organizations below provide members with lists of opportunities and courier brokers.

Air Courier Association, 1767A Denver West Blvd., Golden, CO 80401 (☎800-211-5119; www.aircourier.org). From ten departure cities throughout the US and Canada to major destinations throughout Western Europe, including Frankfurt and Munich (US$130-420 round-trip). One-year membership US$49.

International Association of Air Travel Couriers (**IAATC;** www.courier.org). From 7 North American cities to Western European cities, including London, Madrid, Paris, and Rome. Does not currently offer direct flights to Germany, although cheap intra-continental flights are available on many European airlines. One-year membership US$45.

Courier Travel (www.couriertravel.org). Searchable online database. Multiple departure points in the US to various European destinations, including Berlin, Munich, and Frankfurt. One-time membership fee US$40.

FROM THE UK, AUSTRALIA, AND NEW ZEALAND

The **International Association of Air Travel Couriers** (www.courier.org) often offers courier flights from London to Sydney, and from Auckland to Frankfurt and London. **Courier Travel** (see above) offers flights from London and Sydney.

STANDBY FLIGHTS

Traveling standby requires considerable flexibility in arrival and departure dates and destinations. Companies dealing in standby flights sell vouchers rather than tickets, along with the promise to get you to your destination (or near your destination) within a certain window of time (typically 1-5 days). You call before your specific window of time to hear your flight options and the probability that you will be able to board each flight. You can then decide which flights you want to try to make, show up at the airport at the appropriate time, present your voucher, and board if space is available. Vouchers can usually be bought for both one-way and round-trip travel. You may receive a monetary refund only if every available flight within your date range is full; if you opt not to take an available (but less convenient) flight, you can only get credit toward future travel. Carefully read agreements with any company offering standby flights as fine print can leave you in the lurch. To check a company's service record in the US, contact the **Better Business Bureau** (☎703-276-0100; www.bbb.org).

TICKET CONSOLIDATORS

Ticket consolidators, or **"bucket shops,"** buy unsold tickets in bulk from commercial airlines and sell them at discounted rates. The best place to look is in the Sunday travel section of any major newspaper (such as *The New York Times*), where many bucket shops place tiny ads. Call quickly, as availability is typically extremely limited. Not all bucket shops are reliable, so insist on a receipt that gives full details of restrictions, refunds, and tickets, and pay by credit card (in spite of the 2-5% fee) so you can stop payment if you never receive your tickets. For more info, see www.travel-library.com/air-travel/consolidators.html.

TRAVELING FROM THE US AND CANADA

Some consolidators worth trying are **Rebel** (☎ 800-732-3588; www.rebeltours.com), **Cheap Tickets** (www.cheaptickets.com), **Flights.com** (www.flights.com), and **Travel-HUB** (www.travelhub.com). These are just suggestions to get you started in your research; Let's Go does not endorse any of these agencies. As always, be cautious, and research companies before you hand over your credit card number.

CHARTER FLIGHTS

Tour operators contract charter flights with airlines in order to fly extra loads of passengers during peak season. These flights are far from hassle free. They occur less frequently than major airlines, make refunds particularly difficult, and are almost always fully booked. Their scheduled times may change and they may be cancelled at the last moment (as late as 48 hours before the trip, and without a full refund). And check-in, boarding, and baggage claim for charter flights are often drastically slower. They can, however, be much cheaper than standard flights.

Discount clubs and fare brokers offer members savings on last-minute charter and tour deals. Study contracts closely; you don't want to end up with an unwanted overnight layover. **Travelers Advantage** (☎ 800-835-8747; www.travelersadvantage.com; US$90 annual fee includes discounts and cheap flight directories) specializes in European travel and tour packages.

BY TRAIN

German trains are generally comfortable, convenient, and reasonably swift. Second-class compartments, which seat two to six, are great places to meet fellow travelers. Trains, however, are not always safe; for safety tips, see p. 19. For long trips, make sure you are on the correct car, as trains sometimes split at crossroads. Towns listed in parentheses on European train schedules require a train switch at the town listed immediately before the parenthesis.

You can either buy a **railpass**, which allows you unlimited travel within a region for a given period of time, or rely on buying individual **point-to-point** tickets. Almost all countries give students or youths (usually defined as anyone under 26) discounts on domestic rail tickets, and many also sell a student or youth card that provides 20-50% off all fares for up to a year.

RESERVATIONS. While seat reservations are required only for selected trains (usually on major lines), you are not guaranteed a seat without one (usually US$5-30). You should strongly consider reserving in advance during peak holiday and tourist seasons (at the very latest, a few hours ahead). You will also have to purchase a **supplement** (US$10-50) or special fare for high-speed or high quality trains such as Germany's ICE. InterRail holders must also purchase supplements (US$3-20) for trains like EuroCity and InterCity; supplements are often unnecessary for Eurailpass and Europass holders.

OVERNIGHT TRAINS. On night trains, you won't waste valuable daylight hours traveling and you can avoid the expense of staying at a hotel. However, the main drawbacks include discomfort, sleepless nights, and the lack of scenery. Passengers on overnight trains also face greater vulnerability to theft and assault. **Sleeping accommodations** on trains differ from country to country, but typically you can either sleep upright in your seat (supplement about $2-10) or pay for a separate space. **Couchettes** (berths) typically have four to six seats per compartment (supplement about US$10-50 per person); **sleepers** (beds) in private sleeping cars offer more privacy and comfort, but are considerably more expensive (supplement US$40-150). If you are using a railpass valid only for a restricted number of days, inspect train schedules to maximize the use of your pass: an overnight train or boat journey often uses up only one of your travel days if it departs after 7pm.

SHOULD YOU BUY A RAILPASS? Railpasses were conceived to allow you to jump on any train in Europe, go wherever you want whenever you want, and change your plans at will. In practice, it's not so simple. You still must stand in line to validate your pass, pay for supplements, and fork over cash for seat and couchette reservations. More importantly, railpasses don't always pay off. If you are planning to spend extensive time on trains, hopping between big cities, a railpass will probably be worth it. But in many cases, especially if you are under 26, point-to-point tickets may prove a cheaper option.

MULTINATIONAL RAILPASSES

EURAIL PASSES. Eurail is **valid** in most of Western Europe: Austria, Belgium, Denmark, Finland, France, Germany, Greece, Hungary, Italy, Liechtenstein, Luxembourg, the Netherlands, Norway, Portugal, the Republic of Ireland, Spain, Sweden, and Switzerland. It is **not valid** in the UK. Standard **Eurailpasses**, valid for a given consecutive number of days, are best for those planning on spending extensive time on trains every few days. **Eurailpass Flexi,** valid for any 10 or 15 (not necessarily consecutive) days within a two-month period, is more cost-effective for those traveling longer distances less frequently. **Eurailpass Saver** provides first-class travel for travelers in groups of two or more (prices are per person). **Eurailpass Youth** and **Eurailpass Youth Flexi** provide second-class perks for those under 26.

EURAILPASSES	15 DAYS	21 DAYS	1 MONTH	2 MONTHS	3 MONTHS
1st class Eurailpass	US$605	US$785	US$975	US$1378	US$1703
Eurailpass Saver	US$513	US$668	US$828	US$1173	US$1450
Eurailpass Youth	US$394	US$510	US$634	US$896	US$1108

EURAILPASS FLEXI		10 DAYS IN 2 MONTHS	15 DAYS IN 2 MONTHS
1st class Eurailpass Flexi		US$715	US$940
Eurailpass Saver Flexi		US$608	US$800
Eurailpass Youth Flexi		US$465	US$611

Passholders receive a timetable for major routes and a map with details on possible bike rental, car rental, hotel, and museum discounts. Passholders often also receive reduced fares or free passage on many boat, bus, and private railroad lines.

The **Eurail Selectpass** is a slimmed-down version of the Eurailpass: it allows five to 15 days of unlimited travel in any two-month period within three, four, or five bordering countries. Eurail Selectpasses (for individuals) and **Eurail Selectpass Savers** (for people traveling in groups of 2 or more) range from US$383/325 per person (5 days) to US$850/723 (15 days). The **Eurail Selectpass Youth,** for those aged 12-25, costs US$249-553. You are entitled to the same **freebies** afforded by the Eurailpass, but only when they are within or between countries that you have purchased.

SHOPPING AROUND FOR A EURAIL. Eurailpasses are designed by the EU itself, and can be bought only by non-Europeans almost exclusively from non-European distributors. These passes must be sold at uniform prices determined by the EU. However, some travel agents tack on a US$10 handling fee, and others offer certain bonuses with purchase, so shop around. Also, keep in mind that pass prices usually go up each year, so if you're planning to travel early in the year, you can save cash by purchasing before January 1 (you have three months from the purchase date to validate your pass in Europe).

It is best to buy your Eurail before leaving; only a few places in major European cities sell them, and at a marked-up price. You can get a replacement for a lost pass only if you purchased insurance on it under the Pass Security Plan (US$12). Eurailpasses are available through travel agents, **Rail Europe** (Canada ☎800-361-7245, US 888-382-7245; www.raileurope.com), **Flight Centre** (866-967-5351; www.flightcentre.com), and student travel agencies like STA (see p. 24). It is also possible to buy directly from Eurail's website, www.eurail.com.

INTER RAIL PASSES. If you have lived for at least six months in one of the European countries where Inter Rail Passes are valid, they prove an economical option. The Inter Rail pass allows travel within 30 European countries (excluding the passholder's country of residence), which are divided into eight zones. Passes may be purchased for one, two, or all eight zones. The one-zone pass (€286, under 26 €195) is good for 16 days of travel, the two-zone pass (€396, under 26 €275) is good for 22 days of travel, and the global pass (8 zones; €546, under 26 €385) is valid for a full month. Passholders receive free admission to many museums, as well as discounts on accommodations, food, and many ferries to Ireland, Scandinavia, and the rest of Europe. Passes are available at www.interrailnet.com, as well as from travel agents, at major train stations throughout Europe, and through online vendors (www.railpassdirect.co.uk).

FURTHER READING & RESOURCES ON TRAIN TRAVEL

Info on rail travel and railpasses: www.raileurope.com.

Point-to-point fares and schedules: www.raileurope.com/us/rail/fares_schedules/index.htm. Allows you to calculate whether buying a railpass would save you money.

Railsaver: www.railpass.com/new. Uses your itinerary to determine the best railpass for your trip.

European Railway Server: www.railfaneurope.net. Links to rail servers throughout Europe.

Thomas Cook European Timetable, updated monthly, covers all major and most minor train routes in Europe. Buy directly from Thomas Cook (www.thomas-cooktimetables.com).

Independent Travellers Europe by Rail 2005: The Inter-railer's and Eurailer's Guide. Thomas Cook Publishing (US$19.95).

BY BUS

Though European trains and railpasses are extremely popular, in some cases buses are better option. Amsterdam, Athens, Istanbul, London, Munich, and Oslo are centers for private bus lines that offer long-distance rides across Europe. Often cheaper than railpasses, **international bus passes** allow unlimited travel between major European cities. The prices below are based on high-season travel.

Eurolines, 4 Vicarage Rd., Edgbaston, Birmingham B15 3ES, UK (☎08705 143 219; www.eurolines.com). The largest operator of Europe-wide coach services. Unlimited 15-day (high season UK£195, under 26 and over 60 UK£165; low season UK£149/129); 30-day (high season UK£290/235; low season UK£209/169); or 60-day (high season UK£333/259; low season UK£265/211) travel passes that offer unlimited transit between 35 major European cities.

Busabout, 258 Vauxhall Bridge Rd., London SW1V 1BS, UK (☎0207 950 1661; www.busabout.com). Offers 5 interconnecting bus circuits covering 60 cities and towns in Europe. Unlimited (consecutive-day) Passes, Flexipasses, and Add On Passes are available. Unlimited standard/student passes are valid for 2wk. (US$469/419), 4 weeks (US$739/659), 6wk. (US$919/819), 8wk. (US$1049/939), 12wk. (US$1319/1179), or for the season (US$1649/1469).

 EUROPEAN BORDER CROSSINGS. Thanks to the EU's **freedom of movement** policy, travel within the Schengen Zone is effectively borderless; see **One Europe** (p. 10) for more information. For those moving between Germany and the Czech Republic, see p. 637.

GETTING AROUND GERMANY

BY PLANE

With one-way flights averaging about US$80, it's never been faster or easier to jet set across Germany. In addition to the airlines listed below, **RyanAir** and **easyJet** (p. 26) run flights between German destinations.

Air Berlin: (UK ☎0870 738 88 80; www.airberlin.com). Serves Berlin, Bremen, Cologne/Bonn, Dortmund, Dresden, Düsseldorf, Erfurt, Frankfurt, Hamburg, Hanover, Karlsruhe/Baden-Baden, Leipzig, Münster/Osnabrück, Munich, Nuremberg, Paderborn, Rostock/Laage, Saarbrücken, Stuttgart, and over 50 other destinations across Europe.

Deutsche BA: (Germany ☎01805 35 93 22; www.deutscheba.de). Serves Berlin, Bremen, Cologne/Bonn, Düsseldorf, Dresden, Frankfurt, Hamburg, Hanover, Munich, Nuremberg, and Stuttgart; limited service to other European destinations.

Germania: (Germany ☎01805 73 71 00; www.gexx.de). Service to Berlin, Bremen, Cologne/Bonn, Düsseldorf, Frankfurt, Hamburg, Hanover, Munich, and Stuttgart, as well as 18 other destinations across Europe.

germanwings: (Germany ☎01805 95 58 55; www.germanwings.com). Flights to Berlin, Cologne/Bonn, Düsseldorf, Dresden, Hamburg, Leipzig/Halle, Munich, and Stuttgart, and dozens of other European cities.

Hapag-Lloyd Express: (Germany ☎0180 509 35 09; www.hlx.com). Serves Berlin, Cologne/Bonn, Hamburg, Hanover, Leipzig, Munich, Stuttgart, and 25 other European destinations.

The **Star Alliance European Airpass** offers economy class fares as low as US$65 for travel within Europe to more than 200 destinations in 43 countries. The pass is available to transatlantic passengers on Star Alliance carriers, including Air Canada, BMI British Midland, Lufthansa, and United Airlines, as well as on certain partner airlines. See www.staralliance.com for more information.

BY TRAIN OR BUS

RAILPASSES AND DISCOUNTED FARES

BASIC DISCOUNTS. Deutsche Bahn, the national German rail company, offers some terrific discounts to travelers. **Groups of at least six** can save up to 70% by reserving in advance, and **children** up to age 14 ride free with a guardian. Buyers who purchase tickets at least three days in advance are eligible for the **Sparpreis25** or **Sparpreis50** discounts: Sparpreis25 offers a 25% discount, while Sparpreis50 affords a 50% discount on trips that leave and return on a weekend.

DEUTSCHE BAHN PASS. Designed for tourists, the railpass allows unlimited travel for four to 10 days within a month. Non-Europeans can purchase Deutsche Bahn Railpasses in their home countries and—with a passport—in major German train stations. A second-class railpass costs €160 for four days of unlimited travel and €20 per extra day. The **German Rail Youth Pass,** for tourists under 26, costs €130 for four days and €10 per extra day. The second-class **Twin Pass,** for two adults traveling together, is €240 for four days and €30 per extra day.

BAHNCARD. A great option for those making frequent and extensive use of German trains for more than one month, the **Bahncard25** is valid for one year and entitles you to a 25% discount on all trains (even on already-discounted tickets). Passes are available at major train stations and require a passport-sized photo and mailing address in Germany. A second-class card costs €51.50. A newer **Bahncard50**, offering 50% discounts on tickets, now costs €206 (€103 for students up to 26 years old and senior over 60). Bahncard holders can upgrade to **Railplus** and earn 25% rail discounts across Europe for an additional €15.

REGIONAL TICKETS. Deutsche Bahn offers two regional tickets: **Happy Weekend Tickets** enable up to five adults to travel together on local trains on any single Saturday or Sunday for €30, and **Länder-Tickets** grant up to five adults unlimited travel on a single day within any one of Germany's *Länder*, or provinces (€22-29).

PRAGUE EXCURSION PASS. A useful purchase for holders of Eurail and German Rail passes—neither of which are valid in the Czech Republic—the **Prague Excursion Pass** covers round-trip travel from any Czech border to Prague and back out of the country within a period of seven days (2nd-class US$75, under 26 US$60). Available from **RailEurope** (p. 29) and from travel agencies.

RAIL-AND-DRIVE PASSES. RailEurope offers rail-and-drive passes, which combine two days of car rental with two days of rail travel. Prices range from US$155-320 per person, depending on the type of pass, type of car, number of people traveling, and ticket vendor, so shop around. Additional second-class rail days cost US$51, while extra car rental days run US$49-95.

BUS TRAVEL

The few parts of Germany that are inaccessible by train can often be reached by bus, which can be slightly more expensive than trains for comparable distances. Service between cities and outlying areas runs from the local main bus station, the **Zentralomnibusbahnhof (ZOB),** which is usually near the main train station.

Although **Eurolines** (see **Getting to Germany: By Bus,** p. 30) mostly offers travel between countries, its German routes include Berlin-Hanover and Frankfurt-Munich, as well as routes covering the Romantic Road, Castle Road, and Strasbourg-Reitlingen (Black Forest), all of which are offered through Eurolines' German subsidiary **Deutsche Touring GmbH** (www.deutsche-touring.de).

BY CAR

Cars—especially German cars—offer speed, freedom, access to the countryside, and an escape from the town-to-town mentality of trains. Although a single traveler won't save by renting a car, four usually will. If you can't decide between train and car travel, you may benefit from a combination of the two; some railpass vendors offer rail-and-drive packages (see **Rail-and-Drive Passes**). Fly-and-drive pack-ages are available from travel agents, airlines, and rental agencies.

Before setting off, familiarize yourself with Germany's strictly-enforced driving laws and customs (e.g., although the famed German **Autobahn** (highway) has no official speed limit, drivers traveling in the left lane are expected to change lanes to let faster cars pass). For an informal primer on European road signs and con-ventions, check out www.travlang.com/signs. The **Association for Safe International Road Travel (ASIRT)**, 11769 Gainsborough Rd., Potomac, MD 20854, USA (☎301-983-5252; www.asirt.org), can provide specific information about road conditions.

DRIVING PERMITS AND CAR INSURANCE

INTERNATIONAL DRIVING PERMIT (IDP)

If you plan to drive, you must be over 18 and have a valid driver's license accompa-nied by an International Driving Permit (IDP), an official 10-language translation of your license recognized across the world. Foreign licenses are acceptable for six months after entering Germany, after which a German license is required.

Your IDP, valid for one year, must be issued in your own country before you depart. An application for an IDP usually requires one or two passport-size photos, a current local license, an additional form of identification, and a fee. To apply, contact your home country's automobile association. Be careful when purchasing an IDP online or anywhere other than your home automobile association. Many vendors sell permits of questionable legitimacy for higher prices.

CAR INSURANCE

Many credit cards cover standard insurance, although coverage can be limited or nonexistent overseas (see **Renting: Costs and Insurance**). If you rent, lease, or bor-row a car, you will need a **Green Card,** or **international Insurance Certificate,** to cer-tify that you have liability insurance and that it applies abroad. Green cards can be obtained at car rental agencies, car dealers (for those leasing cars), some travel agents, and some border crossings. Rental agencies may require you to purchase theft insurance in countries that they consider to have a high risk of auto theft.

RENTING

Next to other European countries, the auto-obsessed nation of Germany offers rel-atively affordable car rental. Still, you should expect to pay a pretty penny for the independence of your own ride—factoring insurance and fees for automatic trans-mission into the cost of car rental means that you'll almost certainly be paying at least US$40 per day.

RENTAL AGENCIES

You can generally make reservations before you leave by calling major interna-tional offices in your home country. However, occasionally the price and availabil-ity information they give doesn't jive with what the local offices in your country will tell you. Try checking with both numbers to make sure you get the best price and accurate information. Local desk numbers are included in town listings; for home-country numbers, call your toll-free directory.

To rent a car from most establishments in Germany, you need to be at least 21 years old. Some agencies require renters to be 25, and most charge a "young driver surcharge" to those 24 and under. Rental agencies in Germany include:

Auto Europe: US and Canada ☎888-223-5555; www.autoeurope.com.

Avis: Australia ☎136 333; New Zealand 0800 655111; UK 0870 60 60 100; US/Can-ada 800-331-1212; www.avis.com.

ESSENTIALS

Budget: Australia ☎ 1300 362 848; Canada 800-268-8900; New Zealand 0800 283 438; UK 8701 565656; US 800-527-0700; www.budgetrentacar.com.

Europe by Car: US ☎ 800-223-1516; www.europebycar.com.

Europcar International: US and Canada ☎ 877-940-6900; UK 870 607 5000; www.europcar.com.

Hertz: US ☎ 800-654-3131; www.hertz.com.

Kemwel: US ☎ 877-820-0668; www.kemwel.com.

COSTS AND INSURANCE

Rental car prices start at around US$40 per day from national companies. Expect to pay more for larger cars and for 4WD. Cars with **automatic transmission** can cost substantially more than cars with manual transmission (stick shift), and in some places, automatic transmission (especially 4WD) is hard to find in the first place.

Many rental packages offer unlimited kilometers, while others offer a limited number of kilometers per day with a surcharge per kilometer after that. Return the car with a full tank of gasoline (petrol) to avoid high fuel charges at the end. Be sure to ask whether the price includes **insurance** against theft and collision. Remember that if you are driving a conventional rented vehicle on an **unpaved road,** you are almost never covered by insurance; ask about this before leaving the rental agency. Be aware that cars rented on an **American Express** or **Visa/MasterCard Gold** or **Platinum** credit card in Germany might *not* carry the automatic insurance that they would in your home countries; check with your credit card company. Insurance plans from rental companies almost always come with an **excess** of around €5000 for conventional vehicles; excess ranges up to around €20,000 for younger drivers and for 4WD vehicles. Some rental companies in Germany require you to buy a **Collision Damage Waiver (CDW),** which will reduce or waive the excess in the case of an accident. **Loss Damage Waivers (LDWs)** do the same in the case of theft or vandalism.

LEASING OR BUYING A CAR

For longer stays, leasing can be less expensive than renting; it is often the only option for those ages 18 to 21. The cheapest leases are agreements to buy the car and then sell it back to the manufacturer at a prearranged price; despite the word "buy," these plans do not entail enormous financial transactions. Leases generally include insurance coverage and are not taxed. Expect to pay around US$1100-1800 (depending on size of car) for 60 days. Contact **Auto Europe, Europe by Car,** or **Kemwel** (p. 33) before you go. If you're brave and know what you're doing, **buying** a used car or van in Germany and selling it just before you leave can provide the cheapest wheels for longer trips. You must show proof of insurance before registering or driving your car.

ON THE ROAD

There is no set speed limit on the **Autobahn,** only a recommendation of 130km per hour (81mph). In the car, Germans know only one word: *fast.* Watch for signs indicating right-of-way (usually designated by a yellow triangle). The Autobahn is indicated by an intuitive "A" on signs; secondary highways, where the speed limit is usually 100km per hour (60mph), are accompanied by signs bearing a "B." Germans drive on the right side of the road, and it is always illegal to pass on the right. If a car is coming up behind you in the left lane of the Autobahn, you are expected to move to the right to let the other driver pass you safely. In cities and towns, speeds hover around 30-60kph (18-36mph). Wearing a **seatbelt** is the law in Germany, and children should sit in the rear seat; children under 40 lb. (17kg) should ride only in a specially-designed carseat, available from most car rental agencies. **The legal maximum for blood-alcohol levels is 0.08%.** German police strictly enforce driving laws, and German motorists observe them almost religiously.

> **DRIVING PRECAUTIONS.** When traveling in the summer, bring substantial amounts of **water** (a suggested 5L per person per day) for drinking and for the radiator. For long drives to unpopulated areas, register with police before beginning the trek, and again upon arrival at the destination. Check with the **ADAC** (p. 35) for details. When traveling for long distances, make sure tires are in good repair and have enough air. Bring thorough maps. A **compass** and a **car manual** can also be very useful. You should always carry a **spare tire** and **jack, jumper cables, extra oil, flares,** a **flashlight,** and **heavy blankets** (in case your car breaks down at night or in the winter). If you don't know how to **change a tire,** learn before heading out, especially if you are planning on traveling in lightly-populated areas. Blowouts on dirt roads are exceedingly common. If you do have a breakdown, **stay in your car,** where you'll be most visible.

CAR ASSISTANCE

The **Allgemeiner Deutscher Automobil Club** (ADAC; www.adac.de) is Europe's largest automobile association, offering support to motorists across Germany. Members of partner associations across the world (including the American and Canadian Automobile Associations) can contact the ADAC for emergency assistance (☎0180 222 22 22), although non-German speakers would likely be better served by calling the international helplines of their home organizations.

BY BICYCLE

With a mountain bike, you can do some serious natural sightseeing. Many airlines will count your bike as your second free piece of luggage; a few charge extra (around US$80 one-way). Bikes must be packed in a cardboard box with the pedals and front wheel detached; many airlines sell bike boxes at the airport (US$15-25). Most ferries let you take your bike for free or for a nominal fee, and you can always bring your bike on trains. Some youth hostels rent bicycles for low prices, and Deutsche Bahn often rents bikes at train stations. In addition to **panniers** (US$10-40) to hold your luggage, you'll need a good **helmet** (US$15-50) and a **sturdy lock** (from US$25). For country-specific books on biking through France, Germany, Ireland, and the UK, try **Mountaineers Books,** 1001 S.W. Klickitat Way, Ste. 201, Seattle, WA 98134, USA (☎206-223-6303; www.mountaineersbooks.org).

Blue Marble Travel (Canada ☎519-624-2494, US 215-923-3788; www.bluemarble.org) offers small-group bike tours for ages 20 to 49 in Europe, including one that works its way through northwestern Germany. **CBT Tours,** 2506 N. Clark St. #150, Chicago, IL 60614, USA (☎800-736-2453; www.cbttours.com), offers full-package culinary, biking, hiking, and sightseeing tours (US$2000-2500) to Germany.

BY MOPED AND MOTORCYCLE

Motorized bikes and **mopeds** don't use much gas, can be put on trains and ferries, and are a good compromise between costly car travel and the limited range of bicycles. However, they're uncomfortable for long distances, dangerous in the rain, and unpredictable on rough roads. Always wear a helmet, and never ride with a backpack. Expect to pay about US$20-35 per day; try auto repair shops, and remember to bargain. **Motorcycles** are more expensive and normally require a license, but are better for long distances. Before renting, ask if the price includes tax and insurance, or you may be hit with an unexpected fee.

BY FOOT

The very best of Germany can be seen only by foot. *Let's Go: Germany* features many daytrips, but native inhabitants, hostel proprietors, and fellow travelers are the best source for tips. Germany has many hiking and mountaineering groups, and alpine clubs provide simple accommodations in splendid settings. For more info on Germany's National Parks, see the **Mountains and Mudflats Itinerary,** p. 7.

BY THUMB

 Let's Go never recommends hitchhiking as a safe means of transportation, and none of the information presented here is intended to do so.

No one should hitchhike without careful consideration of the risks involved. Hitching means entrusting your life to a random stranger who happens to stop beside you on the road and risking theft, assault, sexual harassment, and unsafe driving. Hitchhiking at night can be particularly dangerous; experienced hitchers stand in well-lit places. For women traveling alone (or even in pairs), hitching is just too dangerous. A man and a woman are a less dangerous combination. Two men will have a harder time getting a lift; three men will go nowhere. Experienced hitchers pick a spot outside of built-up areas, where drivers can stop, return to the road without causing an accident, and have time to look over potential passengers as they approach. Hitching (or even standing) on the Autobahn itself is illegal: one may only thumb at rest stops or entrance ramps. Finally, success will depend on appearance. Drivers prefer hitchers who are neat and wholesome-looking.

Germany does have a ride-share service, known as the **Verband der Deutschen Mitfahrzentralen,** which pairs drivers with riders; the fee varies according to destination. Not all organizations screen drivers and riders; ask in advance. **Mitfahrzentrale** offices are listed under the **Transportation** header of most large cities. The central website (in German; www.mitfahrzentrale.de) has more information.

KEEPING IN TOUCH

BY EMAIL AND INTERNET

Internet is widely available in Germany, in both wireless and conventionally wired forms. Many hostels offer both, for a fee, and Internet cafés dot many street corners. Expect to pay anywhere from €1-6 per hr. for Internet access; wireless connections are generally more affordable.

Though in some places it's possible to forge a remote link with your home server, in most cases this is a much slower (and thus more expensive) option than taking advantage of free **web-based email accounts** (e.g., www.hotmail.com and www.yahoo.com). **Internet cafés** and the occasional free Internet terminal at a public library or university are listed in the **Practical Information** sections of major cities. For lists of additional cybercafés in Germany, check out www.cybercaptive.com and www.netcafeguide.com.

Increasingly, travelers find that taking their **laptop computers** on the road can be a convenient option for staying connected. Laptop users may also find Internet cafés that allow them to connect their laptops to the Internet. And most excitingly, travelers with wireless-enabled computers may be able to take advantage of an increasing number of **Internet hotspots,** where they can get online for free or for a small fee. Newer computers can detect these hotspots automatically; otherwise, websites like www.jiwire.com, www.wififreespot.com, and www.wi-fihotspot-list.com can help you find them.

BY TELEPHONE

CALLING HOME FROM GERMANY

 PLACING INTERNATIONAL CALLS. To call Germany from home or to call home from Germany, dial the:

1. **International dialing prefix.** To call from **Australia,** dial 0011; **Canada** or the **US,** 011; **Ireland, New Zealand,** or the **UK,** 00; **Germany,** 00.
2. **Country code** of the country you want to call. To call **Australia,** dial 61; **Canada** or the **US,** 1; **Ireland,** 353; **New Zealand,** 64; the **UK,** 44; **Germany,** 49.
3. **City/area code.** Let's Go: Germany lists the city/area codes for cities and towns in Germany opposite the city or town name, next to a ☎. If the 1st digit is a zero (e.g., 020 for London), omit the zero when calling from abroad (e.g., dial 011 20 from Canada to reach London, not 011 020).
4. **Local number.**

You can usually make **direct international calls** from pay phones, but if you aren't using a phone card, you may need to drop your coins as quickly as your words. **Prepaid phone cards** are a relatively inexpensive means of calling abroad. Each one comes with a Personal Identification Number (PIN) and a toll-free access number. You call the access number and follow the directions for dialing your PIN. To purchase prepaid phone cards, check online for the best rates; www.callingcards.com is a good place to start. Online providers generally send your access number and PIN via email, with no actual "card" involved. You can also call home with prepaid phone cards purchased in Germany (see **Calling Within Germany,** p. 38).

Another option is to purchase a **calling card,** linked to a major national telecommunications service in your home country. Calls are billed collect or to your account. To obtain a calling card, contact the appropriate company listed in the table below. Where available, there are often advantages to purchasing calling cards online, including better rates and immediate access to your account. To call home with a calling card, contact the operator for your service provider in Germany by dialing the appropriate toll-free access number (listed in the third column of the table below).

COMPANY	TO OBTAIN A CARD:	TO CALL ABROAD:
AT&T (US)	800-364-9292 or www.att.com	0800 225 5288
Canada Direct	800-561-8868 or www.infocanadadirect.com	0800 888 0014
MCI (US)	800-777-5000 or www.minutepass.com	0800 888 8000
Telecom New Zealand Direct	www.telecom.co.nz	0800 654 210
Telstra Australia	1800 676 638 or www.telstra.com	0800 0800 061

Placing a **collect call** through an international operator can be quite expensive, but may be necessary in case of an emergency.

CALLING WITHIN GERMANY

The simplest way to call within the country is to use either a card- or coin-operated phone. **Prepaid phone cards** (available at newsstands, tobacco stores, and call shops) carry a certain amount of phone time depending on the card's denomination and are generally cost-effective. Phone displays will tell you how much time you have left on your card each time you place a call. These cards can be used to make international and domestic calls.

CELLULAR PHONES

Cell phone retailers are ubiquitous across Germany, and competition among service providers is fierce. German cell phone companies offer two types of service plans: **contract plans,** which offer you a set number of minutes per month for a preset price, and **prepay plans,** which enable you to buy minutes as you use them.

The international standard for cell phones is **Global System for Mobile Communication (GSM).** To make and receive calls in Germany you will need a **GSM-compatible phone** and a **SIM (Subscriber Identity Module) card,** a country-specific, thumbnail-sized chip that gives you a local phone number and plugs you into the local network. Many SIM cards are **prepaid,** meaning they come with calling time included and don't require a monthly plan. **Incoming calls are free.** When you use up the prepaid time, you can buy additional cards or vouchers (available at convenience stores and call shops). For more info on GSM phones, check out www.telestial.com, www.roadpost.com, or www.planetomni.com. Companies like **Cellular Abroad** (www.cellularabroad.com) rent cell phones that work in a variety of destinations, providing a simpler option than picking up a phone in-country; for substantial stays, however, buying a GSM cell phone is a more economical option.

TIP | **GSM PHONES.** Just having a GSM phone doesn't mean you're necessarily good to go when you travel abroad. The majority of GSM phones sold in the United States operate on a different **frequency** (1900) than international phones (900/1800) and will not work abroad. Tri-band phones work on all three frequencies (900/1800/1900) and will operate through most of the world. In addition, some GSM phones are **SIM-locked** and will only accept SIM cards from a single carrier, or from affiliated carriers overseas. You'll need a **SIM-unlocked** phone to use a SIM card from a local carrier when you travel.

TIME DIFFERENCES

Germany is one hour ahead of Greenwich Mean Time (GMT), and observes Daylight Saving Time from late March through late October. The following table relates Germany and other localities at noon GMT.

4AM	5AM	6AM	7AM	NOON	1PM	10PM
Vancouver	Denver	Chicago	New York	London	**BERLIN**	Sydney
Seattle			Boston		Paris	Canberra
San Francisco			Toronto		Rome	Melbourne
Los Angeles					Prague	

BY MAIL

SENDING MAIL HOME FROM GERMANY

Airmail is the best way to send mail home from Germany. **Aerogrammes,** printed sheets that fold into envelopes and travel via airmail, are available at post offices.

Write "par avion," or "*luftpost*" on the front. Most post offices will charge exorbitant fees or simply refuse to send *aerogrammes* with enclosures. **Surface mail** is by far the cheapest and slowest way to send mail. It takes one to two months to cross the Atlantic and one to three to cross the Pacific—good for heavy items you won't need for a while, such as souvenirs or other articles weighing down your pack. These are standard rates for mail from Germany to:

Australia, Canada, New Zealand, and the US: Allow 4-10 days for regular airmail home. Postcards/*aerogrammes* cost €1. Letters up to 20g cost €1.70; packages up to 0.5kg €12, up to 2kg €36.

Ireland and UK: Allow 3-6 days for regular airmail home. Postcards/aerogrammes cost €0.65. Letters up to 20g cost €0.70; packages up to 0.5kg €6, up to 2kg €18.

SENDING MAIL TO GERMANY

To ensure timely delivery, mark envelopes "airmail," "par avion," or "*luftpost*." In addition to the standard postage system whose rates are listed below, **Federal Express** (Australia ☎ 13 26 10, Canada and the US 800-463-3339, Ireland 1800 535 800, New Zealand 0800 733 339, the UK 08456 070 809; www.fedex.com) handles express mail services from most countries to Germany. Sending a postcard within Germany costs €0.45, while sending letters (up to 20g) domestically costs €0.55.

There are several ways to arrange pickup of letters sent to you while you are abroad. Mail can be sent via **Poste Restante** (General Delivery) to almost any city or town in German with a post office, but it not perfectly reliable. Address *Poste Restante* letters like so:

Jürgen FISCHER

Poste Restante

01099 Dresden, GERMANY

The mail will go to a special desk in the central post office, unless you specify a post office by street address or postal code. It's best to use the largest post office, since mail may be sent there regardless. It is usually safer and quicker, though more expensive, to send mail express or registered. Bring your passport (or other photo ID) for pickup; there may be a small fee. *Let's Go* lists post offices in the **Practical Information** section for each city and most towns.

American Express's travel offices throughout the world offer a free **Client Letter Service** (mail held up to 30 days and forwarded upon request) for cardholders who contact them in advance. Let's Go lists AmEx locations for most large cities in **Practical Information** sections; for a complete list, call ☎ 800-528-4800 or visit www.americanexpress.com/travel.

ACCOMMODATIONS

HOSTELS

In 1908, a German named Richard Schirmann, believing that life in industrial cities was harmful to the physical and moral development of Germany's young people, built the **world's first youth hostel** in Altena—a budget dormitory that would make travel possible for urban youth. Many hostels are laid out dorm-style, often with large single-sex rooms and bunk beds, although private rooms that sleep two to four are becoming more common. They sometimes have kitchens and utensils for your use, bike or moped rentals, storage areas, transport to airports, breakfast and other meals, laundry facilities, and Internet access. There can be drawbacks: some

ESSENTIALS

> **A HOSTELER'S BILL OF RIGHTS.** There are certain standard features that we do not include in our hostel listings. Unless we state otherwise, you can expect that every hostel has no lockout, no curfew, a kitchen, free hot showers, some system of secure luggage storage, and no key deposit.

hostels close during certain daytime "lockout" hours, have a curfew, don't accept reservations, impose a maximum stay, or, rarely, require that you do chores.

Hostelling in Germany is overseen by **Deutsches Jugendherbergswerk (DJH)**, Bismarckstr. 8, 32756 Detmold, Germany (☎05231 740 10; www.jugendherberge.de). Its hostels are open to members of DJH or Hostelling International (see below), but travelers can join or buy guest passes at the hostels. DJH has recently initiated a growing number of **Jugendgästehäuser,** youth guest-houses that are generally more expensive, have more facilities, and attract slightly older guests. DJH has absorbed hundreds of hostels in eastern Germany with efficiency, though some still lack the sparkling facilities of their western counterparts. DJH's German-language *Jugendherbergen in Deutschland*, a guide to all federated German hostels, can be purchased at German bookstores and major newsstands, by writing to DJH, or from the **DJH webpage,** which also has pictures, prices, addresses, and phone numbers for almost every hostel in Germany. Contact information can also be found on most German cities' official websites, listed under the tourist office in the **Practical Information** section of cities in this guide. **Eurotrip** (www.eurotrip.com) has information on and reviews of budget hostels and international hostel associations. The **Internet Guide to Hostelling** (www.hostels.com) provides a hostel directory in addition to hostelling and backpacking tips, as does www.hostelplanet.com.

HOSTELLING INTERNATIONAL

Joining the youth hostel association in your own country (listed below) automatically grants you membership privileges in **Hostelling International (HI),** a federation of national hostelling associations. Non-HI members can stay in most HI hostels by purchasing a **guest membership**—a blank card with space for six validation stamps. Each night you'll pay a nonmember supplement (one-sixth the membership fee) and earn one guest stamp; get six stamps and you're a member. A new membership benefit is the **FreeNites program,** which allows hostelers to gain points toward free rooms. Most student travel agencies (p. 24) sell HI cards, which can also be purchased at HI's website (www.hihostels.com), or through any of the national hosteling organizations listed below. All prices listed are valid for **one-year memberships** unless otherwise noted.

Australian Youth Hostels Association (AYHA), 422 Kent St., Sydney, NSW 200 (☎02 9261 1111; www.yha.com.au). AUS$52, under 18 AUS$19.

Hostelling International-Canada (HI-C), 205 Catherine St. #400, Ottawa, ON K2P 1C3 (☎613-237-7884; www.hihostels.ca). CDN$35, under 18 free.

An Óige (Irish Youth Hostel Association), 61 Mountjoy St., Dublin 7 (☎830 4555; www.irelandyha.org). €20, under 18 €10.

Hostelling International Northern Ireland (HINI), 22-32 Donegall Rd., Belfast BT12 5JN (☎02890 32 47 33; www.hini.org.uk). UK£13, under 18 UK£6.

Youth Hostels Association of New Zealand (YHANZ), Level 1, Moorhouse City, 166 Moorhouse Ave., P.O. Box 436, Christchurch (☎0800 278 299 (NZ only) or 03 379 9970; www.yha.org.nz). NZ$40, under 18 free.

Scottish Youth Hostels Association (SYHA), 7 Glebe Cres., Stirling FK8 2JA (☎01786 89 14 00; www.syha.org.uk). UK£6, under 17 UK£2.50.

Youth Hostels Association (England and Wales), Trevelyan House, Dimple Rd., Matlock, Derbyshire DE4 3YH (☎08707 708 868; www.yha.org.uk). UK£15.50, under 26 UK£10.

Hostelling International-USA, 8401 Colesville Rd., Ste. 600, Silver Spring, MD 20910 (☎301-495-1240; www.hiayh.org). US$28, under 18 free.

 BOOKING HOSTELS ONLINE. One of the easiest ways to ensure you've got a bed for the night is by reserving online. Click to the **Hostelworld** booking engine through **www.letsgo.com,** and you'll have access to bargain accommodations from Argentina to Zimbabwe with no added commission.

OTHER TYPES OF ACCOMMODATIONS

HOTELS, GUESTHOUSES, AND PENSIONS

Lower-end **hotel singles** in Germany cost about €25-40 per night, doubles €35-50. The cheapest hotel-style accommodations are places with **Pension, Gasthof, Gästehaus,** or **Hotel-Garni** in the name. Breakfast *(Frühstück)* is almost always included. You'll typically share a hall bathroom; a private bathroom will cost extra. Some hotels offer "full pension" (all meals) and "half pension" (no lunch). If you make **reservations** in writing, indicate your night of arrival and the number of nights you plan to stay. Often it is easiest to make reservations by phone with a credit card.

HOME EXCHANGES AND HOSPITALITY CLUBS

Home exchange offers the traveler various types of homes (houses, apartments, condominiums, villas, even castles in some cases), plus the opportunity to live like a native and to cut down on accommodation fees. For more information, contact **HomeExchange.com,** P.O. Box 787, Hermosa Beach, CA 90254, USA (☎800-877-8723; www.homeexchange.com), or **Intervac International Home Exchange** (☎070 52 93 24 06; www.intervac.com).

Hospitality clubs link their members with individuals or families abroad who are willing to host travelers for free or for a small fee to promote cultural exchange and general good karma. In exchange, members usually must be willing to host travelers in their own homes; a small membership fee may also be required. **Global-Freeloaders.com** (www.globalfreeloaders.com) and **The Hospitality Club** (www.hospitalityclub.org) are good places to start. **Servas** (www.servas.org) is an established, more formal, peace-based organization, and requires a fee and an interview to join. An Internet search will find many similar organizations, some of which cater to special interests (e.g., women, GLBT travelers, or members of certain professions). As always, use common sense when planning to stay with or host someone you do not know.

LONG-TERM ACCOMMODATIONS

Travelers who wish to stay in Germany for an extended period of time may find it most cost-effective to rent an **apartment.** A basic one-bedroom (or studio) apartment in Berlin will start at €250-350 per month. Besides the rent itself, prospective tenants usually are also required to front a security deposit (frequently one month's rent) and the last month's rent. Foreign visitors often find it easier to rent through **Mitwohnzentralen** (homeshare companies), which find rooms for individuals in shared apartments. These companies charge a percentage of each

month's rent as commission; shop around to find the best rates. Check the **Practical Information** sections of cities listed in this guide for information about specific *Mitwohzentralen*.

CAMPING AND THE OUTDOORS

The 26,000 campsites dotting the Alps, forests, beaches, and suburbs of major cities demonstrate Germany's enthusiasm for the outdoors. Hiking trails wind through the outskirts of every German city, and a national network of long-distance trails weaves the country together. The Black Forest, Saxon Switzerland, Harz Mountains and Bavarian Alps are especially well-traversed. The outdoor facilities in Germany are among the best-maintained in the world, usually accessible by public transportation and providing showers, bathrooms, and a restaurant or store. Camping typically costs €3-6 per person with a surcharge for tents and vehicles. Blue signs with a black tent on a white background indicate official sites. For information on campsites across the country, check out the **accommodations** sections of the towns and outdoor areas listed in this guide, or visit the **Great Outdoor Recreation Pages** at www.gorp.com for excellent general information on camping and spending time in the outdoors.

LEAVE NO TRACE. Let's Go encourages travelers to embrace the "Leave No Trace" ethic, minimizing their impact on natural environments and protecting them for future generations. Trekkers and wilderness enthusiasts should set up camp on durable surfaces, use cookstoves instead of campfires, bury human waste away from water supplies, bag trash and carry it out with them, and respect wildlife and natural objects. For more detailed information, contact the **Leave No Trace Center for Outdoor Ethics**, P.O. Box 997, Boulder, CO 80306 (☎800-332-4100 or 303-442-8222; www.lnt.org).

USEFUL RESOURCES

A variety of publishing companies offer hiking guidebooks for both novices and experts. For information about camping, hiking, and biking, write or call the publishers listed below to receive a free catalog. Campers heading to Europe should consider buying an **International Camping Carnet.** Similar to a hostel membership card, it's required at a few campgrounds and sometimes provides discounts. It is available in North America from the **Family Campers and RVers Association** and in the UK from **The Caravan Club.**

ADAC Camping Caravaning Führer (campingfuehrer.adac.de). Offers a wealth of German-language camping information organized by Germany's automobile association.

Alan Rogers, Spelmonden Old Oast, Groundhurst, Kent TN17 1HE, UK (☎0870 405 4055; www.alanrogers.com). Publishes a series of European camping guides and features a searchable online database of campsites, including over 1000 in Germany.

Automobile Association, Contact Centre, Carr Ellison House, William Armstrong Drive, Newcastle-upon-Tyne NE4 7YA, UK (☎08706 000 371; www.theAA.com). Sells *Caravan and Camping Europe* (UK£10) and road atlases for Germany and Europe.

Camping Germany (www.camping-germany.de). Offers information and pictures for campgrounds across the country in sometimes-amusingly flawed English translation.

The Caravan Club, East Grinstead House, East Grinstead, West Sussex, RH19 1UA, UK (☎01342 326 944; www.caravanclub.co.uk). For UK£32, members receive access to sites, insurance services, equipment discounts, maps, and a monthly magazine.

Family Campers and RVers, 4804 Transit Rd., Bldg. #2, Depew, NY 14043, USA (☎ 800-245-9755; www.fcrv.org). Membership (US$25) includes *Camping Today* magazine.

NATIONAL PARKS

The heaviest concentration of parks is in Bavaria and former East Germany. **Winter sports,** especially skiing and tobogganing, are popular in the Berchtesgaden and *Bayerischer Wald* (Bavarian Forest) parks; the Saxon Switzerland and Harz parks in the east are popular for their magnificent **hiking opportunities** among chalk cliffs and forested peaks. Germans are predictably fastidious about their parks, placing strict limits on camping, fire-building, and other activities that could potentially harm the environment.

There are no entrance fees for German parks, although parking can be costly and camping is nearly always restricted to designated campgrounds, which charge around €5-10 per camper per night. Travelers can also stay at huts in some parks, which rarely require reservations and typically cost €10-20. For general information, contact **Nationalpark-Service,** Informationshaus, 17192 Federow, Germany (☎ 039 91 66 88 49; www.nationalpark-service.de). Listings of ranger offices in specific national parks can be found in each park's listing in this book.

WILDERNESS SAFETY

Staying **warm, dry,** and **well hydrated** is key to a happy and safe wilderness experience. For any hike, prepare yourself for an emergency by packing a first-aid kit, a reflector, a whistle, high-energy food, extra water, raingear, a hat, mittens, and extra socks. For warmth, wear wool or insulating synthetic materials designed for the outdoors. Cotton is a bad choice since it dries slowly.

Check **weather forecasts** often and pay attention to the skies when hiking, as weather patterns can change suddenly. Always let someone—a friend, your hostel, a park ranger, or a local hiking organization—know when and where you are going. Know your physical limits and do not attempt a hike beyond your ability. See **Safety and Health** (p. 18) for information on outdoor medical concerns.

WILDLIFE

Germany supports a diverse array of wildlife. While beautiful birds, alpine butterflies, and oodles of fuzzy creatures are sure to delight the wilderness explorer, a few other animals—notably **bears**—are less than cuddly. Always pack trash in a plastic bag and carry it with you until you reach the next trash receptacle. If you do encounter a bear, *do not approach it.* Back away slowly while keeping your eye to the bear; bears are shy of humans and are not likely to attack if they are not threatened. For more information, consult *How to Stay Alive in the Woods*, by Bradford Angier (Black Dog & Leventhal Books, US$10).

CAMPING AND HIKING EQUIPMENT

WHAT TO BUY

Good camping equipment is both sturdy and light. North American suppliers tend to offer the most competitive prices.

Sleeping Bags: Most sleeping bags are rated by season; "summer" means 30-40°F (around 0°C) at night; "four-season" or "winter" often means below 0°F (-17°C). Bags are made of **down** (warm and light, but expensive, and miserable when wet) or of **syn-**

수증(공급받는자용)

진 료 기 간	야간(공휴) 진료
5-21~2007-05-21	■야간 □공휴일

실	환 자 구 분	영 수 증 번 호
	보험외래	20070521-004

여 ③	금 액 산 정 내 역	
기타( )	요양기관기호:	
명 칭	진료비 총액 ④ ((①+②+③)	14,240
전 화 번 호	환자 부담 총액 ⑤ ((①+③)	3,000
팩 스 번 호	기 납부한 금액 ⑥	
e-mail주소	수 납	카 드	3,000
면허종별	금액	현금영수증	
면허번호 ⑦	제	호
하지 아니합니다.	(⑤-⑥) 합 계	3,000

1일 여횟수	총 투약일수	대 체 가 능	용 현금영수증( ) 매직(선.갑.후)	법 시 분복용
			신분확인번호	
			현금승인번호	
			※ 요양기관 임의활용 공간	

양 **전**

기타（　　　）　요양기관기호:　12313254

명　　칭	예인소아과
전 화 번 호	2676-7889
팩 스 번 호	
e-mail주소	

영	면허종별	의　사		
는	면허번호	제	63925	호

하지 아니합니다.

1일 여횟수	총 투약일수	대 체 가 능	용　　　　　　법 매식(전,간,후)　　시　　분복용
1	2		->매번 같이 복용하셔요
3	2		
3	2		
3	2		

thetic material (heavy, durable, and warm when wet). Prices range US$50-250 for a summer synthetic to US$200-300 for a good down winter bag. **Sleeping bag pads** include foam pads (US$10-30), air mattresses (US$15-50), and self-inflating mats (US$30-120). Bring a **stuff sack** to store your bag and keep it dry.

Tents: The best tents are free-standing (with their own frames and suspension systems), set up quickly, and only require staking in high winds. Low-profile dome tents are the best all-around. Worthy 2-person tents start at US$100, 4-person tents US$160. Make sure your tent has a rain fly and seal its seams with waterproofer. Other useful accessories include a **battery-operated lantern,** a plastic **groundcloth,** and a nylon **tarp.**

Backpacks: Internal-frame packs mold well to your back, keep a lower center of gravity, and flex adequately to allow you to hike difficult trails, while **external-frame packs** are more comfortable for long hikes over even terrain, as they carry weight higher and distribute it more evenly. Make sure your pack has a strong, padded hip-belt to transfer weight to your legs. Some models are designed specifically for women. Any serious backpacking requires a pack of at least 4000 cu. in. (16,000cc), plus 500 cu. in. (2000cc) for sleeping bags in internal-frame packs. Sturdy backpacks cost US$125-420, and it doesn't pay to economize. Either buy a **rain cover** (US$10-20) or store all of your belongings in plastic bags inside your pack.

Boots: Be sure to wear hiking boots with good **ankle support.** They should fit snugly and comfortably over 1-2 pairs of **wool socks** and a pair of thin **liner socks.** Break in boots over several weeks before you go to spare yourself blisters.

Other Necessities: Synthetic layers, like those made of polypropylene or polyester, and a pile jacket will keep you warm even when wet. A **space blanket** (US$5-15) will help you to retain body heat and doubles as a groundcloth. Plastic **water bottles** are vital; look for shatter- and leak-resistant models. Carry **water-purification tablets** for when you can't boil water. Although some campgrounds provide campfire sites, you may want to bring a small **metal grate** or **grill.** Also bring a **first-aid kit, pocketknife, insect repellent,** and **waterproof matches** or a **lighter.**

WHERE TO BUY IT

The online and mail-order companies listed below offer lower prices than many retail stores. A visit to a local camping or outdoors store will give you a good sense of the look and weight of certain items before you buy.

Campmor, 28 Parkway, P.O. Box 700, Upper Saddle River, NJ 07458, USA (☎800-525-4784; www.campmor.com).

Cotswold Outdoor, Unit 11 Kemble Business Park, Crudwell, Malmesbury Wiltshire, SN16 9SH, UK (☎08704 427 755; www.cotswoldoutdoor.com).

Discount Camping, 880 Main North Rd., Pooraka, South Australia 5095, Australia (☎08 8262 3399; www.discountcamping.com.au).

Eastern Mountain Sports (EMS), 1 Vose Farm Rd., Peterborough, NH 03458, USA (☎888-463-6367; www.ems.com).

Gear-Zone, 8 Burnet Rd., Sweetbriar Rd. Industrial Estate, Norwich, NR3 2BS, UK (☎1603 410 108; www.gear-zone.co.uk).

L.L. Bean, Freeport, ME 04033, USA (US and Canada ☎800-441-5713; UK 0800 891 297; www.llbean.com).

CAMPERS AND RVS

Renting an RV costs more than tenting or hostelling but less than staying in hotels while renting a car (see **Rental Cars,** p. 32). The convenience of bringing along your own bedroom, bathroom, and kitchen makes RVing an attractive option, especially for older travelers and families with children. During peak season, rental prices for a standard RV are around €700 per week.

Auto Europe, 39 Commercial St., P.O. Box 7006, Portland, ME 04112, USA (☎888-223-5555; www.autoeurope.com). Rents RVs in Berlin and 9 other German cities.

Motorhomes Worldwide, 2/1 Balmoral St., P.O. Box 1518, Frankston, Victoria 3199, Australia (Australia ☎1300 880035; outside Australia 800 8781 1120; www.motorhomesworldwide.com). Rents motorhomes in 18 German cities.

ORGANIZED ADVENTURE TRIPS

Organized adventure tours offer another way to explore the wild. Activities include hiking, biking, skiing, canoeing, kayaking, rafting, climbing, photo safaris, and archaeological digs. Tourism bureaus can suggest parks, trails, and outfitters. Organizations that specialize in camping and outdoor equipment (see **Where to Buy It,** p. 45) also are good info sources. The **Specialty Travel Index** (www.specialtytravel.com) lists dozens of companies offering adventure trips in Germany.

SPECIFIC CONCERNS

SUSTAINABLE TRAVEL

As the number of travelers on the road continues to rise, the detrimental effect they can have on natural environments becomes an increasing concern. With this in mind, Let's Go promotes the philosophy of **sustainable travel.** Through a sensitivity to issues of ecology and sustainability, today's travelers can be a powerful force in preserving as well as restoring the places they visit.

Ecotourism, a rising trend in sustainable travel, focuses on conserving natural habitats and using them to build up the economy without exploitation or overdevelopment. Travelers can make a difference by doing research in advance and by supporting organizations and establishments that pay attention to their impact on their natural surroundings and that strive to be environmentally friendly. Travelers interested in pursuing conservation-oriented volunteer opportunities should consult the **Beyond Tourism** chapter (p. 78).

ECOTOURISM RESOURCES. For more information on environmentally responsible tourism, contact one of the organizations below:

Conservation International, 1919 M St. NW, Ste. 600, Washington, D.C. 20036, USA (☎800-406-2306 or 202-912-1000; www.conservation.org).

Green Globe 21 (☎61 2 6257 9102; www.greenglobe.com).

International Ecotourism Society, 733 15th St. NW, Ste. 1000, Washington, D.C. 20005, USA (☎202-347-9203; www.ecotourism.org).

United Nations Environment Program (UNEP), 39-43 Quai André Citroën, 75739 Paris Cedex 15, France (☎33 1 44 37 14 50; www.uneptie.org/pc/tourism).

RESPONSIBLE TRAVEL

The impact of tourist dollars on the destinations you visit should not be underestimated. The choices you make during your trip can have powerful effects on local communities—for better or for worse. Travelers who care about the destinations and environments they explore should make themselves aware of the social and cultural implications of the choices they make when they travel. Simple decisions such as buying local products instead of globally available ones, paying fair prices for products or services, and attempting to say a few words in the local language can have a strong, positive effect on the community.

Community-based tourism aims to channel tourist dollars into the local economy by emphasizing tours and cultural programs that are run by members of the host community and that often benefit disadvantaged groups. Travelers who pursue this type of tourism also benefit themselves, as socially conscious travel often takes them beyond traditionally touristed areas. An excellent resource for general information on community-based travel is *The Ethical Travel Guide* (UK£13), a project of **Tourism Concern** (☎44 020 7133 3330; www.tourismconcern.org.uk).

TRAVELING ALONE

There are many benefits to traveling alone, including independence and a greater opportunity to connect with locals. On the other hand, solo travelers are more vulnerable targets of harassment and street theft. If you are traveling alone, look confident, try not to stand out as a tourist, and be especially careful in deserted or very crowded areas. Stay away from areas that are not well lit. If questioned, never admit that you are traveling alone. Maintain regular contact with someone at home who knows your itinerary, and always research your destination before traveling. For more tips, pick up *Traveling Solo* by Eleanor Berman (Globe Pequot Press, US$18), visit www.travelaloneandloveit.com, or subscribe to **Connecting: Solo Travel Network,** 689 Park Rd., Unit 6, Gibsons, BC V0N 1V7, Canada (☎604-886-9099; www.cstn.org; membership US$30-48).

WOMEN TRAVELERS

Women exploring on their own inevitably face additional safety concerns, but it's easy to be adventurous without taking undue risks. If you are concerned, consider staying in hostels with single rooms that lock from the inside or in religious organizations with single-sex rooms. Stick to central accommodations and avoid solitary late-night treks or subway rides. Always carry extra cash for a phone call, bus, or taxi. **Hitchhiking** is never safe for lone women, or even for two women traveling together. Look as if you know where you're going and approach older women or couples for directions if lost or uncomfortable. The less you look like a tourist, the better off you'll be. Dress conservatively, especially in rural areas. Wearing a conspicuous **wedding band** sometimes helps to prevent unwanted advances.

Your best answer to verbal harassment is no answer at all; feigning deafness, sitting motionless, and staring straight ahead at nothing in particular will usually do the trick. The extremely persistent can sometimes be dissuaded by a firm, loud, and very public *"Laß mich in Ruhe!"* ("Leave me alone!"). Harassment is never tolerated in public places; head to a crowded area if you feel uncomfortable. Memorize important emergency numbers (**Police** ☎110, **Ambulance and Fire** ☎112), and consider carrying a whistle on your keychain. A self-defense course will both prepare you for a potential attack and raise your level of awareness of your surroundings (see **Self Defense,** p. 20). Also be sure you are aware of the health concerns that women face when traveling (p. 24).

GLBT TRAVELERS

Attitudes toward gay, lesbian, bisexual, and transgendered (GLBT) travelers in Germany are surprisingly accepting. While homophobia persists in rural areas and parts of conservative Bavaria, Germans are generally more tolerant than

Americans and Brits, though not quite as open-minded as the Dutch. The German word for gay is *schwul* (SHVOOL), which refers exclusively to men; lesbians are *lesbe* (LEZ-buh). *Let's Go* provides information on local bisexual, gay, and lesbian culture in **Practical Information** listings and **Entertainment and Nightlife** sections of city descriptions. The epicenter of gay life in Germany (and possibly in all of Europe) is Berlin (p. 107). Other major centers include Hamburg (p. 214), Cologne (p. 278), and Munich (p. 428). While tolerance is still a new concept in Eastern Germany, growing gay scenes have developed in Leipzig (p. 629) and, to a lesser extent, in Dresden (p. 598).

To avoid hassles at airports and border crossings, transgendered travelers should make sure that all of their documents report the same gender. Many countries (including the US, the UK, Canada, Ireland, Australia, and New Zealand) will amend the passports of post-operative transsexuals to reflect their true gender, although governments are generally less willing to amend documents for pre-operative transsexuals and other transgendered individuals.

Women should look for *Frauencafés* and *Frauenkneipen.* It should be stressed that while such cafés are for women only, they are *not* exclusively for lesbians. Of the dozens of regional and national gay and lesbian organizations; two of the largest are the **Bundesverband Homosexualität (BVH)**, Greifswalder Str. 224, 10405 Berlin (☎030 441 24 98), and the **Lesben- und Schwulenverband Deutschland (LSVD)**, Friedrichstr. 165, 10117 Berlin (☎030 201 08 04). Listed below are contact organizations, mail-order catalogs, and publishers that offer materials addressing some specific concerns. **Out and About** (www.planetout.com) offers a weekly newsletter addressing travel concerns and a comprehensive site addressing gay travel concerns. The online newspaper **365gay.com** has a travel section (www.365gay.com/travel/travelchannel.htm), and the German National Tourist Office (www.germany-tourism.co.uk) sports a wealth of resources for GLBT Travelers and distributes the free English-language *Gayfriendly Germany* guide.

Gay's the Word, 66 Marchmont St., London WC1N 1AB, UK (☎44 020 7278 7654; http://freespace.virgin.net/gays.theword/). The largest gay and lesbian bookshop in the UK, with both fiction and non-fiction titles. Mail-order service available.

Giovanni's Room, 345 South 12th St., Philadelphia, PA 19107, USA (☎215-923-2960; www.queerbooks.com). An international lesbian and gay bookstore with mail-order service (carries many of the publications listed below).

International Lesbian and Gay Association (ILGA), Ave. des Villas 34, 1060 Brussels, Belgium (☎32 2 502 2471; www.ilga.org). Provides political information, such as homosexuality laws of individual countries.

ADDITIONAL RESOURCES: GLBT

Spartacus 2005-2006: International Gay Guide. B.G. Verlag (US$33).

Damron Men's Travel Guide, Damron Accommodations Guide, Damron City Guide, and *Damron Women's Traveller.* Damron Travel Guides (US$18-24). For info, call ☎800-462-6654 or visit www.damron.com.

The Gay Vacation Guide: The Best Trips and How to Plan Them, Mark Chesnut. Kensington Books (US$15).

TRAVELERS WITH DISABILITIES

Germany provides services, information, and accessibility to facilities for travelers with *Behinderte* (disabilities). Both national and regional tourist boards provide directories on the accessibility of various accommodations and transportation services. Germany's excellent public transportation systems make most places easily accessible for travelers with disabilities; many buses and subways are wheelchair accessible. A wheelchair icon or a large "B" indicates access. Intersections in major cities have audible crossing signals for the blind.

Rail is probably most convenient mean of travel for disabled travelers in Germany. All ICE, EC, and IC trains are **wheelchair accessible**, and disabled travelers can request free seat reservations; for more information, check out www.bahn.de. All **EuroStar** trains are also wheelchair accessible. **Guide dog owners** should be aware that Germany requires evidence of rabies vaccination from a licensed veterinarian at least 30 days but not more than 12 months before entering the country; a notarized German translation of this certificate is required. Those with disabilities should inform airlines and hotels of their disabilities when making reservations; some time may be needed to prepare special accommodations. Call ahead to restaurants, museums, and other facilities to assess accessibility. For those who wish to rent cars, some major **car rental** agencies (e.g. Hertz) offer hand-controlled vehicles.

USEFUL ORGANIZATIONS

Access Abroad (www.umabroad.umn.edu/access). A website devoted to making study abroad available to students with disabilities. The site is maintained by Disability Services, University of Minnesota, 230 Heller Hall, 271 19th Ave. S., Minneapolis, MN 55455, USA (☎612-626-7379).

Flying Wheels, 143 W. Bridge St., P.O. Box 382, Owatonna, MN 55060, USA (☎507-451-5005; www.flyingwheelstravel.com). Specializes in escorted trips to Europe for people with physical disabilities; plans custom trips worldwide.

Mobility International USA (MIUSA), P.O. Box 10767, Eugene, OR 97440, USA (☎541-343-1284; www.miusa.org). Provides a variety of books and other publications containing information for travelers with disabilities.

Society for Accessible Travel and Hospitality (SATH), 347 Fifth Ave., Ste. 610, New York, NY 10016, USA (☎212-447-7284; www.sath.org). Publishes free online travel information and the magazine *OPEN WORLD* (annual subscription US$13, free for members). Annual membership US$45, students and seniors US$30.

MINORITY TRAVELERS

Germany has a significant minority population composed mainly of about two million Turks. Travelers may notice that some Germans harbor resentment towards this burgeoning population, which first arrived in Germany during the post-WWII years as *Gastarbeiter* (guest workers). Since then, many Turks have settled and prospered in Germany, while others have faced difficulties adjusting to Germany's open society. Tensions between Turks and ethnic Germans can be felt palpably in parts of major cities; in particularly tense neighborhoods, dark-skinned travelers and those of Middle Eastern descent should be especially cautious.

In certain regions, mostly large cities of former East Germany, minority tourists may feel threatened by small but vocal neo-Nazi groups. While they represent only a fraction of the population, neo-Nazi skinheads have been known to attack foreigners, especially non-whites. In these areas, common sense will serve you best.

DIETARY CONCERNS

Although Germany is unapologetically carnivorous, **vegetarianism** has become increasingly popular (see **Food and Drink,** p. 62) in the wake of growing health consciousness and a blooming alternative scene. Nearly six million Germans do not eat meat, and vegetarian restaurants have proliferated in larger cities, while health food shops, such as the well-known **Reformhaus,** provide a large selection of vegetarian and vegan products. *Let's Go* tries to list restaurants that offer vegetarian and vegan choices whenever possible. Many are ethnic restaurants; traditional German eateries often offer very few completely vegetarian dishes. For more information about vegetarian travel, contact:

> **European Vegetarian Union,** Hildegund Scholvien, Friedhofstr. 12, 67693 Fischbach (☎06305 272; www.european-vegetarian.org). Website includes lists of vegetarian- and vegan-friendly brands and restaurants.

> **Vegetarian Association of Germany,** Blumenstr. 3, 30159 Hanover (☎0511 363 20 50; www.vegetarierbund.de).

The travel section of the The Vegetarian Resource Group's website, at www.vrg.org/travel, lists organizations and websites geared toward helping vegetarians and vegans traveling abroad. For more information, visit your local bookstore or health food store, and consult *The Vegetarian Traveler: Where to Stay if You're Vegetarian, Vegan, Environmentally Sensitive,* by Jed and Susan Civic (Larson Publications; US$16), or *Vegetarian Europe,* edited by Alex Bourke (Vegetarian Guides; US$17). Vegetarians will appreciate www.vegdining.com and www.happycow.net. A list of vegetarian restaurants in Germany can be found at www.fleischlos-geniessen.de.

Travelers who keep **kosher** should contact synagogues in larger cities for information on kosher restaurants. Your own synagogue or college Hillel may have helpful lists or books, and a number of Jewish establishments in Germany can be found on the worldwide kosher restaurant database at http://shamash.org/kosher. A good resource is the *Jewish Travel Guide,* edited by Michael Zaidner (Vallentine Mitchell; US$18). Travelers looking for halal restaurants may find www.zabihah.com a useful resource.

OTHER RESOURCES

Let's Go tries to cover all aspects of budget travel, but we can't put *everything* in our guides. Listed below are books and websites that can serve as jumping-off points for your own research.

USEFUL PUBLICATIONS

For books on Germany's culture and history, see **Additional Resources,** p. 77.

> **Atlantik-Brücke,** Magnus-Haus Am Kupfergraben 7, D-10117 Berlin-Mitte. Devoted to promoting mutual understanding (hence "Atlantic Bridge"), it publishes *These Strange German Ways*—a must for any American planning on living in Germany—as well as *Meet United Germany, German Holidays and Folk Customs,* and *Speaking Out: Jewish Voices from United Germany.* Order the books from the Hamburg office (☎030 20 39 830).

> **Culture Shock! Germany,** Richard Lord. Graphic Arts Publishing Co., 1996 (US$13). A readable lowdown on living in Deutschland that isn't afraid to hold your hand.

> **Germany by Bike,** Nadine Slavinski. Mountaineers Books, 1994 (US$15). 20 tours throughout the *Länder,* with information on getting ready to *Tour de...Deutschland.*

> **A Traveller's Wine Guide to Germany,** Kerry Brady Stewart. Traveller's Wine Guides, 1997 (US$18). Exactly what it says it is, by a well-known oenophile.

> **Wicked German,** Howard Tomb. Workman, 1992 (US$5). A little guide to everything you really didn't need to know how to say in German.

WORLD WIDE WEB

ESSENTIALS

 WWW.LETSGO.COM. Let's Go's website features a wealth of information and valuable advice at your fingertips. It offers excerpts from all our guides as well as monthly features on new hot spots in the most popular destinations. In addition to our online bookstore, we have great deals on everything from airfares to cell phones. Our resources section is full of information you'll need before you hit the road, and our forums are buzzing with advice from other travelers. Check back often to see constant updates, exciting new tips, and prize giveaways. See you soon!

THE ART OF TRAVEL

Backpacker's Ultimate Guide: www.bugeurope.com. Tips on packing, transportation, and where to go. Also tons of country-specific travel information.

BootsnAll.com: www.bootsnall.com. Numerous resources for independent travelers, from planning your trip to reporting on it when you get back.

How to See the World: www.artoftravel.com. A compendium of great travel tips, from cheap flights to self defense to interacting with local culture.

Travel Intelligence: www.travelintelligence.net. A large collection of travel writing by distinguished travel writers.

Travel Library: www.travel-library.com. A fantastic set of links for general information and personal travelogues.

World Hum: www.worldhum.com. An independently produced collection of "travel dispatches from a shrinking planet."

INFORMATION ON GERMANY

CIA World Factbook: www.odci.gov/cia/publications/factbook/index.html. Tons of vital statistics on Germany's geography, government, economy, and people.

Das Deutschland Portal: www.deutschland.de. The official German site about Germany, available in English.

Germany Tourism: www.germany-tourism.de. A rich source of information for travelers to Germany, including some stunning panoramic pictures.

Geographia: www.geographia.com. Highlights, culture, and people of Germany.

PlanetRider: www.planetrider.com. A subjective list of links to the "best" websites covering the culture and tourist attractions of Germany.

TravelPage: www.travelpage.com. Links to official tourist office sites in Germany.

LIFE AND TIMES

Germany has never treaded a single well-worn path. With revolutionaries and innovators of strikingly diverse aims, Germany's history appears at once strikingly multifaceted and confoundingly contradictory. Charlemagne first united Europe under a Germanic banner in the ninth century; when a millennium later Adolf Hitler once again brought Europe, nationalism had morphed into racism and genocide. Kant's stern absolutism wound its way into the communist imperatives of Marx and Engels. The ornate intricacy of Beethoven gave way to the aesthetic sparsity of the Bauhaus movement. Today, this enigmatic historical legacy meets with new social, diplomatic, and economic uncertainties brought on by the country's staggeringly quick reunification just 15 years ago. With a population of 82 million including 7 million immigrants, modern Germany again wears its own trail as the country shapes a new identity of social and economic cohesion.

HISTORY

Few national histories are as enigmatic and rife with conflict as Germany's. Documented German history has been a roller coaster of loose alliances and fractured unions since 90 BC, when Roman author Posidonium first called Central European tribes "Germans" *(Germaniae)*. Baffling historical progression that leaps from the enlightened absolute rulers of the 18th century to the brutal National Socialism of the early 20th century have led some scholars to endorse the Sonderweg theory. Literally meaning "special path," this theory argues that, from its earliest days, Germany has developed on a path wholly distinct from the rest of Europe.

58 BC
Roman Empire conquers Germanic tribes.

476 AD
Roman Empire collapses.

800
Charlemagne is crowned Emperor by the Pope.

962
Otto the Great unifies Germanic Franks; proclaimed Holy Roman Emperor.

EARLY GERMAN HISTORY: 58 BC-AD 1517. Around 58 BC, the Roman Republic had expanded its borders to the Rhein, causing pagan clans of the Germanic peoples in Central Europe (including the Saxons, Franks, Frisians, and Thuringians) to join forces for defense. In AD 9, when battles erupted in the Teutoburg Forest (near present-day Osnabrück), the allied Germans scored a resounding homecourt victory against the Romans, earning the nickname "Teutons" and a date to mark the first assertion of a truly Germanic culture. After five centuries of mutual antagonism and several barbarian attacks on Rome, the weakened Roman Empire fell in 476. From 600, Christian missionaries, including Irish-Scottish monks, propogated the vestiges of fourth-century Roman Christianity amidst the Germans.

Without a common enemy to unify them, the disparate clans went their own ways. The **Franks** expanded their power into the Rhein Valley, including part of modern-day France, uniting nearly every Germanic kingdom of Europe three centuries later under the rule of **Charlemagne** (known in Germany as Karl der Große), crowned emperor by the pope in 800. Charlemagne initiated administrative reforms and cultural advancements, reviving European commerce along the way.

Disputes among Charlemagne's sons prompted the **Treaty of Verdun,** which split the empire into three kingdoms. Although German king **Otto I the Great** managed to partially reunify the kingdoms in 962, earning himself the title of Holy Roman Emperor, destructive internal disputes divided the would-be German lands into a fractured feudal society. Otto I initiated a close relationship between the church and the monarchy, but in the **Investiture Crisis** of 1075 the Pope demanded autonomy, specifically in appointing church officials, sparking conflict that ravaged Germany for nearly 50 years. Finally, the **Concordat of Worms** (1122) restored peace by setting up checks and balances between the pope and the king.

War broke out time and again between the dozens of minor dukes and princes vying for power, while the **bubonic plague** of the 14th century killed roughly a third of Europe's population. The **Golden Bull of 1356** declared that seven electors—three archbishops and four secular leaders—should approve the selection of the Holy Roman Emperor. Under the leadership of the **House of Habsburg** (which occupied the throne for five centuries), the empire began to define itself more clearly. Manufacturing and sea trade transformed small North Sea towns into wealthy merchant oligarchies, which banded together in 1358 to form the **Hanseatic League.** This trade federation had outposts as far away as England, Norway and Russia, and grew powerful enough to successfully defeat Denmark in war. Yet while German interests focused on wealthy towns, discontent roiled in rural regions, and outlying areas of the empire slipped out of the Habsburgs' control entirely.

THE REFORMATION: 1517-1700. On All Saints' Day 1517, **Martin Luther,** a monk and professor of Biblical studies at the University of Wittenberg (p. 576), posted his **95 Theses** on the door of the city's castle church, igniting the **Protestant Reformation.** Luther objected to the Roman Catholic Church's practice of selling indulgences—trinkets which relieved the purchaser from purgatory—and insisted that salvation came through God's grace alone. While Luther broke the unity of Western Christianity, his **vernacular translation of the Bible** helped crystallize German dialects into *Hochdeutsch*, a standardized language based on Saxon.

The Reformation soon grew into a political movement, as German electoral princes adopted Lutheranism as a way to restrict the flow of money to the Vatican. Habsburg **Emperor Charles V** (**Karl V**), the most powerful leader since Charlemagne, initially resolved to destroy the subversive doctrine of Lutheranism, but eventually decided to sign the 1555 **Peace of Augsburg**. This treaty granted individual princes the right to choose their territory's official religion, and further dividing the empire.

Charles' successors were less than thrilled with the agreement. When Archduke Ferdinand of Austria tried to impose Catholicism on Bohemia, his Protestant subjects rebelled, throwing a papal representative out a window in the 1618 **Defenestration of Prague.** Fomenting violence between the German Catholics and Protestants escalated as Catholic France sided with the German Protestants to oppose the Habsburgs. The ensuing **Thirty Years' War** (1618-48) was a catastrophic and bloody setback in Germany's development, killing off one-third

1075
Investiture Crisis

1122
Concordat of Worms resolves Investiture Crisis, balancing power between the Pope and the King.

14th Century
Bubonic Plague ravages Germany, killing a third of the population.

1517
Martin Luther nails his 95 Theses to the door of Wittenberg's castle church.

1555
Powerful emperor Karl V signs the Peace of Augsburg, allowing princes to determine the official religion of their own domains.

1618-48
The Thirty Years' War, fought primarily within Germany, involves most of continental Europe in a religious and political struggle that kills one third of Germany's population.

LIFE AND TIMES

1756-63
Brandenburg-Prussia's Fredrick the Great expands his kingdom's borders in the Seven Years' War.

1806
Napoleon conquers the remains of the Holy Roman Empire.

1815
The Congress of Vienna, convened in the wake of Napoleon's defeat, establishes the German Confederation to govern central Europe.

1818
The Prussian-led Zollverein links Northern Germany in a free-trade union, which grows to include most of Germany within two decades.

1848
The failed Revolution of 1848 resulted in the emigration of hundreds of thousands of German liberals as well as profound political instability.

1862
Bismarck is named prime minister of Prussia, and in 1867, chancellor of Germany.

of the population before the **Peace of Westphalia** ended the conflict. This document served as the de facto constitution of the empire until its abolition in 1806.

THE RISE OF BRANDENBURG-PRUSSIA: 1700-1870. After the Thirty Years' War, **Brandenburg-Prussia** was the ascendant state in Germany, with King Friedrich II—known as **Frederick the Great**—at the reins. An enlightened ruler and artistic patron, Friedrich snatched Silesia from the Habsburgs during the **Seven Years' War** (1756-1763), and joined forces with Russia and Austria to partition Poland in 1772. He also linked Brandenburg to Prussia for the first time, piecing together a kingdom for the Habsburgs' dynastic rivals, the **Hohenzollern.**

In 1806, **Napoleon** conquered the remains of the Holy Roman Empire, creating a subservient **Confederation of the Rhein.** After he incorporated hundreds of thousands of German soldiers into his army, a rebellion known as the **Wars of Liberation** ousted Napoleon from Germany (see p. 558). The 1815 **Congress of Vienna** partially restored the pre-war German state system, creating the Austrian-led **German Confederation.** In 1818, Prussia sponsored the **Zollverein,** a customs union linking most of the North German territories in a free trade zone that grew to include most of Germany.

In 1848, as liberal revolution broke out again in France and discontent spread across the rest of Europe, the German Confederation decided to let an elected assembly decide its future. The **Frankfurt National Assembly** drafted a liberal constitution and invited **Friedrich Wilhelm IV** of Prussia to be emperor. He refused to accept a crown with limited authority, and crushed the ensuing revolt with the Prussian army. In 1862, Prussian King Wilhelm I appointed a talented aristocrat named **Otto von Bismarck** as prime minister of Prussia. Bismarck famously exploited a remarkably complex series of alliances and compromises that were frequently dissolved in favor of more violent tactics. His maneuvering initiated the practice of *Realpolitik,* choosing "realistic" political aims and strategies that favor practical compromise over ideological fidelity. Blood and iron, Bismarck proclaimed, were paramount to the creation of a strong, unified German nation. To demonstrate this, he fought Denmark in 1864 and seized control of Northern Schleswig. This offensive led to the **Austro-Prussian War,** which Prussia won in 1866 at Sadowa. In 1867, he disbanded the Confederation and replaced it with the Prussian-dominated **North German Confederation**, of which he then became chancellor.

SECOND REICH: 1871-1914. Realizing that France would never willingly acquiesce to a united Germany under Prussian rule, Bismarck manipulated his neighbor into initiating a war it was almost sure to lose, the **Franco-Prussian War** of 1870. The technologically superior Prussian army swept through France, capturing Emperor Napoleon III and crowning Wilhelm **Kaiser of the German Reich** at the Palace of Versailles. With France out of the way, Bismarck founded the **German Empire** on his own terms in 1871: unification under an authoritarian monarchy.

The so-called conservative empire gained popular support by promoting aggressive nationalism.

Germany industrialized at breakneck speed in the late 19th century, but the aristocratic political system could not keep up. To consolidate power, Bismarck began a series of social initiatives known as the **Kulturkampf,** including unemployment insurance for the working class, but repressed trade unions and imposed sanctions against Catholicism. This tactic allowed Bismarck to quell revolts, but he was forced to resign in 1890 over disputes with the new Kaiser Wilhelm II.

These rapid transitions produced tremendous social friction. To shift the focus from unrest at home, Germany accelerated its foreign adventurism—a policy derisively known as **"Flucht nach vorn"** (escape forward). Disputes over colonial issues left Germany diplomatically isolated in Europe. Though its navy did not yet compare with the British fleet, Germany kept the most powerful army in the world at the turn of the century, prompting Britain, France, and Russia to unite and form the **Triple Entente.** Meanwhile, democratic opposition began to pose a challenge within the regime itself. To the Kaiser and his supporting elite, it appeared that dramatic and militaristic action would be required for self-preservation.

WORLD WAR I: 1914-1918. On the eve of WWI, Europe was balanced in a web of alliances so complex that minor disputes threatened to ignite continental war. The first domino fell in 1914, when a Serbian nationalist assassinated **Archduke Franz-Ferdinand,** Habsburg heir to the Austrian throne. Austria marched on Serbia in immediate retaliation, and Russia ran to the aid of its Slavic ally. After Russia ignored Germany's ultimatum to retreat, Germany united with Austria to form the **Central Powers,** prompting France to mobilize. Germany declared war on France and demanded that the German army be allowed to march through Belgian territory. When Belgium refused, Britain (treaty-bound to defend Belgian neutrality) declared war on Germany. Despite this opposition, Germany advanced through Belgium and northern France, sweeping all of Europe into war.

The German offensive stalled at the **Battle of the Marne.** Four years of agonizing **trench warfare** ensued 50km outside of Paris. The rivals' technologically advanced weaponry--tanks, planes, flame-throwers, and poison gas--caused unprecedented slaughter. In 1917, Germany's policy of unrestricted submarine warfare provoked the U.S. to enter the war on the side of the Allies. A British naval blockade, coupled with the manpower of the US, let the Allies emerge victorious.

THE WEIMAR REPUBLIC: 1918-1933. In late 1918 the German army was on the brink of collapse, refusing to attack in a war they considered lost as riots broke out on the home front. Workers and Socialists spearheaded the revolt in the **November Revolution**. On November 9, 1918, Social Democratic leader **Philipp Scheidemann** declared a republic in Berlin, with **Friedrich Ebert** as its first president. Germany then signed an **armistice** in a railroad car outside of Compiègne, France, on November 11. Following the armistice, France pressed in the **Treaty of Ver-**

1871
Through careful political maneuvering by Bismarck, Germany founded the unified German Empire.

1914
The great powers of Western Europe are plunged into WWI.

1918
The Treaty of Versailles exact harsh reparation payments from Germany, leaving it demoralized and economically vulnerable. The Weimar Republic is declared.

LIFE AND TIMES

sailles for staggering reparation payments, reducing the German army to 100,000 men, and ascribing full blame for the war to Germany. The newborn republic was literally starved into accepting the treaty by an Allied blockade.

Now Germany's oldest political party, the **Social Democratic Party of Germany** (*Sozialdemokratische Partei Deutschlands--SPD*), was historically sympathetic to socialism with a base among both the working and middle classes, and bolstered the newly-forged republic. Feeding on popular unease, the new **Communist Party** (*Kommunistische Partei Deutschlands*— KPD), led by **Karl Liebknecht** and **Rosa Luxemburg,** launched a revolt in Berlin (p. 88). A group of right-wing army veterans launched their own coup d'état under **Wolfgang Kapp;** the workers, however, didn't share their revolutionary fervor, and demonstrated support for the new republic, organizing a force of 50,000-80,000 against the coup. The republic emerged bruised but intact. Its leaders drew up a constitution in **Weimar** (p. 551), the birthplace of German Enlightenment, which now gave its name to the period of intense cultural activity between the World Wars.

By 1922-23, hyperinflation from war debts had become so severe that paying for a loaf of bread physically required a wheelbarrow full of bills. The American **Dawes Plan** staved off total economic collapse by reducing the demand for war reparations. Relative calm and remarkable artistic production ensued, though the old, reactionary order still clung to power in many levels of society. It was during the abortive 1923 **Beer Hall Putsch** uprising in Munich that **Adolf Hitler,** then a frustrated artist and decorated Austrian corporal, was arrested. He received the minimum sentence of five years, but served only 10 months. It was during his imprisonment that Hitler wrote **Mein Kampf** (My Struggle), attacking both Communists and Jews and stressing the importance of *Lebensraum* ("living space"). Hilter came to believe that his party, the **National Socialist German Workers Party** (Nationalsozialistische deutsche Arbeiterspartei-NSDAP, also known as the Nazis), should seize power by constitutional means. Though the Nazi party had nearly quadrupled its membership to 108,000 by 1929, it was still a fringe party, receiving only 2.6% of the vote. The same year, the Great Depression struck, leaving 25% of the population unemployed; membership in the party exploded to over a million. The **SA** *(Sturmabteilung),* its paramilitary arm, grew to match the German army by 1930. Hitler failed in a presidential bid against the aging Franco-Prussian war-hero Paul von Hindenburg in 1932, but parliamentary elections made the Nazis the largest party in the Reichstag. After intense political maneuvering, Hindenburg reluctantly appointed Hitler chancellor of a coalition government on January 30, 1933.

1933
President Hindenburg appoints Hitler chancellor of Germany.

BIRTH OF THE THIRD REICH: 1933-1939. Although Hitler now held the most powerful government post, the Nazi party still had difficulty obtaining a majority in the Reichstag. Politically astute, Hitler used the mysterious **Reichstag fire** one week prior to the elections—then attributed to Communists—to declare a state of emergency and round up his opponents, many of whom were relocated to newly-built **concentration camps.** Within two months of taking control, Hitler convinced the ailing Hindenburg to dissolve the Reichstag and hold new elections, allowing Hitler to invoke **Article 48,** a provision drafted by sociologist Max Weber that granted Hitler the power to rule by decree for seven weeks. During this reign of terror, he curtailed freedom of the press, authorized special security arms (the Special State Police or **Gestapo,** the SA Storm Troopers, and the **SS** Security Police), and brutalized opponents. In the ensuing election on March 5, 1933 the Nazis got 44% of the votes, once again less than a majority. However, they arrested and browbeat enough opposing legislators to secure passage of an **Enabling Act** in 1933, making Hitler the legal dictator of Germany. Hitler proclaimed his rule the **Third Reich,** successor to the Holy Roman Empire (800-1806) and the German Empire (1871-1918).

Vilifying the Weimar government as soft and ineffectual, Hitler's platform played on post-war anxieties. Germany's failing economy forced greater uncertainty upon a country that was largely receptive to ideas of anti-Semitism and German racial superiority, gleaned from centuries of struggle for a national identity in an atmosphere of continental anti-Semitism. Nazi rallies were masterpieces of political demagoguery, and the Nazi emblem, the **swastika** (co-opted from Hindu tradition), appeared everywhere from propaganda films to the fingernails of loyal teenagers. *Heil Hitler* and the right arm salute became a legally required greeting.

To restore the floundering economy, Hitler pushed for massive industrialization, creating jobs in munitions factories. Hitler defied the Versailles Treaty, refusing to pay reparations and beginning rearmament. Next, he annexed Austria—staring down the Western Allies with the infamous "**Anschluß Österreichs**"—in 1938. He demanded territorial concessions from Czechoslovakia, claiming (truthfully) that ethnic Germans comprised the majority of the population in the **Sudetenland**. British Prime Minister Neville Chamberlain assured Hitler in the 1938 **Munich Agreement** that Britain would not interfere with this hostile takeover in exchange for future peace. The Allies continued to tolerate Germany's aggressive expansionism until war was inevitable. Not everyone kept silent, though; **resistance** movements sprang up in Germany, such as the **Weiße Rose** (White Rose) student group.

WORLD WAR II: 1939-1945. On September 1, 1939, German tanks rolled across the eastern border into Poland. Britain and France, bound by treaty to defend Poland, declared war on Germany but did not attack. The Soviet Union likewise ignored the German invasion, having secretly divided up Eastern Europe with Germany under the **Molotov-Ribbentrop Pact.** Within a month, Poland had been crushed by Germany's new tactic of **Blitzkrieg** (literally, "lightning war"); Hitler and Stalin carved it up between themselves. By April 9, 1940, Hitler had overrun Denmark and Norway. A month later, *Blitzkrieg* roared

LIFE AND TIMES

1938
Kristallnacht, an early and brutal display of anti-Semitism, foreshadows the atrocities of the Holocaust, in which 6 million Jews and 5 million homosexuals, Gypsies, Slavs, Soviets, the mentally disabled, and political dissenters were killed.

1939
After steadily annexing territory, Germany invades Poland and initiates WWII.

through Luxembourg and overwhelmed Belgium, the Netherlands, and France. Despite leveling most of the city, the Nazis failed to bomb London into submission in the aerial **Battle of Britain**. Hitler shelved preparations for a cross-channel invasion, turning his attention to the Soviet Union. The German **invasion of the USSR** in June 1941 ended the Hitler-Stalin pact, bringing the Soviets in on the side of France and Britain. Despite the Red Army's overwhelming manpower, the German invasion nearly succeeded. At his apex of power in late 1941, Hitler held an empire from the Arctic Circle to the Sahara Desert and from the Pyrenees to the Urals.

The Soviets suffered extremely high casualties, but *Blitzkrieg* faltered in the Russian winter. Hitler's stubborn refusal to allow a retreat at the bloody battle of **Stalingrad** resulted in the death or capture of over 200,000 troops and represented a crucial turning point on the Eastern Front. Following the bombing of Pearl Harbor, Hitler declared war on the U.S. The Allies began their counterattack in North Africa, and soon Germany was retreating on all fronts. The Allied landings in Normandy on **D-Day** (June 6, 1944) preceded an arduous, bloody advance across Western Europe. The Third Reich's final offensive, the **Battle of the Bulge,** failed in December 1944. As part of the Allies' advance the following February, the **firebombing of Dresden** killed at least 35,000 Germans, mostly civilians and refugees (see Dresden, p. 598). This was one of many lamentable assaults on civilian populations worldwide that exemplified 20th century warfare and the concept of **Total War**. In March 1945, the Allies crossed the Rhine; in April, the Red Army took Berlin. With Soviet troops closing in, Hilter committed suicide along with his long-time mistress and recent wife, **Eva Braun**. The Third Reich, which Hitler had boasted would endure for 1000 years, had lasted only 12.

THE HOLOCAUST. The persecution of the Jews began years before WWII. The racial ideology that had fueled Hitler's rise to power framed history in terms of racial confrontations with absolute winners and losers. Hitler believed that the German *Volk* ("people") would either triumph universally or perish; in his mind, Jews threatened his program of fanatic nationalism, militarism, and belief in the infallibility of the *Führer*. In 1935 the first anti-Semitic **Racial Purity Laws** deprived Jews of German citizenship. On November 9, 1938, known as **Kristallnacht** (Night of Broken Glass), Nazis across Germany destroyed Jewish businesses, burned synagogues, killed nearly 100 Jews, and sent 20,000 more to concentration camps.

Early on, German SS troops massacred entire Jewish towns as they rolled eastward, but as the war progressed, institutions of mass execution were developed as Nazis further expanded the persecution and deportation of minorities under their control. Seven extermination camps—**Auschwitz, Buchenwald** (p. 558), **Chelmno, Treblinka, Majdanek, Sobibor, and Belzec**—and dozens of "labor" camps such as **Bergen-Belsen** (p. 258), **Dachau** (p. 435), and **Sachsenhausen** (p. 151) were operating before war's end. Nearly six million Jews (two-thirds of Europe's Jew-

1945
The Allies defeat Germany and divide the country and its capitol in four distinct zones.

ish population), mostly from Poland and the Soviet Union, were gassed, shot, starved, worked to death, or killed by exposure, along with five million other Soviets, Slavs, Gypsies, homosexuals, the mentally disabled, and political dissenters as part of Hitler's atrocious and systematic "**final solution.**"

OCCUPATION AND DIVISION: 1945-1949. Germans call their defeat at the end of WWII *Nullstunde*—"Zero Hour"—the moment at which everything began again. Germany had suffered an estimated 3.6 million military and 1.3 million civilian casualties, and 5.7 million more civilian deaths followed the war, resulting largely from the mass deportation of Germans from Eastern Europe. The war left Germany desolate, and reconstruction under Allied occupation did not begin until 1948. In July 1945, the U.S., the U.K., France, and the Soviet Union met at **Potsdam** to partition Germany into occupation zones: German territory east of the Oder and Neisse rivers— one quarter of the nation—was confiscated and placed under Soviet and Polish administration, the coal-rich Saarland was put under French control (until 1957), the U.K. held the northwest, and the U.S. occupied the south. Berlin was divided into four sectors and western sectors later united to form **West Berlin,** while the U.S.S.R. controlled **East Berlin**.

The three-pronged Allied program of **Occupation**—demilitarization, democratization, and de-Nazification (including the 1945 war crimes trials in Nuremberg)—proceeded apace, but growing animosity between the Soviets and the Western allies made joint control of Germany difficult. In 1947, the Western Allies merged their occupation zones into a single economic unit, to be rebuilt as a market economy with a huge cash infusions from the American **Marshall Plan.** The Soviets, who suffered immeasurably more in the war, had neither the desire nor the resources to help the East rebuild; instead, they plundered it. The Western Allies ceased their contribution to the East in 1948 and severed the East's economy from the West's by introducing a new currency, the **Deutschmark.** This resulted in a Soviet **blockade** of West Berlin, followed shortly by the full **division of Germany** in 1949.

EAST AND WEST: 1949-1989. Upon division, West Germany established the **Bundesrepublik Deutschland (BRD),** or Federal Republic of Germany, as a provisional government. Its headquarters were seated in the sleepy university town of Bonn. Under Western supervision, the fledgling government drafted a **Basic Law** to safeguard individual rights. The document did not ratify German autonomy, however, as the Allies retained ultimate political authority over the country. The first chancellor of the new government was **Konrad Adenauer,** whose Christian Democratic Union (*Christlich Demokratische Union*—CDU) had won a small parliamentary majority over the Social Democratic Party (*Sozialdemokratische Partei Deuschlands*— SPD) in the 1949 elections. Adenauer pushed to integrate Germany with a unified Europe—a goal that anticipated the creation of the EU—and to reestablish German national self-determination, culminating in the recognition of **West German**

1949
French, American, and British holdings in Germany are consolidated into the autonomous Federal Republic of Germany; East Germany becomes the socialist German Democratic Republic (DDR).

sovereignty by the Western Allies in 1955. Reconstruction helped restore self-esteem in post-war BRD citizens. An influx of *Gastarbeiter* (guest workers) from Turkey and the guidance of economist **Ludwig Erhard** helped transform West Germany into the world's fourth-largest economy by the 1960s.

Meanwhile, the Soviet Union ended free elections after the **Socialist Unity Party** (*Sozialistische Einheitspartei Deutschlands*—SED) suffered a defeat at the hands of the SPD in Berlin ballot boxes. A People's Congress of pre-selected candidates from the SED was "elected" and declared the establishment of the **Deutsche Demokratische Republik (DDR)**, or German Democratic Republic. Berlin housed the new government under SED leader **Wilhelm Pieck.** While the republic paid lip service to guarantees of civil liberties, the SED retained strict controls over citizens of the DDR, causing many to seek refuge in West Germany. Political conditions relaxed after Stalin's death in 1953, but nationalization of industry continued and impossibly high goals resulted in a **worker's revolt** on June 17, 1953, which was quickly crushed by Soviet tanks. In 1955, in response to the BRD's normalization of relations with the West, the DDR joined in signing the **Warsaw Pact.**

1961
The Berlin Wall is constructed.

By 1961, the tally of illegal emigrants from East to West had reached three million. With SED party head **Walter Ulbricht** at the helm, the DDR decided to act; on the night of August 12, the beginnings of the **Berlin Wall** were constructed. By morning, Berliners found themselves blessed with an "anti-fascist protective wall"; however, it was clear that Easterners themselves were being contained. In 1968, Ulbricht signed the DDR's second constitution, jettisoning most democratic rights.

The BRD's miraculous recovery had ground to a halt by 1967, when its first post-war recession loosened the CDU's grip on power. The Social Democrats embraced dynamic young leader **Willy Brandt,** who took control in 1969 and enacted vital reforms and diplomatic achievements. His **Ostpolitik** (Eastern Policy) sought improved relations with the DDR and the rest of the Eastern Bloc. For the first time, many *Wessis* (West Berliners) were permitted to visit their relatives in the East. Brandt won the Nobel Peace Prize in 1971. Meanwhile, East German president **Erich Honecker** maintained East German subservience to the Soviet Union. By the late 1970s, DDR citizens enjoyed the highest standard of living in the Eastern Bloc, but were still far behind the West. The secret police, or **Stasi,** held files on every citizen; one in seven East Germans was a paid informant.

Throughout the 1970s, West Germany continued to prosper. As unemployment mounted, however, the Social Democrats lost popularity. **Helmut Kohl** of the CDU became chancellor in 1982, enacting tight monetary policy and military cooperation with the US. In 1985, **Mikhail Gorbachev** of the USSR, who utilized *glasnost* ("openness"), sent waves of reform throughout the Eastern Bloc—except the DDR. In May 1989, Hungary dismantled its barbed-wire border with Austria. On October 6, Gorbachev attended East Germany's 40th birthday and rebuked Honecker publicly, announcing that the USSR would not interfere with the DDR's domestic affairs. Honecker

1989
The Berlin Wall falls.

resigned; chaos reigned as thousands of DDR citizens escaped to the West via Czechoslovakia. On November 8, the entire DDR *Politbüro* stepped down. One day later, a Central Committee spokesperson announced the **opening of all borders to the West,** including the Berlin Wall.

REUNIFICATION AND ITS AFTERMATH: 1989-2000. The *Wende* ("change" or "turning"), as East Germans call the DDR's end, was the most significant turning point in Germany since WWII; the euphoria of those months is most evocatively expressed by images of Berliners celebrating on the Brandenburg Gate (the symbolic conduit between East and West) and tearing apart the Wall. However, joy soon gave way to disillusionment as the DDR lingered and East and West feuded over the terms of *Wiedervereinigung* (reunification). In March 1990, the CDU-backed **Alliance for Germany** won elections, preserving Kohl's hold on power. On September 12, 1990, the two Germanys and four occupying powers signed the **Four-Plus-Two** treaty, signifying the **end of a divided Germany;** October 3, 1990 marks the date on which the Allies forfeited their occupation rights of Berlin.

Reunification was not conducted on equal terms; the East was absorbed into the structure of the BRD, which then tried desperately to deal with the its counter-part's inefficient industries and institutions. The BRD plunged into its worst recession in history, with unemployment skyrocketing in the East. Westerners resented the inflation and taxes required to rebuild the new federal states, while Easterners had to go without the generous social benefits afforded them by communism. Economic frustrations led to scapegoating of foreigners, punctuated by attacks on immigrants in Mölln and Rostock in 1992 and 1993.

The BRD's post-*Wende* woes led to Kohl's ouster in 1998, after a 16-year run, by **Gerhard Schröder,** who led a coalition of Social Democrats and the **Green Party.** He appointed environmental warrior **Joschka Fischer** as secretary of state, who soon announced that the government intended to shut down all of Germany's nuclear reactors, causing heated tension with France and the UK. In 1999, the government moved from Bonn to Berlin, inaugurating the much-heralded **Berlin Republic.**

TODAY

While average unemployment in Germany hovers around 11%, rates in the former DDR remain almost twice as high. Nevertheless, Germany still boasts **the world's third-largest economy** and is the European Union's industrial heavyweight, giving it tremendous clout. Many Germans believe that the nation should be more isolated, but the country's centrality in the EU keeps it in the thick of international affairs.

POLITICS. 2005 saw the election of Germany's first female chancellor, **Angela Merkel.** Head of the conservative Christian Democrats (CDU), Merkel heads a coalition government with her Christian Social Union of Bavaria (SCU) and the historic SPD. The previous chancellor of 7 years, the Social Democrat

1990
Germany is officially reunified.

1992
The European Union is established.

2005
Germany's first female chancellor, Angela Merkel, is elected.

Schröder, proved unable to shake the economic difficulties that plagued his career. Merkel's coalition plans to cut government spending to combat the growing deficit, and foresees a renewed commitment to NATO and the EU. The hotly contested extension of EU membership to Turkey remains undecided and will remain so for several years; some members of the CDU oppose Turkish membership in part because of the country's questionable human rights standards and anti-Christian persecution.

FOREIGN POLICY. Germany was one of the most outspoken critics of Anglo-American foreign policy in the wake of the terrorist attack of September 11, 2001; American officials called relations "poisoned" and refrained from sending congratulations to Schröder when he was re-elected. But recent ties have become far more cordial: in February of 2004 Schröder and US President Bush issued a joint statement on "The German-American Alliance for the 21st Century." Schröder also accepted French President Jacques Chirac's invitation to the 60th-anniversary commemoration of the Allied D-Day invasion, calling that day a victory for Germany as well as for the Allies. Merkel's coalition government has expressed a renewed commitment to mutli-lateral action, as well as issues of national and international security; the **Coalition Agreement** aims to bolster democracy worldwide, specifically in Eastern Europe, as well as to continue supporting the reconstruction of Afghanistan and the Balkans.

LANGUAGE

Though German, or *Deutsch*, is clearly the language of choice in Germany, don't despair if your *Sprach* (speech) is sub-par. Most people in urban areas, especially younger Germans, are impressively fluent in English. Depending on your German background, you may find it easier to use English as a tourist. Dialects are distinct and disparate—it's no surprise that *Frieslanders* and Bavarians can often barely understand each other (see **Speaking of German,** p. 63).

RELIGION

Germany's legacy as a land of strong Catholic rule under the Holy Roman Empire was followed closely by a long tradition of Protestantism: it was in Wittenberg that Luther nailed his 95 Theses to the church door in 1517. Germany has developed as a Christian country (supported by the government), with the Protestant North and the Roman Catholic South each currently representing about one-third of the country's inhabitants. The total Jewish population in Germany today is well above 100,000. The largest Jewish congregations are in Berlin and Frankfurt, which are together home to over 25,000 Jews. An influx of foreign workers has brought a strong Islamic population; more than three million Muslims, most from Turkey, now live in Germany, and mosques can be found in many cities.

CULTURE

FOOD AND DRINK

German food gets bad press. Maybe it isn't as "gourmet" as French cuisine or "delicato" as Italian fare, but *deutsche Küche* has a robust charm that meat-and-potato lovers find especially satisfying. And if the local food is not to your taste, Germany's cities offer a wide variety of quality ethnic restaurants.

LIFE AND TIMES

Exploring the dialects of everyone's favorite "language"

German is recognized as an official or national language in eight nations: Germany, Switzerland, Austria, Italy, Denmark, Belgium, Luxembourg, and Liechtenstein. It's used by over 100 million people, making it the world's 10th most widely-spoken language. But "German" is not actually a language at all. Even on a good day, a Bavarian farmer and a sailor from Bremen would probably not understand each other, despite their common citizenship. The "German language" is, in fact, a wide group of related but distinct dialects.

So what exactly do the terms "language" and "dialect" actually mean? Most linguists would say that if two people can communicate with each other fairly well, they're speaking the same language. And if those people happen to speak with the same pronunciation, grammar, and vocabulary, they're speaking the same dialect. There are three main language areas in the German-speaking part of Europe, each with countless dialects.

Oberdeutsch (Upper German) is spoken in the mountains (hence "upper") of Austria, Switzerland, Liechtenstein, northern Italy, and southern Germany. People here are fervently proud of their heritage, and hardly ever speak Standard German; you'll probably have trouble understanding their thick accent and musical intonation. Make sure you order a *Maß* (liter) of *Bock* (strong beer), *Goaßmaß* (beer, cola, and cognac), or *Schdamperl* (schnapps) at the bar; if you're a *Saufaus* (strong drinker), you might end up doing a *Schuaplattler* (drunken bar dance). Just remember to use a *Biafuizl* (beer cover) or you'll fall prey to the *Noagerlzuzla* (guy-who-drinks-up-your-beer-while-you're-not-watching). More importantly, don't *froasel* (annoy) any *Eigschnappters* (easily-insulted guys) or you'll get *aufgmischt* (thrashed) in the *Hoisl* (bathroom).

Mitteldeutsch (Middle German) is spoken from Luxembourg to Poland and the Czech Republic, across central Germany. This narrow band has spawned two national languages. *Hochdeutsch* (Standard German) is based on the 16th-century Middle German spoken around Meißen. *Lützebuergesch* (Luxembourgish) is a western Middle German dialect that is now one of the three official languages of the Grand Duchy of Luxembourg (with Hochdeutsch and French).

In the coastal plains of southern Denmark, eastern Netherlands, and northern Germany and Poland, people speak a very different language, variously named *Niederdeutsch* (Low German), *Niedersächsisch* (Low Saxon), *Plattdeutsch* (Flat German), or just *Platt*. English speakers may breathe a sigh of relief in these lowlands; the Platt dialects often sound and look more like English than German. The words for open, water, good, and later, for example, are spelled (but not spoken) the same in both English and Platt (compare with the Hochdeutsch *offen*, *Wasser*, *gut*, and *später*). The huge difference between Platt and Hochdeutsch (Northern Germans can converse more easily with their Dutch neighbors than with other Germans) is leading to Platt's gradual decline; speakers are so self-conscious of their distinct language that most of them prefer to speak Standard German even at home. *Niederdeutsch* resembles English in its refusal to participate in the softening of consonants p, t, and k to f, s, and ch, respectively, a shift that occurred in Mittel- and Oberdeutsch. Where Standard German speakers would say *Schiff* (ship), *weiß* (white), and *brechen* (breaking), northerners might prefer *Schipp*, *witt*, and *breken*.

So how did German reach this fractured state, and why doesn't everyone just speak the same language? The answer is historical: a map of medieval Europe shows that the "German-speaking area" was originally settled by dozens of distinct tribes. Distantly related through ancestry, Franks, Saxons, Burgundians, Thuringians, Alemannes, and Bavarians formed their own kingdoms and spoke their own languages. When dealing with other tribes, officials often turned to Latin: totally foreign, but universally respected.

Not until the kingdoms of central Europe were united under the Holy Roman Empire did the common people get fed up with resorting to Latin to communicate with the next city. Martin Luther picked up on this and boldly translated the Bible from Latin into a local Saxon dialect. He picked this believing it would be the easiest to understand across the whole Empire, which at that time comprised the modern-day nations of Germany, Austria, and Switzerland. His translation formed the base from which later writers slowly shaped a standard German language.

This unifying language, *Hochdeutsch*, is taught in all public schools, and is used in formal situations, the media, and virtually all written documents. Colloquial variations of *Hochdeutsch*, called *Umgangssprachen* (literally, "languages of going around"), introduce regional pronunciation and vocabulary to varying degrees. All Germans are familiar with *Hochdeutsch*, but few of them are ready to trade in their ancient linguistic traditions for national unity. In the past decade, more literature, news, and songs have been published in local dialects, a sign that Germans will likely remain a proudly multilingual people.

Sameer ud Dowla Khan is a graduate student in Linguistics at the University of California, Los Angeles, focusing in phonology. He's loved German in all of its forms since he first heard it spoken, and has been studying it for several years, along with Spanish, Bengali, Chinese, and Arabic.

THE REAL DEAL. Germany is admirably obsessed with conservation and energy efficiency; this sometimes manifests itself in inconvenient ways. For example, most grocery stores don't offer shopping bags. If you plan to buy more than you can carry in your hands, bring your own bag along. *– Amelia Atlas*

Vegetarians should not fear this land of carnivores. Since the 1970s, vegetarianism has steadily gained popularity in Germany. Approximately one-fifth of Germany's population now eats little or no meat, and most cities, and vegetarian and *Biokost* (health food) restaurants and supermarkets are common. Be sure to mention *ich bin Vegetarier(en)* ("I am a vegetarian") when dining, or simply say *kein Fleisch* ("no meat"). As most vegetarian fare relies heavily on cheese, **vegans** may have a more difficult time. For more information, see **Dietary Concerns** (p. 49).

The typical German **Frühstück** (breakfast) consists of coffee or tea with a selection of *Brötchen* (rolls), butter, marmalade, *Wurst* (cold sausage of myriad varieties), *Schinken* (ham), *Eier* (eggs, usually soft- or hard-boiled), *Käse* (cheese), and *Müsli* (granola). **Mittagessen** (lunch) is traditionally the main meal of the day, consisting of soup, sausage or roasted meat, potatoes or dumplings, and a salad or *Gemüsebeilage* (vegetable side dish). **Abendessen** or **Abendbrot** (supper) is a re-enactment of breakfast, with less *Müsli* and coffee, and more wine or beer. **Dessert** after meals is rare, but many older Germans indulge in a daily ritual of **Kaffee und Kuchen** (coffee and cakes), analogous to English "tea-time," at 3 or 4pm.

Germany's bakeries produce a delicious range of **Brot** (bread). *Vollkornbrot* is a heavy whole-wheat, *Roggenbrot* is rye, *Schwarzbrot* (black bread) is a dense, dark loaf, and *Bauernbrot* (farmers' bread) a lighter, slightly sour country recipe. Go to a *Bäckerei* (bakery) and point to whatever looks good. Bread is usually sold as a whole loaf; for half, ask for *ein Halbes*. German bread does not contain preservatives and will go stale the day after its purchase; Germans typically make the *Bäckerei* a daily stop. *Brötchen* (rolls) come in staggering varieties, starting with the simple, white *Wasserbrötchen* and extending to the hearty *Kürbiskernbrötchen* (pumpkin seed rolls). No visit to Germany would be complete without a taste of a *Bretzel*, the south German soft pretzel that puts ballpark vendors to shame, and that in larger bakeries also comes in roll and even baguette shapes.

Aside from breads, the staples of the German diet are *Wurst* (sausage, in dozens of varieties; see **The Best Wurst**, p. 323), *Schweinefleisch* (pork), *Rindfleisch* (beef), *Kalbfleisch* (veal), *Lammfleisch* (lamb), *Huhn* (chicken), and *Kartoffeln* (potatoes). Sampling the various **local specialties** around Germany gives a taste of diverse culinary traditions. In **Bavaria,** *Knödel* (potato and flour dumplings, sometimes filled with meat or jam) are popular, as is *Weißwurst,* a sausage made with milk. Thüringen and northern Bavaria are famed for their succulent grilled *Bratwurst,* a roasted sausage eaten with potatoes or bought from a street vendor clasped in a roll and bathed in mustard and *sauerkraut.* Southwestern Germany is known for its *Spätzle* (rough, twisty egg noodles), and *Maultaschen* (pasta pockets) are popular in **Swabia. Hessians** do amazing things with potatoes; be sure to sample the *grüne Soße* (green sauce). The North and Baltic seacoasts harvest *Krabben* (shrimp) and *Matjes* (herring), as well as other fresh forms of seafood.

When Turks began immigrating to West Germany in the early 1960s, the German palate was first treated to such now-ubiquitous delights as the *Döner Kebap;* thin slices of lamb mixed with cucumbers, onions, and red cabbage in a wedge of *Fladenbrot,* a round, flat, sesame-covered bread. Other well-known Turkish dishes include *Börek,* a flaky pastry filled with spinach, cheese, or meat; and *Lahmacun* (also called *türkische Pizza*), a smaller, zestier version of Italy's staple fast food. Turkish restaurants and *Imbiße,* popular and cheap fast-food stands, also offer *Kefir* (flavored yogurt drinks) and *Baklava* for dessert.

Beer and wine (p. 65) are the popular meal-time **beverages.** *Saft* (juice), plain or mixed with mineral water, is an alternative. Germans do not guzzle glasses of water by the dozen, instead they will sip a (small) glass of carbonated mineral water—ask for *Wasser ohne Gas* to get the non-bubbly kind. If you ask for water in a restaurant, you'll get the expensive bottled type, so be sure to ask for *Leitungswasser* (tap water) if that's what you want.

With very few exceptions **restaurants** expect you to seat yourself. If there are no free tables, ask someone for permission to take a free seat by saying *Darf ich Platz nehmen?* (DAHRF eesh PLAHTS nay-men). In a less formal setting, just say *hallo*. It's standard practice for perfect strangers to plunk down next to you—they may or may not be interested in conversation. At the table, Germans eat with the fork in the left hand and the knife in the right and keep their hands above or resting on the table. While eating, it is polite to keep the tines of your fork pointing down at all times. When you're finished, ask the server *Zahlen, bitte* (TSAH-len, BIT-tuh: "check, please"); it's considered rude to bring customers the bill before they have asked for it. Taxes *(Mehrwertsteuer)* and service *(Bedienung)* are always included in the price, but it is customary to leave a small tip, usually by rounding up the bill to the nearest euro.

Eating in restaurants at every meal will quickly drain your budget. One strategy to save money at restaurants is to stick to the daily fixed-price option, called the *Tagesmenü*. A cheaper option is to buy food in **grocery stores.** University students eat in cafeterias called **Mensen.** Some *Mensen* (singular *Mensa*) require a student ID (or charge higher prices for non-students). In smaller towns, the best budget option is to stop by a bakery *(Bäckerei)* for bread and garnish it with sausage and cheese purchased from a butcher *(Fleischerei* or *Metzgerei)*.

BEER

Beer brewers shall sell no beer to the citizens, unless it be three weeks old; to the foreigner, they may knowingly sell younger beer.
  —German Beer Law, 1466

Germans have brewed frothy, alcoholic malt beverages since the 8th century BC, and they've been consuming and exporting them in prodigious quantities ever since. The state of Bavaria alone contains about one-fifth of all the breweries in the world. Germans drink more than 120L of beer per person every year. According to legend, the German king Gambrinus

WOULD YOU LIKE FRIES WITH THAT?

While Frankfurters happily grill their hot dogs and Berliners savor their donuts, the people of Hamburg get to share their name with the world's most beloved sandwich: the hamburger.

The hamburger's history spans many years and thousands of miles. Although descriptions of ground beef date back to Roman times, the burger's development began in earnest in medieval Russia, where nomadic Tartars ate raw, chopped beef mixed with spices. German sailors observed this practice and, after (mercifully) deciding that the meat should be cooked instead of eaten raw, they brought it back to the docks of Hamburg.

The "Hamburger steak" would have to leave Germany before it could gain a bun. German immigrants brought recipes for the steak (still bunless) with them to America in the 1870s, where it became popular in restaurants. In 1904, an enterprising vendor first served the hamburger on bread at the World's Fair in St. Louis. Its popularity exploded in America in the years before WWI.

The burger in its present form was slow to return to Germany, and many restaurants still serve Hamburger steak without a bun. In spite of the proud tradition surrounding the original dish, most Germans are loathe to surrender the bun, and the hamburger thrives in its modified form.

invented the modern beer recipe when he threw some hops into fermenting malt. During the Middle Ages, monastic orders refined the art of brewing, imbibing to stave off starvation during long fasts. It wasn't long before the monks' lucrative trade caught the eye of secular lords, who established the first *Hofbrauereien* (court breweries).

To ensure the quality of this new phenomenon, Duke Wilhelm IV of Bavaria decreed in 1516 that beer could contain only pure water, barley, and hops. Wilhelm's Purity Law *(Reinheitsgebot)* has endured to this day, with minor alterations to permit the cultivation of Bavaria's trademark wheat-based beers. As a result, German beer contains no preservatives and will spoil relatively quickly. Most German beer is **Vollbier,** containing about 4% alcohol. **Export** (5%) is also popular, and stout, tasty **Bockbier** (6.25%) is brewed in the spring. **Doppelbock** is an strong malt reserved for special occasions. *Ein Helles* gets you a light-colored beer, while *ein Dunkles* can look like anything from Coca-Cola to molasses. The average German beer is maltier and thicker than Czech, Dutch, or American beers (hence the term *"flußiges Brot"*: liquid bread). Generalizations are difficult, however, as each region boasts its own special brew. Here are a few:

BEER	REGION	DESCRIPTION
Altbier	Düsseldorf	dark, top-fermented beer
Berliner Weiße	Berlin	light beer, often served with *Schuß* (raspberry syrup)
Bockbier & Doppelbock	Einbeck (near Hannover)	strong, bottom-fermented, many seasonal versions
Dampfbier	Bayreuth	fruity, top-fermented
Dortmunder Export	Dortmund	mild, bottom-fermented lager
Dunkles Lagerbier	Bavaria	dark lager, strong malt, bottom-fermented
Gose	Leipzig	top-fermented wheat beer with oats
Hefeweizen	Bavaria	wheat beer, more hops than Weißbier
Kölsch	Cologne (Köln)	pale, top-fermented beer (by law, served only in Köln)
Märzen	Bavaria	amber colored lager
Pils (Pilsner)	North Germany	clear, bitter taste (extra hops)
Radler (Alster)	Hamburg	mix of half beer, half lemon-lime soda
Rauchbier	Bamberg	dark and smoky
Weißbier (Weizenbier)	Bavaria/south	wheat beer, smooth and refreshing, rich brown color

The variety of places to drink beer is almost as staggering as the variety of brews. A traditional **Biergarten** consists of outdoor tables under chestnut trees; often, simple food is served as well. In the days before refrigeration, the broad leaves of the trees kept beer barrels cool—now they just shade the beer drinkers. A **Bierkeller** is a subterranean version of the *Biergarten*. To order *ein Bier*, hold up your thumb, not your index finger. Raise your glass to a *Prost* (cheers), make eye contact with your companions, and drink (for more information, see **The Proper Prost**, p. 452). Another option for drinking is the **Gaststätte**, a simple, local restaurant. It's considered bad form to order only drinks at a *Gaststätte* during mealtimes, but at other times friends linger for hours over beers. Many *Gaststätten* have a *Stammtisch* (regulars' table) marked by a flag where interlopers should not sit. The same group of friends may meet at the *Stammtisch* every week for decades to drink and play cards. **Kneipen** are bars where hard liquor is also served.

WINE AND SPIRITS

Although overshadowed by Germany's more famous export beverage, German wines win over connoisseurs and casual drinkers alike. Over 80% of German wines are white, though they vary widely in character. Generally, German wines are

LIVING UNDER GLASS. Most of Germany's beverage bottles—containing everything from cola to beer—are made of glass, and bars will often add a €1-2 *Pfand* (deposit) to the advertised price. Return the bottle, and you'll get your *Pfand* back. Grocery stores have collection bins for the absent-minded, but retail reimbursements are much lower.

sweeter and taste fresher than French, Mediterranean, or Californian wines. Because Germany is the northernmost of the wine-producing countries, the quality of a vineyard's produce can vary considerably with the climate.

Dry wines are labeled *trocken* or *halbtrocken* (literally, half dry), while mild, sweeter wines are called *lieblich*. Only wines with 45g/L of residual sugars can be labeled *süss* (sweet). Cheap wines are classified as *Tafelwein* (table wine) or *Landwein* (superior table wine), while the good stuff (which is still pretty affordable) is *Qualitätswein* (quality wine). The label *Qualitätswein bestimmter Anbaugebiete*, or *Q. b. A.*, designates quality wine from a specific cultivation region. *Qualitätswein mit Prädikat* (quality wine with distinction) denotes an even purer wine derived from a particular variety of grape. The *Prädikat* wines are further subdivided according to the ripeness of the grapes when harvested; from least to most ripe, they are *Kabinett, Spätlese, Auslese, Beerenauslese, Trockenbeerenauslese*, and *Eiswein*. The grapes that produce the *Trockenbeerenauslese* are left on the vine well into winter until they have shriveled into raisins and begun to rot—seriously. During the *Erntefesten* (harvest festivals) of many towns in the Southwest, vintners will sometimes add alcohol to the fresh-pressed, cloudy grape juice to make the intoxicatingly spicy *Neue Süsse* (new sweet wine).

Most vineyards cluster in the Rhein and Mosel valleys, along the Main River in Franconia, and in Baden. Of the dozens of varieties, the most famous are *Riesling, Müller-Thurgau, Sylvaner*, and *Traminer* (source of *Gewürztraminer*). In wine-producing towns, thirsty travelers can stop by a *Weinstube* for samples. In Hessen, the beverage of choice is **Ebbelwei** or **Äpfelwein** (apple wine), a hard cider similar in potency to beer. After a meal, many Germans aid their digestion by throwing back a shot of **Schnapps,** brandy distilled from fruit. **Kirschwasser,** a cherry liqueur from the Black Forest, is the best known and probably the easiest to stomach, but adventurous sorts can experiment with the sublime *Black Haus*, 100-proof blackberry *Schnapps* also from the Schwarzwald. Each year, unsuspecting tourists are lured into buying little green bottles of **Jägermeister,** a pungent take on Germany's numerous herb liqueurs.

CUSTOMS AND ETIQUETTE

Although Germans may seem reserved or even unfriendly, they are not as stand-offish as they may first appear. Germans are very frank and will not hesitate to show disapproval. To the uninitiated this may come across as confrontational, but it stems mostly from honesty. Many Germans consider effusive chumminess insincere, and Americans are often perceived as disingenuous for being overly friendly.

The complex rules of German etiquette may seem excessive; however, most apply only with older Germans and in rural areas. Even so, travelers should bear a few things in mind. In general, Germans are more formal than Americans and Australians, and incredibly big on punctuality. An invitation to a German home is a major courtesy—bring a gift for the hostess. Among the older generations, be careful not to use the informal *du* (you) or a first name without being invited to do so. *Du* is appropriate when addressing fellow students and friends, or with children. In all other circumstances, use the formal *Sie* for "you," as in the question *Sprechen Sie Englisch* (do you speak English)?

Addressing a woman as *Fräulein* is inappropriate in most instances; address all women as *Frau* (followed by a surname). While the average German's language skills are, in general, impressively well-developed, Germans will be more receptive to a traveler who knows at least a little German; learn some before you go (see the **Appendix,** p. 652, for help). In any case, remember at least two phrases: **bitte** (both please and you're welcome; BIT-tuh) and **danke** (thank you; DAHNK-uh).

The first time you see a German standing at an intersection in the rain, no cars in sight, waiting for the "walk" signal, you'll see what a law-abiding nation Germany is. **Jaywalking** is only one of several petty offenses that will mark you as a foreigner (and subject you to fines); **littering** is another. Many tourists also do not realize that the **bike lanes** marked in red between the sidewalk and the road are strictly off-limits for pedestrians. The drinking age is 16 for beer and wine and 18 for hard liquor, although neither is strictly enforced, and it is not uncommon to see young teenagers in a store picking up a bottle of wine for the family dinner. Driving under the influence, however, is a severe offense. **Drug** use has yet to become publicly acceptable, even where penalties are more relaxed (see **Essentials,** p. 18).

ARTS AND CULTURE

Germany is the land of *Dichter und Denker*—poets and philosophers. German humanities have had an enormous influence on the world, in addition to innumerable advances that German research has procured in the natural sciences.

ARCHITECTURE. Churches and castles around Germany manifest stunning Romanesque, Gothic, and Baroque styles, colored by Germany's unique history and geography. The **Romanesque** period, spanning the years 800 to 1300, arose from direct imitation of Roman ruins. Outstanding Romanesque cathedrals can be found along the Rhein at Speyer, Trier, Mainz, and Worms.

Gothic style, characterized by pointed rib vaulting, gradually replaced the Romanesque form between 1300 and 1500. Gothic cathedrals often take the form of a cross, facing east so that the morning sun would shine down onto the altar. The Gothic cathedral at Cologne (p. 278) is one of the most famous structures in Germany. Secular architecture at the end of the Middle Ages is best remembered through the **fachwerk** (half-timbered) houses that still dominate the *Altstädte* of many German cities. In the South, the **Renaissance** influence can be seen in the Augsburg Rathaus (p. 528) and the Heidelberg Schloß (p. 385).

By 1550, Lutheran reforms put a damper on the unrestrained extravagance of cathedrals in the North, while the Counter-Reformation in the Catholic South spurred the new **Baroque** style. The **Zwinger** in Dresden (p. 603) exemplifies Baroque aims of fluidity, contrast, and exaggerated motion. This style eventually reached an opulent extreme with **Rococo**, as exemplified by **Schloß Sanssouci** at Potsdam (p. 156). Versailles set a decadent precedent that influenced Bavarian castles, notably **Herrenchiemsee** (p. 487) and the **Königsschlößer** (p. 464).

Eventually this exuberance ran its course. The late 18th century saw an attempt to bring Greco-Roman prestige to Germany in the form of **Neoclassical** architecture. This style was spurred on by the pomp of **Karl Friedrich Schinkel** (p. 130), state architect of Prussia. The **Brandenburg Gate** and the buildings along **Unter den Linden** Berlin (p. 120) were products of this new, simpler period.

The **Mathildenhöhe** buildings in Darmstadt (p. 331) are products of a much more modern movement, **Jugendstil,** which took its name from *Die Jugend* magazine. This style, strongly influenced by *art nouveau,* spanned the decades before and after the turn of the century. In the 1920s and early 30s, **Walter Gropius** and the **Bauhaus** school of Weimar (p. 551) and Dessau (p. 579) came to the fore, seeking to unite the principles of form and function in sleek glass and concrete buildings.

Hitler disapproved of these new building styles. He named a design school reject, **Albert Speer,** as his minister of architecture, and commissioned hilariously large neoclassical buildings appropriate to the "thousand-year Reich." Many were intended for public rallies, such as the **congress hall** and **stadium** in Nürnberg (p. 540) and the **Olympic Stadium** in Berlin (p. 112). After the war, Soviet architecture began to clutter East Germany, reaching its pinnacle with the 368m high **Fernsehturm** (TV tower) in Berlin (p. 123). Berlin's Karl-Marx-Allee (p. 140) is rich in **Plattenbauen,** the dispassionate pre-fab apartment buildings that can be found throughout eastern Germany. Reconstruction of war-torn Altstadt architecture fostered a revival of old forms across Germany.

New construction since the reunification has once again put Germany on the architectural map, although many buildings were designed by non-German architects. Berlin is home to many high-profile projects, such as Sir Norman Foster's glass dome on the **Reichstag** (p. 126) and the reconstruction of **Potsdamer Platz** (p. 121), anchored by the steel and glass Sony Center. Daniel Libeskind's highly conceptual **Jewish Museum** (p. 146) opened in 2002, and American architect Peter Eisenman's jarring **Holocaust memorial** (p. 126) was unveiled in 2005.

FINE ARTS. German art first broke its Gothic fetters with Renaissance painters like **Matthias Grünewald** and **Hans Holbein the Younger,** who gave depth and realism to secular subjects. Their prolific colleague **Lucas Cranach** went beyond realistic portraits to churn out pieces with historical and mythological themes. **Albrecht Dürer's** series of self portraits were among the first, and most influential, in Western art; his engravings and detailed work *A Young Hare* are highly recognizable .

During the tumult of the **Protestant Reformation** and the Thirty Years' War, the visual arts suffered from lack of financial encouragement in Germany, but by the 19th century German critics were advocating Romantic painters' return to traditional, spiritual German masterworks. This idea easily bled into the melancholy landscapes of **Philipp Otto Runge** and **Caspar David Friedrich,** who painted Rügen's chalk cliffs (p. 182) and the ancient ruins of Eldena.

In the 20th century, German art boomed. **German Expressionism** recalled the symbolist tendencies of Viennese **Jugendstil** and **French Fauvism.** Its deliberately anti-realist aesthetics intensified colors and the representation of objects to project deeply personal emotions. **Die Brücke** (The Bridge) was the earliest Expressionist group, founded in Dresden in 1905. Its artists, especially the celebrated **Ernst Ludwig Kirchner,** used jarring outlines and deep color to make artwork loud and aggressively expressive. A 1911 exhibition in Munich entitled **Der Blaue Reiter** (The Blue Rider), led by Russian emigré **Wassily Kandinsky,** marked the rise of a second Expressionist school. Kandinsky's contribution was a 1910-11 series called *Improvisations*, considered to be among the first totally abstract paintings in Western art. Other members include Swiss painter **Paul Klee,** whose simple style has remained influential throughout the century.

WW I and its aftermath forced politics onto German art. **Max Ernst** started a **Dadaist** group in Cologne expressing artistic nihilism with collage and composition. The grotesque, satirical works of **Otto Dix** juggled Expressionism and Dadaism; ultimately the artist embraced **Neue Sachlichkeit** (New Objectivity), an anti-fascist movement that sought to understand the rapid modernization of life through matter-of-fact representation. Perhaps its best-known proponent, **Max Beckmann**, painted severely posed figures, expressing a tortured view of man's condition. The smaller German **Realist** movement devoted itself to bleak, critical works such as the social reform posters of **Käthe Kollwitz.** Sculptor **Ernst Barlach** infused realism with religious themes, inflaming Nazi censors (p. 172). Other prolific artists to emerge concurrently include **John Heartfield** and the collage artist **Hannah Höch.** The dynamic **Kurt Schwitters** used found objects to construct visceral projects on a large scale, later termed **installations,** including an entire studio entitled **Merzbau.**

Nazism drove most artists and their work into exile. Themes of *Blut und Boden* (Blood and Soil) dominated Nazi visual arts, depicting the mythical union of folkish blood and German soil through idealized images of workers, farmers, and soldiers of the "master race." In 1937, the Nazis' infamous **Entartete Kunst** (degenerate art) exhibit ridiculed pieces by Kandinsky, Kirchner, and other masters by displaying them alongside paintings by psychotics and mental patients.

After the war, German art made a quick recovery. In **East Germany,** state-supported **Socialist Realism** dominated, particularly in Leipzig, while West German art was characterized by **abstraction.** As time went on, installations, "happenings," and other new media art pieces, especially video, edged out painting, although **Sigmar Polke, Gerhard Richter,** and a few other masters kept the medium alive. Richter gained renown for his paintings of photos of the criminal Baader-Meinhof group, entitled *October 15, 1977.* Polke also studied with **Josef Beuys,** known for his performance art happenings, at his **Constructivist sculpture** school at Düsseldorf.

Today, Germany produces and exhibits a huge range of modern art, from video and multimedia installations to avant-garde painting and sculpture. *Kunstfonds* (art funds) have supported artists since 1980, and the modern art school in Leipzig enjoys international renown. Kassel deserves special mention, as it hosts the acclaimed "Documenta" exhibit every five years, showcasing contemporary art in various indoor and outdoor installations throughout the town. Other museums to see are Berlin's **Hamburger Bahnhof** (p. 130), Cologne's **Museum Ludwig** (p. 286), and Düsseldorf's **Kunstsammlung im Ständehaus** (p. 304). **Wolfgang Laib,** a minimalist artist who uses materials from nature, and the unconventional painter **Günter Förg,** are among Germany's dynamic and prolific contemporary artists.

LITERATURE. German literary history begins around 800 with an epic poem describing the fatal struggle between the heroic **Hildebrand** and his son Hadubrand. The next several centuries showed an intriguing mix of Christianity and Germanic myth. As chivalry took hold in Germany, lyric poetry focused on unrequited love emerged, best represented by the work of **Walther von der Vogelweide.** The medieval troubadour performed in this **Minnesang** genre until the mid-13th century, when the **lyric ballad** became popular. The epic poetry tradition continued with the 13th-

Like a Rhein-Stone Cowboy

The German obsession with the American West, with all its inconsistencies and historical baggage, is hard to miss; yet Western-themed bars only hint at a fascination more thoroughly entrenched in the German psyche. In fact, the most successful German-speaking author who ever lived, Karl May, set many of his best-selling works in the American West. One-hundred million of May's books have been sold since the first publication of his "Winnetou" tales in 1893, outsold only by the Bible, and arguably more thoroughly read. The omnipotent narrator of May's legendary Western novels, "Old Shatterhand," (May thought that the "Old" prefix would lend some American flavor) is a German who emigrates to the United States and befriends the Native American Winnetou, a "noble savage" of the highest order. The two travel together through the frontier, far from the reach of the money-grubbing Yankees in Eastern cities.

May was far from the first German author to turn his attention to the Wild West. Johann Wolfgang von Goethe was particularly fascinated by the American frontier, and was a huge fan of James Fenimore Cooper's Western tales. Like Goethe, who never made it across the Atlantic, May had not been to America when he wrote his books. Even when he finally visited the United States in 1908, the farthest west May got was Buffalo, NY, which, despite its name, leads much to be desired in the way of frontier romance.

Instead of documenting an actual phase in American history, his oeuvre functions as an exercise in German benign imperial fantasy. Whereas in the American collective memory the westward push is remembered as a bloody, albeit romantic, struggle for control of a continent, May's escapist and ahistorical tales focus on the unparalleled freedom of frontier life. This sense of liberation through expansive vistas (implicitly contrasted with the relatively densely-settled German lands) is omnipresent in German depictions of the West, from Rudolf Cronau's etchings to director Wim Wenders' photographs. In his first "Winnetou" book, May depicts a world of Germans living in harmony with the Native Americans, devoted caretakers of the West, an imagined surrogate for the colonies they never had.

Despite this element of fantasy, the Germans did have a history of settling in America, one which fed into their countrymen's interest in the West. After the failed democratic revolutions in 1848, thousands of committed German leftists left for the United States, contributing to a rising wave interest in frontier life back at home. Upon visiting America in 1886, German artist Rudolf Cronau returned to Europe with a group of Sioux whom he showed off as part of an immensely popular touring human zoo (*Völkerschau*). In 1896, Buffalo Bill's famed Wild West Show toured Europe, further stoking the German obsession with all things Western.

In 1912, May gave a speech on his life and work to over 2000 enraptured fans in Vienna, including a destitute young artist named Adolf Hitler. Hitler had been a devout May fan his entire life, reading his stories late into the night and regaling Nazi battalions with inspirational accounts of Winnetou and Old Shatterhand. During the Russian campaign, Hitler allegedly said that he wanted the Volga river to be his "Mississippi," drawing an eerie connection between North American notions of manifest destiny and the Nazi's own violent quest for Lebensraum.

While the mind of a genocidal vegetarian is hardly the first place to look for precedent, Hitler was not the only one to infer political significance from May's novels, perhaps explaining their persistent popularity on both sides of the Iron Curtain. Today, *Indianerlager* (Cowboy and Indian clubs) proliferate throughout Germany, though their program of reenactments and education cater to a steadily aging demographic.

In 1974, the German toy company Playmobil debuted a roster of three figures, a trinity familiar to every German schoolchild: the knight, the farmer, and the cowboy. While the cowboy now lives on only in reissues, young Germans still eagerly look westward, now to the latest frontier of gangster rap and fast food. The demand for authentic American burger joints in Germany far outstrips the supply; most places with names like "Route 66 Rock and Roll Drive-In Diner Truck Stop" are owned and run by Germans about as familiar with the American West as Karl May.

Will Payne was the Associate Editor for Let's Go: Germany, Twelfth Edition. He studies History and Literature at Harvard University and spent several years living in Germany.

century **Nibelungenlied,** describing the struggles of the hero **Siegfried.** During the **Reformation** in the late 15th century, **Martin Luther's** translation of the **Bible** in the 1530s laid the foundations for a standardized form of modern German writing.

What Luther did for language, **Martin Opitz** and **Andreas Gryphius** did for poetry a century later, insisting on strict rules for meter and stresses. The first significant German novel, **Hans J. C. von Grimmelshausen's** roguish epic *Simplicissimus*, was written during the Thirty Years' War. The long war hampered German literary efforts, which would slowly revive in the 18th century.

Sentimental, unusually personalized verse arose in the mid-18th century, about the time **Johann Wolfgang von Goethe** was writing his early poetry (p. 554). Goethe's lyrics possessed a revolutionary immediacy and drew on rediscovered folk songs and ballads. His novel *Die Leiden des jungen Werthers* (The Sorrows of Young Werther) drew the attention of Europe to the budding **Sturm und Drang** (Storm and Stress) movement, which would greatly influence early Romantic literature. Goethe later turned to the *Bildungsroman* (coming-of-age tale) and to themes of classicism and orientalism. His masterpieces are numerous; his retelling of the **Faust** legend is often considered the pinnacle of a German literature that had moved to the center of Europe's attention by the time Goethe died in 1832.

In the early 19th century, **Romanticism** gained momentum, with the poetry of **Novalis** and **J. C. Friedrich Hölderlin,** who wrote mythical poetry until he succumbed to insanity. While doing research for a German dictionary, **the Brothers Grimm** documented fairy tales for the first time. **E.T.A. Hoffmann** wrote ghost stories which were later analyzed by Freud (see **Bamberg,** p. 546). Romanticism gave way to realistic political literature around the time of the revolutions of 1848. **Heinrich Heine** was the finest of the **Junges Deutschland** (Young Germany) movement and also one of the first German Jews to achieve literary prominence (see **Düsseldorf,** p. 299). Social dramatists **Georg Büchner** and **Gerhart Hauptmann** achieved great influence around the turn of the century with characteristic *fin-de-siècle* realism.

Hermann Hesse incorporated Eastern spirituality into his writings (his 1922 novel *Siddhartha* became a paperback sensation in the 1960s), while **Thomas Mann** carried the Modernist novel to a high point with *Der Zauberberg* (The Magic Mountain), using the traditional *Bildungsroman* to criticize German culture (see **Lübeck,** p. 193). Also vital to the period were German-language writers living in Austria-Hungary, among them **Rainer Maria Rilke, Robert Musil,** and **Franz Kafka.**

In the years before WWI, Germany produced a violent strain of Expressionist poetry that mirrored developments in painting. The style was suited to depict the horrors of war, though several of its masters were killed in battle. The **Weimar Era** was filled with artistic production. Its most famous novel was **Erich Maria Remarque's** bleak portrayal of the Great War, *Im Westen nichts Neues* (All Quiet on the Western Front). **Bertolt Brecht** presented mankind in its grotesque absurdity through literature (see **Berlin,** p. 128). The Third Reich burned more books than it published; the Nazi attitude toward literature was summed up by Nazi propaganda chief **Joseph Goebbels:** "Whenever I hear the word 'culture,' I reach for my gun."

While the literature of the Weimar period seemed to succeed WWI almost effortlessly, WWII left Germany's artistic consciousness in shambles. To nurse German literature back to health, several writers joined to form **Gruppe 47,** named after the year of its founding. The group included many who would become world-class authors, such as **Günter Grass** and the poet **Paul Celan.** Much of the ensuing literature dealt with the problem of Germany's Nazi past, while the poetry of **Hans Magnus Enzensberger** and the novels of Grass and **Heinrich Böll** also turned a critical eye towards post-war West Germany's repressive, overly-bureaucratic tendencies. The state of letters in the DDR was largely determined by the waxing and waning of government control. Many expatriates, particularly those with Marxist leanings from before the war (such as Brecht), returned to the East with great hopes. But the communist leadership was not interested in eliciting free artistic expression, causing many talented writers to emigrate.

Since reunification, there has been a period of artistic anxiety in the former East as many authors faced scandals over *Stasi* ties. Günther Grass's receipt of the Nobel Prize for Literature in 1999 provided the newly-reunited Germany with its first literary icon and propelled German literati back into an international spotlight. However, the new world of capitalism has filled the shelves of many corner bookstores with translations of American bestsellers, pushing many works by German authors to the side. For happening German literature, look for **W. G. Sebald, Monika Maron, Peter Schneider,** and **Bernhard Schlink.**

PHILOSOPHY. German philosophy is like German *Wurst*: thick and difficult to digest. **Immanuel Kant,** the foremost thinker of the **German Enlightenment,** argued for autonomous rational calculation, positing reason as our highest moral safeguard; we must ask if our motivating principles can at any time be made into a universal law. Meanwhile **Johann Gottlieb Fichte** spearheaded the new **German Idealist** movement, which stressed the importance of a spirit or *Geist* in interpreting experience (p. 558). **G. W. F. Hegel** proposed that history as well as the development of the individual consciousness could be understood as conflicts between thesis and antithesis, which produced synthesis—essentially the idea that from struggle comes growth. (Visit their final resting place, p. 128.) Hegel's view of world history would, after some distortion, eventually provide a theoretical backing for German nationalism. Meanwhile, **Johann Gottfried Herder** pushed for romantic nationalism, asserting that the spirit of a nation could be found in its folklore and peasant traditions. **Karl Marx** turned Hegel around, asserting that class conflict was the stage on which the world was made, profoundly altering the course of 20th-century history and ensuring the long-term profitability of Che Guevara t-shirts.

Similarly controversial, **Friedrich Nietzsche,** influenced by pessimist par excellence **Arthur Schopenhauer,** scorned the mediocrity of "resentful" Judeo-Christian masses and advanced the idea of the *Übermensch* (superman), a man who creates a moral code without reference to the standards of others. Evidence suggests his works were later edited to emphasize their anti-Semitic elements.

Writing around the turn of the century, **Max Weber** announced that the world was trapped in a bureaucratic iron cage and spoke out against the archaic, retarding effect of noble **Junker** society on German agriculture. **Martin Heidegger** made his name with *Sein und Zeit* (Being and Time). This notoriously cumbersome book insists that man understand the significance of questioning the meaning of life in a world where one-sided technology development has led to a crisis of existential alienation. The most celebrated post-war exponent of this school, **Jürgen Habermas,** has criticized German re-unification, citing the danger of joining two nations that had adopted two very different cultures.

MUSIC. A tradition of secular music began in the 12th century with the **Minnesänger,** German troubadours whose technique of singing poetry passed gradually to the **Meistersänger** of the 14th and 15th centuries. Religious reformation ushered in musical changes, with German *cantata* and *oratorio* (sacred and secular forms) becoming the first genres to be composed in the vernacular. **Johann Pachelbel** (best known for his *Canon in D*) worked in the new musical style of the "Passion," a piece centered on the life of a saint. **Georg Friedrich Händel**'s *Messiah* (1742, think "Hallelujah!"), initially considered heretical for using religion in a theatrical setting, has become a staple of choral music (and advertising).

Johann Sebastian Bach (1685-1750) began as a composer of sacred organ music, but eventually moved into the secular world; his *Brandenburg Concerti* were written in an attempt to secure a post as a court composer. Bach's appointment as cantor to Leipzig's largest church, the Thomaskirche in 1723 (p. 633), brought him once again to Lutheran music. During his appointment, Bach composed over 200 cantatas, one for every Sunday. He wrote both the *St. Matthew* and *St. John Passions* during this time, as well as his famous Easter and Christmas Oratorios.

Ludwig van Beethoven's symphonies and piano sonatas bridged Classicism and Romanticism, driven by intense rhythm and emotion. His later string quartets and *Ninth Symphony*, a mammoth orchestral and choral masterpiece, were written in the 1820s, well after he had gone completely deaf. The ethereal nature of **Felix Mendelssohn-Bartholdy** is represented by his overture to *A Midsummer Night's Dream*. **Robert Schuman,** best known for his the piano works and song cycles like the *Dichterliebe* (poet's love), drew inspiration from poetry of Heine and Goethe. **Johannes Brahms** imbued Classical forms with rich Romantic emotion, while the highly nationalistic **Richard Wagner,** the most influential German composer after Beethoven, revolutionized the German opera. He composed many renowned operas—*Tannhäuser, Tristan und Isolde, Der Ring des Nibelungen*—as **Gesamtkunstwerken** (total works of art), unifying music and text, poetry and philosophy. Through the use of a resurfacing *Leitmotif*, Wagner gave signature sounds to certain characters or dramatic actions.

Paul Hindemith headed a group of German Neoclassicists (a school of composing inspired by Russian Igor Stravinsky). They embraced the older, variational forms (such as the sonata) most suited to the abstract aesthetic of the time. Yet at the same time, an anti-Romantic backlash and the unstable Weimar economy encouraged smaller, cheaper musical forms like jazz. A new movement of *Gebrauchsmusik* (utilitarian music) engendered music for amateur players and film scores. **Carl Orff,** Hitler's favorite composer, is known for his *Carmina Burana,* a resurrection of bawdy 13th-century lyrics with a bombastic score. Prior to WWII, music hall works bred the *Singspiel;* satiric operettas with songs of the political avant-garde. **Kurt Weill**'s partnership with Bertolt Brecht mastered the genre with *Die Dreigroschenoper* (Three-Penny Opera) and the universally-known song *Mackie Messer* (Mack the Knife). After the immediate post-war period, largely dominated by schmaltzy *Schlagermusik* (pop music), many exiled musicians returned to Germany to try to revitalize the otherwise unremarkable music scene.

Current German musical tastes dip more into the American and British pop worlds than into the tunes of fellow Teutons. Apart from **Nina Hagen**'s apocalyptic 80s hit *99 Luftballons* and, more recently, **Rammstein's** frightening rock hit *Du Hast*, Germany is best known internationally for its hugely influential **Krautrock** of the 60s and 70s (a blend of rock instrumentation and electronic textures characterized by repetition and sparse lyrics, featuring artists such as **Can, Faust, Kraftwerk,** and **Neu!**), and for having pioneered **techno,** an umbrella term for various kinds of electronic music, from dancefloor dignitaries such as Berlin's **Paul von Dyk** to more cerebral artists like Köln's **Schneider TM.** Germany's techno zenith is the annual **Love Parade** in Berlin (p. 107), when DJs such as **Dr. Motte** (the parade's founder) induce hundreds of thousands of Germans to drop ecstasy and get down.

Apart from techno, Germany enjoys a vital rock scene, with such notable acts as **Die Ärtzte, Einstürzende Neubauten** (Collapsing New Buildings) and **The Notwist** (recently signed to U.S. record label Domino). After becoming a rock sensation in the 60s, Germany's equivalent to The Boss, **Herbert Grönemeyer,** has recently enjoyed a comeback among the younger generations. Influenced by American musical trends, Germans have also begun to dabble in hip-hop and rap, ranging from the wildly popular **Die fantastischen Vier** to the cannabis-inspired tracks of the Hamburg crews **Fünf Sterne Deluxe** and **Fettes Brot.** One of the most prolific homegrown labels, **3p** (from Frankfurt) bills itself as the number one source of *deutsche Soulmusik*. Under its aegis, numerous hip-hop stars, among them **Sabrina Setlur, Xavier Naidoo,** and **Illmatic,** have come to the forefront of the German charts.

Mad-skilled Berlin rapper **Sido** is one of many hip-hop artists whose explicit lyrics are causing a censorship controversy as their songs enjoy increasing popularity.

FILM. The newborn medium of film exploded onto the German art scene in the Weimar era thanks to numerous brilliant directors. *Das Cabinet des Dr. Caligari* (The Cabinet of Dr. Caligari), an early horror film directed by **Robert Wiene,** plays out a melodrama of autonomy and control against sets of painted shadows and tilted walls. **Fritz Lang** produced a remarkable succession of films, including *M.*, *Dr. Mabuse der Spieler*, and *Metropolis*, a dark and brutal vision of the techno-fascist city of the future. Meanwhile, **Josef von Sternberg** extended the tradition into sound with his satiric *Der blaue Engel* (The Blue Angel), based on a Heinrich Mann novel and starring Berlin bombshell **Marlene Dietrich.** Relics of this era are on display at the former **UFA** studio grounds in Potsdam and Babelsberg (p. 158).

Heeding Hitler's prediction that "without motor-cars, sound films, and wireless, (there can be) no victory for National Socialism," propaganda minister **Joseph Goebbels** became a masterful manipulator. Most **Nazi films** were political propaganda and many, such as *Der ewige Jude* (The Eternal Jew) glorified anti-Semitism. The frighteningly compelling films of **Leni Riefenstahl** functioned as propaganda, while taking the art of the documentary to new heights. Her *Triumph des Willens* (Triumph of the Will) documented a Nürnberg Party Rally (p. 534), and *Olympia* recorded the 1936 Olympic Games in Berlin (p. 112).

Film continued to be a vigorous artistic medium in the latter half of the 20th century, with a flood of new cinema in West Germany in the late 60s and the 70s. The renaissance began in 1962 with the **Oberhausen Manifesto,** a declaration by independent filmmakers demanding artistic freedom and the right to create new feature films. **Rainer Werner Fassbinder** told fatalistic stories of people corrupted or defeated by society, including an epic television production of Alfred Döblin's mammoth novel *Berlin Alexanderplatz*. Fassbinder's film *Die Ehe der Maria Braun* (The Marriage of Maria Braun) and **Volker Schlöndorff's** *Die Blechtrommel* (The Tin Drum, based on Günther Grass's novel of the same title) brought the new German wave to a wider, international audience. **Wolfgang Petersen** directed *Das Boot* (The Boat), one of the most famous submarine films ever made. **Wim Wenders's** "road films," such as *Alice in den Städten* (Alice in the Cities) and the award-winning *Paris, Texas*, examine unconventional relationships and freedom of life on the road.

East German film was subject to more constraints than other artistic media due to the fact that all films had to be produced under the supervision of the state-run German Film Corporation (DEFA). **Slatan Dudow** produced the first of the DEFA's films, *Unser täglich Brot* (Our Daily Bread), a paean to the nationalization of industry, as well as *Stärker als die Nacht* (Stronger than the Night), which tells the story of a communist couple persecuted by the Nazis. After a brief post-Stalinist thaw, few East German films departed from the standard format of socialist heroism or love stories. **Egon Günther's** 1965 film *Lots Weib* (Lot's Wife), an overtly feminist exploration of marital breakdown and divorce, was one notable exception. The next year saw **Frank Beyer's** politically daring *Spur der Steine* (Trace of Stones), a reflection on corruption and intrigue in a communal construction project. Beyer later made the critically acclaimed *Jakob der Lügner* (Jacob the Liar), which was nominated for an Oscar. The DDR also devoted a healthy portion of its filmmaking resources to **documentaries,** with **Winfried Junge, Volker Koepp,** and **Jürgen Böttcher** making significant contributions—although most of these films shunned political critique, instead glorifying the East and vilifying the West.

Since the reunification, German film has struggled to create a new identity. Tom Tykwer wowed international audiences in 1998 with stylish, high-energy **Lola Rennt** (Run Lola Run); the film is, to many, iconic of a reunified and postmodernist

Germany, apace with throbbing techno and bodies relentlessly in motion. Wim Wenders's hugely popular documentary **Buena Vista Social Club** celebrates Cuban music and spawned a best-selling soundtrack. Caroline Link's dramatic **Nirgendwo in Afrika** (Nowhere in Africa), follows a Jewish family fleeing to Kenya in 1938. Based on a true story, the film won the 2002 Academy Award for Best Foreign Film. The most successful German movie to date, however, is Wolfgang Becker's **Goodbye, Lenin!,** a nuanced and affecting (not to mention hilarious) portrait of life in the DDR after reunification.

PUBLICATIONS. British dailies, such as the *Times* and *Guardian*, are widely available at newsstands in most cities. The *International Herald Tribune* and the European edition of the *Wall Street Journal* are the most common US papers. American and British armed forces maintain English-language radio stations in Western Germany. German speakers can keep track of things with German-language papers both in print and on the web. Hamburg-based weekly *Der Spiegel* (www.spiegel.de), one of the world's leading newsmagazines, provides reliable coverage of world events. *Die Zeit* (www.zeit.de) is a left-leaning weekly newspaper. The *Frankfurter Allgemeine Zeitung* (www.faz.de) is a more conservative daily, as is the much-respected Munich-based *Süddeutsche Zeitung* (www.sueddeutsche.de). Of course, the tabloid *Bild* (www.bild.de) is far more popular. Radical Berlin offers the liberal newspaper *Berliner Tagesspiegel* (www.tagesspiegel.de) and the leftist *Tageszeitung* (www.taz.de). For a far-leftist spin on the news, check out the daily *Neues Deutschland* (www.nd-online.de).

HOLIDAYS AND FESTIVALS

Stores, museums, and most tourist offices will be closed on the days listed, as the local population either sleeps late or spends the day in church.

2007	2008	HOLIDAY	ENGLISH
Jan. 1	Jan. 1	Neujahrstag	New Year's Day
Jan. 6	Jan. 6	Heilige Drei Könige	Epiphany
Apr. 6	Mar. 21	Karfreitag	Good Friday
Apr. 8	Mar. 23	Ostersonntag	Easter Sunday
Apr. 98	Mar. 24	Ostermontag	Easter Monday
May 1	May 1	Tag der Arbeit	Labor Day
May 17	May 1	Christi Himmelfahrt	Ascension Day
May 27	May 11	Pfingstsonntag	Whit Sunday (Pentecost)
May 28	May 12	Pfingstmontag	Whit Monday
June 7	May 22	Fronleichnam	Corpus Christi
Aug. 15	Aug. 15	Maria Himmelfahrt	Assumption Day
Oct. 3	Oct. 3	Tag der deutschen Einheit	Day of German Unity
Nov. 1	Nov. 1	Allerheiligen	All Saints' Day
Dec. 24	Dec. 24	Heiligabend	Christmas Eve
Dec. 25-26	Dec. 25-26	1. und 2. Weihnachtstagtage	Christmas Day and Boxing Day
Dec. 31	Dec. 31	Silvester	New Year's Eve

LIFE AND TIMES

ADDITIONAL RESOURCES

GENERAL HISTORY

Craig, Gordon. *The Germans*. An excellent picture of modern German society.

Fulbrook, Mary. *Anatomy of a Dictatorship: Inside the GDR, 1949-1989*. A retrospective of the East German state.

Peukert, Detlev. *The Weimar Republic*. Thorough examination of the trends of the inter-war period, such as doing the Charleston and not getting enough to eat.

Schulze, Hagen. *Germany: A New History*. Comprehensive overview of German history from its inauspicious beginnings to the present.

GERMAN CULTURE

Zeidenitz, Stefan and Ben Barkow. *Xenophobe's guide to the Germans*. Everything you ever wanted to know about the German psyche, but were afraid to ask.

Lord, Richard. *Culture Shock! Germany!* An essential guide to Teutonic customs and etiquette. Required reading for anyone planning to live in Germany.

BEYOND TOURISM

A PHILOSOPHY FOR TRAVELERS

As a tourist, you are always a foreigner. While hostel-hopping and sightseeing can be rewarding, you may want to consider going *beyond tourism*. With this chapter, *Let's Go* hopes to promote a better understanding of Germany and to provide suggestions for those who want more than a photo album out of their travels. Whether you find yourself re-creating an Ice Age dwelling on the banks of the Rhein or studying the effects of cultural integration in Berlin, you are sure to have an experience more memorable than any sightseeing tour could offer.

Germany may seem quaint, cold, or quirky at first glance, but a longer stay and a more nuanced interaction with the local culture will afford a broader understanding of today's pressing issues. Discrepancies between the former East and West have created lingering social divides, and German cultural homogeneity has been shattered by an influx of Turkish Muslim immigrants. Religious and cultural tensions pose new and unfolding challenges to volunteer agencies, many of which now prioritize mutual understanding as a means of reforging an inclusive national identity. These new forces are met with old concerns; the preservation of Germany's exquisite monuments and sprawling natural wonders have become a locus of Beyond Tourism activity. The ancient pines of the Black Forest and the plunging earth of the Bavarian Alps remain essential, but vulnerable, national assets.

Those who pursue Beyond Tourism opportunities in Germany will find a well-developed volunteer infrastructure as well as many avenues for finding employment. Germany can be something of a bureaucratic maze, so you'll need either perseverance or enough cash (US$100-7000) to pay for private programs that take care of the paperwork for you. Don't be discouraged if you come up empty-handed after your first few stabs at finding a job—German university students often take time off to do internships, and many organizations can also help you in piggy-backing onto this practice.

VOLUNTEERING

Volunteering can be tremendously fulfilling, especially when combined with the thrill of traveling in a new place. Opportunities are plentiful, well organized, and often structured around workcamps or homestays.

Some volunteer in Germany on a short-term basis, working with organizations that make use of drop-in or once-a-week volunteers. Both participating in and finding drop-in volunteer opportunities require German proficiency. **ParksIT**

WHY PAY MONEY TO VOLUNTEER? Many volunteers are surprised to learn that some organizations require large fees or "donations." While this may seem ridiculous at first glance, such fees often keep the organization afloat, in addition to covering airfare, room, board, and administrative expenses for the volunteers. If you're concerned about how a program spends its fees, request an annual report or finance account. A reputable organization won't refuse to inform you of how volunteer money is spent.

Pay-to-volunteer programs might be a good idea for young travelers who are looking for more support and structure or anyone who would rather not deal with the uncertainty implicit in creating a volunteer experience from scratch.

(www.parks.it/world/DE/Eindex.html) maintains an English-language list of parks and nature reserves.

Those looking for longer, more intensive volunteer opportunities usually choose to work through a parent organization that takes care of logistical details and often provides a group environment and support system—for a fee. These projects often take the form of two- to three-week trips with group lodging and outings. These are generally the most accessible option for those not fluent in German.

ENVIRONMENTAL CONSERVATION

The **Canadian Alliance for Development Initiatives and Projects,** (see Youth and the Community, p. 80), occasionally has similar programs, such as trail maintenance.

Agriventure, Lerchenborg Gods, 4400 Kalundborg, Denmark (☎45 59 51 15 25; www.iaea.de or www.agriventure.com). Organizes agricultural exchanges and home-stays at farms throughout Europe. Prices vary by program.

Bund Jugend, Am Köllnischer Park 1A, 10179 Berlin, Germany (☎030 27 58 65 84; www.bundjugend.de). This eco-friendly group provides information and organizes events for youth in Germany, including volunteer and internship opportunities.

Earthwatch, 3 Clocktower Pl. Ste. 100, Box 75, Maynard, MA 01754, USA (☎800-776-0188 or 978-461-0081; www.earthwatch.org). Arranges 1- to 3-week programs in Europe (occasionally Germany) to promote conservation of natural resources. Fees vary based on location and duration; costs average US$1700 plus airfare.

Willing Workers on Organic Farms (WWOOF), Postfach 210259, 01263 Dresden, Germany (www.wwoof.de). Membership (€18) in WWOOF offers room and board at a variety of organic farms in Germany in exchange for work.

RESTORATION AND ARCHAEOLOGY

One result of the prolonged occupation of Germany after WWII was the haphazard care afforded to the country's war-ravaged historical sights. Volunteers need not have experience to participate in archaeological digs and restoration projects.

Archaeological Institute of America, 656 Beacon St., Boston, MA 02215, USA (☎617-353-9361; www.archaeological.org). The *Archaeological Fieldwork Opportunities Bulletin,* on the website, lists field sites throughout Europe.

Open Houses Network, Goethepl. 9B, D-99423 Weimar, Germany (☎036 43 50 23 90; www.openhouses.de). A group dedicated to restoring and sharing public space (mostly in the former DDR); offers lodging in return for work. 18+ only.

Pro International, Bahnhofstr. 26A, 35037 Marburg, Germany (☎0642 16 52 77; www.pro-international.de). Since 1949, this volunteer organization has brought together youth from around the world to help reconstruct and preserve sites in Germany. Many of their projects also serve local children and the environment. Ages 16-26.

YOUTH AND THE COMMUNITY

AFS Intercultural Programs, AFS International, 71 West 23rd St., New York, NY 10010, USA (☎212-807-8686; www.afs.org). Volunteer opportunities for 18+ travelers to serve local communities, with a separate education program.

Big Friends for Youngsters (Biffy), Tempelhofer Ufer 11, D-10963 Berlin (☎030 25 76 76 12; www.biffy.de). The German arm of the Big Brothers Big Sisters program; provides mentoring for young kids in need of guidance on a longer term basis.

Canadian Alliance for Development Initiatives and Projects, 129-1271 Howe St., Vancouver, British Columbia V62 1R3 Canada (☎1-604-628-7400; www.cadip.org). Offers diverse 2- to 3-wk. programs in Germany, with the aims of peace, tolerance, and community. Program fee roughly US$350.

Elderhostel Inc., 11 Avenue de Lafayette, Boston, MA 92111, USA (☎1-800-454-5768; www.elderhostel.org). Sends volunteers over age 55 around the world to work in construction, research, teaching, and other projects. Roughly US$200 per day plus airfare.

Habitat for Humanity International, 121 Habitat St., Americus, GA 31709, USA (☎229-924-6935, ext. 2551; www.habitat.org). Volunteers build houses in over 83 countries. Periods of involvement range from 2wk. to 3yr. Short-term programs run US$1200-4000.

Service Civil International Voluntary Service (SCI-IVS), SCI Deutscher Zweig e.V., Blücherstr. 14, D-53115 Bonn (☎0228 21 20 86; www.sci-d.de). In the US, SCI USA, 5474 Walnut Level Rd., Crozet, VA 22932, USA (☎/fax 206-350-6585; www.sci-ivs.org). Arranges placement for work in German civil service camps for those 18+. Program fee (including registration) €250.

Volunteers for Peace, 1034 Tiffany Rd., Belmont, VT 05730, USA (☎802-259-2759; www.vfp.org). Grassroots organization arranges 2- to 3-wk. programs for low-income housing, environmental projects, social services, and historic preservation. Registration fee US$250. Must be 18+.

SOCIAL AND POLITICAL ACTIVISM

Amnesty International, Sektion der Bundesrepublik Deutschland e.V., 53108 Bonn, Germany (☎0228 98 37 30; www.amnesty.de). Human rights organization; often has internship and volunteer positions available.

Internationale Begegnung in Gemeinschartsdiensten, e.V., Schlosserstr. 28, D-70810 Stuttgart, Germany (☎0711 649 0263; www.ibg-workcamps.org). Camps bring together Germans and foreigners to promote mutual understanding and tolerance while working on projects that serve the local community.

Mobility International USA, 132 E. Broadway St., Suite 343, Eugene, OR 97401, USA (☎541-343-1284; www.miusa.org). Joins people with and without wide-ranging disabilities to staff international projects of community service and champion disability rights.

DATABASES

Be sure to narrow your search to Germany, as these sights often list projects across the globe.

www.alliance-network.org. Umbrella website that brings together various service organizations from around the world.

www.idealist.org. Provides extensive listings of service opportunities (150+ in Germany alone), with contact info and descriptions.

www.oekojobs.de. German-language listing of environmentally oriented opportunities.

www.umabroad.umn.edu. Run by the University of Minnesota. Offers a searchable database of international programs for working, studying, and volunteering abroad.

www.worldvolunteerweb.org. World-wide venue for advertising volunteer opportunities.

STUDYING

 STUDY VISA INFORMATION. **Residence permits** are necessary for all foreign citizens to study in Germany. For information on obtaining one, see **Essentials** (p. 10)

Study abroad programs range from basic language and culture courses to college-level classes, often for credit. Programs that have large groups of students who speak the same language represent a trade-off. You may feel more comfortable in a community of English speakers, but you will not have the same opportunity to practice German or to befriend other international students. For accommodations, dorm life provides a better opportunity to mingle with fellow students, but there is less of a chance to experience the local scene. If you live with a family, there is a potential to build lifelong friendships with natives and to experience day-to-day life in more depth, but conditions can vary greatly from family to family.

UNIVERSITIES

Most university-level study-abroad programs are conducted in German, although many programs offer classes in English along with beginner-level German language courses. Those relatively fluent in German may find it cheaper to enroll directly in a university, although getting college credit may be more difficult. Fortunately, the EU's **European Credit Transfer System (ECTS)** makes credit transfer manageable: all coursework completed at German universities is translated into a letter grade by ECTS, which then facilitates credit transfer to institutions across the globe. Check with your home university to see if it participates.

Studying abroad in Germany may be complicated by the country's 12-month academic calendar. Winter semester runs from October to March, while summer semester stretches from April to September. You can search **www.studyabroad.com** or **www.studyabroaddirectory.com** for various semester-abroad programs that fit your calendar and meet your other criteria, including your desired location and focus of study.

GERMAN PROGRAMS

Congress-Bundestag Youth Exchange for Young Professionals, 81 United Nations Plaza, New York, NY 10017, USA (☎212-497-3500; www.cdsintl.org/cbyx/cbyxfro-musa.htm). Cosponsored by the German and United States governments, this year-long cultural exchange is geared towards young professionals age 18-24. 75 people are chosen to participate in language immersion, classes, and an internship in Germany; airfare and accommodations are provided. Application deadline Dec. 1.

Deutscher Akademischer Austauschdienst (DAAD), 871 United Nations Plaza, New York, NY 10017, USA (☎212-758-3223; www.daad.org); in Germany, Kennedyallee 50, 53175 Bonn; mailing address Postfach 200404, 53134 Bonn, Germany. Information on language instruction, exchanges, and the wealth of scholarships for study in Germany. Processes foreign enrollment in German universities; also distributes applications and the valuable publication *Grants for Study and Research in Germany*.

OTHER PROGRAMS

IES, 33 N. LaSalle St., 15th fl., Chicago, IL 60602, USA (☎800-995-2300; www.iesabroad.org). Formerly the Institute for European Studies, IES offers college students the opportunity to enroll directly at Berlin's Humbolt-Universität. Participants receive supplementary language instruction and housing with Berlin residents. IES also arranges internships in Berlin. Program fees US$15,000.

International Association for the Exchange of Students for Technical Experience (IAESTE), 10400 Little Patuxent Pkwy. Ste. 250, Columbia, MD 21044, USA (☎410-997-2200; www.aipt.org). Offers 8- to 12-wk. internships in Germany for college students who have completed 2 years of study in a technical field. US$50 application fee.

School for International Training, College Semester Abroad, Kipling Rd., P.O. Box 676, Brattleboro, VT 05302, USA (☎888-272-7881 or 802-257-7751; www.sit.edu/studyabroad). Semester-long program in Germany with a focus on nationalism and ethnic conflict. Tuition US$16,500. Also runs **The Experiment in International Living** (☎800-345-2929; www.usexperiment.org), 3- to 5-wk. summer programs that offer high-school students cross-cultural homestays, community service, ecological adventure, and language training in Germany. US$1900-6000.

LANGUAGE SCHOOLS

Language schools rarely offer college credit, but are a good alternative to university study if you desire a deeper focus on the language or a slightly less rigorous course load. These programs are also good for younger students who might not feel comfortable in a university setting.

BWS Germalingua, Bayerstr. 13, 80335 Munich, Germany (☎089 599 892 00; www.germalingua.com). Part- and full-time language classes in Munich and Berlin for up to 1yr. Full-time 2-wk. courses from €370; night classes from €49 per wk.

Eurocentres, 1901 N. Fort Myer Dr. Ste. 800, Arlington, VA 22209, USA (☎703-243-7884; www.eurocentres.com) or in Europe, Head Office, Seestr. 247, CH-8038 Zurich, Switzerland (☎41 1 485 50 40; fax 481 61 24). Language programs for beginning to advanced students with homestays in Germany.

Goethe-Institut, Dachauer Str. 122, 80637 Munich, Germany; mailing address Postfach 190419, 80604 München (☎89 159 212 00, toll-free from North America 1-888-446-3843; www.goethe.de). Runs German language programs in 14 German cities and abroad; also orchestrates high school exchange programs in Germany. For information, look on the web, contact your local branch (**Australia:** Melbourne, Sydney; **Canada:** Montreal, Ottawa, Toronto; **Ireland:** Dublin; **New Zealand:** Wellington; **UK:** Glasgow, London, Manchester; **US:** New York, Washington, D.C., Boston, Chicago, Atlanta, San Francisco, Los Angeles) or write to the main office. 8-wk. intensive summer course from €1770, with room from €2320 (prices vary by course and city).

Language Immersion Institute, JFT 214, State University of New York at New Paltz, 75 S. Manheim Blvd., New Paltz, NY 12561, USA (☎845-257-3500; www.newpaltz.edu/lii). 2-wk. summer language courses in German. Program fees around US$1000, not including accommodations.

Research in Germany

During my time as a college student in the United States, I took an unforgettable semester off to work at the University of Ulm doing chemistry research. I was interested not only in learning about polypeptides and phenolphthalein, but also in discovering how Germans differ in their approaches to research, academics, and life. I wanted to get to know Germany (and Europe) more intimately than the average tourist, using the city of Ulm as the stronghold from which I would sally forth to other nations.

For centuries, Germany has been known for its rigorous intellectual tradition, especially in the physical sciences. After sitting in on a mind-blowing statistical mechanics lecture in Ulm, I learned that the professor was also deeply interested in history. In particular, he emphasized Einstein's variegate contributions to the field and the fact that Ulm was his birthplace. Germany may have lost some of its academic luster since the times of Boltzmann, Leibniz, and Hegel, but academic research there is still as vital as the flow of the mighty Rhein.

I began my search for a position in a German lab by talking to my academic advisor in the States about potential contacts in Germany. I then emailed these professors my résumé to convey to them my sincere interest. Finding professors who wanted an American protégé ended up being much easier than finding a reliable, sufficient, and legal method of financing my trip. I eventually was lucky enough to come upon a professor whose university could fund my studies, which meant I could stop trying to arrange my own funding through the German Academic Exchange Program (www.daad.de).

Undertaking academic research in Germany had several advantages over participating in a mere study abroad program, the best being that my trip was financed. I also appreciated the interaction afforded by eating with students in their dining hall. During my time in Germany, I lived in university housing with visiting scholars from many different countries, all of whom had very different academic and personal back-grounds, and fascinating stories to tell. The true highlight of my research experience, however, was the opportunity to get involved in intense, focused scholarship, which can be far more intellectually rewarding than the academic dabbling of broad overview classes.

To pursue academic research in Germany, you usually have to be a university student or graduate with a strong interest in a narrow research topic in a rigorous academic setting. In most fields, especially scientific ones, you do not need to speak any German at all, let alone know how to decline an unpreceded adjective in front of a feminine noun in the dative case. Everyone in my lab spoke some heartfelt variant of English, and I was actually required to give my presentations in English.

My six-month stay in Germany was extremely rewarding. Academically, my project succeeded beyond our wildest dreams. I worked hard, but received unending support from my labmates. I survived the student dining hall, sat in on sundry classes, and went to a few raging university parties. But even as we climbed scientific mountains together, I saw firsthand the ways in which German students differed from Americans. One day I arrived at work to find that the students had gone on strike (by refusing to attend classes, a tough move for the industrious Germans) to protest an administrative fee that the university was planning to establish.

While based in Ulm, I also had opportunities to explore Munich and Stuttgart and spend a strenuous but rewarding weekend biking at the glorious Chiemsee in Bavaria. Since I was a wage-earning chemist instead of a starving backpacker, my quick trips to Austria, France, and England had a more generous budget than they otherwise would have, and the superb European train system and new discount airlines helped make them relatively hassle-free. Academic research was a phenomenal way for me to get to know Germany, change the shape of my life for a while, see much of Europe, and even learn a little bit of science.

Barbara Richter was a Researcher-Writer for Let's Go: Austria & Switzerland. A native Austrian now based out of New Jersey, she will be continuing her studies in chemistry and physics at graduate school, though unfortunately not in Germany.

WORKING

 WORK VISA INFORMATION. To work in Germany, non-European Uni-oncitizens will need a **residence permit.** For instructions on securing a permit, see **Essentials** (p. 10).

As with volunteering, work opportunities tend to fall into two categories. Some travelers want long-term jobs that allow them to get to know another part of the world as a member of the community, while others seek out short-term jobs to finance the next leg of their travels. Bilingual English speakers can be a prized commodity within the tourist industry, especially at tourist offices, pubs, cafés, restaurants, and hotels. Other fields such as fast food, agriculture, and nursing (for which you will need further health certification), as well as sectors involving skilled construction labor, can also be traveler-friendly. It is critical that you be aware of your rights as an employee; make sure you have a signed agreement with your employer.

The recruitment of non-EU workers is strictly regulated in Germany. You can consult local, federally run employment offices. These fall under the umbrella of **Bundesanstalt für Arbeit** (Federal Employment Service), through which you can find local agencies (www.arbeitsagentur.de). The best tips on jobs for foreigners often come from other travelers; newspaper listings are another start. Online search engines are increasingly useful. **Career Journal,** (www.careerjournaleurope.com), one of many such engines, is affiliated with the *Wall Street Journal;* it provides a searchable index of jobs, usually in the financial sector, for young professionals dreaming of middle-management jobs abroad.

For US college students, recent graduates, and young adults, the simplest way to get legal permission to work abroad is through **Council Exchanges Work Abroad Programs** (http://us.councilexchanges.org). Affiliated with the Council on International Educational Exchange, they can help you obtain a three- to six-month work permit/visa and provide assistance finding jobs and housing, as well as further resources for student exchanges and volunteering. (Fees run about US$300-425.) Note that working abroad often requires a special work visa (p. 10).

LONG-TERM WORK

If you're planning on spending a substantial amount of time (more than three months) working in Germany, search for a job well in advance. **Internships,** usually for college students, are a good way to segue into working abroad; although they are often unpaid or poorly paid, many say the experience is well worth it. Be wary of advertisements for companies claiming the ability to get you a job abroad for a fee—often the same listings are available online or in newspapers.

Carl Duisberg Gesellschaft e.V. (CDG), Weyerstr. 79-83, 50676 Cologne, Germany (☎0221 209 80; www.cdg.de/english). Professional training for students and young people from Germany and abroad.

CDS International, 871 United Nations Plaza, New York, NY 10017, USA (☎212-497-3500). Arranges 6- to 12-month paid internships for students and recent graduates of accredited US colleges and universities.

International Association for the Exchange of Students for Technical Experience (IAESTE), 10400 Little Patuxent Pkwy., Ste. 250, Columbia, MD 21044, USA (☎410 997 3069; www.aipt.org/subpages/iaeste_us/index.php). 8- to 12-wk. internships in Germany for college students with 2 years of technical study. US$10 application fee.

International Cooperative Education, 15 Spiros Way, Menlo Park, CA, 94025, USA (☎650-323-4944; www.icemenlo.com). Finds summer jobs for students in Germany. Costs include a US$250 application fee and a US$700 fee for placement.

US Armed Forces Civilian Human Resources Agency (CHRA), (www.chra.eur.army.mil). Arranges limited-tenure jobs for Americans at US military bases near Heidelberg, Würzburg, and dozens of other German cities and towns. Employees staff shops, eateries, and recreation centers; for most positions, housing is included or offered at an exceptionally low rate. The **Edelweiss Lodge and Resort,** St. Martin Str. 120, 82467 Garmisch-Partenkirchen (☎88 21 94 40), is a US Armed Forces recreation center near Chiemsee that offers competitive 13-month paid hospitality positions. Round-trip airfare to Germany is included, and housing is available for US$30 per month.

Zentralstelle für Arbeitsvermittlung der Bundesagentur für Arbeit (Central Placement Office), 53107 Bonn, Germany (☎228 71 30). Federal agency that specializes in placing foreigners in German firms.

TEACHING ENGLISH

Teaching jobs abroad are rarely well paid, although some elite private international schools offer competitive salaries. Volunteering as a teacher in lieu of getting paid is a popular option; even then, teachers often receive some sort of a daily stipend to help defray living expenses. In most cases, you must have at least a bachelor's degree to be a full-fledged teacher, although college undergraduates can often get summer positions tutoring. American English is frequently preferred.

Many schools require teachers to have either a **Teaching English as a Foreign Language (TEFL)** certificate or a **Certificate in English Language Teaching to Adults (CELTA),** which can be obtained in Germany or at TEFL and CELTA centers for US$400-1000. Some schools go further and necessitate the **DELTA (Diploma in English Language Teaching to Adults).** Non-certified teachers will have a more difficult time finding jobs, and certified teachers often find higher-paying jobs. Native English speakers working in private schools are most often hired for English-immersion classrooms where no German is spoken. Those volunteering or teaching in poorer, public schools are more likely to be working in both English and German. Placement agencies or university fellowship programs are the best resources for finding teaching jobs. You can also peruse the German yellow pages, **GelbeSeiten** (www.ods.gelbeseiten.de). The alternative is to make contact directly with schools or just to try your luck once you get there.

International Schools Services (ISS), 15 Roszel Rd., P.O. Box 5910, Princeton, NJ 08543, USA (☎609-452-0990; www.iss.edu). Hires teachers for more than 200 overseas schools including Germany; candidates should have experience teaching or with international affairs; 2-yr. commitment expected.

Fulbright English Teaching Assistantship, US Student Programs Division, Institute of International Education, 809 United Nations Plaza, New York, NY 10017, USA (☎212-984-5400; www.iie.org). This highly competitive program sends college graduates to teach in Germany.

Oxford Seminars, 244 5th Ave., Ste. J262, New York, NY 10001, USA (☎212 213 8978; www.oxfordseminars.com). Offers TEFL programs and job placement in Europe.

AU PAIR WORK

Au pairs are typically women (although sometimes men), aged 18-27, who work as live-in nannies, caring for children and doing light housework in foreign countries in exchange for room, board, and a small spending allowance or stipend. One perk of the job is that it allows you to get to know Germany without the high expenses of traveling. Drawbacks, however, often include mediocre pay and long hours of constantly being on duty. Pay can vary widely, but €200-300 per month is considered average. The agencies below are a good starting point.

Au Pair Agentur, Kotten Büsken 87, D-46325 Borken in Westfalen, Germany (☎+49 2862 417 97 45; www.aupair-aus-deutschland.com). German-speaking agency.

Au Pair Worldwide, Lückenweg 18, D-64743 Beerfelden, Germany (☎+49 6068 91 21 68; www.aupair-worldwide.de). Matches international au pairs with German families.

Childcare International, Ltd., Trafalgar House, Grenville Pl., London NW7 3SA, England (☎+44 020 8906; www.childint.co.uk).

InterExchange, 161 Sixth Ave., New York, NY 10013, USA (☎212-924-0446; www.interexchange.org).

SHORT-TERM WORK

Traveling for long periods can be expensive; to offset costs, many travelers try their hand at odd jobs for a few weeks at a time. Although shops and cafes looking for short-term employees during the height of the tourist season sometimes hire foreigners illegally, a work visa is required to obtain legal employment of any sort in Germany (see **Essentials** p. 10). A more popular—and less legally tenuous— option is to work several hours a day at a hostel in exchange for free or discounted room or board. Most often, these short-term jobs are found by word of mouth, or by talking to the owner of a hostel or restaurant. Check out the hostel and food listings in *Let's Go;* the managers of these establishments may be interested in short term help, or they may even be able to point you to others who are looking.

FURTHER READING ON BEYOND TOURISM

Back Door Guide to Short-Term Job Adventures, by Michael Landes. Ten Speed Press, 2002 (US$22).

Green Volunteers, by Ausenda and McCloskey. Universe, 2003 (US$15).

How to Get a Job in Europe, by Sanborn and Matherly. Planning Communications, 2003 (US$22).

How to Live Your Dream of Volunteering Overseas, by Collins, DeZerega, and Heckscher. Penguin Boocaféks, 2002 (US$17).

International Directory of Voluntary Work, by Whetter and Pybus. Peterson's Guides and Vacation Work, 2000 (US$16).

International Job Finder: Where the Jobs Are Worldwide, by Daniel Lauber. Planning Communications, 2002 (US$20).

Invest Yourself: The Catalogue of Volunteer Opportunities, published by the Commission on Voluntary Service and Action (☎646-486-2446).

Live and Work Abroad: A Guide for Modern Nomads, by Francis and Callan. Vacation-Work Publications, 2001 (US$16).

Overseas Summer Jobs 2002, by Collier and Woodworth. Peterson's Guides and Vacation-Work, 2002 (US$18).

Volunteer Vacations: Short-term Adventures That Will Benefit You and Others, by Cutchins and Geissinger. Chicago Review Press, 2003 (US$18).

Work Abroad: The Complete Guide to Finding a Job Overseas, by Hubbs, Griffith, and Nolting. Transitions Abroad Publishing, 2002 (US$16).

Work Your Way Around the World, by Susan Griffith. Vacation-Work Publications, 2003 (US$18).

BERLIN

Berlin is bigger than Paris, up later than New York, wilder than Amsterdam, and more eclectic than London. Simultaneously cosmopolitan, dynamic, and in some regards delightfully oblivious, the city is nearing the end of a profound transition from Newly Reunited Post-Cold War Metropolis to Geographic and Emotional Center of an Eastward-Expanding European Union. Everything in this city of 4.2 million is changing, from the demographics of the diverse population to which *Bezirk* (neighborhood) is currently "in." The long, agonizing period of division and the unanticipated and abrupt reunification in 1989—which saw the Berlin wall literally shattered at the hands of eager civilians—resulted in a turbulent decade filled with euphoria, disillusionment, wild despair, and wilder optimism. In 1999 the federal government moved from Bonn to Berlin, throwing the new capital back into chaos as construction sites sprang up everywhere and droves of bureaucrats provided a sudden contrast to the wayward artists and nihilistic punks that had ruled the city streets. Amid lingering turmoil, ambitious plans for the city's renovation are speeding toward completion. The glass and steel Potsdamer Pl. now towers where the *Mauer* used to stand and the new Hauptbahnhof, Europe's largest train station, connects Berlin—arguably the heart of the EU—to the rest of the continent without the blockades and air corridors that once marred its path. But while Berlin surges ahead as one of Europe's most vibrant cities, memories of the past— both the days of the Nazi regime and the DDR—remain etched in its geography, its architecture, and even in the texture of its daily life.

The ramifications of this transformation are profound, and many Berliners, understandably, are not without ambivalence. Nobel laureate **Günter Grass** goes so far as to contend that Germany shouldn't even have been allowed to reunite. The problem of *Mauer im Kopf* ("wall in the head;" persisting feelings of division) is more prevalent here than anywhere else in the country. *Wessies* (Westerners) resent having to spend so much to give a leg up to their less-affluent eastern neigh-

HIGHLIGHTS OF BERLIN

ABANDON MODESTY AND MODERATION while partaking in Berlin's notorious **nightlife** (p. 106) in the districts of Mitte, Kreuzberg, Prenzlauer Berg, and Friedrichshain, or while experiencing the unparalleled **gay scene** in Schöneberg.

CHECK OUT CUTTING-EDGE ARCHITECTURE, among the best in Europe, on a walking tour that includes an aquarium-cum-elevator and Berlin's newest memorial (p. 124).

ASCEND the sleek spiraling glass dome atop the **Reichstag** (p. 126) and wonder how many other countries have a **solar-powered parliament.**

ABSORB OBSCENE AMOUNTS OF ART by Old Masters and contemporary renegades alike in **Museumsinsel** (p. 128), **Kulturforum** (p. 129), **Dahlem** (p. 152), and **Charlottenburg** (p. 108).

MINGLE WITH HIPSTERS in **Hackescher Markt** before relaxing with a foaming *Milchkaffee* at one of the many cafés in the **Hackeshe Höfe.** (p. 127).

RELIVE THE COLD WAR at **Checkpoint Charlie** (p. 145) or at the longest surviving stretch of the **Berlin Wall,** now the canvas for the **East Side Gallery** (p. 138).

SOAR 368m up from **Alexanderplatz** (p. 123) to view Berlin from the DDR's pride and joy, the **Fernsehturm** (p. 123), or just check the time at home on the **World Clock.**

bors, while *Ossies* (Easterners) resent what they consider an attitude of superiority from the West and disdain its glistening corporate demeanor.

Unlike most major capitals, Berlin has no "downtown" in the traditional sense; instead, the city is composed of many *Bezirke*. These neighborhoods began as individual settlements on the Spree River, growing together over hundreds of years into a city spread out over an area ten times the size of Paris. Neighborhoods struggle to maintain their individuality in the face of increasing integration. Areas that no one would have dreamed of visiting five years ago are now nightlife hotspots, and districts where everyone wanted to live last week will be passé tomorrow. Berlin is the most tolerant Germany city, with a world-famous gay and lesbian scene and few racist crimes. The city's progressive bent extends even into its urban development scheme. But as it rushes into the future, this very dynamism in some regards endangers the preservation of its rich history. In Mitte, controversy rages over plans to tear down the DDR-era Palast der Republik, while the longest remaining portion of Berlin's once ubiquitous Wall is rapidly being defaced by tourist scribblings. Come watch Berlin change before your very eyes, because, as an old German song goes, "*Es gibt nur einmal, und kommt nicht wieder*" (It will only happen once, and never again).

 HOW TO USE THIS CHAPTER. Berlin is best experienced one *Bezirk* at a time. Listings for accommodations, food, sights, museums, and nightlife are grouped together by neighborhood. General information on these aspects of Berlin, as well as shopping, gay and lesbian offerings, and specific listings for camping and entertainment can be found after the practical information below.

HISTORY

THE BEGINNING: LOTS OF WAR

Berlin, now Germany's most populous city, was originally the site of small Slavic settlements in the marshlands along the Havel and Spree Rivers during the early Middle Ages. Berlin takes its name from the Slavonic word *birl*, "swamp." The Saxon duke **Albrecht der Bär** (Albert the Bear) came to power in Brandenburg during the 12th century and removed the Slavs from the region, resettling with immigrants from the west. By the 13th century, the trading posts Cölln and Berlin were founded, and in 1307 the two formally united. The electors of Brandenburg seized control in 1411 and built a capital to match their dreams of glory. With the Edict of Potsdam (1685), **Friedrich Wilhelm** bolstered the city's population by accepting Huguenot and Jewish refugees from newly intolerant France, and in 1701 Berlin became the capital of the Kingdom of Prussia. Berlin flourished as an intellectual hotspot thanks to thinkers such as dramatist **Gotthold Ephraim Lessing,** educators like the **Humboldt brothers,** and the ruler **Friedrich II**—whose penchant for martial pomp and circumstance turned the city into an assortment of broad avenues and grandiose parade grounds. Conquered by **Napoleon** in 1806 and beset by revolution in 1848, the city fell into a decline until **Otto von Bismarck** unified Germany in 1871. Though Berlin was made capital of the fledgling empire, it never became the center of the new nation, and most Germans felt little affection for the capital.

BETWEEN WARS: REBELLION AND POVERTY

WWI and the Allied blockade reduced Berlin to poverty. A popular uprising led to **Kaiser Wilhelm II's** abdication and **Karl Liebknecht's** declaration of a socialist republic with Berlin as its capital on November 9, 1918. Locally, the revolt, led by Liebknecht and **Rosa Luxemburg,** turned into a full-fledged workers' revolution that controlled the city for several days. **Philipp Scheidemann's** rival Social Democratic government enlisted the aid of right-wing mercenaries, the **Freikorps,** to suppress the rebellion and murder Liebknecht and Luxemburg. As Berlin recovered from economic and political instability, it grew into one of the major cultural centers of Europe. Expressionist painting flourished, **Bertolt Brecht** revolutionized new theater techniques, and artists and writers from all over the world flocked to the city. The city's "Golden Twenties" ended abruptly with the 1929 economic collapse, when the city erupted with bloody riots and political chaos.

WAR AGAIN: A CITY DIVIDED

With economic woes came a rise in the popularity of the extremist Nazi party (see **The Weimar Republic,** p. 55). When Hitler took power on January 30, 1933, traditionally left-wing **"Red Berlin"** was not one of his strongholds. Furious at the radical city, Hitler famously declared: "Berliners are not fit to be German!" He finally consolidated control over the city through economic improvements and totalitarian measures, marshalling support for the savage anti-Semitic pogrom of November 9, 1938, known as **Kristallnacht.** Only 7000 members of Berlin's once-thriving Jewish community of 160,000 survived the Holocaust. Berlin suffered acutely during WWII; Allied bombing and the Battle of Berlin leveled one-fifth of the city, killing 80,000 citizens. The pre-war population of 4.3 million was reduced to a mere 2.8 million by 1945. With nearly all healthy men dead or gone, it was Berlin's **Trümmerfrauen** (rubble women) who literally picked up the pieces of the city.

The Allies divided post-war Germany into American, British, French, and Soviet sectors controlled by a joint **Allied Command.** On June 16, 1948, the Soviets withdrew from the alliance and demanded full control of Berlin. Ten days later, they blockaded land and water routes into the non-Soviet sectors; the Allies saved West Berlin from starvation by a massive airlift of supplies called the **Luftbrücke** (or, **Berlin Airlift**). On May 12, 1949, the Soviets ceded control of West Berlin to the Allies.

THE DDR YEARS: CONCRETE AND CHECKPOINTS

On October 5, 1949, the Soviet-controlled German Democratic Republic was formally established (p. 59), with East Berlin as its capital. East Berliners, dissatisfied with their government, staged a **workers' uprising** on June 17, 1953. Soviet tanks overwhelmed the demonstrators, and the only upshot of the day's events was the renaming of a major West Berlin thoroughfare to "Straße des 17. Juni" in a gesture of solidarity between *Ossis* and *Wessis*. Many were convinced to flee the repressive state for West Berlin—200,000 in 1960 alone. On the morning of August 13, 1961, the East German government responded to the exodus of its workforce with the overnight construction of the **Berlin Wall,** a 165km-long "anti-fascist protective barrier," separated families and friends, in some places even running through people's homes. In the early 1970s, a second wall was erected parallel to the first; the space between them was filled with barbed wire, land mines, and glass shards and patrolled by armed East German guards. Known as the **Todesstreifen** (death strip), this wasteland claimed hundreds of lives. The Western Allies responded to West Berlin's isolation by pouring millions of dollars into the city's reconstruction, turning it into *das Schaufenster des Westens* (the shop-window of the West).

While West Berliners elected a mayor, the Allies retained ultimate authority over the city—never officially a part of the Federal Republic—until German reunification in 1990. One perk of its "special status" was West Berliners' exemption from military conscription. Thousands of German artists, punks, homosexuals, and left-wing activists moved to West Berlin to escape the draft, forming an unparalleled alternative scene. The West German government, determined to make a Cold War showcase of the city, directly subsidized Berlin's economy and cultural scene.

BERLIN

THE WALL COMES DOWN

On November 9, 1989—the 71st anniversary of the proclamation of the Weimar Republic, the 66th anniversary of Hitler's Beer Hall *Putsch*, and the 51st anniversary of *Kristallnacht*—a series of popular demonstrations throughout East Germany. The unrest rode on a decade of discontent and a year of rapid change in Eastern Europe, culminating in the opening of the Berlin Wall. Photos of Berliners embracing beneath the Brandenburg Gate that night provided some of the most memorable images of the century. Berlin was officially reunited (and freed from Allied control) along with the rest of Germany on October 3, 1990, to widespread celebration. Since then, the euphoria has evaporated. Resignation to reconstruction has taken the place of the biting criticism and tasteless jokes that were standard just after reunification. After a decade of planning, the Bundestag (German Parliament) finally moved from Bonn to Berlin in 1999, restoring Berlin to its prewar status as the locus of German political power.

■ INTERCITY TRANSPORTATION

Berlin, located on the Prussian plains of northeastern Germany, is rapidly becoming the hub of both domestic and international rail networks. Three hours southeast of Hamburg by train and seven hours north of Munich, Berlin has rail and air connections to most European capitals, including those in Eastern Europe. Nearly all European airlines have frequent service to one of Berlin's airports.

Flights: For information on all 3 of Berlin's airports, call ☎0180 500 01 86. Currently, the 3 airports are combining into 1 (Flughafen Schönefeld to become the Berlin-Brandenburg International Airport), but at least until 2011, **Flughafen Tegel** will remain Western Berlin's main international airport. Take express bus #X9 from Bahnhof Zoo, bus #109 from "Jakob-Kaiser-Pl." on U7, bus #128 from "Kurt-Schumacher-Pl." on U6, or bus TXL from Potsdamer Pl. or Bahnhof Zoo. At the airport, check by the bus platforms for public transportation. **Flughafen Schönefeld**, southeast of Berlin, is used for intercontinental flights and travel to developing countries. Take S9 or S45 to "Flughafen Berlin Schönefeld" or the Schönefeld Express train, which runs every 30min. through most major S-Bahn stations including Bahnhof Zoo, Hauptbahnhof, Ostbahnhof, Alexanderpl., and Friedrichstr. **Flughafen Tempelhof** was slated to close in 2003 but remains open for flights within Europe. U6 to "Pl. der Luftbrücke."

Train Stations: Berlin's massive new **Hauptbahnhof,** which opened just in time for the World Cup in 2006, is now the city's major transit hub, with some international and national trains continuing on to **Ostbahnhof** in the East. **Zoologischer Garten** (almost always called **Bahnhof Zoo**), formerly the West's main station, now connects only to regional destinations. Many trains also connect to **Schönefeld** airport. A number of U- and S-Bahn lines make stops at **Oranienburg, Spandau,** and **Potsdam.** Trains in the Brandenburg regional transit system tend to stop at all major stations, as well as Friedrichstr. and Alexanderpl.

Trains: Every hr. to: **Cologne** (5hr., €93); **Frankfurt** (4hr., €48); **Hamburg** (1½-2hr., €47-58); **Leipzig** (1½hr., €36); **Munich** (7-8hr., €96). Every 2hr. to: **Dresden** (2¼hr., €32); **Rostock** (2¾hr., €31.90). International connections to: **Amsterdam, Netherlands** (6½hr.); **Brussels, Belgium** (8hr.); **Budapest, Hungary** (12hr.); **Copenhagen, Denmark** (7½hr.); **Kraków, Poland** (9½hr.); **Moscow, Russia** (27-33hr.); **Paris, France** (9hr.); **Prague, Czech Republic** (5hr.); **Rome, Italy** (17½-21hr.); **Stockholm, Sweden** (13-16hr.); **Vienna, Austria** (9½hr.); **Warsaw, Poland** (6hr.); **Zurich, Switzerland** (8½hr.). Times and prices change frequently—check at the computers located in the train stations. Under Deutsche Bahn's new pricing system, prices depend on when you book—to save 25-50% or more book **3 weeks to 3 days in advance.**

Rail Information: Deutsche Bahn Information (☎0180 599 66 33; www.bahn.de). Long lines snake out the door of the **Reisezentrum** (Travel Center) in the Hauptbahnhof (open daily 6am-10pm), Bahnhof Zoo (open M-F 6am-10pm, Sa-Su 7am-9pm), and Ostbahnhof. Lines are separated according to whether you need information and reservations or just a quick ticket; be sure to wait in the correct line. All computers can be operated in English or German and accept credit cards only (AmEx/MC/V). **EurAide** (see **Tourist Offices,** p. 96) sells tickets in English.

Buses: ZOB, the central bus station (☎301 03 80), by the Funkturm near Kaiserdamm. U2 to "Kaiserdamm" or S4, S45, or S46 to "Witzleben." Open M-F 6am-9pm, Sa-Su 6am-3pm. Check *Zitty* and *Tip* for deals on long-distance buses, which are slower and cheaper than trains. **Gullivers,** at ZOB (☎311 02 11; www.gullivers.de) and Hardenbergpl. 14 (☎0800 48 55 48 37), often has good deals on buses. Call ahead for promotions. To: **Paris, France** (13hr., €73, students €58); **Vienna, Austria** (10½hr., €57, students €51). Open daily 8am-9:30pm. Shorter hours in winter.

Mitfahrzentralen (Ride Share): Citynetz, Joachimstaler Str. 17 (☎194 44), has a computerized ride-share database. U9 or 15 to "Kurfürstendamm." To: **Hamburg** or **Hannover** (€18); **Frankfurt** (€30.50). Open M-F 9am-8pm, Sa-Su 10am-6pm. Check the magazines *Zitty, Tip,* and *030* for addresses and phone numbers.

Hitchhiking: *Let's Go* does not recommend hitchhiking as a safe mode of transportation. Hitching is rare in Berlin and also illegal at rest stops or anywhere along the highway. Those heading west or south (Hanover, Munich, Weimar, Leipzig) have been known to take S1 or S7 to "Wannsee," then bus #211 to the Autobahn entrance ramp. Those heading north (Hamburg, Rostock) report riding S25 to "Hennigsdorf," then walking 50m to the bridge on the right, or asking for the location of the Trampenpl. Both spots have crowds, but it is said that someone gets picked up every few minutes.

ORIENTATION

The **River Spree** snakes west to east through Berlin, north of the narrower **Landwehrkanal** that flows into it. The vast **Tiergarten,** Berlin's beloved park, lies between the waterways at the city's center. If you see a radio tower it's either the **Funkturm** (pointed and Eiffel-like) in the west or the **Fernsehturm** (with the globe) in the east at Alexanderpl. Major streets include **Kurfürstendamm** (nicknamed the Ku'damm), lined with department stores and running into the **Bahnhof Zoo,** the regional transit hub of West Berlin. The eloquent ruins of the **Kaiser-Wilhelm Gedächtniskirche** are near Bahnhof Zoo, as is the **Europacenter,** one of Berlin's few real skyscrapers.

The grand, tree-lined **Str. des 17 Juni** runs east-west through the Tiergarten, ending at the triumphant **Brandenburger Tor** at the park's eastern border. From here it becomes **Unter den Linden,** flanked by the bulk of Berlin's imperial architecture (**Sights,** p. 120). Next to the Brandenburger Tor is the **Reichstag,** and several blocks south, **Potsdamer Pl.** is shadowed by the glittering **Sony Center** and the towering Deutsche Bahn headquarters. Streets in Berlin are short and frequently change names, and street numbers often climb to the end of the street and then wrap around to the other side, conveniently making the highest- and lowest-numbered buildings across from one another. A map with an index is invaluable here.

> **! SAFETY PRECAUTION.** Berlin is by far the most tolerant city in Germany, and, among major cities, Berlin has the fewest hate crimes per capita and very few neo-Nazi skinheads. However, minorities, gays, and lesbians should exercise caution in the outlying eastern suburbs at night. If you see skinheads wearing dark combat boots (especially with white laces), proceed with caution, but do not panic, and avoid drawing attention to yourself.

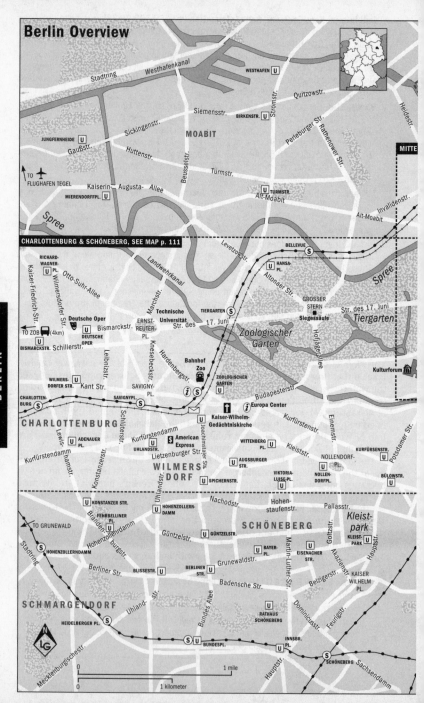

Berlin Overview

WESTHAFEN U

MITTE

Stadtring · Westhafenkanal

Quitzowstr.

Siemensstr. · BIRKENSTR. U · Stromstr.

Perleburger Str. · Rathenower Str.

Heidestr.

JUNGFERNHEIDE U · Sickingenstr.

MOABIT

Gaußstr. · Huttenstr. · Beusselstr. · Turmstr.

TO ✈ FLUGHAFEN TEGEL

Kaiserin- Augusta- Allee

MIERENDORFFPL. U

TURMSTR. U · Alt-Moabit

Invalidenstr.

Alt-Moabit

Spree

CHARLOTTENBURG & SCHÖNEBERG, SEE MAP p. 111

Landwehrkanal

Levetzowstr. · BELLEVUE S

RICHARD-WAGNER-PL. U · Otto-Suhr-Allee

HANSA-PL. U · Altonaer Str.

Spree

Kaiser-Friedrich-Str. · Wilmersdorfer Str.

Marchstr.

GROSSER STERN · Siegessäule · Str. des 17. Juni

Tiergarten

Deutsche Oper 🎭 · Bismarckstr. · Technische Universität · TIERGARTEN S · Str. des 17. Juni

ERNST-REUTER-PL. U

Zoologischer Garten

TO ZOB 🚌 (4km) · DEUTSCHE OPER U

BISMARCKSTR. U · Schillerstr.

Leibnizstr. · Knesebeckstr. · Hardenbergstr.

Bahnhof Zoo

Hoflallee

Kulturforum 🏛

WILMERS-DORFER STR. U · Kant Str. · SAVIGNY-PL. · ZOOLOGISCHER GARTEN

Budapesterstr.

CHARLOTTENBURG S · SAVIGNYPL. · ℹ S

CHARLOTTENBURG

Schillerstr.

Europa Center

Lewishamstr. · ADENAUER PL. U

Kurfürstendamm · UHLANDSTR. U · American Express · Lietzenburger Str.

Kaiser-Wilhelm-Gedächtniskirche

Kurfürstenstr. · Einemstr.

KURFÜRSTENR. U

Kurfürstendamm · Konstanzerstr.

Joachimsthaler Str.

WITTENBERG PL. U · Kleiststr.

AUGSBURGER STR. U

NOLLENDORF-PL. U

NOLLEN-DORFPL. U · Potsdamer Str.

BÜLOWSTR. U

WILMERS-DORF · SPICHERNSTR. U

Uhlandstr.

VIKTORIA-LUISE-PL. U

KONSTANZER STR. U

Nachodstr. · Hohen-staufenstr. · Pallasstr.

Kleist-park

HOHENZOLLERN-DAMM U

FEHRBELLINER PL. U

Brandenburgische Str.

SCHÖNEBERG

Goltzstr. · KLEIST-PARK U

TO GRUNEWALD

Hohenzollerndamm · Güntzelstr. · GÜNTZELSTR. U

Martin-Luther-Str. · Akazienstr. · Hauptstr.

Stadtring

HOHENZOLLERNDAMM S

Berliner Str. · BLISSESTR. U · BERLINER STR. U · Grunewaldstr.

BAYER. PL. U · EISENACHER STR. U

Belzigerstr.

KAISER WILHELM PL.

Badensche Str.

Bundes Allee

Dominicusstr. · Feurigstr.

SCHMARGENDORF · Uhland-str.

HEIDELBERGER PL. S

RATHAUS SCHÖNEBERG U

Mecklenburgischestr.

BUNDESPL. S U

INNSBR. PL. U

SCHÖNEBERG S · Sachsendamm

Haupstr.

0 ————— 1 mile

0 ————— 1 kilometer

BERLIN

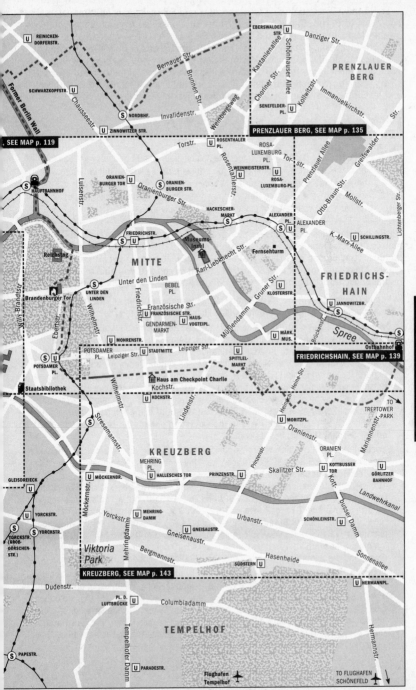

SEE MAP p. 119

REINICKEN-DORFERSTR.

SCHWARZKOPFSTR.

Former Berlin Wall

Chausseestr.

NORDBHF.

ZINNWITZER STR.

Invalidenstr.

Bernauer Str.

Brunnen Str.

Weinbergsweg

Torstr.

Luisenstr.

EBERSWALDER STR.

Danziger Str.

PRENZLAUER BERG

Kastanienallee

Schönhauser Allee

Choriner Str.

Kollwitzstr.

Immanuelkirchstr.

Str.

SENEFELDER-PL.

PRENZLAUER BERG, SEE MAP p. 135

ROSENTHALER

Rosenthalerstr.

ROSA-LUXEMBURG PL.

WEINMEISTERSTR.

Tor

str.

ROSA-LUXEMBURG-PL.

Prenzlauer Allee

Greifswalder

Str.

HAUPTBAHNHOF

ORANIEN-BURGER TOR

ORANIEN-BURGER STR.

Oranienburger Str.

Reichstag

FRIEDRICHSTR.

HACKESCHER-MARKT

Museums-Insel

ALEXANDER PL.

ALEXANDER PL.

Otto-Braun-Str.

Mollstr.

Lichtenberger Str.

SCHILLINGSTR.

K.-Marx-Allee

MITTE

Fernsehturm

Karl-Liebknecht Str.

FRIEDRICHS-HAIN

Brandenburger Tor

UNTER DEN LINDEN

Unter den Linden

BEBEL PL.

Friedrichstr.

Französische Str.

FRANZÖSISCHE STR.

HAUS-VOGTEIPL.

GENDARMEN-MARKT

Gruner Str.

KLOSTERSTR.

Mühlendamm

MÄRK. MUS.

JANNOWITZBR.

Spree

Ostbahnhof

FRIEDRICHSHAIN, SEE MAP p. 139

Willy-Brandt-Str.

Ebertstr.

Brückenstr.

MOHRENSTR.

POTSDAMER PL.

Leipziger Str.

STADTMITTE

Leipziger Str.

SPITTEL-MARKT

POTSDAMER PL.

Staatsbibliothek

Wilhelmstr.

Haus am Checkpoint Charlie

Kochstr.

KOCHSTR.

Lindenstr.

Heinrich-Heine-Str.

MORITZPL.

Oranienstr.

TO TREPTOWER PARK

Marianenstr.

Streesemannstr.

KREUZBERG

MEHRING PL.

HALLESCHES TOR

MÖCKERNBR.

PRINZENSTR.

Prinzenstr.

Skalitzer Str.

ORANIEN PL.

KOTTBUSSER TOR

Kott.

GÖRLITZER BAHNHOF

Landwehrkanal

GLEISDREIECK

YORCKSTR.

YORCKSTR.

YORCKSTR. (GROßGÖRSCHEN-STR.)

Möckernstr.

Yorckstr.

MEHRING-DAMM

MEHRING-DAMM

Mehringdamm

GNEISAUSTR.

Gneisenaustr.

Bergmannstr.

Urbanstr.

SCHÖNLEINSTR.

Bussel Damm

Sonnenallee

Viktoria Park

KREUZBERG, SEE MAP p. 143

Hasenheide

SÜDSTERN

HERMANNPL.

Dudenstr.

PL. D. LUFTBRÜCKE

Columbiadamm

Tempelhofer Damm

TEMPELHOF

Hermannstr.

PAPESTR.

PARADESTR.

Flughafen Tempelhof

TO FLUGHAFEN SCHÖNEFELD

B E R L I N

The former West, including **Charlottenberg** and **Schöneberg,** is still the commercial heart of Berlin. In the former East are the most happening neighborhoods: swanky **Mitte,** hipster-populated **Prenzlauer Berg,** and the newest scenester destination, **Friedrichshain.** Counter-culture-heavy **Kreuzberg** was part of West Berlin but falls geographically in the east. Berlin is rightly called a collection of towns, not a homogeneous city, as each *Bezirk* maintains an individual history and identity. Every year, for example, citizens of Kreuzberg and Friedrichshain battle with vegetables for possession of the *Oberbaumbrücke* on the border between them.

⊑ LOCAL TRANSPORTATION

> **THE REAL DEAL.** If you feel like splurging on a cab but don't want pay the hefty metered rates, ask the driver for a *Kurzstrecke*—a special deal whereby, for only €3, you can travel 2km in any given direction. You probably won't get all the way to your doorstep, but you may get close. The *Kurzstrecke* applies only for cabs that you hail, not those you call. – *Amelia Atlas*

Berlin may be the second largest city in Europe, but with a train pass and a city map it's yours. Maps cost €0.50 at any tourist office or *Fahrscheine* station and include a **transit map** of S-Bahn and U-Bahn lines, enough to get you almost anywhere. Make sure to pick up a *Nachtnetz* (**night bus map**) if you plan to be out past midnight, as most U-Bahn and several S-Bahn lines shut down until about 4am.

Public Transportation: The **BVG** *(Berliner Verkehrsbetriebe)* is one of the most efficient transportation systems in the world. Disruptions in service are rare.

Orientation and Basic Fares: It is futile to try to see all of Berlin on foot. Fortunately, the extensive **Bus, Straßenbahn** (streetcar or tram), **U-Bahn** (subway), and **S-Bahn** (surface rail) systems will get you to your destination safely and relatively quickly. Berlin is divided into 3 transit zones. **Zone A** encompasses central Berlin, including Tempelhof Airport. The rest of Berlin is in **Zone B; Zone C** consists of the outlying areas, including Potsdam and Oranienburg. An AB ticket is the best deal, as you can buy extension tickets for the outlying areas. An *Einzelfahrausweis* (one-way ticket) is good for 2hr. after validation. (Zones AB €2.10, BC €2.30, ABC €2.60. Children under 6 free with an adult, under 14 reduced fare.) **Within the validation period, the ticket may be used on any S-Bahn, U-Bahn, bus, or tram.**

Special Passes: Single tickets are seldom worth purchasing during a visit to Berlin. A **Tageskarte** (AB €5.80, ABC €6) is good from the time of validation until 3am the next day. The **WelcomeCard** (sold at Tourist offices) is valid on all lines for 48hr. (€16) or 72hr. (€22) and includes discounts on select tours. The BVG offers the **CityTourCard,** good within zones AB for 48hr. (€14.90) or 72hr. (€19.90) but with discounts at over 30 attractions. The **7-Tages-Karte** (AB €25.40, ABC €31.30) is good for 7 days of travel. An **Umweltkarte Standard** (AB €67, ABC €83) is valid for 1 month. With proof of study at a Berlin university you can get the **Azubi Karte** (AB €48.50), also good for 1 month. **Bikes** require a supplemental ticket (€1.40 per trip, available at all ticket stations), and are permitted on the U-Bahn and S-Bahn, but not on buses and trams.

Purchasing Tickets: Buy tickets, including monthly passes, from *Automaten* (machines), bus drivers, or ticket windows in the U- and S-Bahn stations. When using an Automat, make your selection before inserting money; note that machines will not give more than €10 change. Also, many machines do not take bills; you may have to save coins or use a ticket window to buy more expensive day or week passes. Some machines accept credit cards. **Validate your ticket** by inserting it into one of the machines marked "hier entwerfen" **before boarding!**

THERE ARE NO FREE RIDES. You may have noticed that getting on and off the U-Bahn, S-Bahn, tram, or bus doesn't involve that ticket that you just bought. Does Berlin public transportation work on the honor system? Of course not! Every so often, plainclothes officials will board your car and ask to see your ticket once the doors close. They accept no excuses for *Schwarzfahren* (riding without paying), and if you fail to produce a validated ticket you'll be slapped with a **€40 fine,** due on the spot if you can't provide identification.

Maps and Information: The BVG's numerous **Fahrscheine und Mehr** (tickets and more) stations have tons of maps. They can be found in most major transfer stations (e.g. Alexanderpl.). **Liniennetz** maps of the U-Bahn, S-Bahn, bus lines, and night bus lines are free. BVG **information line:** ☎ 194 49, open 24hr.; www.bvg.de.

Night Transport: U- and S-Bahn lines generally do not run M-F 1-4am. On F-Sa nights, S-Bahn and U-Bahn lines continue to run, though less frequently. Exceptions are the U4, S45, and S85. An extensive system of approximately 70 **night buses** runs every 20-30min. and tends to follow major transit lines; pick up the free Nachtliniennetz map at a Fahrscheine und Mehr office. The letter **N** precedes night bus numbers. Trams also continue to run at night.

Ferries: Stern und Kreis Schifffahrt, Puschkinallee 15 (☎536 36 00; www.sternund-kreis.de), in Treptower Park. Operates along the Spree Apr.-Oct. Ferries leave from locations daily 10:30am-4:30 on throughout the city, including Friedrichstr., Jannowitzbrucke, and the Nikolaiviertel. Fares (€7.50-16) depend on distance traveled. Pleasure cruises available. Fahrscheine und Mehr offers information.

Taxis: (☎26 10 26, 21 02 02, free 080 02 63 00 00.) Call at least 15min. in advance. Women can request female drivers. Trips within the city cost up to €21.

Car Rental: Most companies have counters at the airports and around Bahnhof Zoo, Ostbahnhof, and Friedrichstr. stations. Offices are also in the Europa Center with entrances at Budapester Str. 39-41. Rates average around €65 for a small car. 19+. **Hertz** (☎261 10 53), open M-F 7am-8pm, Sa 8am-4pm, Su 9am-1pm; **Avis** (☎230 93 70), open daily 24hr.; **4 Rent** (☎355 3003), open M-F 9am-7pm, Sa 9am-4pm.

Bike Rental: Fahrradstation, Dorotheenstr. 30 (☎20 45 45 00; www.fahrradstation.de), is centrally located near the "Friedrichstr." S-Bahn station. Turn in at the parking lot next to STA. €15 per day. Open in summer daily 8am-8pm; in winter M-F 8am-7pm, Sa 10am-3pm. **Prenzelberger Orangebikes** 37 Kollwitz Pl. (☎0163 89 12 64 27), U2 to "Senefelderpl." €5 per day. Open M-F noon-6pm, Sa noon-4pm. **Velomondo,** Motzstr. 12. (☎21 75 30 46), U1-U4 to "Nollendorfpl." €10 per day, €37 per wk. Open M-F 10am-7pm, Sa 10am-2pm. **Deutsche Bahn Call-A-Bike** (☎0700 522 55 22; www.callabike.de) are all over the city. After signing up (€5), call to unlock a bike. It costs €0.7 per min. (up to €15 per day) or €60 per wk. Having a cell phone and a German-language skills is helpful, as you must call to pick-up and drop-off.

▣ PRACTICAL INFORMATION

CITY CODE:	The city code for all of Berlin is ☎030.

TOURIST OFFICES

Now privately-owned, tourist offices provide a narrower range of free services and information than they once did. They still sell a useful **city map** (€1) on which sights and transit stations are clearly marked, and book same-day **hotel rooms** for a €3 fee—room prices start around €30. The monthly *Berlin Programm* (€1.75) lists museums, sights, restaurants and hotels, and opera, theater, and classical music performances. German speakers should get *Tip* (€2.70) or *Zitty* (€2.70) for comprehensive listings of film, theater, concerts, and clubs. *Siegessäule*, *Sergej*, and *Gay-yellowpages* have gay and lesbian event and club listings. English-language movie and theater reviews are in the *Ex-Berliner* (€2), and www.berlin.de has comprehensive information on all aspects of the city.

EurAide (www.euraide.com), in the Hauptbahnhof, across from the McDonald's. Sells rail tickets, maps, phone cards, and walking tour tickets, and gives away much more: general assistance in English and lists of recommended hostels. Arrive early—the office is often packed and doesn't accept phone calls. Open June-Oct. daily 8am-noon and 1-6pm, Nov.-May M-F 8am-noon and 1-4:45pm.

Tourist Info Centers (☎25 00 25; www.berlin-tourist-information.de), reserve rooms for a €3-6 fee, with friendly service in English. A list of campgrounds and pensions is available. Transit maps (free), and city maps (€0.50). From outside Germany, call (☎49 700 TO BERLIN/700 86 23 75 46) or write Berlin Tourismus Marketing GmbH, Am Karlsbad 11, 10785 Berlin. One location is at the **Europa Center,** entrance on Budapester Str. Open M-Sa 10am-7pm, Su 10am-6pm, extended hours Apr.-Oct. Another office is near the **Brandenburger Tor,** S1, S2, or S25 or bus #100 to "Unter den Linden," on your left as you face the pillars from the Unter den Linden side. Open daily 9:30am-6pm. The 3rd location is at the **Alexanderpl. Television Tower** across from the Alexanderpl. station. Open daily 10am-6pm. All locations extend hours Apr.-Oct.

CITY TOURS

Unless otherwise noted, the tours listed below are conducted in English.

■ **Terry Brewer's Best of Berlin** (www.brewersberlin.com) is heavy on information and personal touches. Terry and his guides are legendary for vast knowledge and engaging personalities, making the 8hr. walk well worth it. Tours leave daily from the Australian ice cream shop on Friedrichstr. (S5, S7, S9, S75, or U6 to "Friedrichstr.") The tour picks up guests at hostels Odyssee (p. 138), Circus (p. 117), and Mitte's Backpacker (p. 117). €12. An abridged (4hr.) tour is offered Apr.-Oct. 11am. Also offers nightlife tours (F 8:30pm at the same meeting point, €10).

Insider Tour (☎692 31 49; www.insidertour.com) offers a variety of fun, erudite tours that hit all the major sights. More importantly, the guides' enthusiasm for Berlin is contagious and their accents span the English-speaking world. **The Famous Insider Walk** picks up daily at 10am and (in summer) 2:30pm at the McDonald's outside the Zoo Station. Tours also pick up at Hackesher Markt 30min. later and last 4hr. from there. €12, students and under 26 €10, WelcomeCard or ISIC €9. **Bike tours** meet at Hackesher Markt by the Coffee Mamas at 11am and (in summer) 4pm (€22/19). Also offers themed Red Star (former DDR), Nazi, and Bar & Club Crawl tours.

Original Berlin Walks (☎301 91 94; www.berlinwalks.de) offers a range of English-language walking tours, including "Infamous Third Reich Sites," "Jewish Life in Berlin," and "Discover Potsdam." Their **"Discover Berlin Walk"** (4hr.; €12, under 26 and students €10, WelcomeCard and ISIC €9) is a great way to get acquainted with the city. Guides' knowledge complements their eager attitude. Tours 2½-6hr. meet at 10am at the taxi stand in front of Bahnhof Zoo and 10:30 at the Hackesher Markt Häagen-Dazs. The "Discover Berlin Walk" also meets Apr.-Oct. at 2:30/3pm. Other tours start at €10-12.

New Berlin (☎973 03 97; www.newberlintours.com) offers free tours (on a tips only basis, which means some pandering from the guides) of Berlin's biggest sights, and special tours (Sachsenhausen, Third Reich tour, **pub crawl,** etc.) for a fee. Backpackers with little cash are encouraged to take the tour, but occasionally dislike the cursory nature of the set-up. Tours leave every day from the Brandenburg Gate Starbucks (11am and 1 and 4pm) and the Zoologischer Garten Dunkin' Donuts (10:30am and

12:30 and 3:30pm). A new free **bike tour** runs daily from **Brauhaus Mitte** in the Alex-anderpl. S-Bahn (11am and 4pm; bike rental €7 or free for 1st ten people).

Bus tours: Severin + Kühn's Stadtrundfahrt (☎880 41 90; www.severin-kuehn-berlin.de) hits 14 different sites (2hr.; €15). You can get on and off at any stop all day; tours are led by cassette tape in English, German, and 7 other languages. Tours start at 10am at Ku'damm 216 (in front of Hotel Kempinski) or at their office near Alexanderpl. at Karl-Lie-bnect-Str. 3 and run every 15min. after that. Many other bus tours leave roughly every hr. from near the Hauptbahnhof, Europa-Center, and Gedächtniskirche or from Unter den Linden near the Brandenburg Gate. Most cost about €17 for a full day of sightseeing.

TRAVEL AGENCIES

STA: Books flights and hotels and sells ISIC cards. Branches at: **Dorotheenstr. 30** (☎20 16 50 63). S3, S5, S7, S9, S75, or U6 to "Friedrichstr." Open M-F 10am-7pm, Sa 11am-3pm. **Gleimstr. 29** (☎28 15 133). S4, S8, S85, or U2 to "Schönhauser Allee." Open M-F 10am-7pm, Sa 11am-4pm. **Hardenbergerstr. 9** (☎310 00 40). U2 to "Ernst-Reuter-Pl." Open M-F 10am-7pm, Sa 11am-3pm. **Takustr. 47** (☎852 53 76). Open M-F 10am-6:30pm, Sa 11am-2pm.

EMBASSIES AND CONSULATES

Berlin's construction plans include a new complex to house foreign dignitaries. Though most have moved to their new homes, the locations of some embassies and consulates remain in a state of flux. For the latest information, call the **Auswärtiges Amt Dienststelle Berlin** (☎20 18 60; www.auswaertiges-amt.de) or visit their office on the Werderscher Markt (U2 to "Hausvogteipl.").

Australian Embassy: Wallstr. 76-79 (☎880 08 80; www.australian-embassy.de). U2 to "Märkisches Museum." Open M-Th 8:30am-5pm, F 8:30am-4:15pm.

Canadian Embassy: Leipziger Pl. 27 (☎20 31 20; www.canada.de). S1, S2, or U2 to "Potsdamer Pl." Open M-F 8:30am-12:30pm and 1:30-5pm.

Embassy of Ireland: Friedrichstr. 200 (☎22 07 20; www.botschaft-irland.de). U2 or U6 to "Stadtmitte." Open M-F 9:30am-12:30pm and 2:30-4:45pm.

New Zealand Embassy: Friedrichstr. 60 (☎20 62 10; www.nzembassy.com). U2 or U6 to "Stadtmitte." Open M-F 9am-1pm and 2-5:30pm, F closes at 4:30pm.

British Embassy: Wilhelmstr. 70-71 (☎20 42 70; www.britischebotschaft.de). S1-S3, S5, S7, S9, S25, S75, or U6 to "Friedrichstr." Open M-F 9am-4pm.

American Citizen Services/US Consulate: Clayallee 170 (☎832 92 33; fax 83 05 12 15). U1 to "Oskar-Helene-Heim." After a long debate over the security of proposed loca-tions, the US Embassy is now in the process of moving to a spot next to the Brandenburg Gate, to be completed by 2008. Open M-F 8:30am-noon. Telephone advice available M-F 2-4pm; after hours, call ☎830 50 for emergency advice.

FINANCIAL SERVICES

Currency Exchange: The best rates are usually found at exchange offices with **Wechsel-stube** signs outside, at most major train stations, and in large squares. **ReiseBank**, at the Hauptbahnhof (M-Sa 8am-10pm), at Bahnhof Zoo (☎881 71 17; open daily 7:30am-10pm), and at Ostbahnhof (☎296 43 93; open M-F 7am-10pm, Sa 8am-8pm, Su 8am-noon and 12:30-4pm), is conveniently located, but has poor rates.

Bank and ATM: ATMs are labeled *"Geldautomat."* **Berliner Sparkasse** and **Deutsche Bank** have branches everywhere. Their ATMs usually accept MC/V. **Citibank** has 23 branches in Berlin with 24hr. **ATMs,** including: Friedrichstr. 194-99 (U-Bahn to "Stad-mitte") and Tegel Airport.

BERLIN

American Express: Main Office, Bayreuther Str. 37-38 (☎21 47 62 92). U1 or U2 to "Wittenbergpl." Holds mail and offers banking services. No commission for cashing American Express Traveler's Cheques. Expect out-the-door lines F-Sa. Open M-F 9am-7pm, Sa 10am-2pm. **Branch,** Friedrichstr. 172 (☎204 55 72). U6 to "Französische Str." Same services and hours.

LOCAL SERVICES

Luggage Storage: In the **Hauptbahnhof,** in "DB Gepack Center." €3 for up to 3 bags. In **Bahnhof Zoo,** lockers €3-5 per day, depending on size. Max. 2hr. Open daily 6:15am-10:30pm. 24hr. lockers are also at **Ostbahnhof** and **Alexanderpl.**

Bookstores:

Marga Schöler Bücherstube, Knesebeckstr. 33 (☎881 11 12). S5, S7, S9, or S75 to "Savignypl." Off-beat and contemporary reading material in English. Open M-W 9:30am-7pm, Th-F 9:30am-8pm, Sa 9:30am-4pm.

Hugendubel has that massive-chain-store flavor. Branches at Tauentzienstr. 13 (☎484 484; www.hugendubel.de) by the Ku'damm; Friedrichstr. 83; Karl-Marx-Str. 66; Potsdamer Str. 7; Wilmersdorfer Str. 121. Open M-Sa 9:30am-8pm.

Dussman, Friedrichstr. 90 (☎20 25 11 11). S1-S3, S5, S7, S9, S25, S75, or U6 to "Friedrichstr." Another immense bookstore, with books in English on the 2nd fl. Open M-Sa 10am-10pm.

Libraries: Staatsbibliothek Preußischer Kulturbesitz, Potsdamer Str. 33 (☎26 61). A book for every Berliner; 3.5 million in all. Lots of English-language newspapers. Built for West Berlin in the 1960s, after the Iron Curtain cut off the original *Staabi* at Unter den Linden 8 (☎26 60), next to the Humboldt-Universität (p. 120). Now you can choose between them. Both open M-F 9am-9pm, Sa 9am-5pm; Potsdamer Str. also Sa until 7pm. Day-pass required for entry, €0.50.

EMERGENCY AND COMMUNICATIONS

Police, Pl. der Luftbrücke 6. U6 to "Pl. der Luftbrücke." **Emergency** ☎110. **Ambulance** and **Fire** ☎112.

Crisis Lines: English spoken at most crisis lines.

American Hotline (☎0177 814 15 10). Crisis and referral service.

Berliner Behindertenverband, Jägerstr. 63d (☎204 38 47; www.bbv-ev.de). Advice for the handi-capped. Open M-F 8am-4pm.

Deutsche AIDS-Hilfe, Dieffenbachstr. 33 (☎690 08 70; www.aidshilfe.de).

Drug Crisis (☎192 37). Open M-F 8am-10pm, Sa-Su 2-9:30pm.

Frauenkrisentelefon (☎611 03 33). Women's crisis line. Open M and W noon-2pm, Th 2-4pm.

Lesbenberatung, Kulmer Str. 20 (☎215 2000; www.lesbenberatung.de). Lesbian counseling.

Schwulenberatung, Mommsenstr. 45 (☎194 46). Gay men's counseling.

Schwules Überfall (☎216 33 36). Hotline/legal help for gay violence victims. Open daily 6-9pm.

Sexual Assault Hotline (☎251 28 28). Open Tu and Th 6-9pm, Su noon-2pm.

Pharmacies: Ubiquitous in Berlin. **DominoApotheke,** Tauentzienstr. 13 (☎261 41 42), near Bahnhof Zoo. Open M-F 6am-8pm, Sa 9am-4pm. Pharmacies list a rotating sched-ule of 24hr. service.

Medical Services: The American and British embassies list English-speaking doctors. **Emergency doctor** (☎31 00 31); **Emergency dentist** (☎89 00 43 33). Both 24hr.

Internet Access: Free Internet access with admission to the **Staatsbibliothek** (see **Libraries**). Also try: **Netlounge,** Auguststr. 89 (☎24 34 25 97; www.netlounge-berlin.de). U-Bahn to "Oranienburger Str." €2.50 per hr. Open daily noon-midnight. **Easy Internet** has several locations throughout Berlin: Karl-Marx-Str. 78, Kurfürstendamm 224, Schloßstr. 102, Sony Center, and Rathausstr. 5. **Wireless Internet** access can be found throughout Berlin, both free and charge-based services (see **Essentials,** p. 36).

Post Offices: Joachimstaler Str. 7 (☎88 70 86 11), down Joachimstaler Str. from Bahnhof Zoo and near the intersection with Kantstr. Open M-Sa 9am-8pm. Branches: **Tegel Airport,** open M-F 8am-6pm, Sa 8am-noon; **Ostbahnhof,** open M-F 8am-8pm, Sa-Su 10am-6pm. Most branches are open M-F 9am-7pm, Sa 9am-1pm. **Postal Code:** 10706.

ACCOMMODATIONS

Same-day accommodations in Berlin aren't impossible to find, but you may need to wait until late in the day when establishments have vacancies due to cancellations. If you want to stay in the same place longer than a couple of days or on weekends, reservations are essential. Watch out for the **Love Parade,** when same-day space is impossible to find; prices go up by at least €10 per night and only a few hostels (like **Circus,** p. 117) save beds for the stranded. Book at least two weeks ahead to get a room and two months ahead to have a selection.

For a €3-6 fee, **tourist offices** will find you a room in a hostel, pension, or hotel. Be prepared to pay at least €30 for a single and €50 for a double. Some tourist offices also have the pamphlet *Hotels und Pensionen,* which lists options across the price spectrum.

For stays of a month or more, **Mitwohnzentrale** (home share companies) find rooms in *Wohngemeinschäfte* ("WG," shared apartments). Leases typically require a passport and payment up front for those without a German bank account. Rooms start at €250 per month. Private apartments run at least €350 per month. Mitwohnzentralen charge commission on the monthly rent; the longer the stay, the lower the percentage. **Home Company Mitwohnzentrale,** Joachimstaler Str. 17, is the biggest. Commission is 20% for stays up to one month. (U9 to "Kurfürstendamm." ☎194 45; www.homecompany.de. Open M-Th 9am-6pm, F 9am-5pm, Sa 11am-2pm.) Located in Mitte, **City Mitwohnzentrale,** Linienstr. 111, has pictures of rooms it rents. Commission starts at 25%. (S1 to "Oranienburgerstr." ☎194 30; www.city-mitwohnzentrale.de. Open M-F 10am-6pm, Sa 10am-3pm.) **Erste,** Sybelstr. 53, charges 29% commission, but has a personal touch. (U7 to "Adenauerpl." ☎324 30 31; www.mitwohn.com. Open M-F 9am-8pm, Sa 10am-6pm.) **Fine+Mine,** Neue Schönhauser Str. 20, is in the Hackescher Markt. (☎235 51 20; www.fineandmine.de. Open M-F 10am-7pm, Sa 10am-6pm.)

Another long-term option is to live in a **Wohnheim** (residential hostel). **Studentenwerk** (www.studentenwerk-berlin.de) manages over 40 of these apartments, limited to students studying in Berlin. For interns or youth staying long-term for other reasons, **Wohnheim Berlin Junge Politik** in Charlottenburg offers single rooms starting at €180 per month and apartments at €230 (www.junge-politik-berlin.de).

HOSTELS AND DORMITORIES

HI hostels in Berlin are state-owned and usually clean, reliable, and filled with German school groups. Some impose a curfew or require an access code for late entry. Most require a membership card and charge an extra €3 a night without one. Purchase an **HI card** at any **HI hostel** (see p. 41). If you're looking for a more party-ready crew, crash at a **private hostel,** popular among international travelers. These centers for the young and hip are often located near train stations and nightlife areas and have a turnover rate of two days, so you'll never be bored.

HOTELS AND PENSIONS

Many small pensions and hotels are fairly cheap, particularly since most are amenable to *Mehrbettzimmer,* where extra beds are moved into a large double or triple. However, these benefits are really only for groups of three or more; hotels will not usually allow random individuals to stay together. Most affordable hotels are in western Berlin, though inexpensive options are beginning to appear in the east, notably around Mitte's Oranienburgerstr. The best place to find cheap rooms is Charlottenburg, especially around Savignypl. and Wilmersdorfer Str.

CAMPING

Deutscher Camping-Club runs campgrounds in Wannsee, Spandau, and Köpenick. Reservations are recommended; write to Deutscher Camping-Club Berlin, Geisbergstr. 11, 10777 Berlin, or call in advance. (☎218 60 71; www.dccberlin.de. Sites charge €5.60 per person, €2.50 per child, €4 per tent.) One convenient campground is **Kladow 1 ❶**, Krampnitzer Weg 111-117 (☎365 27 97). Take U7 to "Rathaus Spandau," then bus #135 (dir.: Alt-Kladow) to the end. Switch to bus #234 to "Krampnitzer Weg/Selbitzerstr.," then follow Krampnitzer Weg 500m. A store and restaurant complement the swimmable lake in this far-off suburban locale. (Open year-round. €5.60 per person. Cash only.)

ACCOMMODATIONS BY PRICE

OVER €50 (❺)		Die Fabrik (142)	KB
Art Hotel Connection (114)	SB	✉East Seven Hostel (133)	PB
Frauenhotel Artemisia (109)	CB	Generator (134)	PB
		Heart of Gold Hostel (117)	M
€50 AND UNDER (❹)		Hotel Transit (144)	KB
Hotel-Pension Charlottenburg (108)	CB	JetPAK (114)	SB
Pension Kreuzberg (144)	KB	Jugendherberge Berlin Inter'l HI (114)	SB
		Jugendgästehaus am Wannsee (149)	OD
€35 AND UNDER (❸)		Jugendgästehaus Tegel (149)	OD
Hotel-Pension Charlottenburg (108)	CB	Lette'm Sleep Hostel (133)	PB
✉Jugendhotel Berlincity (113)	SB	✉Mitte's Backpacker Hostel (117)	M
Jugendgästehaus am Zoo (108)	CB		
		€15 AND UNDER (❶)	
€25 AND UNDER (❷)		All in Hostel (138)	FH
A&O Hostel (108)	CB	Backpacker's Paradise (149)	OD
Alcatraz (134)	PB	Eastern Comfort Hostelboat (138)	FH
✉Bax Pax (142)	KB	Globetrotter Hostel Odyssee (138)	FH
✉Bax Pax, Mitte (117)	M	Helter Skelter (117)	M
✉Berolina Backpacker (108)	CB	Hostel X Berger (142)	KB
✉Circus (117)	M	Meininger City Hostel (113)	SB
CityStay Hostel (117)	M	✉Sunflower Hostel (137)	FH
CVJM-Haus (114)	SB	Three Little Pigs (117)	M

AREA ABBREVIATIONS: CB Charlottenburg **FH** Friedrichshain **KB** Kreuzberg **M** Mitte **OD** Outer Districts **PB** Prenzlauer Berg **SB** Schöneberg

◪ FOOD

Food in Berlin is less German than it is cosmopolitan. The city boasts a variety of tasty local options, as well as terrific ethnic food thanks to its Turkish, Indian, Italian, and Thai populations. In early summer, expect an onslaught of the wildly popular *Spargel* (asparagus). Berlin's dearest culinary tradition, however, is breakfast, a gloriously civilized institution often served in cafés well into the afternoon. Relax over a leisurely *Milchkaffee*, a bowl of coffee foaming with milk.

Almost every street in Berlin has its own Turkish restaurant and *Imbiß* (snack bar). Most are open ridiculously late, some 24hr. The *Döner Kebap* (shaved roast lamb or chicken stuffed into a toasted flatbread and topped with vegetables and garlic sauce) has cornered the fast-food market, with *Falafel* running a close second. Another budget option for travelers is to buy sandwiches (usually baguettes) at a local *Bäckerei* or *Konditorei* (€1.50-€2.50). Quality Indian and Italian eateries also abound, and of course the city has its fair share of *Currywurst* and *Bratwurst*. **Aldi, Plus, Spar, Edeka,** and **Penny Markt** are the cheapest supermarket chains, followed by **Bolle, Reichelt,** and the ubiquitous **Kaiser's.** Supermarkets are usually open M-F 9am-6pm and Sa 9am-4pm, though some are open as late as 8pm on weekdays. Bahnhof Zoo's open-air market fires up Saturday mornings on Winterfeldtpl., and almost every neighborhood has its own market. For cheap veggies and huge wheels of *Fladenbrot* (pita bread), hit the kaleidoscopic **Turkish market** in Kreuzberg, along Maybachufer on the Landwehrkanal, every Tuesday and Friday. (U1 or U8 to "Kottbusser Tor.")

FOOD BY TYPE

AFRICAN
Blue Nile (145)   KB ❸
Massai (134)   PB ❸

ASIAN
Chao Grung (115)   SB ❷
Fish and Vegetables (115)   SB ❷
Lemongrass(138)   FH ❷
▨Monsieur Vuong (118)   M ❷
Orchidee (109)   CB ❷
Thai Phiset (134)   PB ❶

CAFÉS
Beth Café (118)   M ❷
▨ Café Berio (114)   SB ❷
▨ Café Bilderbuch (114)   SB ❸
Café Einstein (114)   SB❹
Café-Restaurantion 1900 (134)   PB ❸
Café-Restaurant Miró (134)   PB ❸
Café V (144)   KB ❸
Hannibal (145)   KB ❷
Malzcafé (134)   PB ❸
Restaurant-Café Bleibtreu (109)   CB ❷
Schwarzes Café (109)   CB ❸
Toronto (115)   SB ❸

CONTINENTAL
Assel (118)   M ❸
Dollinger Café-Restaurant (109)   CB ❸
▨Nosh (134)   PB ❸

DESSERT
Melek Backerei (144)   KB ❶

FAST FOOD
Bagels & Bialys (118)   M ❶
Baharat Falafel (115)   SB ❶
Dada Falafel (118)   M ❶
Damas Falafel (109)   CB ❶

GERMAN
▨Die Feinbeckerei (115)   SB ❷
▨Wirsthaus Henne(144)   KB ❷
Weinhaus Hoff (145)   KB ❸

INDIAN
Amrit (118)   M ❸

LATIN AND SOUTH AMERICAN
Art-Café Miró (109)   CB ❸

MEDITERRANEAN
Babel (134)   PB ❶
Bar Tolucci (115)   SB ❸
Cappuccino (138)   FH ❷
Intimes (138)   FH ❸
Mario Pasta Bar (109)   CB ❸
Restaurant Rissani (144)   KB ❶

MENSA/CAFÉTERIA
Mensa TU (109)   CB ❶

AREA ABBREVIATIONS: CB Charlottenburg **FH** Friedrichshain **KB** Kreuzberg **M** Mitte **OD** Outer Districts **PB** Prenzlauer Berg **SB** Schöneberg

BERLIN

◉ SIGHTS

Most of central Berlin's major sights are along the route of **bus #100,** which travels from Bahnhof Zoo to Alexanderpl., passing the Siegessäule, Brandenburg Gate, Unter den Linden, and the Berliner Dom among others. Tickets for individual bus rides quickly add up, but a day pass will save you money (see **Local Transportation,** p. 94). There are only a few places to see **remnants of the Berlin Wall:** a narrow band stands in Potsdamer Pl.; the tremendously popular **Haus Am Checkpoint Charlie** guards another piece (p. 145); the sobering Documentation Center in Prenzlauer Berg has preserved an entire city block (p. 135); and a much-embellished section of the wall in Friedrichshain has become the **East Side Gallery** (p. 138).

🏛 MUSEUMS

Berlin is one of the world's great museum cities, with collections of art and artifacts encompassing all subjects and eras. The **Staatliche Museen zu Berlin (Stiftung Preußischer Kulturbesitz** or **SPK,** or simply **SMB)** runs over 20 museums in four major regions—the **Museumsinsel** (an island of historic museums in the middle of the Spree), **Kulturforum, Charlottenburg,** and **Dahlem**—as well as elsewhere in Mitte and around the Tiergarten. Prices are generally standardized; single costs €6, students €3 for Dahlem and Charlottenburg, €8/4 for Hamburger Bahnhof and the KulturForum, and €12/6 for Museumsinsel. Tickets are valid for all SMB-PK museums in a given complex on the day of purchase. The Drei-Tage-Karte (€15, students €7.50) is valid for three consecutive days. Buy either card at any SMB-PK museum. Admission is free the first Sunday of every month. Non-SMB-PK-affiliated museums tend to be smaller and more specialized, dealing with everything from Käthe Kollwitz to the cultural history of marijuana. *Berlin Programm* (€1.75) lists museums and galleries. See www.smb.museum for further info.

GALLERIES

Berlin has an extremely well-funded art scene, with many first-rate galleries. The work is as diverse as Berlin's cultural landscape and includes everything from early Christian antiques in Charlottenburg to conceptual installations in Mitte. A few good pamphlets, all with maps and available just about anywhere in the city, are: *ARTery Berlin* (€2.50), with complete show listings in English and German; *Berliner Kunst Kalender* (€2); and *Berliner Galerien* (free).

The center of Berlin's gallery world is Mitte, which has more contemporary work than classics; the *Berlin Mitte* pamphlet provides listings and a map. Five times a year, Mitte offers a *Galerienrundgang* tour of the galleries (dates are listed in the pamphlets). On nearby Sophienstr., Gipsstr., Auguststr., Linienstr., galleries pack the streets and *Hinterhöfe* (courtyards hidden behind building facades). Charlottenburg also has a large selection of galleries, many of which tend to be more upscale. Kreuzberg hosts a handful of spaces, and a scene has developed in Prenzlauer Berg off Danziger Str. For gallery listings, see p. 131.

🎭 ENTERTAINMENT

Berlin has one of the world's most vibrant cultural scenes, bustling with exhibitions, concerts, plays, and dance performances. The city generously subsidizes its artists despite recent cutbacks, and tickets are usually reasonable, especially with student discounts. Reservations can be made through the box office. Most theaters and concert halls offer up to 50% off for students who buy at the *Abendkasse* (evening box office), which generally opens 1hr. before shows. Other ticket outlets charge 15-18% commissions and do not offer student discounts. There is a ticket counter in the **KaDeWe.** (p. 105. ☎217 77 54. Open M-F 10am-8pm, Sa 10am-4pm.) Theaters generally accept credit cards, but many ticket outlets do not. Most theaters and operas close from mid-July to late August.

Hekticket, Hardenbergpl. near the Cineplex. (☎23 09 93 33; www.hekticket.de). Last-minute tickets up to 50% off. Open M-Sa noon-7pm. **Branch** at Alexanderpl., Karl-Liebknecht-Str. 12. Open M-F 2-7pm, Sa noon-7pm, closed July to mid Aug.

Berlin Ticket, (☎23 09 93 33; www.berlin-ticket.de). By phone only.

CONCERTS, OPERA, AND DANCE

Berlin reaches its musical zenith in September during the fabulous **Berliner Festwochen,** which draws the world's best orchestras and soloists. The **Berliner Jazztage** in November, featuring top jazz musicians, also brings in the crowds. For tickets (which sell out months in advance) and more information for both festivals, call or write to Berliner Festspiele (☎25 48 90; www.berlinerfestspiele.de). In mid-July, the **Bachtage** feature an intense week of classical music, while every Saturday night in August the **Sommer Festspiele** turns the Ku'damm into a multi-faceted concert hall with punk, steel-drum, and folk groups competing for attention.

The monthly pamphlets *Konzerte und Theater in Berlin und Brandenburg* (free) and *Berlin Programm* (€1.75) list concerts, as do the biweekly *Zitty* and *Tip.* Tickets for the *Philharmonie* and the *Oper* are nearly impossible to get without writing months in advance, except by standing outside before performances with a small sign saying *"Suche Karte"* (seeking ticket)—people often try to unload tickets at the last moment, usually at outrageous prices.

⬛ Berliner Philharmonisches Orchester, Herbert Von Karajanstr. 1 (☎25 48 81 32; www.berlin-philharmonic.com). S1, S2, or S25 or U2 to "Potsdamer Pl." and walk up Potsdamer Str. It may look bizarre, but this yellow building, designed by Scharoun in 1963, is acoustically perfect: every audience member hears the music exactly as it is meant to sound. The Berliner Philharmoniker, led by the eminent Sir Simon Rattle, is one of the world's finest orchestras. It is difficult to get a seat; check 1hr. before concert time or write at least 8wk. in advance. Closed late-June to early-Sept. Box office open M-F 3-6pm, Sa-Su 11am-2pm. Tickets start at €7 for standing room, €13 for seats.

Konzerthaus (Schauspielhaus am Gendarmenmarkt), Gendarmenmarkt 2 (☎20 30 90; www.konzerthaus.de). U2 or U6 to "Stadtmitte." The opulent home of Berlin's symphony orchestra. Last-minute tickets are somewhat easier to come by. No performances mid-July to Aug. Box office open M-Sa 11am-7pm, Su noon-4pm.

Deutsche Oper Berlin, Bismarckstr. 35 (tickets ☎0700 67 37 23 75 46; www.deutscheoperberlin.de). U2 to "Deutsche Oper." Berlin's best and youngest opera. Box office open M-Sa 11am until 1hr. before performance, Su 10am-2pm. Evening tickets available 1hr. before performances. Closed July-Aug. Tickets €10-112. 25% student discounts.

Deutsche Staatsoper, Unter den Linden 7 (☎20 35 45 55; www.staatsoper-berlin.de). U6 to "Französische Str." or bus #100, 157, or 348 to "Deutsche Staatsoper." Eastern Berlin's leading opera company. Box office open M-F 11am-7pm, Sa-Su 2-7pm, and 1hr. before performances. Closed mid-July to Aug. Tickets €5-120; students €12, 1hr. before shows and ½-price on cheaper seats.

Komische Oper, Unter den Linden 14 (☎479 97400; www.komische-oper-berlin.de). U6 to "Französische Str.," or S1, S2, S25 to "Unter den Linden." Started by zany director Walter Felsenstein and now under the direction of Andreas Homoki, the 112-year-old opera is known for fresh versions of the classics. Box office open M-Sa 11am-7pm, Su 1-4pm. Tickets €8-93. 25% student discounts always available 1hr. before curtain.

THEATER

Theater listings, found on the yellow and blue posters in most U-Bahn stations, are available in the monthly pamphlets *Kultur!news* and *Berlin Programm,* as well as in *030, Zitty,* and *Tip.* In addition to the world's best German-language theater, Berlin also has a lively English-language scene; look for listings in *Zitty* or *Tip* that say *"in englischer Sprache"* (in English). A number of privately run companies called *Off-Theaters* also occasionally feature English-language plays. As with concert halls, virtually all theaters are closed in July and August (closings are indicated by the words *Theaterferien* or *Sommerpause*).

Deutsches Theater, Schumannstr. 13a (☎28 44 12 25; www.deutsches-theater.berlin.net). U6, S1, S2, S5, S7, S9, S25, or S75 to "Friedrichstr." Even western Berlin admits it: this is the best theater in Germany. The **Kammerspiel** (☎28 44 12 26) stages smaller, provocative productions. Box office open M-Sa 11am-6:30pm, Su 3-6:30pm. Tickets for Deutsches Theater €5-43, for Kammerspiel €12-30; students €8.

Hebbel-Theater, Stresemannstr. 29 (☎25 90 04 27; www.hebbel-theater.de). U1, U6, or U15 to "Hallesches Tor." The most avant of the avant-garde theaters in Berlin, drawing innovative talent from all over the world. Order tickets from the box office (open daily noon-7pm) on Stresemannstr., or by phone daily 4-7pm, or show up 1hr. before shows. Tickets €10-15, students €6.

Berliner Ensemble, Bertolt-Brecht-Pl. 1 (☎28 40 81 55; www.berliner-ensemble.de). U6 or S1, S2, S5, S7, S9, S25, or S75 to "Friedrichstr." The theater established by Brecht is enjoying a renaissance under the eye of Claus Peymann. Hip repertoire with Heiner Müller, young American playwrights, and Brecht himself. Box office open M-F 8am-6pm, Sa-Su 11am-6pm, and 1hr. before shows. Tickets €2-30, students €7.

Maxim-Gorki-Theater, Am Festungsgraben 2 (☎20 22 11 15; www.gorki.de). U6, S1, S2, S5, S7, S9, S25, or S75 to "Friedrichstr.," or bus #100, 157, or 348 to "Deutsche Staatsoper." Contemporary theater with a wide repertoire. Box office open M-Sa noon-6:30pm, Su 4-6:30pm, and 1hr. before shows. Tickets €12-30, student discounts.

Die Distel, Friedrichstr. 101 (☎204 47 04; www.distel-berlin.de). U6, S1, S2, S5, S7, S9, S25, or S75 to "Friedrichstr." During DDR days, this cabaret was renowned for political satire. As popular as ever, the shows feature lots of snappy dialogue and German slang, making it hard for non-speakers to follow. Box office open M-F noon-6pm and 2hr. before performances. Tickets €11-23; students 25% off 2hr. before performances.

Vaganten-Bühne, Kantstr. 12a (☎312 45 29; www.vaganten.de). U2, U9, S5, S7, S9, or S75 to "Zoologischer Garten." This off-beat venue in a courtyard near the Ku'damm presents a healthy balance of contemporary German plays and classics. Box office open M-W 10am-4pm, Th-F 10am-8pm, Sa 2-8pm. Tickets €9-17, students €7.

Friends of Italian Opera, Fidicinstr. 40 (☎691 12 11; www.thefriends.de). U6 to "Pl. der Luftbrücke." The name of Berlin's leading English-language theater is a joking reference to the mafia in *Some Like It Hot.* A smaller, less well-funded venue, this stage still produces new, experimental works and old favorites like Samuel Beckett and Tennessee Williams. Box office opens at 7pm. Most shows at 8pm. Tickets €8-15.

Volksbühne, Am Rosa-Luxemburg-Pl. (☎24 06 55; www.volksbuehne-berlin.de). U2 to "Rosa-Luxemburg-Pl." High on shock value, low on name recognition. Box office open daily noon-6pm. Tickets €10-30, students €6-15. The Volksbühne also features 2 nightclubs for the proletariat: the Roter Salon and Grüner Salon. Ask permission to eat downstairs with the actors in the **Cantina.**

Prater, Kastanienallee 7-9 in Prenzlauer Berg (☎24 06 55; www.volksbuehne-berlin.de). U2 to "Eberswalder Str." Smaller sister theater to the Volksbühne. Box office open daily noon-6pm and 1hr. before performances (tickets €12, students €6). There's a Biergarten out back (open M-F from 4pm, Sa from noon), and the theater occasionally doubles as a club. Prater also hosts the popular bar and concert venue **Bastard;** check listings.

FILM

On any night in Berlin you can choose from over 150 different films. *O.F.* next to a movie listing means original version (i.e., not dubbed in German); *O.m.U.* means original version with German subtitles. Check *Tip* or *Zitty* for theater schedules. Mondays through Wednesdays are *Kinotage* at most theaters, with reduced prices and further discounts for those with a student ID. The city also hosts the international **Berlinale** film festival (Feb. 8-18, 2007).

Arsenal, in the Filmhaus at Potsdamer Pl. (☎26 95 51 00). U2, S1, S2, or S25 to "Potsdamer Pl." Run by the founders of the *Berlinale,* Arsenal showcases indie films and some classics (€4.50, students €3.50). Frequent appearances by guest directors make the theater a popular meeting place for Berlin's filmmakers.

Filmkunsthaus Babylon, Rosa-Luxemburg-Str. 30 (☎242 59 69; www.babylonberlin.de). U2 to "Rosa-Luxemburg-Pl." Shows classics like *Goodfellas* in the main theater and art films from around the world in the intellectual **Studiokino** (entrance on Hirtenstr.). Main theater M €4.50, Tu-W €5.50, Th-Su €6.50. Studiokino €5.50.

Odeon, Hauptstr. 116 (☎78 70 40 19; www.yorck.de). U4 to "Innsbrucker Pl." One of the 1st English-language theaters in Berlin, Odeon shows mainstream American and British flicks, generally with German subtitles. €7.50, students €7; M €5, Tu-W €6.

CineStar, in the Sony Center, Potsdamer Pl. 4 (☎20 66 62 60). S1, S2, or U2 to "Potsdamer Pl." English-language blockbusters in a huge, glittering theater with seating so steeply graduated you'll fear for your life. Last showing around 11pm, M no late show. M and W €6.50, Tu €4.50, F-Sa €7.50, students €5.50.

Freiluftkino: Berlin buzzes with outdoor movies in summer: **Freiluftkino Hasenheide** (☎30 87 25 10; www.freiluftkino-hasenheide.de), at the Sputnik in Hasenheide park, screens silent films and last year's blockbusters. U7 or U8 to "Hermannpl." **Freiluftkino Kreuzberg,** Mariannenpl. 2 (☎24 31 30 30), screens foreign films. U1 or U8 to "Kottbusser Tor." **Freiluftkino Friedrichshain** (☎29 36 16 29; www.freiluftkino-berlin.de), in Volkspark Friedrichshain, shows modern Hollywood and German films. U5 to "Straußberger Pl." €5.50. Reduced admission M and W. Check schedules online.

🗂 SHOPPING

When West Berlin was a lonely outpost in the consumer wilderness of the Eastern Bloc, West Berliners had no choice but to buy local. Consequently, the city amassed a mind-boggling array of things for sale: if a price tag can be put on it, you can buy it in Berlin. The high temple of consumerism is the seven-story **KaDeWe department store** on Wittenbergpl. at Tauentzienstr. 21-24, the largest department store on the continent. (☎212 10. Open M-F 10am-8pm, Sa 9:30am-8pm.) The sidewalks of the 2-mile-long **Kurfurstendamm,** near Bahnhof Zoo, have at least one big store from every mega-chain you can name.

SECOND HAND. *Zweite Hand* (€2) appears Tu, Th, and Sa with listings for everything under the sun: plane tickets, silk dresses, cats, and terrific deals on **bikes.** Boutiques on **Kastanianallee** and **Oranienburger Str.** sell chic second-hand clothes for first-hand prices. Kreuzberg's strip for used clothing and cheap antiques is **Bergmannstraße.** (Take U7 to "Gneisenaustr.") Get your leather jacket at Made in Berlin, which has funky used stuff for cheap. (Neue Schönhauser Str. 19. ☎89 950. M-Sa noon-8pm.) **Garage,** in Nollendorfpl., has heaps of quirky and vintage used clothing for sale by the kilo. (Ahornstr. 3. ☎211 27 60. Open M-F 11am-7pm, Sa 11am-6pm.) If you simply must have a new old vest to wear clubbing, get to Humana, a city-wide chain. (Schönhauser Allee 58. ☎44 06 333. Open M and W 10:30am-7pm, Tu and F 10:30am-7:30pm, Sa 10:30am-5pm.)

FLEA MARKETS. The market on **Str. des 17. Juni** has the best selection, but the prices are higher than those at other markets. *(S5, S7, S9, or S75 to "Tiergarten." Open Sa-Su 11am-5pm).* **Winterfeldtpl.** overflows with food, flowers, and people crooning Dylan tunes. *(Near Nollendorfpl. Open W and Sa 8am-1pm.)* Sundays in Prenzlauer Berg's **Mauerpark** see a second-hand market take over the park, with everything from food to furniture. Other markets are around **Ostbahnhof** in Friedrichshain *(near Erich-Steinfurth-Str.; S3, S5, S7, S9, or S75 to "Ostbahnhof"; open Sa 9am-3pm, Su 10am-5pm),* on **Am Weidendamm** in Mitte *(S-Bahn or U6 to "Friedrichstr.";* open *Sa-Su 11am-5pm)* and on **John-F.-Kennedy-Pl.** in Schöneberg *(U4 to "Rathaus Schöneberg";* open *F-Su 8am-4pm).*

CDS AND MUSIC. Berlin's enormous electronics store **Saturn** has a respectable CD store in its basement level.. (Alexanderpl. 8. U2, U5, U8, S3, S5, S7, S9, or S75 to "Alexanderpl." ☎24 75 16. Open M-F 9:30am-8pm, Sa 9am-8pm.) If you're looking for used CDs or LPs, snoop around the streets near Schlesisches Str. and Bergmannstr. (U1 or U15 to "Schlesisches Tor.") A variety of used CDs and records are bought and sold at **Cover,** where pop music rules the day. (Turmstr. 52. U9 to "Turmstr." ☎395 87 62. Open M-F 10am-8pm, Sa 10am-4pm.) **Freak Out** features somewhat less mainstream music, ranging from electronica to reggae. The back room contains used CDs and LPs, most around €5. (Prenzlauer Allee 49. U2 to "Eberswald Str." ☎442 76 15. Open M-F 11am-7:30pm, Sa 11am-4pm.)

▣ NIGHTLIFE

Berlin's nightlife is world-renowned absolute madness, a teeming cauldron of debauchery that runs around the clock. Bars typically open at 6pm and get crowded around 10pm, just as the clubs are opening their doors. Bar scenes wind down anywhere between midnight and 6am; meanwhile, around 1am, dancefloors fill up and the lights begin flashing at clubs that keep on pumping beats until dawn, when a variety of after-parties and 24hr. cafés keep up the perpetual motion. In summer months it's only dark from 10:30pm to 4am, so it's easy to be unintentionally included in the early morning crowd, watching the sun rise on Berlin's landmarks and waiting for the cafés to open. From 1-4am on weekdays, 70 **night buses** operate throughout the city, and on Friday and Saturday nights the U- and S-Bahn run on a limited schedule throughout the night. The best sources of information about bands and dance venues are the bi-weekly magazines *Tip* (€2.70) and the superior *Zitty* (€2.70), available at all newsstands, or the free and comprehensive *030*, distributed in hostels, cafés, shops, and bars.

In eastern Berlin, **Kreuzberg's** reputation as dance capital of Germany is challenged nightly as clubs sprout up in **Mitte, Prenzlauer Berg,** and especially southern **Friedrichshain,** just over the bridge. Even so, Kreuzberg remains a reliable nightlife stronghold, with some of the best bars and clubs the city has to offer. Berlin's largest but most touristed bar scene sprawls down pricey, packed **Oranienburger Str.** in Mitte. Prenzlauer Berg, originally the edgy alternative to the trendy Mitte repertoire, has become more expensive and established, especially around **Kollwitzpl., Helmholzpl.,** and **Kastanianallee.** Still, areas around Schönhauser Allee and Danziger Str., such as the "LSD" zone of Lychener Str., Schliemannstr., and Dunckerstr., keep the dream alive. While it has it's own thriving club scene, Prenzlauer Berg's real draw is its all-night bar and café culture. **Friedrichshain,** despite increasing gentrification, boasts edgier venues farther east, often in abandoned factories, as well as a bar scene along Simon-Dach-Str. and Gabriel-Max-Str. Raging dance venues are scattered between the car dealerships and empty lots on Mühlenstr.

In western Berlin, gay nightlife centers around **Nollendorfpl.,** where the crowds are usually mixed and establishments range from relaxed to cruisy. **Gneisenaustr.,** on the western edge of Kreuzberg, offers a variety of ethnic restaurants and some good bars. Closer to the former Wall, a dizzying array of clubs and bars on and around **Oranienstr.** rage all night, every night with a mixed crowd of partygoers: male and female, gay and straight, and everyone from punk to preppy. East Kreuzberg gets even more extreme, with its radical politics and even more radical hairstyles. Currently, it's one of the last battlegrounds in the fight against tenacious clutches of gentrification, yet this only further entrenches its reputation as a hipster hotspot. The Ku'damm is best avoided at night, unless you enjoy fraternizing with drunken businessmen and middle-aged tourists (or are one).

If at all possible, try to hit Berlin during the **Love Parade.** Usually held the third weekend of July, all of Berlin says "yes" to everything (though financial troubles may have changed it forever; see **Screwing with Love,** at right). Prices skyrocket during this weekend of hedonism and insanity. Underground counter-movements such as the **Hate Parade** and the **Fuck Parade,** despite arrests that have hampered the fun in recent years, can be interesting, cheap party alternatives—ask around to find out what's planned. It's also worth mentioning that Berlin has **decriminalized marijuana possession** of up to 8g (see **Drugs and Alcohol,** p. 18). Smoking pot in public is not widely accepted, though it's becoming more common in some clubs—it's pretty easy to tell which ones.

◥ GAY AND LESBIAN BERLIN

With a virtually unparalleled café, club, bar and sex party scene, Berlin is one of the gay capitals of Europe. Indeed, as t-shirt proudly declare, "Berlin ist schwul" (Berlin is gay). During the Cold War, thousands of homosexuals flocked to west Berlin to take part in its left-wing activist scene as well as to avoid West Germany's *Wehrpflicht* (mandatory military service). Even before the war, Berlin was known as a gay metropolis, particularly in the 1920s. **Christopher Isherwood** lived in gay-friendly **Nollendorfpl.** while writing his collection of stories *Goodbye to Berlin*, which later became the musical *Cabaret*. The city's reputation for tolerance was marred by Nazi persecutions of the 1930s and 40s, when thousands of gay and lesbian Berliners were deported to concentration camps. When the Wall fell, Berlin's *Szene* was revitalized by eastern Berlin's formerly oppressed homosexual community and the subsequent surge of new gay and lesbian clubs in the eastern half of the city. All of Nollendorfpl. is gay-friendly, with mixed bars and cafés on the main streets (Goltzstr., Akazienstr., and Winterfeldtstr.), and more flamboyant locales in the "Bermuda Triangle" of Motzstr., Fuggerstr., and Eisenacherstr.

Mann-o-Meter, Bülowstr. 106, at the corner of Else-Lasker-Schüler-Str., offers counseling and information on gay nightlife and long-term living arrangements, in addition to reasonably priced drinks and **Internet** access. (☎216 80 08; www.mann-o-meter.de. Open M-F 5-10pm, Sa-Su 4-10pm.) **Spinnboden-Lesbenarchiv,** Anklamer Str. 38, at the back of the courtyard, tends toward culturally hip lesbian offerings, with exhibits, films, and all kinds of information about current lesbian life. (U8 to "Bernauer Str."

NO WORK, ALL PLAY

SCREWING WITH LOVE

The love is back. Or so claimed the slogan of the 2006 Love Parade, Berlin's renowned all-day techno-rager that returned to the streets after a two year hiatus. Since 1989, Love Parade has been the paragon of all that is bizarre and free-spirited about Berlin. Every year in mid-July roughly one million people descend upon the Tiergarten, decked out in anything from cow print hotpants to, well, almost nothing. Dancers crowd the streets surrounding mobile dance floors commanded by DJs from all over the world. The highlight comes at the end, when cream-of-the-crop international DJs entrance the crowd.

The Love Parade, despite its happy-go-lucky moniker, has had a rocky time of it the past few years. In 2004 and 2005, insufficient funding cancelled the event. Without the "demonstration" legal status it had held until 2001, the Love Parade could, alas, no longer afford to spread the love.

Although it has returned in full force, not everybody is thrilled about Love Parade's jubilant revival. Berlin now also plays home to the "Fuck Parade"—short, not quite cleverly, for "Fuck the Love Parade"—a reaction to Love Parade's increasingly corporate atmosphere that has been palpable every July since 1997. Even so, the Love Parade exemplifies an uninhibited public free-for-all that would only happen in Berlin.

☎448 58 48. Open W and F 2-7pm.) **Lesbenberatung,** Kulmer Str. 20a, has a library, movie screenings, and counseling on lesbian issues. (U7 to "Kleistpark." ☎215 20 00. Open M-Tu and Th 4-7pm, W 10am-1pm, F 2-5pm.)

For up-to-date event listings, pick up a free copy of the amazing *Siegessäule* at virtually any gay establishment, or visit www.siegessaeule.de. Less in-depth, but also useful, is *Sergej*, a free publication for men. The monthly *Blattgold* (€3 from women's bookstores and some natural food stores) has information and listings for women. **Eisenherz Buchladen,** Lietzenburger Str. 9a, has gay- and lesbian-themed books, many of them in English. (☎313 99 36. Open M-F 10am-8pm, Sa 10am-4pm.) Most *Frauencafés* are not exclusively lesbian, but they do offer an all-female setting.

The second half of July is the high point of the annual GLBT calendar of events, when the ecstatic, champagne-soaked floats of the **Christopher Street Day (CSD)** parade line the streets in a 6hr. street party that draws more than 250,000 revelers. The weekend before CSD sees the smaller but no less jubilant **Lesbisch-schwules Stadtfest** (Gay/Lesbian City Fair) at Nollendorfpl.

CHARLOTTENBURG

Originally a separate town founded around the grounds of Friedrich I's imperial palace, Charlottenburg became an affluent cultural center during the Weimar years, home to dozens of fashionable cabarets. For the most part, present-day Charlottenburg is composed of quiet, upscale residential areas that cater to an older crowd, with nightlife options few and far between. The exception to this is the lively area surrounding the Bahnhof Zoo, which includes Berlin's main shopping strip, the Ku'damm, and several notable sights. This stretch—where up-scale department stores, street performers, and punks happily coexist—is the life-blood of the generally tame Charlottenburg.

☛ ACCOMMODATIONS

▨ **Berolina Backpacker,** Stuttgarder Pl. 17 (☎32 70 90 72; www.berolinabackpacker.de). S3, S5, S7, S9, or S75 to "Charlottenburg." This quiet, refined hostel with an ivy-laced facade keeps things elegant with print art in the bunk-free dorms and daisies on the breakfast table. Surrounding cafés and proximity to the S-Bahn make up for its distance from rush of the city. Breakfast €6. Reception 24hr. Check-out 11am. Dorms €13-14; singles €33; doubles €44; triples €48. Nov.-Apr. €4 less. AmEx/MC/V. ❶

A&O Hostel, Joachimstaler Str. 1-3 (☎0800 222 57 22; www.aohostels.com), 30m from Bahnhof Zoo. Reliably cheap dorms in prime locations. Lobby, bar, and rooftop terrace are packed at night. **Branches** in Mitte and Friedrichshain. Breakfast €5, included for private rooms. Sheets €3. Internet access €2.50 per hr. Reception 24hr. 16-bed dorm from €14; smaller dorms €15-17, with showers €20-24; singles €43-76; doubles €44-86; prices lower in winter. MC/V. ❶

Jugendgästehaus am Zoo, Hardenbergstr. 9a (☎312 94 10; www.jgh-zoo.de), opposite the Technical University *Mensa*. Take bus #245 to "Steinpl.," or walk from Bahnhof Zoo down Hardenbergstr. (not Hardenbergpl.). Tucked away in a quiet, late 19th-century building, Jugendgästehaus am Zoo contains 85 beds in simple rooms. The prices and location are hard to beat. Reception 24hr. Check-out 10am. Lockout 10am-2pm. 4- to 8-bed dorms €17, over 27 €20; singles €25/28; doubles €44/47. Cash only. ❸

Hotel-Pension Charlottenburg, Grolmanstr. 32/33 (☎88 03 29 60; www.hotel-pension-charlottenburg.de). S3, S5, S7, S9, or S75 to "Savignypl." All of this pension's 17 rooms have TV and phones; some have private shower. Breakfast included. Check-out 11am. Singles €38-58; doubles €68; triples €90 . MC/V, cash preferred. ❸

Frauenhotel Artemisia, Brandenburgische Str. 18 (☎873 89 05; www.frauenhotel-berlin.de). U7 to "Konstanzer Str." Pricey but rare—an elegant hotel for women only, the first of its kind in Germany. Outdoor terrace provides a sweeping view of Berlin. Speiseraum serves drinks (5-10pm) and complimentary breakfast. Reception 9am-10pm. Singles €59, with bath €79; doubles €89/104. Extra bed €23. Ages 3-8 €10 per night, under 3 free. Discounted rates for longer stays; your birthday night is free if you pay for 2 other nights. Check website for more specials. AmEx/DC/MC/V. ❺

◪ FOOD

Schwarzes Café, Kantstr. 148 (☎313 80 38). S3, S5, S7, S9, or S75 to "Savignypl." Exposed brick walls, frescoes, and absinthe on the menu give Schwarzes a bohemian feel. Locals flood this 2-fl. café at night. Breakfast (€4.90) served around the clock. Open 24hr. (except Tu 3am-11am). Cash only. ❸

Damas Falafel, Goethestr. 4 (☎37 59 14 50). Frequented by students and businessmen, this small restaurant, more upscale than your average falafel joint, is a vegetarian haven in a city of carnivores. The *falafel* (€3-5) and *makali* (mixed grilled vegetables; €3.30) are particularly popular, and deservedly so. Don't forget to load up on free *Zimttee* (cinnamon tea). Open daily 11am-11pm. Cash only. ❶

Mario Pasta Bar, Leibnizstr. 43 (☎324 35 16). Warm, personable place where a menu is rarely offered—instead, the cook helps guests select their meal. Delicious hand-made pasta (€6.50-9.50) or meat (€16.50). Open M-Sa noon-midnight. Cash only. ❸

Orchidee, Stuttgarter Pl. 13 (☎31 99 74 67; www.orchidee-restaurant.de). Orchidee groups its pan-Asian menu by cuisine; reading the menu is like traveling to four different countries at once. Lunch special (11am-4pm) with ½-price sushi or free appetizer with any entrée (€5.50-11). Open M-Sa 11am-midnight, Su 3pm-midnight. Cash only. ❷

Restaurant-Café Bleibtreu, Bleibtreustr. 45 (☎881 47 56). S5, S7, S9, or S75 to "Savignypl." Gilt mirrors, classic film posters, and a London phone booth decorate this local favorite. International food and vegetarian plates €5-6. Breakfast buffet Sa-Su €6 per person. Open daily 9:30am-1am. AmEx/MC/V. ❷

Art-Café Mirò, Stuttgarter Pl. 14 (☎32 90 74 04). S3, S5, S7, S9, or S75 to "Charlottenburg," or U7 to "Wilmersdorfer Str." This restaurant exhibits local artists and poets, but the creativity doesn't stop there: the leopard-print seats and international tapas, declared *Kunstwerke* (works of art; €2-6), tend to surprise diners. Breakfast buffet (€8) served 7-11am, entrées €4.50-14. Lunch menu €6 noon-3pm. Open 24hr., kitchen closes 1am. AmEx/MC/V, min. €7. ❸

Dollinger Café-Restaurant, Stuttgarter Pl. 21 (☎323 87 83). S3, S5, S7, S9, or S75 to "Charlottenburg" or U7 to "Wilmersdorfer Str." Located on a quiet neighborhood corner opposite a playground, this laid-back spot packs locals into its ample outdoor seating. The trendy exposed brick and huge wire globe above the bar keep things worldly. Traditional dishes €8-13. All-day breakfast €3-8. Open daily 9am-2am. Cash only. ❸

Mensa TU, Hardenbergstr. 34 (☎311 22 53). U2 to "Ernst-Reuter Pl.," bus #245 to "Steinpl.," a 10min. walk from Bahnhof Zoo. The mightiest *Mensa* in Berlin (behold its huge neon sign). Offers 3 entrée choices and vegetarian options. Meals €2-4, students €2-3. Cafétéria downstairs has slightly higher prices. *Mensa* open M-F 11am-3pm (last entry 2:40pm). Cafétéria open M-F 9:30am-6pm. Cash only. ❶

◉ SIGHTS

During the city's division, West Berlin centered around Bahnhof Zoo, the station that inspired U2's "Zoo TV" tour. (U-Bahn line U2 runs through the station—clever, no?) The area surrounding the station is dominated by a slew of department stores and peepshows intermingled with souvenir shops and more G-rated attractions.

Charlottenburg and Schöneberg

▲ ACCOMMODATIONS

A&O Hostel, **19**
Art Hotel Connection, **36**
Berolina Backpacker, **12**
CVJM-Haus, **34**
Frauenhotel Artemisia, **45**
Hotel-Pension
  Charlottenburg, **30**
JetPAK, **44**
Jugendgästehaus am Zoo, **8**
Jugendherberge Berlin
  International (HI), **32**
Jugendhotel Berlincity, **53**
Meininger City Hostel, **46**

🍴 FOOD & DRINK

Ali Baba, **29**
Art-Café Mirò, **13**
Baharat Falafel, **49**
Bar Tolucci, **47**
Chao Grung, **54**
Cafe Berio, **41**
Café Einstein, **42**
Café Bilderbuch, **51**
Damas Falafel, **9**
Die Feinbeckerei, **55**
Dollinger Café-Restaurant, **14**
Fish and Vegetables, **50**
Mario Pasta Bar, **27**
Mensa TU, **7**
Orchidee, **15**
Restaurant-Cafe Bleibtreu, **28**
Schwarzes Café, **17**
Toronto, **57**

🍸 BARS
& ★ NIGHTLIFE

A-Trane, **11**
Abraxas, **16**
Connection, **35**
Hafen, **38**
Heile Welt, **40**
Mister Hu, **52**
Neue Ufer, **56**
Quasimodo, **18**
Slumberland, **48**
Tom's Bar, **39**

● SIGHTS

Aquarium, **22**
Elefantentor, **21**
Gay Memorial, **37**
Kaiser-Wilhelm-
  Gedächtiskirche, **31**
Siegessäule, **6**

🏛 MUSEUMS

Akademie der Künste, **4**
Bauhaus-Archiv, **23**
Bröhanmuseum, **3**
Brücke Museum, **43**
Erotik Museum, **20**
Gemäldegalerie, **25**
Käthe-Kollwitz Museum, **33**
Kunstgewerbemuseum, **24**
Neue Nationalgalerie, **26**
Museum Berggruen, **2**
Museum Für Fotografie, **10**
Schloß Bellevue, **5**
Schloß Charlottenburg, **1**

ZOOLOGISCHER GARTEN. Germany's oldest zoo houses around 14,000 animals of 1500 species, most in open-air habitats. Feeding times are posted at the gate. The second entrance is the famous **Elefantentor** (across from Europa-Center), a decorated pagoda of pachyderms standing at Budapester Str. 34. *(Open daily May-Sept. 9am-6:30pm; Oct.-Feb. 9am-5pm; Mar.-Apr. 9am-5:30pm. €11, students €8, children €5.50. Combination ticket to zoo and aquarium €16.50/13/8.50.)*

AQUARIUM. Within the walls of the Zoo, but independently accessible, is the Aquarium, with three floors of fish, reptiles, amphibians, and insects. Check out the psychedelic jellyfish tanks, filled with translucent sea nettles, or the mudskipper, a fish that can live on land. *(Budapester Str. 32. Open daily 9am-6pm. €11, students €8, children €5.50. See above for Aquarium-Zoo combo tickets.)*

KAISER-WILHELM-GEDÄCHTNISKIRCHE (KAISER WILHELM MEMORIAL CHURCH). Nicknamed "the hollow tooth" (*Hohler Zahn*) by Berliners, this shattered church has been left in its jagged state as an eerily beautiful testament to the fallout of warfare. Finished in 1895 in a neo-Romanesque/Byzantine style, the church has a striking interior lined with cracked, colorful mosaics. Inside is a small exhibit showing what the church used to look like, as well as horrific photos of the city in the wake of WWII. More impressive still is the **New Church** juxtaposed against the remains of the old. Consecrated in 1962 and separated into a disconnected nave and tower, this modern building's cold exterior makes its stunningly fragmented blue stained glass interior all the more surprising. In the summer, Berlin's youth, salesmen, and street performers gather in front of the church to hang out, sell their wares, and play bagpipes and sitars. *(☎218 50 23. Exhibit open M-Sa 10am-4pm. Church open daily 9am-7pm.)*

MUSEUM FÜR FOTOGRAFIE. The former Landwehr-Casino building became a museum in June 2004, devoted principally to displaying the work of Helmut Newton in ever-changing guises. In the former brick ballroom on the third floor, rotating exhibits join the alternating collection of Newton's quasi-pornographic photos. *(Jebensstr. 2, directly behind the Zoo station. ☎20 90 55 66. Open Tu-Su 10am-6pm, Th until 10. €6, students €3. SMB Museum cards accepted.)*

BEATE UHSE EROTIK MUSEUM. The world's largest sex museum contains over 5000 sex artifacts from around the world, primarily from the 17th to 20th centu-

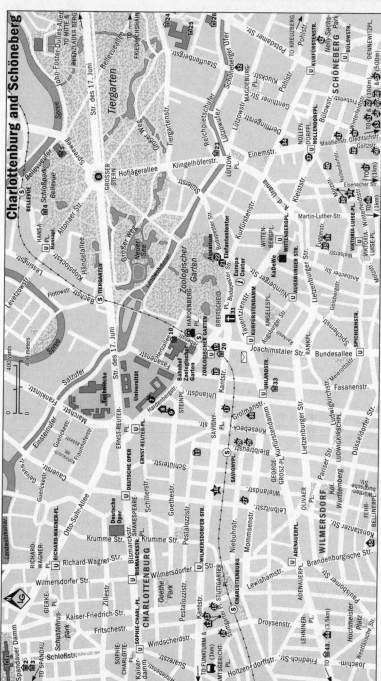

BERLIN

ries. A small exhibit describes the life of **Beate Uhse,** a pilot-turned-entrepreneur who pioneered Europe's first and largest sex shop chain. The gift shop on the ground floor gives people the chance to buy a little something to remind them of their visit. *(Joachimstalerstr. 4. ☎886 06 66. Open daily 9am-midnight. €5, students €4.)*

SCHLOß CHARLOTTENBURG. The broad Baroque palace, which was commissioned by Friedrich I in the 17th century for his second wife Sophie-Charlotte, stands impassively at the end of a beautiful, tree-lined esplanade in northern Charlottenburg. The *Schloß*'s extensive grounds include the Neringbau (or Altes Schloß); the palace proper, which contains many rooms filled with historic furnishings (much of it reconstructed as a result of war damage) and gratuitous gilding; the Neuer Flügel, which includes the marble receiving rooms and the more sober royal chambers; the Neuer-Pavillon, a museum dedicated to Prussian architect Karl Friedrich Schinkel; the Belvedere, a small building housing the royal family's porcelain collection; and the Mausoleum, the final resting spot for most of the family. Stroll the Schloßgarten behind the main buildings, an elysium of small lakes, footbridges, fountains, and meticulously manicured trees. *(Take bus #M45 from Bahnhof Zoo to "Luisenpl./Schloß Charlottenburg" or U2 to Sophie-Charlotte Pl. ☎320 92 75. Altes Schloß open Tu-F 9am-5pm, Sa-Su 10am-5pm. €8, students €5; accessible only with tour (in German, with written translations available in English and French). Upper floor, same hours, €2/1.50. Neuer Flügel open Tu-F 10am-6pm, Sa-Su 11am-6pm. €5/4. Neuer Pavilion open Tu-Su 10am-5pm; €2/1.50. Belvedere open Apr.-Oct. Tu-Su 10am-5pm; Nov.-Mar. Tu-F noon-4pm and Sa-Su noon-5pm. €2/1.50. Mausoleum open Apr.-Oct. Tu-Su 10am-noon and 1-5pm. €1. Schloßgarten open Tu-Su 6am-10pm. Free. Combination tickets include admission to everything except the Altes Schloß, €9/7.)*

OLYMPIA-STADION. At the western edge of Charlottenburg, the Olympic Stadium is one of the most prominent legacies of the Nazi architectural aesthetic. It was erected for the 1936 Olympic Games, in which African-American Jesse Owens triumphed over Nazi racism, winning four gold medals. Hitler refused to congratulate Owens because of his skin color, but there's now a Jesse-Owens-Allee to the south of the stadium. Film buffs will recognize the complex from Leni Riefenstahl's controversial film *Olympia* while others will simply know it as the sight of the 2006 World Cup final. The *Glockenturm* (bell tower) provides a great lookout point and holds an exhibit on the history of German athletics. *(S5, S7, or U2 to "Olympia-Stadion." For Glockenturm S5 or S7 to "Pichelsburg." Open Apr.-Oct. 9am-6pm. €3.)*

🏛 MUSEUMS

▓MUSEUM BERGGRUEN (MOUNTAIN GREEN MUSEUM). Subtitled "Picasso and his Time," this museum contains three floors of the consummate Cubist's work. The bottom floor exhibits works that influenced the artist, including African masks and late French Impressionist paintings by Matisse; the top floor showcases paintings by Bauhaus teacher Paul Klee and Alberto Giacometti's surreally elongated sculptures. *(Schloßstr. 1. The state-run Sammlung Berggruenmuseum is near the Schloß Charlottenburg. Take bus #M45 from "Bahnhof Zoo" to "Luisenpl./Schloß Charlottenburg" or U2 to "Sophie-Charlotte Pl." ☎32 69 58 11. Open Tu-Su 10am-6pm. €8, students €3. Audio guide free. Day card available.)*

KÄTHE-KOLLWITZ-MUSEUM. Through both World Wars, Käthe Kollwitz, a member of the Berlin *Sezession* (secession) movement and one of Germany's most prominent modern artists, protested war and the condition of the working class through her harsh pen marks. Here you'll find three floors of her drawings, posters, and self-portraits, in addition to a rotating exhibit. *(Fasanenstr. 24. U1 to "Uhlandstr." ☎882 52 10. Open M and W-Su 11am-6pm. €5, students €2.50.)*

BRÖHANMUSEUM. This sleek building is full of *Jugendstil* (Art Nouveau) and Art Deco paintings, houseware, and furniture. The ground floor consists of several ensembles of furniture, complete with accompanying paintings from the same time period (1889-1939). The first floor is a small gallery dedicated to the Modernist Berlin *Sezession* painters, and the top floor houses special exhibitions. *(Schloßstr. 1a, next to the Berggruen. ☎ 32 69 06 00; www.broehan-museum.de. Open Tu-Su 10am-6pm. Usually €5, students €4. Prices depend on special exhibits. First W of month free.)*

� NIGHTLIFE

Charlottenburg's quiet cafés and music venues cater to the 30-something set. It's a nice place for a mellow evening, but the real parties are eastward.

Quasimodo, Kantstr. 12a (☎ 312 80 86; www.quasimodo.de). U2, S5, S7, S9, or S75 to "Zoologischer Garten." Beneath a huge café, this spacious venue showcases soul, R&B, and jazz. Cover for concerts €8-20. Tickets available from 5pm at the café upstairs or from Kant-Kasse ticket service (☎ 313 45 54); cheaper if reserved in advance. Concerts start at 11pm. Check website for schedule. Cash only.

A-Trane, Bleibtreustr. 1 (☎ 313 25 50; www.a-trane.de). S3, S5, S7, S9, or S75 to "Savignypl." Red curtains and dim lights. There's little chatting: the jazz fans are here for the music. Cover €7-15, student discount €2. M-F 9pm-2am, Sa-Su 9pm-late; music from 10pm. Usually closed Su. Tables can be reserved online in advance. Cash only.

Abraxas, Kantsr. 134 (☎ 312 94 93). U7 to "Wilmersdorferstr." You won't find any techno in this club; instead, prepare yourself for Latin, Jazz, African, and Brazilian music. Popular since the 80s, Abraxas caters to a slightly older clientele in a relaxed and friendly atmosphere. Cover €5 weekends, weekdays free. Open W-Sa 10pm-late.

SCHÖNEBERG AND WILMERSDORF

South of the Ku'damm, Schöneberg and Wilmersdorf are middle-class residential districts noted for their world-class restaurants and shopping. The kind of place where breakfast is an institution rather than a meal and locals lounge for hours in a seemingly endless supply of cafés, the *Bezirk* of Schöneberg has managed to retain the feel of a self-contained neighborhood while incorporating itself into the greater city. The area around Nollendorfpl., where even the military store is draped with rainbow flags, is the nexus of Berlin's gay and lesbian community, and the streets surrounding Hauptstr. are home to a sizable Turkish population. The birthplace of Marlene Dietrich and former stomping grounds of Christopher Isherwood, Schöneberg has a decidedly mellow, contented atmosphere.

⌂ ACCOMMODATIONS

▨ **Jugendhotel Berlincity,** Crellestr. 22 (☎ 78 70 21 30; www.jugendhotel-berlin.de). U7 to "Kleistpark." or "Yorckstr." Dark blue accents the blond wood furniture and floors while art and funky light fixtures line the halls. Some have a view of the TV tower over the hostel's courtyard. Popular with frenetic school groups. Breakfast included. Free Internet access. 6-bed rooms €25.50-27.50; singles €38, with bath €55; doubles €60/79; triples €84/99; quads €108/118. AmEx/MC/V. ❸

Meininger City Hostel, Meininger Str. 10, Shöneberg (☎ 666 36 100 or 0800 634 64 64; www.meininger-hostels.de). U4, bus #146 or N46 to "Rathaus Schöneberg." Walk toward the Rathaus tower on Freiherr-vom-Stein-Str., turn left on Martin-Luther-Str., then right on Meininger Str. Lively atmosphere and superb value in a hostel that has its own terrace, beer garden, and pool table. Also branches at **Hallesches Ufer** and **Tempelhofer Ufer**

with same rates. Breakfast buffet and sheets included. Locker keys €5 deposit. Reception 24hr. Book in advance. Large dorms €14; 5- to 6-bed dorms €15-16; singles €25; doubles €40; quads €68. Flash a copy of *Let's Go* for a 10% 1st night discount. MC/V. ❶

JetPAK, Pücklerstr. 54, Dahlem (☎83 26 011; www.jetpak.de). Near the border of Wilmersdor. U3 to "Fehrbelliner Pl." or U9 to "Güntzelstr.," then bus #115 (dir.: Neuruppiner Str.) to "Pücklerstr." Walk 5min. west on Pücklerstr. to the edge of the park and follow the sign. Hidden in an old Wehrmacht military complex in the Grunewald forest, this casual hostel has a summer-camp feel that defies its history and justifies the distance. Outdoor ping-pong table and basketball hoop. Linen €3. Breakfast €3. Free Internet access. Dorms €14-16; singles €25; doubles €40. Cash only. ❷

CVJM Jugendgastehaus, Einemstr. 10 (☎264 10 88; www.cvjm-berlin.de). U1, U2, U4, or U15 to "Nollendorfpl." Despite the low prices, guests here seldom have to sleep in a room with strangers. Especially popular with school groups, so reserve well ahead. Breakfast buffet included. Breakfast included. Sheets €4. Reception M-F 8am-5pm. Quiet hours 10pm-7am and 1-3pm. Keys are available for curfew-free revelry. €23 per person; singles €30; doubles €50. Cash only. ❷

Jugendherberge Berlin International (HI), Kluckstr. 3 (☎257 99 808, www.jh-berlin-international.de). U1 to "Kurfürstenstr." Feels like sleeping in your grade school—cafeteria breakfast and kids included—but with a big-screen TV, table tennis, and large common room. Bikes €10-€15. Internet access €3 per hr. Breakfast included. Lockers and laundry available. Key deposit €10. Reception and café 24hr. After midnight, the door opens every 30min. Lockout 11am-1pm. Dorms €21, over 27 €24; 3-5 person room €19/23.10; doubles €24/28. MC/V. ❷

Art-Hotel Connection, Fuggerstr. 33 (☎210 21 88 00; www.arthotel-connection.de). U1, U2, or U15 to "Wittenbergpl.," off Martin-Luther-Str. For **men only**. Located above the club Connection (p. 116), on the 3rd fl. of an apartment building, this hotel caters to a gay crowd seeking to take advantage of all the craziness Berlin's gay scene has to offer. 16 unique rooms, all with phone, TV, and shower; 3 even have slings and other sex toys. Singles €55-85; doubles €70-110. Cheaper in winter, with advanced booking, or for stays over 3 nights. Cash only. ❺

◖ FOOD

To experience Schöneberg's relaxed café culture, look no farther than the intersection of **Maaßenstr.** and **Winterfeldstr.**

▨ **Café Bilderbuch**, Akazienstr. 28 (☎78 70 60 57; www.cafe-bilderbuch.de). U7 to "Eisenacher Str." Fringed lamps, oak bookcases, and fat, colorful sofas give Café Bilderbuch the feel of a Venetian library. The tasty brunch baskets, served around the clock, reach their pinnacle in a sumptuous Sunday buffet (€8). From Oct.-Apr. you can dance to swing and jazz music at the Su afternoon Tantzee. Open M-Th 9am-1am, F-Sa 9am-2am, Su 10am-1am. Kitchen open 9am-11pm. Cash only. ❸

▨ **Café Berio**, Maaßenstr. 7 (☎216 19 46; www.cafe-berio.de). U1, U2, U4, or U15 to "Nollendorfpl." Always jam-packed with locals, this 2-fl. Viennese-style café tempts passerby off the street with its unbeatable breakfast menu (€3.50-8.50). Of special note is the business lunch (€4.50 for entrée and drink, M-F noon-2pm). Open M-Tu and Su 8am-midnight, F-Sa 8am-1am. Cash only. ❷

Café Einstein, Kurfurstenstr. 58 (☎261 50 96; www.cafeeinstein.com). U1, U2, U3, or U4 to "Nollendorf Pl." A bit pricey and not exactly off the beaten track, but Berlin's premier Viennese coffee shop earns its reputation by dishing out class German breakfasts (€5-10) in an elegant wood-panelled interior or, if you prefer, an outdoor garden. Entrées €12-18. Open daily 9am-1am. AmEx/MC/V. ❹

Die Feinbäckerei, Vorbergstr. 2 (☎81 49 42 40; www.feinbaeck.de). U7 to "Kleistpark." Like Die Feinbäckerei's pub-like interior, its Swabian cuisine is unassuming and traditional. The *Spätzle* (noodles; €6.50) and the M-F noon-5pm special (€5 for any entrée) cannot be beat. Open daily from noon. Cash only. ❷

Bar Tolucci, Eisenacherstr. 86 (☎214 16 07; www.bar-tolucci.de). U7 to "Eisenacherstr." This tastefully understated Tuscan restaurant pays homage to the Italian filmmaker Bertolluci by decorating the walls with images from his films (and of course with the terrible pun). The small garden is a perfect place to enjoy a leisurely meal (entrées €6-12, pizza from €4). Open M-Sa noon-1am, Su 10am-1am. MC/V. ❸

Baharat Falafel, Winterfeldtstr. 37 (☎216 83 01). U1-U4 to "Nollendorfpl." This isn't your average Döner stand—it's all about falafel. Your choice of 3 or 5 chick-pea balls in a fluffy pita, with veggies and sesame, mango, or chili sauce (€2.50/3). Plates from €6, complete with hummus, tabouleh, and aubergine pasta. Wash it down with fresh-squeezed *Gute-Laune Saft* (good mood juice) for €1.50. Open daily noon-2am. Cash only. ❶

Toronto, Crellestr. 17 (☎781 92 30). U7 to "Kleistpark." An airy café with a sunny paint-job, Toronto's international cuisine appeals to locals from its residential milieu who want to read the paper while enjoying a quiet lunch (€5.40-8.80). Try the *Tagesmenu*, a 3-course meal for €10-12. Open M-Sa 9am-midnight, Su 10am-11pm. AmEx/MC. ❸

Fish and Vegetables, Goltzstr. 32 (☎215 74 55). U1, U2, U4, or U15 to "Nollendorfpl." Order generous portions (€4-6) of the eponymous food groups from a little counter in the back of this tasty Thai spot and enjoy them on the checkered tables outside. Their dishes, especially the ones with *Kokosmilch* (coconut milk), are tastier than the decor is tasteful. Open M-Th and Su 11am-11pm, F-Sa 11am-midnight. Cash only. ❷

Chao Grung, Vorbergstr. 8 (☎881 53 69). U7 to "Kleistpark." Sculptures of women at prayer greet you at the door of this relaxed Thai restaurant. Spicy noodle dishes (€6-8) in a quiet residential section of Schöneberg. Plentiful outdoor seating. Lunch special with soup and entrée €6.50. Open daily noon-11pm. Cash only. ❷

👁 SIGHTS

FEHRBELLINER PLATZ. This square was erected by the Nazis as a vision of the fascist architectural future. The austerely regular, prison-like blocks were model apartment houses; to get the full effect, try to imagine a city full of them. More optimistically, a park extends from the square. *(U3 or U7 to "Fehrbelliner Pl.")*

GRUNEWALD. In summer, this 745-acre birch forest, the dog-walking turf of many a Berliner, provides an ideal retreat from the heat and chaos of the city. About a kilometer into the wood, the **Jagdschloß**, a restored royal hunting lodge, houses paintings by German artists like Graff and Cranach. The one-room hunting museum in the same building displays cabinets full of weapons, racks of antlers, mounted wild boars, and everything from goblets to tea sets adorned with hunting scenes. *(Am Grunewaldsee 29. U3 or U7 to "Fehrbelliner Pl.," or S45 or S46 to "Hohenzollerndamm," then bus #115 (dir.: Neuruppiner Str.) to "Pücklerstr." Walk west 5min. on Pücklerstr. and continue straight into the forest to reach the lodge. ☎813 35 97. Open May 15-Oct. 15 Tu-Su 10am-5pm; open for weekend tours Oct.16- May 14 11am, 1 and 3pm. €2, students €1.50; with tour €3/2.50.)*

BRÜCKE MUSEUM. This museum features four rooms of bright, fierce paintings from the *Brücke* school, a short-lived component of German Expressionism whose name (literally "the bridge") emphasizes its connection to other European schools of art, such as Art Nouveau. *(Bussardsteig 9. U3 or U7 to "Fehrbelliner Pl." then bus #115 (dir.: Spanische Allee/Potsdamer Chaussee) to "Pücklerstr." Follow the signs* *down Pücklerstr., Fohlenweg, and Bussardsteig.* ☎*831 20 29; www.bruecke-museum.de. Open M and W-Su 11am-5pm. €4, students €2.)*

GAY MEMORIAL. Just outside the Nollendorfpl. U-Bahn station, heading in the Kleiststr. direction, stands an unassuming and unmarked memorial to gay victims of the Holocaust. It takes the form, incongruously, of a bright, multi-colored sculpture of a pencil jutting straight up from the sidewalk, surrounded by a bench.

 NIGHTLIFE

BARS AND CLUBS

🏖 **Slumberland,** Goltzstr. 24 (☎216 53 49). U1-U4 to "Nollendorfpl." Palm trees, rotating art from Africa and, yes, a real sand floor that will transport you to the Bahamas. Listen to Bob Marley while drinking a tall Hefeweizen (€3). The secret to the frappes is coffee crystals. Open M-F and Su from 6pm, Sa from 11am. Cash only.

Mister Hu, Goltzstr. 39 (☎217 21 11; www.misterhu-berlin.de). U1-U4 to "Nollendorfpl." Green bead lights and a bar made of rocky tiles lend this energetic bar a certain mystique. Happy hour daily5-8pm, Su all mixed drinks €4.50, including concoctions like "G-thang" (cachaca, guava syrup, grenadine, maracuja, and grapefruit). Open M-Th and Su 5pm-4am, F-Sa 5pm-5am, Sa from 11am in summer. Cash only.

GAY AND LESBIAN

🏳️‍🌈 **Hafen,** Motzstr. 19 (☎214 11 18; www.hafen-berlin.de). U1-U4 to "Nollendorfpl." The 8 owners take turns at the bar, surrounded by their own art on the walls, as DJs spin their favorites. The mostly male, but not restricted, crowd jams the surrounding sidewalk in summer. "Weekly pub quiz" M at 10pm (1st M of the mo. in English). Drinks €2.50-7.50. Open daily 8pm-late. Cash only.

Heile Welt, Motzstr. 5 (☎21 91 75 07). U1-U4 to "Nollendorfpl." Despite the addition of 2 enormous, quiet inner sitting rooms, Heile Welt's clientele still pack the bar and spill into the street. Mostly male crowd during "prime time," more mixed in the early evening and early morning. Open daily 6pm-4am, sometimes later. Cash only.

Neue Ufer, Hauptstr. 157 (☎78 95 79 00). U7 to "Kleistpark." Formerly *Anderes Ufer* (The Other Shore), this long-running café has become "the new shore" and abandoned the rainbow ship that once decorated the interior. But the beer (€2.30-3.50) and coffee (€1.50-2.80) still flow and the mood is still mellow. Open daily 8am-2am. Cash only.

Connection, Fuggerstr. 33 (☎218 14 32; www.connection-berlin.de). U1 or U2 to "Wittenbergpl." The name says it all. Find your soulmate (or 1-night stand) in the disco, then go downstairs to dimly lit, labyrinthine **Connection Garage** to "get acquainted." First F of the month mixed, otherwise men only. Cover €7, including 1st drink. Open F-Sa from 11pm. Cash only.

Tom's Bar, Motzstr. 19 (☎213 45 70; www.tomsbar.de). U1-U4 to "Nollendorfpl." Gay men don't come to Tom's for a relaxed drink; they come to take advantage of the vast dark room below. Th DJs spin techno and house. Open daily from 10pm. Cash only.

MITTE

Mitte, once the heart of Berlin, is home to most of the city's Imperial architecture. The district was split down the middle by the wall, and much of it languished in disrepair during the DDR days, but the wave of revitalization that swept post-wall Berlin hit Mitte first. It still boasts a first-rate nightlife, but the best clubs have closed (they were the illegal ones, as every good Berliner knows) as the city's nightlife culture *sweeps* farther East. Mitte may have received a final coat of polish, but you can still find devastated war wrecks squeezed in among grandiose Prussian palaces, glittering modern constructions, swank galleries, and stores so hyper-trendy they only sell one thing—messenger bags, acid-tone sweaters, or rugs with words on them.

ACCOMMODATIONS

Mitte's Backpacker Hostel, Chausseestr. 102 (☎28 39 09 65; www.backpacker.de). U6 to "Zinnowitzer Str." The apex of hostel hipness, with a gregarious English-speaking staff and themed rooms, from "Aztec" to the more scandalous "Temptation." The social common room is lined with antique theater seats. A pickup spot for **Terry Brewer's Tours** and **Insider Tours** bike tours (p. 96). Bike rental €10 per day. Internet access €3 per hr. Sheets €2.50. Laundry €5. Reception 24hr. Dorms €13-18; singles €29-30; doubles €43-56; triples €60-63; quads €76-80. €1-2 less in winter. AmEx/MC/V. ❶

BaxPax Downtown Hostel/Hotel, Ziegelstr. 28 (☎251 52 02; www.baxpax-down-town.de). S1, S2, or S25 to "Oranienburger Str." or U6 to "Oranienburger Tor." This gleaming new hostel, the sleeker sibling of the Kreuzberg branch, is the height of budget luxury. Brightly painted dorms, an outdoor lounge, and a roof-top bar with a kiddie pool make it the perfect summer hangout. Internet access €3 per hr. Breakfast €4.50. Laundry €5. Dorms €16-21; singles €30-45; doubles €48-88; triples €66. MC/V. ❷

Circus, Rosa-Luxemburg-Str. 39-41 (☎28 39 14 33; www.circus-berlin.de). U2 to "Rosa-Luxemburg-Pl." Close to Alexanderpl., Circus was designed with the English-speaking traveler in mind, complete with laundry, Internet access (€0.05 per min.), nightlife info, a large bar, and booking services. Wheelchair-accessible. Another, larger **Circus,** at Rosenthaler Pl. on Weinbergsweg 1a, has similar facilities and prices. **Terry Brewer's Tours** stops at both locations, and **Insider Tours** bike tour stops at the Rosenthaler branch, which rents bikes for €12 per day. Breakfast €2-5. Sheets €2. 24hr. reception and bar. 4- to 8-bed dorms €17-19; singles €33, with shower €45; doubles €50; triples €63. Cheaper in winter. MC/V. ❷

CityStay Hostel, Rosenstr. 16 (☎23 62 40 31; www.citystay.de). S5, S7, S9, or S75 to "Hackescher Markt" or U2, U5, or U8 to "Alexanderpl." A playful, detail-oriented hostel that has ample amenities—an all-night bar, courtyard BBQs, clean dorms, private showers—only paces from central sights. Kitchen facilities. Breakfast €4. Sheets €2.50. Laundry €5. Internet access €3 per hr.; wireless free. Dorms €17-21; singles €34-45; doubles €50-62; quads €84. Cash only. ❷

Heart of Gold Hostel, Johannisstr. 11 (☎29 00 33 00; www.heartofgold-hostel.de). S1, S2, or S25 to "Oranienburger Str." or U6 to "Oranienburger Tor." Designed in tribute to *The Hitchhiker's Guide to the Galaxy,* this kooky hostel is clean and space-age. Breakfast €3.50. Laundry €3. Internet access €0.50 per 10min. Reception 24hr. 6-bed dorms €17; 4-bed dorms €19; 3-bed dorms €21; singles €40; doubles €56. MC/V. ❷

Three Little Pigs, Stresemannstr. 66 (☎32 66 29 55; www.three-little-pigs.de). S1, S2, or S25 to "Anhalter Bahnhof" or U2 to "Potsdamer Pl." Located in a red brick building off a sunny courtyard, this friendly hostel is only minutes from the glistening Potsdamer Pl. Simple rooms spruced up with potted plants. Breakfast €4. Linen €2.50. Free Internet access. Reception 24hr. Dorms €13-14; doubles €22; triples €60; quads €72. €2 lower per person in winter. AmEx/MC/V. ❷

Helter Skelter, Kalkscheunestr. 4-5 (☎28 04 49 97; www.helterskelterhostel.com). S1, S2, or S25 to to "Oranienburger Str." or U6 to "Oranienburger Tor." A great location in the center of the Oranienburger Str. nightlife with a haphazard, casual feel. **Terry Brewer's Tours** pick up guests daily at 10:15am. Breakfast buffet €3. Sheets €2. Internet €0.50 per 5min. 24hr. reception and bar. Call at least 2-3 days ahead. 8- to 12-bed dorms €14; 6- to 7-bed €17; doubles €50; triples €63; quads €80. MC/V. ❶

Berlin Mitte

 FOOD

🍲 **Monsieur Vuong,** Alte Schönhauser Str. 46 (☎30 87 26 43; www.monsieurvuong.de). U2 to "Rosa Luxembourg Pl." Extremely popular among local professionals. Serves 2 different delicious Vietnamese dishes every day—one with chicken and rice and the other with meat and noodles—in a bright red and yellow interior. Fresh fruit drinks. Entrées €6.40. Open M-Sa noon-midnight, Su 2pm-midnight. Cash only. ❷

Dada Falafel, Linienstr. 132 (☎27 59 69 27). U6 to "Oranienburgertor." Located just off of Oranienburger Str. Caters to executives during the day and clubgoers at night. Most popular at this takeout joint, with limited seating and an even more limited menu, are the *falafel* and *schawarma* (€3). Open daily 10am-2am; F-Sa until 3am. Cash only. ❶

Bagels & Bialys, Rosenthalerstr. 46 (☎283 65 46). S5, S7, S9, or S75 to "Hackescher Markt." Because even Dada closes sometimes. An array of sandwiches with international brio: ciabatta, *shawarma*, and bagels, with a selection and prices (€2.50-4) that are hard to beat. Open 24hr. Cash only. ❶

Beth Café, Tucholskystr. 40 (☎281 31 35), just off Augustr. S-Bahn to "Oranienburger Str." A favorite of the local Jewish community, Beth Café serves quality kosher dishes and classics like bagels with lox and cream cheese (€2.50). Other dishes €3-8. Open M-Th and Su 11am-10pm, F 11am-5pm in summer, to 3pm in winter. AmEx/MC. ❷

Assel, Oranienburger Str. 21 (☎24 04 88 99). S-Bahn to "Oranienburger Str." One of Mitte's oldest restaurants, Assel is popular with a younger crowd. Dimly lit basement bistro and bar where pencil drawings line the walls. A rotating menu that has everything from Tex-Mex to pasta (€8-13) to breakfast. Open daily 10am-late. Cash only. ❸

Amrit, Oranienburger Str. 50 (☎28 88 48 70; www.amrit.de). S1, S2, or S25 to "Oranienburger Str." People naturally congregate in the lively outdoor dining area at this sleek Indian restaurant with garish lights and leather seats. Entrées (€6.50-13) can be split, and vegetarians will not be disappointed. Tip is included, according to the fine print. Open M-Th and Su noon-2am, F-Sa noon-4am. The original location in Kreuzberg (Oranienstr. 202-203; ☎617 55 50) has the same hours. AmEx/MC/V. ❸

Berlin Mitte

BERLIN

◉ SIGHTS

UNTER DEN LINDEN

Unter den Linden, one of the best known boulevards in Europe, was the spine of Imperial Berlin. During the DDR days, it was known as the "idiot's mile," because it was often all that visitors saw, giving them little idea of what the eastern part of the city was really like. Beginning in Pariser Pl. in front of the Brandenburger Tor, the street runs east through Bebelpl. and the Lustgarten and still, for many tourists, serves as the face of Berlin with its stretches of tourist shops and what remains of the city's dignified imperial architecture. *(S1, S2, or S25 to "Unter den Linden." Bus #100 runs the length of the street every 4-6min.)*

⬛ BRANDENBURGER TOR (BRANDENBURG GATE). Berlin's only remaining gate was built by Friedrich Wilhelm II in the 18th century as an image of victory, although in recent years in a stab of political correctness this has been rephrased as "the victory of peace." It later became the symbol of the divided city: situated in the center of the city along the Wall, it was once a barricaded gateway. Today, it is the most powerful emblem of reunited Germany. The Room of Silence in the northern end of the gate provides a non-denominational place for meditation and reflection.

PARISER PLATZ. Ringed since 1735 by impressive Hohenzollern palaces, including the Stadtpalais, this area suffered acutely in WWII when all but a few of the venerable buildings were destroyed. Since then, massive reconstruction has taken place, including the renovation of the **Hotel Adlon**, once the premier address for visiting dignitaries and celebrities and, more recently, the site of the infamous Michael Jackson baby-dangling incident. *(The square in front of the Brandenburger Tor.)*

RUSSIAN EMBASSY. Rebuilding the edifices of the rich and famous wasn't a big priority in the workers' state of the DDR. The exception was Berlin's largest embassy, which covers almost an entire city block. While the *Palais* reverted to being just another embassy at the end of the Cold War (the huge bust of Lenin that once graced its red star-shaped topiary was quietly removed in 1994), you can still marvel at the imposing building from behind the iron fencing. *(Unter den Linden 65.)*

DEUTSCHE STAATSBIBIBLIOTHEK (GERMAN STATE MUSEUM). The quite stately library's shady, ivy-covered courtyard, accentuated by lounging intellectuals, provides a pleasant respite from the urban bustle. *(Unter den Linden 8. ☎26 60. Library open M-F 9am-9pm, Sa 9am-5pm. Free Internet access with admission ticket. Admission €0.50.)*

HUMBOLDT-UNIVERSITÄT. Just beyond the Staatsbibliothek lies the H-shaped main building of Humboldt University, whose hallowed halls have been paced by the likes of Hegel, Einstein, Bismarck, the Brothers Grimm, and Karl Marx. In the wake of the post-1989 internal ideological *Blitzkrieg*, in which many departments were purged of socialist leanings, international scholars have descended upon the university to take part in its dynamic renewal. Budding socialists can peruse the works of Marx and Lenin at the book vendors outside, under the statue of a triumphant **Frederick the Great.** *(Unter den Linden 6.)*

NEUE WACHE. The New Guardhouse was designed by Prussian architect **Karl Friedrich Schinkel** in unrepentant Neoclassical style. During the DDR era, it was called the "Memorial to the Victims of Fascism and Militarism," even as goose-stepping East German soldiers stood guard outside. Closed after reunification, the building reopened in 1993 as a war memorial. The remains of an unknown soldier and an unknown concentration camp victim are buried inside with earth from the camps at Buchenwald and Mauthausen and from the battlefields of Stalingrad, El

Alamein, and Normandy. A copy of Käthe Kollwitz's sculpture *Mutter mit totem Sohn* (mother with dead son) conveys the solemnity of the space and serves as a memorial to victims of war of all kinds. *(Unter den Linden 4. Open daily 10am-6pm.)*

BEBELPLATZ. On May 10, 1933, Nazi students burned nearly 20,000 books here by "subversive" authors such as Heinrich Heine and Sigmund Freud—both Jews. A plaque in the center of the square is engraved with Heine's eerily prescient 1820 German epigram: "Wherever they burn books, eventually they will burn people too." Underneath the square rests a memorial, visible through a glass window on the ground in the center, in the form of a stark white room lined with empty book shelves. On the west side of the Platz, the building with the curved facade is the **Alte Bibliothek.** Once the royal library, it is now home to Humboldt's law faculty. On the other side of the square is the **Deutsche Staatsoper,** one of Berlin's three opera houses, fully rebuilt after the war from original sketches by Knobelsdorff, the architect who designed Schloß Sanssouci in Potsdam (p. 156). The distinctive blue dome at the end of the square belongs to the **St.-Hedwigs-Kathedrale.** Completed in 1773 as Berlin's first Catholic church built after the Reformation, it was destroyed by American bombers in 1943. Originally designed after the Roman Pantheon, the church was rebuilt in the 1950s in a more modern style. Organ concerts draw visitors on Wednesday at 3pm. *(Cathedral open M-Sa 10am-5pm, Su 1-5pm. Free.)*

ZEUGHAUS. This heavily ornamented pink building is the former military museum and hall of fame of the Prussian army. Now it houses the **Museum of German History.** *(Unter den Linden 2. ☎ 20 30 40.)*

AROUND POTSDAMER PLATZ

POTSDAMER PLATZ. Built under Friedrich Wilhelm I as an approximation of Parisian boulevards, Potsdamer Pl. was designed for the primary purpose of mobilizing troops quickly. The commercial and transport hub of pre-war Berlin, the square was caught in the death strip between East and West during the Cold War. After reunification, Potsdamer Pl. became the new commercial center of a united Berlin, and achieved infamy in the 1990s as the city's largest construction site. Today its cutting-edge, wildly ambitious architectural designs make for metallically spectacular sightseeing. The complex of buildings overlooking Potsdamer Str. includes the towering **Deutsche Bahn headquarters,** the glossy ◪**Sony Center,** and an off-kilter glass recreation of Mt. Fuji that covers the courtyard enclosed by cafés, shops, and a movie theater. *(U2, or S1, S2, or S25 to "Potsdamer Pl.")*

FÜHRERBUNKER. Near Potsdamer Pl., unmarked and inconspicuous, is the site of the bunker where Hitler married Eva Braun and then ended his life. During WWII, it held 32 rooms including private apartments and was connected to Hitler's chancellery building, since destroyed. Plans to restore the bunker were shelved for fear that the site would become a shrine for radical groups, so all there is to see now is a dirt expanse and the occasional tourists still seeking the long-destroyed building. *(Under the parking lot at the corner of In den Ministergarten and Gertrude Kolmar Str.)*

GENDARMENMARKT

Several blocks south of Unter den Linden, this gorgeous Platz was considered the French Quarter in the 18th century, when it became the main settlement for Protestant Huguenots fleeing persecution by "Sun King" Louis XIV. During the last week of June and the first week of July, the square becomes an outdoor stage for open-air classical concerts. *(U6 to "Französische Str." or U2 or U6 to "Stadtmitte.")*

DEUTSCHER DOM. Gracing the southern end of the square, the Dom is not currently used as a church but instead houses **Wege Irrwege Umwege** ("Milestones, Setbacks, Sidetracks"), an exhibition tracing German political history from despotism to democracy. *(Gendarmenmarkt 1. ☎ 22 73 04 31. Open Tu-Su June-Aug. 10am-7pm; Sept.-May 10am-6pm. Free.)*

FRANZÖSISCHER DOM. Built in the early 18th century by French Huguenots, the Dom now holds a restaurant and small museum on the Huguenot diaspora. The tower offers a sweeping view of the city. *(Gendarmenmarkt 5. ☎ 229 17 60. Open Tu-Su noon-5pm. Tower open daily 9am-7pm. Museum €2, students €1. Tower €2/1.50.)*

MUSEUMSINSEL (MUSEUM ISLAND)

After crossing the Schloßbrücke over the Spree, Unter den Linden becomes Karl-Liebknecht-Str. and cuts through the **Museumsinsel** (museum island), home to five major museums and the **Berliner Dom.** Take S3, S5, S7, S9, or S75 to "Hackescher Markt" and walk toward the Dom. Or, pick up bus #100 along Unter den Linden and get off at "Lustgarten." For information on the **Altes Museum, Pergamon, Bodemuseum,** and **Alte Nationalgalerie,** see **Museums,** p. 128.

▧ BERLINER DOM. This elegantly bulky, multiple-domed cathedral, one of Berlin's most recognizable landmarks, proves that Protestants can design buildings as dramatically as Catholics. Built during the reign of Kaiser Wilhelm II in a faux-Renaissance style, the cathedral suffered severe damage in a 1944 air raid. Today's church is the result of a 20-year process of reconstruction. Look for the Protestant icons (Calvin, Zwingli, and Luther) that adorn the decadent interior, or soak in a glorious view of Berlin from the top of the cupola. Helpful guides welcome you with information and multi-lingual tours. *(Open M-Sa 9am-8pm, Su noon-8pm, closed during services 6:30-7:30pm. Free organ recitals W-F at 3pm. Frequent concerts in summer; buy tickets in the church or call. M-Sa 9am-8pm, Su 10am-8pm. ☎ 20 26 91 36. Combined admission to Dom, crypt, tower, and galleries €5, students €3.)*

LUSTGARTEN. This immaculate green stretch, where students sun themselves and children splash in the fountain, is bounded by the Karl Friedrich Schinkel-designed **Altes Museum** to the north and the **Berliner Dom** to the east. The massive granite bowl in front of the museum was meant to adorn the main hall, but didn't fit through the door. Now the bowl sees daily indignities as policemen shoo away children who treat it as a playground.

SCHLOßPLATZ. Known as Marx-Engels-Pl. during the days of the DDR, this square houses the glaring, amber-colored **Palast der Republik,** where the East German parliament met, and is the former site of the **Berliner Schloß,** the Hohenzollern family palace. In 1990, city authorities discovered that the Palast was full of asbestos and shut it down for renovations. Plans exist, with maximal irony, to convert it into an international business school. Remarkably, the *Schloß* survived the war, only to be demolished by DDR authorities in the 1950s in censure of its royal excess. The Platz houses a small exhibit chronicling the history of the *Schloß*, as well as the city's plans to rebuild the palace. The **Staatsrat,** the temporary office of the federal chancellor, currently resides on the site—its modern facade has a slice of the old palace embedded in it. The East German government preserved this section because **Karl Liebknecht** proclaimed a German socialist republic from its balcony. The government has decided to rebuild the facade rather than restore the old Communist city hall, frustrating some Berliners who would rather see history, even a grim one, maintained. *(Across the street from the Lustgarten.)*

MARX-ENGELS-FORUM. Across the river from Museumsinsel on the south side of Karl-Liebknecht-Str. stands a memorial of steel tablets, imprinted with photographs, dedicated to the world-wide workers' struggle against fascism and imperialism. Bulbous statues of Marx and Engels preside over the oft-graffitied tablets, while stone reliefs of struggling workers circumscribe the memorial. The park and the street opposite Karl-Liebknecht-Str. together used to be known as the Marx-Engels-Forum. Rather than rename the park, the city has left it nameless.

ALEXANDERPLATZ AND NIKOLAIVIERTEL

Karl-Liebknecht-Str., which divides the Museuminsel, leads into the monolithic Alexanderpl. Behind the Marx-Engels-Forum, the preserved cobblestone streets of Nikolaiviertel (Nicholas' Quarter) stretch towards Mühlendamm. Take U2, U5, or U8, or S3, S5, S7, S9, or S75 to "Alexanderpl."

FERNSEHTURM (TV TOWER). The tremendous and bizarre tower, the tallest structure in Berlin at 368m, was originally intended to prove East Germany's technological capabilities (though Swedish engineers were ultimately brought in when construction faltered); as a result, the tower has acquired some colorful, politically infused nicknames, among them the perennial favorite "Walter Ulbricht's Last Erection" (p. 59). Look at the windows when the sun is out to see the cross-shaped glint pattern known as the *Papsts Rache* (Pope's Revenge), so named because it defied the Communist government's attempt to rid the city of religious symbols. An elevator whisks tourists up and away to the magnificent view from the spherical node (203m), and a slowly rotating café one floor up serves international meals for €7-13. (☎ 242 33 33. Open daily Mar.-Oct. 9am-11pm; Nov.-Feb. 10am-midnight. €8, under 16 €3.50.)

ALEXANDERPLATZ. Formerly the bustling heart of Weimar Berlin, this plaza was transformed in East German times into an urban wasteland of fountains and prefab office buildings, including some concrete-block classics. In the 1970s, the grey drear was interrupted by enormous neon signs with declarations like "Medical Instruments of the DDR—Distributed In All the World!" in order to satisfy the people's need for bright lights and semblances of progress. Today chain stores like **Kaufhof** have replaced the signs and serve as a backdrop for the affairs of bourgeois German shoppers, tourists, and hurried commuters stopping for a snack.

MARIENKIRCHE. The church is Gothic, the altar and pulpit Rococo, the tower Neo-Romantic: the result of centuries of additions to the original structure. Relatively undamaged during the war, this church still holds relics from other nearby churches that used it as a shelter. Knowledgeable guides explain the artifacts, as well as the painting collection, mainly comprising works from the Dürer and Cranach schools. (☎ 242 44 67. Open daily in summer 10am-6pm, in winter 10am-4pm.)

BERLINER RATHAUS (BERLIN CITY HALL). The city hall is called the *Rotes Rathaus* (red city hall) for its brick color, not the politics of the government that used it in the DDR days. Now the seat of Berlin's municipal government, the building is often mobbed by schoolchildren who come on field trips to watch legislation in action. (Rathausstr. 1. Open M-F 9am-6pm. Call ☎ 90 26 25 23 for guided tours. Free.)

SCHEUNENVIERTEL AND ORANIENBURGER STRAßE

Northwest of Alexanderpl., near Oranienburger Str. and Große Hamburger Str., is the **Scheunenviertel** (Barn Quarter), once the center of Berlin's Orthodox Jewish community. Prior to WWII, wealthier and more assimilated Jews tended to live in Western Berlin, while Orthodox Jews from Eastern Europe settled in the Scheunenviertel. The neighborhood shows evidence of Jewish life back to the 13th century (though the Jews were expelled from the city several times before WWII, once for allegedly causing the Black Death). Today, the Scheunenviertel is known more for its teeming masses of outdoor cafés than for its historical significance, but the past few years have seen the opening of Judaica-oriented bookstores and kosher restaurants. (S1, S2, or S25 to "Oranienburger Str." or U6 to "Oranienburger Tor.")

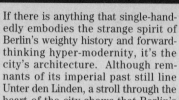

If there is anything that single-hand-edly embodies the strange spirit of Berlin's weighty history and forward-thinking hyper-modernity, it's the city's architecture. Although remnants of its imperial past still line Unter den Linden, a stroll through the

START: Radisson Hotel on Karl-Liebnecht-Str.

FINISH: Sony Center on Potsdamer Pl.

DURATION: 1½-3 hours

WHEN TO GO: Late afternoon

heart of the city shows that Berlin's reputation for edginess and artistry is well deserved. The construction cranes puncturing the skyline mean that while the buildings listed here may represent some of the greatest feats in contemporary architecture, they are in fact only the beginning of Berlin's steamroll toward a new kind of cosmopolitan future.

1 AQUADOM. In the lobby of the Radisson Hotel, built in a square formation around a central courtyard, towers a massive elevator shaft, and not just any elevator shaft: a roughly five-story cylindrical aquarium on a concrete foundation, with thousand of colorful fish swirling about in sparkly blue water. While you have to pay entrance to the neighboring aquarium to ride up the "AquaDom," simply ask the concierge's permission to enter the building and get a glimpse.

2 LUSTGARTEN (PLEASURE GARDEN). This is a typical Berlin contrast between the formidably old and jarringly new. You'll find yourself surrounded on one side by the **Altes Museum** (p. 129), designed by imperial architect Karl Friedrich Schinkel, and the towering **Berliner Dom** (p. 122). On the other, Schloßplatz holds the modern **Staatsrat,** a federal government building, which incorporates a fragment of the old facade.

3 DEUTSCHES HISTORY MUSEUM. One of the newest additions to Berlin's trove of cultural treasures, I.M. Pei's 2004 masterpiece stands hidden behind the **Zeughaus** on Unter den Linden and houses the temporary exhibits of the German History Museum (p. 130). The building, however, tends to outdo its contents. A conical glass structure with an upward-spiraling staircase, links the different floors, which can be glimpsed through the curved glass facade. The new marble supports blend into the more traditional segments of the old building, framing the glass entrance hall. The interior, largely visible from outside, contains crisscrossed, multi-tiered walkways leading to different floors of the museum. In back, imposing marble is interrupted by a triangular balcony with a window overlooking a single tree, while the front contains an indentation resembling a half-column, perhaps a contemporary reference to the imperial structures along neighboring Unter den Linden.

4 INTERNATIONALES HANDELSZENTRUM, FRIEDRICHSTR., AND SCHIFFBAUER-DAMM. From the museum, continue away from Under den Linden and turn left on Dorotheen-str. As you follow this to Friedrichstr., you'll pass the **Internationales Handelszentrum** (Trade Center), built in 1978 and among the most prominent features of the Berlin skyline. Heading right on Friedrichstr., take in the wavy glass-plated facade at **#148** before crossing the Spree and heading left on Schiffbauerdamm, which is lined with a mish-mash of modern buildings.

5 GOVERNMENT COMPLEX. Schiffbauerdamm will lead you to some of Berlin's most unusual architectural marvels. Opposite the glass-domed **Reichstag** (p. 126) spans a stretch of government buildings dating from 1997-2003: they begin with the **Marie-Elisabeth Lüders Building,** designed by Stephen Braunfels and home to the Bundestag's library; cross over the river to Braunfels' **Paul Löbe Building,** which holds the Bundestag's many commities; and culminate in the **Federal Chancellery,** the hyper-modern structure imagined by Axel Schultes and Charlotte Frank and best known for the huge circular windows on its sides. The contrast between fluid shapes and sharp angles in these buildings make them totally unlike normal bureaucratic architecture, with its habitual stiffness. The walkway over the Spree, an area once located in the death strip, symbolizes a newly reunified Germany. To the northwest, you can spot the shimmering Hauptbahnhof, the largest train station in Europe.

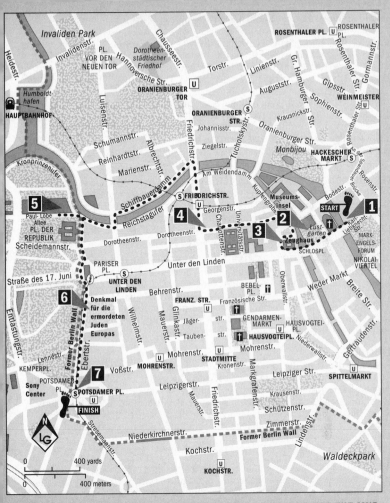

☐ DENKMAL FÜR DIE ERMORDETEN JUDEN EUROPAS (MEMORIAL FOR THE MURDERED JEWS OF EUROPE). Cutting across the top of the Tiergarten, you'll reach this new memorial, opened in 2005 and designed by Peter Eisenman (p. 126). It spans 19,000 square meters and allows you to walk unsteadily on the wavy ground between rectangular slabs of concrete. Their varying heights, coupled with the uneven walkways, will probably leave you feeling (appropriately) unsettled.

☐ POTSDAMER PLATZ. Welcome to the glittering hub of modern Berlin, surrounded by an array of towering contemporary buildings, with more on the way. Most strikingly, the **Deutsche Bahn Tower** commands attention with its curved glass front, jutting upward at an abrupt angle. Next door, the triangular **Sony Center** (p. 121) lures spectators with its courtyard arena, covered in a strangely asymmetrical structure resembling a circus tent.

NEUE SYNAGOGE. This huge building, modeled after the Alhambra, was designed by Berlin architect Eduard Knoblauch. The synagogue, which seated 3200, was used for worship until 1940, when the Nazis occupied it and used it for storage. Amazingly, the building survived *Kristallnacht*—the SS torched it, but a local police chief bluffed his way past SS officers to order the fire extinguished. The synagogue was later destroyed by bombing, but its restoration, largely financed by international Jewish organizations, began in 1988. The sanctuary's beautiful, gold-laced domes were opened to the public in 1995. Too big for Berlin's remaining Jewish community, the striking building is no longer used for services and instead houses an exhibit chronicling its history as well as that of the Jewish community that once thrived in the surrounding neighborhood. *(Oranienburger Str. 29. ☎88 02 83 00. Open May-Aug. M and Su 10am-8pm, Tu-Th 10am-6pm, F 10am-5pm; Sept.-Apr. M-Th and Sa-Su 10am-6pm, F 10am-2pm. A series of security checks is required to enter. €3, students €2. Dome €1.50/€1.)*

ALTER JÜDISCHER FRIEDHOF (OLD JEWISH CEMETERY). Obliterated by the Nazis, the cemetery now contains only the restored gravestone of the Enlightenment philosopher and scholar Moses Mendelssohn; the rest is a quiet park. In front, a prominent plaque marks the site of the **Jüdisches Altersheim** (Jewish Old-age Home), which served as a holding place for Jews before their deportation to concentration camps. *(At the end of Große Hamburger Str., near Oranienburger Str.)*

JÜDISCHE KNABENSCHULE (JEWISH BOYS' SCHOOL). Next to the cemetery on Große Hamburger Str. stands Berlin's oldest **Jewish school**, where Moses Mendelssohn taught. The plaque on the side of the school memorializes Mendelssohn, "the German Socrates," who translated the Hebrew Bible into German and supported the integration of Berlin's Jewish and non-Jewish communities. Corresponding with his progressive outlook, the school's enrollment was half-Jewish. The building was reopened as a school in 1992, and its student body is still mixed.

TIERGARTEN

In the center of Berlin, the lush **Tiergarten** provides welcome relief from the urban chaos around it. Stretching from Bahnhof Zoo in the west to the Brandenburg Gate in the east, the vast landscaped park was formerly used by Prussian monarchs as a hunting and parade ground. Today, it's frequented by strolling families, elderly couples, and, at night, cruising gay men. **Straße des 17. Juni** bisects the park from west to east, connecting Ernst-Reuter-Pl. to the Brandenburg Gate. The street is the site of many *Demos* and parades; in early July, the park hosts the serious partying (i.e., widespread sex) of the Love Parade (p. 107).

■THE REICHSTAG. The current home of Germany's governing body, the *Bundestag*, the Reichstag has seen some critical moments in history. Here, in 1918, Philipp Scheidemann proclaimed "*Es lebe die Deutsche Republik*" ("Long live the German Republic"), and in 1933 Adolf Hitler used a fire here as an excuse to declare a state of emergency and seize power. In 1997, a glass dome was added to the top, built around the upside-down solar cone that powers the building. A walkway spirals up the inside of the dome, leading visitors through panoramic views to the top. Throngs of tourists wait in line to get there, but the patient are well rewarded with innovative architecture and a famous view of the city. *(☎22 73 21 52; www.bundestag.de. Open daily 8am-midnight; last entrance 10pm. Free.)*

DENKMAL FÜR DIE ERMORDETEN JUDEN EUROPAS (MEMORIAL FOR THE MURDERED JEWS OF EUROPE). This new and prominent memorial opened in the spring of 2005, after years of anticipation and controversy. Designed by abstract architect Peter Eisenman and spanning an entire block, the sight uses 2711 concrete stelae—large rectangular columns of concrete varying in height—

and wavy, uneven pathways to immerse people in an environment of instability and reflection. Underground, an information center transports people from the theoretical to the real, with blunt displays on the history of the Holocaust. The memorial makes a effort to treat this tragedy on the level of individual history, lest the scale of it cloud our memory, by telling the stories of specific families and, in the most stirring room, casting the names of victims one by one onto four walls. *(Cora–Berliner-Str. 1, at the corner of Behrenstr. and Ebertstr. near Brandenburg Gate. ☎26 39 43 36; www.stiftung-denkmal.de. Open daily 10am-8pm, last entry 7:15pm. Free.)*

AROUND THE REICHSTAG. The huge white and blue residence was reportedly a source of embarrassment to former Chancellor Schröder, who wished to keep a low profile. Tourists aren't permitted inside. The **Palais am Pariser Pl.**, directly north of the Brandenburg Gate, used to be the site of a castle; enter the courtyard to find Stephen Balkenhol's startling 1998 statue *Großer Mann mit kleinem Mann* (Big Man with Little Man). *(Across the lawn to the right the new Federal Chancellery.)*

SIEGESSÄULE (VICTORY COLUMN). In the heart of the Tiergarten, this slender 70m monument commemorates Prussia's crushing victory over France in 1870. The statue at the top—Victoria, the goddess of victory—is made of melted-down French cannons. In a less-than-subtle affront to the French, the Nazis moved the monument here in 1938 from its former spot in front of the Reichstag in order to increase its height and visibility. Climb the monument's 285 steps for a panorama of the city. *(Großer Stern. Take bus #100 or 187 to "Großer Stern" or S5, S7, or S9 to "Tiergarten." Accessible via the stairs at the West corners around the traffic circle. ☎391 29 61. Open Apr.-Nov. M-F 9:30am-6:30pm, Sa-Su 9:30am-7pm; Nov.-Mar. M-F 10am-5pm, Sa-Su 10am-5:30pm. €2.20, students €1.50.)*

SOWJETISCHES EHRENMAL (SOVIET CENOTAPH). At the eastern end of the Tiergarten, a Soviet memorial rises (yes, in western Berlin) above a pair of red star-emblazoned tanks, the first two to enter Berlin in 1945. This memorial honors the Soviet soldiers who lost their lives storming the city; an estimated 2500 soldiers are buried at the end of the park. *(Bus #100 to "Pl. der Republik.".)*

OTHER SIGHTS IN MITTE

◼ DIE HACKESCHE HÖFE. A complex of buildings built in the early 1900s as a combination of offices, workshops, factories, and apartments, these eight gorgeous inter-connected courtyards have been thor-

THE LOCAL STORY

PASTRY OR PRESIDENT?

"All free men, wherever they may live, are citizens of Berlin. And therefore, as a free man, I take pride in the words: *Ich bin ein Berliner.*" Ending his speech with these words on June 26, 1963, the 15th anniversary of the Berlin Airlift, John F. Kennedy assured a crowd of 1.5 million West Berliners of the Allies' continued commitment to protect their city.

But JFK's final four words, the product of a last-minute decision to utter something in German, have left some linguistic confusion in their historical wake. Some skeptics insist that Kennedy actually called himself a jelly doughnut (in German, *ein Berliner*). The difference between a citizen of Berlin and a pastry depends on the article *"ein"* (a), which a native German speaker would omit when expressing place of origin. Thus, a German from Hamburg would say, "Ich bin Hamburger," while a hamburger, if it could talk, might tell you "Ich bin ein Hamburger" before disappearing down your esophagus. Natives point out that in Berlin the pastry is called a *Pfannkuchen,* and that Kennedy's version is grammatically valid.

The site of the speech now houses Berlin's municipal government, and still remains open to tourists.

(John-F.-Kennedy-Pl. U4 to "Rathaus Schöneberg." ☎75 60 70 20. Open daily 10am-6pm.)

oughly restored. It now features theaters, bars, trendy shops—and above all else—cafés pleasantly sequestered from the hubbub of the streets. *(Rosenthaler Str. 40/41. www.hackesche-hoefe.com.)*

BERTOLT-BRECHT-HAUS. If any one man personifies the maelstrom of Berlin's political and aesthetic contradictions, it is **Bertolt Brecht** (p. 69), who lived and worked in this house from 1953 to 1956. "There is a reason to prefer Berlin to other cities," the playwright once said, "because it is constantly changing. What is bad today can be improved tomorrow." The **Literaturforum im Brecht-Haus** on the second floor sponsors exhibits and lectures on artistic and metropolitan subjects. *(Chausseestr. 125. U6 to "Oranienburger Tor" or "Zinnowitzer Str." ☎283 05 70 44. Obligatory German tours every 30min., max. 8 people, Tu-F 10-11:30am, Th also 5-6:30pm, Sa 9:30am-1:30pm; every hr. Su 11am-6pm. €3, students €1.50.)*

DOROTHEENSTÄDTISCHER FRIEDHOF (DOROTHEEN MUNICIPAL CEMETERY). Attached to Brecht's house is the cemetery where he and his wife, Helene Weigel, are buried; their graves marked by simple stones bearing only their names. Other famous personages interred in the cemetery include Karl Friedrich Schinkel, Heinrich Mann, and Georg Hegel and JohannFichte, who lie side by side in the middle of the yard. A map near the entrance points out locations of notable graves, not to be confused with the conjoined French cemetery. *(Open daily May-Aug., Mar., and Oct. 8am-8pm, Dec.-Jan. 8am-4pm, Feb. and Nov. 8am-5pm, and Apr. and Sept. 8am-7pm.)*

SCHLOß BELLEVUE. This *Schloß*, finished in 1786, was the first palace in Berlin to be built in the classical style. Used as a guest house by the Nazis, the complex was severely damaged in WWII but reconstructed in the 1950s and now serves as the official residence of the federal president in Berlin. It is closed to the public. *(Spreeweg 1. S5, S7, S9, or S75 to "Bellevue" or Bus 100 to "Schloß Bellevue." ☎200 00.)*

HI-FLYER BALLOON. Tethered to the ground near Potsdamer Platz, this hot-air balloon rises 150m into the air every 15min. for a bird's-eye view of the surrounding area. *(At the corner of Wilhelmstr. and Niederkirchnerstr. ☎226 67 88 11; www.air-service-berlin.com. Open summer M-Th and Su 10am-10pm, F-Sa 10am-12:30am; winter M-Th and Su 11am-7pm, F-Sa 11am-8pm. €19, students €10.)*

KOPPENPLATZ. This square is home to a simple yet stunning monument to Nelly Sachs, a Jewish Berliner who shared the Nobel Prize for literature in 1966. No men on horseback, no walls of names, just a table with an overturned chair and a line of her poetry pays tribute to her flight from Berlin in 1940. *(At the corner of Große Hamburger Str. and Linienstr. U8 to Rosenthaler Pl.)*

🏛 MUSEUMS

MUSEUMSINSEL (MUSEUM ISLAND)

The Museumsinsel holds the treasures of Germany in five separate museums. These temples of culture, built in the 19th and 20th centuries, are separated from the rest of Mitte by two arms of the Spree. Many of the museums are undergoing extensive renovation: the **Bodemuseum** will be closed until October 2006 and the **Neues Museum** should reopen in 2009, when it will house the collection currently in the Ägyptisches Museum. *(S3, S5, S7, S9, or S75 to "Hackescher Markt" or bus #100 to "Lustgarten." ☎20 90 55 55. All national museums, unless otherwise noted, open Tu-Su 10am-6pm, Th until 10pm. Free audio guides in English. Admission to each is €8, students €4. All sell a 3-day card good for admission to every museum; €15, students €7.50.)*

▨ PERGAMONMUSEUM. One of the world's great ancient history museums, the Pergamon dates from the days when Heinrich Schliemann and other zealous 19th-century German archaeologists dismantled the remnants of collapsed empires the world over and sent them home for reassembly. Named for Pergamon, the city in present-day Turkey from which the enormous **Altar of Zeus** (180 BC) was taken, the museum features gargantuan pieces of ancient Mediterranean and Near Eastern civilizations from as far back as the 10th century BC. The colossal blue **Ishtar Gate** of Babylon (575 BC) and the Roman **Market Gate of Miletus** are just two more massive pieces in an collection that also includes Greek, Assyrian, and Far Eastern art. *(Bodestr. 1-3. ☎ 20 90 55 77. €10, students €5. Last entry 30min. before closing.)*

ALTE NATIONALGALERIE (OLD NATIONAL GALLERY). After extensive renovations, this renowned museum is open to lovers of 19th-century art. Everything from German Realism to French Impressionism; Caspar David Friedrich and Camille Pisarro are but two names in an all-star cast. *(Am Lustgarten. ☎ 20 90 58 01.)*

ALTES MUSEUM (ANCIENT MUSEUM). At the far end of the Lustgarten, in the stately columned building designed by Schinkel, the Altes Museum is surprisingly untouristed. The lower level contains a permanent collection of ancient Greco-Roman (especially Etruscan) decorative art. The contents of a former Egyptian museum provide for a surprisingly rich Eastern collection. Upstairs, temporary exhibits, often similarly involving archaic artifacts, await. *(Lustgarten. ☎ 266 36 60.)*

KULTURFORUM

The **Tiergarten-Kulturforum** is a complex of museums at the eastern end of the Tiergarten, near the Staatsbibliothek and Potsdamer Pl. Students and local fine arts aficionados swarm throughout the buildings and on the multi-leveled courtyard in front. *(S1, S2, or S25 or U2 to "Potsdamer Pl." and walk down Potsdamer Str.; the museums will be on your right on Matthäikirchpl. ☎ 20 90 55 55.)*

■ **GEMÄLDEGALERIE (PICTURE GALLERY).** One of Germany's most famous museums, and rightly so. It houses an enormous collection of 2700 13th-18th century masterpieces by Italian, German, Dutch, and Flemish masters, including works by Dürer, Rembrandt, Rubens, Vermeer, Raphael, Titian, and Botticelli. *(Stauffenbergstr. 40. ☎ 266 29 51. Open Tu-W and F-Su 10am-6pm, Th 10am-10pm.)*

NEUE NATIONALGALERIE (NEW NATIONAL GALLERY). This sleek building, designed by Mies van der Rohe, contains creative temporary exhibits in the glass entrance hall and gallery downstairs. Plans are in the

THE HIDDEN DEAL

SAMMLUNG HOFFMANN

From the gallery-filled streets of Mitte to the state-curated collections at the KulturForum, it's almost impossible to visit Berlin without taking in some of its masterpieces. While everyone knows that museums boast some of the city's most cutting-edge work, most tourists miss the major exhibition of modern art that lies hidden in, of all places, a private residence on Sophienstr.

In 1968, Rolf and Erika Hoffmann began to purchase contemporary art and have since amassed an impressive collection. The Hoffmanns have turned their Mitte home into a veritable museum—which they call "an experiment in living among art."

Every Saturday, the family opens up their home in order to share their love of art. They rotate the works on display every summer, but the living room, with a large Frank Stella piece permanently on the wall, marks the heart of the collection. The work features everything from neon installations to video art to painting. Tours are required, so if you are planning to spend a Saturday roaming between the galleries along Sophienstrasse, Augustr., and Linienstr., remember to call ahead: it's not every day that you get to see great art and great real estate all rolled into one.

(Sophienstr. 21 (☎ 28 49 91 20; www.sophie-gips.de). Open Sa 11am-4pm. German only, but guides can speak English. €6.)

works to move its formidable permanent collection of 20th century art, including works by Warhol, Munch, Kirchner, and Beckmann, to a yet-to-be determined space. *(Potsdamer Str. 50, just past the Kulturforum. ☎ 266 26 51. Open Tu-W and F 10am-6pm, Th 10am-10pm, Sa-Su 11am-6pm.)*

KUNSTGEWERBEMUSEUM (MUSEUM OF DECORATIVE ARTS). This museum highlights masterpieces of design, from spoons and tables to carpets and boxes. A crazy congregation of chairs, including a shopping-cart-turned-recliner, makes the contemporary exhibit unique. *(☎ 266 29 02. Open Tu-F 10am-6pm, Sa-Su 11am-6pm. €8 with Tiergarten museum ticket, students €4. No independent tickets.)*

KUNSTBIBLIOTHEK/KUPFERSTICHKABINETT (ART LIBRARY/ETCHING CABINET). A stellar collection of lithographs and drawings by Renaissance masters, including many Dürers and Goyas, and Botticelli's fantastic illustrations for the *Divine Comedy. (☎ 266 29 02. Library open M-F 9am-8pm. Tours Su at 3pm. Free.)*

OTHER MUSEUMS IN MITTE AND TIERGARTEN

⬛HAMBURGER BAHNHOF: MUSEUM FÜR GEGENWART (MUSEUM FOR THE PRESENT). Berlin's foremost collection of contemporary art, with a colossal 10,000 square meters of exhibition space lies in this converted train station. The museum features several quite whimsical works by Warhol, as well as pieces by Twombly and Kiefer and more challenging temporary exhibits. The vastness of the rooms and the stark white walls create excellent conditions for observation. *(Invalidenstr. 50-51. S3, S5, S7, S9, or S75 to "Hauptbahnhof" or U6 to "Zinnowitzer Str." ☎ 39 78 34 11. Open Tu-F 10am-6pm, Sa 11am-8pm, Su 11am-6pm. €8, students €4, Th free 2-6pm.)*

ANNE FRANK ZENTRUM. Tucked away in a little courtyard, this center is dedicated to the fight against discrimination and prejudice, particularly anti-semitism. The permanent exhibit "Anne Frank—A Story for Today" features a timeline of her short life. Moving films about Frank and the Holocaust play continuously. *(Rosenthaler Str. 39. ☎ 24 04 88 64; www.annefrank.de. Open Tu-Su noon-8pm. €3.50, students €2.)*

SCHINKELMUSEUM. In Berlin, if it's made of stone, Karl Friedrich Schinkel likely designed it; the lovely Friedrichwerdersche Kirche is no exception. It houses 19th-century French and German sculpture and an exhibit on the Prussian architect's life and work in its renovated interior. *(Werderscher Markt, on the corner of Oberwallstr., south of Unter den Linden. U2 to "Hausvogteipl." ☎ 208 13 23. Open Tu-Su 10am-6pm. Free.)*

INDEPENDENT MUSEUMS

⬛DEUTSCHES HISTORISCHES MUSEUM. Thorough exploration of German history from Neanderthals to Nazis, complete with art, artifacts, and detailed explanations. Rotating exhibitions examine the last 50 years with large quantities of DDR art in the "painting-of-a-happy-faced-worker" vein. Behind the main building stands its modern antidote, a new wing of temporary exhibits designed by I. M. Pei that further bolsters Berlin's reputation for cutting edge architecture. *(Unter den Linden 2. S3, 5, 7, 9, or 75 to "Hackescher Markt." ☎ 20 30 47 50. Open daily 10am-6pm. €4.)*

KUNST-WERKE BERLIN (BERLIN WORKS OF ART). Under the direction of Mitte's art world luminary Klaus Biesenbach, this former margarine factory now houses studio space, a matrix of rotating contemporary exhibitions, a slide linking parts of the building, and a tranquil garden café. Check the website for current shows. *(Auguststr. 69. U6 to "Oranienburger Tor." ☎ 243 45 90; www.kw-berlin.de. Exhibitions open Tu-Su noon-7pm, Th noon-9pm. €6, students €4.)*

FILMMUSEUM BERLIN. This museum chronicles the development of German film with a special focus on older works like Fritz Lang's *Metropolis*. The contrast between old film (whole rooms are devoted to such icons as Leni Riefenstahl and Marlene Dietrich) and new provides insight into the evolution of the medium over time and the exhibits (with English captions) are fascinating. Even the architecture, with its ultra-futuristic mirrored entrance, is worth seeing. *(Potsdamer Str. 2; 3rd and 4th fl. of the Sony Center. S1, S2, S25 or U2 to "Potsdamer Pl." ☎ 300 90 30; www.film-museum-berlin.de. Tickets sold on the ground fl. Open Tu-Su 10am-6pm, Th noon-8pm. €6, students €4, children €2.50.)*

MARTIN-GROPIUS-BAU. Walter Gropius's uncle Martin designed this neo-Renaissance museum as a tribute to the industrial arts. The style is anything but Bauhaus-slick—the ornate fixtures are absolutely decadent. The array of temporary exhibits on subjects ranging from photography to archaeology are well-organized and often compelling enough to justify the price of admission. *(Niederkirchnerstr. 7. U2 or S1 or S2 to "Potsdamer Pl." ☎ 25 48 60; www.gropiusbau.de. Open M and W-Su 10am-8pm. Admission depends on exhibit; around €5-10, students €3-6.)*

DEUTSCHE GUGGENHEIM BERLIN. Located in a renovated building across the street from the Deutsche Staatsbibliothek, this joint venture of the Deutsche Bank and the Guggenheim Foundation features new exhibits of modern and contemporary art every few months. *(Unter den Linden 13-15. ☎ 202 09 30; www.deutsche-guggenheim.de. Open daily 11am-8pm, Th until 10pm. €4, students €3; M free.)*

BAUHAUS-ARCHIV MUSEUM FÜR GESTALTUNG (BAUHAUS ARCHIVE MUSEUM FOR DESIGN). A must-visit for Bauhaus fans, this building was designed by Bauhaus founder Walter Gropius and houses changing exhibits of paintings, sculptures, and—of course—that famous furniture. *(Klingelhöferstr. 14. Bus #100, 187, 200, or 341 to "Nordische Botschaften/Adenauer-Stiftg" or U1, U2, U3, or U4 to Nollendorf Pl. ☎ 254 00 20. Open M and W-Su 10am-5pm. W-F €6, students €3, Sa-M €7/4.)*

TOPOGRAPHIE DES TERRORS. Housed in the crumbling torture bunkers discovered beneath the former Gestapo headquarters, a comprehensive exhibit of photographs and documents details the Nazi party's rise to power and the atrocities that occurred during the war. English audio guides are available to clarify the text-heavy accounts. Along the outside perimeter of the exhibit stand 200m of the Berlin Wall, a graffitied memorial to the city's divided past. *(S1 or 2, or U2 to "Potsdamer Pl." ☎ 25 48 67 03. Open daily May-Sept. 10am-8pm, Oct.-Apr. 10am-dark. Free.)*

HANFMUSEUM (HEMP MUSEUM). Catering to the curious and the devoted, this museum details the medical and textile uses of hemp, as well as the debate over its legality. *(Mühlendamm 5. U2 to "Klosterstr." ☎ 242 48 27; www.hanfmuseum.de. Open Tu-F 10am-8pm, Sa-Su noon-8pm. €3, students €2.)*

GALLERIES

AKADEMIE DER KÜNSTE (ACADEMY OF ART). This 300-year-old institution has been the core of Berlin's art community for years, promoting a variety of media: film, literature, painting, photography, music, architecture, performing arts, and more. The Akademie sponsors a variety of prizes and hosts exhibitions in its Hanseatenweg location. A new **branch,** at Pariser Pl., contains the Akademie archives and five additional exhibition halls. *(Hanseatenweg 10. S3, S5, S7, S9, or S75 to "Bellevue," or U9 to "Hansapl." ☎ 39 07 60; www.adk.de. Open Tu-Su 11am-8pm. Last Su of the month free. Exhibits range from free to €7, students €4.)*

BERLIN

NEUER BERLINER KUNSTVEREIN. This organization puts art into the hands of the public. Besides hosting a gallery space, it sponsors the weekly "Treffpunkt NBK," a series of lectures, discussions with artists, performances, and more. It also lends contemporary works to Berlin residents for €0.50 per month through the **Artothek,** and has myriad videos available to the public via the **Video-Forum.** *(Chausseestr. 128-129. ☎ 280 70 20; www.nbk.org. Gallery open Tu-F noon-6pm, Sa-Su 2-6pm.)*

📷 NIGHTLIFE

The Mitte nightlife scene centers around **Hackescher Markt** and **Oranienburgerstr.** (also, incidentally, the city's most conspicuous prostitution drag). The strip offers a great deal of fun, but is filled well-touristed bars and clubs. If you'd prefer to get off the beaten track, head to the outskirts of Mitte or the Eastern *bezirke.*

Week-End, Alexanderpl. 5 (www.week-end-berlin.de), on the 12th fl. of the building with the neon "Sharp" sign overlooking the city. A rising staple of the Berlin club scene, where house music fuels the dance floor until the sun rises over the block-housing of East Berlin. Wheelchair accessible. Cover €6-8. Open Th-Sa from 11pm. Cash only.

Café Moskau, Karl-Marx-Allee 34. (☎288 78 89 10). U5 to "Schillingstr." Lodged in a former East German dinner cabaret, more chic than some of its neighbors, Café Moskau packs its dancefloor with hip-hop fanatics and electro-junkies alike. Sundays belong to GMF, a popular gay party with some women and straight men in the mix. Cover €7-13. Open Sa and sometimes F from 11pm-6am, Su from 10pm-5am. Cash only.

Tacheles, Oranienburger Str. 54-56 (☎282 61 85). U6 to "Oranienburger Tor" or S1, S2, or S25 to "Oranienburger Str." or night buses N6 or N84. Housed in a bombed-out department store and the adjacent courtyard, this edgy complex boasts a motif of graffiti and scrap metal artwork. A playground for artists, punks, and curious tourists, the labyrinth of rooms leads into several art galleries, movie theaters, and balcony bars. Flickering films broadcast onto the building across the street, a metal dragon breathes fire in **Café Zapata,** and there's an occasional rave. Opening times for the theater and galleries vary, as do rave dates; check www.tacheles.de. For theater tickets, call ☎28 09 68 35. Café Zapata open daily noon-4am. **Offen Bar Konzept** on the top floor serves drinks with a view (and a breeze) starting every day at 8pm. Cash only.

Kaffee Burger, Torstr. 60 (☎28 04 64 95; www.kaffeeburger.de). U2 to "Rosa-Luxemburg-Pl." This awesomely oblivious retro bar and club with a tinge of DDR-era backwardness draws an eclectic crowd with its wide variety of nightly parties, especially on bimonthly "Russian Disco" night. Live bands Th 10pm. Cover weekdays €1, F-Sa €5-6. Open M-Th and Su 7pm-late, F 8pm-late, Sa 9pm-late. Cash only.

Zosch, Tucholskystr. 30 (☎280 76 64). U6 to "Oranienburger Tor." Refreshingly far from the crowded Oranienburger Str. scene and hidden behind layers of ivy, this place fills to the corners every night. Bright bar on the ground fl. with couch and café tables fills up with Mitte-dwellers just looking to relax. The basement has live music, fiction and poetry readings, and a darker bar. Performances (and crowds) vary widely from day to day. Dixieland jazz W. Open M-F from 3:30pm, Sa-Su from noon. Cash only.

2BE-Club, Ziegelstr. 23 (☎89 06 84 10; www.2be-club.de). S1, S2, or S25 to "Oranienburger Str." or U6 to "Oranienburger Tor." This touristed club lures committed dancers to the indoor dancefloor with deep-bassed hip-hop. In the more casual outdoor area, reggae beats and fake palms feel decidedly out of place in Berlin. F-Sa ladies free until midnight. Cover €7.50-8. Open F-Sa from 11pm, sometimes W. Cash only.

Strandbar Mitte, Monbijoustr. 3. S3, S5, S7, S9, or S75 to "Hackescher Markt." In Monbijoupark, across from the Bodemuseum. Filled with beach chairs and a huge pit of sand, this bar radiates California sunshine. The sound system blasts hits as locals enjoy beer (€2.50-3.50) and mixed drinks (€4-7). Open summer only, daily from 10am.

VEB-OZ, Stadtbogen 153, Monbijoupark (www.veb-oz.de). Under the S-Bahn tracks just west of Hackescher Markt. The name stands for Verkehrsberuhigte Ost Zone, and though it's recently moved from Oranienburger Str., it took its kitschy East German paraphernalia along for the ride. The new location may be somewhat tiny, but that doesn't keep crowds from pouring in for live music and foosball. Open daily from 6pm. Cash only.

Delicious Doughnuts, Rosenthaler Str. 9 (☎28 09 92 74; www.delicious-dough-nuts.de). U8 to "Rosenthaler Pl." This backpacker hangout's curvacious design draws you into one of the loungeable booths. Other facilities include pinball and a pocket-sized dancefloor. Shades keep early-morning stragglers protected from the sun. Cover €3 weekdays, F-Sa €5. Open daily from 10pm-late, weekends until noon. Cash only.

Sage Club, Kopenicker Str. 76 (☎27 59 10 82; www.sage-club.de). U8 or night bus N8 to "Heinrich-Heine-Str." A decadent haven for the trendy, where women dressed as gothic angels perch along the walls (no, those aren't statues...) and some bartenders unabashedly bare all. The wooden patio, open F-Sa, has porch swings, couches, and a pool. Th punk/indie, F funk/disco/R&B, Sa-Su house. Cover €5-13. Open Th from 10pm, F-Su 11pm-9am. The packed "Sage Market" is open Su noon-10pm. Cash only.

b-flat, Rosenthaler Str. 13 (☎28 38 68 35; tickets 283 3123; www.b-flat-berlin.de). U8 to "Weinmeisterstr." or S3, S5, S7, S9, or S75 to "Hackescher Markt." Enter off the adjoining courtyard. Live jazz and acoustic nightly in a sleek, dimly lit bar with pictures of musicians lining the walls. W Free music. Cover €8. Open daily from 8pm. Cash only.

PRENZLAUER BERG

Though largely overlooked during post-war reconstruction efforts, *Prenzlberg* (as locals call it) has been transformed in recent years from a heap of crumbling, graffiti-covered buildings into perhaps the trendiest of Berlin's *Bezirke*. Attracted by low rents, thousands of students and artists moved into the neighborhood after reunification; today, the streets are owned by well-dressed first graders and their effortlessly hip young parents, and studded with cool but costly second-hand clothing stores. Everything in Prenzlauer Berg used to be something else, including the expats who drop English phrases in neighborhood cafés. Scrumptious brunches unfold every Sunday in what were once butcher shops, a former power plant stages thoughtful furniture exhibitions, and students cavort in breweries-turned-nightclubs. Relics of Prenzlberg's past life are disappearing, but café-bar owners know shabby chic when they see it: mismatched sofas and painted advertisements for cabbage remain the decorating standard. Prenzlberg is the bar scene to Friedrichain's club culture: if you prefer drinking against a backdrop of studied cool to gyrating in the dark, this is your spot.

ACCOMMODATIONS

East Seven Hostel, Schwedter Str. 7 (☎93 62 22 40; www.eastseven.de). U2 to Senefelderpl. A new, relaxed hostel on a quiet street. The orange facade and classy paint job are as upbeat as the light-filled, bunkless (!) dorms. Kitchen facilities. Linen €3. Laundry €4. Internet €0.50 per 20min. Dorms €15-17; singles €32; doubles €46; triples €60; quads €72. Lower rates in winter. Cash only. ❷

Lette'm Sleep Hostel, Lettestr. 7 (☎44 73 36 23; www.backpackers.de). U2 to "Eberswalder Str." With its street-level common room and easy-going staff, you could mistake Lette'm Sleep for one of the cafés lining Helmholtzpl. The big kitchen, complete with comfy red couches, is the social nexus of this 48-bed hostel. Free Internet. Wheelchair accessible. Sheets €2. 4- to 7-bed dorms €17-20; doubles with sheets €49. 10% discount (15% in winter) for stays over 3 nights. Lower prices in winter. AmEx/MC/V. ❷

Alcatraz, Schönhauser Allee 133a (☎ 48 49 68 15; www.alcatraz-backpacker.de). U2 to "Eberswalder Str." Tucked away in a spray-painted courtyard, Alcatraz offers 80 beds in small rooms. The "chill out room" is quite the hangout after dark, and the location is convenient for late nights in Mitte or Prenzlberg. Bike rental €5. Free Internet access. Kitchen facilities. Reception 24hr. Dorms in summer €16-18; in winter €12-14; singles €40/€30; doubles €50/42; triples €66/54; quads €100/84. MC/V. ❷

Generator, Storkower Str. 160 (☎ 417 24 00; www.generatorhostels.com). S8, S9, or S85 to "Landsberger Allee." It's the blue and white building just right of the Syringenstr. exit. Although a bit out of the way, this tremendous hostel, decorated with a metallic sheen to match its industrial trappings, is the largest hostel in Berlin. Internet €3 per hr., free wireless. Breakfast included. Laundry €5. Dorms in summer €15-25, €10-22 in winter; singles €38-48/€32-40, doubles €56-62/€42-50; triples €72-90/€48-57; quads €92-118/€64-84. AmEx/MC/V. ❷

⌂ FOOD

Prenzlauer Berg is an area flooded with all manner of restaurants, particularly at the borders of **Hemholzpl.** and **Kollwitz Pl.** Eating out is quite common here; on most Sundays, when virtually every restaurant serves brunch, you'll be hard-pressed to find an outdoor spot.

▨ **Nosh,** Pappelallee 77 (☎ 44 04 03 97; www.nosh-berlin.de). U2 to "Eberswalder Str." A fresh little concept restaurant amid Prenzlberg's run-down sophistication. "Borderless cooking" brings bagels topped with pesto-olive spread (€3), pad thai (€7.50) and the Brighton breakfast (€6.50) together on one menu. Nosh's baked goods (€1.50-2.50), in particular, are not to be missed. Free wireless Internet access. Open daily 10am-late. Kitchen closes at midnight, 11pm Su. Cash only. ❸

Café-Restaurant Miró, Raumerstr. 29 (☎ 44 73 30 13). U2 to "Eberswalder Str." A quiet Mediterranean café whose calm atmosphere and fresh entrées (€8-11) capture the region perfectly. The back room, a candlelit lair complete with overstuffed pillows, is surprisingly difficult to leave. Breakfast €4.50-7.50, soups €3-3.50, large appetizers and salads €4-9. Open 10am-late. Kitchen closes at midnight. ❸

Babel, Kastanienalle 33 (☎ 44 03 13 18). U2 to "Eberswalder Str." Locals obsessed by Babel's falafel (€3-5) keep this neighborhood Middle Eastern joint busy at all hours. Grab your food to go, or lap up the large portions under the garlic dangling from the ceiling. Open daily 11am-midnight. Cash only. ❶

Thai Phiset, Pappelallee 19 (☎ 44 04 49 29), on Raumerstr. U2 to "Eberswalder Str." The cheapest lunch in Prenzlberg that still comes on a plate. Noodle dishes from €2.80, chicken €3.20-4.50. Open daily 11am-11pm. Cash only. ❶

Café Restauration 1900, Husemannstr. 1 (☎ 442 24 94; www.restauration-1900.de), at Kollwitzpl. U2 to "Senefelderpl." A fashionable set frequents this ideally located café. The salad for 2 (€18.80) challenges conventional notions of what "salad" should include. Those on a budget can take advantage of the brunch buffet on weekends (€7.80; 10am-4pm). Open daily 10am-late. Kitchen closes at midnight. MC/V. ❸

Malzcafé, Knaackstr. 99 (☎ 44 04 72 27; www.malzcafe.de). U2 to "Eberswalder Str." Frescoes and, oddly, burlap potato sacks, decorate this restaurant with international cuisine (€3-9.80). Sa brunch buffet (€6.10) includes unlimited cake. Open daily 10am-midnight. Brunch Sa-Su. Cash only. ❸

Massai, Lychener Str. 12 (☎ 48 62 55 95; www.massai-berlin.de). U2 to "Eberswalder Str." African art and carved wooden chairs alongside a menu ranging from traditional Sudanese bean dishes (€7) to the more adventurous crocodile filet (€17.50). Many vegetarian options. Banana beer €3.30. Open daily noon-2am. AmEx/MC/V. ❸

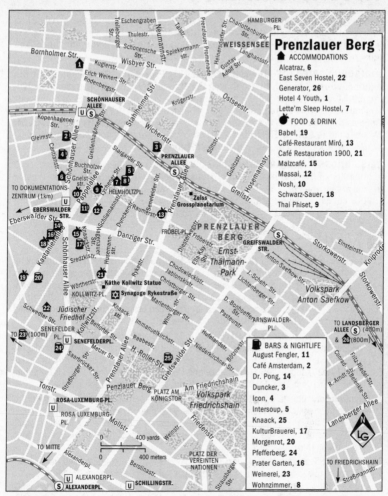

Prenzlauer Berg

⌂ ACCOMMODATIONS

Alcatraz, 6
East Seven Hostel, 22
Generator, 26
Hotel 4 Youth, 1
Lette'm Sleep Hostel, 7

🍎 FOOD & DRINK

Babel, 19
Café-Restaurant Miró, 13
Café Restauration 1900, 21
Malzcafé, 15
Massai, 12
Nosh, 10
Schwarz-Sauer, 18
Thai Phiset, 9

🍸 BARS & NIGHTLIFE

August Fengler, 11
Café Amsterdam, 2
Duncker, 14
Dr. Pong, 3
Icon, 4
Intersoup, 5
Knaack, 25
KulturBrauerei, 17
Morgenrot, 20
Pfefferberg, 24
Prater Garten, 16
Weinerei, 23
Wohnzimmer, 8

BERLIN

🔗 SIGHTS

BERLINER MAUER DOKUMENTATIONZENTRUM (BERLIN WALL DOCUMENTATION CENTER). A museum, chapel, and an entire city block of the preserved Berlin Wall—two concrete barriers separated by the open Todesstreife (death strip)—combine to form a controversial memorial to "victims of the communist tyranny." The **museum** assembles a comprehensive record of all things wallrelated; exhibits include historic photos, film clips, and sound bites. Climb up the spiral staircases for the full effect of the desolate scene below you. (*Bernauer Str. 111. U8 to "Bernauer Str." Open Apr.-Oct. Tu-Su 10am-6pm, Nov.-Mar. Tu-Su 10am-5pm. Free.*)

KOLLWITZPLATZ. This little triangle of greenery is a nexus of Prenzlauer Berg's café scene, populated by young couples and, on Saturdays, an upscale 🛒**market**

selling everything from hand-made pasta to freshly pressed apple juice. The Platz centers on a statue of famed visual artist **Käthe Kollwitz** (p. 112). The monument has been painted a number of times in past years in acts of affectionate vandalism, most notably with big pink polka-dots. *(U2 to "Senefelderpl.")*

JÜDISCHER FRIEDHOF (JEWISH CEMETERY). Prenzlauer Berg was one of the major centers of Jewish Berlin during the 19th and early 20th centuries. The ivy-covered Jewish cemetery on Schönhauser Allee contains the graves of composer Giacomo Meyerbeer and painter Max Liebermann. *(Enter by the "Lapidarium." Open M-Th 8am-4pm, F 8am-1pm. Men must cover their heads.)* Nearby, **Synagoge Rykestraße**, Rykestr. 53 is one of Berlin's loveliest synagogues. It was spared on *Kristallnacht* thanks to its inconspicuous location.

ZEISS-GROSSPLANETARIUM. In 1987 this planetarium opened as the most modern facility of its kind in the DDR. Though compared to its peers in the West it seems about as technologically advanced as a **Trabi**, it can still show you the stars. Call or check the web for show times. *(Prenzlauer Allee 80. S4, 8, or 85 to "Prenzlauer Allee"; it's across the bridge. ☎42 18 45 12; www.astw.de. €5, students €4.)*

☕ NIGHTLIFE

⊠ Intersoup, Schliemannstr. 31 (☎23 27 3045; www.intersoup.de). U2 to "Eberswalder Str." This craftedly shabby bar eschews big name drink brands and popular music in favor of worn 70s furniture, soup specials (€4.50-5), and retro floral wallpaper. Downstairs, the small club "undersoup" keeps things wild with live music dance parties (most W and Sa), karaoke, occasional films and, if you can believe it, puppet theater (M and Tu). DJs most nights. Club cover max. €3. Open daily from 4pm. Cash only.

Morgenrot, Kastanienallee 85 (☎44 31 78 44; www.cafe-morgenrot.de). U2 to "Eberswalder Str." Candy-print wallpaper and funky print art lure young hipsters off the Kastanianallee strip. By day, it's a vegetarian restaurant, by night, there are frosty vodka shots (€3.20) and a €4.50 *Milchkaffee* and cake deal. Th-Su brunch buffet 11am-4pm. Open Tu-Th 10am-1am, F 10am-3am, Sa 11am-3am, Su 11am-1am. Cash only.

Wohnzimmer, Lettestr. 6 (☎445 54 58; www.wohnzimmer.de). U2 to "Eberswalder Str." The name means living room, and they aren't kidding. With wood-beam floors, a bar that resembles an old-fashioned kitchen, and glassware cabinets along the walls, you'll feel right at home as you settle into a velvet armchair for a mixed drink (€4-5). Open daily 10am-4am. Cash only.

The Weinerei, at Zionkirch pl. next to the sushi restaurant. This unmarked local secret offers cheap self-service wine in an atmosphere of eclectic elegance. To drink, insert a euro into the bizarre ceramic bird on the bar in exchange for a glass. When you leave, you decide how much to pay and leave the amount in the vase. Hours vary. Cash only.

August Fengler, Lychener Str. 11 (☎44 35 66 40; www.augustfengler.de). U2 to "Eberswalder Str." Most Prenzlberg nightlife is either dirty or disposable, but this homey café-bar, with paintings and elegant lampshades, manages to avoid both extremes. DJs spin daily. Open daily from 7pm, music starts at 10pm. Cash only.

Duncker, Dunckerstr. 64 (☎445 95 09; www.dunckerclub.de). S8, S41, or S85 to "Prenzlauer Allee." This intense club draws crowds with its insider vibe: M and Su goth, Tu hippie, Th live bands, F-Sa varies. Grill in back. Ring the bell for entry. Cover €2.50-4, Th often free. Open M-Tu and Th-Su 8pm-late. Heats up around 1am. Cash only.

Dr. Pong, Eberswalderstr. 21 (www.drpong.net). U2 to "Eberswalder Str." An arena-like intensity pervades the atmosphere of this ping-pong stadium-turned-bar. Players gather paddles in hand, while the more impatient drink amid the care-worn paraphernalia in back. Drinks €3.50-4.50. Open M-Sa 8pm-late, Su from 4pm. Cash only.

Icon, Cantianstr. 15 (☎48 49 28 78; www.iconberlin.de). U2 to "Eberswalder Str." Plenty of dancing in brick underground tunnels, and just enough light, provided by surreal projections, to flirt. Frequented by a young crowd. Cover €6-10, Tu €3. Tu electro, F hip-hop/indie, Sa drum'n'bass. Tu from 11pm, F-Sa from 11:30pm. Cash only.

Prater Garten, Kastanienallee 7-9 (☎448 5688; www.pratergarten.de). U2 to "Eberswalder Str." Giant chestnut trees overhang sprawling picnic tables and umbrellas at Berlin's oldest beer garden. Outdoor theater and TV. Bratwurst €2. Beer €2.20-3.10. Open in good weather Apr.-Sept. M-Sa from 6pm, Su from noon. Cash only.

KulturBrauerei, Knaackstr. 97 (☎441 92 69; www.kulturbrauerei.de). U2 to "Eberswalder Str." A dauntingly massive party space in a former brewery. This expansive village of *Kultur* houses the popular clubs **Soda, nbi,** and **Kesselhaus,** the concert venue **Franz,** a beer garden, a Russian theater, upscale cafés, a cinema, and an art school. Dance floors and stages abound. Music includes hardcore, *Ostrock*, disco, techno, reggae, *Schlager,* and more. Cover (from €1.50) varies wildly among venues.

Pfefferberg, Schönhauser Allee 176 (☎44 38 33 42; www.pfefferberg.de). U2 or night bus N58 to "Senefelderpl." *Biergarten,* nightclub, cinema, and live music venue. A summery spot for a drink; heats up on weekends with a clubbier ambience and after-hours parties. Cover €5-8. Open M-F from noon, Sa-Su from 3pm. Club open F-Sa. Cash only.

Schwarz-Sauer, Kastanienallee 13/14 (☎448 56 33; www.schwarzsauer.de). U2 to "Eberswalder Str." A jam-packed neighborhood hang-out with a mirror-plated wall. Crowds spill out into the street and the promise of breakfast until 5pm keeps them coming back by day. Open daily 8am-6am. Cash only.

Café Amsterdam, Gleimstr. 24 (☎448 07 92). S8, S41, S42, or S85 or U2 to "Schönhauser Allee." Romantic and quieter than some of its overflowing neighbors, with gilt-framed paintings and sweet, creamy cocoa. Gay friendly. Pasta dishes (€6-7) until 11:30pm. Brunch Sa-Su from 10am. Open daily 3pm-1:30am. Cash only.

FRIEDRICHSHAIN

As the alternative scene follows low rents ever eastward and farther from the geographical center of the city, Friedrichshain is becoming its new temple. While this *Bezirk* still retains much of its DDR atmosphere, from the pre-fab apartment houses and gray concrete to the massive remains of the Wall, some of its longstanding proponents complain that gentrification has found its way even here. The bustling bar scene, second-hand clothing stores, and ethnic merchants that have always kept the neighborhood lively give way at night to the new wave of Berlin club culture colonizing its old industrial sites. The oppressive architecture of central axis Frankfurter Allee is overtaken by more traditional residential areas, while the main drag for the young populace is Simon-Dach-Str., covered with sun-soaked outdoor seating and crowds of chic 20-somethings. Farther north, Rigaerstr. is a stronghold of Berlin's legendary underground, home to squatter bars, makeshift clubs, and sidewalk punks. Even as it steps increasingly into the limelight, Friedrichshain continues to meet the future with an individual flair to ensure that its place at the cutting edge isn't purely a matter of geography.

ACCOMMODATIONS

If you want to stay near Friedrichshain's legendary nightlife, keep an eye out for "Warschauer Str.," which can be reached from the U15, S3, S5-7, S9, and S75.

Sunflower Hostel, Helsingforser Str. 17 (☎44 04 42 50; www.sunflower-berlin.de). Relaxed eclectic, featuring a leafy and bright orange lounge. Spotless dorms are a marked contrast to the studied chaos of the common areas. The staff knows the nightlife scene unbelievably well. Internet €0.50 per 20min. Breakfast €3. Sheets and locks €3 deposit each. Laundry €4.50. Reception 24hr. 5-6 bed dorms Mar.-Oct. €15, Nov.-Feb.€12.50; 7-8-bed €13/10; singles €35/30; doubles €45/38; triples €57/51; quads €68/60. 7th night free. ISIC discount 5%. MC/V. ❶

Globetrotter Hostel Odyssee, Grünberger Str. 23 (☎29 00 00 81; www.globetrotterhostel.de). Convenient base for nightlife "sightseeing." Rooms with psychedelic swirls of paint, an outdoor courtyard, and a pool table by the bar make this a backpacker favorite. Bar open until dawn. Internet access €0.50 per 20min. Breakfast €3. Sheets included with deposit. Reception 24hr. Reserve a couple weeks ahead. 8-bed dorms in summer €13, in winter €10; 6-bed dorm €15/12, doubles €45/39, with shower €52/46; triples €57/48; quads €68/56. 7th, 13th, and 14th nights free. MC/V. ❷

Eastern Comfort Hostelboat, Mühlenstr. 73-77 (☎66 76 38 06; www.eastern-comfort.com). Enter through the first opening in the **East Side Gallery** (p. 138). Those willing to brave narrow corridors and cramped quarters will be reward with Berlin's most adventurous hostel: a docked boat. The truly bold can sleep outside on the deck for the cheapest river-view in town. Breakfast €3. Sheets €5. Internet €2 per hr. Tent/open-air €10; dorm €14; 1st class singles €58, 2nd class €42; doubles €72/50; triples €57; quads €68. 2-night bookings only during weekends. MC/V. ❶

All in Hostel, Grünberger Str. 54 (☎288 76 83; www.all-in-hostel.com). A sparkling new hostel that, with 400 beds, anticipates the rising demand for Friedrichshain's booming nightlife scene. Sleek, minimalist aesthetic revolves around a metal-frame spiral staircase. Breakfast included. Internet access €1 per 20min. 8-bed dorms €10.25; 4-6 bed €18-30; singles €55-63; doubles €66-76. AmEx/MC/V. ❶

◖ FOOD

The following restaurants can be reached on the U5 at the "Frankfurter Tor" stop.

Cappuccino, Simon-Dach-Str. 7 (☎292 64 57). A frantically popular Italian joint frequented by locals. Quality pastas and pizzas (€3-4.50) in cave-like interior splashed with colored light. Rinse with a flaming sambucca shot, free with a main dish if you're lucky. Open M-F 10am-1am, Sa-Su noon-1am. Cash only. ❷

Intimes, Boxhagener Str. 107 (☎29 66 64 57). This Greek spot is the perfect place to start an evening along Simon-Dach-Str. Sizeable portions and numerous vegetarian options. An adjoining cinema plays European Indie flicks. Meals €6-11. Su brunch 10am-4pm (€8). Open daily from 10am. Kitchen open 10am-midnight. Cash only. ❸

Lemongrass, Simon-Dach-Str. 2 (☎200 56 975). The zest lacking from the decor has been saved for the food: classic Thai specialities cooked within view make this a neighborhood favorite. Entrées €5.50-8. Open daily noon-midnight. Cash only. ❷

◉ SIGHTS

▨**EAST SIDE GALLERY.** The longest remaining portion of the Berlin Wall, this 1.3km stretch of cement slabs and asbestos also serves as the world's largest open-air art gallery, unsupervised and, on the Warschaur Str. side, open at all hours. The murals are not remnants of Cold War graffiti, but rather the organized efforts of an international group of multi-national artists who gathered here in 1989 to celebrate the end of the city's division. It was expected that the wall would be destroyed and the paintings lost, but in 2000, with this portion still standing, many of the same artists reconvened to repaint their work, covering the scrawlings of tourists. Unfortunately, the new paintings are once again being rapidly eclipsed by graffitied scribblings. *(Along Mühlenstr. Take U1 or U15 or S3, S5-S7, S9, or S75 to "Warschauer Str." or S5, S7, S9, or S75 to "Ostbahnhof" and walk back toward the river. www.eastsidegallery.com.)*

BERLIN

Friedrichshain

▲ ACCOMMODATIONS
All in Hostel, 6
Eastern Comfort Hostelboat, 18
Globetrotter Hostel Odyssee, 3
Sunflower Hostel, 12

♦ FOOD & DRINK
Cappuccino, 9
Intimes, 2
Lemongrass, 5

● SIGHTS
East Side Gallery, 17
Gedenkstätte
Normannenstraße, 1

BARS & NIGHTLIFE
Astro-Bar, 8
Berghain/Panorama Bar, 4
Cassiopeia, 15
Die Busche, 19
Dachkammer Bar, 10
Euphoria, 7
Habermeyer, 14
Maria am Ostbahnhof, 13
Matrix, 16
Paule's Metal Eck, 11

LICHTENBERG

Gedenkstätte
Normannenstraße

Stadtpark

FRANKFURTER ALLEE

FRANKFURTER TOR

FRIEDRICHSHAIN

WARSCHAUER STR.

East Side
Gallery

OSTBAHNHOF

Spree

SCHLESISCHES
TOR

WEBERWIESE

STRAUSBERGER PL.

NÖLDNERPL.

RUMMELSBURG

OSTKREUZ

TO VOLKSPARK
FRIEDRICHSHAIN (50m)

TO PRENZLAUER
BERG

TO MITTE

0   200 yards
0   200 meters

FROM THE ROAD

I EAT BEATS
FOR BREAKFAST

So proclaims the t-shirt of the boy bopping arrhythmically in front of me at Maria am Bahnhof, a hotspot in the Friedrichshain club scene. Yes, I am at a techno concert—my first—and am trying to learn the particularities of dancing to something that has neither lyrics nor a recognizable melody (not that I can dance under any circumstances, to be fair).

More difficult, even, than learning the nuances of moving to electronic music is knowing what its various sub-categories mean. As I researched Berlin, I would frequently learn that a club played, say, "drum and bass" on Fridays and "electro" on Saturdays. I would give a confident nod and record this information while secretly having no idea what these were, my taste being generally confined to faux-obscure indie pop. So for those who are looking to test the waters of Berlin nightlife but are equally clueless about its fiendish electronic music culture, I can offer some info, if not some dance moves:

Drum and Bass – Also called "dnb," this form is mostly a product of British rave culture. The quick drum beats and complex bass lines are the most prominent sonic elements. Influenced by hip-hop, it is usually mid-tempo and can involve samples or synthesized bass lines.

FORSCHUNGS- UND GEDENKSTÄTTE NORMANNENSTRAßE. The Lichtenberg suburb harbors perhaps the most hated and feared building of the DDR regime: the headquarters of the East German secret police, the **Staatssicherheit** or **Stasi**. During the Cold War, the *Stasi* kept dossiers on some six million of their own citizens, in a country of only 16 million people. On January 15, 1990, a crowd of 100,000 Berliners stormed and vandalized the building to protest the police state. Since a 1991 law returned the records to the people, the "Horror Files" have rocked Germany, exposing millions of informants—and wrecking careers, marriages, and friendships—at all levels of German society. Today, the building maintains its oppressive Orwellian drear and much of its worn 70s aesthetic. The exhibit displays the extensive offices of **Erich Mielke** (the loathed Minister for State Security from 1957 to 1989), a large collection of tiny microphones and hidden cameras used for surveillance by the *Stasi*, and a replica of a *Stasi* prison cell. *(Ruschestr. 103, Haus 1. U5 to "Magdalenenstr."* ☎ *553 68 54; www.stasimuseum.de. Exhibits in German. Recommended English info booklet €3. Open M-F 11am-6pm, Sa-Su 2-6pm. €3.50, students €2.50.)*

KARL-MARX-ALLEE. The cornerstone of the East German National Construction Program, Karl-Marx-Allee became a showcase of the infant Communist government in the early 1950s, when it was known as Stalinallee. Billed as Germany's "first socialist road," the broad avenue, widened in the 1960s to accommodate grandiose military parades, is flanked by scores of pre-fab gems, climaxing with the "people's palaces" at Strausberger Pl. *(U5 to "Strausberger Pl.")*

▶ NIGHTLIFE

BARS AND CLUBS

▓ Berghain/Panorama Bar, Am Wriezener Bahnhof (☎29 00 05 97; www.berghain.de). S3, S5, S7, S9, or S75 to "Ostbahnhof." Heading up Str. der Pariser Kommune, take the third right into what looks like a parking lot. An "it" club that actually deserves its reputation, Berghain is as much an architectural feat as is a late night spectacle. Spaced out techno-fiends pulse to the music reverberating beneath the towering ceilings of this former power plant. Cover €6-10. Open Th-Sa from midnight. Check schedule online. Cash only.

Maria am Ostbahnhof, Am der Schillingbrücke (☎21 23 81 90; www.clubmaria.de). S-Bahn to "Ostbahnhof." From Stralauer Pl. exit, take Str. der Pariser Kommune to Stralauer Pl., follow it right along the wall. Turn left at the bridge and look for the red lights by the water. Tucked away by the river in an old factory, this club embodies the industrial legacy of Friedrichshain's scene. Grey-toned murals line the wall and rickety wooden crates and converted speakers serve as seating. Sizeable—and full—dance floor. Mostly electronic music, occasional punk and reggae. Beer €2.50. Cover €10. Open F-Sa 11pm-late, weekdays for concerts and events only. Cash only.

Habermeyer, Gartnerstr. 6 (☎29 77 18 87; www.habermeyer-bar.de). U5 to "Samariterstr." Retro stylings and soft red lighting from funky lamps complement nostalgic New Wave DJ. Foosball table in back lends a competitive edge to the otherwise chill atmosphere. Mixed drinks €5.40-6.80. Open daily 7pm-late. Cash only.

Matrix, Warschauer Pl. 18 (☎29 36 99 90; www.matrix-club.de). U1 or S3, S5, S7, S9, or S75 to "Warschauer Str." No, the pounding sound of the bass from underneath the station isn't only in your head—4 dancefloors and multiple bars extend through the caverns under the tracks. The stylish can opt for a mixed drink (€4.50-7.50) in the VIP lounge. No sneakers. Cover €3-6. 18+, bring ID. Open M-Sa 10pm-late. Cash only.

Astro-Bar, Simon-Dach-Str. 40 (www.astro-bar.de). U5 to "Frankfurter Tor." The rough edges of this retro-space locale are obscured by plenty of 70s plastic robots. Back room with many mod things to sit on and many mod things sitting on them. DJs spin anything from R&B to electronica. Mixed Drinks €4.50-5.50. Open daily from 6pm. Cash only.

Cassiopeia, Revaler Str. 99 (☎29 36 29 66; www.cassiopeia.de). U- or S-Bahn to "Warschauer Str." A sprawling nightlife oasis in an abandoned train factory, this club/beer garden has outdoor couches that provide a respite from the packed dancefloor. Beer €2-3. Cover €3-10. Open F-Sa from 11pm, check schedule for weekdays. Cash only.

Knaack, Greifswalderstr. 224 (☎442 70 60; www.knaack-berlin.de). Tram #2 to "Metzer Str." 4-floored Knaack has an enviable infrastructure, with music ranging from disco to rock and punk—virtually everything but techno. Live music on "wide-open Wednesdays," with free entrance before 11pm, billiards upstairs, occasional karaoke contests. Internet €1 per hr. M karaoke. Dance floors open F-Sa 10pm and sometimes W at 11pm. Cover €1 10-11pm, from 11pm €5. Cash only.

Dachkammer Bar (DK), Simon-Dach-Str. 39 (☎296 16 73). U5 to "Frankfurter Tor." Draped vines give this bar a rustic feel, along with plenty of brick, wood, and comfy places to relax. Quieter than its neighbors, DK is the place for mixed drinks (€5-8), snacks (from €3.50), and conversation, provided you don't mind the people making out at the next table. Open daily noon-late. Cash only.

Electro – Shorthand for "electro funk," this brand of electronic hip-hop, sometimes traced all the way back to German stalwarts Kraftwerk (p. 74), relies heavily on drum machines, synthetic bass lines, and elaborate sonic reverberations. It often takes on futuristic themes. Lyrics are digitally remastered in order to make the voices sound mechanical.

House – A form of electronic dance music in which the 4/4 beat is heavily accentuated by the drum, House tends to have a Latin influence and often tries to approximate the experience of live music, sampling everything from pop to jazz. Although the drum accents vary in their placement, the uptempo beat structure stays relatively consistent.

Techno – With computerized sequences that layer different rhythms and syncopations, Techno is generally more melodic than its counterparts. It tends to use exclusively inorganic sounds.

Trance – Using the high degree of repetition common to melodic song structures, Trance often builds up a steady crescendo using recurring synthesizer phrases. A bass drum catches the down beats while minor scales add variety. Occasionally, though not often, vocal layers are added to the mix.

—Amelia Atlas

Paule's Metal Eck, Krossener Str. 15 (☎291 16 24; www.paules-metal-eck.de). U5 to "Frankfurter Tor," at Simon-Dach-Str. A well-executed fake heavy metal bar—don't let the chihuahua skeletons or the hooded monk over the door scare you from the foosball tables. Drinks €2.10-6.70. Open 4pm-late. Cash only.

Euphoria, Grünberger Str. 60 (☎29 00 46 83). U5 to "Frankfurter Tor," on the corner of Simon-Dach-Str. A bright-orange hot spot full of dripping candles. Creatively named mixed drinks (€4.50-8) are the way to go: bomb down an "Autobahn" or replenish your "Red Power." Open daily 9am-late. Cash only.

GAY AND LESBIAN

Die Busche, Warschauer Pl 18 (☎296 08 00; www.diebusche.de). U-Bahn or S-Bahn to "Warschauer Str." East Berlin's famous disco in the DDR days is still a color-saturated haven of dance. Incongruous rotation of techno, top 40, and German *Schlager* to a mixed crowd. W night is a great midweek option as most other gay/lesbian clubs close. Cover €2-6. Open W 10pm-5am, F-Sa 10pm-7am, Su 10pm-4am. Cash only.

KREUZBERG

Across the Spree and over the wall from Freidrichshain, Kreuzberg is West Germany's dose of counter-culture. A center of Berlin's alternative *Szene*, Kreuzberg's only certainty is unpredictability. In the 1960s and 70s, much of the area was occupied by *Hausbesetzer* (squatters) until a conservative city government forcibly evicted most of them in the early 80s. The ensuing riots threw the city into chaos; during President Reagan's 1985 visit to Berlin, authorities so feared protests from Kreuzberg that they cordoned off the whole district. This *Bezirk*'s anti-establishment reputation belies its incredible diversity. Home to an especially large segment of the city's immigrant and ethnic population, Kreuzberg boasts a staggering array of sidewalk food stands, fruit vendors, and cafés. Its increasing trendiness has attracted a wave of gentrification in the form of yuppies and sober government workers, particularly in the western half; farther east, the neighborhood remains as forward-looking as ever. Kreuzberg defiantly rejects stereotypes, presenting instead a kaleidoscopic mix of people who keep the dynamic scene alive with a tireless supply of partiers.

🏠 ACCOMMODATIONS

🛏 **Bax Pax,** Skalitzer Str. 104 (☎69 51 83 22; www.baxpax.de). U1 or U15 to "Görlitzer Bahnhof," right across the street. Run by the same friendly people as Mitte's Backpacker Hostel. At the start of mighty Oranienstr., with a pool table, roomy common spaces, walls painted with film reels, and a bed inside an antique VW Bug (ask for room 3). Kitchen facilities and an outdoor terrace. Internet €3 per hr. Sheets €2.50. Breakfast €4. Reception 24hr. Big dorms €15; 7- to 8-bed dorms €16; 6- to 7-bed dorms €16; singles €30; doubles €46; triples €60; quads €72. AmEx/MC/V. ❷

Hostel X Berger, Schlesische Str. 22 (☎695 18 63; www.hostelxberger.com). U1 or U15 to "Schlesisches Tor," or night bus #N65 to "Taborstr." This social hostel provides perfect access to one of the most up-and-coming areas in Kreuzberg. Roomy, barebones dorms off hallways painted with bright blocks of color. Female-only dorms available. Free Internet access. Reception 24hr. Sheets €2. Dorms €11-13, depending on size; singles €25; doubles €36; triples €48; quads €56. Cash only. ❶

Die Fabrik, Schlesische Str. 18 (☎611 71 16; www.diefabrik.com), next to Hostel X Berger. Frequented by a slightly older clientele, this former factory now has spacious rooms and a classy leather and glass lounge. Easy access to Kreuzberg nightlife. Internet €1 per 20min. Reception 24hr. Dorms €18; singles €38; doubles Th-Sa €58/Su-W €52, with private bath €62/54; triples €78/69; quads €92/84. Cash only. ❷

BERLIN

Kreuzberg

▲ ACCOMMODATIONS

Bax Pax, **17**
Die Fabrik, **26**
Hotel Transit, **2**
Hotel X Berger, **28**
Pension Kreuzberg, **1**

Heinz Mincki, 25
Junction Bar, 7
Mas Y Mas, 10
Clash, **6**
Rose's, **14**
SchwuZ, **5**
SO36, **15**
Club der Visionaere, **23**
Francken, **12**
Freischwimmer, **27**

Weinhaus Hoff, **21**
Wirtshaus Henne, **9**
■ BARS & NIGHTLIFE
Ankerklause, **16**
Bateau Ivre, **13**
Barbie Dienhoff's, **24**
Watergate, **22**
Wild at Heart, **19**

■ FOOD & DRINK
Blue Nile, **3**
Café V, **20**
Curry 36, **4**
Hannibal, **16**
Melek Bäckerei, **11**
Sarod's Thai Restaurant, **8**
Rissani, **18**

East Side Gallery

Spree

OSTBAHNHOF Ⓢ

TO FRIEDRICHSHAIN

TO MITTE

TO DEUTSCHES
TECHNIKMUS. (200m)

LUFTBRÜCKE(30m)▼
TO PL. DER

Viktoria-
park

Volkspark
Hasenheide

CONTROVERSY IN THE CROSSWALK

If you're lost in Berlin and have, remarkably, lost sight of the towering Fernsehturm, the easiest way to decide if you're in eastern or western Berlin is not to pull out your map, but to look at the pedestrian traffic lights. When you cross the streets in most of western Berlin, you'll see a standard crossing light: a green walking man indicating "go," and a red standing man indicating "stop." In eastern Berlin, the crossing light figures are more robust. The green walking man strides jauntily forward into the bright, egalitarian future with his hat cocked back; the red standing man throws both arms fully to his sides.

The crossing-man of eastern Berlin, known as the *Ampel-Männchen,* or "little traffic-light guy," was created by traffic psychologist Karl Peglau in 1961 during the days of the DDR. Its cheerful design was meant to appeal to children, but it quickly developed followers of all ages.

When the city was reunified, plans were made to standardize the symbols. Distraught eastern Berliners, however, started a "Save the *Ampel-Männchen*" campaign; not only did the little man remain on traffic lights, but he cropped up on a whole host of paraphernalia. Even as the city moves beyond its past divisions, the *Ampel-Männchen* allows the East to preserve a small shard of its prior identity as it is increasingly folded into the West.

Pension Kreuzberg, Großbeerenstr. 64 (☎251 13 62; www.pension-kreuzberg.de). U6 or U7, or night bus #N19 to "Mehringdamm." Elegant, old-fashioned staircases, a cheery yellow breakfast room and antique iron stoves. Neighborhood is lively, even for Kreuzberg. Breakfast included. Reception 8am-9pm. Shared rooms €22.50 per person; singles €41, with private bathroom €60; doubles €55/68. AmEx/MC/V. ❷

Hotel Transit, Hagelberger Str. 53-54 (☎789 04 70; www.hotel-transit.de). U6 or U7, or night bus #N19 to "Mehringdamm." Modern rooms and dorms with bath overlooking a sunny courtyard in this hostel. Gay-friendly, but a mixed crowd. Internet €0.10 per min. Breakfast included. Reception 24hr. 3- to 6-bed dorms €21; singles €62; doubles €72; 3- to 6-bed rooms €30 per person. AmEx/MC/V. ❷

🍴 FOOD

Kreuzberg is packed with small restaurants and cafés, and no shortage of kebab stands. But if you're looking for the best deal, the **Turkish market** along Maybachufer (Tuesday and Friday until 6:30pm) is not to be missed. From fresh meat to cured olives, it's a jumble of enticing sights and smells.

🏅 Wirtshaus Henne, Leuschnerdamm 25 (☎614 77 30; www.henne-berlin.de). U1 or U15 to "Kottbusser Tor." Though this slightly secluded German restaurant does serve other dishes (€2.50-6), virtually everyone orders the famous *Brathänchen* (fried chicken), arguably the best in Berlin. While it has a small beer garden, the real charm is in its dark wood interior, with plaid tablecloths and antique lanterns. Always packed, so reserve in advance. Open Tu-Su 7pm-late. Cash only. ❷

Café V, Lausitzer Pl. 12 (☎612 45 05). U1 or 15 to "Görlitzer Bahnhof." Berlin's oldest vegetarian restaurant, featuring vegan and fish entrées in a romantic yellow interior with additional street-side seating. Top-of-the-line entrées from the bottom of the food chain include, among other tempting options, spinach balls in cheese sauce (€8.80) and an array of specials (€6-8). Open daily 10am-2am. Cash only. ❸

Restaurant Rissani, Spreewaldplatz 4-6 (☎616 24 933). U1 or 15 to "Görlitzer Bahnhof." The best Middle Eastern food in the neighborhood. Moroccan and Lebanese specialties conveniently located near Görlitzer Park; obvious pre-, post-, or mid-party stop. Open M-Th and Su noon-3am, F-Sa noon-5am. Cash only. ❶

Melek Bäckerei, Oranienstr. 28 (☎612 01 958). U1, U8, or U15 to "Kottbusser Tor." Popular sweets shop has Turkish pastries for pocket change. 100g baklava €0.75. Open 24hr. to accommodate sugar cravings of late-night partygoers. Cash only. ❶

Weinhaus Hoff, Reichenberger Str. 116 (☎342 08 13; www.weinhaus-hoff.de). U1 or U15 to "Görlitzer Bahnhof." Rich Swabian specialties in an out-of-the-way German wine shop lined with bottles and vines. Pork filet with mushroom cream and *Spätzle* is a house specialty (€7.50). Open daily 5pm-midnight. Cash only. ❸

Blue Nile, Tempelhofer Ufer 6 (☎25 29 46 55). U1 or 15 to "Möcknerbrücke," or U6 to "Hallesches Tor." The chairs may look like they're on loan from a hospital waiting room, but the service is friendly and the (literally) heaping portions are more than enough. Meals come on *injera,* a spongy Ethiopian sourdough bread. Vegetarian or meat combos (€9) big enough to share. Open daily 3pm-midnight. MC/V. ❸

Hannibal, (☎611 23 88) corner of Wienerstr. and Skalitzerstr. U1, U12, or U15, or night bus #N29 to "Görlitzer Bahnhof." Hanging beads, floral armchairs, and "alligator crossing" signs are among the wacky miscellany of this popular restaurant. Good for a leisurely breakfast (from €4.20), massive Hannibal burger (€6.50), or fruit smoothie (€3). Open M-Th 8am-3am, F-Sa 8am-4am, Su 9am-3am. MC/V. ❷

👁 SIGHTS

▓GÖRLITZER PARK. Built on the graffiti-coated ruins of an old train station, Gorlitzer Park now sports lush greenery and a ceaseless supply of neighborhood hipsters. It manages to be both shabby and stylish, perfectly embodying the spirit of Kreuzberg itself. In the center, you'll find a large basin, marked by a bizarre iron sculpture and bisected by a bike path. What remains of the old station building is now a café, **Station Park,** complete with beach chairs; next door a club keeps the park raging even after sunset. *(Café open M-F 11am-10pm, Sa-Su 10am-10pm.)*

AROUND MEHRINGDAMM. The broad thoroughfare of Mehringdamm runs through a vibrant, quickly gentrifying part of Kreuzberg. Around Chamissopl., Bergmannstr. holds an especially large number of cafés, second-hand clothing stores, and used music shops, while the quieter, cobblestone Fidicinstr. is lined with an unmollested stretch of traditional, ornamented German appartment buildings. To the north is the nightlife hotspot Gneisenaustr., filled with bars and clubs. On the other side of Mehringdamm, the forested **Viktoriapark** contains Kreuzberg's namesake, a 66m hill featuring Berlin's only waterfall, and an artificial one at that. Further south down Mehringdamm is the **Platz der Luftbrücke,** a flower-ringed field with a monument known as the **Hungerharke** (hunger rake) representing the three air corridors and dedicated to the 78 pilots who lost their lives in the 328 days of the Berlin Airlift. *(U6 to "Platz der Luftbrücke" or U6 or 7 to "Mehringdamm.")*

EASTERN KREUZBERG. The **Landwehrkanal,** a channel bisecting Kreuzberg, is where the Freikorps threw Rosa Luxemburg's body after murdering her in 1919 (p. 55). The tree-dotted strip of the canal near Kottbusser Damm, **Paul-Linke-Ufer,** is sedate and shady, popular with families and runners. *(U8 to "Schönleinstr.")* This ethnic part of town—especially near **Schlesisches Tor** and the former Wall—is rich in Balkan and Turkish restaurants, and, more recently, a booming nightlife scene. The **Oberbaumbrücke** spanning the Spree was once a border crossing into East Berlin; it now serves as an entrance to Friedrichshain's nightlife scene, complete with public art projects. *(U1 or U15 to "Schlesisches Tor.")*

ORANIENSTRAßE. This colorful mix of cafés, bars, and stores boast a more radical element: the May Day parades always start on Oranienpl., the site of frequent riots in the 1980s. Revolutionaries jostle shoulders with Turkish families, while an anarchist punk faction and a boisterous gay and lesbian population make things interesting after hours (see **Nightlife,** p. 147). Restaurants, clubs, and shops of staggering diversity beckon to passersby. The Western end culminates in **Oranienplatz,** a small park stretching toward the dauntingly large, green-domed church Michaelkirshe. *(U1 or U15 to "Kottbusser Tor" or "Görlitzer Bahnhof.")*

BERLIN

KREUZBERG DOTH PROTEST TOO MUCH

Kreuzberg, more than any Berlin *Berzirk*, stands out for its diversity, but there is one day per year that manages to unify the eclectic neighborhood. May 1, the German equivalent of labor day, sees the area transformed into a massive political protest. "A protest of what?" you might ask. Well, that's entirely up to you.

Reflecting the unusual combination of solidarity and singularity that defines Kreuzberg, the protests on May 1 are a time to represent whatever political issue has been pushing your buttons and to continue Kreuzberg's tradition of civil disobedience. Massive crowds take to the street, calling for everything from workers' rights to Kurdish independence.

Although recent years have seen comparatively little destruction, the May Day protests have a charged history. In 1987, when the neighborhood was still the counter-cultural hotbed of West Berlin, full-fledged riots broke out. While May Day protests take place across Germany, they are most indelibly associated with this area. So even if the protests are more moderate than they were in wall-era Berlin, unless you're willing to end up in a heap of overturned cars or desperate to plead your cause, May 1 might be a good time to leave the megaphone at home and avoid Kreuzberg.

🏛 MUSEUMS (INDEPENDENT)

■ THE MAUERMUSEUM: HAUS AM CHECKPOINT CHARLIE. From its beginnings as a 2½-bedroom apartment, this eccentric museum at the famous border-crossing point has become one of Berlin's most popular attractions. A strange blend of earnest Eastern sincerity and glossy Western salesmanship, the museum is a wonderfully cluttered collection of artwork, newspaper clippings, and photographs documenting the history of the wall and displaying all types of devices used to get over, under, or through it. The exhibits detail how women curled up in loudspeakers, men attempted to crawl through spike-laden gates, and student groups dug tunnels with their fingers, all in an attempt to reach the West. Surrounding shops sell all things Wall-related, while the unassuming station itself is overshadowed by two large photos of an American and a Russian soldier looking into "enemy" territory. *(Friedrichstr. 43-45. U6 to "Kochstr." ☎ 253 72 50; www.mauer-museum.de. Museum open daily 9am-10pm. German-language films with English subtitles every 2hr. from 9:30am. €9.50, students €5.50. Audio guide €3.)*

■ JÜDISCHES MUSEUM BERLIN. Architect Daniel Libeskind's design for the zinc-plated Jewish Museum is fascinating even as an architectural experience. No two walls are parallel, creating a sensation of perpetual discomfort. Underground, three symbolic hallways—the Axis of the Holocaust, the Axis of Exile, and the Axis of Continuity—are intended to represent the trials of death, escape, and survival. The labyrinthine "Garden of Exile" replicates the dizzying effects of dislocation and the eerie "Holocaust Tower," a giant, asymmetrical concrete room nearly devoid of light and sound encourages reflection. Exhibits feature works by contemporary artists, memorials to victims of the Holocaust, and a history of Jews in Germany. Enter at the top of the stairs from the Axis of Continuity. *(Lindenstr. 9-14. U6 to "Kochstr.," or U1, U6, or U15 to "Hallesches Tor." ☎ 308 78 56 81. Open daily 10am-8pm, M until 10pm. €5, students €2.50. Special exhibits €4.)*

DEUTSCHES TECHNIKMUSEUM. Sporting an airplane on the roof, this colossal museum includes aged trains, a history of film technology, and full-size model ships through which you can actually wander. Across the parking lot, another building features a collection of classic cars, music makers, a plethora of science experiments involving optical illusions, and—best of all—a revolving playhouse. The new aeronautical wing documents the history of flight and its displays range from life-size planes to a whole room full of engines. Some exhibits are in English. *(Trebbiner Str. 9. U1, U2, or U15 to "Gleisdreieck," or U1, U7, or U15 to "Möckernbrücke." ☎90 25 40; www.dtmb.de. Open Tu-F 9am-5:30pm, Sa-Su 10am-6pm. €4.50, students €2.50. Some special exhibits require extra fees. 1st Su of the mo. free.)*

MÄRKISCHES MUSEUM. Two millennia of Berlin artifacts are displayed in this museum, a towering brick building structured like a church. The museum contains a permanent exhibition entitled "Look at this city!" that traces the cultural history of Berlin from the Middle Ages to the present. *(Am Köllnischen Park 5. U2 to "Märkisches Museum." Take Wallstr. past Inselstr.; it's on the right. ☎30 86 60; www.stadtmuseum.de. Open Tu and Th-Su 10am-6pm, W noon-8pm. €4, students €2. W reduced fee .)*

SCHWULES MUSEUM (GAY MUSEUM). A series of exhibitions that shed light on the past and current lifestyles of gays and lesbians. A permanent exhibit traces the history of homosexuals in Germany from 1800 to 1970. A collection of homoerotic art captures society's changing attitude toward homosexuality over time. *(Mehringdamm 61. ☎69 59 90 50. Open Tu-F 2-6pm, Sa 2-7pm. €5, students €3.)*

▮ NIGHTLIFE

Although clubs are emerging throughout the rest of eastern Berlin (namely Friedrichshain) Kreuzberg is still a nightlife *Bezirk*, full of options for virtually every demographic. Although there is no shortage of bars, Oranienstr. and Schlesishes Str. have the densest and coolest stretches of nightlife offerings.

BARS AND CLUBS

▨ **Club der Visionaere,** Am Flutgraben 1 (☎695 18 944; www.clubdervisionaere.de). U1 or U15 to "Schlesisches Tor" or night bus #N65 to "Heckmannufer." From the multiple languages drifting through the air to the people settled on ground-cushions, Club der Visionaere has a decidedly backpacker vibe. Those looking for the best view of the water can take in the torch-light from a raft attached to the terrace or dance along as a DJ spins house inside. Beer €3. Open M-F 3pm-late, Sa-Su noon-late. Cash only.

▨ **Heinz Minki,** Vor dem Schlesischen Tor 3 (☎695 33 766; www.heinzminki.de). U1 or U15 to "Schlesisches Tor" or night bus #N65 to "Heckmannufer." A *biergarten* that, shockingly, is actually a garden. Plush drapery lines the small interior, but the real fun is to be had outside. Patrons pound their beers (0.5L, €3.10) at long tables under hanging colored lights and surrounded by greenery. Gourmet pizza €2.60. Open daily noon-late; check website for shorter winter hours. Cash only.

Ankerklause, Kottbusser Damm 104 (☎693 56 49; www.ankerlause.de). U1 or U8 or night bus #N8 to "Kottbusser Tor." Patrons spill out onto the curb or sip their beers in diner-style booths at this canal-side bar. Features an impressive jukebox collection of indie and classic rock. Terrace overlooking the water provides an alternative to the dancefloor. 0.5L Pilsner €3. Th parties €2 cover. Open daily 9am-late. Cash only.

Freischwimmer, vor dem Schlesischen Tor 2 (☎61 07 43 09; www.freischwimmer-berlin.de). U1 or 15 to "Schlesisches Tor," or night bus #N65 to "Heckmannufer." A mess of waterside tables tangled in roses—indoors or outdoors—and strewn with chubby sofas and tables on floating rafts. Seems to stretch out almost infinitely along the bank. Food until midnight, F-Sa until 1am. Su brunch (€8.20, 11am-4pm). Open M-F from noon, Sa-Su from 11am. Cash only.

Franken, Oranienstr. 19a (www.franken-bar.de). U1, 12, or 15 to "Görlitzer Bahnhof." Air-drumming bartenders dish out daily cocktail specials (small €2.60, large €4.10) at this local hangout. The bizarre blend of decorative flourishes, from a totem pole to punk-rock posters, and overflowing crowds keep the atmosphere scruffily vibrant. Occasional live music. Open daily from 8pm. Cash only.

Watergate, Falckensteinstr. 49 (☎61 28 03 94; www.water-gate.de). U1 or U15 to "Schlesisches Tor." One of the hippest clubs in Berlin, with 2fl., ceiling lights that double as video screens, and rotating DJs. The view of the Spree from the "Water Floor" lounge and terrace is unbeatable. Occasionally exclusive. Crowds pick up at 2am. Cover W €6, F-Sa €10. Open W and F 11pm-late and Sa midnight-late. Cash only.

Wild at Heart, Wiener Str. 20 (☎611 70 10; www.wildatheartberlin.de). U1, U12, or U15 to "Görlitzer Bahnhof." A red cave of decadence: shrines to Elvis, Chinese lanterns, fuzzy hearts, flaming booths, tiki torches, and glowing tigers. Pierced and punked clientele enjoy an impressive selection of whiskey (€4.70). Live bands usually 4 times per wk., almost always Sa and Su. Open daily from 8pm. Cash only.

Bateau Ivre, Oranienstr. 18 (☎61 40 36 59). U1, U12, or U15 to "Görlitzer Bahnhof." Locals relax over coffee or beer (from €2) at this bistro-bar before letting loose at neighboring clubs, making tables a hot commodity. In the morning, weary clubbers stagger in for breakfast after a long night (around €5). Open daily 9am-late. Cash only.

Junction Bar, Gneisenaustr. 18 (☎694 66 02; www.junction-bar.de). U7 to "Gneisenaustr.," or night bus #N4 or N19 to "Zossener Str." Small but energetic venue for American music, with nightly shows on an intimate subterranean stage. Take a break at **Junction Café** upstairs (open 11am-2am). Live rock, soul, funk, jazz, or blues M-Th and Su from 9pm, F-Sa 10pm. DJs start M-Th and Su 11:30pm, F-Sa 12:30am. Cover €5-6 for live music. Cover for DJs M-Th and Su €3, women free; F-Sa €4. Open daily 8pm-5am. Cash only.

Mas Y Mas, Oranienstr. 167 (☎61 65 81 78). U1, U12, or U15 to "Kottbusser Tor." Gold-striped walls, chandeliers, and sultry Latin music. Those who prefer conversation to chaos will enjoy the darkly elegant atmosphere. Fantastic drinks have names like "Income Tax" or "Wedding Bells" (€7). Mixed Drinks €4 at Happy hour (daily 6-9pm and 1-2am, and all day W). Open daily 5pm-late. Cash only.

GAY AND LESBIAN

Most bars and clubs are on and around Oranienstr. between Lausitzer Pl. and Oranienpl. Take U1, U8, U12, or U15 to "Kottbusser Tor" or U1, U12, or U15 to "Görlitzer Bahnhof." After hours, night bus #N29 runs the length of the strip.

▨ **Rose's,** Oranienstr. 187 (☎615 65 70). U1 to "Görlitzer Bahnhof." Marked only by "Bar" over the door. It's Liberace meets Cupid meets Satan. A friendly, mixed gay and lesbian clientele packs this intense and claustrophobic party spot all night. The voluptuous dark-red interior is accessorized madness, boasting hearts, glowing lips, furry ceilings, feathers, and glitter. Vodka tonics (€5) and attitude. Open daily 10pm-6am. Cash only.

SchwuZ, Mehringdamm 61 (☎62 90 880; www.schwuz.de). U6 or U7 to "Mehringdamm." Enter through **Sundström,** a popular gay and lesbian café. Features 2 dancefloors and a lounge area with its own DJ in an unground lair lined with pipes and disco lights. Music varies from alternative to house depending on the night (check *Siegessäule*), every 2nd F of the month is for lesbians. Frequented by a relatively young crowd. Cover €5 before midnight, €6 after. Open F-Sa from 11pm. Cash only.

Barbie Deinhoff's, Schlesisches Str. 18 (www.bader-deinhoff.de). U1 or U15 to "Schlesisches Tor," or night bus #N65 to "Heckmannufer." Catch a glimpse of the flashy pink interior through the crowds that pour out onto the sidewalk at the neighborhood lesbian bar. Inside, a friendly barstaff, a drink menu jokingly advertising phone sex, and rotating art exhibits. Shots €2-2.50. Open M-Th 6pm-2am, F-Sa 6pm-6am. Cash only.

OUTER DISTRICTS

Berlin's outer districts, primarily residential neighborhoods surrounded by greenery, provide a pleasant respite from the bustle of the metropolis. The vast **Treptow** park is a relaxing locale for summer lounging, Berlin goes to the beach at **Wannsee,** and **Oranienburg** contains the grim former **Sachsenhausen** concentration camp. **Dahlem's** suburban streets are home to affluent professionals, the sprawling **Freie Universität,** and one of Berlin's federal museum complexes. **Spandau** is one of the oldest parts of Berlin and in many ways remains a stubbornly independent city, with a lively pedestrian zone, stately archaic houses, and glitzy car dealerships. Neighboring **Steglitz** is remarkable only for its trendy shopping district (U9 to "Schloßstr.") and expansive botanical garden. All of these districts are 20-50min. by train from the heart of the city and make good daytrips.

ACCOMMODATIONS

TEGEL

Backpacker's Paradise, Ziekowstr. 161 (☎433 86 40; www.backpackersparadise.de). U6 to "Alt-Tegel," then bus #222 or night bus #N22 (dir.: Alt-Lübars) to "Titusweg." Or, take the S25 to "Tegel" and walk 20m right out of the station to catch the #222. Nightly campfires, hot showers, and a free-spirited vibe in a little yard behind the *Jugendgästehaus*. Space is nearly always available. The *Kantine* serves a breakfast buffet (€2.50) and cheap snacks. Free Internet access. Lockers €1. Laundry €4. Reception 24hr. Open June to Aug. €8 gets you a blanket and foam pad in a 20-person tent, €1.50 more provides a cot to put them on. Cash only. ❶

Jugendgästehaus Tegel, Ziekowstr. 161 (☎433 30 46; JGH-Tegel@t-online.de). A dignified red brick building with an institutional, boarding-school feel to it. Free Internet access. Breakfast and sheets included. Reception 7:30am-11pm. Singles €27; doubles to 8-bed dorms €19.90 per person. Under 27 only. Cash only. ❷

WANNSEE

Jugendgästehaus am Wannsee (HI), Badeweg 1 (☎803 20 34; www.jugendherberge.de). S1 or S7 to "Nikolassee." From the main exit, cross the bridge, continue through the park, and head left on Kronprinzessinweg; Badeweg will be on your right after 5min. Many German school groups frequent this pseudo-dorm with a lake view, 30min. from central Berlin. Breakfast and sheets included. Key deposit €10. Reservations recommended. €21, over 27 €24. AmEx/DC/MC/V. ❷

SIGHTS

For excursions to Potsdam, see **Brandenburg** (p. 154).

WANNSEE

Most Berliners think of the town of Wannsee, on a lake of the same name, as the beach. Wannsee has long stretches of sand along the Havel-Uferpromenade, and the roads behind the beaches are crowded with vacation villas. To reach the locally beloved baths, **Strandbad Wannsee,** take S1 or S7 to "Nikolassee," cross the bridge in front of the main exit, continue through the park, and follow the signs down the road. Getting to the beach along the Uferpromenade is more complicated: walk along Am Großen Wannsee to Haveleck. Or, take bus #218 from the Wannsee station to "Pfaueninsel," backtrack to Pfaueninsel-Chaussee, and take it to Uferpromenade, which will appear on your right. On summer weekends, a special bus shuttles bathers from the train station. The beach fills up absurdly early with German families; be prepared to battle the crowds for choice spots. Most of Wannsee's sights can be reached from the "Nikolassee" S-Bahn station. *(Baths open May-Aug. M-F 10am-7pm, Sa-Su 8am-8pm. €4, students €2.50.)*

BERLIN

PFAUENINSEL. The banks of Peacock Island (the second largest island in Berlin) served as the perfect setting for Friedrich Wilhelm II's "ruined" castle, where he and his mistress could romp for hours. Far more impressive than this underwhelming fortification, however, are the perfectly manicured orchards and trails that open out to views of the lake. A flock of the island's namesake fowl roams about the gardens. *(Take bus #218 from the S-Bahn station to "Pfaueninsel" and wait for the ferry. Castle open daily May-Aug. 8am-8pm; Apr. and Sept. 8am-6pm; Oct. 9am-5pm; Nov.-Feb. 10am-4pm. Castle admission €3, students €2.50. Castle by tour only, on the half hour.)*

HAUS DER WANNSEE-KONFERENZ. Wannsee's reputation is tarnished by the memory of the notorious **Wannsee Conference** on January 20, 1942. Leading officials of the SS completed the details for the implementation of the "Final Solution"—including the deportation and murder of all of Europe's Jews—in the **Wannsee Villa,** formerly a Gestapo intelligence center. In January 1992, the 50th anniversary of the Nazi death-pact, the villa reopened as a museum with permanent Holocaust exhibits and a documentary film series. The villa is incongruously lovely, and the exhibit is gripping. *(Am Großen Wannsee 56-58. Take bus #114 from the S-Bahn station to "Haus der Wannsee-Konferenz." ☎ 805 00 10. Open M-F 10am-8pm. Free.)*

GLIENICKER BRÜCKE. At the southwestern corner of the district, this bridge crosses the Havel River into Potsdam and the former DDR. Closed to traffic in Cold War days, it was the spot where East and West once exchanged captured spies. The most famous such incident traded American U2 pilot Gary Powers for Soviet spy Ivanovich Abel. For sights on the other side of the bridge, see p. 157. *(Bus #316 from the S-Bahn station (dir.: Glienicker Brücke-Potsdam) to the end.)*

WANNSEE CRUISES. Two ferry companies run boats from the Wannsee waterfront behind the park. Boats set sail once or twice an hour, though the ferries' leisurely pace means that they're meant more as pleasure cruises than efficient transportation. *(Head left on Kronprinzessinweg from S-Bahn station "Wannsee" and go down the stairs on the right. Call Stern und Kreis at ☎ 803 87 50 or Reederverband at ☎ 803 87 53 for details. Most cruises €8-13.)*

TREPTOW

SOWJETISCHES EHRENMAL. This powerful Soviet War Memorial is a mammoth promenade built with marble taken from Hitler's Chancellery. The Soviets dedicated the site in 1948, honoring the millions of Red Army soldiers who fell in what Russians call the "Great Patriotic War." Massive granite slabs along the walk are adorned with quotations from Stalin and depictions of terrifying war scenes, while the colossal bronze figure at the head of the promenade symbolically crushes Nazism underfoot. Even the trees are designed to bow toward this gargantuan stoic soldier; the total effect is a little grandiose, but manages to convey a sense of the power the Soviet Union once held in the city. Buried beneath the trees surrounding the monument are the bodies of 5000 unknown Soviet soldiers who died in the Battle of Berlin in 1945. *(S4, S6, S8, S9, or S85 to "Treptower Park." Turn left on Puschkinalle and follow the signs; it's about 900m down.)*

TREPTOWER PARK. On the banks of the Spree, this relaxed stretch of green contains more than just the Soviet Memorial. **Stern und Kreis,** which runs ferry tours along the river, is based here, as are several shops and waterfront cafés. Berliners come to the park to picnic, throw boomerangs, or stretch out semi-nude on the grassy expanse. Also in the park is the **Figurentheater,** where wooden puppets perform a variety of *Märchen* (fairy tales). Follow the yellow signs. *(Puschkinallee 16a. ☎ 53 69 51 50. Performances €4.30–9.)*

ORANIENBURG AND SACHSENHAUSEN

KZ SACHSENHAUSEN. The small town of Oranienburg, just north of Berlin, was home to the Nazi concentration camp Sachsenhausen, where more than 100,000 Jews, communists, intellectuals, gypsies, and homosexuals were killed between 1936 and 1945. The **Gedenkstätte Sachsenhausen,** a memorial preserving the remains of the camp and recalling those imprisoned in it, was opened by the DDR in 1961. Some of the buildings have been preserved in their original forms, including sets of cramped barracks, the cell block where particularly "dangerous" prisoners were kept in solitary confinement and tortured daily, and a pathology department where Nazis performed medical experiments on inmates both dead and alive. However, only the foundations of **Station Z** (where prisoners were methodically exterminated) remain. A stone monolith commemorating the camp's victims stands sentinel over the wind-swept grounds and several small museums. **Barracks 38 and 39,** the special "Jewish-only" barracks torched by neo-Nazis in 1992 and since reconstructed, feature displays on daily life in the camp during the Nazi period. The jail block contains a **museum** that will re-open in late 2007. The museum buildings and industrial yard contain broader exhibits on the history of Sachsenhausen, both as a concentration camp and a memorial site. A DDR slant is still apparent; the main museum building features Socialist Realist stained-glass windows memorializing "German Anti-Fascist Martyrs." Even more than the exhibits, the blunt gray buildings, barbed-wire fencing, and vast, bleak spaces express the camp's brutality and despair. *(Str. der Nationen 22. S1 (dir.: Oranienburg) to the end (40min.). Then either use the infrequent bus service on lines #804 and 821 to "Gedenkstätte" or take a 20min. walk from the station. Follow the signs from Straslsunderstr., turn right on Bernauer Str., left on Str. der Einheit, and right on Str. der Nationen. ☎ 03301 20 00; www.gedenkstaette-sachsenhausen.de. Open daily Mar. 15-Oct. 14 8:30am-6pm; Oct. 15-Mar. 14 8:30am-4:30pm. Last entry 30min. before closing. Museums closed M. Free. Audio guide €3.)*

SPANDAU

ZITADELLE. Rising sternly from the water, this Renaissance citadel is accessible only by a single stone bridge and was considered impregnable in the 16th and 17th centuries. During WWII, the Nazis used the fort as a chemical weapons lab, and in 1945 the Allies employed the Zitadelle as a prison to hold war criminals before the Nuremberg Trials. Nowadays the citadel is a sort of wistful ghost town filled with old field-cannons, statues, a **medieval history museum,** and a variety of art galleries. The solid brick facade is overgrown with ivy, and the ramparts are carpeted in fields of grass. The thickly fortified **Juliusturm** (Julius Tower), dating c. 1200, is Spandau's unofficial symbol. *(Am Juliusturm. Take U7 to "Zitadelle" and follow the signs. ☎ 354 94 42 00. Open Tu-F 9am-5pm, Sa-Su 10am-5pm. Last entry 30min. before closing. Museum and tower €2.50, students €1.50.)*

STEGLITZ

BOTANISCHER GARTEN. The Botanischer Garten is one of the best botanical gardens in the world, featuring everything from orderly English gardens and Japanese koi ponds to vast greenhouses (lush even in winter). The seemingly endless pathways provide an escapist retreat from the hectic pace of city life. *(Königin-Luise-Str. 6. S1 to "Botanischer Garten." Follow the signs from the S-Bahn station; entrance on Unter den Eichen. ☎ 83 85 01 00. Open daily May-July 9am-9pm; Apr. and Aug. 9am-8pm; Sept. 9am-7pm; Mar. and Oct. 9am-6pm; Feb. 9am-5pm; Nov.-Jan. 9am-4pm; Last entry 30min. before closing. €5, students €2.50; 2hr. before closing €2/1.)*

BERLIN

🏛 MUSEUMS

SMB-PK DAHLEM

The **Museen Dahlem** consists of three museums, all housed in one building in the center of Dahlem's Freie Universität. The **Museum Europäischer Kulturen,** also part of the complex, is located a couple of blocks away. One ticket (€6, students €3) provides access to all three, which are also free on Thursdays 4hr. before closing.

■ **ETHNOLOGISCHES MUSEUM (MUSEUM OF ETHNOLOGY).** The Ethnology Museum dominates the main building and richly rewards a trek to Dahlem. The exhibits are stunning, ranging from huge pieces of ancient Central American stonework to African elephant tusk statuettes. Most surprising are the enormous, authentic boats from the South Pacific and model huts that you can actually enter. While smaller, the **Museum für Indisches Kunst** (Museum for Indian Art), housed in the same building, is no less fascinating, featuring ornate gilded shrines and brightly painted murals. The **Museum für Ostasiatisches Kunst** (Museum for East Asian Art) also has a noteable collection, including many fanciful tapestries. *(U1 to "Dahlem-Dorf" and follow the "Museen" signs to get to the main building. ☎830 14 38. Open Tu-F 10am-6pm, Sa-Su 11am-6pm. Th free 4hr. before closing.)*

MUSEUM EUROPÄISCHER KULTUREN (MUSEUM OF EUROPEAN CULTURES).

This museum complex holds the permanent exhibit "Cultural Contacts in Europe," which uses pictures to show how European cultures developed through communication with each other. *(From the main building, turn right out the front door onto Lansstr. Turn left onto Takustr., right onto Königin-Luise-Str., and left onto Im Winkel. The museum is on the left where the road forks. Also accessible from within the Ethnologisches Museum. ☎83 90 12 87. Open Tu–F 10am-6pm, Sa-Su 11am-6pm.)*

🔊 NIGHTLIFE

TREPTOW

 Insel, Alt-Treptow 6 (☎533 71 69; www.insel-berlin.net). S6, S8, S9, S41 of S42, to "Treptower Park," then bus #265 or N65 from Puschkinallee to "Rathaus Treptow." Enter through the park at the corner of Alt-Treptow. The club, located on an island in the Spree River, is a tower of 3 stories crammed with gyrating bodies, multiple bars, riverside beach chairs, an open-air movie theater, and a café with hammocks. Club cover W free, Th-Sa €4-6. Club open W from 7pm, F-Sa from 10 or 11pm; time varies, check the website. Café open Sa-Su from 2pm. Movies M-Tu, Th, Su; €8. Cash only.

BRANDENBURG

Completely surrounding Berlin, the *Land* of Brandenburg is a perfect
escape from the sprawling urban behemoth resting at its center. The
infamous Hohenzollern family emerged from the province's forests to
become the rulers of Prussia, leaving their mark on the region in the
shape of more than 30 stunning palaces. The castles attract their share
of visitors to Brandenburg, especially the sprawling **Sanssouci,** at only
a 30min. train trip away, a favorite jaunt for native Berliners.

HIGHLIGHTS OF BRANDENBURG

RINSE AWAY the (figurative) grit of Berlin with a visit to the refreshingly lavish **Park
Sanssouci** (p. 156) in regal **Potsdam** (p. 154).

LOUNGE IN A GONDOLA on the winding canals near tiny **Lübbenau** (p. 160), under
the trees and among the ghosts of the swampy **Spreewald** (p. 160).

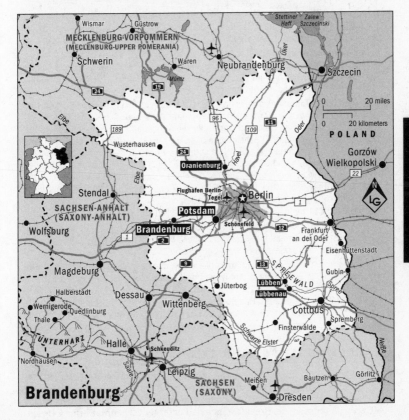

POTSDAM
☎ **0331**

Visitors disappointed by Berlin's distinctly unroyal demeanor can get their Kaiserly fix by taking the S-Bahn to Potsdam (pop. 146,000), the glittering city of Friedrich II (the Great). While his father, Friedrich Wilhelm I (the "Soldier King"), wanted to turn Potsdam into a huge garrison of the tall, tall men he had kidnapped to serve as his toy soldiers, the more aesthetically minded Friedrich II beautified the city. His additions include Schloß Sanssouci and the surrounding park, and the nearby Neues Garten with its Marmorpalais. Potsdam was Germany's "Little Hollywood" in the 1920s and 30s, when the suburb of Babelsberg played a critical role in the early film industry. A 20-minute air raid in April 1945 brought Potsdam's glory days to an end. As the site of the 1945 Potsdam Conference, in which the Allies divvied up the country, Potsdam's name became synonymous with German defeat. After hosting Communist Party fat cats for 45 years, the 1000-year-old city gained independence from Berlin in 1991, recovering its eminent status as capital of the *Land*. Much of the residential city has been renovated to create long boulevards adorned with gateways and historic buildings. Today, the city moves at a leisurely pace, its palaces and avenues swelling with curious visitors.

⊏▐ ⁊ TRANSPORTATION AND PRACTICAL INFORMATION

Trains: S7 runs to Potsdam's Hauptbahnhof, as does the RE1 from Berlin's Friedrichstr., Alexanderpl., and other major stations (40min. or 25min., €2.60). Trains every hr. to: **Dessau** (1½hr., €24.90); **Leipzig** (2½hr., €36.50); **Magdeburg** (1½hr., €26.40).

Public Transportation: Potsdam is in Zone C of Berlin's BVG transit network. It is also divided into its own subdivisions of A, B, and C; special Potsdam-only tickets can be purchased on any bus or tram (€1.10, valid 1hr.; all-day €3.60). The **Berlin Welcome Card** (€22) is also valid in Potsdam.

Bike Rental and Tours: Potsdam is best seen by bike, and bike rental places often map out the best way to see all the sights. ▉**Potsdam Per Pedales,** (☎0331 748 00 57; www.pedales.de) rents them out from their main location at Rudolf-Breitscheid-Str. 201, in the "Griebnitzsee" S-Bahn station or on the S-Bahn platform at Potsdam Hauptbahnhof. From the former, pay to take your bike on the S-Bahn (special bike pass €1.20 at any BVG ticket office). Bike tours in English (reserve ahead) and German (€10, students €8; bike rental €8; €6 audio guide.) **Canoe** and **kayak** rental €28 per day. Open daily Easter-Apr. M-F 9am-6:30pm, Sa-Su 9am-7pm. **Cityrad** rents bikes right across from the Hauptbahnhof (Babelsbergerstr. exit). (☎0177 82 54 746 0331 27 06 210. €11 per day. Open M-F 9am-7pm, Sa-Su 9am-8pm).

Tourist Office: Brandenburger Str. 3 (☎505 88 38) by Brandenburg Gate. The office sells cheap city maps and books rooms (from €15). Open Apr.-Oct. M-F 9am-6pm, Sa-Su 9:30am-4pm; Nov.-Mar. M-F 10am-6pm, Sa-Su 10am-2pm.

Tours: The tourist office runs 3½hr. tours of the city, inquire at the office. **Original Berlin Walks** has 5-6hr. walking tours that leave from the taxi stand outside Berlin's Bahnhof Zoo May-Sept. Su 9:45am. €15, students €11.20. **Bus tours** leave from the Filmmuseum, Breitestr. 1a, and the Hauptbahnhof Tu-Su at 11am. €14, students €11; with admission to Sanssouci €16. Other tours (€8) have narrower themes.

Post Office: Pl. der Einheit. Open M-F 9am-6:30pm, Sa 9am-1pm. **Postal Code:** 14476.

█ ACCOMMODATIONS AND CAMPING

Potsdam has limited budget accommodations. **Jugendherberge Potsdam (HI) ❷,** Schulstr. 9, located in Babelsberg, is a hostel one S-Bahn stop from the Potsdam Hauptbahnhof. Head left out of the S-Bahn station and take the first left. (☎030 264 9520; www.jh-potsdam.de. Breakfast included. Internet €2 per hr. Dorms €15; sin-

BRANDENBURG

Potsdam

🍴 FOOD & DRINK
Kashmir Haus, **1**
Slam, **2**

TO SCHLOSS
CECILIENHOF
(800m)

Marmorpalais

Neuer Garten

Heiliger See

Am Neuen Garten

TO SCHLOßPARK GLIENICKE,
GLIENICKER BRÜCKE (1km)

HOLLÄNDISCHES
VIERTEL

Französische
Kirche

Babelsberger Str.

Cityrad

Potsdam
Hauptbahnhof

TO KAPELLE
ALEXANDER
NEWSKI (300m)

Hebbelstr.

Kurfürstenstr.

BASSIN-
PLATZ

Französische Str.

Altes
Rathaus

Obelisk

Puschkinallee

Russische
Kolonie

Am Schragen

Friedrich-Ebert-Str.

Neuener
Tor

Jägerstr.

Kirche St.
Peter und Paul

Am Bassin

Am Kanal

Am Alten Markt

Lange Brücke

Nikolaikirche

Filmmuseum

Schloßstr.

PLATZ DER
NEUEN EINHEIT
AM NEUEN
MARKT

TO WISSENSCHAFTPARK
ALBERT EINSTEIN (1km)

Jägerallee

Yorckstr.

Dortustr.

Breite Str.

Jägertor

Hegelallee

Guttenbergstr.

Gutenbergstr.

Brandenburger Str.

Charlottenstr.

Lindenstr.

Neustädter
Havelbucht

Triumphtor

Obeliskportal

Brandenburger
Tor

Schopenhauerstr.

LUISEN-
PLATZ

Friedenskirche

Allee Nach Sanssouci

Dampfmaschinen-
haus

Pappelallee

Gregor-Mendel-Str.

Ruinenbergstr.

Voltaireweg

Bildergalerie

Neptur-
grotte

Schloß
Sanssouci

Zur Historische Mühle

Neue
Kammern

Sizilianischer
Garten

Nordischer
Garten

Mahlgarten

Am Grünen

Lennéstr.

Feuerbachstr.

Zeppelinstr.

Große
Fontäne

Rosengarten

BRANDENBURGER
VORSTADT

Bornstedter Str.

N

400 yards
400 meters

An der Orangerie

Orangerie

Botanischer
Garten

Hauptallee

Chinesisches
Teehaus

Ökonomieweg

Maschinen-
teich

Maschinen-
teich

Maulbeerallee

Park
Sanssouci

Römische
Bäder

Schloß
Charlottenhof

Geschwister-Scholl-Str.

Eichenallee

Drachenhaus

Antikentempel

Freundschafts-
tempel

Hippodrom

Lindenavenue

Fasanerie

Lindstedter Weg

Neues
Palais

Am Neuen Palais

Bahnhof
Park Sanssouci

Almundstr.

Ribbeckstr.

gles €21, over 27 €24; doubles €34. In winter all rooms €15 per person. Cash only.) Another option is in **Wannsee** (p. 149), 10min. away by S-Bahn. The hostels in central Berlin are also a short train ride away. Hotels are scarce, but the tourist office finds private rooms and has a list of campgrounds in the area. **Campingplatz Sanssouci-Gaisberg ❶**, An der Pirschheide 41, is on the scenic banks of the Templiner See. Take regional train #94 or 95 to "Bahnhof Pirschheide" and call to get a ride over. (☎951 09 88. Phone reception 8am-1pm and 3-8pm. Wash €3.50. Dry €3.50. €8.20 per person, €1 per child.)

⬛ FOOD

Bright, renovated **Brandenburger Str.**, the local pedestrian zone, encompasses many of the city's restaurants, fast-food stands, and markets. The dozens of cafés near Brandenburger Tor are lovely but pricey, as are parts of Friedrich-Ebert-Str. and the **Holländisches Viertel** (see **Sights,** p. 156), lined with chic cafés. Head to the **flea market** on Bassinpl. for fresh produce. (Open M-F 9am-6pm.) In the Hauptbahnhof is a massive **Kaufland** grocery store. (Open daily 6am-8pm.) **Siam ❷**, Friedrich-Ebert-Str. 13, prepares tasty Thai food (€5-8) right before your eyes in a bamboo-heavy interior. (☎200 92 92. Open daily noon-11pm. Cash only.) Away from the touristed bustle of Brandenburgerstr., **Kashmir Haus ❸**, Jägerstr. 1, offers Indian food in a trapestry-draped setting. The weekday lunch special (from €4, 11am-4pm) is an unbeatable deal. (☎870 95 80. Open daily 11am-11pm. Cash only.)

◉ SIGHTS

A good investment for sightseeing is a **day ticket** (€15, students €10, families €25.50), valid and available at all castles in Potsdam with the exception of Sanssouci, which requires separate admission.

PARK AND SCHLOß SANSSOUCI

◧**PARK SANSSOUCI.** Schloß Sanssouci's 600-acre "backyard," a testament to the size of Friedrich II's treasury and the diversity of his aesthetic tastes, has two distinct areas to explore. Half of the park is done in Baroque style—straight paths intersecting at topiaries and statues of nude nymphs arranged in geometrically pleasing patterns—and the other half is in the rambling, rolling style of English landscape gardens. The sheer magnitude of the park—encompassing wheat fields, rose trellises, and lush, immaculate gardens—makes it a compelling place to spend an afternoon. For information on the park's many attractions, from Rococo sculptures to beautiful fountains, head to the visitors center next to the windmill behind the *Schloß*. (☎969 42 00. Open daily Mar.-Oct. 8am-10pm; Nov.-Feb. 9am-8pm.)

SCHLOß SANSSOUCI. The park's main attraction, the Versailles-esque *Schloß*, sits atop a landscaped hill. Designed by **Georg Wenzeslaus von Knobelsdorff** in 1747, the yellow palace is small and airy, adorned with rich depictions of Dionysus and other Greek gods. Tours of the castle in German leave every 20min.; the final tour (5pm) usually sells out by 2pm during the high season. An English-language tour, led by the tourist office, includes only the main *Schloß*. Inside the castle, the style is cloud-like French Rococo—all pinks and greens with gaudy gold trim. Friedrich, an unrepentant Francophile until his death, built the exotic **Voltairezimmer** (Voltaire Room), decorated with carved reliefs of parrots and tropical fruit, in honor of Voltaire, though the writer never stayed here. The library reveals another of Friedrich's eccentricities: whenever he wanted to read a book, he had a copy printed for each of his palaces—*en français*, of course. Friedrich's remains, which were spirited away to a salt mine near Tübingen in 1945 to save them from the Red Army, were returned to the grounds in 1991, and now lie under six plain flagstones (although, to be technical, five of the six are for each of his favorite dogs) next to the *Schloß*. Behind the place, the extensive, multi-tiered grounds culminate in an elegant fountain. *(Bus #695 to "Schloß Sanssouci." ☎ 969 41 90. Open Tu-Su Apr.-Oct. 9am-5pm; Nov.-Mar. 9am-4pm. Mandatory tours €8, students €5.)*

NEUES PALAIS. At the opposite end of the park, the New Palace is the largest and latest of the park's four castles. Commissioned by Friedrich the Great to emphasize Prussia's power after the Seven Years' War, this 200-room ornate pink *Schloß* features royal apartments, festival halls, and the impressive **Grottensaal**, whose shimmering walls are literally coated with seashells. *(☎ 969 42 55. Open Apr.-Oct. M-Th and Sa-Su 9am-5pm; Nov.-Mar. Sa-Th 9am-4pm. €5, students €4. Tours €1 extra in summer.)*

OTHER BUILDINGS IN THE PARK. Next to the Schloß Sanssouci is the **Bildergalerie** (Picture Gallery), whose collection of Caravaggio, van Dyck, and Reubens crams a long hall of massive and elaborate canvases. *(☎ 969 41 81. Open mid-May to mid-Oct. Tu-Su 10am-5pm. €2, students €1.50. Tour €1.)* On the other side of *Schloß* lies the **Neue Kammern** (New Chambers), a former guest house and recital hall. The ball and festival rooms are lavishly decorated; check out the Hohenzollern porcelain in a gold-trimmed closet room. *(Open mid-May to mid-Oct. Tu-Su 10am-5pm; Apr. to mid-May Sa-Su 10am-5pm. €2, students €1.50. Tour €1.)* The stunning **Sizilianischer Garten** (Sicilian Garden) is next door. Overlooking the park from the north, the pseudo-Italian **Orangerie** is famous for its 67 dubious Raphael imitations that replace originals swiped by Napoleon. *(Open mid-May to mid-Oct. Tu-Su 10am-12:30pm and 1-5pm. Mandatory tours €3, students €2.50. Tower only €2.)* Romantic **Schloß Charlottenhof,** whose park surroundings were a Christmas gift from Friedrich Wilhelm III to his son Friedrich Wilhelm IV, melts into landscaped gardens and grape arbors to the south. *(Open mid-May to mid-Oct. daily 10am-5pm.)* Nearby are the **Römische Bäder** (Roman baths), alongside a reedy pond with a miniature bridge. Meant to provide a contrast to the Italian villas, the gold-plated **Chinesisches Teehaus** stands complete with a parasol-wielding rooftop Buddha and 18th-century *chinois* porcelain inside. *(Open mid-May to mid-Oct. Tu-Su 10am-5pm. €1)* The plainer, almost industrial-looking **Friedenskirche** at the east entrance of the park contains the graves of Friedrich Wilhelm IV and his wife Elizabeth below glittering mosaics.

OTHER SIGHTS

NEUER GARTEN. Running alongside the Heiliger See, Potsdam's second park contains several royal residences. **Schloß Cecilienhof,** built in the image of an English Tudor manor, houses exhibits on the **Potsdam Treaty,** signed at the palace in 1945. Visitors can see numerous Potsdam Conference items, including the table at which the Big Three bargained over Europe's fate, and can stand in the very room Stalin used as his study. *(☎ 969 42 44. Open Tu-Su Apr.-Oct. 9am-5pm; Nov.-Mar. 9am-4pm. €4, students €3. Tours in summer €1.)* The garden also contains the **Marmorpalais** (Marble Palace), the marble-intensive palace that Friedrich II commissioned in 1786 as the centerpiece of the park. Many odd little buildings are scattered throughout the grounds, including a replica of an Egyptian pyramid formerly used for food storage. *(Take bus #692 to "Schloß Cecilienhof." Marmorpalais open Apr.-Oct. Tu-Su 10am-5pm; Nov.-Mar. Sa-Su 10am-4pm. €4, students €3. Tour extra €1 in summer.)* At the far end of the park, beachgoers bare all by the lake. Another palace-park, **Schloßpark Glienicke** contains a casino as well as its namesake, **Schloß Glienicke,** a mediocre yellow-green affair built by Karl Friedrich Schinkel in 1828 for Prince Karl of Prussia. The nearby **Mauerweg** (Wall Path) follows the 160km route along which the Wall separated West Berlin from the surrounding DDR territory. *(Take tram #93*

BRANDENBURG

to "Glienicker Brücke" and continue along Berliner Str. to the bridge; the castle is just on the other side to the left. Open mid-May to mid-Oct. Sa-Su 10am-5pm.) A walk back on Berliner Str. leads to the **Glienicker Brücke** (a.k.a. "The James Bond Bridge"), which was swallowed up by the death strip between the DDR and West Berlin. Closed to traffic until 1989, it was instead used for the exchange of spies, and was known rather ironically as the "Bridge of Unity." It can also be reached from Wannsee (p. 149). Across the water you can see **Schloß Babelsberg** and the **Maschinenhaus,** and on the other side is the more distant **Heilandskirche.**

RUSSISCHE KOLONIE. In the beginning of the 19th century, General Yorck brought 500 Russian soldiers to Prussia, and Friedrich Wilhelm III, a great fan of Russian culture and handsome soldiers, discovered that many of them had singing talent. Unfortunately, only 12 of the original group were left by the 1820s. To mitigate the depressing atmosphere, Friedrich III built each soldier a small, shingled wooden house trimmed with ornate carvings. The nearby pink, onion-domed **Kapelle Alexander Newski,** designed by Schinkel, was also intended as compensation. *(Tram #90, 92, or 95 to "Puschkinalle;" follow the street north.)*

FILMMUSEUM. Housed in an old orangerie that once held Friedrich's stables, this museum documents Potsdam's days as a film mecca, with artifacts like Marlene Dietrich's costumes, as well as a silent film archive and a small **movie theater.** *(On the corner of Breite Str. and Schloßstr. ☎ 271 81 12; www.filmmuseum-potsdam.de. Open daily 10am-6pm. €4, students €2.50. Movies from 6pm. Theater open daily noon-1am. €4.50, students €3.50. €3 during "blue hour" W-Su beginning at 5pm.)*

HOLLÄNDISCHES VIERTEL. Friedrich's attempt to import Dutch craftsmen to beautify the city produced the Dutch Quarter, which lies in the center of the town around Friedrich-Ebert-Str. Though it fell into disrepair during the mid-20th century, the neighborhood was revitalized when entrepreneurs converted the beautiful old buildings into a row of shops and restaurants in 1990.

NIKOLAIKIRCHE. Toward the waterfront, the impressive dome of the Nikolaikirche rises above its neighbors. On closer inspection, the dome and the granite cube it sits on don't seem to match. While the topping is light and spacious, the interior was renovated à la DDR with glass and sound-tiles that somehow dampen the aesthetic impact. In front stands an **obelisk** decorated with sphinxes and ram skulls, dedicated to Schinkel. *(Am Alten Markt. ☎ 270 86 02. Open daily 10am-7pm. Vesper music Su 10pm.)*

FILMPARK BABELSBERG. Back in the Golden Age of European cinema, the **UFA-Fabrik** in Babelsberg was *the* German studio, giving Marlene Dietrich, Hans Albers, and Leni Riefenstahl their first big breaks. Fritz Lang also made *Metropolis* here. That said, this amusement park has little to do with film, and little beyond the lunch-counter *Wurst* is particularly German. Still, the park is fun and very family-conscious, with rides and huge walk-through exhibits geared toward children. *(August-Bebel-Str. 26-53. Take S7 to "Babelsberg," then bus #690 to "Filmpark" or take bus #601 or 690 to the same stop from Potsdam Hauptbahnhof. ☎ 721 27 50; www.filmpark.de. Open Apr.-Oct. daily 10am-6pm, last entry 5pm. €17, students €15.50.)*

BRANDENBURG AN DER HAVEL   ☎ 03381

When Albert "the Bear" chose Brandenburg (pop. 74,000) "on the Havel" for the site of his cathedral in 1165, the small, unpretentious town had to deal with sudden prominence, reluctantly growing to assume a central political role in the region. In the end, Brandenburg's slow pace triumphed over the commercial demands imposed by its key river-side location. These days, the town has reclaimed its more peaceful past, cultivating an atmosphere light-years away from its urbane neighbor as residents spend their time fishing by the Havel or strolling the Altstadt's cobblestone streets. The province's namesake moves at a leisurely gait and invites you to do the same along its scenic waterways.

🖂🚆 TRANSPORTATION AND PRACTICAL INFORMATION. Brandenburg is on the Magdeburg-Berlin regional express line, the RE1, with frequent **Trains** to Berlin (45min., €6) and Magdeburg (1hr., €13.40). Visitors from Berlin should consider buying a day ticket valid on all Berlin and Brandenburg public transportation (€11.40), or the **Brandenburg Ticket** (for up to 5 people, €24). The **tourist office,** Steinstr. 66/67, is at the tram stop "Neustädtischer Markt." From the station, cross Am Hauptbahnhof, walk along Große Gartenstr., and follow it right onto Jakobstr., which becomes Steinstr. The staff books rooms for free, distributes English maps and brochures, and runs **walking tours** (1hr., May-Sept. Sa-Su at 11am, €3) and **boat tours,** which leave several times per day from near the Jahrtausendbrücke at the end of Hauptstr. (☎208 769; www.stadt-brandenburg.de. Boat tours €5-6. Open May-Sept. M-F 10am-7pm, Sa-Su 9am-3pm; Oct.-Apr. Sa 10am-2pm.) The Steinstr. and Neustädtischer Market areas are the town's main thoroughfare, while Hauptstr. offers more commercial shopping and chain stores.

🛏🍴 ACCOMMODATIONS AND FOOD. There's no youth hostel in Brandenburg, but private rooms are abundant and cheap—ask at the tourist office for a brochure or look for *Zimmer frei* signs. Hidden behind a café directly on Steinstr. is the **Pension Blaudruck ❷**, Steinstr. 21, with six small, charming rooms adorned with paintings and stray ivy creeping in from the window. The proprietors dress in blue and the courtyard is full of hanging chickens and laundry. Enter through the passage into the courtyard at #21. (☎22 57 34; www.blaudruck-designe.de. Reserve ahead. Singles €20; doubles €40, suites €50, extra beds €5. Cash only.) By a quiet canal between the Altstadt and train station, **Pension "Haus am Jungfernsteig" ❸**, Kirchhofstr. 9/Jungfernsteig 6a, run by a kindly violinist couple, has spacious rooms with TV, skylights, and shared bathrooms. (☎20 15 11; www.pensionhaus-am-jungfernsteig.de. Breakfast included. Singles €26; doubles €47; triples €64.50. AmEx/MC/V.) **Seecamp Malge ❶**, in the woods 20min. from the city center, has about 40 tent sites and provides instant access to the beach. Take Bus B from Große Gartenstr. to "Malge" (check the schedule to make sure it goes all the way there; it's the last stop), cross the train tracks, and bear left heading into the park, past the restaurant stands, to find the campground. By bike, take Steinstr. southwest out of the city, follow it straight when the main road branches off, and look for signs to turn right for Malge. (☎66 31 34. Reception 9am-1pm and 3-5pm. Open Apr.-Oct. €5 per person, €4-8 per tent. Cash only.)

The main café and *Imbiß* (snack bar) scenes are on **Steinstr.** and perpendicular to **Hauptstr.**, which also features an open-air **farmer's market** behind the Katharinenkirche. Along Mühlendamm, dockside cafés and snack stands let you sample the region's fresh-caught fish. (Open M-F 7am-5pm, Sa 7am-noon.) **Nummer 31 ❷**, Steinstr. 31, offers gourmet pizzas in a traditional German setting for €3-5. (☎22 44 73; www.nommer31.de. Open M-Sa from 11am, Su from 5pm. Cash only.) The **Kartoffelkäfer ❷**, Steinstr. 56, serves tasty meals based on every possible variation of the potato. The outdoor café is a short walk from Neustädtischerer Markt. (☎22 88 04. Entrées €5-9. Open daily 11am-midnight.)

◪ SIGHTS. Brandenburg's sights can be found along Steinstr. and its extension. Begin your tour of the **Neustadt** at the end of Steinstr. with the 14th-century **Steintorturm** (Stone Gate Tower), which holds a maritime history museum with displays on each level of the tower. Brave the steep, narrow spiral staircase for a view of the Havel and pedestrian Brandenburg. (☎20 02 65. Tower open Tu-F 9am-5pm

BRANDENBURG

and Sa-Su 10am-5pm. €3, students €1, families €5.) Work your way up the street to the cluttered, rooms of DDR paraphenalia the **nOstalgie-Museum,** Steinstr. 52. (☎22 06 20. Open Tu-Su 10am-noon and 1-6pm. €1.50.) The 14th-century **St. Katharinenkirche,** on the corner of Neustädter Markt, is a beautiful example of North-German *Backstein* (glazed brick) Gothic, now pockmarked by war damage. (Open M-Sa 10am-4pm, Su 1-4pm.) Walking through Molkenmarkt, across the river and along St. Petri will bring you to the famed **Dom St. Peter und Paul,** Burghof 11, a cathedral currently housing a rotating exhibition. Artwork is placed in the aisles with surprising abandon. The church is also adorned with its own art; architect **Friedrich Schinkel** couldn't resist adding a few touches like the "Schinkel-Rosette" and the window over the entrance. The **Dommuseum** inside displays an array of old clothing, local-history treasures, and medieval books. (☎211 22 21. Open M-Tu and Th-Sa, Sa 10am-5pm, W 10am-noon, Su 11am-5pm. €3, students €2.) Across the street, the **Petrikapelle** has gone from church to contemporary art gallery. (☎20 03 25. Open M-Tu and Th-F 10am-4pm, W 10am-noon, Sa 10am-5pm, Su 11am-5pm.)

For those with time to spare, Brandenburg's Altstadt, across the Havel, has even more centuries-old buildings (including towers from the 12th-century walls), fewer glossy storefronts, and a quieter, more reserved feel. From St. Katharinenkirche, head down Hauptstr. across the river. For 500 years, a 6m statue of the epic hero Roland has stood here in front of the Rathaus. Farther afield, the modern and comically phallic Friedenswarte tower, on the Marienberg, directly uphill from Am Marienberg, provides a great view of the contrasting antiquity surrounding it. (Open Apr.-Oct. Tu-Su 10am-5pm. €2, students €1.)

SPREEWALD (SPREE FOREST)

The Spree River splits apart 100km southeast of Berlin and branches out over the countryside in an intricate maze of streams, canals, meadows, and primeval forests stretching over 1000sq. km. The Spree Forest's tiny villages were first settled in the Middle Ages, and the folklore is an especially rich tradition. The **Sorbs,** Germany's native Slavic minority, originally settled the region and continue to influence its cultural identity (**The Absorbing Sorbs,** p. 620).

This popular vacation spot for Berliners is known for its ubiquitous canals, earning the region the title "Venice of the North." Farmers row to their fields and children paddle home from school. The fields and forests teem with owls, otter, deer, and foxes, ensuring that even a fleeting walk through the woods remains interesting and strikingly idyllic. Because the forest is now recognized as a *Biosphärreservat* (a biosphere nature reserve) by the UN, some sections are off-limits to the public; other sections are closed during mating and breeding seasons but not tourist season. Camping spots abound, bicycles can be rented everywhere, and excellent hiking trails and footpaths weave through the peaceful forest. Each local tourist office has information on leisure activities and advice on how to be environmentally responsible in protected areas.

Lübben and Lübbenau, two tiny towns that open into labyrinths of canals, are popular destinations that lie within daytrip-range of Berlin, while nearby Cottbus is the area's largest transporation hub. The forest is divided into two sections: the Unterspreewald, has extensive bike paths, while the Oberspreewald, surrounding Lübben and Lübbenau, is a web of rivers and canals best explored by boat.

LÜBBENAU ☎03542

Tiny Lübbenau (pop. 7000) is the most famous of the Spreewald towns and deservedly so—its interwoven canals and roads seem worlds away from the modernizing cities around it. For tourists, the village serves as a springboard for trips into the kingdom of the *Irrlichter* (will o' the wisp). The landscape here is dense with waterways, and has more gondolas than houses. Buried in the forest, the neighboring village **Lehde** has tiny houses with straw roofs and a museum that recreates life as it once was for the Spreewald Sorbs.

TRANSPORTATION AND PRACTICAL INFORMATION. Trains go to: **Berlin** (1¼hr., 2 per hr., €9.60); **Cottbus** (25min., every hr., €4.60); **Lübben** (10min., 2 per hr., €1.80). For a **taxi** call ☎31 53 or 836 88. **Kowalsky's,** near the station at Poststr. 6, rents **bikes.** (☎28 35. €7 per day. Open M-F 9am-12:30pm and 2-6pm, Sa 9am-noon, Su call in advance.) Rent a **kayak** at the campsite (p. 161) or at **Franke,** Dammstr. 72., down the walkway over the bridge. From the station, turn right down Bahnhofstr. and left at Dammstr. (☎27 22. Paddleboats €2-5 per hr. Open Apr.-Oct. daily 8am-7pm.) **Hannemann,** Am Wasser 1, rents **boats** at the other port. Follow Spreestr. to the end, cross the bridge, and continue to the next bridge. (☎36 47. 1-seaters €3-4 per hr. Call ahead to reserve a boat. Open daily Apr.-Oct. 8am-7pm.) The **tourist office,** Ehm-Welk-Str. 15, at the end of Poststr., has maps and finds rooms for a €3 fee. (☎36 68; fax 467 70. Open May-Oct. M-F 9am-6pm, Sa 9am-4pm; Nov.-Apr. M-F 9am-4pm.) The **post office** is at Kirchpl. 6. (Open M-F 9am-6pm, Sa 9am-noon.) **Postal Code:** 03222.

ACCOMMODATIONS AND FOOD. Though the closest hostel is in **Lübben,** 10min. away by train (p. 162), finding a room isn't a problem in friendly Lübbenau. Check for *Zimmer frei* signs, particularly common along Poststr., or ask for the *Gastgeberverzeichnis* brochure at the tourist office. Between the train station and the center of town, **Pension Zur Linde** ❸ offers carpeted rooms with plush comforters. (☎46 792. Breakfast included. Singles €23; doubles €38. Cash only.) On the road to Lehde and surrounded by water, **Campingplatz "Am Schloßpark"** ❶ has 125 tent plots with cooking and bathing facilities on-site, as well as a convenience store. (☎35 33; www.spreewaldcamping.de. Bikes €6 per day; single boats €15 per day. Reception 7:30am-12:30pm and 2-9pm. €5 per person, €2.50 per child, €5-6 per tent. 2- to 8-person bungalows €19-44. Cash only.)

For cheap food—and pickles, beets, and beans by the barrel—check out the *Imbiße* (snack bars) and stands along the **Großer Hafen.** Cheerful yellow **Café Fontane** ❸ dishes out delicious local cuisine just behind the church at Ehm-Wehk-Str. 42; try a salad with baguette (€7-9) or spring for the *Heringsfilet nach Hausfrauen Art* (herring à la housewife; €8). Homemade cakes make dessert a must. (Open daily from 11:30am. Cash only.) **Spreewald Idyll** ❷, Spreestr. 13, serves regional specialties like *Grützwurst* with potatoes (€6.20), fish dishes, and salads (€2.40-6) within spitting distance of the Kleiner Hafen on an outdoor patio. (☎14 22 51. Open M-Sa 10am-10pm, Su 10am-9pm. Cash only.)

SIGHTS AND HIKING. The Altstadt is a 10min. walk from the station. Go straight on Poststr. until you reach the marketplace and the Baroque **Nikolaikirche.** (Open May-Oct. M-F 2-4pm.) The requisite **Schloß** is now a handsome (and expensive) hotel and restaurant with lush grounds open to the public. Across the marketplace in the gatehouse (a prison until 1985) is the ▇**Spreewaldmuseum,** Topfmarkt 12, which gives a historical overview of the Spreewald and its customs. (☎24 72. Open Apr. to mid-Oct. Tu-Su 10am-6pm. €3, students €2.) The **Haus für Mensch und Natur** (House for Man and Nature), Schulstr. 9, has a free exhibit on the local ecosystem. (Open Apr.-Oct. daily 10am-5pm.)

Gondola tours of the forest depart from the **Großer Hafen** and the **Kleiner Hafen** (larger and smaller ports, respectively). The Großer Hafen, along Dammstr. a block behind the church, offers a wider variety of tours, including 2 and 3hr. trips

BRANDENBURG

to Lehde. The boats take on customers starting at 9 or 10am and depart when full (about 20 passengers) throughout the day. **Genossenschaft der Kahnfährleute,** Dammstr. 77a, is the biggest company. (☎22 25. Open Mar.-Oct. daily 9:30am-6pm. 2hr. round-trips to Lehde €7, children €3.50; 3hr. €9/4.50; 5hr. tour of the forest €12.50/6.25.) From the Kleiner Hafen, less-touristy but nearly identical wilderness trips are run by the **Kahnfährmannsverein der Spreewaldfreunde,** Spreestr. 10a. (☎40 37 10; kahn@spreewald-web.de. Open Apr.-Oct. daily 9am-6pm. Tours 2-10hr.; 4-5hr. tours recommended. €7-20, children €3-10.)

It's only a hop and a paddle from Lübbenau to the haystacks and thatched-roof houses of **Lehde,** a UNESCO-protected landmark that is accessible by foot (15min.), bike, or boat. Follow the signs from the Altstadt or Großer Hafen, or take a boat from the harbor. The **Freilandmuseum** (Open-Air Museum), a recreated 19th-century village, portrays a time when entire Spreewalder families slept in the same room and newlyweds literally went for a "romp in the hay." Follow the signs to Lehde; it's just behind the aquarium and over the bridge. (☎24 72. Open Apr. to mid-Sept. daily 10am-6pm. €3, students and seniors €2, children €1.) Just before the bridge to the museum lies the **Fröhlichen Hecht ❷** (Jolly Pike), Dorfstr. 1, a large café, restaurant, and *Biergarten* with a patio right on a river. Enjoy a *Kartoffel mit Quark* (potatoes with curd cheese) in a special Spreewald sauce (€6.50) as gondolas drift. (☎27 82; www.zumhecht.come. Open daily 11am-7pm.)

LÜBBEN ☎03546

With canals and trails fanning out from all ends, little Lübben (pop. 14,700) fills with German tourists milling around the colorful Altstadt and gliding by in kayaks, canoes, and gondolas. Lübben offers easy access to wooded bike paths and hiking trails, as well as a ceaseless supply of juicy *Gurken* (pickles, the region's specialty) and fresh fish that make for a woodland picnic.

🖪🚺 TRANSPORTATION AND PRACTICAL INFORMATION. Trains go to: **Berlin Ostbahnhof** and other major stations (1hr., 2 per hr., €8.40); **Cottbus** (30min., every hr., €6); **Lübbenau** (10min., 2 per hr., €1.80). For a **taxi** call ☎48 12 or 30 39. Rent **bikes** at the tourist office (€5.50 per day, €4 each subsequent day). The **tourist office** is at Ernst-von-Houwald-Damm 15. From the station, head right on Bahnhof-str., make a left when it dead-ends onto Luckauer Str., veer left onto Lindenstr., and cross the two bridges; the office will be on the right, on the *Schloßinsel* across the bridge. The staff finds private rooms (€15-40) for a €3 fee. After hours, they post a list of private rooms outside the entrance. (☎30 90 or 24 33; fax 25 43. Open Apr.-Oct. daily 10am-6pm; Nov.-Mar. M-F 10am-4pm.) The **post office** is at Poststr. 4. (Open M-F 9am-6pm, Sa 9am-noon.) **Postal Code:** 15907.

🖪🖸 ACCOMMODATIONS AND FOOD. The Jugendherberge Lübben (HI) ❶, Zum Wendenfürsten 8, is in a field at the edge of town. To get there, follow Bahnhofstr. to its end and turn left on Luckauer Str. Turn right on Burglehnstr. before the big crossing and right again on Puschkinstr., which becomes Cottbusser Str. After 1.5km, take a left on Zum Wendenfürst, and follow it for another 1.5km. Signs point the way. Though remote, the hostel is dreamy—surrounded on one side by a river and on the other by a stretch of hayfields—and offers easy access to wilderness paths in addition to a playground, ping-pong, and canoes. (☎30 46; www.jh-luebben.de. Sheets €3.30. Reception 9am-7pm. Dorms €14. Campsites €9.50. Cash only.) For convenience, **Pension am Markt ❸,** Hauptstr. 5, can't be beat. Each large room has a kitchen and fold-out couches. (☎32 72; pension-am-markt@gmx.net. Breakfast included. Singles €35; doubles €50-60; 1- to 4-person apartments €30 per person.) To get to **Spreewald-Camping Lübben ❶,** follow the directions to the Jugendherberge until Puschkinstr., and then turn left at the sign. (☎ 70 53; www.spreewald-camping-luebben.de. Boat rental €3.50 per hr., €20 per day; for campers €2.70/16. Bike rental €6.50 per day. Reception 7am-1pm and 3-10pm. Open mid-Mar. to Oct. €6 per person, €3.50-4.50 per tent.)

While in Lübben, be sure to sample the Spreewald's pickled delicacies, famous throughout Germany. **Gurken Paule ❶,** at the entrance to the tourist office plaza on the *Schloßinsel,* is an outdoor stand offering the freshest of the Spreewald's unique pickle assortment: *Salzdillgurken* (dill), *Senfgurken* (mustard), *Gewürzgurken* (spicy), and sundry other varieties. They're sold by weight, averaging about €0.50 per pickle and €2.50 per jar. (Open daily 9am-6pm.) More varied local cuisine and evening music ranging from *Schlager* to country can be found at **Bubak ❸,** Ernst-von-Houwald-Damm 9, named after the Sorbian bogeyman famed for carrying naughty children off into the forest. Sample the *Gurken-Kartoffelsuppe* (pickle-potato soup; €2.80) or an entrée for €5.50-15. (☎ 18 61 44. Open M-F 11:30am-3pm and 5:30-10:30pm, Sa-Su 11:30am-10:30pm.)

◙ ⚠ SIGHTS AND OUTDOOR ACTIVITIES. The Altstadt's architectural pride is the newly restored **Paul-Gerhardt-Kirche,** named for the most famous German hymn writer since Martin Luther. (Open May-Aug. W 10am-noon and 3-5pm.) Gerhardt is buried inside (no one knows quite where) and immortalized outside in stone. The entrance to Lübben's forested park, **Der Hain,** is at the end of Breite Str., which begins where Haupstr. ends. To the south, the **Schloßinsel,** an island whose park is more impressive than the palace also located there, houses the tourist office, docks, and pricey cafés. The **Schloß** contains an exhibit on Lübben's history and culture. (Open May-Sept. Tu-Su 10am-6pm; Oct.-Apr. W-F 10am-4pm, Sa-Su 1-5pm.) Most of Lübben's attractions are in the forests surrounding the town. The **Fährmannsverein "Lustige Gurken" Lübben/Spreewald,** Ernst-von-Houwald-Damm 15 on the *Schloßinsel,* offers boat trips exploring the Spreewald. (☎ 71 22; www.lustige-gurken.de. Open daily 9am-4pm. 1-7hr., €7-15.) The **Fährmannsverein "Flottes Rudel,"** at the end of the parking lot across Lindenstr. from Am Spreeufer, offers boat and barge trips with picnics starting daily at 10am. (☎ 82 69; www.flottesrudel.de. 2-8hr. tours €7-18.) You can rent **kayaks** or **canoes** at **Bootsverleih Gebauer,** Lindenstr. 18. From Luckauer Str., turn right on Lindenstr. before the tourist office. (☎ 71 94; www.spreewald-bootsverleih.de. ID required. Open daily Apr.-Oct. 9am-7pm. 1-person kayaks €4 per hr., €2.50 per additional hr., €16 per day.)

MECKLENBURG-VORPOMMERN (MECKLENBURG-UPPER POMERANIA)

Nature takes center stage in sparsely populated Mecklenburg-Vorpommern. Over 1700 lakes lie nestled between thick forests and peaceful towns, stretching northward to breathtaking cliffs and sandy beaches along the Baltic Sea coast. A popular tourist destination at the turn of the 20th century, Mecklenburg-Vorpommern (especially the islands of Rügen and Usedom) has been rediscovered by the west in the wake of reunification. Even now, dramatic Hanseatic architecture continues to emerge from rubble as restoration continues in Germany's poorest *Land*.

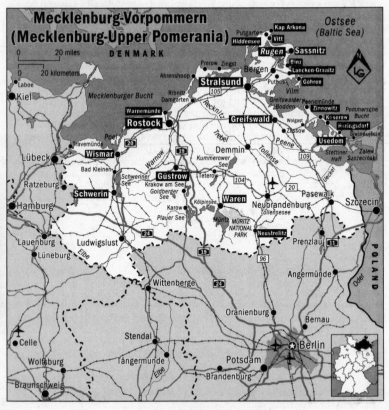

HIGHLIGHTS OF MECKLENBURG-VORPOMMERN

SUN YOURSELF as you revel in nature on the car-less island of **Hiddensee** (p. 188).

HIKE the white chalk cliffs of **Jasmund National Park** (p. 182).

STEP BACK into the Middle Ages in **Stralsund** (p. 179), birthplace of the glazed brick Gothic architectural style.

SCHWERIN
☎ **0385**

Founded in 1018, Schwerin (pop. 98,000) is the grandfather of Mecklenburg-Vorpommern's cities, and is now capital of the province. Encircled by lakes and largely free of communist "architectural innovations," Schwerin's *Schloß* and well-preserved townhouses lend the town a regal flair. The undeniable cultural center of the *Land*, Schwerin hosts dozens of art festivals and concerts every year, and is home to some of the region's finest traditional cuisine.

TRANSPORTATION AND PRACTICAL INFORMATION

Schwerin is on the Magdeburg-Rostock rail line and is accessible from all major cities on the Baltic coast. **Trains** run every hour to Berlin (2½hr., €28-39); Lübeck (1¼hr., €11.70); and Rostock (1¼hr., €13.40). An efficient system of **buses** and **trams** covers the city and outlying areas (single ride €1.30, day pass €4). The city's two **Räder Center** shops, at Schusterstr. 3 and in the train station, rent **bikes,** recommend trails, and lead personal tours. (☎500 76 30. M-F €6 per day, Sa-Su €7. Rentals mid-Apr. to Oct. daily 9am-6pm.)

The **tourist office,** Am Markt 14, books hotel rooms for free and leads 1½hr. German-language walking tours (daily 11am, €4.50). From the train station, go right on Grundthalpl. and continue as it turns into Wismarsche Str.; take a left on Arsenal, a right on Mecklenburgstr., and another left on Schmiedestr. (☎592 52 12; www.schwerin.com. Open Apr.-Sept. M-F 9am-7pm, Sa-Su 10am-6pm; Oct.-Mar. M-F 9am-6pm, Sa-Su 10am-4pm.) Do **laundry** at **Schnell & Sauber,** on Pl. der Freiheit. (Wash €3 per 6kg. Dry €0.50 per 12min. Open daily 6am-11pm.) An **Apotheke,** Puschkinstr. 61/65, is just off the Markt. (☎59 37 90. Open M-F 8am-6pm, Sa 9am-12:30pm.) **Internet** access is available at **InCa,** on Wismarsche Str., across from **Zum Stadtkrug** (€2.50 per hr., students €2; open daily 11am-11pm), and at **Netz-Games,** Ritterstr. 1, on the corner of Salzstr. (☎593 69 60. €0.50 per 10min., €2 per hr. Open M-F 2pm-midnight, Sa-Su 4pm-midnight.) The **Stadtsbibliothek** (municipal library), Wismarsche Str. 144, also offers Internet access. (☎590 19 21. €2 per hr. Open M-W and F 10am-6pm, Th 2-7pm, Sa 9am-1pm.) The main **post office** is at Mecklenburgstr. 4-6. From the Markt, go down Schmiedestr. and turn right. (Open M-F 8am-6pm, Sa 9am-noon.) **Postal Code:** 19053.

ACCOMMODATIONS

Family-run **Zimmervermietung Familie Kuhnert ❷,** Voßstr. 44, is in the blue house next to Café Bernstein (p. 166). Take bus #10 or 11 from the train station to "Alter Friedhof" and cross the street at the intersection. While the back facade of the building is still pocked from WWII grenades, the inside is all comfort, with bright rooms, cheerful bedspreads, and TVs. (☎79 79 79. Breakfast €5. Singles €20-30, €250-350 per month; doubles €30-40/400. Cash only.) The always-booked **Jugendherberge (HI) ❷,** Waldschulweg 3, is 3km south of town in the woods by the lake. From the station, take a right on Wismarschestr. to Marienpl. Take bus #14 to the end of the line at "Jugendherberge" and take the road into the woods; the hos-

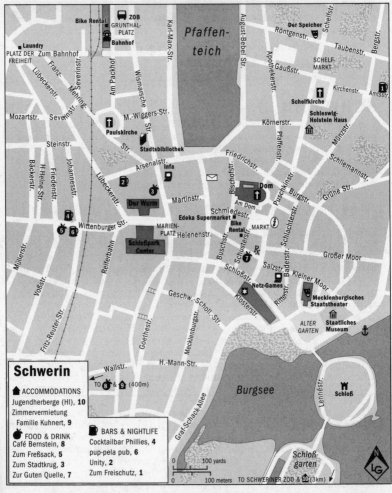

Schwerin

▲ ACCOMMODATIONS
Jugendherberge (HI), **10**
Zimmervermietung
  Familie Kuhnert, **9**

🍴 FOOD & DRINK
Café Bernstein, **8**
Zum Freßsack, **5**
Zum Stadtkrug, **3**
Zur Guten Quelle, **7**

🍸 BARS & NIGHTLIFE
Cocktailbar Phillies, **4**
pup-pela pub, **6**
Unity, **2**
Zum Freischutz, **1**

TO ❽ & ❾ (400m)

0 — 100 yards
0 — 100 meters
TO SCHWERINER ZOO & 🏠❿ (3km)

tel is on the left. (☎326 00 06; fax 326 03 03. Breakfast and sheets included. Reception 4pm-midnight. Curfew midnight. Full board packages available. Dorm beds €18, under 27 €15. Cash only.)

🍴 FOOD

Fast-food joints proliferate in **Der Wurm,** a mall on Marienpl. whose courtyard paths resemble a worm. (Open M-F 9:30am-7pm, Sa 9:30am-4pm.) The neighboring **Schloßpark Center** is a larger, more modern shopping complex with similar food options. Schwerin's coziest micro-brewery, **⬛Zum Stadtkrug ❸**, Wismarschestr. 126, serves German specialties and award-winning beer. The local brew, *Schweriner Altstadtbräu* (€1.70 for 0.25L), complements an intimidating *Brauhauspfanne* (pig roll, smoked turkey, lung sausage, sauerkraut, and vegetables; €9.95).

(☎593 66 93. Open daily 11am-1am. Cash only.) At **Zur Guten Quelle ❸**, Schusterstr. 12, dark wood, red vinyl, and DDR-style furniture rule. Try the *Matjes* (herring; €6.96-8.65), the restaurant's specialty. (☎56 59 85. Entrées €8-13. Open daily 11am-midnight. Cash only.) Potato lovers shouldn't miss the gigantic stuffed potatoes (€3.30-6.50) at **Zum Freßsack ❸**, Wittenburgerstr. 52, at the corner of Voßstr. The restaurant's romantic charm stems from its name—it means "At the Feedbag"—and from the obscure Mecklenburg specialties it serves, like *gepökeltes Eisbein* (pickled pig's knuckles on sauerkraut; €8.50). (☎760 71 72. M-Th and Su 11:30am-10pm, F-Sa 11:30am-midnight. AmEx/DC/MC/V.) Relax in the friendly atmosphere of **Café Bernstein ❷**, Voßstr. 44. Take bus #10 or 11 from the train station to "Alter Friedhof" and cross the street at the intersection. The café is full of people sipping iced drinks and delicious *Milchkaffee* (coffee with cream; €2.40) served in giant bowls. (Open daily 9am-3am. Cash only.) Buy groceries at **Edeka,** Schmiedestr. 10, just off the Markt. (Open M-F 8am-8pm, Sa 8am-4pm.)

⊙ SIGHTS

Schwerin's fairy-tale **Schloß**, on an island south of the city center, is a glitzy amalgamation of grandiose building styles. Begun in the 1500s, the castle was expanded in the 19th century, when it served as the seat of the Duchy of Mecklenburg. The exterior's gold-capped towers are partially shrouded by ongoing restoration, but the inside still shines. Mahogany inlay floors lead through ornate chambers to the grand throne room, with its marble columns and wall-to-wall ornamentation. A sweeping view of the castle grounds can be had from atop the hill at the far end of the adjoining *Schloßgarten*. (☎525 29 20. Open mid-Apr. to mid-Oct. daily 10am-6pm; mid-Oct. to mid-Apr. Tu-Su 10am-5pm. €4, students €2.50, families €7.) On the other side of the *Schloß*, the **Alter Garten,** now used for outdoor concerts, was the site of mass demonstrations preceding the downfall of the DDR in 1989. The adjacent **Staatliches Museum** (State Museum) houses a remarkable collection of 15th- to 19th-century Dutch and German art, including works by Rembrandt, Rubens, and Cranach the Elder. A room full of Barlach statues and extensive Duchamp holdings will please fans of modernism. (☎595 80. Open Apr. 15-Oct. 14 daily 10am-6pm; Oct. 15-Apr. 14 Tu-Su 10am-5pm. €6, students €4, families €12. German-language tours W 3pm and Su 11am and 3pm.) Uphill from the Alter Garden, the nearest spire is the 13th-century Gothic **Dom.** Many of the church's treasures, including its 42 altars, were lost when the Dom was redecorated in Neo-Gothic style at the beginning of the 19th century. Restoration of the Dom to early Gothic style took place from 1970 to 1988. The church's striking Gothic triumphal cross comes from Wismar's Marienkirche, which was demolished in 1961. (Open M-Sa 10am-4:30pm, Su noon-4:30pm. Tower €1.50, children €0.50.) In front of the Rathaus on the Markt, a towering **lion statue** painted with amusingly irreverent scenes pays tribute to Schwerin's founder, **Henry the Lion.** The **Schleswig-Holstein-Haus** has small, rotating exhibitions that have included sketches by Picasso and Dalí. (Puschkinstr. 12. ☎55 55 27. Open daily 10am-6pm. Prices vary; typically €3, students €2.) Animals cavort at the **Schweriner Zoo.** Take tram #1, 2, or 3 (dir.: Hegelstr.) to "Zoo." From Bernhard-Schwentener-Str. turn left onto Am Grünen Tal. The highlight of the zoo is its waterfowl exhibit. (☎39 55 10; www.zoo-schwerin.de. Open Apr.-Oct. M-F 9am-5pm, Sa-Su 9am-6pm; Nov.-Feb. daily 10am-3pm; Mar. daily 10am-4pm. €7.50, students and children €3.50.) In summer, **ferries** leave every hour from the docks between the *Schloß* and the museum to tour the Schweringersee lake, including a loop around **Kaninchenwerder** (Rabbit Haven). (Departures Tu-Sa 10am-5pm. €9.50-13, children €4) North of the Markt, the smaller **Pfaffenteich** lake offers a walk spotted with statues.

🎵 🎭 ENTERTAINMENT AND NIGHTLIFE

The cream-pillared building next door to the Staatliches Museum is the **Mecklen-burgisches Staatstheater Schwerin,** which puts on the most elaborate and expensive plays, ballets, and symphonies in town. (☎530 01 23. Tickets €13-59.) Buy tickets for most shows through **Ticketservice am Markt** in the tourist office. (☎56 05 00. Open M-F 9am-7pm, Sa 10am-noon.) Schwerin's best sights often double as perfor-mance spaces; in the summer, the steps of the museum are converted into an opera stage, and in the nearby *Schloß,* the throne room is transformed into a regal venue for monthly concerts (€26, students €18). **Der Speicher,** Röntgenstr. 20-22, airs cult films and hosts book readings and folk music shows. (Entrance on Schelf-str. ☎51 21 05, tickets 761 901 901 or at **Ticketservice,** Wittenburger Str. 118.)

Most Schwerin bars are open daily, closing around midnight on Sundays and later on weekends. Pick up a free copy of *piste* (in German) at the tourist office for reviews and listings of clubs and parties. **Zum Freischutz,** Am Ziegenmarkt 11, a popular bar near the Speicher, covers its dimly illuminated walls with an odd com-bination of Beethoven portraits, stuffed ravens, and butterflies. The crowd is young and the beer (€2) is good. (☎56 86 55. Open daily from 6pm. Cash only.) The Altstadt empties at night, but the party continues at **Unity,** Arsenalstr. 35, where an intimate setting and overstuffed sofas make for house-party ambience. (☎550 98 30. Beer €1.80-2.60. Glühwein €2.05. Open daily from 6pm. Cash only.) The cozy **pup-pela pub** is just down Wittenburgerstr. from Zum Freßsack. The adobe-style walls and wooden decorations make this a cross between the Wild West and old Schwerin. (Beer €1.50-3. Open Tu-Sa from 9pm. Cash only.) Across the street, join Schwerin's glamorous at **Cocktailbar Phillies,** Wittenburgerstr. 51, for mixed drinks (€6.50-8) and Cuban cigars (€4.50) from an extensive list. (☎71 31 01. Open daily from 8pm. Free outdoor movies in summer Su 10pm. Cash only.)

MECKLENBURGISCHE SEENPLATTE (MECKLENBURG LAKE PLAIN)

When things got hectic in Berlin, Chancellor Otto von Bismarck found refuge in the beauty of the Mecklenburgische Seenplatte, the lowland lake district of south-ern Mecklenburg-Vorpommern. The region's landscapes are a product of Ice Age glacial activity; hundreds of lakes are scattered about the Seenplatte, lined by wet-lands and deciduous forests. A popular destination for the past century, the area fills with hikers, bikers, and paddlers during the summer.

MÜRITZ NATIONAL PARK

In the heart of the Seenplatte, Müritz National Park boasts thick forests, rolling grasslands, and over 100 lakes. The relatively compact park is easily accessible from small towns around it, and the park's bike trails, hiking paths, and abundant wildlife make it well suited to nature enthusiasts of all levels of expertise.

✴ ORIENTATION

The two separate regions of Müritz National Park are west and east of **Neustrelitz.** The much larger western area is bordered on the west by **Lake Müritz,** Germany's largest freshwater lake. At the northwestern corner, the port town of **Waren** (p. 171) is a major jumping-off point for tourists. The park's southwestern quarter, mostly wetland, is home to much of its wildlife. The remainder of the western por-

Müritz National Park

○ TRAILS

Green Left (10km), **6**
Müritz-Nationalpark-Weg
  (163km), **4**
Purple Flower (10km), **2**
Purple Mushroom (6km), **5**
Red Squirrel (11km), **3**
Yellow Bird Bike Trail, **7**
Yellow Butterfly (8.5km), **1**

tion is forest interspersed with expansive fields and sparkling lakes. Müritz's eastern region has more hills and is thickly forested, but is also dotted with lakes and brooks. The **Hirschberg,** not exactly looming at a mere 143.5m, is the highest point in the park. Other major towns around the park are **Kratzeburg,** in the center of the western region; **Speck,** west of Kratzeburg; **Federow,** on the north edge of the park southeast of Waren; and **Serrahn,** somewhat west of center in the eastern region. Maps of the park (€5.50) are highly recommended and available at all national park information offices and local tourist offices.

▆ TRANSPORTATION

Nearly everyone gets to the park through Neustrelitz or Waren, both of which are on the Berlin-Rostock rail line. **Trains** shuttle between Waren and Neustrelitz every 2hr., stopping in Kargow, Klockow, and Kratzeburg (€5.70). The **Müritz-Nationalpark-Ticket** runs **buses** every hr. 9am-4pm (July-Aug. until 5pm) from Waren to Federow, Speck, and Boek. The line also includes a boat that connects Waren, Klink, and Roebel on the Müritz lake. Buy tickets on board buses or boats or at tourist information centers. (Day ticket €6.50, students and children €3, families €13; with unlimited boat travel €13/6/26. 3- and 7-day passes also available. Check the schedule: many tours are free with purchase of these passes.) Renting a **bike** is an efficient way to be mobile in Müritz itself. Rental stores are ubiquitous, even in the smaller towns like Boek, Schwarzenhof, and Carpin.

MÜRITZ NATIONAL PARK AT A GLANCE	
AREA: 322sq. km.	**HIGHLIGHTS:** Imposing oak forests, rare birds, and Germany's largest freshwater lake.
CLIMATE: Relatively dry weather and mild temperatures year-round.	
FEATURES: Largely flat, forested terrain dotted with marshes and lakes.	**CAMPING:** Only on designated campsites, most outside the park.
GATEWAYS: Waren (p. 171) and Neustrelitz.	**FEES AND RESERVATIONS:** Free entry to park. Camping fees vary.

MECKLENBURG-
VORPOMMERN

🛈 PRACTICAL INFORMATION

National Park Information Centers: Hiking maps (€5.50), brochures, and advice are available at Müritz National Park's *Nationalparkinformation* offices:

Waren, Am Teufelsbruch (☎66 27 86). Follow the directions to Ecktannen (p. 172) but stay on Am Seeufer as it becomes Specker Str., then turn left on Am Teufelsbruch at the park sign. Or, take Waren's bus #1 to "Schabernack" at the end of the line. Open May-Sept. daily 9:30am-5pm.

Neustrelitz, Am Tiergarten (☎03981 20 32 84). Take Marienstr. from the train station past the *Opfern des Faschismus* monument on your right. Veer left onto Friedrich-Wilhelm-Str. Continue past the traffic circle and follow signs. Wheelchair accessible. Open May-Oct. daily 10am-5pm.

Nationalparkamt Müritz, Schloßpl. 3, 17237 Hohenzieritz (☎039824 25 20; www.nationalpark-mueritz.de), is the office to contact for information before you arrive.

Branches are located in Boek, Federow, Kratzeburg, Schwarzenhof, Serrahn, Speck, and other locations throughout the region. Check www.nationalpark-mueritz.de for more information.

Tours: Free themed walking and biking tours of the park, including family tours, are available May-Oct. Tours last 1½-5hr., most around 3hr., and depart several times a day. For a list of dates, durations, and meeting points, visit the park website or any park center.

Emergency: Police ☎110. **Ambulance** and **fire** ☎112.

🏕 CAMPING

Camping is permitted only in designated campgrounds. *Camping im Land der Tausend Seen,* which lists campgrounds within and near the park, is available at tourist offices. Waren (p. 171) offers visitors several options. Travelers interested in Müritz East should contact the Neustrelitz **tourist office,** Strelitzer Str. 1. (☎25 31 19; Open May-Sept. M-F 9am-6pm, Sa-Su 9:30am-1pm; Oct.-Apr. M-Th 9am-noon and 1-4pm, F 9am-noon.) Within the park itself, signs lead from the Kratzeburg train station to **Campingplatz "Naturfreund" am Käbelicksee ❶,** Dorfstr. 3, on a secluded lake shore. (☎039822 202 85. Boat rental €3-6 per hr. Reception 8:30am-6pm. Open Apr.-Oct. €4.50 per person, €2-4 per tent.)

🏞 OUTDOOR ACTIVITIES

HIKING. Trails in Müritz are marked by colored images; many trails share symbols and are differentiated only by the location of their trailheads. Grünow is the best starting point for trails in the east, while the trails in the west begin in many different towns. The extensive booklet *Wandern im Müritz-Nationalpark,* available at park information centers, describes all the trails and has color maps (€12). **In high-protection areas in the core zone of the park, you may not leave the marked trails.** Some of the good trails include:

🔲 **Rotes Eichhörnchen** (Red Squirrel; 11km). To reach the trailhead, leave Kratzeburg on the road leading to highway B-193 (dir.: Neustrelitz); the beginning of the trail will appear on your left, across from a small parking area. A local favorite that passes several of Müritz's lakes. The trail has a closed loop in the north: 2hr. takes you around the little lily-padded **Wienpletschsee** and then by the banks of the Müritz and Binnenmuritz, where the *Strandpromenade* (boardwalk) is scalloped with tiny beach alcoves.

Violetter Pilz (Purple Mushroom; 6km). Follows the coastline of the Müritzsee from starting point Boek, providing good opportunities to spot wildlife. In fall, wild swans are everywhere, while in summer, fish-hawks hunt for lunch on the water.

Gelber Schmetterling (Yellow Butterfly; 8.5km). Follow Strandstr. past site of the Waren Jugendherberge to reach the trailhead. In the north near Waren, this trail makes a circuit around the Feisnecksee, with grassy fields and views of the lake. The small *Burgwallinsel* in the middle of the lake is a remnant of a former Slavic settlement.

Grünes Blatt (Green Leaf; 10km). Beginning from Grünow in Müritz East, this path meanders through rolling country hills, forests, and along lakeside paths.

> **OF MOORS AND MOSQUITOES.** Müritz's location amid swampy lakes may be pleasant for you, but it's even more exciting for mosquitoes. Use bug spray and wear long pants while hiking to avoid a day of futile swatting.

BIKING. Bike routes are nearly as common as hiking trails; some recommended ones are the **Gelber Vögel** (Yellow Bird) near Grünow, the **Violette Blüme** (Purple Flower) south of Waren, and the comprehensive 163km **Müritz-Nationalpark-Weg.** The road to Federow is good for biking, and the town of Federow itself is an excellent gateway to the park. From Neustrelitz, there are several ways to enter the western section. To get to the heart of Müritz West, bike on road B-193 in the direction of Penzlin (signs indicating this road begin at the town's main traffic circle on Strelitzer Str.) and then fork left to Kratzeburg, as indicated by road signs. The road to Userin, on the southern border of the park (in the opposite direction of Penzlin), leads to a number of trails that veer north into Müritz West. To get to Serrahn, in Müritz East, take B-198 from Neustrelitz east in the direction of Carpin and fork right at the sign. Following the signs on the road will get you to Grünow, another springboard for trips into the eastern area of the park.

WATERSPORTS. The stretch of the Havel River between the Käbelicksee and the Granzinersee has the most scenic canoeing in Müritz. **Bootsvermietung Hecht,** Dalmsdorf 6, just outside of Kratzeburg, rents canoes, kayaks, and rowboats. (☎ 039822 202 41; www.kanu-hecht.de. Boats €6-17 per 4hr.) Sailing and windsurfing are popular on the Müritzsee; rentals are readily available in Boek.

WAREN ☎ 03991

Waren's beautifully situated marina and cheerful atmosphere make it a hot spot for German vacationers. The town (pop. 22,400) overflows with accommodations and provides an ideal base for exploring Müritz.

◪◪ TRANSPORTATION AND PRACTICAL INFORMATION. Trains head to Berlin (2hr., every hr., €20-21) and Rostock (1hr., every 2hr., €12.90). For a **taxi** call ☎ 12 22 55. **Bikes** can be rented at **Zweirad Karberg,** off the Neuer Markt at Lange Str. 46. (☎ 66 60 80. €4-7 per day.) Other outdoor gear can be bought at **Sport-Assmuß,** Friedensstr. 17. (☎ 66 52 33. Open M-F 9am-6pm, Sa 9am-4pm.) Waren's **tourist office,** Neuer Markt 21, books rooms (from €25) for free. From the train station, turn right onto the footpath and follow it under the overpass at Schweriner Damm; go left on Friedensstr. and left again on Langestr. (☎ 66 61 83; www.waren-tourismus.de. Open daily May-Sept. 9am-8pm; Oct.-Apr. 9am-6pm.) All accommodations in Müritz charge a daily *Kurtaxe* of €1, which entitles you to discounts on local attractions and services. A **pharmacy, Löwen-Apotheke,** Neuer Markt 21, is next to the tourist office. (☎ 66 61 53. Open May-Oct. M-F 8am-6:30pm, Sa 8am-1pm; Nov.-Apr. M-F 8am-6pm, Sa 8am-1pm.) Do **laundry** at **Waschsalon Wirbelwind,** Strandstr. 1. (☎ 66 26 63. Wash and dry €8. Open M-F 9am-6pm, Sa 9am-2pm.) Options for **Internet** access are limited and prices are high. The **Waren Jugendclub,** Alter Feuerwache at the edge of the Alter Markt, charges €0.05 per minute. (☎ 66 45 48. Open M-F 1-8pm, every 2nd weekend of the month 2-8pm.) The **Stadtbibliothek** (Municipal Library), Zum Amtsbrink 9, charges €2 per 30min. (☎ 18 15 310. Open M-Tu and F 10am-6pm, Th 10am-7pm, Sa 10am-1pm.) The **post office** is at Neuer Markt 19. (☎ 67 39 30. Open M-F 9am-6pm, Sa 9am-noon.) **Postal Code:** 17192.

▐▐▐ ACCOMMODATIONS AND FOOD. The most convenient campground is **Campingplatz Ecktannen ❶**, on Fontanestr., near the lake. Take bus #3 (dir.: Ecktannen) to the last stop. (☎66 85 13. Reception daily May-Sept. 8am-10pm; Apr. and Oct. 8am-6pm; if you arrive later, camp outside the gate and check in the next day. Open April-Oct. €5.10 per person, €3-4 per tent. Cash only.) The **Pension Zur Fledermaus ❸**, Am Teufelsbruch 1, has rooms with a meadow view in an unbeatable location 3km from the harbor in the north of the park. Follow the directions to Waren's National Park Information Center (p. 170), and continue another 1km along the dirt road. (☎66 32 93; www.pension-fledermaus.de. Breakfast included. Singles €27; doubles €48; triples €72. Bath €3 extra; add €3 for 1-night stays. Beds without breakfast €13. AmEx/MC/V.) To get to Waren's recently reopened **Jugendherberge (HI) ❷**, An der Feisneck 1a, follow Am Seeufer out of the center of town. The hostel is right before the intersection with An der Feisneck. (☎77 66 70. Breakfast and sheets included. €22.15 per night, under 27 €19.15. Cash only.)

Buy **groceries** at **Edeka**, Neuer Markt 23. (Open M-F 8am-7pm, Sa 8am-2pm, Su 9am-2pm.) On Tuesdays and Fridays, a local **market** sells food (9am-5pm). **Langestraße** and **Neuer Markt** in Waren's Altstadt are crammed with bakeries and *Imbiße* (snack bars). Budget-conscious diners can enjoy a waterfront view at **Schnitzel-König ❷**, Strandstr. 3. Tasty *Schnitzel* dishes (€5.50-7.50) complement occasional live music. Vegetarian options are largely limited to baked potatoes (€3.30-4.90). (☎66 90 11. Open daily from 11am. Cash only.)

▐▐▐ SIGHTS AND OUTDOOR ACTIVITIES. The **Müritzeum**, Friedensstr. 5, has been presenting the natural history of the area through 1866. Enjoy the how-to on stuffing birds and small mammals and visit the aquarium showcasing local fish. (☎63 63 80; www.mueritzeum.de. Open daily May-Sept. 10am-6pm, Jul.-Aug. Th 10am-9pm; Nov.-Mar. Tu-Su 10am-4pm; Apr. and Oct. 10am-5pm. Admission €4, students €2.50, children €1.50.) **Boat tours** of the lake are offered by **Warener Schifffahrtsgesellschaft**, Am Stadthafen (☎12 56 24; www.warener-schifffahrt.de), **Müritzwind Personenschifffahrt**, on Strandstr. (☎66 66 64; www.schifffahrt-mueritzwind.de), and the **Weiße Flotte Müritz**, Kietzstr. 17 (☎12 26 68; www.mueritzschifffahrt.de). Tours run 1-7hr. (€5-20, children ½-price.) To tackle the waters yourself, visit **Eastside** (☎73 50 61), next to Campingplatz Ecktannen, which rents kayaks, small dinghies, catamarans, and windsurf boards. Follow Strandstr. as it becomes Kietzstr. and then Gerhart-Hauptmann-Allee, to get to the **Volksbad**, a grassy beach with a dock where swimming is permitted.

GÜSTROW ☎03843

Despite its winding bike trails and a striking Renaissance *Schloß*, Güstrow (pop. 34,000) is most famous for its collection of paintings and sculptures by prolific 20th-century artist Ernst Barlach. A longtime resident of Güstrow, Barlach fiercely opposed German militarization, filling the town with pacifist sculptures and causing the Nazis to condemn his work as *"Entarte Kunst"* (degenerate art). The rows of abandoned, crumbling buildings scattered throughout the inner city are signs of a continuing economic slump, but Güstrow's Altstadt is slowly regaining its sparkle as a result of the EXPO 2000 urban renewal project.

▐▐ TRANSPORTATION AND PRACTICAL INFORMATION. Central Güstrow is south of the **train station.** Follow Eisenbahnstr. three blocks until it becomes Lindenstr., then turn left onto Pferdemarkt. **Trains** run to Rostock (30min., every hr., €4.60) and Waren (30min., every 2hr., €9.10). Güstrow's **tourist office,** Domstr. 9, books rooms for free. (☎68 10 23; fax 68 20 79. Open May-Sept. M-F 9am-7pm, Sa 9:30am-4pm, Su 10am-4pm; Oct.-Apr. M-F 9am-6pm, Sa 9:30am-1pm.) **Walking**

tours, hosted by the tourist office, leave Franz-Parr-Pl. daily at 11am. (May 15-Oct. 3. €2, students €1. Call ahead for tours in English.) **Rats-Apotheke,** Am Markt 24, is the local **pharmacy.** (Open M-F 8am-6pm, Sa 9am-noon.) **Internet** access is available at **Lennys Computer,** Gleviner Str. 23. (€1 per hr. Open M-F 10am-1pm and 2-6pm, Sa 9:30am-1pm.) The **post office** is at Pferdemarkt 52-56. (Open M-F 9am-6pm, Sa 9am-noon.) **Postal Code:** 18271.

⌐⌐⌐ ACCOMMODATIONS AND FOOD. Güstrow's gorgeous **Jugendherberge (HI) ❷,** Heidberg 33, is 5km from town, serviced by buses #205, 224, and 252, which run only five times per day (€1.90; last bus around 5pm). The hostel lies at the edge of the woods and is surprisingly luxurious, boasting modern 1- to 4-bed rooms, most with bath and some with TV, and a public lakefront beach only ten minutes down the road. (☎84 00 44. Breakfast and sheets included. Curfew 10pm. €19.50-21, under 27 €18-21. Cash only.) For cheap, quick food, *Imbiße* (snack bars) of various sort abound on Pferdemarkt. At the heart of Güstrow, **Café Central ❷,** Neuer Markt 35, offers pizza (€5-8), pasta (€5-7), ice cream (€0.70-3.90), and more to hungry crowds on the patio. (☎68 68 98. Cash only.) Try the 150-year-old **Café Küpper ❶,** Domstr. 15, for delicious and reasonably priced German *Kaffee und Kuche* (coffee and cake). (☎68 24 85. Cash only.)

◪ SIGHTS. Güstrow's 13th-century **Dom,** on the southwest side of town, houses Barlach's most famous sculpture, *Der Schwebende Engel* (the hovering angel), created as a tribute to the victims of WWI. The statue was first cast in 1926, but was publicly melted into bullets by the Nazis in 1941. After WWII, a plaster cast of the statue was unearthed in West Germany and the angel was restored and rededicated to the victims of both wars in 1952. (Open M-Sa 10am-5pm, Su after services and 2-4pm. Free.) The white Renaissance **Schloß** rises above as you walk back toward Domstr. The palace's *Festsaal* (Ballroom) has a forest mural with antlers sprouting out of the walls, and the upper floors house Renaissance art from Italy, Germany, and the Netherlands. The basement is filled with altars and suits of armor from the Middle Ages. Lavender scents waft in through windows overlooking the manicured **Schloßgarten** surrounded by shrub archways. (☎75 20. Open Apr. 15-Oct. 14 daily 9am-5pm, Oct. 15-Apr. 14 Tu-Su 9am-5pm. €3, students €2, families €6. German tours daily 11am and 2pm; €1.50, students €1.) On the west side of town, the **Gertrudenkapelle,** Gertrudenpl. 1, houses a collection of Barlachs in an octagonal white chapel. (☎68 30 01. Open Apr.-Oct. daily 10am-5pm; Nov.-Mar. Tu-Su 11am-4pm. €3, students €2.) On the Neuer Markt, in the **Pfarrkirche St. Marien,** a folding golden altar crafted by Brussels artist **Jan Borman** in 1522 displays over 180 sculpted figures. (Open June-Oct. M-Sa 10am-5pm, Su 2-4pm; Nov.-May M-Sa 10am-noon and 2-4pm, Su 2-4pm. Tower €1, students €0.50.) Barlach's **Atelierhaus** (Studio), Heidberg 15, contains the world's largest collection of his works, including some 300 sculptures, in the house in which they were created. Next door, the elegant *Ausstellungsforum* hosts passing exhibits related to Barlach's life. The exhibit is a 1hr. walk from the Altstadt, next to the Jugendherberge, so renting a bike is the best way to visit. Head down Gleviner Str. from the Marktpl. and continue as it turns into Plauer Str. until you see the "Barlachweg" signs. Take this path around the lake past the grassy beach; continue 100m through the woods and the museum will be on the left. (☎844 00. Open Apr.-Oct. daily 10am-5pm, Nov.-Mar. Tu-Su 10am-5pm. €4, students €3.)

WISMAR
☎ 03841

After destruction wrought by WWII and years of neglect under socialist rule, massive restoration efforts in Wismar (pop. 45,000) are finally underway. The Altstadt, containing the largest marketplace in Northern Germany and ringed with magnificent churches, is rapidly regaining its former beauty. A founding member of the Hanseatic League in the 1300s, Wismar was later conquered by Sweden and expanded into the largest fortress in Europe. The 1903 end of Swedish rule is commemorated by the annual Schwedenfest, a celebration of Swedish culture held during the third week of August. For its historical and architectural significance, Wismar has been designated a UNESCO World Heritage Site.

◤◢ ORIENTATION AND PRACTICAL INFORMATION. Wismar's shipping industries are north of the **Alter Hafen** (Old Harbor) at the **Wismarbucht** (Wismar Bay). To the east of the Altstadt on Bahnhofstr. is the park **Lindengarten**. The **Bahnhof** lies at the northern edge of the Altstadt. Trains run every hr. until 10pm to Rostock (40min., €9.10) and Schwerin (40min., €5.50). The **ZOB** (bus station) is a block away (single ride €1, day pass €3). Bus #430 runs to the beaches of nearby Poel ("Timmendorf Strand," 1-2 per hr. until 6pm, €3.90). The **tourist office,** Am Markt 11, in the southwest corner of the Markt, books rooms for free, provides maps, and offers guided tours in German. (☎251 30 25; www.wismar.de. Open daily 9am-6pm. 2hr. tours Apr.-Oct. daily 10:30am, Sa and Su also 2pm. €4, students €3.) A bulletin board outside the office lists rooms.

◤◖ ACCOMMODATIONS AND FOOD. The new **Jugendherberge (HI) Wismar ❷** is accessible by bus lines B/D, C, or E to "Phillip-Müller-Str./Kinderkrankenhaus." Backtrack one block, and turn left on Juri-Gagarin-Ring. (Rents bikes. Breakfast included. Dorms €17.65, over 27 €20.65. Cash only.) The Alter Hafen area, the center of Wismar's nightlife, has seafood restaurants aplenty. Not far from the Schabbelhausmuseum is the unpretentious **Fischrestaurant "Seehase" ❸**, Altböterstr. 6, which specializes in local seafood. Try the beer-battered *Seelach* for €9.25. (☎28 21 34; www.fischrestaurant-seehase.de. Open M-F from 11am, Easter-Oct. Sa 11am-9:30pm, Nov.-Easter Sa-Su 11am-3pm. Cash only.) The popular Altstadt bar **Der Schlauch**, Lübsche Str. 18, bills itself as a place for "jazz, art, and companionship," with lots of Irish whiskies and beer (€1.60-3.80). (☎20 06 55. Open daily 7pm-1am. Cash only.) **Kellerkassel**, Lübsche Str. 26, is a cozy cellar bar down the street. (Open Tu-Sa from 8pm. Cash only.)

◗ SIGHTS. Of Wismar's many churches, **St.-Georgen-Kirche** has been a construction site for over a decade now, and will remain so until 2010 when Germany's largest church restoration will finish. Although the exterior remains obscured by scaffolding, the interior of the church has been partially reopened, and contains an exhibition on Christian history and the church's Gothic architecture. (Open daily 10am-8pm. Free.) All that remains of the nearby **St.-Marien-Kirche,** severely damaged by bombing in 1945 and all but demolished by the DDR in 1960 for "political reasons," is the imposing (and inaccessible) 81m tower. The bells still toll every 15min., and during the summer months, concerts and exhibitions are held outside. The Gothic **St.-Nikolai-Kirche** survived WWII intact, and houses portions of the interiors of St.-Georgen-Kirche and St.-Marien-Kirche that were removed from the two churches shortly before the bombings, including a 15th-century altar from St. Marien. Construction on the St.-Nikolai-Kirche began in the 14th century, but after the tower collapsed in 1703, much of the church was rebuilt in the Baroque style. (Open daily May.-Sept. 8am-8pm; Oct. and Apr. 10am-6pm; Nov.-Mar 11am-4pm. Requested donation €1.) The **Heilige-Geist-Kirche,** the Altstadt's other major church, has medieval art, an ornately painted altar and organ, stained glass, and a year-round nativity scene. The attached "Lange Haus" originally served as a hospital. (From the Markt go 3 blocks west on Lübschestr. Open M-Sa 10am-6pm, Su after services until 6pm. Requested donation €1.)

The Marktpl.'s dizzying variety of architecture is a record of Wismar's history of destruction and reconstruction. The **Rathaus** was rebuilt in 19th-century Neoclassical style after the roof collapsed in 1807 and destroyed most of the original building. In 1992 the roof collapsed again, requiring another renovation. The basement of the Rathaus has an exhibit on the city's history. (Open daily 10am-6pm.) Across the Marktpl., the **Wasserkunst,** an ornate Dutch Renaissance style well-house completed in 1602, was the village spigot for almost 300 years. Near St. Nikolai, the **Schabbelhausmuseum,** Schweinsbrücke 8, is the city's historical museum, with medieval artifacts and works by local artists. (☎28 23 50. Open Tu-Su May-Oct. 10am-8pm; Nov.-Apr. 10am-5pm. €2, students €1, under 18 free. F free.)

ROSTOCK
☎0381

A victim of socialist industrial ambitions after WWII, the port city of Rostock (pop. 200,000), the largest in sparsely populated Mecklenburg, was reconstructed but never fully restored. Fortunately, most of the concrete eyesores erected during the DDR-era are relegated to the city's suburbs, and hints of Rostock's thriving past as a member of the Hanseatic League can still be glimpsed downtown. Rostock's university, the oldest in the Baltic region, infuses the city with youthful energy, contributing to a thriving nightlife. Tourists flock to the charming resort town of Warnemünde, whose wide, sandy beaches are just minutes away.

MECKLENBURG-VORPOMMERN

Rostock

🏠 ACCOMMODATIONS
City-Pension, **6**
Hanse-Hostel, **7**
Jugendgästeschiff Rostock, **5**
Jugendherberge Warnemünde, **1**
Pension Am Doberaner Platz, **9**

🍎 FOOD & DRINK
Café Central, **8**
Kettenkasten, **2**
Mensa, **12**
Salsarico, **3**

🍷 NIGHTLIFE
Calamaris, **4**
diesseits, **10**
Studentenkeller, **11**

▐ TRANSPORTATION

Trains: To: **Berlin** (2½hr., every 2hr., €32); **Dresden** (5¼hr., every 2hr., €64); **Hamburg** (2½hr., every hr., €28); **Schwerin** (1hr., every hr., €13); **Stralsund** (1hr., every hr., €12); **Wismar** (1¼hr., every hr., €9).

Public Transportation: Trams #5 or 6 run from the train station to the Altstadt. Single bus/tram ticket €1.60, *Tageskarte* (day ticket) €3.20. To get to the **bus station** for lines to smaller towns, leave the train station through the Südstadt exit. Bus service slows after 10pm; after midnight, the *Fledermaus* (bat) buses run to a few central stops approx. every hr.

Ferries: Boats for **Scandinavia** leave from the **Überseehafen** docks. **TT-Line** runs to **Trelleborg, Sweden.** (☎045 02 81 03 48; www.TTLine.com. 5hr.; 2-3 per day; round-trip from €60, children and students from €30.) **Scandlines** sails to **Gedser, Denmark.** (☎207 33 17; www.scandlines.de. 2hr.; 3 per day; one-way €10, children €5.)

Bike Rental: Radstation, Am Bahnhof (☎252 39 90), to the right from the Hauptbahnhof's north exit. €7 per day. Open M-F 10am-6pm, Sa 10am-1pm.

◀✦ 🛈 ORIENTATION AND PRACTICAL INFORMATION

Rostock lies on the Warnow River, slightly more than 10km inland from the Baltic Sea. The city's main attractions are within the **Altstadt**, which is bordered to the north by the Warnow, and encircled on the other three sides by segments of the old city wall. Stretching across the Altstadt from **Kröpeliner Tor** in the west to the Rathaus in the east is **Kröpeliner Straße**, the city's main pedestrian zone and shopping district, also home to the city's university. Many of the city's cafés and bars are to the west of the Altstadt in the lively student quarter near **Doberaner Pl.** The **Hauptbahnhof** is south of the Altstadt. The beaches of **Warnemünde** lie 11km to the northwest of Rostock, where the Warnow river meets the Baltic Sea.

Tourist Office: Neuer Markt 3 (☎381 22 22; fax 381 26 01), in the post office building. From the train station, take tram #5 or 6 to "Neuer Markt." The staff books rooms for €3 and leads 1½hr. **tours.** (May-Oct. M-Sa 2pm, Su 11am. €4. Available in English for groups on request.) Open June-Aug. M-F 10am-7pm, Sa-Su 10am-4pm; May and Sept. M-F 10am-6pm, Sa-Su 10am-4pm; Oct.-Apr. M-F 10am-6pm, Sa-Su 10am-3pm.

Currency Exchange: Deutsche Bank, Kröpeliner Str. 84 (☎456 50), changes traveler's checks. **ATMs** downstairs. Open M-Tu and Th 9am-6pm, W 9am-1pm, F 9am-3pm.

Library: Kröpeliner Str. 82. Open M-Tu and Th-F 10am-6pm, W noon-6pm, Sa 9am-1pm.

Gay and Lesbian Resources: rat + tat, Leonhardstr. 20 (☎45 31 56; www.schwules-rostock.de). Open Tu 10am-6pm, Th 1-6pm, and by appointment.

Emergency: Police ☎110. **Ambulance** and **Fire** ☎112.

Pharmacy: Rost Apotheke, Neuer Markt 13 (☎493 47 47). Open M-F 8am-6pm, Sa 8am-1pm.

Internet Access: Treffpunkt, Am Vögenteich 23 (☎643 80 67), inside the Ostseesparkasse building. €1.50 per 30min. Open 9am-7pm.

Post Office: Neuer Markt 3-8. Open M-F 9am-6pm, Sa 9am-noon. **Postal Code:** 18055.

▐ ACCOMMODATIONS

▨ **Hanse-Hostel Rostock,** Doberaner Str. 136 (☎128 60 06; www.hanse-hostel.de). Tram #5 to "Volkstheater." A 15min. walk from the Altstadt, this convivial hostel has a lively kitchen and a TV lounge stocked with board games. Breakfast €4. Laundry €2.50 wash,

Are you aiming for a budget vacation?

With Cellular Abroad, talk is not only cheap, *it's free.*

Unlimited FREE incoming calls and no bills or contracts for overseas use!

1-800-287-5072
www.cellularabroad.com

€1.50 dry. Internet access €0.50 per 30min. Check-out 11am. 8-bed dorms €12; singles €24. ISIC discount 10%. MC/V. ❶

Jugendgästeschiff Rostock: MS Georg Buchner (HI), Am Stadthafen 72 (☎670 03 20). Take tram #5 to "Kabutzenhof," turn right onto Am Kabutzenhof, walk until you reach the water (5min.). A converted cargo ship, now permanently docked in Rostock's harbor, serves as a 50-bed youth hostel. Beautiful waterfront views and a wood-paneled officers' mess hall make up for the distance from town. Breakfast included. Sheets €4. Dorms €15, over 27 €19.50. ❷

Jugendherberge Warnemünde (HI), Parkstr. 47 (☎54 81 70), 1km west of the Warnemünde harbor; take bus #36 or 37 to "Warnemünde Strand." Near the beach, housed in the bottom floors of a former weather tower. The 40 rooms with bath and 20 with hallway facilities fill up quickly. In-room Internet access €1 per 10min. Breakfast included. Dorms €21.15, over 27 €25.15. ❷

City-Pension, Krönkenhagen 3 (☎252 22 60). Located directly in the Altstadt, this comfortable house has rooms with TV, radio, and bath. Sauna (fee applies) and exercise facilities in the building. Breakfast included. Wheelchair accessible. Check-in 2pm. Check-out 10am. Singles €40-58; doubles €60-96. ❹

Pension Am Doberaner Platz, Doberanerstr. 158 (☎49 28 30; fax 492 83 33). Take tram #3 or 6 to "Doberaner Pl." and follow the signs down the driveway. Large, quiet rooms come with shower, breakfast, and TV. Located near the student quarter, steps away from public transport. Singles €46; doubles €69. ❹

🍴 FOOD

Neuer Markt, on Steinstr. across from the Rathaus, fills with produce vendors. (Open M-F 8am-5pm, Sa 8am-1pm.) For groceries, try **Spar,** at the corner of Paulstr. and Hermannstr. (Open M-Th 8am-7pm, F 8am-8pm, Sa 8am-2pm.) The bakeries on **Kröpeliner Straße** sell cheap sandwiches and pastries. In **Warnemünde,** dozens of more expensive restaurants lining the harbor serve the bounty of the sea.

Salsarico, Am Leuchtturm 15 (☎319 35 65), just down the street from the lighthouse in Warnemünde. Tasty, though not particularly authentic, Mexican food (€9-13) and a variety of tequilas (€2-3). Lounge in wicker chairs as rows of mechanized fans send a welcome breeze. M unlimited chicken (€8), W steak (€8). Th 8-11pm free wine for women. Happy hour daily 5-6pm. Open M-F from 1pm, Sa-Su from noon. Cash only. ❸

Café Central, Leonhardstr. 22 (☎490 46 48), fills with a 20-something crowd that spills out into the street. Take in the creative artwork on the walls over light pasta dishes (€4-8) or come for a drink (€2-4) later. Open M-Sa 9am-2am, Su 10am-2am. Cash only. ❷

Kettenkasten, Am Strom 71 (☎512 48), in Warnemünde. Tourists eat *Ostseeheringe* (herring; €11.50) and other fish, accompanied by maritime tunes on the accordion (W-Su 8-10pm; cover €2). Open M-F noon-midnight, Sa-Su 11am-midnight. Cash only. ❹

Mensa, St.-Georg-Str. 104-107, near the Leibnizpl. tram stop, in the basement of the cream stucco *Studentenwerk* building. Super-cheap cafeteria lunches (€1-4) feed a university crowd. Open M-F 11:15am-2pm, Sa noon-1:30pm. Cash only. ❶

👁 SIGHTS

KRÖPELINER STRAßE. Rostock's main pedestrian mall runs west from the Rathaus to 12th-century **Kröpeliner Tor,** the former town gate. Although much of the city was destroyed in WWII, many of the half-timbered and glazed-brick houses along this stretch have been restored. The main buildings of **Rostock University,** the oldest in Northern Europe, are located near the middle of Kröpeliner Str., sur-

MECKLENBURG-VORPOMMERN

rounding the massive Rococo fountain at Universitätspl. Next to the university, along the remains of the city wall, is the **Kloster zum heiligen Kreuz,** a restored cloister founded by the Danish Queen Margaret in 1270. It now houses the **Kulturhistorisches Museum,** featuring medieval artifacts, an exhibit on life in the cloister, and a selection of local landscape paintings from the early 20th century. *(Open Tu-Su May-Sept. 10am-6pm; Oct.-Apr. 11am-5pm. €3, students €1.)*

ZOO. During WWII, Rostock housed some of its zoo's animals in public offices; the apes were guests of the police station. Since then, the zoo has grown to include over 2000 animals, especially arctic and aquatic species. *(Tram #3 or 6 to "Zoo." ☎ 208 20. Open daily Apr.-Oct. 9am-7pm; Nov.-Mar. 9am-5pm. www.zoo-rostock.de. €9, children €5.)*

MARIENKIRCHE. In the final days before the fall of the Berlin Wall, services at this 13th-century brick basilica overflowed with political protesters who came for the sermons of **Pastor Joachim Gauck.** In one of his bolder gestures, Gauck publicly chastised the *Stasi* (secret police) by calling out the names of those he could identify from the pulpit. After reunification, Gauck was entrusted with the difficult job of overseeing the fate of the *Stasi* archives. The highlight of the church's interior is the 12m high **astronomical clock** contracted in 1472. The intricate mechanical workings display the date, time, and positions of the sun and moon. At noon, a set of miniature apostles pop out, traveling around a figure of Jesus in circular procession. *(At the end of Kröpeliner Str. near the Neuer Markt. May-Sept. M-Sa 10am-6pm, Su 11am-5pm; Oct.-Apr. M-Sa 10am-12:15pm and 2-4pm, Su 11am-noon. Requested donation €1. Organ concerts July-Sept. W 8pm. Tours daily 11am; €1, students €0.50.)*

ALTER MARKT. The Alter Markt is old in name alone; since bombs leveled the whole area, all the buildings, including the church, have been built anew. Reconstruction of the magnificent **Petrikirche** began in the 1950s, but it was not until 1994 that the church's lofty spire was restored. Visitors can ascend the tower by stair or elevator for a view of all of Rostock. *(Open June-Aug. daily 10am-7pm; Apr.-May and Sept.-Oct. daily 10am-5pm; Nov.-Mar. M-F 10am-4pm, Sa-Su 10am-5pm. Tower €2.)*

SCHIFFFAHRTSMUSEUM (NAVIGATION MUSEUM). Paintings, photographs, and models tell the story of Rostock's maritime past from Vikings to today. *(August-Bebel-Str. 1. ☎ 25 206 21. Open Tu-Su May-Sept. 10am-6pm; Oct.-Apr. 11am-5pm. €3, students €1.)*

JEWISH ROSTOCK. Rostock was once home to a substantial Jewish population. Soon after coming to power, Nazis razed the synagogue on Augustenstr. and began deportations. The town's small **Jewish cemetery** was damaged in the war; in the 1970s, the government turned the remaining gravestones face-down to create the city's **Lindenpark.** Pressure from the international community convinced the city to right most of the stones and add a memorial in 1988, though gravestones are still scattered in the underbrush on the park's fringes. *(Take tram #3 or 6 or bus #24 to "Saarpl.," then walk south through the park.)*

WARNEMÜNDE

S-Bahn or Fledermaus bus to "Warnemünde." (20min., 4 per hr. 4:45am-8:30pm.) Less frequent service during the night. Rostock tram/bus day ticket is valid for the ferry across the Warnemünde harbor.

To the north of Rostock is the beach town of **Warnemünde.** Warnemünde's **Alter Strom** (Old Harbor) rings with the sounds of fishing boats and clicking cameras. Across the bridge from the Bahnhof, stands sell snacks and trinkets along the waterfront promenade. **Tourist information** is at Am Strom 59. *(☎ 54 08 00; fax 548 00 30. Open Jun.-Aug. M-F 9am-6pm, Sa-Su 10am-4pm; Sept.-Oct. and Mar.-May M-F 10am-6pm, Sa-Su 10am-4pm; Nov.-Feb. M-F 10am-5pm, Sa 10am-3pm.)* Climb the **lighthouse** by the Alter Strom for a view of shores stretching far into the distance. *(Open daily May-*

Sept. 10am-7pm. €2, students €1, families €4.) Walk long enough, and you can disrobe at the town's **nude beaches** (look for *FKK* or *free body culture* signs at beach entrances). Just off Kirchenpl., the **Heimatmuseum** (Local History Museum ■), Alexandrinerstr. 31, gives an overview of life in the tiny, colorful houses here. *(Open Apr.-Oct. Tu-Su 10am-6pm; Oct.-Mar. W-Su 10am-5pm. €3, students and children €1.)* Though summer brings beach parties nearly every weekend, the largest celebrations hit during the **Warnemünde Woche** in July, when the town hosts a sailing regatta.

❊ ⬛ FESTIVALS AND NIGHTLIFE

Every August, the extravagant **Hanse Sail** festival attracts over a million visitors to ogle at tall ships, dance, and drink. Rostock also hosts the largest **Christmas market** in the north of Germany (annually Nov. 22-Dec. 22). At night, Rostock's students come out to play, congregating along Kröpeliner Str., Wismarische Str., and Barnstorfer Weg. Check out *Rostock Szene*, which lists local clubs and performances, and *Nordost Eventguide*, which covers clubs across Mecklenburg-Vorpommern. Both are free at the tourist office.

▨ **Studentenkeller,** Universitätspl. 5 (☎45 59 28; www.studentenkeller.de). Entrance on Schwaansche Str., across from the Marriott. The nexus of Rostock's university crowd, which fills the large brick cellar and attached garden. The *Keller* hosts DJs, parties, and movies most nights; check the website for a schedule. Open Tu-Th from 9pm, F-Sa from 10pm. Cover Tu-Th €1, F-Sa €1.50. Cash only.

diesseits, Margaretenstr. 41 (☎203 68 95), serves pastas and steaks (€4-8) at outdoor tables that line the quiet Margaretenpl. The bar heats up at night, and has a long list of mixed drinks (€3-5). Breakfast M-Sa 9am-4pm, Sunday brunch 10am-3pm (€8). Open daily 9am-1am. Cash only.

Calamaris, Am Leuchtturm 3 (☎510 68 78), in Warnemünde, down the stairs from the lighthouse. Somewhat kitschy nautical decor complements fish (€6-12) and beer (€2-3). Open daily from 11:30am. Cash only.

STRALSUND ☎03831

Stralsund (pop. 60,000) is famous for the distinctive red brick Gothic architecture pervading its lively Altstadt. Founded in 1234, the city became an instrumental member of the Hanseatic League, amassing great wealth. Stralsund came under Swedish rule after the Thirty Years' War before being annexed by Prussia in 1815. Although the city was heavily damaged by air raids in WWII, reconstruction efforts have maintained the architectural integrity of the Altstadt. In 2002, the city, in conjunction with nearby Wismar, was recognized as a UNESCO World Heritage Site. Sadly, a slumping economy in the wake of reunification has left many of the city's historic buildings to decay, but tourism is now blossoming thanks to its upbeat atmosphere and its proximity to pristine Hiddensee.

⬛ TRANSPORTATION

Trains: To: **Berlin** (3½hr., 2 per hr., €32); **Binz** and **Sassnitz** on Rügen (both 1hr., every hr., €9); **Hamburg** (3-4hr., every hr., €34-44); **Rostock** (1hr., every hr., €12).

Buses: Intercity buses depart from the ZOB at **Frankenwall,** in the south of the Altstadt. Take Tribseer Damm right from the train station and then another right at the split onto Frankenwall. Within Stralsund, bus #1 circles the Altstadt. Lines #2-6 serve the Altstadt and the outskirts of town. Single ride €1.50, 9hr. day pass €3.50.

Ferries: Reederei Hiddensee (☎0180 321 21 50) runs 3 times per day to **Kloster, Vitte,** and **Neuendorf** on Hiddensee (round-trip €16-17, children €7-9, bikes €7.50).

Bike Rental: Fahrradverleih, Tribseer Damm 75 (☎30 61 58). To your right as you exit the train station. From €4.50 per day. Open M-F 9am-5pm, Sa 9am-1pm.

✳ 🛈 ORIENTATION AND PRACTICAL INFORMATION

Stralsund's historic **Altstadt** sits on a small island, bordered to the south and west by the **Frankenteich** and **Knieperteich,** two large natural ponds, and to the east by the **Stralsund,** a strait separating Rügen Island from the mainland. Two of 11 city gates remain, the **Kütertor** in the west and the **Kniepertor** to the north. A segment of the old city wall stretches between them. Stralsund's main pedestrian zone, **Ossen-reyerstraße,** runs north-south through the center of the Altstadt from the **Alter Markt** towards the **Neuer Markt.** The distinctive spires of the town's three main churches are landmarks that simplify navigation within the Altstadt. Stralsund's train station lies near the Altstadt's southwest corner across the Tribseer Damm.

Tourist Office: Alter Markt 9 (☎246 90; fax 24 69 22). From the train station, turn right on Tribseer Damm and follow the signs just past the Rathaus (10min.). Or take bus #4 to "Kütertor." Distributes free maps, finds rooms for €3, and rents **audio guide tours** (€5) of the Altstadt in English, German, and Swedish. Themed walking tours depart May-Sept. daily 11am and 2pm (€3-7.50, students €2-4.50). Open May-Sept. M-F 9am-7pm, Sa 9am-2pm, Su 10am-2pm; Oct.-Apr. M-F 10am-5pm, Sa 10am-2pm.

Emergency: Police ☎110. **Fire** and **Ambulance** ☎112.

Pharmacy: Tribseer Damm 6 (☎29 23 28), across the street from the train station. Open M-F 8am-6pm, Sa 8am-noon.

Internet Access: Internet- and EisCafé MATRIX, Wasserstr. 8-9. €4 per hr. Open daily 1-11pm. Access also available at one terminal in the **tourist office.** €0.50 per 10min., €2.50 per hr.

Post Office: Neuer Markt 4. Open M-F 9am-6pm, Sa 9am-noon. **Postal Code:** 18439.

▛ ACCOMMODATIONS

Pension Cobi, Jacobiturmstr. 15 (☎27 82 88; www.pension-cobi.de), by St. Jakobi on Böttcherstr. Located in one of the Altstadt's quiet residential neighborhoods, this pension has brightly lit, basic rooms with TV and bath. Breakfast included. Singles €37-45; doubles €46-69. Cash only. ❹

Hotel Schweriner Hof, Neuer Markt 1 (☎28 84 80, reservations 739 37 32; www.schweriner-hof.de). A stone's throw from the Marienkirche, this hotel has large rooms with TV, bath, radio, and minifridge. Breakfast included. Reception 7am-10pm. Singles €40-60; doubles €55-88; triples €66-117. AmEx/MC/V. ❹

Jugendherberge Stralsund-Devin (HI), Strandstr. 21 (☎49 02 89). From the station, take bus #3 to the end of the line at "Devin" (20min., €1.50). Take the path that veers right into the woods, continue on the trail to the left of the *Kurhaus-Devin,* and turn left when you hit Strandstr. (5min.). Located in the seaside village of Devin, this tired-looking hostel occupies 20 buildings near the beach. Breakfast included. Reception 7:30am-10:30pm. Check-in 3-7pm. Dorms €17.15, over 27 €20.15. MC. ❷

▟ FOOD

Stock up on **groceries** at **Edeka-Neukauf,** on the corner of Rudolf-Breitscheid-Str. and Mariakronstr. (Open M-F 8am-7:30pm, Sa 7am-6pm.) The many restaurants near the harbor serve fresh seafood late into the night, while cheaper bakeries and sidewalk cafés line Ossenreyerstr. and both Neuer and Alter Markt.

Fischermann's, An der Fährbrücke 3 (☎29 23 22). This massive restaurant and bar sprawls onto the pier. Fish dishes €8-14. Open daily 10am-2am. Cash only. ❸

Hansekeller, Mönchstr. 48 (☎70 38 40), occupies a Renaissance-era basement where customers relish regional specialties such as fish, duck, and *Sauerfleisch* (sour cured meat; €9.50-14). Come hungry. Open daily 11am-11pm. AmEx/DC/MC/V. ❸

Salsarico, Frankenstr. 7 (☎66 60 50). While the Mexican food served here (entrées €7.90-15.90) could hardly be considered authentic, south-of-the-border decor and imported Mexican beers (€2.50-2.90) provide a complete change of atmosphere from surrounding Stralsund. Popular bar late at night. Open daily 11am-1am. Cash only. ❸

◉ SIGHTS

▥ DEUTSCHES MUSEUM FÜR MEERESKUNDE UND FISCHEREI (THE GERMAN MUSEUM FOR OCEANOGRAPHY AND FISHING). At Germany's largest oceanographic museum, located in the former St. Katharinen monastery between Alter and Neuer Markt, mackerel and mussels have taken the place of monks and manuscripts. The museum is home to four aquariums, including a display of the Baltic and North Sea fishes and a tide pool environment. *(On the corner of Mönchstr. and Böltcherstr. ☎265 00. Open daily June-Sept. 10am-6pm; Oct.-May 10am-5pm. Feedings Sa-Su 11am. €6.50, students €4.50, families €17.)*

▥ KULTURHISTORISCHES MUSEUM (CULTURAL HISTORY MUSEUM). Sharing St. Katharinen with the Meeresmuseum, this wide-ranging collection covers all aspects of Stralsund's history. Collections range from Stone and Bronze Age artifacts to a series of rooms furnished in historical styles (including a DDR-style living room). The highlight of the collection is the spectacular Goldschatz von Hiddensee, a set of intricate gold jewelry created by the Vikings of Schleswig in the 9th century. The treasure washed up on the shores of nearby Hiddensee between 1873 and 1874, and contains 596 grams of pure gold. *(☎287 90. Open July-Oct. daily 10am-5pm; Nov.-June closed M. €4, students €2, families €8.)*

ALTER MARKT (OLD MARKET). As the name would suggest, the Alter Markt is surrounded by some of Stralsund's oldest buildings. The well-preserved 14th-century *Backsteingotik* facade of the **Rathaus** sports coats-of-arms from members of the Hanseatic League, including Stralsund's trademark green-and-gold 12-point stars. An inner courtyard opens to the street on all sides of the building. Next to the Rathaus, **St. Nikolaikirche,** the oldest parish church in Stralsund, has watched over the town since the 13th century. The church's interior glows with fresh paint and recently restored altarpieces. Efforts are underway to replace the missing second spire, destroyed in WWII. *(☎29 71 99. Open Apr.-Sept. M-Sa 10am-5pm, Su 2-4pm; Oct.-Mar. M-Sa 10am-noon and 2-4pm, Su 2-4pm.)*

NEUER MARKT (NEW MARKET). After the wealthier half of Stralsund built St. Nikolai, merchants from the other part of town responded by erecting the **Marienkirche** on Neuer Markt. The city's most impressive church, this late-Gothic colossus is best known for its rare mid-17th-century Stellwagen organ, under repair through 2008. The largest and best preserved of its kind in the world, its pipes range from 8mm to 10m. *(Concerts every second W 8pm, around €8-10.)* Climb 100m to the top of the church tower for a spectacular view of Stralsund. *(Open May-Sept. M-F 9am-6pm, Sa-Su 10am-5pm; Oct.-Apr. daily 10am-5pm. Tower €4, students and children €2.)*

JOHANNISKLOSTER. This Franciscan monastery, built in 1254, is one block up Külpstr. from the Alter Markt. Within the red-brick Gothic hallways are 14th-century mosaics, murals, and the town archives. On the upper floor, the unique *Raucherboden* (smoking attic) once housed stoves that vented directly into the chimneyless attic, helping to preserve the wooden beams of the rafters and impart the distinctive smoky smell that is still noticeable today. *(Open May-Oct. W-Su 10am-6pm. €2.10, students €1.70, families €4.)* Next to the monastery is the former **Johanni-skirche;** destroyed in 1944, the ruins now host occasional open-air concerts and theater performances. The monastery courtyard contains a dramatic Ernst Barlach sculpture in which Mary holds the stiff body of her dead son, who wears a war helmet; their bodies form a cross. In the public courtyard outside is a **memorial** to Stralsund's lost Jewish community. Originally in the Apollonienmarkt, near the former site of the synagogue, it was placed in the cloister after it was vandalized by neo-Nazis in 1991. A permanent swastika remains. *(Outer courtyard free.)*

ST. JAKOBIKIRCHE. At the eastern end of Böttcherstr., St. Jakobi is the third of Stralsund's monumental churches. It was damaged in 1944 and during the DDR days, the organ pipes were removed and used as rain gutters. Financial constraints have hampered restoration efforts. The crumbling church hosts frequent theatrical performances and concerts. *(☎29 04 02. Open daily 11am-6pm. Free.)*

RÜGEN ISLAND

In the Baltic Sea northeast of Stralsund, Germany's largest island is a natural paradise of white beaches, rugged chalk cliffs, beech forests, meadows, heaths, and swamps. Ancient stone burial sites and monuments scattered about the island are remnants of Rügen's stone age past. In the AD 5th century, the Teutonic tribes inhabiting the island were pushed out by the Slavs. The Danes came to the island 500 years later, converting the Slavs to Christianity. Briefly under Swedish control, Rügen eventually became part of Prussia. *Fürst* (Prince) Wilhelm Malte I was the first to introduce bathing tourism to the island in the early 1800s, and by the beginning of the 20th century the island was a favorite destination for nobility. The fall of the Berlin Wall opened up Rügen to a flood of westerners, and the island is quickly becoming one of Germany's favorite vacation destinations, attracting throngs of bikers, hikers, and beachgoers.

Trains leave Stralsund—the mainland gateway to Rügen—for Binz and Sassnitz (1hr., every hr., €9) via Bergen, an unattractive transportation hub in the center of the island. **Buses** connect Stralsund with Rügen's largest towns, and a **ferry** runs from Stralsund to Schaprode, near Hiddensee, on Rügen's west coast. Most visitors drive onto the island; public transportation tends to be expensive. To get to Kap Arkona in the north or Göhren in the south, you'll have to take an **RPNV** bus from Bergen or Sassnitz. (☎03838 194 49. Every hr.; €3-7, day pass €9.) The **Rasender Roland,** a narrow-gauge rail line with historic steam locomotives, runs every 2hr. from Putbus to Göhren (€8) with stops in many spa towns; however, with a top rate of 30km per hr., the railway is more of a tourist attraction than a means of transportation. The best way to appreciate Rügen's stunning scenery and picturesque towns is by hiking and biking. Although the whole island is crisscrossed and circled by trails, the best are found along the eastern coast in Nationalpark Jasmund, NSG Granitz, the Mönchgut Peninsula, and on Hiddensee Island to the west. There are 21 campgrounds in Rügen, with the majority to the southeast on the Mönchgut Peninsula.

JASMUND NATIONAL PARK

Carved by massive glaciers 12,000 years ago, Jasmund's jagged, white *Kreideklippen* (chalk cliffs) drop into an emerald-green sea. Due to erosion, the sheer faces of the tooth-like cliffs hang precariously over the stormy coast. Fortunately, the roots of the

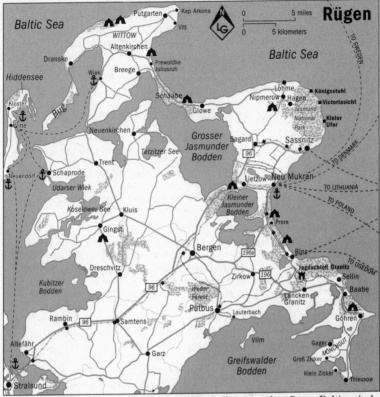

red beech trees above the cliffs help the chalk to weather fierce Baltic winds, although nature can at times overpower these safeguards, sending sections of chalky rock into the sea (see **Dissolving Landscapes**, p. 185). These 5000-year-old groves, as well as miles of canopied forest (the Baltic's largest), and the highest cliffs on the German coast make Jasmund Rügen's most attractive landscape.

⬛ TRANSPORTATION

Rügen is small enough that no matter where you stay, getting to the park will not take long. Trains run from Stralsund to Sassnitz, the gateway to the park. Once in

JASMUND NATIONAL PARK AT A GLANCE

AREA: 30sq. km.

CLIMATE: Frequent alternation between sun and rain. Warm, sunny summers; wet and windy winters.

FEATURES: Chalk cliffs, beech forests, wet grasslands, sandy beaches.

GATEWAY: Sassnitz

HIGHLIGHTS: Imposing cliff formations, like the arresting Königsstuhl (118m).

CAMPING: Forbidden within the park.

FEES AND RESERVATIONS: Admission fee at selected sights. Camping reservations recommended in summer. Parking €1.50-8.

Jasmund, bikes and feet are the best modes of transportation, as trails are plentiful and well-marked. Many of the more scenic coastline trails are off-limits to bikes because of numerous stairways. Buses #20 and 23 run from the Sassnitz train station to within 100m of the park's most famous site, the **Königsstuhl** (King's Throne). (2 per hr. in summer, until 5:40pm; €1.55.) Private cars are not permitted on the 3km stretch of road leading to the Königsstuhl. Drivers must park their cars in Hagen and take the #19 "Pendelbus" shuttle to the Königsstuhl (every 10min. in summer, €2.40) or walk the trail.

ORIENTATION AND PRACTICAL INFORMATION

Jasmund is a peninsula of Rügen that is nearly an island itself, flanked by the Großer Jasmunder Bodden on the west and the Baltic Sea on the east. The national park is at the easternmost tip of the peninsula, stretching between the towns of Sassnitz in the south and Lohme in the north. Twelve km of chalk cliffs descend over 100m into the sea along the coast and Stubnitz plateau, while beech forests, orchids, springs, lakes, moors, and ancient gravesites ornament the areas inland. Hiking and biking trails run throughout the park.

Emergency: Police ☎110. **Fire** and **Ambulance** ☎112.

Climate: Summer is the best time to come, as temperatures are generally warm enough for hikers to wear shorts and t-shirts. Surprise rain-showers spring up year-round.

Ranger Stations: The brand-new **Nationalpark-Zentrum am Königsstuhl** (☎038392 66 17 66; www.koenigsstuhl.com), by the entrance to the Königsstuhl lookout point, has maps and information on hand. Multimedia exhibits highlight the history and ecology of the park. Open daily Easter-Oct. 9am-7pm; Nov.-Easter 10am-5pm. Exhibits €6, children €3. The #6 ("Wedding") parking lot in Sassnitz is also staffed daily 9am-6pm.

Gear: Light hiking boots are adequate for the trails here. Bike trails are mostly bumpy cobblestone paths, so a mountain bike and an extra tire tube are recommended. Rain gear is a good idea at any time of year.

Tours: Free 2hr. German-language tours of the Königsstuhl area leave from the Hagen parking lot daily at 11am. Adler Schiffe (☎038378 477 90) runs **ferries** past the Jasmund Park shoreline, departing daily from Göhren, Sellin, and Binz. (2½-4hr., €12-15.)

CAMPING

The closest campsite to the park is **Wald-Camping-Nipmerow** ❶, 4km west of Königsstuhl. Take bus #20 or 23 from the Sassnitz station (dir.: Königsstuhl) to "Nipmerow." Most buses do not make the complete trip; be sure to ask before boarding. Otherwise, get off at "Königsstuhl," take bus #19 "Pendelbus" to Hagen, then hike the remaining 2km to reach the campground in Nipmerow. (☎038302 92 44. Bike/tent rental available. Reception 7am-6pm, but arrive anytime and check in the next morning. From €20 for 2 adults, 1 child, and 1 tent in summer.)

HIKING

KÖNIGSSTUHL HOCHUFERWEG. The park's signature trail is an 8.1km, 3hr. hike that starts in the #6 ("Wedding") parking lot in Sassnitz at the end of Weddingstr. and runs the length of the park's coastline, with other trails branching off it. The trail leads fairly easily from one scenic lookout to the next, often over enormous flights of stairs. When hiking, you can follow the white blazes with blue horizontal stripes painted on trees, but the signs at trail crossings or maps from the ranger station are more reliable. Six hundred meters into the trail, the **Piraten-**

schlucht offers a chance to make for the beach, but the trail continues on to the **Kieler Bach** lookout several kilometers farther. From there, you can walk the next stretch along the rocky water's edge or head back up the trail to the **Victoriasicht** lookout. This little balcony over the cliff offers a dramatic view with fewer tourists than the famous **Königsstuhl** 0.5km farther. If you follow the mob there, you'll have to pay the cost of admission to the Nationalpark-Zentrum (p. 170), and the view is only slightly better than what you can see from Victoriasicht for free. According to local legend, the first man to climb the crumbling cliff face to this chair-like formation became king of Rügen—hence *Königsstuhl* or "king's throne."

HERTHASEE. Running from the Hagen parking lot to the Königsstuhl beneath the shelter of red beech trees, this 3km trail offers an alternative to the shuttle bus. Two kilometers into the walk is the **Herthasee,** a lake named after the German harvest goddess. According to myth, Hertha drowned her mortal servants in this lake, and their spirits are said to gather on the banks each night. The **Herthaburg,** a U-shaped earth wall built by the Slavs in the 7th century, still stands near the shore.

BINZ ☎ 038393

Blindingly white seaside villas with frilly gables and wide balconies embody the *Bäderarchitecktur* (spa architecture) of Rügen's largest, liveliest, and most elegant resort town (pop. 5500). Nudists enjoy Binz's clothing-optional *FKK* (free body culture) beaches, tastefully situated at the end of town. Jazz crooners and oompah bands make frequent appearances on the stage by the Kurplatz pier.

Accommodations in Binz fill up quickly and run €5-10 more than those on other parts of the island. *Ferienwohnungen* (vacation apartments) are the best options, but only for couples or groups staying for a minimum of three days. The most cost-effective accommodations (doubles €40-70 per night) line the narrow alley at the eastern edge of Binz that climbs the Klünderberg. The little homes are opposite a quiltwork slope of individual garden plots, and the view of the Schmachter lake to the south is stunning. The room squeeze doesn't spare Rügen's youth hostel, **Jugendherberge Binz (HI)** ❷, Strandpromenade 35. Judging by its location and gourmet breakfast, one could mistake the hostel for a luxurious beach hotel, although mobs of German schoolchildren correct that mistake. (☎ 325 97; www.jugendherberge-binz.de. Breakfast included. Curfew 11pm but access code available. Dorms €21; over 27 €25.) If the hostel in Binz is full, you

DISSOLVING LANDSCAPES

Chalk it up to the natural forces of wind and water, but the cliff formations that inspired German painter Caspar David Friedrich's famous painting *Kreidefelsen auf Rügen* now lie dissolved in the Baltic Sea. The Wissower Klinken, formerly one of the top attractions of Rügen's Jasmund National Park, fell off into the water on February 25, 2005.

Officials blamed the cliffs' demise on unusually drastic spring weather conditions. Just as seasonal weather changes create potholes in road surfaces, the transition from winter to spring created enormous cracks in the precipice. Water in the cliffs froze, expanded, and then thawed, critically weakening the crags. While the cliffs (one of only four such formations in the world, along with those in Dover, Étretat, and on the Danish island of Mon) are prone to physical changes in the spring, this was the first time that such a well-known vista had disappeared. Over 50,000 cubic meters of chalk cliff slid into the sea, coloring it white for weeks as the chalk dissolved into the surrounding water.

Now, those desperate to see the Wissower Klinken will have to settle for Friedrich's rendition, currently held in Switzerland. Fortunately, however, visitors to the park can still console themselves with the dramatic view from the Königstuhl and the remaining 12km of chalk cliffs.

can try the **Jugendherberge Sellin (HI)** ❷, Kiefernweg 4, a block away from the train station in the neighboring resort town of Sellin. (☎0381 77 66 70. Breakfast included. Dorms €27. Cash only.) Also in Sellin, **Haus Sellin** ❷, Wilhelmstr. 9, occupies a historic gabled home along the town's main promenade. (☎038303 153; www.haus-sellin.de. Singles €26-48; doubles €42-94. Cash only.) At the end of Zepplinstr., **Edeka Neukauf**, Schillerstr. 5, sells **groceries**. (Open M-Sa 8am-8pm, Su noon-6pm.) Binz also teems with restaurants, bars, and ice cream stands. The **Strandcafé Binz** ❸, Strandpromenade 29, sells tasty pizza, pasta, and herring to the tune of €6-9. (☎327 45. Open daily from 11am. MC/V.) **Taverne "Minos"** ❸, Strandpromenade 38, oozes *ouzo*, Greek music, and tantalizing food, with gyros (€8.90), grill specialties and *moussaka* (€9.70). (☎148 88. Open M-F from 4pm, Sa-Su noon-3pm and 5pm-late.)

Pauli's Radshop, Hauptstr. 9a, rents bikes from €6 per day. (☎669 24. Open daily 9am-6pm.) The **Fremdenverkehrsverein**, Paulstr. 2, books rooms and provides basic information about the town. To get there, make a right on Dollahner Str., which becomes Jasmunder Str. Turn left on Zeppelinstr. and take an immediate right onto Paulstr. (☎66 57 40; www.gastgeber-binz.de.) To find the **Rügener Reiselotse Zimmervermittlung & Touristinformation**, Proraer Chaussee 3g, which also books rooms and provides local information, head right out of the station and veer right at the next street onto Proraer Chaussee. (☎337 89; www.reiselotse.com. Open M-Sa 10am-6pm.) For a **taxi**, call ☎03838 25 26 27. A **laundromat, SB Waschsalon**, is at Proraer Chaussee 3c. (Wash €4. Dry €1 per 13min. Open daily 6am-11pm.) The **post office** is at Zeppelinstr. 7. (Open M-F 10am-1pm and 2-5pm, Sa 9:30am-12:30pm.) **Postal Code:** 18609.

GRANITZ AND GÖHREN ☎038308

The 🏰**Jagdschloß Granitz**, in the dense Granitz forest, is an odd, castle-like hunting lodge designed in 1836 by Prussian architect **Friedrich Schinkel,** whose unmistakable creations can be seen all over the island. Built on top of the Tempelberg hill, its 38m tower offers a panorama of the island. Faint of heart, beware: 164 animal heads are mounted in the **Jagdmuseum** (Hunting Museum), and antlers have been crafted into chairs and chandeliers. The Roland rail line stops at the Jagdschloß, as does the **Jagdschloßexpress**, which leaves from the *Seebrücke* in Binz (☎338 80 for price, times, and reservations). From the Roland "Jagdschloß" stop, head uphill on the trail off to the right to reach the castle. To walk or bike the 5km from Binz, take the red-striped trail near the top of the Klünderberg hill in eastern Binz. (Open May-Sept. daily 9am-6pm; Oct.-Apr. Tu-Su 10am-4pm. €3, students €2.50.) Heading south from the "Jagdschloß" stop to the village of Lancken-Granitz, you'll pass prehistoric graves from 2300 BC; larger ones lie southwest of town. The Roland's final stop is **Göhren** (pop. 1300), on the easternmost tip of the forested **Mönchgut Peninsula**, settled by monks in the 13th century. The city sits on a hill, with a view of Greifswald across the sea from the church off Strandstr. **Hiking** and **biking trails** lead through the beaches, forests, and hills of the **Zickerschen Berge.**

An excellent two hour bike trip follows the well-marked trail from Göhren through Theissow to Klein Zicker on the tip of the peninsula. Catch the bus back from Klein Zicker, or retrace the route to return to Göhren. Göhren's main attractions are the **Mönchguter Museen**, four tiny museums scattered about the town. The first of these, the **Heimatmuseum** (Local History Museum) describes the geology of the Mönchgut peninsula and traces the evolution of Göhren from a fishing village to a tourist resort. A block away, the **Museumshof** exhibits antique farming machinery. On Thiessower Str., off Strandstr., the **Rookhus** has a display of fishing equipment inside a historic building. Farther down the hill on Theissower Str., you can peer inside the cargo hold of the 20m-long boat-cum-museum **Museumsschiff Luise,** or learn knot-tying skills in the summer every Wednesday 10am-noon. (☎21 75. Heimatmuseum and Museumshof: open daily mid-Apr. to May and Sept. to mid-Oct. 10am-5pm; mid-Oct. to mid-Apr. 10am-4pm. Rookhus: June-Aug. 10am-2pm; mid-Apr. to May and Sept. to mid-Oct. 11am-2pm. Museumsschiff: July-Aug. 10am-5pm; Apr.-June and Sept.-Oct. 10am-1pm. Each museum €3, adults with *Kurkarte* or students €2.50; day card for all 4 museums €8/6, families €15.)

Göhren's campground, **Regenbogen Camp Göhren ❶,** is one block to the right of the train station, near the beach. The site boasts a restaurant, cinema (€6), **laundromat,** and **Spar grocery.** (☎901 20; www.regenbogen-camp.de. Reception M-Th and Su 8am-9pm, F-Sa 8am-10pm. €4.90 per person, €7.90-10.60 per tent, less in low season. Reservations possible only for stays of 3 or more days. V.) For a hot meal try **Zum Leuchtfeuer ❷,** Max-Dreyer-Str. 6, an inexpensive restaurant close to the center of town. From Strandstr., turn onto Max-Dreyer-Str.; the restaurant is up the hill on the left. Fish and meat dishes range €6-9. (Open daily 11:30am-2pm and from 5pm; Apr.-Oct. only evenings. Cash only)

Navigating Göhren is simple; almost everything is on or near **Strandstraße.** To get to the town center from the train station, turn left and take Bahnhofstr. until it turns into Strandstr., then follow it up the hill. Frequent **buses** connect Göhren to Binz, Bergen, Sassnitz, and Klein Zicker (€3-6). The **Fahrradverleih,** Kastanienallee 9, rents touring **bikes** for €4 and mountain bikes for €5. (☎254 06. Open daily 9am-12:30pm and 5-6:30pm.) To get to the **tourist office,** Poststr. 9, follow Strandstr. from the train station up the hill as it turns into Poststr.; the office is on the right. (☎667 90; www.goehren-ruegen.de. Open M-F 9am-6pm, Sa 9am-noon.) The **Fremdenverkehrsverein,** Berliner Str. 8, a block past the Kurverwaltung, books rooms. (☎259 40; info@zimmervermittlung-goehren-ostsee.de.) A **Pharmacy** is at Strandstr. 3. (☎910 20. Open M-F 8am-12:30pm and 2:30-6pm, Sa 9am-noon.) The **post office** is inside the **Edeka** grocery store at the corner of Strandstr. and Waldstr. (Store open M-F 8am-7pm, Sa-Su 8am-1pm and 4-6pm.) **Postal Code:** 18586.

KAP ARKONA AND VITT
☎038391

At Rügen's northernmost extreme, the dramatic **Kap Arkona**—Germany's only cape—lies on the charming half-island of Wittow (in the local *Plattdeutsch,* or Low German, it means "land of the wind"). Quieter and less accessible than Rügen's southern regions, Wittow is carpeted with wildflowers. Near Kap Arkona is the tiny fishing village of **Vitt,** with 13 reed homes. Before reunification, the three lighthouses on Kap Arkona were part of a restricted area belonging to the DDR's National People's Army. The short, rectangular **Schinkelturm** (Schinkel Tower), designed by architect Karl Friedrich Schinkel, was built in 1827. It guarded the DDR's sea borders, but has been open to the public since 1993. Next door, the **Neuer Leuchtturm** (New Lighthouse) towers above the other two lighthouses, offering the best views. (Schinkelturm open daily 10am-7pm. Neuer Leuchturm open daily 11am-6pm. Neuer Leuchtturm €3, Schinkelturm €2.) From the two lighthouses, you can make the steep descent to the beach via the wooden steps of the **Königstreppe.** The nearby **Marinepeilturm** (Naval Pinpointing Tower) was built in 1927 and rigged to listen in on British radio communications. The tower now houses art exhibits along the stairway spiraling up to the observation deck. (Open daily 10am-6pm. €2, students €1.50.) Next to the Marinepeilturm is the **Slawischer Burgwall,** the remains of an old Slavic fortification. (Open daily 10am-5:45pm. €1.)

The **Campingplatz Altenkirchen ❶** is 2km east of Altenkirchen. (☎129 65; www.camping-auf-ruegen.de. Reception 9am-noon and 3-6pm. Open Apr.-Oct. €3-5 per adult, €2-3 per child, tents €3.50-8.) Dining options in the area are limited, but there are a few pleasant outdoor cafés in Vitt, and fishermen usually smoke and sell their catch at the town's tiny harbor.

MECKLENBURG-VORPOMMERN

Buses run every hr. from Sassnitz (#13, 40min., €4.85) to Altenkirchen, where you can transfer to bus #11 to "Putgarten" (15min., €1.40), 1.5km away from the cape and its lighthouses. The 1km walk along the coast between Kap Arkona and Vitt is jaw-dropping: in spring and summer, flowering bushes and brilliant red poppies carpet the hills. The gorgeous 4.6km loop between Putgarten, Kap Arkona, and Vitt is ideal for biking. Rent **bikes** by the tourist office. (Open daily 10am-6pm. €2.50 per hr., €5 per 3hr., €7 per day.) You may prefer the painfully slow *Arkonabahn*, a tourist train that connects these destinations for a modest fee. (30min. round-trip; 2 per hr.; €2 one-way to either Kap Arkona or Vitt from Putgarten, or €3 round-trip to both, children 6-13 €0.50/1.50.) **Horse-drawn carts** also make the loop at a leisurely pace (1½hr.; 2 per hr.; €10, children €4). The combination souvenir shop and **tourist office,** in Putgarten's parking lot, 300m down the road from the bus stop in the direction of Altenkirchen, books rooms. (☎41 90; www.kap-arkona.de. Open M-F 9am-5pm, Sa 10am-5pm, Su 11am-5pm.)

▶ DAYTRIP FROM RÜGEN: HIDDENSEE   ☎038300

West of Rügen is Hiddensee, called in *Plattdeutsch "das söte Länneken"* (the sweet little island). The majority of it is now part of the protected **Nationalpark Vorpommersche Boddenlandschaft** (Vorpommern Lagoon National Park), and Hiddensee remains the same sliver of unadulterated natural beauty that drew Sigmund Freud, Albert Einstein, and Thomas Mann to its shores. Automobiles are prohibited—even garbage trucks are horse-drawn—so bikes rule the island.

Hiddensee makes a superb daytrip from Stralsund or Rügen. You can easily see the entire island in a day on **bike.** *Fahrradverleih* (bike rentals) are hard to miss; the standard rate is €6 for a 5-speed. Since many of the island's roads are either muddy country trails or sandy beach paths, a mountain bike with fat tires and plenty of gears is best. **Reederei Hiddensee** (☎03831 26 81 38) operates ferries from Stralsund to Hiddensee's three towns: Neuendorf, Vitte, and Kloster (90min.; round-trip €14-18 including Hiddensee *Kurkarte;* bikes €6.50/7.50), as well as ferries from Schaprode, on Rügen. (Round-trip to Vitte €14.80, ages 4-14 €8.60, families €42.50.) To get to Schaprode, take bus #410 from Bergen. (30min., €3.40.)

Vitte (pop. 650) is Hiddensee's main town and home to the island's best beaches. As Hiddensee has neither a hostel nor a campground, visit the **tourist office,** Norderende 162, in Vitte, to book a room. (☎642 26; www.seebad-insel-hiddensee.de. Open May-Sept. M-F 8:30am-5pm, Sa-Su 10am-noon; Oct. M-F 8:30am-4pm; Nov.-Mar. M-F 9am-3pm.) The **National Park Information Center,** Norderende 2, at the northern edge of Vitte on the way to Kloster, can provide further assistance, and displays the unique geology of the island. (☎680 41. Open daily in summer 10am-4pm; in winter 10am-3pm.) In Vitte, you can catch lunch at **Godewind,** Süderende 53, before you start exploring. Try the fresh fish (€8-14), and a glass of *Sanddorn-saft,* a rust-colored, honey-like local specialty drink (€3.50), also available in bottled form from many stores on the island (€3-6 per bottle, €8-13 for the alcoholic variant). Buy **groceries** at **Edeka Markt** a block from the Vitte Harbor on Wallweg. (☎66 00. Open M-F 8am-7pm, Sa 8am-6pm, Su 1-5pm.)

GREIFSWALD   ☎03834

Graced with one of Germany's oldest and smallest universities, Greifswald (pop. 55,000) belongs to its students. Small gold plaques throughout the historic college town commemorate 545 years worth of professors, and the cobblestone streets swarm with students on bikes. Even in the summer, students populate the handful of bars tucked between the historic churches of the remarkably well-preserved Altstadt, which was never a target of Allied air raids.

◘ ⃞ ORIENTATION AND TRANSPORTATION. Greifswald is the easternmost city on Germany's Baltic coast, 60km west of the Polish frontier. Signs of life in Greifswald are confined to the Altstadt, home to all of the city's historic architecture and the majority of the restaurants and nightlife. **Trains** run to: Berlin (3½-4hr., every hr., €29-45); Rostock (1¾hr., every 2hr., €16-21); Schwerin (3hr., every 2hr., €27); Stralsund (20min., 1-2 per hr., €6-9). The **bus station (ZOB)** is across from the train station. (Single ride €1.50, daypass €3.50.) To get a **taxi**, call ☎ 50 22 22. Rent **bikes** at **Zweirad Kruger,** Gützkowerstr. 81-82, on the way to the hostel from the station. (☎ 50 22 68; www.zweirad-kruger-greifswald.de. Bikes from €5 per day. Open M-F 9am-6pm and Sa 9am-noon.)

◪ ⃞ PRACTICAL INFORMATION. At the **tourist office** in the Rathaus am Markt, book a room for free or get a free map of the Altstadt. (☎ 52 13 80; www.greifswald.de. Open May-Sept. M-F 9am-6pm, Sa 10am-2pm; July-Aug. also Su 10am-2pm. Oct.-Apr. M-F 9am-5pm.) Do **laundry** at **Schnell und Sauber,** Gützkowerstr. 19. (Wash €3. Dry €0.50 per 15min. Open daily 6am-11pm.) A **pharmacy** is at Markt 1. (☎ 21 38 or 25 35. Open M-F 7:30am-6:30pm, Sa 9am-noon.) Find **Internet** access at **Mowie's Internet Café,** on the corner of Hans-Beimler-Str. and Anklamer Str. (Open M-F 9am-6:30pm, Sa 9am-12:30pm. €2.50 per hr.) The **post office** is down the street at Markt 15-19. (Open M-F 9am-6pm, Sa 9am-noon.) **Postal Code:** 17489.

⃞ ⃞ ACCOMMODATIONS AND FOOD. Greifswald's clean and basic **Jugendherberge Greifswald (HI) ❷,** Pestalozzistr. 11-12, is 15min. from the Altstadt. From the station, take a right on Bahnhofstr., a right on Gützkowerstr., then a left on Pestalozzistr. (☎ 516 90; fax 51 69 10. Breakfast (7:30-9am) included. Reception 7am-10pm. Dorms €25.90, under 27 €21.90.) Ritzy cafés line the cobblestone Markt in front of the Rathaus. Nearby, **Das Sofa ❷,** Bruggstr. 29, has light pasta and pizza (€4), lots of comfy sofas, and a kitschy film motif. (☎ 89 95 51. Open daily from 11am. Cash only.) **Café Malanders ❶,** Lange Str. 49, inside the Soziokulturelles Zentrum, offers small entrées for €2-3. (☎ 89 95 51. Open Tu-Th 11:30am-5pm, F 11:30am-4pm. Cash only.) **Café Caspar ❷,** Fischstr. 11, serves tasty breakfasts (€3-5), baguettes (€4), and salads (€5-7) in a self-consciously sophisticated environment, and doubles as a bar at night. (☎ 89 13 00. Open daily from 9am. Cash only.)

◙ SIGHTS. Stretching high above the Greifswald skyline is the **St. Nikolaikirche,** Domstr. 54. Around the tower of this 14th-century basilica, a small viewing platform is accessible by a narrow, 60m spiral staircase. Like the rest of the Altstadt, the church survived WWII partly because a German general risked death by surrendering the city to the Soviets in April of 1945. (☎ 26 27. Open Su after 10am services; May-Oct. M-Sa 10am-4pm; Nov.-Apr. M-F 11am-3pm. €1.50, students €1. Tours W 2pm, €2.) The cannonballs that struck the east wall of the 13th-century **St. Marienkirche,** Friedrich-Löffler-Str. 68, during a war with Brandenburg in 1678 are still lodged there. The early Gothic interior is worth a look. (☎ 22 63. Open June-Oct. M-F 10am-5pm, Sa 10am-2pm, Su 10:45am-noon; Nov.-Apr. M-F noon-1pm, Su 10:45am-noon; May M-F 10am-noon, Su 10:45am-noon. Free.) The **Karzer,** Rubinenstr. 1, are prison cells in the basement of the main university building which were used to punish students for various offenses, including chasing "strange women" and drinking too much. The rowdiest served sentences of up to 10 days, although by the early 20th century it was common practice to let student prisoners out for a few hours each day to eat and socialize. Some of the best parties were purportedly held in *Karzer* cells—students would climb walls and through the windows. (☎ 86 11 22. Call for hours.) The **Gemäldegalerie** (Picture Gallery), Mühlenstr. 15, displays a large collection of paintings from the Romantic and Impressionist eras, including a Van Gogh. (☎89 43 57. Open Tu-Su 10am-6pm. €4.50, students €2.50. Audio guides in English, German, Polish, and Swedish.) Near the train station, the university's modest **Botanischer Garten**, Münterstr. 11, features pleasant gardens and a greenhouse with lush hanging vines and spiky cacti. (☎86 11 30. Open year-round M-F 9am-3:45pm; May-Sept. Sa-Su 1-6pm; Oct.-Nov. and Apr. Sa-Su 1-4pm; Dec.-Mar. Sa-Su 1-3pm.)

▓ **NIGHTLIFE.** At night, students flock to **Domburg**, Domstr. 21, with deep-red, high-backed sofa chairs and walls swathed in white cloth. (☎77 63 51. Happy hour 7-10pm. mixed drinks €3.50. Open in summer M-F from 11am, Sa-Su from 2pm; in winter Sa-Su from 2pm. Cash only). At **CoMiX**, Steinbeckerstr. 30, student bartenders mix on both floors. (☎88 45 99. Open M-F noon-3am, Sa 3pm-3am, Su 5pm-3am. Cash only.) **Pariser**, Kapaunenstr. 20, was founded in 1991 in an abandoned building and runs, among other projects, a bar with a made-from-scratch feel, where bold guests can sign up to DJ. (☎85 55 89. Open W-Su from 8pm.)

USEDOM ISLAND

During the 19th century, Usedom was a favorite vacation destination for Germany's elite, earning it the nickname "Berlin's bathtub." Depression and war temporarily scattered the tourists, but their beach toys—enormous, gaudy houses and long piers—remain. Today, the island is the playground of the *petite bourgeoisie;* a swarm of upper-middle-class families fills the beaches and rents rooms in restored palaces. A hilly bike trail spans the island's sun-dappled woods, showing off Usedom's natural beauty and offering access to secluded warm-water beaches.

◧ TRANSPORTATION

Usedom lies at the northeastern corner of Germany; the easternmost portion of the island belongs to Poland. Tourists fill the island in July and August, so it's a good idea to reserve rooms in advance. Usedom is connected to the national rail system through the **Usedomer Bäderbahn (UBB)**, which runs the length of the island, connecting all its towns to Greifswald and Stralsund. A UBB day pass costs €15. **Adler-Schiffe** (☎038378 477 90) runs **ferries** daily from Usedom's resorts to Binz on Rügen Island (3½hr., €21). The price of a *Kurkarte*, required for beach access, is automatically added to your accommodation bill (€2 per day; under 18 €1).

ZINNOWITZ   ☎038377

Commercially upscale, this resort town is packed with a diverse crowd of beachgoers. The **Sportschule ❷**, Dr.-Wachsmann-Str. 30, caters to sports teams, but opens up its big, airy dorms to individuals as well. The track, handball court, and ping-pong tables are free for guests. (☎422 68; fax 422 80. Breakfast €6. Book well in advance. Dorms €20, €18 for each night past the 4th. Cash only.) Just down the street, the expansive **Campingplatz Pommernland**, Dr.-Wachsmann-Str. 40, rents **camping plots ❶** and has several new but expensive **bungalows ❹**. (☎403 48; fax 403 49. Reception daily 8am-noon and 2-9pm. Camping €5.25 per person, €4.25 per student, €4-6 per tent. Less for low season and longer stays. Bungalows: doubles €80; quads €100; 6-person €110.) Restaurants line Neue Strandstr. and the Strandpromenade, while the **Edeka Neukauf** supermarket, Neue Strandstr. 38, sells groceries perfect for a beach picnic. (Open M-F 8am-8pm, Sa 8am-8pm, Su noon-6pm.)

Trains run to Greifswald (1hr., every 2hr., €8) and Stralsund (1½hr., every 2hr., €12.20). For a **taxi** call ☎405 67. At the corner of Neue Strandstr. and Dünenstr., the **Kurverwaltung** (Spa Administration), Neue Sandstr. 30, books rooms for free.

(☎49 20; fax 422 29. Open M-F 9am-6pm, Sa-Su 10am-3pm.) They also offer **bike tours** that leave from the office. (M 9:30am, Tu and Th 10am. €3, with *Kurkarte* €1.50.) Rent **bikes** at **Fahrradverleih Meister Betrieb,** Dr.-Wachsmann-Str. 5. (☎428 69. May-Aug. €4, Sept.-Apr. €3. Open daily 8am-noon and 1-7pm.) There is a **pharmacy** at Neue Strandstr. 39. (☎421 66. Open July-Aug. M-F 8am-7pm, Sa 8:30am-1pm; Sept.-June M-F 8am-6pm, Sa 8:30am-noon.) The **library,** in the back of the Kurverwaltung building at Neue Strandstr. 30, offers **Internet** access (€1.02 per 15min.; open M-F 9am-6pm, Sa-Su 10am-3pm), as does the **Zinnowitz Internet Café,** Neue Strandstr. 16. (☎398 90. First 12min. €1, €0.083 per additional min. Open M-F 10am-7pm, Sa 2pm-7pm; May-Sept. also Su 2-7pm.) The **post office** is at Neue Strandstr. 38. (Open M-F 8am-6pm, Sa 8am-noon.) **Postal Code:** 17454.

KOSEROW ☎038375

At Usedom's narrowest point, forests of moss-covered trees fall onto stunning beaches in what is, refreshingly, the least touristed of Usedom's resort towns. Koserow's central location on the island makes it a good base for hiking and biking excursions. A short climb to **Streckelsburg,** the island's highest point (58m), affords a beautiful view. While nearly every house in the small town advertises rooms for rent, they are usually booked well in advance. **Wald und Meer,** above the beach on the west end of town 1km from Hauptstr., at the end of Forster-Schrödter-Str., runs a large **pension ❹** with bare dorm-style accommodations in the **Radlercamp ❷.** (☎26 20; www.koserow.de. Breakfast included. Sheets €5. Camp: beds €18. Pension: singles €48; doubles €31-41 per person. Cash only.) **Campingplatz Am Sandfeld ❶** has the best view on the island. By the station end of Hauptstr., take a right onto Siemensstr. and follow the signs for 15min. (☎207 59; fax 214 05. Laundry €2.50 per hr. Reception 8am-1pm and 3-10pm. Open Apr.-Sept. €5 per person, €4-6 per tent, €2.50 per car. Cash only.) A **Netto** supermarket, Hauptstr. 67, sells groceries. (Open M-Sa 7am-8pm, Su noon-6pm.) The best places to eat in Koserow are the bakeries along Hauptstr. and the *Salzhütten* by the pier, where fishermen packed herring during the 19th century, and where **Udo's Fischräucherei ❷** now smokes delicious salmon and sells *Fischbrötchen* (fish rolls; €1-2) and fish plates for €3.50-7. (Open 10am-5:30pm. Cash only.)

Trains run to Greifswald (1½hr., every 2hr., €9.60) and Stralsund (1¾hr., every 2hr., €13.80). For a **taxi** call ☎202 07. **Fahrrad Ortmann,** Bahnhofstr. 2, rents **bikes.** (☎213 60. €3-5 per day. Open M-F 9am-noon and 2-6pm, Sa 9am-noon.) The **tourist office,** Hauptstr. 21, has free maps. (☎204 15; www.seebad-koserow.de. Open July-Aug. M-F 9am-6pm, Sa-Su 9am-noon; May-June and Sept. M-F 9am-6pm; Jan.-Apr. and Oct.-Mar. M-F 9am-4pm, Sa 9am-noon.) The **Zimmervermittlung** (Accommodations Bureau), Hauptstr. 11, finds rooms for free. (☎210 62; fax 210 64. Open M-F 9am-5pm, Sa 9am-noon.) Most services line Hauptstr., which connects to the train station via Bahnhofstr.: a **pharmacy, Apotheke,** Schulstr. 1b (☎20 71; open M-F 8am-6pm, Sa 8am-noon); **Internet** access at **Hotel Nautic,** Hauptstr. 46e (open daily 8am-10pm; €4.60 per hr.); and a small **post office,** Hauptstr. 49a, near the train station. (Open M-F 8:30am-12:30pm and 2:30-5:30pm, Sa 9-11am.) **Postal Code:** 17459.

HERINGSDORF ☎038378

Heringsdorf has long been the most elite of Usedom's resort towns, illustrated by the rows of ornate villas that line the waterfront. It was a favorite vacation spot of **Kaiser Wilhelm I,** who paid his first visit in 1820. His house, at Delbrückestr. 6, is privately owned, but you can see it from the street. Although Heringsdorf was a popular destination for dignitaries straight through the DDR years, interest has spurted in the wake of reunification. The town's tourist trade thrives at its new pier, the busy shops lining the **Platz des Friedens,** and the long beachfront promenade. To get to the Platz, which lies at the heart of Heringsdorf, turn left on Bülowstr. from the station, right on Friedenstr., and follow it to the end. A kilometer down the beach at Maxim-Gorki-Str. 13, **Villa Irmgard,** the former home of Russian writer **Maxim Gorki,** is now a museum housing Gorki's personal possessions, an exposition on the history of Heringsdorf, and interesting temporary exhibits upstairs. (☎223 61. Open Apr.-Oct. and around Christmas Tu-Su noon-6pm; Nov.-Mar. Tu-Su 10am-4pm. €4, with *Kurkarte* €3, ages 6-14 €2.)

During the high season (July-Aug.), it's virtually impossible to find accommodations in Heringsdorf; most vacationers reserve early in the year. The ideally located **Jugendherberge Heringsdorf (HI) ❷,** Puschkinstr. 7, occupies a set of old beach houses between Heringsdorf and Ahlbeck. From the train station, turn right on Liehrstr. and follow the signs right onto Delbrückestr. (☎223 25; www.jh-heringsdorf.de. Breakfast included. Reception 7am-10pm. Curfew 10pm. Reservations required. €19.50, over 26 €23.50.) If the hostel is full, call or email the **Zimmervermittlung** (Accommodations Bureau) for rooms (☎447 10; zimmervermittlung@dreikaiserbaeder.de). Food in Heringsdorf is generally expensive and aimed at an older crowd, though many cafés have terraces with amazing beach views. **Terrassen Kaffee ❸,** Kulmstr. 29, serves traditional German dishes (€8-14) on a patio with a lovely view of the ocean. (☎225 40. Open daily 11:30am-11pm. Cash only.)

Most tourist services cluster around the Platz. **Trains** run to Greifswald (2hr., every 2hr., €12.50) and Stralsund (2¼hr., every 2hr., €16.70). For a **taxi,** call ☎229 92. Rent a **bike** at **Fahrradverleih Elegant,** Kulmstr. 26a. (☎223 14. €5 per day. Open daily 9am-6pm.) Heringsdorf's **tourist office** is at Kulmstr. 33. (☎24 51; fax 24 54. Open M-F 9am-6pm, Sa-Su 10am-3pm.) The **police station** is down the street at Seestr. 12 (☎110). A **pharmacy, Apotheke Heringsdorf,** is at Seestr. 40. (☎25 90. Open M-F 8am-6:30pm, Sa 8am-12:30pm.) At Seestr. 17, find **Internet** access at **Kaiserbäder I-Café** (☎330 86; open Tu-Th noon-8pm, F-Sa 2-8pm) and a **post office.** (☎228 80. Open M-F 9am-noon and 2-6pm, Sa 9am-noon.) **Postal Code:** 17424.

SCHLESWIG-HOLSTEIN

 The only *Land* to border two seas, Schleswig-Holstein bases its past and present livelihood on the trade generated at its port towns. Between the western coast of the North Sea and the eastern coast of the Baltic, the velvety plains are populated primarily by sheep and bales of hay. Although Schleswig-Holstein became a Prussian province in 1867 following Bismarck's defeat of Denmark, the region retains close cultural and commercial ties with Scandinavia. Linguistically, Schleswig-Holstein is also isolated from its southern neighbors by its various dialects of *Plattdeutsch* (literally, "flat German") and, to a lesser extent, the Dutch-like Frisian spoken throughout the *Land*. The most noticeable difference is the greeting *Moin* or *Moin moin*, a *Plattdeutsch* salutation used all day.

HIGHLIGHTS OF SCHLESWIG-HOLSTEIN

BARE ALL on the barren dunes of the island **Sylt** (p. 206), Germany's favorite beach.

SCRUTINIZE sailboats from all over the world during **Kiel's Kieler Woche** (p. 200).

SAVOR legendary marzipan from **Lübeck's I.G. Niederegger Marzipan Café** (p. 195) while listening to the strains of the world's largest mechanical organ echo through the magnificent **Marienkirche** (p. 197).

LÜBECK ☎ 0451

At night, a medieval aura lingers in the shadowy facades of Lübeck's old homes and around the steeples of its many churches. In its heyday, the city was capital of the Hanseatic League, controlling trade across Northern Europe. Later it was home to literary giants Heinrich and Thomas Mann, who had a tempestuous relationship with the local bourgeoisie. The city still has a tendency to rest on its glorious past, understandably—meticulous post-WWII reconstruction has refashioned Lübeck into an engaging medieval town. It may no longer be a center of political and commercial influence, but tourists still flock to Lübeck (pop. 215,000) for its history, famous marzipan, and red-blonde *Duckstein* beer.

▄ TRANSPORTATION

Trains: Every hr. to: **Berlin** (3½hr., €36-66); **Hamburg** (45min., €11); **Kiel** (1¼hr., €13); **Rostock** (2hr., €18); **Schwerin** (1¼hr., €11).

Ferries: Many ferries run tours of the canals out of the waterfront on An der Obertrave and An der Untertrave. **Quandt-Linie,** An der Obertrave (☎777 99), cruises around the Altstadt, canal, and harbor from the bridge in front of the Holstentor. €7, students €5.50. May-Oct. daily every 30min. 10am-6pm; less frequent in the low season.

Public Transportation: The Altstadt is easily seen on foot, though Lübeck also has an excellent bus network. The **ZOB** (central bus station) is across from the train station. Single ride €1.50-2.15, children €0.85-1.20; day pass €7. To reach the Lübeck airport,

take bus #6 (dir.: Blankenese/Seekamp) to "Flughafen." Direct questions to the **Service Center am ZOB** (☎888 28 28). Open M-F 5am-8pm, Sa-Su 9am-4pm.

Car Rental: Hertz, Willy-Brandt-Allee 1 (☎70 22 50), near the train station. From €49 per day. Open M-F 7am-6pm, Sa 7am-1pm, Su 9-10am.

Bike Rental: Jugendwerkstatt Leihcycle, Schwartauer Allee 39 (☎426 60), in a back courtyard. €5 per day. Open M-F 9am-5pm, Sa 10am-noon.

🛈 PRACTICAL INFORMATION

Tourist Office: Holstentorpl. 1 (☎88 22 33, €0.12 per min.; fax 409 19 92), next to the Holstentor. The informed staff books rooms for free, dispenses city maps (€0.90), offers Internet access (€3 per hr.), and sells the **Happy Day Card,** which provides unlimited access to public transportation and discounted admission to many museums. Open June-Sept. M-F 9am-7pm, Sa 10am-3pm; Oct.-Nov. and Jan.-May M-F 9:30am-6pm, Sa 10am-3pm; Dec. M-F 9:30am-6pm, Sa 10am-2pm.

Tours: Red **LVG Open-Air-Stadtrundfahrt** buses provide tours of the city, leaving every hr. from the "Kohlmarkt/Wahmstr." stop. July-Aug. daily 11am-4pm; June and Sept. Sa-Su only. €5.50, children €3.80, families €14.50.

Currency Exchange: Deutsche Bank, Kohlmarkt 7 (☎14 90). Open M-Tu and Th 8:30am-6pm, W 8:30am-1pm, F 8:30am-4:30pm. 24hr. **ATM** at post office.

Laundromat: McWash (☎ 702 03 57), on the corner of An der Mauer and Hüxterdamm. Wash €3.90 per 7kg, soap included. Dry €0.80 per 15min. Open M-Sa 6am-9pm.

Emergency: Police, Mengstr. 18-20 *(☎ 110).* **Fire** ☎ 112. **Ambulance** ☎ 192 22.

Women's Resources: Rape Crisis Center: Musterbahn 3 (☎ 70 46 40). Open M 9am-1pm, Tu and Th 4-6pm. Phone consultations M and W-F 9am-1pm, Tu and Th 4-6pm.

Pharmacy: Adler-Apotheke, Breite Str. 71 (☎ 798 85 15, after hours 710 81). Open M-F 8:30am-7pm, Sa 9am-6pm.

Post Office: Königstr. 44-46. 24hr. **ATM.** Open M-F 8:30am-6:30pm, Sa 8:30am-1pm. **Postal Code:** 23552.

ACCOMMODATIONS AND CAMPING

▓ **Rucksack Hotel,** Kanalstr. 70 (☎70 68 92; www.rucksackhotel-luebeck.de). Bus #1, 11, 21, or 31 to "Katharineum." This popular hostel is a member of a collective of communalist, eco-friendly shops in a former glass factory. Breakfast €3. Sheets €3. Free wireless Internet access. Reception 10am-1pm and 5-9pm. 6- to 10-bed dorms €13; doubles with bath €40; quads €60-68. Student discount in winter. Cash only. ❶

Jugendherberge Lübeck-Altstadt (HI), Mengstr. 33 (☎ 702 03 99; fax 770 12). Typical hostel, unbeatable location. Breakfast included. Reception 7am-midnight. Lockout midnight; guests 18+ can get a key. Dorms €17.90, over 27 €20.90; singles and doubles from €22.90/25.90. €1 per night discount for stays of 3+ nights. MC/V. ❷

Jugendherberge Lübeck "Vor dem Burgtor" (HI), Am Gertrudenkirchhof 4 (☎334 33; www.djh-ris.de), off Travemünder Allee. This large, recently renovated hostel 15min. from the town center brims with activity. Breakfast included. Internet access €0.50 per 5min. Laundry €2.60. Dorm beds €16.80, over 27 €19.80. AmEx/DC/MC/V. ❷

Baltic Hotel, Hansestr. 11 (☎855 75; www.baltic-hotel.de). Cheerfully bright rooms with phone and TV. The owner is a veritable encyclopedia of Lübeck's history. Breakfast included. Reception 7am-10pm. Singles from €38; doubles from €68. MC/V. ❹

Sleep-In (CVJM), Große Petersgrube 11 (☎719 20; www.cvjm-luebeck.de). This cozy lodge is run by a Christian organization. The pub downstairs often echoes with jazz. No locked rooms or lockers. Breakfast €4. Sheets €4.50. Key with €10 deposit. Check-in before 7pm. Reception M-F 8am-8pm, Sa-Su 8am-8pm. 4- to 8-bed dorms €12.50 (includes sheets); doubles €20-40; 2-person apartments from €50. Cash only. ❶

Campingplatz Lübeck-Schönböcken, Steinrader Damm 12 (☎89 30 90), 3km west of the city. From the ZOB, take bus #7 to "Schönböckener Hauptstr." Showers, washing machines, and cooking facilities. €4.50 per person, €2 per child, €5 per site. ❶

FOOD

While the rest of Germany swims in beer, Lübeck drowns in coffee. Lübeck's cafés stay open into the wee hours of the morning and become the nightlife venue of choice. The hippest, most popular cafés line **Mühlenstraße** in the eastern part of the city. A local specialty is *Lübecker Marzipan,* a sweet, colored almond paste molded into different shapes. Buy groceries at **Aldi,** just north of Hundestr. on Kanalstr. (Open M-F 8am-8pm, Sa 8am-5pm.)

▓ **Café Affenbrot,** Kanalstr. 70 (☎721 93), on the corner of Glockengießerstr. A vegetarian café and *Biergarten,* Affenbrot is part of the same cooperative as Rucksack Hostel. Sit at tables crafted from antique sewing machines. Organic dinners €4-8. Breakfast €3.50-9. Open daily 9am-midnight. Kitchen closes at 11pm. Cash only. ❷

▓ **I.G. Niederegger Marzipan Café,** Breitestr. 89 (☎530 11 26). This famous confectionery shop and café is *the* place to eat marzipan cake (€1.95), sample marzipan-flavored

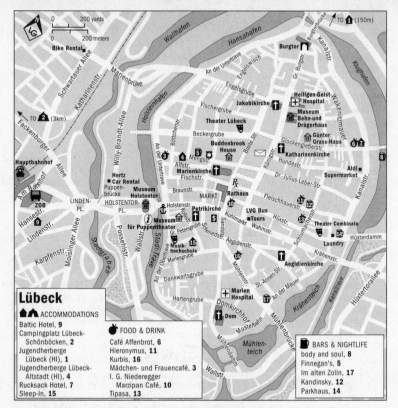

Lübeck

■▲ ACCOMMODATIONS

Baltic Hotel, **9**
Campingplatz Lübeck-
   Schönböcken, **2**
Jugendherberge
   Lübeck (HI), **1**
Jugendherberge Lübeck-
   Altstadt (HI), **4**
Rucksack Hotel, **7**
Sleep-In, **15**

🍎 FOOD & DRINK

Café Affenbrot, **6**
Hieronymus, **11**
Kurbis, **16**
Mädchen- und Frauencafé, **3**
I. G. Niederegger
   Marzipan Café, **10**
Tipasa, **13**

🍷 BARS & NIGHTLIFE

body and soul, **8**
Finnegan's, **5**
Im alten Zolln, **17**
Kandinsky, **12**
Parkhaus, **14**

ice cream, or buy candies shaped like pigs, jellyfish, or the town gate (cheaper at the counter than in the café). The **Marzipan Salon,** a free exhibit dedicated to the history and preparation of the sweet, is located upstairs. Café and Salon both open M-F 9am-7pm, Sa 9am-6pm, Su 10am-4pm. AmEx/MC/V. ❷

Kurbis, Mühlenstr. 9 (☎707 01 26). Though a *Kurbis* (pumpkin) theme pervades the decor, no gourds are on the menu. Pastas and *Pfanne* (pan-cooked meals topped with cheese) €7-8. Many vegetarian options. Open M-Tu and Th 11am-1am, F-Sa 11am-2am. Kitchen closes 30min. earlier. AmEx/DC/MC/V. ❸

Tipasa, Schlumacherstr. 12-14 (☎706 04 51). The cave art on the walls adds neolithic charm to this student haunt. Pizza €4-7, meat dishes €8-10. The *Tipasa-Topf* (€6.60) is a zesty tomato, beef, mushroom, and pepper stew. *Biergarten* out back. Open M-Th and Su noon-1am, F-Sa noon-2am. Kitchen closes 30min. earlier. MC. ❸

Hieronymus, Fleischhauerstr. 81 (☎706 30 17; www.hieronymus-restaurant.de). Long menu of pan-European cuisine. The massive fireplace, dark lighting, and wooden beams are thoroughly 15th-century. Lunch specials (€5-8) M-F before 5pm. Meat dishes €8-15, pizzas €4-7. Open M-Th and Su noon-1am, F-Sa noon-2am. Cash only. ❸

Mädchen- und Frauencafé, An der Untertrave 97 (☎122 57 46; m-f-z@versanet.de), on the 2nd fl. Friendly women-only café with more meeting than eating, hosting frequent breakfast chats, girls' clubs, literature discussion groups, and discos. Check the door for postings about events and opening times.

SIGHTS

The streets of Lübeck are filled with small surprises. Be on the lookout for the hundreds of blue signs (all with English translations) describing the history of many of Lübeck's buildings. In the northeastern section of the Altstadt, you can find dozens of narrow passages, or *Gänge*, which lead from the street into beautiful courtyard gardens. ☎ 92 92 00 is the hotline for most of the city's museums.

HOLSTENTOR (HOLSTEN GATE). Between the Altstadt and the station is Lübeck's 15th-century city symbol, the imposing Holstentor. Inside, you can read about the city's rise to prominence while exploring the tower's massive walls, gun bays, and limestone troughs for dumping hot tar on the enemy. Ironically, Napoleon, the only invader since its construction, entered the city from the north, bypassing the gate entirely. *(☎ 122 41 29. Open Apr.-Sept. daily 10am-5pm; Oct.-Mar. Tu-Su 10am-5pm. €4, students and seniors €2, families €8.)*

MARIENKIRCHE. The Marienkirche's two brick towers dominate the Lübeck skyline. Construction of the church began around 1200 in the Romanesque style, but it was completed as a Gothic cathedral in 1350. The gigantic building, which houses the largest mechanical organ in the world, sustained heavy damage during WWII; the effects of the attacks are still visible. A giant bronze bell, warped and splintered, lies embedded in the shattered marble floor where it fell during the air raids of 1942. Pictures of the church's famous **Totentanzbild,** an intricate mural depicting the "dance of the dead," hang in the left apse, where the original, lost in the fires that followed the attacks, once stood. To the left of the pews is the church's newly restored astronomical clock. On your way out, take a peek at the little devil sitting just outside the main door. Legend has it that the devil helped build the church, thinking it was to be a bar. When he realized his mistake, locals only prevented him from destroying the church by building a bar across the street, in the Rathauskeller. *(Open daily in summer 10am-6pm; in winter 10am-4pm. Suggested donation €1. Tours June-Sept. W and Sa 3:15; Apr.-Oct. Sa only. €3.50, students €2.50.)*

RATHAUS. Lübeck's beloved city hall, at the center of the Altstadt, is a somewhat schizophrenic conglomeration of three contrasting architectural styles. The original building, constructed in the 13th century, is the portion with the striking glazed black and red brick. New wings were added in the 14th and 15th centuries. *(Admission only with tour (in German). M-F 11am, noon, and 3pm. €2.60, students €1.50.)*

BUDDENBROOKHAUS. Author **Thomas Mann,** who won the Nobel Prize in 1929, set his novel *Buddenbrooks* in this house, where he and his brother **Heinrich** were raised. It now houses a museum dedicated to the life and works of the brothers. Special events are held during the summer, including a "literary walk" through Lübeck on Sundays from June to August. *(Mengstr. 4, beside the Marienkirche. ☎ 122 41 92. Open daily 10am-6pm; Jan. 11am-5pm. Some exhibits captioned in English. Walks last 2hr., €8. Admission €5, students €2.60; combo ticket with Günter Grass-Haus €7/4.)*

DOM. Founded by Henry the Lion in 1173, Lübeck's oldest church is guarded by a distinctive lion statue. Approach the church from the north on Fegefeuer and you'll be able to say you walked through Purgatory (the literal translation of the street's name) to reach the cathedral. *(Domkirchhof, at the southernmost end of the inner island. ☎ 747 04. Open daily 10am-6pm. Free. Organ concerts July-Aug. F 5pm; €6, students €4.)*

PETRIKIRCHE. An elevator climbs 50.5m to the viewing platform inside the 13th-century steeple for a sweeping, windy view of the Altstadt and Lübeck's many spires. The nave of the church exhibits modern art. *(East of the Rathaus on Schmiederstr. Church open Tu-Su 11am-4pm. Tower open daily Apr.-Oct. 9am-7pm; Mar. and Nov. 11am-5pm; Dec. 9am-7pm. Requested donation €2. Tower €2.50, students €1.50.)*

THE LOCAL STORY

PUPPETMAN

Fritz Fey, owner of Lübeck's Puppet Theater Museum (p. 198), talks about his inspirations.

I always liked traveling and meeting people from other countries—I was fascinated by the Orient and by India from the time I was a boy. I got a job at a television studio as a cameraman. I loved my job; it gave me the chance to travel all around the world—we made documentary films. While traveling, I had the chance to meet puppet players, and I found out that the tradition is very old, and that it exists in nearly every country. As I learned more, my interest increased.

I started my collection in 1971, and invested everything that I earned into it. After exhibiting my collection a few times, the idea came to me to create a museum. I eventually got the chance to rent a small house for the museum in Lübeck. I have expanded the collection every year since then... We still have about 20 times more figures than there is space to display...

My vision is to make this a haven for children and those fascinated by the history of theater. I want the museum to become an island in Lübeck's old city—a place for international friendship, where people see the figures from their culture displayed among figures from all over the world, as part of a larger tradition aimed at creating beautiful things and bringing happiness to people.

JAKOBIKIRCHE. Traditionally a place of worship for seafarers, the whitewashed, high-ceilinged church has bronze chandeliers, a large marble altarpiece depicting the death of Jesus, and an enormous wooden organ with detailed pictures of the saints. *(North of the Rathaus on Breitestr., near Koberg. Open M 10am-4pm, Tu-Su 10am-6pm. Requested donation €1. Organ concerts W 5pm, F 7pm, and Sa 5pm. €4, students €2.)*

THEATERFIGURENMUSEUM (THEATER FIGURE MUSEUM). Exquisitely detailed hand, string, shadow, and stick puppets from across the globe pack the museum's five floors, forming the largest such collection in the world. Check out the fully-preserved Chinese theaters or ask to hear the barrel organs, which the owner will happily play for you. Across the street, the puppet theater puts on daily performances at 3pm (€4), and Sa also at 6 or 7:30pm (€8, students €6.50). *(Kolk 14. Just below the Petrikirche. ☎786 26. www.tfm-luebeck.com. Open daily Apr.-Sept. 10am-6pm; Oct. 10am-4pm; Nov.-Mar. 10am-3pm. €3, students €2.50, children €1.50.)*

MUSEUM BEHN- UND DRÄGERHAUS. In this 18th-century house is an exhibition of furnishings from the early 19th century, a collection of Impressionist and Realist art, and a unique display of historical musical instruments. Also on display are portraits by Edvard Munch, statues by Ernst Barlach, and a violin fitted with trumpet tubes. The artists' cooperative in the **sculpture garden** outside showcases local artists. *(Königstr. 9-11. ☎122 41 48. Open Tu-F 10am-6pm, Sa-Su 11am-6pm. €4, students €2, ages 6-18 €1, families €7.)*

GÜNTER GRASS-HAUS. The cousin of the Buddenbrookhaus, this museum contains a visually enticing presentation of bronze sculpture, sketches, and watercolors created by acclaimed author and Nobel laureate **Günter Grass,** who lived in Lübeck for many years. Grass makes occasional appearances for readings and special events. *(Glockengießerstr. 21. Open daily Apr.-Dec. 10am-6pm; Jan.-Mar. 11am-5pm. Admission €4, students €2.20; combo ticket with Buddenbrookhaus €7/4.)*

🎵 ENTERTAINMENT

Lübeck is world-famous for its Saturday **organ concerts** at the Jakobikirche (5pm) and the Marienkirche. (6:30pm. €6, students €4. See *Musik in Lübecks Kirchen,* available at both churches, for full schedule.) The city's music academy, the **Musikhochschule,** Gr. Petersgrube 17-29, plays frequent free concerts, often of professional caliber. (☎150 50; www.mh-luebeck.de.) For entertainment listings (in German), pick up *Heute, Piste, Szene, Zentrum,* or (for women) *Zimtzicke* at the tourist office, or grab *Ultimo* at any bar. Lübeck's two main theaters offer student discounts, but are closed from July to August. The huge **Theater Lübeck,** Beckergrube 16, puts up operas, symphonies, and plays. (☎745 52; www.theaterluebeck.de. Tickets €15-36; students from €5. Box office open Tu-F 10am-6:30pm, Sa 10am-1pm, and 30min. before shows.) The smaller **Theater Combinale,** Hüxstr. 115, shows avant-garde works. (☎788 17. Tickets €8-14.)

🔲 NIGHTLIFE

Most of the better *Diskotheken* (dance clubs) are scattered around the perimeter of the Altstadt. Avoid the northwestern part of the island along the waterfront late at night, when drug dealers and addicts frequent the area.

Parkhaus, Hüxterdamm at Kanalstr. (☎70 72 557; www.parkhaus.tv). This 3-story club boasts 2 dancefloors, a classy lounge, and a rooftop "beach" in summer. Beer approx. €2.50, mixed drinks €4.50-8. Th ladies' night; women get up to €20 of free drinks. 21+. M no cover, Th €5, F-Sa €4. Open M and Th-Sa 10pm-late. Cash only.

Finnegan's, Mengstr. 42 (☎711 10). Irish pub serving Guinness and other dark, yeasty beers (€3-4) to 30-something locals and backpackers from the Emerald Isle. Live music W, F, and Sa at 9pm. Open Tu-Sa 7pm-late. Cash only.

body and soul (☎706 06 00; www.bodyandsoul.de). On a boat at the corner of Kanalstr. and Höhe Glockenstr. Climb the red-carpeted gangplank to join students dancing to hip-hop, pop, and rock. Cover approx. €4. Open Tu and Sa 10pm-late, F 10:30pm-late.

Kandinsky, Fleischhauerstr. 89 (☎702 06 61). More than 30 tables in the street, a mile-long drink list of teas, coffees, and beer (€2-3), and live jazz every Tu night (except during the summer). Snug environment and gold walls attract a mostly student crowd. Open M-Th and Su 1pm-1am, F-Sa 1pm-2am. Cash only.

Im alten Zolln, Mühlenstr. 93 (☎723 95). Don't come here for a visa: the "old customs office" is now decked out with classy wood paneling and a grand piano. Beer €2-4, mixed drinks €5-6. Open daily noon-1am. Cash only.

HOLSTEINISCHE SCHWEIZ (HOLSTEIN SWITZERLAND)

PLÖN   ☎04522

Amid the ancient glacial moraines of wooded *Holsteinische Schweiz*, Plön (pop. 13,000) is situated in the middle of lake country. The town balances on a land bridge between the Kleiner Plöner See and the Großer Plöner See, where the sparkling waters and the opportunities to paddle, sail, and fish lure school groups and nature lovers alike. The red brick steeple of Plön's central church and the white facade of its elegant castle dominate the quiet town.

🔲🔲 TRANSPORTATION AND PRACTICAL INFORMATION. Trains run every hr. to: Eutin (15min., €7); Kiel (30min., €5); Lübeck (40min., €7). For a **taxi,** call ☎26 00, 35 35, or 88 88. Rent **bikes** at **Wittich,** Lange Str. 39. (☎27 48. €6 per day. Open M-F 9am-6pm, Sa 9am-2pm.) Bike trails loop around the lakes. Rent **boats** at the **Kanucenter Plön,** Ascheberger Str. 76, on the campground. (☎41 43; www.lustaufkanufahren.de. €5 per 2hr. Open daily 9am-7pm.) **Großer Plöner Seerundfahrt** chugs around the lake from the dock on Strandweg. (Daily 10am-5pm. Round-trip €8, students €4.50, children €4.) The **tourist office,** Lübeckerstr. 20, is near the train station. The staff distributes maps and books rooms (€15-50) for free. (☎509 50; www.ploen.de. Open in summer M-F 9am-6pm, Sa-Su 10am-1pm; shorter hours in winter.) **Internet** access is available at the **library**. (€1.50 per 30min. Open M-F 9:30am-1:30pm and 3-6pm.) The **post office**, Lange Str. 18, is off the walkway near the square. (Open M-F 9am-1pm and 2-6pm, Sa 9am-12:30pm.) **Postal Code:** 24306.

◪◩ ACCOMMODATIONS AND FOOD. Plön's **Jugendherberge (HI) ❶**, Ascheberger Str. 67, is 2km outside of town. Take bus #360 (every hr.) to "Spitzenort." With a beach volleyball court, a soccer field, and ping-pong and picnic tables by the shores of the Großer Plöner See, this enormous hostel attracts noisy school groups. (☎25 76; fax 21 66. Breakfast included. Check-out 9am. Lock-out 10pm-7am, but key available. Dorms €14.10, over 27 €17.10.) **Hotel Zum Hirschen ❸**, Bahnhofstr. 9, opposite the station, has small, clean rooms with phone and TV. (☎24 23. Breakfast included. Singles €30-37; doubles €54-68. Discounts for extended stays.) On the road right before the hostel, **Naturcamping Spitzenort ❶**, Ascheberger Str. 76, has grassy spots on the water. (☎27 69; www.spitzenort.de. €5 per person, €2.30 per child age 4-14, €4.50-6.50 per tent. Reduced rates in low season. AmEx/DC/MC/V.) **Lange Straße** is full of cafés. **Eisenpfanne ❸**, Lange Str. 47, serves the massive *Plöner Teller* (€11), a local specialty with three kinds of fried fish. They also serve German-influenced Greek, Italian, and Balkan fare. (☎22 90. Main dishes €8-12. Open daily 11am-11pm. Kitchen 11am-10:30pm. Cash only.) **Antalya-Grill ❷**, Lange Str. 36, offers grill platters (€7), spicy Turkish pizzas (€4-7), and *Döner kebap* (€2.50-4). (☎39 82. Open M-F 11am-1am, Sa-Su 11am-2am. Cash only.) **Sky**, Markt 1, sells groceries. (Open M-F 8am-8pm, Sa 8am-8pm, Su 11am-6pm.)

◪ SIGHTS. Though it is now a private boarding school, Plön's late Renaissance **Schloß** is still the most noticeable building in town. The path in front of the palace affords a spectacular view of the town. Wooded trails lead away from the castle to the stately brick **Prinzenhaus** and the **Schloßgarten**. Built in 1744, the Priznehaus is now a museum detailing the history of the *Schloß*. (☎509 50. Obligatory tours May-Sept. W 11:30am, Sa and Su 3, 4pm; Nov.-Apr. Su 11:30am. €3, children €2, families €6.50.) To the southwest, the **Prinzeninsel** (Prince Island), in the Großer Plöner See, is separated from the mainland by a tiny canal spanned by a foot-bridge. Down the eastern slope of the Schloßberg is Plön's small 19th-century **Rathaus**. Though the nearby **Nicolaikirche** has a Baroque exterior, the inside was remodeled during the 1960s in a jarringly angular style. (Open daily 10am-4pm.) Housed in a former apothecary, the **Museum des Kreises** (Museum of Circles), Johannisstr. 1, at the intersection of Hamburger Str. and Lange Str., displays 17th-century glassware and prehistoric artifacts. (☎74 43 91. Open mid-May to Sept. Tu-Su 10am-noon and 2-5pm; Jan. to mid-May Tu-Sa 2-5pm. €1.50, students €1.) Across the street, the **Johanniskirche's** uneven brick and copper construction has the subtle elegance and rustic flavor of a folk church. (Open Tu-F 10am-noon and 2-6pm, Sa-Su 10am-noon and 2-5pm. Free.) Far east of the town center between the two lakes, the **Parnaßturm**, a former lookout tower, provides a view well worth the 20min. climb up Rodomstorstr. (Open Easter-Oct. 9am-7pm. Free.)

KIEL ☎0431

Site of the 1936 and 1972 Olympic sailing events, the waters around Kiel fill with sailboats and ocean liners. The city's fascination with ships cluminates in the Kieler Woche, which turns the harbor into a massive party and floods the town with music and beer (information ☎90 19 05). During the rest of the year, this city of 250,000 quiets down considerably. Residents ignore the somewhat plain down-town and keep their eyes on the sea and the gigantic Nord-Ostsee-Kanal.

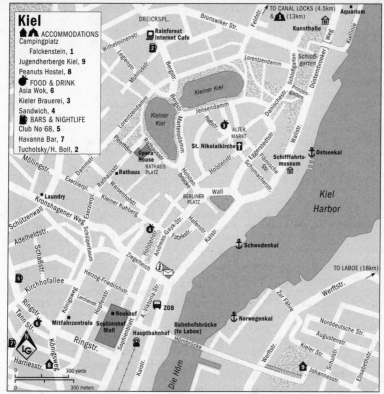

Kiel

▲▲ ACCOMMODATIONS
Campingplatz
    Falckenstein, 1
Jugendherberge Kiel, 9
Peanuts Hostel, 8
🍴 FOOD & DRINK
Asia Wok, 6
Kieler Brauerei, 3
Sandwich, 4
🍺 BARS & NIGHTLIFE
Club No 68, 5
Havanna Bar, 7
Tucholsky/H. Boll, 2

📧 **TRANSPORTATION. Trains** run every hr. to: Flensburg (1¼hr., €13); Hamburg (1¼hr., €15); Lübeck (1¼hr., €12). **Buses** and **ferries** cost €2.10 for the shortest rides; **Tageskarte** (1-day €6.20; all zones €9.90) and the **KielCard** (one day, bus only €8.90, bus and ferries €11.50), which includes discounts at local museums, are also offered. Call ☎750 00 for a **taxi.** Most **ferries** leave from the west side of the harbor (port information at www.port-of-kiel.de). **Stena Line,** on the west side near the station at **Schwedenkai,** runs to Sweden. (☎01805 91 66 66; www.stenaline.de. Departures daily at 7:30pm arrive in Göteborg at 9am the next morning. €70, add €20 per person for a basic bed; less in off-season) The posh **Color Line** at **Norwegenkai,** on the opposite side of the harbor, sails to Oslo. (☎73 00 300; www.color-line.com. Daily 2pm. 2-person cabins €156-360; less on weekdays and in off-season.) Boats bound for Kaliningrad and the Baltics leave from **Ostuferkai.**

📋 **PRACTICAL INFORMATION.** Kiel's **tourist office,** Andreas-Gayk-Str. 31, is two blocks north of the train station. The staff books rooms for a €3 fee. (☎01805 56 56 700; www.kiel-tourist.de. Open M-F 9am-6pm, Sa 10am-2pm.) **Laundry** can be done at **Waschcenter,** Exerzierpl. on Ziegelteich or Kirchofsallee. (Wash €3.50. Dry €0.50 per 12min. Both open daily 6am-10pm.) For **Internet** access, cross the Kleiner Kiel lake to the **Rainforest Internet Café,** Bergstr. 17. (€0.70 per 15min; 9am-noon €0.50 per 15min. Open daily 9am-4am.) The **post office,** Stresemannpl. 1-3, is just past the train station. (Open M-F 9am-7pm, Sa 9am-2pm.) **Postal Code:** 24103.

🏠🍴 **ACCOMMODATIONS AND FOOD.** The tiny, apartment-style **Peanuts Hostel ❷**, Harriesstr. 2, has a cozy kitchen and living room. (☎ 364 2208. www.peanuts-hostel.de. Reception 8:30-11am and 5-9pm. 4-bed dorms €17; 2-bed €20; singles €28. Cash only.) **Jugendherberge Kiel (HI) ❷**, Johannesstr. 1, has spacious quads surrounding surround an interior courtyard. Take bus #11 to "Kieler Str." (☎ 73 14 88; fax 73 57 23. Breakfast included. Reception 7am-1am. Check-out 9:30am. Curfew 1am. Dorms €16.80, at least 2 nights €15.50, over 26 €19.80/15.50. Cash only.) **Campingplatz Falckenstein ❶**, Palisadenweg 171, is 13km from the center. Take bus #501 or 502 (dir.: Strande) to "Preis." Follow the signs, for 25min. (☎ 39 20 78; www.campingkiel.de. Open Apr.-Oct. €4.35 per person, €5-7.50 per site.)

Neukauf, on the ground floor of the Sophienhof Mall, sells **groceries** (open M-F 8am-8pm, Sa 8am-6pm), as do the produce stands along Holstenbrücke, the country's oldest designated *Fußgängerzone* (pedestrian zone). Enjoy traditional fare at the ⬛**Kieler Brauerei ❸**, Alter Markt 9, which serves dark suds (€3-4), roasted sausages, and potatoes. Watch the *Bräumeister* tending the copper tanks upstairs or examine the giant brew vats in the basement. (☎ 90 62 90. Entrées €7-10. Open M-Th and Su 10am-midnight, F-Sa 10am-late. MC/V.) Find a culinary change of pace at **Asia Wok ❷**, Ringstr. 47, which serves pan-Asian dishes. (☎ 99 07 554. Entrées €5-7. Open M-Sa 11am-10pm, Su 4-10pm.) On Europapl., **Sandwich ❶**, Holstenstr. 92, sells diminutive versions of its namesake (€1.50-3) amid zebra-patterned sofas. (Open M-Sa 6:30am-5pm, Su 8:30am-4pm. Cash only.)

🔲 **SIGHTS.** Kiel, where the 99km-long **Nord-Ostsee-Kanal** enters the Baltic Sea, has the world's largest *Schleusen* (canal locks). (Bus #11 to "Wik-Kanal," then take the free ferry that runs every 15min. Walk right 10min. along Kanalstr. from the ferry dock to the Schleuseninsel. Or, take bus #91 to "Schleuse." Tours 1½hr.; 9 and 11am, 1 and 3pm. €3, students €2.) Running from the *Schloßgarten*, the **Kiellinie** pedestrian walkway offers spectacular views. Near the Kiellinie's southern end, the **Kunsthalle** (Art Hall), Düsternbrooker Weg 1, exhibits Greek and Roman statues. Upstairs exhibits include works by German impressionists and 20th-century artists. (☎ 880 57 56. Open Tu-Su 10:30am-6pm, W 10:30am-8pm. Sculpture gallery free. Upstairs exhibits €5, students €3.) North of the Kunsthalle, along the Kiellinie at the Institut für Meereskunde, is a small **Aquarium.** (Open Apr.-Sept. 9am-7pm, Oct.-Mar. 9am-5pm, €2, children and students €1.50.) Along the waterfront, the **Schifffahrtsmuseum** (Maritime Museum), Wall 65, brings Kiel's maritime history to life. Model boats and photographs recreate German trading vessels and Nazi warships. (☎ 34 28. Open mid-Apr. to mid-Oct. daily 10am-6pm; mid-Oct. to mid-Apr. Tu-Su 10am-5pm. Requested donation €3, students and children €1.50, families €6.) At the north end of the pedestrian zone, the **St. Nikolaikirche** towers over the Alter Markt. (Open M-F 10am-6pm, Sa 11am-3pm. Free.)

🎵 **NIGHTLIFE.** Clubs and bars line Bergstr. Descend into the labyrinthine **Tucholsky/H. Boll**, Bergstr. 17, and its rooms of billiards, foosball, air hockey, and dancing. (Drinks €1-4. Open daily 8pm-4am. F-Sa €1-4 cover.) **Havanna Bar**, Harmesstr. 65, provides a more grown-up atmosphere. (☎ 67 94 036. Mixed drinks €5-8. Tu ½-price drinks. Tu-Sa 7pm-late, Su 5pm-late. Cash only.) Relax in genuine leather seats from old Mercedes at **Club N°68.** (☎ 61 739. Beer €2.20-3.70. Open daily 6pm.)

WATTENMEER NATIONAL PARK (SCHLESWIG-HOLSTEIN)

Schleswig-Holstein's Wattenmeer National Park is one of three such parks in Germany, the other two located farther down the coast in Hamburg and Lower Saxony. The *Watt* refers to the mud—miles and miles of it—that sustains a wide variety of unique plant and animal life. The region is filled with small towns that label themselves health resorts, capitalizing on the invigorating salt-laden air that circulates through the region and the purported curative properties of the mud. The Wattenmeer National Park witnesses a seasonal migration of birds and tourists alike, with resort towns more than tripling in population during the summer.

WATTENMEER NATIONAL PARK AT A GLANCE	
AREA: 2850sq. km. **CLIMATE:** Mild summers, wet winters. Windy year-round. **FEATURES:** Sandy beaches, *Wattenmeer* mud flats, grassy dunes, historical towns, spas.	**HIGHLIGHTS:** Guided *Watt* hikes, extensive network of bicycle paths, relaxing on Sylt and Amrum's wide beaches. **GATEWAYS:** Tönning, St. Peter-Ording. **CAMPING:** Not allowed within the park, but common on its fringes.

☀ ORIENTATION

Wattenmeer National Park stretches along Schleswig Holstein's western coast, situated on the North Sea. **Tönning,** (p. 205) in the central region of the park, is a good place to begin exploring. Twenty-five kilometers to the west, the resort town of **St. Peter-Ording** (p. 205) offers access to Wattenmeer wildlife and a spectacular beach that extends for miles. To the northwest lie the North Frisian Islands, including **Sylt** and **Amrum,** with beautiful white sand beaches on their western shores and wide stretches of Wattenmeer tidal flats on their sheltered eastern sides.

▣ ⁊ TRANSPORTATION AND PRACTICAL INFORMATION

Trains provide easy access to nearly all national park towns and sights along the coast. Most trains within the greater Wattenmeer National Park area are **NOB** (Nord-Ostsee-Bahn) regional trains; tickets for these can be purchased onboard. **Bus** connections are less frequent and less extensive than train connections. The region's bus terminals often lack information centers, so plan ahead and inquire about bus routes in town or decipher the posted schedules on your own.

Emergency: Police ☎ 110. **Fire** ☎ 112.

Information Centers: Schutzstationen (protection stations) are on each of the islands and in major mainland coastal towns. The staff offer guided tours of the *Watt*. (See city listings for locations and contact info.) Additionally, information pavilions—part of the **Besucherinformationssystem (BIS)**—are at the beginning of many paths in the region. Contact the **Wattenmeer Information Line** (☎04861 616 70; www.wattenmeer-nationalpark.de) for further details..

Boat Tours: Adler-Schiffe (☎04842 90 00 30; www.adler-schiffe.de) offers 2½hr. seal bank excursions (€12-13), while Reederei Rahder (☎04832 36 12; www.rahder.de), conducts 2½-6hr. tours from Büsum to the seal habitat in Dithmarschen (€11-19).

⌂ ACCOMMODATIONS

Youth hostels dot the North Sea coast. In addition to the hostels described in the city listings, other **HI hostels** in the region are listed here (prices are per night and exclude *Kurkarte;* over age 26 add €3-4):

Büsum, Dr.-Martin-Bahr-Str. 1, Büsum (☎04834 933 71). €15.60.

Heide, Poststr. 4, Heide, on Holstein Island (☎0481 715 75). €14.10.

Husum, Schobüller Str. 34, Husum (☎04841 27 14). €15.60.

WHAT IS THIS WATT? Created by the radical fluctuation of tides, the Wattenmeer is an area of mudflats stretching along the North Sea from the Dutch to the Danish coasts. The Watt is classified into three unique bands: the *Sandwatt*, as its name suggests, includes the sandy part of the shore where sea worms burrow to hide from predatory birds. Farther inland, the *Mischwatt*, a bank of mixed sand and mud, teems with species from bacteria to mussels. Extending to the highest water line is the charcoal-black *Schlickwatt*, where only the most resilient organisms live in the oxygen-poor mud that is marketed to health-seekers as a nutrient-rich skin treatment. A relatively rare ecosystem, the Wattenmeer habitat supports some 3200 different types of animals. Among the most visible are the mussels that filter the ocean water, the fish that stock the plankton-rich waters with their eggs, the birds that feast at low tide on creatures trapped in shallow pools, and the seals that frolic on sandbanks just offshore.

Niebüll-Deezbüll, Deezbüll Deich 2, Niebüll (☎04661 93 78 90). €16.85.
Niebüll-Mühlenstraße, Mühlenstr. 65, Niebüll (☎04661 93 78 90). €16.85.
Wyk auf Föhr, Fehrstieg 41, Wyk, on Föhr Island (☎04681 23 55). €15.60.

■ OUTDOOR ACTIVITIES

WATTWANDERN (WATT HIKES). When the tides ebb, the mud flats of the Watt are exposed, making it possible to walk across the terrain. To arrange a tour, call the National Park Service (☎04861 616 70) or a nearby *Schutzstation*. Private companies also offer tours. **Adler-Schiffe** leads walks across the Watt between the islands of Amrum and Föhr. The 2½hr. trip departs from Nordstrand, near Husum, and includes the cost of ferry rides to and from the islands. (☎04842 900 00. €24, children €13.50.) **Reederei Rahder** (see **Boat Tours**) offers 2hr. guided hikes of the Watt in the vicinity of Büsum. If you insist on striking out independently, pick up a tide chart and seek advice from one of the information centers.

WATT SAFETY. *Let's Go* does not recommend hiking the Watt without a guide. Tour guides are familiar with tidal patterns, and can steer you away from dangerous quicksand. Always heed markings: orange balls forbid entrance, yellow flags warn that a sandbank will be submerged at high water, and green flags encourage caution at high tide. Watch for protected sanctuaries, and be alert to changing tides.

BEACHES AND SWIMMING. Most costal towns levy fees called *Kurtaxe* for beach access. The cost varies, but is generally €1.50-3 per day for adults, €0.50 for children. Hotels and pensions in the area automatically add the cost of the *Kurkarte* to your bill. Guests not staying overnight can purchase a day card granting beach access for roughly the same cost. Swimming is allowed at all beaches in the park, although the water can be uncomfortably cool year-round. Nude beaches are common and are marked with signs labeled *FKK Strand*, a reference to the *Freier Körper Kultur* ("free body culture") association.

HIKING AND BIKING. Biking is an incredibly popular and effective way to explore the park, both on the mainland and the islands. The park has a broad network of paved and gravel trails, and the powerful North Sea wind can send you flying along at exhilarating speeds—or slow progress to a painful crawl. Hiking trails crisscross the park as well; visit the local information centers for maps. For information on renting bikes, see individual town listings below.

TÖNNING   ☎04681

The charming little town of Tönning (pop. 5000) is an easily accessible gateway to the Wattenmeer. From the town square, white fish painted on the sidewalk past the harbor lead to the **Multimar Wattforum**, Am Robbenberg, a combined museum, aquarium, and research station. (☎96 20 38; www.multimar-wattforum.de. Open daily Apr.-Oct. 9am-7pm; Nov.-Mar. 10am-6pm. €8, children €5.50.) Tönning is also home to a pleasant **Schloßgarten**, which faces the market square.

To reach the **Jugendherberge Tönning ❶**, Badallee 28, turn left from the train station and follow Badallee for 15min. The building doubles as an environmental center and offers programs on *Watt* biology. (☎04861 12 80. Breakfast included. Excluding *Kurkarte* €15.60, over 27 €19.60.) Halfway to the hostel, **Camping Eiderblick ❶**, Strandweg 19, is small and on the water. (☎04861 15 69. Laundry €2. Dry €2. €3 per adult, €2 per child, €5 per tent. AmEx/MC/V.) Restaurants near the market are generally less expensive and offer more variety than those along the harbor. Steps away from the train station, **Peper's Fischerhütte ❸**, Westerstr. 17, serves fresh local fish for €8-14. (☎68041. Open Tu-F 11:30am-2pm and 5-10pm, Sa 5-10pm, Su 11am-2pm and 5-10pm). **Fischimbiß ❷**, am Hafen 33, serves tasty fish sandwiches and plates (€2-9). (☎740. Open M-F 9am-6:30pm, Sa-Su 10am-7pm; later in summer. Cash only.) To stock up on **groceries**, visit the **SPAR**, Am Markt 8, located in the main square. (Open M-F 7:30am-6pm, Sa 7:30am-12:30pm.)

NOB regional **trains** run every hr. to St. Peter-Ording (25min., €3), and Husum (30min., €3.50). The city center is 5min. to the right of the train station. Across the square, near the church, is the **tourist office**, Am Markt 1. (☎614 20. Open May 15-Sept. 30 M-F 9am-noon and 2-5pm, Sa 10am-noon; Oct.-May 14 M-Th 9am-noon and 2-4pm, F 9am-noon.) Accommodations listings (€0.50) are available outside the office door. The main **National Park Information Center**, at Schloßgarten 1, is primarily an administrative center, but the staff can help you plan your itinerary. (☎04861 61 60; www.wattenmeer-nationalpark.de.)

ST. PETER-ORDING   ☎04683

St. Peter-Ording (pop. 4000) consists of three parts: St. Peter-Bad to the northwest, St. Peter-Dorf in the middle, and St. Peter-Böhl to the south. The most beautiful beachfront is accessible from St. Peter-Bad. A **bike path** extends several miles along the dike from the Ording-Hus, Dreilanden 5, north of St. Peter-Bad. For those looking to avoid the chilly water and stiff ocean breeze, the **Dünen-Therme**, directly off Am Kurbad, offers aromatic Swedish saunas and therapeutic pools. (☎99 91 61; www.duenen-therme.de. Open Apr.-Oct. M-Sa 9:30am-10pm, Su 10am-7pm, €5.70 per 2hr., students €3.30, plus €3.10 for sauna access.)

Hotel rooms in St. Peter-Ording are expensive and hard to come by in summer; most private pensions only rent by the week. Offering a bit of luxury at moderate expense, the **Strand Hotel Garni ❺**, Im Bad 16, has huge rooms a block from the beach. (☎969 60. Breakfast included. Reception until 10pm. Singles €62; doubles €70-90. Cash only.) **Camping Rönkendorf ❶**, Böhler Landstr. 171 in St. Peter Böhl, is area's largest campground. (☎51 95. €3 per adult, €2 per child, €6 per tent.) The long strip along Im Bad in St. Peter-Ording is lined with restaurants. For personable atmosphere, head to the cluttered living-room-cum-bar **Benen Diken ❸**, Badallee 29, near Dorf. Traditional skillet-cooked *Pfanne* meals (€9-12) and asparagus are the specialties, but fish (€8-13) is also popular. (☎15 50. Open daily 11:30am-2pm and from 5pm.) For **groceries**, try **Spar**, Dorfstr. 39 in St. Peter Dorf. (Open M-Sa 8am-8pm, Su 9am-4pm.)

Trains run every hr. to: Berlin (5hr., €84); Hamburg (3hr., €35); Hanover (5hr., €63); Tönning (25min., €3). To reach St. Peter-Bad from the train station, take the shuttle bus that meets the arriving trains. Alternatively, cross Eiderstedter Str. and follow the dirt path through the woods until it reaches Im Bad (5min.). The **tourist office** is in the "Dünen-Therme" building, and offers room booking and tour packages. (☎99 90. Open M-F 10am-4pm, Sa-Su 10am-2pm.) **Branches** are in Ording, Dorf, and Süd. A *Kurkarte*, available with an overnight stay, provides free access to the town's bus service. The **Wattenmeer Park Info Station** (☎53 03), Schulstr. 1, in Dorf on the Markt, runs daily Watt tours. The **post office** is at Nordergeest 5. (Open M-F 9am-12:30pm and 1:30-6pm, Sa 9am-1pm.) **Postal Code:** 25826.

SYLT ISLAND   ☎04651

The windswept island of Sylt, with miles of trails, 39km of white sand beaches, and traditional thatched-roof Frisian houses, has long been Germany's favorite vacation spot. Westerland, the island's largest city and its transportation hub, was founded as a resort town in the middle of the 19th century. Long regarded as a playground for the rich, the island is now the destination of choice for everyone from the biggest German celebrities to the nation's most typical vacationing families. Trains from the mainland cross the 10km-long Hindenburgdamm to deposit eager tourists at the beach. Others arrive by ferry to the town of Hörnum, at the extreme south end of the island, or to List, which is Germany's northernmost town. North of List, the dunes of the slender Ellenbogen peninsula separate the Wattenmeer from the open ocean. Bike paths, which run parallel to the highway or shake through the dunes, connect the island's towns parallel to the highway or snaking through the dunes. Affluent vacationers congregate in Kampen, just north of Westerland, while everyone else spreads out along the island's beaches, where vacationers sit in wicker "beach baskets" to shield them from the stiff North Sea breeze, while they watch windsurfers battle the surf.

🖪🖪 TRANSPORTATION AND PRACTICAL INFORMATION. Trains run from Westerland to: Flensburg (2½hr., €19); Hamburg (3hr., €29); Hanover (5hr., €61); Tönning (1½hr., €14). **Buses** with bike racks circuit the island, leaving the ZOB terminal to the left of the train station. (3 per hr. Single trips €1.45-5.95, day card €12.40, families €17.50.) **Ferries** run from List harbor to Havneby on the Danish island of Rømø. Call **Rømø-Sylt Linie** in List for reservations. (☎0180 310 30 30; www.sylt-faehre.de. 1hr.; 7-12 per day 5:30am-7:15pm; €7.50, children €5.) **Adler-Schiffe,** Boysenstr. 13, Westerland, runs daytrips to Amrum or Fohr. Buy tickets 30min. in advance at the ticket booth at the Hörnum harbor (☎88 12 97), and try to board early. (☎987 00; www.adler-schiffe.de. Open daily 9am-5:30pm, round-trip €20, children €12.) Sylt's **bus** company **SVG** offers a variety of tours around the island and its neighbors. (☎83 61 00. Departs Apr.-Nov. M-F from the Westerland ZOB.) For bike rentals, the most convenient is **Fahrrad am Bahnhof** at the station, across from track 1. (☎58 03. €6-10 per day, €26-47 per wk. Open daily 7am-7pm.) The **tourist office** in the train station books rooms for a €16 fee plus deposit for stays longer than one night, and the big bulletin boards in front of the station also list available rooms. (☎99 88.) There is another tourist office in Hörnum (Strandweg 2. ☎962 60; www.hoernum.de. Open M-F 9am-5pm, Sa-Su 9am-1pm; in winter M-Th 9am-4pm, F 9am-1pm). A **pharmacy, Friesen Apotheke,** is on Friedrich Str. next to the grocery store. (☎51 69. Open M-F 8:30am-6:30pm, Sa 8:30am-1pm.) Use the **internet** at **Stadtbücherei Westerland,** Alte Post, Stephanstr. 6b, across from the Rathaus. (☎227 10. €1 per 20min. Open M-Tu 10am-noon and 3-6pm, Th 10am-8pm, F 10am-noon, Sa 8:30am-noon.) The **post office,** Kampende 11, has a 24hr. **ATM.** (Open M-F 7am-6pm, Sa 7am-1pm.) **Postal Code:** 25980.

🖪🖪 ACCOMMODATIONS AND FOOD. For rooms in List, call ☎952 00; in Hörnum, ☎96 26 26; in Kampen, ☎46 98 33. Sylt has three youth hostels. **Jugendherberge**

Hörnum (HI) ❷, Friesenpl. 2, is a standard hostel set among the gentle *Südspitz* dunes 10min. from the water. From the ZOB, take bus #2 (dir.: Hörnum Hafen) to "Hörnum-Nord" and continue 2min. along Rantumer Str., turning left at the *Jugendherberge* sign. (Reception 5-10pm. Dorms €15.60, over 27 €18.60. *Kurtaxe* €0.50, over 27 €2.20. D/MC/V.) Sylt's newest hostel, **Jugendherberge Westerland "Dikjen Deel" ❷**, Fischerweg 36-40 near Westerland, is primarily a tent site for youth groups, but the main building contains 50 beds. (☎835 78 25. Breakfast included. Reception 9am-noon and 4-7pm. Dorms €15.60, over 27 €18.60. *Kurtaxe* €2.90. MC/V.) Three kilometers northwest of List, **Jugendherberge Mövenberg ❷** is a monolithic complex settled alone on the edge of Nördsylt, the island's largest nature preserve. Catch bus #1 (dir.: List Hafen) from the Westerland ZOB and take it to the end of the line (€3.60). From mid-April to early November you can change to bus #5 to "Mövenberg" (7 per day); otherwise, return to the second intersection before the bus stop, turn right, and follow the *Jugendherberge* sign for 35min. School groups love the hostel's proximity to the youth beach. (☎87 03 97; fax 87 10 39. Breakfast included. Reservations recommended. Open Feb.-Oct. Dorms €15.60, over 27 €19.60, plus *Kurtaxe*.) Camping is an affordable alternative to the expensive pensions and hotels. Near the beach and minutes away from ritzy Kampen, **Campingplatz Kampen ❶**, Möwenweg 4, is one of Sylt's most appealing sites. (☎420 86; www.campen-in-kampen.de. Reception in summer 8am-1pm and 3-6pm; otherwise 8am-1pm and 3-5pm. Cash only.) Dining options on Sylt cater to the luxury automobile crowd that frequents the island. Kampen, also known as "Whiskey Alley" is lined with expensive bars and cafés. The cash-conscious head to **Toni's Restaurant ❸**, Norderstr. 3, (☎258 10; open daily 11:30am-midnight) serving comparatively cheap examples of traditional German cuisine (€5.80-13). Near the train station in Westerland is **grocery** store **Edeka**, Wilhelmstr. 6. (Open M-F 8:30am-7pm, Sa 8:30am-6pm, Su 11am-1:30pm and 3:30-6pm.)

🏔🄼 SIGHTS AND OUTDOOR ACTIVITIES. The best way to explore the 39km-long island is by bicycle. The main **bike path** hugs the highway, making it good for inter-town travel, while smaller dirt and gravel paths meander through the dunes, with alternating views of the ocean, flowering hills, and dense heath below. The most spectacular view is from atop **Uwedüne,** the island's highest point, located near Kampen. Western Sylt offers sparsely populated beaches, including the nude beach **Bühne 16.** *Kur-*

ON THE MENU

OSTFRIESENTEE

In a country otherwise famous fo its beers, East Frisians are prou of, nay, obsessed with, their tea These tiny islands in the Nortl Sea produce aromatic stron black tea blend called *Ostfriesen mischung*, with variations ii strength including *Buenting Thiele*, and *Onno Behrens*. Tea i commonly served with breakfast in the mid-afternoon, and in the mid-evening.

While the East Frisians brev their tea the conventional way (a teaspoon of leaves per cup anc one for the pot), they serve it ir an unusual ceremony. First, large blocks of rock candy callec *kluntjes*, made from white sugar are placed in each cup. Tea i poured in through a strainer; as the *kluntje* melts you can hear a distinct crackling. The beverage i topped with cream through a spe cially shaped spoon that trace the inside rim of the teacup so that the cream slowly forms a cloud, or *en wulkje*.

Under no circumstance shoulc you stir your tea. This serving method ensures that the first si is especially creamy, while subse quent sips bring increasingl strong tea. A good host will neve let guests see the bottom of thei cups until their *kluntjes* are com pletely melted; it is not unusual tc drink four or five cups in one sit ting. If you've had your fill before the *kluntje* has melted, signa your satiation by putting your tea spoon into the cup--you certainl won't have any other use for it!

taxe (visitor's taxes) for most beaches are €2-3. Beginner **windsurfers** flop around on the eastern side of the island, while the more experienced brace themselves against the cold, turbulent water of the unprotected western side at **Wenningstedt, Hörnum,** and **List.** List is also an excellent base for hikers and bikers wishing to explore the trails leading into the remote dunes of Ellenbogen, 8km north of town. The Wattenmeer Park's **Schutzstation Hörnum,** 100m south of bus stop "Steintal," offers information about the region and leads a variety of Watt-related activities (☎88 10 93. Open daily Apr. 1-Oct. 31 10am-noon and 3-6pm; Dec. 23-Jan. 6 10am-noon and 2-4pm). Westerland's new **Aquarium,** Gaadt 33, is filled with fish from the North Sea and more tropical locales. (Bus A from the ZOB to "Schützenpl." ☎836 25 22. Open daily 10am-7pm. €11, children €7.) Next to the aquarium, the **Aussichtspunkt** (Outlook) provides a panoramic view of the beach to the west and the sprawling city to the east.

AMRUM ISLAND ☎04682

Although it is the smallest of the North Frisian Islands, Amrum possesses all of Sylt's beauty and charm, in a quieter, more personal environment. The island's main attractions are, not surprisingly, nautical: lighthouses and some of the wildest beaches in Europe.

⌨⍰ TRANSPORTATION AND PRACTICAL INFORMATION. Boats to the town of Wittdün, run by **Adler-Schiffe,** leave from Hörnum on Sylt and Nordstrand, near Husum. (☎04842 900 00; www.adler-schiffe.de. Hörnum to Wittdün 50min. 11:55am and 5:10pm. Round-trip €19, children €13.50.) For more frequent service, the **Wyker Dampfschiffs-Reederei** goes to Wittdün from Dagebüll harbor, next door to Dagebüll's train station. (☎01805 08 01 40; www.faehre.de. 5 per day; €7.80, round-trip €15.80.) At the southern end of the island is the town of **Wittdün,** which is home to Amrum's ferry terminal. Following the main road north, you can reach the island's four other towns: Süddorf, Steenodde, Nebel, and Norddorf. Amrum's **bus lines** connect the towns (Apr.-Nov. single rides €1.30-2.20, day ticket €7.40). **Bikes** are available for rent all over the island, but prices go up the closer you are to Wittdün and the ferry. (A good price is around €3 per ½-day, €5 per day.) The **tourist office,** Am Fähranleger, is on the road across from the ferry terminal. (☎940 30; www.amrum.de. Open M-F 9am-5pm, Sa 9:30am-12:30pm.) The Wattenmeer National Park's **Schutzstation Wittdün** (☎27 18), Mittelstr. 34, is near the hostel and offers guided tours of the Watt (€4, children €2). Though the danger of **quicksand** pits makes it advisable to take a guided tour, at low tide some hikers cross the Wattenmeer to the neighboring island, **Föhr.** Do **laundry** at **Marlene's Münz Wasch,** Inselstr. 56, about 700m from the ferry landing. (Wash €3. Dry €2. Open daily 8am-8pm.) The entrance to the **post office,** Hauptstr. 30, is actually on Inselstr. (Open M-Tu and Th-F 9am-noon and 2:30-6pm, W and Sa 9am-noon.) **Postal Code:** 25046.

⌨⌂ ACCOMMODATIONS AND FOOD. Book far ahead to stay anywhere on the island in the summer. To get to ◪**Haus Eckart ❷,** Mittelstr. 20, walk away from the ferry dock past Inselstr. on V-Quedens-Weg, then turn right on Mittelstr. Family-run since 1902, the home offers easy beach access, a garden perfect for picnicking, and occasional in-house yoga seminars run by the cheery owner. (☎20 56; www.haus-eckart.de. Breakfast included. Dorms €16; singles €27; doubles €44.) **Jugendherberge Wittdün ❷,** Mittelstr. 1, 100 yards before House Eckart, has large, clean rooms, some with beach views. (☎20 10. Breakfast included. Internet access €1 per 10min. Reception 8:15-9:15am, noon-1pm, and 5-7pm. Open Apr.-Nov. Dorms €15.60, over 27 €19.60. Kurtaxe €2.50.) **Campingplatz Amrum ❶,** Inselstr. 125, Wittdün, is nestled in the dunes and has its own *Biergarten.* (☎22 54;

www.amrum-camping.de. Check-in 9:30am-12:30pm and 4:30-6pm. Tents €5-9, €6.50 per person, €5-9 per tent, plus *Kurtaxe*. Cash only.) Restaurants in Wittdün tend to be fairly expensive, but there are two **SPAR** supermarkets on Inselstr., close to the docks. (Open M-F 7:45am-12:30pm and 2:30-6pm, Sa 7:45am-noon and 2-5pm.) Those with a sweet-tooth should sample the dainty *Friesenwaffeln* (waffles with plum sauce and whipped cream; €2.60) or down an invigorating *Eiergrog* (egg, sugar, and hot rum; €4.90) in Nebel's time-tested **Friesen-café ❷**, Vasterstigh 7. (☎966 20. Open daily 11:30am-6pm.) A block from Wittdün's ferry dock, **Restaurant Klabautermann ❹**, Inselstr. 13, serves big portions of reasonably priced fish and meat (€8-14), next door to the restaurant's private bowling alley. (☎21 39. Open daily 11am-1:30pm and 5-9:30pm.) In the evening, crowds fill **Die Blaue Maus,** Inselstr. 107 in Wittdün. This cozy pub is Amrum's most beloved bar; it even has its own bus stop. (☎20 40. Open F-Tu 6pm-3am, W 6pm-2am, kitchen open until 1am. MC/V.)

🖪 🖊 SIGHTS AND OUTDOOR ACTIVITIES.

Wittdün has a pleasant main street, Hauptstr., as well as a souvenir- and *Imbiß*-free **Strandpromenade** (beach walkway). To the west lies the **Kniepsand,** a wild stretch of North Sea beach. Between the *Kniepsand* and the towns lies a strip of grassy dunes crisscrossed by hiking trails and crowned by the **Amrumer Leuchtturm,** the tallest lighthouse on Germany's North Sea coast. (Open Apr.-Oct. M-F 8:30am-12:30pm. €5, with *Gastkarte* €2, children €0.50.) The *Aussichtsdünen* (lookout dunes) along the island's trails, offer similarly breathtaking views of the island. **Nebel,** a village of traditional thatch-roof Frisian houses, is unquestionably the cultural center of the island. The **Mühlenmuseum** (Windmill Museum), in an old thatched windmill, has exhibits on the history of Amrum and its lighthouse. (☎38 89. Open Apr.-Oct. M-Sa 10am-noon and 2:30-5pm, Su 2-5pm. €3, children €1.) Amrum's Frisian culture is exhibited inside the **Ömrang Hüüs,** Waaswai 1. The 18th-century captain's home captures the harshness of life in austere Nordfriesland—in the tiny closet bedroom, the whole family slept sitting up to keep from freezing during the night. (☎10 11. Open M-Sa 3-5pm, early May to late Oct. also M-F 10am-noon. Donation requested.) **St. Clemens,** Nebel's small church, is also worth a visit. Outside Nebel, two trails run to Norddorf. The **forest trail** (7.9km, marked by green triangles) cuts through the western portion of the island, while the more scenic **Wattenmeer trail** (7.4km, marked by yellow dots), runs across the villages and open pasture along the east shore of the

---

10 4 2 6 1
7 8 9 5 3

TOP TEN LIST

HOW TO BE A GERMAN TOURIST

Relaxing on a beautiful German beach, you realize you're the only foreigner around. To fit in among native holiday-makers, learn what every German tourist already knows:

10. Nordic walking. The addition of ski poles turns mere walking into a veritable sporting event.

9. Driving. Roar down the Autobahn to make sure pedestrians take waiting for the "walk" signal seriously.

8. Tents. Going to the beach? Then a sun-protective half-open tent of sorts is an absolute must.

7. Lunch. Whether it's 40 degrees or 90, no meal is complete without the apparition of meat and some form of potatoes.

6. Bikes. The best means of transportation around, as sidewalks reserve paths for cyclists.

5. Bike helmets. According to German custom, these are rarely worn. (*Let's Go* isn't convinced that this is a good idea.)

4. Open container laws. Germans have never put these three words together, so finish that *Bier* wherever you want.

3. Hiking. Not to be attempted half-heartedly; appropriate shoes, socks, and hats should be worn.

2. Jogging. Unlike hiking, anything goes—loafers, polo shirts, or shorts even Richard Simmons would be ashamed of.

1. Nudity. Nothing special here, whether in the communal showers of a youth hostel or on the beach. Staring, however, is discouraged.

island. Cut left on the smaller paths that branch off the green triangle path to reach the 2km-wide *Kniepsand* beaches.

SCHLESWIG ☎ 04621

One of the oldest towns in Northern Europe, Schleswig has held the Schlei river in its horseshoe embrace since around AD 800. Over the centuries Schleswig was strengthened by the Vikings and the **Gottorfer** dukes, small-time nobles who set themselves up in a showy island castle. Though the grandeur of the past is now confined to museums and the swords of the Vikings are sheathed under meters of earth, Schleswig remains a careful steward of its cultural heritage. Every two years, the city hosts an elaborate **Viking Festival,** complete with longboats and reen-actments, drawing crowds from afar. (Look for the next one in August 2008.)

▐ TRANSPORTATION

Trains every hr. to: Flensburg (30min., €6.30); Hamburg (2hr., €19.70); Kiel (50min., €8.90). **Buses** run from the train station to the **ZOB** (bus station), on the corner of Königstr. and Plessenstr. (Single rides €1.20, day ticket €3.60.) For **taxis,** call ☎333 33 or 50 60. Rent **bikes** at **Radsport Splettstößer,** Bismarckstr. 13. Take Plessentstr. away from the water up the hill until it turns into Bismarckstr. It's just past Lutherstr. on the left. (☎241 02. €4.50 per day. Open M-F 8:30am-12:30pm and 1:30-6pm, Sa 8:30am-12:30pm.)

◆▐ ORIENTATION AND PRACTICAL INFORMATION

Unlike most German towns, Schleswig centers on its **bus terminal** rather than its train station. The train station, a 20min. walk or 5min. ride on the #1, 2, 3, 6, or 7 buses from the Altstadt, is to the south of the Schlei River, across the inlet. On the other side of the Schlei, a few hundred meters north of the bus station, the pedestrian shopping street **Stadtweg** runs through the town center. South of Stadtweg, paved paths, parks, and cafés line the waterfront. Halfway between the bus and train stations is the expansive **Schloß Gottorf,** while east of the yacht harbor the **Altstadt** and the fishing village of **Holm** remain in pristine condition. The **tourist office,** Plessenstr. 7, is up the street from the harbor; from the ZOB, walk down Plessenstr. toward the water. (☎98 16 16, room reservations 98 16 17; fax 98 16 19. Open May-Sept. M-F 9:30am-6:30pm, Sa 9:30am-12:30pm; Oct.-Apr. M-Th 10am-4pm, F 10am-1pm.) Do **laundry** at **Waschcenter,** Stadtweg 70. (Wash €3.50. Dry €0.50 per 12min. Open M-Sa 6am-10pm.) The **post office,** with a 24hr. **ATM,** is just off Stadtweg at Poststr. (Open M-F 9am-6pm, Sa 9am-12:30pm.) **Postal Code:** 24837.

▐ ◖ ACCOMMODATIONS AND FOOD

The **Jugendherberge (HI) ❶,** Spielkoppel 1, is near the center of town. Take bus #2 to "Schwimmhalle." The facilities are standard issue, but just seconds from a park with a commanding view of Schleswig's jumbled rooftops and the Schlei's swirling waters. (☎238 93. Breakfast included. Reception 7am-1pm and 5-11pm. Curfew 11pm. Dorms €14.10, over 27 €16.60; singles €18.10/21.10. MC/V.) **Hotel Schleiblick ❹,** Hafengang 4, overlooks the harbor. Tucked away on a sidestreet, this hotel offers bright, airy rooms with baths. (☎234 68. Breakfast included. Singles €36; doubles €63. Prices lower in the off-season. Cash only.) The **Wikinger Campingplatz ❶,** Am Haithabu, is a spacious, though windy, campsite on the water. The Vikings set up camp near here over 1200 years ago, when they established their settlement at Haithabu in AD 800. (☎324 50; www.camping-haithabu.de. Closed Nov.-Mar.

Reception in summer 8am-10pm; in winter 8-11am and 4-6pm. €3.50 per person, €2 per child, €6 per tent. Cash only.) Closer to the Altstadt, fresh and cheap seafood can be found in the *Imbiße* along Am Hafen. The Stadtweg is also lined with cheap eateries. Watch beer brewing at Schleswig's own **Asgaard-Brauerei ❸**, Königstr. 27, where descendants of Eric the Red nurture big copper tubs of suds. Look for the converted beer-dispensing fire engine parked outside. (☎ 292 06. Meals €9-10; beer €2-3. Open M-Th 5pm-midnight, F 5pm-2am, Sa 10am-2am, Su 11am-midnight. Cash only.) The **Fischrestaurant Schleimöwe ❸**, Süderholmstr. 8, serves excellent fish straight from the Schlei, with a waterfront view of the quaint village of Holm. (☎ 234 09. Entrées €8-15. Open M-F 11:30am-2pm and 5-10pm.)

👁 🏛 SIGHTS AND MUSEUMS

A 20min. walk along the harbor from the Altstadt or a quick ride to "Oberlandesgericht" on buses #1, 2, 4, or 5 brings you to the 18th-century **◪Schloß Gottorf**, home to the **Landesmuseen** (State Museums). These six museums are Schleswig's primary attraction owing to the incredible breadth of the collections. On the ground floor of the *Schloß*, the left wing contains altarpieces, religious statues, a Gutenberg Bible, and the *Schloßkapelle* (castle chapel). Works by Dutch masters fill the hall to the right of the entrance, while a collection of furnishings, porcelain, and silver are exhibited in the rear. In the Art Nouveau display on the second floor, even the carpets are part of the exhibit. Ascending further, you reach the **Archäologisches Landesmuseum** (State Archeology Museum), which showcases prehistoric artifacts from Schleswig-Holstein and around the world. Across from the castle, the Kreuzstall and adjacent buildings house the **Museum des 20. Jahrhunderts** (20th Century Museum), an extensive collection devoted to the works of 20th-century artists. In particular, the **Gallerie der Klassische Moderne** (Classical Modern Gallery) exhibits the paintings, sketches, and sculpture of contemporary Germans. The **outdoor sculpture museum,** in the park surrounding the castle, showcases other modern works. (☎ 81 32 22. Open Apr.-Oct. daily 10am-6pm; Nov.-Mar. Tu-F 10am-4pm, Sa-Su 10am-5pm. Admission to everything €6, students €3, families €13.)

A few minutes away from Schloß Gottorf, on the south side of the harbor, is the **Stadtmuseum Schleswig** (Municipal Museum), Friedrichstr. 9-11, which houses a display on the history of Schleswig-Holstein, a series of special exhibits, and **Das Teddy Bär Haus,** a collection of teddy bears spanning 100 years. (☎93 68 20; www.stadtmuseum-schleswig.de. Open Tu-Su 10am-5pm. Admission €3; students, children, and seniors €1.50; families €5.50.) A typical assortment of shops and department stores lines **Stadtweg,** the main pedestrian zone. Schleswig's hilly Altstadt, a few blocks above the harbor, is crisscrossed by cobblestone streets and dwarfed by the **St. Petri Dom.** The bird's-eye view from its 12th-century tower will take your breath away, if you still have any after the 240-stair ascent. The highlight of the church is Brüggemann's incredibly intricate **Bordesholmer Altar.** Choral and organ concerts take place here in the summer. (Open May-Sept. M-Sa 9am-5pm, Su 1:30-5pm; Oct.-Apr. M-Sa 10am-4pm, Su 1:30-4pm. €1 suggested donation. Tower €2, children €1. Summer concerts W evenings at 8pm; usually free.) The **Holm,** an old fishing village where a ring of miniature houses and a tiny church are carefully tended, begins east of Knud-Laward-Str.

From the harbor, a 20min. journey across the Schlei will bring you to the **Wikinger Museum Haithabu** (Haithabu Viking Museum). Ferries leave from Stadthafen am Dom, dock #2, every hr. 12:30-4:30pm. (€2, under 12 and students €1.50; round-trip €3.50/2.50.) Follow the signs along the winding path to the cluster of buildings housing the museum. Many of the artifacts displayed inside were found right next door at Haithabu, the site of Schleswig's first Viking settlement. Don't miss the hall containing the full-size frame of a partially reconstructed longboat. (Open Apr.-Oct. daily 9am-5pm; Nov.-Mar. Tu-Su 10am-4pm. €4, students and children €2.50, families €9.)

FLENSBURG   ☎0461

Minutes from the Danish border, Nordic Flensburg (pop. 75,000) has some of the best sailing in Germany. Separated from the industrial harbor to the north, Flensburg's Altstadt drinks in the mild scene of sea and sails from its windswept cafés and restaurants. Spared from all but two bombs in WWII, Flensburg's medieval architecture and churches remain in near-perfect condition. In 1945, Flensburg played reluctant host to an SS army on the cusp of surrender, briefly making the city the Nazi provisional capital. On curving cobblestone and brick pedestrian streets, crowds of young Germans and Danes take advantage of the city's cosmopolitan flair over home-brewed *Flensburger Pilsener.*

🖪🖊 **TRANSPORTATION AND PRACTICAL INFORMATION. Trains** travel from Flensburg to: Copenhagen, Denmark (4hr., every 2hr., €46); Hamburg (2hr., 1 per hr., €22); Kiel (1¼hr., 1 per hr., €13); Schleswig (30min., 1 per hr., €6). To get to the **ZOB** (bus station) from the train station, turn right at the end of the Bahnhofstr., and take the left fork that curves as Süderhofenden for two blocks. **Buses** leave for Denmark every 20min. from gate B4 (20min., €1.50). Flensburg's **public transportation** system saves a lot of uphill walking in town (single trip €1.50, day pass €4.70). A few blocks from the ZOB, Nordlicht Reisen's **Hansalinie** sails round-trip to **Glücksburg.** (☎04631 617 10; www.nordlicht-reisen.de. 1hr.; every 2hr. 9:30am-5:30pm, return every 2hr. 10:30am-6:30pm; round-trip €5, children €4.) To reach the **tourist office,** Rathausstr. 1, go to the corner of Norderhofen and Rathausstr. near the ZOB. The staff at this site will gladly book rooms for free. (☎909 09 20; www.flensburg.de. Open July-Sept. M-F 9am-6pm, Sa 10am-1pm; Oct.-June M-F 9am-1pm and 3-6pm.) Local services include: **Waschcenter,** Angelburgerstr. 45 (wash €3.50; dry €0.50 per 12min.; open daily 6am-2am); **police,** Norderhofenden 1 (☎110, non-emergency ☎484 41 10); **post office,** Bahnhofstr. 40. (Open M-F 7am-6pm, Sa 8am-1pm.) **Postal Code:** 24939.

⌂⌂ ACCOMMODATIONS AND FOOD. In the leafy Volkspark northeast of the Altstadt, Flensburg's **Jugendherberge (HI) ❷**, Fichtestr. 16, sits between two centers of learning: Heldenheim Universität and a Marines training ground. To reach the hostel from the ZOB, take bus #2, 3, 5, or 7 to "Stadion," then follow the signs past the stadium. Standard hostel fare in 2-, 4-, and 6-bed flavors. (☎377 42; fax 31 29 52. Breakfast included. Reception 7:30am-2pm and 4-10pm. Dorms €15.40, over 27 €18.40. Cash only.) A bargain compared to the overpriced hotels on Süderhofenden, economy-chain **ETAP Hotel ❸**, Süderhofenden 14, offers rooms with TV and bath near the bus station. (☎48 08 920; www.etaphotel.com. Reception M-Sa 6:30-11am and 5-10pm, Su 7-11am and 5-10pm. Singles €36; doubles €44; less in low-season. AmEx/DC/MC/V.) Cheap *Currywurst* joints, bakeries, and ice cream parlors coexist with the boutiques of the pedestrian zone. The popular **Nordermarkt** is filled with classy cafés and bars. For coastal specialties from a different region head to **Côté Bretagne ❸**, Rote Str. 14, and try genuine Breton *galettes* (buckwheat crêpes; €6.30-8.90) or more substantial traditional French meat dishes like the *canard confit* (€14.80). (☎318 6868; www.cote-bretagne.com. Café open daily 9am-5:30pm, restaurant noon-3pm and 5:30-10pm, wine and cheese bar 5:30-11pm. AmEx/MC/V.) As you head north on Schiffbrücke, the streets become seedier, but hold the city's best bars and clubs. **Hansen's Brauerei**, Schiffbrücke 16, serves home-brewed beer by the meter (12 drinks lined up along a meter-long board for €15). (☎222 10. Open M-Th and Su 11:30am-1am, F-Sa 11:30am-2am. MC/V.)

◪ SIGHTS. Flensburg surrounds the harbor formed by the inland banks of the Flensburger Förde; streets run up from the water's edge into the hills. The **Kapitänsweg** (Captain's Path) connects the city's major historical sites. In the Südermarkt, the 14th-century **Nikolaikirche** boasts an impressively large organ and a series of post-Reformation paintings of comparable magnitude. One painting shows Christ crucified when viewed from one angle, and from another angle depicts him rising from the dead. (Open daily 9am-6pm. Free. Tours of the tower July to mid-Sept. Sa at noon.) Up Große Str., beyond the Nordermarkt, is the larger **Marienkirche**, with modern stained-glass windows and a spectacular two-story Baroque altar depicting the Last Supper. (Open in summer M-Sa 10am-5pm; in winter 10am-4pm. Free.) The **Marientreppe**, across from Norderstr. 50, gives a panoramic glimpse of Flensburg and Denmark from atop its 146 stairs. In the **Schiffahrtsmuseum** (Maritime Museum), Schiffbrücke 39, four packed floors document Flensburg's nautical history, its role in Denmark's once-thriving Caribbean trade, and its long-touted production of rum. (Open Apr.-Oct. Tu-Su 10am-5pm; Nov.-Mar. Tu-Su 10am-4pm. €4, students €1.50, families €8.) Nearby, at Norderstr. 157-163, is **Phänomenta**, Germany's first hands-on science center, where over 150 experiments allow for painless learning. See how much pedaling it takes to power a TV, or witness waves traveling down a coil. (www.phaenomenta-flenstburg.de. Open June-Sept. M-F 10am-6pm, Sa-Su 11am-6pm; Oct.-May M-F 9am-5pm, Sa-Su 11am-6pm.) Near Südermarkt, the **Deutsches Haus**, Friedrich-Ebert-Str. 7 (☎01805 969 00 00) and the **Theater Flensburg**, Rathausstr. 22, put on plays, artsy films, and concerts. (☎0461 14 10 00; www.sh-landestheater.de. Box office open M-F 10am-1pm and 3-6pm, Sa 10am-1pm.) Up the hill from the city theater is Museumsberg, upon which sit the two buildings containing the **Städtische Museen** (Municipal Museums). The bottom floor of the **Heinrich-Sauermann-Haus** contains Flensburg's **Naturwissenschaftliches Museum** (Scientific Museum), with hundreds of stuffed birds, mammals, and insects on display. The upper floors house a series of furnished rooms filled with artifacts of Schleswig-Holstein's cultural history. The adjacent building, the **Hans-Christiansen-Haus** Museumsberg 1, contains a unique collection of 19th-century paintings by regional artists and a collection of modern art. (☎85 29 56. Open Tu-Su 10am-5pm; Nov.-Mar. 10am-4pm. €4, students €1.50; F €2.50/1 from 1pm.)

SCHLESWIG-HOLSTEIN

HAMBURG

Water shapes every aspect of life in the harbor city of Hamburg, Germany's second-largest city. Joggers and walkers flock to the Alster lakes to enjoy the area's beauty, while the bustling port on the Elbe floods the city with new people, ideas, and trade. The many canals that cross Hamburg reflect images of spectacular church steeples alongside modern facades. A walk through the city is a walk over water—with a grand total of 2478 bridges, Hamburg has more than Venice.

A hub for commerce since its early history, Hamburg was a founding member of the Hanseatic trade league in the 13th century. Overland trade from the Baltic Sea brought prosperity in the 16th century, leading to the establishment of the first German stock exchange here in 1558. By the 17th century, Hamburg's influence had spread, and it gained the title of "Free Imperial City" in 1618. Along with Berlin and Bremen, it is one of the three remaining city-states among Germany's 16 *Länder*. Hamburg still values its autonomy, which, along with great sea-trade wealth, has seen the city through many hardships.

The Great Fire of 1842 leveled the entire downtown, but a massive rebuilding effort resurrected the city as an industrial-age powerhouse in naval construction and home of the Hamburg-America Line, then the world's largest shipping firm. In WWII, a series of air raids once again turned the downtown to rubble. Over 50,000 tenants of the crowded buildings on the waterfront were killed in a single strike in July of 1943. Thanks to a massive reconstruction effort begun in the 1960s, Hamburg has restored many of its most beloved buildings.

Today's Hamburg is progressive, cosmopolitan, and accepting. The city is Germany's most diverse, with large ethnic populations including many Turkish and Portuguese residents. The district of **St. Georg** is also home to a flourishing gay scene. As the cultural center of Germany, Hamburg houses world-renowned opera and theater companies and many of the country's finest museums. Hamburg's venues hosted The Beatles before they were famous, and a thriving independent and experimental music scene exists today. At night, tens of thousands of revelers flock to the infamous red-light district of the **Reeperbahn,** and bars and pubs throughout the city fill up nearly every night of the week.

HIGHLIGHTS OF HAMBURG

DANCE UNTIL DAWN in the midst of **Hamburg's** spectacular nightlife (p. 231).

BARGAIN for the freshest fish in the **Land** while listening to local rock bands play on Sunday morning at the **Fischmarkt** (p. 225).

MARVEL at the works of the old masters and contemporary artists in the museums along the **Kunstmeile.**

✈ INTERCITY TRANSPORTATION

Flights: Air France (☎018 05 83 08 30) and **Lufthansa** (☎018 03 80 38 03) service Hamburg's **Fuhlsbüttel Airport** (☎507 50). **Jasper Airport Express** buses (☎040 22 71 060) run from the Kirchenallee exit of the Hauptbahnhof directly to the airport (25min.; every 15min. 4:40am-8:20pm, then every 20min. 8:20-9:20pm; €5, under 13 €2). Alternatively, you can take U1 or S1/S11 to "Ohlsdorf," and then an **express bus** to the airport (every 10min. 4:30am-11pm, every 30min. 11pm-1am; €2.50, children 6-14 €0.90).

Trains: The **Hauptbahnhof** has connections every hr. to: **Berlin** (1½hr., €47); **Copen-hagen, Denmark** (5hr., €76); **Frankfurt** (3½hr., €93); **Hanover** (1½hr., €36); and **Munich** (6hr., €115). The efficient staff at the **DB Reisezentrum** sells tickets. Open M-F 5:30am-10pm, Sa-Su 7am-10pm. Or, purchase them online at www.bahn.de. **Dammtor** station is near the university; **Harburg** station is south of the Elbe; **Altona** station is to the west of the city; and **Bergedorf** is to the southeast. Most trains to and from Schleswig-Holstein stop only at Altona. Frequent local trains and the S-Bahn connect the stations. **Lockers** are available for €1-6 per day.

Buses: The **ZOB** is across Steintorpl. from the Hauptbahnhof. Terminal is open M-Th 5am-10pm, F-Sa 5am-midnight, Su 5am-10pm. **Autokraft** (☎280 86 60) goes to **Berlin** (3¼hr., 10-12 per day, €24). **Gulliver's** (☎253 28 978) to **Amsterdam, Netherlands** (5½hr., daily, €36); **London, England** (14½hr., daily, €72); and **Paris, France** (12hr., daily, €60). Discount rates for students and children.

Ride Share: Mitfahrzentrale Citynetz, Ernst-Merck-Str. 12-14 (☎24 85 95 25; www.citynetz-mitfahrzentrale.de). To: **Berlin** (€15.50); **Cologne** (€24); **Frankfurt** (€18); **Munich** (€37). Open M-F 9:30am-6:30pm, Sa 9:30am-2pm.

◪ ORIENTATION

Hamburg lies on the northern bank of the Elbe river, 100km from the North Sea. The ideally situated harbor has shaped the city's growth. Hamburg's center is between the Elbe and the nearby Alster lakes, **Außenalster** and **Binnenalster,** which are formed by the confluence of the Alster, Bille, and Elbe rivers. Lush parks, including the beautiful **Planten un Blomen** (p. 224), skirt the western boundary of downtown and arch northward from the **Landungsbrücken** (piers) of **St. Pauli** all the way to the western shore of the Alster lakes. The **Hauptbahnhof** lies at the eastern edge of the city center, along Steintorwall. Bisecting the downtown, the **Alsterfleet canal** separates the **Altstadt** on the eastern bank from the **Neustadt** on the west. The city's best museums, galleries, and theaters are located within these two districts.

Extending from the Kirchenallee exit of the Hauptbahnhof, the predominantly gay district of **St. Georg** follows the Außenalster's east bank. Here, the seediness of the Hansapl. area near the station falls away to a quiet café scene along the Lange Reihe. Outside the Hauptbahnhof's main exit on Steintorwall is the **Kunstmeile** (Art Mile), a row of museums extending from the Alster Lakes to the banks of the Elbe. Perpendicular to Steintorwall, **Mönckebergstr.,** Hamburg's most famous shopping street, runs westward to the **Rathausmarkt.** The Neustadt's **Hanseviertel,** nestled between Rathausmarkt and Gänsemarkt, is crammed with banks, shops, galleries, and auction houses. The area's glamor turns window-shopping into high art, while the nearby *Fleete* (canals) give the quarter a Venetian charm. North of the city center, the **university** dominates the **Dammtor** district and the western portion of **Rotherbaum,** sustaining a vibrant community of students and intellectuals. To the west of the university, young designers and trendy stores promise future sophistication for the **Karoviertel.** Farther west, the **Schanzenviertel** is a politically active community that inhabited by artists, students, and a sizable Turkish population. The **Altona** district was once a Jewish community and, in the 17th century, an independent city ruled by Denmark, but as power shifted these groups were ousted. Altona's bustling pedestrian zone, the **Ottenser Hauptstr.,** runs west from the Altona station. Hamburg's wealthiest neighborhoods, such as **Winterhude** and **Harvesthude,** line the shores of the Außenalster. Toward the west, **Eppendorf** is home to the most beautiful outdoor markets in the city. At the southwest end of the city center, an entirely different atmosphere reigns along the Elbe in **St. Pauli,** where the raucous **Fischmarkt** (fish market) takes place blocks away from the infamous **Reeperbahn,** home to Hamburg's sex trade and most of its clubs.

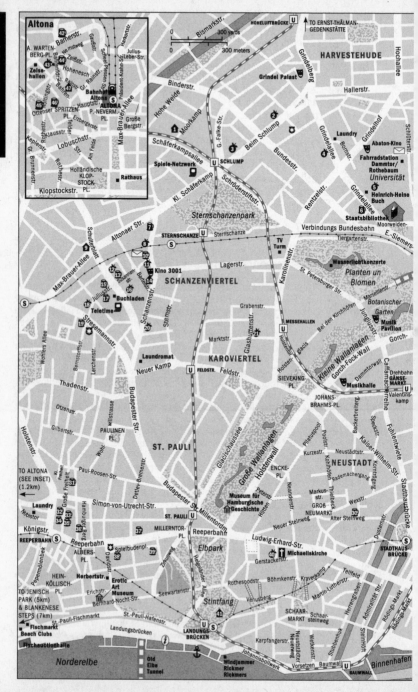

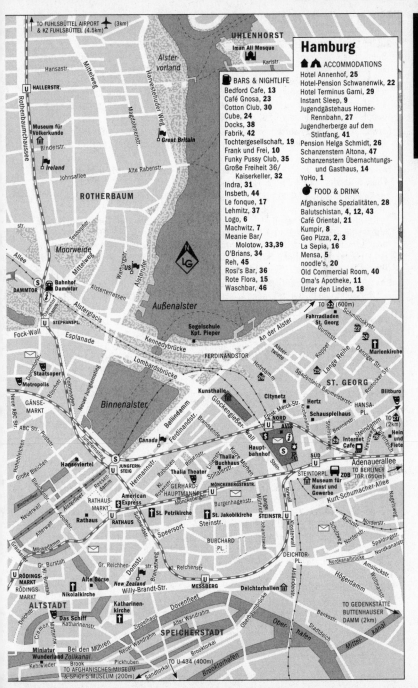

TO FUHLSBÜTTEL AIRPORT ✈ (3km)
& KZ FUHLSBÜTTEL (4.5km)

UHLENHORST

Iman Ali Mosque

Hamburg

🏨🏠 ACCOMMODATIONS

Hotel Annenhof, **25**
Hotel-Pension Schwanenwik, **22**
Hotel Terminus Garni, **29**
Instant Sleep, **9**
Jugendgästehaus Horner-
Rennbahn, **27**
Jugendherberge auf dem
Stintfang, **41**
Pension Helga Schmidt, **26**
Schanzenstern Altona, **47**
Schanzenstern Übernachtungs-
und Gasthaus, **14**
YoHo, **1**

🥘 FOOD & DRINK

Afghanische Spezialitäten, **28**
Balutschistan, **4, 12, 43**
Café Oriental, **21**
Kumpir, **8**
Geo Pizza, **2, 3**
La Sepia, **16**
Mensa, **5**
noodle's, **20**
Old Commercial Room, **40**
Oma's Apotheke, **11**
Unter den Linden, **18**

🍸 BARS & NIGHTLIFE

Bedford Cafe, **13**
Café Gnosa, **23**
Cotton Club, **30**
Cube, **24**
Docks, **38**
Fabrik, **42**
Tochtergesellschaft, **19**
Frank und Frei, **10**
Funky Pussy Club, **35**
Große Freiheit 36/
Kaiserkeller, **32**
Indra, **31**
Insbeth, **44**
Le fonque, **17**
Lehmitz, **37**
Logo, **6**
Machwitz, **7**
Meanie Bar/
Molotow, **33,39**
O'Brians, **34**
Reh, **45**
Rosi's Bar, **36**
Rote Flora, **15**
Waschbar, **46**

HAMBURG

⊑ LOCAL TRANSPORTATION

Public Transportation: HVV operates an efficient U-Bahn, S-Bahn, and bus network. Short rides within downtown cost €1.55, one-way in greater Hamburg €2.50; 9hr. pass €4.90, 1-day €5.80, 3-day €14.40. The **Hamburg Card** provides unlimited access to public transportation, reduced admission to museums, and discounts on bus and boat tours for groups of 1 adult and up to 3 children under 12. (Available at tourist offices. €7.30 per day, €15 for 3 days) The **Group Card** provides the same benefits for up to 5 people of any age. (1-day €13, 3-day €23.)

Ferries: Alster-Kreuz-Fahrten (☎357 42 40) runs between 9 stops on the Binnen- and Außenalster daily 10am-6pm. €1.30 per stop; €6.50 for 5 stops or more; €8.50 for all 9; children ½-price.

Taxis: All Hamburg taxis charge the same (expensive) rates. **Autoruf,** ☎44 10 11. **Taxi Funk & Service,** ☎ 61 11 22. **Taxi Hamburg,** ☎666 666.

Car Rental: Avis (☎32 87 38 00), in the Hauptbahnhof near track #12. Cars from €273 per wk., with insurance and 24hr. emergency assistance. International reservations ☎018 05 55 77 55. Open M-F 7:30am-9pm, Sa 8am-6pm, Su 10am-6pm. **Hertz,** Kirchenallee 34-36 (☎280 12 01, international reservations 018 05 33 35 35), is across the street and to the left. Cars from €305 per wk., including insurance. Open M-F 7am-9pm, Sa 8am-8pm, Su 10am-8pm. **Europcar A-2,** Holstenstr. 156 (☎306 82 60; www.europecar.de), U3 to "Feldstr." Open daily 24hr.

Boat Rental: Segelschule Kpt. Pieper, An der Alster/Atlantikstieg (☎24 75 78; www.segelschule-pieper.de), directly across from the Hotel Atlantic at the foot of the Kennedybrücke on the Außenalster. Paddleboats and rowboats €12 per hr.; sailboats for up to 6 people €15-18 per hr. Open daily 10am-9pm.

Bike Rental: Fahrradladen St. Georg, Schmilinskystr. 6 (☎24 39 08), is off the Lange Reihe towards the Außenalster. €8 per day; €56 per wk. with a €50 deposit. Open M-F 10am-7pm, Sa 10am-1pm. **Fahrradstation Dammtor/Rothebaum,** Schlüterstr. 11 (☎41 46 82 77), rents for the best price in Hamburg. €3 per day. Open M-F 9am-6pm.

⑦ PRACTICAL INFORMATION

CITY CODE: The city code for all of Hamburg is ☎**040.**

TOURIST AND FINANCIAL SERVICES

Tourist Offices: Hamburg's main tourist offices supply free English-language maps and pamphlets. All sell the **Hamburg Card** (p. 218). The **Hauptbahnhof office,** in the *Wandelhalle* near the Kirchenallee exit (☎30 05 12 01; www.hamburg-tourism.de), books rooms for a €4 fee. Open daily 7am-10pm. The **St. Pauli Landungsbrücken office** (☎30 05 12 03; fax 31 35 78), between piers 4 and 5, is less crowded than the Hauptbahnhof office. Open Oct.-Mar. daily 10am-5:30pm; Apr.-Sept. M, W, Su 8am-6pm, Tu and Th-Sa 8am-7pm. The English-speakers on the **Hamburg Hotline** (☎30 05 13 00) book rooms (€4), sell event tickets, and answer questions. Open daily 8am-8pm.

Tours: Information booths for many tours are located at the St. Pauli Landungsbrücken and in the Hauptbahnhof.

Top-Tour Hamburg (☎641 37 31; www.top-tour-hamburg.de). Top-Tour operates several sightseeing tours on double-decker buses throughout Hamburg, leaving from the Kirchenallee exit of the Hauptbahnhof and the St. Pauli Landungsbrücken, every 30min. daily Apr.-Oct. 9:30am-5pm; fall and winter tours are less frequent. If a sight seems particularly intriguing you can hop off the bus and catch the next one after a more thorough inspection. For a tour in English, ask as you board. €9.50, children €4.75.

Stattreisen Hamburg (☎ 430 34 81; www.stattreisen-hamburg.de). Offbeat 2hr. neighborhood and themed walks, with titles such as "Reeperbahn by Night," "Merchants and Catastrophes Downtown," and "Neon lights, Seedy Bars, and Catholics in St. Pauli." Most tours are given in German; however, English tours are offered on a less-frequent basis. Call for times and locations, or ask at the tourist office. €6-10.

Alster-Touristik (☎ 357 42 40; www.alstertouristik.de), on Jungfernstieg by the Außenalster. Walk to the Außenalster or take the U1 or U2, or S1 or S3 to "Jungfernstieg." 50min. boat rides around the lakes. Tours leave daily Apr.-Oct. every 30min. 10am-6pm, €10, under 16 €5. Also offers more expensive trips through the city's canals as well as a tour that goes all the way to Bergedorf.

Stadtrundfahrten Hamburg (☎ 792 89 79), at the Hauptbahnhof's Kirchenallee exit, offers a variety of tours on red double-decker buses and a small train. Apr.-Oct. daily every 30min. 9:30am-5pm; Nov.-Mar. M-F every hr. 10am-4pm. €13, under 12 free.

Jogging Tours (☎ 439 87 80; www.touristjogging.com). A variety of jogs around the Altstadt, St. Pauli, or the Neustadt, 7-10km. €19 per hr.

Consulates: Most consulates flank the ritzy neighborhoods on the western shore of Außenalster, Harvestehuder Weg, and the smaller streets branching off of them. **Canada:** Ballindamm 35 (☎ 460 02 70), between Alestertor and Bergstr. U1 or S1-3 to "Jungfernstieg." Open M-F 9:30am-12:30pm. **Ireland:** Feldbrunnenstr. 43 (☎ 44 18 61 13). U1 to "Hallerstr." Open M-F 9am-1pm. **New Zealand:** Domstr. 19 (☎ 442 55 50), on the 3rd fl. of Zürich-Haus. U1 to "Messberg." Open M-Th 9am-1pm and 2-5:30pm, F 9am-1pm and 2-4:30pm. **UK:** Harvestehuder Weg 8a (☎ 448 03 20). U1 to "Hallerstr." Open M-Th 9am-4pm, F 9am-3pm. **US:** Alsterufer 26-28. S11, S21, or S31 to "Dammtor." (☎ 41 17 11 00). Open M-F 9am-noon.

Currency Exchange: ReiseBank, (☎ 32 34 83), 2nd fl. of the Hauptbahnhof near the Kirchenallee exit, arranges money transfers for Western Union, cashes traveler's checks (1% commission with a min. €4 for American Express and a min. €6 for other types), and exchanges currency for a steep 4-5% fee, plus a fixed charge of €3-5. Open daily 7:30am-10pm. ReiseBank also has branches in the Altona and Dammtor train stations. For better rates, try one of the dozens of exchanges and banks (most of which are open M-F 9am-5pm) near the Hauptbahnhof or downtown.

American Express: Rathausmarkt 10 (☎ 30 39 38 11). U3 to "Rathaus." Across from the bus stop, on the corner of Hermanstr. All banking services. Mail (letters only) held for members up to 5wk. Open M-F 9:30am-1pm and 2-6pm, Sa 10am-3pm.

LOCAL SERVICES

Home Share: Mitwohnzentrale Homecompany, Schulterblatt 112 (☎ 194 45; www.hamburg.homecompany.de), U3, S21, or S31 to "Sternschanze." Apartments available for 1 month or more. Passport and deposit of 1st month's rent required. Open M-F 9am-1pm and 2-6pm, Sa 9am-1pm.

Bookstores: Thalia-Buchhaus, Spitalerstr. 8 (☎ 48 50 11 22), U2 to Mönkebergstr., is one of the city's largest bookstores. **Heinrich-Heine Buch,** Grindelallee 26 (☎ 441 13 30), has an excellent travel section and a decent selection of English-language novels. Open M-F 9:30am-7pm, Sa 10am-4pm. **Buchladen,** Schulterblatt 55 (☎ 439 13 49), in the heart of the Sternschanze area, has about 100 English novels. Open M-F 9:30am-6:30pm, Sa 10am-4pm.

Library: Staats- und Universitätsbibliothek, Von-Melle-Park 3 (☎ 428 38 22 33; www.sub.uni-hamburg.de). Hamburg's university library contains a good English-language collection. Open to the public M-F; hours vary by department. Computers on the 2nd fl., although Internet access is limited to library cardholders.

Gay and Lesbian Resources: St. Georg is the center of the gay community. Try picking up the useful, free *hinnerk* magazine and *Friends: The Gay Map* from **Café Gnosa,** Lange Reihe 93 (p. 233). Other organizations include: **Hein und Fiete,** Pulverteich 21 (☎ 24 03 33). Walk down Steindamm Str. away from the Hauptbahnhof, turn right on

Pulverteich and look for a rainbow-striped building. Open M-F 4-9pm, Sa 4-7pm. **Magnus-Hirschfeld-Centrum,** Borgweg 8 (☎ 27 87 78 00). U3 to "Borgweg." Daily films and counseling sessions, and an evening café, **Feelgood Café** (☎ 27 87 78 01). Open M-Th 5-11pm, F 5pm-late, Su 3-10pm. The center operates hotlines for gays (☎ 279 00 69, M-F 2-6pm, Tu-W also 7-10pm) and lesbians (☎ 279 00 49, W 7-9pm).

Laundromat: Schnell und Sauber, Grindelallee 158. S21 or S31 to "Dammtor," then bus #5. Wash €4 for 6kg, soap included. Dry €0.50 per 10min. Open daily 7am-10:30pm. Other locations at Pferdemarkt 27 and Nobistor 34 have the same prices and hours. Sip a beer while laundering your clothes at **Waschbar** (p. 233).

EMERGENCY AND COMMUNICATIONS

Emergency: Police, ☎ 110. From the Kirchenallee exit of the Hauptbahnhof, turn left and follow signs for "BGS/Bahnpolizei." Also on the **Reeperbahn** at the corner of Davidstr. and Spielbudenpl. and in the courtyard of the Rathaus. **Fire and Ambulance:** ☎ 112.

Rape Crisis Line: ☎ 25 55 66. Open M and Th 9:30am-1pm and 3-7pm, Tu 9:30am-1pm and 3-4pm, W 3-4pm. English-speaking staff available. The **Seelsorge Center** (☎ 31 65 43) near the Reeperbahn also takes calls Tu and Th-F 10:30am-5:30pm.

Pharmacy: Senator-Apotheke, Hachmannpl. 14 (☎ 32 75 27 or 33 92 92). English-speaking staff. Open M-F 7am-8pm, Sa 8am-4pm.

Internet Access: Internet Café, Adenauerrallee 10 (☎ 28 00 38 98), directly across from the ZOB, offers one of the best deals in town. €0.50 for 30min. Open daily 10am-11:55pm. **Teletime,** Schulterblatt 39 (☎ 41 30 47 30), in the heart of the Sternschanze district. €0.50 per 15min. Open M-F 10am-10pm, Sa-Su 10am-7pm. Near the U3 "Schlump" stop, **Spiele-Netzwerk,** Kleiner Schäferkamp 24, (☎ 45 03 82 10) costs €2 for 30min., €3 per hr., and is open later (daily 10am-2am). **Branch** with same prices near U2 "Mundsburg" at Hamburger Str. 1 (☎ 22 92 71 36) is open daily 10-4am.

Post Office: At the Kirchenallee exit of the Hauptbahnhof. Open M-F 8am-6pm, Sa 8:30am-12:30pm. **Postal Code:** 20099.

ACCOMMODATIONS

The vibrant **Schanzenviertel** area, filled with students, leftist dissidents, and a large ethnic community, houses two of the city's best backpacker hostels near many excellent, inexpensive cafés and shops. More expensive hotels are plentiful around the **Binnenalster** and eastern **Außenalster.** A slew of small, relatively cheap pensions (often renting by the hour) line **Steindamm, Steintorweg, Bremer Weg,** and **Bremer Reihe,** around the Hauptbahnhof. The area has its share of drug addicts, prostitutes, and wannabe mafiosi, but the hotels are, for the most part, safe. There are nicer budget options north of the Bahnhof around **Ernst-Merck-Str., Holzdamm,** and **Lange Reihe.** The tourist office's free *Hotelführer* can help direct you.

HOSTELS AND CAMPING

▨ **Schanzenstern Übernachtungs- und Gasthaus,** Bartelsstr. 12 (☎ 439 84 41; www.schanzenstern.de). U3, S21, or S31 to "Sternschanze." In the middle of the electrifying Schanzenviertel, the Schanzenstern maintains bright, hotel-like rooms on the upper floors of a renovated pen factory. Wheelchair accessible. Breakfast €4-6. Reception 6:30am-2am. Reserve ahead in summer. Dorms €18; singles €36; doubles €51; triples €61; quads €74; quints €92. Cash only. ❷

▨ **Instant Sleep,** Max-Brauer-Allee 277 (☎ 43 18 23 10; www.instantsleep.de). U3, S21, or S31 to "Sternschanze." Guests reading books from the improvised library or cook dinner in the communal kitchen before retiring to airy rooms. Helpful, bilingual staff. Sheets €2. Internet access €1 per 30min. Lockers €5 deposit. Reception 8am-2am. Check-out 11am. Dorms €15-18; singles €28; doubles €44; triples €60. Cash only. ❷

Schanzenstern Altona, Kleiner Rainstr. 24-26. (☎39 91 91 91; www.schanzenstern-altona.de), close to Altona Station. Just as nice as its Schanzenviertel counterpart. Dorms €18; singles €40; doubles €55-65; triples €70; quads €80. Cash only. ❷

Jugendherberge auf dem Stintfang (HI), Alfred-Wegener-Weg 5 (☎31 34 88; www.djh.de/jugendherbergen/hamburg-stintfang). U3, S1, or S3 to "Landungsbrücke." Bunk beds, checkered curtains, and views of the nearby woods create a camp-style feel. Breakfast (7-8:30am) included. Dinner buffet €5. Laundry €3.50. Reception 12:30pm-12:30am. Lockout 2-6:30am. Dorms €18.80-20.30, over 27 €3 extra per night. Discounts for stays of more than 5 nights. D/MC/V. ❷

Jugendherberge Horner-Rennbahn (HI), Rennbahnstr. 100 (☎651 16 71; www.jugendherberge.de/jh/hamburg-horn). U3 to "Horner-Rennbahn," then bus #23 to Tribünenweg; hostel is 150m farther. Far from Hamburg's center, but extremely clean and secure. Breakfast (7-9am) included. Internet access €1 per 10min. Max. 10-night stay. Check-in noon-1am. Check-out 7-9:30am. Curfew 2am. Dorms €18.80, over 27 €21.80; less for longer stays. Family rooms €17-20 per person. Cash only.❷

Campingplatz Rosemarie Buchholz, Kieler Str. 374 (☎540 45 32; www.camping-buchholz.de). From Altona station, take bus #183 to "Basselweg" (20min., 2-3 per hr. 5am-midnight), then walk 100m farther. Tightly packed with campers, surrounded by houses, and just off a busy road. Breakfast €4. Showers €1. Reception 8am-1pm and 2-10pm. Quiet hours 10pm-7am. Check-out noon. €4.80 per person, €8-11 per tent. ❶

HOTELS AND PENSIONS

▨ **Hotel Annenhof,** Lange Reihe 23 (☎24 34 26; www.hotelannenhof.de). Built in 1901, the rooms in this building exude a charm not often found at this price. High ceilings, moldings, brightly colored walls, and hardwood floors enhance very inviting rooms, some with shower. Singles €40; doubles €70; triples €100; quads €130. Cash only. ❹

YoHo - The Young Hotel, Moorkamp 5 (☎28 41 910; www.yoho-hamburg.de). U2 or U3 to "Schlump." A team of young architects used glass, steel, and mood lighting to transform this turn-of-the-century villa into a destination for the style-conscious crowd, with details like bold curtains and bowls of floating red roses. Free Internet access and cable TV. Breakfast €10. Reception M-F 6am-midnight, Sa-Su 6:30am-midnight. Singles €80, under 26 €57; doubles €87/€67. AmEx/DC/MC/V. ❺

Hotel-Pension Schwanenwik, Schwanenwik 29 (☎220 09 18; www.hotel-schwanenwik.de). Bus #6 to "Mundsburger Brücke." Beautiful lakeside rooms are quiet and spacious. Some with private showers. Breakfast included. Free wireless Internet access. Reception until 10pm. Singles €46-75; doubles €66-95. AmEx/DC/MC/V. ❹

Pension Helga Schmidt, Holzdamm 14 (☎280 83 90; www.klickinfo.de/pension-schmidt-hamburg). Located in a decent neighborhood only 2 blocks from the Hauptbahnhof. The rooms, though dated (pastel florals and light-colored wood abound), have phone and TV; some have private shower. Reception 8am-10pm. Breakfast €6. Singles €35-37; doubles €55-65; triples €82. AmEx/DC/MC/V. ❸

Hotel Terminus Garni, Steindamm 5 (☎280 31 44; www.hotel-terminus-hamburg.de). Although located at the foot of the somewhat-seedy Steindamm, the hotel itself is clean and secure. Large rooms with TV, phone, and shower. Wheelchair accessible. Breakfast included. Reception 24hr. Singles €40-65; doubles €66-96. AmEx/DC/MC/V. ❸

◨ FOOD

While traditional German beer, bread, cheese, and *wurst* still hold sway here, Hamburg's seaside location and diverse population have had a formative influence on its food. The specialty is fish, the king of them herring—grilled as *Brathering* or pickled as *Matjes* and served on a sandwich bun. The Portuguese community of

Hamburg serves its own seafood dishes in the area between the Michaeliskirche (p. 223) and the river, while Turkish *Imbiße* (snack bars) serve cheap *Döner Kebap* and falafel wraps. In early spring when asparagus is in season, it's hard to find a restaurant that doesn't serve *Spargelcremesuppe* (asparagus cream soup), and late summer sees a similar burst in *Blumenkohl* (cauliflower) dishes. For the sweet tooth, *Rote Grütze* is a beloved pudding made of red berries, usually served with vanilla sauce. Small markets selling cheap fresh fruit and Persian flatbread line Suzannestr. in the Schanzenviertel. And if you dig deep enough, you just might be able to find a hamburger or two (see **Would You Like Fries With That?**, p. 65).

SCHANZENVIERTEL

The Schanzenviertel overflows with fruit stands, Asian *Imbiße*, and avant-garde cafés. **Schulterblatt, Susannenstr.**, and **Schanzenstr.** host a slew of funky restaurants.

La Sepia, Schulterblatt 36 (☎ 432 24 84). Portuguese restaurant prepares some of the city's tastiest and most affordable seafood. From 111am-5pm, €5 gets you grilled tuna with carrots and potatoes, fresh bread, and soup. For dinner, try a heaping *paella* (€12-14). Lunch €4-6. Dinner €7.50-22. Open daily noon-3am. AmEx/MC/V. ❸

Unter den Linden, Juliusstr. 16 (☎ 43 81 40). Join happy couples and intellectuals reading complimentary papers (in German). Enjoy *Milchkaffe* (coffee with milk; €3.30), breakfast (€4.30-7), or monster salads (€3.50-6.80) in a relaxed atmosphere underneath—as the name suggests—the linden trees. Open daily 10am-1am. Cash only. ❷

noodle's, Schanzenstr. 2-4 (☎439 28 40). Serves up excellent noodle dishes like fettucini with salmon and dill sauce (€9) and generous salads. By day, the restaurant maintains a coffee shop feel, while at night it becomes a trendy bar. Beer €3-5. Open M-Th and Su 10am-1am, F-Sa 10am-3am. Cash only. ❷

Oma's Apotheke, Schanzenstr. 87 (☎43 66 20). Drawing its name from the bar made up of apothecary's drawers, Oma's draws crowds with its curious mixture of German, Italian, and American cuisine. *Schnitzel* platter €7.50; hamburger with a 1 lb. of fries €6.60. Open daily 9am-1am, F-Sa until 2am or later. Cash only. ❷

Café Oriental, Markstr. 21a (☎42 10 29 95). Be transported into the markets of Marrakesh by this artsy café's dark wood, woven carpets, and hanging lamps. Locals come for the "yogitee," honey tea with cinnamon mountains of milk foam (€2.50-3). Also offers breakfast and a variety of entrées, including oriental wraps (€3.50) and pastas (€4.50-€5). Open daily 10am-1am, later on weekends. Cash only. ❷

Kumpir, Schanzenstr. 95 (☎430 976 04). Baked potatoes in all possible incarnations, ranging from Moroccan-style spuds to more traditional versions (€2.90-3.30). Many vegetarian options. Open M-Th and Su noon-midnight, F-Sa until 1am. Cash only. ❶

UNIVERSITY

Slightly cheaper establishments can be found in the university area, especially along **Rentzelstraße, Grindelhof,** and **Grindelallee.**

Mensa, Von-Melle-Park 5. S21 or S31 to "Dammtor," then bus #4 or 5 to "Staatsbibliothek" (1 stop). Student crowd, massive plates of cafeteria food, and a bulletin board of events listings. Meals €1.55-2 with student ID. Non-students add up to €1. Open M-Th 10am-4pm, F 10am-3:30pm. Limited summer hours. Cash only; **ATM** in building. ❶

Geo Pizza aus dem Holzbackofen, Beim Schlump 53 (☎45 79 29). U2 or U3 to "Schlump." Geo has vegetarian options, but carnivorous diners will melt for the Inferno Pizza's blend of jalapeños, red peppers, beef, onions, salsa, and corn (€7.30). Pizzas €4-8. Open M-Th 11am-midnight, F 11am-1am, Sa-Su noon-1am. Branch at Beim Schlump 27 has a slightly smaller menu. Open daily 11:30am-midnight. Cash only. ❷

ELSEWHERE IN HAMBURG

In **Altona,** the pedestrian zone along Ottenserstr. next to the train station is packed with ethnic food stands and produce shops. A decidedly younger and more boisterous crowd eats and drinks at Altona's **A.-Wartenberg-Pl.** In a pinch, the shopping arcade at the **Hauptbahnhof** has about a dozen fast-food joints (open daily 6am-11pm). **Lange Reihe,** in the heart of **St. Georg,** offers good but overpriced Portuguese, Italian, and Spanish restaurants. **Gänsemarkt** and **Gerhard-Hauptmann-Pl.** have decent options in the city center.

Balutschistan, Bahrenfelderstr. 169 (☎390 22 29) on A.-Wartenberg-Pl. in Altona, corner of Friedensalle. Serves beautifully prepared Pakistani food in a quiet, elaborate environment. Enjoy the *Kofta curry lichi* (vegetable balls in curry with sweet lichee fruit and almonds; €9.50) and the pink, nutty *doodh* soda (€3). Entrées €8-15, lunch plates €5-6. Open daily noon-midnight. Additional locations at Schulterblatt 88 (☎43 36 61) and Grindelallee 91 (☎41 28 02 46) have the same hours. Cash only. ❸

Old Commercial Room, Englische Planke 10 (☎36 63 19), directly across from St. Michaeliskirche. The name is English but the atmosphere and food is authentic Hamburg at this century-old institution. Sample one of the many seafood specialties (€14-17) or the highly-touted *Labskaus* (pickled beef brisket mixed with mashed potatoes and a fried egg). The restaurant has hosted celebrities including Berlin's ex-mayor Willy Brandt, the Beatles, and Jon Bon Jovi. The throne-like toilet in the men's bathroom is a work of art. Open daily 11am-midnight; kitchen opens at noon. AmEx/MC/V. ❹

Afghanische Spezialitäten (☎280 27 58), on the corner of Steindamm and Pulverteich. This *Imbiß*-style Afghan grill serves a variety of creative *kebaps* and rice dishes. The strong of heart wash down the huge *Kabeli Osbaki* (brown rice with raisins, lamb, and meat sauce; €6) with thick *dogh* (bitter buttermilk drink with mint and pickle bits; €1). Open daily 10am-10pm. Cash only. ❷

◉ SIGHTS

ALTSTADT

GROßE MICHAELISKIRCHE. Affectionately called "Michael" by the Hamburgers, the tower of the gargantuan 18th-century Michaeliskirche is a symbol of the city. The church has had a tumultuous past, having been destroyed numerous times by lightning, accidents, and Allied bombs. Guarded by a dashing, Satan-crushing St. Michael, the newly renovated church's wide nave and scalloped walls often function as a venue for a evening concerts and performances. The tower affords the best view of Hamburg and an elevator can cut the 462-stair climb to only three flights. A small exhibition about the history of the church is housed in the crypt. (☎37 67 81 00. *Open daily May-Oct. 9am-8pm; Nov.-Apr. 10am-5pm. Church €2 suggested donation, tower €2.50. Organ music daily Apr.-Aug. at noon. Movie on the history of the church every hr. M-Sa 12:30-3:30pm, every 30min. Su 11:30am-3:30pm, €2.50. Crypt open June-Oct. daily 11am-4:30pm; Nov.-May Sa-Su 11am-4:30pm. €1.50. Discounts with Hamburg Card.*)

RATHAUS. With six more rooms than Buckingham Palace, the 1897 Hamburg Rathaus, which replaced the one destroyed in the Great Fire of 1842, is an imposing sight. Its lavishly furnished chambers contain intricate mahogany carvings, gigantic murals, and spectacular chandeliers. The building still serves as the seat of both city and state government, and the Rathausmarkt out front holds constant festivities, ranging from political demonstrations to medieval fairs. (☎428 31 24 70. *Tours of the Rathaus in German every 30min. M-Th 10am-3pm, F-Su 10am-1pm. Tours in English every hr. M-Th 10:15am-3:15pm, F-Su 10:15am-1:15pm. €1.50, under 14 €0.50.*)

MÖNKEBERGSTRAßE. Hamburg's glossiest shopping zone stretches from the Rathaus to the Hauptbahnhof. Two anachronistic spires punctuate the street. The first belongs to the **St. Petrikirche,** the oldest church in Hamburg, which survived WWII entirely intact but still suffers from damage done when Napoleon wintered his horses here in 1813. The 123m-high platform in the tower makes it the highest climbable tower in Hamburg, but the 544-step journey is only for the enthusiastic. (☎ 32 57 400. Tower open M-Sa 10am-5pm, Su 11:30am-4pm. €2, under 15 €1, under 10 free.) The second tower belongs to **St. Jakobikirche,** known for its 14th-century Arp-Schnittger organ. (☎ 30 37 370. Open M-Sa 10am-6pm.)

NIKOLAIKIRCHE. The blackened spire of this neo-Gothic ruin, destroyed during Allied air raids in July of 1943, has been preserved as a memorial for the victims of war and persecution. Empty frames for stained-glass windows and half-ruined walls greet visitors. An exhibition underneath the glass pyramid in the former apse of the church displays chilling photos of Hamburg and other cities bombed during WWII, including Coventry and Warsaw. (Exhibition open M-F 10:30am-5:30pm. €2, students €1.50, children €1.) Behind the church lies a labyrinthine maze of canals and bridges surrounding the **Alte Börse** (Old Stock Exchange). The spires of buildings along nearby **Trost-Brücke** sport copper models of clipper ships—a testament to Hamburg's enduring connection to the sea. (Just south of the Rathaus, off Ost-West-Str.)

SPEICHERSTADT (WAREHOUSE CITY). East of the docks, near the copper dome of the **St. Katherinenkirche,** is the historic warehouse district of Speicherstadt. These elegant, late 19th-century brick storehouses are still used today, holding carpets, electronics, and other goods. The tiny **Afghanisches Kunst- und Kulturmuseum** (Afghani Art and Culture Museum), built in 2002, is dedicated to portraying an Afghanistan that no longer exists through a series of life-size dioramas depicting carpet-making and porcelain-repairing, photo exhibits, and artifacts from daily life. End the visit with a cup of complimentary Afghan tea. Some explanations are in English. (Am Sandtorkai 32. From St. Katherinenkirche, cross the street and continue over the Jungfernbrücke and the Neuerwegsbrücke, then turn right on Am Sandtorkai. ☎ 37 82 36; www.afghanisches-museum.de. €3, students €2.50, under 12 €1.50. Open daily 10am-5pm.) Upstairs, **Spicy's Gewürzmuseum**—which bills itself as "the only Spice Museum in the world"—appeals to epicurians with its collection of 500 years' worth of seasonings. The museum allows visitors to touch, smell, and taste 50 different spices and features exhibits on their origins and uses. (☎ 36 79 89. Open June-Oct. daily 10am-5pm; Nov.-May Tu-Su 10am-5pm. €3, under 13 €1.)

ELSEWHERE IN CENTRAL HAMBURG

PLANTEN UN BLOMEN. This large expanse of gardens is one among a crescent of parks that extends from the TV tower to the Dammtor station and south to St. Pauli. The stunning flower displays and relative quiet lure families and romantics to the park, where they can wander for miles on scenic paths (S21 or S31 to "Dammtor." Open daily 7am-11pm). The park houses the largest Japanese garden in Europe and also contains a botanical garden with an array of exotic plants. (Open Mar.-Oct. M-F 9am-4:45pm, Sa-Su 10am-5:45pm; Nov.-Feb. M-F 9am-3:45pm, Sa-Su 10am-3:45pm.) Children can enjoy three playgrounds, a water slide, giant chess sets, and water-jet soccer, a minigolf course, and a trampoline. Daily 3pm performances by groups ranging from Irish step dancers to Hamburg's police choir fill the outdoor *Musikpavillion* from May to September. The nightly *Wasserlichtkonzerte* draws crowds to the lake, with choreographed fountains and underwater lights (May-Aug. 10pm; Sept. 9pm). By long-standing tradition, septuagenarians go to dance and find late love at the two park cafés on Wednesday and weekends.

FISCHMARKT. A Hamburg tradition since 1703, the Sunday morning Fishmarket is an anarchic mass of charismatic vendors hawking fish, produce, flowers, and clothing. Early risers mix with Reeperbahn partyers who head straight to the marketplace after a long night of revelry. Whether you like pastries, fish sandwiches, or beer for breakfast, this is the perfect place to find them delicious and cheap. Bands of varying style entertain shoppers with loud rock music from the stage of the fish auction hall. *(S1, S3, or U3 to "Landungsbrücken" or S1 or S3 to "Königstr." or "Reeperbahn." Open Su Apr.-Oct. 5-10am; Nov.-Mar. 7-10am.)*

ST. PAULI LANDUNGSBRÜCKEN. Hamburg's harbor, the second largest port in Europe, lights up at night with ships from all over the world. Although crowded with tourists and lined with *Imbiße*, the piers provide an exceptional view of the Hamburg harbor, and are a starting point for most cruises and tours. **Kapitän Prüsse** gives tours of the harbor departing every 30min. from Pier 3. *(S1, S3, or U1 to "Landungsbrücken."* ☎ *31 31 30. 1hr.; daily in summer 9am-5pm, in winter 9am-4pm; German only; €10, ages 5-14 €5.)* **HADAG** offers elaborate cruises of outlying areas from Pier 2. *(*☎ *311 70 70. Times and prices vary by cruise.)* Docked at Pier 1 is the tri-masted, 97m-long **Windjammer Rickmer Rickmers.** Constructed in 1896, the ship has been renamed five times and served as many different roles. It transported nitrates, was confiscated while anchored in neutral Portugal during WWI, and then served as a Portuguese cadet training ship before finally coming to rest in the harbor as a museum. All quarters have been painstakingly restored to the original 1890s decor. The ship houses a large special exhibit space, an account of the vessel's unique history, and a café. *(*☎ *319 59 59. Open daily 10am-5:30pm. €3, students €2.50, families €7. Discounts with Hamburg card.)* Behind pier 6, inside the building with the large copper cupola, is the entrance to the **Old Elbtunnel,** completed in 1911. Cars and pedestrians descend 23.5m in an elevator, then travel through the two 426.5m-long tubes running under the Elbe. Benches on the other side offer an impressive view of the Hamburg skyline. *(Pedestrians: open daily, free. Cars: open M-F 5:30am-8pm, €2.)*

ALSTER LAKES. Just north of downtown, the Alster river, flowing from Schleswig-Holstein, expands into the two Alster lakes before converging with the Elbe. Follow the elegant promenades around the **Binnenalster** *(U1, U2, S1 or S3 to "Jungfernstieg")* or join the joggers and bikers near the larger **Außenalster** *(S21 or S31 to "Dammtor").* On a beautiful day, sailboats, crewshells, and windsurfers can be rented (p. 218). On the far northeastern shore of the Außenalster, the brilliant blue **Iman Ali Mosque** is home to the world's largest circular rug.

BEYOND THE CENTER

BLANKENESE STEPS. Hamburg is home to more millionaires than any other German city, and most reside in Blankenese, a western suburb on the Elbchausee. Dozens of narrow, cobbled staircases wind down to the shore around the area's impressive terraced homes and immaculate gardens. Stroll along the Strandweg by the shore; it offers an eviable view Hamburg's harbor. Or, grab a coffee in the main square and admire the preppy populace. *(S1 or S11 to "Blankenese." From the station go right, take the 1st left on Blankenese Bahnhofstr., and head straight until the road hits a "T" and you see the river. Or take a HADAG boat from the St. Pauli Landungsbrücken.)*

KZ NEUENGAMME. A concentration camp where 110,000 people were forced into labor between 1938 and 1945, Neuengamme was built in an idyllic agricultural village east of Hamburg. Close to 55,000 of its inhabitants died from overwork or execution. In 1948, some of the buildings were cleared to make way for a new German prison, closed in 2006. A mile-long path, constructed in 1989, begins at the **Haus des Gedenkens,** a memorial building containing banners and books inscribed with the names and death-dates of the victims. The path skirts the remains of the camp's

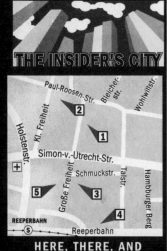

HERE, THERE, AND EVERYWHERE: THE BEATLES IN HAMBURG

The Beatles got their first break when a promoter landed them a gig in Hamburg. The experience they gained performing in clubs here played an integral part in shaping the group, and by the time they returned to England they were well on their way to stardom.

1 **64 Große Freiheit:** John, Paul, George, and Pete Best played their first Hamburg shows at the **Indra** (p. 232), beginning August 17, 1960. The 8hr. gigs were grueling and the pay was poor, but the group learned how to keep audiences satisfied. A plaque at the front of the building commemorates the group's performances.

2 **33 Paul-Roosen-Str.:** while playing at the Indra, the Beatles slept in tiny quarters upstairs at the **Bambi Kino,** the blue-gray house. Look for the small plaque on the door.

3 **36 Große Freiheit:** after the police shut down the rough-

brick-making factory, passes labor barracks, and finally leads to the former **Walther-Werke** factory, with its exhibit about the history of the camp, including recorded testimony from survivors. *(Jean-Dolidier-Weg 39. S21 to "Bergedorf," then bus #227 to "Jean-Dolidier-Weg." Bus runs from Bergedorf M-Sa every hr., Su every 2hr. ☎428 96 03. Museum and memorial open Apr.-Sept. M-F 9:30am-4pm, Sa-Su noon-7pm; Oct.-Mar. M-F 9:30am-4pm, Sa-Su noon-5pm. Path open 24hr. Tours Su noon and 2pm.)*

JENISCH PARK. This park, and the museums within, sit upon a beautiful swath of green running up from the Elbe. **Ernst-Barlach-Haus,** the plain, white building, contains many of the Expressionist artist's most esteemed wood-carvings. It also hosts changing exhibits on other artists and occasional concerts. *(☎82 60 85. S-Bahn to "Klein-Plottbek," go left on Jürgensallee, then right on Baron-Vought-Str. Follow the signs. Open Tu-Su 11am-6pm. Free tour (in German) Su 11am. €5, students €3.50, families €7.)* Fifty paces from the Barlach Haus is **Jenisch Haus,** former residence of Hamburg's famous senator, Martin Jenisch. Many of the rooms are used to display the orginal furnishings that Jenisch and his wife had there; crystal chandeliers, ornate furniture and paintings of ancestors abound. There's also an art collection and a special exhibition space. *(☎82 87 90. Open Tu-Su 11am-6pm. Tours Su noon and 3pm €2. €5, students €3.50. Combination tickets €7 for both museums.)* Directly across from the S-Bahn station, you can also visit the beautiful **Botanical Gardens,** whose expansive grounds center around a large pond. *(Open daily 9am-8pm. Free.)*

U-434. The world's largest non-nuclear sub now resides in Hamburg. After being decommissioned in 2002, the ship was purchased from the Russian navy and towed to the harbor where it now stands open to curious tourists. A visit affords a glimpse at a piece of Cold War history. The 90m-long ship and its 84-man crew were stationed off the American coast on reconnaissance missions from 1976-1978, after which the ship served on patrols of the North Sea. The maze of pipes and instruments will fascinate the mechanically-inclined, although this attraction is not for the claustrophobic. Tours offered in German only. *(Vermannstr. 23c. Shuttles to the ship (€3 round-trip) leave from the St. Pauli Landungsbrücken; call ☎32 00 49 34 for details. Otherwise, it is a 25min. walk from "Messberg" (U1) along pedestrian-unfriendly streets: heading towards Katherinenkirche, turn left over the 1st bridge and continue over 3 more until you reach Booktor, which becomes Versmannstr. Continue walking for 15min.; this museum will be on your right. www.u-434.de. Open Apr. 1-Oct. 3 M-Th 10am-6pm, F Su 9am-7pm; Oct. 4-Mar. 31 daily 10am-6pm. €8, students €6, families €18. Tour €3.)*

HAGENBECK'S TIERPARK. Founded in 1907 by the enthusiastic and slightly eccentric collector of exotic animals Carl Hagenbeck, Hamburg's zoo maintains its quirky character today. Animals wander about the park freely, while children clamber up the inside of the man-made mountain at the center of the park to gaze down on the many lions, tigers, and elephants. *(U2 to "Hagenbeck's Tierpark." ☎540 00 10; www.hagenbeck.de. Open daily 9am-6pm. €14.50, ages 4-16 €8.50.)*

SCHLOß BERGEDORF. A medieval castle that has been rebuilt several times over the years, Schloß Bergedorf today is an unassuming brick building, redeemed by its tower, moat, and pastoral charm. Inside the Castle is the **Museum für Bergedorf und die Vierlande,** which chronicles daily life in the area and the role of the Vierlande canal, which passes through Bergedorf, in conveying food to Hamburg. Several castle rooms replicate 19th-century interiors, while the basement houses a small collection of old firearms, suits of armor, and torture devices. *(S21 to "Bergedorf." Exit the station following the "Ausgang City" sign, turn left on Weidenbaumsweg, right on Holstenstr. then left immediately after the church. Open Apr.-Oct. Tu-Th and Sa-Su 10am-6pm; Nov.-Mar. Tu-Th and Sa-Su 10am-4pm. €3, students €1.50, under 18 free.)*

GEDENKSTÄTTE BULLENHUSER DAMM. In among the warehouses, the Janusz-Korczak School and its adjoining rose garden serve as a memorial to the 20 Jewish children who underwent "medical testing" at KZ Neuengamme and were brought to the school and murdered only hours before Allied troops arrived in Hamburg on April 20, 1945. Visitors are invited to plant a rose in memory of the victims, whose photographs line the fence of the flower garden. Inside the school, a small exhibition tells the story of the children and those locals who tried to save them. *(Bullenhuser Damm 92. S21 to "Rothenburgsort." Follow the signs to Bullenhuser Damm along Ausschläger Bildeich, over the bridge. The garden is on the far left side of the intersection with Grossmannstr.; the school is through the garden, 200m farther. ☎428 13 10; www.www.kz-gedenkstaette-neuengamme.de. Rose garden open 24hr. Exhibition open Th 2-8pm, Su 10am-5pm. Free.)*

KZ FUHLSBÜTTEL. Within weeks of coming to power in 1933, the Nazis began detaining political opponents at this prison. Over the next 12 years, its ranks swelled with Hamburg's resistance fighters, communists, gypsies, gays, beggars, and prostitutes. A small German-language exhibit in the gatehouse profiles some of the prison's victims, and a reconstructed solitary cell provides a chilling glimpse into life at the prison. *(Suhrenkamp 98 in Torhaus. S1, S11, or*

and-tumble Indra, the Beatles moved down the street to the **Kaiserkeller** (p. 231), where they played shows from Oct. 4 to Nov. 30, 1960. It was here that the group first met drummer Ringo Starr, who joined them when Pete Best fell ill. A sign on a pillar outside the door marks this bit of history.

4 136 Reeperbahn. After spending time in Liverpool, the Beatles returned to Hamburg to play the **Top-Ten-Club.** They lived upstairs while playing the gigs, which lasted from April 1 to July 1, 1961. The club has since changed its name several times, most recently to **La Rocca.**

5 39 Große Freiheit. The Beatles played their final Hamburg show on New Year's Eve 1962 at the **Star Club.** The recordings were later released as the famous "Star Club Tapes." From the Kaiserkeller, go through the archway and look to the left, immediately inside the arch. A guitar-shaped marker denotes the site where the building housing the Star stood until a 1987 fire destroyed it.

U1 to "Ohlsdorf." From the "Im Garten Grund" exit, follow signs. Go past the main entrance to the prison, then take a left on Fuhlsbütter Damm, which becomes Suhrenkamp. The entrance is on your left. ☎428 13 15 27. Open Su 10am-5pm. Talks by survivors and other witnesses every Su 11am and noon. Free.)

ERNST-THÄLMANN-GEDENKSTÄTTE (ERNST THÄLMANN MEMORIAL). In 1923, Communist leader Ernst Thälmann led a march on police headquarters, setting off a riot that left 61 protestors and 17 policemen dead. Thälmann was later murdered by the Nazis, becoming the DDR's first martyr. His life history is chronicled in this small German-language museum geared toward those with a strong interest in the history of German communism. *(Tarpenbekstr. 66, at Ernst-Thälmann-Pl. U1 to "Hudtwalck-erstr." Turn right on Hudtwalckerstr., go over the bridge, turn right on Ludolfstr. and walk 10min. until the intersection with Tarpenbekstr. ☎47 41 84. Open W-F 10am-5pm, Sa 10am-1pm. Donation requested.)*

🏛 MUSEUMS

Many of Hamburg's finest museums are located along the **Kunstmeile,** running from from the Alster Lakes to the Elbe. The **Hamburg Card** (p. 218) provides discounted admission to most museums, excluding the Deichtorhallen, Harry's Hamburger Hafen Basar, and the Erotic Art Museum. Hamburg also has a thriving contemporary art scene; pick up a list of current gallery exhibits at any tourist office. The free newspaper *Museumswelt Hamburg,* available at tourist offices, lists museum exhibitions and events. Unless specified, museums are closed on Mondays and open 10am-6pm the rest of the week, and until 9pm on Thursdays.

🖼HAMBURGER KUNSTHALLE (HALL OF ART). It would take days to fully appreciate this expansive art museum, regarded as one of the finest in Germany. The collection covers seven centuries, and is organized chronologically. Highlights include a set of medieval altars, works by Rembrandt and other 17th-century Dutch painters, and a large Impressionist gallery. The lower level houses temporary exhibitions. The connected four-level building, **Galerie der Gegenwart** (Gallery of the Plesant), houses the museum's contermporary art holdings. *(Glockengießer-wall. Turn right from the "Spitalerstr./City" exit of the Hauptbahnhof and cross the street. ☎428 13 12 00; www.hamburger-kunsthalle.de. €8.50, students €5, families €14.)*

🖼MUSEUM FÜR KUNST UND GEWERBE (MUSEUM OF ART AND INDUSTRY). The exhibitions at Hamburg's applied arts museum spans nations and centuries. A huge exhibit containing over 430 historical keyboard instruments such as harpsichords, clavichords, and hammer-klaviers illustrates the development of the modern piano and showcases some of the more picturesque fantasies of instrument makers, evident in the elaborate oils decorating lids and benches. The museum also has an extensive photography collection, an impressive Art Nouveau display, and a treasure-trove of antique gold jewelry. Some galleries are closed due to construction through 2008. *(Steintorpl. 1. 1 block south of the Hauptbahnhof. ☎428 134; www.mkg-hamburg.de. €8; students, Hamburg Card holders and seniors €5; under 18 free.)*

DEICHTORHALLEN HAMBURG. Hamburg's contemporary art scene thrives inside these two former fruit markets, which house photography, paintings, and film installations. Each season brings new exhibits to the large, vaulted halls. The recently renovated south hall will be hosting an exhibit on the Körber-Foto-Award, given to young photographers each summer. *(Deichtorstr. 1-2. U1 to "Steinstr." Follow signs from the U-Bahn station; look for 2 entwined iron circles. ☎32 10 30; www.deichtorh-allen.de. Open Tu-Su 11am-6pm. Each building €7, students €5, families €9.50. Combination ticket to both halls €12/8/16.50. Combined ticket €4.50 Tu after 4pm. Under 18 free.)*

HAMBURGER MUSEUM FÜR VÖLKERKUNDE (ETHNOGRAPHY MUSEUM). From African masks to an entire Maori house, this museum of world cultures is an anthropologist's paradise. The exhibit on nationalism and the creation of a European culture is especially interesting in light of contemporary European politics. *(Rothenbaumchaussee 64. U1 to "Hallerstr." ☎ 01805 30 88 88, €0.12 per min.; www.voelkerkundemuseum.com. €7, with Hamburg Card €1.50, students €3.50, under 18 free.)*

MUSEUM FÜR HAMBURGISCHE GESCHICHTE (HISTORY MUSEUM). On the edge of the Große Wallanlagen gardens near St. Pauli, this four-story complex provides an interesting, if somewhat scattered, overview of Hamburg's history. The museum features the largest model train display in Western Europe and the top floor chronicles the history of Hamburg's Jews. *(Holstenwall 24. U3 to "St. Pauli." ☎ 4281 32 23 80. Open Tu-Su 10am-5pm. €7.50, with Hamburg Card €5, students €4, families €12. F €4, families €6.)*

EROTIC ART MUSEUM. Not for the prudish, this museum occupies four floors, containing everything from the *Kama Sutra* to Victorian pornography and gigantic Russian dolls in varying degrees of undress. Drawings by Picasso and John Winston Lennon add prestige and propriety to an otherwise shocking display. The top floor features an exhibit on the history of Hamburg's own Reeperbahn. *(Bernhard-Nocht-Str. 69. S1 or S3 to "Reeperbahn." ☎ 317 47 57; www.erotic-art-museum.de. 16+. Open M-Th and Su noon-10pm, F-Sa noon-1am. €8, students €5.)*

MINIATUR WUNDERLAND HAMBURG. This small museum—perfect for those under 12 or with an undying interest in model trains—revels in all things tiny. On the fourth floor of a warehouse in the Speicherstadt, a 9000m model railroad winds its way through miniature versions of Hamburg, the Alps, Scandinavia, and America, complete with centimeter-high people and more than 700 trains. Go early to avoid the hordes of children dragging their parents along. *(Kehrwieder 2, Block D. U3 to "Baumwall," cross the left of the 2 bridges (Niederbaum Brücke), turn left on Kehrwieder, and walk 1½ blocks. ☎ 300 51 555; www.miniatur-wunderland.de. Open M and W-F 9:30am-6pm, Tu 9:30am-9pm, Sa-Su and holidays 8:30am-8pm. €9, under 16 €4, children under 1m tall free with adult.)*

❧ ENTERTAINMENT

In addition to the regular offerings of music, theater, and film, Hamburg's Rathausmarkt and other locations often host lively street fairs, especially during the summer. Hamburg owes its prosperity to Friedrich Barbarossa, who granted the town the right to open a port on May 7, 1189. The city still celebrates this with the **Hafengeburtstag** (Harbor Birthday, May 11-13, 2007), which attracts 1.5 million people to watch the ship parade and fireworks and to party onshore. During April, August, and November the **Heiligengeistfeld** north of the Reeperbahn transforms into the **"Dom,"** a titanic amusement park bursting with beer and wild partying.

MUSIC

The **Staatsoper,** Große Theaterstr. 36, houses one of the best **opera** companies in Germany. The associated **ballet** company is considered the dance powerhouse of the nation. (☎ 35 68 68. U2 to "Gänsemarkt." Open M-Sa 10am-6:30pm and 1½hr. before performance. Tickets €4-146.) **Orchestras** abound: the Philharmonie, the Norddeutscher Rundfunk Symphony, and Hamburg Symphonia all perform at the **Musikhalle** on Johannes-Brahms-Pl. (U2 to "Gänsemarkt.") The Musikhalle (☎ 34 69 20; www.musikhalle-hamburg.de) also hosts **chamber music** concerts on a regular basis, and the occasional jazz performance. Hamburg's churches (see **Sights,** p. 223) offer a wide variety of classical concerts, often for free.

PLIÉ FOR PENNY-PINCHERS

Since Director John Neumeier's 1973 arrival to the Hamburg Ballet, the prestige of the group has grown exponentially. The exceptional ballet company puts on everything from Balanchine's *Jewels* and *Romeo and Juliet* to Neumeier's own choreographies.

Enthusiasts come from as far as Japan and the United States just to see Neumeier's ballet. While a front-row orchestra seat to one of his performances can run as high as €146, the ballet can be yours for as little as €4. At the top of the theatre there are 12 standing room tickets. Although they are definitely in the nose-bleed section, these "seats" afford a perfect view of the stage—better than what those paying 20 times as much can see—and the smug satisfaction that can only come from paying so little for something so opulent.

According to regulars, these tickets are often still available the day of the performances. To guarantee yourself a seat—especially for premieres—however, reserve a few days in advance.

(The Hamburg Ballet box office is located at Grosse Theaterstr. 25 (U1 to "Stephansplatz" or U2 to "Gänsemarkt"). ☎ 35 68 68; www.hamburgballet.de. Open M-Sa 10am-6:30pm and 90 minutes before performances.)

Live music of all genres prospers in Hamburg. Superb traditional jazz swings at the **Cotton Club** and **Indra** (see **Nightlife**, p. 231). On Sunday mornings, musicians talented and otherwise play at the **Fischmarkt**. Rock groups jam at **Große Freiheit** and **Docks** (p. 231). The renowned **Fabrik**, in Altona (p. 233), features everything from funk to punk. The magazine *Szene* (€3) has an exhaustive listing of events. During the summer, big name bands come to the **Stadtpark** (☎ 41 80 68; www.karsten-jahnke.de). The **West Port Jazz Festival,** Germany's largest, runs in mid-July. Call the Konzertkasse (☎ 32 87 38 54) for information.

THEATER AND FILM

Most theaters sell reduced-price tickets to students at the regular box office as well as at the evening box office, generally open 1hr. before performances. In July and August, many theaters close down, but only to make way for the summer arts festivals; pick up a schedule of programs at one of the tourist offices.

The acclaimed **Deutsches Schauspielhaus,** Kirchenallee 39, is directly across from the Hauptbahnhof. The theater presents contemporary international works interspersed with the masterpieces of Shakespeare and Sophocles. (☎ 24 87 13; www.schauspielhaus.de. Box office open M-Sa 10am-7pm or showtime. Student tickets from €7.50.) The satellite **Polittburo,** Steindamm 45, puts on more experimental performances to a young, intellectual crowd. (☎ 28 05 54 67. Open 1hr. before showtime. Tickets also available at the Deutsches Schauspielhaus. €5-20.) The **English Theater,** Lerchenfeld 14, entertains both natives and tourists with its English-language productions. (U2 to "Mundsgurg." ☎ 227 70 89. Performances M-Sa 7:30pm; matinees Tu and F 11am. Box office open M-F 10am-2pm and 3:30-7:30pm, Sa 3:30-7:30pm, and 1½hr. before show. Tickets €23-28, matinees €15, lower prices available online.) **Thalia,** Alstertor 1, sets up adventurous avant-garde musicals, plays, and staged readings. (S21 or S31 to "Mönckebergstr." ☎ 32 81 44 44.) Regular performances are also held in the **Hamburger Kunsthalle.** The German **cabaret** tradition lives on at several venues, including **Das Schiff,** at Holzbrückestr. 2. (Head east 1 block on Ost-Weststr. then turn right—it's docked at the bridge, unless it's off touring. ☎ 69 65 05 60.)

Metropolis, Dammtorstr. 30a, is a nonprofit cinema showing new independent films and revivals from all over the globe (☎ 34 23 53). **Kino 3001,** Schanzenstr. 75, shows artsy alternative and international flicks (☎ 43 76 79). An intellectual crowd packs **Abaton-Kino,** Allendepl., and its adjoining café for classics and new releases in English and German (☎ 41 32 03 20;

www.abaton.de). In Altona, the **Zeise Kinos,** Friedensalle 7-9, projects films in the open-air courtyard of Altona's Rathaus on warm evenings (☎39 90 76 37). The **Grindel Palast,** Grindelberg 7a, screens American blockbusters in English (☎44 93 33. €7.50, Tu €4. Student discount).

🅟 NIGHTLIFE

The Sternschanze and St. Pauli areas host Hamburg's unrepressed nightlife scene. The infamous **Reeperbahn,** a long boulevard that makes Las Vegas look like the Vatican, is the backbone of St. Pauli. Sex shops, strip joints, peep shows, and other establishments seeking to satisfy every lust compete for space with fast-food stands and regular theaters. On weekends, this street doesn't sleep, as discos and bars stay open nearly through the night. Though the Reeperbahn itself is reasonably safe for both men and women, it is not recommended for women to venture onto some of the less populated side streets alone. **Herbertstr.,** Hamburg's "official" prostitution strip, runs parallel to the Reeperbahn; its bright red barrier opens only to men 18+, but prostitutes surround the area and nearby Davidstr. The industry is legal and regulated: all the prostitutes on Herbertstr. are licensed and required to have health inspections. If you attract unwanted attention, simply ignore it or respond with a firm *"Nein."* Despite some seedy offerings, the area contains many of the city's best bars and clubs and young, energetic crowds.

Those who'd rather avoid the hypersexed Reeperbahn should head north to the trendy, ethnic streets of the **Schanzenviertel.** Unlike St. Pauli, this area is dominated by cafés where students drink beers and enjoy the outdoors. Filled with spectacular graffiti that crosses the boundary into "public art" and posters that could be the products of high-end design schools, the neighborhood is steeped in creative energy. Much of Hamburg's **gay scene** is located in the **St. Georg** area, near **Berliner Tor** and along **Lange Reihe.** Gay and straight bars in this area are more welcoming and classier than those in the Reeperbahn. In general, clubs open late and close late, with some techno and trance clubs remaining open past daybreak. *Szene,* available at newsstands (€2.50), lists events, while the German-language gay magazine *hinnerk* and the more condensed *Gay Map* list gay and lesbian events. Though bars are not as picky, you must be at least 18 to enter most clubs.

ST. PAULI

The uncontestable heart of St. Pauli's—and all Hamburg's—nightlife scene is the seedy Reeperbahn. Take U3 to "St. Pauli" or S1 or S3 to "Reeperbahn."

Große Freiheit 36/Kaiserkeller, Große Freiheit 36 (☎317 77 80; www.grossefreiheit36.de). The Beatles played here during their early years. Today, young people and couples pour in to hear everyone from Radiohead to the Roots. 3 bars answer revelers' thirst (beer €2.50-3.80). Foosball and pool tables downstairs. Cover €5-6, live bands €10-30. Live music or DJ usually 10:30pm-5am. Frequent free entry until 11pm—get your hand stamped and you can return later. Cash only.

Docks, Spielbudenpl. 19 (☎317 88 30; www.docks.de). Off the Reeperbahn, between Davidstr. and Taubenstr. A massive dancefloor, oil drum tables, and an alter ego as a movie theater make the Docks unique and popular. Drinks €1-8. Cover €4-8, sometimes €1 or free for students and women. Open F-Sa from 10 or 11pm. Cash only.

Meanie Bar/Molotow, Spielbudenpl. 5 (☎31 08 45; www.molotowclub.com). A basement club, Molotow lives at the fringes of Hamburg's club scene. 70s decor and music, live bands, and good dancers keep this small club rocking. Upstairs, Meanie Bar (open daily 9pm-late) is more relaxed. Molotow cover €3-4, live bands €8-15. Open F-Sa 11pm-late, from 8pm for concerts. Cash only.

HAMBURG AT THE BEACH

All of Germany's best beach resorts—Rügen, Sylt, Amrum—have one thing in common: they're located near...well...a beach. Lack of proximity to sand and surf, however, isn't enough to stop the denizens of Hamburg from enjoying a day of lazy relaxation. Since 2003, a new phenomenon has been taking the city by storm: "beach clubs" have emerged and multiplied.

Admittedly, the view may be a little different from that which beach-goers are used to; most of Hamburg's beach clubs are located on the banks of the Elbe river, affording loungers a perfect view of Hamburg's industrial port. Nevertheless, open spots are hard to come by on a sunny day, as everyone from families to hip 20-somethings pack the clubs. The Schanzeviertel goes one step further than the Elbe clubs, distilling the beach experience down to just one element: sand. (That's all you'll find there, given the Schanzeviertel's lack of proximity to actual water.)

The **Hamburg City Beach Club,** Große Elbstr. 134, is open daily from 11:30am-midnight. **Lago Bay,** Große Elbstr. 150, is open M-Th and Su noon-11pm, F-Sa noon-midnight. In the Schanzeviertel, **Central Park,** Max-Brauer-Allee, is open M-Th and Su 10am-11pm, F-Sa 10am-midnight.)

O'Brians, Große Freiheit 13 (☎86 69 09 25) One of the many Irish bars in St. Pauli, O'Brian's distinguishes itself from its neighbors with its small dance area in the back playing classics from "99 Red Balloons" to Madonna. Live music M-W and Su. F-Sa Happy hour 10pm-midnight. Open daily from 7pm. Cash only.

Rosi's Bar, Hamburger Berg 7. Normalcy 1 block off the Reeperbahn? Yup. The crowd packs this *richtige Kneipe* (authentic bar) to enjoy retro furniture, cheap beer (€2.20-2.70), and W-Su live DJ. Open M-Th and Su 9pm-4am, F-Sa 9pm-6am. Cash only.

Cotton Club, Alter Steinweg 10 (☎34 38 78; www.cotton-club.de). U3 to "Rödingsmarkt." A Hamburg institution for over 45 years, this intimate club draws an older crowd for boisterous jazz, dixie, and swing. Cover from €5. Open M-Th 8pm-midnight, F-Sa 8pm-1am, Su 11am-3pm. Shows at 8:30pm. AmEx/MC/V.

Indra, Große Freiheit 64 (☎0174 49 74 61 23; www.indramusikclub.com). The newly formed Beatles played here in 1960, as ubiquitous photos attest. The club now draws younger crowds with blues, hip-hop, and R&B. Cover only for concerts. Open summer W-Su 6pm-late (music starts around 11pm), otherwise 11pm-late. Cash only.

Lehmitz, Reeperbahn 22 (☎31 46 41). A strange mix of students and tatooed punks gather around the clock for €2 beers. Corrugated-metal bar and long tables spill out onto the sidewalk. Loud thrashing music W and F-Sa. Open daily 24hr. Cash only.

Funky Pussy Club, Große Freiheit 34 (☎31 97 75 90; www.funkypussyclub.de). Don't let the stripper poles scare you away; this isn't one of the Reeperbahn's sketchier clubs. Several bars, a large dance floor, and typical club music. Cover Th €5 (free for students and women until midnight), F-Sa €7. Open Th-Sa from 11pm. Cash only.

SCHANZENVIERTEL
Student cafés fill the Schanzenviertel. Take U3, S21, or S31 to "Sternschanze."

Bedford Café, Schulterblatt 72 (☎43 18 83 32), on the corner of Schulterblatt and Susannesstr. College students and 20-somethings pack the inside, outside, and whole street corner—one of the trendiest bars in the Schanzenviertel. Salads and sandwiches €3.30-4.80. Beer €2-3.40. Mixed drinks €5-6. Open daily 10am-late. Cash only.

Frank und Frei, Schanzenstr. 93 (☎43 48 03), across from Oma's Apotheke. The feel of an English pub, but with German *bier*. Standard bar food (croques, pasta) €4.40-8. Beer €2.35-4.50. Mixed drinks €5.65-6.50. Open daily from 11am. Cash only.

Logo, Grindelallee 5 (☎410 56 58; www.logohamburg.de). Keeps the college crowd cultured with its eclectic lineup of folk rock, samba, and tribadelic techno. Cover €4-15. Doors open 8pm; music starts 9pm, check website or call for schedule. Cash only.

Machwitz, Schanzenstr. 121 (☎43 81 77). Get in on a feisty game of foosball in the back room between beers (€2.30). Students mix with an older crowd. Open M-Th and Su noon-3am, F-Sa noon-5am. Cash only.

Le Fonque, Juliusstr. 33 (☎430 75 15; www.fonque.de). Mellow but cool with live DJs every night. Drinks (€2-5). Open daily from 9pm. Cash only.

Rote Flora, Schulerblatt 71 (☎439 54 13). This hotbed of community activism is a weekday café and weekend concert venue. Drum'n'bass and punk concerts F-Sa around 10pm; crowds arrive after midnight. Café open M-F 6-10pm.

Tochtergesellschaft, Stresemannstr. 60 (☎43 63 77). S21 or S31 to "Holstenstr." Visitors disconcerted by the Reeperbahn find relief at this quiet, friendly bar and meeting place. Going on its 30th year (2007), this bar is for women only, except F when everyone is invited. Open daily 6pm-midnight. Cash only.

ALTONA

With lively, but less rowdy, cafés and bars, Altona is a calmer alternative to the craziness of St. Pauli. Take S1, S3, or S31 to "Altona."

🌊 **Fabrik,** Barnerstr. 36 (☎39 10 70; www.fabrik.de). This former weapons factory, complete with a rusted-out crane on top, now cranks out beats instead. For years, crowds have packed the 2-level club to hear big-name rock acts and an eclectic mix of other bands, with styles ranging from latin to punk. Music nearly every day, beginning at 9pm. Every 2nd Sa of the month "Gay Factory" attracts a mixed crowd. Tickets €18-30. Live DJ most Sa nights at 10pm, cover €7-8. Cash only.

Waschbar, Ottenser Hauptstr. 56. (☎017 92 32 59 18). Gleaming, state-of-the-art machines and well-stocked bar make this a far cry from your usual laundromat. Residents crowd Waschbar at night, when you can start the evening off with a beer (€2-2.90), hot chocolate (€2), or light fare (€4-7) while your clothes sit in one of the washers (€3 per 6kg, soap €0.50) or dryers (€0.50 per 15min.). Happy hour M-Th and Su 7-10pm (mixed drinks €4) and F-Sa 8-11pm (mixed drinks €4.50). Live DJ 4 nights per wk. Open daily 9am-1am, F-Sa 9am-2am or later. Cash only.

Insbeth, Bahrenfelder Str. 176 (☎390 19 24). The over-the-top decor defies categorization, but the 3-room café is a comfy hangout spot, especially popular for its cheap, tasty breakfast (1 *brötchen* with cold cuts €2, 1st cup of coffee included), served daily 10am-2:30pm. Open daily from 10am. Cash only.

Reh, Nöltingstr. 84 (☎99 99 22 09). This elegant green-and-gold bar with modern lines is well loved by Altona locals. Serves a variety of exotic mixed drinks (€6-8) and beer (€1.80-3.50) to a mixed clientele. Open daily 9:30am-2am. Cash only.

ST. GEORG

The center of Hamburg's gay scene can be reached by following Ernst-Merck-Str., which runs along the Hauptbahnhof's norther facade, to Lange Reihe.

Cube, Lange Reihe 88 (☎017 33 13 66 32; cube-hamburg@web.de). Mixed bar in the heart of St. Georg provides a relaxed alternative to the raucous pubs near the Reeperbahn. Mixed drinks €2-8. Open daily from 7pm. Cash only.

Café Gnosa, Lange Reihe 93 (☎24 30 34; www.gnosa.de). A social focal point for the gay community of St. Georg. Serves drinks (€2-5), appetizing desserts (€3-5), and tasty light entrées (€5-9) in a bright, comfortable atmosphere to 20-somethings of mixed orientation. Free gay publications like *hinnerk* and *Hamburg's Gay Map* available. Open M-Th and Su 10am-1am, F-Sa 10am-2am. Cash only.

NIEDERSACHSEN (LOWER SAXONY) AND BREMEN

Niedersachsen extends from the Ems River in the west to the Harz Mountains in the east, and from the North Sea down to the hills of central Germany. The deep forest around the Weser that inspired Grimm Brothers' fairy tales has retreated in the face of agriculture—a train ride through the region is a blur of corn and barley fields, windmills, and languid cows. In the remote East Frisian islands, fishermen still cling to their traditional language and culture, while the cities to the south constantly strive to outdo one another with new subway lines, shopping centers, and skyscrapers. The sea-faring cities of Bremen and Bremerhaven have united to make up Germany's smallest *Land*, an extremely popular and diverse summertime destination.

HIGHLIGHTS OF LOWER SAXONY AND BREMEN

EXPLORE the independent *Land* of **Bremen** (p. 259) and its feisty residents, **liberal** political climate, and uncontainable **nightlife** in the student-dominated **Viertel.**

PEDAL along beautifully barren island trails in the **East Frisian Islands** (p. 267) before hitting the **superb beaches.**

SUBLATE THE PSYCHOLOGICAL IMMEDIACY OF ABSTRACT EXPRESSIONISM and other complicated things with the modern art at the **Sprengel Museum** in Hanover (p. 234).

SMELL THE ROSES in the **Herrenhausen** gardens, the wild animals at the **Erlebnis-Zoo Hannover** (p. 239), or **Hanover's** sweaty nightlife scene (p. 245).

WALK ON WATER on the mud flats of the North Sea in the **Wattenmeer National Park** (p. 270).

HANNOVER (HANOVER) ☎0511

Hanoverian **George I** ascended the British throne in the 18th century, making the past three centuries of "English" royals *Deutsch* by lineage. The German-British connection endowed Hanover (pop. 515,000) with prominent status and numerous English gardens. Broad avenues, pedestrian zones, and parks make the city a model of effective urban planning. Add to that a famous opera house, expansive museums, numerous summer outdoor festivals, and vibrant nightlife, and the result is a cosmopolitan dreamboat on the river Leine. The 2000 World's Fair left a shining exhibition hall, new municipal facilities, and improved tourist services in its wake, and the city, saturated with modern art, remains abuzz at all hours.

▐ TRANSPORTATION

Available at the tourist office and hostel, the **Hannover Card** provides public transportation within the city and to the airport, as well as admission or discounts at several museums (1 day €9; 3 days €15; group ticket for up to 5 people €17/29). The card is valid from 7pm the day before use and the entire 24hr. of the day of use, so plan ahead and buy your ticket one day early.

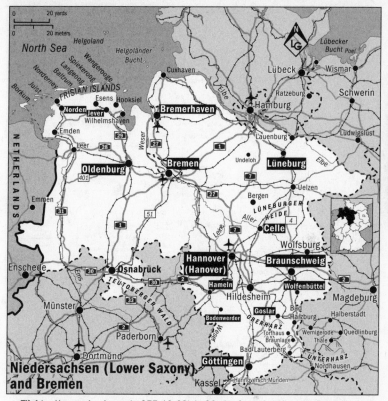

Niedersachsen (Lower Saxony) and Bremen

Flights: Hanover's airport (☎977 12 23) is 30min. from the Altstadt. *Schnellbuslinie* (express bus) #60 and the S-Bahn run from the Hauptbahnhof to the airport. (M-F every 20min. 5am-10:30pm; Sa-Su every 30min. 5:30am-10:30pm. €5.)

Trains: Trains leave at least every hr. to: **Berlin** (2hr., €49-57); **Frankfurt** (2½hr., €65); **Hamburg** (1½hr., €29-34); **Munich** (9hr., €95-111). International service to **Amsterdam, Netherlands** (4½-5hr., €56-61);

Public Transportation: ÜSTRA, Hanover's mass-transit system, is extremely efficient. Pick up a free map of the U-Bahn and bus lines at the tourist office or the aluminum stand at the "Raschpl." bus stop behind the station. Stand open M-W and F 8am-6pm, Th 8am-7pm, Sa 9am-2pm. Buy tickets at machines or from drivers. Hanover has 3 zones with varying prices. *Kurzstrecke* (3 stops) €1; single ride €1.80-3.50, ages 6-11 €1; day ticket €3.30-5.30; group ticket for up to 5 people €6.60-10.60. The Altstadt and Mitte are both in Zone 1. **If your ticket does not have the date printed on it, you must punch it in a blue machine or risk a €40 fine.** For more information and maps, call or stop by the ÜSTRA customer service booth (☎16 68 22 38) in the Kröpcke station. Open M-W and F 8am-6pm, Th 8am-7pm, Sa 9am-2pm.

Taxis: Taxi Ruf (☎ 214 10), or **Funk Taxi Zentrale** (☎38 11).

Bike Rental: Fahrradstation, Femroderstr. 2 (☎353 96 40), to your left as you exit the train station. €7.50 per day, €45 per wk., €25 deposit. Open M-F 6am-11pm, Sa-Su 8am-11pm.

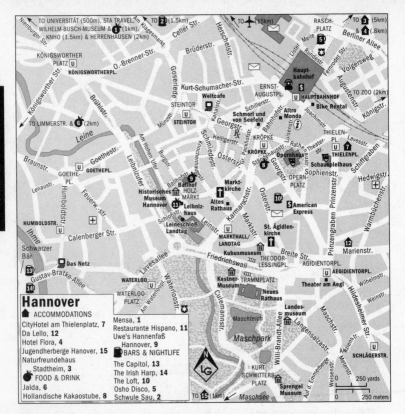

Hannover

ACCOMMODATIONS
CityHotel am Thielenplatz, **7**
Da Lello, **12**
Hotel Flora, **4**
Jugendherberge Hanover, **15**
Naturfreundehaus
Stadtheim, **3**
FOOD & DRINK
Jalda, **6**
Hollandische Kakaostube, **8**

Mensa, **1**
Restaurante Hispano, **11**
Uwe's Hannenfaß
Hannover, **9**
BARS & NIGHTLIFE
The Capitol, **13**
The Irish Harp, **14**
The Loft, **10**
Osho Disco, **5**
Schwule Sau, **2**

✦ 🛈 ORIENTATION AND PRACTICAL INFORMATION

In Old Saxon, *Hon overe* meant "high bank," referring to the city's position on the river **Leine**. The Hauptbahnhof is in **Mitte,** the heart of Hanover. Bahnhofstr. leads to the landmark **Kröpcke Café** and eventually south into the Altstadt. Below sprawls the underground **Passerelle,** a mall-like cave of cheap diners and souvenir shops. Behind the station is **Raschpl.,** home to a disco, film, and club scene. A pedestrian zone connects most of the center, including the shopping districts along **Georgstr.** and the Altstadt. The vibrant student quarter surrounding the university to the northwest of the city center is often overlooked. West of Mitte and just south of the university, **Limmerstr.** runs through **Linden,** historically a working-class area and now home to many artists and immigrants.

Tourist Office: Hanover Information, Ernst-August-Pl. 8 (☎ 123 45 111). Across the street from the station, in the Spardabank building. Friendly staff find rooms for a €2.50-6.50 fee (free by phone ☎ 12 34 55 55), provide maps (€0.30) and information on cultural events, sell tickets to concerts and exhibits, and run a full travel agency. Free hotel list available. Open M-F 9am-6pm, Sa 9am-2pm; May-Sept. also Su 9am-2pm. The **tourist office** offers 12 themed tours (€3-15), including "Hanover's Cemeteries" and "Animal Magic." (☎ 16 84 97 34.) To experience Hanover fully, follow the ▨ **Red**

Thread, a 4km walking tour along a painted red line connecting all the sites. The *Red Thread Guide* (€2), available from the tourist office, details the tour in English.

Budget Travel: STA, Callinstr. 23 (☎131 85 31), in the same building as the *Mensa.* Open M-Th 9am-5pm, F 9am-4pm, Sa 10am-1pm.

Currency Exchange: ReiseBank, to the left just before the main exit of the train station. Open M-Sa 8am-9pm, Su 9am-9pm.

American Express: Georgstr. 54 (☎368 10 03), near the opera house inside ReiseLand. Travel agency and full card member services. Mail held up to 4wk. for card members and Traveler's Cheque clients. Open M-F 9am-noon and 1-6pm, Sa 10am-1pm.

Bookstore: Schmorl und von Seefeld, Bahnhofstr. 14 (☎367 50), has a tremendous selection of English-language novels. Open M-Sa 9:30am-8pm.

Gay and Lesbian Resources: ☎194 46; www.Hanover.gay-web.de. The main hub to hotlines, events, resources, and parties.

Women's Resources: Rape Crisis Line ☎33 21 12. **Shelter** ☎66 44 77.

Laundromat: Münz Waschcenter, at the corner of Hildesheimer Str. and Siemensstr. From the station take U1, U2 or U8 (dir.: Aegidientorpl.) to "Altenbekener Damm." Backtrack 1 block; it's on the left. Wash €3.50. Dry €1 per 15min. Open daily 6am-11pm, last wash 10pm.

Emergency: Police ☎110. **Fire** ☎112. **Ambulance** ☎192 22.

Pharmacy: Europa Apotheke, Georgstr. 16 (☎32 66 18; fax 363 24 63), walk down Bahnhofstr. and turn right on Georgstr.; it's 150m down on the left. Assistance available in several languages. Open M-Sa 8am-8pm.

Medical Services: EMS ☎31 40 44. **Medical Information** ☎31 40 44.

Internet Access: Weltcafe Telefon & Internet Cafe, on Kanalstr. (☎21 35 91 01) off the Georgstr. pedestrian zone near Steintor. Access the **Internet** (€1.25 per 30min.) or call home for cheap (€0.10 per min. to US/Canada/UK). Open M-Sa 9am-midnight.

Post Office: Right of the train station exit. Open M-F 9am-7pm, Sa 9:30am-2pm. **Postal Code:** 30159.

🏠 ACCOMMODATIONS

There is a dearth of budget accommodations in Hanover; finding a place to stay means nabbing a spot in the youth hostel or *Naturfreundehaus.* Otherwise, try calling the **reservation hotline** (☎811 35 00) or the tourist offices (p. 236). If all else fails, staying in the hostels in nearby Braunschweig, Hamelin, or Celle is cheaper than settling for one of Hanover's royally priced hotels.

Hotel Flora, Heinrichstr. 36 (☎38 39 10; www.hotel-flora-hannover.de), in the center of town 10 min. from the station. Take the back exit and turn right on Berliner Allee, then left on Henrichstr. Carpeting, serene paintings, TV in every room, and attentive breakfast (included) feel like home just minutes from the Raschpl. Reception 8am-8pm. Dogs €7.50. Singles €32-42; doubles €55-75; triples €67-84. AmEx/MC/V. ❸

Jugendherberge Hanover (HI), Ferdinand-Wilhelm-Fricke-Weg 1 (☎131 76 74; jh-hannover@djh-hannover.de). Located near the Maschsee and 500m from the soccer stadium but far from nightlife options. U3 or U7 (dir.: Wettbergen) to "Fischerhof/Fachhochschule." From the stop, walk 10m back, turn right, cross the tracks, follow the path as it curves, and cross Stammestr. Go over the enormous red footbridge and turn right. Hostel is 50m down the road on the right. The Cadillac of youth hostels—spacious rooms with balconies, an airy dining room, and a fully stocked bar. 6-, 4-, and 2-bed, and single rooms available. Internet access €0.10 per min. Breakfast included. Reception 7:30am-1am. After 1am, doors open every hr. on the hr. €19.50-22.50. MC/V. ❷

CityHotel am Thielenplatz, Thielenpl. 2 (☎32 76 91; info@smartcityhotel.com). From the station, turn left onto Joachimstr. and go 1 block to Thielenpl. Prime location a few hundred yards behind the Opernhaus. Luxurious lobby and 150 beds in well-maintained, furnished rooms, all with TV and bath, some with panoramic views of the city. Breakfast €5. Check-out 11:30am. Singles €38-119; doubles with shower €65-149. MC/V. ●

Naturfreundehaus Stadtheim, Hermann-Bahlsen-Allee 8 (☎69 14 93; www.naturfreundehaeser-nds.de/hannover.html). U3 (dir.: Lahe) or U7 (dir.: Fasanenkrug) to "Spannhagengarten." Walk back to the intersection and follow Hermann-Bahlsen-Allee to the left for 5min.; follow the sign to your right into the narrow path. An environmentally friendly hostel with small rooms in the outskirts of town. Breakfast included. Reception 8am-noon and 3-10pm. Singles €25, over 27 €29. Cash only. ●

◐ FOOD

Hanover offers plenty in high culture, and growing options in cuisine. The pedestrian zone's expensive cafés cater to tourists—even the beloved **Kröpke** diner, a favorite local meeting place for the last 50 years, has been bought out by ice cream tsar Mövenpick. Find **groceries** at **Euro-Spar** by the Kröpke U-Bahn stop (open M-Sa 7am-8pm) or walk from the Hauptbahnhof to the **Markthalle,** affectionately known as "the belly of Hanover," a food court where varied snacks, meals, and booze await. (Open M-W 7am-8pm, Th-F 7am-9pm, Sa 8am-5pm.) Along Limmerstr., restaurants and *Imbiße* (snack bars) serve up cheap international flavors.

■ **Uwe's Hannenfaß Hanover,** Knochenhauerstr. 36 (☎32 16 16), in the timber-framed house once home to Hanover's master brewer. Decor as heavy and dark as the vittles. The house-brewed *Hannen Alt* (€3.65 for 0.5L) accompanies steaming potato casserole *Niedersachsenschmaus* (€5), *Jägerschnitzel* (€6.50), and other specialties. Open M-Th and Su 4pm-2am, F 4pm-4am, Sa noon-4am. AmEx/MC/V min. €25. ●

■ **Hollandische Kakaostube,** Standehausstr. 2-3 (☎30 41 00), features a dozen awe-inspiring hot chocolates (€3-6) and a truly decadent assortment of cakes. Try the *mohrenkof* (merengue filled with hazelnuts and enrobed in chocolate; €1.85), or the rich marzipan cake (€2.20). The classy gold-accented dining room features a Titanic-esque winding staircase. Open M-F 9am-7:30pm and Sa 8:30am-6pm. Cash only. ●

Jalda, Limmerstr. 97 (☎212 32 61). Take U10 (dir.: Ahlem) to "Ungerstr.". Serves popular Italian, Greek, and Arabic dishes, soups, pizza, and salads (€5-10). Weekdays bring 3-course lunch specials (€7). Eat dinner by candlelight to funk beats. Open M-Th and Su 11:30am-11pm, F-Sa 11:30am-1am. Cash only. ●

Mensa, Callinstr. 23 (☎768 80 35). U4 or 5 to "Schneiderberg/W.-Busch-Museum." Take a right up Schneiderbergstr., just past the pedestrian bridge in the green-trimmed building on the left. A bright cafeteria that welcomes both eat-and-go or stay-and-linger types. Meals €3-4. Open M-F 11:30am-2:30pm. Cash only. ●

Restaurate Hispano, Holzmarkt 6 (☎363 16 17), next door to Leibnizhaus, serves flavor-soaked Spanish tapas (€5.90-9), steaming paella (€11), and an extensive selection of Iberian wines. Eat dinner by dim candlelight on lace tablecloths indoors, or enjoy the shady outdoor patio. Open M-Sa 5:30-11:30pm. Cash only. ●

◉ SIGHTS

■ **HERRENHAUSEN GARDENS.** In 1714, the crown of the United Kingdom was handed to **George I,** son of Hanover's Princess Sophie, in order to maintain Protestant rule in Britain. His descendants reigned over both Hanover and the UK until 1837, when the Hanoverians refused to accept the rule of Queen Victoria. The city owes much to Princess Sophie, who built the three Herrenhausen gardens. Here, Sophie waited to inherit the crown from Queen Anne, only to die just weeks too soon. The centerpiece of the gardens is the Baroque **Großer Garten,** where the striking geometry of the intricately-laid paths in the landscaping manifests itself in square trees and spiral bushes, all overseen by godly statues. The **Große Fontäne,** one of Europe's highest fountains, builds to an astounding 80m and sprays unwitting downwind bystanders with cool mist. At the end of August, a dazzling fireworks contest adds to the spray in the sky. *(Fountain spurts Apr.-Oct. M-F 11am-noon and 3-5pm, Sa-Su 11am-noon and 2-5pm. Garden open daily Apr. to mid-Oct. 9am-8pm; mid-Oct. to Mar. 8am-dusk. Entrance €4, including admission to Berggarten. Concerts and performances June-Aug.; ☎ 16 84 12 22.)* The wide-open meadows and broad, tree-lined paths—perfect for running or biking—of the **Georgengarten** might convince you that you are hundreds of kilometers from anything resembling a city. *(Open 24hr. Free.)* The **Berggarten** has an indoor **rainforest** with a winding path ascending through the canopy amid tropical birds and butterflies. *(Berggarten open same hours as Großer Garten. €2. Rainforest open June-Aug. M-Th 10am-6pm, F 10am-10pm, Sa-Su 10am-8pm; Sept.-Oct. and Apr.-May M-Th 10am-5pm, F-Su 10am-8pm; Nov.-Mar. M-Th 10am-4pm, F-Su 10am-6pm. €8.50, students €5.50. Combination ticket €10, students €7.50, children €5.)*

■**ERLEBNIS-ZOO HANOVER.** More than 2500 animals live at this "experience zoo" specially designed to give visitors the sensation of observing wildlife in nature. Themed areas include the **African Sambesi,** the **Indian Jungle Palace,** and **Gorilla Mountain.** The swift lory, a colorful tropical bird, might decide to perch on your head inside the **Tropical House.** Swarms of people, dogs, and strollers fill the zoo on sunny summer afternoons. All shows free with admission. *(Adenaueralle 3. ☎ 28 07 41 63; www.zoo-hannover.de. Take U11 to "Zoo." Open daily Mar.-Oct. 9am-6pm; Nov.-Feb. 10am-4pm. €16, children €11.50, under 4 free; dogs €6.)*

NEUES RATHAUS. On the outskirts of the Altstadt, built over swampland and filled in with piles of beech trees, is the spectacular Neues Rathaus. Don't be fooled by the palatial turn-of-the-century style: this beauty is indeed the new city hall, painstakingly recreated by Hanoverians after WWII. Inside, models depict the city in 1689, 1939, 1945, and today. Take the famous slanted elevator up the tower and view the city from 98m. *(Open May-Sept. M-F 9am-6:30pm, Sa-Su 10am-6:30pm. Elevator runs M-F 9:30am-6:30pm, Sa-Su 10am-6:30pm, ticket sales until 6pm. €2, students €1.50.)*

ALTSTADT. Post-war reconstruction and the recent development boom for the World's Fair have given much of the city center a decidedly modern feel. However, many older sights still stand in Hanover's **Altstadt,** a 15min. walk from the train station. Walk down Bahnhofstr. and continue as it becomes Karmarschstr.; take a right on Knochenhauerstr. Immediately to the right is Hanover's **Altes Rathaus.** Used for official purposes until 1913, it now serves as a shopping center. Just past the Altes Rathaus, the 14th-century brick **Marktkirche** towers over Hans-Lilje-Pl. *(Open daily 10am-6pm; check for concerts.)*

LEIBNIZHAUS. A beautifully restored Baroque mansion, this house, which cost over €11 million to restore, was home to brilliant mathematician, philosopher, man of letters, and royal advisor Gottfried Wilhelm Leibniz until his death in 1716. *(Holzmarkt 5. ☎ 62 44 50 for opening times. Free.)*

ST. ÄGIDIENKIRCHE. Across the street from Leibnizhaus is the magnificent **Leineschloß,** seat of the Diet of Niedersachsen. Farther down Leinstr., the road leads to the ivy-covered **St. Ägidienkirche,** a powerful monument kept in the state that WWII left it. Colored squares of glass suspended in empty window frames symbolize elaborate stained-glass designs that once filled them, and memorial plaques and rough-hewn timber crosses serve as reminders of the folly of war. *(Open 24hr. Free.)*

🏛 MUSEUMS

⬛ SPRENGEL MUSEUM. A 20th-century art lover's dream, with works by Beckmann, Dalí, Chagall, Klee, Magritte, Moore, Picasso, Turrel, and hometown hero Kurt Schwitters. Exhibits include *Schwitters and Friends* (through 2007). One modernist installation holds you in a pitch-dark space for 5min. so your mind can become attuned to the light that is actually there. *(Kurt-Schwitters-Pl. At the corner of the Maschsee and Maschpark, near the Neues Rathaus. ☎ 16 84 38 75; www.sprengel-museum.de. Open Tu 10am-8pm, W-Su 10am-6pm. Permanent collection €3.50, students €2; with special exhibits €7/4.)*

⬛ KESTNER-MUSEUM. August Kestner, Hanover's emissary to Rome, began this collection with Egyptian and Greco-Roman artifacts he picked up abroad: miniature figurines, ancient Mediterranean glassware, and a sofa shaped like enormous lips. You needn't be a chair enthusiast (though who isn't?) to appreciate the intriguingly large chair collection. *(Trammpl. 3. Next to the Neues Rathaus. ☎ 16 84 21 20; www.kestner-museum.de. Open Tu-Su 11am-6pm, W until 8pm. €3, students €1.50; F free.)*

HISTORISCHES MUSEUM HANNOVER. Catch a glimpse of everyday life and folklore in Niedersachsen over the centuries, chronicled by items such as a 10th-century fortress replica and Nazi regalia. Paintings, family trees, and ornate carriages attempt to unravel the convoluted relationship between the British and Hanoverian monarchies. *(Pferdestr. 6, next to the Leibnizhaus. ☎ 16 84 23 52. Open Tu and Th 10am-7pm, W and F-Su 10am-5pm. €3, students and children €2, under 12 free; F free.)*

WILHELM-BUSCH-MUSEUM. Busch was the 19th-century German cartoonist responsible for **Max und Moritz,** troublemakers who have simultaneously amused and frightened German children into good behavior for generations. This small museum contains original sketches and paintings, and hosts rotating exhibits of children's book illustrations and caricatures. *(Georgengarten 1. U4 (dir.: Garbsen) or bus #5 (dir.: Stöcken) to "Schneiderberg/W. Busch Museum." ☎ 16 99 99 16; www.wilhelm-busch-museum.de. Open Tu-F 11am-5pm, Sa-Su 11am-6pm. €4.50, students and children €2.50.)*

LANDESMUSEUM (MUNICIPAL MUSEUM). The playful displays inside this child-friendly cultural museum include a vivarium of exotic lizards and fish, a non-European ethnology exhibit (jumbles of African masks, Oceanic weaponry, and Inuit huts), Neanderthal skulls, and paintings by Lieberman, Rubens, and Monet. *(Willy-Brandt-Allee 5. ☎ 980 75; www.nlmh.de. Open Tu-Su 10am-5pm, Th until 7pm. €4, students €3, children €1.50, free F 2-5pm.)*

KUBUSMUSEUM. This Hanoverian artists' co-op shows contemporary art with origins ranging from local to international in a large one-room gallery on the second floor. *(Theodor-Lessing-Pl. 2, near the Ägidienkirche. ☎ 16 84 57 90. Open Tu-F 11am-6pm, Sa-Su 11am-4pm. €3, students €2.)*

🏵 FESTIVALS

If you're within a 100km radius of Hanover the first week in July, detour to its **Schützenfest** (marksmanship festival), the largest such *fête* in the world. Every summer since 1539, Hanoverians have congregated—weapons in hand—to test their marksmanship before retreating to the beer gardens. The 10-day festival in early July comes complete with parade, fireworks, and amusement park rides, but its main attraction is the *Lüttje Lage*, a feisty traditional drink: you down the contents of two shot glasses simultaneously, holding them side by side in one hand and trying not to spill; one glass contains *Weißbier*, the other *Schnapps*. This party is a mere warm-up for the **Maschseefest** (late July to early Aug.), which provides another wild mix of concerts, masked balls, and street performances. Hanoverians let loose at the **Altstadtfest** the first or second weekend in August. The **Flohmarkt** (flea market) on the **Leibnizufer** hits town every Saturday 7am-2pm.

🎭 🎵 ENTERTAINMENT AND NIGHTLIFE

More than 20 theaters supply Hanover with ballet, opera, drama, and musicals. The four largest are the **Opernhaus,** Opernpl. 1; the **Ballhof,** Ballhofstr. 5; the **Schauspielhaus,** on Theaterpl.; and the **Theater am Ägi,** on Ägidientorpl. Tickets for most shows (from €10) are sold at the tourist office (ticket line ☎30 14 30). The monthly *Hannover Vorschau* and *Hannover Live,* free at the tourist office, list theater shows and more. The Opernhaus provides its own free guide to opera and ballet. **KNHO,** Schaufelder Str. 30 (☎70 38 14; www.kino-im-sprengel.de), near the university, shows art-house flicks. Take U6 or 11 to "Kopernikusstr."

When the sun goes down, Hanover lights up with an array of packed cafés and sweaty discos. The university crowds swarm **Linden-Nord,** the area beginning at Goethepl. and running along Limmerstr., filling the cafés and *Kneipen.* For parties, snoop around the *Mensa* for signs, or check *Prinz* (€1) or *Schädelspalter* (€2.50), both available at the tourist office and newsstands. The free *MagaScene* (www.magascene.de) lists clubs and concerts. For live music, check out **The Capitol** (p. 241) or **Altro Mondo,** Bahnhofstr. 8 (☎32 33 27), in the City-Passage. (Tickets can be purchased at ☎41 99 99 40.)

🏛 **The Loft,** Georgstr. 50a (☎473 93 10), near Kröpcke. The mood-lighting at this hip spot draws packs of students on weekends. Go through the alleyway to enter this chic bar or its companion bistro **Masa.** Enjoy falafel (€3.50) and milkshakes (€3) by candlelight or next to the waterfall in the garden. Happy hour M-Th and Su 8-9pm, F-Sa 1-2am. Masa open daily noon-1am. Loft open daily 8pm-2am, F-Sa until 4am. Cash only.

The Capitol, Schwarzer Bär 2 (☎929 88 18; tickets 44 40 66). U9 to "Schwarzer Bär," and walk back toward the river. Loosen up in a sea of bumping bodies. F nights "Dancing Queen" or "Destiny's Child" (discount with student ID). Sa nights the disco moves to the main hall to make way for live indie rock bands. Cover €2-5. Open F 10pm-3am, Sa 10pm-6am. Cash only.

The Irish Harp, Schwarzer Bär 1 (☎336 06 06). Across the street from The Capitol, take a break from disco fever and share a Guinness (€3.50) with Irish and English expats in this laid-back pub. Live Irish ensemble Su at 5pm. Battle the locals on quiz night, in German and English, M 9pm. Open Su-Th 5pm-1am, F-Sa 5pm-3am. Cash only.

Osho Disco, Raschpl. 7L (☎34 22 17). At the round, banner-covered building just behind the train station, DJs spin everything from house to Frank Sinatra. Rest your feet upstairs with the dolphins. Every W is "Forever Young"—ages 30+ no cover. 18+. Cover €5-10, including one drink. Open W-Su from 10pm. Cash only.

Schwule Sau, Schaufeldstr. 30 (☎700 05 25). U6 or U11 to "Kopernikusstr.," exit left on An der Lutherkirche and turn right on Schaufeldstr. It's on the left, entrance on the far side of the building. Popular gay and lesbian bar in the university district. On good nights, the 3-person sofa can seat 15. Tu ladies only. W men only. Tea Su afternoons. Open T-Sa from 9pm, Su from 2pm. Cash only.

GÖTTINGEN ☎0551

Home to Europe's first free university, Göttingen (pop. 123,000) is a college town to the core. Its alumni include Otto von Bismarck, J.P. Morgan, and the Brothers Grimm, but its real fame comes from the sciences. Over 40 Nobel laureates have studied or worked here, including Max Planck (the father of quantum mechanics) and Werner Heisenberg (the head of the Nazi atomic bomb project, rumored to have secretly sabotaged the process). Completely independent of the German government since its inception, the university has historically taken extreme political positions—far left in 1734, reactionary right in the 1920s, and back again to the left in the 1950s, earning its reputation as a *rote Uni* (red university).

⌐ TRANSPORTATION

Trains: Every hr. to **Berlin** (2½hr., €62). 2 per hr. to: **Frankfurt** (2hr., €34); **Hamburg** (2hr., €53); **Hanover** (1hr., €20); **Kassel** (1hr., €16).

Public Transportation: Most city buses stop at the central "Markt" in 1 direction and "Kornmarkt" in the other. Single ride with 1 transfer €1.70. Day tickets (€4) good for 24hr. from the time of purchase, available on any bus. Most buses run until 11pm.

Taxis: Taxi Night & Day ☎ 650 00.

Car Rental: Europcar, Groner Landstr. 17a (☎ 54 71 90). Open daily M-F 7:30am-midnight. Prices start at around €50.

Bike Rental: Fahrrad-Parkhaus (☎ 599 94), to the left facing the station's main exit. Bikes from €11 per day. Open M-Th 5:30am-10pm, F-Su 5:30am-11pm.

◼✷ 🛈 ORIENTATION AND PRACTICAL INFORMATION

The Altstadt, encircled by an ancient wall, is bisected by Weenderstr. At the center are the **Altes Rathaus** and **Wilhelmspl.**, the original site of the university.

Tourist Office: Markt 9 (☎ 49 98 00; www.goettingen-tourismus.de), in the Altes Rathaus. From the station, cross Berliner Str. to perpendicular Goetheallee, follow it several blocks as it becomes Prinzenstr., and turn right onto Weender Str. In the Markt, climb the stairs to find free maps and room booking, along with **city tours** (1½hr., in English the 1st and 3rd Sa of the month at 11am, €5.50). Open Apr.-Oct. M-F 9:30am-6pm, Sa-Su 10am-4pm; Nov.-Mar. M-F 9:30am-1pm and 2-6pm, Sa 10am-1pm.

Currency Exchange: Commerzbank, Prinzenstr. 2 (☎ 40 80). Open M-W 9am-4pm, Th 9am-6pm, F 9am-3:30pm.

Laundromat: Wasch-Salon, Ritterplan 4, opposite the Städtisches Museum. Wash €2.50, soap €0.50. Dry €0.50 per 12min. Open M-Sa 7am-10pm.

Emergency: ☎ 110. Non-emergency **police,** Groner Landstr. 51, ☎ 49 10. **Fire** ☎ 112.

AIDS Hotline: AIDS-Beratung ☎ 400 48 31.

Pharmacy: Universitäts-Apotheke, Markt 6 (☎ 588 49). Helping students cure headaches, choler, and "other illnesses" since 1734. Open M-F 9am-7pm, Sa 9am-4pm.

Internet Access: Red Sea Telecafe, Prinzenstr. 18 (☎ 488 36 37). €0.50 per 15min. Open M-Sa 10am-11pm, Su noon-11pm.

Post Office: Heinrich-von-Stephan-Str. 1, to the right facing the train station. Open M-F 8am-6pm, Sa 9am-1pm. **Branch** near the city center at Groner Str. 15/17. Open M-F 9am-6pm, Sa 10am-1pm. **Postal Code:** 37073.

▐ ACCOMMODATIONS

Jugendherberge (HI), Habichtsweg 2 (☎ 576 22; fax 438 87). Bus #6 (dir.: Klausberg) to "Jugendherberge," across the street and down the path. Helpful staff and a pool table. Breakfast and sheets included. Internet €0.10 per min. Key deposit €10. Reception 6:30am-midnight. Curfew midnight, or get a key with a €15 deposit. Check-out 9am. Dorms €21.60, under 27 €18.60; singles €24.60/21.60. AmEx/MC/V. ❷

Göttingen

▲ ACCOMMODATIONS
Hotel Garni Gräfin
  Holtzendorff, **4**
Hotel-Gaststätte
  Berliner Hof, **1**
Jugendherberge (HI), **2**

🍎 FOOD & DRINK
Claudio, **11**
Schucan, **7**

Villa Cuba, **10**
Zentral-Mensa, **3**

🍷 BARS & NIGHTLIFE
Blue Note, **9**
Cafe Kollektiv
  Kabale, **12**
Electro Osho, **6**
Irish Pub, **5**
Trou, **8**

Hotel-Gaststätte Berliner Hof, Weender Landstr. 43 (☎38 33 20; www.berlinerhof.de). Bus #15 from the station (dir.: Steffensweg) to "Kreuzbergring." Or walk left from the station up Berliner Str. and turn left on Weender Str. Friendly staff offers simply decorated rooms with TV and phone. Large 3-bedroom suites (€77) are ideal for families or groups. Breakfast included. Reception 8am-11pm. Singles €34, with shower €38; doubles with showers €64. AmEx/MC/V. ❸

Hotel Garni Gräfin Holtzendorff, Ernst-Ruhstrat-Str. 4 (☎639 87; fax 63 29 85). From the station, take bus #13 (dir.: Esebeck) to "Florenz-Sautorius-Str." Continue in the direction of the bus and take the 1st left. In a somewhat distant industrial area, but a courtyard garden offers relief from the drab neighborhood. Many rooms have TV. Breakfast included. Singles €29-39, with bath €45; doubles €45-50/65. ❸

🍴 FOOD

Göttingen's most appetizing produce comes from its two main **fruit markets**—one adjacent to the Deutsches Junges Theater (Tu, Th, Sa 7am-1pm), and the other in the square in front of the Rathaus, open only during the summer (Th 2-8pm). Bakeries and snack stops line **Weender Str.** and **Jüdenstr.** The streets surrounding **Wilhelmspl.** have a variety of pizza joints and other restaurants that cater to the local student population.

Villa Cuba, Zindelstr. 2 (☎488 66 78). Behind Kirche St. Johannis. The stucco interior, thatched roof above the bar, and imported Cuban beer will send you on a mini-vacation to Havana. The food is plentiful and surprisingly authentic. Tapas €4-5, delicious Creole specialties €5-10. Open M-Th and Su 10am-2am, F-Sa 10am-3am. ❸

Schucan, Weender Str. 11 (☎48 62 44). The toucans painted on the ceiling are as colorful as the creative fruit-garnished ice cream dishes (€2-5) at this lively, tropical-themed café. Open M-F 10am-11pm, Sa-Su 11am-midnight. ❷

Zentral-Mensa, Pl. der Göttinger Sieben 4 (☎39 51 51). Follow Weender Landstr. onto Pl. der Göttinger Sieben, turn right into the university complex, and walk until you reach the mammoth *Studentenwerk* on the left. Meals €1.80-3.80 for students, non-students €4.05. Open M-F 9am-2:15pm, Sa 10am-2pm. The **Café Central** sells baguettes and pastries (€1-2). Open M-Th 9am-7:30pm, F 9am-6:30pm. ❶

Claudio, Lange Geismarstr. 39 (☎481 13 41), near Kornmarkt, serves ice cream and dessert. The *Kugeln* (€0.60) comes in more than 15 flavors. Open M-F 9am-7pm, Sa 9:30am-4:30pm. ❶

◉ SIGHTS

ALTES RATHAUS. Built in the 13th century, the Altes Rathaus and its courtyard once formed the focal point of the city. The 19th-century murals in the lobby were painted during the only renovation the Rathaus has seen. Outside, students, tourists, and street musicians gather around the Gänseliesel fountain.

BISMARCK SIGHTS. The **Bismarckhäuschen,** built into the city wall in 1459, is a tiny stone cottage. Here, the 17-year-old law student **Otto von Bismarck** took up residence after authorities expelled him from the inner city for overzealous partying. On display is his 1832-1833 class schedule, as well as his wooden student ID. *(From the Markt, walk down Zindelstr. and follow it as it becomes Nikolaistr.; just before the intersection with Bürgerstr., turn right by the bus stop onto the footpath on top of the wall; the house is on your left. ☎48 62 47. Open Tu 10am-1pm, Th and Sa 3-5pm. Free.)* The **Bismarckturm** (Bismarck Tower) in the Hainberg forest east of town affords a great view of the city. *(Im Hainberg. Bus #9 to "Hainbundstr.," then continue up the hill, following Bismarckstr. as it winds into the woods. After about 1km, watch for signs pointing to the tower, on your left. ☎561 28. Open Sa-Su 11am-6pm. Free.)*

MEDIEVAL CHURCHES. Göttingen is home to several notable churches. Inside the **Jacobikirche,** the modern and the ecclesiastical collide: geometric stained-glass windows (1997) face off against more traditional turn-of-the-20th-century ones. An optical illusion makes candy-colored columns appear to dance. *(Corner of Prinzenstr. and Weender Str. ☎575 96. Open daily 11am-3pm. Free. Tower open Sa from 11am. €2.)* Behind the Altes Rathaus stands the fortress-like **Kirche St. Johannis,** whose 301-step tower housed students for 80 years. The church is undergoing renovations until 2007. *(☎48 62 41. Open M-F 11am-noon, Sa 10am-noon. Tower open Sa 2-4pm.)*

GEORG-AUGUST-UNIVERSITÄT. The esteemed university, established in 1737, fills an area bounded by Weender Landstr., Humboldtallee, and Nikolausberger Weg, just northeast of town.

STÄDTISCHES MUSEUM (MUNICIPAL MUSEUM). The museum gives a detailed examination of the city over the last few millennia. Jewelry from the Bronze Age and 1950s furniture fill out a benign history, while medieval torture devices and a model of a child dressed in Hitler youth regalia are considerably more chilling. *(Ritterplan 7. 1 block north of the Jakobikirche on Jüdenstr. ☎400 28 43. Open Tu-F 10am-5pm, Sa-Su 11am-5pm. Permanent exhibit €1.50, students €0.50; temporary exhibits €1.50/1.)*

SYNAGOGUE MEMORIAL SCULPTURE. On Untere Maschstr., the steel sculpture stands over the site where a Göttingen synagogue was razed in 1938. The silver structure has plaques listing the names of Jews from the synagogue who died during WWII. Viewed from above, the memorial forms a Star of David.

🎵 ENTERTAINMENT

Deutsches Theater, Theaterpl. 11 (☎49 69 11; www.dt-goettingen.de), presents classics, contemporary plays, and improv. Tickets from €8. Box office open M-F 10am-1:30pm and 5-8pm, Sa 11am-2pm, and 1hr. before shows.

Junges Theater, Hospitalstr. 6 (☎49 50 15). This edgy but top-notch alternative theater presents a new outlook on both classic and innovative works. Box office open Tu-Sa 11am-2pm and 1hr. before shows. Tickets €10, students €7.

Cinema: American blockbusters and German-language flicks play at **Cinema,** Weender Str. 58 (☎588 88), or at the gigantic **Cinemaxx** complex (☎521 22 00) behind the train station. The artsy **Lumière,** Geismarer Landstr. 19 (☎48 45 23), housed in Café Kabale (p. 245), is more cosmopolitan.

🌃 NIGHTLIFE

Trou, Burgstr. 20 (☎439 71). This 500-year-old, candle-lit cellar has been Göttingen's most intimate watering hole for 45 years. People cluster around barrels amid light jazz. A specialty is *Altbierbowle mit Erdbeeren* (strawberries in a 0.3L-bowl of *Diebels* beer; €2). Open M-Th 7:30pm-2am, F-Su until 3am.

Irish Pub, Mühlenstr. 4 (☎456 64), winner of Guinness' "Most Entertaining Pub" award. Popular student bar with lots of Guinness and live Irish music nightly at 10pm (summer 3 times per wk.). 18+. Open daily 3pm-3am.

Blue Note, Wilhelmspl. 3 (☎469 07), under the Aula. The most diverse venue for music and fun in the Altstadt. A different theme every day (jazz, reggae, and African pop are favorites). W Latin music, Sa salsa dancing, both no cover. Other nights €2.50, concerts (at least once per wk.) €4-16. Open W and F-Sa 9pm-4am.

Café Kollektiv Kabale, Geismarlandstr. 19 (☎48 58 30; www.cafe-kabale.de). Far outside the old city past the Neues Rathaus (15min.); watch for the sign on your left. Hidden behind a stone wall and tall trees, this café brims with art, film, food, and drink. Call for schedule of theme parties, art exhibitions, and poetry readings. Tu Lesbian bar 8:30pm. Open M-F 4pm-1am, Sa 2pm-1am, Su 10am-1am.

GOSLAR   ☎05321

Tiny Goslar (pop. 45,700) is one of Niedersachsen's most historically and culturally prominent cities. Spared from WWII air raids by a proclamation of neutrality, historic Goslar overflows with fountains, sculptures, and ornate palaces. The town's beauty and proximity to the Harz Mountains draw intimidating crowds of tourists, but the town retains the charm that once lured Goethe and Henry Moore.

🚆 TRANSPORTATION AND PRACTICAL INFORMATION

Trains roll to: Brunswick (45min., every hr., €5.60); Göttingen (1¼hr., every hr., €13.40); Hanover (1½hr., 2 per hr., €13.40). The hub of an extensive bus network, Goslar is a convenient gateway to the region (ticket €1.80, *Tageskarte* (day pass) €4). **Hotel Der Achtermann,** Rosentorstr. 20 (☎700 09 99), rents bikes even to nonguests (€10 per day); as you walk out of the station, turn left. The **tourist office,**

Markt 7, across from the Rathaus, books rooms (from €20) for free and sells maps. From the station, turn left onto Rosentorstr; follow it as it winds to the right, turns into Hokenstr., and leads to the Marktpl. The office is on your left. (☎780 60; www.goslar.de. Open May-Oct. M-F 9:15am-6pm, Sa 9:30am-4pm, Su 9:30am-2pm; Nov.-Apr. M-F 9:15am-5pm, Sa 9:30am-2pm.) Themed **tours** (€3-5) depart regularly from the Marktpl. The **post office** is to the right of the train station at Klubgartenstr. 10. (Open M-F 8:30am-6pm, Sa 9am-12:30pm.) **Postal Code:** 38640.

ACCOMMODATIONS AND FOOD

The half-timbered **Jugendherberge (HI) ❷**, Rammelsberger Str. 25, is a bit of a hike; it's best to take bus #808 from the train station (dir.: Bergbaumuseum) to "Theresienhof." (every hr. until 6pm). Continue along in the same direction, and take a sharp left up the hill at the white "Jugendherberge" sign (5min.). Once the luggage is off your back, the walk from Marktpl. becomes pleasant. Take the twisty Bergstr. from the church southwest until it ends at Clausthaler Str. Cross the intersection and follow the signs for the hostel down Rammelsberger Str. (25min.). Rooms are small but provide a good view of the mountains and surrounding farmland. For an additional €5, you can claim a double as a private single. (☎222 40; fax 413 76. Breakfast and sheets included. Reception 7am-10pm, call if arriving later. Curfew 10pm, but keys to the front door are available without deposit. Dorms €19.50, under 26 €16.50.) **Campingplatz Sennhütte ❶**, Clausthaler Str. 28, is 3km from town along the B241 highway; bus #830 (dir.: Hahnenklee or Clausthal-Zellerfeld) to "Sennhütte" (6min., 1-2 per hr.) This site is a short hike from a lake, with a kiosk, WC, and laundry room. (☎224 98. €3.50 per person, €2.50 per tent, €2 per car. MC/V.) The town has a weekday **market** (Tu-F 8am-1pm) and the beautiful surrounding square is ringed with pricey restaurants. **Markt Treff ❷**, Fleischscharren 6 (☎30 67 61), serves German favorites (€4-6) like *Currywurst* with french fries, at prices that put the other outdoor cafés to shame. Cheaper *Imbiße* (snack bars) abound in Goslar, especially along Hokenstr.; *Imbiße* meals run €2-4. Music, beer, and the local 20-something crowd converge at **Brauhaus Wolpertinger ❸**, a *Biergarten* that is part of a restaurant complex set in a 16th-century courtyard just off Marstallstr. (Open M-F noon-2pm and 5pm-midnight, Sa noon-2am, Su 10am-midnight; closing times approximate. MC/V.). The nearby **Kö Musik-Kneipe**, Marktstr. 30, offers free **Internet** access. (☎268 10. Open M-Th 4pm-2am, F-Sa 4pm-3am. AmEx/MC/V.)

SIGHTS

Guarded by a pair of bronze Brunswick lions, the austere ⬛**Kaiserpfalz**, Kaiserbleek 6, is a massive Romanesque palace that served as the ruling seat for 11th- and 12th-century emperors. Its glory was short-lived, however, as the palace was abandoned and subsequently converted into a prison. By the 19th century it had fallen into disrepair, but a romantic infatuation with the Middle Ages led a group of Prussian aristocrats to restore it to its prior majesty. The interior of the **Reichssaal** (Imperial Hall) is plastered with jaw-dropping murals displaying carefully selected incidents from German history. In the palace's **Ulrichskapelle**, Heinrich III's heart lies inside a massive sarcophagus, while the stone entrance still bears evidence of its stint as town jail. (☎311 96 93. Open daily Apr.-Oct. 10am-5pm; Nov.-Mar. 10am-4pm. Last entry 30min. before closing. €4.50, children €2.50.)

Each day in the market square, figures of court nobles and miners dance to the chiming bells on the treasury roof in the **Glocken-und-Figurenspiel** (bell and figure routine, 9am, noon, and 6pm). Behind the Rathaus loom the two towers of the reconstructed 12th-century **Marktkirche**. The church contains the stained-glass saga of St. Cosmas and St. Damian, 3rd-century twin doctors and martyrs. In classic Roman excess, the saints were drowned, burned at the stake, stoned, and cru-cified. (☎229 22. Tours M and Sa 12:30 and 3:30pm. Open daily Apr.-Oct. 10am-5pm; Nov.-Mar. 10am-4pm. Free.) On the way back from the Kaiserpfalz the fantas-tic ◪**Musikinstrumente- und Puppenmuseum,** Hoher Weg 5, feels like the inside of a children's book. The owner, once a musical clown in a traveling circus, has spent over 50 years assembling Germany's largest private instrument collection, and the sheer number of dolls is nothing short of astounding. (☎269 45. Open daily 11am-5pm. €3, children €1.50.) The media-drenched **Mönchehaus,** Mönchestr. 1, houses racy video displays, and cutting-edge modern art exhibitions in a traditional half-timbered home. The museum annually awards the prestigious *Kaiserring* prize to a modern artist based on a vote by the townspeople; recipients include Henry Moore, Willem de Kooning, and Cindy Sherman. (☎295 70; www.moenchehausmu-seum.de. Open Tu-Sa 10am-5pm, Su 10am-1pm. €3, students €1.50.)

HAMELN (HAMELIN) ☎05151

In the 700 years since the *Rattenfänger* (Pied Piper) last strolled out of town, his talents have kept this once-obscure German village in the limelight. On June 26, 1284, after Hamelin (pop. 58,000) failed to pay the piper his rat-removal fee, he walked off with 130 children in thrall. Today, this legend of the Pied Piper draws tourists as steadily as his flute drew rodents. Rats are back in town, but nobody's complaining—this time, they are made of bread and marzipan. In addition to the day's worth of sights in the city itself, Hamelin is a gateway to the region; buses connect nearby countryside castles and the villages tucked between them.

◪◪ TRANSPORTATION AND PRACTICAL INFORMATION

Hamelin bridges the Weser River and is 45min. from Hanover by **train** (2 per hr., €9.10). **Flotteweser,** Deisterallee 1 (in the same building at the tourist office), runs **ferries** up and down the Weser to Bodenwerder, Holzminden, and Hannoversch Münden. (☎93 99 99; www.flotte-weser.de. Operates May-Oct. Call for schedule. 1hr. trip €6, children €3; 2hr. €9.50/3.) For a **taxi,** call ☎74 77, 33 38, or 122 00. Rent **bikes** from **Troche Fahrrad-Shop,** Kreuzstr. 7. (☎136 70. €10 per day; €45 per week. Open M-F 9:30am-12:45pm and 2:30-6pm, Sa 9:30am-12:30pm.) The **tourist office,** Deisterallee 1, on the Bürgergarten, books rooms (from €20) for free and lists hotels and pensions. From the station, cross Bahnhofpl., make a right on Bahn-hofstr., and turn left on Deisterstr., which becomes Deisterallee. (☎95 78 23; www.hameln.de. Open May-Sept. M-F 9am-6:30pm, Sa 9:30am-4pm, Su 9:30am-1pm; Oct.-Apr. M-F 9am-6pm, Sa 9:30am-1pm.) **Tours** leave from the tourist office. (M-Sa 2:30pm, Su 10:15am. €4, children €2.) To reach the Altstadt, cross the road just beyond the tourist office. **Matthias Buchhandlung,** Bäckerstr. 56, has English paperbacks. (☎947 00. Open M-F 9am-7pm, Sa 9am-6pm.) Access the **Internet** at **Witte,** Kopmanshof 69. (☎994 40. €2 per 30min.) The **post office** is on Stubenstr., a block past the Markt. (Open M-F 8am-6pm, Sa 8am-1pm.) **Postal Code:** 31785.

◪ ACCOMMODATIONS

Hamelin's tourist boom has spawned a large number of pensions, listed in a detailed free brochure provided by the tourist office. The best deal is probably **Gästehaus Alte Post ❷,** Hummenstr. 23, in the Altstadt, offering colorful rooms complete with Picasso prints, TV, phone, and clock radio. (☎434 44; ottokater@aol.com. Breakfast included. Reception 11:30am-2:30pm and 5pm-mid-night; call ahead to arrange other times. Check-out 11am. Singles €25-35; doubles €50-65. Cash only.) The scenic **Jugendherberge (HI) ❶,** Fischbeckerstr. 33, sits on a bend in the Weser River, a 20min. walk north of the Altstadt. From the station, take bus #5 or 20 to "Langer Kreis/Jugendherberge," then backtrack 100m and look for the sign on your right. (☎34 25; fax 423 16. Breakfast included. Reception 12:30-1:30pm (if you call ahead) and 5-9pm. Curfew 10pm, key available with €15 deposit. €15.20, over 27 €18. MC/V.) Southeast of the city center on the shores of Tönebon Lake, **Campground Jugendzeltplatz** ❶, Tönebonweg 8, has warm showers and a sauna. Take bus #44 or 51 (only runs a few times per day) to "Südbad." (☎262 23. Reception 8am-8pm. Open May-Sept. €3 per person.)

🖸 FOOD

Hamelners stock up on fruit, vegetables, and other treats at the open-air **market** on the *Bürgergarten*. (W and Sa 8am-1pm.) The streets of the Altstadt around Osterstr. and Pferdemarkt are lined with restaurants and cafés, but the chances of finding a bargain are slim, particularly on *Osterstr.* Some good deals wait along Bäckerstr. near the Münster or in the alleys branching off from the touristy café area. **Mexcal** ❸, Osterstr. 15, serves excellent, if unexpected, German-Mexican meals and inexpensive lunch specials (noon-3pm; burritos, rice, and drink €5). (☎428 06. Dinners €6-10. Happy hour 3-6pm and 11pm-close mixed drinks €4. Open daily noon-midnight. Cash only.) Little crusty souvenir bread-rats are €1.70 at the excellent bakery in the **Schmelz Reformhaus**, Osterstr. 18, in the Altstadt. It carries all-natural foodstuffs in a town otherwise filled with cellophane-wrapped candy. (Open M-F 8:30am-6pm, Sa 8:30am-3pm.)

👁 SIGHTS

If you want to make your own escape from rats, you may have to venture out of the compact Altstadt: the Piper motif is ubiquitous. A small exception is the **Bürgergarten,** near the tourist office, where the locals relax and play life-size chess. (Open daily 7am-10pm.) At Rathauspl. is the **Theater Hameln,** featuring a musical about the Piper and other theater, opera, and dance. (Information and tickets ☎91 62 22 or 91 62 20, or from the tourist office. Box office open Tu-F 10am-7pm, Sa 10am-3pm.) One-hundred meters away, the **Leisthaus**, Osterstr. 8-9, is where the **Museum Hameln** exhibits an eclectic collection of pieces from Hamelin's history, among them some fossils, 1960s rock albums with the Piper theme, and a cane with a hidden *erotisches* skeleton—use your imagination. (☎20 22 15. Open Tu-Su 10am-4:30pm. €3, students and children €1.50.) The *Rattenfänger* tale is enacted zealously by the community theater every Sunday at noon in a *Freilichtspiel* (open-air play) outside the 17th-century **Hochzeithaus (Wedding House)** on Osterstr., as well as in ▧ **RATS: Das Musical,** every Wednesday, 4:30pm, in the same place. (May-Sept., weather permitting. Free.) At 9:35am, the **Glockenspiel** (bell routine) on the **Hochzeithaus** (Wedding House) plays the haunting *Rattenfängerlied* (Pied Piper song); at 11:45am the *Weserlied;* and at 1:05, 3:35, and 5:35pm, a tiny stage emerges from the Hochzeithaus and "rats" circle around a wooden flautist. The **Glashütten Hameln** (Glassworks), Pulverturm 1, provides respite from the ubiquitous piper obsession with a glass-blower's workshop upstairs. (☎272 39; www.gladblaeserei.de. Open M-F 9:30am-1pm and 2-6pm, Sa 9:30am-2pm, Su 10am-5pm. Workstation entrance €1, children €0.80.) Removed from Piperville, the **Schloß Hämelschenburg** 12km to the south comes with horses, brooks, a water-wheel, and a pond full of huge goldfish. To get there, take bus #40 from "Münster" on the south edge of the Altstadt toward Emmerthal (30min., every hr., €2). This Weser Renaissance-style moated castle, built in 1588, shelters gargoyles next to a trail with panoramic views of the countryside. (☎05155 95 16 90. Open Apr.-Oct. Tours every hr. Tu-Su 10am-noon and 2-5pm. €5, students €2.50. Admission only with tour.) For **hiking**, try one of the trails that laces the woods, meadows, and hills of the area surrounding the castle. For routes ranging from 5-14km, check out the map next to the bus stop or pick up a hiking map at the tourist office (€7).

⚡ DAYTRIP FROM HAMELIN

BODENWERDER

Take bus #520 (dir.: Stadtoldendorf) to "Weserbrücke, Bodenwerder," from the train station or from "Münster," on the edge of the Altstadt (40min.; every hr., Sa-Su every 2hr.; €5.50).

Deep forests of hundred-year-old trees engulf small clusters of wood-frame houses along the banks of the Weser river in this cyclist haven. It was in this small village that the legendary soldier, wanderer, and liar **Baron von Münchhausen** finally settled down. His tall tales of riding on cannon balls and flying with a team of ducks are now immortalized in statues all over the town. Near the tourist office, Münchhauspl. has Bodenwerder's one sight: the 200-year-old **Münchhausen-Museum Bodenwerder**. On display are a few of the Baron's personal effects, including the pistol he used to shoot his horse down from a steeple. (☎405 41. Open daily Apr.-Oct. 10am-noon and 2-5pm. €2, children €1.50). On the second Saturday of August, Bodenwerder sets the Weser ablaze with its pyrotechnic **Festival of Lights.** Head to the ⚡**Rodelbahn**, Grüne Schleite 1, for the chance to **toboggan** down the mountain on a railed track. Follow the signs in town, or from the tourist office, head away from the river. (☎93 48 00; www.rodelpark.de. 1 ride €2, 3 rides €5.60, under 16 €1.50/4. Open Apr.-Oct. 10am-6pm. Beer garden May-Aug. 10am-7pm.) Though there are many **bike trails** right along the Weser, the best route is to follow the road left or right from the Weserbrücke bus stop. **Trails** leave from behind the Jugendherberge (on the left as you climb the hill), or from across the river.

A great way to see the countryside is to rent a **bike** from **Karl-Heinz Greef**, Danziger Str. 20. From the end of Große Str. go left on Mühlentor, take the 5th right, and then the first left. (☎33 34. €8 per day. €40 per wk. Open Mar.-Oct. daily 8:30am-6pm.) The **tourist office**, Weserstr. 3, sells maps (€3) of the trails in the area and a biking map (€10) of northwest Germany. (☎405 41; fax 61 52; www.bodenwerder.de. Open Apr.-Oct. M-F 9am-12:30pm and 2-5pm, Sa 10am-12:30 pm).

BRAUNSCHWEIG (BRUNSWICK)   ☎0531

In 1166, Henry the Lion erected Brunswick's now-emblematic lion statue, built Burg Dankwarderode, and inaugurated the city's growth into a thriving religious and commercial center. Today, in addition to its stunning cathedrals and museums, Brunswick (pop. 245,000) draws national attention for its 130-year-old soccer tradition, thriving shopping centers, and cosmopolitan nightlife.

▐ TRANSPORTATION

Trains: Brunswick is on the Hanover-Berlin line. To: **Berlin** (1½hr., 1 per hr., €46); **Hanover** (45min., 2 per hr., €14); **Magdeburg** (1¼hr., 2 per hr., €17).

Public Transportation: A thorough system of **trams** and **buses** covers Brunswick and its environs (including **Wolfenbüttel**, p. 254). Pick up a **free map** at the tourist office. For information call ☎383 20 50 or stop by the information center right in front of the Hauptbahnhof. Single-ride ticket, valid for 1½hr. and any number of transfers is €1.80. Daypass €4.20. Most buses make their final run around 11:30pm; select trams run until 2am on weekends.

Taxis: ☎555 55.

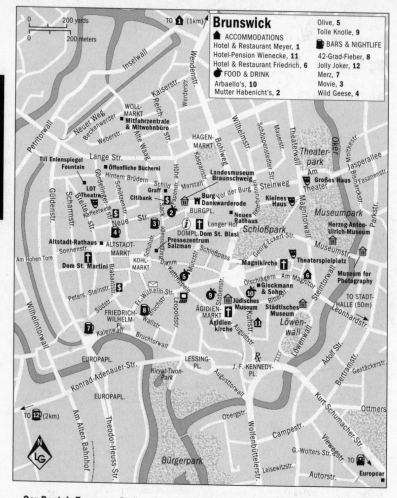

Brunswick

🏠 ACCOMMODATIONS
Hotel & Restaurant Meyer, 1
Hotel-Pension Wienecke, 11
Hotel & Restaurant Friedrich, 6
🍴 FOOD & DRINK
Arbaello's, 10
Mutter Habenicht's, 2

Olive, 5
Tolle Knolle, 9
🍸 BARS & NIGHTLIFE
42-Grad-Fieber, 8
Jolly Joker, 12
Merz, 7
Movie, 3
Wild Geese, 4

Car Rental: Europcar, Berliner Pl. 3 (☎ 24 49 80), across from the train station. Open daily 7:30am-midnight. Prices from €62 per day.

Bike Rental: Glockmann + Sohn, Ölschlägern 29 (☎ 469 23). Open M-F 9:30am-6:30pm, Sa 10am-2pm.

🧭 🔢 ORIENTATION AND PRACTICAL INFORMATION

Many of Brunswick's streets and pedestrian walkways end in forks without street signs; navigate using buildings marked on city maps instead of unmarked streets. The city center is an island ringed by the **Oker** river. The renovated **Hauptbahnhof** is a short way from the city, connected to the south-east corner (called **John-F.-Kennedy-Pl.**) by the busy **Kurt-Schumacher-Str.** North on Augusttstr. are **Ägidienmarkt** and **Bohlweg**, the wide eastern boundary of the pedestrian zone. Turn left at Langer Hof to get to the Rathaus. Most trams and buses pass through "Rathaus/Bohlweg" stops (downtown) or "JFK-Pl./K.-Schumacher-Str." (15min. from the station). Trams #1 and 2 go to all these stops.

Tourist Office: Next to Dom St. Blasi at the corner of Vor der Burg and Dompl. (☎470 20 40; www.braunschweig.de). Open M-F 10am-7pm, Sa 10am-4pm. May-Sept., also Su 10am-12:30pm. Staff finds rooms (from €25) and hands out maps for free.

Currency Exchange: Dresdner Bank, Neuestr. 20, near the Altstadtmarkt. 24hr. **ATM.** Open M-Tu and Th 9:30am-6pm, W 9:30am-4pm, F 9:30am-1pm.

Bookstore: Graff, a block from the Burgpassage on the corner of Sack and Schild, sells English-language paperbacks. Open M-Sa 9:30am-8pm. AmEx/MC/V.

Emergency: Police ☎110. **Ambulance** ☎192 22. **Fire** ☎112.

Pharmacy: Apotheke am Kennedy-Pl., Auguststr. 19, corner of Kurt-Schumacherstr. (☎439 55). Open M-F 8:30am-6pm, Sa 8:30am-1pm.

Internet Access: Telecafé, on Friedrich-Wilhelm-Str. €1.50 per hr. Open daily 9am-11pm.

Post Office: Berlinerpl. 12-16, to the right of the train station. Open M-F 8:30am-7pm, Sa 9am-1pm. **Branch** at Friedrich-Wilhelm-Str. 3. Open M-F 9am-7pm, Sa 9am-1pm. **Postal Code:** 38106.

ACCOMMODATIONS

Pick up *Hotels und Gaststätten* (in German, free) at the tourist office for a listing of accommodations and cafés.

Hotel & Restaurant Meyer, Wenderring 18 (☎34 03 63; fax 33 68 67). Bus #429 (dir.: Hamburger Str.) or 439 (dir.: Weststadt Donaustr.) to "Maschpl." It's the 2nd building on your right. This family-run hotel offers comfortable rooms with cable TV. Breakfast included. Singles €23-25.50, with bath €46; doubles €41-46/62. ❷

Hotel & Restaurant Friedrich, Am Magnitor 5 (☎417 28). In the Magniviertel, by the Städtisches Museum. Friendly chatter from cafés below drifts through the windows into bright, airy rooms right out of *Home & Country;* top floor doubles have sofas and large bathrooms. TV and stereo in every room. Restaurant (entrées €4-15) open daily 5pm-midnight. Singles €35; doubles €52. ❸

Hotel-Pension Wienecke, Kuhstr. 14 (☎464 76; www.koehler-wienecke.de). From the station, walk up Kurt-Schumacher-Str. to JFK-Pl. Bear right onto Auguststr. and then Kuhstr. (15min.). Rooms have private bathroom, fridge, and TV. Breakfast included. Singles €35-40, with bath €47-75; doubles with bath €65-99. ❹

FOOD

Bars and *Imbiße* (snack bars) along **Bohlweg** serve pizzas, salads, soups, and small sandwiches at reasonable prices. The Altstadt hosts an open produce market each week (W and Sa 8am-1:30pm). The open **Kohlmarkt** area, southeast of the Altstadt-markt in the city center, bustles with many pleasant, but not cheap, cafés and restaurants. Late-night cavorters head to the Turkish delis on **Friedrich-Wilhelm-Str.,** near the clubs and bars of the pedestrian zone.

Mutter Habenicht's, Papenstieg 3 (☎459 56), near the tourist office. Century-old model airplanes, sleds, mini-blimps, and other toys adorn this 136-year-old German restaurant's homey wooden interior. Entrées (€7-12) include the delicious namesake dish, the Toast Mutter Habenicht (€7.85). Open daily 11am-midnight. Cash only. ❸

Arbaello, Ritterstr. 2 (☎422 44), just down the block from Hotel-Pension Wienecke. The deliciously extensive breakfast menu makes this friendly bistro-bar a morning hotspot. Great weekday lunch specials (€3-5). Open in summer M-Th 9am-midnight, F-Sa 9am-1am, Su 10pm-midnight; in winter M-Th and Su until 11pm. Cash only. ❷

Tolle Knolle, Stobenstr. 15-16 (☎437 33), near the "Bohlweg/Damm" stop. At this bar and restaurant, potatoes rule. Potato soups, potato omelets, potato salads, baked potatoes, even "Potatoes of the World" (€3-14). Open M-Sa 11:30am-3pm and 5:30-11pm, Su 11:30am-3pm and 5:30-10pm. ❷

Olive, Münzstr. 9 (☎356 43 95). This congenial restaurant offers the cheapest *Döner kebap* around (€2.50). Open daily 24hr. Cash only. ❶

⬡ SIGHTS

Offshoots of the Oker river surround the oldest part of the city—the Altstadt—where many of the city's medieval sights ring the cobbled **Burgpl.**

DOM ST. BLASI. In 1173, the conceited Henry began construction of the Dom—situated in the southwest corner of Burgpl.—as a monument to himself. Midway through 22 long years of construction, the designs were altered to suit a new, edgy Gothic style just in from France. Although the older interior arches retain Romantic curves, the later exterior windows bend with the sharp angles characteristic of Gothic cathedrals. Fading frescoes cover the ceilings, illustrating the lives of Christ and Mary. The original stone grave plate portraying Henry and his consort Mathilde stands in front of the altar and their sarcophagi rest in an otherwise nondescript **crypt.** *(Dom open daily 10am-5pm. Free. Crypt €1; children free.)*

DOM ST. MARTINI. Built concurrently with the Dom St. Blasi, this cathedral's magnificent interior includes a Baroque communion altar and a pulpit decorated with sculptures of the "Wise and Foolish Virgins." Wise were the virgins who held their lamps upright as they waited for their grooms, foolish were those who let their lamps tip and got left in the dark. *(An der Marktkirche 10, next door to the Altstadt-Rathaus. Open Tu-F 10am-1pm and 3-5pm, Sa 10am-5pm, Su 10am-noon and 3-5pm. Free.)*

LÖWENWALL. The obelisk in the center, flanked by lions and splashing fountains, is a monument to city nobles who died in the Napoleonic Wars. *(Walk up Kurt-Schu-macher-Str. from the train station; the Löwenwall will be on your right just before you reach JFK-Pl.)*

⬛ MUSEUMS

HERZOG-ANTON-ULRICH MUSEUM. One of the first on the continent to welcome the public, this museum houses a small but eye-popping collection of great Western art (mostly Dutch Masters), as well as rotating shows of art and handiwork from all over the world. *(Museumstr. 1. From the pedestrian zone, walk across Bohlweg and down Georg-Eckert-Str., which turns into Museumstr. Or, ride tram #5 to "Museumstr." ☎122 50. Open Tu and Th-Su 10am-5pm, W 1-8pm. €2.50, students €1.30.)*

BURG DANKWARDERODE. This 19th-century reconstruction of Henry's castle exhibits his medieval collections of tapestries and religious and secular art, including a mantel owned by emperor Otto IV in 1200. The **Rittersaal** (knights' hall) has golden frescoes of Henry and his favorite knight, guarded by the original Brunswick lion. *(Burgpl. ☎12 15 26 18. Museum open Tu and Th-Su 11am-5pm, W 1-8pm. Rittersaal open Tu and Th-Su 10-11am, W 2:30-4pm. €3, students €1.30.)*

LANDESMUSEUM: JÜDISCHES MUSEUM (JEWISH MUSEUM). Having inherited furniture and an altar rescued from Brunswick's crumbling synagogue in

Hornburg, the Jewish museum has carefully reconstructed the synagogue's main sanctuary in a serene, if slightly ironic, setting (the museum sits in a Gothic monastery). Relics of German Jewish culture complete the collection, with a small exhibit on the British liberation of Bergen-Belsen. *(Hinter Ägidien, facing the Ägidienkirche. Walk along the far right side and through the iron gate. ☎ 12 15 26 61. Open Tu-F and Su 10am-5pm. €2.50, students €1.30.)*

LANDESMUSEUM BRAUNSCHWEIG (BRAUNSCHWEIG STATE MUSEUM). The Landesmuseum has three branches in town and one in Wolfenbüttel. The primary collection is in the Vierweg-Haus, and ranges from equine armor to Victorian dollhouses; the museum also has a collection of Hitler-inspired dolls' books and other WWII-era playthings. *(Burgpl. 1., across from the tourist office. ☎ 121 50. Open Tu-W and F-Su 10am-5pm, Th 10am-8pm. Vierweg-Haus €1.50; combination ticket to all 4 branches €2.50.)*

MUSEUM FÜR PHOTOGRAPHIE. This constantly evolving museum hosts the work of a different contemporary artist every few months. The small building is full of light, and its avant-garde attitude is a nice break from the heavy-duty history of the town. *(Helmstedter Str. 1. Just down Museumstr. from the Ulrich museum. Or, take bus #413 or 443 to "Steintor." ☎ 750 00. Open Tu-Su 1pm-6pm. €2.50, students €1.50.)*

🎵 ENTERTAINMENT

Brunswick's theatrical scene first blossomed in 1772 with the premiere of Lessing's Emilia Galotti. The monumental **Staatstheater** (☎ 123 45 67), with three houses built in the Florentine Renaissance style, now hosts around 30 premieres every year. The **Großes Haus**, Am Theater (☎ 484 28 00), is the largest of the three; the other two are the **Kleines Haus,** Magnitorwall 18 (☎ 484 28 00) and the **Theaterspielpl.,** Hinter der Magnikirche 6a (☎ 484 27 97). Tickets for all three theaters available at the Großes Haus box office M-F 10am-6:30pm, Sa 10am-2pm, and 1hr. before performances.) Several free German-language monthly magazines offer details on local events: *Subway, Da Capo, Cocktail,* and *Braunschweig Bietet.*

🍸 NIGHTLIFE

For traditional German bars, check out the intersection of Sack, Vor der Burg, and Schuhstr., where bars like the popular cinema-themed **Movie** attract locals nightly. (☎ 437 26. Open daily 9am-2am.) At the Irish pub **Wild Geese**, Goerdelingerstr. 49, a couple blocks from the Altstadtmarkt, James Joyce quotes and

LOCAL LEGEND

DE-LIONIZING HENRY

When Adolf Hitler turned to the long-deceased Henry the Lion for help in the 1930s, he received quite a surprise. To sustain his program of extreme German nationalism, Hitler emphasized legendary heroes who glorified German history and the power of the Aryan man. Henry—the militant founder of Brunswick and Munich—fit the bill perfectly, and to channel the leader's strength and spirit, Hitler decided to have his body publicly exhumed.

On the prescribed day, Henry's coffin was ceremoniously opened. Flushed with excitement at first, the Nazis soon realized that the skeleton they had unearthed was a woman's. Apparently, the corpse of Henry's wife Mathilde lay in his sarcophagus, and he in hers. A simple mistake, of course, so the Nazis turned to Mathilde's coffin, anticipating the wonders they could work by showing the German people, and the world, a powerful conqueror like Henry.

After the second coffin creaked open, the Nazis gazed dumbfoundedly at the skeleton inside. To be sure, it was a man's corpse this time, but that of a man just under five feet tall with uneven legs. Instead of a beacon of German strength, the Nazis had found a five-foot tall man with a limp, buried in the wrong sarcophagus. A disappointment to say the least, Henry was not at all the sort of Aryan hero the Nazis needed.

black-and-white pictures of Ireland hang from the walls as locals enjoy beer (€4) in the jovial atmosphere. (☎449 34. M Student night. Th karaoke. F-Sa live music. Open M-Th 5pm-1am, F 5pm-2am, Sa 2pm-2am, Su 4pm-midnight.) For dancing, check out the clubs around **Europapl.** At the corner of Gieseler and Kalenwall, students and 20-somethings fill the huge **Merz** complex. The first floor houses the **Merz** bar; the second, the well-stocked, popular **Soleile** bar; the third, the hip-hop playing, energetic **Vibe** disco; the fourth, the exotic **Schwannsee** (Swan Lake), bathed in red lights, whose ladies' night on the first Friday of the month draw gargantuan crowds. (Gieseler Str. 3. ☎181 28. Cover €3 for all except Schwannsee (€4). Open Th-Sa 9pm-3am.) Outside the Altstadt, the loud, titanic **Jolly Joker** disco attracts a younger crowd (16 to early 20s) with three dance floors, a *Biergarten*, fast food, movies, and more bars than you can count. (Broitzemer Str. 220. Tram #5 or 6 to "Jodebrunnen." 0800 244 42 55. Cover varies. Open Th-Sa 10pm-late.)

⚜ DAYTRIP FROM BRUNSWICK: WOLFENBÜTTEL

Catch bus #420 or 421 (€2.65) or the train (10min., 2 per hr., €2.40) from Brunswick's Hauptbahnhof. Phone code ☎05331.

It's not hard to believe that until a few centuries ago Wolfenbüttel (pop. 53,600)—only a few kilometers from Brunswick—was the more prominent cultural center. Developed with care by the literature-loving dukes of Braunschweig-Lüneburg, Wolfenbüttel's resilient castle, a scenic "Little Venice" system of canals, and collection of medieval manuscripts (the largest in the world) set it apart.

To get to the **tourist office,** Stadtmarkt 7, exit the station and turn left on Bahnhofstr., continuing as it becomes Kommissstr. Continue straight onto Wasserweg (a pedestrian path) and follow it to the *Markt*; it's on the left. The office lists accommodations and gives city information, including maps, in English. (☎862 80; www.wolfenbuettel-tourismus.de. Open M-F 9am-6pm, Sa 9am-1pm.)

Once the site of a gate through the city's protective wall, the pink, towerless **Trinitatskirche** in the *Holzmarkt* looks more like a palace than a church; only a viewing of the elaborate interior, with three levels of balconies and a prominent altar, reveals its true purpose. (Open Tu 11am-1pm, W 11am-1pm and 2-4pm, Th 3-5pm, Sa 11am-4pm.) The red **Schloß,** home to a museum and a high school, has the foundation of a 13th-century fortress, but its current appearance is pure Baroque, with a beautifully proportioned 17th-century clock tower. A tour through the painstakingly recreated front rooms of the **Schloßmuseum,** Schloßpl. 13, is like walking through a life-size royal dollhouse. (☎924 60. Open Tu-Su 10am-5pm. €3, students €2.) The *Schloß*'s courtyard hosts open-air performances nearly every day from mid-June to mid-July. Get tickets at the *Braunschweiger Zeitung* office in Wolfenbüttel, Löwenstr. 6 (☎800 10).

Medieval and Renaissance books line the walls of the ⚜ **Herzog-August-Bibliothek.** Founded by Duke Julius in the 16th century, bookworm **Duke August** transformed the collection into Europe's largest library. The library made the most expensive book purchase in history in 1983 when it shelled out over €2.5 million for the stunning **Evangeliar Heinrichs des Löwen,** a gospel drawn up in the late 12th century at the request of Henry the Lion; a facsimile is on display. Intellectual greats Leibnitz and Lessing were head-librarians here. Lessing loved the library so much that he lived next door. The **Lessing House** displays early editions of the playwright's *Nathan der Weise* and countless personal letters. (☎80 82 13; www.hab.de. Library and Lessing House open Tu-Su 10am-5pm.) Across from the castle is the 17th-century **Zeughaus,** whose magenta, high-gabled facade belies its former role as an armory. (Open M-F 8am-8pm, Sa 9am-1pm. Combination ticket to Lessing House and Zeughaus €3, students €2, under 19 €1, families €6.)

LÜNEBURGER HEIDE (LÜNEBURG HEATH)

Germany's literary greats have often written about the heather-carpeted Lüneburger Heide, which stretches between the Elbe and Aller rivers. The delicate *Heidenröslein* (heath rose) found a role in one of Goethe's *Lieder*, while Heine once compared a lady's bosom to the "flat and bleakly desolate" landscape of the *Heide*. Careful preservation efforts, including a ban on cars, have allowed the *Heide* to remain the largest moor in Europe. The most important regional towns are **Lüneburg** and **Celle.** The staff at the **AG Urlaub und Freizeit auf dem Lande,** Lindrooperstr. 63, 27283 Verden (☎04231 966 50; www.bauernhofferien.de), provides information on the *Heide's Heu-Hotels* (hay hotels), functioning barns with rooms that farmers rent out to travelers for around €10. They take their name from the hay on which travelers rest (bring a sleeping bag), but all have showers and toilets, and many are surprisingly luxurious.

To see the greater *Heide*, traveling by **bike** is your best option. The tourist offices in Lüneburg and Celle have information on self-guided and group tours. Maps outline the Heath's major bike tours. The most popular is an 80km route that follows main roads through the expansive woods and pastures near Lüneburg and neighboring Harburg. The tour is marked only with tiny white and green bicycle signs, so bring a map. **Horseback** tours are also offered at a number of local farms. The best source of **hiking** information is not tourist offices, but bookstores.

LÜNEBURG ☎04131

Lüneburg (pop. 71,000) made its money during the Middle Ages by supplying nearby trading centers like Lübeck and Hamburg with the salt needed for shipping, storing, and seasoning fish. Although "salt shocks" no longer pose a threat to the world economy and Lüneburg's broader influence has faded, neither the industry nor the town are obsolete. Salt is channeled into the city's famed rejuvenating baths, and the town, with its brick Altstadt and elegant half-timbered houses, retains an ancient grace. Streets are marked by an upscale sophistication, brimming with boutiques and chic cafés. It was here that Lüneburg native Heinrich Heine penned one of Germany's greatest Romantic poems, *Die Lorelei*.

◪◪ TRANSPORTATION AND PRACTICAL INFORMATION

Lüneburg serves as the transportation center of the *Heide*. **Trains** run to: Hamburg (30min., 2 per hr., €11); Hanover (1-2hr., every hr., €19.80-23); Lübeck (1hr., every hr., €11.70). The city's **bus** terminal is directly outside the train station. (Single ride €1.40, 9hr. pass €4.65.) Summon a **taxi** by dialing ☎520 25 or 520 77, or find one at the main square on Am Sande. The only place to rent **bikes** is **Radspeicher am Bahnhof,** Bahnhofstr. 4. (☎26 63 58. €5 per 3hr., €10 per day. €100 deposit and ID required. Reservations recommended. Open M-F 6am-8pm, Sa-Su 9am-6pm.) The **tourist office,** Am Markt, is next to the Rathaus and books rooms for free. From the train station, turn right and then make a left on the first street, Bleckeder Landstr., which becomes Lünertorstr. At the end, turn left on Bardowickerstr. (☎207 66 20; www.lueneburg.de. Open M-F 9am-6pm, also May-Oct. Sa-Su 9am-4pm; Nov.-Apr. Sa-Su 9am-2pm.) **Tours** of the Altstadt leave from the office. (1½hr., May-Oct. daily 11am, Sa also 2pm; Nov.-Apr. Sa 11am. €5, students €4.) Tickets to shows and concerts can be bought at **LZ Kartenverkauf,** Am Sande 17. (Open M-F 9am-5pm, Sa 9am-1pm.) **Deutsche Bank,** Bardowickerstr. 6, is a block from the Rathaus. (Open M 9am-1pm and 2-4pm, Tu and Th 9am-1pm and 2-6pm, W 9am-1pm, F 9am-

2:30pm.) Do **laundry** at **Schnell und Sauber,** Rote Str. 9. (Wash €3.50 per 6kg. Dry €0.50 per 15min. Open daily 6am-10pm.) There is a **pharmacy** at Grapengießerstr. 48, just off Am Sande. (Open M-F 8:30am-7pm, Sa 8:30am-4pm.) **Internet** access is available at the **Volkshochschule Lüneburg (VHS),** on the corner of Haage Str. and Rote Str. (Open M-Th 8:30am-6pm, F 8:30am-3pm.) The **post office** is at Sülztorstr. 21. (Open M-F 8:30am-6pm, Sa 9am-1pm.) **Postal Code:** 21335.

ACCOMMODATIONS AND FOOD

Hotels fill up when the *Heide* blooms from July to September. The **Jugendherberge Lüneburg (HI) ❶,** Soltauer Str. 133, caters mostly to groups and is booked months in advance. Take bus #11 (dir.: Rettmer/Häcklingen; M-Sa 6am-7:30pm and Su 1-7:30pm; €1.40) to "Scharnhorststr./DJH." (☎418 64; fax 457 47. Breakfast included. Beds from €14.60, over 27 €16.50. Cash only.) **Das Stadthaus ❹,** Am Sande 25, may lighten your wallet, but its location is unbeatable, with a spectacular view of Am Sande square and the Johanniskirche. (☎444 38; www.das-stadthaus.de. Breakfast included. Singles €49-68; doubles €82-92; triples €108. Cash only.) There are a number of official **campgrounds** along the Elbe and in the wooded suburbs; contact the tourist office for further information.

Schroederstr. and the city squares are lined with restaurants and cafés serving local *Lüneburger Pilsner.* **Sand Passage,** Am Sande 8, sells **groceries.** (Open M-F 8:30am-6:30pm, Sa 8:30am-2:30pm.) **Central Café ❸,** Schroederstr. 1, offers a broad menu in a dark-wooded, big-windowed tavern a block from the Markt. Try fish and chips (€6.50), pasta (€5-8), or the ample breakfast buffet (€9.95). (☎40 50 99. Open M-Th 8am-2am, F-Sa 8am-3am, Su 10am-1am.) **Brau und Tafelhaus Mälzer ❸,** Heiligengeiststr. 43, capitalizes on its beers (€2.20, pitcher €9), as patrons young and old crowd the streetside *biergarten.* (☎477 77. M-F lunch buffet €6.90. Pastas €6.80-8.20. Meat entrées €9-13.50. Open daily from 11am. Cash only.)

SIGHTS AND ENTERTAINMENT

The fruits of the salt trade are evident in the **Rathaus,** Am Markt, where gold statues stand outside. You'll have to take a tour (in German) to see the fancifully painted interior. (☎30 92 30. Tours Apr.-Dec. daily at 10, 11:30am, 1, 2:30, and 3:30pm; Jan.-Mar. Tu-Sa 10, 11:30am, 1:30, 3pm. €4.50, students €3.50.) The **Deutsches Salzmuseum** (German Salt Museum), Sülfmeisterstr. 1, is a sleek, dimly lit shrine to the city's 1000 years of salt production. From the Rathaus, follow Neue Sülze to Salzstr.; follow the signs past the Neukauf supermarket. (☎450 65. Open May-Sept. M-F 9am-5pm, Sa-Su 10am-5pm; Oct.-Apr. daily 10am-5pm. €4.60, students €3.50, families €11. German tours M-F 11am, 12:30, 3pm; Sa-Su 11:30am and 3pm. €1.80, children €1.10, families €3.) On the way back to town is the **Brauerei-museum** (Brewery Museum), Heiligengeiststr. 39, housed in a 500-year-old former brewery. The museum explores every aspect of the brewing process, from the complex purifying machine at the top to the gigantic **wort kettle** at the bottom. (☎448 04. Open Tu-Su 1-4:30pm. Free.)

Lüneburg's giant churches make navigation easy. At Bardowicker Str. and Lünerstr. on the edge of the Rathauspl., **St. Nicolai's** flying brick buttresses set the church apart. (☎243 07 70. Open daily 9am-5pm. Suggested donation €1. Frequent organ concerts; check www.kirche-lueneburg.de for schedule. €6, students €4 during the summer.) Cobbled side streets with ivy-covered houses and boutiques lead to the Gothic **Michaeliskirche,** on Johann-Sebastian-Bach-Pl. in the Altstadt. The imposing brick, wood, and ceramic church was built in 1418 on a foundation of salt. The massive sandstone-colored pillars have warped considerably since then, so the interior of the church may induce vertigo. A young Bach sang in the choir here from 1701 to 1702. (☎314 00. Open M-Sa 10am-5pm, Su 2-5pm; Oct.-Apr. until 4pm only.) **Johanniskirche**, Am Sande, soars over late 13th-century walls sheltering a Gothic altar and Baroque organ. (☎445 42. Open M-Th 10am-5pm, F-Sa 10am-6pm, Su 9am-5pm; in winter shortened hours and closed M. Free 30min. organ concerts in summer M-F 12:30pm. Summer tours of the tower Sa-Su 1 and 3pm.) The town's old **Wasserturm** (water tower) offers a panoramic view of the city. Take the elevator up to the top, then meander down the stairs past exhibits on water and the environment. (Open Apr.-Oct. daily 10am-6pm; Nov.-Mar. Tu-Su 10am-5pm. Evening cultural events every full moon. €3.30, students €2.30.)

A trip to the old **Kloster Lüne** makes for a nice 20min. walk. Take Bardowicker Str. out of the town center, then turn right on Stadtring and make a left on Bockelmannstr. On the far side of the street, walk through the forest to the cloister. The site is also home to Lüneburg's **Teppich Museum** (Carpet Museum), a collection of historic rugs and tapestries. (☎52 38. Grounds open in summer daily until 6pm. Museum open Apr.-Oct. 15 Tu-Sa 10:30am-noon and 2:30-5pm, Su 11:30am-noon and 2:30-5pm. Museum €3, students €2. Combo €6/4. Tours €4/3.) At night, locals fill the cafés and bars along picturesque Am Stintmarkt. Partiers park themselves at the large **Garage** club, Auf der Hude 74-80, a 15min. walk from the Altstadt. (☎358 79; www.discothek-garage.de. Drinks €2-4. Cover €3; free after 4am. Open F-Sa from 10pm, June-Aug. also W.)

CELLE ☎05141

The powerful prince electors of Lüneburg moved to Celle (pronounced "TSEL-luh"; pop. 71,000) in 1398 after the Lüneburg War of Succession and stayed here until 1705 when the last duke died. During those 307 years, the royalty lavished funds on their home, building a massive castle and promoting the city's growth. The innumerable well-maintained half-timbered houses that line Altstadt used to be taxed based on the number of diagonal beams on their facades, which quickly became esoteric status symbols. The town is an convenient base for visiting the Bergen-Belsen concentration camp.

🖃🛈 TRANSPORTATION AND PRACTICAL INFORMATION. Trains run twice per hr. to Brunswick (1½hr., €12.50) and Hanover (45min., €8.10). Rent **bikes** at **Fahrradverleih Am Bahnhof**, Bahnhofstr. 27. (€7.50 per day; €40 per week. Open M-F 8:30am-1pm and 3-6pm, Sa 9am-1pm.) The **tourist office**, Markt 14-16 in the Altes Rathaus, reserves rooms for free and sells tickets for the theater at the *Schloß* (see **Sights**, p. 258). From the train station, walk up Bahnhofstr., which becomes West-cellertorstr., then turn left onto Poststr., which becomes Markt. (☎12 12; www.region-celle.de. Open mid-May to mid-Oct. M-F 9am-7pm, Sa 10am-4pm, Su 11am-2pm; mid-Oct. to mid-May M-F 9am-5pm, Sa 10am-1pm.) **Tours** in German start from the bridge in front of the *Schloß*. (1½hr. May-Oct. and Dec. M-Sa 2:30pm, Su 11am. Apr. and Nov. Sa 2:30pm and Su 11am; €4, children €2.50.) **Decius**, at the corner of Markt and Neue Str. next to the Rathaus, carries English-language paperbacks. (Open M-F 9am-7pm, Sa 9am-4pm.) **Internet** access is available at **Spiel-Treff**, Am Heiligen Kreuz 7. (€0.50 per 7½min., €4 per hr. 18+. Open M-Sa 8am-11pm, Su 11am-11pm. Cash only.) The **post office**, Runde Str. 8, near Schloßpl., has a 24hr. **ATM.** (Open M-F 8:30am-6pm, Sa 8:30am-1pm.) **Postal Code:** 29221.

🖪🕻 ACCOMMODATIONS AND FOOD. Budget travelers in Celle compete with school groups for limited space. The **Jugendherberge (HI) ❶**, Weghausstr. 2, covered with sky-blue siding and located near an aromatic cow pasture, brings you oh-so-close to nature. From the train station, take bus #3 (dir.: Boye) to "Jugendherberge." Or walk along the pedestrian path to the left, which becomes

Biermannstr., turn left on Bremer Weg, and take the first right onto Petersburgstr.; it's on the left after 20min. (☎532 08; jh-celle@djh-hannover.de. Breakfast included. Reception until 10pm. Curfew 10pm, deposit €10 for a key. Dorms €15, over 26 €17.50. Cash only.) **Hotel zur Herberge ❸,** Hohe Wende 14, offers stylishly simple, well-outfitted rooms with TVs, phones, and showers, albeit at some distance from town. From the tourist office, go left and immediately turn left, walk through the Markt—which becomes Hehlentorstr.—and walk straight for 30min., then turn right onto Hohe Wende and continue until the sign. Or, take bus #5 from Schloßpl. (dir.: Vorwerk) and get off at "Harburger Heer Str.," continuing in the direction of the bus to the intersection where Hohe Wende begins. (☎20 81 41; www.nacelle.de. Breakfast included. Singles €42; doubles €58; triples €85. MC/V for min. 2-night stays.) **Campingplatz Silbersee ❶** is 7km northeast of the town. Take bus #6 (dir.: Vorwerk) to "Silbersee." (☎312 23. €3.50 per person. Reception 9am-1pm and 3pm-8pm. Cash only.)

Cafés have cropped up all over the Altstadt. **Alex's Antikcafé ❷,** Schuhstr. 6, in a secluded patio combines simple food—baguettes and pastas (€4-6)—with myriad old doodads. (☎236 36. Open M-Sa 8:30am-6pm, Su 9am-6pm. Cash only.) On the other side of the Altstadt, **Millennium ❷,** Bergstr. 16-17, is an inexpensive restaurant by day and an Irish pub by night. The salad (€4.50) is only slightly less tempting than the authentic fish'n'chips (€2.50). British tabloids plaster the ceiling. (☎21 70 16. Open daily 10am-11pm, F-Sa until midnight. Cash only.)

◪ **SIGHTS.** Some of the city's finest houses are tucked down alleys; wander any of the smaller streets radiating from Schloßpl. or Großer Pl. in the Altstadt. The **oldest house** in the area, at Am Heiligen Kreuz 26, was built in 1526. Celle's landmark **Herzogschloß,** Schloßpl. 13, which stretches out just west of the Altstadt directly across from the Bomann-Museum, has foundations dating to 1292 and grounds with a willow-draped pond. Inside is a macabre exhibit of artifacts pertaining to executions and a section devoted to the history of the kingdom of Hanover. (☎55 07 14. Open Tu-Su 10am-5pm. Mandatory 50min. tours for castle rooms Apr.-Oct. Tu-Su 11am-3pm on the hour; Nov.-Mar. 11am and 3pm. €3.50, students €2.50.) The **Stadtkirche** hosts concerts and art exhibits, as well as regular services. (☎77 35. Church open Tu-Su 10am-6pm. Tower open Apr.-Oct. Tu-Su 10-11:45am and 12:15-4:45pm. Suggested donation €1, children €0.50.) In the Altstadt, the **Rathaus** is richly wrought in the Weser Renaissance style. Right across the road, figures from Celle's colorful history mark the hour on the **Glockenspiel** (bell routine; daily every hr. 10am-6pm). The **Bomann-Museum Celle,** Schloßpl. 7, has rooms modeled after early Cellean houses, a history of the town and the *Heide* (including an exhibit on Celle's famed *Zwieback* and a room of live heather), and modern art. (☎123 72. Open Tu-Su 10am-5pm. €3, students €2.) The 1740 Baroque **Synagogue,** Im Kriese 24, is one of the nation's oldest standing places of Jewish worship and a memorial to Celle's once-thriving Jewish community. (☎55 07 14. Open Tu-Th 3-5pm, F 9-11am, Su 11am-1pm. Free.)

▇ **DAYTRIP FROM CELLE: BERGEN-BELSEN**

Take bus #11 from the train station to "Belsen-Gedenkstätte." (1hr 15min., M-F 12:05 and 1:36pm, return 4:54 and 5:34pm. €5.20.) ☎05051 60 11. Open daily 9am-6pm.

The Bergen-Belsen **concentration camp** was founded in 1940 as a labor camp for prisoners of war. For five years, 20,000 Soviet prisoners were held here, performing futile, torturous tasks like rolling heavy stones up and down hills, or refilling ditches they had just dug. In January 1945, the POW camp was dissolved and the SS took over, bringing in thousands of Jews, homosexuals, and political dissidents from Auschwitz and other concentration camps. For four months, tens of thousands of people lived in cramped conditions and suffered through mindless torture. Over 35,000 died of hunger and typhoid fever, including **Anne Frank,** whose symbolic gravestone is near the Jewish memorial. In total, Bergen-Belsen claimed more than 100,000 lives. In the documents building near the entrance, a permanent exhibit displays the history of the camp and shows a film made by British liberation forces. At the camp boundary, a gap in the trees shows where the fence once stood. Though the grounds of the camp contain no original buildings (they were burned after liberation to prevent the spread of disease), recent excavations have begun to reveal the foundations of buildings that have been covered over. Grass-covered mounds of mass graves can be found throughout the site. A path through the woods (20min.) leads to the memorial cemetery for Russian POWs. A stone obelisk commemorates the 30,000 Jewish victims, and a wall is inscribed with memorial phrases in the languages of the victims. Self-guided tours for the camp are available in several languages.

BREMEN ☎0421

Bremen (pop. 550,000) can boast not only of having been a member of the Hanseatic league, but also of having been expelled from it, after citizens made a bonfire of Hanseatic documents. Despite its rebellious flair, Bremen has done an exceptional job of preserving the relics of its past; unlike many other German towns—which suffered tremendous damage during WWII—Bremen retains much of its medieval architecture. The historic Rathaus and Dom dominate the city, and the *Schnoorviertel*, with myriad winding alleyways and tiny red brick homes, provides a fascinating, if touristy, glimpse into its medieval heart. Bremen today, though relatively small, is surprisingly lively—its renowned cultural institutions and busy bar scene rival cities several times as large.

▎ TRANSPORTATION

Flights: Flughafen Bremen (☎559 50) is 3.5km from the city center; take S6 (15min.). Frequent flights to the East Frisian Islands and major German and international cities.

Trains: 2 per hr. to: **Bremerhaven** (1hr., €9.40); **Hamburg** (1-1½hr., €18.30-22); **Hanover** (1-1½hr., €18.70-27); **Osnabrück** (45-75min., €18.50-22).

Public Transportation: VBN runs an integrated system of trams and buses across the city. 1 ride €2.05, day pass €5. In the round building opposite the Hauptbahnhof, an **information center** has tickets and transportation maps. Open daily 7am-7pm.

Ferries: Hal Över, Schlachte 2 (☎33 89 89; www.hal-oever.com), runs boats to suburbs and towns on the Weser, ending in Bremerhaven. (3½hr. May-Sept. Sa 8:30am and Su 9:30am; June-Aug. also W and Th 8:30am. €13.50, round-trip €21.50, students and children half-price.) Also offers 1½hr. harbor tours May-Sept. 5 times daily; Apr. and Oct. 3 times daily; Mar. 3 times Sa-Su. (€8.50, students €6.50, children €4.50.)

Taxis: ☎140 14. **Frauen Nachtaxi** (☎133 34) runs taxis for women daily 6pm-6am.

Bike Rental: Radstation (☎178 33 61), between the Hauptbahnhof and Übersee Museum. €9 per day, €35 per week. Open M-F 6am-10pm, Sa-Su 9am-8pm.

▎ ▎ ORIENTATION AND PRACTICAL INFORMATION

Where the Weser River meets the North Sea, Bremen's four neighborhoods await: the tourist-filled **Altstadt,** containing most sights and the oldest architecture; the **Alte Neustadt,** a residential neighborhood south of the Weser; the **Schnoor,** an old neighborhood-turned-shopping-village; and the **Viertel,** a student quarter filled with college kids, clubs, and cheap food. Avoid the area around Ostertorsteinweg and Am Dobben late at night. An **EntdeckerCARD Nordwest,** available at the tourist office, offers free entrance to several attractions in Bremen and the rest of the region, as well as free public transportation within Bremen, and on certain regional train segments. (Valid for 72hr.; €42, children €28.)

Tourist Office: The central office (tourist hotline ☎01805 10 10 30, €0.12 per min.; www.bremen-tourismus.de) in the Altstadt on Obernstr. at the Liebfraukirchenhof. Tram #2 or 3 to "Obernstr." Has free maps of the city center, makes room reservations for free, and sells tickets for concerts and festivals. Open M-W 9:30am-6:30pm, Th-F 9:30am-8pm, Sa-Su 9:30am-4pm. **Branch** in the Hauptbahnhof. Open M-F 8am-8pm, Sa-Su 9:30am-6pm. **Walking tours** of the Altstadt leave daily from the central office. (2hr.; daily 2pm, Apr.-Sept. also Sa 11am; €6.50.)

Consulate: UK, Herrlichkeit 6 (☎59 07 01). Open M-F 9am-noon and 2:30-3:30pm. For visa or passport questions, contact Düsseldorf (p. 299).

Currency Exchange: Reisebank, in the Hauptbahnhof. Exchanges currency and wires money via **Western Union.** Open daily 8am-8pm.

Bookstore: Thalia, Sögestr. 36-38 (☎30 29 20), in the pedestrian zone; helpful staff will lead you to the English paperbacks. Open M-F 9:30am-8pm, Sa 9:30am-6pm.

Gay and Lesbian Resources: Rat- & Tat-Zentrum, Theodor Körnerstr. 1 (☎70 00 07). Take tram #2 or 3 to "Theater am Goethepl.," and continue on, veering right onto St.-Pauli-Str. Information about gay events. Open M, W, F 11am-1pm, Tu 3-6pm. Also in the building is **AIDS Beratungsstelle** (☎70 41 70). Open M, W, F 11am-1pm, Tu 3-6pm.

Women's Resources: Info pertinent to women travelers is available on the web at www.gesche.bremen.de. The tourist office sells women's city maps for €1.

Laundromat: Schnell und Sauber, Vor dem Steintor 105. Take Tram #2, 3, or 10 to Brunnenstr. Wash €3.50 per 7kg. Dry €0.75 per 15min. Open daily 6am-11pm.

Emergency: Police ☎110. **Fire** and **Ambulance** ☎112.

Pharmacy: Päs Apotheke, Bahnhofspl. 5-7 (☎144 15). Straight from the Hauptbahnhof's main exit, on the right side of the Platz. M-F 8am-6:30pm, Sa 8am-2pm.

Internet Access: Internet Center Bremen, Bahnhofspl. 22-28 (☎277 66 00), in the DGB building to the left of the main entrance. €1 per 20min. Open M-Sa 10am-10pm, Su noon-8pm. Also at **Lift Internetcafé,** Weberstr. 18 (☎774 50), just off Ostertorsteinweg. Tram #2 or 3 to "Wulwesstr." €1.60 per hr. Open daily 2pm-midnight.

Post Office: Domsheide 15 (☎367 33 66), near the Markt. Open M-F 8am-7pm, Sa 9am-1pm. **Branch,** Bahnhofspl. 21, left of the train station. Open M-F 9am-8pm, Sa 9am-1pm. **Postal Code:** 28195.

🏠🏕 ACCOMMODATIONS AND CAMPING

🏨 **Bremer Backpacker Hostel,** Emil-Waldmann-Str. 5-6 (☎223 80 57; www.bremer-backpacker-hostel.de). A 5min. walk from the Hauptbahnhof. From the main exit, turn left on An der Weide, turn right onto Löningstr., and make another right onto Emil-Waldmann-Str. Kitchen and common room with TV and Internet access (€1 per 30min.). 5- to 7-bed rooms €17; singles €28; doubles €45; triples €61; quads €76. ❷

Pension Weidmann, Am Schwarzen Meer 35 (☎498 44 55; weidmann@white-pleasure.de). Take tram #2, 3, or 10 to "St. Jürgen-Str." and follow the left fork (Am Schwarzen Meer) for 2 blocks; pension is on the right. Decor is dated, but rooms have plush comforters, coffee-makers, refrigerators, and TV. Breakfast included. Call ahead. Non-smoking rooms available. Singles from €21; doubles from €42. Cash only. ❷

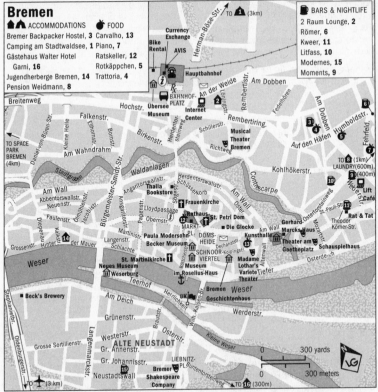

Bremen

▲ñ ACCOMMODATIONS   🍴 FOOD

Bremer Backpacker Hostel, **3**
Camping am Stadtwaldsee, **1**
Gästehaus Walter Hotel
  Garni, **16**
Jugendherberge Bremen, **14**
Pension Weidmann, **8**

Carvalho, **13**
Piano, **7**
Ratskeller, **12**
Rotkäppchen, **5**
Trattoria, **4**

🍸 BARS & NIGHTLIFE

2 Raum Lounge, **2**
Römer, **6**
Kweer, **11**
Litfass, **10**
Modernes, **15**
Moments, **9**

Jugendherberge Bremen (HI), Kalkstr. 6 (☎16 38 20; www.jugendherberge.de/jh/bremen). Bus #26 or 27 or Tram #1 to "Am Brill." With all the charm of a large, institutional building filled with giant schoolgroups, this hostel makes up for its lack of architectural innovation with cleanliness, location, game room, and terrace. Breakfast included. Dorms €20.90, over 26 €23.90. MC/V. ❷

Gästehaus Walter Hotel Garni, Buntentorsteinweg 86-88 (☎55 80 27; www.hotel-walter.de). Tram #4-6 to "Theater am Leibnizpl." Left onto Buntentorsteinweg. Large rooms with hardwood floors in a quiet neighborhood. Breakfast included. Singles €35-45; doubles €55-68. Book ahead. AmEx/DC/MC/V. ❹

Camping: Camping an Stadtwaldsee, Hochshulring 1 (☎841 07 48; contact@camping-stadtwaldsee.de). Tram #8 to "Kulenkampfallee," then bus #28 to "Campingpl." Shaded campground near the university. Showers and electricity included. €4.40-6.60 per site, €4.70 per adult, €2.85 per child. ❶

🍴 FOOD

For cheap eats, try the open-air **market** in front of the Rathaus (daily 8am-2pm) or follow the bronze pig statues to the take-out cafés on **Sögerstraße** in the Marktpl. Cheap bakeries and *Imbiße* (snack bars) crowd around the **Hauptbahnhof.** To escape the tourist mob, head to **Auf den Häfen,** where even locals get lost in the tiny cobblestone alleys crammed with gourmet restaurants and trendy bars. Student pubs proliferate farther east in the **Viertel** and around **Ostertorsteinweg** (see **Nightlife**, p. 265). The immensely popular **Schlachte**, on the banks of the Weser, is home to a long stretch of bars and restaurants with huge outdoor seating areas. For groceries, there is a **EuroSpar** at the back of the train station. (Open M-Sa 8am-8pm.)

▧ Piano, Fehrfeldstr. 64 (☎785 46). Take tram #2, 3, or 10 to "Sielwall" and walk a block toward the Altstadt; it's on your right. Students and locals flock to this neighborhood institution for coffee, conversation, huge breakfast spreads (€2.60-8.70), and pizzas (€5-8). Open daily from 9am. Breakfast M-F until 4pm, Sa-Su until 5pm. Cash only. ❷

Trattoria, Auf den Häfen 12-15 (☎70 03 35). Take tram #10 to "Humboldtstr." and turn right on Auf den Häfen and then right again down the corridor beneath the neon sign. Ideal for a warm summer evening, this Italian bistro has excellent pastas (€7-9) and appetizing, if somewhat more expensive, meat dishes (€13-21). Cash only. ❸

Rotkäppchen, Am Dobben 97 (☎754 46). Tram #10 to "Humboldtstr." Heaping lunch specials (€6-7), weekend breakfast buffets (€5.50-8.50), and light salads, crêpes, and veggie meals (€4-9). Open daily 10am-2am. Cash only. ❷

Carvalho, Kolpingstr. 14 (☎336 50 80). Tram #2-6 or 8 to "Domsheide," 2 blocks behind the post office. Combines colorful tapas (€4-12) and specialty dishes (€9-17) with good sangria and a decorative style halfway between art deco and 1950s Cuba. Open daily from 6:30pm. ❸

Ratskeller, Am Markt 1 (☎32 16 76), in the basement of the Rathaus. Tram #2 or 3 to "Obernstr." German wine has been served in these vaulted chambers since 1405. Massive wine casks date to the 1800s. Try one of the 650 wines (€4-6 per glass), or treat yourself to a meal. German specialties like *Jungschweinsbralen* (suckling pig roast; €13-21). Lunch special €6.90. Open daily 11am-midnight. AmEx/MC/V. ❹

⊙ SIGHTS

ST. PETRI-DOM. A survivor of WWII, the 1200-year-old St. Petri Dom was excavated from 1973 to 1976 and subsequently restored to its medieval glory. The interior now explodes with color, its canopied vaults embellished by wall paintings. If you look closely, you can see the "Bremen Church Mouse," a tiny rodent carved into a pillar near the south entrance to the choir. *(Sandstr. 10-12. ☎36 50 40. Cathedral open M-F 10am-5pm, Sa 10am-2pm, Su 2-5pm. Free. Tower open Easter-Oct. €1, children €0.70.)* In a corner of the cathedral is the **Dom Museum,** home to original 15th-century paintings and the remains of 900-year-old silk attire, recovered from the bodies of entombed archbishops unearthed during the archaeological dig. *(☎365 04 41. Open Apr.-Oct. M-F 10am-4:45pm, Sa 10am-1:30pm, Su 2-4:45pm; Nov.-Mar. M-F 11am-4pm, Sa 10am-1pm, Su 2-5pm. Call in advance for English tours. €2, students and children €1.)* Walk around and behind the church into the **Bibelgarten,** which provides the only access to the macabre **Bleikeller** in the basement of the Dom. Here, an assortment of mummified corpses have been on display for three centuries; it's not for the squeamish. *(Open M-F 10am-5pm, Sa 10am-2pm, Su 2-5pm. €1.40, children €0.70.)* Just past the Domshof, turn left on Domsheide to reach the **Schnoorviertel,** Bremen's district of historic, tiny red-roofed houses, which now hosts many shops and restaurants of various cuisines.

RATHAUS. Bremen's Altstadt surrounds the striking Renaissance-era Rathaus. The hall and surrounding square are largely preserved in their original states, since the English WWII bomber assigned to obliterate the area deliberately missed his target. On the west side of the Rathaus is Gerhard Marcks's famous 1951 sculpture *Die Musikanten*—the town's symbol—which portrays the Grimms' famed donkey, dog, cat, and rooster. *(Tram #3 or 4 to "Obernstr." Required 45min. tours M-Sa 11am, noon, 3, 4pm. €4, children and students €2. Buy tickets at tourist office.)*

BECK'S BREWERY. Guides usher wide-eyed beer aficionados through this giant brewery, explaining the drink's Sumerian origins and inspiring awe with mind-boggling statistics (e.g., Beck's annual export of 320 million liters). The 2hr. tour ends with a tasting challenge and two free rounds of beer for the winners. The free beer itself is worth more than the cost of admission; don't miss the bitter regional specialty, Haake Beck, or the family's newest member, Beck's Gold. *(Am Deich 18-19. Tram #1-3 or 8, or bus #25, 26, or 27 to "Am Brill." Cross the Bürgermeister-Smidt Bridge, then turn right on Am Deich. Walk toward the Stephan Bridge to get to the Visitors Center. ☎ 50 94 55 55; www.becks.de. Tours Apr.-Dec. every 1½hr. Th-F 11am-5pm, Sa 9:30am-5pm; Jan.-Mar. Th-Sa 12:30, 2, 3:30, 5pm. 2pm tours in English. €7.50. 16+.)*

BÖTTCHERSTRAßE. A project of Ludwig Roselius, millionaire inventor of decaffeinated coffee, this street was transformed from a cramped artisans' quarter to a graceful harmony of Art Nouveau and Expressionist architectural elements. It houses two of the city's most interesting museums: the **Museum im Roselius-Haus** (p. 264) and the **Paula Modersohn-Becker Haus** (p. 264). Tourists huddle every day at noon, 3, and 6pm awaiting the **Böttcherstraße Glockenspiel** (bell routine).

 MUSEUMS

KUNSTHALLE (HALL OF ART). Bremen's excellent art collection includes paintings and sculptures dating from the 15th century to the present. Modern interpretations of old classics are interspersed throughout the galleries. The museum's best holdings are those of the German Expressionists and French Impressionists, although the museum's Delacroix and medieval paintings are impressive as well. *(Am Wall 207. Tram #2 or 3 to Theater am Goethepl. ☎ 32 90 80. Open Tu 10am-9pm, W-Su 10am-5pm. €5, students €2.50.)*

NEUES MUSEUM WESERBURG BREMEN. Almost all of this museum's collection is privately owned, allowing it to display an evolving array of works by contemporary artists from across the globe. Captions in both English and German. *(Teerhof 20. Off the Bürgermeister-Smidt Brücke on an island in the Weser River. Tram #1-3, 8, or bus #25, 26, or 27 to "Am Brill." ☎ 59 83 90. Open Tu-F 10am-6pm, Sa-Su 11am-6pm. Tours daily in German; €7, students and children €4. €5, students and children €3.)*

THE NON-MUSICIANS NOT FROM BREMEN

In the center of Bremen stands a statue of four animals: a donkey, a cat, a dog, and a rooster. While they are known to the world as the Bremen town musicians, they never visited that town, and according to the Grimm brothers, musical ability did not rank high among their talents. As the story goes, the foursome ran away from masters intent on killing them in their old age and met on the road to Bremen. There, like so many modern-day runaways on the way to the big city, they idealistically decided to support themselves by becoming town musicians in the town of Bremen.

Before making it to Bremen, however, they stumbled upon a pack of robbers enjoying a meal in a modest house. As the animals were all hungry, they began playing. None of the animals had any musical talent (do you know any dogs that can play the guitar?), but it hardly mattered—the foursome only wanted to drive the robbers away with their painfully off-pitch playing. It worked, and the animals moved in to finish off the meal. The robbers, although frightened by the dreadful cacophony, returned to retake their home that night. When the animals fought them off the second time, it wasn't with horrible music but with tooth and claw. Having permanently rebuffed the bandits, the quartet decided to stay in this house, never even setting foot in Bremen.

MUSEUM IM ROSELIUS-HAUS. Tapestries, pious icons, carved dark wooden furniture, nothing is missing to complete this showcase of medieval upper middle class life. *(Böttcherstr. 6-10. Tram #2-6 or 8 to "Domsheide." ☎ 336 50 77. Open Tu-Su 11am-6pm. €5, students and children €3. Includes admission to Paula Modersohn-Becker Haus.)*

ÜBERSEE MUSEUM. This museum delivers a *"Weltreise im Minutentakt"* (quick trip around the world), with displays ranging from a Shinto garden to a South Sea fishing village. When you're finished with the life-size wildlife dioramas and artifacts, head upstairs for an exhibit on the history of Bremen, Bremerhaven, and the container shipping business. *(Bahnhofspl. 13, next to the train station on the right. ☎ 16 03 81 01. Open Tu-F 9am-6pm, Sa-Su 10am-6pm. €6.50, students €4.50, children €2.50.)*

PAULA MODERSOHN-BECKER HAUS. Celebrating the work of Modersohn-Becker, this museum is the first ever dedicated to a female artist. Her pre-Expressionist paintings are accompanied by works of other German artists such as **Bernard Hötger,** the architect responsible for many of Böttcherstr.'s buildings. *(Böttcherstr. 6-10. Tram #2-6 or 8 to "Domsheide." ☎ 336 50 77. Open Tu-Su 11am-6pm. Tours Su 11:30am and W 6pm. €5, students €3. Includes admission to Roselius Haus.)*

BREMEN GESCHICHTENHAUS IM SCHNOOR (HISTORIC HOUSE). Take a tour through this museum in a typical Schnoor house, as characters from Bremen's past guide you through the history of their city with the aid of videos, dioramas, and more. *(Wüste Stätte 10. ☎ 33 626 50. Open daily 10am-6pm. €3.90, students €2.20, ages 6-17 €1.90. Call ahead for English tours.)*

GERHARD-MARCKS-HAUS. Devoted to contemporary sculpture, this elegant indoor and outdoor sculpture garden features works by Marcks (1889-1981), creator of Bremen's famous *Die Musikanten* (p. 262), along with changing exhibitions of avant-garde sculpture. *(Am Wall 208, next to the Kunsthalle. ☎ 32 72 00. Open Tu-Su 10am-6pm. Tours Th 5pm. €3.50, students and children €2.50.)*

🎵 ENTERTAINMENT

Known for operas, musicals, and dance, the 900-seat **Theater am Goetheplatz,** Am Goethepl. 1-3, is the city's largest theater. Take tram #2 or 3 to "Theater am Goethepl." Its sister, the **Schauspielhaus,** Ostertorsteinweg 57a, behind the Theater am Goethepl., presents new drama. Tickets for both range €12-50 and must be purchased at the Theater am Goethepl. (☎ 365 33 33. Open M-F 11am-6pm, Sa 11am-2pm.) The **Musical Theater Bremen,** Richtweg 7-13, favors musicals. Take tram #4, 6, or 8 to "Herdentor"; purchase tickets by calling ☎ 35 36 37. The **Bremer Shakespeare Company,** in the Theater am Leibnizplatz, enjoys an unrivaled national reputation for its productions of some obscure English playwright. Take tram #4-6 to "Theater am Leibnizpl." (☎ 50 03 33. Box office open Tu-Sa 3-6pm. Tickets €7.50-16.)

The last two weeks of October find Bremen residents drinking beer and eating tubs of lard cakes during the colorful **Freimarkt** fair—an annual event since 1035. Bremen also hosts big concerts in the **Stadthalle** (☎ 35 36 37; box office open M-F 8am-6pm, Sa 9:30am-1pm), located behind the train station, and in the **Weserstadion** (☎ 491 31 10). Summertime brings performances to parks around the city; a children's production of Bremen's famous fairy tale takes place on the main Platz every Sunday at noon. Check the tourist office, the theaters, or the free German-language publication *Bremer Umschau* for schedules and prices. Many magazines list events in German. *Foyer,* free at many museums, details theater, music, film, and art events. *Belladonna* lists cultural events of special interest to women. The indispensable *Prinz* provides monthly party listings and the lowdown on the Bremen scene (€1 at the tourist office and newsstands). *Partysan,* a Hamburg magazine free at many cafés, also lists big parties in Bremen.

■ NIGHTLIFE

To experience Bremen's raucous pub culture, head for the **Viertel;** for slightly more touristed, multi-floor clubs, hit the **Rebertiring,** across from the Hauptbahnhof.

Modernes, Neustadtswall 28 (☎ 50 55 53; www.modernes.de). Tram #1 or 8, or bus #26 or 27 to "Hochschule Bremen," backtrack 1 block, and turn right on Neustadtswall. In a gutted movie theater, this popular disco hosts everything from flamenco concerts to Depeche Mode parties. Retractable roof makes way for a starry canopy on warm nights. Cover €3.50-4.50. Special events €9. Disco open F-Sa 11pm-4am.

Litfass, Ostertorsteinweg 22 (☎ 70 32 92). Tram #2 or 3 to "Wulwesstr." A late-night bastion of alternative chic in bar form, with a big outdoor terrace and open facade. Open M-Th and Su 10am-2am, F-Sa 10am-4am. Cash only.

2 Raum Lounge, Auf den Häfen 12-15 (☎ 745 77). Next to Trattoria, this bar offers a huge variety of mixed drinks (€5-8.50) among trendy 60s-inspired decor. Cash only.

Moments, Vor dem Steintor 65 (☎ 792 66 33; www.club-moments.de). Tram #2 or 3 to "Sielwall," and another 1½ blocks farther. A mixture of live music and dance-hall fun. Hosts events such as Turkish music nights. Open Th-Sa 10pm-6am.

Römer, Fehrfeldstr. 31 (☎ 794 65 98), 2 blocks off Ostertorsteinweg. Tram #2, 3, or 10 to "Sielwall Station"; follow Fehrfeldstr. to its end. Long bar and big dance floor with a young crowd. Mostly independent and alternative music, with an occasional splash of hip hop. Mixed drinks €5-6. Happy hour 11pm-midnight, beer €1.50, mixed drinks €3. F-Sa cover €2-4. Open Tu-Th 10pm-2am, F-Sa 10pm-4am. Cash only.

Kweer, Theodor Körnerstr. 1 (☎ 70 00 08). Tram #2 or 3 to "Theater am Goethepl.," and right onto St.-Pauli-Str. Though Bremen isn't known for gay nightlife, the relaxed atmosphere of this intimate café and bar attracts a crowd of regulars. All proceeds go to AIDS education. Open 1st and 3rd Tu of the month and every W 8pm-midnight, F 8pm-1am, Su 3-6pm.

▶ DAYTRIP FROM BREMEN

BREMERHAVEN

From Bremen, take the train (45min., 1-2 per hr., €9.40) or the ferry (p. 259). From the Hauptbahnhof take bus #502, 505, 506, 508, or 509 to "Grosse Kirche," and then walk one block behind the Columbus Center (opposite the church) to the Seemeile, where Bremerhaven's more worthwhile attractions are located.

Flooded with maritime culture, the port city of Bremerhaven (pop. 118,000) was established in the 18th century to handle the ever-increasing number of ships that couldn't make the shallow passage down the Weser River to Bremen. Bremerhaven today is proud of its maritime legacy; the **Seemeile** (sea mile), by the water, is home to Bremerhaven's major tourist attractions. The **◪Deutsches Schiffahrtsmuseum** (German Maritime Museum) brings the history of boats alive through varied models and full-sized boats, most memorably the Hansekogge, a carefully reconstructed Hanseatic merchant ship dating to the 14th century. Once you've done enough looking, go down to the basement, where you can drive remote control ships, or visit the museum ships docked outside. Across the docks, clamber through the hatches of the 1945 **Technikmuseum U-Boot Wilhelm Bauer,** one of the few German WWII submarines that was neither sunk nor scrapped. Man a periscope, examine torpedo tubes, see the frogmen sluice, and feel the claustrophobia of the living quarters. *(Hans-Scharoun-Pl. 1. ☎ 047 14 82 070. Museum open Apr.-Oct. daily 10am-6pm; Nov.-Mar. Tu-Su 10am-6pm. Ships and U-Boat open Apr.-Oct. only. Museum and ships €5; students, seniors, and children €3.50, family €12. U-Boat €3, ages 6-17 and seniors €2.)*

NIEDERSACHSEN AND BREMEN

OLDENBURG ☎0441

First settled as early as 1108, the city of Oldenburg (pop. 158,000) was spared destruction in the Thirty Years' War due largely to Count Anton Günther, who built the most beautiful horses in Germany. Oldenburg today has more to offer—Frisian culture runs deep, and is actively preserved by its people. Though the city's varied museums and bustling pedestrian shopping zone fill daily with tourists, it is easy to overlook the city's other gems, including the winning neighborhood west of Alexanderstr., the unassuming cemetery, and the lush Schloßgarten.

◨ ? TRANSPORTATION AND PRACTICAL INFORMATION

Trains to: Bremen (30-50min., 3 per hr., €6-9); Jever (1hr., every hr., €9-11); Osnabrück (1½hr., 1-2 per hr., €16-22). The old, moated city is along an offshoot of the Weser River and is the take-off point for excursions to East Frisia. For a **taxi** call ☎22 55. **Rent bikes** at the **Fahrradstation,** adjoining the back of the train station. (☎218 82 40. €7 per day; €3 per day after 3rd day. Open M-Sa 6am-11pm, Su 8am-11pm.) The **tourist office,** Kleine Kirchenstr. 10, is located in center of town and hands out maps and finds rooms for free. From the train station, go right on Moslestr., continue as it becomes Heiligengeistwall, then Theaterwall, and turn left on Bergstr. (☎018 0593 83 33; www.oldenburg-tourist.de. Open M-F 10am-6pm, Sa 10am-2pm.) **Internet** access is at **Telecafé,** Ritterstr. 15, at the corner of Mühlenstr. (☎95 50 40. 1st hr. €2, then €1 per hr. Open M-Sa 9am-8pm, Su 11am-8pm.) Two blocks away, **Teleking,** Staustr. 18, near the corner of Poststr., stays open later. (☎217 62 39. €2 per hr. Open daily 10am-10pm, Sa until 11pm.) The **post office** is to the left of train station. (Open M-F 8am-6:30pm, Sa 9am-1pm.) **Postal Code:** 26123.

◪ ◖ ACCOMMODATIONS AND FOOD

The **Hotel Hegeler ❸,** Donnerschweer Str. 27, is a convenient stop for the weary traveler. Exit from the rear of the station and turn left on Donnerschweer Str. (☎875 61. Breakfast included. Singles €25-47, with bath €47; doubles €55/80. Cash only.) The city's **Jugendherberge (HI) ❷,** Alexanderstr. 65, is 1.5km from the station. Take bus #302 or 303 to Von-Finckh-Str. or take a right out of the train station, pass the post office on your right and continue straight until you reach Staulinie. Cross the street, take a right, and go straight until Pferdemarkt. Go left at the fork in the road onto Alexanderstr.; it's on the left. This concrete complex offers inexpensive, no-frills rooms. (☎871 35; www.djh.de/unterweser. Breakfast included. Reception 5am-11pm. Curfew 10pm, key available. Dorms €16; singles €22; doubles €40. MC/V.) **Pension Helga Bundkiel ❸,** Friedrich-Ruder Str. 30, is a 15min. walk through the Schloßgarten from the city center. Kept by a middle-aged couple, this pension offers well-furnished rooms in a quiet residence overlooking a park. From the train station, take bus #301, 314, 322, or 324 to "Schloßwall" and continue along Elisabethstr. until it intersects Friedrich-Ruder Str. (☎123 40. Singles €30; doubles €40; discounts for longer stays. Breakfast €5. Cash only.)

To get to the rose-covered facade of ▨**Marvin's ❷,** Rosenstr. 8, head up Bahnhofstr. from the train station, and go left on Rosenstr. You'll arrive at an inimitable local hangout with an entertaining menu. Purists stick to "Moon Trip" or "First Aid," from the drinks menu (from €1.30). Choose from a selection of salads, soups, pizzas, and sandwiches for €2.50-7.70. (Open M-Th and Su 7pm-2am, F-Sa 8pm-3am. Cash only.) **Tandour ❷,** Staustr. 18, lets you scribble your order of savory gyros, pastas, or lunch specials (€2.50-7) on scraps of paper and bring them to the counter to be cooked. (☎170 75. Open daily 11am-midnight. Cash only.) **Picknick ❸,** Markt 6, across from the church and Rathaus, cooks regional specialties, like *Rievkoochen* (potato pancakes with applesauce; €4.50). (☎273 76. Open M-Sa from 10am. Cash only.) Check out Wallstr. for a selection of cheap late-night pizza, *kebap*, and pasta places. Oldenburg's market overwhelms the **Rathaus** square with fresh produce (Tu, Th, Sa 8am-2pm).

👁 SIGHTS

Purchase a 🏛**Museumskarte** for €6 from the tourist office or from any museums to gain admission to all sites listed below. The **Landesmuseum für Kunst und Kulturge-schichte** (State Museum for Art and Cultural Heritage) combines three museums, all near the Schloßgarten: the *Schloß*, Augusteum, and Prinzenpalais. The yellow **Schloß**, Schloßpl. 26, presents the city's history using early reliefs depicting executions in the Middle Ages, 17th-century armor, Nazi propaganda, and 1950s cocktail dresses. Don't miss the paper theater display on the top floor. Head down Damm to find the **Augusteum**, Elisabethstr. 1, which houses paintings by the "old masters" of Germany, France, Italy, and the Netherlands from the 12th century onward. Across the street, the **Prinzenpalais**, Damm 1, contains a modern collection, including works by German Expressionists and a room devoted to **Franz Radziwill** canvases. (All 3 museums: ☎220 73 00; www.landesmuseum-oldenburg.de. Open Tu-F 9am-5pm, Th until 8pm, Sa-Su 10am-5pm. Combined ticket €3; students, seniors, and children €1.50.) Walk another 300m to get to the **Landesmuseum für Natur und Mensch** (State Museum for Man and Nature), Damm 38-44, a pink building which formerly housed the Grand Duke's state library from 1846, containing spearheads, mastodons, and other ghosts of Oldenburg's primeval past. (☎924 43 00; www.naturundmensch.de. Open Tu-Th 9am-5pm, F 9am-3pm, Sa-Su 10am-5pm. €3, students and children €1.50.) At the other end of the pedestrian zone, just off Moslestr., the **Stadtmuseum** (Municipal Museum), Am Stadtmuseum 4-8, preserves color-coordinated, stately rooms. The attached **Horst-Janssen-Museum** hosts rotating exhibits on the prolific 20th-century printmaker. (☎235 29 81; www.oldenburg.de/stadtmuseum; www.horst-janssen-museum.de. Both museums open Tu-Su 10am-6pm. Stadtmuseum €1.50, students €0.75. Horst-Janssen-Museum €3.50/1.50. Combined ticket €4/2.25.)

🎵🎭 ENTERTAINMENT AND NIGHTLIFE

Cinemaxx, Stau 79-85, is a modern cinema that features a different current English release each week. (☎217 70; www.cinemaxx.de. Shows M around 8pm and W around 5pm, check online for exact times. €4.50-7.) Nightlife in Oldenburg is centered around **Wallstr.** where casual cafés and sedate awnings give way to streetside *Kneipen* (bars). **Der Schwan**, Stau 34, across from Kaiserstr., is a beer garden with occasional live music. Boats cross the harbor while patrons down cheap beer (€3 per 0.5L) under strings of white lights. (☎261 89. Breakfast buffet served until noon; M-F €5.30, Sa €7, Su €9. Cash only.) Open daily 9am-2am, F-Sa until 3am.) **Cubes,** Baumgartenstr. 2, is a chic restaurant-lounge that transforms into a bar with special club nights. Trendy patrons nursing elaborate mixed drinks (€4.50-8) relax on the large leather sofas before giving in to the lure of hip-hop and pop beats from the dancefloor. (☎326 122. Open M-Sa from 5pm. Cash only.)

OSTFRIESLAND (EAST FRISIA)

Germany's North Sea shoreline and the seven sandy islands strung like pearls a few kilometers off its coast conceal some of the most rewarding—and oft-overlooked—natural and cultural wonders of western Germany. The flat landscape

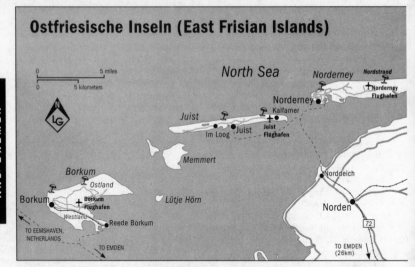

Ostfriesische Inseln (East Frisian Islands)

North Sea

unfolds into North Sea, dotted with windmills, seemingly impenetrable clouds, and foreboding seascapes; this stunning visual wonder throws into sharp relief the neighboring bustle of river valleys and modern skylines. The seafaring Frisians, whose dialect is a close linguistic relative to English, treasure their strong tea, which is customarily served in elaborate porcelain sets over sugar candies called *Kluntje*. A traditional tea ceremony may be filling (it's impolite to drink fewer than three cups), but there's always room for the region's culinary delicacies. Try some *Ostfriesische Rosinenstütten*, a sweet raisin loaf, on display in every bakery, or the unforgettable *Bohnensuppe* (literally, bean soup), which has nothing to do with beans, and is in fact made with raisins, brandy, and sugar. Though buses and trains in the area are often inconvenient, miles of unspoiled beaches, green fields, and rolling dunes compensate for the planning required.

JEVER   ☎ 04461

Jever received city rights 450 years ago from its patroness, Lady Mary, who commissioned art, building fortifications, and a school. The town's modern patron, if recognized begrudgingly by its residents, is the nationally famous local brewery, serving up some of the most refreshing beer in Germany. A regional **rail line** runs to Jever from **Oldenburg** and **Osnabrück** (2½hr., every hr., €16). For a **taxi** call ☎30 30. The **tourist office,** Alter Markt 18, across from the *Schloß*, books rooms for free. From the train station, follow Anton-Günther-Str. to the right, turn left at Mühlenstr. and it will be near the Schloßpl. on the left. (☎710 10; www.stadt-jever.de. Open Mar.-Oct. M-F 9am-6pm; Sa 9am-1pm; Nov.-Feb. M-F 9am-5pm.) From the office, signs indicate the way to major sights. Near the Alter Markt, the **post office** is on Kattrepel. (Open M-F 9am-5:30pm, Sa 9am-12:30pm.) **Postal Code:** 26441.

⬛**Im Schmidz Pension** ❹, Alter Markt 2, matches convenient location with snug comfort and personal touches in the center of town. (☎75 90 36. Breakfast included. Singles €38; doubles €70; 10-15% discount for multiple nights. Cash only.) The **Jugendherberge Jever (HI)** ❶, at Mooshütterweg 12, is well-situated and offers inexpensive rooms. From the train station, take a right onto Anton-Günther-Str. and turn left on Mooshütterweg. (☎35 90; jugendherberge-jever@t-online.de.

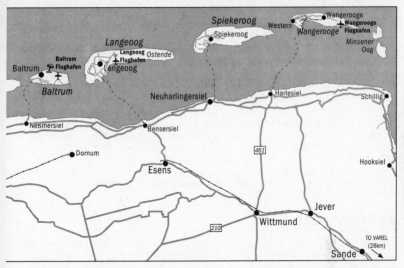

Breakfast and sheets included. Check-in M-F and Su 5-5:30pm, Sa 5:30-6pm; late check-in 9:45pm or call from the front desk. Curfew 10pm, key available. Open Apr.-Oct. €12.70, over 27 €15.50. Cash only.)

⦿Balu ❸, Kattrepel 1a, just across from the post office and tucked in a quiet courtyard off the Altstadt, cooks African specialty dishes like yam wings and plantains, as well as a range of other distinctive finger foods (€10-13). *Salat à la Rosemarie* (€10), with chicken, avocado, orange slices, and warm pita bread, is life-affirmingly good, and draws a loyal local following. (☎70 07 09. Open daily 10am-10pm. Cash only.) A rare late night option in Jever is **La Casetta Pizzeria ❷,** Bahnhofstr. 44. If the selection of 34 pizzas on the menu doesn't satisfy your tastes, try the pasta (€6.70). (☎725 89. Entrées €3-8. Open daily noon-3pm and 5pm-midnight. Cash only.)

North of the Altstadt, the **Freisisches Brauhaus,** Elisabethufer, is a futuristic glass brewing complex that puts Jever on the map—and on tap—all over northern Germany. To reserve **tour** tickets or purchase the essential Jever survival gear (sweatshirt, sun visor, watch, and beer mug), head for **Der Jever-Shop,** Elisabethufer 18. (☎137 11; www.jever.de. Open M-F 9am-7pm, Sa 9am-5pm. 45min. German tours begin at half past every hr. €6.50, including a souvenir mug and 2 glasses of beer. Sa tours go to museum only.) Most *Jeverische* dismiss *pilsner* as their claim to fame by insisting that their finest offering is the castle across from the tourist office. Each room in the salmon-colored, 15th-century **Schloß** details a facet of East Frisian heritage, from intricate traditional tea sets to 18th-century clothing. (☎96 93 50; www.schlossmuseum.de. Open Tu-Su 10am-6pm; May-Sept. also M 11am-5pm. €3, students €1.50, children €1. Tower €1.) Outside, the **Lady Mary Statue** is the city's enduring monument to its beloved patroness. Just outside the castle entrance at the Hof von Oldenburg is a **Glockenspiel,** which goes off every hr. from 11am-noon and 3-6pm, releasing figurines from Jever's history through its trap doors. The cheerful characters, among them Lady Mary and a Russian Empress, extend their hands in greeting. On Kirchpl., the **Stadtkirche** is a product of the citizens' dedication; after it burned down, they reconstructed and modernized it. The ornate brick facade of the Renaissance **Rathaus** is a few blocks away from the main square.

WATTENMEER NATIONAL PARK (NIEDERSACHSEN)

Twice daily, tides rush out of the Wattenmeer National Park, laying kilometers of the ocean floor completely exposed. The Frisian Islands make up one component of a much large and ecologically diverse wonder.The delicately sloping continental shelf along the coast that creates this dramatic ebb and flow sustains a unique ecology at Wattenmeer, the westernmost of Germany's three Wattenmeer parks (p. 270). Dunes formed here millions of years ago, protecting the islands from erosion and the flora and fauna from salt water. Hundreds of local plant and insect species interact in the protected island interiors, while various fish, birds, and invertebrates have evolved to thrive on the surrounding ocean floor mudflats (see **What is this Watt?**, p. 204). Familiar with the intricacies of the Watt terrain and timing of the tides, local experts lead popular **Wattwanderung** (Watt walk) groups out onto the flats during low tides, describing this specialized ecosystem as everyone enjoys a romp in the mud.

✳ ORIENTATION

The National Park stretches along the coast from the **Ems** to the **Weser Rivers.** It includes the coastline as well as the seven **East Frisian Islands.**

> **WATT NOT TO DO.** A few rules apply throughout the park. First, **always keep at least 500m from seals.** Your approach will frighten them and as they flee they are likely to hurt their sensitive underbellies. Second, **do not venture off marked trails within the park** between April and July—you'll disturbed protected bird nesting areas. Third, in areas labeled "Schutzzone I: Ruhezone," **never leave the marked trails at any time of year.** These areas, which make up more than 60% of the park, are especially protected, and you will be **fined** if a ranger catches you anywhere in these areas. Venturing indepedently across the mudflats is generally ill-advised, as the tide rushes in all at once and you can easily get caught in a tidal channel. Let a guide lead you through the intricacies of the unique ecosystem.

▣ TRANSPORTATION

Trains run to Norden and Norddeich from Bremen (2-2½hr., every hr., €26) and Oldenburg (1½-2hr., every hr., €16). Only two mainland ports are accessible by train: **Emden,** the ferry port for Borkum, and Norddeich, the ferry port for Norderney and Juist. The departure points for all other islands lie in a string of tiny ports on the coast, all connected by the costly **Bäderbus,** which runs on a sparse schedule from Norden to Carolinensiel. Be advised: the Bäderbus is not scheduled to connect with departing ferries. The ferry companies servicing **Baltrum** run a separate bus from the Norden train station which is conveniently timed with the ship. Pick up a bus schedule from the train station in Norden and **plan at least a day ahead,** or you may get stuck waiting for hours with no bus or ferry. Watch for new ferry services; companies sometimes run inter-island trips. In general, unless you want to take a tiny, vibrating **plane** for €40-150 (which can get you to all islands except Spiekeroog), you can't travel between islands—you must return to the mainland. To learn all the ins and outs of your chosen island, buy its brochure (in German only) at a regional tourist office. These pamphlets contain extensive accommodations listings and full explanations of local attractions.

⚡ PRACTICAL INFORMATION

Information Centers: A series of **National Park Häuser** offer information and tours; locations include **Baltrum** (p. 273) and **Norderney** (p. 274). Town information centers also have transportation and hiking information, as well as accommodations listings.

Tours: The National Park Häuser offer themed nature tours. Private guided tours of the Watt are also available; see individual town listings.

Climate and Seasonality: The best time to visit is summer, when the weather is typically mild and the migrating birds have arrived. Keep in mind, however, that North Sea weather is a tad temperamental; windy and rainy days are not uncommon even during peak tourist season (July-Sept.). The salt marsh flora bloom late July to early Aug.

NORDEN ☎ 04931

Norden is the transportation hub for excursions around East Frisia.

📠⚡ TRANSPORTATION AND PRACTICAL INFORMATION. Trains travel to Emden (every hr., € 6) and Norddeich (2 per hr., €2), and the Bäderbus provides easy access to most other port towns from which to access all the islands. The train station is 2km from the city center; from the station follow Bahnhofstr. to the right and veer right at the fork onto Neuer Weg. At the pedestrian zone, turn left on Osterstr. to the main market square. Visit the **tourist office,** Am Markt 36, inside the Teemuseum, for transportation information or free room (from €25) reservations. (☎98 62 01. Open M-F 9am-12:30pm and 2-5pm, Sa 9am-4pm.) Turn right at the market to find the post office. (Open M-Sa 8:30am-12:30pm, M-F also 2:30-5:30pm.) **Postal Code:** 26506.

📠📶 ACCOMMODATIONS AND FOOD. Hotel Smutje ❹, Neuer Weg 89, has impeccably clean and comfortable large rooms with bath near the marketplace. (☎942 50. Breakfast included. Singles €39; doubles €58. Discounts for longer stays. Cash only.) Sample East Frisian specialties at **Café Ten Cate ❷,** Osterstr. 153 (☎24 20), where strong *Ostfriesentee* sold by the pot (€7) or the indulgent *Bohnensuppe* (€4.50) will leave you with a surprising buzz. (Open daily 6am-6:30pm. Cash only.) A block away, **Das Kleine Pizzastübchen ❷,** Neuer Weg 121 (☎53 34), near the corner of Osterstr., dishes out generous portions of pizza, gyros, pasta and salad (€3-7). (Open M-Sa 11am-10pm. Cash only.) Across the street, **Mittelhaus ❶,** Neuer Weg 11 (☎97 18 81), has apple strudel and baguettes (€2.70-3), beer (€1.65), and coffee-liquor drinks (€3.50). (Open daily 10am-1am. Cash only.)

📷 SIGHTS. A couple blocks off Neuer Weg, the **Rathaus,** Am Markt 15, looks across the market green at the imposing tower of the 15th-century **Ludgerikirche.** The intricate woodwork and pleasant blue pews inside are lovingly tended by Norden's townspeople. (Open Apr.-Sept. M 10am-12:30pm, Tu-Su 10am-12:30pm and 3-5pm. Organ concerts every W 8pm. €5, students €3.50.) Experience the church's **Glockenspiel** (Bell Routine) at 9am, noon, 3, or 6pm. The East Frisian fascination with tea is explained at the **East Frisian Teemuseum,** Am Markt 36, in the old Rathaus on the southwest side of the market. The museum houses myriad teacups, pots, and silverware associated with northern German tea culture, and features exhibits on historical and modern customs of taking tea. For €1, participate in an East Frisian **tea ceremony** (July-Sept. W 2pm). The **Heimatmuseum** (Local History Museum) in the same building covers the other elements of East Frisian culture, including dike construction and shoemaking. (☎121 00; www.teemuseum.de. Both museums open Mar.-Oct. Tu-Su 10am-5pm; July-Aug. also M 2-5pm. Joint admission €3, students and children €1.50.) For some treasures of the sea, try the **Muschel-&-Schnecken-Museum** (Shell and Snail Museum), In der Gnurre 40, a collection of shells inside an old windmill just off Bahnhofstr. (☎126 15. Open Apr.-Oct. Tu-F 2:30-6pm. €1.50, children €0.50.)

A couple blocks off Neuer Weg, the **Rathaus**, Am Markt 15, looks across the market green at the imposing tower of the 15th-century **Ludgerikirche**. The intricate woodwork and pleasant blue pews inside are lovingly tended by Norden's townspeople. (Open Apr.-Sept. M 10am-12:30pm, Tu-Su 10am-12:30pm and 3-5pm. Organ concerts every W 8pm. €5, students €3.50.) Experience the church's **Glockenspiel** (Bell Routine) at 9am, noon, 3, or 6pm. The East Frisian fascination with tea is explained at the **East Frisian Teemuseum**, Am Markt 36, in the old Rathaus on the southwest side of the market. The museum houses myriad teacups, pots, and silverware associated with northern German tea culture, and features exhibits on historical and modern customs of taking tea. For €1, participate in an East Frisian **tea ceremony** (July-Sept. W 2pm). The **Heimatmuseum** (Local History Museum) in the same building covers the other elements of East Frisian culture, including dike construction and shoemaking. (☎121 00; www.teemuseum.de. Both museums open Mar.-Oct. Tu-Su 10am-5pm; July-Aug. also M 2-5pm. Joint admission €3, students and children €1.50.)

NORDDEICH ☎04931

The busy port of Norddeich, 3km north of its sister city of Norden, is a more logical base camp for budget travelers, offering affordable accommodations, easy access to the ferry network, and spectacular seascapes along a string of beaches.

⌐✈ TRANSPORTATION AND PRACTICAL INFORMATION. The convenient **train** station is **Norddeich-Mole**, which is the end of the line. To reach town, follow the crowds uphill and over the dike to the right. Badestr. runs parallel to the dike and intersects Dörper Weg after 800m. **Ferries** leave Norddeich two-three times daily for Norderney and Juist. Pick up schedules in the ferry ticket offices outside of the train station. **Bike** rental shops line Dörper Weg; many also rent **go-carts** from €3 per hr. (Bikes about €7 per day, €25 per week; ID required.) The patient staff at the Norddeich **tourist office**, Dörper Weg 22, finds rooms for free, hands out ferry schedules, gives information about **Watt tours**, and offers the only **Internet** access (€4.50 per hr.; €10 deposit) for miles. (☎83 75 200; www.norddeich.de. Open M-F 9am-5pm, Sa 10am-5pm, Su 10am-1pm.) For a **taxi**, call ☎80 00. The **post office** is in the Fernseh Hemken building on Frisiastr., which intersects Badestr. near the train station. **Postal Code:** 26506.

⌐⌐ ACCOMMODATIONS AND FOOD. The town's **Jugendherberge (HI) ❶**, Strandstr. 1, is excellent for those lucky enough to snatch a reservation: it's cheap, clean, and right in the center of town. From Badestr., turn left just past the Hotel Regina Maris; the hostel is on the next corner on the left. The main hostel compound is generally filled with school groups, but the adjacent *Blockhütten* (pine cabins) provide some escape. (☎80 64; fax 818 28. Breakfast included. Reception 5-8pm. Book weeks, preferably a season in advance. €14, over 27 €17. €5.80 to pitch your own tent in the backyard. MC/V.) **Hotel Seeblick ❸**, Badestr. 11, provides snug rooms near the beach at unbeatable prices. (☎80 86; fax 16 84 84. Breakfast included. Reception 8am-10pm in the restaurant below. June-Sept. singles €25; doubles €45. Oct.-Apr. 10% discount. Cash only.) **Gästehaus Merlan ❷**, Kakteenweg 7, just off of Deichstr., has roomy doubles and red-bricked apartments, each with cable TV, radio, and private bath. (☎816 30; fax 816 15. Reservations strongly recommended. Doubles €48, including breakfast; 2- to 6-person apartments €23 per person. Cash only.) **Nordsee-Camp ❶**, Deichstr. 21, is 20min. farther down Badestr., which becomes Deichstr. It has impressive views (though dike-side camping gets chilly), a cheap bar, and a not-so-cheap grocery store on the grounds. (☎80 73; fax 80 74. Reception until 10pm. Open mid-Mar. to Oct. €2.60 per person, €6.80 per day. *Kurtaxe* €1.50.) ◪**Diekster Köken ❸**, Deichstr. 6 (☎822 42), serves fresh regional fare that attracts locals and tourists alike. Specialties include delicious potato pancakes (€3-15), served with almost anything, and fresh seafood (€12-20). (Open daily 9am-10pm. MC/V.)

◙ **SIGHTS.** At the **Seehundstation,** Dörper Weg 22, in the park behind the tourist office, injured North Sea seals are rehabilitated before their return to the wild. Get up close and personal with the playful sea critters, who entertain with their under-water acrobatics on the other side of a glass wall. (☎89 19; www.seehundstation-norddeich.de. Open daily 10am-5pm. €2, children €1, family €5.)

BALTRUM ISLAND ☎ 04939

The smallest of the Frisian Islands with only 500 residents, Baltrum is dominated by bold wildlife—rabbits and pheasants regularly emerge from the brush to size you up. A ban on motor vehicles creates a much-treasured silence, broken only by the occasional animal call or clopping of horse hooves. Houses are numbered in the order they were built, which seems charming until you have to find one.

◧◪ **TRANSPORTATION AND PRACTICAL INFORMATION.** To reach Baltrum, take the **ferry** company bus from the Norden train station to **Neßmersiel.** Ferry times vary greatly, as the boats can only travel this route close to low tide. The first ferry leaves for Baltrum anywhere between 6am and 2:30pm, the last ferry returns between 2 and 9:30pm. (June-Nov. 2-3 per day. Open-ended return €21, children €10. Daytrip €16/7.50.) **Buses** leave Norden about 1hr. before the ferry (€6 round-trip). Check the schedule at the information signs at the market square in Norden or www.wattfuehrer.com. For more information, call the ferry company, **Reederei Baltrum Linie** (☎913 00.) The **tourist office,** in the Rathaus, Nr. 130, books private rooms and helps coordinate transportation to the island. Turn right at the harbor exit and then take the third left; it's near the end of the road on the left. (☎800; www.baltrum.de. Open M-F 9am-noon, Sa-Su 10am-noon.) For essential **hiking** tips and bird-call lessons, head to the **National Park Haus,** Nr. 177, to your right as you leave the harbor. (☎469. Open Tu-F 10am-noon and 3-7pm, Sa-Su 3-7pm.) ◪**Watt tours** between the island and the mainland during low tide are quite popular. For tour times, call a local *Wattführer* or look for signs at the tourist office. **Family Ortelt** runs tours for Baltrum, Norderney, Langeoog, and Spiekeroog in German supplemented with some essential English. (☎04933 17 06; www.wattfuehrer.com. 2½hr. €20, children €13, including ferry.) Hansjürgen Barow also leads a tour to the mainland in German. (☎918 20. 2½hr. €21, children €13, including ferry.) The **post office** is across the street, Nr. 43. (Open M-F 9am-noon and 3-5pm, Sa 9am-noon.) **Postal Code:** 26579.

◧◪ **ACCOMMODATIONS AND FOOD.** To get to **Haus Störtebeker ❷**, Nr. 167, from the National Park Haus, turn right and take the third left, between two brick walls. Take the next right; it will be on your right, overlooking the water. All rooms have full size beds and huge windows. (☎295; www.stoertebeker-baltrum.de. Kitchen available. Singles €25. Call in advance as reception times vary. Cash only.) **Jugendbildungsstätte ❶** lets you camp within the National Park. Turn right immediately after the harbor and continue for 1.5km along the bike path. (☎04941 99 11 64. Cot and tent included. Open June-Sept. €7 per person, €5.50 per child.

Kurkarte €2.30/0.50. Cash only.) For cheap eats, **Strandcafé ❷**, Nr. 70, contains a cafeteria-style restaurant serving pizza, salads, pasta, sausages, and potatoes (all items under €10) and is apparently staffed by every teenager on the island. Go past Haus Störtebeker until the road forks, stay left, and continue until you reach the sand dunes at the end of the road. (☎200. Open daily 10am-midnight. Closed M in off-season.) Where the road splits after Haus Störtebeker, **Kiek Musikkniepe**, Nr. 123, lights up with late entertainment and occasional live music. (☎89 60. Open daily from 9pm. Cash only.)

▧ **HIKING.** To get to the trailhead from the **National Park Haus,** take a right and continue for 600m. Take the fourth left (just past the pond on your right) and then the first right. Follow the path as it curves to the right before a large off-white house. From there take an immediate left and then the following left; take the stairs over the large sand dune with its peak enclosed by faded green fences and continue east on the middle path for 400m. Stay left when the path merges as you enter the *Ruhezone* after another 300m. From here, there are two hiking options options. For a short hike (1¾hr.), continue straight for 500m and make a right onto the riding and hiking path marked alternately with red and green markers. The trail eventually brings you back to the road from which you began. For a long hike (3hr.), go left toward the beach; from there you can walk through the sand dunes or parallel to the dunes along the beach. For the dunes, take the first right. For the beach, walk until you hit the sand, then turn right. Both paths head east to the end of the island. Once there, you can either double back the way you came or take the **Watt Trail;** which is **only accessible within 1hr. of the tide;** check with the **National Park Haus.** Taking this trail adds at least 1hr. to the long hike; make sure you budget enough time to emerge before the tide rushes in. If you hike the Watt trail in the other direction, be careful not to miss the trailhead coming back into town. To enter the Watt trail eastward, go to the *Jugendstätte* campground, then fork right, curving around to the south. When you hit the Watt, lose your shoes, roll up your pant leg, and enjoy the 1hr. slosh east through the mud.

NORDERNEY ISLAND   ☎04932

The holiday destination of Otto Van Bismarck and Heinrich Heine, Norderney celebrates tourist success despite its status as the youngest of the seven East Frisian islands, with postcard and beach-bucket shops and some of the best-maintained trails in the National Park. Though only 6500 people call the island home, tides of sunburned Germans swell the population to 60,000 on warm days. The entire eastern half of the Norderney is a wildlife refuge within the park.

▦▧ **TRANSPORTATION AND PRACTICAL INFORMATION. Ferry Company Frisia** runs from Norddeich to Norderny. (☎04931 98 70 in Norden; ☎91 30 in Norderney; www.reederei-frisia.de. 1hr., 9-13 per day. 1st departure July-Aug. daily 6:30am; Sept.-June Sa-Su 7:15am. Last return between 6 and 7:15pm. Check schedules online and at the Norddeich tourist office for exact times. Round-trip €15.) For a **taxi,** call ☎23 45 or 33 33. A bike is essential for getting around; be sure to walk it through pedestrian zones designated by blue and white signs. Two **bike rental** shops are located just beyond the harbor. **Dicki Verleih** is on Gorch-Fock-Weg and also at Jann-Berghaus-Str. 62 in the town center. (☎33 78. €1.50-2 per hr., €6.50-8 per day. Open daily 9am-6pm.) **Reinke's Fahrradverleih am Hafen,** Hafenstr. 1, is 300m down Hafenstr. as you step off the ferry. (☎13 26. Open daily 9am-6pm. €1.50-2 per hr., €5.50-6.50 per day.) To spend the night, line up early at the busy **tourist office,** Bülowallee 5, at the end of Hafenstr. The staff, who speak only German, find rooms (typically over €50) for a €4.50 fee or free by phone. (☎918 50;

fax 824 94. Open M-F 9am-12:30pm and 2-6pm, Sa 10am-3pm, Su 11am-2pm.) Information about exploring the island can be found at the **National Park Haus,** directly on your left as you leave the ferry, which sells maps (€2), teaches about the local wildlife (in German), and displays stuffed birds. (☎20 01. Open May-Oct. Tu-Su 10am-6pm, Nov.-Apr. Tu-F 10am-5pm, Sa-Su 2-5pm.)

ACCOMMODATIONS AND FOOD. Norderney has two youth hostels, both of which are relatively expensive and fill up early. To get to the centrally located **Jugendherberge Südstraße (HI) ❷**, Südstr. 1, turn right on Deichstr. just outside the harbor, then turn onto Südstr.; it's on the right. This small house is one of Germany's oldest hostels, offering minimalist eight- to 14-bed dorms. (☎24 51; fax 836 00. Full board included. Reception 5-5:30pm. Reserve in advance. Open Mar.-Oct. Dorms €22.20, after 3 nights €20.40; over 27 €25/23.20; all prices include *Kurtaxe*. Cash only.) **Hotel Aquamarin ❸**, Friedrichstr. 5, has sparkling cerulean rooms and a sunny veranda. (☎928 50; www.hotel-aquamarin-norderney.de. *Ostfriesiche* Breakfast (assortment of cheese, smoked fish, eggs cooked to order, and tea) €10. All rooms €35-60 per person. D/MC/V.) The main campsite on the island is **Camping Booken ❶**, Waldweg 2. (☎448; fax 478. Wash €3, dry €3. €6.40 per person, €4.50 per tent. Showers €0.50 from 9pm-9am, otherwise free. Cash only.)

Norderney's restaurants are pricey (entrées €12-20), and come adorned with fake lobsters and fish netting. The most enthusiastically recommended seafood in town is at **Bootshaus ❸**, Am Hansendamm 1. From the ferry dock walk around the harbor; it's on the other end. The fresh crab soup (€5.20) is creamy and delicious. (☎28 50. Entrées from €7.20. Open daily from 11am. Kitchen closes 10pm.) For the perfect afternoon pick-me-up, stop by **Café Marienhohe**, Am Weststrand, for *Ostfriesentee* by the cup (€2.10) and a slice of *Rosinenstütten* (sweet raisin pastry; €2.50). (☎686. Open M-Sa 8am-8pm. Cash only.) For groceries, try **Plus**, Hafenstr. 6, 200m from the harbor exit. (Open M-Sa 8am-8pm, Su 10am-3pm.)

SIGHTS AND HIKING. The town's tiny 16th-century **Evangelische Inselkirche** (Evangelical Island Church) sits in the center of town near the end of Bülowallee. Model ships hang from the bright orange ceiling, and contrasting white trim adds elegance to the straight-backed pews. (Open M-Th 8am-5pm, Su after the service until 5pm. Free.) Away from town, the dunes and beaches of the eastern half of the island are part of the national park. Areas designated **FKK** for *Freier Körper Kultur* ("free body culture") are nude beaches. To go for a **Watt tour**, call local expert seaman Kurt Knittel (☎04931 30 96; www.mit-kurt-ins-watt.de); his tour is 2½hr. and includes a bus from Norddeich to Neßmersiel, an explanation of sea creatures along the walk to Norderney (in German), and a ferry ticket back to Norddeich. (€21; pick up a schedule at the ferry office or call for departure times.) There are three good ways to see the island: a bike trail, a medium hike, or a long hike. All three begin by leaving the bike shop and traveling down Deichstr. past the large industrial cylinders on your right. As you round the long curve in the road, cross the street and take the path above the dike. The trail curves sharply to the left 300m later; follow it and walk along the right side for another 500m past the golf course. If you want to do the **⊠bike trail,** look for a sign for Trail 4 on your right. Cross onto Trail 4, which will take you along the coast. After 5km, you'll ride into **Parkplatz Ostheller.** Look for the bike path on your left as you go down the ramp from the dike trail. Take this path to the lighthouse. If you keep going straight, you can return to town (12km, under 2hr.). Continue, make a right onto Trail 2. After about 1km it stops abruptly, but breaks off another 50m to your right leading into the town of Norderney. Once in town, take Emsstr. past rows of houses, and through the pedestrian zone and Fannenstr. Make a left on Poststr., which will eventually bring you to the harbor (17km, 3½hr.).

To **hike,** follow the bike trail to Parkpl. Ostheller, park your bike, and walk up the ramp over the dike. Trail 5 begins to the right. Continue on Trail 5 for 3km until you reach the **Möwendune,** a wooden lookout tower. Piles of stacked rocks designate the way. Loop around the tower to head back to the parking place (1km biking, 6km hiking, 2½-3hr. total). For a longer hike, continue on Trail 5 past the Möwendune to the end of the island. Here, a large colony of seals calls Norderney's tip home. Continue down the beach to the left, keeping the trail markers in sight. With the Möwendune on your left, walk toward the tip from the beach. Turn right on the trail and head to the parking lot (14km, 4½-5hr.).

BORKUM ISLAND   ☎ 04922

Lodged in an inlet halfway between Germany and the Netherlands, Borkum, the largest of the seven islands, is where industrious Germans go to do nothing. Though in the summer months the island sees too many tourists chasing too few beds, the atmosphere is festive and laid-back—tiny painted trains cart vacationers through a serene, flower-filled landscape to the bustling town at the far end of the island. Every year, Borkum's beaches send home thousands of pale Germans with vicious sunburn as a tell-tale souvenir, but still they return.

🖪🏢 TRANSPORTATION AND PRACTICAL INFORMATION. AG-EMS (☎01805 18 01 82; www.ag-emes.de; office in the Emden train station open M-F 8:30am-5pm) runs a **ferry** from Emden's *Außenhaven* (outer harbor) to the island (2hr.; June-Sept. 2-3 per day; morning ferry departs for Borkum at 7:15am; last return ferry leaves Borkum Apr.-Dec. 4:30pm; Jan.-Mar. 1:30pm. Open-ended return €34.50. Ticket window opens 1hr. before departure.) You can get to the island in half the time on the **catamaran.** (1hr.; first departing ferry Apr.-Dec. 9:15am; Jan.-Mar. 12:30pm. Last return ferry 5:30pm, 4:30pm Jan.-Mar. Round-trip €37.50.) On Borkum, unless you are staying at the hostel, take the train to town (fare included in ferry ticket). In town, rent **bikes** at the **Fahrradverleih** in the train station with an ID or credit card. (☎30 90. €2.10 per hr., €7.20 per day. Open M-Sa 7am-6pm, Su 8:30am-6pm.) Borkum's **tourist office,** Am Georg-Schütte-Pl. 5, across from the train station in town, books rooms for free. (☎93 30; www.borkum.de. Open M-F 9am-12:30pm and 2-5:30pm, Sa 10am-noon and 2-5pm; Su 11am-noon and 2-5pm.)

🖪🍴 ACCOMMODATIONS AND FOOD. Overnight accommodations in Borkum are usually available only with reservations at least a month in advance and up to three months in advance for summer weekends. The reliable **Jugendherberge (HI) ❷,** Reedestr. 231, a 5min. walk from the dock, prefers guests to confirm by email at least one month in advance. (☎579; jh-borkum@djh-unterweser-ems.de. Full board included. Curfew 10:30pm, key available. Closed Dec. Dorms €19.20, over 27 €21.50; singles €34; doubles €67.50; *Kurtaxe* €2.50. MC/V.) **Pension Stella-Maris ❷,** Alte Schulstr. 9, is just around the corner from the station; follow Strand-str. and take the first right. Snug rooms with wicker wardrobes and slanted paneled ceilings await. (☎26 14. Breakfast included. Singles €20-24; doubles €48-66. Call ahead for reception. Cash only.) **Insel-Camping ❶,** Hindenburgstr. 114, is 15min. from the train station. Even pitching a tent may require reservations. (☎10 88; fax 42 34. €12.50 per person, tent included. *Kurtaxe* €2.50.) Restaurants line Bismarckstr. A hip crowd snacks on baguettes, wraps, and desserts among the leopard-skin bar stools of **Café Coffee? Bar ❷,** Bismarckstr. 16 (☎92 42 86. Salads, pastries, baguettes, soups €2-7. Open daily 9am-2am. Cash only.)

🖪 SIGHTS. Although Borkum's **beaches** are the real draw, the island also offers some indoor attractions good for a few hours of fun. Though the 19th-century **Alter**

Leuchtturm (Old Lighthouse) on the island's eastern shore no longer operates, tourists can still ascend the attractive brick tower to savor the panoramic views. From the station, follow Strandstr. until it ends and turn right on Wilhelm-Bakker-Str. (Open M, W, Sa 10am-noon; July-Sept. also F 10am-noon. €1.50, students €1.) One block past the lighthouse, the **Heitmatmuseum** displays interesting articles of island culture, including a full whale skeleton and a knot collection that would make any sailor proud. (☎48 60. Open Apr.-Oct. Tu-Su 10am-noon and 3-5pm; Nov.-Mar. Tu and Su 3pm-5pm. Tours Apr.-Oct. W 5pm; €4. Museum €3, children €1.50.) On the grassy knoll just behind the train station, the **Neuer Leuchtturm,** successor to the old lighthouse, is also open for your stair-climbing enjoyment. (Open daily 10-11:30am and 3-4:30pm; Apr.-Oct. also M, W, F-Sa 7-9pm. €1.50, students €1.)

The **bike loop** on Borkum (25km) connects numerous trails along the way, allowing for shorter hikes over the sand dunes. Begin the trail at the beachfront in town and follow the Strandweg path to the right, hugging the shoreline until you reach the sand dunes. This path winds up to the northern shore and follows the beach all the way to the easternmost tip of the island. From here the *Deich-und Salzwiesenweg* path continues to your right, bringing you out of the dunes, through grassy plains, across the main highway, and to the far southern shore. The path then follows the coast to the right and meets up with Strandweg, leading back to town.

NIEDERSACHSEN AND BREMEN

NORDRHEIN-WESTFALEN (NORTH RHINE-WESTPHALIA)

In 1946, the victorious Allies attempted to expedite Germany's recovery by merging the traditionally distinct regions of Westphalia, Lippe, and the Rheinland to unify the economic and industrial nucleus of post-war Germany. The resulting *Land*, Nordrhein-Westfalen, defies all German stereotypes. A dense concentration of highways and rail lines forms the infrastructure of the most heavily populated and economically powerful region in Germany, where an industrial boom during the late 19th century sparked social democracy, trade unionism, and revolutionary communism. The enormous wealth of the region continues to support a multitude of cultural offerings for the citizens of and visitors to its lively urban center, even in the face of high unemployment and recession. While industrial squalor may have inspired the philosophy of Karl Marx and Friedrich Engels, the natural beauty of the Teutoburg mountains (p. 314), coupled with the intellectual energy of Cologne and Düsseldorf (p. 299), have spurred writers from Goethe to Heine.

HIGHLIGHTS OF NORDRHEIN-WESTFALEN

SLURP UP CHOCOLATE from an special fountain (or *Kölsch*) in **Cologne** (Köln, p. 278), internationally renowned for its striking **Dom.**

PAY YOUR RESPECTS at **Beethoven's birthplace** (in Bonn, p. 288) and **Aachen's** (p. 295) collection of **Charlemagne's body parts,** or visit **Münster's** (p. 310) **Leprosy Museum**. Despite the body count, these hip university towns are alive and well.

STRUT WITH STYLE down the "Kö"—a glitzy strip of designer boutiques in **Düsseldorf** (p. 299), the nation's undisputed fashion cop. By night, its citizens retire to the procession of over 500 *Kneipen* (the "longest bar in the world") lining the city's Altstadt.

KÖLN (COLOGNE)   ☎ 0221

Founded as a Roman colony (*colonia*, hence Köln) in 32 BC by Agrippina, wife of Roman Emperor Claudius, Cologne was Petrarch's "city of dreams" when the rest of Germany was just wilderness. Cologne's modern prosperity camouflages the staggering damage it sustained in WWII, when relentless air raids crumbled 90% of the city center. Looming over the city skyline, the legendary Dom serves as a reminder of a turbulent past; though it eclipses all other churches in Gothic splendor, discolored stones mark old war wounds. The cathedral miraculously remained intact despite the 14 bombs that struck its north end, and currently sees 22,000 visitors daily. Today, Cologne is North Rhein-Westphalia's largest city and its cultural center, with a wide range of world-class museums and theatrical offerings. The city's long history includes a variety of traditionally extravagant festivals and celebrations. Each year, *Karneval* plunges Cologne into a frenzy of parades, costume balls, and intoxication for the week before Lent. Meanwhile, locally brewed *Kölsch* beer helps to instill a festive mentality all year, and the city's expanding nightlife scene indulges eclectic tastes of the university crowd, whose presence keeps the city buzzing 24 hours a day.

Nordrhein-Westfalen (North Rhine-Westphalia)

⌐ TRANSPORTATION

Flights: Flights depart from **Köln-Bonn Flughafen.** Flight information ☎018 03 80 38 03; www.koeln-bonn-airport.de. S13 leaves the train station M-Fevery 20min., Sa-Su every 30min. Shuttle to **Berlin** 24 per day 6:30am-8:30pm.

Trains: Berlin (4½hr., every hr., €75-90); **Düsseldorf** (30min.-1hr., 5-7 per hr., €9-17); **Frankfurt** (1¼-2hr., 2 per hr., €35-55); **Hamburg** (4hr., 2-3 per hr., €63-78); **Munich** (4½-5hr., 1-2 per hr., €85-110). International Service to: **Amsterdam, Netherlands** (2½-3½hr., 2 per hr., €37-47); **Paris, France** (4hr., every 2 hr., €87-120).

Ferries: Köln-Düsseldorfer (☎208 83 18; www.k-d.com) begins its popular Rhein cruises here, at the end of Salzg. Sail to **Koblenz** (€34, €37 round-trip) or see the castles along the Rhein to **Mainz** (€46/€53). Ships to **Bonn** (€10.80/12.80) offer a scenic alternative to trains. Children ages 4-13 travel for €3.20 on cruises, seniors ½-price M and F. Many trips are covered by Eurail and German railpasses.

Public Transportation: VRS offices have free maps of the S- and U-Bahn, bus, and tram lines; 1 office is downstairs in the Hauptbahnhof, at the U-Bahn station. Major terminals include the **Hauptbahnhof, Neumarkt,** and **Appellhofpl.** Single ride €1.20-8, depending on distance. Day pass €5.50. The *Minigruppen-Ticket* (from €7.50) allows up to 5 people to ride M-F 9am-midnight and all day Sa-Su. Wk. tickets €12-20.

Gondolas: Kölner Seilbahn, Rhiehlerstr. 180 (☎547 41 84), U17-U19 (dir.: Ebertpl./ Mülheim) to "Zoo/Flora." Float over the Rhein from the Zoo to the Rheinpark, enjoying the spectacular cityscape. €3.80, children ages 4-12 €2.20; round-trip €5.50/€3. Open Apr.-Oct. daily 10am-6pm, last ride 5:45pm.

Taxis: Funkzentrale, ☎28 82.

Car Rental: Hertz, Bismarckstr. 19-21 (☎515 08 47). Open M-F 7:30am-6pm, Sa 8am-noon. **Avis, InterRent Europcar,** and **Alamo** also have airport offices.

Bike Rental: Kölner Fahrradverleih, Markmannsg. (☎0171 629 87 96), in the Altstadt. €2 per hr., €10 per day, €40 per wk.; €25 deposit. Open daily 10am-6pm.

Ride Share: Citynetz Mitfahrzentrale, Maximilianstr. 2 (☎194 40). Turn left from the back of the train station. Open daily 9am-7pm.

Hitchhiking: *Let's Go* does not recommend hitchhiking. Opportunities in Cologne are limited; hitchers have been known to look for rides at the train station or the airport.

✳ 🞄 ORIENTATION AND PRACTICAL INFORMATION

Eight bridges cross the Rhein; nearly all the sights are on the western side of the river. The **Altstadt** (also called the **Innenstadt**) is split into two districts: **Altstadt-Nord** near the main train station, and **Altstadt-Süd** just south of the Severinsbrücke. The convenient **Köln WelcomeCard,** sold at the tourist office, gives generous discounts on city museums, Rhein cruises, and bike rentals as well as free use of public transportation (1-day card €9; 2-day card €14; 3-day card €19).

Tourist Office: KölnTourismus, Unter Fettenhennen 19 (☎22 13 04 10; www.koelntourismus.de), opposite the Dom, has free city maps and books rooms for a €3 fee. The €1 booklet "*Köln im* [month]" gives city info and event schedules. A €2 brochure has maps and overviews of all sights. Open M-Sa 9am-9pm, July-Sept. 9am-10pm; Su 10am-6pm.

Budget Travel: STA Travel, Zülpicher Str. 178 (☎44 20 11). U8 or U9 to "Universität." Makes ISICs and books flights. Open M-F 10am-6pm, Sa 11am-2pm.

Currency Exchange: At the Reisebank in the train station. Open daily 7am-10pm. Also at the tourist office.

American Express: Burgmauerstr. 14 (☎925 90 10), near the Dom. Open M-F 9am-6pm, Sa 10am-1pm.

Bookstore: Gonski, Neumarkt 18a (☎20 90 90). Great selection of English bestsellers and classics on the 5th fl. Open M-Sa 9:30am-8pm.

Women's Resources: Frauenamt, Markmansg. 7 (☎22 12 64 82), has a friendly staff ready to field questions. Open M-Th 8am-4pm, F 8am-noon.

Mitwohnzentrale (Room Share): Im Ferkulum 4, finds apartments for long stays. (☎194 40. Open daily 8am-8pm.)

Laundromat: Eco-Express Waschsalon, at the corner of Richard-Wagner-Str. and Händelstr. Wash €2. Soap €0.50. Dry €0.50 per 10min. Open M-Sa 6am-11pm. **Waschsalon,** Severinstr. 74. Wash €3. Dry €0.50 per 10min. Open M-Sa 6am-11pm.

Emergency: Police ☎110. **Fire and Ambulance** ☎112. A police station is located at Maximinenstr. 6 (☎299 61 30), behind the train station.

Pharmacy: Apotheke im Hauptbahnhof, at the back of the train station, near platform 11 (☎139 11 12). Open M-F 6am-8pm, Sa 9am-8pm.

Internet Access: Telepoint Callshop & Internet C@fe, Komödenstr. 19 (☎250 99 30), by the Dom. €1.50 per hr. Open M-F 8:30am-midnight, Sa-Su 9am-midnight. **Branch:** Fleischmengerg. 33 (☎397 52 46), near Neumarkt. €1 per hr. Open M-F 8:30am-midnight, Sa-Su 10am-midnight.

Post Office: At the corner of Breite Str. and Tunisstr. in the *WDR-Arkaden* shopping gallery. Open M-F 9am-7pm, Sa 9am-2pm. **Postal Code:** 50667.

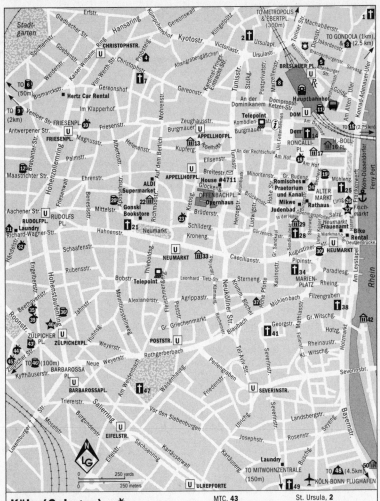

NORDRHEIN-WESTFALEN

Köln (Cologne)

🏠🏠 ACCOMMODATIONS
Campingplatz Poll, **48**
Das Kleine Stapelhäus'chen, **26**
Hotel Am Rathaus, **24**
Hotel Berg, **5**
Hotel Heinzelmännchen, **37**
Hotel Im Kupferkessel, **4**
Jugendgästehaus Köln-Riehl, **3**
Jugendherberge Köln-Deutz, **15**
Pension Jansen, **31**
Station Hostel for Backpackers, **8**

🍴 FOOD & DRINK
Brauhaus Früh am Dom, **18**
Café Magnus, **36**
Café Orlando, **35**
Eis Café Firenze, **23**
Engel Bät, **39**
Feynsin, **44**
Ganesha, **32**
Päffgen-Brauerei, **10**

🍸⭐ BARS & NIGHTLIFE
Alter Wartesaal, **11**
Cent Club, **40**
Cuba Bar, **46**
Das Ding, **45**
Gloria, **20**
Hotel Timp, **30**
M20, **12**

MTC, **43**
Papa Joe's Jazzlokal, **27**
Pitter, **19**
Stadtgarten, **6**
Underground, **9**

🕇 CHURCHES
Alt St. Alban, **28**
Dom, **14**
Groß St. Martin, **25**
St. Aposteln, **21**
St. Georg, **41**
St. Gereon, **7**
St. Kunibert, **1**
St. Maria im Kapitol, **34**
St. Maria Lyskirchen, **38**
St. Pantaleon, **47**
St. Severin, **49**
St. Ursula, **2**

🏛 MUSUEMS
Käthe-Kollwitz-Museum, **22**
Imhoff-Stollwerck-Museum, **50**
Museum Ludwig, **16**
Museum Schnütgen, **33**
NS-Dokumentations-Zentrum, **13**
Römisch-Germanisches Museum, **17**
Schokoladen-museum, **42**
Wallraf-Richartz Museum, **29**

ACCOMMODATIONS AND CAMPING

Cologne's hotels fill up and charge more from March to October, when trade winds blow conventioneers into town. The main hotel haven is **Brandenburger Str.**, on the less exciting side of the train station. Looking for last-minute rooms during *Karneval* is an exercise in futility—book up to a year ahead.

Station Hostel for Backpackers, Marzellenstr. 44-56 (☎912 53 01; www.hostel-cologne.de). Abuzz with backpackers, boasting a social and relaxed in-house bar (*Kölsch* €2). Breakfast €3. Towels €1 with €5 deposit. Laundry €4. Free Internet access. Reception 24hr. Check-in 2pm. Check-out noon. 4- to 6-bed dorms €17-21; singles €27-30; doubles €45-52; triples €72. Cash only. ❷

Pension Jansen, Richard-Wagner-Str. 18 (☎25 18 75), on the 3rd fl. U1, U6, U7, U12, or U15 to "Rudolfpl." Close to nightlife hotspots. Pension with social atmosphere, sky-high ceilings, and shared bathrooms. The resident pet bunny befriends all. Breakfast included. Singles €31-42; doubles €62. Discount for longer stays. Cash only. ❸

Jugendherberge Köln-Deutz (HI), Siegesstr. 5 (☎81 47 11; www.koeln-deutz.jugendherberge.de), just over the *Hohenzollernbrücke*. U1 or 7-9 to "Deutzer Freiheit." Exit the station toward Siegesstr.; the hostel is 100m ahead. This newly-built, massive, and family-oriented hostel with minishop offers superbly clean rooms, all with shower and toilet. Breakfast and sheets included. Laundry €1. Internet access €4 per hr. Reception 24hr. Dorms €23.50; singles €39.80; doubles €59.80. MC/V. ❷

Das Kleine Stapelhäus'chen, Fischmarkt 1-3 (☎272 77 77; www.koeln-altstadt.de/stapelhaeuschen.com).An old-fashioned *Rheinisch* inn with a green-and-pink front, featuring carved oak bed frames. Reception in the restaurant below. Breakfast included. Singles €39-51, with shower or full bath €52-81; doubles €64-85/€90-141. MC/V. ❹

Hotel Heinzelmännchen, Hohe Pforte 5-7 (☎21 12 17; hotel.koeln@netcologne.de). Bus #132 (dir.: Frankenstr.) to "Waidmarkt." Fairy-tale pictures decorate the quiet rooms of this family-run hotel. Breakfast included. Reception 6am-10pm. Singles €40-45; doubles €65-70; triples €80-85. Discounts for stays over 2 nights. MC/V. ❹

Hotel Im Kupferkessel, Probsteig. 6 (☎270 79 60). Spacious, simple rooms with TV and telephone. Breakfast included. Singles €30-49; doubles €66. AmEx/MC/V. ❸

Jugendgästehaus Köln-Riehl (HI), An der Schanz 14 (☎76 70 81; jh-koeln-riehl@djh-rheinland.de). U17-U19 (dir.: Ebertpl./Mülheim) to "Boltensternstr." Or, walk along the Rhein on Konrad-Adenauer-Ufer as it becomes Niederländer Ufer and finally An der Schanz (40min.). Carpeted rooms with baths at a tree-lined location along the Rhein, if farther from the nightlife. Breakfast included. Reception 24hr. Dorms €25.30; singles €38.10; doubles €61.20. HI members only. MC/V. ❸

Hotel Am Rathaus, Bürgerstr. 6 (☎257 76 24; www.hostel-am-rathaus-koeln.de). On your right as you stand on the front porch of the Rathaus, demonstrating the true value of location. Reception in the bar below. Breakfast included. Singles €38, with bath €43; doubles €58/62; triples €75. AmEx/MC/V. ❸

Campingplatz Poll, Weidenweg (☎83 19 66), southeast of the Altstadt on the Rhein. U16 to "Heinrich-Lübke-Ufer," cross the bridge (15min.). Reception 8am-noon and 5-8pm. Open mid-Apr. to Oct. Tent sites €8. Extra person €5. MC/V. ❶

FOOD

Cologne's local cuisine centers on sausage, but also offers hungry visitors delicious *Rievkooche*—slabs of fried potato to dunk in *Apfelmus* (apple sauce). Don't pass through without sampling the city's smooth *Kölsch* beer. Local brews include *Sion*, *Küppers*, *Früh*, *Gaffel*, and the devout *Dom*. Cheap restaurants and cafés packed with students line **Zülpicher Str.** Take U8 or U9 to "Zülpicher Pl." Mid-priced ethnic restaurants are concentrated around the perimeter of the Altstadt, particularly from Hohenzollernring to Hohenstaufenring. The city's best deals are found in the Turkish district on Weideng. North of Ebertpl., an **open-air market** on **Wilhelmsplatz** takes over the **Nippes** neighborhood. (Open M-Sa 8am-1pm.) **ALDI**, Richmodstr. 31, is a no-frills supermarket. (Open M-F 9am-7pm, Sa 8am-4pm.)

🏮 **Päffgen-Brauerei,** Friesenstr. 64-66 (☎13 54 61). U3-U6, U12, or U15 to "Friesenplatz." A local favorite since 1883. Legendary *Kölsch* (€1.25) is brewed on the premises and enjoyed in cavernous halls; bring your friends—the room seats 600. Meals €2-20. Open daily 10am-midnight. Kitchen open 11:30am-11pm. Cash only. ❸

🏮 **Engel Bät,** Engelbertstr. 7 (☎24 69 14). U8 or U9 to "Zülpicher Pl." Scrumptious sweet and savory crêpes (€2-8) and myriad vegetarian and dessert options. Anything that can fit in a crêpe will be added upon request. Open daily 11am-midnight. Cash only. ❷

🏮 **Café Orlando,** Engelbertstr. 7 (☎23 75 23; www.cafeorlando.de). U8 or U9 to "Zülpicher Pl." With tapestry-covered benches, stained glass lamp. Breakfasts from €3.10, salads €5.50-6.80, and mixed drinks €3.50-4.80 draw a devoted following of students who squeeze in at all hours. Free wireless Internet. Open daily 9am-midnight. Cash only. ❷

Café Magnus, Zülpicherstr. 48 (☎24 16 14 69). U8 or U9 to "Zülpicher Pl." Though students dominate the night scene, locals of all ages come here for artfully prepared meals (from €4), and the surprising multitude of vegetarian options (€5-7). Open M-Th 8am-3am, F-Sa 8am-5am, Su 8am-1am. Cash only. ❷

Ganesha, Händelstr. 26 (☎21 31 65), at the corner of Richard-Wagner-Str. U1, U6, U7, U12, or U15 to "Rudolfpl." This elaborately draped restaurant offers a range of Indian specialties, including chicken vindaloo (€9). A favorite with curry-obsessed Germans. Entrées €7-12. Open daily 6pm-midnight, Tu-Su also 12:30-3pm. AmEx/DC/MC/V. ❸

Brauhaus Früh am Dom, Am Hof 12-16 (☎261 32 11). A trip to Cologne isn't complete without a visit to Früh am Dom or Päffgen. The combination of well-priced *Kölsch* (€1.35) and pleasantly persistent waiters is sure to take effect in no time. Pricier, meatheavy options focus on regional specialties (€8-18). Open daily 8am-midnight, kitchen closes at 11:45pm. MC/V. ❸

Feynsinn, Rathenaupl. 7 (☎24 09 210). U8 or U9 to "Zülpicher Pl." Swanky university crowds chatter under a star-studded ceiling and over an endless menu of drinks and Italian entrées. Breakfast served M-F until 4pm, Sa-Su until 5pm. Open daily 9am-1am, Sa-Su from 10am. MC/V. ❸

🔘 SIGHTS

🏛 DOM

*Across from the train station. ☎52 19 77. Open daily 6am-7:30pm. **Tours** in German M-Sa 11am, 12:30, 2, and 3:30pm; Su 2 and 3:30pm; in English M-Sa 10:30am and 2:30pm, Su 2:30pm. €4, children €2. Dom free. **Tower** open daily May-Sept. 9am-6pm; Mar.-Apr., and Oct. 9am-5pm; Nov.-Feb. 9am-4pm. €2, students €1. **Domschatzkammer** open daily 10am-6pm; €4, students €2. **Diözesanmuseum** open M-W and F-Su 11am-6pm. Free.*

This structure has dominated Cologne since its erection in 1880. With its colossal spires, a canopied ceiling towering 44m above the floor, and 1350sq. m of exquisite stained glass casting a harlequin display of colored light, the cathedral is the perfect realization of High Gothic style. Evidence of the Cologne Bishopric reaches back to the 4th century, suggesting that multiple structures have existed at the site of current cathedral. At 157m, the Dom was the tallest building in the world for four years until the US's Washington Monument eclipsed it in 1884. Today, construction continues to repair the damage wrought by WWII and centuries of pollution, pigeons, and acid rain. Beneath the scaffolding permanently affixed to its spires, the body of the cathedral is being meticulously replaced with new stone. As you cross the threshold, a section of original stone is on display to the right side of the nave, its once-intricate detail blunted by weather and war.

Inside, a chapel to the right of the choir houses a 15th-century **triptych** painted by Stephen Lochner to represent the city's five patron saints. St. Ursula and her bevy of female attendants (a whopping 10,000 virgins, according to legend) dominate the left wing, St. Gereon the right, and in the center, the Three Kings pay tribute to a newborn Christ. Silver, gold, and thousands of encrusted jewels ornament the **Shrine of the Magi,** which reportedly holds the remains of the Three Kings. Transplanted to Cologne by an archbishop in 1164, the reliquary demanded an appropriately opulent building to house this treasure; construction began on the cathedral in 1248. The shrine's golden front depicts the Three Kings bringing their gifts, and careful observation shows that a fourth king has snuck into the back of the scene. This is Germany's own **Holy Roman Emperor Otto IV,** who donated the gold and thereby earned patron saint status. To see a model of the Dom's predecessor, move to the opposite side of the choir, where a floor mosaic depicts the former cathedral. The **Chapel of the Cross** holds the world-famous, 10th-century ▨**Gero Crucifix,** the oldest intact sculpture of **Christus patiens** (a crucified and deceased Christ with eyes shut). Nearby, a doorway leads into the **Domschatzkammer** (treasury), which holds the requisite clerical artwork and reliquaries: thorn, cross, and nail bits, as well as pieces of 18 saints.

Back at the entrance, 15min. and 509 steps are all it takes to scale the **Südturm** (south tower) and peer down at the river below. Catch your breath at the **Glockenstube** (about three-quarters of the way up), a chamber for the tower's nine bells. Four of the bells date from the Middle Ages, but the 19th-century upstart known affectionately as **Der Große Peter** (at 24 tons, the world's heaviest swinging bell) is loudest. Those who prefer the view from below can attain a sense of the tower's immenseness; the plant-like statue located directly opposite the front door is a scale replica of the cathedral's crowning pinnacles. Find more ecclesiastic treasures in the **Diözesanmuseum,** just outside the south portal in the red building. The allure of the cathedral illuminated from dusk to midnight is irresistible, drawing natives and tourists to the expansive **Domvorplatz** to admire it.

INNENSTADT

In the shadow of the cathedral, the **Hohenzollern** bridge empties out onto a promenade flanked by equestrian statues of the imperial family. A monumental flight of stairs leads from the Rhein to **Heinrich-Böll-Pl.** and its cultural center (see **Museums,** p. 286), a complex of modern architecture that complements the Dom. Farther on, the squares and crooked streets of the **Altstadt** and old **Fischmarkt** district open onto paths along the Rhein; the café patios give way to an expanse of grass along the river, providing a venue for musicians and repose for tourists.

HOUSE #4711. In the 18th century, Goethe noted "How grateful the women are for the fragrance of *Eau de Cologne.*" The recipe for this revolutionary water was presented to its first manufacturer, Wilhelm Mühlens, on his wedding day in 1792. Though it was once prescribed as a potable curative containing 80% alcohol, today it is treasured merely for its scent, which is supposed to enhance one's senses. Genuine bottles say *Echt kölnisch Wasser* (real Cologne water) and have a "4711" label. The name comes from Mühlens's residence, called House #4711 under a Napoleonic system that abolished house names because it confused soldiers. The home now functions as a boutique, where a corner fountain bubbles with the scented water and elegantly attired attendants dole out small samples. The free upstairs museum has a full history of the famous fragrance. *(Glockeng., at the intersection with Tunisstr. Open M-F 9am-7pm, Sa 9am-6pm.)*

RATHAUS. Bombed in WWII, Cologne's city hall has been reconstructed in its original mongrel style. A Gothic tower stands guard over Baroque cherubs encircling an ornate 1570 Renaissance arcade, the only part that survived the war. The tower is a diverse array of historical and cultural figures; Marx and Rubens loom above rows of popes and emperors. The *Glockenspiel* plays daily every hour from noon-6pm. *(Open M-Th 7:30am-4:15pm, F 7:30am-12:15pm. Free.)*

RÖMISCHES PRAETORIUM UND KANAL. Classical historians and *Ben Hur* fans will be impressed by the excavated ruins of the former Roman military headquarters. In addition to offering access to the nearby baths, this underground museum displays remnants of Roman idols and an array of rocks left by early inhabitants. *(Open Tu-Su 10am-5pm, €1.50, students €0.75.)*

MIKWE JUDENBAD. Look through the Louvre-like glass pyramid to the left as you exit the Rathaus. Underneath it is a 12th-century Jewish ritual bath that burrows 15m to groundwater. Once the center of one of the oldest Jewish communities in Germany, it was destroyed in 1349 when the Jews were driven out of the city. To enter, deposit your passport at the Praetorium. *(Open Tu-Su 10am-5pm, Free.)*

CHURCHES

The Romanesque period saw the construction of 12 churches in a rough semi-circle around the Altstadt, each containing the holy bones of saints to protect the city. Though dwarfed by the splendor of the Dom, these churches attest to the glory and immense wealth of what was the most important city north of the Alps. In addition to those below, other Romanesque churches include **Alt St. Alban** (Martinstr. 39), **St. Maria in Lyskirchen** (An Lyskirchen 10), **St. Georg** (Georgspl. 17), **St. Pantaleon** (An Pantaleonsberg 2), **St. Severin** (Im Ferkulum 29), **St. Kunibert** (Kunibertsklosterg. 2), and **St. Aposteln** (Neumarkt 30).

ST. GEREON. This magnificent rose-colored medieval church was constructed in the 11th century over the remains of its patron **St. Gereon,** a Roman soldier who refused to kill fellow Christians. Its decagon structure contains a gilt mosaic of a sword-wielding David tackling oafish Goliath. *(Gereonsdriesch 2-4. ☎ 13 49 22. Open M-Sa 9am-6pm, Su 1:30-6pm; decagon open M-Sa 10am-noon and 3-5pm, Su 3-5pm. Free.)*

ST. URSULA. North of the Dom, this church commemorates Ursula's attempts to maintain celibacy despite her betrothal. This was easier after she was struck by an arrow in 383 when an untimely arrival in Cologne put her and 11,000 of her chaste companions in the midst of a Hunnish siege. Relics and more than 700 skulls line the walls of the **Goldene Kammer.** *(Ursulapl. 24. ☎ 13 34 00. Open M 9am-noon and 1-5pm, W-F 10am-6pm, Sa-Su 11am-6pm. Church free. Kammer €1, children €0.50.)*

GROß ST. MARTIN. Along with the Dom, **Groß St. Martin** defines Cologne's skyline. Near the Rathaus in the Altstadt, the church was reopened in 1985 after near destruction in WWII. The interior is tiled with mosaics from the Middle Ages, and crypts downstairs house an esoteric collection of stones and diagrams. *(An Groß St. Martin 9. ☎ 257 79 24. Open M-Sa 10am-6pm, Su 2-4pm. Church free. Crypt €0.50.)*

ST. CÄCILIEN. This church dates back to the 9th century, but after many centuries and post-WWII restorations it is no longer used for services, and instead holds the **Museum Schnütgen,** a collection of religious artifacts and artwork. *(Cäcilienstr. 29. ☎ 22 12 23 10. Accessible only through Museum Schnütgen, p. 286.)*

ST. MARIA IM KAPITOL. Possessing Germany's second largest crypt, this church, built in 1030 above a Roman capitol temple, also features 11th-century door panels whose reliefs detail the life of Christ. *(Marienpl. 19. Entrance around the corner on Kasinostr. ☎ 21 46 15. Open M-Sa 9am-6pm, Su 11:30am-5pm.)*

🏛 MUSEUMS

NEAR THE DOM

🖼 **MUSEUM LUDWIG.** In Heinrich-Böll-Pl., this museum features works by virtually every big-name artist of the 20th century, including displays of pop art, photography, and one of the world's largest Picasso collections. *(Bischofsgartenstr. 1, behind the Römisch-Germanisches Museum. ☎ 22 12 61 65. Open Tu-Su 10am-6pm, first F of the month 10am-10pm. €7.50, students €5.50.)*

WALLRAF-RICHARTZ MUSEUM. Recently relocated to accommodate its growing collection, the pastel galleries of this museum are lined with masterpieces spanning the Middle Ages through Post-Impressionism. *(Martinstr. 39. ☎ 22 12 11 19. Open Tu 10am-8pm, W-F 10am-6pm, Sa-Su 11am-6pm. Free German tours W 4:30pm and Su 11:30am. Call ahead for English tours, min. 10 people. €5.80, students and children €3.30, children under 7 free. Special exhibitions €1.)*

RÖMISCH-GERMANISCHES MUSEUM (ROMAN-GERMANIC MUSEUM). Discovered in 1941 during the excavation of an air raid shelter, a 3rd-century **Dionysus Mosaic** is the foundation for this extensive collection. Three floors of artifacts filled with ancient toys, gambling dice, and Roman statues illuminate Cologne as a Roman colony. *(Roncallipl. 4., next to the Dom. ☎ 22 12 44 38. Open Tu-Su 10am-5pm. German tours Su 11:30am. €4.50, students and children €2.70.)*

ELSEWHERE IN COLOGNE

🖼 **IMHOFF-STOLLWERCK-MUSEUM (CHOCOLATE MUSEUM).** This museum not only demonstrates how to make hollow chocolate soccer balls, but also displays artifacts from the first cultures who cultivated (and revered) the cocoa bean in Central and South America. Salivate at every step of production, from rainforests of cocoa trees to the gold fountain that spurts a stream of free chocolate samples. *(Rheinauhafen 1a. Near the Severinsbrücke. Proceed under the Deutzer Bridge and take the 1st footbridge to the bit of land jutting into the Rhein. ☎ 931 88 80. Open Tu-F 10am-6pm, Sa-Su 11am-7pm. Last entry 1hr. before closing. Museum €6, students, seniors, and children €3.50.)*

KÄTHE-KOLLWITZ-MUSEUM. The world's largest collection of sketches, sculptures, and prints by the brilliant artist and activist (p. 69). Dark and deeply moving images chronicle the struggle of common life and pains of personal loss against the stark black-and-white landscape of early 20th-century Berlin. *(Neumarkt 18-24. Take U1, U3, U7-U9, U16, or U18 to "Neumarkt." ☎ 227 23 63. Open Tu-F 10am-6pm, Sa-Su 11am-6pm. German tours Su at 3pm. €5, students €1.50.)*

NS-DOKUMENTATIONS-ZENTRUM. Once Cologne's Gestapo headquarters, this museum now portrays the city as it was during the Nazi regime. The *Mutterkreuz*, an award given to mothers of three or more children for doing their part to help build a strong Nazi state, is on display. Explore prison cells in the basement, where political prisoners memorialized themselves in over 1200 wall inscriptions, including poems of protest, simple calendars, love letters, and self-portraits. English translations are available. *(Am Appellhofpl. 23-25. ☎ 22 12 63 32. Open Tu-F 10am-4pm, Sa-Su 11am-4pm. €3.60, students €1.50.)*

MUSEUM SCHNÜTGEN. Showcasing one of the world's largest collections of medieval art with over 5000 Romanesque and Gothic stone sculptures and 2000 works in silver, gold, ivory, and bronze, this museum is a bastion of ecclesiastical art from its very beginnings. Also included is an extensive collection of stained glass windows, tapestries, and priestly fashions. *(Cäcilienstr. 29. In St. Cäcilien, p. 285. ☎ 22 12 23 10. Open Tu-F 10am-5pm, Sa-Su 11am-5pm. €4.20, students €3.)*

FESTIVALS AND ENTERTAINMENT

Cologne explodes in festivity during ▓**Karneval,** in the literal sense of the word: a week-long pre-Lenten "farewell to flesh" (from the Latin *carnivale*). Celebrated in the hedonistic spirit of the city's Roman past, *Karneval* is made up of 50 neighborhood processions in the weeks before Ash Wednesday. **Weiberfastnacht** (Feb. 15, 2007), is the first major to-do: the mayor mounts the platform at Alter Markt and abdicates leadership of the city to the city's *Weiber* (a regional, untranslatable, and unabashedly politically incorrect term for women). In a demonstration of power, the women then traditionally find their husbands at work and chop their ties off. In the afternoon, the first of the big parades begins at Severinstor. The weekend builds up to the out-of-control parade on **Rosenmontag,** the last Monday before Lent (Feb. 19, 2007). Everyone dresses in costume and gets and gives a couple dozen *Bützchen* (*Kölsch* dialect for a kiss on the cheek). While most revelers nurse their hangovers on Shrove Tuesday, pubs and restaurants set fire to the straw scarecrows hanging out their windows.

Cologne has more than 30 theaters, including the **Oper der Stadt Köln** and **Kölner Schauspielhaus** near Schilderg. on Offenbachpl. (☎22 12 84 00. Open M-F 10am-7:30pm, Sa 11am-7:30pm. Tickets €8-55.) **KölnTicket,** in the same building as the Römisch-Germanisches Museum (p. 286), also sells tickets for the opera as well as other venues, from Cologne's world-class **Philharmonie** to open-air rock concerts. (☎28 01; www.koelnticket.de. Open M-F 10am-7pm, Sa 10am-4pm. Tickets €30-150.) **Metropolis,** Ebertpl. 19, plays new releases in their original language, and children's movies dubbed in German. (☎739 12 45. Shows daily from 2pm, on weekends from 1:45pm. Last screenings start around 10pm. €4-7, all shows €4 on Th.)

▓ NIGHTLIFE

Roman mosaics dating back to the AD 3rd century record the wild excesses of the city's early residents, but Cologne has come a long way: instead of grape-feeding and fig-wearing, life here focuses on a more sophisticated bump-and-grind. Many bars and clubs change their music nightly; the best way to know what you'll get is to pick up *Kölner* (€1) from newsstands. The closer to the Rhein or Dom you venture, the more quickly your wallet will empty. After dark, in **Hohenzollernring,** crowds of people move from theaters to clubs and finally to cafés in the early hours of the morning. Students congregate in the **Bermuda-Dreieck** (Bermuda Triangle), bounded by **Zülpicherplatz, Roonstraße,** and **Luxemburgstraße** The center of gay nightlife runs up **Matthiasstraße** to **Mühlenbach, Hohe Pforte, Marienplatz,** and up to the Heumarkt area by **Deutzer Brücke.** Radiating westward from **Friesenplatz,** the **Belgisches Viertel** (Belgian Quarter) is dotted with more expensive bars and cafés.

At the various *Brauhäuser,* where original *Kölsch* is brewed, servers will greet you with a forthright "Kölsch?" and then bring glass after glass until you fall under the table or cover your glass with a coaster. Unless your waiter keeps a tally, make sure that the lines on your coaster correspond to the number of beers you actually drink—otherwise, they might count on the fact that you won't be able to count.

▓ **Papa Joe's Jazzlokal,** Buttermarkt 37 (☎257 79 31; www.papajoes.de). Papa Joe's has a legendary reputation for great music and good times, drawing locals and expats alike. Local groups play traditional jazz 6 days per wk. Drinks are pricey, but a 0.4L *Kölsch* (€3.60) goes a long way. Add your business card or expired ID to the informal collage that adorns the perimeter of the bar. Open M-F 7pm-1am, Sa-Su 7pm-3am. Live jazz M-Sa 10:30pm-12:30am; linger afterwards and buy the band a round. Cash only.

▓ **Cent Club,** Hohenstaufenring 25-27 (www.centclub.de). Near Zülpicher Pl. U8 or U9 to "Zülpicher Pl." Rivaling **Das Ding** across the street, this student disco features more dance (hip-hop, pop, dance classics) and less talk, with the appeal of enticingly inexpensive drinks (€0.50 shooters, €1 mixed drinks, €1.50 beers). Open M-Sa from 9pm. Cover €5, M and Tu free. Cash only.

Stadtgarten, Venloerstr. 40 (☎952 99 40). From Friesenpl. follow Venloerstr. for several blocks. 2 clubs in 1 location: downstairs plays techno and house; upstairs concert hall hosts live jazz. Cover €5-8. Open M-Th 9pm-1am, F-Sa 9pm-3am. Cash only.

Das Ding, Hohenstaufenring 30-32 (☎24 63 48). Smoky and dedicated to drinking, this popular and eclectic student bar and disco has dirt-cheap alcohol specials (€1 and under). W 70s and 80s night. Open Tu, Th, Su 9pm-3am; W 9pm-2am; F-Sa 9pm-4am. Cover €5. Student ID required. Cash only.

Alter Wartesaal, Johannisstr. 11 (☎912 88 50; www.wartesaal.de). In the basement of the train station, this enormous dance floor fills with trendily clad 20-somethings. Cover €8. Disco open 10pm-5am most nights. AmEx/MC/V.

M20, Maastrichter Str. 20 (☎51 96 66). Distinguished DJs deliver some of the city's best drum'n'bass, rock, and punk. Open daily 10pm-2am, F-Sa until 4am. Cash only.

MTC, Zülpicherstr. 10 (☎240 41 88). Take U8 or U9 to "Zülpicher Pl." Frequent live bands, generally of the rock and indie-pop persuasion. Cover €5, includes 1 drink; on concert night €5-15. Open daily from 10pm-late. Cash only.

Underground, Vogelsangerstr. 200 (☎54 23 26). U3 or U4 to "Venloer Str./Gürtel." Catering to an alternative student crowd, this beer garden transforms into a typical club when it's not hosting live experimental music. Open daily from 10pm. Cash only.

Cuba Bar, Zülpicherstr. 25 (☎21 60 280). U8 or U9 to "Zülpicher Pl." Having adopted Che Guevara as its eccentric mascot, this lounge and bar plays reggaeton and salsa and offers similarly-inclined drinks. Bartenders are known to sing along as they pour your speciality mixed drink (€3.50-4.50). Open daily 5pm-3am. Cash only.

GAY- AND LESBIAN-FRIENDLY

☒ **Hotel Timp,** Heumarkt 25 (☎258 14 09; www.timp.de), opposite the "Heumarkt" U-Bahn stop. This outrageous club and hotel is an institution for travesty theater. A mixed crowd comes nightly for the gaudy, glitter-filled cabarets. No cover, but your 1st drink is €8, weekends €13. Open daily from 11pm. Shows daily from 1-4am. AmEx/MC/V.

Gloria, Apostelnstr. 11 (☎25 44 33; www.gloria-theater.com). A former movie theater, this popular café, theater, and occasional club is at the nexus of Cologne's trendy gay and lesbian scene. Call for a schedule of themed parties. Cover €7-30, may include show ticket. Open M-Sa 10am-11pm, until 5am on party nights. MC/V.

Pitter, Alter Markt 58-60 (☎258 31 22). Warm evenings bring a primarily gay crowd to the outside patio of this easygoing pub. Open daily noon-1am. Cash only.

BONN   ☎0228

Known derisively for the past 50 years as the *Hauptdorf* (capital village), Bonn (pop. 312,000) was basically a non-entity before falling into the limelight by chance. Konrad Adenauer, the Federal Republic's first chancellor, resided in the suburbs, and the occupying Allied powers made Bonn the "provisional capital" of the Western Occupation Zone before they named it capital of the fledgling Republic. The summer of 1991 brought headlines of "Chaos in Bonn" as Berlin fought to reclaim the seat of government. By the narrowest of margins, Berlin won, and in 1999, the Bundestag packed up and moved east. Though Berliners joke that Bonn is "half the size of a Berlin cemetery and twice as dead," it is the perfect combination of a forward-thinking university and a sparkling, historical Altstadt. Bonn's exceptional museums bolster an ever-eclectic cultural scene at Bonn's main market and at its avant-garde events.

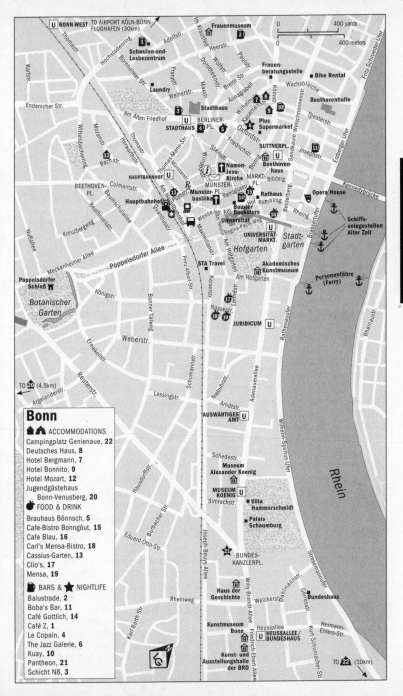

U BONN-WEST TO AIRPORT KÖLN-BONN
FLUGHAFEN (30km)

Frauenmuseum **2**

Schwulen-und-
Lesbezentrum **1**

Frauen-
beratungsstelle

Bike Rental

Laundry

Beethovenhalle

Stadthaus **3**

8
Kässenstr. **7**
9
10

U BERLINER-
STADTHAUS **4** PL.

Plus
Supermarket **5**

SUTTNERPL.

Beethoven-
haus **11**

Namen-
Jesu-
Kirche

MARKT-
PL.

HAUPTBAHNHOF U

Münster-
basilika **15**

Münster-
PL. Rathaus
Rathausg. **14**
Bouvier
Bookstore

Opera House

Hauptbahnhof **15**

Universität **16**

Schiffs-
anlegestellen
Alter Zoll

UNIVERSITÄT-
MARKT.
Stadt-
garten

Hofgarten

STA Travel

Akademisches
Kunstmuseum

Personenfähre
(Ferry)

Poppelsdorfer
Schloß

Botanischer
Garten

17

18 19 JURIDICUM U

TO **20** (4.5km)

AUSWÄRTIGES
AMT U

Bonn

🏕🏠 ACCOMMODATIONS
Campingplatz Genienaue, 22
Deutsches Haus, 8
Hotel Bergmann, 7
Hotel Bonnito, 9
Hotel Mozart, 12
Jugendgästehaus
  Bonn-Venusberg, 20
🍴 FOOD & DRINK
Brauhaus Bönnsch, 5
Cafe-Bistro Bonngôut, 15
Cafe Blau, 16
Carl's Mensa-Bistro, 18
Cassius-Garten, 13
Clio's, 17
Mensa, 19

🛏 BARS & ⭐ NIGHTLIFE
Balustrade, 2
Boba's Bar, 11
Café Gottlich, 14
Café Z, 1
Le Copain, 4
The Jazz Galerie, 6
Kuay, 10
Pantheon, 21
Schicht N8, 3

Museum
Alexander Koenig

MUSEUM
KOENIG U

Villa
Hammerschmidt

Palais
Schaumburg

21
BUNDES-
KANZLERPL.

Rhein

Haus
der
Geschichte

Bundeshaus

Kunstmuseum
Bonn

HEUSSALLEE/
BUNDESHAUS U

Kunst- und
Ausstellungshalle
der BRD

TO **22** (10km)

⊟ TRANSPORTATION

Flights: Köln-Bonn Flughafen (☎ 02203 40 40 01 02). Bus #670 runs from the train station (every 30min. 5am-10pm; €3, children €1.50).

Trains: To: **Cologne** (20min., 5 per hr., €5-8); **Frankfurt** (2hr., 3 per hr., €25-32); **Koblenz** (45min., 3 per hr., €8-13).

Public Transportation: Bonn is linked to Cologne and other riverside cities by the **VRS** S-Bahn and U-Bahn network. Areas are divided into zones; the farther you go, the more you pay. Single tickets (€1.20-5.60) and day tickets (€5.50-12.10) are available at *Automaten*. With the *Minigruppenkarte* (€8.30-23 per day) 5 people can ride M-F after 9am and all day on weekends. Stop by the **Reisezentrum** in the train station or go to the tourist office to pick up a free transit map. Open M-Sa 6am-10pm, Su 7am-10pm. The **Bonn Regio WelcomeCard** covers public transportation (see below).

Taxis: Funkzentrale ☎ 55 55 55.

Bike Rental: Radstation, Quantiusstr. 26 (☎ 981 46 36), behind the train station. €5-7 per day, €30 deposit. Open M-F 6am-11:30pm, Sa 7am-11:30pm, Su 8am-11:30pm. **Kurscheid**, Römerstr. 4 (☎ 63 14 33). €8 per day; €11 weekend special. Also rents cars (€55-90 per day). ID required. Open M-Sa 7am-7pm, Su 9am-1pm and 3-7pm.

⊠ PRACTICAL INFORMATION

Tourist Office: Windeckstr. 1 (☎ 775 000; www.bonn.de), off Münsterpl. near the cathedral. Staff doles out free maps, offers sightseeing bus tours (mid-Apr. to Oct. W-Su 2pm; Nov. to mid-Dec. and Jan. to mid-Apr. Sa only; €13), runs walking tours (Sa 11am, free), and books rooms via phone for a €2 fee or online for free (☎ 910 41 70). Open M-F 9am-6:30pm, Sa 9am-4pm, Su 10am-2pm. **Bonn Regio WelcomeCard,** available at the tourist office, covers public transportation into the Cologne area (M-F after 9am; all day Sa-Su) and admission to more than 20 museums in Bonn and the surrounding area (1-day €9, 2-day €14, 3-day €19; family €18/28/38).

Bookstore: The mammoth **Bouvier**, Am Hof 28-32 (☎ 72 90 10), has a wide range of foreign books on the top floor. Open M-F 9:30am-8pm, Sa 10am-8pm. MC/V.

Gay and Lesbian Resources: Schwulen- und Lesbenzentrum, Am Frankenbad 5 (☎ 63 00 39; www.zentrumbonn.de), at the far left corner of the Mobil Autoöl parking lot. From Münsterpl., follow Windeckstr., which becomes Sternstr. Walk across Berliner Pl. to Bornheimer Str. and take a right on Adolfstr.; Am Frankenbad is down the street on the left. **Counseling** and **gay assault hotline** (☎ 194 46) open M-Tu 7-9pm, W 5-9pm.

Women's Resources: Frauenberatungsstelle, Kölnstr. 69 (☎ 65 95 00). Open M and Th 5-7:30pm, W and F 10am-noon. Pick up *Frauen in Bonn* at the tourist office.

Laundromat: Eco-Express Waschsalon, Bornheimer Str. 56 (☎ 560 26 03). Wash 6-10am €1.50, 10am-11pm €2. Dry €0.50 per 10min. Open M-Sa 6am-11pm.

Emergency: Police (☎ 110), inside the train station. **Fire** and **Ambulance** ☎ 112.

Pharmacy: Bahnhof-Apotheke, Poststr. 19 (☎ 65 30 66). Open M-W and F 8am-7pm, Th 8am-8pm, Sa 9am-6pm.

Internet Access: Cheap access can be found at **Bonner Internet Café & Tele-Service,** Maximilianstr. 26. €2 per hr. Open M-Th 8am-1am, F-Sa 8am-2am, Su 9am-1am.

Post Office: Münsterpl. 17. Open M-F 9am-8pm, Sa 9am-4pm. **Postal Code:** 53111.

◪◩ ACCOMMODATIONS AND CAMPING

▨ **Deutsches Haus,** Kasernenstr. 19-21 (☎ 63 37 77; info@hotel-deutscheshaus.net). On a quiet residential street connecting busy squares (Münsterpl. and Berlinerpl.), this value hotel offers simple rooms with TV, and private bath. Complimentary breakfast in a tulip-filled room. Reception 6am-11pm. Singles €34-38.50, with bath €35-41; doubles€60-77, triples €66-99. MC/V. ❸

Jugendgästehaus Bonn-Venusberg (HI), Haager Weg 42 (☎28 99 70; jgh-bonn@t-online.de). Take bus #621 (dir.: Ippendorf Altenheim) to "Jugendgästehaus," or bus #620 (dir.: Venusberg) to "Sertürnerstr." Turn left on Haager Weg and walk 10min. A modern hostel in the suburbs with a bar and clean rooms with bath. Wheelchair accessible. Breakfast included. Laundry €4. Curfew 1am. Dorms €21.50; singles €35.70; doubles €51.20. MC/V. ❷

Hotel Bergmann, Kasernenstr. 13 (☎63 38 91; ajbergmann@web.de). Elegant rooms in a Victorian-embellished home. Call ahead for reservations. Breakfast included. Singles €35; doubles €50. Cash only. ❸

Hotel Bonnito, Kölnstr. 45 (☎63 80 89; info@bonnito.de). Right around the corner from the Hotel Bergmann. Functional rooms with phones, private bath, TV, and colorful sheets. Entrance to the right of the Spanish restaurant below. Breakfast €8. Reception 7am-10pm. Singles €40; doubles €70; triples €90. Cash only. ❹

Hotel Mozart, Mozartstr. 1 (☎65 90 71; www.hotel-mozart-bonn.de). Piano in the front foyer, large, trim rooms, and Viennese elegance in a sedate neighborhood. Breakfast included. Singles €41-80; doubles €60-95. AmEx/MC/V. ❹

Campingplatz Genienaue, Im Frankenkeller 49 (☎34 49 49). U16 to "Bad Godesberg," then bus #613 (dir.: Giselherstr.) to "Guntherstr." Turn left on Guntherstr. and right on Frankenkeller. Rhein-side camping in suburban Mehlem, 40min. from the city. Reception 9am-noon and 3-10pm. €5.10 per person, €3-5 per tent. Cash only. ❶

◱ FOOD

The **market** on **Münsterplatz** teems with haggling vendors and determined customers. At the end of the day, voices rise and prices plummet. (Open M-Sa 8am-6pm.) **Plus** supermarket is on Oxfordstr. 26. (Open M-Sa 8am-8pm.) There is a **food court** in the Kaufhof on Münsterpl. (Open M-F 9:30am-8pm, Sa 9am-4pm.)

▨ **Cassius-Garten**, Maximilianstr. 28d (☎65 24 29; www.cassiusgarten.de), at the edge of the Altstadt facing the station. Take a break from meaty German specialties at this fresh, sunny veggie bar. 50 kinds of salads, noodles, hot entrées, soups, desserts, and whole-grain baked goods, all €1.50 per 100g. Terrace, booth, and rear garden seating. Open M-F 9am-10pm, Sa 9am-6pm. MC. ❷

▨ **Clio's**, Lennestr. 6 (☎20 94 972; www.clios.de). This casual and intimate bookstore-café is not your neighborhood Barnes and Noble. Inside, comfortable booth and bar seating and walls lined with shelves filled with philosophy, literature, and social science texts attract students who catch up over cappuccinos (€0.90) and beers (€1.50). Open M-F 10:30am-6:30pm, Sa 10:30am-3pm. Cash only. ❷

Café-Bistro Bonngôut, Remigiusstr. 2-4 (☎65 89 88). Revel in sleek furniture and floor-to-ceiling windows as you indulge in meaty entrées (€10-15) or dessert crêpes (€3.50-4.50). Huge breakfasts (€5-10) served M-F until noon, Sa until 1pm, Su until 3pm. Open M-Sa 9am-1am, Su 10am-midnight; kitchen open until 11:30pm. MC/V. ❸

Carl's Mensa-Bistro, Nassestr. 15, has cheap restaurant-quality meals (i.e., ridiculous amounts of pasta) served cafeteria-style. Chili and burritos €3-4. *Bratwurst* €2.60. Salad €0.65 per 100g. Open M-Th 10:30am-10pm, F 10:30am-3pm. Cash only. ❷

Brauhaus Bönnsch, Sterntorbrücke 4 (☎65 06 10), pours its own *Bönnsch* (€2.10 for 0.2L), the smooth-as-butter illegitimate son of Cologne's *Kölsch*. At this busy restaurant, *Bönnsche Flammkuchen* (Bonn Flaming Cakes), made from an old Alsatian recipe, come in many delicious varieties, including vegetarian (€8-10). Open M-Th 11am-1am, F-Sa 11am-3am, Su noon-midnight. Cash only. ❸

Café Blau, Franziskaner Str. 5. Crowds of students flock to this pastel café across from the university. If you can get the attention of the waitstaff, you can have your fill of tasty pasta and salad (€3-6). Breakfast from €1.20. Open daily 9am-1am. Cash only. ❷

Ⓖ SIGHTS

While most of Bonn's bureaucracy has been packed up and shipped out, the hulls remain. These erstwhile seats of power have a historical novelty factor, but Bonn's more interesting sights include its many museums and castles.

■**BEETHOVENHAUS.** Attracting music aficionados of all sorts, Beethoven's birth-place hosts a fantastic collection of the composer's personal effects, with over 1000 manuscripts, primitive hearing aids, and his first violin. The ghost haunts Bonn annually during the **Beethoven Festival** (mid-Sept. to mid-Oct.). The first fête, in 1845, was a riot, with Franz Liszt brawling with French nationalist Louis Berlioz while King Ludwig's mistress Lola Montez table-danced. This historic 18th-century residence is one of the few preserved from its era. *(Bonng. 20. ☎ 981 75 25; www.beethoven-haus-bonn.de. Open Apr.-Oct. M-Sa 10am-6pm, Su 11am-6pm; Nov.-Mar. M-Sa 10am-5pm, Su 11am-5pm. Last entry 30min. before closing. €4, students €3.)*

RATHAUS. This voluptuous birthday cake of a Baroque building is frosted with pastel pink, blue, and gold trim, providing a backdrop for countless celebrity photo-ops: from these steps Charles de Gaulle, John F. Kennedy, and Elizabeth II have all charmed the crowds. In the absence of foreign dignitaries, the scenic Rathaus now provides a performance space for concerts and town presentations.

MÜNSTERBASILIKA. Three stories of arches within arches yield to a gorgeous gold-leaf mosaic inside the impressive basilica. A 12th-century cloister laced with crossways and passages branches off under the doorway labeled "Kreuzgang." Keep an eye out for the incongruous blue-red windows, designed by expressionist Heinrich Campendonk. *(Münsterpl., or Gerhard-von-Are-Str. 5. ☎ 63 33 44. Open daily 7am-7pm. Cloister open daily 9am-5pm. Free.)*

BUNDESHAUS (FORMER GERMAN PARLIAMENT). In its heyday, this Bauhaus-inspired structure earned the title of "least prepossessing parliament building." Its transparent walls were meant to mark a new German democracy where the gover-nors felt their responsibility to the people. *(Take U16, U63, or U66 to "Heussallee" or bus #610 to "Bundeshaus." Mandatory tour Sa-Su 2 and 3pm; free tickets in the tourist office.)*

PALAIS SCHAUMBURG. This gated and guarded structure was home to Konrad Adenauer, Germany's first chancellor and Bonn's guiding light. The less impres-sive **Denkmal,** in the Bundeskanzlerpl. outside the *Palais,* was also erected in Ade-nauer's honor, though arguably by people with strange ideas of honor: the 2m hollow-cheeked bust looks like it was lifted from a pirate flag. Engraved into his cranium are allegorical figures: various animals, a pair of hands, and two French cathedrals. *(Adenauerallee 135-141. Take U16, U63, or U66 to "Museum Koenig.")*

OTHER SIGHTS. Forty-thousand students study in the **Kurfürstliches Schloß,** the huge 18th-century palace that is now the center of **Friedrich-Wilhelms-Universität** (also called **Universität Bonn**). The *Schloß* leads to the open grassy spaces and tree-lined walkways of the **Hofgarten** and **Stadtgarten,** gathering places for students, pic-nickers, and dog-walkers. To see Bonn's "other" palace, stroll down Poppelsdorfer Allee to the 18th-century **Poppelsdorfer Schloß.** The palace boasts a French facade, an Italian courtyard, and a beautifully manicured **botanical gardens.** It also houses the **mineralogy museum.** *(Museum open W 3-5pm, Su 10am-5pm. €2.50, students €1.50, under 17 free. Gardens open Apr.-Sept. M-F 9am-6pm, Su 9am-1pm; Oct.-Mar. M-F 9am-4pm. Greenhouses open M-F 10:30am-noon and 2-4pm; Apr.-Sept. also Su 9am-1pm. Free.)*

MUSEUMS

The **"Museum Mile"** begins at the **Museum Alexander Koenig.** Take U16, U63, or U66 to "Heussallee" or "Museum Koenig." The **WelcomeCard** (p. 290) gives free admission to all museums listed below.

■HAUS DER GESCHICHTE (MUSEUM OF HISTORY). This museum provides a microcosmic study of a nation grappling with its past and future, beginning in the broken landscape of 1945, and culminating in a chronicle of modern issues. Along the way, enjoy the artful exhibits, including Konrad Adenauer's first Mercedes, rubble of the Berlin Wall, the first German green card granted to a foreigner, and a genuine moon rock. *(Willy-Brandt-Allee 14.* ☎ *916 50. Open Tu-Su 9am-7pm. Free.)*

KUNSTMUSEUM BONN (ART MUSEUM OF BONN). Unveiled in 1992, this immense building designed by Berlin architect Axel Schultes houses an even more impressive collection of 20th-century German art. Highlights include the genre-defying canvases of Richter, cameo works by Warhol and Duchamp, and an extensive selection of oils and sketches by local expressionist Macke. *(Friedrich-Ebert-Allee 2.* ☎ *77 62 60. Open Tu and Th-Su 10am-6pm, W 10am-9pm. €5, students €2.50. With Kunstmuseum Bonn and Ausstellungshalle €10/5.)*

KUNST- UND AUSSTELLUNGSHALLE DER BRD (ART AND EXHIBITION HALL OF THE FEDERAL REPUBLIC OF GERMANY). This modern hall has no permanent art collection; scheduled shows vary widely, and the hall hosts films, concerts, and theatrical performances. The striking building is a defining element of the Bonn skyline with its three sharp cone spires and 16 columns flanking the *Ausstellungshalle* (designed to represent Germany's federal states). See website for rotating exhibition info. *(Friedrich-Ebert-Allee 4.* ☎ *917 12 00; www.bundeskunsthalle.de. Open Tu-W 10am-9pm, Th-Su 10am-7pm. €7, students €3.50. F 9am-7pm free for students.)*

MUSEUM ALEXANDER KOENIG. If taxidermy had a *Louvre*, this would be it. The recently renovated zoology museum displays superb specimens in natural poses amid detailed dioramas, with a focus on conservation and revival. A vivarium has live lizards in the basement. *(Adenauerallee 160.* ☎ *912 20. Open Tu-Su 10am-6pm, W until 9pm. €3, students €1.50.)*

FRAUENMUSEUM (WOMEN'S MUSEUM). This museum is the first of its kind world-wide, featuring over 700 works that span centuries of female artists, including Yoko Ono. *(Im Krausfeld 10.* ☎ *69 13 44. U61 to "Rosental/Herrstr." Open Tu-Sa 2-6pm, Su 11am-6pm. €4.50, students €3.)*

AKADEMISCHES KUNSTMUSEUM (ACADEMIC ART MUSEUM). A world's worth of classical Greco-Roman masterpieces resides in Germany's largest collection of plaster casts. Includes casts of Venus de Milo, the Colossus of Samos, and Laocöon. *(On the far side of the Hofgarten, facing the Kurfürstliches Schloß.* ☎ *73 77 38. Originals collection open Tu and Su 10am-1pm, Th 4-6pm. Casts collection open M-W, F, Su 10am-1pm, Th 10am-1pm and 4-6pm. Closed in Aug. Guided tours Su 11am. €1, students free.)*

🅢 NIGHTLIFE

Of Bonn's monthly nightlife glossies, *Schnüss* (€1), available at all newsstands, is unbeatable and more complete than the free *Szene Bonn.* The tourist office sells tickets to most of Bonn's extensive theater offerings through **BonnTicket.**

■ The Jazz Galerie, Oxfordstr. 24 (☎ 65 06 62). There's no jazz to be found at this rowdy bar and disco, popular with swank youths. Cover Th €5, F-Sa €7.50; includes 1 drink. Open Tu and Th 9pm-3am, F-Sa 10pm-5am. Cash only.

Balustrade, Heerstr. 52 (☎63 95 96). Enjoy a beer (€2-2.50) or *caipirinha* (Brazilian mixed drink; €4.50) at this hip bar. Monthly theme nights include beach, snowball, and jungle parties. Open M-Th 7pm-1am, F-Sa from 7pm. Cash only.

Pantheon, Bundeskanzlerpl. 2-10 (☎21 25 21; www.pantheon.de), in the shadow of an enormous Mercedes logo. Follow Adenaueallee out of the city until you reach Bundeskanzlerpl. This popular club also hosts concerts, stand-up comedy, and art exhibits. Website lists shows and events. Cover €6.50-8. Disco open 11pm-late. MC/V.

Café Gottlich, Fürstenstr. 4 (☎65 99 69). Modern decor and casual atmosphere rule at Café Gottlich, which is a popular student scene. Serves drinks (€2-5) and beer (€1.30-3.60) long into the wee hours. Open M-Th 9am-2am, F-Sa 9am-4am, Su 10am-2am. Cash only.

Schicht N8, Bornheimer Str. 20-22 (☎963 83 08). This quirky Bonn standby rocks with a different kind of party every night. Tu theme nights (such as karaoke), Th ladies night (free entry before midnight and half-price drinks for women). Cover Th-Sa €4. Open Tu-Th and Su 10pm-3am, F-Sa 10pm-5am. Cash only.

Kuay, Theaterstr. 2 (☎96 96 39 00). Trendy 20- and 30-somethings fill this bar into the wee hours of the morning, but its best "night" is its Su morning afterparty. Open daily 9pm-3am, F-Sa 9pm-late, after-hours party Su 6am. Cash only.

GAY AND LESBIAN

Café Z, in the **Schwulen- und Lesbenzentrum** (p. 290). This upstairs bar with colorful wall art is the center of gay and lesbian life in Bonn. M Gay night, Tu lesbian party, W youth group (ages 16-27), and Th mixed. Open M-Th 8pm-midnight. Cash only.

Boba's Bar, Josephstr. 17 (☎65 06 85). A relaxed bar drawing a lively and varied crowd of mostly gay men. Open daily 8pm-3am. Cash only.

Le Copain, Thomas-Mann-Str. 3a (☎63 99 35). Comfortable bar serving cheap drinks (beer €1.25) to men of all ages. Open daily 4pm-1am. Cash only.

▶ DAYTRIP FROM BONN

KÖNIGSWINTER AND DRACHENFELS

The ruins can be reached from Bonn and Königswinter, the town in the valley below. From Bonn, take U66 (dir.: Königswinter/Bad Honnef) to "Königswinter Fähre" (30min., every 10min., €3.60). Or take the **Bonner Personen Schifffahrt** *ferry (☎0228 63 63 63; 4-8 per day; €5.50, round-trip €7.50). From Königswinter, follow Drachenfelsstr. (about 45min. uphill), or take the* **Drachenfelsbahn.** *(Drachenfelsstr. 53. €8.50, round-trip €10.)*

"The castled crag of Drachenfels frowns o'er the wide and winding Rhein," wrote Lord Byron in *Childe Harold's Pilgrimage.* According to the *Nibelungenlied* (p. p. 72) and local lore, epic hero **Siegfried** slew a █dragon who once haunted the crag. Siegfried then bathed in the dragon's blood and would have been invincible if not for the bare spot left by a leaf on his back. The **Nibelungenhalle,** where the dragon once devoured its prey, is now home to scale-covered creatures big and small—a newly opened **reptile zoo** is located halfway between the museum and the ruins. (Open mid-Mar. to mid-Nov. daily 10am-6pm, mid-Nov. to mid-Mar. Sa-Su 11am-4pm.) The Drachenfels' little brother **Schloß Drachenburg** (☎02223 90 19 70), a newly renovated 19th-century castle, flaunts its ornate turrets just uphill from Nibelungenlied. The castle's neo-Gothic style features interlacing patterns, intricate panelling, and oil murals. Check out the Nibelung wall painting featuring Siegfried in scenes from the epic and at other eccentricities, such as antlered furniture and a dummy organ. (Grounds open Apr.-Nov. Tu-Su 11am-6pm. Guided tour required; call ahead for reservations. €2.50, children €1.)

AACHEN
☎ 0241

Aachen (pop. 257,000) bustles day and night in four different languages, exuding a youthful internationalism in spite of its age. Bordering Belgium and the Netherlands, with the Dutch town of Maastricht just a few minutes away, Aachen has been tossed between empires for centuries, retaining historical treasures from each. The Romans took advantage of the city's hot springs and turned the town into a recreational center, building thermal baths. The ruins of the baths have long since been built over, but visitors can still relax as the Romans did at Aachen's modern spa. The capital of Charlemagne's Frankish empire in the eighth century, Aachen has preserved his palace and cathedral—and fragments of his body.

TRANSPORTATION

Trains: To: **Cologne** (1hr., 2-3 per hr., €12.50). The **Airport Aixpress shuttle** stops at **Elisenbrunnen** en route to the Düsseldorf and Köln/Bonn Airports. Daily every 60-90min. 3:30am-7pm).

Public Transportation: The main **bus station** is on the corner of Peterskirchhof and Peterstr. Tickets are priced by distance; one-way trips run €1-6. *24-Stunden* tickets provide a full day of unlimited travel within Aachen from €5, though most attractions are within comfortable walking distance.

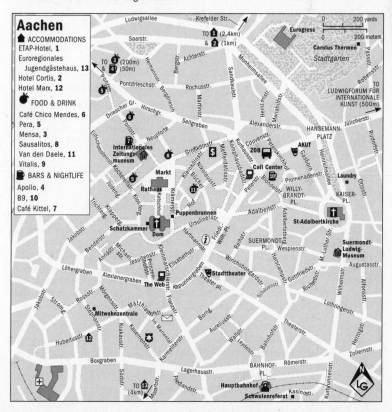

Aachen

🏠 ACCOMMODATIONS
ETAP-Hotel, **1**
Euroregionales
  Jugendgästehaus, **13**
Hotel Cortis, **2**
Hotel Marx, **12**

🍎 FOOD & DRINK
Café Chico Mendes, **6**
Pera, **5**
Mensa, **3**
Sausalitos, **8**
Van den Daele, **11**
Vitalis, **9**

🍸 BARS & NIGHTLIFE
Apollo, **4**
B9, **10**
Café Kittel, **7**

🛈 PRACTICAL INFORMATION

Tourist Office: (☎180 29 60; fax 180 29 30). From the train station, cross the street and head up Bahnhofstr., turn left on Theaterstr., which becomes Theaterpl., then right on Kapuzinergraben, which becomes Friedrich-Wilhelm-Pl. The office is in the Atrium Elisenbrunnen on your left. Also a stop for most city buses. The helpful staff dispenses maps, runs playful themed tours in English (call ahead), and finds rooms for free. Open M-F 9am-6pm, Sa 9am-2pm; Apr.-Dec. also Su 10am-2pm.

Currency Exchange: Citibank, Großkölnstr. 64-66 (☎470 34 80), near the Rathaus. €3 fee and 3.5% commission. Open M-F 9am-1pm and 2-6pm.

Room Share: Mitwohnzentrale, Stefanstr. 56 (☎194 45). Finds lodging for long stays. Open M-Th 9am-1pm and 2-5pm, F 2-5pm.

Gay and Lesbian Resources: Schwulenreferat, Kasinostr. 37 (☎346 32). Office open Th noon-2pm. Café open Tu, F, and Su 7:30am-midnight.

Laundromat: Münz Washcenter, Heinrichsallee 30. Wash €1. Dry €0.50 per 15min. Open M-Sa 6am-11pm, last wash at 10pm.

Emergency: Police Kasernenstr. 23 (☎110). **Fire** and **Ambulance** ☎112.

Internet Access: Call Center & Internet Café, Peterstr. 11, near the main bus station. Wireless access €3 per hr. Open M-Sa 10am-11pm, Su 1-11pm. **The Web,** Kleinmarschierstr. 74-76. €4 per hr., F-Sa after 11pm €2.50 per hr., Su €3 per hr. Open M-W 11am-11pm, Th 11am-midnight, F-Sa 11am-3am, Su noon-10pm.

Post Office: An den Frauenbrüdern 1. Open M-F 9am-6pm, Sa 9am-2pm. **Postal Code:** 52062.

🛏 ACCOMMODATIONS

Many hotels close in January; check with the **Mitwohnzentrale** (see **Room Share**).

Euroregionales Jugendgästehaus (HI), Maria-Theresia-Allee 260 (☎71 10 10; jh-aachen@djh-rheinland.de). From the "Finanzamt" stop on Lagerhausstr. take bus #2 (dir.: Preusswald) to "Ronheide." Pristine rooms in a hilltop hostel next to a pasture. Reservations recommended. Breakfast and sheets included. Wash €2. Dry €1.50. Curfew 1am. Dorms €21.50; singles €37; doubles €55. Cash only. ❷

Hotel Marx, Hubertusstr. 33-35 (☎375 41; www.hotel-marx.de). Well-kept rooms near the Altstadt, and a duck pond in back. Breakfast included. Check-out noon. Singles €34-49; doubles €62, with bath €77. MC/V. ❸

Hotel Cortis, Krefelderstr. 52 (☎997 41 10; fax 99 74 14). Bus #51 to Rolandstr. Walk to the end of the street and turn left. Hotel is next to the gas station. Comfortable B&B near the city center offers cable TV in every room. Reception until midnight. Singles €28; doubles €50-55, with shower and bath €61. MC/V. ❸

ETAP-Hotel, Strangenhäuschen 15 (☎91 19 29; fax 15 53 04). From the bus station, take bus #51 to "Strangenhäuschen," then walk back to the end of the street and turn left; it's on the left. A clean chain hotel 25min. from the city center. Breakfast €4.90. Reception M-Sa 6:30-11am and 5-10pm, Su 7-11am and 5-10pm. Automated check-in the afternoon. Check-out noon. Singles €35; doubles €42. AmEx/MC/V. ❸

🍴 FOOD

Food in Aachen has a distinctly international character; here, quiche and crêpes meet *Wurst* and *Kartoffeln* (potatoes). Aachen's specialties include popular desserts *Reisfladden*, a rice pudding cake often served with strawberries or cherries, and *Printen*, spicy gingerbread biscuits from an old Belgian recipe.

Sausalitos, Markt 45-47 (☎40 19 37). This Mexican bar and restaurant is one of Aachen's most popular haunts for the young and hip, with red lighting, leather booths, and a central location. The gigantic bar, occupying an entire wall, serves jumbo drinks like "Killer Cool Aid" (€8.40) and "Mega Mojito" (€11) and the best enchiladas, tacos, and burritos for miles (€7-13). Open daily noon-1am, F-Sa until 2am. MC/V. ❸

Van den Daele, Büchel 18 (☎357 24), just off the Markt. This café and bakery occupies the oldest house in Aachen, built in 1655. Enjoy a homemade selection of Aachen's famed local delicacies (€2.50). Customized English, French, and Dutch breakfasts €5-11. Open M-Sa 9am-6:30pm, Su 11am-6:30pm. DC/MC/V. ❷

Café Chico Mendes, Pontstr. 74-76 (☎470 01 41), located inside the Katakomben Studentenzentrum, is the Catholic College's lively café (food €4-6). Neon green bar and over 80 board games provide hours of entertainment. Cheap beer F-Su 6-8pm and all night M. Open M-Th 4:30pm-1am, F-Su 6pm-1am. Kitchen open 6-10pm. Cash only. ❷

Vitalis, Kockerellstr. 12 (☎40 12 050), has a health-conscious menu featuring seemingly endless varieties of salads (€3-5.50), soups (€2.80), and fresh-squeezed juices (€1.50-3.50), all of which are custom-tailored to your order. Open M-F 10am-6pm, Sa 11am-4pm. Cash only. ❷

Pera, Pontstr. 95 (☎409 37 80). Minimalism reaches new heights here, but not on the drinks list. Sample one of their Mediterranean dishes (from €3.50) or splurge on an ornate Su brunch (€10.80). Lunch buffet €6. Open M-Th 11am-1am, F-Sa 11am-2am, Su 10am-1am. Su brunch 10am-3pm. Cash only. ❹

Mensa, Turmstr. 3 (☎80 37 92), in the teal-trimmed building on Pontwall, near the Ponttor. Look for the sign "Studentenwerk Aachen." Cafeteria style meals €1.50-7. Open M-F 11:30am-2pm. Cash only. ❷

👁 SIGHTS

In AD 765, the Frankish King Pepin the Short liked to unwind at the hot springs north of Aachen's city center. After assuming power, his son **Charlemagne** (**Karl der Große,** p. 52) made the family's former vacation spot the capital of a rapidly expanding kingdom, casting a long shadow of Carolingian influence.

📷 DOM. With its three-tiered dome, intricate marble inlays, and dazzling blue-gold mosaics, the Aachen city cathedral rings with echoes of Charlemagne's "second Rome." Inaugurated in AD805 as his palace chapel, the magnificent Dom is said to fall under the emperor's protection to this day—in WWII, a bomb aimed at the cathedral was apparently deflected by a statue of Charlemagne. For 700 years after his death, new Holy Roman Emperors traveled to this cathedral to be crowned and to sit in the simple throne still displayed upstairs, linking themselves to the greatest king Europe had ever known. The ornate gold filigree and Gothic stained glass are the modest attempts of these rulers to join in his glory. Though Charlemagne was originally buried in the "Proserpina Sarcophagus" (located in the Schatzkammer), today his remains reside in the jewelled reliquary behind the altar. (☎470 91 27. Visiting hours M-Sa 7am-7pm, Su 1-7pm, except during services. Services M-F 7am, 10am; Sa-Su 7, 8, and 10am Call ahead to book group tours. Access above the 1st fl. by guided tour only.)

SCHATZKAMMER (CATHEDRAL TREASURY). Regarded as the most important ecclesiastical treasury north of the Alps, and containing one of the largest collections of late antique and early medieval devotional art (i.e., gold stuff to put bones in), the Schatzkammer's reliquaries are said to contain everything from John the Baptist's hair to nails and splinters from the true cross and Christ's scourging rope. Charlemagne is also divided among numerous containers. The most famous likeness of him, a gold-plated silver bust, was made in Aachen in 1349 and donated by Emperor Charles IV. *(Klosterpl. 2. ☎ 47 70 91 27. Open M 10am-1pm, Tu-Su 10am-5pm, first Th each month 10am-10pm. Last entry 30min. before closing. €4, students, seniors, and children €3. Tours €3.50/3.)*

MARKTPLATZ. The 14th-century stone **Rathaus,** which looms over the wide Marktpl. and offers a great view of the Dom, was built on the ruins of Charlemagne's palace. The upstairs **Coronation Hall** contains his sabre, and is garnished with larger-than-life (literally) 19th-century frescoes of military scenes. On the facade stand 50 statues of German sovereigns, 31 of whom were crowned in Aachen. *(☎ 432 17 10. Open daily 10am-1pm and 2-5pm. Last entrance 30min. before closing. €2, students and children €1.)* The **Puppenbrunnen,** a fountain of interactive bronze figures with movable joints that invite passersby to contort their shapes, portray Aachen's townspeople. *(At the intersection of Krämerstr. and Hofstr.)*

🏛 MUSEUMS

LUDWIGFORUM FÜR INTERNATIONALE KUNST (FORUM FOR INTERNATIONAL ART). Aachen has focused its cultural energies on acquiring cutting-edge visual arts, with the Ludwigforum at the center of this endeavor. In addition to hosting impressive international exhibits, the museum explores artistic expression in all media. Exhibits from the permanent collection rotate monthly. **Space,** underneath the museum, is a forum for modern dance, music, and theater. *(Jülicher Str. 97-109. Bus # 1, 16, or 52 to "Lombardenstr." ☎ 180 70. Open Tu-Su noon-6pm. Last entry 30min. before closing. Free German tours Su noon. €3, students €1.50. Events at Space €7-18.)*

INTERNATIONALES ZEITUNGSMUSEUM (INTERNATIONAL PRESS MUSUEM). Housed in a 15th-century building and serving as the registry office of the world press since its founding in 1886, this museum stores more than 165,000 different international newspapers from the 17th century to the present, covering the revolutions of 1848, the World Wars, the day Hitler died, and the fall of the Berlin Wall in 1989. The museum also has a reading room of current papers. *(Pontstr. 13. Up the street from the Markt. ☎ 432 45 08. Open Tu-F 9:30am-6pm. Free. Call ahead for free tours.)*

SUERMONDT-LUDWIG-MUSEUM. This museum's rotating exhibits showcase everything from Etruscan vases to photography, and its permanent collection specializes in religious works from the Middle Ages through the Baroque era. *(Wilhelmstr. 18. ☎ 47 98 00. Open Tu-Su noon-6pm, W until 9pm. Last entry 30min. before closing. Free tours Su 3pm and W 7:30pm. Museum €3, students and children €1.50.)*

🎵 🎭 ENTERTAINMENT AND NIGHTLIFE

Aachen has a lively theater scene, led by the **Stadttheater,** on Theaterpl. in the central city. *(☎ 478 42 44; www.theater-aachen.de. Box office open M-Sa 11am-2pm, 5-7pm, and 30min. before performances. Tickets €8-20; up to 40% discount for students.)* A small strip of newer, edgier theaters lines Gasborn, spearheaded by the **Aachener Kultur- und Theaterinitiative (AKuT),** Gasborn 9-11 *(☎ 274 58).* **Apollo,** Pontstr. 141-149, has a multi-screen cinema, mellow terrace café, space-age underground *Kneipe* (pub), and a grab-and-go bar outside for pre-movie beer runs. *(☎ 900 84 84. Café open Tu-F noon-8pm, Sa 9am-2pm. Kneipe open M-Th and Su noon-midnight, F-Sa noon-1am. Cash only.)*

Most nightlife in Aachen centers on **Pontstraße** and **Pontwall.** The free *Klenkes Magazin,* available at newsstands, has movies and music listings. The thorough *Stonewall TAC,* available in cafés and at newsstands, lists gay and lesbian events. **Café Kittel,** Pontstr. 39, maintains a dedicated student following with a beer garden and trendy waitstaff. Posters smother the door with announcements for live music and parties. (☎365 60. Open Su-Th 10am-2am, F-Sa 10am-3am. Cash only.) **B9**, Blondelstr. 9, is crowded even mid-week, and spins Top 40s for dance-happy twenty-somethings. Posters give their weekly program of events, including Freaky Friday and Student Night. Crowds line up 1hr. early for Tuesday Free Beer—€4.50 cover for all you can drink 10pm-midnight. (Drinks €2-3.50. Cover weekdays €2, weekends €4. Open M-Th 10pm-4am, F-Sa 10pm-5am. Cash only.)

DÜSSELDORF ☎0211

As Germany's fashion and corporate hub, the capital of densely populated North Rhein-Westphalia crawls with German businessmen and style mavens. Founded in the 13th century, Düsseldorf (pop. 573,500) has thrice rebounded after pummelings in the Thirty Years' War, the War of Spanish Succession, and WWII. Today, it is Germany's *"Hautstadt,"* a pun on *Hauptstadt* (capital) and the French *haute*, as in *haute couture*. The stately, modern metropolis has an Altstadt that features graceful promenades and a boisterous nightlife along the Rhein. Just beyond the riverbank is the Königsallee ("the Kö"), a kilometer-long catwalk that sweeps down both sides of the old town moat. By day, the social scene revolves around sipping espresso in Kö boutiques. By night, cast-away remnants of propriety (and sobriety) litter the streets as thousands of Düsseldorfers flock to the 500 pubs lining the Altstadt for glasses of local *Alt* beer.

! Summer is low season for Düsseldorf's tourist industry; from August to April the city swarms with trade fairs. Hotels often double prices. Reserve accommodations at least a month ahead and confirm the price of your room upon arrival.

TRANSPORTATION

Flights: S7 and a Lufthansa shuttle travel from the main train station to **Flughafen Düsseldorf.** Call ☎421 22 23 for flight information. Open 5am-12:30am.

Trains: To: **Berlin** (4½hr., 2 per hr., €72-88); **Frankfurt** (2hr., 3 per hr., €41-64); **Hamburg** (4hr., 2 per hr., €60-72); **Munich** (5-6hr., 2-3 per hr., €92-112). It's cheaper to take the S-Bahn to **Aachen, Cologne,** and **Dortmund.**

Public Transportation: The **Rheinbahn** (☎582 28) includes U-Bahn, trams, buses, and the S-Bahn. Single tickets €1.10-8 depending on distance. A *Tagesticket* (€7-20) is the best value—up to 5 people can travel for 24hr. on any line. Düsseldorf's S-Bahn is integrated into the regional **VRR** system, which connects most surrounding cities.

Taxi: ☎333 33, 999 99, or 21 21 21.

Car Rental: Hertz, Immermannstr. 65 (☎35 70 25). Open M-F 7am-6pm, Sa 8am-noon. **Avis,** Berliner Allee 26 (☎865 62 20). Open M-F 7:30am-6pm, Sa 8am-noon.

Ride Share: Mitfahrzentrale, Bismarckstr. 88 (☎194 40). Open daily 9am-7pm.

Bike Rental: Zweirad Egert, Ackerstr. 143 (☎66 21 34). S6 (dir.: Essen) to "Wehrbahn." Turn right from the exit on Birkenstr., then right on Ackerstr. and walk 10min. Call ahead to check availability. Bikes €7.50 per day, €12 per weekend. €35 deposit and ID required. Open M-F 10am-6:30pm, Sa 10am-2pm.

PRACTICAL INFORMATION

Tourist Office: Immermannstr. 65 (☎172 02 28; www.duesseldorf-tourismus.de). Walk up and to the right from the train station and look for the Immermannhof building. Free German monthly *In Düsseldorfer* details local goings-on. Open for event ticket sales (their 12% fee is better than a 20% surcharge at the door) and information M-F 8:30am-6pm, Sa 9am-12:30pm, or call the Düsseldorf ticket hotline ☎01805 64 43 22. Books rooms for free (€5 during fairs) M-F 9:30am-6:30pm, Sa 9:30am-2pm. **Branch office,** Berliner Allee 33 (☎300 48 97), inside the Kö-Gallerie shopping mall. Open M-F 10am-6pm.

Consulates: Canada and **UK,** Yorckstr. 19 (☎944 80). Open M-F 8:30am-12:30pm, F also 1:30-4:30pm. **US,** Willi-Becker-Allee 10 (☎788 89 27). Open M-F 9am-5pm.

Currency Exchange: ReiseBank, in the station. Open M-Sa 7am-10pm, Su 8am-9pm.

American Express: Inside the main tourist office. Open M-F 9:30am-1pm and 1:30-5:30pm, Sa 10am-1pm.

Room Share: Mitwohnzentrale, Immermannstr. 24 (☎194 45).

Bookstore: Stern-Verlag, Friedrichstr. 24-28 (☎388 10). Paperbacks in many languages plus Internet access (€3 per hr.). Open M-F 9:30am-8pm, Sa 9:30am-6pm.

Women's Resources: Frauenbüro, Mühlenstr. 29 (☎899 36 03), 3rd fl., entrance next to Mahn-und-Gedenkstätte. Open M-Th 8am-4pm, F 8am-1pm; call for appointments.

Gay and Lesbian Resources: Cafe Rosa Mund, Lierenfelderstr. 39 (☎99 23 77; www.rosamund.de). Events for gays and lesbians. **Aids-Hilfe Zentrum,** Oberbilker Allee 310 (☎77 09 50; www.duesseldorf.aidshilfe.de). S6 to "Oberbilk" or U74 or U77 to "S-Bhf. Oberbilk." Open M-Th 10am-1pm and 2-6pm, F 10am-1pm and 2-4pm.

Laundromat: Wasch Center, Friedrichstr. 92, down the street from the "Kirchpl." Wash €3. Soap €0.50. Dry €0.50 per 10min. Open M-Sa 6am-11pm, last load 10pm.

Emergency: Police ☎110. **Ambulance** and **Fire** ☎112. Emergency **doctor** ☎192 92.

Police: Heinrich-Heine-Allee 17 (☎870 91 13).

Pharmacy: Apotheke im Hauptbahnhof. Open M-F 7am-8pm, Sa 8am-4pm. Emergency ☎01 15 00.

Internet Access: Internet shops line Graf-Adolf-Str., and **g@rden** (p. 306) offers access.

Post Office: Konrad-Adenauer-Pl., to the right of the tourist office. Open M-F 8am-6pm, Sa 9am-2pm. Limited service M-F 6-8pm. **Branch** in Hauptbahnhof open M-F 7am-6:30pm. **Postal Code: 40210.**

ACCOMMODATIONS AND CAMPING

▧ **Backpackers Düsseldorf,** Fürstenwall 180 (☎302 08 48; www.backpackers-duesseldorf.de), lives up to its claim as "the cleanest hostel in the world." Take bus #725 (dir.: Lausward/Franziusstr.) from the station to "Kirchpl." Fully equipped kitchen, proximity to most sights, and a youthful clientele make this a rare find in Düsseldorf. Breakfast, lockers, linen, and Internet access included. Reception 8am-9pm. Check-out noon. Reservations recommended for summer weekends. Dorms €22. MC/V. ❷

Jugendgästehaus Düsseldorf (HI), Düsseldorfer Str. 1 (☎55 73 10; jh-duesseldorf@djh-rheinland.de). Take U70 or U74-U77 (dir.: Heinrich-Heine-Allee) to "Lügpl.," then walk to "Belsenpl." and take bus #835 or 836 (dir.: Graf-Adolf-Pl.) to "Jugendherberge." Clean and reliable, catering mostly to school groups. Reception 7am-1am. Curfew 1am; doors open every hr. on the hr. 2-6am. Dorms €24; singles €35.60; doubles €58.20. €3.10 per night HI discount. Cash only. ❸

Jugendherberge Duisburg-Wedau (HI), Kalkweg 148e (☎0203 72 41 64; www.jh-duisburg@dmx.net). S1 or S21 to "Duisburg Hauptbahnhof," then bus #934 to "Jugendherberge." These dorm beds are too far from the city to accommodate wild nights, but are reliable and inexpensive. Breakfast included. Sheets €3.60. Wash and dry €2 each. Reception 8am-10pm. Closed mid-Dec. to mid-Jan. Curfew 1am. €15.60, over 27 €18.30. 10% discount for stays over 2 nights. Cash only. ❷

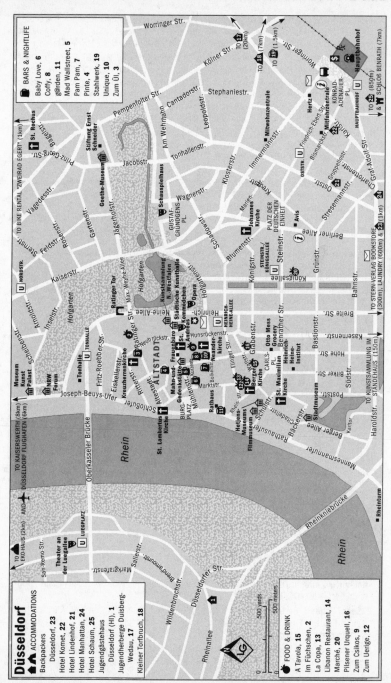

BARS & NIGHTLIFE
Baby Love, 6
Coffy, 8
g@rden, 11
Mad Wallstreet, 5
Pam Pam, 7
Pinte, 4
Stahlwerk, 19
Unique, 10
Zum Ül, 3

Düsseldorf

ACCOMMODATIONS
Backpackers
  Düsseldorf, 23
Hotel Komet, 22
Hotel Lindenhof, 21
Hotel Manhattan, 24
Hotel Schaum, 25
Jugendgästehaus
  Düsseldorf (HI), 1
Jugendherberge Duisberg-
  Wedau, 17
Kleiner Torfbruch, 18

FOOD & DRINK
A Tavola, 15
Im Füchschen, 2
La Copa, 13
Libanon Restaurant, 14
Marché, 20
Pilsener Urquell, 16
Zum Csikos, 9
Zum Uerige, 12

Hotel Lindenhof, Oststr. 124 (☎36 09 63; fax 16 27 67). Spacious rooms in the center of town with informative reception, TV, phone, and private bath. Lavish breakfast included. Check-in and check-out noon. Singles €45; doubles €65. MC/V. ❹

Hotel Schaum, Gustav-Poengsen-Str. 63 (☎311 65 10; fax 31 32 28). From the train station, exit left on Graf-Adolf-Str., follow the first left along the tracks to Gustav-Poengsen-Str. Or, take the S-Bahn 1 stop to "Düsseldorf-Friedrichstadt," exit on Hüttenstr., and take the first left on Gustav-Poengsen-Str. Smoking rooms with TV, and phone, and bathrooms provide a comfortable retreat from the bustle of downtown. Breakfast included. Singles from €30; doubles from €50. MC/V. ❹

Hotel Manhattan, Graf-Adolf-Str. 39 (☎602 22 50; www.hotel-manhattan.de), 4 blocks from the station. The mirror-plated reception hallway reflects neon signs and Coca-Cola posters into infinity. Cozy rooms with TV and phone. Breakfast included. Reception 24hr. Singles from €36; doubles from €57. MC/V. ❸

Kleiner Torfbruch (☎899 20 38). S-Bahn to "Düsseldorf Geresheim," then bus #735 (dir.: Stamesberg) to "Seeweg." Pitch your palace and live like a king. Open Apr.-Oct. Reception 8am-8pm. €4 per person, €5 per tent. Cash only. ❶

🍴 FOOD

There are rows of cheap pizzerias, *Döner kebap* and waffle stands, and Chinese diners reaching from **Heinrich-Heine-Allee** to the Rhein. The **Markt** on Carlspl. has foreign fruits and a local favorite, *Sauerbraten* (pickled beef). (Open M-F 9am-6pm, Sa 9am-4pm.) **Otto Mess** is a popular **grocery** chain; the most convenient location is at the corner of Carlspl. in the Altstadt. (Open M-F 8am-8pm, Sa 8am-6pm.)

La Copa, Bergerstr. 4 (☎323 88 58). Traditional Spanish restaurant serving 50 tasty types of *tapas* (€2-9). Go with a crowd to sample as many as you can, and rinse with sangria (€7 per L). Open daily 11am-midnight. DC/MC/V. ❷

Zum Uerige, Bergerstr. 1 (☎86 69 90). This heavy-wood, heavy-food restaurant competes with Im Füchschen for the best beer in town. Breezy *Rheinisch* nights can be savored over a *Schlösser Alt* or one of their own *Uerige* beers. Meals from €2. Open daily 10am-midnight. Kitchen open M-F 6-9pm, Sa 11am-4pm. Cash only. ❷

Zum Csikos, Andreasstr. 9 (☎32 97 71; www.csikos.de). This colorful little *Kneipe* (bar) is bursting with character and Hungarian cuisine. Though some brave the bear meat, less experimental taste buds will revel in the tasty *Gulyassuppe* (Hungarian stew; €5). Open Tu-Su 6pm-midnight, F-Sa until 1am. Closed Aug. Cash only. ❷

Marché, Königsallee 60 (☎32 06 81), downstairs in the Kö-Galerie mall. Well-stocked with salad, pasta, and meat options, this cafeteria-style restaurant provides a rarity: cheap food on the Kö. Entrées from €3.50. Buffet daily 6pm to close (€11.80). Open M-F 8am-9pm, Sa-Su 8am-8pm. Cash only. ❷

Im Füchschen, Ratinger Str. 28 (☎13 74 70). A popular favorite with the local after-work crowd. *Blutwurst* (blood sausage) and Mainz hand cheese (€3.50) go well with Im Füchschen's own delicious beer, *Füchsenbier* (€1.35 per 0.25L). Open daily 9am-midnight, F-Sa until 1am. Cash only. ❷

Libanon Restaurant, Bergerstr. 19-21 (☎13 49 17). A touch of the exotic. Splurge on the *Masa* (5 course menu; €29) or join the early birds and eat anything on the menu for half-price during the day. Meals €8-20. W-Sa belly dancing from 9pm. Open daily noon-midnight. AmEx/DC/MC/V. ❹

Pilsener Urquell, Grabenstr. 6 (☎13 13 67). The local outlet of a Czech brewery specializes in Eastern European dishes (€4-12). Open M-Sa 10am-1am, Su 4pm-midnight. Kitchen open M-F 10am-3pm and 5-11pm, Sa noon-11pm, Su 4-10pm. MC/V. ❷

A Tavola, Wallstr. 11 (☎13 29 23). Score a seat on the outdoor patio and delight in bottomless bread baskets, meticulously prepared pastas (most €7.50-9), and an Italian-speaking waitstaff. The tomato-smothered bruschetta (€4.90) is a culinary wonder. Open daily noon-3pm and 6-11pm. DC/MC/V. ❸

👁 SIGHTS

KÖNIGSALLEE (KING'S AVENUE). The glitzy Königsallee (known as the "Kö"), just outside the Altstadt, embodies the vitality and glamour of wealthy Düsseldorf. While it doesn't have the fashion-center status of Milan or New York, it packs in enough boutiques and pretension to fill Fifth Avenue. Its title (which means King's Avenue) actually originated as an attempt to placate an angry King Wilhelm IV after he was hit with a piece of manure. Stone bridges span the river that runs down the middle, which trickles to a halt at the toes of an ornate statue of the sea god Triton. Midway up is the highbrow **Kö-Galerie**, a marble-and-copper shopping mall showcasing one sleek, chic store after another. *(Head 10min. down Graf-Adolf-Str. from the train station.)*

SCHLOß BENRATH. Originally built as a retreat and hunting lodge for Elector Karl Theodor, this 18th-century palace is one of the latest examples of Rococo architecture in western Europe. Though the architect used strategically placed mirrors and false exterior windows to make the pink castle appear larger than it is, the vast French gardens and central fountain put the building in perspective. Walk along the reflecting pool behind the castle or explore the tree-lined paths in the park. *(Benrather Schloßallee 100-106. S6 (dir.: Köln) to "Schloß Benrath." ☎899 38 32. Castle open Tu-Su mid-Apr. to Oct. 10am-6pm; Nov. to mid-Apr. 11am-5pm. Tours on the hr., in English if requested. €4, students and children €2.)*

HEINRICH-HEINE-INSTITUT. Beloved poet **Heinrich Heine** is Düsseldorf's melancholic son. His birthplace and homestead are marked by plaques, and every third restaurant and fast-food stand bears his name. This institute is the official shrine, with a collection of manuscripts, Lorelei paraphernalia, and an unsettling death mask. *(Bilker Str. 12-14. ☎899 55 71; www.duesseldorf.de/kultur/heineinstitut. Open Tu-F and Su 11am-5pm, Sa 2-5pm. €2, students €1.)*

HOFGARTEN. At the upper end of the Kö, the Hofgarten park—the oldest public park in Germany and the model for Munich's English Garden—is an oasis of lush green. Stroll to the eastern end of the garden, where the 18th-century **Schloß Jägerhof** houses the **Goethe-Museum** (p. 305) behind white iron gates. The Neoclassical **Ratinger Tor** gatehouse leads into the garden from Heinrich-Heine-Allee.

THE LOCAL STORY

TURNING TRICKS

Düsseldorf may be a modern city focused on efficient business and the latest fashions, but one of its historical legacies—the cartwheel—has less refined, dizzier roots. Although thought to originate in a 1288 battle in which Düsseldorf defeated Cologne (see **Battling Beers**, p. 306), the first cartwheel wasn't officially recorded until 1583. During a royal wedding celebration, local boys impressed the guests with their ability to spin down the street head over heels, and the town's children have been spinning head over heels ever since.

Cartwheels came into prominence in the late 19th century as young boys discovered that adults were willing to part with a penny for a good enough trick. The *Radschlägebrunnen* (Cartwheel Fountain), erected in 1954 in the middle of Burgpl., celebrates the cartwheel's local origins.

Today, cartwheelers are scattered across the city—mostly just as statues, key chains, and pictures on tour buses. But every year during the last week in June, the local youth once again take their sport to the streets. An annual tradition since 1937, *Radschlägen Turnier* is a competition to seek out both the fastest and the most stylish cartwheels in town. Around 500 boys and girls descend on Königsallee to show off in front of the crowds and compete in 20m cartwheel races.

KAISERWERTH. North on the Rhein in tiny Kaiserwerth are the ruins of Emperor Friedrich Barbarossa's palace. Built in 1184, it was the most important fortress on the Rhein before being destroyed by the French in 1702 during the War of Spanish Succession; only the gloomy frame remains. Some fearless travelers climb the ruins at night (with the aid of flashlights) and check out the blinking lights of the Rheinturm, a huge clock tower over 8km away. From bottom to top, the dots represent one second, 10 seconds, 1min., 10min., 1hr., and 10hr. *(Take U79 to "Klemenspl.," then follow Kaiserswerther Markt left to the Rhein, turn left, and walk another 150m.)*

EKO-HAUS. Across the Rhein from the Altstadt, the EKO-Haus celebrates Düsseldorf's Japanese population (one of the largest in Europe) with a beautiful garden, temple, and cultural center that hosts frequent tea ceremonies and readings from Buddhist texts. *(Brüggener Weg 6. Take U70 or U74-U77 to "Barbarossapl." Follow Arnulfstr., turn right on Kirchweg and then left on Brüggener Weg. Take the path to the left that leads to a small gate.* ☎ *577 91 80; www.eko-haus.de. Open Tu-Su 1-5pm. €2.50, students €1.50.)*

🏛 MUSEUMS

Düsseldorf takes pride in its many museums, especially the collections of contemporary art from the last century. Museums cluster around **Ehrenhof** above the Altstadt and **Grabbeplatz** near the center. The **Düsseldorf WelcomeCard** (available at the tourist office) includes entrance to major museums, as well as free public transportation and other discounts. (One-day card €9; 2-day card €14; 3-day card €19.)

▨ **K21: KUNSTSAMMLUNG IM STÄNDEHAUS (ART COLLECTION IN THE ESTATE HOUSE).** Once home to the *Land*'s parliament, this enormous building reopened in April 2002 as the companion museum to the Kunstsammlung Nordrhein-Westfalen, focusing on experimental art from the late 20th century onward. A box fan swinging like an erratic pendulum greets you as you prepare to delve into the most progressive styles the art world has to offer. Featuring prolific modern artists such as Sigmar Polke and Katharina Fritsch, each exhibit has German and English captions. *(Ständehausstr. 1. Take tram #704, 709, or 719 to "Graf-Adolf-Pl." Walk 1 block down Elisabethstr. and turn right on Ständehausstr.* ☎ *838 16 00; www.kunstsammlung.de. Open Tu-F 10am-6pm, Sa-Su 11am-6pm, 1st W of month until 10pm. €6.50, students €4.50; combined K21/K20 ticket €10/8. German and English audio guides €1.)*

▨ **FILMMUSEUM.** Generations of movie madness are chronicled through demonstrations of early animation, dubbed clips from notable directors, film cuttings, dioramas, and lots of Greta Garbo. Impress your friends with excellent shadow puppets or transport yourself using blue screen technology. The Black Box theater (p. 305), in the same complex, specializes in recent cult flicks. *(Schulstr. 4. between Carlspl. and the Rhein.* ☎ *899 22 32. Open Tu-Su 11am-5pm, W until 9pm. €3, students €1.50.)*

▨ **K20: THE KUNSTSAMMLUNG NORDRHEIN-WESTFALEN (THE REGIONAL ART COLLECTION).** Within this black glass edifice, skylights lavish sunshine on Matisse, Picasso, Surrealists, and Expressionists. The collection of works by Düsseldorfer Paul Klee is one of the most extensive in the world. The museum hosts rotating exhibits of modern art and film. *(Grabbepl. 5. U70, U74-U79 or tram #706, 713, or 715 to "Heinrich-Heine-Allee."* ☎ *838 11 30. Open Tu-F 10am-6pm, Sa-Su 11am-6pm, 1st W of month 11am-10pm. Tours W 3:30pm, Su 11:30am. €3, students €1.50.)*

HETJENS-MUSEUM. Connected to the Filmmuseum, the Hetjens-Museum fills four floors with 8000 years of ceramics, including intricate Islamic tilework, 19th-century porcelain pets, and Precolumbian American relics. *(Schulstr. 4.* ☎ *899 42 10. Open Tu and Th-Su 11am-5pm, W until 9pm. €3, students €1.50; exhibitions €1 extra.)*

STÄDTISCHE KUNSTHALLE (MUNICIPAL ART GALLERY). Across the square from K20 is a gallery of rotating modern art exhibits. The stove-pipe on the museum is a piece by Joseph Beuys meant to symbolize the link between art and the real world. *(Grabbepl. 4. ☎899 62 43; www.kunsthalle-duesseldorf.de. Open Tu-Sa noon-7pm, Su 11am-6pm. Admission depends on exhibit; usually €5, students €4.)*

MUSEUM KUNST PALAST (PALACE OF ART). A dizzying display that mingles masterworks of antiquity with modern creations. On the ground floor, glassware, tapestries, and some astonishingly intricate locks memorialize 11 centuries of aristocratic decor. The museum's rotating contemporary exhibits lie beyond stained-glass windows. The newly designed Robert-Schumann-Saal complex features theatrical and musical performances. *(Ehrenhof 4-5. ☎899 24 60; www.museum-kunst-palast.de. Open Tu-Su 11am-6pm. Tours Th and Su 3pm. €6, students and children €3.50.)*

NRW FORUM. Dedicated to works that combine art and industry, the Forum's past exhibits have included Herb Ritts's portraits, Verner Panton's retro furnishings, and Frank Miller's comic book art. *(Ehrenhof 2. ☎892 66 90. Open Tu-Su 11am-8pm, F until midnight. €5.50, students €3.50.)*

STADTMUSEUM (MUNICIPAL MUSEUM). This museum recounts the history of Düsseldorf from the pre-historic to the aftermath of WWII. Also featured are works by the Young Rheinland group and a Napoleon room. *(Berger Allee 2. ☎899 61 70. Take tram #704, 709, or 719 to "Poststr." or U-Bahn to "Heinrich-Heine-Allee." Open Tu-Su 11am-5pm, W and Sa 11am-9pm. €2.60, students and children €1.30.)*

MAHN- UND GEDENKSTÄTTE (JEWISH MEMORIAL). Through photographs, videotapes, and audio-taped interviews, the Gedenkstätte documents the persecution of Jews during the Nazi era. Established as a memorial in 1987, this museum addresses the Christian Churches' and workers' movements as well as racial persecution. *(Mühlenstr. 29. ☎899 62 05. Open Tu-F and Su 11am-5pm, Sa 1-5pm.)*

GOETHE-MUSEUM. Goethe only visited Düsseldorf for four weeks in 1792, but this museum houses the world's largest collection of artifacts related to his life, with 1000 exhibits from a collection of 50,000 original testimonials. *(Jakobistr. 2. In Schloß Jägerhof. Tram #707 or bus #752 to "Schloß Jägerhof." ☎899 62 62. Open Tu-F and Su 11am-5pm, Sa 1-5pm. Library open Tu-F 10am-noon and 2-4pm. €2, students and children €1.)*

🎵 🎭 ENTERTAINMENT AND NIGHTLIFE

Folklore holds that Düsseldorf's 500 pubs make up *die längste Theke der Welt* (the longest bar in the world). Every night, pubs in the Altstadt are standing-room-only by 6pm, and foot traffic is shoulder-to-shoulder by nightfall. The young, tourist-friendly **Bolkerstraße** and **Flingerstraße** are jam-packed with street performers of the musical and beer-olympic varieties, while mature locals head to **Ratingerstr.** Though the Altstadt makes a casual setting for all ages, the city's debutantes flaunt their designer purchases in upscale bars and clubs; don't expect to mingle if you don't dress the part. Clubbers should watch their valuables while hanging out around Charlottenstr. after nightfall. *Prinz* (€3) is Düsseldorf's fashion bible; it's often free at the youth hostel. *Facolte* (€2), a gay and lesbian nightlife magazine, is available at most newsstands.

Kommödchen is a tiny, extraordinarily popular theater behind the Kunsthalle on Kay-und-Lore-Lorentz-Pl. (☎32 94 43. Box office open M-Sa 11:30am-8pm, Su 5-8pm.) To avoid a service charge, purchase ballet and opera tickets at the **Opernhaus,** Heinrich-Heine-Allee 16a. (☎890 82 11. Box office open M-F 10am-8pm, Sa 10am-6pm, and 1hr. before each performance. Tickets €8-59.) **Black Box,** Schulstr. 4 (☎899 24 90), off Rathausufer along the Rhein, serves the art-film aficionado with

BATTLING BEERS

Drinking beer is generally a simple affair; however, while indulging in Düsseldorf, never forget one simple rule of thumb: never, under any circumstances, order a *Kölsch*. The rationale behind this dictate is twofold. Legally, according to the 1985 Kölsch Convention, this special beer can only be served within a 20mi. radius of Cologne. More important, though, is the long-standing rivalry between Düsseldorf and its upstream neighbor Cologne.

Historians date the rift back to 1288 when Count Adolf vom Berg (of what was then Duseldorp) led 6000 troops into battle against the Archbishop of Cologne in one of the bloodiest spectacles of the Middle Ages. Locals say that mere jealousy fuels the hatred: Cologne resents the fact that its protégé has become an international corporate and fashion headquarters, while Düsseldorf remains envious of the art, history, and Dom it will never have.

Others argue that the fierce competition is founded on more serious grounds: beer. Nothing elicits town pride more than the local brew: Cologne boasts a gold fountain of *Kölsch* (known by its gold color and subtle, fruity flavor), while Düsseldorf prides itself on its coppery reservoirs of *Altbier* (bitter and thick). Fortunately, travelers can experience (and taste) the charms of both cities, which are less than an hour of train travel apart. Just keep your preferences to yourself.

foreign flicks in their original format (€5, students €4). Tickets for all events are available by phone, at the box office, or from the tourist office.

■ **Mad Wallstreet,** Kurzestr. 6 (www.madwallstreet.de). A play on the market economy: prices listed on flatscreens show fluctuating drink prices every 300 seconds throughout the night. The law of drunken supply and demand means prices of popular drinks soar as others plummet. Prices crash to historical lows on Black Fridays (beer €0.90, shooters €1.90, mixed drinks €2.90). Packs a loyal crowd of trendy youths every weekend. Open F-Sa 10pm-3am. Cash only.

Unique, Bolkerstr. 30 (☎323 09 90). Instead of joining in the endless beerfest with neighboring bars, this aptly named, red-walled club focuses on the music and draws a young, trendy crowd with deeper pockets. Cover €5-10. Open W-Sa from 10pm. MC/V.

Pam-Pam, Bolkerstr. 32 (☎854 93 94). This minimally lit basement disco is filled to overflowing by midnight, yet the crowds keep coming. Dance the night away to house, rock, pop, and plenty of American music. Open daily 9pm-5am. Cash only.

Zum Ül, Ratinger Str. 16 (☎32 53 69). The quintessential German *Kneipe*, and a dime a dozen in Düsseldorf. The crowd congregating out front renders the street impassable; inside people of all ages down glasses of *Füchschenbier* (€1.40 for 0.2L). Open daily 10am-1am, Sa-Su until 3am. Cash only.

Coffy, Mertensg. 8 (☎868 16 50). Hipsters at this popular bar and disco drape themselves across cubical cushions or assemble in the cavernous downstairs dance hall. In the summer, the bar moves to the square outside Tonhalle 3-11pm. Cover F-Sa €3. Café open daily from noon. Disco open F-Sa 11pm-4am. MC/V.

Baby Love, Kurzerstr. 2 (☎828 43 45). This favorite practically pulsates with dancing and music. W reggae and R&B, Th punk, F-Sa techno. Open Tu-Th 9pm-3am, F-Sa 10pm-late. Cash only.

Stahlwerk, Ronsdorfer Str. 134 (☎73 03 50; www.stahlwerk.de). U75 to "Ronsdorfer Str." This classic 2fl. factory-turned-disco packs in 1500 or more of the city's most divine for events like their famous 80s nights and Diebels beer parties. Dress to impress and don't plan to leave before the city starts to wake up. Cover €4-6. Open F-Sa and the last Su of the month from 10pm. Cash only.

g@rden, Rathausufer 8 (☎86 61 60). A futuristic café with Internet access (€2 per 30min., €3 per hr.), a view of the Rhein, and DJs who spin everything from R&B to techno on request. Checking email never felt so cool. Open Mar.-Sept. Café open 10am-1am. Club open from 9pm on 1st and 3rd Sa of the month. MC.

RUHRGEBIET (RUHR REGION)

On the banks of the Ruhr River, this region leapt from obscurity to industrial powerhouse when factories began cropping up all over in the mid-19th century. As the Industrial Revolution swept across Europe, the pace at which train tracks, rail cars, and guns streamed from these factories increased, catapulting the region into industrial preeminence in just 25 years. During this time, mounting economic pressures, coupled with labor strikes and Marxist rhetoric, kindled fears of Communist revolt; the popular moniker "Red Ruhr" had little to do with the water color. Still, residents remained loyal to the government; the region was felled not by revolution but by Allied bombing in WWII. Today it boasts an unrivaled sense of regional unity and high quality of life. Named the European Capital of Culture 2010, the Ruhrgebiet, spearheaded by Essen, will focus on the theme of transformation in and through culture as it plays host to a bevy of international events.

ESSEN ☎0201

For a millennium after the Bishop of Hildesheim founded a nunnery on the premises in AD 852, Essen remained just another German cathedral town. By the eve of WWI, however, it had become the industrial capital of Germany, thanks to seemingly limitless deposits of coal and iron. Essen capitalized on the utter annihilation inflicted by Allied air raids, reinventing itself as a city free of soot and full of culture. Though today visitors benefit from revamped historical sights and an outstanding museum, the city maintains its reputation as the industrial cornerstone of the Ruhr with shiny skyscrapers and rows of chain stores.

TRANSPORTATION AND PRACTICAL INFORMATION. Trains go to Düsseldorf (30min., 5 per hr., €10) and Dortmund (45min., 3 per hr., €9). U-Bahn and tram rides cost €1-1.85, depending on distance; day tickets costs €6.70. The **tourist office,** Am Hauptbahnhof 2, opposite the station, books rooms and dispenses maps for free. (☎ 194 33; www.essen.de. Open M-F 10am-7pm, Sa 10am-6pm.) **Internet** access is at **Web & Call,** Hachestr. 5, one block to the left of the train station. (€2 per hr. Open daily 9am-11pm.) The **post office** is on Willy-Brandt-Pl. across from the station. (Open M-F 8am-7pm, Sa 8:30am-3:30pm.) **Postal Code:** 45127.

ACCOMMODATIONS AND FOOD. The **Jugendherberge (HI) ❷,** Am Pastoratsberg 2, is in the middle of a quiet forest in Werden, a suburb noted for its eighth-century Abteikirche and Luciuskirche, the oldest parishes north of the Alps. Take S6 to "Werden" (25min.) and bus #190 to "Jugendherberge." Rooms are standard but far from the city. (☎49 11 63; jh-essen@djh-rheinland.de. Breakfast and sheets included. Reception 7am-10pm. Curfew midnight. Dorms €19; singles €30; doubles €50. MC/V.) The comfortable **Hotel Kessing ❸,** Hachestr. 30, is close to the train station and has a TV in every room; go left as you exit the station on Hachestr. (☎23 99 88. Breakfast included. Singles €35, with shower €45, with bath €45; doubles with bath €75. Cash only.) Camp at **Stadt-Camping Essen-Werden ❶,** Im Löwental 67, on the west bank of the Ruhr. Take the S6 to "Werden," then walk under the bridge and continue straight. The campground is on the left. (☎49 29 78. Reception 7am-1pm and 3-9pm. €4 per person, €8 per tent. Cash only.) The youthful **Porscheplatz,** near the Rathaus, mixes outdoor cafés with cheap mall food. Take the U-Bahn to "Porschepl." Nearby **Kennedyplatz** is lined with full-service restaurants, all with outdoor seating perfect for taking in the crowd. Next door, the university-sponsored bar/restaurant **KKC ❷,** Universitätsstr. 2, hosts occasional parties and serves up more varied but equally inexpensive food (€2-8) and drinks.

(☎205 02. Open M 9am-8pm, Tu-F 9am-midnight. Cash only.) Across the street, **Beaulongerie ❶**, Segerothstr. 81, offers delicious foot-long sandwiches (€3-4) on fresh-baked baguette or ciabatta bread. (☎32 62 12. Open M-Sa 10am-10pm. Cash only.) The **Mensa ❶**, Segerothstr. 80, is in the yellow-trimmed cafeteria at the university. Take the U11 or U17 to "Universität," exit to "Segerothstr.," head toward the rail overpass; the *Mensa* is on the left. (☎18 31. Open M-F 11:15am-2pm. Meals €2.50-6. Cash only.) A **supermarket** can be found in the basement of **Kaufhof** on Willy-Brandt-Pl. across from the station. (Open M-F 8am-8pm, Sa 9am-5pm.)

◪ **SIGHTS.** The **Museumszentrum,** Goethestr. 41, houses two museums. Take tram #101, 107, or U11 to "Rüttenscheider Stern," follow signs to the Museumzentrum, and continue north on Rüttenscheiderstr., then turn left on Kuhrstr. and right onto Goethestr. Or, walk down Hachestr. from the train station, turn left on Bismarckstr., and the museum is 500m on the right. Unrivaled among Essen's modern attractions is its internationally renowned ▨**Museum Folkwang** (☎884 53 00; www.museum-folkwang.de), a stunning collection featuring defining works from the repertoire of every important German artist of the 19th and 20th centuries. The Folkwang's **Fotographische Sammlung** takes on camera work from the early days, with photographs capturing the grit of urban life in the Ruhrgebiet.

Also worth a look is the attached **Ruhrlandmuseum** (☎884 50 10), which has display of fossils, gemstones, and Egyptian artifacts, in addition to an exhibit on the geology, industry, and social history of the Ruhr in its industrial heyday. Visitors can live a day in the life of a miner without dirtying their hands by peeking at sundry paraphernalia, tools, and medical evaluations surrounding an old mining elevator. (Both museums open Tu-Su 10am-6pm, F until midnight. Single admission €5, students and children €3.50. Combined admission €8/5.50.)

Nineteenth-century arms and railroad mogul **Alfred Krupp** perfected steel-casting in industrial Essen. **Villa Hügel,** Hügel 15, the longtime Krupp family home (or rather, palace), was given to the city in the 1950s to brighten the company's image, once tarnished by its Nazi affiliation. Inside, the museum details the history of this illustrious man, his family, and his business. Even the gargantuan Victorian mahogany staircases and intricate carvings pale in comparison to the rotating exhibits that fill the mansion's main hall with exotic artifacts from afar. (S6 to "Essen-Hügel." ☎61 62 90. Museum open Tu-Su 10am-6pm, grounds open 8am-6pm. €1, under 14 and seniors free. Check concert schedule at tourist office.)

Built as a nunnery in the ninth century and presently the cathedral of the bishopric of Essen, the **Münsterkirche,** near the city center on Burgpl., served as the focus of life for centuries. Today, its octagonal towers are dwarfed by Essen's industrial edifices, but the cloistered string of flowering courtyards and hexagonal crypts continue to impress. Next to the choir, a candlelit shrine surrounds the 1000-year-old, doll-like *Goldene Madonna*—the church's most cherished item and the oldest three-dimensional sculpture of the Virgin Mary in the world. (☎220 44 19. Open daily 7:30am-6:30pm. Free. Treasury open Tu-Sa 10am-5pm, Su 12:30-5pm. €3, students €1.50.) Though Nazis gutted Essen's **Alte Synagogue,** Steeler Str. 29, in 1938, the largest synagogue north of the Alps now serves as a memorial to Jews oppressed and murdered by the regime. The ground floor presents German Jewish history from the Middle Ages through the "Final Solution," as well as "Stages of Jewish Life," while temporary exhibits on the second floor portray life during the Nazi regime. Exhibits are in German and English. (Take the U-Bahn to "Porschepl." and follow the signs to the Schützenbahn; as you head south on the Schützenbahn, the synagogue is on your left. ☎884 52 18 or 884 52 23. Open Tu-Su 10am-6pm. Free.) Across the street, the **Theaterplatz,** site of the **Grillo theater,** along with the **Rathaus theater** at Porschepl., hosts a range of productions. (☎812 22 00. Box office in the Rathaus open M-F 10am-5pm, Sa 10am-1pm.)

NORDRHEIN-WESTFALEN

DORTMUND ☎0231

Dortmund's fame for steel and coal production made it a prime target for bombing raids during WWII. The city (pop. 587,000) has been since rebuilt with a mix of small family-owned shops and large department stores, blending the languid gait of medieval charms with the modern sheen of convenience. Spacious parks found just outside the city center complete its suburban appearance. Budget flights from the nearby airport make Dortmund a requisite stopover for many travelers.

■🖪 TRANSPORTATION AND PRACTICAL INFORMATION. Trains to: Cologne (1¼-1½hr., 2-3 per hr., €15); Düsseldorf (1hr., 3 per hr., €12); Münster (50min., 3 per hr., €9); Hanover (2hr., 2 per hr., €33). The **airport shuttle** departs from the train station every hr. 4:30am-10:30pm (25min., €5). U-Bahn and tram rides cost €1-1.80; day tickets €6.70. The **tourist office**, Königswall 18a, across from the station, books hotel rooms for free and hands out info on city sights and €0.50 maps of the Altstadt. Detailed tourist maps of the area are also available. (☎18 99 91 12; www.dortmund-tourismus.de. Open M-F 9am-6pm, Sa 9am-1pm.) Rent **bikes** next door at **Fahrradvermietung**. (€8 per day, €30 deposit. Open M-F 5:30am-11pm.) Find English **books** on the second floor of **Mayersche Bücher**, on the corner of Hansastr. and Westenhellweg. (Open M-F 9:30am-8pm, Sa 9am-8pm.) Do **laundry** at **Eco-Express Waschsalon**, Burgwall 17; follow Königswall left from the train station until it becomes Burgwall. (Wash €1.50, soap €0.50. Dry €1 per 15min. Open daily 6am-11pm, last wash 10pm.) The **post office** is at Kurfürstenstr. 2, behind the train station. (Open M-F 7:30am-8pm, Sa 8am-3:30pm.) **Postal Code:** 44137.

🖪🛏 ACCOMMODATIONS AND FOOD. Ruhgebiet.de ❷, Lindemannstr. 78, in a residential neighborhood filled with lively cafés and bars outside the city center, offers two- to eight-person dorms with ultra-modern kitchen, TV lounge, free laundry, wireless Internet access, and the most social lodgings in Dortmund. Take the U-Bahn to "Kreuzstr." (10min. from train station). (☎95 29 977; www.ruhgebiet.de. Sheets €2.50, breakfast buffet €5. Dorms €17-24; multiple nights discount. Cash only.) The **Jugendgästehaus Adolph Kolping (HI) ❷**, Silberstr. 24-26, offers clean and secure rooms centrally located in the Altstadt. Follow Königswall left from the train station, turn right on Hansastr., and right on Silberstr. (☎14 00 74. Breakfast included. Reception 24hr. Dorms €19.90; singles €30; doubles €50. MC/V.) **Hotel Carlton ❸**, Lütge-Brückstr. 5-7, provides basic rooms with TV and bath in the Altstadt. From Hansastr. turn left on Lütge-Brückstr.; it's on the left. (☎52 80 30. Breakfast included. Singles €30-45; doubles €60-90. Cash only.) **Pension Göhler ❸**, Sudermannstr. 40, has bright rooms with private bath outside the city center. Take the U-Bahn to "Kampstr.," and then tram #403 or 404 (dir.: Dorstfeld) to "Heinrich-str." and backtrack to Sudermannstr. Or, follow Königswall right from the train station, turn right on Rheinische Str. and left on Sudermannstr. (25min.). (☎16 44 49. Singles €29; doubles €45. 10% discount for week-long stays. Cash only.)

Many pricey restaurants line the streets in central Dortmund, where the locally brewed *Hövels* is the beer of choice. Younger residents dine at the eateries lining **Bruckstr.** to the north of the city center. One that shouldn't be passed up is **🖪Boomerang ❸**, Kuckelke 20, an Australian restaurant and pub with superb food. Tackle the emu burger (€8) or wrangle an entire crocodile steak (€18.50). Pizza and pasta (€5.50-6.50) are available for more timid taste buds. From Hansastr., turn left on Friedhof and left again at Kuckelke. (☎586 29 11. M all you can eat. Open daily 11am-midnight, F-Sa until 1am. DC/MC/V.) **Mongo's ❹**, Lindemannstr. 80, cooks custom-tailored casseroles on a Mongolian grill. Choose your meat—including rabbit, lamb, duck, and kangaroo—and unlimited sides for an all-you-can-eat feast (from €14.50). Ample non-meat options include salmon, tilapia, halibut, mus-

sels, and tofu. (☎58 44 950. Open daily 5pm-midnight, Su also noon-4pm. MC/V.)
ALEX ❷, Ostenhellenweg 18-21, maintains a hip atmosphere under brightly colored
chandeliers. Located in the C&A building, this café/bar has salads, baguettes, and
hot entrées, all €3-8. (☎589 78 50. Open daily 8am-1am. Cash only.)

◪ SIGHTS. Dortmund has numerous parks in the vicinity of the Altstadt. **West-falenpark,** 2km southeast, is known for the magnificent rose gardens that cover its
gentle hills. Several playgrounds on the east end of the park keep children occupied for hours. Ascend **Florianturm,** the 212m radio tower, for a view of the city or
a bite to eat at the rotating restaurant. Take U45 or 49 to "Westfalenpark," or U41
or 47 to "Märkische Str." (☎502 61 00. Open daily 10am-11pm. €1.80, children €1.
Florianturm €1.50. Combination ticket €3.10, children €2.50.)

MÜNSTER ☎0251

Long ago, the citizens of Münster (pop. 956,000) chose the crowing cock as their
city symbol—and rightly so: the people here have a little more swagger and a lot
more fun than residents of most towns their size. Locals meet nightly for dinner
and a drink to celebrate almost anything—Wednesdays, for instance—especially
in the student-filled *Kuhviertel* (cow quarter). The promenade encircling the city
center and surrounding parks teems with joggers, dog-walkers, and people taking
the scenic route to work. As capital of the Kingdom of Westphalia, Münster witnessed the treaty that ended the Thirty Years' War and defined the borders of German states for centuries. Residents never tire of retelling the story of the 1648
Peace of Westphalia over a beer.

▟ TRANSPORTATION

Flights: Flughafen Münster-Osnabrück, to the northeast of the city, has flights to major
European cities. Bus #S50 shuttles between the train station and the airport. **Flight
information:** ☎02571 940.

Trains: To: **Cologne** (2hr., 2-3 per hr., €23-28); **Düsseldorf** (1½hr., 2-3 per hr., €18-25);
Emden (2hr., 1-2 per hr., €24-29).

Car Rental: Hertz, Weseler Str. 316 (☎773 78). Weekly rates start at €270, including
insurance. Open M-F 7:30am-6pm, Sa 7:30am-1pm.

Bike Rental: Radstation (☎484 01 70), in front of the station. Look for the big glass triangle. €6 per day, €25 per wk. Open M-F 5:30am-11pm, Sa-Su 7am-11pm.

Ride Share: Mitfahrzentrale AStA, Schloßpl. 1 (☎405 05). Open M-F 9am-4pm.

▟ ✦ ORIENTATION AND PRACTICAL INFORMATION

Münster is at the confluence of the lower channels of the Ems River, in the midst
of the Münsterland plain. The concentric Promenade encircles the Altstadt to the
west of the train station.

Tourist Office: Heinrich-Brüning-Str. 9 (☎492 27 10; www.tourismus.muenster.de). Just
off the Marktpl. From the station, cross Bahnhofstr. and head into the Windhortstr.
pedestrian zone. Veer right as the street becomes Stubeng.; the office is on your left as
Stubeng. crosses Klemenstr. Books rooms for free and offers tours and theater tickets.
German tours daily 11am, English tours Sa 11am. €5, children, students, and seniors
€4. Open M-F 9:30am-6pm, Sa 9:30am-1pm.

Budget Travel: STA Travel, Frauenstr. 25 (☎41 43 90), makes ISICs. Open M-F 10am-6pm, Sa 10am-2pm.

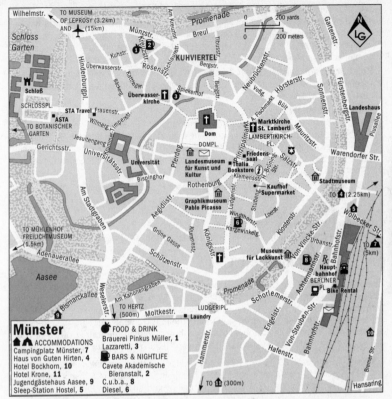

NORDRHEIN-
WESTFALEN

Münster

ACCOMMODATIONS
Campingplatz Münster, **7**
Haus von Guten Hirten, **4**
Hotel Bockhorn, **10**
Hotel Krone, **11**
Jugendgästehaus Aasee, **9**
Sleep-Station Hostel, **5**

FOOD & DRINK
Brauerei Pinkus Müller, **1**
Lazzaretti, **3**

BARS & NIGHTLIFE
Cavete Akademische
Bieranstalt, **2**
C.u.b.a., **8**
Diesel, **6**

Bookstore: Thalia Bücher, Prinzipalmarkt 24 (☎41 86 00). A decent selection of English paperbacks and classics. Open M-F 9:30am-8pm, Sa 9:30am-4pm.

Laundromat: Münz Waschcenter, Moltkestr. 5-7. Wash €3.50, soap included. Dry €0.50 per 15min. Open M-F 6am-11pm. Last wash 10pm.

Emergency: Police, Alter Steinweg 26 (☎110). **Fire** and **Ambulance** ☎112.

Pharmacy: Bahnhofs-Apotheke, Bahnhofstr. 24. Open daily 9am-9pm. Emergency after-hours pharmacy ☎455 48.

Internet Access: PTT Call Shop & Internet Café, Bahnhofstr. 8-10, directly across from the train station. €2 for 30min., €3 per hr. Open daily 9am-10pm.

Post Office: Berliner Pl. 35-37. To the left as you exit the train station. Open M-F 8am-7pm, Sa 8am-1pm. Another **branch,** Dompl. 6-7, is across from the Dom. Open M-F 9am-7pm, Sa 8:30am-2pm. **Postal Code:** 48143.

🏠🏕 ACCOMMODATIONS AND CAMPING

Sleep-Station Hostel, Wolbecker Str. 1 (☎482 81 55; www.sleep-station.de). Next to the train station, this no-fuss-or-frills hostel is perfect for the mobile traveler. Fully equipped kitchen, free lockers, and a common room abuzz with backpackers. Reception 8am-8pm. Check-out noon. Dorms €18; singles €32; doubles €52. Cash only. ❷

Jugendgästehaus Aasee (HI), Bismarckallee 31 (☎53 02 80; jgh-muenster@djh-wl.de). Bus #34 (dir.: Roxel) to "Hoppendamm." Overlooking the Aasee, this friendly hostel has in-room bath, sheets, Internet, and a pool table. Bike rental €5 per day (€10 deposit). Breakfast included; other meals €6.90. Reception 7am-1am. Lockout 1am, doors open for 5min. on the hr. 2-6am. Dorms €21.70; singles €37; doubles €59; quads €87. MC/V. ❸

Hotel Bockhorn, Bremer Str. 24 (☎655 10). Rooms with TV, close to the city's club scene. Breakfast included. Reception 24hr. Singles €35, with bath €50; doubles €60/90. AmEx/D/MC/V. ❸

Haus vom Guten Hirten, Mauritz Lindenweg 61 (☎378 70). Bus #14 to "Mauritz Friedhof." A 40min. walk from the rear of the train station: turn left on Bremer Str., right on Wolbecker Str., left on Hohenzollernring, right on Manfred-von-Richthofen-Str., and left on Mauritz Lindenweg. Managed by the Church, this "bed & bike" hotel offers suites big enough to debunk ideas of church asceticism. Breakfast included. Reception 6am-9pm. Singles €32; doubles €54; triples €77. Cash only. ❸

Hotel Krone, Hammerstr. 67 (☎738 68). Bus #1 or 9 to "Josephkirche." Above a chic restaurant, this small family- and pet-friendly hotel has large, if worn, rooms. Singles €37; doubles €60. Cash only. ❹

Campingplatz Münster, Wolbecker Str. 7 (☎31 19 82). Bus R22 or R32 to "Freibad," near the pool. Reception 8am-midnight. €4 per person, €4-7 per tent. Cash only. ❶

◘◙ FOOD AND NIGHTLIFE

The plaza in front of the Dom hosts a **farmer's market** (W and Sa 7am-1:30pm). Fridays 12:30-6pm you'll find the organic produce market **Biomarkt** there. The student district, **Kuhviertel**, hides cheap eateries and cafés. Bars line the streets opposite the *Schloß*, and clubs reign between the train station and the harbor, while large party venues litter **Hafenweg**. Münster has frequent concerts; buy tickets at the tourist office or box office. (☎41 46 71 00. Open Tu-F 9am-1:30pm and 3:30-7pm, Sa 9am-1pm.)

Diesel, Windthorstr. 65 (☎579 67), in the Altstadt, at the intersection of Windthorstr., Stubeng. and Lörstr. Trendy types nurse mixed drinks over pizzas (€4-7) in a smoky pub filled with Keith Haring art. A gas pump stands guard and James Brown provides the soundtrack. Open daily 10am-1am. Kitchen open until 10pm. Cash only. ❷

Brauerei Pinkus Müller, Kreuzstr. 7-10 (☎451 51). Across the street from the Cavete, this enormous beer hall brims with locals and *Original Pinkus Alt* (€1.80 per 0.25L). Deep thoughts may very well hide within the overlapping inscriptions carved into the tables by less well-mannered patrons. Open M-Sa 11:30am-midnight. Cash only. ❷

Cavete Akademische Bieranstalt, Kreuzstr. 38 (☎457 00). Founded in 1959, the first student pub in Westphalia serves homemade spinach noodles smothered in thick sauces (€6-8) in a dark, cavernous atmosphere. Open daily 7pm-1am. Kitchen closes M-Th and Su 11:30pm, F-Sa 12:30am. Cash only. ❷

C.u.b.a., Achtermannstr. 10-12 (☎548 92; www.cuba-muenster.de). A late-night hotspot for the alternative crowd, this 2-floor cultural center, club, and *Kneipe* (pub) throws specialty parties W and Sa. Open daily 6pm-1am. Kitchen open until 11pm. MC/V.

Lazzaretti, Spiekerhof 26 (☎48 42 333). This stylish bistro and outdoor patio is a popular student haunt by day and home to a young after-work crowd by night. Pasta €6-12. Giant sundaes €4-7. Open daily 10am-11pm. DC/MC/V.

◉ SIGHTS

▨ **DOM.** The heart of Münster's religious community is the huge **St. Paulus-Dom** in the center of the Altstadt. Though the church was founded under the direction of

Charlemagne in AD 792, the cathedral standing today dates from the 13th century, now beautifully restored after WWII bombings. A stone from the similarly bombed Cathedral of Coventry stands in the entryway, carrying a wish for mutual forgiveness between Britain and Germany. Inside is the pulpit where Bishop Clemens von Galen delivered three courageous sermons against the Nazi program of euthanasia for so-called "incurables." Fearing revolt if he arrested the popular bishop, Hitler took out his frustration by sending 37 priests and clergy to concentration camps in von Galen's place; 10 of them died there. Transcripts of his sermons can be purchased in English or German at the treasury. An exceptional feat of artistry and intellectual precision, a 16th-century **astronomical clock** dominates the choir ambulatory. Adorned with hand-painted zodiac symbols, the clock will operate until the year 2071, when its calendar will end and restart at the year 1540. Meanwhile, it continues to keep accurate time, trace the movement of the planets, and play a merry Glockenspiel (Carousel with the Three Magi and chimes) tune. *(M-Sa noon and Su 12:30pm.)* A wide selection of diocesan vestments in the basement displays church fashion from the late Middle Ages. *(Dom open daily 6:30am-6pm. Free. Courtyard open Tu-Sa 9am-6pm, Su 2-6pm. Free. Treasury open Tu-Su 11am-4pm. €1, students €0.50.)*

MARKTKIRCHE ST. LAMBERTI. Münster's piety shows its macabre side at the Marktkirche St. Lamberti, where three cages hang above the clock face. In 1535 one cage held the corpse of anabaptist zealot Jan van Leiden, who ordered the town's citizens to relinquish all property and be rebaptized as polygamists. The menacing cages still hang as a "reminder." Following a tradition dating to 1481, the watchman—who occupies the "highest office" in Münster—plays a copper horn every 30min. from 9pm-midnight, daily except on Tuesday. *(Kirchherrng. 3, off the Prinzipalmarkt. ☎ 448 93. Free concerts 1st Sa of the month at noon.)*

PROMENADE. When Goethe's carriage used to turn onto the Promenade encircling Münster's Altstadt, he would slow it and smell the flowers. In the west, the Promenade meets the Schloßgarten, where centuries-old trees continue to grow, moss-covered and gnarled. The Baroque **Schloß**, designed by local architect Johann Conrad Schlaun, is part of Wilhelmsuniversität. *(Open daily Apr.-Sept. 7am-7pm; Oct.-Mar. 7am-8pm.)* Don't miss the **botanical gardens** behind the *Schloß.* *(☎ 832 38 27. Open daily mid-Mar. to mid-Oct. 8am-5pm; mid-Oct. to mid-Mar. 8am-4pm.)*

FRIEDENSSAAL (HALL OF PEACE). Beside the gabled houses of Prinzipalmarkt, the Friedenssaal commemorates the end of the Thirty Years' War. Within these hallowed halls, the Spanish-Dutch Peace of Westphalia was signed in 1648. Fortunately, all important artifacts were stored away in the coutryside during WWII, so after renovations it was possible to bring the hall to its original splendor. Inside, guarded by a golden cockerel, a centuries-old human hand is on display—no one seems to know why. *(Open Tu-Su 10am-5pm. €1.50, children and students €1.)*

🏛 MUSEUMS

Münster treasures its historical and cultural artifacts in a well-maintained **Landesmuseum,** but its real gems are the small collections. Ask the tourist office for information about these offerings, including the **Railway Museum, Carnival Museum,** and **Museum of Organs,** all in nearby suburbs.

LANDESMUSEUM FÜR KUNST UND KULTUR (STATE MUSEUM FOR ART AND CULTURE). Spiraling around a central atrium, a series of modern galleries include visions of Franz Marc's paradise and a procession of Kirchner canvases (one of which is positioned sideways at the artist's request). A separate wing explores religious art from the Middle Ages to the Baroque period and hosts traveling exhibitions. *(Dompl. 10. ☎ 59 07 01. Open Tu-Su 10am-6pm. €3.50, students €2.10, children €2.)*

LEPRAMUSEUM (LEPROSY MUSEUM). It's a little far, but the novelty factor never wears thin and the exhibits (all strictly hands-off) possess unique appeal. Highlights include playful leper puppets. *(Kinderhauser Str. 15. Northwest of the Altstadt; take bus #6, 9, or 17 to "Kristiansandstr."* ☎ *285 10. Open Su 3-5pm. Call for other days. Free.)*

GRAPHIKMUSEUM PABLO PICASSO. This museum houses over 800 of Picasso's lithographs, making it a near-complete collection of the artist's lithographic works. It also features a large selection of Picasso's colleagues, including Braque, Matisse, Miro, Chagall, and Leger. *(Koenigstr. 5.* ☎ *414 47 10; www.graphikmuseum-picasso-muenster.de. Open Tu–Su 10am-6pm. €3, students €2.)*

MÜHLENHOF-FREILICHTMUSEUM (MILL-YARD OPEN AIR MUSEUM). This open-air museum allows visitors to sample daily life in an 18th-century farm town with 25 rural half-timbered buildings from all parts of the region dating from the 17th to the 19th century. The pungent odor of strung sausages saturates an old miller's cottage, but you can savor a less meaty picnic on a millstone dating back to 1868. Loaves of indestructible *Schwarzbrot* (brown bread; €2) and authentic wooden clogs (€12) for purchase. *(Theo-Breider-Weg 1, near the Aasee and Torminbrücke.* ☎ *98 12 00. Open mid-Mar. to Oct. daily 10am-6pm, last entry 5pm; Nov. to mid-Mar. M-Sa 1-4:30pm, Su 11am-4:30pm, last entry 4pm. €4, students and seniors €2.50, children €2.)*

MUSEUM FÜR LACKKUNST (MUSEUM OF LACQUERED ART). This museum presents a selection of the highly refined lacquered crafts of East Asia and Islamic art from India and Persia. Statues and vases fill perfectly polished cases, and ornate furnishings seem to glow with abalone and mother-of-pearl inlays. Visiting exhibits glisten the basement. *(Windthorststr. 26, just off the Promenade.* ☎ *41 85 10. Open Tu noon-8pm, W-Su noon-6pm. €3, students €2. Free Tu.)*

STADTMUSEUM (MUNICIPAL MUSEUM). Abounding with ancient vases, courtly frocks, and models of the evolving history, this museum follows Münster from its inauspicious beginning early in the eighth century. *(Salzstr. 28. Open Tu-F 10am-6pm, Sa-Su 11am-6pm. Free.)*

DETMOLD ☎ 05231

Though Detmold (pop. 74,000) may not boast as many attractions as neighboring cities, the town is an ideal base for exploring the *Teutoburger Wald*. Serene pastures fold into dips in the forested landscape, providing a relaxing backdrop for die-hard nature-lovers and bicyclists in warm weather.

🖿🗹 **TRANSPORTATION AND PRACTICAL INFORMATION. Trains** run to: Bielefeld (45min., 1-2 per hr., €10); Münster (2hr., every 2hr., €18); Osnabrück (1¼hr., every hr., €15). The **tourist office,** Rathaus am Markt, will help you explore the region. From the station, head left on Bahnhofstr., turn right on Paulinenstr., then left on Bruchstr. into the pedestrian zone, and walk another 5min. to the peach Rathaus. The tourist office is on the right side of the building. For longer hikes, ask for the green *Hermannsland* map (€8), a detailed trail map with elevations, or the *Wanderschuh* (free), a basic guide that gives hike distances and durations. The staff books rooms for free. (☎ 97 73 28; www.detmold.de. Open M-F 10am-6pm, Sa 10am-2pm.) Altstadt **tours** (in German) leave from the main entrance of the Residenzschloß. (Apr.-Oct. Sa 10am, Su 11am. €2, students €1.) The tourist office offers free audio guide in English. Save money with an *extraTour* ticket (€14.50, children €5.90), valid at the Hermannsdenkmal, Adlerwarte, Vogel- und Blumenpark, Residenzschloß, and Landesmuseum. Use the **Internet** at **Internet-Bistro,** Lange Str. 84. Turn left out of the tourist office and walk straight; it's on the left. (☎ 98 11 12. €2.50 per 30min.

Open M-F 1-10pm, Sa noon-8pm, Su 2-10pm.) The **post office** is between the station and the pedestrian zone, on the corner of Paulinenstr. and Bismarckstr. (Open M-F 8am-6pm, Sa 8am-12:30pm.) **Postal Code:** 32701.

▲▶ ACCOMMODATIONS AND FOOD. In addition to the regular pack of school children, the **Jugendherberge Detmold ❷**, Schirrmannstr. 49, houses Socke the mule, who meanders quietly around the isolated stucco house and its orchard setting. Expect breezy and standard rooms. From Bussteig 3 at the train station, take bus #704 (dir.: Hiddesen; 1-2 per hr.) to "Auf den Klippen," and walk 10min. down the road across the street from the stop. Or, take the 45min. walk from the station: turn right on Paulinenstr., right on Freiligrathstr. (which becomes Bandelstr.), left on Bülowstr., right on Schützenberg, and right on Schirmannstr. (☎247 39. Breakfast included. Reception until 10pm. Curfew 10pm, but keys are available. Dorms €17. Cash only.) A few blocks from the Rathaus, find luxurious accommodations at **Hotel Nadler ❹**, Grabbestr. 4. Rooms are bright and spacious, with new furniture, cable TV, and phone. (☎924 60; www.hotel-nadler.de. Breakfast included. Singles €29-44; doubles €65-76; triples €92. MC/V.)

Buy fresh produce at the **market** in front of the Rathaus. (Open Tu, Th, Sa 7am-2pm.) A variety of delicious crêpes, soups, and salads await at **Knollchen ❶**, Lange Str. 21. (☎283 99. €2-4. Open M-F 10am-7pm, Sa 10am-4pm. Cash only.) Down the street at **Fuchsbau ❷**, Lange Str. 13, get your fill of baguette sandwiches (€2-5), *Schnitzel*, and pasta from the straw-hut bar (€4-7). Pizzas are €4 from 5-8pm. (☎280 22. Open M-F 5-11pm, Sa noon-3pm and 5-11pm, Su 5-11pm. Cash only.)

◨ SIGHTS. Most of Detmold's activities lie beyond the city limits, but cannons still arm the courtyard of the **Fürstliches Residenzschloß**, a Renaissance castle in the town's central park. (☎700 20. Obligatory 40min. tours daily on the hr. 10am-4pm, except 1pm; Apr.-Oct. also 5pm. €3.50, children €2.) Other sights unfold across the countryside. It's not hard to walk from sight to sight, though bus #792 (dir.: Scheider) shuffles sight-seers between locations, leaving from *Bussteig* (bus rise) 6 at the train station once per hr. on weekends, and on weekdays at 8:10, 9:10am, and 3:10pm. (Day ticket for following sights €7.10, 5 people €11.10; excluding Externsteine €3.70, 5 people €6.60). There are also many trails that crisscross the Teutoburger Wald, hiking opportunities between sights. A good place to start is the **Adlerwarte**, a nature trail featuring more than 80 birds of prey. Time your arrival to catch a free falcon flight exhibition. Take bus #792 or 701 (€1.65) from Detmold (dir.: Weidmüller/Berlebeck) to "Adlerwarte." (☎471 71. Open mid-Mar. to mid-Nov. daily 9:30am-5:30pm. Displays noon and 3pm. May-Sept. also 4:30pm. €4, children €2.) For emus instead of eagles, follow signs on the trail (about 30min.) behind the Adlerwarte to the relaxing **Vogel- und Blumenpark** (Bird and Flower Park), home to ostriches and peacocks. Bus #792 or 782 (€1.65) gets you there if you prefer not to hike. Take it from Detmold to "Vogelpark." (☎474 39. Open mid-Mar. to Oct. daily 9am-6pm. €4.50, students €3.50, children €2.50.) The main road in front of the park left toward the **Hermannsdenkmal** (about 30min.) commemorates the victory of the Germanic chief Hermann over the Romans. Complete with winged helmet, the statue wields a 7m sword with the disconcerting inscription, "German unity is my power; my power is Germany's might." Research continually relocates the battle site; the only consensus is that the colossus does not mark it. (Bus #792. Open daily Mar.-Oct. 9am-6:30pm; Nov.-Feb. 9:30am-4pm. €1.50, children €0.50.) At the Hermannsdenkmal, a number of marked **hiking** trails head out in various directions; the path from Hermann's front left leads into wooded hills, while the one on his right side leads back to Detmold.

Also among the hills south of town, massive pillars of rock at **Externsteine** emerge incongruously from the surrounding forest. Cleaved out of the mountains during an ice age, the exposed rock faces were carved and etched by people long ago to mark celestial events. Atop one of the towering cliffs, **Grave Rock** appears to teeter precariously close to the edge, prepared to tumble and earn its name. Actually quite stable, the rock won't be going anywhere for a while. Take bus #792 or 782 (€3.30) to "Abzweig Externsteine." (Stairways open Apr.-Oct. daily 9am-6pm. €1.50, students €1.) Detmold's **Westfälisches Freilichtmuseum** (Westphalian Open Air Museum) is miraculously untouristed: spread over 80 hectares, this outdoor museum consists of more than 100 restomred and rebuilt 17th- to 19th-century German farm buildings. Horse-drawn carriages take visitors from the entrance to the museum's far end. (€1.50, children €1.) Take bus #792 or 701 (dir.: Weidmüller/Berlebeck) to "Freilichtmuseum." (☎70 61 05. Open Apr.-Oct. Tu-Su 9am-6pm. Last entrance 5pm. €5, students €3.50, children €2.)

HESSEN (HESSE)

Prior to the 20th century, Hessen was known for exporting mercenary soldiers to rulers such as King George III, who enlisted them to put down an unruly gang of colonials across the Atlantic in 1776. Today, Hessen's ivy-clad castles and immense steeples find their modern analog in the region's ultramodern skyscrapers. Hessen is the busiest economic center in the country, led by the unsparing financial behemoth of Frankfurt. Overshadowed by its capital, the rest of understated Hessen attracts little attention from tourists, leaving the medieval charisma of Marburg and the more modern offerings of Kassel blessedly off the beaten path.

HIGHLIGHTS OF HESSEN

LAND at **Frankfurt's** busy airport (p. 317), and stay for the **Römerberg**, fast-paced nightlife, and superb museums.

PARTY ALL NIGHT LONG in the hip university town of **Marburg** (p. 333), which influenced the writings of the **Brothers Grimm** and has spawned a racy youth culture.

SEE IT TO BELIEVE IT in **Wilhelmshöhe Park,** where waterfalls and castles complement the curious cosmopolitanism of **Kassel** (p. 338).

FRANKFURT AM MAIN ☎069

Though Frankfurt may lack some of the traditional architecture of many German cities, its modern and post-modern buildings perfectly complement its older cathedrals and half-timbered houses. It is said that while fleeing the Saxons, Charlemagne and his Franks saw a deer crossing the Main River in a shallow *Furt* (ford) and followed the animal to safety on the opposite bank, where Charlemagne proceeded to found a city. In 1356, Frankfurt rose to prominence when the Golden Bull of imperial law made it the site of emperors' elections and coronations until the Holy Roman Empire dissolved. Frankfurters have been leaving their indelible mark on Western culture ever since. Goethe and Anne Frank lived here, and the Oppenheim and Rothschild families built up Frankfurt's economic power.

Ten years after Allied bombers destroyed much of the city in March 1944, Frankfurt received a concrete makeover, paid for by the countries that had ruined it. Today, skyscrapers loom over crowded streets and dark-suited stock traders scurry about. It's easy to see how Frankfurt acquired the nicknames "Bankfurt" and "Mainhattan"—the EU's bank is even based here. Frankfurt has a reputation for being the most Americanized city in Europe, but the government works to preserve the city's rich history. Though it remains a transportation blip for most travelers, Frankfurt spends more on cultural attractions than any other German city.

▐ TRANSPORTATION

Flights: The busy **Flughafen Rhein-Main** (☎01805 372 46 36) welcomes hundreds of airplanes and thousands of travelers from all over the world daily. From the airport, Schnellbahn (S-Bahn) trains S8 and S9 travel to the Frankfurt Hauptbahnhof every 15min. Buy tickets (€3) from green ticket machines marked *Fahrkarten* before boarding. Most public transportation and trains to major cities depart from Terminal 1. Take the free bus (runs every 15min), or walk through the skyway, to reach the terminal from the main airport. Taxis to the city center (around €20) can be found outside any terminal.

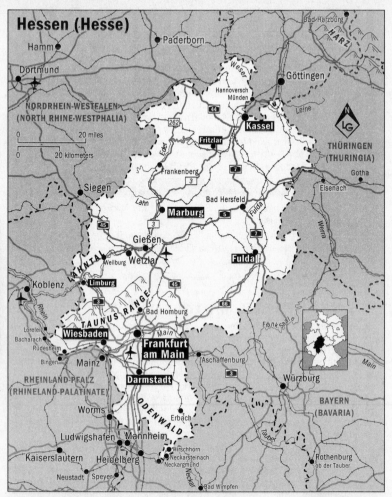

Hessen (Hesse)

HESSEN

Trains: ☎018 05 19 41 95 for reservations and information. Trains from Frankfurt's **Hauptbahnhof** to: **Amsterdam** (4hr., every 2hr., €98); **Berlin** (5-6hr., 2 per hr., €98); **Cologne** (2½hr., every hr., €75); **Hamburg** (3½-5hr., 2 per hr., €93); **Munich** (3½-4½hr., 3 per hr., €55); **Paris** (6-8hr., 4 per day, €82.60).

Ride Share: Stuttgarter Str. 12 (☎23 64 44). Take a right on Baseler Str. at the side exit of the Hauptbahnhof (track 1) and walk 2 blocks. Arranges rides to **Berlin** (€30), **München** (€89), and elsewhere. Open M-F 8am-6:30pm, Sa 8am-4pm, Su 10am-4pm.

Public Transportation: Single-ride tickets valid for 1hr. in 1 direction, transfers permitted (€1.70; 6-9am and after 4pm €2). Eurail passes valid only on S-Bahn trains. For unlimited access to the S- and U-Bahn, trams, and buses, the *Tageskarte* is valid until midnight the day of purchase. (€4.70, children €2.80). **Passengers without tickets face a €40 fine.** At the Hauptbahnhof, long distance trains depart the main level, while the

면허종별	의 사
면허번호	제 63925 호

...성명(...)... 하지 아니합니다.

1일 투여횟수	투여일수	대체 가능	용법 매식(전.간.후) 시	법 본부용
3	3			
3	3			
3	3			
3	3			
3	3			

S-Bahn leaves the lower level. Escalators to the U-Bahn are in the shopping passage **(Einkaufspassage)**. Trams #11, 16, 17, 20, and 21 pass by the island platform outside the entrance, while buses #35, 37, and 46 leave to the right of the main entrance.

Taxis: ☎23 00 01, 23 00 33, or 25 00 01. €1.38-1.53 per km.

Boat Rides: Several companies offer Main tours, departing near the Römerberg (1-2hr.; 2 per hr.; €6.20-8.20, children €3.20). **Primus Linie** also cruises to wine towns along the Main, including Rüdesheim and Loreley (☎13 38 37 01 12; www.primus-linie.de).

Bike Rental: Deutsche Bahn (DB) runs the citywide bike rental, **Call a Bike.** These bikes (with the red DB logo) are found throughout the city. To rent, call the service hotline (☎0700 05 22 55 22; www.callabike.de.), dial 0, and ask for an English-speaking operator for further instructions. €0.07 per min. or max. €15 per day. Credit cards only.

Hitchhiking: Let's Go does not recommend hitchhiking as a safe mode of transport and it is not encouraged in Germany. However, hitchers report that those heading south to Munich take buses #36 or 960 from Konstablerwache to the Autobahn interchange. Those heading to Cologne or Düsseldorf take S1 or S8 to "Wiesbaden Hauptbahnhof," then S21 (dir.: Niedernhausen) to "Auringen-Medenbach," and turn right, walk 800m, and take the access road to the Autobahn rest stop.

HIGH CULTURE, LOW BUDGET. The Frankfurt Card, available at tourist offices and travel agencies, allows unlimited travel on trains and buses including the airport line. It also gives discounts on 21 museums, the Palmengarten, zoo, city tours, river cruises, and ▨ free drinks with meals at restaurants. (1-day €8, 2-day €12.) The Museumsufer Ticket gets you in to 26 museums for two days (€12, students €6, family €20). See **Museums,** p. 325 for more info.

HESSEN

⊞ ORIENTATION

A sprawling collage of steel, concrete, glass, and scaffolding, Germany's fifth-largest city bridges the **Main** (pronounced "mine") 35km east of its confluence with the Rhein. The train station is at the end of Frankfurt's red-light district (Kaiserstr. and environs, one of the world's largest), where Baseler Str. and Düsseldorfer Str. converge on airline offices, banks, licensed brothels, and bookstores. From the station, the city center is a 20min. walk down Kaiserstr. or Münchener Str., which lead to the Altstadt. North of the river, the Altstadt has the well-touristed **Römerberg** square. Take U4 (dir.: Seckbacher Landstr.) to "Römer" or walk down Liebfrauenstr. from **Hauptwache** (S1-6, S8, or S9, or U1-3, U6, or U7). The commercial heart of Frankfurt, north of Römer, is an expanse of department stores, ice cream vendors, and beer gardens stretching along Zeil from Hauptwache to **Konstablerwache** in the west (one S-Bahn stop farther) and to **Opernplatz** in the east (U6 or U7 to "Alte Oper"). Students, cafés, and services cluster northwest around the university in **Bockenheim.** Take U6 or U7 to "Bockenheimer Warte." On the southern bank of Main, **Sachsenhausen** draws shoppers and lovers of *Äpfelwein* (applewine, a Hessen specialty) alike to the bustling Schweizer Str., while art aficionados lovers flock to the myriad museums along the Main (U1-3 to "Schweizer Pl.")

⊞ PRACTICAL INFORMATION

TOURIST AND FINANCIAL SERVICES

Tourist Office: (☎21 23 88 00; www.frankfurt-tourismus.de), in the Hauptbahnhof, next to the main exit. Brochures, tours, and free maps. Books rooms for a €3 fee; free if you call or email ahead. Open M-F 8am-9pm, Sa-Su and holidays 9am-6pm. A **branch,** at Römerberg 27, also books rooms. Open M-F 9:30am-5:30pm, Sa-Su 10am-4pm.

Tours: Depart daily 10am and 2pm (in winter only 2pm) from the Römerberg tourist office, and 15min. later from the Hauptbahnhof tourist office. Tours last 2¼hr. 8 languages offered. €25, students €20, under 12 €10.

Budget travel: STA Travel, Bockenheimer Landstr. 133 (☎70 30 35; www.statravel.de), near the university. U-Bahn to "Bockenheimer Warte," turn around after leaving the U exit and then left on Bockenheimer Landstr. Books national and international flights and sells ISICs (p. 11). Open M-F 10am-6pm, Sa 11am-2pm.

Consulates: Australia, Neue Mainzer Str. 52-58 (☎90 55 80). Open M-Th 9am-4:30pm, F 9am-4pm. **US:** Giebener Str. 30 (☎753 50; fax 75 35 22 77). Open M-F 7:30-11:30am; closed holidays and last Th of every month.

Currency Exchange: At any bank. Banks in the airport and the Reise Bank open daily 7:30am-10:30pm) in the station have slightly worse rates, but, unlike most banks, stay open during the weekend.

American Express: Theodor-Heuss-Allee 112 (☎97 97 10 00; fax 97 97 15 00). Exchanges currency, handles Travelers' Cheques, and arranges hotel reservations and car rentals. Open M-F 9:30am-6pm, Sa 10am-2pm.

LOCAL SERVICES

Bookstore: British Book Shop, Börsenstr. 17 (☎28 04 92). Classics, Shakespeare, popular novels, and nonfiction in English. Open M-F 9:30am-7pm, Sa 9:30am-6pm.

Gay and Lesbian Resources: The **Switchboard,** Alte Gasse 36 (☎283 53; switchboard@frankfurt.gay-web.de), contains a gay infodesk, as well as the **Café der AIDS-Hilfe Frankfurt,** a popular bar/café run by the local AIDS foundation. Take the U- or S-Bahn to "Knostablerwache," or Bus 36 to "Alte Grasse." Open Tu-Th 7pm-midnight, F-Sa 7pm-1am, Su 7-11pm. Another solid resource is the **AIDS Anonyme Beratungsstelle** (Aids Anonymous Information Center; ☎21 24 32 70; www.gesundheitsamt.stadt-frankfurt.de). The **Rosa Hilfe Frankfurt,** (☎194 46) also has a gay and lesbian hotline. Open Su 6-9pm. In an emergency, call ☎0171 174 57 21.

Laundromat: Waschsalon, Wallstr. 8, near Haus der Jugend in Sachsenhausen. Wash €3 (soap included). Dry €0.50 per 15min. Open daily 6am-11pm. **Miele Washworld,** Moselstr. 17, is just a 10min. walk from the Hauptbahnhof. Small wash €4; large €8 (soap €0.50). Dry €1 (€1.80 for large loads) per 15min. Coin-op machine. Open M-Sa 6am-11pm.

EMERGENCY AND COMMUNICATIONS

Emergency: ☎110. **Fire** and **Ambulance:** ☎112.

Women's Helpline: ☎70 94 94. More information at the Frankfurt Forum (see below).

AIDS hotline: ☎405 86 80.

Disabled Travelers: Transportation access info at www.vgf.ffm.de. **Frankfurt Forum,** Römerberg 32 (☎21 24 00 00), publishes a guide to accessible locations in Frankfurt. Open M and W 10am-4:30pm, Tu and Th 10am-6pm, F 10am-2pm.

Pharmacy: Abstexpress is in the train station's **Einkaufspassage** (☎271 14 20). Open M-F 6am-midnight, Sa 7am-midnight, Su 8am-midnight. After hours, call ☎192 92 for medical emergencies.

Internet Access: Alpha, in the Hauptbahnhof's gambling salon, past track 24 on the north side. €2.50 per hr. Open 24hr. To your right outside of the Hauptbahnhof, **PTT Multi-Media-Story,** Baseler Str. 65, offers cheap Internet access (€2.50 per hr.) and long-distance calling (daily 8:45am-midnight). Elizabethstr. directly behind the Haus der Jugend and Kaisterstr. across from the Haupbahnhof are both packed with Internet-Telefon stores.

Frankfurt

ACCOMMODATIONS
City Camp Frankfurt, 2
Fennis Fuchser, 14
Haus der Jugend, 20
Hotel an der
Gallusvarte, 13
Hotel-Pension Bruns, 4
Stay & Learn Hostel, 16

FOOD & DRINK
Adolf Wagner, 23
Bitter Zart, 17
Da Rosario, 15
Eiscafé de Nardi, 19
Frankfurt Imbiß, 21
IMA Multibar, 5
Kleinmarkthalle, 12
Mensa, 1
Mozart Cafe, 11
Zum Gemalten Haus, 22

BARS & NIGHTLIFE
Blue Angel, 7 -
The Cave, 8
Clubkeller, 24
Cocoon Club, 3
Der Jazzkeller, 6
King Kamehameha
Club, 18
Odeon, 9
U Bar, 10

HESSEN

Post Office: Goethe Platz, walk 10min. walk down Taunusstr. from the Hauptbahnhof, or take the U- or S-Bahn to "Hauptwache" and walk south to the square. Open M-F 9:30am-7pm, Sa 9am-2pm. **Filiale Frankfurt 2,** Zeil 90/Schäferg. (☎13 81 26 21), inside the Karstadt department store. U- or S-Bahn to "Hauptwache." Take a right on Zeil with your back to the church until you see the Karstadt building. Open M-Sa 9:30am-8pm. **Postal Code:** 60313.

ACCOMMODATIONS AND CAMPING

In the financial center of Europe, deals are rare, and trade fairs make rooms scarce. The **Westend/University** area has a few budget options. There are also hostels under 45min. away: **Darmstadt** (p. 330), **Mainz** (p. 354), and **Wiesbaden** (p. 328).

■ **Haus der Jugend (HI),** Deutschherrnufer 12 (☎610 01 50; www.jugendherberge-frankfurt.de). Bus #46 from the station to "Frankensteiner Pl." Its location along the Main and in front of the pubs and cafés of the old Sachsenhausen district makes it popular with student groups and young travelers. Affable staff. Breakfast (7am-9am) and sheets included. Check-in 1pm. Check-out 9:30am. Curfew 2am. Locks available for €5 deposit. Some private bathrooms. Dorms from €20, under 27 from €15. MC/V. ❷

Stay & Learn Hostel, Kaiserstr. 74 (☎24 75 130; info@room-frankfurt.de). In the heart of the action—and the red light district—this airy hostel is a popular and convenient option. Internet €1 per hr. Free laundry, free bag storage. Dorms €17-20; singles €40; doubles €50; triples €75. Prices rise during trade fairs. MC/V. ❷

Hotel-Pension Bruns, Mendelssohnstr. 42 (☎74 88 96; www.brunsgallus-hotel.de). U4 to "Festhalle." Ring the bell; it's on the 2nd fl. In the wealthy but far-flung Westend area near the *Uni*, Bruns has 9 Victorian rooms with high ceilings, hardwood floors, and cable TV. Free breakfast in bed. Singles €40-45; doubles €50-55; triples €66-75; quads €88-105. Cash only. ❸

Hotel-Pension Gölz, Beethovenstr. 44 (☎74 67 35; www.hotel-goelz.de). U6 or U7 to "Westend." One street north of Pensions Backer and Bruns. Quiet, attractive rooms with TV, phone, and couches, some with balconies overlooking the surrounding ivy-covered houses. Big breakfast included. Singles €50; doubles €81; triples €96. MC/V. ❹

Fennis Fuchser, Mainzer Landstr. 95 (☎25 38 55). Near the Hauptbahnhof, this hotel is a convenient place to crash. From the station, take a left on Düsseldorfer Str., walk 2 blocks, and take a left on Mainzer Landstr.; the hotel is 1 block down on the left. Enter through the dim bar downstairs (meals €4-15). Special rates for stays longer than 1 night. Singles €20; doubles €38; triples €60. Cash only. ❷

City Camp Frankfurt, An der Sandelmühle 35b (☎57 03 32; www.city-camp-frankfurt.de). U1-U3 to "Heddernheim," leave through the unmarked exit, take a left at the Kleingartnerverein sign and continue down the road until you reach the Sandelmühle sign. Cross the stream and turn left, following the signs until you reach the campground. Reception Nov. to Feb. 4-8pm; Mar. to Oct., 9am-1pm and 4-8pm. €5.50 per person, €2.30 per child, €3.50 per tent. Showers €1 per 4min. Cash only. ❶

FOOD

Frankfurters love sausages and beer, but they have their own regional specialties as well: Goethe's favorite, *Handkäse mit Musik* (cheese curd with raw onions); *grüne Sosse* (a green sauce with various herbs, usually served over boiled eggs or potatoes); and *Äpfelwein*. Large mugs (0.3L) of apple wine should never top €2 and are most frequently enjoyed in **Sachsenhauser,** the old district of Frankfurt.

Just a few blocks from the Haus Der Jugend is a well-stocked **HL Markt,** Dreieichstr. 56 (open M-F 8am-8pm, Sa 8am-4pm), while **Alim Markt,** Münchener Str. 37, is near the Hauptbahnhof (open M-F 8:30am-7:30pm, Su 8am-2pm). The most reasonably priced meals are around the university in **Bockenheim** and nearby **Westend** (U6 or U7 to "Bockenheimer Warte"), and many pubs in **Sachsenhausen** serve food at a decent price. Take U1-3 to "Schweizer Pl." Bockenheim and the **Zeil** attract carts and stands.

THE BEST *WURST*

So you're finally in Germany and itching to sink your teeth into your first authentic German *Wurst*. With over 1500 varieties, you'll have plenty of choices. All have one thing in common: German law mandates that sausages can only be made of meat and spices. If it has cereal filling, it's not *Wurst*.

Bockwurst: This tasty sausage is commonly roasted or grilled at street stands, and is served dripping with ketchup and mustard in a *Brötchen* (roll). Although *Bock* means billy-goat, this *Wurst* is made of ground veal with parsley and chives. Complement your *Bockwurst* with some *Bock* beer.

Thüringer Bratwurst: Similar to the *Bockwurst*, the *Bratwurst* has a little pork too, plus ginger and nutmeg.

Frankfurter: Unlike the American variety, the German *Frankfurter* can only have this name if made in Frankfurt. It's made of lean pork ground into a paste and then cold smoked, which gives it that orange-yellow coloring.

Knockwurst: Short and plump, this is served with *sauerkraut*. It's made of lean pork and beef, with a healthy dose of garlic.

Weißwurst: Cream and eggs give this "white sausage" its pale coloring. *Weißwurst* goes with rye bread and mustard.

Currywurst: A great late-night snack, this pork *Bratwurst* is smothered in a tomato sauce and sprinkled with paprika and curry.

■ **Kleinmarkthalle,** on Haseng. between Berliner Str. and Töngesg. Make your own lunch in this 3-story warehouse of bakeries, butchers, and vegetable stands. Cutthroat competition among the many vendors pushes prices down. Enough meat and sausage to feed a small nation (possibly Monaco). Open M-F 8am-6pm, Sa 8am-4pm. Cash only. ❶

■ **Da Rosario,** Ottostr. 17 (☎24 24 81 82). Giovanna Bono serves up huge pizzas (from €4) and endearingly hectic atmosphere at this small pizzeria. Open daily noon-midnight. Cash only. ❷

Bitter Zart, Domstr. 5 (☎94 94 28 46). This famous sweets shop sells some of the best chocolates (from €3 per 100g) and *gelee frÜdde* (from €2.50 per 100g) in the city. The hot chocolate suits any season. Open M-F 10am-7pm, Sa 10am-4pm. Cash only. ❷

Adolf Wagner, Schweizer Str. 71 (☎61 25 65). Saucy German dishes (€5-17) and some of the region's most renowned *Äpfelwein* (€1.40 per 0.3L) keep the patrons of this famous corner of old Sachsenhausen jolly. Sit elbow-to-elbow with storied regulars. Tasty vegetarian options include salad with mushrooms and apples (€8). Open daily 11am-midnight. Cash only. ❸

Mozart Cafe, Töngesg. 23-25 (☎29 19 54). Lauded by locals, Mozart serves a variety of foods like delicately made *Spargel* (white asparagus), only available in May and June, and a selection of pastas, salads, and heaping desserts. Famously huge breakfasts. Meals €4.90-6.80. Open M-Sa 8am-10pm, Su 9am-10pm. MC. ❷

Zum Gemalten Haus, Schweizer Str. 67 (☎61 45 59). The long tables of this jovial Sachsenhausen institution have seen generations of locals savor *Wurst* and *Kraut* (from €3), and homemade *Äpfelwein* (€1.70). Open W-Su 10am-midnight. V. ❸

IMA Multibar, Klein Bockenheimer Str. 14 (☎90 02 56 65). This fast-paced and hip bar/café combo on the back streets off of Zeil offers delicious smoothies (€3.50), and wraps (€4-7.30) with fresh vegetables. Drinks from €7. MC/V. ❸

Frankfurt Imbiß, Wallstr.18 (☎ 66 36 84 74), behind the Haus der Jugend. With a handful of tables, this haven of simple and affordable dining provides relief from the otherwise-expensive Sauchsenhausen district. Rich *kartoffelsalat* (potato salad). Open M-Th noon-8pm, F noon-4pm, Sa 2-4pm, Su 2-8pm. Cash only. ❷

Mensa, U6 or U7 to "Bockenheimer Warte." Follow signs for "Palmengarten Universität." Exit to "Mensa" and take the first left before STA travel. The *Mensa* is across the courtyard to your right. The third floor draws penny-pinching students to its state-run cafeteria. Guest meals €2.80-4.30. Open M-F 11am-6:30pm. Cash only. ❶

🅖 SIGHTS

Much of Frankfurt's historic splendor lives on only in memories. After the Allied bombing of 1944 destroyed everything but the cathedral, the industrious Frankfurters engineered the resurrection as a testament to both pre- and postmodern times. A walk around town quickly reveals the resulting architectural variety.

RÖMERBERG. A voyage through Frankfurt should begin in this central area of the Altstadt, among the half-timbered architecture and medieval-looking fountains that appear on postcards of the city. To celebrate the 13 coronations of German emperors held in the city, the Statue of Justice in the center of the square once spouted wine. Today, she only offers pigeons some much-needed refreshment.

RÖMER. At the west end of the Römerberg, the gables of Römer have marked the site of Frankfurt's city hall since 1405. It was also the original stop on the Main for the merchants who began the city's long trade tradition. The building's upper floors are open to the public, including the **Kaisersaal,** a former imperial banquet hall adorned with portraits of 52 German emperors, from Charlemagne to Franz II. *(Entrance from Limpurgerg. Open daily 10am-1pm and 2-5pm. German tours every hr. €2.)*

ARCHÄOLOGISCHEN GARTEN. Between the Dom and the rest of the Römerberg are the Schirn Kunsthalle and a plantless "garden" of crumbled building foundations dating back to the 2000-year-old Roman settlement. Two plaques provide explanations in German.

DOM. East of the reconstructed Römerberg stands the only major historical building in the city center that escaped WWII bombings. The red sandstone Gothic cathedral contains large paintings along the walls and elaborate altarpieces. The seven electors of the Holy Roman Empire chose emperors here, and the Dom served as the site of coronation ceremonies from 1562 to 1792. Reconstruction of the viewing tower atop the Dom should be finished by 2008. The Dom Museum inside the main entrance has architectural studies of the Dom, intricate chalices, and the ceremonial robes of imperial electors. *(☎ 13 37 61 86. Open Tu-F 10am-5pm, Sa-Su 11am-5pm. German tours Tu-Su 3pm; €3, students €2. Admission €2/1.)*

GOETHEHAUS. Goethe was born in Frankfurt in 1749, found his first love (a girl named Gretchen, said to be the inspiration for the Gretchen/Margarete character in *Faust*), and penned some of his best-known works here, including *The Sorrows of Young Werther.* For lukewarm Goethe fans, the house is little more than a typical 18th-century showroom for a well-to-do family, refurbished with the family's original belongings, many of which the renowned author hated. The memorable writing chamber, puppet-show room, and personal library should not be missed. The **Goethe Museum** next door traces the progression of Goethe's portraits and artistic tastes and sensibilities throughout his life. *(Großer Hirschgraben 23-25, northwest of the Römer. ☎ 13 88 00. Open M-F and Sa 10am-6pm, Su 10am-5:30pm; last Sa of month 10am-8pm. Tours in German daily 2pm and 4pm. Audio guides in German or English €2, 2 people €6.50. Admission €5, students €2.50, families €8.)*

PAULSKIRCHE. St. Paul's Church stands directly across Braubachstr. from the Römerberg. The church was the site of the 19th century's last chance for constitutional government over a united Germany (p. 54). Here, the liberal bourgeoisie sided with order in the face of peasant revolts in 1848 and watched the slaughter of their one-time political allies. Non-history-buffs will enjoy a conference center and a political memorial to German democracy, as well as a highly acclaimed mural spanning the cylindrical inner wall. (☎ 21 23 85 26. Open daily 10am-5pm. Free.)

PALMENGARTEN. Tourists and a variety of native and exotic birds take refuge in the sprawling grounds of this garden in the northwest part of town. The garden's greenhouses contain seven different "worlds," from the tropics to frozen wastes, and provide a relaxing place to watch the summer's impromptu performers. (Palmengartenstr. 1. U6 or U7 to "Bockenheimer Warte." ☎ 21 23 39 39. Open daily Feb.-Oct. 9am-6pm; Nov.-Jan. 9am-4pm. €5, students €2.50, families €9.50; with special exhibits €7/3/15.)

MAIN TOWER OBSERVATION DECK. With cocktail in hand, see the city and much of Hessen from nearly 250m up in the dominant fixture of the Frankfurt skyline. (Neue Mainzer Str. 52-58; ☎ 36 50 47 77; open Mar.-Oct. M-Th and Su 10am-9pm, F-Sa 10am-11pm; Nov.-Feb. M-Th and Su 10am-7pm, F-Sa 10am-9pm.)

ALTE NIKOLAIKIRCHE. This church raises its modest spires south of the Römerberg. With foundations dating back to the 11th century, this church was named for **St. Nicholas of Myra** in order to protect it from bad weather and flooding. Gothic sandstone sculptures adorn the exterior, and the sparse interior hosts occasional organ concerts. (Open daily Apr.-Sept. 10am-8pm; Oct.-Mar. 10am-6pm. Free.)

▥ MUSEUMS

Pick up a **Frankfurt Card** or a Museumsufer Ticket (p. 319) for museum savings, or go on the last Saturday of the month, when most museums are free.

MUSEUMSUFER

The **Museumsufer,** also known as **Schaumainkai,** hosts an eclectic range of museums housed in opulent 19th-century mansions and more contemporary buildings on the south bank of the Main between the Eiserner Steg and the Holbeinsteg. The Museumsufer is also home to Frankfurt's **Museumsuferfest,** a huge cultural celebration thrown annually in July with art showings, music, and general revelry along the Main. Frankfurt also has nearly 50 commercial **art galleries** clustered around Braubachstr. and Saalg.

▧ **STÄDEL.** This museum presents seven centuries of art, from Van Eyck, Botticelli, Dürer, Rembrandt, and Vermeer to an extensive collection of Impressionist and Expressionist art. Some notable names include Monet, Renoir, and Picasso. There is also a comprehensive collection of post-war graphic prints and paintings in changing exhibitions. (Schaumainkai 63, between Dürerstr. and Holbeinstr. ☎ 605 09 80. Open Tu and F-Su 10am-5pm, W-Th 10am-9pm. Audio guides available in English and German, €2. €8, students €6, family €16, under 12 free. Last Sa of the mo. free.)

DEUTSCHES FILMMUSEUM. Observe the progression of film from a 19th-century obsession with optical illusions to the first pictures of the Lumière Brothers. On the second floor, a nickelodeon plays silent comedy classics to the delight of school children and young adults. Themed screenings highlight specific directors, localities, and genres. All captions are in German. (Schaumainkai 41. ☎ 21 23 88 30; www.deutsches-filmmuseum.de. Open Tu, Th-F and Su 10am-5pm; W 10am-9pm; Sa 2-9pm. Tours Su 3pm. €2.80, students €1.30. Last Sa of the mo. free. Films €5.50/4.50.)

ARCHITEKTURMUSEUM. This museum highlights German architecture over the past decade, plus classical and modern city models. A permanent exhibit links the history of architecture to the evolving social and cultural structures of the past 8000 years with a handful of intricate models. (Schaumainkai 43. ☎ 21 23 88 44. Open Tu and Th-Su 11am-6pm, W 11am-8pm. German tours Sa-Su 3pm. €6, students €3.)

MUSEUM FÜR KOMMUNIKATION. Guarded by a sheep fashioned from telephone cords, this museum is dedicated to the importance of communication technology. Go behind the scenes at the post office, learn how telegraphs and telephones work, and trace the rise of radio, television, and the Internet. Interactive displays are in German; English audio guides available. *(Schaumainkai 53. ☎ 606 00. Open Tu-F 9am-5pm, Sa-Su and holidays 11am-7pm. €2, children €1. Guided tours Su 2pm and W 3pm.)*

MUSEUM DER WELTKULTUREN (MUSEUM OF WORLD CULTURES). This site holds rare collections from Indonesia, Africa, the Pacific, and the Americas. **Galerie 37,** a small gallery of rotating, ethnically themed exhibitions, is connected to the museum. *(Schaumainkai 29. ☎ 21 23 57 55; www.mdw.frankfurt.de. Open Tu, Th-F, and Su 10am-5pm; W 10am-8pm; Sa 2-8pm. €3.60, students €2. Last Sa of the mo. free. Galerie 37 ☎ 21 23 57 55. Same opening times. Prices vary with exhibition.)*

LIEBIEGHAUS. The pillared building and gardens contain antique, medieval, Renaissance, Baroque, Rococo, and Classical statues, friezes, and other sculpted material. *(Schaumainkai 71. ☎ 21 23 86 15. Open Tu and Th-Su 10am-5pm, W 10am-8pm. Call ☎ 21 23 86 15 for tour information. €4, students €2.50. Last Sa of the mo. free.)*

MUSEUM FÜR ANGEWANDTE KUNST (MUSEUM OF APPLIED ARTS). Displays arts and crafts from around the world. The collection includes handiwork from the Ming dynasty to Baroque Frankfurt. The building itself rivals the work it contains for beauty and is a principal attraction of the waterfront. *(Schaumainkai 17. ☎ 21 23 40 37. Open Tu-Su 10am-5pm, W 10am-9pm. €5, students €2.50. Last Sa of the mo. free.)*

ELSEWHERE IN FRANKFURT

■**MUSEUM FÜR MODERNE KUNST (MUSEUM OF MODERN ART).** Blocks from the Dom, this highly stylized post-modern "slice of cake" building provides an ideal setting for the modern art within. The museum rotates through its permanent collection of European and American art from the 1960s to the present, and prides itself in special exhibits of new and unknown artists and forms. *(Domstr. 10. ☎ 21 23 04 47; www.mmk-frankfurt.de. Open Tu and Th-Su 10am-5pm, W 10am-8pm. €6, students €3.)*

SCHIRN KUNSTHALLE. With no permanent exhibits, the Schirn morphs up to 10 times a year to every imaginable genre—anything from a sedate Baroque gallery to an experimental photodocumentary. *(Next to the Dom. ☎ 299 88 20; www.schirn.de. Open Tu and F-Su 10am-7pm, W-Th 10am-10pm. €4-10, varies by exhibit; student discounts.)*

STRUWWELPETER-MUSEUM. Revel in the erring but resilient ways of Struwwelpeter, Germany's favorite nursery-rhyme rapscallion. Unkempt children worldwide have learned to heed the strange but resonant rhymes of Heinrich Hoffmann, translated to English by Mark Twain. The enthusiastic staff and comprehensive collection of "Peterphenelia" make this a must-see. *(Benderg. 1. Entrance next to Archäologisches Garten. ☎ 28 13 33. Open Tu-Su 11am-5pm. Free.)*

JÜDISCHES MUSEUM (JEWISH MUSEUM). Chronicling Jewish life in Frankfurt from the Middle Ages to the modern world, this museum houses a model of the 15th-century Jewish ghetto (*Judengasse*) as well as cultural artifacts documenting settlement, persecution, and ultimate emancipation in the 19th and 20th centuries. It also explores the November pograms and *Kristallnacht*, when the synagogues were burned and over 10,000 Jews from Frankfurt were deported or committed suicide. An unexpected mammoth and giant whale are on display. *(Kurt-Schumacher-str. 10 Untermainkai 14-15. ☎ 297 74 19 21 23 50 00. Open Tu and Th-Su 10am-5pm, W 10am-8pm. €2.60, students €2.)*

NATURMUSEUM. The largest natural history museum in Germany attracts the largest school groups in Frankfurt to its impressive works of taxidermy and giant whales. Preserved birds and an array of dinosaur skeletons seem as cool as they did when you were a child. *(Senckenberganlage 25. U6 or U7 to "Bockenheimer Warte."* ☎ *754 20. Open M-Tu and Th-F 9am-5pm, W 9am-8pm, Sa-Su 9am-6pm. €6, students €3.)*

🎵 🎭 ENTERTAINMENT AND NIGHTLIFE

When it comes to entertainment, Frankfurt features first-rate ballet, theater, and opera heavily subsidized by the city. There are two major theaters. The **Alte Oper,** Opernpl. (U6 or U7 to "Alte Oper;" ☎ 134 04 00; www.oper-frankfurt.de), a magnificent classical building rebuilt in the 1980s, offers a full range of classical music (tickets €11-110), while the **Oper Frankfurt** (☎ 212 02; www.oper-frankfurt.de) displays premier German opera. The **Städtische Bühne,** Untermainanlage 11 (U1-4 to "Willy-Brandt-Pl"; ☎ 21 23 71 33), stages ballets, operas, and experimental renditions of traditional German plays. For productions in English, the **English Theater,** Kaiserstr. 34 (☎ 24 23 16 20; www.english-theatre.org) near the Hauptbahnhof, puts on comedies and musicals. **Die Komoedie,** Neuer Mainzerstr. 14-18 (U1-4 to "Willy-Brandt-Pl;" ☎ 28 45 80; www.diekomoedie.de), produces lighter theatrical fare. Shows and schedules of the city's stages are detailed in several publications, including *Fritz* and *Strandgut* (free at the tourist office), and the *Journal Frankfurt* (€2), available at any newsstand and online at www.journal-frankfurt.de. Students can often buy tickets at reduced prices (from €5) 1hr. before a show. For ticket information for most venues, call **Frankfurt Ticket** (☎ 134 04 00).

For drinks, head to the **Sachsenhausen** district between Brückenstr. and Dreieichstr. for rowdy pubs and taverns specializing in local *Äpfelwein*. The complex of cobblestone streets centering on **Grosse** and **Kleine Rittergasse** teems with cafés, bars, restaurants, and gregarious Irish pubs. While nightlife is occasionally fickle, Frankfurt has many thriving clubs and prominent DJs, mostly between Zeil and Bleichstr., and near Hanauer landstr. In general, things don't heat up until after midnight. Wear something dressier than jeans—unless they're really sweet jeans—if you plan to get past the picky bouncers. Most clubs are 18+; cover runs €5-16.

Odeon, Seilerstr. 34 (☎ 28 50 55). Look for the whitewashed medieval villa with cut-out octopi on the door and ornate pillars. This 2-fl. club vibrates with house, soul, and hip-hop. Theme nights: M hip-hop, Th student night (special drinks ½-price and free buffet from 11:30pm), F 27+, Sa Wild Card. M and Th-F drinks ½-price until midnight. Cover €5, students €3 on Th only. Open M-Sa from 10pm. Cash only.

King Kamehameha Club, Hanauer Landstr. 192 (☎ 48 00 370; www.king-kamehameha.de). With intricate timber rafters, exposed brick, and a raging dance floor, this club lures Frankfurt's young partygoers for resident DJs and the occasional jazz show. Watch your step near the indoor stream. Th 9pm-3am, F-Sa 10pm-4am. Cash only.

Cocoon Club, Nordenstr. 30b (☎ 900 20 590; www.cocoonclub.net). This popular club epitomizes ultra-hip German nightlife and features star DJs, actual cocoons for socializing, vaguely intergalactic decor, and a green foam VIP pod. The neighboring **Micro** serves food in an equally fanciful and crowded setting. Dress to kill. Cocoon Club open F-Sa 9am-6am; Micro open T-Th 7pm-3am. Cover €10-15. AmEx/MC/V.

Clubkeller, Textorstr. 26 (☎ 66 37 26 97; www.clubkeller.com). Down Elizabethstr. from the Haus der Jugend. A small bar/club with low brick-arched ceilings, cheap beer (€2-2.50), hard liquor (vodka shots €2), and lively clientele. Call ahead for the theme of the night. Cover €3. Open daily from 8:30pm. Cash only.

Der Jazzkeller, Kleine Bockenheimer Str. 18a (☎ 28 85 37; www.jazzkeller.com). Founded in September 1952, the oldest jazz club in Germany has hosted many masters, including Dizzy Gillespie. Popular events include W jazz jam sessions and F dance mix. Cover €4-15. Open W-Sa from 9pm, Su from 8pm. Cash only.

Blue Angel, Brönnerstr. 17 (☎28 27 72; www.blueangel-online.de). Techno music and flashing lights dominate the interior of the liveliest gay club around, a Frankfurt institution for 30yr. Ring the bell to enter. Crowds arrive after 1am. Cover €5. Usually open daily 11pm-late, 24hr. straight from 2am Sa. Cash only.

U Bar, Roßmarkt (www.u60311.net), enter through the abandoned subway station on the corner of Goethepl. Frankfurt's best DJs, and some international stars, spin in this old subway station. When the whole station is open for the weekend, it spans the entire breadth of subterranean Goethepl. F night lines start at 9pm. Cover €6-15. Open from 10pm. F-Su Techno/house club opens 11pm. Cash only.

WIESBADEN   ☎0611

Wiesbaden—home to thermal springs and the historic Kurhaus casino—was the playground of European aristocrats and intellectual luminaries alike throughout the 19th century. Brahms and Wagner drew inspiration from the city's unfailing greenery, and Russian novelist Fyodor Dostoevsky wrote much of his work in its surrounding foothills. Today, this very modern state capital of Hessen has retained its distinctive flair for the elegant, from the simple cobblestone streets of the bustling Marktpl. to the inspired architecture of the State Theater.

🖪🔁 TRANSPORTATION AND PRACTICAL INFORMATION. Frequent trains to: Frankfurt (45min., €6.40); Heidelberg (1½hr., €20); Koblenz (1½hr., €14.70); **Mainz** (15min., €7). Wiesbaden is a convenient daytrip from Mainz (p. 354), as the two cities share a **public transportation** system. Wiesbaden's **tourist office**, Marktstr. 6, down Bahnhofstr. from the train station, books rooms for free and offers city bus tours and guided walks (€5.50, children €3.50). (☎17 29 930 or 194 33; www.wiesbaden.de. Open Apr.-Oct., M-F 10am-6:30pm, Sa 9am-6pm, Su 11am-3pm; Nov.-Mar., M-F 10am-6pm, Sa 9am-3pm.) **Internet** access can be found at **Universnet** (€2 per hr.), Schwalbacher Str. 45. Take bus #15 (dir. Graselbeg) or 4 (dir. Kohlkeck) to "Kirchgasse." Exit left off the bus and walk two blocks ahead. Open daily 11am-11pm. The **post office**, Wilhelmstr. 47, is next to the Staatsstheater. (Open M-F 9am-12:30pm, 2-6pm; Sa 9am-12:30pm.) **Postal Code:** 65001.

🖪🗀 ACCOMMODATIONS AND FOOD. The ⛊**Jugendherberge (HI)** ❷, Blücherstr. 66, has colorful common space, reliable beds, and a hospitable staff. Take bus #14 (dir.: Klarental) to "Gneisenaustr." Turn left as you step off the bus and walk 200m up the street. (☎44 90 81; wiesbaden@djh-hessen.de. Breakfast included. Reception until 10pm. Check-in 2pm. Loosely-enforced quiet time 10pm. Midnight curfew, but keys are available for a €20 deposit. 6-bed dorms €19; singles €27; doubles €44. Cash only.) To reach the **Ring-Hotel** ❹, Bleichstr. 29, take the Hauptbahnhof take bus #1 (dir.: Dürenpl.) to "Bleichstr." This family-owned hotel once housed renowned musicians like Jimi Hendrix and Tom Jones, and today features clean, simple rooms near the pedestrian zone. (☎949 02 77. Breakfast included. Singles €55; doubles with shower and TV €75. Prices vary with trade fairs. MC/V.)

The pedestrian zone around the Marktpl. is brimming with pubs, restaurants, fruit stands, bakeries, and cafés. To its north, Goldg. is packed with Italian restaurants (pizza/pasta €4-10). **Aurum Mediterrane** ❷, Goldg. 16, is especially festive, with large windows onto the street and outdoor dining options. (☎302 880. Cash only.) Mauerg., home to many economical seafood and German restaurants, is your best bet for lunch. The jolly staff at **Ludwig** ❸, Wagemannstr. 33, serves up Bavarian specialties like *Leberkäse* or *Weißwurst* for under €12. Eat on the 18th-century wood tables set over cobblestone streets. (☎30 64 75. Open Tu-Th and Su, noon-midnight; F-Sa noon-1am. Cash only.) **The Irish Pub**, Michelsberg 15, rocks with live music every night from 9pm, offers enormous Irish breakfasts (under

€12) Su 11am-3pm, and serves drinks until the wee hours. Monday-Wednesday and Sunday shot specials (4 shots for €5), Tuesday karaoke with karaoke-enabling €1.50 tequila shots, and Th cocktail specials (all €4.50). (☎30 08 49. Open M-Th 5pm-1am, F 5pm-2am, Sa 3pm-2am, Su 11am-1am. Cash only.)

◘ **SIGHTS.** On the other side of the Kurhaus is the stately **Staatstheater,** whose Rococo foyer and auditoriums are inscribed with the rather demanding instruction *Der Menscheit Würde ist in Eure Hand gegeben, bewahret Sie* ("The dignity of mankind is in your hands, preserve it"). The Staatstheater and neighboring **Kleines Haus** present ballets, operas, and plays for as little as €5.50. (☎13 23 25. Box office for both open Tu-F 11am-6pm, Sa-Su 11am-1pm, and 1hr. before performances.) Across Wilhelmstr. from the Staatstheater, the **World's Biggest Cuckoo Clock** is topped by a giant moose head. The birds strut and fret every 30min. from 8am-8pm. Toward the train station on Friedrich-Ebert-Allee, the **Museum Wiesbaden** houses temporary exhibits of modern German art in addition to its permanent collection. (☎335 22 50; www.museum-wiesbaden.de. Open Tu 10am-8pm, W-Su 10am-5pm. €4, students and seniors €2.) The neo-gothic **Marktkirche** is on the Markt near the tourist office. Organ concerts (Sa 11:30am) are followed at noon by a 30min. carillon concert on the church's 21-ton, 49-bell glockenspiel. (Open Tu-W and F-Sa 10am-12:30pm, Th 3:30-5:30pm.)

The **Neroberg,** a low hill at the north end of town, provides bucolic alternative to the bustle of Wiesbaden's pedestrian zone. Take bus #1 to "Nerotal" and walk or take the Nerobergbahn hydraulic funicular to the summit of the 254m hill crowned by the Neroberg tower. (☎780 23 98. Funicular open May-Aug. daily 9:30am-8pm; Apr. and Sept. W noon-7pm, Sa-Su 10am-7pm; Oct. W and Sa-Su noon-6pm. €2, round-trip €2.80; families €5.60.) Head down the hill to take a dip in the *Opelbad* (swimming pool) or enjoy the scenery and tan with the locals. (☎172 98 85. Open 7am-8pm. €6, after 5pm €4; students €4.) A bit farther down the mountain is the **Russische Kirche,** a richly ornamented Russian Orthodox church modeled after the Cathedral of Christ the Redeemer in Moscow. The 1885 gold-domed church contains rich tapestries, decadent altars, and the tomb of Elizabeth of Nassau, niece of a Russian tsar. (Open Apr.-Oct. daily 10am-5pm; Nov.-Mar. Sa noon-4pm, Su 10am-4pm. €1, children €0.50.)

◪◧ **ENTERTAINMENT AND NIGHTLIFE.** In early June, the **Kurpark** and Wilhelmstr. fill with a cultural extravaganza known as the **Theatrium** street festival, and in mid-August the pedestrian zone celebrates the local wines of the Rheingau regions during the **Rheingauer Weinwoche** festival. More beer, music, and general revelry can be found during **Folkore im Garten, Mosburgfest,** and **Taunusstrassenfest,** which occur over two successive weekends in late August and early September. If you've always wanted to try your luck at a game of chance, then dig up your nicest clothes (or rent a jacket and tie there for €2.50) and head for the **Kurhaus Casino** in the Kurpark. Game demonstrations on F and Sa (10 and 11pm) are a perfect chance to-win a few chips risk-free (☎53 61 44; www.spielbank-wiesbaden.de. 18+. Slots open daily noon-4am, table games 2:45pm-4am. Entry €2.50.) Or, flout dress codes and get down and dirty with the slots next door at **Kleines Spiel,** the longest hall in Europe with pillar supports. (18+. Open daily 1pm-4am. Entry €1.) The Kurhaus Casino complex, situated off Wilhelmstr., is bordered on two sides by the expansive **Kurpark.** (Take bus #1 or 8 to "Kurhaus/Theater.")

The Irish Pub, Michelsberg 15, rocks with live music every night from 9pm, offers enormous Irish breakfasts (under €12) Su 11am-3pm, and serves drinks until the wee hours. M-W and Su shot specials (4 shots for €5), Tu karaoke with karaoke-enabling €1.50 tequila shots, and Th cocktail specials (all €4.50). (☎30 08 49. Open M-Th 5pm-1am, F 5pm-2am, Sa 3pm-2am, Su 11am-1am. Cash only.)

DARMSTADT ☎ 06151

Nestled among winding streets and parks, the Technical University and the German Academy of Language and Literature distinguish Darmstadt (pop. 140,000) from a dozen other sleepy towns like it. While the university grants Darmstadt a youthful vigor year-round, the German Academy commands the whole nation's attention once a year by awarding of the Georg-Büchner Prize, Germany's highest literary honor. The formidable intellectual and artistic legacy of the Academy adds to Darmstadt's cultural pretensions, many of which live on only in memories and lost luminaries. Nonetheless, the city displays some superb *Jugendstil* (Art Nouveau) architecture, and its museums remain largely untouristed and peaceful.

▐▀ TRANSPORTATION

Frequent **trains** and the S3 run from Frankfurt to Darmstadt (30min., every hr., €7). Local **S-Bahn** and **bus** tickets cost €1.30, children €0.80; day pass €2.80/1.70; week pass €8.40. For a **taxi,** call **Funk** (☎ 194 10). Rent **bikes** at **Minigolf,** next to the pond; take S1 to "Prinz-Emil-Garten." (☎ 66 40 90. Bikes €4 per day. Mini-golf €1.50, students €1. Open M-F 8am-8pm, Sa-Su 2-8pm.)

▐▊ PRACTICAL INFORMATION

The **ProRegio tourist office** (look for the "info & tickets" shop) on the Luisenpl., in the pavilion adjacent to the fountain, books rooms for a €4 fee (free by phone or email), sells area maps (€0.60), and provides free city maps and hotel guides. (☎95 15 013; www.proregio.darmstadt.de. Open M-F 9:30am-7pm, Sa 10am-3pm; in summer and Christmas-time Sa 9:30am-6pm) Another branch is on Am Carre 4a, off Luisenstr. (☎95 15 00). The **Darmstadt Card** allows free public transportation and reduced museum entrance fees (1-day €6, 2-day €9). **STA Travel,** Alexanderstr. 37-39, handles all student travel needs and sells ISIC cards. (☎225 22. Open M-F 9:30am-6pm, Sa 9:30am-1pm.) For books, visit **The British Shop,** Mauerstr. 2, right off Alexanderstr. (☎753 80. Open M 3-6:30pm, Tu-F 11:30am-1:30pm and 3-6:30pm, Sa 10:30am-2pm.) Walk away from Luisenpl. and the tourist office to find **Up 2 Date,** 12 Luisenstr., which offers **Internet** and telephone access (€2 per hr. Open daily 10am-11pm). The **post office** is opposite the tourist office in Luisenpl. (Open M-F 7am-6:30pm, Sa 8am-12:30pm.) **Postal Code:** 64283.

▐▘ ACCOMMODATIONS

The **Jugendherberge (HI) ❷,** Landgraf-Georg-Str. 119, has spotless rooms and friendly service. Take Bus L (dir.: Ostbahnhof) to "Woog." (☎452 93; fax 42 25 35. Breakfast included. Lockers €5 deposit. Reception until 1am. Check-in 9:30am-10pm, later with reservation. Curfew 1am. Dorms €22.30; singles 28.70; doubles €50.60. Cash only.) The hostel overlooks swimming hole **Großer Woog,** an artificial lake. (Open daily mid-May to mid-Sept. 9am-8pm. Last entry 7pm. €1.80, students €1. Showers €0.50.) **Zentral Hotel ❹,** Schuchardstr. 6, is pricier, but its affable staff and soothing atmosphere are worth it. From Luisenpl., walk along Luisenstr. with the Luisencenter Mall on your right; turn left onto Schuchardstr. (☎264 11 12; fax 268 58. Breakfast included. Singles €50-57; doubles €52-87. AmEx/MC.)

▐▘ FOOD

Eating in Darmstadt can be pricey, but **Markthalle Caree,** across the street from the Zentral Hotel, is a wonderland of bakeries, fruit stands, Chinese groceries, and

Imbiße. (Open M-F 11am-10pm, Sa 11am-8:30pm, but fruit and vegetable vendors leave earlier.) Every morning except Sunday, Marktpl. is crowded with fruit and sausage vendors. A few inexpensive restaurants can be found at the beginning of Landgraf-Georg-Str., west of the *Schloß*. The university **Mensa ❶** also dishes out cheap meals. With your back to the northern side of the *Schloß*, cross Alexander-str., then take a right and walk past the yellow Staatsarchiv and the first university building on your left. Turn left down the stairs, then right into the University's Otto-Bernd-Halle. The entrance is through the glass doors behind the hall, on the second floor. A decent selection of snacks is available for €0.85-4. (Open during the school year M-Th 11am-2:30pm, F 11am-2pm. Cash only.) Right in front of the *Schloß*, loungers at the outdoor tables of the green **Bormuth Café Haus am Markt ❷** enjoy quirky sundaes (€2.90-4.70) and fresh baked goods (€4-8) while taking in the bustle of the Marktpl. (Open M-F 7:30am-7pm, Sa 7:30am-6pm, Su 10:30am-6pm. Cash only.) **Ratskeller Hausbrauerei,** am Markpl. 8, serves up beer brewed in-house from shiny copper vats (.25L for €1.50) and *Wurst, Braten,* and *Frankfurt-ers* (€4.50-7). (☎264 44. Open daily 10am-1am. MC.)

🜚 SIGHTS

🔲**MATHILDENHÖHE (THE MATHILDE HEIGHTS).** The mecca of Darmstadt's *Jugendstil* architecture (p. 68), this artists' colony on a hill west of the city was founded by Grand Duke Ernst Ludwig in 1899. The Duke fell in love with *Jugendstil* and invited seven artists to build a "living and working world" of art, financing the transformation of the urban landscape into the predecessor to Art Deco. While the *Jugendstil* school formally disbanded after WWII, the city has committed itself to the upkeep of the resplendent environs of the Mathildenhöhe's museums, chapels, and fountains. *(Walk east from the Luisenpl. along Erich-Ollenhauer-Promenade, or take bus F to "Lucasweg/Mathild." and take a right on Lucasweg.)* Like a monstrous jukebox, the **Hochzeitsturm** (wedding tower) atop the Mathildenhöhe was the city's wedding present to Ernst Ludwig in 1908. The 48m tower offers a view of Darmstadt. *(Open Mar.-Oct. Tu-Su 10am-6pm. €1.50, students and children €0.50.)* The **Museum Künstlerkolonie** to the southeast of the tower houses Art Nouveau furniture and modern art. *(Alexandra Weg 26. ☎13 33 85. Open Tu-Su 10am-5pm. €3, students €2, families €6.)* The **Russische Kapelle,** a gilded onion-domed Russian Orthodox church, is south of the tower. The chapel was imported stone by stone from Russia at the behest of the last Tsar Nicholas II when he married Darmstadt's Princess Alexandra. Its foundations were built on earth from every state in the Russian empire so it would stand on Russian soil. Because of its association with the martyred royal family, it is a pilgrimage site for Russian Orthodox Christians in the diaspora. *(Nikolaiweg 18. ☎42 42 35. Open daily 10am-4pm. €0.80, students €0.60.)*

🔲**WALDSPIRALE (FOREST SPIRAL).** An architectural feat of biomorphic shapes and fanciful colors, this project was originally conceived by famous Austrian architect Friedensreich Hundertwasser on a restaurant napkin. The resulting building was largely faithful to this sketch, rejecting straight lines and instead opting for whimsical, sediment-like coloring. The building, completed just months after the artist's death in 2000, contains apartments, office space, and a restaurant. *(At the corner of Bad Nauheimer Str. and Friedberger Str.)*

ROSENHÖHE (THE ROSE HEIGHTS). Don't be fooled by the overgrown lawns and sprawling evergreens of the park's perimeter: the terraced fish pools, ivy-covered arches, and age-old perennials of the center rose garden make it one of the most pristine parks in Germany. The somber Mausoleum houses the tombs of the grandducal family of the city. *(Enter at the corner of Seitersweg and Wolfskehlstr.)*

BRAUN MUSEUM. The home of the Braun design collection showcases the evolution of the company's appliances since 1955—everything from Aunt Ulrike's blender to Uncle Franz's cutting-edge electric razor. *(Eugen-Bracht-Weg 6. Right off Alexandraweg near Mathildenhöhe.* ☎ *42 48 81. Open Tu-Sa 10am-6pm, Su 10am-1pm. Free.)*

SCHLOß. The gigantic coral-and-white palace is smack-dab in the middle of the city. Built between 1716 and 1727, it was modeled after Versailles by a wistful Frenchman. Since WWII, the *Schloß* has served as a public university library and police station. A small museum tucked in the eastern wing holds 17th- to 19th-century ducal clothing and furniture. *(*☎ *24 03 53. Open M-Th 10am-1pm and 2-5pm, Sa-Su 10am-1pm. Obligatory 45min. tour leaves every hr.* €2.50, *students* €1.50.*)* Local students and families relax in the **Herrngarten,** a lush garden north of the *Schloß* that is a haven for frisky dogs and frumpy ducks. In its northeastern corner is the even more exquisite **Prinz-Georg-Garten,** arranged in a highly geometrical Rococo style. *(Open daily Mar.-Oct. 7am-7pm; Nov.-Feb. 8am-5pm.)* Next to it, the **Porzellanschlößchen** (little porcelain castle) displays an extensive china collection. *(Schloßgartenstr. 10.* ☎ *71 32 33. Open M-Th 10am-1pm and 2-5pm, Sa-Su 10am-1pm.* €2.50, *students* €1.50.*)*

◨ NIGHTLIFE

Darmstadt parties annually the first weekend in July during **Heinerfest** with beer, music, and a raucous carnival in the city's center. For the rest of the year, jazz, rock, poetry, and boxing can be had at **Central Station,** Platz der Deutschen Einheit 21. From the tourist office on Marktpl., follow Luisenstr. and take the first left. This three-story cultural center showcases a dizzying variety of talents and in peak season (winter), it hosts acts almost every night. The website lists the latest attractions. *(*☎ *80 94 60; www.centralticket.de. Hours vary. Closed Aug.)* In the center, locals recommend **Nachrichten-Treff,** Elisabethenstr. 20, for cheap beer (€2.10) and laid-back atmosphere. From Luisenpl. take Luisenstr. and make the first right onto Elisabethenstr. *(*☎ *238 23. Open daily 9pm-1am. MC/V.)* For late-night bar-hopping, take buses K, U, or H to "Kopernikus Pl.," then walk down the Lauteschlägerstr.

LAHNTAL (LAHN VALLEY)

The peaceful Lahn River flows through this verdant valley, and the hills on either side of it are dappled with vineyards, quiet hamlets, and German families in search of outdoor fun. Every spring and summer, campgrounds and hostels fill with people who have come to take advantage of the hiking, biking, and kayaking available along the Lahn. Rail service runs regularly between Koblenz in the west and Gießen at the eastern end of the valley, as well as between Frankfurt and Limburg. Visit local bookstores to pick up hiking maps, and inquire at town tourist offices for locations of bike and boat rentals.

LIMBURG AN DER LAHN ☎ 06431

Limburg an der Lahn (pop. 35000) serves much the same function today as it did during the Middle Ages: a stop for merchants traveling from Cologne to Frankfurt. With the most important train station between Koblenz and Gießen, Limburg is an excellent base for exploring the Upper Lahn Valley. **Trains** run every hour to **Gießen, Frankfurt,** and **Koblenz** making Limburg a popular weekend getaway for these city-dwellers. Largely unscathed by WWII, the Altstadt is a maze of narrow, brick streets that provide a backdrop for all things bucolic. The little town's pride is the **St. Georg-Dom,** a stunning cathedral that towers over the Altstadt. The landmark red-and-white structure is a unique combination of Romanesque and Gothic styles filtered through the traditional German architectural sensibility, and the result might be the biggest, holiest *Fachwerkhaus* (half-timbered house) you'll ever see. Inside are a number of well-preserved frescoes and devotional artworks. From the train station, follow Bahnhofstr. until it ends in the Altstadt and take a left on Salzg. Take a sharp right onto the Fischmarkt and from there follow Domstr. for 25min. all the way up to the Dom. (☎29 53 32. Open daily Apr.-Oct. 9am-6pm; Nov.-Mar. 9am-5pm. Tours M-F at 11am and 3pm, Sa at 11am, Su at 11:30am. Free.) Next to the cathedral, the **Diözesanmuseum und Domschatz** (Diocesan Museum and Cathedral Treasury), Domstr. 12, displays a small, impressive collection of medieval religious artifacts dating from the 12th century, including jewel-encrusted crucifixes and elaborate robes. (☎29 53 27. Open Easter-Nov. Tu-Sa 10am-5pm, Su 11am-5pm. €2, students €1.)

The **Jugendherberge (HI) ❷**, Auf dem Guckucksberg, in Eduard-Horn-Park, provides spacious rooms, pristine facilities, and a friendly staff at its hilltop location. From the station, turn right and take the stairs down to an underpass, then take the left exit toward Frankfurter Str. Follow Im Schlenkert right until it empties onto a larger road, and take this until Frankfurter Str. forks off on the left. Stay right and keep on up the hill to the hostel (40min.). Or take bus #603 from Hospitalstr. (dir.: Am Hammerberg; every hr. 8am-6pm) to "Jugendherberge." (☎414 93; fax 438 73. Breakfast included. Reception 2-10pm. €17, over 27 €20.) To avoid the pricey hotels in town, call local couple Herr and Frau Hantl, who offer comfortable **Privatzimmer ❸**, Walderdorffstr. 25. From the station, take a left on Weiersteinstr., and after two blocks bear left on Parkg.; Walderdorfferstr. will be on your right. The rooms are large and outfitted with private bathrooms, but they fill fast. (☎38 05. Breakfast included. Singles €31; doubles €58.) **Lahncampingplatz ❶** is on the far bank of the Lahn, just outside the Altstadt. Follow directions to the Dom until the Fischmarkt, then bear left (instead of right on Domstr.) along Fahrg. downhill to Brückeng. and the Lahnbrücke. On the other side of the Lahn, turn right onto Schleusenweg and walk 10min. along the Lahn to the campground. (☎226 10. Reception M-F 8am-1pm and 3-10pm, Sa 8am-1pm and 3-5pm, Su 8am-1pm. Open May-Oct. €4 per person. €3 tents.)

The tangle of narrow streets below the Dom are filled with cheap (but still over-priced) bakeries offering sweets and sandwiches. Just off the Fischmarkt, ▓**Bodega Dali Loco ❸**, Rütsche 11, serves homemade bread and a wide range of dinner options (€8.50-20). Savor delicious tapas (€2-6) and the suspicion that you've stepped into Spain. (☎288 606. Open daily 11am-midnight. AmEx/DC/MC/V.) **Da Sandro ❷**, Schiede 26, offers pizza and pasta dishes in an upscale restaurant for low prices (€4-7). From the Bahnhof, turn left and walk along Weiersteinstr. and take the right side of the fork onto Schiede. (Open Tu-Su noon-2:30pm and 6pm-midnight. Cash only.)

The **tourist office,** Hospitalstr. 2, offers a guide to the town and provides a list of rooms. Exit the station, turn left, and turn right on Hospitalstr. The office is at the intersection with Grabenstr. The office is poorly marked; walk in the *Verkehr-samt* from Hospitalstr., and it's on the right. (☎61 66. Open M-F Apr.-Oct. 9am-5pm; Nov.-Mar. 10am-4pm) The **post office** is at the corner of Grabenstr. and Eschhöfer Weg. (Open M-F 8:30am-5:30pm, Sa 9am-12:30pm.) **Postal Code:** 65549.

MARBURG ☎06421

In 1527, Landgrave Philip founded the world's first Protestant university in Marburg (pop. 78,000), an isolated town on the banks of the Lahn River. The university has produced an illustrious list of alumni, including Martin Heidegger, T.S. Eliot, Richard Bunsen (of burner fame), and the Brothers Grimm. It seems that nothing here is at a right angle—teetering rows of *Fachwerkhäuser* (half-timbered houses) look as though they will topple into the Lahn at any moment. The city's snug perch between mountains and river provides a dramatic setting where tourists and students alike enjoy watersports, cafés, monuments, and nightclubs.

TRANSPORTATION AND PRACTICAL INFORMATION

Trains: To **Cologne** (3hr., 2 per hr., €34-41); **Frankfurt** (1hr., every hr., €12-15); **Hamburg** (3½hr., 6 per day, €60-68); **Kassel** (1½hr., 2 per hr., €15-20).

Public Transportation: Buses run throughout the city. Single tickets €1.50.

Taxis: Funkzentrale (☎477 77).

Tourist Office: Pilgrimstein 26 (☎991 20; www.marburg.de). Bus #1, 2, 3, 5 or 6 to "Rudolphspl.," and exit to the north along Pilgrimstein; the office is on the left. Or, walk across the bridge straight out of the train station, turn left on Elisabethstr. as you pass the post office, and continue straight (10min.). Provides maps, books rooms for free, sells theater tickets, and offers a variety of city tours in German (€3). English tours available if arranged 2wk. in advance. Open M-F 9am-6pm, Sa 10am-2pm.

Banks: 24hr. **ATM** at **Deutschebank,** at the corner of Pilgrimstein and Biegenstr.

Bookstore: N.G. Elwert, Pilgrimstein 30 (☎17 09 34), 1 block from Rudolphspl., has a sophisticated selection of English books. Open M-F 9:30am-7pm, Sa 9:30am-5pm.

Women's Resources: Autonomes Frauenhaus, Alter Kirchainer Weg 5 (☎16 15 16). Open M and W 10am-1pm, Th 4-7pm.

Laundromat: Waschcenter, at the corner of Gutenbergstr. and Jägerstr. From the HI hostel, cross the wooden bridge, then another bridge, turn left on Frankfürterstr. and quickly hang a right on Gutenbergstr. Wash €3. Soap €0.50. Dry €0.50 per 15min. Open daily 8am-midnight, closed Su during school holidays.

Emergency: Police ☎110. **Fire** ☎112.

Internet Access: Internet Treff, Pilgrimstein 27 (☎92 47 05), right across from the tourist office. Choose from a variety of hot and cold drinks (€1.50-3) while surfing the web (€1.50 per 30min.). Open M-Sa 10am-2am, Su noon-1am.

Post Office: Bahnhofstr. 6. A 5min. from the train station. Open M-F 9am-6pm, Sa 9am-12:30pm. **Postal Code:** 35037.

ACCOMMODATIONS AND CAMPING

Marburg boasts more than 30 hotels and pensions, but competition hasn't done much to keep prices down. Plan ahead if you intend to spend less than €30.

Jugendherberge (HI), Jahnstr. 1 (☎234 61; marburg@djh-hessen.de). Bus C (dir.: Marburg Stadtwerke P+R) to "Auf der Weide," backtrack and turn right into a street that becomes 2 bridges (one metal, one wooden). From the tourist office, go to Rudolphspl.; cross the bridge and turn right on the river path; the hostel is on the left (40min.). Scenic location, close to town. Large rooms, some with bath. Breakfast included. Reception 7:30am-11:30pm. Keys available with ID or €25 deposit. Dorms €21.50. Cash only. ❷

Tusculum-Art-Hotel, Gutenbergstr. 25 (☎227 78; www.tusculum.de). Follow Universitätsstr. from Rudolphspl. and take the 1st left on Gutenbergstr. Many tourists visit modern art museums, but here you can feel like you're staying in one. Each room is decorated with a different theme—bathroom fixtures can get pretty ridiculous. Reception 4-9pm; call ahead to arrange other times. Singles €37; doubles €66, with shower €74; triples €82.50. Cash only. ❹

Hotel und Gasthaus Zur Sonne, Market 14 (☎171 90; fax 17 19 40), on the Markt in a 1569 *fachwerk* (half-timbered) building. Location, history, delicately painted furniture, breakfast buffet, and kind owners make this a good base for exploring Marburg. Office closed M. Reception 8am-midnight. Singles €41-51; doubles €77-87. AmEx/MC/V. ❹

Camping: Lahnaue, Trojedamm 47 (☎213 31; www.lahnaue.de), on the Lahn River and close to the city center. Follow directions to the hostel and continue downriver another 5min. €5 deposit for use of electricity and showers. Laundry €2.50. The **Terrassencafé** has moderately priced food and drink near the minigolf course. Open Apr.-Oct. €4 per person, €3 per tent. Cash only. ❶

◪ FOOD

Marburg's cuisine caters to its students, with *Wurst*, pizza, *Kebap*, and the omnipresent *Marburger* beer. The streets around the Markt are full of cafés serving inexpensive sandwiches. **ALDI** supermarket has **groceries;** from Rudolphpl. take Universitätstr. and turn left on Gutenbergstr. (Open M-F 9am-7pm, Sa 8am-4pm.)

Bistro-Café Phönix, Am Grün 1 (☎16 49 69). Tucked in a short alley between Rudolphspl. and Universitätsstr., this bistro-bar serves pizzas, salads, and baguettes for €3-6. Ice-cold piña coladas €5. Open M-Th 6pm-1am, F-Sa 6pm-3am. Cash only. ❷

Café Barfuß, Barfüßerstr. 33 (☎253 49), is packed with locals and students. Big breakfast menu (€3-8) served until 3pm, and the unique (if not slightly intimidating) *Fladenbrot*-meets-pizza 'Fetizza.' The booths and picnic tables, as well as the laid-back staff, make this the kind of place to sit all afternoon. Open daily 10am-1am. Cash only. ❷

Havana, Am Grün 58 (☎16 49 60), tucked off the street next to a canal. A student hot spot with tapas, baked roll-ups, and dozens of mixed drinks (€4-8). Happy hour daily 7-9pm. Open daily 6pm-1am, F-Sa 6pm-2am, Su 6pm-midnight. Cash only. ❸

Café Vetter, Reitg. 4 (☎258 88) A 90-year-old cake shop proud of its terrace on the edge of the Oberstadt. Live piano music Sa-Su afternoons in good weather (Sa 5pm, Su 3pm). Cake and coffee €5. Chocolates, marzipan, and gourmet tea for sale. Open M and W-Sa 8:30am-6:30pm, Tu 11am-6:30pm, Su 9:30am-6:30pm. Cash only. ❷

◉ SIGHTS

UNIVERSITÄTSMUSEUM FÜR BILDENDE KUNST (UNIVERSITY MUSEUM FOR VISUAL ARTS). The university's impressive little collection of 19th- and 20th-century German painting and sculpture is housed in a modest building that belies the quality of the works. Pieces by Paul Klee and Otto Dix compete with temporary exhibits of provocative modern work and a section on Expressive Realism and the lost generation of artists who matured during the Nazi period. *(Biegenstr. 11. ☎282 23 55. Open Tu-Su 11am-1pm and 2-5pm. €2, students €1.)*

LANDGRAFENSCHLOß. The exterior of this castle, which sits on the Gison cliffs, looks almost as it did in 1500 when it was a haunt of infamous Teutonic knights. In 1529, Count Philip brought rival Protestant reformers **Martin Luther** and **Ulrich Zwingli** to his court to convince them to reconcile. Inside, the *Schloß* has been completely re-made into the **Museum für Kulturgeschichte** (Museum for Cultural History), which exhibits Hessian history and art, including wooden shields and ornate crosses. The basement holds a 7th-century skeleton and recently unearthed 9th-century wall remnants The **Landesherrschaft** (Provincial Rule) floor is a war buff's dream come true. Behind the *Schloß* is a quiet garden that provides views in all directions. *(From Rudolphspl. or Markt take bus #16 (dir.: Schloß) to the end, or hike the 250 steps from the Markt. ☎282 23 55. Open Tu-Su Apr.-Oct. 10am-6pm; Nov.-Mar. 11am-5pm. Last entry 30min. before closing. €2.60, students €1.)*

HESSEN

ELISABETHKIRCHE. Save some ecclesiastic awe for the oldest Gothic church in Germany, modeled on the French cathedral at Reims. The name of the church honors the town patroness, a widowed child-bride (engaged at 4, married at 14, dead by her 20s) who took refuge in Marburg, founded a hospital, and snagged sainthood four years after her death. The reliquary for her bones is the centerpiece for the elaborate choir, which is like a church-within-a-church, so overdone it's glorious. The somber brown interior is illuminated by glowing stained-glass windows. *(Elisabethstr. 3. With your back to the train station, walk down Bahnhofstr. 10min. and turn left on Elisabethstr. ☎655 73. Open Apr.-Sept. M-Sa 9am-6pm, Su 11:15-5pm; Oct.-Mar. daily 10am-4pm. Church free; reliquary €2, students €1.50.)*

RUDOLPHSPLATZ. The modern university building was erected in 1871, but the original Alte Universität on Rudolphspl. was built on the rubble of a monastery conveniently empty after Reformation-minded Marburgers ejected the resident monks. The enormous stone building stands at the foot of the big hill, anchoring the Altstadt that spreads up and out behind it. The **Aula,** or main hall, bears frescoes illuminating Marburg's history, but you can see it only by reservation (call ☎991 20). The nearby houses are former fraternities, and the topsy-turvy state of their frames attest to a proud, *Bier*-soaked tradition.

OTHER SIGHTS. In front of the 16th-century Gothic **Rathaus** is the **Markt,** a plaza surrounded by open-air cafés and shops. To get there, take the **Altstadt Aufzug** elevator between the tourist office and the bookstore, or wind up the steep hill from the Alte Universität. Even farther up the hill, the 13th-century **Lutherische Pfarrkirche St. Marien** features amber-colored stained glass and an elaborate organ. The view overlooking the old city rivals the one from the *Schloß* perched near the top of the hill. *(Lutherische Kirchhof 1. ☎252 43. Open daily 9am-5pm. Free organ concerts Oct.-July Sa 6:30pm.)* Down Kugelg., the 15th-century Catholic **Kugelkirche St. Johannis** (Sphere Church) owes its peculiar name not to its shape but to the *cuculla* (hats) worn by the religious order that founded it. Back down by the river, visit the newly relocated **Kunstverein** (Art Association), a cavernous gallery that hosts temporary exhibitions of contemporary art and an annual show of local artists. *(Biegenstr. 1. ☎258 82; www.marburger-kunstverein.de. Open Tu and Th-Su 11am-5pm, W 11am-8pm. Free.)*

🎵 📻 ENTERTAINMENT AND NIGHTLIFE

Marburg's upper village alone has over 60 bars and clubs. Live music, concert, theater, and movie options appear in the weekly *Marburger Express*, available at bars and pubs. Posters plaster the main streets to announce larger events. The **Hessisches Landestheater** hosts an array of theatrical and dance productions. Ask for a program of upcoming performances at the tourist office, and buy tickets at the Stadthalle, Biegenstr. 15. *(☎256 08; www.hlth.de. Open M-F 9am-12:30pm and 4:30-6pm.)* There are a number of movie theaters; **Marburger Filmkunsttheater,** Steinweg 4, shows old American hits and more unusual recent releases. One movie per week is not dubbed; check out the website or posters by the door. *(☎672 69 or 626 77; www.marburgerfilmkunst.de.)* The first Sunday in July, costumed citizens parade onto the Markt for the rowdy **Frühschoppenfest** (Morning Beer Festival). Drinking officially kicks off at 11am when the brass rooster on top of the Rathaus flaps its wings. Unofficially, the barrels of *Alt Marburger Pils* are tapped at 10am when the ribald old *Marburger Trinklieder* (drinking ballads) commence.

Bolschoi Café, Ketzerbach (☎622 24). From Rudolfspl. walk up Pilgrimstein to the Elizabethkirche and turn left on Ketzerbach; it's at the end of the block. The decor is pure communist kitsch: red candles, walls, and ceiling, and 20 kinds of vodka (€1.50-3),− you might find some Comerades in debauchery. Open M-Sa 8pm-2am. Cash only.

Discothek Kult, Temmlerstr. 7 (☎941 83). Bus #A1 (dir.: Pommernweg) or A2 (dir.: Cappeler Gleiche) to "Stadtbüro." This warehouse is the place to dance the night away with Marburg's teens on one of 3 dance floors, to bass-throbbing techno, hip-hop, or oldies, or join the 20-somethings at any of the 4 bars. Lots of different theme nights; call for the schedule. Cover €2-4. Open Tu-W 9pm-3am, F-Sa 9pm-4am. Cash only.

Hinkelstein, Markt 18 (☎242 10). This medieval cellar now features tunes from the Kinks and the Stones. A blue jeans-friendly pub with a sturdy cast of regulars at the bar sipping beer (€3 for 0.5L). Walking uphill from the Markt, it's on the left. Open M-Th and Su 7pm-3am, F-Sa 7pm-5am. Cash only.

FULDA   ☎0661

Only 30km from the former East-West border, Fulda (pop. 63,000) gained notoriety during the Cold War as the most likely target for a Warsaw Pact invasion, earning it the undesirable nickname "Fulda Gap." The city's central location changed from burden to asset as reunification turned Fulda into a transportation hub. Its palace and castle do not draw overwhelming crowds leaving the beautiful Baroque quarter and gardens refreshingly free of tourist clichés.

🖪🚪 TRANSPORTATION AND PRACTICAL INFORMATION. Fulda offers good rail connections from its strategic location. **Trains** to: Frankfurt (1hr., 2-3 per hr., €25-31); Hamburg (3hr., 2 per hr., €67-77); Kassel (1½hr., 2 per hr., €17); Nuremberg (1½hr., every hr., €35); Weimar (2hr., every hr., €40). Public transit consists of two **bus** fleets, with the hub located up the stairs to your left as you step outside the train station. The **tourist office** (☎102 18 14; www.tourismus-fulda.de) is across the intersection from the *Schloß*. It distributes maps and tour booklets and books rooms for free. (Open M-F 8:30am-6pm, Sa 9:30am-4pm, Su 10am-2pm. Tours Apr.-Oct. daily 11:30am; Nov.-Mar. Sa-Su 11:30am; call ahead for English. €2.50, children €1.50.) Find an **ATM** at the **Sparkasse** on Rabanusstr. Do **laundry** at **Wash n' Dry,** Floreng. 18. From behind Stadpfarrkirche, take Steinweg, which becomes Floreng. (Wash €3.60. Dry €0.80 per 15min. Open daily 7am-10pm.) The **post office** is on Heinrich-von-Bebra Pl. (Open M-F 8am-6pm, Sa 8am-1pm.) **Postal Code:** 36037.

🖪🗋 ACCOMMODATIONS AND FOOD. Fulda's **Jugendherberge (HI) ❷,** Schirmannstr. 31, can be reached from the train station by bus #5052 or 1B to "Stadion." Proceed 5min. up the hill; it's on the left. Its small size, purple halls, and attentive staff make for a restful experience. (☎733 89; fulda@djh-hessen.de. Breakfast included. Curfew 11:30pm. Dorms €16, over 27 €18.70; singles €20/22.50; doubles €39/45. Cash only.) The ebullient Frau Kremer maintains technicolor accommodations at the **Gasthaus Kronhof ❸,** Am Dronhof 2, behind the Dom just outside the old city walls. Take bus #7, AS 5, or AS 12 to "Hinterburg/Am Kronhof" and continue down Kronhofstr. Ask for one of the top floor singles that open onto the roof deck, complete with flowers and lawn furniture. (☎741 47. Breakfast included. Singles €23-41; doubles €55-75. Cash only.) For something a bit more upscale, try the family-run **Hotel Garni Peterchens Mondfahrt ❺,** Rabnusstr. 7. Posh rooms include cable TV, phone, modem connection, and cosmically decorated bed linens. (☎90 23 50; Harnier@t-online.de. Breakfast included. Singles €58-68, F-Sa €48-58; doubles €78-98/58-78; family suites €88-108. MC/V.)

Mercado ❷, Gemüsemarkt 15, offers a different vegetarian meal every day, as well as staples like veggie burgers, all for €3-5. To get there, from the Stadtschloß, follow Friedrichstr. past the Stadtpfarrkirche and down Mittelstr. and take a right into Gemüsemarkt. (☎229 88. Open M-F 9am-6pm, Sa 9am-4pm. Cash only.) Taking a left past the church down Marktstr. brings you to the **Buttermarkt,** where cheap dinner options abound. **Vini & Panini ❸**, Steinweg 2-4, is a Italian delicatessen tucked between Karstadt and Pfarrkirche. Enjoy gourmet pasta or risotto (€6-12) or sip fine wine (from €4) among innumerable bottles of olive oil. Extensive dessert menu. (☎774 93. Open M-Sa noon-2am, kitchen until 11pm. DC/MC/V.)

◙ SIGHTS. Prince-abbots reigned in Fulda for 700 years, leaving behind a glorious, if small, Residenz palace. Built in 1706 as the centerpiece of the town, the historical **Stadtschloß** now contains offices and a one-room exhibit on Fulda's Nobel Prize-winning **Carl Braun**, inventor of the television tube. Particularly striking are the **Spiegelsäule** (mirror rooms) and the **Fürstensaal**, ringed with paintings from Greek mythology. One corner room has 420 mirrors and 46 tiny paintings. Every Friday morning the castle closes for Fulda's wedding ceremonies, held here because the *Schloß* serves as the de facto city hall. Entrance to the castle also includes access to the **Schloßturm** (tower), where you can look out over the town. To reach this yellow behemoth from the train station, head down Bahnhofstr. and turn right onto Rabnusstr. Enter across from the tourist office. (Castle open M-Th and Sa-Su 10am-6pm, F 2-6pm; last tower entrance 5:30pm. Castle and tower €2.50, students €1.50. Tower only €1/0.50.) Behind the palace is the luxurious **Schloßpark** lined with terraces; just beyond the fountain sits the 18th-century **Orangerie**, a striking structure topped with golden pineapples, originally built to house the royal garden of imported lemon trees, now a ritzy cafe and convention center. The Baroque **Floravase** sculpture graces the steps of the Orangerie.

Across the street from the *Schloß* is the stunning 18th-century **Dom,** which houses the tomb of St. Boniface. An 8th-century English monk and missionary known as "the apostle of Germany," Boniface founded the Fulda abbey in 744. Dozens of alabaster saints and cherubs are scattered among marble pillars and gilded alcoves, including a plaster skeleton posing near the pulpit. (Open daily 8am-7pm. Free.) To the left of the cathedral is the **Dommuseum,** with an array of Baroque relics and other sacred items. (Open Apr.-Oct. Tu-Sa 10am-5:30pm, Su 12:30-5:30pm; Nov.-Mar. Tu-Sa 10am-12:30pm and 1:30-4pm, Su 12:30-4pm. €2.10, students €1.30.) To the right of the Dom is one of Germany's oldest and most unusual churches, the medieval **St. Michaelskirche,** built in 820. Take the stairs to the right of the circular sanctuary to enter the eerie, twisting crypt. (Open daily Apr.-Oct. 10am-6pm; Nov.-Mar. 2-4pm. Free.)

KASSEL ☎0561

After Napoleon III and his soldiers were captured in the Battle of Sedan in 1870, the Aacheners jeered *"Ab nach Kassel"* (off to Kassel) at the crestfallen monarch as he was marched into Kassel's **Schloß Wilhelmshöhe.** Since then, Kassel (pop. 194,000) has developed into a city of modern architecture, unique museums, and artsy citizens. From bizarre castles and monuments to sweeping vistas, Kassel offers plenty to draw the curious in search of an unusual locale. The **documenta,** an international exhibition of contemporary art held every five years, will bring Kassel into the limelight in 2007 (June 16-September 23). The project is designed to reconcile the German public with modernity after years of Nazi barbarism and Germany's failed Enlightenment-era revolution.

🚆 TRANSPORTATION

Trains: From Bahnhof Wilhelmshöhe-Kassel to: **Berlin** (3hr., 2 per hr., €74); **Düsseldorf** (3½hr., every hr., €38-45); **Frankfurt** (2hr., 2 per hr., €41-49); **Hamburg** (2½hr., 2 per hr., €57-65); **Munich** (4hr., every hr., €78-87).

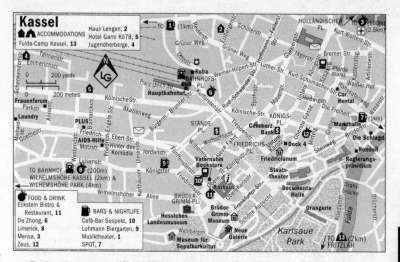

Kassel

▲▲ ACCOMMODATIONS
Fulda-Camp Kassel, **13**
Haus Lengen, **2**
Hotel Garni Kö78, **5**
Jugendherberge, **4**

FOOD & DRINK
Eckstein Bistro &
  Restaurant, **11**
Da Zhong, **6**
Limerick, **8**
Mensa, **3**
Zeus, **12**

🍺 BARS & NIGHTLIFE
Cafè-Bar Suspekt, **10**
Lohmann Biergarten, **9**
Musiktheater, **1**
SPOT, **7**

Ferries: Personenschifffahrt Söllner, Die Schlagd/Rondell (☎ 77 46 70; www.personen-schiffahrt.com), offers daily 3hr. Fulda Valley tours May to mid-Sept. 2pm and W, Su, and holidays 9:30am (leaves Hannoversch Münden at 3pm). One-way to Hannoversch Münden €11, round-trip €17; children €6/8

Public Transportation: Kassel's sophisticated system of buses and trams is integrated into the **NVV.** Tickets are priced by distance; single rides range from €1.25 (up to 4 stops) to €2.50 (anywhere in Kassel). The **Multiticket** (€5) is valid for 2 adults and 3 children throughout Kassel. The **Kassel Card,** available at the tourist office, gives free public transportation and tours, and museum discounts. 1-day card €7, 3-day €10; 2 people €10/13; 4 people €15/19.

Taxis: ☎ 881 11.

Bike Rental: FahrradHof, Bahnhof Wilhelmshöhe (☎ 31 30 83). €10 per day, €40 per wk. Open M-F 9am-1pm and 2-6:30pm; Apr.-Oct. Sa 9am-3pm; Nov.-Mar Sa 9am-1pm.

✳ 🔢 ORIENTATION AND PRACTICAL INFORMATION

When Deutsche Bahn chose Kassel to be an InterCity Express connection, they rebuilt **Bahnhof Wilhelmshöhe-Kassel** to its streamlined contemporary specs. While the new station elevated Kassel's status as a connected urban hub, it also had the effect of taking a lot of the action away from the old city center, since it is at the far western end of Wilhelmshöhe Allee at the edge of an enormous park (see **Sights,** p. 341). The old Hauptbahnhof overlooks the economically depressed downtown area. Now marketed as more of a cultural center than a train station, it has been outfitted with postmodern adornments, including the popular Gleis 1 nightclub and one of the documenta exhibitions, the **Caricatura** (p. 342). IC, ICE, and some IR trains stop only at Wilhelmshöhe, but frequent trains and tram #7 shuttle between the stations. Trams #1-4 run between the Altstadt and the Wilhelmshöhe areas. Be careful walking along the underground walkway in the tram station alone after dark. **Treppenstr.,** Kassel's original pedestrian zone (the first in all of Germany), takes you from the hill from the front of the station and to **Obere Königsstr.,** the main pedestrian zone and condensed site of major shops and eateries.

Tourist Office: Main office is in the Rathaus, Obere Königstr. 8 (☎70 77 07; www.kassel.de). The hip, young staff book rooms for a €2.50 fee and offer free maps. Smaller **branch** in the the Kassel-Wilhelmshöhe Allee station provides the same services (☎340 54; fax 31 52 16). Ask about the **Kassel Card,** which gives free public transportation and tours, and museum discounts. Both offices open M-F 9am-6pm, Sa 9am-2pm.

Currency Exchange: Commerzbank, Königspl. 32-24 (☎789 90). 24hr. **ATM.** Open M and F 9am-4pm, Tu and Th 9am-6pm, W 9am-1pm.

Bookstore: Buchhandlung Vaternahm, Obere Königsstr. 7 (☎78 98 40). Broad selection of English paperbacks. Open M-F and Su 9:30am-8pm, Sa 9:30am-6pm.

Women's Resources: Frauenforum, Annastr. 9 (☎77 05 87). **Mädchenhaus,** Annastr. 9 (☎717 83).

Laundromat: Wasch-Treff, Friedrich-Ebert-Str. 83, near the HI hostel. Wash €3.50. Dry €0.50 per 12min. Open M-Sa 5am-midnight.

Emergency: Police ☎110. **Fire** and **Ambulance** ☎112.

AIDS-Hilfe: Motzstr. 4 (☎10 85 15; www.kassel.aidshilfe.de), in a small complex of medical facilities. Open M-W and F 10am-1pm, Th 1-4pm.

Hospital: Klinikum Kassel, Mönchebergstr. 41-43 (☎98 00; www.klinikum-kassel.de).

Internet Access: Red Sea Telecafé, Fünffensterstr. 9 (☎70 33 40), has computers and comfy office chairs around the corner from the Rathaus. €1.50 per hr. Open daily 9am-9pm, F-Sa until 10pm. **@Internet,** Untere Königsstr. 72, halfway between Königpl. and the Universität on the 2nd fl. €2 per hr. Open daily noon-8pm.

Post Office: Untere Königsstr. 95, between Königspl. and the university. Open M-F 8am-6pm, Sa 8am-1pm. **Branch** at the corner of Friedrich-Ebert-Str. and Bürgerm. Brunner-Str., has the same hours. **Postal Code:** 34117.

ACCOMMODATIONS AND CAMPING

Jugendherberge am Tannenwäldchen (HI), Schenkendorfstr. 18 (☎77 64 55; kassel@djh-hessen.de). From Bahnhof Wilhelmshöhe take tram #4 (dir.: Lindenberg) to "Annastr." Or, take the bus to "Jugendherberge." Spacious cafeteria, clean rooms, and a good location. Breakfast included. Sheets €4. Internet access €2 per hr. Reception 9am-11:30pm. Curfew 12:30am, but code available. Dorms €19.50; singles €28; doubles €50.40. Cash only. ❷

Hotel Garni Kö78, Kölnische Str. 78 (☎716 14; www.koe78.de). From the Hauptbahnhof, exit through the *Südausgang,* walk up the stairs, and turn right on Kölnische Str. Coming from Bahnhof Wilhelmshöhe, follow the directions to the Jugendherberge above, and from the tram stop walk up Annastr. Turn right onto Kölnische Str. Handsome brick townhouse with several spacious rooms, many with balconies overlooking a garden behind the building. Most rooms have cable TV and phone. Breakfast included. Reception 7am-10pm. Singles €32, with bathroom and shower €41-51; doubles €51/61-75. MC/V. ❸

Haus Lengen, Erzberger Str. 23-25 (☎188 01; www.koe78.de). Lengen features quiet, cozy rooms in a home a mere 10min. from the city center. Breakfast included; call ahead for reception. Singles €25-28; doubles €35-41; all with shared bath and sauna room. Cash only. ❸

Camping: Fulda-Camp Kassel, Giesenallee 7 (☎224 33). Bus #16 (dir.: Aüstadion) from Königspl. or #25 (dir.: Lindenberg) from Kirchweg on Wilhelmshöher Allee to "Damaschkebrücke." Located on the Fulda, south of Karlsaue. Reception 7am-10pm. Open Mar.-Oct. €4 per person, €2.50 per child, €6 per tent. Cash only. ❶

◖ FOOD

Friedrich-Ebert-Str., the upper part of **Wilhelmshöher Allee**, and the area around **Königspl.** all have supermarkets, bakeries, *Imbiße* (snack bars), and cafés sprinkled among department stores and fashion boutiques. **Plus** is a cheap supermarket at the corner of Friedrich-Ebert Str. and Bismarckstr. (M-Sa 8am-8pm). The **Markthalle,** a block from the Fulda off Brüderstr. hosts an indoor and outdoor ◼market with delectables of different nationalities (Th-F 7am-6pm, Sa 7am-1pm).

◪ **Limerick,** Wilhelmshöher Allee 116 (☎77 66 49; www.restaurant-limerick.de), proves that the jack of all trades can be master of many. Pan-European menu boasting 237 appetizers and entrées. The pizza list alone (60 in total, €2.60-6.70) is broken down by meat, vegetarian, poultry, and seafood categories. 25 beers on tap and a large variety of fixed 4-course lunches (€4.90-7.90) attract loyal crowds. Open M-Th 11am-1am, F-Sa until 2am, Su until midnight. Cash only. ❷

Eckstein Bistro & Restaurant, Obere Königsstr. 4 (☎71 33 00), at the corner of Fünffensterstr. Pizzas and veggie meals (€5-9). Well known for its steak specials €12.70. Lunch €5.10. Open daily 11am-midnight. AmEx/MC/V. ❷

Zeus, Entenanger 4 (☎173 53), works wonders with every variety of the pita (€6-12). Try their zucchini and calamari omelette (€6.90) amid the plaster busts and stained glass windows. Leave room for the baklava (€3.33). Open daily noon-1am. Cash only. ❸

Da Zhong, Kurfürstenstr. 8 (☎739 88 53), downhill from the Hauptbahnhof. Lavish, crimson decor and a laughing Buddha at the entrance sets the mood for Chinese specialties, served near a goldfish pond. Though main courses cost €7-12, the lunch (€5.40) or dinner buffets (€8.80) are excellent ways to fill up for less. Try the lychee wine (€2.60). Open daily 11:30am-3:30pm and 5:30-11pm. AmEx/DC/MC/V. ❸

Mensa, on Arnold-Bode-Str. (☎804 31 32) Walk down Unter-Königsstr. from the pedestrian zone or take tram #1 to "Holländischer Pl." Cross through the underground passage and veer right on Diagonale, which cuts through campus. €2.50-4, students €1 off. Lunch M-F 11:30am-2:15pm. The **Moritz-Restaurant** (☎804 33 90), in the same building, serves a more elaborate lunch with much shorter lines. €4, students €3. open M-F 11am-2:30pm. **Studentwerke-Pavillon** is a cheap café just around the corner on Diagonale. Open M-Th 8am-5pm, F 8am-3pm. ❶

◖ SIGHTS

The Rathaus area is home to various museums, many of which are devoted to Kassel's pride and joy: **documenta** (held every five years; June 16-Sept. 23, 2007). The area around the Schloß Wilhelmshöhe offers an adventurous jaunt into German history. The **Staatliche Museen Kassel—Schloß Wilhelmshöhe, Ballhaus, Hessisches Landesmuseum, Neue Galerie,** and **Orangerie**—are covered by the *Tageskarte* (day card), for sale at any of the museums (€7, students €5).

DOCUMENTA AND RATHAUS AREA

For the past 50 years documenta has showcased cutting-edge art in a month-long festival that takes over the town. Exhibitions explore the role of contemporary art within global culture, usually with an emphasis on politics and social conscience; the projects ask whether art can help us gain access to what is essential in contemporary life. Though it only happens every five years, the international event leaves indelible marks on Kassel. Several works from past documentas have become permanent exhibitions: visit Claus Oldenburg's *Pick-axe* and Joseph Beuys's *7,000 oak trees,* both from Documenta VII in 1982.

HESSEN

MUSEUM FÜR SEPULKRALKULTUR (SEPULCHRAL MUSEUM). An ultramodern structure houses death-ritual-related paraphernalia. The museum strives to "arrest the taboo process which surrounds the subject of 'death and dying' in today's world, and open it to public discussion." Painted skulls, mourning garb, elaborate crucifixes, spliced organs in plexiglass, and monuments are sure to satisfy anyone's morbid curiosity. *(Weinbergstr. 25-27. ☎91 89 30. Open Tu-Su 10am-5pm, W 10am-8pm. €4, students €2.50.)*

MUSEUM FRIEDRICIANUM. The large yellow Friedricianum is the oldest public museum on the continent. During documenta years, it functions as the central exhibition hall; in off years it houses work from past festivals, as well as other exhibitions of modern art. *(Friedrichspl. 18. ☎707 27 20. Open W-Su 10am-6pm, Th until 8pm. Single exhibition €4, students €3; entire museum €6/4. W Free.)*

NEUE GALERIE (NEW GALLERY). Whatever the documenta leaves in its wake, the Neue Galerie picks up and puts on display. Their well-rounded collection also includes paintings dating back to the 1700s and important works from the "Neue Sachlichkeit" movement. *(Schöne Aussicht 1. ☎70 96 30. Open Tu-Su 10am-5pm. €3.50, students €2.50. F free.)*

BRÜDER GRIMM-MUSEUM (BROTHERS GRIMM MUSEUM). Rooms are filled with drawings and cutouts of characters from the famous tales, as well as large busts and personal effects that bring to life the men who wrote down many blithesome and often frightening German folktales. *(Schöne Aussicht 2, across from the Neue Galerie. ☎787 20 33; www.grimms.de. Open daily 10am-5pm. €1.50, students €1.)*

KUBA. Short for KulturBahnhof, it houses **Caricatura,** the self-proclaimed "gallery for bizarre art." Nothing is off-limits—missing limbs and scatological humor are the main currency at this off-color museum. *(Bahnhofspl. 1. ☎77 64 99. During exhibitions, Caricatura open Tu-F 2-8pm, Sa-Su noon-8pm. €3, students €2.)*

KARLSAUE. This English garden has sprawling lawns along the Fulda. At its southern tip is the **Insel Siebenbergen,** Karlsaue's unique "Island of Flowers." *(From Königspl., hop on bus #16 (dir.: Auestadion) to "Siebenbergen.")* The **Orangerie,** in a yellow manor house at the north end of the park, contains the mechanical and optical marvels and a planetarium of the **Astronomy and Technology Museum.** *(Karlsaue 20c. ☎70 13 20. Open Tu-Sa 10am-5pm. €3.50, students €2.50. F free. Planetarium shows in German Tu, Th, Sa 2pm; W and F 3pm. €3-5, students €3-4.)*

HESSISCHES LANDESMUSEUM (HESSEN REGIONAL MUSEUM). Surprises at this museum include 16th-century leather-and-gold Spanish hangings, a rare depiction of the Battle of Austerlitz, a wallpaper printer, and a letter from Goethe to Schiller mentioning a wallpaper order. The museum houses several other collections, including prehistoric artifacts. *(Brüder-Grimm-Pl. 5. In the yellow building near the Rathaus. ☎31 68 03 00. Open Tu-Su 10am-5pm. €3.50, students €2.50. F free.)*

▨ WILHELMSHÖHE (WILHELM HEIGHTS)

The Wilhelmshöhe area is a hillside park that must be seen to believed. Impeccably manicured gardens and emerald lawns surround one enormous castle, while another sits crumbling on a wooded hill above. Towering over both castles by a few hundred meters is a Greek titan, visible from miles away. To fully experience this city escape allow yourself a full afternoon, good walking shoes, and willingness to wander off the paved paths. From Bahnhof Wilhelmshöhe, take tram #1 to Wilhelmshöhe, at the eastern end of the park.

SCHLOß WILHELMSHÖHE. The rulers of Kassel once called this mammoth building home. Napoleon III was imprisoned here after the Battle of Sedan. Although the main wing was rebuilt in the aftermath of WWII, the museums inside continue to impress. The **Antikensammlung und Gemäldegalerie Alte Meister** (Antique Collection and Picture Gallery of Old Masters) collection includes works by Rembrandt and Rubens, and the pride of the town—Dürer's *Elsbeth Tucher*, featured on the former 20-*Deutschmark* bill. A tour through the **Museumsschloß** reveals the palace's extravagant private rooms. *(From the tram stop, walk under the overpass, and take the path straight or right. ☎ 937 77. Gemäldegalerie open Tu-Su 10am-5pm. Museumsschloß open Tu-Su Mar.-Oct. 10am-5pm; Nov.-Feb. 10am-4pm. Obligatory tours every hr., last tour 1hr. before closing. Each museum €3.50, students €2.50.)*

SCHLOß LÖWENBURG. Landgrave Wilhelm IX of Kassel, a Teutonic Don Quixote obsessed with the year 1495 and fancying himself a time-displaced knight, built this architectural fantasy, complete with a moat and drawbridge, for his concubine in the 18th century. To make it look crumbling and medieval, Wilhelm demanded rapidly deteriorating basalt as the construction material and dictated that some stones should be left missing. This plan was too successful; the castle has passed the "weathered" stage and is starting to fall apart. The ever-eccentric Wilhelm also sent the architect to Britain to study castles for two years and requested the inclusion of a Catholic chapel in the *Schloß* to date it to before the Reformation, though he himself was a Protestant. *(Facing up the hill at Schloß Wilhelmshöhe, take the path to the left of the pond; go left when it ends at the paved road. ☎ 935 72 00. Open Tu-Su Mar.-Oct. 10am-5pm; Nov.-Feb. 10am-4pm. Obligatory tours on the hr. 10am-3pm. €3.50, children €2.50.)*

HERKULES. Kassel's most imposing emblem stands atop a massive pedestal, jeering at conquered giant Encelades, whose head pokes out of the rocks at the top of the cascades. All told, the structure is 108m tall—even from the base, you can see for miles. If you're not exhausted by the climb up the hill and hundreds of steps, you can climb onto Herkules's pedestal and up into his club. *(Access to the base of the statue free. Pedestal and club open mid-Mar. to mid-Nov. daily 10am-5pm. €2, students €1.25.)*

⚑ ENTERTAINMENT AND NIGHTLIFE

The stretch along Friedrich-Ebert-Str. and Obere Königsstr., between Bebelpl. and Königspl., is home to numerous bars and clubs; the free monthly magazines *Fritz* and *Xcentric* list schedules of parties at most of the city's clubs. **Bali** (☎ 71 05 50; www.balikinos.de) in the Hauptbahnhof shows movies in their original language. Kassel hosts an outdoor film festival every summer behind the Museum Friedricianum at the **Dock 4** theater (www.filmladen.de; info and ticket sales at the Bali). Shows (€6.50, students €6; all tickets €4.50 on M) range from the likes of *Fahrenheit 9/11* to *Star Wars*. The **Staatstheater** (☎ 109 43 33) on Friedrichspl. hosts plays, concerts, operas, and ballet from mid-Sept. to early July.

Lohmann Biergarten, Königstor 8 (☎ 701 68 75). One of Kassel's oldest beer gardens, and the only one open late. Serves beer (€3 for 0.5L) and *Äpfelwein* (€1.70), and some creative—and even alarming—variations on *Schnitzel* (€5-6.50). Open daily 11am-1am, kitchen until 11pm. Cash only.

Café-Bar Suspekt, Fünffensterstr. 14 (☎ 10 45 22). A popular hangout where 20-somethings linger over drinks and enjoy the laid-back ambience. Perpetually dim lighting, even by day, overpower even the most insistent clock. By day a pleasant café (Tu-Su 1-8pm), at night a bar (Tu-Su 8pm-1am, F-Sa until 2am). Cash only.

SPOT, Ölmühlenweg 10-14 (☎ 562 09; www.spot-kassel.de). Take tram #4 or 8 (dir.: Kaufungen Papierfabrik) to "Hallenbad Ost," backtrack 10m toward the city, and turn right on the path through the parking lot. Move to techno and hip-hop on 3 dance floors, or hit the quieter front bar. Cover €3-6. Most nights open 10pm-late. Cash only.

HESSEN

Musiktheater, Angersbachstr. 10 (☎ 840 44). Bus #14 or 18 to "Drei Brücken," or #27 to "Naumburgerstr.," or follow Schenkendorfstr. as it curves left and over the tracks. A party mecca where eternal 20-somethings congregate. 3 massive dance floors fill 2 city blocks. Theme areas include "Hell's Kitchen" (heavy metal) and the Gothic "Dark Place." The area is dimly lit and sparsely traveled; use caution or take public transportation. Cover €2-7. Open W 8:30pm-3am, F-Sa 10:30pm-5am. Cash only.

⚡ DAYTRIP FROM KASSEL

FRITZLAR

An ideal afternoon jaunt from Kassel, accessible from either of its stations by train (40min., 3-4 per day, €6.50) or bus #50 (45-60min.; M-F 1 per hr., Sa-Su 3 per day; €5).

Fritzlar was named *Frideslar* (Place of Peace) in 723, when St. Boniface chopped down the huge **Donar's Oak,** the pagan religious symbol of the Thor-worshipping Chatti tribe. The "Apostle of Germany" used the timber to build his own wooden church, which today is the **Petersdom.** Heinrich (Henry) I was proclaimed king here in 915, inaugurating the medieval Holy Roman Empire. Since then, this diminutive medieval town has become happily isolated from the main routes of commerce. Fritzlar is content as a town of half-timbered houses, cobbled streets, and slow-gaited ambience on the **Märchenstraße,** the German Fairy Tale Road. The gem of Fritzlar is the 12th-century Petersdom, with its golden altar, stained-glass windows, and sizable treasury, which includes the 11th-century diamond- and pearl-covered **Heinrichkreuz** (Cross of Heinrich) and precious robes and relics. A statue of the axe-toting Boniface stands in the square just outside the Dom. (Dom open M-F 8am-noon and 2-6pm, Sa-Su 9am-noon and 1-5pm. Free. Treasury and crypt open May-Oct. M 2-5pm, Tu-F 10am-noon and 2-5pm, Sa 10am-noon and 2-4:30pm, Su 2-4:30pm; Nov.-Apr. M and Su 2-4pm, Tu-Sa 10am-noon and 2-4pm. €2, students €1.) On the western end of the medieval city wall, the austere 39m **Grauer Turm** (Grey Tower) is the tallest defense tower in Germany. (Open Apr.-Oct. daily 9am-noon and 2-5pm. €0.25) On the way to the tower from the Markt you'll pass the **Hochzeitshaus** (Wedding House), which has hosted weddings and festivals since the 16th century. Fritzlar spawns big festivals; the **Pferdemarkt** (Horse Market) happens from the second Tuesday to the next Sunday every July and the **Altstadtfest** (Old Town Festival) occurs the third weekend of every other August (Aug. 17-18, 2007). Both inspire a mad array of *Lederhosen*, traditional music, and *steins*.

The **tourist office,** Zwischen den Krämen 5, next to Fritzlar's Rathaus, built in 1109, is the oldest official building in Germany. Make a left out of the train station and a quick right on Gießener Str., following it up the hill until it reaches Marktpl., then go left on Zwischen den Krämen. (☎ 98 86 43; www.fritzlar.de. Open M 10am-6pm, Tu-Th 10am-5pm, F 10am-4pm, Sa-Su 10am-noon.) Town tours in German (min. 5 people) leave from the Rathaus. (1½hr. Mid-Apr. to mid-Oct. Tu-Sa 10:30am, Su 11am. €2.50, under 14 free.)

RHEINLAND-PFALZ (RHINELAND-PALATINATE) AND SAARLAND

With plunging hills, enfolded hamlets, and a surfeit of worn castle ruins, Rheinland-Pfalz appears stuck in the Middle Ages. The fatal call of Lorelei sirens and the fireside folklore of *Nibelung* treasure echo across the dramatic landscape. The region is not without actual nourishment—the vineyards of the Rhein and Mosel valleys produce world-famous wines. The Rheinland has had power since its electors chose the kings of the Holy Roman Empire, and the Saarland's minerals have been the envy of Germany and France for centuries.

HIGHLIGHTS OF RHEINLAND-PFALZ

BIKE OR HIKE the **Mosel Valley** (p. 357), which keeps up the German tradition of gorgeous, ubiquitous castles surrounded by endless vineyards.

RELIVE ANCIENT ROME in 2000-year-old **Trier** (p. 360), which makes the typical German *Schloß* seem like a sandcastle.

DILIGENTLY SAMPLE every wine produced along the cliffs of the lush Rhein Valley (p. 350).

KOBLENZ ☎ 56068

Koblenz (pop. 107,000) sits at the point where the Rhein and Mosel rivers meet, which led the Romans to name the city *confluentes* (confluence), and also explains why the city has been coveted by every empire seeking to conquer Europe in the last two millenia. Before reunification, Koblenz was West Germany's largest munitions dump, but the blasts that light up the city now are decorative—Koblenz turns into a flaming spectacle during Rhein in Flammen (May 9, 2007).

⌨ TRANSPORTATION

Trains: Koblenz is on the line connecting Frankfurt to Cologne. To: **Bonn** (30min., 3 per hr., €4.20-8.40); **Cologne** (1½hr., 4 per hr. €10-14); **Frankfurt** (1½-2hr., 2-3 per hr., €12.50-26); **Mainz** (1hr., 3 per hr., €9); **Trier** (1½-2hr., 2-3 per hr., €16).

Public Transportation: 10 main bus lines cruise around the city and suburbs for €1.25-3 per ride. **Zentralpl.**, serviced by all bus lines, offers the most convenient access to the Altstadt. Purchase tickets from the driver.

Taxis: Taxi Koblenz ☎ 330 55 or **Funk Taxi** ☎ 121 51

Bike Rental: Biking the Rhein and Mosel valleys is an excellent way to take in the sights. **Fahrradhaus Zangmeister,** Am Löhrrondell (☎ 323 63), rents bikes for €8 per day, €45 per wk. ID required. Open M-F 10am-8pm, Sa 8am-2pm.

✴ 🛈 ORIENTATION AND PRACTICAL INFORMATION

Koblenz's sights are clustered in the strip of Altstadt between the **Deutsches Eck** (a spit of land jutting into the Mosel and Rhein) and the **Markt.** The train station lies farther inland, but busy **Löhrstraße**, lined with shops, runs from there to the Markt.

Rheinland-Pfalz (Rhineland-Palatinate) and Saarland

Tourist Offices: Bahnhofpl. 17 (☎ 100 43 99; www.koblenz.de), across from the train station, hands out boat schedules and maps, as well as booking hotel rooms for free. Open May-Oct. M-F 9am-7pm, Sa-Su 10am-7pm; Nov.-Apr. daily until 6pm. Another **branch** in the Rathaus (at the entrance to Jesuitenpl.) offers the exact same services and has the same hours.

Bookstore: Reuffel, Löhrstr. 62, fills 3 stories on Koblenz's main shopping street. Current mainstream English books on the top floor.

Laundromat: Eco-Express Waschsalon, on the corner of Rizzastr. and Löhrstr. Wash €3. Dry €0.50 per 10min. Soap included. Open daily 6am-11pm, last wash 10pm.

Emergency: Police, Moselring 10-12 (☎ 110). **Fire** and **Ambulance,** ☎ 112.

Pharmacy: Medico Apotheke, Bahnhofpl. 6 (☎ 91 46 60; fax 91 46 622), is directly in front of the train station, a short walk just beyond the buses. Open M-F 8am-6:30pm, Sa 9am-1pm.

Internet: Chatpoint, Am Plan 10. Palm trees, funky booths, and plastic dolphins. Baguettes (€2-4), and pizza (€4). Landline and wireless €3 per hr. Open M-Th 10am-midnight, F-Sa until 2am, Su noon-midnight.

Post Office: To the right of the train station exit. Open M-F 7am-7pm, Sa 8:30am-1:30pm. **Postal Code:** 65068.

ACCOMMODATIONS AND CAMPING

Rooms in Koblenz are expensive, so if you want to avoid the long, dreary hike to the outer reaches of town, make reservations early.

Hotel Jan von Werth, Von-Werth-Str. 9 (☎365 00). This classy family-run establishment is inexpensive living with a touch of elegance—and one of the best values in Koblenz. Large breakfast included. Reception 6:30am-10pm. Check-out 10am. Singles from €28, with shower and toilet €41; doubles from €53/62; triples €60-70. MC/V. ❸

Hotel Sessellift, Obertal 22 (☎752 56; fax 768 72), next to the "Obertal" bus stop; take bus #8 or 9. Though a bit far from town, this hotel offers basic, functional rooms with showers. Breakfast included. Singles €25; doubles €42; triples €60. Cash only. ❷

Jugendherberge Koblenz (HI), (☎97 28 70; fax 972 87 30), is in the fortress Festung Ehrenbreitstein (p. 348) 118m above the Rhein. Short on amenities and far-flung, but great views of the valley. Take bus #8 or 9 from the bus station to "Ehrenbreitstein." To hike there, follow the main road along the Rhein side of the mountain, following the DJH signs. Within minutes you'll come to a path leading to the Festung (20min. steep uphill walk); after dark, the hike can be tricky. The *Sessellift* (chairlift) is a block farther. (Easter-May and Oct. 10am-4:50pm, June-Sept. 9am-5:50pm; €4.50, round-trip €6.50; students and hostel guests €2.50/3.50). Breakfast included. Reception 7:15am-10pm. Curfew 11:30pm. Dorms €16.50; doubles €44. MC/V. ❷

Campingplatz Rhein-Mosel, Am Neuendorfer Eck (☎827 19), across the Mosel from the Deutsches Eck. Cross the river by ferry (€0.80). Reception daily 8am-10pm. Open Apr.-Oct. 15. €4.50 per person, €2.50 per site. Cash only. ❶

FOOD AND NIGHTLIFE

The **Rizza Obst und Gemüse** grocery store, Rizza Str. 49, provides an assortment of fruit and necessities. (Open M-F Sa 7am-7pm, Su 7am-2pm.)

Taquitos, Münzpl. 12 (☎46 94; www.taquitos.de), has a Latin American menu and is always crowded at night. Tasty tapas (€2-3.50) are cheap and varied. Try the shrimp with olive oil and garlic (€2.50), and wash it down with your favorite tropical mixed drink (€7). Opens daily noon-late; ½-price mixed drinks 5-7pm daily. MC. ❷

Kaffeewirtschaft, Münzpl. 14 (☎914 47 02). Crimson and navy walls, candlelight, and fresh roses set the scene at this hip bar and café. Local seasonal entrées (€8-14). Open M-Th 9am-midnight, F-Sa 9am-2am, Su 10am-midnight. MC/V. ❸

Café Galleria Bistro & Pizzeria, Emil-Schüllerstr. 45 (☎337 58), left of the train station. Leisurely meals of pizzas and pastas from €5 in this bright, classy café. Open daily 10:30am-midnight, F-Sa until 3am. ❷

Markt-Stübchen, Am Markt 220 (☎755 65), down the hill from the hostel, a block from the chairlift. Casual atmosphere with seasonal specials (€7 or less). Open M-Tu, Th, Su 11am-midnight; W 11am-2pm; F 4pm-1am; Sa 11am-1am. Cash only. ❷

Café Bistro in der Mehlgasse, Mehlg. 12 (☎144 57). Sandwiches on tasty ciabatta bread (€4.50-6), fresh salads (€3.50-7), rotating soup menu (€3.40-5.50), and a relaxed pace. Open daily 9:30am-11pm, F-Sa until midnight. Cash only. ❷

Salatgarten, Gymnasialstr. 10-12 (☎364 55). Stuff your plate with a medley of salad mixes, hot entrées, pasta, and dessert at this salad-bar style restaurant where every 100g of food costs €1.49. Open M-F 10am-7pm, Sa 10am-4pm. Cash only. ❷

Sugar Ray's, Münzpl. 15 (☎42 19), features neon, and rock and roll. Eat beforehand—this place specializes in "liquid bread," as the Germans call it: beer (€2). Mixed drinks (€4-9, M-Th and Su €3.50). Open M-Th and Su 8pm-1am, F-Sa 8pm-2am. Cash only.

SIGHTS

FESTUNG EHRENBREITSTEIN. Towering over the town, this 12th-century fortress, completed in 1828, offers a bird's-eye view of the clear Mosel as it blends into the muddy Rhein. Stay at the **Jugendherberge Koblenz,** the hostel actually located in the fortress (p. 347), or pop up for to marvel at the defensive pits and portcullises on the grounds. *(45min., tours from tourist office every hr. Apr.-Oct. 10am-5pm; €1.10. English translation sheet free. Fortress €1, students €0.60, hostel guests free.)*

DEUTSCHES ECK (GERMAN CORNER). The Rhein, the Mosel, and German nationalism converge at the Deutsches Eck, 100m from the pier where ships leave for Rhein or Mosel cruises. This area allegedly witnessed the first stirrings of the German nation in 1216 when the Teutonic Knights settled here. Erected in 1897, the large monument at the top of the steps stands in tribute to Kaiser Wilhelm I for his forced resolution of the internal conflicts of the German Empire. The 14m equestrian statue of the Kaiser that once topped the monument was toppled in 1945 and replaced by a duplicate in 1993. Beginning in 1953, the corner also became know as Mahnmal der Deutschen Einheit (Monument of German Unity) as a reminder of the bonds still shared by a divided East and West Germany.

CHURCHES. Koblenz's Altstadt is dotted with churches, many of which received post-WWII facelifts. The 12th-century **Florinskirche** was used as a slaughterhouse during the Thirty Years' War. *(Open daily 11am-5pm. Free.)* Nearby, Baroque towers rise above the intricate latticework of the **Liebfrauenkirche,** whose choir windows depict women's roles in the Passion of Christ. *(Open M-Sa 8am-7pm, Su 9am-8pm. Free.)* More stained-glass windows hide behind a masterful *Rheinisch* facade in the modern interior of the **Jesuitenkirche** on the Marktpl. *(Open daily 7am-6pm. Free.)* The 19th-century **Herz-Jesu-Kirche** dominates the city center and looks down upon the **Schängelbrunnen,** where a statue of a young boy spits water on passersby every two minutes. *(Church open daily 7:30am-7pm. Free.)* On the other side of the train station, **St.-Josef-Kirche** is awash in yet more stained glass. *(Open daily 9am-6pm. Free.)*

BLUMENHOF. In the understated gardens next to Museum Ludwig, there is more national braggadocio to be had, though this time not on the part of the Germans. Here, an overconfident Napoleon erected the fountain to commemorate the "certain impending victory" in his Russian campaign. The Russians, after routing the French army, added the mocking inscription "seen and approved."

 MUSEUMS

Koblenz's Museums are outstanding and diverse, and a 4-day pass (€5.10), available at tourist offices and museums, gets you into all those listed below, as well as the **Festung Ehrenbreitstein, Schloß Stolzenfels,** and the **Wehrtechnische Studiensammlung** (Military Technology Museum).

MUSEUM LUDWIG IM DEUTSCHHERRENHAUS. Just behind the Deutsches Eck, this art museum showcases modern French artists and presents high-caliber exhibitions every six to eight weeks. The original building was erected by the Teutonic Knights who settled in Koblenz in 1212. Regular tours are insightful. The permanent collection is on the second floor. *(Danziger Freiheit 1. Behind the Mahnmal. ☎ 30 40 40. Open Tu-Sa 10:30am-5pm, Su 11am-6pm. €2.50, students €1.50.)*

MITTELRHEINMUSEUM (CENTRAL RHINE MUSEUM). This museum's floors of art are devoted to religious sculpture and a number of romantic landscapes depicting the Rhein Valley, through Gothic, Renaissance, and contemporary periods. The 2nd floor holds changing exhibits. *(Florinsmarkt 15-17 next door to the Florinskirche. ☎ 129 25 20. Open Tu-Sa 10:30am-5pm, Su 11am-6pm. €2.50, students €1.50, children free.)*

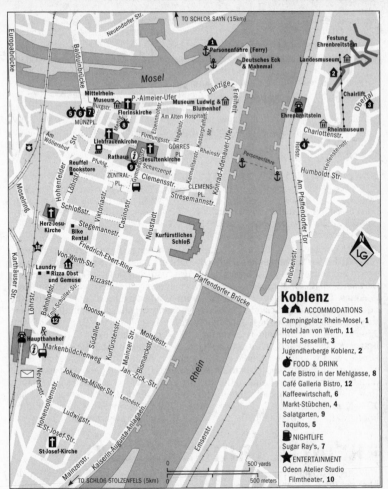

Koblenz

🏠🏕 ACCOMMODATIONS
Campingplatz Rhein-Mosel, 1
Hotel Jan von Werth, 11
Hotel Sessellift, 3
Jugendherberge Koblenz, 2

🍎 FOOD & DRINK
Cafe Bistro in der Mehlgasse, 8
Café Galleria Bistro, 12
Kaffeewirtschaft, 6
Markt-Stübchen, 4
Salatgarten, 9
Taquitos, 5

🍺 NIGHTLIFE
Sugar Ray's, 7

⭐ ENTERTAINMENT
Odeon Atelier Studio
Filmtheater, 10

RHEINLAND-PFALZ

LANDESMUSEUM KOBLENZ (KOBLENZ STATE MUSEUM). A collection of shiny antique automobiles and regional artifacts, including huge wooden wine-presses. Located in the **Festung**. (*Hohe Ostfront, in Festung Ehrenbreitstein.* ☎970 30. *Open daily Easter to mid-Nov. 9:30am-5pm. Last entry 30min. before closing.* €2, students €1.50.)

RHEINMUSEUM. This museum is devoted to all things *Rheinisch*. Four floors of maritime history and more model boats than you ever wanted to see. (*Charlottenstr. 53a. Bus #9 or 10 to "Charlottenstr."* ☎97 42 44. *Open daily 10am-5pm.* €3, children €2.)

📷 DAYTRIPS FROM KOBLENZ

SCHLOß STOLZENFELS

Take bus #650 (dir.: Boppard) from the train station to "Stolzenfels Mitte" (10min., 2 per hr., €2), then walk 10min. up the winding Schloßweg. Information ☎0180 522 13 60. *Koblenz tourist office ☎ 0261 100 43 99. Obligatory 45min. tours in German (English translation sheet €0.50). Open daily Easter-Sept. 10am-6pm; Jan.-Easter and Oct.-Nov. 10am-5pm. 10am-6pm. Last entry 1hr. before closing. €2.60, students €1.30, children €1.*

Five kilometers south of Koblenz, the orange Schloß Stolzenfels sprawls with the typical decadence one might expect of a 13th-century stronghold turned 19th-century summer residence for the Prussian royal family (after its destruction during a French siege). Since King Wilhelm IV died in 1863, the only people to stay in the castle have been refugees from Koblenz during WWII. Glossy imported fabrics, paneled ceilings, intricate antiques, and mirrors adorn every room. See the merging of medieval and Romantic styles inside the chapel, enhanced by the apse mural and meticulous cast-iron staircase. The **pergola garden,** garnished with dangling flowerpots, rose-shaded trellises and languishing statues, feels like an Italian villa.

SCHLOß SAYN AND BUTTERFLY GARDEN

Take bus #8 (dir.: Bendorf/Sayn; 30min., 1-2 per hr., €3.15) from the train station or Zentralpl. to "Sayn Schloß"). The castle is next to the bus stop and the butterfly garden is inside the park at the left. Castle museum (☎ 02622 902 40; www.sayn.de) and butterfly garden (☎ 02622 154 78) open Mar.-Sept. 9am-6pm, Oct-Nov. 10am-5pm. €6, children €4. Falconry show Mar.-Oct. Tu-Su at 5pm. €3.50, children €2.50.

Relive your playground days in clouds of colorful wings in the tropical paradise of the █Garten der Schmetterlinge (Butterfly Garden). Inside the **Schloßpark,** this glass house has more than just butterflies; turtles, fish, and birds fill the streams and dart across paths. Visitors who arrive early may see butterflies breaking from their cocoons. The garden also contains playgrounds and a mini golf course. Across the street is the dignified **Schloß Sayn.** The Sayn family originally lived in the 12th-century castle at the top of the hill, but left after it was ruined in the Thirty Years' War. After returning in the mid-19th century, they bought the medieval palace at the bottom of the hill and had it redone in the popular neo-Gothic style by François Girard, who would later become chief architect of the Louvre. Inside, the Sayn-Wittgenstein family history is told through the unique perspective of its female members. The castle is home to the **Rheinische Eisenkunstguss Museum** (Rhein Cast Iron Museum), commemorating an iron foundry. *(Open Mar.-Oct. 9am-6pm, Oct-Nov. 10am-5pm; €3, students, €2.)* Further up the hill, the **Falconry** opens up in the afternoon. At the crest of the hill, the ruins of **Burg Sayn** look over the Rhein Valley.

RHEINTAL (RHINE VALLEY)

Though the Rhein River runs from Switzerland all the way up to the North Sea, the Rhein of the poetic imagination exists in the 80km gorge from Bonn to just north of Mainz. Here 12th- and 16th-century castles crown steep bluffs overlooking the river, and minor estuaries cut through the hills in search of larger waters. Of all places along the Rhein, none has captured the imaginations of poets and artists like the Lorelei Cliffs. Towering above some of the narrowest plunges of the river, these cliffs are home to the golden-haired siren immortalized in Heinrich Heine's 1823 poem "Die Lorelei." Heine, however, cannot claim sole credit for the river's resonance: Wagner paid homage to the mythical legacy in his "Der Ring des Nibelungen" opera cycle, and British Romantic artists captured its jagged beauty in violent brushstrokes.

Two different train lines (one on each bank) plod along this stretch of the Rhein. The line on the west bank runs between Koblenz and Mainz and hugs the water's edge, providing superior views. Many choose to skip the large tourist crowds and experience the landscape by boat. The **Köln-Düsseldorfer (KD) Line** and **Bingen Rüdesheim Line** cover the stretch three to four times per day during the summer.

FSH

LH
Prolactin
GH
IGF-1

□ HBV DNA(LMHA)
□ HAV Ab IgG
□ HAV Ab IgM
□ HCV Ab(EIA)
□ Chlamydia Ab IgG

전용채취를 사용하여 주세요.

□ Cytology

기 타 검 사
□ HLA B27 PCR
□ Deoxypyridinoline(DPD)

추가항목검사 Code

추가그룹검사 Code

A	B	C	D	E	F
G	H	I	J	K	L
M	N	O	P	Q	R
S	T	U	V	W	X
Y	Z

(의뢰)(법인) 필립심상의학연구소 Tel.02)517-1728

LORELEI CLIFFS AND CASTLES

Though it was the Lorelei maiden who once drew sailors to the shores of this rugged region, her hypnotic song is now unnecessary; today, hordes of travelers are seduced by scenery alone. Hillsides rise from the Rhein, cloaked in slanting vineyards, romantic villages, and restored medieval castles. Tour buses trickle in from the towns of **St. Goarshausen** and **St. Goar. Trains** run to St. Goarshausen from Cologne (1½hr., €23) and Mainz (1½hr., €16) and to St. Goar from Cologne (1½hr., €22) and Mainz (1hr., €9.70). These two towns host the spectacular **Rhein in Flammen** fireworks celebration in mid-September. St. Goarshausen, on the east bank, provides access to the Lorelei statue and the infamous cliffs. Facing the Rhein, follow the signs on Rheinstr. left to the statue's peninsula. For the cliffs, take the stairs across the street from the peninsula (45min.).

In St. Goarshausen (city code ☎06771), the **tourist office,** Bahnhofstr. 8, hands out free maps and local listings. (☎91 00; www.loreley-touristik.de. M and Sa-Su 9:30am-noon, M also 2-4:30pm; Th 2-4:30pm; F 2-5:50pm.) The **police station,** Bahnhofstr. 12 (☎932 70; emergency ☎110), is a few doors down. Thirty minutes up the Lorelei Cliffs, the hostel **Jugendheim Loreley** ❶ lures travelers with its spectacular location, only to drown them in crashing waves of schoolchildren. From Rheinstr., follow the signs for the Jugendheim up into the hills. (☎26 19; tuhe@loreley-herberge.de. Breakfast included. Sheets €3.50. Curfew 10pm. €8.50 per person. Call ahead for doubles. Cash only.) **Nassauer Hof** ❸, Bahnhofstr. 22, offers bright, tidy rooms near the river. (☎80 28 40; www.nassauer-hof-loreley.de. Breakfast included. Singles €33-38; doubles €48-58. Cash only.) To reach **Campingplatz Loreleystadt** ❶ from the station, face the Rhein and go right on Rheinstr. to Rheinpromenade (☎25 92.

The Rhein

TO DÜSSELDORF

Köln (Cologne)

0 ___ 10 miles
0 ___ 10 kilometers

Köln-Bonn Flughafen

Wesseling   Lülsdorf

Bonn

Sieg

Königswinter
Drachenfels

Altenahr
Ahrweiler
Bad Honnef
Remagen   **Unkel**
Bad Neuenahr
Erpel
Ahr   Kripp   **Linz**

Schloß Arenfels
Bad Hönningen

Rhein

R H E I N   V A L L E Y

Laacher See

Andernach   Neuwied
Schloß Sayn
Sayn

Koblenz

Burg Eltz
Moselkern
Mosel

Schloß Stolzenfels   Lahnstein
Lahn
Boppard   Braubach
Bad Salzig   L A H N   V A L L E Y
Burg Maus
Burg Rheinfels   **St. Goarshausen**
St. Goar   Burg Katz
Oberwesel

Burg Stahleck
Bacharach

Niederheimbach | Name | City Served by Ferry Service |

Burg Rheinstein

Burg Klopp   Rüdesheim   TO FRANKFURT
Bingen   Rhein   Wiesbaden

TO NAHE VALLEY   Nahe   **Mainz**

€4.80 per person, €2.60-4.50 per tent.) To be closer to the famed cliffs, try **Campingplatz Auf der Loreley ❶**. Follow signs from the Lorelei statue. (☎430. €5 per person, €10.50 per tent.) Directly above St. Goarshausen, the dark **Burg Katz** (Cat Castle) stands just a few kilometers downstream from its quadroped nephew **Burg Maus** (Mouse Castle). Though all of Burg Katz is a privately-owned B&B (rooms from €250) closed to sightseers, Burg Maus, at the end of a very strenuous 1¼hr. hike, contains an eagle and falcon court and offers demonstrations daily at 11am and 2:30pm (also at 4:30pm on public holidays and Su) from May to the beginning of October. If you're lucky, you can watch falcons snatch rats off the heads of small children. (☎76 69. €6.50, children €5.50.)

The "Loreley V" **ferry,** the oldest family-run ferry in Germany, crosses the river to and from St. Goar (phone code 06741), another base for Lorelei explorations. (Ferries M-F 6am-11pm, Sa-Su from 7am. €1.30.) St. Goar's **tourist office,** Heerstr. 86 in the pedestrian zone, books rooms for free. (☎383; www.st-goar.de. Open M-F 8am-12:30pm and 2-5pm, Sa 10am-noon.) The **Jugendherberge (HI) ❶**, Bismarckweg 17, is 10min. from the station. With your back to the tracks, follow Oberstr. left. At the end of Oberstr., make a left under the bridge. Bismarckweg is the next right. Close to the castle, this cheap hostel packs in beds with admirable efficiency. (☎388; st-goar@diejugendherbergen.de. Breakfast and sheets included. Reception 8-9am, 5-6pm, and 7-8pm. Curfew 10pm, but keys are available. Dorms €13.50. Cash only.) **Hotel Hauser ❸**, Heerstr. 77, has central, spotless rooms with balconies facing the boat docks. (☎333; www.hotelhauser.de. Breakfast included, plus discounts on meals at the restaurant downstairs. Singles €26-38; doubles €55-60. Cash only.) The view from the cliffs on this, the eastern side of the Rhein, is spectacular. The beautiful, age-worn **Burg Rheinfels** (☎383) is a sprawling, half-ruined castle with underground passages—it doesn't get more *romantisch* than this. Beware of slippery slopes. (Open daily mid-Mar. to mid-Oct. 9am-6pm and mid-Oct. to Nov. 9am-5pm; Dec. to mid-Mar. Sa-Su 11am-5pm. €4, children €2, families €10. Bring a flashlight, or buy a candle in the museum for €0.50.)

BACHARACH   ☎06743

Bounded by a lush river promenade, a resilient town wall, and dramatically sloping vineyards, Bacharach retains an irrepressible sense of identity in the face of increasing tourist traffic. Renovated Tudor-style houses surround the popular market square, and narrow alleyways contain wine cellars and taverns alike. Once home to a stone altar to Bacchus (hence the town name), today Bacharach fills with pilgrims journeying to worship at the town's numerous *Weinkeller* and *Weinstuben* (wine cellars and pubs), tucked between, and sometimes directly within, historic half-timbered houses. Every second or third weekend in June, the nearby town of Bacharach-Steeg hosts the **Gteeger Weinblütenfest,** a festival replete with free wine tasting, fireworks over the Rhein, and live music. Festivities inevitably spread to Bacharach, which holds its own annual **Kulinarische Sommernacht** on the fourth weekend in August. Within the **Altes Haus,** whose half-timbered perfection has acquired minor fame, this family-owned business makes its own wine on the premises. Entrées are €5-15; wine with cheese €3-8. (☎12 08. Open M-T and Th-F 1-11pm, Sa-Su from noon. Cash only.) On Oberstr., up the steps next to the late-Romanesque **Peterskirche,** is the 14th-century **Wernerkapelle,** the ghost-like Gothic skeleton of a chapel that took 140 years to build but only a few hours to destroy in the Palatinate War of Succession of 1689.

To start the steep 15min. trek, take a right out of the station pathway, turn left at the Peterskirche, and take any of the marked paths leading up the hill to the fanciful ⛻**Jugendherberge Stahleck (HI) ❷**. A converted 12th-century castle, many rooms, some individually named and all with beds fitted with colorful sheets, directly overlook the Rhein Valley. (☎ 12 66; fax 26 84. Breakfast included. Bagged lunches and dinners available (€5.50). Many rooms have private bathrooms. Reception 7:30am-7:30pm. Check-in at the bar until midnight. Check-out 9:30am. Curfew 10pm. Reservations recommended. Dorms €17. MC/V.) For those weary of uphill treks, a charming mother-son duo runs two centrally-located pensions. Frau Dettmar owns the spacious and flowery **Haus Dettmar ❷**, Oberstr. 8, above the Stadt Café. All rooms have showers, toilets, cable TV, and refrigerators. (☎ 26 61; fax 91 93 96. Reception M-Sa 10am-6pm. Rooms €17-30. Price reductions for longer stays. Cash only.) Just down the road is Jürgen's smaller, but convenient **Hotel Am Markt ❹**, Oberstr. 64. (☎ 17 15; fax 91 90 48. Doubles €50. Cash only.) Turn right from the station (downhill towards the river), then walk south for 10min. to reach **Campingplatz Bacharach ❶**, directly on the Rhein. Reception is at the bar. (☎ 17 52. €5 per person, €3 per tent, €6 per site. Cash only.) The price is right at the ▧**Café Restaurant Rusticana ❸**, Oberstr. 40, where an elderly German couple serves three-course meals of regional dishes for €6-11. The legendary apple strudel (€3) is baked daily from recipe of the owner's Romanian grandmother. (☎ 17 41. Open May-Oct. M-W and F-Su noon-9:30pm. Cash only.) Try some of the Rhein's best wines (from €2) and cheeses (€3.10-6.50) at **Die Weinstube ❸**, Oberstr. 63. (Open M-F from 1pm and Sa-Su from noon. Cash only.)

The **tourist office**, Oberstr. 45, is near the town center and offers **Internet** access (€0.50 per 5min.) and books rooms for free. (☎ 91 93 03. Open Apr.-Oct. M-F 9am-5pm, Sa-Su 10am-1pm; Nov.-Mar. M-F 9am-noon.) In this largely cash-only town, an **ATM** and **currency exchange** can be found at the **Volksbank**, Blücherstr. 19. (M-Tu and Th 8:30am-noon and 1-4:30pm; W and F 8:30am-1pm.) Take the first left off Oberstr. after the tourist office.

RÜDESHEIM

☎ **06722**

With sloping terraced vineyards and sharp cuts of the Nahe estuary on the western bank, it is little wonder that Rüdesheim is the most touristed town in the Rheintal. Still the center of the **Rheingau** wine-producing region, Rüdesheim was so well loved by the Ancient Romans that they hung around as unwanted visitors for a few hundred years before the Franks displaced them in the AD fifth century. Yet large portions of this arcadian village escape the unrelenting search for marketable nostalgia: narrow back-alleyways lie untouched and all but the most conveniently placed castles remain largely unvisited. A giant figure of Germania wielding the Emperor's crown and the imperial sword looms high above the town on the 38m **Niederwald Monument.** Erected on the establishment of the Second Reich in 1871, the frieze features legions of aristocrats pledging loyalty to the Kaiser, while emblems of war and peace stand guard. The panoramic views from the monument stretch far into the Rhein River Valley. A **Seilbahn** (chairlift), Oberstr. 37, runs to the statue from the top of Christoffelstr. but is no match for a brisk walk; take a left directly before the tourist office. (10min. each way. Open Apr. daily 9:30am-4:30pm; May-Aug. M-Th 9:30am-6pm, F-Su 9:30am-7pm; Aug.-Mar. daily 9:30am-5pm. €4, round-trip €6, children €2/3.) To reach the monument by foot (35min.), walk towards the station on Oberstr. and turn onto Feldtor, which winds through terraced vineyards toward the monument. Bordered on both sides by a small vineyard, the idyllic 12th-century **Brömserburg** castle, Reinstr. 2, is a **wine museum,** featuring wine technology from the Stone Age onward, with a focus on the traditions of the Rheingau region. From the station or ferry docks, walk 2min. toward town along Rheinstr. Ask for details about their wine tasting tours. (☎ 23 48. Open daily mid-Mar. to Oct. 9am-6pm. Last admission 5:15pm. €3, students and children €2.) The famous "Sträußche" symbol (a wreath hanging above the entryway) marks the *Strausswritschafts* (wine pubs) and garden taverns that pack the famous **Dros-**

RHEINLAND-PFALZ

selg. alley. For relief from the heavily-touristed Niederwalddenkmal, pay a visit to the 60 monastic nuns at the comely **Benedictine Abbey of St. Hildegard.** Follow Oberstr. past the tourist office, take a left on Zum Niederwald-Denkmal, and turn right onto the winding Klosterweg 500m up. If you prefer a milder walk, follow the signs for the **Brahmsweg** from the station and see the vineyards from which Johannes Brahms drew inspiration for his 3rd Symphony. Every third weekend in August, the drinking center of the city shifts from Drosselg. to the nearby Markpl., which hosts the **Rüdesheim Wine Festival.** Up Drosselg. to the left are signs for ◨**Siegfried's Mechanisches Musikkabinett,** Oberstr. 27-29. The myriad self-playing musical instruments from the 18th to 20th centuries put the generic ballerina-in-a-box to shame. Mandatory 45min. tours (English or German) are led by women in traditional 19th-century garb. Visitors can even play the instruments themselves. (☎492 17. Open Mar.-Dec. daily 10am-10pm. €5.50, students €3.) The **Mittelalterliches Foltermuseum,** Oberstr. 49-51, displays the entire history of medieval torture devices up through the times of the infamous German witchhunts. Bloodied mannequins abound. (☎475 10. Open daily Apr.-Nov. 10 10am-6pm. €5, students €4.)

The family-oriented **Jugendherberge (HI) ❷,** Jugendherberge 1, has simple, clean rooms a steep 30min. walk above town. From the station, walk down Rheinstr. and take a left on any street you please. At Oberstr., turn right. Bear left at the fork onto Germaniastr. and follow it to Kuhweg and the Jugendherberge signs. **Taxis** (€7-9) leave from the tourist office, and are worth the extra money for travelers with heavy luggage. (☎27 11; rudesheim@djh-hesssen.de. Breakfast included. Curfew 11pm. Dorms €16.20; doubles €41.40. Cash only.) **Campingplatz am Rhein ❶** has riverside plots, well-kept flower gardens, clean bathrooms and washing facilities, and a swimming pool nearby. From the station, walk past town along the river (15min.). (In summer ☎25 28, in winter ☎25 82. Reception 8am-10pm. €4.30 per person, €4.70 per tent. Cash only.)

The **tourist office,** Geisenheimerstr. 22, is 10min. from the station. Facing the Rhein, take a left, walk down Rheinstr. and continue on Bleichstr.; turn left at the bus park and the office will be on your right. The staff books rooms for free. Ask about biking tours throughout the region. (☎194 33; www.ruedesheim.de. Open mid-Apr. to Oct. M-F 9am-6:30pm, Sa-Su 11am-5pm; Nov. to mid-Apr., M-F 11am-5pm.) The **post office,** Geisenhermer Str. 16 (open M-F 8am-12:30pm and 1:30-6pm, Sa 8am-2pm), is two blocks toward the city center from the tourist office and next to **Internet-telecafé.** (€3 per hr. Open daily 9am-7pm.)

MAINZ   ☎06131

The unlikely marriage of Mainz (pop. 190,000) and Johannes Gutenberg dates back to the 1455 invention of the movable-type printing press. What the couple lacks in youth it makes up in intensity: scarcely a block passes without a statue or museum of Gutenberg, nor a year without a fair in his honor. His name finds its way onto so many storefronts that you'd think he owns the place. Fortunately for the cultural diversity of the capital of Rheinland-Pfälz, however, he does not; the city features a busy network of shopping streets, a stunning cathedral, and a thriving riverfront.

▟ TRANSPORTATION

Trains run to: Frankfurt (30min., €9); Heidelberg (1½hr., €14.70); Koblenz (1hr., €14.70). Mainz shares a **public transportation** system with Wiesbaden; to get there, take bus #6. The Köln-Düsseldorf **ferry** docks in Mainz and departs from the wharfs on the other side of the Rathaus. (☎23 28 00; www.k-d.com.) To: Köln (2hr., €48.50). For a **taxi,** call ☎91 09 10. **Bicycles** are available at ASM in CityPort, Binger Str. 19 (☎23 86 20; www.asm-mainz.de).

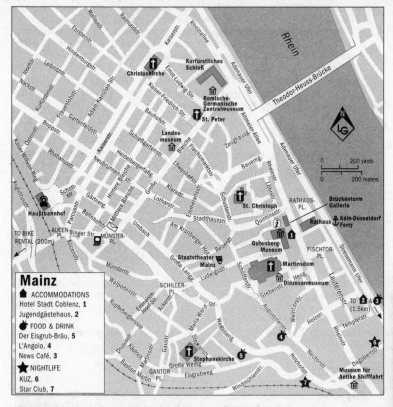

Mainz

▲ ACCOMMODATIONS
Hotel Stadt Coblenz, **1**
Jugendgästehaus, **2**

🍴 FOOD & DRINK
Der Eisgrub-Bräu, **5**
L'Angolo, **4**
News Café, **3**

⭐ NIGHTLIFE
KUZ, **6**
Star Club, **7**

RHEINLAND-PFALZ

✈ ❓ ORIENTATION AND PRACTICAL INFORMATION

Streets running parallel to the Rhein are marked with blue nameplates, while streets perpendicular to the river have red ones. The **tourist office** in Brückenturm has free maps, conducts **tours** (2hr.; Sa 2pm, May-Oct. also W and F 2pm; in German and English; €5) and reserves rooms for a €2.50 fee. (☎28 62 10; www.info-mainz.de/tourist. Open M-F 9am-6pm, Sa 10am-3pm.) The **Mainz Card** grants access to all museums, one day of free transportation, a free city tour, and various other benefits (€9.95, families and groups up to 5 €25). The **AIDS-Hilfe hotline** (☎22 22 75) has the scoop on GLBT life in the city. **Internet** access is available in the **Internet-Callshop,** 3 Münster Pl. (Open daily 10am-11pm.) The **post office** is a block down Bahnhofstr. from the station. (☎0800 222 62 24. Open M-F 8am-6pm, Sa 8:30am-12:30pm.) **Postal Code:** 55001.

🏠 ACCOMMODATIONS

The tourist office maintains a comprehensive list of private apartments and single rooms available for rent (from €18) in and around the city. Inquire about rooms with the English-speaking hosts at the office.

Jugendgästehaus (HI), Otto-Brunfels-Schneise 4 (☎853 32; www.DieJugendherbergen.de), is in Weisenau in a corner of the Volkspark. Take bus #62 (dir.: Weisenau) or 63 (dir.: Laubenheim) to "Viktorstift/Jugendherberge" (10min.) and follow the signs. Bright, clean rooms with private bath and generous common area make the trek worthwhile. Breakfast included. Reception 6:30am-10pm. 4- to 6-bed rooms €17.50; singles €27; doubles €48. MC/V. ❷

Hotel Stadt Coblenz, Rheinstr. 49 (☎629 04 44; www.stadtcoblenz.de). Go through the Havana Restaurant to get to reception. Moderately priced rooms just 4min. from the Dome. Breakfast included. Singles €40; doubles €60-70; triples €80. MC/V. ❹

FOOD

In warm months, butchers and farmers peddle goods in an outdoor **market** near Mainz's cathedral, on the Dompl. (Tu and F-Sa open 7am-2pm.) At night, wonderful smells waft through Augustinerstr., with meals under €6. If you're in a hurry, stop on any street-corner for a pretzel or mini-pizza (€0.50-1.25) from a **Ditsch** stand, or grab a *Kebap* (€2-3.50) from an ethnic restaurant along the backstreets.

Der Eisgrub-Bräu, Weißlilieng. 1a (☎22 11 04). A popular, wood-tinged spot on the edge of the Altstadt, with the motto *"Bier Erleben"* (experience beer). Beer is brewed in large copper vats and served without refiltering (€2.70 for 0.4L). Entrées €5-13. Breakfast buffet daily 9am-noon (€2.90); lunch buffet M-F 12:30-4pm (€5.10). Open M-Th and Su 9am-1am, F-Sa 9am-2am. MC/V. ❸

News Café, Göttelmannstr. 40 (☎98 98 37), may be far from the city center, but is an ideal backyard to the hostel, overlooking one of the most popular parks in the city. Sandwiches €5-8.50. Entrées—including large pasta dishes—under €10. Open M-Th 11:30am-2am, Sa-Su 10am-2am. Cash only. ❷

L'angolo, Augustinerstr. 8 (☎23 17 47), is a reliable bistro among swarms of Augustinerstr. cafés. Serves cheap beer (€2) and simple dishes (from €4). Cash only. ❷

SIGHTS

MARTINSDOM. In the heart of Mainz is the resting place of the archbishops. The colossal sandstone cathedral has withstood wars and renovations since the 10th century. The extravagant tombstones line the walls, under a stained-glass timeline from AD 975. (☎25 34 12. Open Mar.-Oct. Tu-F 9am-6pm, Sa 9am-2pm, Su 1-2:45pm and 4-6:30pm; Nov.-Feb. M-F 9am-5pm, Sa 9am-4pm, Su 12:45-3pm and 4-5pm. Free.)

STEPHANSKIRCHE. The Gothic Stephanskirche, on a hill south of the Dom, was almost completely destroyed by WWII bombs and later reconstructed using the original stones. From 1978 until just before his death in 1985, Russian expatriate artist **Marc Chagall** made nine stained-glass windows that give the church an eerie soft blue glow. The biblical themes symbolize the Abrahamic bond between Jews and Christians and a pledge of international peace between France and Germany. (On Stefansberg. ☎23 16 46. Open M-F 10am-noon and 2-5pm, Sa 2-5pm. Free.)

KIRCHE ST. CHRISTOPH. The reputed site of Gutenberg's baptism was gutted by fire in WWII. Bare walls are a reminder of war's cultural casualties. (On Christofsstr.)

▥ MUSEUMS

GUTENBERG-MUSEUM. Johannes Gutenberg, father of movable type, is immortalized at the **Gutenberg-Museum,** which contains copies of the Gutenberg Bible, several of the printer's letters, and a replica of his workshop. A collection of printing presses, typesetting machines, letterpresses, and 4000 years worth of printing paraphernalia set the famous lithographer in context. Every hour, the staff prints a page from the Bible using a duplicate of the original press. *(Liebfrauenpl. 5, across from the Dom. ☎ 12 26 44. Open Tu-Sa 9am-5pm, Su 11am-3pm. €3.50, students €2.)*

DIÖZESANMUSEUM (DIOCESAN MUSEUM). Adjacent to the Martinsdom, the museum looks out on a pleasant courtyard and houses changing exhibitions on religious themes. The permanent collection includes well-preserved Gothic sculptures and brilliant illuminations. *(Enter at the back of the Dom or from Domstr. ☎ 25 33 44. Open Tu-Su 10am-5pm. €3; students €1.50.)*

OTHER MUSEUMS. The **Römisch-Germanisches Zentralmuseum** (Roman-Germanic Central Museum), housed in the Kurfürstliches Schloß on the bank of the Rhein, traces human existence from prehistory to the Middle Ages with period artifacts. *(☎ 912 40. Open Tu-Su 9:30am-4:30pm. Free.)* The **Museum für Antike Schifffahrt** displays remnants and replicas of Roman ships recovered near Mainz, in addition to shipbuilding displays. *(Neutorstr. 2b. ☎ 28 66 30. Open Tu-Su 10am-6pm. Free.)* A comprehensive collection of art and archaeology from Roman to modern times is housed in the **Landesmuseum.** *(Bauhofstr. 3. ☎ 28 57 25. Open Tu 10am-8pm, W-Su 10am-5pm. €2.50, students €1.50. With special exhibits €8/3.)*

▣ ❈ NIGHTLIFE AND FESTIVALS

The popular **KUZ (Kulturzentrum),** Dagobertstr. 20b, packs dancefloors with locals. Take bus #90 to "Holzturm," face the shopping center across the street, and turn right; turn left on Dagobertstr. *(☎ 28 68 60; www.kuz.de.)* A 60s throwback popular even among Frankfurters, **Star Club,** Holzhofstr. 1, draws internationally renowned DJs with its geometrically daring decor. *(☎ 60 38 71; www.starclub-records.de. Cover Th and Su €3, F €4, Sa €6. Open Th-Su 9pm-late, F-Sa 9am-6am.)*

On the third weekend in June, Mainz celebrates **Johannisnacht,** three days of revelry, Gutenberg style. The Altstadt fills with wine, sausage, and music by day, and the luminescent Rhein is showered with fireworks by night. More revelry and booze accompany **Fastnacht** (Mardi Gras; www.mainzer-fastnacht.de). The **Grosses Haus** of the **Staats Theater** produces opera, concerts, and ballet. The **Klein Haus** offers dramatic production. (Gutenberpl. ☎ 28 510. Student tickets from €5.50.)

MOSELTAL (MOSEL VALLEY)

Before its inevitable surrender to the Rhein at Koblenz, the Mosel River meanders slowly past sun-drenched hills, scenic towns, and ancient castles. The slopes can't compete with the Rhein's narrow gorge, but the less-touristed vineyards on the Moseltal's gentle hillsides have been pressing quality wines since the Romans first cultivated them 2000 years ago. The only local complaints are that summers are too dry and winters too wet. The valley's scenery is best viewed by boat, bus, or bicycle—the train between Koblenz and Trier cuts through unremarkable countryside rather than following the river. Passenger boats no longer make the complete run, but companies run daily trips along shorter stretches in summer.

COCHEM ☎ 02671

Like many German wine-making villages, Cochem is often overrun by busloads of elderly Germans looking for the quaint, idyllic village of yesteryear. But Cochem's vineyard-covered hills and the many-turreted Reichsburg Castle, towering over the sleepy town, can't be cheapened. The bustle found in the town square extends to the narrow, brick-laden streets that radiate from the town center.

▐▜ TRANSPORTATION AND PRACTICAL INFORMATION. Unlike much of the Mosel Valley, Cochem is easily accessible by **train** from Koblenz (1hr., 2-3 per hr., €8) and Trier (1hr., 2 per hr., €9). Although Cochem is equidistant from the two cities, the route from Koblenz is more scenic, hugging the Mosel and affording spectacular views. The **tourist office,** Endertpl. 1, next to the bus station, books rooms for free. From the train station, go to the river and turn right. (☎600 40; www.cochem.de. Open Apr.-Oct. M-Th 9am-5pm and F 9am-6pm; May to mid-July also Sa 9am-3pm; mid-July to Oct. also Sa 9am-5pm and Su 10am-noon; Nov.-Mar. M-F 9am-1pm and 2-5pm.) The **police station** is at Moselstr. 31. (☎98 40; **emergency** ☎110. Open 24hr.) Find **Internet** access at **Murphy's @ Internet Café,** on Endertstr. 11 and Moselpromenade 7. (€1.60 per 30min. Open Mar.-Oct. daily 1pm-midnight; Nov.-Feb. M-F 7pm-midnight, Sa-Su 1pm-midnight.) The **post office** is at the corner of Ravenestr. and Josefstr. (Open M-F 9am-5pm, Sa 9am-noon.) **Postal code:** 56812.

▐▐ ACCOMMODATIONS AND FOOD. Cochem's ▨**Jugendherberge (HI)** ❷, Klottener Str. 9, is 15min. from the train station on the opposite shore and offers stunning views of the Mosel. Cross the Nordbrücke to the left as you exit the station; the hostel is next to the bridge on the right. (☎86 33; fax 85 86. All rooms have shower and toilet. Breakfast included. Free wireless Internet access. Dorm beds €17.50; singles €31; doubles €46. MC/V.) Spacious rooms await at **Gästehaus Zum Onkel Willi** ❹, Endertstr. 39, a family-operated guesthouse and restaurant. Welcoming service mitigates the inconvenience of the distance from the town center. (☎73 05; www.zum-onkel-willi.de. Breakfast included. Singles €40; doubles with bath €60. Cash only.) Down the street from Gästehaus Zum Onkel Willi, **Hotel Holl** ❹, Endertstr. 54, combines standard, bright, and comfortable rooms with a restaurant serving steaks and *Schnitzel.* (☎43 23; www.hotel-holl.de. Breakfast included. Singles €36; doubles €52. Cash only.) **Gästehaus Bambeg** ❷, Schloßstr. 5, offers commodious rooms uphill on your way to the Reichsburg. (☎70 56; fax 98 01 28. Breakfast included. Singles €22; doubles €34-38. Cash only.) If you've got your own tent and don't mind the mosquitoes, walk down the path below the hostel to the **Campingplatz am Freizeitzentrum** ❶ on Stadionstr. (☎44 09; fax 91 07 19. Laundry €1. Bike rental €7.50 per day. Reception 8am-9pm. Open Easter-Oct. €4 per person, €4 per campsite, €5 tent rental with €10 deposit. Cash only.)

Weinhexenkeller ❸, on Hafenstr. across the Moselbrücke and immediately to the left. Vegetables are few and far between at this outpost of traditional German food (€5-9) and Mosel wine. Live music, dancing, and Bacchus-inspired decor complete the atmosphere. (☎977 60. June-Aug. music begins daily 7pm; Sept. F-Su 7pm. Open M-F 11am-1am, Sa-Su 10am-2am. MC.) At **Filou** ❸, down Bernstr., sample homemade potato cakes smothered in cheese and veggies (€9), or splurge on one of the rich desserts. Lounge in their indoor/outdoor seating. (Open daily 9am-6pm. MC.) On the Marktpl. next to the bridge, the **Café-Restaurant Mosella** ❸ offers both contemporary and traditional fixed menus (€8-13). (Open daily Apr.-Oct. 9am-10pm. Cash only.) **La Baia Ristorante Pizzeria** ❷, Liniusstr. 4, near the Moselbrücke, serves reliable pizza and pasta (€5-11) on a second-floor terrace. (☎80 40. Open M-Th and Su 11:30am-2:30pm and 5-11:30pm, F-Sa until midnight. Cash only.)

▐▐ SIGHTS AND ENTERTAINMENT. The neo-Gothic **Reichsburg** dominates the valley from 100m above the Mosel. The view more than warrants the 15min. climb along Schloßstr. from the Marktpl. A 19th-century refurbishment salvaged the original, which was nearly destroyed in the 11th century. The only way to see the castle interior is with one of the effusive tour guides. (☎255. Open daily Mar.-Nov. 9am-5pm. 40min. tour, written English translations available; last tour at 4pm. €4.50, students €4, children €2.50.) Another popular hillside attraction is the **Sesselbahn** (chairlift) on Endertstr. The lift brings visitors to the family-friendly

Wildpark (30min. walk from the top), which has thrill rides and wildlife, as well as the **Pinnerkreuz,** a lone cross on a high peak illuminated by 10,000-watt bulbs at night. (☎98 90 63; www.wildpark-daun.de. Lift runs July-Aug. 9:30am-7pm; Sept.-Oct. 10am-6pm; Oct to mid-Nov. 10am-5pm. €4, round-trip €6; children €2.50/4.) For **hiking** *sans* crowds, try the under appreciated trails across the street from the Sesselbahn. Follow the stone steps to a trail that ends at the hill's summit, then head down the opposite side, turn left on the highway, and follow the trail branching off with the sign for "Maria Hell" (*"hell"* is German for "brightly colored"). The 2hr. hike leads through vineyards with marvelous views of Cochem's castle. If you haven't tired of theme-park-style thrills, head across the river and follow the *Freizeitzentrum* signs to reach the gigantic **Schwimmbad**, a complex of pools, saunas, jacuzzis, and waterslides 5min. north of the *Nordbrücke*, the bridge near the train station. (☎979 90. Indoor pool open daily 10am-10pm. Outdoor pool open daily June-Aug. 10am-6:30pm. €10.70, students €6.70, ages 6-11 €4.60, under 6 free. Outdoor pool only €3, students €2.) **Historischer Gewölbekeller,** Schlossestr. 4, on the street leading to the Reichsburg, is a wine cellar reputedly carved around 1450. Since 1982, winegrowner Walter Oster has presented his award-winning wines, home-made liqueurs, mustards, and brandies for tasting and for sale. Try wine of any quality (€1.50 for 0.2cL serving) inside the candlelit store. (☎026 75; www.weingutoster.de. Open daily 10am-6:30pm.) The **Weinwoche** (wine week; May 24-29, 2007) runs 1½ weeks after *Pfingsten* (Pentecost) and showcases some of the Mosel's best vintages. On the last weekend of August (Aug. 23-26, 2007) the **Heimat-und-Weinfest** peaks in a dramatic fireworks display.

⚑ DAYTRIP FROM COCHEM: BURG ELTZ. Originally constructed in the 11th and 12th centuries, **Burg Eltz** was one of the few castles in the Rheinland to escape destruction by Louis XIV's troops in the 17th century. Though the castle's secluded valley location didn't hurt, the Eltz family claims it was their ancestors' diplomacy that kept the castle intact. This political savvy was stretched thin in the 1330s when Baldwin, Elector of Trier, decided to tighten the law within his land. Two years of rock-slinging later, the Eltz family surrendered to Baldwin's terms: they retained the castle, but served him as vassals. Today the Eltz family still has rooms in the castle but lives elsewhere, leaving more of the Burg open to tourists. The shadowed forest path snakes along a stream, culminating in the sudden appearance of the Gothic monument in the valley floor. The castle's interior can only be seen on a tour; guides point out medieval armory, Chinese porcelain, decaying tapestry, and spiral staircases. The recreations of castle life are exceptional, in particular, explanations of medieval bedding and plumbing. Dazzling gold and silver pieces can be found in the **Schatzkammer** (Treasury), which is separate from the tour. (☎02672 95 05 00; www.burg-eltz.de. Open daily Apr.-Oct. 9:30am-5:30pm. Tours every 40min. English-language tours if you call ahead (min. 15 people); English translation sheet €0.50. Tour €6, students €4.50; last tour departs 5:30pm. Schatzkammer €2.50/1.50.) Two cafeteria-style eateries provide local dishes and wines on site. The nearest town connected to Burg Eltz by **train** is Moselkern. (20min., every hr., €3.15.) With your back to the train station, head right on Oberstr. through town until Oberstr. passes under a bridge and becomes a slightly winding road along the Eltz brook. The road ends at **Ringelsteiner Mühle**—from here, the path through the woods is well marked. The mildly strenuous hike to the Burg (45min.) provides views of the river. The castle is accessible by foot or car.

BEILSTEIN   ☎02673

A tiny hamlet of half-timbered houses, crooked cobblestone streets, and about 350 residents, Beilstein takes pride in being the smallest official town in Germany.

Cochem's historical rival as the most powerful town along the Mosel, spared in WWII, Beilstein has provided the idyllic backdrop to several movies and political summits, including that which established the European Economic Community (now the European Union). By day, Beilstein's natural charm draws a tourist crowd that gives the town the illusion of size, but after 6pm, crowds subside. **Burg Metternich** (of the same family as the 19th-century Austrian statesman) is the local castle; though little of the castle survived the French sacking in 1689, the tower's view is truly memorable. (☎936 39. Open daily Apr.-Oct. 9am-6:30pm. €2, students €1, children €0.50.) The Baroque **Karmelitenkirche,** also on the hill, has an intricately carved wooden altar and houses the **Schwarze Madonna von Beilstein,** a 16th-century Montserrat sculpture left behind by Spanish troops reintroducing Catholicism to the region. (Open daily 9am-7pm. Free.)

Hotels fill up quickly for October's grape harvest, so call well in advance. At **Hotel Gute Quelle ❸,** Marktpl. 34, the cordial staff will show you to a cozy room with private bath. (☎14 37; fax 13 99. Breakfast included. Reception 7am-7pm. Doubles €60-70. Cash only.) **Klapperburg ❸,** Bachstr. 33, offers spacious rooms on this slanting street and serves complimentary breakfast in the café below. (☎14 17. Reception and café open 8am-6pm. Singles €35; doubles €55; triples €75. Cash only.) **Winzerschenke ❸,** An der Klostertreppe 29, has comfortable doubles with bath not far from the Karmelitenkirche. (☎13 54; fax 96 23 71. Breakfast included. Singles €28; doubles €38. Cash only.) The **Klostercafé ❸,** outside the church, offers traditional food (€5-12), Mosel wine, and a view that tops both. (☎16 74 or 16 53. Open daily 9am-7pm. Cash only.) **San Donato ❷,** Fürst-Metternich-Str. 28, sells pizza and pasta dishes (€4-12) along with fish and vegetarian specials. (☎90 00 69. Open daily 11am-midnight. Cash only.)

The town can be reached by **bus** #716, which departs from the bus station at Endertpl. in Cochem (15min.; M-F 14 per day, Sa 5 per day, Su 3 per day; €3). The boats of **Personenschifffahrt Kolb** also go to Beilstein. (☎15 15. 1hr.; May-Oct. 5 per day; €8, round-trip €11.)

TRIER ☎0651

The oldest town in Germany, Trier (pop. 100,000) has weathered more than two millennia in the western end of the Mosel Valley. Founded by the Gallo-Celtic Treveri tribe and seized by the Romans during the reign of Augustus, Trier reached its zenith in the early 4th century as the capital of the Western Roman Empire and a major center for Christianity in Europe. This rich historical legacy, coupled with the tiered vineyards of the surrounding valley, attracts throngs of tourists who crowd the streets of Trier all day and night. Unfazed by the surfeit of crumbling Roman ruins, Trier remains at its core a bustling university city catering to a large and highly visible student population.

▶ TRANSPORTATION

Trains: To: **Cologne** (2½hr., 2-3 per hr., €24); **Koblenz** (1½hr., 2 per hr., €16); **Luxembourg** (45min., every hr., €11); **Saarbrücken** (1½hr., 2 per hr., €13).

Buses: Although most sights are within walking distance of the town center, buses run everywhere. Prices vary. A Trier Card may save you money (see **Practical Information**).

Taxis: Taxi-Funk ☎120 12.

Bike Rental: Fahrradservicestation (☎14 88 56), in the main train station building on track 11. From €7.50 per day with €30 deposit. Open daily May-Oct. 9am-7pm, Nov.-Apr. 9am-5pm. Reservations recommended for groups.

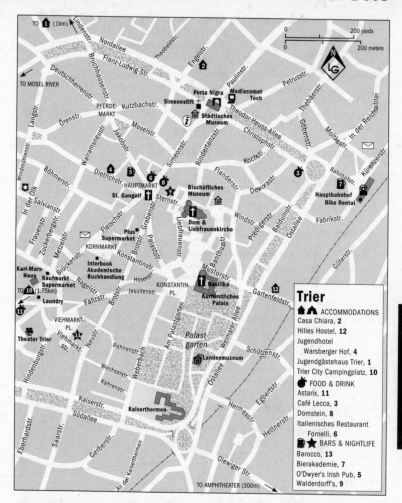

RHEINLAND-PFALZ

Trier

▲▲ ACCOMMODATIONS
Casa Chiara, **2**
Hilles Hostel, **12**
Jugendhotel
 Warsberger Hof, **4**
Jugendgästehaus Trier, **1**
Trier City Campingplatz, **10**

● FOOD & DRINK
Astarix, **11**
Café Lecca, **3**
Domstein, **8**
Italienisches Restaurant
 Fornelli, **6**

■★ BARS & NIGHTLIFE
Barocco, **13**
Bierakademie, **7**
O'Dwyer's Irish Pub, **5**
Walderdorff's, **9**

ORIENTATION AND PRACTICAL INFORMATION

Trier lies on the Mosel River fewer than 50km from the Luxembourg border. The entrance to the Altstadt, the **Porta Nigra** (Black Gate) is a 5min. walk from the train station down Theodor-Heuss-Allee or Christophstr. A **Trier Card,** available at the tourist office, offers free inner-city bus fare and discounts on museums and Roman sites over a three-day period (€9, family card €15).

 Tourist Office (☎97 80 80; www.trier.de), right in the shadow of the Porta Nigra, runs English tours Sa at 1:30pm (€6, students €5). Open Apr.-Oct. M-Sa 9am-6pm, Su 10am-3pm; Nov.-Dec. and Mar. M-Sa 9am-6pm, Su 10am-1pm; Jan.-Feb. M-F 10am-5pm, Sa 10am-1pm.

Bookstore: Interbook Akademische Buchhandlung, Kornmarkt 3 (☎97 99 01). Small selection of English paperbacks. Open M-F 9am-7pm, Sa 9am-6pm.

Laundry: Wasch Salon, Brückenstr. 19-21, down the street from Karl Marx's old house. Wash €5. Dry €2 per 30min. Open daily 8am-10pm.

Emergency: ☎110. **Police Station,** Salvianstr. 9 (☎977 90). Open 24hr.

Internet Access: Mediacomet Technologies, Theodor-Heuss-Allee at Porta-Nigra-Platz 4 (☎145 54 62). €1 per hr. Open M-F and Su 11am-10pm.

Post Office: on Bahnhofpl. Open M-F 8:30am-7pm, Sa 8:30am-1pm. **Postal Code:** 54292.

ACCOMMODATIONS AND CAMPING

Hilles Hostel, Gartenfeldstr. 7 (☎710 27 85; www.hilles-hostel-trier.de). This family-run hostel offers bright, festive decor, and the opportunity to leave your photo on the wall. All rooms have bath. Fully-stocked kitchen. Dorms from €15; doubles €32-38; quads €64, homestays from €400 a month. Laundry €2. Internet €1. MC/V. ❷

Jugendgästehaus Trier (HI), An der Jugendherberge 4 (☎292 92; fax 146 62 30). Bus #2, 8, 12, or 87 (dir.: Trierweilerweg or Pfalzel/Quint) to "Zur Laubener Ufer," and walk 10min. downstream along the river embankment. Or, from the station, follow Theodor-Heuss-Allee as it becomes Nordallee and forks right onto Lindenstr.; at the bank of the Mosel, turn right and follow the path along the river (30min.). Sterile riverside rooms with shower and toilet. Breakfast and sheets included. Reception 7am-10pm. Singles €32; doubles €46; quads €70. MC/V. ❸

Jugendhotel/Jugendgästehaus Warsberger Hof im Kolpinghaus, Dietrichstr. 42 (☎97 52 50; fax 975 25 40). Unbeatable location, with halls crowded with boisterous students until late. Internet €5 per hr. Reception 8am-11pm. Reserve ahead. Hostel dorms €16, sheets €2.50; hotel singles €25; doubles €42, sheets included. Cash only. ❷

Casa Chiara, Engelstr. 8 (☎27 07 30; www.casa-chiara.de), has comfortable rooms with private baths and cable TV. Generous brunch included. Internet €2 per hr. Reception from 6:30am. Singles €50-60; doubles €80-95; triples €110. Cash only. ❺

Trier City Campingplatz, Luxemburger Str. 81 (☎869 21). From Hauptmarkt, follow Fleischstr. to Brückenstr. to Karl-Marx-Str. to the Römerbrücke. Cross the bridge, head left on Luxemburger Str., and then left at the camping sign. Showers available. Open Apr.-Oct. Reception M and Sa-Su 8-11am and 4-6pm; Tu-F 8-11am and 4-8pm. €4.50 per person, €2.50-4.50 per tent. Cash only. ❶

FOOD

For **groceries,** head to **Kaufmarkt,** at the corner of Brückenstr. and Stresemannstr. (open M-F 8am-8pm, Sa 8am-4pm), or check out **Plus,** Brotstr. 54, near the Hauptmarkt (open M-F 8:30am-8pm, Sa 8:30am-6pm).

Astarix, Karl-Marx-Str. 11 (☎722 39). Squeezed in a passageway, Astarix can be reached from the Trier Theater area or by walking down Brückenstr. toward the river. Customers spill out onto the terrace of this laid-back restaurant to enjoy heaping portions of Italian staples served by a hip waitstaff. Salads and baguettes €2.60-5.40; pastas and pizzas €3.50-5.40. Open daily 11am-11:30pm. Cash only. ❷

Café Lecca, Bahnhofspl. 7 (☎994 98 30; www.cafe-lecca.de). Just across from the train station; offers weary travelers a pick-me-up, whether their drink of choice be steamed milk with honey (€1.40), cappuccino (€1.40-2.80), or Long Island Iced Tea (€7). Coffeehouse by day and trendy bar by night with booth, bar, and outdoor terrace seating.

Flatscreen TVs and free wireless Internet access. Beers €2. Sandwiches and desserts €1.50-3.30, mixed drinks €5-7. Open daily 9am-late. Cash only. ❸

Italienisches Restaurant Fornelli, Jakobstr. 34 (☎ 433 85), serves up large, scrumptious pizza (€5-7), pasta dishes (€6-9), and *gelato* (€1.40-3.50) for lunch and dinner crowds. Open daily 11:30am-11pm. Cash only. ❸

Domstein, Hauptmarkt 5 (☎ 744 90; www.domstein.de). A decadent option with unbeatable views of the Dom. Inside, the rich mahogany walls are decorated with oil paintings of Trier. The menu offers several cheese plates (€8.20) and wine flights (€5.50), each with a sampling of five local Rieslings. Try the salmon in Riesling sauce with leafy spinach and pine kernels (€14.20). Open daily 11:30am-9:30pm. MC. ❹

🕲 SIGHTS

History enthusiasts will want to pick up a one-day combination ticket valid at all Roman monuments (€6.20, students €3.10).

PORTA NIGRA. Trier is full of Roman history, the most impressive remnant of which is the Porta Nigra (Black Gate). This massive sandstone construction, held together only by iron clamps, was originally light yellow, but now stands tarnished by years of weathering and pollution. Built in the AD 2nd century, the gate was an entrance to the city until a local archbishop named it a church and pilgrimage site in the 11th century. It has survived relatively unscathed over time, though Napoleon's troops melted the metal roof into bullets. Climb to the top for a great view of Trier from the north. (☎ 754 24. Open daily Apr.-Sept. 9am-6pm; Oct.-Mar. 9am-5pm; Nov.-Feb. 9am-4pm. Last entry 30min. before closing. €2.10, students €1.60.)

DOM. This cloister-complex 11th-century cathedral shelters the tombs of archbishops. The *Tunica Christi* (Holy Robe of Christ) is rumored to be enshrined at the eastern end of the cathedral. Tradition holds that this relic was brought to Trier from Jerusalem around AD 300 by St. Helena, mother of Emperor Constantine. The *Tunica* is shown to the public only on rare occasions, usually once every 30 years. Near the south end of the cathedral, outside the doorway, stands a fractured granite pillar supposedly cracked by the devil himself. Also within the Dom, the **Schatzkammer** holds a treasury of holy relics. Behind the cathedral is the **Bischöfliches Dom- und Diözesanmuseum,** a surprisingly modern building showcasing large archaeological collections and restored frescoes. (☎ 710 52 55. Dom open daily Apr.-Oct. 6:30am-6pm; Nov.-Mar. 6:30am-5:30pm. Admission free. Tour €3, children €1. Schatzkammer open Apr.-Oct. M-Sa 10am-5pm, Su 2-5pm; Nov.-Mar. M-Sa 11am-4pm, Su 2-4pm. €1.50, children €0.50. Diözesanmuseum, Windstr. 6-8. Open M-Sa 9am-5pm, Su 1-5pm; Nov.-Mar. closed M. €2, students €1.)

AMPHITHEATER. A short walk from the city center, the Trier Amphitheater dates from the 2nd century and bears witness to the famed Roman tradition of gladiatorial games. Seating 20,000, this venue would have hosted shows with jesters, exotic animals, and grown men—losing often meant death. The amphitheater is now a stage for city productions; check with **Theater Trier** performance listings. (The signs will lead you to a 10min. walk uphill from the Kaiserthermen along Olewiger Str. Open daily Apr.-Sept. 9am-6pm; Oct. and Mar. 9am-5pm; Nov.-Feb. 9am-4pm. Last entry 30min. before closing. €2.10, students €1.60.)

KAISERTHERMEN (IMPERIAL BATHS). Though vivid when viewed from above, the ruins of 4th-century Roman baths are most memorable for gloomy, underground passages remaining from the ancient sewer network. Paths intersect everywhere, making it easy to get lost. (Enter through the Palastgarten. Open daily Apr.-Sept. 9am-6pm, Oct.-Mar. 9am-5pm; last entry 30min. before closing. €2.10, students €1.60.)

LIEBFRAUENKIRCHE. Adjacent to the Dom is the magnificent Gothic Liebfrauen-kirche, the earliest Gothic church in Germany, built over the foundations of a Roman basilica. Angular red- and blue-patterned stained-glass windows dominate the plain interior. *(Liebfrauenstr. 2. ☎ 425 54; fax 403 13. Open daily Apr.-Oct. 7:30am-6pm; Nov.-Mar. 7:30am-5:30pm; tour available with purchase of Dom tour.)*

KARL-MARX-HAUS. The walls of Karl's humble birthplace are plastered with arti-cles, photographs, and other memorabilia interesting to die-hard Marxists and social scientists. Copies of the Communist Manifesto abound. *(Brückenstr. 10. ☎ 430 11. Open Apr.-Oct. M 1-6pm, Tu-Su 10am-6pm; Nov.-Mar. M 2-5pm, Tu-Su 10am-1pm and 2-5pm. Audio guides available in English €2, students €1.)*

AROUND THE BASILIKA. Built as a throne room for Emperor Constantine, the Basilika is the only remaining Roman brick structure in Trier. This towering build-ing served as a palace and church before it was heavily damaged by bombing dur-ing WWII. Unadorned walls and simple wood benches reveal little of its former splendor. *(Open Apr.-Oct. M-Sa 10am-6pm, Su noon-6pm; Nov.-Mar. Tu-Sa 11am-noon and 3-4pm, Su noon-1pm. Free.)* Next door is the bubble-gum pink **Kurfürstliches Palais,** a former residence of the archbishops and electors of Trier that today houses municipal government offices. The lavish landscaping of the **Palastgarten** com-pletes the Rococo motif. On the eastern edge of the garden lies the **Rheinisches Landesmuseum** (Roman Archaeological Museum), a terrific collection of Roman sculpture, mosaics, and even an Egyptian mummy. Check out the meticulous model of 4th-century Trier. *(Weimarer Allee 1. Open M-F 9:30am-5pm, Sa-Su 10:30am-5pm; Nov.-Apr. closed M. Audio guides available in English. €2.50, students €0.50)*

SIMEONSTIFT. An 11th-century monastery inside the Porta Nigra's courtyard, the Simeonstift holds the **Städtisches Museum,** renovated until 2007 to include a com-prehensive and interactive summary of 2000 years of Trier history. Temporary exhibits continue to display Ancient artifacts. *(☎ 718 14 59. Open Mar.-Oct. daily 9am-5pm; Nov.-Feb. Tu-F 9am-5pm, Sa-Su 9am-3pm. €2.60, students €1.50.)*

🎵 🎭 ENTERTAINMENT AND NIGHTLIFE

Several annual festivals spice up Trier's atmosphere. The **Altstadtfest** (June 22-24, 2007) brings live music, wine, and beer to the streets during the fourth weekend in June. The second weekend in July brings the **Moselfest** (July 13-15, 2007), with Sat-urday night fireworks over the water, and the first weekend in August welcomes the **Weinfest** (Aug. 3-5, 2007) in the nearby town of Olewig. The **Weihnachtsmarkt** (Nov. 21-Dec. 22, 2007) of the Christmas season is also known as "Glühwein-markt" to the local college students because of the featured spiced wine version of the local vintage. The **Theater Trier,** Am Augustinerhof, has three stages and a wide variety of shows. *(☎ 718 18 18; www.theater-trier.de.* Tickets €8-28. Box office open Tu-F 9:30am-2pm and 3:30-8pm, Sa 10am-12:30pm.) Pubs and clubs of all fla-vors fan out from the Hauptmarkt, with dense collections on **Judengasse** and the **Pferdemarkt.** Check out www.lifestyle-tr.de for party and concert information.

Walderdorff's (☎ 994 44 12; www.walderdorffs.de), across from the Dom. At night the mellow café surrenders to throngs of dancers crowding the underground disco. Beer €2. Mixed drinks €5.50-9. Cover €5. Café/bar open M-Th 9:30am-1am, F 9:30am-2am, Sa 10am-2am, Su 10am-1am. Disco open W and F-Sa 10pm-4am. Dancing starts around 12:30am; crowds pack in around 2am. Website lists additional events. MC.

Barocco, Viehmarktpl. 10 (www.barocco.de). For unremitting partiers, this relaxed bar and club combo offers decadent velvet couches, ginormous works of art, and Romanesque pillars. ½-price mixed drinks 6-9pm. F Salsa night 10pm-2am, Sa Hip-hop. Open daily 10:30am-1am, F-Sa until 4am; F-Sa cover €3. MC.

O'Dwyer's Irish Pub, Jakobstr. 10 (☎495 39; www.irish-pub.de), fills up with American and English crowds on regular theme nights, including "U2 Tuesdays" (free Guinness or Bailey's every time a U2 song is played). M Karaoke at 9pm (€2, students €1.50), Su trivia at 9pm. Su and Th cheaper drinks (€0.50 less) for students. Open M-Th and Su 11am-1am, F-Sa until 2am. AmEx/MC/V.

Bierakademie, Bahnhofstr. 28 (☎994 31 95). With 100 beers and numerous local wines, Bierakademie is all about the drinks—just ask the venerable connoisseurs. Foosball, billiards, and darts in back. Open M-Sa noon-1am, Su 3pm-midnight. Cash only.

SAARBRÜCKEN ☎0681

For centuries, proximity to the French border and rich natural resources have involved Saarbrücken (pop. 179,000) in countless wars, leaving virtually none of its Altstadt intact and clearing the way for rampant industrialization. Today, Saarbrücken's downtown marries French markets, ethnic restaurants, and innumerable car manufacturing outposts. The impressive glare of chain stores and sleek glass-and-steel architecture belies the perpetual upheaval of construction. From its expanding cityscape to its progressive punk population, the capital of Germany's smallest *Land* features all the flavor of an urban center, minus the tourists.

TRANSPORTATION AND PRACTICAL INFORMATION

Saarbrücken is connected by **train** to **Trier** (1½hr., 2 per hr., €13), **Frankfurt** (2½hr., every 2hr., €27.20), and **Mannheim** (1½hr., 2 per hr., €19). The **tourist office,** Reichstr. 1, across from the station to the right of the McDonald's, books rooms for free. (☎93 80 90; www.die-region-saarbruecken.de. Open M-F 9am-6pm, Sa 10am-4:30pm.) Do **laundry** at **Waschhaus,** Nauwieserstr. 22, two blocks east of the Rathaus (wash €3; dry €0.50 per 10min.; open daily 8am-10pm) or **Münz-Waschsalon,** Eisenbahnstr. 8, across the street from the Ludwigspl. (Wash €3. Dry €0.50 per 10min. Open daily 7am-10pm.) The **police station** is at Karcherstr. 5. (☎96 20; **emergency** 110. Open 24hr.) **Internet** is at **Phone Center,** Bahnhofstr. 104 (☎876 46 84; €2 per hr.; open daily 10am-11pm), and the **post office** is to the right when you exit the train station. (Open M-F 9am-6pm, Sa 9am-1pm.) **Postal Code:** 66111.

ACCOMMODATIONS AND FOOD

The **Jugendgästehaus Europa (HI) ❷,** Meerwiesertalweg 31, is a 25min. walk from the station. Head downhill and to the left along Kaiserstr.; take a left onto Dudweilerstr., and then a right onto Meerwiesertalweg. Or take bus #69 (€1.50; dir.: Uni-Campus) to "Prinzenweiher" and backtrack 70m to the hostel. This secluded modern hostel has private bathrooms, a lively café/bar, and a touch of whimsy: each bed comes with a pack of gummy bears. (☎330 40; www.diejugendherbergen.de. Breakfast, towels, and sheets included. Reception 7:30am-1am. Curfew 1am, key available upon request. Dorm beds €17.50; singles €32; doubles €46; quads €70. MC.) Nearby, **Gästehaus Weller ❸,** Neugrabenweg 8, offers larger rooms with shower, phone, fridge, and TV. To take the 20min. walk from the station, head downhill and to the left along Kaiserstr., left onto Ursulinenstr., right on Mozartstr., continue on to Schumannstr., take a left on Fichtestr., and cross the bridge to Neugrabenweg. (☎37 19 03; fax 876 47 60. Reception in corner restaurant M-F 6am-11pm, Sa 6am-10pm, Su 6am-9pm. Singles €39; doubles €59; triples €75. MC.) **Hotel Schloßkrug ❸,** Schmollerstr. 14, at the corner of Bruchwiesenstr., has spacious rooms with shower and TV. 15min. from the station. Head downhill and to the left along Kaiserstr., left onto Ursulinenstr., right on Richard-Wagner-Str., and right on Schmollerstr. Or take tram #1 to Landespl. (☎367 35; fax 37 50 22. Singles €31, with shower and bath €39; doubles €61, with shower €66, with bath €69. MC.) **Campingplatz Saarbrücken ❶**, Am Spicherer Berg, is far from the station (approx. 45 min.) walk. Take bus #42 to "Spicherer Weg," then cross Untertürkheimstr. and head uphill on Spicherer Weg. (☎517 80. Reception 7am-1pm and 3-10pm. Open Mar.-Oct. €5 per person, €8 per campsite.)

The pedestrian Bahnhofstr. boasts Paseo-style *al fresco* restaurants and numerous stands with both snacks and more substantive produce. For cheaper and fresher options, walk to the end of Bahnhofstr. and take the escalator down to **Diskonto Passage,** under Bahnhofstr. near Dudweilerstr., home to a fanciful candy shop and stands overflowing with inexpensive seasonal goods. The streets around **St. Johanner Markt** brim with beer gardens and ethnic restaurants; students and the elderly flock to this area for its concentrated dining and shopping options. The **fresh produce market** is open M, W, F 8am-3pm. A handful of ethnic restaurants can be found between Rotenbergstr., Richard-Wagner-Str., Dudweilerstr., and Großherzog-Friedrich-Str., a nighttime hotspot for college students. While you're there, stop by the funky ▨**Fleur de Biere ❷**, Cecilieustr. 3. Don't worry if after a few French specialty beers you see miniature boats, volcanoes, and a plastic frog suspended from the ceiling—they were there when you got there. (☎355 33. Open daily 8pm-1am. Cash only.) The laid-back **Schnokeloch ❷**, Kappenstr. 6, has standing bar-style "seating" and serves *Flammekuchen* (a delicious Alsatian twist on pizza, €5.80) and salads for €5-7. (☎333 97. Open M-F noon-2:30pm and 6pm-1am, Sa noon-1am, Su 6pm-1am. Cash only.) **Tierlieb ❸**, Cecilieustr. 12, features an entirely vegan menu of satisfying pasta and salad dishes garnished with pesto, olive oil, or fresh herbs (€5.50-6.90). Diners can opt for the *klein* size for any dish and pay one euro less. (☎764 897; www.bistrorant-tierlieb.de. Open M-F 11:30am-3pm and 5-9pm, Sa and Su 11:30am-3pm and 5-11pm. MC.)

◉♫ SIGHTS AND ENTERTAINMENT

Saarbrücken couches pretty pieces of old Europe in a leisurely *dolce vita* atmosphere. The details on the bronze doors of the Baroque-style **Basilika St. Johann** have faded since its 1758 construction, and now it's difficult to tell whether the engraved figures are writhing in hell-fire or ecstatic with heavenly bliss. Take Kappenstr. from the market and turn right onto Katherinen-Kirche-Str.; the church is on the left. (Open daily 9pm-5pm. Free.) A walk along Am Stadtgraben leads to the **Saarland Museum,** a complex which houses the **Moderne Galerie,** Bismarckstr. 11-19, featuring a fantastic selection of Impressionist, Surrealist, and Cubist art. The **Alte Sammlung,** Karlstr. 1, across the street, contains regional work from the Middle Ages to the late 19th century, including a collection of medieval Madonnas, French porcelain, and silver beer steins; attached is the **Künstlerhaus,** which highlights promising regional artists. (☎996 40. All museums open Tu-Su 10am-6pm, W until 10pm. All three museums €1.50, students and children €1. Special exhibits €8, students €3.50.) Children and adults can take a reprieve at **Tifliser Pl.** on Saarstr., next to the river. Captain the playground boat, relax on a swing, or unpack a picnic on the large, stone tables. The tame **Saarbrücker Schloß,** on the other side of the Saar river, has been transformed many times since its Renaissance construction and now sports a towering glass facade. It currently houses offices of local officials. (☎50 63 13. Open M-F 8:30am-noon and 2-6pm, Sa-Su 10am-6pm. German tours Sa-Su at 3pm. Free.) The Schloßpl. is officially the ▨**Platz des unsichtbaren Mahnmals** (Place of the Invisible Reminder). From 1990 to 1992, students at a nearby art school dug up stones in the plaza, carved the names of Jewish cemeteries on their undersides, and replaced them carved side down. The 2146 commemorative stones make up the center of the path leading out from the *Schloß.*

Two museums surround the town plaza. To the south, adjacent to the *Schloß*, the **Historisches Museum Saar** (Museum of Regional History) includes a disturbing collection of war propaganda and a prison cell once used by WWI secret police, with graffiti in Russian and German. (☎506 45 01; www.historiches-museum-saar.de. Open Tu, W, F, and Su 10am-6pm; Th 10am-8pm; Sa noon-6pm. €2.50, students €1.50.) To the north, the **Museum für Vor- und Frühgeschichte** (Museum of Prehistory and Early History), Schloßpl. 16, holds a Celtic countess's grave and jewelry from the 4th century BC. (☎95 40 50; www.historisches-museum-saar.de. Open Tu-Sa 9am-5pm, Su 10am-6pm. Free.)

WORMS ☎06241

Worms (pop. 81,000) was immortalized as the city whose imperial council, the Diet of Worms, sent Martin Luther into exile for refusing to renounce his heretical doctrine that religious truth existed only in scripture. There are numerous Jewish memorials and synagogues scattered throughout the city, which served as a cultural center before the Holocaust. A historical town with a crowded pedestrian zone by day, Worms quiets down at night in the shadow of its stately monuments.

📲 TRANSPORTATION AND PRACTICAL INFORMATION. Frequent **trains** run to Mainz from Worms (45min., 2 per hr., €7.60-11.70) and to Frankfurt (€10). The **tourist office,** Neumarkt 14, is in a complex across the street from the Dom St. Peter. (☎250 45; www.worms.de. Open M-F 9am-6pm, Sa 9:30am-1:30pm. Nov.-Mar. closed Sa.) A variety of walking **tours** (in German) are available from March to October. Ask at the tourist office for details. (€4, children €2. Private tours available, €58.) **Exchange money** at the **Deutsche Bank** down Wilhelm-Leuschner-Str. from the station. (Open M-Tu 8:30am-12:30pm and 2-4pm, W 8:30am-2pm, Th 8:30am-12:30pm and 2-6pm, F 8:30am-12:30pm and 2-3:30pm.) The **police station,** Hagenstr. 5, is near the city council building. (☎85 20; **emergency** ☎110. Open 24hr.) **Internet Café** is across Neumarkt from the tourist office. (€1 per hr. Open daily 9am-11pm.) To reach the **post office,** continue along Neumarkt from the tourist office and take a right 2½ blocks into the Kaiser Passage shopping center in Markt Pl. (Open M-F 9am-8pm, Sa 9am-4pm.) **Postal Code:** 67547.

🍴 ACCOMMODATIONS AND FOOD. To get to centrally located **Jugendgästehaus (HI) ❷,** Dechaneig. 1, follow Bahnhofstr. right from the station to Andreasstr., and turn left. The hostel will be to your left across from the Dom. A pink staircase spirals upward to yellow hallways and bright three- to six-bed rooms, each with bath. (☎257 80; fax 273 94. Breakfast and sheets included. Reception 7am-11pm. Doors lock at 11pm, but keys are available. Dorms €17.50; singles €32.30; doubles €46. MC/V.) Kriemhilde ❸, Hofg. 2, is just off Neumarkt in the shadow of the Dom, and doubles as a quiet restaurant and *weinstube* (wine room) in the early evening. All rooms have cable TV, radio, and television. (☎911 50. Breakfast included. Singles €48, doubles €57-70, triples €85. Cash only.) Though many believe the famous Nibelungen treasure is lost forever under the Rhein, the family that owns **Hotel Boos ❸,** Mainzerstr. 5, claims to have found it. From the train station, walk down Siegfriedstr. and turn left. Pastel rooms have private bath and cable TV in this pleasant hotel. The stained-glass windows of the breakfast room, pieced together by the owner and his son, chronicle the *Nibelungenlied* for which the town is famous (see **Treasure and Trysts,** p. 368). (☎94 76 39; www.hotel-boos.de. Singles €38; doubles €56; triples €72; quads €88. Cash only.) The university **Mensa ❶** serves predictable cafeteria food (from €1). Turn right as you exit the station, go right across the first bridge, walk down Friedrich-Ebert-

f the *Nibelungenlied* can be rusted, budget-strained back-backers in Worms need look no arther than the nearby Rhein to eplenish their supply of cash: the nedieval epic claims that the greatest treasure ever known is still buried beneath the river.

According to the legend, Worms vas home to the Burgundian prin-:ess Kriemhild and her older brother Gunther. Several versions of the narrative exist, but most agree that Siegfried, slayer of the dragon Fafnir and owner of the Nibelungenschatz (a treasure of unsurpassed worth), set out to court Kriemhild after hearing of her unsurpassed beauty. Gunther con-sented to the marriage only after Siegfried helped him beguile Brün-hild, the Queen of Iceland.

Much later, when the two men, along with their wives, reunited, a spat between the two queens led o Siegfried's death. The Nibelun-genschatz was thrown into the Rhein outside of Worms, and both Gunther and Kriemhild perished in subsequent attempts to recover it. The *Nibelung* story was later made famous in Wagner's "Ring" cycle, and also influenced Tolk-en's *The Lord of the Rings*. You can check out the details at the Nibelungen Museum.

Nibelungen Museum. Fisher-pförtchen 10. ☎ 20 21 20. Open Tu-Su 10am-5pm, F 10am-10pm. €5.50, students €4.50.)

Str., and turn left after eight blocks on Erenburger Str. It's 1½ blocks up on your right, through the uni-versity gates. (Open M-F 9am-7pm. Student ID required. Cash only.) Otherwise, **Café Schmitz ❸**, on Weckerling Pl. provides patio seating near the Dom. Enjoy pasta (€6-8) and soup (€4-4.50), or choose from a long list of drinks. (☎ 41 35 35. €5-9. Open M-Th and Su 10am-1am, F-Sa 10am-2pm.)

🔲 **SIGHTS.** The site of Luther's confrontation with the Diet is memorialized at the **Lutherdenkmal.** The 1868 statue, three blocks southeast of the station along Wilhelm-Leuschner-Str., is inscribed with the words, "Here I stand. I have no choice. May God help me. Amen." Luther never actually said these words; after leaving the trial, he said, "I am finished!" He was then "kidnapped" by friends who knew that he was an open target for murder and escaped safely. Across the walkway toward the Dom, the **Kunsthaus Heylshof** showcases 15th-century glass paintings, Rococo por-celain, and tortoiseshell furniture. Renaissance Ger-man and Dutch paintings include Rubens' *Madonna with Child*. Contemporary works are in the base-ment. (Open May-Sept. Tu-Su 11am-5pm; Oct.-Apr. Tu-Sa 2-5pm. €2.50, students €1.) Aging trees spread their branches above the **Heylshofgarten** between the museum and Dom.

Crowning Worms with its distinctive Romanesque spirals, the **Dom St. Peter** rises from ancient Celtic foundations. Balthasar Neumann designed the high altar in the 18th century. (Open daily Apr.-Oct. 9am-5:45pm; Nov.-Mar. until 4:45pm. Donation requested.) The legendary *Nibelungenlied* (p. 72), a German myth primarily associated with Worms and linked to the rise of German nationalism in the 19th century, is the focus of the modern **Nibelungen Museum.** The many intricacies, ambiguities, and mis-interpretations of the bloody legend, exploited by German rulers from the Kaiser to Hitler, are illumi-nated through an interactive retelling of "Treasure at the Bottom of the Rhein." Follow Petersstr. until you reach the town wall and turn right. (☎ 20 21 20. Open Tu-Th and Sa-Su 10am-5pm, last entry 3:15pm; F 10am-10pm. €5.50, students €4.50; price includes mandatory headset available in multiple languages.)

The 1000-year-old **Heiliger Sand,** one of the oldest Jewish cemeteries in Europe, is the resting place of rabbis, martyrs, and a few celebrities. Enter through the gate on Willi-Brandt-Ring, just south of Andreas-str. On the opposite end of the Altstadt, the cobble-stone streets around **Judeng.** are all that remain of the 1000-year legacy of Worms's Jewish community (once known as "Little Jerusalem"), which prospered during the Middle Ages but disappeared completely during the Holocaust. The **Synagoge,** just off Judeng., traces its foundations back to 1175, when it was rebuilt after the First Crusade. It remained the spiritual and cultural center of Jewish learning north of the Alps until *Kristallnacht* (Nov. 10, 1938), when the it was torched by the Nazis (p. 56). In 1961 it was rebuilt, and, with no substantive Jewish community left in Worms to use it, today the building commemorates the Jews of Worms lost in the Holocaust. (Open daily Apr.-Oct. 10am-12:30pm and 1:30-5pm; Nov.-Mar. 10am-12:30pm and 1:30-4pm. Required head coverings available at the door.) Behind the synagogue is the **Jüdisches Museum** in the **Raschi-Haus,** which presents a chronology of Worms's Jewish population and original commentary by the 11th-century Talmudic scholar Rabbi Shlomo Ben-Yitzhak, better known as Rashi. A 10min. video is available in English upon request. (☎ 853 47 01. Open Tu-Su 10am-12:30pm and 1:30-5pm. €1.50, students €0.80.)

🎵 **ENTERTAINMENT. 80's Club,** Judeng. 11-13, lies in the historic area around Worms's erstwhile Jewish community. This popular bar pounds with disco and different DJs every Friday and Saturday. (☎ 238 50 19. Open M-Th 7pm-2am, F 7pm-5am, Sa 8-5am, Su 8-2am. Cash only.) Late nights transform the electric blue bar of **Ohne Gleichen,** Kriemhildenstr. 11, into an aquarium of tropical drinks (mixed drinks €6, €10.50 for two). Turn right down Bahnhof and walk three blocks. (☎ 41 11 77. Open daily 9am-1am. Cash only.) The Worms open-air **jazz festival** takes place in early July each summer, while the **Backfischfest** brings a wine-soaked party of 70,000 people to Worms for nine days starting the last weekend in August. The recently inaugurated **Nibelungen-Festspiele** fills the weeks before the Backfischfest with theater events and further interpretations of the *Nibelungenlied.*

SPEYER   ☎ 06232

Speyer's political star rose when the Salian dynasty came to the German throne in the 11th century. This city once hosted meetings of the Imperial Diet, including the 1529 meeting at which the name "Protestant" was coined; today, it boasts the largest Romanesque cathedral in Germany. Burned to the ground by the French in 1689, the town was steadily rebuilt and escaped destruction in both World Wars. Today, this city of quiet parks and curving alleys serves as a gateway both to the Palatinate Forest and the wine region centered in Neustadt. The old town bustles with hikers and schoolchildren during the day only to ease into early evenings.

🚆 **TRANSPORTATION AND PRACTICAL INFORMATION.** Frequent **trains** run to Ludwigshafen (25min., 2 per hr., €4.50) and Mannheim (30min., every hr., €4.50). A **shuttle bus** (line #565) runs the length of the city (every 10min.; shuttle day ticket €1, other buses approx. €2 per ride, but vary by stop). The **tourist office,** Maximilianstr. 13, two blocks before the Dom, has free maps and accommodations listings. Take bus #565 to "Maximilianstr." (☎ 14 23 92; www.speyer.de. Open M-F 9am-5pm; also Apr.-Oct. Sa 10am-3pm and Sun 10am-noon, Nov.-Mar. Sa 10am-2pm.) The **police office** is near the Dom, Maximilian Str., 6. (**Emergencies** ☎ 110.) Find **Internet** access at **Medien Paradies,** Bahnhofstr. 11. (Open M-F 9:30am-10pm, Sa 10am-10pm, Su noon-9pm. €3 per hr.) The **post office** is on Wormser Str. 2. (Open M-F 8:30am-6pm, Sa 8:30am-12:30pm.) **Postal Code:** 67346.

🏠 **ACCOMMODATIONS AND FOOD.** Speyer is blessed with the incredible new **Jugendgästehaus Speyer (HI) ❷,** Geibstr. 5, which has a sunbathers' park, a backyard *Fußball* field, and a nearby beach, open most summer nights (free entry). The sunny rooms have sweet touches, including fruit and gummy welcome packages. Take the city shuttle (line #565) to "Freibad/Jugendherberge." (☎615 97; www.DieJugendherbergen.de. Breakfast and sheets included. Reception daily 7:30am-7:30pm. Curfew M-Th and Su 11pm, F-Sa midnight. Dorms with bath €18; singles €24.50; doubles €27.50; 28+ add extra €5.50. Cash only.) The soft blue exterior of **Pension Grüne Au ❸**, Grüner Winkel 28, has rooms outfitted with grand-motherly care. Take Bus #562 from the train station to "Eselsdamm," turn right as you step off, cross Eselsdamm and continue on Grüner Winkel. (☎721 96; fax 29 28 99. Reception closed 2-5pm and Sa. Singles €29, with bath €37; doubles €45/55; triples €60/70. MC.) North of Maximilianstr., excellent restaurants line **Korng.** and **Große Himmelsg.**, while **Fischmarkt** and **Königspl.** often fill with fresh produce and small vendors on weekdays and Saturdays. The wine cellar **Zur Alten Münz ❸**, Korng. 1a, just off Maximilianstr. and three blocks from the Dom, serves *Pfälzen* specialities from *Saumagen* (stuffed pig's stomach) to *Pfälzer Leibgericht* (favorite dishes, €7.50-15) in a quaint 18th-century residence. (☎797 03. Open daily Apr.-Oct. 11am-midnight; Nov.-Mar. 11am-3pm and 5pm-midnight.)

◳ **SIGHTS.** Since the 11th century, the immense **Kaiserdom** has been the symbol of Speyer, and was recently named an UNESCO World Cultural Heritage sight. Imposing busts and statues line the entryway, and the towering arcades of the inner dome are some of the highest in Germany. The crypt cradles the remains of four German kings, and those of four Holy Roman Emperors and their wives. The cathedral is undergoing renovations until 2008. (☎10 22 98. Open Apr.-Oct. M-Sa 9am-7pm, Su noon-6pm; Nov.-Mar. M-Sa 9am-5pm, Su 1:30-5pm. Call ☎100 92 18 for morning tours in German.) South of the Dom, the **Historisches Museum der Pfalz**, Dompl., gives an overview of Palatinate history—including exhibits on wine and the Romans—and hosts highly touted special exhibits on subjects from pop art to Napoleon. Among the exhibits are the exquisite *Domschatzkammer* (treasury) and the oldest bottle of wine in the world—a slimy remnant of not-infrequent AD third-century Roman revelry. (☎132 50. Open Tu-Su 10am-6pm, W 10am-8pm. €4, children €3.) From the Dom, take Kleine Pfaffeng. one block to reach the **Juden-bad**, a 12th-century Jewish *mikvah* (ritual bathhouse) that is as much a memorial as it is a site for Jewish cold-bathing rituals. (☎14 23 92. Open Apr.-Oct. daily 10am-5pm. €2, children €1.) Maximilianstr., Speyer's main thoroughfare, spreads westward from the Dom, culminating in the **Altpörtel**, a five-story village gate and significant remnant of the city's medieval fortifications. Climb the stairs inside for a complete view of the city. (Tower open Apr.-Oct. M-F 10am-noon and 2-4pm, Sa-Su 10am-5pm. €1, students €0.50.) From the Altpörtel, a southward jaunt on Gilgenstr. leads to the **Josefskirche** (open Apr.-Oct. M-Sa 9am-7pm, Su noon-6pm; Nov.-Mar. M-Sa 9am-5pm, Su 1:30-5pm) and, across the street, to the Gothic arches and oddly sombre stained glass of the **Gedächtniskirche**. (Open M-Sa 10am-noon and 2-6pm, Su 2-6pm.) A short walk back toward the Dom along Ludwigstr. leads to the **Skulpturengarten**, just off of Heydenreichstr. The **Technikmuseum**, Geibstr. 2, fills a gigantic warehouse with airplanes, trains, and boats (including a German U-boat from WWII), many of which visitors can climb into and explore. The museum also has an **IMAX theater** (☎67 08 50) and an "adventure-simulator." Take bus #565 to "Technikmuseum," or walk through the garden behind the Dom until you see the Technikmuseum sign. (☎670 80. Open daily 9am-6pm, Sa-Su 9am-7pm. €12, children €10; IMAX €8/6; combination ticket €16/12.)

THE GERMAN WINE ROAD

Stretching 85km through Germany's most productive grape-growing region, the *Wienstrasse* (Wine Road) runs through to vineyards and small villages. With Palatinate vineyards producing more wine than any other region in Germany, there is no alternative but many join in the slight inebriation that pervades. And if the torrent of wine from near-weekly festivals doesn't get to you, the intoxicating beauty of the Palatinate Forest, Haardt Mountains, and resplendent castles will.

NEUSTADT AN DER WEINSTRAßE ☎06321

Bordering the Palatinate forest and the Haardt mountains, Neustadt and its surrounding villages are the midpoint of the German Wine Road and the easiest to reach: trains run to Mannheim (20min., 3-4 per hr., €8.20) and Saarbrücken (2hr., 1-2 per hr., €14). From the bloom of the almond trees to the crowning of the German Wine Queen in the autumn, Neustadt lives and breathes wine in the shadow of the Palatinate Forest. The nine surrounding villages are as integral to the city's viticulture as its historic Markpl., and hourly buses run to most of them from the Hauptbahnhof. Customers who intend to buy wines at the family-owned *Weingüter* (wine-producing estates) may taste them at will; an official tasting, usually including 7-9 wines and food, will last 1-3hr. and begin at €7.

In Haardt, at **Weingut Probsthof,** Probstg. 7, the Zimmermann family takes guests on a tour of traditional German viticulture with generous tastings of wines (€3-5) from their own vineyards; they often assume intent to buy. Take bus #512 to "Haardt, Winzer," walk up the street, and turn right. If the following 10min. hike doesn't suit you, stop at any number of other *Weinstubes* (wine taverns) along the way. (☎63 15. Usually open M-Sa 8am-6pm. Cash only.) **Diedesfeld Schönhof,** Weinstr. 600, has similar tastings at its in-house restaurant. Ride bus #501 to "Diedesfeld" and walk up the street. (☎861 98; fax 868 23. Usually open daily 9am-6pm, call ahead for an English-speaking attendant and special hours. Cash only.) In town, the glass cases of **Haus des Weines,** Rathausstr. 6, hold hundreds of bottles of regional specialties, most of which are open to tasting. (☎35 58 71. Open Tu-F 10am-1pm and 2:30-6:30pm, Sa 9:30am-2pm. Cash only.)

Though the use of the site dates back to Roman times, the **Hambacher Schloß** was built in the 11th century and later flourished as a retreat for Speyer Bishops. An event of regional attention, "Hambach Festival," held by local vintners, made the *Schloß* the site of a protest for freedom and national unity led by 20,000 citizens in 1832. An hourly bus (#502) runs from the Hauptbahnhof, but the moderately sloped 30min. trail starting from the end of Waldstr. affords vistas of the Palatinate landscape. (☎96 13 28. Open Mar.-Nov. daily 10am-6pm. Last entry 5:30pm. Castle grounds free. Castle €4.50, students €1.50, families €9.50. Audio guides €3, guided tours available by prior arrangement from €45.) The **tourist office,** Hetzelpl. 1, across from the train station, sells hiking maps (€6) of the Palatine forest. (☎92 68 92; www.neustadt.pfalz.com. Open May-Oct. M-F 9:30am-6pm, Sa 10am-noon; Nov.-Apr. M-F 9:30am-5pm.) Neustadt's longe youth hostel, the **Jugendgästehaus Neustadt ❷,** Hans-Geiger-Str. 27, has sparkling two- and four-bed rooms with steep purple ladders and a café/bar and cafeteria on-site. From the train station, walk left, angling back past the post office and across the footbridge. Follow signs uphill on Alter Viehberg, turn left on Kiesstr., then head right on Hans-Geiger-Str. (☎22 89; www.djh-info.de. Breakfast included. Reception 8am-11pm. Dorms €17.50; singles €27; doubles €24. 28+ extra €5.50. MC/V.) **Bistro am Markt ❷,** left off Hauptstr. coming from the train station, across from the fountain, serves large salads (€5.80-13.90) and soups (€3.90). (Open M-Th 9am-1am, F-Sa 9am-2am, Su 10am-1am. Cash only.) Smaller cafés line the maze of alleyways spread out around Metzerg. and Kunigundenstr., as well as Kartoffelmarkt. and Julius Pl. around Marktpl. The **police station** is at Karl-Helferich-Str. 11. (☎85 40; **emergency** ☎110. Open 24hr.) **Internet** is across from the tourist office on Hauptstr. The **post office,** Bahnhofstr. 2, is next to the train station. (Open M-F 9am-6pm, Sa 9am-12:30pm.) **Postal Code:** 67434.

BAD DÜRKHEIM ☎ 06322

While Dürkheim (the *Bad*, though not as damning in German, is rarely used) is best known for its vineyards and natural thermal baths, the nearby Palatinate Forest affords energetic hikers over 12,000km of marked trails and the unspoiled beauty of an UNESCO biosphere reserve. **Römerpl.** and **Stadtpl.**, in front of the train station, form the center of the old city. To the south of Stadtpl. stands a sculpture of a phoenix, symbolizing Dürkheim's rebirth after WWII. The **Kurpark** just past Römerpl. features acres of aging sculptures and flowers. The **Salinarium**, outside the Kurpark, has a pool and sauna. (☎ 93 58 65. Open M-Tu and Th 9am-10pm, W 6:45am-10pm, F 9am-11pm, Sa 9am-8pm, Su 9am-8pm. €5, children €2.50.) Located a block away from the Kurzentrum exit of the Kurpark is the **Große Faß**, the largest wine barrel in the world. With a capacity of 1,700,000L, it eclipses even the *Faß* in Heidelberg (p. 385), though it only contains a small, but lively, café. Head across the street for wine tasting at **Weingut Fitz-Ritter**, Weinstr. Nord 51, whose garden is one of the most critically acclaimed on the German Wine Road. (☎ 53 89. Open M-F 8am-noon and 1-6pm, Sa 10am-4pm, or by appointment.) For over 570 years, Dürkheim has hosted the **Wurstmarkt**, the world's largest wine festival where locals and tourists indulge in wine halls and along the traditional *Schubkärchlers* (wheeled carts) lining the streets. (2nd and 3rd weekends in Sept.) The **Gradierbau Salina** lies near the salinarium. Here, brine springs to the surface and is pumped up and across a 330m long wall before trickling down what look like giant fish gills. The thick surrounding air tastes like the ocean and allegedly does wonders for your respiratory system. (Open mid-Apr. to Oct. M 1-6pm, Tu-Su 10am-6pm. €1.50, 10 tickets €12, or sit for free at one of the public benches nearby.) One kilometer from the town center is the **Pfalzmuseum für Naturkunde**, devoted to the earliest inhabitants of the region. (☎ 941 30. Open Tu and Th-Su 10am-5pm, W 10am-8pm. €2, students €1.30.) **Schloß Limburg**, 2km west of Römerpl. (follow the blue stripes from the cemetery), now lies in ruins, but at various times housed Celtic princes, Salian dukes, and Benedictine monks.

The **Jugendgästehaus St. Christopherus-Haus ❷**, Schillerstr. 151, is a 20min. walk uphill, but worth it. From the train station, turn left and follow Leningerstr. and continue along Schillerstr. The *Haus* is on your left. The multi-bed rooms fill quickly with school groups. (☎ 631 51; www.christophorus-haus.de. Sheets and breakfast included. Lockout 10pm, key available. Singles €20, students €17. Cash only.) **Campingpark Bad Dürkheim ❶**, In den Almen 3, is next to a lake. Take bus 488 from the Hauptbahnhof. (Every hr. ☎ 613 56; fax 81 61. Reception open daily 8am-1pm and 3-10pm. €5 per person, €9 per site. Electricity €2. Cash only.)

The **tourist office** is at Kurbrunnenstr. 14. Cross the plaza in front of the train station and continue onto Kurgartenstr. Go through the park, turn right, and watch for "Kurzentrum." They book rooms and massages for free, and sell hiking maps for €6-8. (☎ 956 62 50; www.bad-duerkheim.de. Open M-F 9am-7pm, Sa-Su 11am-3pm.) The **police station** is on Weinstr. Süd. (☎ 96 30; **emergency** ☎ 110. Open 24hr.) The **post office** is across from the station at Mannheimerstr. 11a. (Open M-F 8am-6:30pm, Sa 8am-1pm.) **Postal Code:** 67098.

BADEN-WÜRTTEMBERG

Once upon a time, the states of Baden, Württemberg-Hohenzollern, and Württemberg-Baden were all independent. When the Federal Republic was founded in 1951, the Allies combined the states into Baden-Württemberg. However, the Badeners and the Swabians (never "Württembergers") still proudly proclaim their distinct regional identities. Today, two powerful German stereotypes—the brooding romantic of the Brothers Grimm and the modern *homo economicus* exemplified by Mercedes-Benz—battle it out in Baden-Württemberg. Pretzels, cuckoo clocks, and cars were all pioneered here, and the region is as diverse as its exports. Rural customs live on in the bucolic hinterlands of the Schwarzwald (Black Forest) and the Schwäbische Alb, while the modern capital city of Stuttgart celebrates the ascendancy of the German industrial machine. The province also plays home to the ritzy resort of Baden-Baden, the Bodensee (Lake Constance—Germany's Riviera), and the historic university towns of Freiburg, Tübingen, and Heidelberg, each with its own distinctive youthful flair.

HIGHLIGHTS OF BADEN-WÜRTTEMBERG

SPOT THE ALPS or roam among the manicured gardens of **Mainau,** on the **Bodensee** (p. 419), tropical for Germany, with wind-swept beaches and turquoise waters.

HIKE through thick stretches of spruce forest in the **Schwarzwald** (p. 412); its towering mountains and serene lakes extend from **Freiburg** (p. 404) to **Baden-Baden** (p. 402).

SOAP UP in the indulgent mineral baths and lush **Schloßgarten** of **Stuttgart** (p. 373), sleek corporate home of Mercedes and Porsche.

SCRAMBLE OVER CASTLE RUINS with local brew in hand at **Heidelberg's** (p. 381) crumbling **Schloß.**

PUNT along the lazy Neckar in **Tübingen** (p. 390), a world-renowned university town.

STUTTGART
☎0711

It would be a mistake to take the sleek modern buildings and speeding sportcars of Stuttgart (pop. 591,000) at face value: Porsche, Daimler-Benz, and a slew of other corporate powerhouses keep the city rich, fast-paced, and sparkling, but the main thoroughfares and shopping streets are never too far from manicured gardens and ornate fountains. The city's famous mineral baths draw old and young to its healing waters, and the castles of Ludwigsburg and bucolic calm of forest and vineyards are just a short train ride away.

⊏ TRANSPORTATION

Flights: Flughafen Stuttgart (☎01805 94 84 44; flight information 948 33 88). Take S2 or S3 (30min., €2.90).

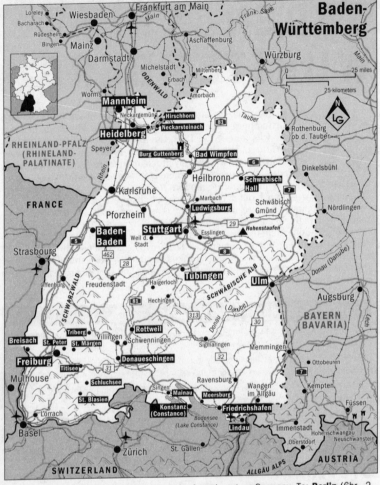

Trains: Stuttgart is the transportation hub of southwestern Germany. To: **Berlin** (6hr., 2 per hr., €112); **Frankfurt** (1-2hr., 2 per hr., €34-49); **Munich** (2½-3½hr., 2 per hr., €31-46). International Service to: **Basel, Switzerland** (3½hr., 2-4 per hr., €48-60); **Paris, France** (8hr., 4 per day, €82-97).

Ferries: Neckar-Personen-Schifffahrt (☎54 99 70 60; www.neckar-kaeptn.de). Boats leave the Bad Cannstatt dock by Wilhelma Zoo. Take U14 (dir.: Remseck) to "Wilhelma." Ships cruise the Neckar 5-6 times daily Easter-Oct. €7-20.

Public Transportation: Single ride from €1. A 4-ride *Mehrfahrkarte* is €6.30-22.40; a *Tageskarte*, valid 24hr. on all trains and buses, is €5.10-10.50. A **3-day tourist pass** (€8.50-14) is available at the tourist office and most hotels.

Car Rental: Offices in the station at track 16 for: **Avis** (☎223 72 58; fax 229 15 26); **Hertz** (☎226 29 21; fax 226 27 10); **Sixt/Budget** (☎223 78 22; fax 223 78 24). At least 1 office open M-F 7am-9pm, Sa 7:30am-9pm, Su 7:30am-9pm.

Bike Rental: Rent a Bike, Kronenstr. 17 (☎209 90), in Hotel Unger. €9.50 per 6hr., €13 per day; students €6/8. Bikes can go on the U- and S-Bahn for the price of a children's ticket except M-F 6-8:30am and 4-6:30pm; never on buses.

Ride Share: Mitfahrzentrale Stuttgart West, Lerchenstr. 65 (☎636 80 36 and 194 48). Bus #42 to "Rosenberg/Johannesstr." Open M-F 9am-6pm, Sa 10am-1pm.

⚑🛈 ORIENTATION AND PRACTICAL INFORMATION

The heart of Stuttgart is an enormous pedestrian zone cluttered with shops and restaurants. **Königstr.** and the smaller **Calwerstr.** are the main pedestrian thoroughfares; from the train station, Königstr., along with a host of other streets and squares, is accessible by the underground **Arnulf-Klett-Passage.** Calwerstr. picks up steam after the Schloßpl. To the left sprawls the tranquil **Schloßgarten,** to the right the thriving business sector, including **Rotebühlplatz,** two blocks right from the end of Königstr. The **Stuttcard** (€17.50, without transportation €12) offers three days of city transportation, admission to most museums, and discounts for guided tours, theaters, mineral baths, the zoo, and other sights.

Tourist Offices: I-Punkt, Königstr. 1A (☎222 80; www.stuttgart-tourist.de), in front of the escalator in the Klett-Passage. Daily tours of the city in German or English (11am-12:30pm; €6). Contains an **ATM.** Open Apr.-Oct. M-F 9am-8pm, Sa 9am-6pm, Su 11am-6pm, Nov.-Mar. daily 1-6pm. **Tips 'n' trips,** Lautenschlagerstr. 22 (☎222 27 30; www.tips-n-trips.de), hands out youth-oriented pamphlets on the hottest clubs, affordable lodgings, and popular cafés. Affable staff. Open M-F noon-7pm, Sa 10am-2pm.

American Express: Arnulf-Klett-Pl. 1 (☎226 92 67; fax 223 95 44). Cashes checks. Open M-F 9:30am-noon and 1-6pm, Sa 10am-1pm.

Gay and Lesbian Resources: Weißenburg, Weißenburgstr. 28a (☎640 44 94; www.zentrum-weissenburg.de). Café open M-F 7-10pm, Su 3-10pm.

Women's Resources: Fraueninformationzentrum (FiZ), Landhausstr. 62 (☎26 18 91; fax 28 26 74). Open M and W-Th 9am-1pm.

Bookstore: Erlkönig, Nesenbachstr. 52 (☎63 91 39), named for the famous Goethe poem. Open M-F 10am-8pm, Sa 10am-4pm.

Laundromat: Lavo'Magic, Katherinenstr. 21d (☎259 98 48). U-Bahn to "Rathaus." Wash €3.50. Dry €0.50 per 10min. Open M-F 9am-8pm, Sa 9am-10pm.

Emergency: ☎110. **Police,** Hauptstätterstr. 34 (☎89 90 31 00). **Fire** ☎112.

Pharmacy: Bahnhof, Königstr. 4 (☎29 02 14). Open M-F 8am-8pm, Sa 9am-8pm.

Hospital: Katharinehospital, (☎27 80) Kriegsbergerstr. 60, near the train station.

Internet Access: Call Shop, Charlottensstr. 17. €1.50 per hr. Open daily 10am-8pm.

Post Office: Inside the train station, Arnulf-Klett-Pl. 2. Open M-F 8:30am-6pm, Sa 8:30am-12:30pm. The **branch** at Bolzstr. 3 does not hold mail. Open M-F 8am-7pm, Sa 9am-2pm. **Postal Code:** 70173.

🏠🏕 ACCOMMODATIONS AND CAMPING

Hotels around the pedestrian zone and train station cater to customers paying top euro—call ahead for better deals. Most of Stuttgart's budget beds are on the two ridges surrounding the downtown area and are accessible by tram. **Tips 'n' trips** (see **Tourist Offices,** p. 375) can help you find cheap accommodations. In general, the best deals are to be found in Stuttgart's suburbs, easily reached by the S-Bahn: try the **hostel** in Ludwigsburg, Gemsenbergstr. 21 (☎07141 515 64; dorms €17.40-20.10 for first night, €14.30-17 thereafter), or Haus Birkach in Birkach. (☎0711 45 80 40; www.hausbirkach.de. Singles €32; doubles €60.)

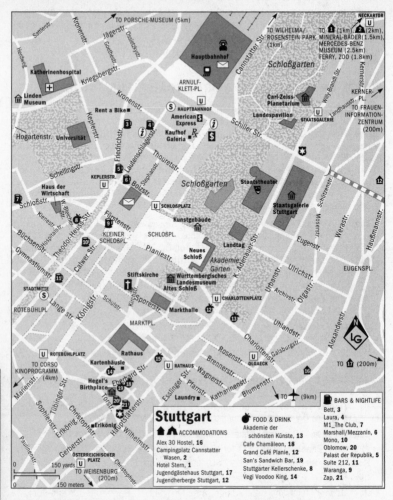

Stuttgart

▲▲ **ACCOMMODATIONS**

Alex 30 Hostel, **16**
Campingplatz Cannstatter
  Wasen, **2**
Hotel Stern, **1**
Jugendgästehaus Stuttgart, **17**
Jugendherberge Stuttgart, **12**

🍎 **FOOD & DRINK**

Akademie der
  schönsten Künste, **13**
Cafe Chamäleon, **18**
Grand Café Planie, **12**
San's Sandwich Bar, **19**
Stuttgarter Kellerschenke, **8**
Vegi Voodoo King, **14**

🍸 **BARS & NIGHTLIFE**

Bett, **3**
Laura, **4**
M1_The Club, **7**
Marshall/Mezzanin, **6**
Mono, **10**
Oblomow, **20**
Palast der Republik, **5**
Suite 212, **11**
Waranga, **9**
Zap, **21**

▓ **Alex 30**, Alexanderstr. 30 (☎ 838 89 50; www.alex30-hostel.de). Tram #15 (dir.: Ruhbank) to "Eugenspl." 5min from the Schloßpl. An international clientele crashes in bright, hip rooms with funky walls at the top of a fickle staircase. Breakfast €6. Sheets €3. 3- to 5-bed dorms €19; singles €020-29; doubles €50. MC/V. ❷

Jugendgästehaus Stuttgart (IB), Richard-Wagner-Str. 2 (☎ 24 11 32; jgh-stuttgart@internationaler-bund.de). Tram #15 (dir.: Ruhbank) or night bus #N8 to "Bubenbad." Take the next right; the hostel is on the right. Comfortable rooms with views of the city fill quickly with an international crowd. Breakfast and sheets included. Dinner M-Th €7. Laundry facilities. Key deposit €10. Reception 24hr. Dorms €17.85; singles €21; doubles €18.50 per person. Bath €5. 1-night stays add €2.50. AmEx/MC/V. ❷

Jugendherberge Stuttgart (HI), Haußmannstr. 27 (☎ 664 74 70; www.jugendherberge-stuttgart.de). Take tram #15 (dir.: Ruhbank) to "Eugenspl." Walk uphill and take a left at the sign. The entrance is through the glass tower, attached by a bridge to the hillside; take the elevator down to the 5th fl. A lively mix of nationalities shack up in 4- or 6-bed rooms, most with city views. Reserve more than a week ahead by email, otherwise by phone. Internet access €0.50 per 5min. Breakfast and sheets included. Locks €5. Reception 24hr. Use night bell at back door 1-5am. 1st night dorms €23.30, under 27 €20.30; additional nights €19.40/17.40. Cash only. ❷

Hotel Stern, Neckarstr. 215a (☎269 69 41; sternhotel@gmx.de), is 5min. from the station and city center. U1 or U14, or tram #2 to "Metzstr." Close to the mineral baths, with tastefully outfitted rooms and a friendly Italian staff. Breakfast and TV included. Singles €35-50; doubles €58; triples €68. AmEx/MC/V. ❸

Campingplatz Cannstatter Wasen, Mercedesstr. 40 (☎55 66 96; www.campingplatz-stuttgart.de), in Bad Cannstatt. S1 (dir.: Daimler-Stadion). Turn back and follow Mercedesstr. to the tree oasis across from the parking lot. Reception daily Apr.-Oct. 7am-noon and 2-10pm; Nov.-Mar. 8-10am and 5-7pm. Wash €4.50. Dry €2.80. Shower €2. €5 per person, €2.20 per child, €2.20 per car, €3.10-6.50 per campsite. MC/V. ❶

FOOD

Stuttgart's Swabian cuisine is some of the best in Germany. *Spätzle* (thick egg noodles) and *Maultaschen* (pasta pockets filled with meat and spinach) are two delicious regional specialties. Reasonably priced restaurants lie along the pedestrian zone between **Pfarrstr.** and **Charlottenstr.**, while **Rotebühlpl.** and **Kronenstr.** has more *Imbiße* (snack bars). A more alternative and stylish—but still inexpensive—brand of *Imbiße* (serving fresh made sandwiches and vegetarian wraps) can be found in the **Eberhardstr.** area near Hegel's birthplace. The basement of the **Kaufhof Galeria** at Königstr. 6 has a **supermarket** (open M-F 9:30am-8pm, Sa 9am-8pm).

Stuttgarter Kellerschenke, Theodor-Heuss-Str. 2a (☎29 44 45; fax 223 72 49), under the Gewerkschaftshaus. Vines wind over lightly colored rafters, while backlit windows lend a gentle glow to the neat tables. Swabian specialties from €5.50. Daily specials are a good deal at €5.20-11.50. Open M-F 10am-11pm. Cash only. MC/V. ❸

Grand Café Planie, Charlottenpl. 17 (☎29 25 53), serves up large German breakfasts (€3.60-11.70) a block from the Schloßpl. The wicker chairs in the large patio fill with group conversations from morning to night. Open daily 7am-10pm. ❸

San's Sandwich Bar, Eberhardstr. 47 (☎236 57 60). Fresh sandwiches with plenty of veggie options (€2.70-3.50), along with a mix of yogurt (€1.80) and drinks. Home-made brownies are delicious. Open M-F 8:30am-10pm, Sa 10am-7pm. Cash only. ❷

Akademie der schönsten Künste, Charlottenstr. 5 (☎24 24 36). U-Bahn to "Charlottenpl." High ceilings, art-decked walls, and a shaded garden draw visitors of all ages to this restaurant-bar. Entrées €1.50-7.50. Open M-Th 6am-midnight, F 6am-1am, Sa 9am-1am, Su 9am-6pm. Kitchen closes 10pm. Cash only. ❸

Café Chamäleon, Eberhardstr. 35 (☎96 01 210). Popular café sells baked goods, coffee, and a small selection of appetizing dishes (€3.20-7.50). Lunch menu €4.81, vegetarian €2.81. Open M-F 6:15am-8pm, Sa 6:15am-6pm, Su 10am-6pm. Cash only. ❷

Vegi Voodoo World, Steinstr., serves up veggie wraps in a semi-psychedelic, *Imbiß*-style eatery. A popular student lair. Open M-W 11:30am-12:30am, Th 11:30am-2am, F 11:30am-4am, Su 1pm-12:30am. Cash only. ❷

SIGHTS

MINERALBÄDER (MINERAL BATHS). Stuttgart boasts amazing mineral baths, formed from Western Europe's most active mineral springs. The 22 million liters of spring water pumped out every day are said to have curative powers. All the baths offer a spectacular array of pools, saunas, and showers. Loll in the **Mineralbad Leuze,** an official healthcare facility. *(Am Leuzebad 2-6. U1 or tram #2 to "Mineralbäder." Past the volcano-like geyser-fountains.* ☎ *216 42 10. Open daily 6am-9pm. Day card €14, students €10. 2hr. soak €5.50, ages 3-18 €3.80; 4hr. €7/5.40.)* **Mineralbad Berg** is less expensive and less luxurious. *(Am Schwanenpl. 9. U1 or U14 or tram #2 to "Mineralbäder."* ☎ *923 65 16. Open M-F 6am-8pm, Sa 6am-7pm, Su 6am-1pm. Day card €6, under 16 €5. Last entry in both baths 1hr. before closing.)*

SCHLOßGARTEN. Almost 20% of Stuttgart is under a land preservation order, resulting in something known as "the green U," crowned by the **Schloßgarten,** Stuttgart's principal municipal park. Running from the station south to the Neues Schloß and northeast to the Neckar, the Schloßgarten is crammed with fountains and flowers. The huge **Rosensteinpark,** at the north end of the Schloßgarten, holds the **Wilhelma,** a zoological and botanical garden containing 9000 species of animals and plants. *(Take U14 (dir.: Remseck) to "Wilhelma."* ☎ *540 20. Open daily 8:15am-dusk. €10.20, after 4pm and Nov.-Feb. €7; ages 6-17 €5.10/3.50. German guidebooks €3.30.)*

SCHLOßPLATZ. The Schloßgarten runs to Schloßpl., off Königstr., to the elegant Baroque **Neues Schloß,** where the mythological figures guard the stodgy bureaucrats working inside. The 16th-century **Altes Schloß,** across the street on Schillerpl., offers a graceful, colonnaded Renaissance courtyard, where local professional and amateur orchestras often perform free of charge. The **Württembergisches Landesmuseum** (p. 379) is inside.

CARL ZEISS PLANETARIUM. Stuttgarters stargaze at the city's Planetarium, named after one of the most famous telescope manufacturers in the entire galaxy. Enjoy shows with German voiceovers, visual effects, and spacey background music. *(Willy-Brandt-Str. 25. U1, U4, U9, or U14 or tram #2 to "Staatsgalerie."* ☎ *162 92 15. Shows Tu and Th 10am and 3pm; W and F 10am, 3, and 8pm; Sa-Su 2, 4, and 6pm. €5, students €3.)*

HEGEL'S BIRTHPLACE. The first and second floors of this unassuming house provide historical context for, and trace the evolution of, the work of this "European phenomenon." *(Eberhardstr. 53, a couple blocks east from the end of Königstr. Take S1-6, U14, or tram #2 or 4 to "Rotebühlpl. (Stadtmitte)."* ☎ *216 67 33. Exhibit in German, brochures in English. Open M-W and F 10am-5:30pm, Th 10am-6:30pm, Sa 10am-4pm. Free.)*

🏛 MUSEUMS

▨ STAATSGALERIE STUTTGART (NATIONAL GALLERY). A superb collection in two wings: the stately paintings in the **old wing** date from the Middle Ages to the 19th century, while the **new wing** contains a first-rate collection of moderns including Picasso, Kandinsky, and Dalí. *(Konrad-Adenauer-Str. 30-32.* ☎ *47 04 00; www.staatsgalerie.de. Open Tu-W and F-Su 10am-8pm, Th 10am-9pm; 1st Sa of the month 10am-midnight. Tours €3, students €1.50. Museum €8/6, ages 13-20 €2, under 13 free. Permanent exhibits free W. Audio guide €4, students €3, with €10 deposit.)*

▨ MERCEDES-BENZ MUSEUM. Visitors are led on a comprehensive journey through automotive history in this sleek museum. A century's worth of gleaming automobiles—from Gottlieb Daimler's and Karl Benz's first experiments to the showy prototypes of tomorrow—will make even the most lukewarm car-enthusiast drool. *(Mercedesstr. 100. S1 (dir.: Plochingen) to "Gottlieb-Daimler-Stadion." Continue on Mercedesstr. and look for signs.* ☎ *173 00 00; www.mercedes-benz.com/museum. Open Tu-Su 9am-6pm, ticket counter closes at 5pm. €8, students €4, under 15 free. Factory tour free.)*

LINDENMUSEUM STUTTGART (LINDEN TREE MUSEUM). This museum features arts and crafts collections from America, the South Seas, Africa, and Asia, and friendly personnel with intimate knowledge of every exhibit. The rapidly rotating exhibitions—ranging from Aboriginal art to Japanese calligraphy and flower arrangements—are of special note. *(Hegelpl. 1. 10min. west of the train station on Kriegsbergstr. Bus #40, 42, or 43, or U14 to "Hegelpl." ☎202 23; www.lindenmuseum.de. Open Tu and Th-Su 10am-5pm, W 10am-8pm. €3, students €2. W after 5pm free, except special exhibits.)*

WÜRTTEMBERGISCHES LANDESMUSEUM. Located in the Altes Schloß, this museum details the culture of the Swabian region and people, with an emphasis on local archaeology. Excellent exhibits on Bronze Age Celtic metalwork, along with well-worn weaponry and crown jewels. The ticket also allows entry to a collection of musical instruments located at Schillerpl. 1. *(Schillerpl. 6. ☎279 34 98; www.landesmuseum-stuttgart.de. Open Tu-Su 10am-5pm. €3, students €2, under 14 free.)*

KUNSTGEBÄUDE (ART BUILDING). Houses the **Württembergischer Kunstverein's** temporary exhibits. The gallery features contemporary art in a variety of media, from digitized presentations and reader-response writeups to photographic concept art. *(Schloßpl. 2, across from Altes Schloß. Both museums open Tu and Th-Su 11am-6pm, W 11am-8pm. Special exhibits €3-8, students €2-4. Obligatory cloak room €0.50.)*

PORSCHEMUSEUM. Even though it's a glorified showroom, Porsche fans will enjoy gawking at this conglomeration of sexy curves. For a factory tour, call well in advance. *(Porschestr. 42, in Stuttgart-Zuffauhausen. S6 (dir.: Weil der Stadt/Leonberg) to "Neuwirtshaus (Porschepl.)"; exit the station to the right; cross the intersection and take a left on Moritz-Horkheimer-Str. ☎911 56 85. Open M-F 9am-4pm, Sa-Su 9am-5pm. Free.)*

🎵 🎭 ENTERTAINMENT AND NIGHTLIFE

The **Staatstheater,** across the plaza from the Neues Schloß, is Stuttgart's most famous theater, with operas, ballets, plays, and concerts. (Reservations ☎20 20 90; www.staatstheater-stuttgart.de. Box office open M-F 10am-6pm, Sa 10am-2pm, and 1hr. before performances. Tickets €8-155; student tickets €8-12.) **Corso Kinoprogramm,** Hauptstr. 6 in Vaihingen (☎73 49 16; www.corso-kino.de; U1, U3, U6, or U8 to "Schillerpl."), shows undubbed films.

The **Stuttgarter Weindorf** (Wine Village) is the largest wine festival in Germany. From late August to early September, wine lovers descend upon Schillerpl., Marktpl., and Kirchstr. to sample Swabian specialties and 350 kinds of wine. Beer gets two weeks in the spotlight during the 160-year-old **Cannstatter Volksfest,** a fair on the Cannstatter Wasen (last week of Sept. and first week of Oct.). The **Christopher Street Day** (☎0179 464 46 94) gay and lesbian festival occurs the last week in July.

Stuttgart's nightlife runs the gamut from calm lounges to techno-filled clubs. The somewhat pricey sit-down cafés along **Königstr.** and **Calwerstr.** are packed in the early evening, while the real nightlife follows a chic, Benz-driving crowd to the innumerable sidewalk lounges on **Theodor-Heuss-Str.** The club scene doesn't pick up until after midnight, but when it does, **Theodor-Heuss-Str., Rotebühlpl.,** and **Eberhardstr.** are the most popular areas. **Tips 'n' trips** (see **Tourist Offices,** p. 375) publishes comprehensive guides to the evening scene in German and English. For more on current events, see the monthly *Lift* (www.lift-online.de), also available at Tips 'n' trips. For gay nightlife, check *Schwulst* (www.schwulst.de).

Suite 212, Theodor-Heuss-Str. 15 (☎253 61 13; www.suite212.org). The streets and couches in front of this simple bar-lounge are packed with beer-guzzling and martini-sipping hipsters on weekends, while a quieter crowd frequents the street chairs by day. Soothing yet disconcertingly addicting soundless art-films play above the bar. DJ and video-mixing on weekends. Beer €2.50-3, mixed drinks €6.50-8. Open M-W 11am-2am, Th 11am-3am, F-Sa 11am-5am, Su 2pm-2am. Cash only.

Bett, Friedrichstr. 23a (☎284 16 67). Jungle-deco walls surround the 20-something and younger crowd filling the dance floor of this bar/club late into the night. The canopied beds out back are crowded with perennial late-night loungers. Bar area open daily 3pm-1am, while the club pulses with house and hip-hop F-Sa 11pm-late. Cash only.

Oblomow, Torstr. 20 (☎236 79 24). The pounding bass and occasional live DJs play to more seated guests than hardcore dancers, but the atmosphere is lively and convivial nonetheless. Snacks €3-6 (served 3pm-4am); drinks €3-8. Live DJs 11pm Sa. Open daily 3pm-7am, or until the last straggler leaves. Cash only.

Zap, Hauptstätter Str. 40 (☎23 52 27; www.club-zap.de), entrance from the back in Josef-Hirn-Pl. Marble-heavy club houses a glittering dance floor, packed late into the night. W Happy hour 9-11pm. Th Live music. Cover Th €8, students €6; W 21+ €4. Sa hip-hop night. Open W 9pm-3am, Th 9pm-2am, F 11pm-5am, Sa 10pm-6am. MC/V.

M1_The Club, Seidenstr. 20 (☎284 79 40; www.m1-theclub.com), downstairs across from the HL Markt, in middle of the Bosch Areal complex. Take U2, U4, U9, or U14 to "Berliner Pl.," continue to the intersection, then turn right and follow the noise through the commercial passageway. Bubbling accents and 2 fl. of house, techno, and hip-hop. Beer €3.50. Cover €10. Open Th-Sa from 9pm. MC/V.

Palast der Republik, Friedrichstr. 27 (☎226 48 87). Circular wooden pavilion blasts music for the after-hours aficionados who congregate on the sidewalk with alarming density. Beer €2-3. Open M-Tu 11am-2am, Th-Sa 11am-3am, Su 2pm-1am. Cash only.

Waranga, Kleiner Schloßpl. 13-15 (☎99 79 92 66; www.waranga.de), overlooks the Schloßpl. Grab a beer and sit on the famous steps down to Königstr. Open weekdays 11am-1am, weekends until 3am. MC/V.

▶ DAYTRIPS FROM STUTTGART

LUDWIGSBURG
From Stuttgart, take S4 (dir.: Marbach) or S5 (dir.: Bietigheim; 20min., 4 per hr., €2.90) to "Ludwigsburg."

This town sprang up in the early 18th century, when Duke Eberhard Ludwig of Württemberg decided that what he needed more than anything else was a residential castle in the duchy's new capital. Though Eberhard, poor dear, died before its completion, Ludwigsburg was brought to life in the middle of nowhere. A 1½hr. guided tour is the only way to see the curiosities inside the opulent Baroque **Residenzschloß,** including Ludwig's 3m-long bed and the rest of the lavish gold, marble, and velvet interior. From the train station, walk down the street to the right of the bank, then go right at the intersection. At the end, take a left on Schloßstr., and look for signs. (☎07141 18 64 40. Open mid-Mar. to Oct. daily 10am-6:30pm, last entry 5pm; Nov. to mid-Mar. 10am-noon and 1-4pm. German-language tours in summer daily every 30min.; in winter M-F 4 per day, Sa-Su 8 per day. English-language tours in summer M-Sa 1:30pm, Su 11am, 1:30, and 3:15pm. €5, students €2.50; combined ticket with gardens and Schloß Favorite €13/6.50.) The castle, often called "the Swabian Versailles," is situated in an expansive 30-hectare garden that earned the title **Blühendes Barock,** or "blooming Baroque." (☎07141 97 56 50. Open Mar.-Oct. daily 7:30am-8:30pm. €7, students €3.30.) Inside, a perennial **Märchengarten** features scenes from major fairy tales in a large park of wild vegetation. (Open daily 9am-6pm.) The **Schloß Favorite,** behind the Residenzschloß garden, is an excellent destination for a stroll or picnic. (☎07141 18 64 40. Open mid-Mar. to Oct. daily 10am-12:30pm (last entry noon) and 1:30-

5pm; Nov. to mid-Mar. 10am-12:30pm (last entry noon) and 1:30-4pm. Guided tours in German every 30min. €2.50, students €1.20.) If you're not Schloß-ed out, stop to pet the wild deer (at your own risk) as you continue through the **Favoritenpark.** (Open daily Apr.-Aug. 8am-7pm; Sept.-Oct. 9am-6pm; Nov.-Jan. 9am-4pm; Feb.-Mar. 9am-5pm. Free.) The third Ludwig palace, the Rococo **Monrepos,** is privately owned and contains a hotel. (1½hr. from entrance.)

Ludwigsburg's **tourist office,** Marktpl. 6, has free maps and guides. (☎ 07141 91 75 55. Open M-F 9am-6pm, Sa 9am-2pm.) Consult the computerized map across the street from the Bahnhof to get your bearings, then walk straight down Myluisstr.

MARBACH

To get here from Stuttgart, take S4 to its terminus (30min., 2 per hr., €3.90).

Friedrich Schiller, the famous 18th-century philosopher best known for his work ethics and aesthetics, was born amid the modest gardens and orchards of Marbach, a fact that is difficult to ignore when everything from drug stores to hair salons in this tiny town bears his name. The alleys and streets are quaint but confusing, so check out the map near the Rathaus, or pick one up for yourself at the information booth inside. Die-hard devotees visit the **Schiller-Geburtshaus,** Niklastorstr. 31, where Schiller was born in 1759. The display consists of some Schiller documents and artifacts from his family's time in the house. (☎ 175 67. Open daily 9am-5pm. €2, students €1.) To get to the stately **Schiller-Nationalmuseum,** Schillerhöhe 8-10, from the Geburtshaus, head uphill. Take a left at the top, go through the arch and take an immediate right. After the alley, head to the intersection and go right, then continue straight. It offers a detailed account of Schiller's life and work, and also looks at his Swabian contemporaries. Out front, a formidable statue of Schiller looks out over the **Schillerhöhe,** the garden complex maintained in his memory. Every Nov. 10, the town—and, most importantly, its children—surround the statue in celebration of the author's birthday. (☎ 84 80. Open M-Tu and Th-Su 10am-6pm, W 10am-8pm. Exhibits in German. €3, students €1.50.) Between the Geburtshaus and the Nationalmuseum you'll pass the **Marktpl.** and the tiny **Bürgerturm,** a guard tower from the 16th century that is now a jewelry shop. **Oberer Torturm** (Upper Gate Tower), at Marktstr. up the hill from the Geburtshaus, houses a small museum detailing the history of the "Upper City Gate" and other town fortifications. (Opne daily 11am-5pm. Free on weekdays, small fee on weekends.) Downhill, the **Rathaus,** Markstr. 23, has information on walking tours, hotels, and restaurants. (☎ 10 20; www.schillerstadt-marbach.de. Open M 7:30am-noon, 1:15-6pm; Tu-Th 7:30am-noon, 1:15-4:30pm; F 7:30am-12:30pm.)

HEIDELBERG   ☎ 06221

Over the years, this sun-drenched town on the Neckar and its crumbling *Schloß* have called to scores of writers and artists: Mark Twain, Wolfgang von Goethe, Friedrich Hölderlin, Victor Hugo, and Robert Schumann, to name a few. During the summer, roughly 32,000 tourists answer the call every day. Even in the off season, legions of camera-toting fannypackers swell Hauptstr., where postcards and t-shirts sell like hotcakes and every sign is posted in four languages. The incessant buzz of tourism, however, does little to detract from Heidelberg's beautiful hillside setting, bustling waterfront, and unique and legendary nightlife centered on student-packed, pub-lined streets, and gritty clubs. In many ways, Heidelberg (pop. 142,000) epitomizes the paradigmatic German university town, reckoning with the crushing weight of history, the fun-loving disaffection of a student population, and the ever-evolving effort to market itself in souvenir-size to foreigners.

⌐ TRANSPORTATION

Trains: To: **Frankfurt** (50min., 2 per hr., €18-22); **Mannheim** (16-20min., 2 per. hr., €6); **Stuttgart** (40min., every hr., €21-28).

Ferries: Rhein-Neckar-Fahrgastschifffahrt (☎201 81), on the southern bank in front of the *Kongresshaus*, runs up the Neckar to Neckarsteinach and back (3hr., every 1½hr. Easter-Oct. 19 9:30am-4:50pm; €9.50, children €5.50), and all over Germany.

Public Transportation: Single **bus** ride prices vary (around €2) with destination. Day passes (€5, €8 for 2-5 people) valid on all trams and buses for 24hr. from the time stamped. Tickets purchased on Sa are valid until Su midnight.

Taxis: ☎30 20 30.

Bike Rental: Eldorado, Neckarstaden 52 (☎654 44 60; www.eldorado-hd.de). €15 per day. Open Tu-F 9am-noon and 2-6pm, Sa 10am-6pm, Su 2-6pm.

Boat Rental: Bootsverleih Simon, (☎41 19 25; www.bootsverleih-heidelberg.de). On the north shore of the Neckar by Theodor-Heuss-Brücke. 3-person boat €6 per 30min. Open daily 11am-dusk.

Hitchhiking: *Let's Go* does not recommend hitchhiking as a safe mode of transportation; those who do hitch reportedly wait at the western end of Bergheimer Str.

■ ⟨? ORIENTATION AND PRACTICAL INFORMATION

About 20km east of the Neckar's confluence with the Rhein, Heidelberg stretches along the river for several kilometers, with almost all of the city's attractions in the eastern quarter. To get to the Altstadt from the Hauptbahnhof, take any bus or tram to "Bismarckpl.," where **Hauptstraße** leads into the city's heart. Heidelberg has a huge population of fierce bicyclists—stay out of the red bike lanes. A **Heidelberg Card,** which includes use of public transit and admission to most sights, is available at the tourist office (2-day card €14, families €26; 4-day card €21).

Tourist Office: (☎13 881 21; www.cvb-heidelberg.de), in front of the station. Books rooms for €3 plus a small deposit, and sells maps (€1) and hotel/sights information pamphlets (€1). Pick up a copy of the magazines *Meier* (€1) or *Heidelberg Aktuell* (€1) to see what's up. Open Apr.-Oct. M-Sa 9am-7pm, Su 10am-6pm; Nov.-Mar. M-Sa 9am-6pm. Additional offices in the **Rathaus** (open M-Sa 11am-5pm, Su 1-5pm) and at **Neckarmünzpl.** (☎137 40). Open daily June-Sept. 9am-6pm; Oct.-May 10am-4pm.

Currency Exchange: Sparkassen on Universitätspl. and Bismarckpl. Open M-F 7:30am-8pm, Sa 9am-5pm, Su 9am-1pm. There's also a **Reise Bank** in the Hauptbahnhof.

English-Language Bookstores: Piccadilly English Shop, Kurfürstenlage 62 (☎16 77 72), through the Kurfürsten-Passage across from the Hauptbahnhof. Small selection including bestsellers and books on tape. Open M-F 10am-7pm, Sa 10am-6pm.

Women's Resources: Emergency hotline ☎582 54.

Laundry: 2 blocks down Kettelg. from Hauptstr. Open M-Tu and Th-F 10am-1pm and 2-6pm, W noon-2pm and 3-6pm, Sa 10am-3pm. €8.50 per load.

Emergency: ☎110. **Fire** and **Ambulance** ☎112.

Police: Römerstr. 2-4 (☎99 17 00).

AIDS Hotline: ☎194 11.

Internet Access: Star Coffee, Hauptstr. 129, has free wireless Internet with any purchase (drinks from €2). Open M-F 8am-9pm, Sa 9am-9pm, Su 11am-8pm. **Internet City,** Ketteng. 8, has Internet access for €1 per hr. Open daily 9am-11pm.

Post Office: Sofienstr. 8-10. Open M-F 9:30am-6pm, Sa 9:30am-1pm. **Postal Code:** 69115.

Heidelberg

ACCOMMODATIONS
Camping Haide, **17**
Camping Heidelberg-Schlierbach, **16**
Jugendherberge (HI), **1**
Hotel Garniam Kornmarkt, **24**
Hotel Kranich, **4**
Merlin, **5**
Hotel-Pension Berger, **8**
Hotel-Pension Elite, **6**
Pension Jeske, **23**

FOOD & DRINK
Cafe Del Caffe, **18**
Cedars, **14**
Hemingway's, **9**
Goldener Anker, **11**
Mensa, **13**
Persepolis, **26**
Sylvie, **20**

BARS & NIGHTLIFE
Alex Bar, **22**
Cave 54, **25**
Destille, **21**
Havana Club, **12**
Nachtschicht, **3**
O'Reilly's, **7**
Schwimmbad Musikclub, **2**
Star Coffee, **15**
VaterRhein, **10**
Vetter, **19**

BADEN-WÜRTTEMBERG

🔣🔣 ACCOMMODATIONS AND CAMPING

In summer, save yourself a major headache by arriving early in the day or calling ahead. If you're out of options, consider basing out of a nearby town; the pensions at Hirschhorn (p. 388) are particularly rewarding. 🔲**Haus La Belle** ❸, Hauptstr. 38, is aptly named: Frau Schernthaner's two rooms are bright and spacious, with soft bedcovers, wood floors, and tall, white-curtained windows overlooking the crooked street one story beneath. (☎14 00. Breakfast included. Singles €30; doubles €60. Cash only.) There are **youth hostels** ❷ in **Neckargemünd**. (20-30min. away. ☎06223 21 33. Breakfast included. Dorms €17; singles €24.50; doubles €39. MC/V.) Also, try **Zwingenberg** ❷, 45min. away on the edge of the Odenwald forest. (☎06251 759 38. Breakfast included. Dorms €16, singles €17.)

🔲 **Pension Jeske,** Mittelbadg. 2 (☎237 33; www.pension-jeske-heidelberg.de). From the Hauptbahnhof, bus #33 (dir.: Ziegelhausen) or #11 (dir.: Karlstor) to "Rathaus/Kornmarkt." The bedstands and closets of each room were individually handpainted with traditional German ornamentation by the late Frau Jeske. The cheapest, friendliest, and best located lodgings in town. Reserve far in advance. Reception 11am-1pm and 5-7pm. Doubles €40, with bath €60; triples €60/75; quints €100. Cash only. ❹

Jugendherberge (HI), Tiergartenstr. 5 (☎65 11 90; www.jugendherberge-heidelberg.de). From Bismarckpl. or the Hauptbahnhof, bus #33 (dir.: Zoo-Sportzentrum) to "Jugendherberge." This neighbor to the Heidelberg Zoo also teems with wildlife in the form of schoolchildren. Small pub serves beer and snacks 6pm-midnight. Partial wheelchair access. Breakfast included. Locker deposit €2. Required key deposit €10. Reception until 2am. Check-out 10am. Reserve at least 1wk. ahead. Dorms €20.30, over 27 €23.30; singles or doubles add €5 per person. MC/V. ❷

Hotel Kranich, Kranichweg 37a (75 63 14; www.hotel-kranich-heidelberg.de), offers reasonably priced rooms close to the town center. From the Hauptbahnhof, take tram #1 or 4 (dir.: Betriebshof), get off at the 1st stop, and take tram #2 (dir. Eppelheim) to "Kranichweg." Walk the rest of the way, or take bus #26 to "Heimgarten." Breakfast €5. Singles €35-45; doubles €50-65; triples and quads from €65. MC/V. ❹

Hotel-Pension Berger, Erwin-Rohde-Str. 8 (☎40 16 08), is outside of town, but the friendly staff and peaceful garden and swimming pool out back are worth the bus ride (#12 to "Mönchhofstr."). Singles €40-75; doubles €75-95. Cash only. ❹

Hotel-Pension Elite, Bunsenstr. 15 (☎257 34; www.hotel-elite-heidelberg.de), 4 blocks south of Bismarckpl. Elegant rooms with bath, TV, and cheerful drapes. Complementary breakfast amid lush greenery and bright flowers. Parking €3. Singles €68; doubles €78; triples €88; quads €98. €20 per additional person. Show your *Let's Go* for a €5 discount. MC/V €3 surcharge. ❺

Hotel Garni am Kornmarkt, Kornmarkt 7 (☎243 25; www.hotelamkornmarkt.de), stands in the shadow of the *Schloß* just off the Marktpl. Most of the bright and tastefully decorated rooms overlook the gold-crowned Madonna. Take bus #33 to "Rathaus/Bergbahn." Singles €45-75; doubles €75-125; triples and quads €130-140. MC/V. ❹

Camping: Haide (☎06223 21 11; camping-haide.de), on the banks of the Neckar. Bus #35 (dir.: Neckargmünd) to "Orthopädisches Klinik," then cross the river, turn right, and walk for 20min. Bike rental €8 per day. Wash €2.60. Dry €1.60. Reception 8-11:30am and 4-8pm. Open Apr. 11-Oct. 31. €4.70 per person, €3 per tent or RV, €1 per car. Cabins €13. Showers €0.50 per 5min. Electricity €2 per night. Cash only. ❶

Camping: Heidelberg-Schlierbach (☎80 25 06; www.camping-heidelberg.de), between Ziegelhausen and Neckargemünd. Bus #35 (dir.: Neckargemünd) to "Im Grund." Café open 7am-10pm. Wash and dry €5. Bike rental €5 per day. Reception 6am-10pm. €5.50 per person, €3 per child, €2.50-6 per tent, €2 per car, €12 per caravan. Cash only. ❶

FOOD

Most of the restaurants around Hauptstr. are pricey, but the *Imbiße* (snack bars) are cheaper. Just outside the central area, historic student pubs offer good values. Grocery stores can be found in Marktpl. and on adjoining sidestreets; **Alnatura**, Bergheimer 59-63, is a health foods store. (☎61 86 34. Open daily 9am-8pm.)

Hemingway's Bar-Café-Meeting Point, Fahrtg. 1 (☎16 50 33; www.hemingways-hd.de). This patio restaurant along the Neckar is well-shaded. Lunch menu M-F 11:30am-2:30pm (from €4.10). Open M-Th and Su 9am-1am, F-Sa 9am-3am. Cash only. ❷

Syvlie, Steing. 11 (☎65 90 90), is the affordable highlight of a bustling street, near Untere Str. and the river. Italian specialties and regional salads €5.50-9.90. Grilled *paninis* €3.50. Open daily 10am-1am. Cash only. ❷

Goldener Anker, Untere Neckar 52 (☎18 42 25), near the Alte Brücke. This quaint *fachwerk* (half-timbered) house offers a traditional German lunch menu M-Sa 11:30am-2:30pm (€5.90-6.50). Dinner (€7-17) served M-Sa 6-11:30pm. AmEx/MC/V. ❷

Cedars, Hauptstr. 105 (☎18 09 09), is a popular Lebanese restaurant tucked behind a tiny entryway off Hauptstr. Vegetarian and meat-filled wraps served late into the night. Open daily 11am-midnight. Cash only. ❷

Merlin, Bergheimer Str. 85 (☎65 78 56). The tables of this calm café spill out onto an untouristed sidewalk away from the rush of Hauptstr. The sorcery-themed breakfast menu (€4-10.20) includes the Harry Potter and the Merlin (served M-F 10-11:30am, Sa-Su 10am-3pm). Lunch menu M-F 11:30am-3pm (from €5.80). Open M-Th and Su 10am-1am, F-Sa 10am-3:30am. AmEx/MC/V. ❷

Persepolis, Zwingerstr. 21 (☎16 46 46), serves up Persian food at prices impossible to find elsewhere in the Altstadt. Open M-Sa 11am-8pm. Cash only. ❷

Mensa "Zeughaus," in the stone fortress on Marstallstr. Bus #35 to "Marstallstr." €0.90 per 100g. Open M-Sa 11:30am-10pm. A popular **café** next door serves snacks and beer (€1.70). Open M-Sa 11:30am-1am. **Branch** on Grabeng. 18, across from Alte Universität. A CampusCard, needed to pay at most cafeterias, can be obtained at **Info Café International,** Grabeng. 18, for €5 deposit. The outer walls are covered with fliers for frat parties and general debauchery. Open M-Th 9am-4pm, F 9am-3pm. Cash only. ❷

◎ SIGHTS

▧**HEIDELBERGER SCHLOß.** The crown jewel of a striking city, the *Schloß* stands careful watch over the armies of tourists below. Its construction began early in the 14th century, and after 1329 it housed the Prince Electors, whose statues remain in front of the entrance. Over a period of almost four centuries, the castle's dwellers commissioned additions ranging in style from Gothic to High Renaissance. Thrice destroyed, twice by war (1622 and 1693) and once by nature (lightning in 1764), the castle became a popular subject for Romantic artists, who depicted tension between the ruins and the thriving forest. The cool, musty wine cellar houses the **Großes Faß,** the largest wine barrel ever used, holding 221,726L and topped by a dance floor; the **Kleines Faß** holds a mere 125,000L. The **Deutsches Apotheken-Museum** chronicles the history of German pharmaceutical research in caverns fitted with centuries-old glassware, scales, and medicine counters. The *Schloß* is accessible by a steep path or the **Bergbahn,** one of Germany's oldest cable cars, which runs from the "Bergbahn/Rathaus" bus stop to the castle. *(Trams depart from the parking lot next to the bus stop every 10min. Mar.-Oct. daily 9am-8pm; every 20min. Nov.-Feb. daily 9am-6pm. Take bus #11 (dir.: Karlstor) or #33 (dir.: Ziegelhausen) to "Rathaus/Bergbahn." Cable car round-trip €5. Castle ☎53 84 21. Grounds open daily 8am-6pm,* *last entry 5:30pm. Guided tours every hr. M-F 11am-4pm, Sa-Su also 10am; in English every hr. M-F 11:15am to 4:15pm, Sa-Su also 10:15am; €4, students €2. Schloß, Großes Faß, and Pharmaceutical Museum €3, students €1.50. English audio guides €3.50.)*

UNIVERSITÄT. Heidelberg is home to Germany's oldest (est. 1386) and most prestigious university. The oldest remaining buildings border the stone lion fountain of the Universitätspl. Other university buildings dot the western Altstadt. The **Museum der Universität Heidelberg** traces the university's long history; in the same building is the **Alte Aula,** Heidelberg's oldest auditorium. *(Grabeng. 1. ☎54 21 52. Open Tu-Su Apr.-Sept. 10am-6pm, Oct. 10am-4pm, and Nov.-Mar. closed Su. 10am-4pm. €2.50, students €2; also includes Studentenkarzer.)* Before 1914, students were exempt from prosecution by civil authorities; instead, naughty youths were tried and punished by the university faculty. Guilty students were jailed—most often for drunken revelry and thumbing their noses at police—in the **Studentenkarzer.** It wasn't much of a prison even in its early years, but by the late 19th-century it was little short of a madhouse: students could receive food packages from friends and family (alcohol was not forbidden), attend classes, and return to the "jail" at their leisure. By the early 1930s, not to have spent some time in the Karzer was a mark of shame. Today, the walls are covered with colorful graffiti painted by students with stove soot and contraband crayons. *(Augustinerg. 2. ☎54 35 54.)* The **Bibliothek** (Library) has a collection of medieval manuscripts. *(Plöck 107-109. ☎54 23 80. Open M-W 9am-5pm, Th 9am-6pm, Sa 9am-1pm. Free.)*

PHILOSOPHENWEG (PHILOSOPHER'S PATH). This favorite stroll of famed thinkers Goethe, Lugwig Feuerbach, and Ernst Jünger stretches along the Neckar, high on the side of the **Heiligenberg,** and offers views of the city. On top of the *Berg* are the ruins of the 9th-century **St. Michael Basilika,** the 13th-century **Stefanskloster,** and an **amphitheater** built under Hitler on the site of an ancient Celtic gathering place. *(To the west of the Karl-Theodor-Brücke, in the direction of the Theodor-Hüss-Brücke. Take tram #1 or 3 to "Tiefburg," for the longer route. Or use the steep, stone-walled footpath 10m west of the Karl-Theodor-Brücke, across from the #34 or 734 bus stop "Alte Brücke Nord.")*

KURPFÄLZISCHES MUSEUM. The museum features an extensive collection of oil paintings by local and regional artists from the 18th and 19th centuries, as well as an impressive archaeology exhibit in its bottom levels. Elsewhere in the museum you'll find well-preserved works of art by Albrecht Dürer and elaborate models of Roman soldiers on the march. *(Hauptstr. 97, near Universitätspl. ☎58 34 00. Open Tu-Su 10am-6pm. €3, students €1.80; Su €1.80/1.20.)*

KARL-THEODOR-BRÜCKE (ALTE BRÜCKE). No trip to Heidelberg would be complete without a walk along the northern bank of the Neckar. On both sides of the Karl-Theodor-Brücke, plump statues of the bridge's namesake, the prince who commissioned the bridge as a symbol of his modesty, stand guard. At night, the bridge provides a view of the illuminated *Schloß.*

MARKTPLATZ. The Altstadt centers on the Marktpl., a cobbled square where a contemplative Hercules directs water at **Hercules' Fountain.** In the 15th century, "witches" and heretics were burned at the stake here; now legions of tourists savor steak in outdoor cafés. Two of the oldest structures in Heidelberg border the square. During Louis XIV's invasion of the town, terrified inhabitants fled to the 14th-century **Heiliggeistkirche,** now used for Protestant worship. For a great view of the town and the surrounding mountains, climb the tower's 204 steps. *(Open M-Sa 11am-5pm, Su 1-5pm. Church free; tower €1.)* Opposite the church's southern face is the ornate 16th-century facade of the **Haus zum Ritter,** a local hotel and restaurant since 1705. The stately **Rathaus** stands at the far end of the square, and the Baroque Madonna statue in the adjacent Kornmarkt is a little-known gem.

🎵 ENTERTAINMENT

The first Saturdays in June and September and the second Saturday in July draw giant crowds to fireworks in front of the *Schloß*. The **Faschingsparade** (carnival) cavorts through the city on Shrove Tuesday (Feb. 20, 2007; Feb. 5, 2008). The **Handschuhsheim Fest** lures revelers the third weekend in June, while the **Schloßfestspiele Heidelberg** features a series of concerts and plays at the castle from late June to early August. (☎582 00 00 or www.heidelberger-schlossfestspiele.de for tickets.) For the last weekend in September, the **Heidelberger Herbst** brings a medieval market to the Altstadt, which later hosts the **Weihnachtsmarkt** for the month before Christmas.

🍷 NIGHTLIFE

The **Marktpl.** is the hub of the action; most nightspots fan out from here. 🌙**Untere Str.**, on the Neckar side of the Heiliggeistkirche, boasts the densest conglomeration of bars in the city. During fair weather, drunken revelers fill the narrow way until 1 or 2am. **Steing.**, off the Marktpl. to the Neckar, is a bit less rambunctious but equally lively earlier in the evening. **Hauptstr.** also harbors a fair number of higher-end venues, and a few dot the north side of the river as well.

Nachtschicht (☎43 85 50, infoline 438 55 22; www.nachtschicht.com), in Landfried-Komplex. Walk through the Kurfürstenlage-Passage opposite the Hauptbahnhof, cross the street, and walk through the parking lot past the abandoned factory. The club is on the right, in a basement space that would be spartan but for the writhing student bodies packing the dance floor. Cover €3.50; M and F students €1.50. Open M and Th-Sa 10pm-4am, W 10pm-3am. Cash only

Cave54, Krämerg. 2 (☎278 40). This jazz club's cavernous dungeon, connected to the tiny entry floor by a tight, spiraling steel staircase, fills with students during jam sessions. Cover €3. Open daily 10pm-3am, from 8:30pm during live shows. Cash only.

Destille, Unterstr. 16 (☎228 08). A tree (fake, but you'd never guess it) grows out of this forest-themed bar. Students drink themselves silly with quirky shots, including vodka with Pop Rocks (from €2). Open M-Th and Su noon-2am, F-Sa noon-3am. Cash only.

Schwimmbad Musikclub, Tiergartenstr. 13 (☎47 02 01; www.schwimmbad-musik-club.de), across the river from the Altstadt. Close to the youth hostel. 4 levels of live music, dancing, and movies attract a crowd, particularly on weekends. Club classics and house F nights. Open W-Th 8pm-3am, F-Sa 9pm-4am. Cash only.

ON THE MENU

TAP THAT

Although droves of tourists visit Germany to guzzle its renowned beer, few understand the intricacies of German *Bierkultur*. Beer is typically served by the quart (*Maß*, ask for *"Ein Maß, bitte,"*) and sometimes by the pint (*Halb-Maß*). A **Helles** is a pale, often Bavarian, lager. Those looking for a bitter, less malty beer with more alcohol order the foam-crowned **Pilsener**, and often search far and wide for the perfect head.

Similar to an English shandy, a **Radler** (bikers brew) is a 50-50 blend of *Helles* and sparkling lemonade, so named because the inventor sought to mitigate the inebriation of the crazed cyclists passing through his pub. **Weißbier** is a cloudy, strong beer made with malted wheat (*Weizen*), while **Rauchbier** acquires its distinctive smoky taste from malted barley.

Even the toasted, malty lager, **Dunkeles**, is not the strongest beer. If you're in the mood for severe inebriation, try a **Bock** (strong beer) or a **Doppelbock** (even stronger). These potent beers are often brewed by monks, as they are rich enough to sustain them through religious fasts. Piety has never looked so enticing.

There are over 1000 German breweries producing thousands more brands of German beer each year. With a liquor pool that big, you'll have more than enough opportunities to lift a glass and shout *"Prost!"*

Casa Del Caffé, Steing. 8/5 (☎299 69; www.casa-del-caffe.com), is as much a coffee-house as a bar, and is one of the few places in town that is as peaceful at night as it is in the early morning hours. Quietly conversing friends and newspapers readers overlook the alley. Open M-Th 7am-1am, F-Sa 7am-3am, Su 8am-1am. Cash only.

Vetter, Steing. 9 (☎16 58 50; www.brauhaus-vetter.de), sells liters of beer brewed in the huge copper vat adjoining the bar. Take a bottle up to the illuminated castle at night, or sip from a *stein* along the busy street (€4 for 0.5L, with €1.50 deposit, or "Pfand," for bottle/mug). Open daily 11am-1am. Cash only.

Alex Bar, Kettelg. 9, is a rowdy bar just off the Marktpl. By midnight most customers are quite boisterous; by 2am they are dancing on tables. Open daily from 11am. Cash only.

Havana Club, is a popular salsa club near the Neckar. Every Th Salsa, and Merengue with live DJs from 10pm; F-Sa typical hip-shaking music from 10pm. Cash only.

VaterRhein, Untere Neckarstr. 20-22 (☎213 71). A popular spot for late-night binge-eating (spaghetti €1.70) feeds students until 2am. Open daily 8pm-3am. Cash only.

◪ DAYTRIPS FROM HEIDELBERG

NECKARSTEINACH

Take the S-Bahn RheinNeckar, S1 or S2 to "Neckarsteinach" (20min., 2-3 per hr.).

Some 14km upstream from Heidelberg, Neckarsteinach is a small village made famous by its four castles. The castles were built during the 12th and 13th centuries by the Steinachs, feudal tenants of the Bishop of Worms. The two western-most castles stand romantically in ruins, while the two to the east have been rebuilt in the traditional style of the nobility—commoners are not allowed inside. All lie along 3km of the north bank of the Neckar, and can be reached by foot via the **Burgenweg.** From the train station, turn right on Bahnhofstr. and follow it about two blocks past the tourist office on Haupstr. to where a brick path labeled "Schloßsteige" veers up the mountain. At the top, the two renovated castles are on the right; to the left, a path leads back down to the road and then up again to the **Hinterburg.** The grassy battlements of the fortress have seen better days, but the valley view from by the unlit lookout tower are worth the rather spooky climb. The fourth castle, the Schwalbennest, is the more visible and well preserved of the two ruins; to get there from the Hinterburg, follow the path uphill to the right and watch for signs. Fireworks burst above the town on the second Saturday after Pentecost in June and on the last Saturday in July for the **Vierburgenbeleuchtung** (four-castle lighting).

To stay, visit the **tourist office** (inside Schreibwaren), Hauptstr. 15, which lists private rooms. (☎920 00; www.neckarsteinach.com. Open M-Tu and Th-F 8:30am-12:30pm and 2:30-6pm, W 8:30am-12:30pm, Sa 8:30am-1pm.)

BURG GUTTENBERG

*To reach Burg Guttenberg, take the train from Neckargemünd (**Neckar Valley,** p. 389). Get off at "Gundelsheim Neckar," head southeast on the tracks, take the 1st right, cross the bridge past the campsite, and follow the signs for 2km along the road (30min.).*

Thirty kilometers south of Hirschhorn, the well-preserved **Burg Guttenberg** towers above a museum detailing its 800-year history. (☎06266 910 20 388; www.burg-guttenberg.de. Open Apr.-Oct. daily 10am-6pm. Museum and castle €4, ages 6-16 €3.) Also within the castle walls is an **aviary** for eagles and vultures, maintained by prominent ornithologist Claus Fentzloff. Each day, Fentzloff sends eagles and vultures flying inches above the heads of the crowds to pluck chicks out of the sky, while he launches into lengthy scientific explanations in German. Get a seat by the railing to see the birds soar over the valley. (☎07063 95 06 50; www.greifenwarte.de. Apr.-Oct. 11am and 3pm; Mar. and Nov. 3pm only. €9.)

NECKARTAL (NECKAR VALLEY)

The Neckar Valley—a swath of the Oden Forest sliced by the Neckar—reaches from Heilbronn to Heidelberg. Centuries ago, a series of enterprising royals decided to build castles to "protect merchants from pirates," and reaped hefty tolls for their services. Today, their castles dot the hilltops of the Neckartal, forming part of the **Burgenstraße** (Castle Road) that stretches from Mannheim to Prague.

Two train lines connect Heidelberg and Heilbronn, with stops in the small towns along both sides of the valley. Local buses also traverse the Neckar Valley, but trains are one- and three-day passes (€8/22 for 5 people) from Heidelberg are valid for connections in the valley; check at the train station in Heidelberg for details. One of the best and most popular ways to explore the valley is by biking along the many well-maintained routes. In Hirschhorn, **Josef Riedel**, Hainbrunner Str. 6 (☎20 18), rents bikes for €6 per day. The **Rhein-Neckar Fahrgastschifffahrt** runs **boat tours** from Easter to Oct. 19 between Heidelberg, Neckargemünd, Neckarsteinach, Hirschhorn, and Eberbach.

BAD WIMPFEN   ☎07063

The medieval towers and church steeples of Bad Wimpfen (pop. 40,000) rise above the Neckar just south of Heilbronn, shading the modest fountains and winding streets of an Altstadt largely free of tourists. The steep and fickle streets of the **Altstadt** are a 5min. walk from the train station. Follow Karl-Ulrich-Str. and make a right onto Hauptstr. at the first fork, or take the steep hiking trail to the right of the station, go up the stairs at the top and follow the old wall until you find an entrance. Next to the **Roter Turm** (Red Tower; open Sa-Su 10am-5pm; free), the **Pfalzkapelle** hosts the **Kirchenhistorisches Museum** (Ecclesiastical History Museum), which exhibits artifacts from the town's monastery and churches, including two Luther Bibles. (Open mid-Apr. to mid-Oct. Sa-Su 10am-5pm. €1, students €0.70.) The principal feature of Bad Wimpen's skyline—and of the town's postcards—is the **Blauer Turm** (blue tower), Burgviertel 9. Panoramic views of the town and environs await at the top. (☎89 68. Open Apr. to mid-Oct Tu-Su 10am-6pm. €1, under 16 €0.50. Pay at the top.) The **Galerie der Stadt** (Municipal Gallery), Hauptstr. 45, features a small exhibit on contemporary artwork, while the **Reichstädtisches Museum** (Municipal Empire Museum) recounts the history of Bad Wimpfen. (☎95 03 13. Both open Easter-Oct. Tu-Su 10am-5pm; Nov.-Easter 10am-noon and 2-5pm. Gallery free. Museum €1.50, students €1. Tours 2nd Sa of month at 3pm.) The showrooms—packed with piggy paraphernalia and play-things—of the world's only **Schweine Museum** (Swine Museum), Kronengäßchen 2, have quieted down considerably ever since the once tiny Timmy, a real piglet, became too fat to haul along to the exhibits. But vegetarians and swine enthusiasts alike need not fear: Timmy is alive and well, and the museum continues to document the role of swine (a good luck symbol in Germany) with collectors' items and charms. (Beside Hauptstr. 67. ☎66 89. Open daily 10am-5pm. €2.60, students €1.30.) A **museum pass** is available to the Museum in Steinhaus, Museum in Alten Spital, Ödenburger Heimatmuseum, and Museum in der Pfalzkapelle (€3, students €2).

Contradicting Benedictine stoicism, **Gästehaus der Benediktinerabtei Grüssau ❸**, Lindenpl. 5. has large, comfortable rooms, a few with bath. From the station, turn away from town and follow the main road to Wimpfen im Tal for 15min. The monastery is on the left. Call or email at least one day ahead. (☎97 04 23; www.abtei-gruessau.de. Singles €30; doubles €54. Cash only.) **Hotel Garni Neckarblick ❹**, Erich-Sailer-Str. 48, will pick you up from the train station if you call; or, take a right from the Hauptbahnhof, follow Hauptstr. to Erich-Salier-Str., and hang a right. Walk for 15min. along the street as it curves around the hillside; the hotel is on the right. Wake up to lapping fountains, a lush green garden, and breakfast overlooking the Neckar and valley below town. Victorian accented rooms have TV and bath. They rent **bikes** for €12 per day, and will pick you up at the end of the bike tour. (☎96 16 20; www.neckarblick.de. Breakfast included. Call ahead. Singles €48; doubles €82-87; triples €98-105; special prices for stays longer then 3 days. Cash only.) **Dobel's Maultaschen ❸**, Hauptstr. 61, achieves local fame with its regional take on pasta (€3.90-8.10). (☎82 12. Open M-Sa 10am-10pm, Su 9am-10pm. Cash only.) **Gästhaus Hirsch ❸**, Hauptstr. 88, serves filling entrées with salad for €7. (☎86 88. Open M and W-Su 11am-2:30pm and 5-10pm.)

The **tourist office** in the train station finds reasonable private rooms and dispenses maps and town information with friendly efficiency. (☎972 00; www.bad-wimpfen.de. Open Nov.-Easter M-F 9am-1pm and 2-5pm; Easter-Oct. M-F 9am-6pm, Sa-Su 10am-12:30pm and 1-2:30pm.) **Postal Code:** 74206.

TÜBINGEN   ☎07071

The smiling punters packing the Neckar River along the town's edge give the first inkling of Tübingen's unique vibrancy. A town that loves its river promenades almost as much as its students, Tübingen is young and energetic, which comes as no surprise when nearly half the town's residents are affiliated with the 500-year-old *Uni*. Even the Altstadt is more students' lair than austere historic center in the city awarded the title of "highest quality of life in Germany."

◰ TRANSPORTATION

Trains and buses: Tübingen is well connected to **Stuttgart** (by bus or train, 1hr., 2 per hr., €10) and many small towns in the Schwäbische Alb.

Taxis: ☎92 05 55 and 243 01.

Bike Rental: Radlager, Lazarettg. 19-21 (☎55 16 51). €7-10 per day. Open M, W, F 9:30am-6:30pm; Tu and Th 2-6:30pm; Sa 9:30am-2:30pm; in winter Sa until 1pm.

Boat Rental: Bootsverleih Märkle, (☎315 29), on the river under the tourist office. €7.50-12.50 per hr. Open Apr.-Sept. daily 11am-dusk.

◪ PRACTICAL INFORMATION

Tourist Office: An der Neckarbrücke 1 (☎913 60; www.tuebingen-info.de), on the Neckarbrücke. From the front of the station, turn right, walk to Karlstr., turn left, and walk to the river. City maps available. **Tours** (in German) €3.50, children €1.50. Ask for a schedule. Call ahead for English tours. Open M-F 9am-7pm, Sa 9am-5pm.

Women's Resources: Frauencafé, Karlstr. 13 (☎328 62), in the magenta house 1 block from the station, has a women-only night spot on the 2nd fl. Call for hours.

Bookstores: The 400-year-old **Osianderische Buchhandlung,** Wilhelmstr. 12 (☎920 111 29; www.osiander.de), occasionally hosts English authors. Open M-W 9am-7pm, Th-F 9am-8pm, Sa 9am-6pm. **UK,** Kronenstr. 6, is just off the Marktpl. and buys and sells new and used English books. Open M-F 10am-6pm, Sa 10am-4pm.

Laundromat: Waschsalon, Mühlstr. 20 (☎36 08 41). Wash €3.80 per 6kg, €6 per 10kg. Dry €1 per 10min. Cappucino €0.90. Open M-Sa 7am-10pm.

Emergency: Police ☎110. **Fire** and **Ambulance** ☎112.

Pharmacy: Apotheke am Marktbrunnen (☎220 16) is in the Marktpl. Open M-F 8:30am-6:30pm, Sa 8:30am-1pm.

Tübingen

🏠🏠 ACCOMMODATIONS
Hotel Meteora, 2
Jugendherberge (HI), 12
Rappenberghalde, 11

🍴 FOOD & DRINK
Istanbul, 13
Die Kichererbse, 4
El Chico, 10
Krumme Brücke
  Schnitzelakademie, 5
Mensa, 1
Wurstküche, 3

🍷 BARS & NIGHTLIFE
Foyer Blaue Brücke, 14
Jazzkeller, 8
Marktschenke, 7
Schloß Café Culture
  Club, 9
Sudhaus, 15
Tangente-Night, 6

Internet Access: Mühlstr. 14. €2.50 per hr. Open M-Sa 10am-10pm, Su noon-10pm.

Post Office: Europapl. 2, 100m to the right of the station. Open M-F 8am-6:30pm, Sa 8:30am-1pm. **Postal Code:** 72072.

🏠 ACCOMMODATIONS AND CAMPING

Jugendherberge (HI), Gartenstr. 22/2 (☎230 02; www.jugendherberge-tuebingen.de). Bus #22 (dir.: Neuhaldenstr.) to "Jugendherberge." A rare hostel that fills with more prospective university students than school children, with a breakfast terrace overlooking the lively riverbanks. Breakfast included. Lockers €2 deposit. Internet access €1 per 15min., with limited wireless near reception. Reception M-Sa 7am-noon, 1-3:30pm, 4:30-7pm and 7:30pm-midnight; Su from 4pm. Curfew midnight, but key is available for a €15 deposit. Dorms 1st night €20.90, 27+ €22.30; thereafter €17.10/21.60. Singles and doubles, some with shower, add at least €5. MC/V. ❷

Hotel Meteora, Weizsäckerstr. 1 (☎227 35; www.hotel-meteora.de). Follow Wilhelmstr. past the university and turn right on Weizsäckerstr. Or take bus #1 or 7 to "Pauline-Krone-Heim" and walk back 1 block. Friendly management, clean facilities, and a Greek/Swabian restaurant. All rooms with phone and TV. Breakfast included. Singles €31, with shower €36-48; doubles €59-78; triples €72-93. MC/V. ❸

Camping: Rappenberghalde (☎431 45; www.neckarcamping.de). Follow Neckarhalde away from town until Hirschauerstr. and finally Rappenberghalde (25min.). Or take bus #9 to "Rappenberg" and follow the river to your left. Bike rental €4.50 per day. Wash €2.10. Dry €2.10. Reception daily 8am-12:30pm and 2:30-10pm. Open Mar. to mid-Oct. €5.30 per person, €3.60 per child, €1.70 per site, €4.10 per tent, €4.80 per caravan, €2.60 per car. Cash only. ❶

🍴 FOOD

Tübingen's superb restaurants seduce students and tourists alike. Most inexpensive eating establishments cluster around **Metzgerg.** and **Am Lustnauer Tor.** Modern *Imbiße* (snack bars) crowd Kornhausg., and there is a **market** on Am Markt (M, W, F 7am-1pm).

Krumme Brücke Schnitzelakademie, Kornhausstr. 17B (☎224 66). This pleasant, 300-year-old restaurant near the Rathaus serves up Swabian specialties, including sizable *Schnitzel* (€3-8.30). Open daily 11am-3pm and 5-11pm. Cash only. ❸

El Chico, Gartenstr. 4 (☎55 02 56). This popular café dishes out Mexican specials along the Neckar, near the winding pedestrian district. The food professes a "fiesta in every bite," which very well may be true. Open daily noon-late. AmEx/MC/V; €20 min. ❷

Wurstküche, Am Lustnauer Tor 8 (☎927 50). A spreading tree protrudes from the steep slope just off Lustnauer square, providing the perfect canopy for tables laden with steaming *Kaserspätzle* (€8) and other traditional German foods (€8.50-11). Open daily 11am-midnight. MC/V. ❸

Istanbul, Karlstr. 1 (☎36 79 80), on the other side of the Neckar from El Chico. A wide variety of vegetarian dishes (€2.70-7). Open daily noon-midnight. Cash only. ❷

Die Kichererbse, Metzgerg. 2 (☎521 71). Prepares fresh Middle Eastern vegetarian meals for €3-6. Open M 11am-6:30pm, Tu-F 11am-7pm, Sa 11am-4pm. Cash only. ❷

👁 SIGHTS

SCHLOß HOHENTÜBINGEN. This 11th-century castle stands atop the hill in the center of town. A dark tunnel and staircase on the far side of the courtyard lead through the castle wall to a view of the surrounding valley second only to that of the Wurmlinger Kapelle. (*Accessible from Am Markt. Castle grounds open daily 7am-8pm. Free.*) Occupied by various university institutes, the *Schloß* is also home to the excellent **Museum Schloß Hohentübingen,** the largest university museum in Germany and, at 2000 sq. meters, one of the largest collections of archaeological artifacts in Europe. Egyptian and East Asian coins, crafts, and curiosities figure as prominently as remnants of Europe's primeval and early modern past. A sizable (approximately 350 pieces) collection of copies of Greek statues fills the bottom level. (*Enter at Burgsteig inside courtyard. ☎297 73 84. Open W-Su May-Sept. 10am-6pm; Oct.-Apr. 10am-5pm. Classical casts open until 4pm. €4, students €2. Tours Su 3pm; €2.*)

STIFTSKIRCHE. The 15th-century church serves as the focal point of the Altstadt's winding alleys. In the **chancel** are the tombs of 14 members of the House of Württemberg, arranged in four rows from east to west. Life-size stone sculptures of the deceased top the memorials, while the stained glass windows fill the room with eerie glow. The church **tower** offers a rewarding view after the steep climb. (*☎431 51. Open daily 9am-5pm. Chancel and tower open Easter through Thanksgiving W, Sa, Su 11am-5pm. Organ concerts July-Aug. Th 8pm. €1, students €0.50.*)

WURMLINGER KAPELLE. This modest, sunbleached chapel—whose naked simplicity is as moving as some of the most imposing cathedrals of Germany—crowns a hill otherwise covered in grapevines and green meadows with sweeping views of the surrounding countryside. *(Follow Kapellenweg to the hill from the Schloß, then continue up the hill through the vineyards; at the 1st fork take a left, then a right at the 2bd fork (6km); ask at the tourist office for the walking map "Tübingen Promenades 2." Or, take bus #18 (dir.: Rotten-burg) to "Hirschau Kirchpl." (10min., every hr. M-F, every 2hr. Sa-Su, €1.50.) Chapel open May-Oct. Su 10am-4pm; Nov.-Apr. call ☎221 22.)*

HÖLDERLINTURM (HÖLDERLIN TOWER). The 18th- and 19th-century poet Friedrich Hölderlin, increasingly emotionally and mentally disturbed in his old age, spent the final 36 years of his life in this tower. The first floor of the museum is dedicated to his impact on contemporary German literature, while the second floor houses an extensive collection of his translations and original compositions, and is viewable upon request. *(Below Bursag. on the river. ☎220 40. Museum tours Sa and Su 5pm. Open Tu-F 10am-noon and 3-5pm, Sa-Su 2-5pm. €2.50, students €1.50.)*

PLATANENALLEE (SYCAMORE ALLEY). The buildings of the **Neckarfront** are best viewed from this quiet tree-lined avenue that runs the length of the man-made island on the Neckar. Punting trips down the Neckar are available from university students; inquire at the tourist office. *(Boats seat 12. M-F and Su €52 per hr., Sa €55.)*

OTHER SIGHTS. Across from the **Stiftskirche** is the unassuming **Buchhandlung Heckenhauer Antiquariat** (Heckenhauer Antique Bookstore), where **Hermann Hesse** worked from 1895 until 1899. The old-fashioned store sells rare books. *(Holzmarkt 5. ☎230 18; www.heckenhauer.de. Open M-F 2-6pm, Sa 11am-3pm.)* On the way from the church to the castle, don't miss the gilded rostrum of the **Rathaus,** Am Markt. The nearby **Kornhaus** contains the **Stadtmuseum** (Municipal Museum), with exhibits on the city's history from the 15th to 20th centuries. *(Kornhausstr. 10. ☎204 17 11. Open Tu-Su 11am-5pm. €2.50, students and children €1.50, group tours €35.)* Above the river is the **Evangelisches Stift** (Evangelist monastery), Klosterberg 2. This theology dorm once housed such luminaries as Kepler, Hölderlin, and Hegel.

🎵 🎭 ENTERTAINMENT AND NIGHTLIFE

Tübingen's laid-back nightlife befits its tranquil location along the Neckar; a walk along its streets at night yields not pulsing house music, but the sounds of heated conversations over coffee and beer. In warm weather, the stairs and fountain on Am Markt fill quickly with a young student crowd. For after-hours transportation, the **Nachtbus** leaves Lustnauer Tor (Th-Sa 12:45-2:45am), or call **Nacht-SAM** to pick you up (☎340 00). Tübingen also has two major theaters: the progressive **Zimmer-theater,** Bursag. 16. (☎927 30; open M-F 10am-5:30pm, Sa 10am-12:30pm, and 1hr. before shows; tickets also available at Buchhandlung Osiander, Wilhemstr. 12, and Verkehrsvereih, Necakarbrücke 1.) and the **Landestheater,** Eberhardstr. 6. (☎931 31 49; www.landestheater-tuebingen.de. Open Tu-F 2-7pm, Sa 10am-1pm.)

Schloß Café Culture Club, Burgsteige 7 (☎96 51 53), near the *Schloß*. This retro-fitted student lair is decorated with an eclectic mix of couches, old church pews, and other slapdash furnishings. Live music on weekends, poetry readings, jam sessions, open mics, and more. Board games and drinks abound. Beer €2.40-2.70. Mixed drinks from €5.20. Open M-Th and Su 11am-2am, F and Sa until 3am. Cash only.

Sudhaus, Hechinger Str. 203 (☎746 96; www.cityinfonetz.de/sudhaus). Bus #3 or 5 or night bus #N95 to "Fuchsstr.," then go under the busy road. This "socio-cultural center" in a former brewery hosts wacky art films, dance parties, and live acts. Schedules are plastered all over town. Cover €5-16. In the summer, head to **Takco Biergarten** instead. Open May-Aug. 11:30am-11pm. **Takco Bar** (☎76 07 67) opens its small dance floor and bar (€7-9) year-round F-Su 10pm-3am. Cash only.

Tangente-Night, Pfleghofstr. 10 (☎230 07), at the corner of Lustnauer Tor. A student hangout for evening beers or morning reading over coffee. Beer €1.90-2.90. Mixed drinks €6. W Techno DJ 9pm. M Karaoke and student night. Open daily in summer 4pm-3am; otherwise 10am-3am. Cash only.

Foyer Blaue Brücke, Friedrichstr. 12 (☎53 82 44). Take bus #3 or night bus N87 to "Blaue Brücke." This 2fl. disco, which once housed French officers, now attracts an even more party-oriented crowd. Beer €2.10-3.30. Mixed drinks €4.50-5. Cover €5. Open F-Sa 10pm-3am. Cash only.

Jazzkeller, Haagg. 15½ (☎55 09 06). From jazz to funk to salsa and back again, in a small, woody bar/club near Am Markt. There's also a disco downstairs, with live gigs W from 9pm Sept.-June only (€3-4). Sa and Tu Happy hour 7-11:30pm with €1.50 beer and €3 mixed drinks. Open daily from 7pm. Cash only.

Marktschenke, Am Markt 11 (☎220 35). Popped pink collars are not in short supply at this chic, modern bar. *Hefeweizen* (€2.90 for 0.5L). Open M-Th 9am-1am, F-Sa 9am-2am, Su 10am-1am. Cash only.

MANNHEIM   ☎0621

The alphanumeric street names of Mannheim (pop. 307,000) are straight out of a game of Battleship, and its historic treasures are undergoing extensive renovation. However, the tangled web of tram cables above Mannheim's cobbled streets typify the cultural and physical anachronisms of modern German cities. This commercial powerhouse is a convenient, if slightly less picturesque, base for visiting Heidelberg while avoiding crowds of tourists.

▐**?** TRANSPORTATION AND PRACTICAL INFORMATION

Trains run to Frankfurt (1hr., 2 per hr., €13.40) and Stuttgart (40min., every hr., €20). **Trams** cost €2, children €1.30. The **tourist office,** Willy-Brandt-Pl. 3, on your left across from the station, distributes free maps and info on accommodations and cultural events. (☎10 10 11; www.tourist-mannheim.de. Open M-F 9am-7pm, Sa 10am-1pm.) A **laundromat, Waschinsel,** is on Seckenheimer Str. 8, 2½ blocks northeast of the station. (Wash €3.70. Dry €2.20. Open M-F and Su 8am-8pm, Sa 9am-4pm.) A **pharmacy, Bahnhof-Apotheke,** is at block L15, across from the station and to the left. (☎12 01 80. Open M-F 7am-8pm, Sa 8am-8pm.) Use the **Internet** at **Chat Corner,** #16-17 L14, two blocks from the train station. Start an account on the machine to your right through the doors and enter username and password into a computer to get online. (€1 per 20min. Open daily 9am-3am.) **Star Coffee,** Sofienstr. 33, has free wireless with any purchase. (Open M-W 7am-9pm, Th-F 7am-11pm, Sa 8:30am-11pm, Su 9am-9pm.) The **post office,** Willy-Brandt-Pl. 13, is one block east of the station. (Open M-F 9am-6pm, Sa 9am-noon.) **Postal Code:** 68161.

▟ ORIENTATION

Mannheim is on a peninsula at the junction of the Rhein and Neckar. The **Innenstadt** is bounded by a horseshoe road, known as **Parkring** to the west, **Luisenring** to the northwest, **Friedrichsring** to the northeast, and **Kaiserring** to the east. **Bismarckstr.** connects the southern ends. The train station is outside the southeast corner. **Kurpfalzstr. (Planken)** and **Breite Str.** bisect the horseshoe, divided into a grid of 144 blocks: each block is named by a letter and number; blocks along Kurpfalzstr. have increasing numbers the farther away from the central axis. Blocks to the west of Kurpfalzstr. are name south to north by letters **A** through **K,** with streets to the east lettered **L** through **U.** East of Kaiserring, streets assume regular names.

🏠🍴 ACCOMMODATIONS AND FOOD

Mannheim's **Jugendherberge (HI) ❷**, Rheinpromenade 21, has small rooms and aging facilities, but compensates with a convenient location 10min. from the station. Walk through the underground passage from the tracks at the east end of the station and take a left up the stairs at the very end. Cross the street, walk left past the big glass building, cross the tracks, and, with the park on your right, continue down Rennershofstr. past Gontardstr. Turn right onto Rheinpromenade; the hostel is in a small enclave 1½ blocks up. Tram #7 (dir.: Neckarau) to "Lindenhofpl." drops you off in front of glass building. (☎82 27 18; www.jugendherberge-mannheim.de. Breakfast 7:30-8:30am included. Key deposit €10. Reception 7-9:30am and 4-10pm. Strictly-enforced check-out 9am. Dorms €16.80, over 27 €19.80; additional nights €13.10/16.70. Singles €25.20, over 27 €26.20; doubles €43.20/49.20. MC/V.) **Goldene Gans ❸**, Bismarckpl. 7/Tattersallstr. 19, two blocks northeast of the train station, opens onto Bismarckpl. during the day, but after midnight the entrance is around the corner. This inn, atop a small restaurant (most dinners €6.80-14.80), offers blue-floored, sunny rooms, many with large bath. (☎42 20 20. Breakfast included. Reception M-Sa 6am-midnight, Su 7am-6pm. Singles €50-80; doubles €65-95; triples €85-120. MC/V.)

Bakers and grocers gather at the **market** in the square at the intersection of Kurpfalzstr. and Kirchstr. in the center of the city grid. (Open Tu, Th, Sa 7am-1:30pm.) Fresh vegetables and fruit can be found in the area even outside of market hours. For an array of local and vegetarian specialities (€6-9), head to the **Kurfürst ❸**, #15 R1, one block east of the Marktpl. (☎262 75. Open daily 9am-11pm. MC/V.) The cheapest meals in town (€4.70-5) are at the **Studentenwerk Mannheim Mensa ❶**, behind the Residenzschloß in the southwest corner (open M-F 11:30am-2pm), and the adjacent **cafeteria.** (Sandwiches €1-1.80. Open M-Th 8:30am-4pm, F 8:30am-3:45pm.) **Murphy's Law Irish Pub ❸**, a block from the Hauptbahnhof, has regular theme nights with drink discounts. (Open M-Th and Su 5pm-2am, F-Sa 5pm-3am. Cash only.) **Flic Flac**, #12 B2, is a local student favorite. Decorated as a 1920s Zeppelin, this bar has a daily Happy hour after 9pm, Monday €5.90 pasta buffet, and Thursday live bands. (☎225 53. Open M-Th and Su 9am-1am, F-Sa until 2am. MC/V.) Blocks **G2** through **J6** have a dense array of *Imbiße* (food stands) and ethnic restaurants, where meals are generally €3-7.

👁 SIGHTS

The bustling **Paradepl.,** with its Baroque fountain, is the heart of Mannheim. Restaurants, department stores, cafés, and movie theaters surround the square and extend along the pedestrian zones on Breite Str. and Planken. At the end of Planken is the city's emblematic masterpiece, the elegant sandstone **Wasserturm**—said to be "the most beautiful water tower in the world"—and the surrounding gardens on **Friedrichspl.** South of Friedrichspl. is the **Kunsthalle**, Friedrichspl. 4, a museum surveying art from the mid-19th century to today, including works by Manet, Van Gogh, and Beckmann, in addition to modern sculpture, and themed art-film shorts. (☎293 64 50. Open Tu-Su 11am-6pm. €7, students €5.) The giant **Kurgürtliches Residenzschloß**, the largest Baroque palace in Germany, now houses the **Universität Mannheim** and a small museum, which will return bigger and better when it reopens in 2007. The pink-striped **Schloßkirche** entombs Karl Phillip's third wife, Violante von Thurn und Taxis. (☎213 63. Open Apr.-Oct. Tu-Su 10am-5pm; Nov.-Mar. Sa-Su 10am-5pm. Free.) The huge **Reiss-Engelhorn-Museen,** around block C5, northwest of the *Schloß*, has buildings dedicated to archaeology, ethnology, and natural science. (☎293 31 50; www.rem-mannheim.de. Open Tu-Su 11am-6pm.

BADEN-WÜRTTEMBERG

Tours Su 3pm; German audio guides from €3. €7, under 18 €2.50.) The recently restored **Jesuitenkirche,** between the museum and the *Schloß* at block A4, was built for the Pfalz court's return to Catholicism. (Open daily 8am-noon and 2-5pm.)

On the other side of the Innenstadt, several blocks northeast of the Wasserturm, lies the 100-acre **Luisenpark.** (☎127 090. Open daily Nov.-Feb. 9am-9pm; Mar.-Oct. 9am-sunset. Entry €4, winter €2.50; students €1.50/1.) The greenhouses, flower gardens, aviary, zoo, water sports, afternoon concerts, and boat rides offer something for everyone. South of Luisenpark, seven blocks due east of Friedrichspl. on the **Augustanlage,** lies the terrific **Landesmuseum der Technik und Arbeit,** Museumstr. 1, which displays the inner workings of big, creaky, rusty things through the lens of technological, social, and economic history. Take tram #6 to "Landesmuseum." (☎429 88 39. Open Tu and Th-F 9am-5pm, W 9am-8pm, Sa-Su 10am-6pm. €3, students €2, families €6. W afternoon free.) The **Museumsschiff "Mannheim"** floats in the Neckar, just by the Kurpfalzbrücke. Once the steamer *Mainz,* which sank in 1956 and was dredged from the murky Rhein, this museum now houses a history of navigation. (☎156 57 56. Open Su and holidays 10am-6pm. €3, families €6.)

SCHWÄBISCHE ALB (SWABIAN JURA)

The limestone plateaus, sharp ridges, and pine-forested valleys stretching from Tübingen in the north to the Bodensee in the south are collectively known as the Schwäbische Alb. This roughly-hewn landscape is scenic yet stubborn and relatively secluded compared to some of the more mountainous regions of the South. Lofty ruins crowning the peaks are all that remain of fortifications erected by the once powerful dynasties that held the region. The **Schwäbische Albstr.** (Swabian Jura Road) bisects the plateau, crossing the Romantic Road at Nördlingen (p. 528). A web of trails serves hikers; maps are available at regional tourist offices in most towns. Train service to many points is roundabout and spotty; plan to make use of the local bus routes and keep track of schedules.

SCHWÄBISCH HALL ☎0791

The relatively undiscovered riverside village of Schwäbisch Hall (pop. 35,000) sits on steeply sloping hills enclosed by lush forests. Sunlight reflects off the red roofs of tilting half-timbered houses during hot summer days, while the bustling Marktpl. hides in the shade of a towering church steeple and Tudor-style homes. If the ancient Altstadt and winding alleys somehow fail to provide ample diversion for visitors, the town's numerous summer festivals, thrown with a contagious local fervor, will almost certainly do the trick.

◄► TRANSPORTATION AND PRACTICAL INFORMATION

Schwäbisch Hall has two **train** stations. The **Hauptbahnhof** is close to town, but the more important station is in **Schwäbisch Hall-Hessental,** on the main rail line to Stuttgart (1¼hr., every hr., €6.70). Bus #2 connects the two stations (15min., 2-3 per hr., €1.50). All **bus** lines stop at "Am Spitalbach Ost" or "West," a few blocks northwest of the tourist office. **Stadtbus KundenCenter,** Am Spitalbach 4, sells *Tageskarten* (€4.50), valid all day or all weekend on buses (☎97 19 00. Open M-F 9:30am-6:15pm, Sa 9am-1:30pm.) For a **taxi,** call ☎61 17. **Kocherflotte,** on the river by Haalpl., rents boats. (☎430 64. €6 per hr. Open May to mid-Oct. daily noon-6pm.) Schwäbisch Hall's **tourist office,** Am Markt 9, has free maps, room lists, and a richly illustrated ▧**town guide.** (☎75 12 16; www.schwaebischhall.de. Open May-Sept. M-F 9am-6pm, Sa-Su 10am-3pm; until 8:30pm during *Freilichtspiele* (p. 397); Oct.-Apr. M-F 9am-5pm.) The **Dresdner Bank,** Neue Str. 9, has a 24hr. **ATM.** The **Hirsch-Apotheke pharmacy** is on Gelbingerg. 18. (Open M-F 8am-12:30pm and 2-6pm, Sa 8:30am-12:30pm.) Check email at **PTT Telecafé,** Marktstr. 15. (Tu-Sa 10am-10pm, Su-M noon-10pm. €0.50 per 20min., €1.50 per hr.) The **post office** is on Hafenmarkt 2. (Open M-F 9am-noon and 2-5:30pm, Sa 9am-noon.) **Postal Code:** 74523.

◼◼ ACCOMMODATIONS AND FOOD

Schwäbisch Hall's **Jugendherberge (HI)** ❷, Langenfelder Weg 5, is beyond the Michaelskirche on the Galgenberg., accesible by bus #1 or 5 at the "Schwäbisch Hall Hölzmarkt." Follow Crailsheimer Str. up 200m from the church and take a left on Ziegeleiweg, then another left on Langenfelder Weg, or head through the stone arch at the corner of Ziegeleiweg. The hostel, in the orange building on the left, offers serene accommodations behind an overgrown stone terrace and garden. Beware the wily little lizards out back. (☎410 50; www.jugendherberge-schwaebisch-hall.de. Excellent breakfast buffet included. Reception 5-10pm, but call if arriving later than 7pm. Dorms €17.90, over 27 €20.90; singles €22.90/25.90; doubles €28.90/30.90. Reduced prices for stays over 1 night. Cash only.) **Gasthof Krone** ❷, Klosterstr. 1, offers basic, clean rooms. Follow the street to the right of Michaelskirche all the way up and around the corner on the right or take bus #1 or #5 to "Schwäbisch Hall Hölzmarkt." (☎60 22. Breakfast included. Singles €25-30; spacious doubles with bath €45-55; triples €55-65. Cash only.) There is a **Campingplatz** ❶ at Steinbacher See. Take bus #2 to "Steinbach/Mitte" (5min., 2-3 per hr., €1.40), then turn back and follow the signs up and to the left. (☎29 84. Reception 7am-1pm and 3-10pm. €9 per site with tent. Showers €0.50. MC/V.) Try one of many fruit shakes, mixed drinks, and beers (€1.60-9.90) on the slightly tilting terrace of **Warsteiner Ilge's** ❷, Im Weiler 2, overlooking the Kocher River. (☎716 84. Open M-F 11am-1am, Sa-Su 10am-1am. Cash only.) Restaurants along **Gelbinger G.** offer a variety of cuisines, including Swabian specialties at **Sonne** ❸, Gelbinger G. 2. (☎97 08 40. Entrées €7-12.50. Open Tu-Su 11:30am-2pm and from 5:30pm. AmEx/MC.) **Olli's Café & Bar** ❷, Untere Herng. 2, down the steep alley from Marktpl., serves up breakfasts (€1.20-14) and sandwiches (€2.50-5.80). Cap off your meal the old-school way—with a stogie (€3.50-17). (☎941 37 90; www.ollis-cafe-bar.de. Open M-Th 11am-1am, F 11am-2am, Sa 10am-2am, Su 3pm-1am. MC/V.)

◉ ♫ SIGHTS AND ENTERTAINMENT

On summer evenings from mid-May to mid-August, the **Freilichtspiele,** a series of plays running the gamut from Shakespeare to Brecht, are performed at several locations in Hall, including the steps of the Michaelskirche, the Kunsthalle Würth, and the Haller Globe theater on the river island. Contact the tourist office for tickets. (☎75 16 00. €4-27.50. Student discounts.) On the weekend of Pentecost (May 27, 2007; May 11, 2008), Schwäbisch Hall celebrates the **Kuchen- und Brunnenfest,** during which the town echoes with drums and trumpets, while locals don 16th-century salt refiner costumes and dance jigs around a 100 lb. cake. During the **Sommernachtsfest** (last Sa in Aug.), 30,000 candles are set alight in patterns along the Ackeranlage and around town while fireworks explode overhead.

ALTSTADT. Thrice charred by fires, Hall's half-timbered center was built in the 18th century. The Romanesque tower and Gothic nave of the **Michaelskirche** sits atop a steep set of stone stairs; five bells within, installed (much to the town's delight) during the 2006 Jakobimarkt, clang every hour. The church is Lutheran thanks to local **Johannes Brenz,** the reformer who converted Hall to Protestantism in the 1520s. Organ music often echoes in the church (check board for concert information), rattling the pile of human bones and skulls in the medieval ossuary—pass to the right of the altar to gaze into the underground mass grave. The **Turmzimmer** atop the church's tower provides a great view of the town. *(Open Mar. to mid-Nov. M 2-5pm, Tu-Sa 9am-5pm, Su 11am-5pm. Tower €1, students €0.50.)*

KLOSTER GROßCOMBURG. Steinbach, the only suburb of Hall that remained Catholic during the Reformation, holds Kloster Großcomburg, a former castle and 11th-century Benedictine monastery. Today, the cloister houses the **Staatliche Akademie Comburg** (National Academy of Comburg), a museum, and a small café. From inside, the 460m wall has peep holes for views of the valley, but you must take a German **tour** to see the museum and gilded interior of the reconstructed Baroque church. *(Take bus #2 (5min., 2-3 per hr., €2) to "Steinbach/Mitte." Cross the street, head back toward the town and take an immediate sharp right onto the Bildersteige path up the hill. ☎93 81 85. Café open Tu-Su 1-5pm. Tours Apr.-Oct. Tu-F 11am, 1, 2, 3, 4pm; Sa-Su 2, 3, 4pm. Nov.-Mar. by appointment. €2.30, students €1.20, family pass €5.80.)*

HÄLLISCH-FRÄNKISCHES MUSEUM (HELLISH FRANKISH MUSEUM). Filling eight stories of the Romanesque Keckenturm, this museum's well-worn timber frame is almost as antiquated as many of the items it has on display. Paintings, sculptures, and an extensive china collection provide insight into seven centuries of town history. The paneled walls of the *Betraum* (praying room) form one of Germany's most important pieces of Jewish art, and the museum's 200 illustrated targets (many of them adorned with intricate allegories) from the 18th and 19th centuries bring the art of archery to a whole new level. *(Im Keckenho. ☎75 13 60 or 75 12 89; info@schwaebischhall.de. Open Tu and Th-Su 10am-5pm, W 10am-8pm. €2.50, students €1.50, families €5.50.)*

HOHENLOHER FREILANDMUSEUM (HOHENLOHER OPEN-AIR MUSEUM). In nearby Wackershofen, this museum reenacts life in a German agricultural village with 51 authentic low-ceilinged houses set in the scenic countryside. Watch broad-shouldered flannel-wearing farmers weave wicker baskets and peak at little piglets suckling in fragrant hay. Most weekends from April to November have special events, ranging from a southern German cheese market to the "Schwäbisch-Hällischen pig day" and traditional Swabian dancing. *(Take bus #7 from Spitalbach West to "Freiland Museum" (15min.; M-F 3 per hr., Sa-Su less frequent; €1.55). Or, hike trail #3 (1½hr.) from central Hall to the museum. ☎97 10 140. Open late Mar. to Apr. and Oct. to early Nov. Tu-Su 10am-5pm; May-Sept. Tu-Su 9am-6pm; June-Aug. M-Su 9am-6pm. Tours €4; call 2wk. early to arrange English tours, €28. €5.50, students €3.50, families €11.50.)*

THE WÜRTH GALLERY. This gallery contains a healthy dose of modern and contemporary German art. *(Lange Str. 35, across the river. ☎94 67 20; www.kunst-wuerth.com. Open daily 10am-6pm. €5, students €3. M Free. English audio guide €4.)*

ULM ☎0731

When Napoleon designated the Danube as the border between Württemberg and Bavaria, Ulm was split into two distinct cities, Ulm and Neu-Ulm. Brochures claim that they are Siamese twins, but it's pretty clear that the younger sibling got the shaft. The looming peak of the Münster, the tallest church steeple in the world, provides a fantastic backdrop to a lively pedestrian district crowded with shopping bags and beer mugs. Ulm is also known for science, having raised both Albert Einstein and Albrecht Berblinger, the "tailor of Ulm," known for his 1811 attempt at human flight that landed him in the Danube.

🚆 TRANSPORTATION AND PRACTICAL INFORMATION. Ulm is connected by **train** to all of southern Germany, with trains to Munich (1½-2hr., 2-3 per hr., €22-30) and Stuttgart (1hr., 2-3 per hr., €14-22). **Public transport** costs €1.70 per ride, children €1. A day ticket, valid for four adults (a child counts as half an adult) on the day of purchase, is €7. The **tourist office**, Münsterpl. 50 in the Stadthaus, books rooms for free, sells city guides (€0.50), and offers **tours** of Ulm in German (€6, students and disabled €3, families €11); arrange in advance for English. (☎161 28 30; www.tourismus.ulm.de. Open M-F 9am-6pm, Sa 9am-1pm. May-Dec. also Sa 9am-4pm, Su 11am-3pm.) An **ATM** is at the **Citibank** behind the Stadthaus. Pharmaceutical supplies can be found at **Neue Apotheke**, Bahnhofstr.13, toward the tourist office from the Bahnhof. (☎659 50. M-F 8am-7pm, Sa 8:30am-5pm.) Free **Internet** access can be found on the second and third floors of the **Stadtbibliothek** (Municipal Library), the modern glass building behind the Rathaus. (☎161 41 00. Open Tu-F 10am-7pm, Sa 10am-2pm.) The **post office**, Bahnhofpl. 2, is to the left of the station. (Open M-F 8:30am-6:30pm, Sa 9am-1pm.) **Postal Code:** 89073.

🛏️🍴 ACCOMMODATIONS AND FOOD. Ulm's **Jugendherberge Geschwister Scholl (HI) ❷**, Grimmelfinger Weg 45, was named in memory of Ulm's Hans and Sophie Scholl, members of the Weiße Rose resistance movement who were executed by the Nazis in 1943 (p. 56). Rooms are tight but clean, if a little out of the way. Take bus #1, 3, 4, 7, 8, 9, or 10 from the train station to "Ehinger Tor," and change to bus #4 or 8 (dir.: Kuhberg) to "Kuhberg Schulzentrum." Walk through the underpass just up the road and follow the "Jugendherberge" signs for 5min. (☎38 44 55; info@jugendherberge-ulm.de. Breakfast and sheets included. Lunch €4.60, lunch and dinner €7.80. Lockers €5 deposit. Reception 7-10:30am and 4-10:30pm. Curfew 10:30pm; key available with €20 deposit. €17.90, over 27 €20.90. Additional nights €17.70/14.70. MC/V.) The age-old Münster towers over the modern **Münster-Hotel ❸**, Münsterpl. 14, to the left of the Münster through the square. Enjoy yellow and blue rooms in a great location, but beware the early bells. (☎/fax 641 62. Breakfast included. Singles €30-40; double €55-70; triple €85. Cash only.) The rust-red building next to the Münster houses the family-kept **Hotel Anker ❸**, Rabeng. 2, with small but cozy rooms, most with shower, toilet, and windows overlooking the Münsterpl. Breakfast included. (☎632 97. Singles €30-40; doubles €50-75, triples €72-80.)

A farmers' **market** crops up on Münsterpl. (W and Sa mornings 7am-1pm). Sandwich-serving bakeries and *Imbiße* (snack bars) dominate the Ladenpassage in front of the train station and line the way to the Münster along Bahnhofstr. and Hirschstr. For the most variety, try the territory between Neue Str. and the river, or the streets just off Münsterpl. For **groceries** head to **Plus**, Münsterpl. 15. (Open M-Sa 8am-8pm.) **Asiatisches Schnellrestaurant ❷**, Münsterpl. 14, serves up huge and affordable portions of Asian fare. (☎153 73 71. Open daily 11am-9pm.) **Ulmer Münz Café ❸**, across from the Schiefes Haus, serves a small selection of dishes (€3-11.90) or afternoon drinks in Ulm's former mint. (☎151 78 87. Open Tu-Su 11am-10pm. Closed Jan. Cash only.) Part of Hotel Anker, the **Spanische Weinstube ❷** serves Spanish, Bavarian, and Swabian specialities and many salads; daily specials start at €5.90. (☎632 97. Open Tu-Su 11:30am-3pm and 5:30-10:30pm. Cash only.)

⬛ SIGHTS. At 161m, the steeple topping the **◩Münster** is the tallest in the world. During the Middle Ages, wealthy guild members decided to fund the building of the cathedral, and in 1377 the foundation stone was laid. Many generations passed away before the enormous steeple was completed, 513 years later. Ulm became Protestant in the early 1500s, and many altars and ornate decorations were destroyed. Among those saved was *The Man of Sorrows*, a stone sculpture of

BADEN-WÜRTTEMBERG

Christ by 15th-century sculptor Hans Multscher, next to the front portal of the cathedral. (☎967 50 23. Church open daily July-Aug. 9am-7:45pm; Apr-June and Sept. 9am-6:45pm; Mar. and Oct. 9am-5:45pm; Nov.-Feb. 9am-4:45pm. Tower closes 1hr. earlier. €3, children and students €2.50.)

The white building that houses the tourist office is also home to the **Stadthaus** (City Hall). Designed by New Yorker Richard Meier, its postmodern style, in conspicuous contrast to the Gothic Münster, raised great controversy among Ulm's residents. The basement holds archaeological and historical exhibits on the Münsterpl. (Open M-W and F-Sa 9am-6pm, Th 9am-8pm, Su 11am-6pm. Free.)

Toward the river on Neue Str., the **Rathaus**, built in 1370, is decorated with brilliant murals and an elaborate astronomical clock dating from 1540. The old **Fischerviertel** (Fishermen's Quarter), down Kroneng. from the Rathaus, is full of half-timbered houses, cobblestone streets, and primitive footbridges over slow-moving streams. One of the oldest houses in Ulm, the **Schiefes Haus** (Crooked House), at Schwörhausg. 6, is now a hotel.

Across from the Rathaus to the East is the **Ulmer Museum**, Marktpl. 9, which features art from the Middle Ages on, archaeological remnants of the area's past, and alternating exhibitions of contemporary and classic paintings. (☎161 43 30. Open Tu-Su 11am-5pm, special exhibits also Th 11am-8pm. €3, students €2, families €4. F Free. Tours Th 6pm.) The **Deutsches Brotmuseum** (German Bread Museum), Salzstadelg. 10, documents 6000 years of bread-making and hunger, and waxes philosophical about "the *Leitmotif* of Man and Bread." (☎699 55. Open daily 10am-5pm, W 10am-8:30pm. Last entry 1hr. before closing. €3, students €2, families €8.) Max Bill's red-marble monument on Bahnhofstr., marks **Albert Einstein's birthplace;** the house itself gave way long ago to a modern cube of a bank.

On even years, during the **International Danube Festival,** the riverbanks fill with handcraft and food stalls, artists, and musicians from the countries that lie on the river's way to the Black Sea. (Early July. ☎96 99 69 02; www.donaufest.de.) The mayor's annual oath to uphold the town constitution is an excuse for another round of festivities on the Danube during **Schwörmontag** (3rd M in July).

KARLSRUHE ☎0721

By German standards, Karlsruhe (Karl's Rest; pop. 284,000) was born yesterday. In 1715, Markgrave Karl Wilhelm built a castle retreat; inspired in his sleep, legend has it, by a vision of a star-shaped city, he placed his castle at the center of radially extending streets. Today, the lively city is home to Germany's two highest courts, the Bundesgerichtshof (Federal Supreme Court) and the Bundesverfassungsgericht (Federal Constitutional Court), as well as Germany's oldest technical university, to which it owes much of its youthful bustle and cultural diversity.

◰☎ TRANSPORTATION AND PRACTICAL INFORMATION

From the **train station,** the town center is a 25min. walk along Ettlinger Str. and Karl-Friedrich-Str., or a tram ride to "Marktpl." or "Europapl." (€2 per ride, 24hr. ticket €4, press "city" on the machine). For a **taxi,** call ☎914 94. The **tourist office,** Bahnhofpl. 6, across the street from the station, books rooms and distributes *Karlsruhe Extra,* a free, annually updated guide in English with great maps. (☎37 20 53 81; www.karlsruhe.de/tourismus. Open M-F 9am-6pm, Sa 9am-1pm.) A **branch office,** Karl-Friedrich-Str. 22, provides the same services, but is closer to town center. (☎37 20 53 76; tickets 250 00. Open M-F 9:30am-6:30pm, Sa 10am-3pm.) The Karlsruhe **WelcomeCard,** available at the tourist office, covers city transportation for two days during the week or three on weekends, and reduces admission to all museums for two days (€10). **Laundromat Waschhaus** is at the corner of

Scheffelstr. and Sophienstr. (☎243 81 67. Wash €3.50 per 6kg, soap €0.50. Dry €0.50 per 10min. Open M-Sa 6am-11pm.) A central **pharmacy** is **Stadt Apotheke,** Karlstr. 19. (☎235 77. Open M-F 8am-7:30pm, Sa 9am-6pm.) **Internet** access is available at the **Internet Café ARENA,** Sophienstr. 82. (☎893 30 20. Open M-Sa 10am-midnight, Su 11am-midnight.) The **post office** is inside the Post Galerie on Europapl. (Open M-F 9:30am-8pm, Sa 9:30am-4pm.) **Postal Code:** 76133.

ACCOMMODATIONS AND FOOD

Karlsruhe's **Jugendherberge (HI) ❷,** Moltkestr. 24, is close to the *Schloß* and the surrounding heart of Karlsruhe, but far from the train station. Take tram #1 or 6 to "Europapl.," then walk to the end of Karlstr. and follow the signs (10min.). The sunny, spacious hostel is on the right, set back from the street. (☎282 48; www.jugendherberge-karlsruhe.de. Breakfast included. Reception 7:30-9am, 9:30am-noon, 4-8pm, and 8:30-10:30pm. Curfew midnight; house key available with €5 deposit. 2-, 4-, or 6-bed dorms €18, over 27 €20. Add €5 for singles or €10 for doubles. Cash only.) **Pensions Zebra** and **Am Zoo ❸,** Ettlingerstr. 33, share an entrance and offer comfortable rooms close to the station and the Marktpl. (Zebra ☎352 47 01, Am Zoo 336 78; pension.zebra@freenet.de. Singles €26-44; doubles €42-65. Cash only.) Chestnut cupboards and simple chandeliers adorn **Hotel Handelshof ❹,** Reinhold-Frank-Str. 46a, next to Mülburger Tor. (☎91 20 90; HotelHandelshof@aol.com. All rooms with bath, phone, and TV. Breakfast included. Singles €42-53; doubles €58-73. AmEx/V.) Camp at **Turmbergblick ❶,** Tiengererstr. 40, in Durlach. Take tram #1 to "Durlach Turmberg," then turn back, take a right, and follow the signs. (15min. ☎49 72 36; www.azur-camping.de. Laundry €3. Dry €3. Reception 9am-1pm and 3-10pm. Open year-round. Prices vary from €5.50-7.50 per person, children €4-6, site €6-9e, €2.50-4.50 per car. Cash only.)

Ludwigspl. is lined with cafés, many of which are open until 1am. *Imbiße* (snack bars) and ice-cream shops line Kaiserstr. and Marktpl. (burgers and *Wurst* €2-3). Buy produce at the **market** on Marktpl. (Open mid-Jan. to mid-Nov. M-F 9am-6pm, Sa 9am-2pm.) Just off the Markpl., **Café Zero ❶,** Kaiserstr. 133 (☎38 06 31), offers a congenial atmosphere, elaborate ice cream (under €5), and surprisingly filling snack foods. (Open M-Sa 10am-1am, Su noon-1am. Cash only.) Stainless steel fans whir inside **Unikat ❷,** Kaiserstr. 57, a pub and *Biergarten* with angel silhouettes cast by orange lighting. Large soups from €2; regional specialties, including *Spätzle,* €4.80-9. (☎384 31 12. Beer €2-3.90. Open M-Th 11am-1am, F-Sa 11am-3am, Su 5pm-1am. Kitchen open 11am-3pm and 5-11pm. Cash only.) **Lehner's Wirtshaus ❷,** Karlstr. 21a, has tulips hanging upside down from the ceiling and rough-cut benches as simple as its tasty fare. (☎249 57 20; www.lehners-wirtshaus.de. Happy hour from 10:30pm. Open daily 11am-1am. Cash only.)

SIGHTS AND FESTIVALS

In Karlsruhe, all roads lead to the classical yellow **Schloß** north of Marktpl. The well-kept **Schloßgarten** stretches out behind the castle for nearly half a kilometer. (Open daily until 10pm. Free.) The *Schloß* houses the **Badisches Landesmuseum** (Federal State Museum of Baden), whose extensive permanent collection of antiques includes 18th-century armor and weaponry, Roman statuary, and the flashy **Türkenbeute,** a documentation of Turkish invaders replete with life-size horses and hulking mannikins. (☎926 28 28. Open Tu-Th 10am-5pm, F-Su 10am-6pm. €4, students €3, families €8, free F after 2pm.) Around the corner, the **Kunsthalle** (Art Center), Hans-Thomas-Str. 2, and the **Kunsthalle Orangerie** (Art Center Orangerie), Hans-Thomas-Str. 6, are two art museums with collections as complete as museum visitors are lacking. European paintings, sketches, and sculptures from the late Gothic to 19th century adorn the Kunsthalle while the Orangerie (under construction until 2007) contains a smaller collection of modern art. (☎926 33 59. Both open Tu-F 10am-5pm, Sa-Su 10am-6pm. €4, students €2.50. Orangerie only €2.50/1.50.) Just through the park from the Kunsthalle lies the **Botanischer Garten**, a reprieve from the hectic city. (Open year-round Tu-F 9am-noon and 1-4pm; Apr.-Sept. also Sa-Su 10am-noon and 1-5pm; Oct.-Mar. Sa-Su 10am-noon and 1-4pm.) The **Museum beim Markt** (Museum near the Market), Karl-Friedrich-Str. 6, is dedicated to design and illustration after 1900, featuring a particularly fascinating Art Deco collection. It also contains some gilded furniture and busts. (☎926 65 20. Open Tu-Th 11am-5pm, F-Su 10am-6pm. €2, students €1, families €4. F free after 2pm if there are no special exhibits. Combo ticket with Badisches Landesmuseum €4/3/8.) On the upper floors of a former mansion, the recently renovated **Prinz-Max-Palais**, Karlstr. 10, has a display of local history with the alleged first bicycle in the world. (☎133 42 34. Open Tu, F, Su 10am-6pm, Th 10am-7pm, Sa 2-6pm. Free, special exhibitions from €3.) Poets like von Scheffel and Hebel inhabit the adjoining **Museum für Literatur**. (Same hours and prices as Prinz-Max-Palais.)

In late May, the appetizing **Brigande-Feschd** brings a huge display of dishes from local restaurants to Marktpl. Two weeks later, *steins* are the standard at **Unifest,** the largest free open-air concert in Germany.

BADEN-BADEN ☎07221

Once a romping ground for the Roman legions in the first century, the warm waters of Baden-Baden (pop. 54,000) found a new, more refined clientele among the nobility of 19th-century Europe. The city has remained the "summer capital of Europe" for the well-to-do, as the *nouveaux riches* and minor royalty of today continue to mingle in the elegant casino and bathe in the mineral spas. Such languid charm and practiced hedonism comes at a price, however, and the luxury baths might tempt even the strictest of budget travelers to spend more than usual.

▐▋ TRANSPORTATION AND PRACTICAL INFORMATION

The **train station** is 5km from town. Walk 1½hr. along a path, or take **bus** #201, 214, 216, 244, or 245 (dir.: Stadtmitte) from the station to "Leopoldspl." (€2; day pass €4). **Trains** to: Frankfurt am Main (1½hr., every hr., €25); Mainz (2hr., 2 per hr., €24); Munich (4hr., every 2hr., €69); Stuttgart (1½hr., every hr., €24). For a **taxi** call ☎621 12. The **tourist office** is inside the Trinkhalle on Kaiserallee. Take bus #201 to "Hindenburgpl." (☎27 52 00; www.baden-baden.de. Open M-Sa 10am-5pm, Su 2-5pm.) The **laundromat** is at Scheibenstr. 14. (☎248 19. Wash €4. Dry €3 per 5min. Open M-Sa 7:30am-9pm.) Get cash at the **ATM** in the **Dresder Bank,** Lichtentaler Str. 27, near Augustapl. (Open M, W, F 9:30am-1pm, 2-4pm; Tu and Th 9:30am-1pm, 2-6pm.) The local **pharmacy, Bernhardas Apotheke,** is at the "Grosse-Dollen-Str." bus stop near the hostel. (Open M-F 8am-1pm, 2:30-6:30pm; Sa 8am-1pm.) @, **Rheinstr. 23,** has **Internet** access for €2 per hr. (Open daily 10am-midnight.) The **post office,** is in the Wagener store next to Hindenburgpl. (Open M-F 9:15am-7pm, Sa 9:15am-6pm.) **Postal Code:** 76530.

▟ ACCOMMODATIONS

Rooms in the center of town are expensive with few exceptions, and all hotels charge the *Kurtaxe* of €2.80 per day per person. The modern **Jugendherberge Baden-Baden (HI) ❷**, Hardenbergstr. 34, is between the station and the town center. Take bus #201, 205, 206, or 216 to "Große-Dollen-Str." (€2) and follow the signs uphill for 10min. The rooms are tightly packed but clean, and some have small rooftop balcony. (☎522 23; jh-baden-baden@t-online.de. Sheets and breakfast included. Reception every hr. on the hr. 5-11pm. Curfew 11:30pm; key available for €25 deposit. Dorms €17.90, over 27 €20.90. Additional nights €17.70/14.70. Cash only.) **Hotel am Markt** ❸, Marktpl. 18, has comfy rooms in an ideal location between the Friedrichsbad and the Stiftskirche, close to the spas and a 5min. walk to the casino. (☎270 40; www.hotel-am-markt-baden.de. Breakfast included. Reception 7am-10pm. Singles €30/32, with shower €41/47; doubles €58-80. Cash only.) The green and red exterior of **Hotel Laterne** ❹, Gernsbacher Str. 10-12, houses luxurious rooms in a 300-year-old half-timbered house a few meters below the Rathaus. (☎299 99; fax 383 08. Breakfast included. Singles €40-70; doubles €65-85. AmEx/MC/V.) **Altes Schloß** ❸, Alter Schloßweg 10, gives you a chance to live like the rich and famous in a wing of the **Hohenbaden** castle. The rooms are comfortable, and the atmosphere priceless. It's a 1hr. uphill trek on gravel roads, so a taxi (about €18 from the station, €12 from the town center) is recommended. (☎269 48; fax 39 17 75. Breakfast included. Singles €35, additional nights €28; doubles €70/56; 1- to 4-person apartments €40/33 per person. AmEx/MC/V.)

🔆 FOOD

Most restaurants are far from cheap, but a string of bakeries and cafés line Gernsbacherstr. off Leopoldpl. For **groceries,** head to the **Nahkauf** supermarket, Rheinstr. 20, near the Grosse-Dollen-Str. bus stop. (☎96 70 07. Open M-F 8am-7pm, Sa 8am-4pm.) **Heinz Vogel,** just off Leopoldpl., sells delicious local cheeses and jams. (Open M-F 8:30am-6pm, Sa 7:30am-1pm.) **Sindbad's Kebap-Haus** ❶, Seilerstr. 5, off Augustapl., sells Turkish meals for €2-8. (☎335 84. Open daily 11am-1am. Cash only.) A wooden cock marks the hidden entrance of **Cockelstub** ❷, Kreuzstr. 2 , near Leopoldpl. Daily specials include a delicious *Flammkuchen* (€6.40) and rich *Gulachesuppe* (€3.50). (Open M-F and Su 11am-2am, Sa 11am-3am. Cash only.)

🔆 SPAS

Baden-Baden's history as a resort goes back nearly two millennia, but the springs are still going strong. The ⚑**Friedrichsbad,** Römerpl. 1, is a high-domed 19th-century bathing palace where visitors are parched, steamed, soaked, scrubbed, doused, and pummeled by trained professionals for 3hr. Fifteen tubs of varying temperatures, as well as saunas, showers, and hot rooms, round out the treatment, after which clients are lathered in cream and wrapped up in blankets for a 30min. nap. Mark Twain put it best: "Here at Friedrichsbad you lose track of time within ten minutes and track of the world within twenty." (☎27 59 20; www.roemisch-irisches-bad.de. Open M-Sa 9am-10pm, Su noon-8pm. Last entry 2hr. before closing. Baths are coed; M and Th men and women bathe separately. Standard Roman-Irish bath €21, with soap and brush massage €29.) The modern marble **Caracalla-Thermen,** Römerpl. 1, next door, is cheaper, and attracts locals to its bathing pools, whirlpools, and steam baths. Bathing suits required, except in the saunas upstairs. Towel rental €5. (☎27 59 40; www.carasana.de. Open daily 8am-10pm. Last entry 9pm. Thermal bath €12 per 2hr., €14 per 3hr.) The **Hardberg public swimming pool** next to the hostel has a giant slide and five pools. (Open May-Sept. daily 10am-8pm in good weather. Last entry 7pm. €3; students €2; families €5-6.50.)

🔆 🔆 SIGHTS AND HIKING

When they're not busy preening themselves at the baths, Baden-Baden's affluent guests head to the oldest **casino** in Germany, which movie star Marlene Dietrich called the "most beautiful casino in the world." You must be 21 in order to gamble here, men must wear a coat (rentals €8) and tie (€3), and women must avoid jeans or tennis shoes. (☎302 40; www.casino-baden-baden.de. Open M-Th and Su 2pm-2am, F-Sa 2pm-3am. Entrance fee €3, min. bet €2.) There is no dress code for the **slot machine wing** downstairs (same hours as casino; €1 entrance fee), or for the casino tour. (Tours 9:30-11:45am; €4, children €2.) In a city with as wealthy a cliental as Baden-Baden, it goes without saying that its **Festspielhaus** attracts some of the biggest names in the classical music world, from Lang Lang to Anne-Sophie Mutter. (☎301 31 01; www.festspielhaus.de. Past the Trinkhalle from the casino. Ticket-service open M-F 10am-6pm, Sa and Su 10am-2pm. Student discounts.) Next to the casino, the terra-cotta tiles of the pillared **Trinkhalle** cover a marble fountain, souvenir shop, and a gallery of murals immortalizing local legends. The *Heilwasser* (healing water) is allegedly good for your health. (Open daily 10am-6:30pm. Free.) Those curious about the history of the famous *badekultur* will enjoy the **Römische Badruinen** (Roman Bath Ruins), a well-preserved hygienic bath from Roman times, today partly covered by the modern Friedrichsbad. (☎27 59 34; www.badruinen.de. Open daily Mar. 16-Nov. 14 11am-1pm and 2-5pm; Nov. 15-Mar. 15 2-5pm. €2, under 14 €1.) A few blocks in the opposite direction, down the paths of the verdant Lichtentaler Allee, the **Staatliche Kunsthalle** (National Arts Center) has modern art. (☎30 07 63; www.kunsthalle-baden-baden.de. Open Tu-Su 11am-6pm, W 11am-8pm. €5, students €4.) Just next door, the **Museum Frieder Burda,** Lichtentaler Allee 8b, presents its own rotating exhibits on modern art, sculpture, and architecture. (☎39 89 80; www.museum-frieder-burda.de. Same hours as the Kunsthalle. Admission €8, students €6.) For a pretty view of the surrounding valleys, head up the steep **Schloßstaffeln** stairwell from Marktpl. to the **Neues Schloß.** Once the home of the Margraves of Baden, the castle is now a private residence. For an exquisite view extending across the Rhein plain to the French frontier, head to the 11th century **Altes Schloß.** Its stately ruins, the **Ruine Hohenbaden,** are accessible by the **trail** starting from behind the Neues Schloß. From the trailhead, the Altes Schloß will be visible on your left. Take any trail up through the meadow, keeping an eye out for the Altes Schloß arrows painted on stones. For even more breathtaking views of the surrounding landscape, and to check out daring climbers, proceed to the **cliffs** ("Felsen" trails) above the Altes Schloß. Several trails connect the castle and the end of bus line #214 at **Eberstenburg** (about 15min. to Leopoldspl., 1-2 per hr., last bus down around 8pm).

Longer **hiking** trails traverse the 668m **Merkur** peak east of town. Take bus #204 or 205 from Leopoldpl. to "Merkurwald," then hike to the top, where a slew of trails plunge into the Schwarzwald. At the bottom, the 37km, more-or-less level **Panoramaweg** (marked by white signs with a green circle) connects the best lookout points. For a general idea of the trails pick up the "Outline map" at the tourist office (€1.50); for more serious hiking buy one of the tourist maps (€5).

FREIBURG IM BREISGAU ☎0761

Tucked in the western edge of the Black Forest, Freiburg (pop. 214,000) hums with activity at all hours. Home to a renowned jazz house as well as a university population, this metropolis is the darling child of Baden-Württemburg. Chairs spill out of boisterous cafés onto medieval cobblestones, and streams spread their cooling web through the city. Complementing the urban din, untouched countryside lies minutes from town, where hiking trails crisscross the rippled forest floor.

▐ TRANSPORTATION

Trains: To **Basel** (1hr., 3 per hr., €11-16) and **Karlsruhe** (1¾hr., every hr., €20-29).

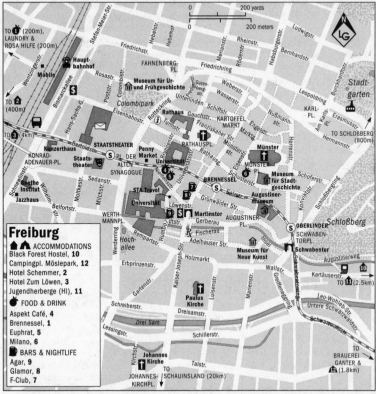

Freiburg

⬆︎🏠 ACCOMMODATIONS
Black Forest Hostel, **10**
Campingpl. Möslepark, **12**
Hotel Schemmer, **2**
Hotel Zum Löwen, **3**
Jugendherberge (HI), **11**

🍴 FOOD & DRINK
Aspekt Café, **4**
Brennessel, **1**
Euphrat, **5**
Milano, **6**

🍸 BARS & NIGHTLIFE
Agar, **9**
Glamor, **8**
F-Club, **7**

Public Transportation: Single fare on Freiburg's bus and tram lines €2. *Regio24* day pass €4; 2 people €7.20. Most transportation stops at 12:30am, but a system of **night buses** covers major stops through the night (€4 per ride; €2 with day pass; F-Su every hr. 1:30-4:30am). The trams stop at the train station, on the overpass to the right. Bus and tram route names are being revised; check the most up-to-date map upon arrival.

Taxis: ☎ 55 55 55.

Bike Rental: Mobile, Wentzingerstr. 15 (☎ 292 79 98), the round wooden structure under the overpass. €7.50 per 6hr., €10 per day. Open daily 5:30am-1:30am.

Hitchhiking: *Let's Go* does not recommend hitchhiking as a safe mode of transportation. Hitchers have been known to take public transit to departure points: for points north, tram #2 (dir.: Zähringen) to "Reutebachg." and walk back 50m; for points east: tram #1 (dir.: Littenweiler) to "Maria-Hilf-Kirche."

✳︎🔋 ORIENTATION AND PRACTICAL INFORMATION

The city's sights and restaurants are concentrated in the Altstadt, a 10min. walk from the Hauptbahnhof down tree-lined Eisenbahnstr. to Rathauspl.

Tourist Office: Rotteckring 14 (☎ 388 18 80; www.freiburg.de). Take the underpass from the station, then walk 2 blocks down Eisenbahnstr. Books rooms for a €3 fee and has free city maps. 24hr. automated displays in front of the office and the train station can help you find lodging as well. Open June-Sept. M-F 9:30am-8pm, Sa 9:30am-5pm, Su 10am-noon; Oct.-May M-F 9:30am-6pm, Sa 9:30am-2pm, Su 10am-noon.

Currency Exchange: The closest to the Hauptbahnhof is the **Volksbank** across from the main entrance. 24hr. **ATM.** Open M-W and F 8:30am-4pm, Th 8:30am-6pm. **Volksbank** at the Martinstor has an **exchange** machine and **ATMs.** Open daily 6am-1am.

Gay and Lesbian Resources: Rosa Hilfe, Eschholzstr. 19 (☎251 61 and 0152 02).

Laundromat: Wasch&Fun, Egonstr. 25 (☎28 72 94), behind the train station. Wash €3, soap €0.50. Dry €2. For €5.50 they will wash, dry, and fold your laundry for you; pick it up the next day. Open M-Sa 9am-10pm; laundry service until 5pm.

Emergency: Police: ☎110. **Fire** and **Ambulance:** ☎112.

Rape Crisis Hotline: ☎285 85 85.

Pharmacy: Apotheke, Bertoldstr. 8 (☎07 61), is near Kaiser-Joseph-Str. Open M-F 8:30-7pm, Sa 9am-6pm.

English Bookstore: Walthari, Bertoldstr. 28 (☎38 77 70; www. bookworld.de). Open M-F 9am-7pm, Sa 9:30am-6pm.

Internet Access: Planet Internetcafé, Kartäserstr. 3-7, near the Schwabentor. €3 per hr. Open M-Sa 9am-midnight, Su 11am-midnight.

Post Office: Eisenbahnstr. 56-58 1 block straight ahead from the train station. Open M-F 8:30am-6:30pm, Sa 9am-2pm. **Postal Code:** 79098.

ACCOMMODATIONS AND CAMPING

Black Forest Hostel, Kartäuserstr. 33 (☎881 78 70; www.blackforest-hostel.de). Take tram #1 (dir. Littenweiler) to "Oberlinden.," walk through the medieval city gate and turn left down Kartäuserstr. Look for the anchor, inner-tube, and signs to the hostel. This congenial and wacky hostel is a rare find in the Black Forest. Kitchen, comfy common room, and piano ensure entertainment into the early morning. Bike rental €5 per day. Linen €2.50, sleeping bags are encouraged. Internet access available. Reception 7am-1am. Check-out 11am. Dorms €13-21; singles €27; doubles €44. Cash only. ❶

Hotel Zum Löwen, Breisgauer Str. 62 (☎809 72 20; fax 840 23). Take tram #1 to "Padua-Allee," then bus #19, 31 or 32 to "Kirchbergstr." or backtrack 20m along the tracks and walk down Breisgauer Str. toward Lehen for 5min. Marble floors, spacious rooms, and friendly French owners belie the budget prices. Enter through the parking lot; the front door leads to a more expensive guesthouse. Breakfast included, most rooms with TV. Singles €30-35; doubles €55-85. MC/V. ❸

Jugendherberge (HI), Kartäuserstr. 151 (☎676 56; www.jugendherberge-freiburg.de). Bus #1 to "Lassbergstr." Take a left and then a right on Fritz-Geiges-Str. The signs will take you from there (800m). Rampant schoolchildren in packed, brightly colored rooms. In-house disco or movie nights. Breakfast and sheets included. Reception every hr. on the hr. Check-in 1pm. Curfew 2am. Dorms €19, over 27 €22.50; doubles €49; additional nights discounted. Cash only. ❷

Hotel Schemmer, Eschholzstr. 63 (☎20 74 90; www.hotel-schemmer.de). Behind the Hauptbahnhof; over the overpass, past the church and to the left. Elegant rooms, some with balconies. Breakfast included. Reception M-F 7am-7pm, Sa-Su 7-11am and 4-7pm. Singles €34-39, with shower €39-45; doubles €51-62; triples €65-78; quads €85. AmEx/MC/V. ❸

Campingplatz am Möslepark, Waldeseestr. 77 (☎767 93 33; www.camping-freiburg.com). Tram #1 (dir. Littenweiler) to "Stadthalle." Head south on Möslestr., cross the tracks, and keep going straight on Waldseestr. past the park (about 15min.). Ideally situated near hiking trails and the *Waldkurbad* (M-Sa 9:30am-11pm, Su

9:30am-10pm). Wash and dry €6.65. Reception 8am-noon and 2:30-10pm. Open Mar.-Oct. €5.80 per person, €2-2.60 per child. €5.90 per plot, add €3 for a car. Internet access €2.50 per 30 min., €3.50 per hr. MC/V. ❶

FOOD

With more than 23,000 university students to feed, Freiburg overflows with budget options. During the daytime, the **Freiburger Markthalle,** next to the Martinstor, is home to foodstands serving ethnic specialties (€3-7). The main entrance is one block up on Grünwälderstr. (☎38 11 11. Open M-F 7am-7pm, Sa 7am-4pm.) **Pennymarkt,** Bertoldstr. 25, provides a typical assortment of groceries and household supplies. (Open M-Sa 7am-8pm.)

Brennessel, Eschholzstr. 17 (☎28 11 87), behind the Hauptbahnhof, serves specialties from ostrich to pancakes (€1.80-9.20) among funk-inflected walls and free-floating jazz. Open M-Sa 6pm-1am, Su and holidays 5pm-1am. Kitchen open until 12:30am, limited menu after 11:30pm. Cash only. ❷

Euphrat, Niemensstr. 13, prepares tasty Middle Eastern plates and wraps (€2.50-6.50). Open M-F 11am-midnight, Sa 11am-1am, Su noon-midnight. Cash only.❷

Aspekt Café, Bertoldstr. 26 (☎367 47), is a bar/café near the Altstadt popular with students and locals. The perfect place for a drink (from €2), snack (from €2), or simple yet satisfying breakfast (from €3). Free wireless Internet access. Open M-F 8am-1am, Sa 9am-1am, Su 10am-midnight. Cash only. ❷

Milano, Schusterstr. 7 (☎337 35), 1 block from Münsterpl. With its leather and brass interior, this *ristorante* feels more upscale than it costs. Delicious pizza (€5-7.50) and pasta (€5.50-11) served with Italian flair. Open daily 11am-midnight. MC/V. ❷

SIGHTS

In only one night in 1944, the Allies finished the bombing job the *Luftwaffe* had mistakenly started, obliterating most of the Altstadt. Since then, the citizens of Freiburg have painstakingly recreated the city's architecture and public spaces.

MÜNSTER. Freiburg's pride and joy is its stunning cathedral, which towers 116m over the Platz. With sections constructed between the 13th and 16th centuries, this architectural melange immortalizes in stained glass the different medieval guilds that financed its construction. Trudge up 209 steps to the ticket counter (the windows on the way up afford a free view), then climb 126 more to ascend the tower. The cathedral is worth a second visit at night, when the bell tower and haunting spires loom half-illuminated over the square below. *(☎298 59 63. Open M-Sa 9:30am-5pm, Su 1-5pm. Tours M-F 2-3pm, Sa-Su 2:30-3:30pm. Tower open M-Sa 9:30am-5pm, Su 1-5pm. €1.50, students €1, under 12 €0.50.)*

SCHLOßBERG. From the Schwabentor, take the overpass across the busy Schloßbergring and climb the **Schloßberg** for a superb view of the city. Or, reach the **Oberer Schloßberg** on the cable car from the Stadtgarten at Leopoldring. *(Open Apr.-Oct. daily 11am-7pm, closed first M of every month; Nov.-Mar. W-Su 11am-5pm. €2.10, round-trip €3.60; ages 4-14 €1.60/2.60.)* To get to the top on foot, start at Schloßbergring across from Hermannstr. (20min.).

AUGUSTINERMUSEUM. Offering a comprehensive cultural history of the Upper Rhine, the Augustiner impresses with medieval sculpture, paintings, and tapestries, and numerous depictions of 18th century *Schwarzwald* (Black Forest) life. *(Augustiner at Augustinerpl. in an old monastery 2 blocks south of the Münster. ☎201 25 21 or 201 25 31. Open Tu-Su 10am-5pm. Free. Special exhibitions subject to fee.)*

MUSEUM FÜR UR- UND FRÜHGESCHICHTE (MUSEUM FOR PRIMORDIAL AND EARLY HISTORY). The early Victorian Colombischlößle overlooks vineyards and flowers. Inside, countless odds and ends track the history of the South Baden region from the stone age to medieval times. *(Rotteckring 5. In Colombipark across from the tourist office. ☎ 201 25 71. Open Tu-Su 10am-5pm. €3, student €1.50. English guide €2.)*

OTHER SIGHTS. On the south side of Münsterpl. is the red **Kaufhaus,** a merchants' hall dating from the 1500s. Two medieval gates stand within blocks of each other in the southeast corner of the Altstadt. The **Schwabentor,** at the bottom of the Schloßberg, houses a museum of tin figurines illustrating the numerous battles in the area. *(☎ 243 21. Open mid-May to Sept. Tu-F 2:30-5pm, Sa-Su noon-2pm. €1.20, students €0.50, children €0.30.)* The **Martinstor,** which served as a revolutionary barricade in the politically tumultuous year of 1848, has since been hijacked by a less revolutionary presence: a lively McDonald's.

🎵 🎭 ENTERTAINMENT AND NIGHTLIFE

Freiburg is a city of wine and music, awash in *Weinstuben* (wine taverns) and *Kneipen* (pubs), though clubs are less abundant. For current events listings, drop by the *Badische Zeitung* office, Bertoldstr. 7, off Universitätstr., where you can buy tickets for upcoming fêtes. *(☎ 555 66 56. Open M-F 9am-7pm, Sa 9am-2pm.)* The **Freiburger Theater,** Bertholdstr. 46, holds plays, ballets, musicals, and concerts (student tickets from €7). *(☎ 201 28 53; www.theaterfreiburg.de. Ticket office open Tu-F 10am-6pm, Sa 10am-1pm.)* The **Freiburger Weinfest** is held on Münsterpl. the first weekend in July. Sample some 400 different vintages (€1.50-3 per glass) to live swing music. The two-week international **Zelt-Musik-Festival** (tent music festival; late June to early July) brings big-name classical, rock, and jazz acts to two circus tents at the city's edge. Tickets (€8-20) sell fast and can be bought over the phone (☎ 50 40 30) online (www.zmf.de), or through the *Badische Zeitung* office. Take tram #5 to "Bissierstr." and catch the free shuttle to the site.

Freiburg's nightlife keeps pace with its students—afternoon cafés become pubs and discos by night. The scene centers around the streets near the city gate on Kaiser-Joseph-Str.—**Niemensstr., Löwenstr., Humboldtstr.**—and nearby alleyways.

Glamour, Kaiser-Joseph-Str. 248 (☎ 28 54 777), next to Martinstor. 1 room dedicated to American and German Top 40, another to hip-hop, and a 3rd—white-walled and more intimate than the other 2—to a calmer mix. 4 separate bars. Drinks from €2.50. Open M and W-Sa from 11pm. Cash only.

F-Club, Kaiser-Joseph-Str. 244, is just around the corner from Glamour and provides a less elaborate, but equally lively, lounge, bar, and dance floor 3 nights per week. Cover usually €3. W student night 10pm-4am. F hip-hop 11pm-5am. Special house act 10pm-5am. Cash only.

Agar, Löwenstr. 8 (☎ 38 06 50; www.agar-disco.de), near Martinstor. Beer €3. Drinks €5.50. The expansive dancefloor attracts a boisterous student crowd Tu nights (free with student ID). Th 80s night; other nights range from house to hip-hop. 18+. Cover Tu, Th, Su €3, F-Sa €4. Su over 30 free. Open Tu and Th 10pm-3am, F-Sa 11pm-4am, Su 10pm-2am. Last entry 1hr. before closing. Cash only.

🥾 HIKING

Freiburg's plentiful accommodations and accessible by train make it a superior base for hikes in the Black Forest. **Mountain biking** trails also traverse the hills; look for symbols with bicycles (maps €3.50-6 at tourist office). The **Schwarzwaldverein** office, Schloßbergring 15, provides trail information. (☎ 38 05 30; www.schwarzwaldverein.de. Open M-Th 8am-noon and 2-4pm, F 8am-noon.)

A good starting spot in Freiburg is **Schauinsland.** Take tram #4 (dir.: Günterstal) to "Dorfstr." (15min. from Hauptbahnhof; 1 per 10min.), then bus #21 to "Talstation" (7min., 2 per hr.). From the station, take the red circle trail to the top (3hr.), or ride the spectacular 3.6km **Schauinslandbahn.** On top is the **Bergwelt Schauinsland,** with a wildlife park and the ▧ **Museums-Bergwerk** (Mining Museum), where visitors don helmets, head lanterns, and working gloves before descending slippery metal ladders into the mountain. The tour explores 800 years of mining history with demonstrations and detailed descriptions of the muddy, narrow passages, huge caverns, and harrowing drops. Wear closed-toe, waterproof shoes that can get dirty. (☎264 68; 45min. family tours; more comprehensive 1½ and 2½hr. tours. July to Sept. 15 shorter tours M, Tu-Th, F. May-June and mid-Sept. to Oct. longer tours W, Sa, Su 11am and 2pm; shorter tours every hr. 11:30am-3:30pm. €18.70/24.) The museum also offers an eight kilometer downhill roller ride and hiking and biking trails (☎29 29 30). (Schauinslandbahn runs Oct-July 9am-5pm, July-Sept. 9am-6pm. €7.50, students €6.50; round-trip €7.50/6.50. Roller ride €23, available Sa, Su, and holidays May-Oct 10am-5:30pm.) Take the red-dot trail down (2hr.). Nordic walking are tours €25 per person (☎07 61). Simple maps are free at the bottom. Slightly longer, the yellow circle trail from the top of the mountain connects "Schauinsland Gipfel," "Rappeneck," and "Kappel," after which you can take the bus #17 back to Freiburg (4hr.). A **Rundweg** also takes you from the top station in a panoramic circle around the top (1hr.). Trails around Schauinsland are loaded with forested vistas of Freiburg and the Black Forest.

For a **day hike,** part of the red-diamond **Westweg Pforzheim-Basel** to Feldberg runs just a couple of hours from Schauinsland. The hike requires about 7hr. from **Schauinsland** to **Feldberg-Bärental** and shows a cross-section of the Black Forest—cow pastures, barns, and soaring trees. Particularly noteworthy are the scenic meadows and thick forest between Feldberg and Notschrei. To reach the trail from Schauinsland top station, take a right and head down the driveway to the parking lot. Follow the blue diamond trail to Halden and keep going; it meets the red-diamond Westweg between Halden and Notschrei (3-4hr.).

⚡TIP **GRABBING THE WEED BY ITS THORNS.** There is a reason German hikers wear those untrendy wool socks hiked up to their knees: a little weed known as **Brennessel** (stinging nettles). These waist-high weeds grow in clusters across Germany, and are recognizable by long, saw-toothed leaves and furry yellow bunches. The leaves and stems are covered with needle-like thorns that snag the flesh and inject formic acid, the same poison in bee and ant stings. A few minutes later, the spot will burn unmercifully and develop a **tingling red rash with white circular bumps.** The pain will stop in around 20min., and the rash, which doesn't spread, will disappear in a day or so on its own. The pulp of the plant's leaves, if rubbed on a sting immediately, is said to prevent the rash from forming. Needless to say, it's advisable to put a layer of cloth or paper between your skin and the leaves you are mushing. During WWI, the German army used fibers from the plant to make uniforms, and more recently, Italian designers have been using nettles to make (non-stinging) blue jeans.

BADEN-WÜRTTEMBERG

▶ DAYTRIP FROM FREIBURG: ST. PETER AND ST. MÄRGEN

Bus #7216 runs from Freiburg to St. Märgen via St. Peter, but the more common route requires a train ride along the Freiburg-Titisee line to "Kirchzarten" (3rd stop), from where bus #7216 heads to St. Peter (25min., 1-2 per hr.). A 24hr. RegioKarte (€6), valid for both buses and trains, is the best deal for round-trips from Freiburg. Only half the buses continue on to St.

Märgen (15min., last bus usually around 7:40pm, €2); always check with the driver. Schedules are only a rough guide, so don't stray far from the bus stop.

Deep in a valley of cow-speckled hills 17km from Freiburg are St. Peter and St. Märgen. Five kilometers above the pastures of St. Peter, the small village of St. Märgen commands a bird's-eye view of the valley, one obscured only by the occasional grove of trees and passing cloud. With links to all major Black Forest trails, the town rightly calls itself a *Wanderparadies*. Most of the trails are marked from Hotel Hirschen (on Landfeldweg), uphill from the bus stop. A challenging local trail leads to the **Zweibach waterfall;** follow signs with a black dot on a yellow field (15km, 4-5hr.). To reach the start of the trail from the town center, walk along Feldbergstr., turn left on Landfeldweg, and follow signs for the Rankmühle.

Bike rentals are available at **Stihldienst Saier,** on Rankhofstr. 28, uphill past the gas station. (☎07669 279. Bikes €5-13 per day. Open M-F 8am-12:30pm and 2-6pm, Sa 8am-noon.) The **tourist office** is in the Rathaus 100m from the "Post" bus stop, downhill to the right of the Volksbank. A hiking trail map awaits at the bus stop for latecomers (☎07669 91 18 17; www.st-maergen.de. Open M-F 9am-12pm, 2-5pm; Sa 9am-12pm.) A 24hr. **ATM** is at **Sparkasse,** on Feldbergstr. 2 near the bus stop. There are **public restrooms** in the Rathaus.

St. Peter, slightly closer to Freiburg and surrounded by patches of black forest pine, is distinguished from a handful of other small towns dotting the pastureland below St. Märgen by its famous cathedral. The green domes of the city's **Klosterkirche** rise above the expansive skyline, while a gilded gaggle of flute and violin playing babies top the mauve marble structures within the church. Take the tour to see the inside of the abbey and its striking library. (☎07660 910 10. Open during the day. Tours in German Su 11:30am, Tu 11am, Th 2:30pm. €3.) Many well-marked hiking paths begin at the tourist office and abbey. A relatively easy and scenic 8.5km path leads to St. Märgen; follow the blue diamonds of the **Panoramaweg** past Vogesenkapelle and Kapfenkapelle. From the abbey, make a sharp right alongside the Klosterkirche, heading for the Jägerhaus, before crossing the highway. The trail meanders through the dark evergreen-scented forest into vast wildflower meadows with stunning views of surrounding peaks. A tiny chapel dedicated to travelers and decorated with chalk paintings of cows inside is a great rest stop about halfway through (2-2½hr.).

The **tourist office** is in the Klosterhof. Get off the bus at Zähringereck; the office is up the hill in front of the church under the *Kurverwaltung* sign. (☎07660 91 02 24; www.st-peter-schwarzwald.de. Open May-Oct. M-F 9am-noon, 2-5pm; July-Aug. also Sa 10am-noon.) For latecomers, a **reservations** phone is out front, but beware the 3min. time limit. **Zähringer Apotheke,** Zähringer Str. 12, is by the bus stop. (Open M-F 9am-12:30pm and 2:30-7pm, Sa 9am-12:30pm.) **Public restrooms** are under the Rathaus next to the tourist office.

BREISACH AND THE KAISERSTUHL ☎07667

Twenty-five kilometers west of Freiburg, Breisach (pop. 14,000) is separated from French Alsace by the Rhein. The Altstadt, a part of which is elevated above the surrounding countryside, is surrounded by hills and unending vineyards. Near Breisach is the Kaiserstuhl, a clump of lush hills that used to be volcanoes, which now attract hikers with unique flora and fauna usually found in warmer climes.

■ **TRANSPORTATION. Trains** arrive from Freiburg (30min., usually every 30min., €4.60). The Freiburg-Breisach train also stops at the towns of Ihringen and Wasenweiler, hubs for hiking the Kaiserstuhl's southern fringes. A slightly tenuous **bus** system handles the route straight into the hills; check the schedule at the Breisach Hauptbahnhof (☎361 72; www.suedbadenbus.de). **Funbike Breisach**, Metzgerg. 1 next to the tourist information office, rents bikes. (Open daily 9am-noon. €10 per day, €25 per 3 days, or €40 per week. Bring a passport and €50 deposit per bike, which need to be returned by 6-7pm.) Jaunts along the Rhein in big white **boats** are available through **Breisacher Fahrgast-Schiffarht**, Rheinuferstr., on the Rhein. Occasional trips to: Basel (€45, children €23); Colmart (€26/13); Strassburg (Strasbourg), France (€45/23.) Buy tickets at the dock or tourist office. (☎94 20 10; www.bfs-info.de. Open Apr.-Sept. Tu-Sa 9am-1pm and 2:30-5:30pm; Oct.-Mar. Tu-F 9am-1pm; boats leave around 11:30am, 2, and 3:15pm. 1 or 2hr. rides €7.50-9, children €3.50-4.50, families €16-24; check the webpage for schedule.)

⚠ PRACTICAL INFORMATION. For hiking, biking, and town maps, visit the Breisach **tourist office**, Marktpl. 16. From the train station, turn left onto Bahnhofstr., follow Neutorpl. right from the rotary intersection, keep the fountain on your right, and go down Rheinstr. into the Marktpl. The office books rooms for €1 and sells hiking and biking maps of the Kaiserstuhl and environs (€1.50-7.90). (☎94 01 55; www.breisach.de. M-F Apr.-Oct. 9am-12:30pm and 1:30-6pm, Sa 10am-1pm; Nov.-Mar. M-F 9am-12:30pm and 1:30-5pm.) The **Volksbank**, across from the station, has an **ATM**. (Bank open M and F 8am-noon and 2-4:30pm, Tu and Th 8am-noon and 2-6pm, W 8am-noon; ATM open daily 5am-midnight.) **Stadt-Apotheke pharmacy**, Neutorstr. 2, is down the street from Marktpl. (☎218. Open M-F 8am-6:30pm, Sa 8am-1pm.) Follow the "Postamt" signs for the **post office**, Richard-Müller-Str. 3a. (Open M-F 9am-12:30pm and 2:30-6pm, Sa 9am-12:30pm.) **Postal Code:** 79206.

🏠🍴 ACCOMMODATIONS AND FOOD. The whitewash shingles of Breisach's **Jugendherberge ❷**, Rheinuferstr. 12, enclose rough-cut stone staircases and rooms, many with a view of the Rhein. From the train station, walk toward and past the tourist office to the Rhein. Take a left and follow the signs. (15min. ☎76 65; www.jugendherberge-breisach.de. Internet €0.07 per min. Wash €3. Reception 7am-11pm. Curfew 11:30pm, but housekey available for €10 deposit. Call ahead to reserve. Dorms €20.30, €17.10 for each additional night. Add €3 for over 27.) A farmer's **market** sets up on Marktpl. (Sa 9am-1pm). For some *Flammkuchen* (German variant of pizza, with a cream-based sauce) and appetizers (€3.30-6) try **Humpen ❷**, Neutorstr. 20. (☎91 26 25. Open M-Th and Su 11am-midnight, F-Sa 11-2am; closed Su in winter. Cash only.)

🏛🥾 SIGHTS AND HIKING. Breisach's **St. Stephansmünster** towers dramatically over a steep riverfront promontory crowded with clapboard houses. Constructed between the 12th and 15th centuries, the church's interior is plain compared to nearby cathedrals, but remnants of frescoes suggest a rich history. The wooden altar, the work of the 16th-century Master Hans Loy, is intricate, without the gilded gaudiness of other altars. Take a look at the unusual open crypt supporting the base of the choir area; since the hilltop was too small for the cathedral, it was extended with this space. The stone wreath of thorns around the central pillar is a war memorial. (Church open daily in summer 9am-6pm; in winter 9am-5pm.)

The **Radbrunnenallee** runs from the Münster to the **Schloßberg** garden, which has panoramic views of the countryside. The entrance to the garden is off Tullag., next to Kapuziner Hotel. Down the hill in the 17th-century **Rheintor**, the **Museum für Stadtgeschichte**, Rheintorpl. 1, contains a large collection of artifacts, including 3000-year-old ceramics and chain-link skivvies from 15th-century northern Italy. (☎70 89. Open Tu-F 2-5pm, Sa and Su 11:30am-5pm. Free.) The most famous of the Kaiserstuhl's trails (maps €5-7) is the **Kaiserstuhl Nord-Südweg**, which braves the overgrown hills and valleys, forging from Ihringen 16km northward to Endingen.

BADEN-WÜRTTEMBERG

From the Ihringen train station, turn left and walk past Hotel Luise; the first trail-post is on your right. The Nord-Südweg is marked by a blue diamond on a yellow field. The last leg of the 108km long **Querweg Donaueschingem-Breisach** also winds through the hills; the trail is marked by a red diamond on yellow. For information on these and other trails, visit the Breisach tourist office, where a clear map of the Kaiserstuhl is available for €4.50.

🎭 **ENTERTAINMENT.** In summer, the Schloßberg garden becomes a theater for the annual Festspiele, hosting plays most weekends between mid-June and mid-September. (Tourist office sells tickets, ☎90 77 60. €8-12, students €7-11.) Breisach also hosts the Weinfest Kaiserstuhl und Tuniberg, during the last weekend in August, when local wines are sipped on the banks of the Rhein. Wine connoisseurs can register for a tour of Badischer Winzerkeller, Zum Kaiserstuhl 16 (☎90 02 70), one of the largest wine cellars in Europe. The cellar is a one kilometer walk east of town. From the train station, go right on Bahnhofstr. and head to the very end of Im Gelbstein (3-7 samples €3-5).

SCHWARZWALD (BLACK FOREST)

The Black Forest comprises the famous and mysterious tangled expanse of ever-green covering the southwest corner of Baden-Württemberg. It is no wonder that the Schwarzwald—so named for the eerily pervasive darkness under its canopy of vegetation—inspired so many of the macabre German fairy tales popular to this day: its murky caves, impenetrable thickets, and clever squirrels assume an unsettling quality even in daylight, what little makes it to the needled ground. Today, many of the region's erstwhile authentic specialties—from cuckoo clocks to *Leder-hosen*—have become kitsch, thanks to the ubiquitous kiosks and souvenir shops lining the streets and otherwise scenic trails.

Myriad trails wind through the hills, leading willing hikers into secluded parts of the forest. Skiing is wildly popular in the area; the longest slope is at Feldberg, near Titisee. The main entry points to the Schwarzwald are Freiburg, in the center; Baden-Baden to the northwest; Stuttgart to the east; and Basel, Switzerland, to the southwest. Rail lines encircle the perimeter, with only two train lines cutting through the region. Bus service is more thorough, but is slower, less frequent, and occasionally erratic.

HOCHSCHWARZWALD (HIGH BLACK FOREST) ☎07655

The towering spruces, broken only by an few, still lakes, blanket the region's mountainous landscape and lonely, largely untouristed, mountain villages. The best source of information for the area is the **Schwarzwaldverein** office in Freiburg, Ludwigstr. 23. (☎01805 66 12 24. Open M-Th 8am-noon and 2-4pm, F 8am-noon.).

At 1493m, **Feldberg** is the Schwarzwald's tallest mountain. The **tourist office,** Kirchg. 1, offers information about Feldberg and other ski slopes in the area. (☎80 19; www.feldberg-schwarzwald.de. Open Tu-F 10am-6pm, Sa-Su 10am-noon.) The Westweg Pforzheim-Basel runs over the Feldberg as well. From the Feldberg-Bärental train station follow the blue circle trail to the glacial Feldsee (2hr.), then pick up the red diamond Westweg to the Feldberg (2hr.). The **Feldbergbahn** ski lift will carry you part of the way (€6, children €4.50; lift open daily 9am-5pm). On a clear day, the Swiss Alps are visible, along with an unfenced drop into the Feldsee. Paths extend from the top, including trails to Titisee. The 30min. hike back down to the ski lift station is magnificent in the early summer, when it winds through the

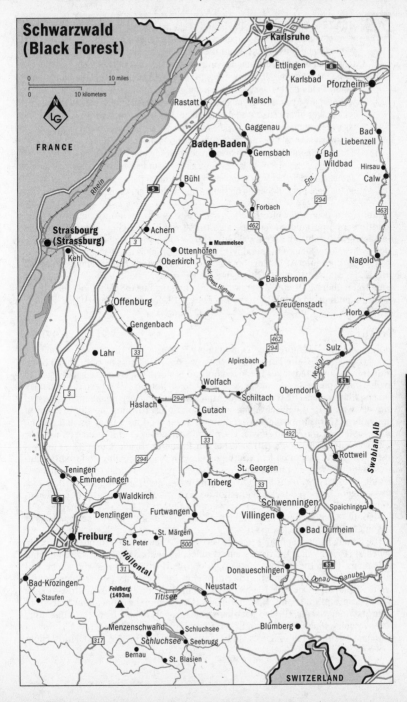

**Schwarzwald
(Black Forest)**

0 — 10 miles
0 — 10 kilometers

FRANCE

Karlsruhe

Ettlingen

Karlsbad

Pforzheim

Rastatt

Malsch

Gaggenau

Baden-Baden

Gernsbach

Bad
Liebenzell

Bad
Wildbad

Hirsau

Calw

Bühl

Enz

294

463

Forbach

462

■ Mummelsee

Strasbourg
(Strassburg)

Achern

3

Ottenhöfen

Oberkirch

Black Forest Highway

Nagold

Kehl

Rhein

5

Baiersbronn

Freudenstadt

Horb

Offenburg

Gengenbach

462
294

Sulz

Lahr

33

Alpirsbach

Neckar

81

Wolfach

3

Haslach

294

Schiltach

Oberndorf

Gutach

33

492

Rottweil

Swabian Alb

294

St. Georgen

Teningen

Emmendingen

Triberg

33

Schwenningen

Spaichingen

Waldkirch

Furtwangen

Villingen

Denzlingen

St. Märgen

Bad Dürrheim

Freiburg

St. Peter

500

Höllental

31

Donaueschingen

Donau (Danube)

81

Bad-Krozingen

Feldberg
(1493m) ▲

Neustadt

Staufen

Titisee

Menzenschwand

Schluchsee

Blumberg

317

Schluchsee

Seebrugg

Bernau

St. Blasien

SWITZERLAND

> **BLAZES OF GLORY.** The Schwarzwald may be a hiker's paradise, but its labyrinth of twisting trails can quickly become a tangled hell. The *Schwarzwald-verein* (Black Forest Association) has set up a system of markers for the major trails. **Red or part-red diamonds on a white field** mark the north-south summit trails, including the 285km Westweg Pforzheim-Basel odyssey. **Diamonds on yellow fields** denote east-west trails, the longest of which is the 178km, Quer-weg Freiburg-Bodensee. Together with the **blue diamond** trails that mark access routes, these trails involve a lot of climbing. The *Schwarzwaldverein* is introducing **yellow diamond** markers for the major local trails to complement local mark-ing systems. Local trails are often eccentrically named, but a **Rundweg** is always a loop; a **Seerundweg,** which follows the shoreline of a lake, will be less taxing. Paths with views of the landscape are called **Panoramaweg.** After trail junctions and intersections, look for a trail marker 50m down the path to confirm you are on the right track. If there is no sign at the intersection, continue straight.

meadows of fragrant white *Edelweiß* ("white noble," a mountain flower) and wildflowers. Sporadic bus service also runs from Titisee via the train station to **Feldbergerhof,** right next to the ski lift. (Bus #7300; 15min., about 6 per day, €2. Dec.-Apr. also a **Skibus,** €13 per day.) The tourist office is in the ground floor of the Feldbergerhof hotel. At 1234m above sea level, Feldberg's **Jugendherberge Hebelhof (HI) ❷,** Passhöhe 14, may be the highest in Germany. Take the Freiburg-Seebrugg train to Feldberg-Bärental (1 per hr., €4.35), then the bus to "Hebelhof." (☎0 76 76; www.jugendherberge-feldberg.de. Sheets €3.10. Reception 8am-10pm. Curfew 10:45pm. Dorms €19.20, over 27 €22.20. Cash only.)

TITISEE   ☎07651

Don't be alarmed if more gray hairs than green trees grace the streets beyond the small train station—the Titisee (TEE-tee-zay; pop. 12,000) is one of the most beau-tiful, if most touristed, lakes in the region, and is worth the crowds (usually easy to avoid) that mob the beach and pedestrian zone on hot days. Between the **Hintergar-ten** and **Himmelreich** (Heavenly Kingdom) train stops, in a gap of sky in the midst of tunnels, watch for the **Hirschsprung,** a statue of a stag crowning the cliff in a part of the valley. According to legend, a deer once escaped its hunter by making the impossible leap across the chasm. The placid **Seerundweg** (1½hr.) is nice for a stroll.

Titisee's **Jugendherberge (HI) Veltishof am Titisee ❷,** Bruderhalde 27, is more a mountain lodge than a typical youth hostel, with wood paneling and rustic paint-ings lining the walls. Continue on Strandbadstr. past the tourist office or take bus #7300 (every 1-2hr. until 6pm) to "Jugendherberge." (2km out of town. ☎238; www.jugendherberge-titisee-veltishof.de. For reception, ring the bell 8:30am-10pm. Dorms €18, over 27 €21; subsequent nights €14.70/17.70. *Kurtaxe* €1. Cash only.) Contact the tourist office for details regarding Titisee's **campgrounds ❶** and many **private rooms** (from €13).

The 30min. train ride from Freiburg (every hr., €4.60) glides through the scenic **Höllental** (Hell's Valley). Titisee's **tourist office,** Strandbadstr. 4, books rooms and sells maps. From the station, hang a right onto Parkstr., left across the square and another right on Strandbadstr. The office is in the *Kurhaus* (☎980 40; www.titi-see.de. Open May-Oct. M-F 10am-6pm, Sa 11am-1pm, Su 10am-noon; Nov.-Apr. M-F 8am-noon and 1:30-5pm.) Hiking trails start in front of the office. Rent **boats** from vendors along Seestr. Guided **boat tours** (in German) depart from the same area, run by **Bootsverleih Schweizer.** (☎82 14. €4 per 25min., children €1.50.) There's a **pharmacy** on the corner of Seestr. and Jägerstr. (☎82 02. Open M-F 8:30am-12:30pm and 2:30-6:30pm, Sa 8:30am-2:30pm.) Get online at the **Internet Café,** Parkst. 10, across from the station. €1 per 15min. Open M-F 9am-noon, 2-8pm, Sa 2-8pm.)

ST. BLASIEN   ☎07672

St. Blasien (pop. 3000) is, on the surface, one of many sleepy towns tucked into the forested hills around the twin lakes of Schluchsee and Titisee. What sets the village apart, however, is not its placid stream, nor its surfeit of hiking trails in the surrounding hills, but rather the town's monumental **Dom,** third only in size to St. Peter's in Rome and Les Invalides in Paris. Dating back to the 9th century, the immaculate white marble pillars and arches within have weathered a peasants' revolt, four fires, and a rather nasty incident involving two deranged monks. (Open daily May-Sept. 8:30am-6:30pm; Oct.-Apr. 8:30am-5pm. Donation requested.) In the same building as the tourist office is the **Museum St. Blasien,** with exhibits on the Dom's religious and secular history, as well as the distinctive wood-carvings, culture, and natural surroundings of the town. (☎414 37. Open Tu-Su 2:30-5pm; closed Nov. 2-Dec. 25. €1.60, students €0.50. June-Aug. concerts every Tu and Sa 8:15pm.) From the end of August to the first week of September, St. Blasien hosts **wood-carving contests.** Trails wind through the virgin wilderness of St. Blasien's surrounding mountains. **Philosophenweg** (Philosopher's Path) offers an excellent view of the Dom. From the Rathaus, follow Hauptstr. to Friedrichstr., then take a left on Bötzbergstr. and another left onto Philosophenweg (45min. round-trip). The other leg of the fork at the end of Bötzbergstr., **Blasiwälder Weg** (marked by a blue diamond), leads to the "Kletteranlage" climbing rocks and the Windberg creek (1½hr. round-trip). On the other side of town, more trails scale the idyllic **Holzberg.** From the **Kurgarten** next to the Dom, take **Tuskulumweg** and head through the tunnel, following the blue diamond markers.

The cheapest night's stay in St. Blasien is **Hotel Garni Kurgarten ❷,** Fürstabt-Ger-bert-Str. 12, across from the tourist office. Most rooms have balconies facing the Dom and Rathaus, some have TV, and all are well lit, clean, and snug. (☎527. All rooms with showers. Singles €22; doubles €44-56. €1.35 *Kurtaxe* per person. Cash only.) The nearest hostel, along with many private rooms, is in **Menzen-schwand.** (10km away. Bus #7321, 15min., runs M-F almost every hr. until 6:45pm, Sa 6:15pm, Su 5pm, but check the schedule plaques to be sure. €2.25.) There, the **Jugendherberge Menzenschwand (HI) ❷,** Vorderdorfstr. 10, offers cheap lodgings in an authentic wood chalet. (☎07675 326. Breakfast included. Reception 5-9pm. Dorms €17.90, over 27 €20.90. Additional nights €14.70/17.70. *Kurtaxe* €0.50. Cash only.) Contact the Menzenschwand **tourist office,** Hinterdorfstr. 15, near the "Hirschen/Hintertor" bus stop and Rathaus. (☎07675 930 90. Same hours and website as the St. Blasien office.) If ever there were a place for a bag lunch, St. Blasien is it: restaurants are not cheap and fill up quickly with elderly sightseers. If a sit-down meal is a must, **Tränke ❷,** Todtmooserstr. 8, serves pizzas and pastas for a decent price. (☎10 30. Cash only.)

A 20min. **bus** ride (#7319, every hr., €2.75) connects St. Blasien with Seebrugg and the train system. The **tourist office,** Am Kurgarten 1-3, has hiking maps (€5), a free town map, and a room catalog. From the main bus station, cross Umgehu-ngsstr., turn right and head for the "Haus des Gastes." The tourist office is inside. (☎414 30; www.st-blasien-menzenschwand.de. Open M-F 10am-noon and 3-5pm; May-Sept. also Sa 10am-noon.) A **pharmacy** is on Hauptstr., across from the Rathaus. (☎515. Open M-F 9am-1pm and 2:30-6:30pm, Sa 9am-12:30pm.) The **Sparkasse** across the street has an **ATM.** (Open M-W 8:30am-noon and 2-4:30pm, Th 8:30am-noon and 2-6pm, F 8:30am-4:30pm. The **post office** is in the Quelle shop on Hauptstr. 45. (Open M-F 8:30am-5:30pm, Sa 8:30-12:30pm.) **Postal Code:** 79837.

CENTRAL BLACK FOREST

TRIBERG   ☎07722

Tucked in a lofty valley 670m above sea level, the tiny but heavily touristed village of Triberg (pop. 5000) is well-known for its waterfalls, the highest in Germany. Spruce forests cover the steep hills around the town, and a well-marked series of trails provide a comprehensive, if cardiovascularly taxing, cross-section of the Central Black Forest. On the hour, the village echoes—for better or for worse—with the sounds of cuckoo clocks, for which the town is known.

▐▀▚ TRANSPORTATION AND PRACTICAL INFORMATION. Trains travel from Triberg to Freiburg (€18-26) and Donaueschingen (€4-12). Call ☎55 33 for a **taxi.** Triberg's **tourist office,** Wallfahrtsstr. 4, is connected to the Schwarzwald Museum, across from the entrance to the waterfalls. From the station, turn right on Bahnhofstr. and follow the signs: cross the bridge, go under it, and head up steep Fréjusstr., which turns into Hauptstr. Or, take any **bus** to Marktpl. (€2). (☎86 64 94; www.triberg.de. Open daily 10am-5pm.) **Sparkasse** at Marktpl. has an **ATM.** The **Stadt-Apotheke pharmacy,** Am Marktpl., is right next to the Rathaus. (☎45 37. Open M-F 8:30am-12:30pm and 2:30-6:30pm, Sa 8:30am-12:30pm.) **Postal Code:** 78098.

▐▛▐▟ ACCOMMODATIONS AND FOOD. Many private rooms and holiday apartments are available at good prices; ask for a list at the tourist office. A stay in any hotel in the Triberg area will get you the **Schwarzwald Gästekarte,** which provides free transportation (bus and train) within 50km of the city for the duration of your stay. Ask individual hotels about up-to-date details and offers. Close to the center, the friendly family who runs **Hotel Zum Bären ❷,** Hauptstr. 10 (on the way into town from the station), goes far out of their way to make guests feel comfortable and cared for. Rooms are clean and most have showers. (☎44 93; fax 47 43. Breakfast included. Singles €26, students €21-22; doubles €49/40-44; triples €64/60; student-only quads €74. Cash only.) The town's **Jugendherberge (HI) ❷,** Rohrbacher Str. 35, sits (far) up a (steep) mountain and offers plunging views of two valleys, although the staff is inattentive. Climb straight up Friedrichstr. (which turns into Rohrbacher Str.) from the tourist office (at least 30min.). A taxi from the station costs about €7. (☎41 10; www.jugendherberge-triberg.de. Internet €0.10 per min. Breakfast included. Reception 5-7pm and 9:45pm. Curfew 10pm, key available. €17.40, over 27 €20.10; additional nights €17/14.30. Mostly 4- or 6-bed dorms, but some doubles available at no extra charge. Cash only.) *Imbiße* (snack bars) around the entrance to the **Wasserfall** park or down Hauptstr. toward the train station offer cheap food. **Zur Lilie ❹,** Wallfahrtstr. 3, near the waterfalls, serves an array of homemade Black Forest speciality baked-goods (€2.30-2.70), including the locally famous Black Forest cake (cherry sponge cake, often served soaked in sherry or a cherry-flavored liquor; around €3). (☎44 19. Open daily from 11:30am to around midnight. Cash only.)

◪ SIGHTS. The **Gutacher Wasserfal** is technically the highest waterfall in Germany; in reality, it is more a inclined stream, bubbling over smooth, green-velvet rocks broken in relatively small but vertical drops. Hemingway found under the towering spruce trees in 1922, but the steep **Kaskadenweg** ("Cascade Trail," 1hr. round trip, marked with a squirrel symbol) draws fewer obnoxious family groups than the longer, less strenuous **Kulturweg** and **Naturweg.** (Park always open and lighted until midnight. Admission 9am-7pm. €1.50, under 18 €0.50, families €3.50.) The signs for the **Wallfahrtskirche** point along Kulturweg to the small Pilgrimage church, Maria in der Tanne, where, according to legend, the pious have been miraculously healed since the 17th century. (☎45 66. Closes around 6 or 7pm.) At the tiny *Bergsee* (mountain lake) uphill from the church, rent rowboats (€1.50 per 30min., under 14 €1.20) or paddleboats (€4.50 per 30min.) from the kiosk. (Usually open M-W and F-Su 8:30am-7pm.) Cross the main road onto Kroneckweg and follow the **"Panoramaweg"** signs for hiking trails with a view of the valley. The **Schwarzwald Museum,** Wallfahrtsstr. 4, back in town, is just across the street and left from the waterfalls. This museum is packed with Black Forest history and culture, including nearly 100 mechanical musical instruments, wood carvings, and, of course, more black forest cuckoo clocks than you could possibly need to see. (☎44 34; www.schwarzwaldmuseum.de. Open daily 10am-5pm. Closed Nov. 15-Dec. 15. €4, students and ages 14-18 €2.50, ages 5-13 €2.) There is, it seems, no upper limit to the superlative "biggest." The "world's biggest cuckoo clock" of Wiesbaden lives in peaceful harmony with the "world's biggest cuckoo clock" in St. Goar, just as the "world's biggest cuckoo clock" on the one side of Triberg is perfectly fine with the "world's biggest cuckoo clock" on the other. The first and the oldest is a bit out of town toward Schonach on L109. (☎46 89. Open daily 9am-noon and 1-6pm.) Another is 15min. away from the train station and accompanied by a **museum;** turn left on Bahnhofstr. and then continue on Franz-Göttler-Weg. After the road below enters a tunnel, take the next right, down to the clock park. (☎962 20. Clock is outside the building. Museum is open Easter-Oct. M-Sa 9am-6pm, Su 10am-6pm; Nov.-Easter M-Sa 9am-6pm. €1.50. Audio guide €1.)

The region's surroundings ensure rewarding hikes. Numerous trail signs on the outskirts of town point the way to a portion of the Pforzheim-Basel **Westweg** (red diamond trail markers; access via blue diamond markers). The tourist office sells maps for hiking (€6-8), biking (€4-6), and mountain biking (€4-6).

DONAUESCHINGEN ☎0771

Ever since a 10-year-old Mozart visited Donaueschingen (pop. 20,000) on his way from Vienna to Paris, musical luminaries and travelers alike have stopped here to pay homage to the mythical source of the Danube (and the local *Fürstenberg* beer). The Donaueschingen of today is small and quiet, but well positioned for forays in the Black Forest, the Bodensee region, and the Wutach Schlucht.

▐▌ TRANSPORTATION AND PRACTICAL INFORMATION. Trains connect Donaueschingen to Triberg (40min., every hr., €5.60-10), and Rottweil (40min., every hr., €4.30-5.40). The **tourist office,** Karlstr. 58, helps find rooms (from €15). Follow Josefstr. (on the right side of the Bahnhof) for 10min. and turn left at Karlstr. (☎85 72 21; www.donaueschingen.de. Open May-Oct. M-F 9am-6pm, Sa 10am-noon; Nov.-Apr. M-F 9am-5pm.) The office gives info on the city's annual **Musiktage,** a modern music festival usually scheduled for the third week in October. Get cash at the **ATM** at the **Baden-Württembergische Bank,** across the street on Schulstr. Stock up on all things pharmaceutical at **Hof Apotheke,** Karlstr. 40. (Open M-Tu and Th-F 8:30am-12:30pm and 2:30-6:30pm, Sa 8:30am-12:30pm.) **Internet** is available at the **Stadtbibliothek,** at Max-Rieple-Pl. behind and below the tourist office. (☎85 72 45. €2 per hr. Open W-Th 2-6pm, Tu and Sa 9am-noon, F 9am-1pm.) The **post office** is on the corner on Schulstr. 5-7. (Open M-F 9am-noon and 2-6pm, Sa 9am-noon.) **Postal Code:** 78166.

▐▌ ACCOMMODATIONS AND FOOD. Find respite at **Hotel Bären ❸**, Josefstr. 7-9, on the way from the train station to town. (☎25 18. Breakfast included. Check-in 4:30pm. Large singles €25; doubles €50, with bath €65. Cash only.) Head to **City Markt,** Karlstr. 44a, for groceries. (Open M-F 7:30am-7pm, Sa 7am-4pm.) The pale pink house behind the "Diana" Fountain (featuring the chaste huntress and her faithful hound) houses **Fürstenberg Bräustüble ❸**, Postpl. 14, which serves up a wide assortment of meaty salads (€4.20), sausages, and *schnitzel* (€5-17). Beer from the *Fürstenberg* brewery next door is €1.90-2.40. (☎36 69. Open M-Tu and Th-Su 11am-midnight, kitchen 11am-2pm and 6-10pm. Cash only.)

⬛ SIGHTS. Donaueschingen's somewhat dubious claim to fame is its status as the "source" of the 2860km Danube, the second-longest river in Europe. The river officially begins east of the city center, but the Fürstenberg princes decided to overlook this minor detail and glorify a spring (from which a somewhat pitiful stream flows into the Brigach) in the garden of their **Schloß Fürstenberg** instead. The **Donauquelle** (source of the Danube) couldn't be farther removed from the "Beautiful Blue Danube" of Strauss Jr.'s Vienna: it's a round sandy basin encased in 19th-century stonework, located (just incidentally, of course) next to the souvenir booth. The French-inflected architecture of the *Schloß* contains an assortment of tapestries and marble befitting the splendid princes of its past. (Garden open 24hr. from May-July. Tours by appointment; ☎85 72 21. Admission €10.) Across the street, the **Fürstlich-Fürstenbergische Sammlungen** (Royal Fürstenberg Collections), Karlspl. 7, juxtaposes a 19th-century collection of Fürstenberg paraphernalia with exhibits of contemporary art. (☎865 63. Open Mar.-Nov. Tu-Th 10am-1pm and 2-5pm, Su and holidays 10am-5pm. Last entry 12:30 and 4:30pm. €5, students €4, family €10.) The museum, *Schloß*, and spring—indeed, anything worth seeing in the town—are all within a 10min. walk of the train station; follow the signs.

If the Fürstenberg decor leaves you envious, you can at least get royally smashed on a world-famous lager from **Fürstliche Fürstenberger Brauerei**, Postpl. 1-4, the complex behind Poststr. (☎862 06. M-F 1½hr. brewery tours followed by 1hr. of beer tasting. €4, students €2. Call at least 2 weeks in advance for reservations.) The tourist office sells a map (€12), and recommends possible routes. Hikers can also take heart: the Schwarzwald rings the western edge of town and the 108km **Schwarzwald-Kaiserstuhl-Rhein Querweg** to Breisach begins at the train station.

ROTTWEIL ☎0741

High on a lush plateau above the Neckar valley and near the Swabian Alps, Rottweil (pop. 18,000) is the oldest settlement in Baden-Württemberg. While the city's main contributions to civilization have included flameless gunpowder and a pugnacious breed of canines, the patchwork cathedral—constructed in four distinct styles over four centuries—and rainbow of facades lining the streets suggest anything but a warlike past. Generally quiet and artsy throughout the year, the town goes wild during the annual *Fasnet* celebration, when 4000 *Narren* (fools) storm the city in wooden masks and extravagant costumes. The procession occurs the two days preceding before Ash Wednesday.

◪◪ TRANSPORTATION AND PRACTICAL INFORMATION. Most **train** journeys require a transfer at nearby **Donaueschingen** (40min., 2 per hr., €10). The train station lies in the valley 20min. below the town center. Turn right after exiting the station, head uphill, and cross the bridge; Hauptstr., the town center, is the second block on your left (10min.). Or take **bus** #1 from the train station to "Friedrichspl." (€1). Rent **bikes** at Alfred Kaiser, Balingerstr. 9, at the end of the bridge leading out of town from Hauptstr. (☎89 19. From €15 per day, €30-50 per weekend. Open M-W 9am-12:30pm and 2-6:30pm, Th-F 9am-12:30pm and 2-7pm, Sa 9am-3pm.) The **tourist office**, Hauptstr. 21-23, reserves rooms and offers maps, an English city guide, and *Freizeit Spiegel*, a publication detailing artistic offerings in the area (all free). Free city tours start here May-Oct. Sa 2:30pm; call one week ahead to reserve. (☎49 42 80; www.rottweil.de. Open Apr.-Sept. M-F 9:30am-5:30pm, Sa 9:30am-12:30pm; Oct.-Mar. M-F 9:30am-12:30pm and 2-5pm.) For cash, head to the **ATM** at Hauptstr. 26 (opposite the tourist office), or to any number of banks along Hochbrücktorstr. **Untere Apotheke**, Hochbrücktorstr. 2, is the central **pharmacy.** (☎77 75. Open M-F 8am-6:30pm, Sa 8am-1pm.) Surf the **Internet** at **CyNet**, Bruder-schaftg. 2-4, in the Neues Rathaus. (☎49 43 53. €2 per hr. Open M, W, F 4-9pm.) The **post office** is at Königstr. 12. (Open M-F 8:30am-12:30pm and 2-6pm, Sa 9am-noon.) **Postal Code:** 78628.

▐▌ ACCOMMODATIONS AND FOOD. Ask at the tourist office about private rooms, many of which are more comfortable, better-situated, and less expensive. **Pension Goldenes Rad ❷**, Hauptstr. 38, above a serene restaurant, offers nice rooms in a central location. (☎74 12. Breakfast included. Reception M-Tu and Th-Su 11:30am-2pm. Singles €25; doubles €45. Cash only.) Save money on food by head-ing across the bridge to the intersection of Königstr. and Stadionstr., or buy **grocer-ies** from **Edeka Neukauf Maier**, Kriegsdamm 7-9. (Open M-F 8:30am-8pm, Sa 8am-4pm.) **Rotuvilla ❸**, Hauptstr. 63, serves wood-oven pizzas (€3.50-10.20) and other Italian dishes in a folksy, half-timbered dining room. (☎416 95. Open M and W-Su 11:30am-2pm and 5pm-midnight. Cash only.)

◧ SIGHTS. Rottweil's fanatic adherence to tradition is not limited to festivals. The town is a living architecture museum, its buildings graced with historic murals, colorful facades, and rich wood trimmings. The **Schwarzes Tor**, built in 1230 and enlarged in 1571 and 1650, guards the Altstadt. At the summit of the hill, the 54m **Hochturm** watchtower offers a stunning view all the way to the Swabian Alps. To scale it, pick up the key to the tower from the tourist office (or at Café Schädle on weekends) in exchange for €1 and an ID. Across Hauptstr. from the tourist office and the Gothic **Altes Rathaus** is the **Stadtmuseum**, Hauptstr. 20, which houses wooden masks from the *Fasnet* celebrations and a still-valid 15th-century defense treaty between Rottweil and 13 Swiss towns. (☎942 96 34. Open Tu-Su 10am-noon. €1.) Behind the Altes Rathaus, the Gothic **Heilig-Kreuz-Münster** (Cathedral of the Holy Cross) houses an array of gilded lanterns that are carried through town in the annual **Corpus Christi** procession. Subject to the winds of architectural fancy, this cathedral was tossed from 12th-century Romanesque to 15th-century Gothic to 17th-century Baroque and back to 19th-century Gothic revivalist. Behind the pas-tel pink Rococo **Predigerkirche**, the **Dominikanermuseum**, on Kriegsdamm, is modern only in appearance. The museum houses a collection of medieval icons and a sur-prisingly captivating exhibit on Rottweil's Roman past, highlighted by a an AD 2nd-century 570,000-tile mosaic. (☎78 62. Open Tu-Su 2-5pm. €2.) To find the stone decorations of the medieval **Kapellenturm** (Chapel Tower) off Hochbrücktor-str., drop by the tiny **Lorenzkapelle**, Lorenzg. 17, constructed in the 1330s. (☎942 96 33. Open Tu-Su 2-5pm. €1.) From the tower, you can glimpse the **Neckar Valley** (p. 389) and the crooked houses of **Lorenzg.**

BODENSEE (LAKE CONSTANCE)

Germany may be lacking in bleached stucco and lapus-tinged waters. However, as the pine thatching of the Black Forest thins, the landscape opens into the **Bod-ensee**, a strikingly beautiful and expansive crystalline lake. In this stretch of south-ern Baden-Württemberg, potted palms line the streets, public beaches are filled with sunbathers tanning to a melanomic crisp, and business is conducted with profoundly un-German casualness. Set against snow-capped Alps and dense woods, the Bodensee is a must-see natural gem of Germany.

Getting to the region by **train** is easy; Constance and Friedrichshafen have direct connections to many cities in southern Germany. Rail transport within the region requires long rides and occasionally tricky connections because no single route encircles the lake. The bright white boats of the **BSB** (Bodensee-Schiffs-Betriebe; Constance office ☎28 13 98) and other ferries, known collectively as the **Weiße Flotte,** provide a calmer alternative. Ships leave every hr. from Constance and Friedrichshafen for ports around the lake. The **BodenseeErlebniskarte** gives discounts on most transportation, sights, and tours. (www.bodensee-tourismus.com. €49 for 3 days, €63 per wk.; ages 6-15 €29/39.)

KONSTANZ (CONSTANCE) ☎07531

At the mouth of the Rhein, Constance (pop. 29,000) rubs elbows with Switzerland and Austria. Its location saved the elegant university town from bombardment in WWII, as the Allies were leery of accidentally striking its neighbors. The unique location has lent the city cultural diversity with an international flair. Its crooked streets wind around delicate Baroque and Renaissance facades in the central part of town, while gabled and turreted 19th-century houses emanate gentility along the river promenades. The green waters of the Bodensee lap the beaches and harbors while, farther out, countless sailboats and ships cruise the waters.

⌗ TRANSPORTATION

Tickets for the **BSB** ship line to Meersburg (€4), Mainau (€5.20), and beyond are on sale on board or in the building behind the train station, Hafenstr. 6. (☎364 03 89; www.bsb-online.com. Open Apr.-Oct. M-Th 8am-noon and 1-4pm, F 8am-noon and 1-5pm.) **Giess Personenschifffahrt** (☎07533 21 77; www.moewe-konstanz.de) runs boats every 40min. from Dock 2 to Freizeitbad Jakob and Freibad Horn (p. 423; both €2, round-trip €5). **Buses** in Constance cost €1.80 per ride, €3 for a *Tageskarte* (1-day card), and €4.50 covers two adults, children, and a dog. For a **taxi,** call ☎222 22. The curiously-named **Taxi Seeteufel** (Taxi Sea-Devil; ☎449 44) will take you anywhere in the city for €5. A stay of two or more nights in the city requires a €1 *Kurtaxe* per adult per night. This gets you **Gästekarte** coupons, providing free transit within Constance and discounts on sights. Rent **paddleboats** (from €4 per 30min., €7 per hr.) or **motorboats** (from €14/24) at **Marc Fluck Bootsvermietung,** Am Gondelhafen, by the Stadtgarten. (☎218 81. Open Apr.-Oct. daily 10am-dusk.) Rent **bikes** from **Kultur-Rädle,** Bahnhofpl. 29. (☎273 10. Open M-F 9am-12:30pm and 2:30-6pm, Sa 10am-4pm. Easter-Sept. also Su 10am-12:30pm. €10 per day, less for consecutive days.)

⌗ PRACTICAL INFORMATION

The tiny but friendly **tourist office,** Bahnhofspl. 13, to the right of the train station, provides a helpful walking map (€0.50) or a city map with index (€1). The staff finds private rooms (€21-30) for a €2.50 fee (usually a min. 3-night stay), and hotels. Ask about rooms in the nearby monastery. (☎13 30 30; www.konstanz.de. Open Apr.-Oct. M-F 9am-6:30pm, Sa 9am-4pm, Su 10am-1pm; Nov.-Mar. M-F 9:30am-12:30pm and 2-6pm.) The **Deutsche Bank** across from the station exchanges currency and has a 24hr. **ATM.** (Open M-W 9am-4:30pm, Th 9am-6pm, F 9:30am-4:30pm.) Get beach reading at the **English Bookshop,** Münzg. 10. (☎150 63; www.englishbookshop.de. Open daily 9am-6pm.) Do **laundry** at **Waschsalon & Mehr,** Hofhalde 3. (☎160 27. Wash €4.50, soap €0.60. Dry €3.50. Open M-F 10am-7pm, Sa 10am-4pm.) **Internet** access is at the **Telecenter,** Bahnhofpl. 6, across from the station. (☎28 42 66. €3 per hr. Open daily 9am-10pm.) The **post office,** Marktstätte 4, is also near the station. (Open M-F 8:30am-6pm, Sa 9am-noon.) **Postal Code:** 78462.

Bodensee (Lake Constance)

BADEN-WÜRTTEMBERG

ACCOMMODATIONS

Searching for last-minute lodging in Constance can prove to be a significant strain on the nerves and the purse. Hostels and guesthouses fill fast in this popular of summer getaway, and most budget options are to be found in smaller villages (from Tägerwilen to Güttingen) 20-30min. away by train.

Jugendherberge Kreuzlingen (HI), Promenadenstr. 7 (from Germany ☎+41 71 688 26 63; from Switzerland 071 688 26 63). South of the Swiss border in Kreuzlingen, but closer to downtown than the Constance hostel, it commands the tip of a lakefront hill and features cushy furniture and a multilingual staff. From the train station, turn left, then left again to cross the tracks, turn right, and go through the parking lot to the border checkpoint "Klein Venedig." Walk along Seestr. until the sharp right curve. Instead of following the street, continue on the gravel path between the children's park and the bushes through the field up past the gardens and fountains to the gray building. The hostel rents bikes for €10 per day, kayaks for €8 per hr. Breakfast included. Reception 8-10am and 5-9pm. Closed Dec.-Feb. €28.50 per person per room. AmEx/MC/V. ❸

Jugendherberge Otto-Möricke-Turm (HI), Zur Allmannshöhe 18 (☎322 62; www.jugendherberge-konstanz.de). Not within walking distance, but this former water tower has a terrific view. Take bus #4 from the train station to "Jugendherberge"; turn back and head uphill on Zur Allmannshöhe. Breakfast included; dinner €4.50, compulsory for stays over 1 night. Sheets €3.10. Reception Apr.-Oct. 8am-noon and 3-10pm; Nov.-Mar. 8am-noon and 5-10pm. Lockout 9:30am-noon. Curfew 10pm, housekey for €20 deposit. Call at least 2 months ahead. €23.10, over 27 €26.10; additional nights €22.90/19.90. AmEx/MC/V. ❷

Pension Gretel, Zollernstr. 6-8 (☎45 58 25; www.hotel-gretel.de). Offers bright, pine-trimmed rooms for a price that belies their superb location. Breakfast included. Call at least a month ahead in summer. Singles €35; doubles €50-68; triples €84; quads €92; extra bed €18. Apr.-Oct. around €10 more per person. Cash only. ❸

DKV-Campingplatz Brudehofer, Fohrenbühlweg 50 (☎313 88; www.campingkonstanz.de). Take bus #1 to "Staad," and walk for 10min. with the lake to your left. The campground is on the waterfront. Reception closed noon-2:30pm. €3.50 per person, €2 per child, €3.10-4.50 per tent, €7 per RV, €0.50 per bike, €2.60 per car. Warm showers €1. Cash only. ❶

FOOD

Find **groceries** in the basement of the Karstadt department store, on Augustinerpl. and Blätzlepl. (☎12 31 58; open M-F 9:30am-8pm, Sa 9:30am-7pm) and fresh vegetables and fruit at **Örk Feinkost,** Hohenhausg. 2. (☎216 28.) A stroll through the small streets surrounding the Münster's northern side, the oldest part of Constance, reveals a busy alternative scene, with health-food stores, left-wing graffiti, and student cafés.

Fachhochschule Mensa, stands in a modern building on Webersteig, overlooking the Rhein. An ISIC is required for a meal card; ask in the cafeteria downstairs. The hassle is worth it—meals cost only €4.70-5.30. Open M-F 11am-1:45pm. Cafeteria open M-Th 7:30am-4pm, F 7:30am-2pm. Cash only. ❶

Café Zeitlos, St.-Stephans-Pl. 25 (☎18 93 84). Cooks all meals (€5.10-7.70) with local ingredients. All-you-can-eat brunch Su 10am, €12.50. Weekly beer specials. Snacks €2.50-3.60. Open daily 10am-1am, kitchen 10am-3pm and 6-10pm. Cash only. ❷

Latinos ❸, Am Fischmarkt 78 (☎17399; www.latinos.de.). Crosses Mexican with German cuisine, serving up a wide assortment of vegetarian options (from €6.80), soups (from €4.50), and house wrap specials (€7.20-14.50). Open daily 10am-1am. ❸

◎ ⌒ SIGHTS AND BEACHES

Constance's **Münster,** built over the course of 600 years, has a 76m soaring Gothic spire (under construction until late 2006) and a display of ancient religious objects. Don't miss the *Kreuzgang* frescoes, downstairs to the left of the crypt. Climb the **Münsterturm** for an excellent view of the city, Bodensee, and distant Alps. (Church open M-F 10am-5pm, Sa-Su 12:30-5pm. Münsterturm €2, closed Sa.) The late-16th century frescoes of the **Rathaus,** Kanzleistr. 15, off Wessenbergstr., illustrate the religious and martial history of the city; in the courtyard, enter the first tower to the left with the "Historische Bilder" sign. Farther south, off Bodanstr., the 13th-century **Schnetztor** shows off its proud layers of battlements, guarding a network of busy shopping streets behind. Choose from two idyllic promenades to enjoy the view across Lake Konstanz: **Rheinsteig,** along the Rhein, or **Seestr.** on the lake across the bridge. The tree-filled **Stadtgarten,** next to Constance's main harbor, gives an unbroken view of the Bodensee and of the voluptuous *Imperia* statue guarding the harbor. In her arms high above the sea she balances two figures—one wearing a crown representing world power, and the other a papal tiara symbolizing the Church. Across the Rhein from the Altstadt, near the "Sternenpl." bus stop, is the **Archäologisches Landesmuseum,** Benediktinerpl. 5, an assemblage of ancient things from Baden-Württemberg's long-lost past—everything from old town walls and pots to reassembled skeletons and spearheads. (☎ 980 40. Open Tu-Su 10am-6pm. €3, students €2, families €6.) Visit the aquatic critters of the Rhein at the **Sea-Life Museum,** Hafenstr. 9, on the way to the Swiss border. Beginning with an ice cave, the museum traces the history of sea life, with a special focus on the Bodensee region. Exhibits include a large trout tank and a walk-though shark tunnel. (☎ 12 82 70. Open July-Sept. daily 10am-7pm; May-June and Oct. daily 10am-6pm; Nov.-Apr. M-F 10am-5pm, Sa-Su 10am-6pm. Last entry 1hr. before closing. €11, students €10, ages 3-14 €8.50.)

Constance boasts a number of **public beaches;** all are free and open May to September. **Freibad Horn** (take bus #5) is the largest and most crowded; it has a nude section enclosed by hedges. In inclement weather, immerse yourself in **Bodensee Therme Konstanz,** Wilhelm-von-Scholz-Weg 2, near Strandbad Horn, a modern pool complex with thermal baths, saunas, and sun lamps. Take bus #5 to "Bodensee Therme Konstanz." (☎ 611 63. Open daily 9am-9pm. €4.60, students €3.) Closer to town, go for a dip at the **Kur- und Hallenbad,** Spanierstr. 7, on the north bank of the Rhein, between the bridges. (☎ 662 68. Outdoors open May-Aug. daily 9am-9pm; indoors open mid.-Sept. to mid.-May Tu 2-6pm, W 6:45-7:45am and 3-7pm, Th 2-9pm, F 6:45-7:45am and 2-7pm, Sa 1-6pm, Su 9am-noon. €2.30, students €1.70.)

◪ DAYTRIPS FROM CONSTANCE

MAINAU

Take bus #4 (dir.: Bettingen) to "Mainau" (20min., 1-2 per hr., €2), or a boat from behind the train station (1hr., every 1-2hr., €9). Island (www.mainau.de) open daily Apr.-Oct. 7am-8pm; Nov.-Mar. 9am-6pm. Apr.-Oct. €11.90, students €6, under 16 €4, over 65 €11, families €24; ½-price after 4pm, free after 7pm; Nov.-Mar. €5.50, students €4, children free.

The island of **Mainau** is all one richly manicured garden, the result of the horticultural prowess of generations of Baden princes and the Swedish royal family. A lush arboretum, exotic birds, and huge flower animals surround the pink 13th-century Baroque palace and church built by the Teutonic Knights. Now thousands of tourists scamper across the footbridge from Constance to pose with the peacocks and take in an unparalleled view of the Bodensee amid 25 varieties of butterflies.

MEERSBURG

Reach Meersburg by boat (30min.; 1-2 per hr., last boat around 6:30pm; €3.80), or by bus #7395 from Friedrichshafen (30min.; 2 per hr., last return around 7:30pm; €2.50). An accommodation service is available at ☎440 41 00, or at the Tourist Office, Kirchstr. 4. (☎44 04 00; www.meersburg.de.) Open M-F 9am-12:30pm and 2-6pm, Sa 10am-1pm.

Glowering over the Bodensee, the medieval fortress **Burg Meersburg** is the center-piece of this town and was formerly displayed on the 20-*Deutschmark* bill. The first watchman moved into **oldest inhabited castle** in 628 and the fortress displays fully furnished chambers and dungeons primarily from the 16th-18th centuries. Also on display are the living quarters of **Annette von Droste-Hülshoff**, generally rec-ognized as Germany's greatest female poet. (☎800 00. Open daily Mar.-Oct. 9am-6pm; Nov.-Feb. 10am-6pm; last entry 30min. before closing. €6, students €5.10, chil-dren €3; with a tour of the tower Apr.-Nov. 1 €8/6.80/5.)

In the 18th century, a prince bishop rejected King Dagobert's **Altes Schloß** and commissioned the sherbert-pink Baroque **Neues Schloß** up the hill on Schloßpl., which now houses the town's art collection in the **Schloßmuseum**. The **Dorniermu-seum** has models of Dornier airplanes, while the **Stadtische Gallery** (Municipal Gal-lery) has a collection of Romantic paintings, many of a vain variety, detailing the beauty of the Burg. (☎440 49 00. Open Apr.-Oct. daily 10am-1pm and 4-6pm. €4; students and Guest Card holders €3; families €8/6; children €1. Combo card with entrance to the Weinbaum Museum and the Stadtmuseum €5/4.)

The privately owned **Zeppelinmuseum**, Schloßpl. 8, hidden halfway down the stairs by the Burg Meersburg water wheel, is staffed by dedicated and knowledge-able Zeppelin devotees eager for visitors. The world's largest collection of Zeppe-lin memorabilia is stuffed into 1½ tiny rooms and bound to delight dirigible devotees. (☎79 09. Open Mar.-Nov. daily 10am-6pm. €3, children €2.)

FRIEDRICHSHAFEN   ☎07541

A former Zeppelin construction base, Friedrichshafen (pop. 14,000) had trouble getting back off the ground after Allied bombings in 1944. The town was finally rebuilt with broad waterfront promenades, which today are some of the longest on Lake Constance. The city's tree-lined boulevards—only slightly less crowded than those of Constance—break onto sweeping panoramas of the jagged Alps by day, while at night the twin orbs of the Schloßkirche's onion-domes stand half-illumi-nated against a pastel sky. The city's flagship attraction is the superb **◪Zeppelinmu-seum**, Seestr. 22, which details the history of the flying dirigibles from the earliest martial kites of the Netherlands to the US Army's current fleet (see **It's a Bird, It's a Plane, It's...**, p. 425). The 16 intricate scale models on the first floor are dwarfed by the 33m reconstruction of a section of the Hindenburg. (☎380 10; www.zeppe-lin-museum.de. Open May-Oct. Tu-Su 9am-5pm; Nov.-Apr. 10am-5pm. Last entry 30min. before closing. English audio guide €3. €7.50, students €3, family €13.) Afterward, climb the spiralling metal **tower** by the dock, off Seestr. and across from Salzstr., to improve your view. On the other side of the Zeppelin Museum, the tiny **Kunstverein** (Art Association) presents the work of current young artists in special exhibitions. (☎219 50; www.kunstverein-friedrichshafen.de. Open Tu-F 2-5pm, Sa-Su 11am-5pm. Free.) The spires in the east belong to the exquisite **Schloßkirche** on Klosterstr. Take Friedrichstr. away from town and turn left on Olgastr. and then immediately right on Klosterstr. (☎213 08; www.evkirche-fn.de. Open mid-Apr. to Oct. M-Th and Sa 9am-5pm, W 2:30-6pm, F and Su 11am-6pm.) The beach is at the **Strandbad**, Königsweg 7, replete with a pool and volleyball nets. (☎280 78. Open daily mid-May to mid-Sept. in good weather 9am-8pm. €1.40, children €0.70.)

Cycling is a popular alternative to the nautical tendencies of the region, and a nexus of popular **biking trails** can be found in Friedrichshafen. Of particular note is the 260km **Bodensee-Radweg**, which encircles the entire Bodensee. The path is marked by signs depicting a cyclist with a blue back tire—ask at any tourist office for maps (usually free) and a list of campsites and hotels along the way.

Friedrichshafen's **Jugendherberge Graf Zeppelin (HI)** ❷, Lindauer Str. 3, named after the first Zeppelin to circumnavigate the world, is clean, recently renovated, 50m from the water, and only occasionally overrun by hoards of schoolchildren. From the Hafenbahnhof, walk 10min. down Eckenerstr. away from Buchhornpl. From the Stadtbahnhof, walk left down Friedrichstr., and continue onto Eckenerstr. (20min.). Or take bus #7 to "Eberhardstr." (☎724 04; www.jugendherberge-friedrichshafen.de. Breakfast included. Wash €3.10. Locker deposit €2. Reception 7-9am, 3-7:30pm and 8:30-10pm. Lockout 9am-noon. Curfew 10pm, key available for guests over 18. €20.30 for 1st night, €17.10 per night thereafter. Cash only.) Weary travelers can find an even cheaper night's rest across the street at the campsite **Cap Rotach** ❶, Lindauerstr. 2, a low hedge away from the lapping waves of the Bodensee. (☎734 21; www.caprotach.de. Wash €3. Reception 8am-noon and 2:30-10pm. Closed from 10pm-8am. €5.50 per person, €4 per child. Singles available for €38, doubles €53. MC/V.) For **groceries,** head to **Lebensmittel Fehl** on the corner of Seestr. and Salzg. (Open M-F 8am-6:30pm, Sa 8am-5pm. AmEx/MC/V.) **Naturkost am Buchhornplatz** ❶, Buchhornpl. 1, serves vegetarian food , and sells a wide variety of health foods and vitamins. (☎243 35. Salads €1.70-3.45. Lunch specials €2.90. Baked goods €0.85-3.10. Open M-F 9:30am-6pm, Sa 10am-2:30pm.) A number of expensive and more traditional German restaurants line Seestr. along the Bodensee. Try the vine-covered **Stadtmauer** ❸, Seestr. 14, for everything from pizza (around €5-10) to *Bodenseeflechen* (or *Blaufelchen*, the white fish of the Bodensee; under €8). (☎281 40. Cash only.)

There are two train stations in Friedrichshafen: the main **Stadtbahnhof** and the **Hafenbahnhof** at the docks behind the Zeppelinmuseum. **Trains** connect the two stations (2-4 per hr., €1.50), but walking is nearly as fast and more scenic. Trains run to Freiburg (1-3hr., 1-2 per hr., €27.20-30.90); Lindau (20-40min., 2 per hr., €4.60); and Munich (3-4hr., 1-2 per hr., €30.20-41). Bus #7395 runs every 30min. during the day from the Stadtbahnhof to Meersburg (€2.50), and frequent boats run to Meersburg and Lindau. For the boat to Constance (1½hr., every 2hr., €8.50), buy tickets on board, at the **ticket counter** next to the Zeppelinmuseum, or at the ticket machines. (☎971 09 00. Open Apr.-Oct. daily 8:30am-5:40pm; Nov.-Mar. M-F 8:30am-12:30pm and 1:30-4:40pm, Sa 8:20am-1pm.)

THE LOCAL STORY

IT'S A BIRD, IT'S A PLANE, IT'S...

Almost every city in Southwest Germany has a street named after the Graf Zeppelin, the rigid airship that beloved engineer Hugo Eckener (so popular that Hitler considered him a threat and banned all mention of him in the press) piloted around the globe from 1928-1938. It was named after Count Ferdinand Graf con Zeppelin, a slightly stuffy but brilliant engineer who flew the world's first untethered airship, the LZ-1, for 17 minutes on July 2, 1900.

While dirigible contraptions had been used worldwide since the early 1800s in the military, it was not until 1910 that Germany's first commercial airship, the Zeppelin-designed Deutschland, got off the ground. The German government commissioned 67 ships during WWI; only 16 survived the war, but most of their target cities survived their attacks: the horrendous inaccuracy of their bombing led the British to believe that the Germans were targeting English cows.

After post-war restrictions were lifted, Germany built the greatest Zeppelins in history, including the Graf Zeppelin and the Hindenberg, which exploded while landing on May 6, 1937, killing 35 passengers. After this catastrophe (caused in part by the US government's refusal to sell safe helium gas to Nazis) and with the start of WWII, the age of the cloud-boat was forever over.

Rent **boats** at the **Bootsvermietung Christiane** by Seestr., but don't shoot for Constance, and watch the skies. (☎28 96 32. Paddleboats €7.50 per hr., motorboats €20-25 per hr. Open May-Sept. daily 9am-dusk.) Rent **bikes** from **Zweirad Schmid,** Ernst-Lehmann-Str. 12. (☎218 70. From €10.50 per day, additional days from €7.50. Open M-F 8am-12:30pm and 2-6pm, Sa 9am-12:30pm.) The **tourist office,** Bahnhofpl. 2, in the striped building left of the Stadtbahnhof, has maps and biking routes, and books rooms for a €3 fee. (☎300 10; tourist-info@friedrichshafen.de. Open Nov.-Mar. M-Th 9am-noon and 2-4pm, F 9am-noon; Apr. and Oct. M-Th 9am-noon and 2-5pm, F 9am-noon; May-Sept. M-F 9am-6pm, Sa 9am-1pm.) **Internet** access is at **Call Shop,** Friedrichstr. 75, to the left of the Stadtbahnhof. (Open M-Sa 10am-9pm, Su 11am-9pm. €2 per hr.) The **post office** is opposite the tourist office. (Open M-F 8:30am-12:30pm and 2-6pm, Sa 9am-12:30pm.) **Postal Code:** 88045.

LINDAU IM BODENSEE   ☎08382

The tiny island of Lindau (pop. 24,000) distills, in many ways, all that the Bodensee region has to offer. Connected to the mainland by a narrow causeway, the town is more in the Bodensee than on it; the Alps loom large across the waters, and Switzerland and Austria are visible across—and readily accessible from—the shoreline. The innumerable cafés, souvenir shops, and harbor promenades, charming and calm in the early morning and late evening, are overrun by tourists rushing to catch the last boat back to Constance in the evening.

🖪🖪 TRANSPORTATION AND PRACTICAL INFORMATION. **Ferries** link Lindau with Constance, usually stopping at Friedrichshafen, Mainau, and Meersburg along the way (3½hr.; 3-6 per day; €11.20 to Constance, €4.60 to Friedrichshafen). Or take the **train** to Constance (1-2hr., every hr., €15.70) or the bus to Friedrichshafen (30min., €2.50). **Public transport** in Lindau costs €1.50 per ride or €3.50 for a 24hr. ticket (families €2.60/6). Rent **bikes** at the train station. (☎212 61. €4-11 per day. Open M-F 9am-1pm and 2-6pm, Sa 9:30am-1pm; May-Sept. in good weather also Su 9am-noon.) A string of **Boat** vendors line the shore on the Kleiner See between the island and the mainland. (☎55 14. Motorboats €25 per hr.; row- and paddleboats €6-8 per hr. Open late Mar. to Oct. 9am-9pm.) The **tourist office,** Ludwigstr. 68, across from the station, finds rooms for €3. (☎26 00 30; www.lindautourismus.de. Open mid-June to mid-Sept. M-F 9am-6pm, Sa-Su 10am-2pm; Apr. to mid-June and early Sept. to Oct. M-F 9am-1pm and 2-6pm, Sa 10am-2pm; Nov.-Mar. M-F 9am-noon and 2-5pm.) **Tours** leave from the office at 10am. (Tu and F in German, M in English. €5, students and overnight guests €4. Audio guide €7.50.) The **Bodenseebank,** across the street at Maximilianstr. 27, offers **currency exchange** and an **ATM.** (Open M-W and F 9am-noon and 2-4pm, Th 9am-noon and 2-5:30pm.) Do **laundry** at **Lindauer Wäschecenter,** Holdereggenstr. 21A. (☎66 98. Wash €6.15. Dry €5.15. Open M-F 9am-12:30pm and 2:30-6:30pm.) The **Lindauer Internet Café** provides Internet access across and to the left from the Bahnhof. (€4 per hr. Open M-F 10am-8pm, Sa 10am-6pm, Su 11am-6pm.) The **post office** is 50m to the left of the station. (Open M-F 8am-noon and 1:30-5:30pm, Sa 9am-noon.) **Postal Code:** 88131.

🖪🖪 ACCOMMODATIONS AND FOOD. All accommodations in Lindau charge a *Kurtaxe* of €1.40 per person per night. The modern **Jugendherberge (HI) ❷,** Herbergsweg 11, lies across the Seebrücke. Cross the bridge, turn right onto Bregenzer Str., right again on Kolpingstr., and left onto Herbergsweg after the Limare indoor swimming pool (20min.). Or, take bus #1 or 2 from the train station to "Anheggerstr./ZUP," then bus #3 (dir.: Zech) to "Jugendherberge." Spacious post-and-beam dorms attract a number of noisy youth and musical groups in the summer months. (☎967 10; www.lindau.jugendherberge.de. Breakfast included. Wash

€1.50. Dry €1.50. Reception 7am-10pm. Curfew midnight, door code available. €19.80-20.50. MC/V.) **Hotel Pension Noris ❸,** Brettermarkt 13, has white-walled rooms right off the promenade. (☎36 45. Large, delicious breakfast included. All rooms with bath. Singles €32-35; doubles €70-75.) **Park-Camping Lindau Am See ❶,** Frauenhofer Str. 20, is 3km to the east on the mainland, within spitting distance of the Austrian border. *Let's Go* does not recommend spitting at Austria. Take bus #1 or 2 to "Anheggerstr./ZUP," then bus #3 (dir.: Zech) to the next-to-last stop, "Laibl-achstr."; exit the bus and turn right, then left onto the large Bregenzer Str., where the campground is marked. (☎722 36; www.park-camping.de. Reception 8am-noon and 2-8pm. €5-6.50 per adult, €1.50-2.60 per child, €1.50-2.50 per tent, €5-8 for vehicle. Electricity €2.50. Grocery store and restaurant open daily 7am-9pm.) Get you French fill at **Insel Bar Café Bistro ❸,** Maximilianstr. 42, which serves a wide array of crêpes (€4.60-6.90), soups (€3.90-5.20), and baguettes (from €3.90), ice cream dishes (€2.80-5.20). (☎50 17. Open M-Sa 10am-7pm, Su 11am-7pm. Cash only.) **Patio, Eat & Art Gallery ❸,** off of Maximilianstr. toward the harbor on Krumg., is a chic restaurant doubling as an art gallery, whose glossy bar is frequented by a young crowd. Large pasta dishes are €12.80-15.80. (☎94 30 789. Open Tu-F noon-2:30pm and 6-10pm, Sa 11am-2:30pm and 6-10pm. Cash only.)

🌄🏖 **SIGHTS AND BEACHES.** The 14th-century gabled houses on **Maximilian-straße** form the center of town. On Maximilianstr., the **Altes Rathaus** is a blend of stylized frescoes, completed in 1436. The muraled **Cavazzen-Haus** in the Marktpl. houses the **Stadtmuseum** (Municipal Museum), which displays a collection of furni-ture and art, ranging from French porcelain and bureaus to portraits of pompous-looking nobles. (☎94 40 73. Open Apr.-Oct. Tu-F and Su 11am-5pm, Sa 2-5pm. €2.50, students €1, families €5. Tours 2:15 and 3pm from Apr.-Oct. €2.50, stu-dents €1.50. Combined ticket €4/2, families €5.) Cross Marktpl. and compare the ornate interior of the Catholic **Stiftskirche,** on the right, with the more sober Evan-gelical **Kirche St. Stephan.** A walk down **In der Grub** leads to the Rapunzel-esque **Die-bsturm** (Thieves' Tower). The medieval **Peterskirche** next door, now a memorial to all victims of the World Wars, contains the only surviving murals by Hans Holbein the Elder. At the harbor, the yellow-topped **Mangturm,** a 12th-century lighthouse, keeps watch over the waves of tourists but does not let any inside. Climb the new lighthouse at the harbor entrance for a great view of the lake and the Alps (on clear days). (Open late Mar. to early Nov. daily 10am-sunset. €1.60, children €0.50.) A walk along the waterfront from the Mangturm leads to unobstructed views of the lake, and to the **Pulverschanze** (Gun Powder Tower), an erstwhile mil-itary fortification. If you're in the Lindau area from late July to late August, ask about the **Bregenzer Festspiele,** an extravagant opera over the Austrian border in Bregenz. Huge crowds have gathered in past years to see *Die Zauberflöte, Porgy and Bess,* and *La Bohème* staged on a platform over the Bodensee. (☎+43 55 74 40 76; www.bregenzerfestspiele.com. Tickets from €26-€413, and sell quickly.)

Lindau has four major beaches, the biggest and busiest of which is **Eichwald,** with three heated pools and a slide. Walk to the east along Uferweg for 30min. or take bus #1 or 2 to "Anheggerstr./ZUP," then bus #3 to "Kamelbuckel." (☎55 39. Open daily May-Sept. 9:30am-8pm. Last entry 1hr. before closing. €3, ages 6-18 €2.) **Römerbad,** on the island left of the harbor, is the smallest and most casual beach. (☎68 30. €2.50, ages 6-18 €2. Warm showers €0.50.) To reach the quieter **Lindenhofbad,** take bus #1 or 2 to "Anheggerstr./ZUP" and then bus #4 to the end; then take the hedged road uphill. (☎66 37. Römerbad and Lindenhofbad both open June to mid-Aug. daily 10am-8pm; May-Sept. M-F 10:30am-7:30pm, Sa-Su 10am-8pm. Last entry 1hr. before closing. €2.50, ages 6-18 €2. Warm showers €0.50.) The luxurious heated pool of **Strandbad Bad Schachen** is also in the Lindenhofpark. (Open May-Aug. daily 9am-7pm. Daypass weekends €9.50, weekdays €7.)

BAYERN (BAVARIA)

Bavaria is the Germany of Wagnerian opera, medieval fairy tales, and Teutonic myth. From tiny forest villages to stately Baroque cities along the Danube and castles perched high in the Alps, the region attracts more visitors than any other part of the country. When foreigners conjure up images of Germany, they are thinking of Bavaria: land of beer gardens, sausage, and *Lederhosen*. But tourists soon discover that there is much more to Germany's largest federal state than the cliches it indulges. From international powerhouses like BMW and Audi to thriving university towns; from the burgeoning Turkish population to scattered Jewish immigrant communities, Bavaria is much too dynamic to be regarded as an open-air museum.

It's true that the region's residents have always been Bavarians first and Germans second. Through wars with France and Austria, Otto von Bismarck pulled Bavaria into his orbit, but it remained its own kingdom until 1918. Local authorities still insist upon using the *Land*'s proper name: *Freistaat Bayern* (Free State of Bavaria). On a local level, Franconians, upper Bavarians and Swabians take great pains to assert their unique cultures. Despite such long-standing cultural identities, modern cosmopolitanism is combining with historical preservation to animate the truly individual character of Germany's southernmost state.

HIGHLIGHTS OF BAVARIA

ABSORB the culture, and the Bier, of Munich (p. 428) during the notorious Oktoberfest (Sept. 22-Oct. 7, 2007; Sept. 20-Oct. 5, 2008; p. 455), or check out the city's sleek bars, lively museums and garden three times the size of New York's Central Park.

BEAR WITNESS to Germany's Nazi past at the **Dachau** memorial, **Nuremberg's** Nazi ruins (p. 534) and **Berchtesgaden's Eagle's Nest** (p. 476).

BIKE for a week in stunning natural surroundings from the gorgeous pastel stucco town of **Eichstätt**, or check out fossils in the **Altmühltal Nature Park** (p. 500).

CHUG extra-strength monks' brew at **Andechs**, a hilltop monastery still serving the 12% alcohol beer it has produced since the 16th century (p. 456).

DISCOVER the medieval splendor of the **Romantic Road** (p. 520). For more feudal fun, try the castles in **Burghausen** (p. 490) and **Landshut** (p. 492).

DRINK MILK practically straight from the cow in the spectacular **Berchtesgaden National Park** (p. 470), a stunning setting for hikes and other outdoor activities.

REALIZE YOUR CINDERELLA FANTASIES among King Ludwig II's extravagant Königsschlößer (p. 464) or at his "cozy" hunting lodge on the Chiemsee (p. 484).

MÜNCHEN (MUNICH) ☎089

Tourists who step past the stereotypes of *Lederhosen* and pot-bellied conservatives will be pleasantly surprised to discover that Munich (pop. 1,248,000) is both the sleek southern capital of German affluence and the leafy home of true German

Bayern (Bavaria)

merriment. The city's unique cosmopolitan attractions and its long-standing tradition of enjoying beer, life, and nature (in that order) make it a place both relaxing and stimulating. World-class museums, handsome parks and architecture, and a rambunctious art scene conspire to create a city of astonishing vitality.

Even in the depths of winter, citizens meet in outdoor beer gardens to discuss art, politics, and (of course) *Fußball*. A bubbling mixture of sophistication and earthy Bavarian *Gemütlichkeit* (coziness) keeps the city awake at (almost) all hours. The people of Munich party zealously during *Fasching*, Germany's own Mardi Gras (Jan. 7-Feb. 20, 2007), shop with abandon during the *Weinachtsmarkt* (Christmas Market; late Nov. to early Dec.), and imbibe unfathomable quantities of beer during the legendary *Oktoberfest* (Sept. 22-Oct. 7, 2007; Sept. 20-Oct. 5, 2008; see p. 455 for more information). Although crowded during *Oktoberfest*, Munich is accessible for budget travelers year-round, with an abundance of hostels, a stellar public transportation system, and parks ripe for an afternoon of free relaxation.

HISTORY

Although Munich stands as the eternal *Hauptstadt* (capital) of southern Germany, the city was actually founded by a Northerner. In 1158 Henry the Lion built Munich to control the only bridge over the Isar River and, with it, the profitable salt trade. Soon Munich came under the rule of the **Wittelsbachs,** who controlled

TO 1 (750m)

TO 2 (500m)
11 (1km)

3

THERESIENSTR. U

Enhuberstr.

Steinheilstr.

Luisenstr.

Theresienstr.

Heßstr.

Neue
Pinakothek

TO OLYMPISCHE PARK (3km)
& BMW MUSEUM (3km)

Dachauer Str.

Gabelsbergerstr.

Schleißheimer Str.

Rottmanstr.

Augustenstr.

R.-Wagner-Str.

13

Theresienstr.

Arcisstr.

Alte
Pinakothek

Barer Str.

Theresienstr.

TO SCHLOß
NYMPHENBURG,
BOTANICHER
GARTEN (4.5km),
15 (3km), 16 (2km),
17 (4.5km)
& 18 (1.5km)
19

Volkstheater

Cinema
STIGLMAIERPLATZ U

Brennerstr.

Gabelsbergerstr.

Hauptschule für
Musik und Theater
20

Pinakothek
der Moderne

Nymphenburgerstr.
Second
Hand Sports
Cinema München

Lenbachhaus

KÖNIGSPL. U

KÖNIGSPL.

Glyptothek

Markuskirche

Prinz-Ludwig-Str.

TO 21 (6.5km)

22

Karlstr.

Luisenstr.

Meiserstr.

Antikensammlung

Obelisk

KAROLINENPLATZ

Universitäts
Hospital

Türkenstr.

Jägerstr.

Oskar-von-Miller-Ring

Finkenstr.

Seidlstr.

Dachauer Str.

Marsstr.

Sophienstr.

Barer Str.

Amerika Haus

Max-Joseph-Str.

Ottostr.

Brennerstr.

23

Hirtenstr.

TO 25 (250m), 27 (3km)
& 28 (4.5km)

Elisenstr.

Alter
Botanischer
Garten

MAXIMILIANS-
PLATZ

SALVATORPLATZ

30

Arnulfstr.

29

City Mitwoh
Bike Rental

HAUPTBHF. S

LENBACHPLATZ

KARLSPL. U

Pranner-str.

American
Express

PROMENADEPLATZ

Prielmayerstr.

Justizpalast

Pacellistr.

Kard.-Faulhaber-Str.

Hauptbahnhof
Car Rental
BAHNHOF-
PLATZ

Maxburgstr.

Maffeistr.

Bahnhofs-
mission

DB CallBikes

Schützenstr.

Löwen-grube

HAUPTBHF. U

KARLSPLATZ (STACHUS)

KARLSPL. S

Bayerstr.

TO 33 (250m), 34 (2km)

International
Phone World

Schlosserstr.

Adolf-Kolping-Str.

Neuhauser Str.

Michaelskirche

Kaufingerstr.

Frauenkirche

FRAUEN-
PLATZ

39

München
Ticket

Neues i
Rathaus

MARIENPL. S

Weinstr.

37

36

Senefelderstr.

Schwanthalerstr.

Deutsches
Theater

Herzogspitalstr.

Herzog-

Damen-
stiftstr.

Eisenmannstr.

Rosenstr.

Peterskirche

TO 35 (500m)

Landwehrstr.

Schillerstr.

43

Sonnenstr.

Wilhelm-Str.

Josephspitalstr.

Brunnstr.

Hackenstr.

Hackenstr.

Rosental

Rindermarkt

Münchener
Stadtmuseum

TO 44 (100m), &
THERESIENWIESE [OKTOBERFEST] (250m)

Asamkirche

Kreuzstr.

Sendlinger Str.

45

Duftstr.

ST. JAKOBS
PLATZ

Schmidtstr.

Klosterhofstr.

Oberanger

Unterer Anger

Schrannenhalle

58

Pettenkoferstr.

Goethestr.

Sendlinger
Tor

SENDLINGER
TOR U

Blumenstr.

Kreuzstr.

Blumenstr.

Unterer Anger

Blumenstr.

Cornelliusstr.

Matthäus-
kirche

Klinikum Innenstadt

Nußbaumstr.

Lindwurmstr.

Thalkirchner Str.

Pestalozzistr.

Müllerstr.

Blumenstr.

Müllerstr.

Staatstheater am
Gärtnerplatz

31

Laundry

0   250 yards
0   250 meters

Hans-Sachs-Str.

60

Jahnstr.

Fraunhoferstr.

Kienzestr.

TO 32 (50m)

TO 63 (3km), 64 (2km), 65 (5km),
66 & TIERPARK HELLABRUNN ZOO (3km)

BAYERN

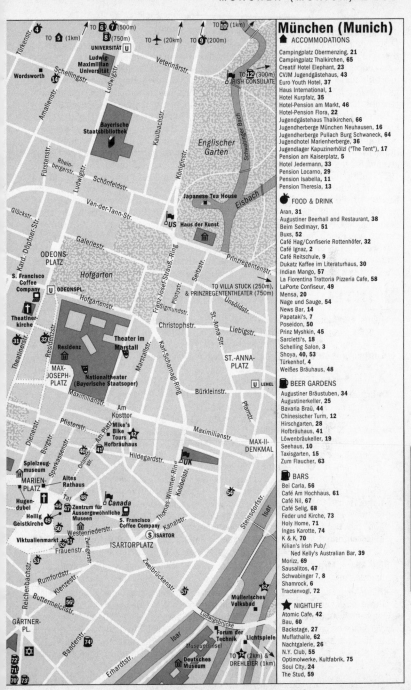

München (Munich)

ACCOMMODATIONS

Campingplatz Obermenzing, 21
Campingplatz Thalkirchen, 65
Creatif Hotel Elephant, 23
CVJM Jugendgästehaus, 43
Euro Youth Hotel, 37
Haus International, 1
Hotel Kurpfalz, 35
Hotel-Pension am Markt, 46
Hotel-Pension Flora, 22
Jugendgästehaus Thalkirchen, 66
Jugendherberge München Neuhausen, 16
Jugendherberge Pullach Burg Schwaneck, 64
Jugendhotel Marienherberge, 36
Jugendlager Kapuzinerhölzl ("The Tent"), 17
Pension am Kaiserplatz, 5
Hotel Jedermann, 33
Pension Locarno, 29
Pension Isabella, 11
Pension Theresia, 13

FOOD & DRINK

Aran, 31
Augustiner Beerhall and Restaurant, 38
Beim Sedlmayr, 51
Buxs, 52
Café Hag/Confiserie Rottenhöfer, 32
Café Ignaz, 2
Café Reitschule, 9
Dukatz Kaffee im Literaturhaus, 30
Indian Mango, 57
La Fiorentina Trattoria Pizzeria Cafe, 58
LaPorte Confiseur, 49
Mensa, 20
Nage und Sauge, 54
News Bar, 14
Papataki's, 7
Poseidon, 50
Prinz Myshkin, 45
Sarcletti's, 18
Schelling Salon, 3
Shoya, 40, 53
Türkenhof, 4
Weißes Bräuhaus, 48

BEER GARDENS

Augustiner Bräustuben, 34
Augustinerkeller, 25
Bavaria Bräu, 44
Chinesischer Turm, 12
Hirschgarten, 28
Hofbräuhaus, 41
Löwenbräukeller, 19
Seehaus, 10
Taxisgarten, 15
Zum Flaucher, 63

BARS

Bei Carla, 56
Café Am Hochhaus, 61
Café Nil, 67
Café Selig, 68
Feder und Kirche, 73
Holy Home, 71
Inges Karotte, 74
K & K, 70
Kilian's Irish Pub/
    Ned Kelly's Australian Bar, 39
Morizz, 69
Sausalitos, 47
Schwabinger 7, 8
Shamrock, 6
Tractenvogl, 72

NIGHTLIFE

Atomic Cafe, 42
Bau, 60
Backstage, 27
Muffathalle, 62
Nachtgalerie, 26
N.Y. Club, 55
Optimolwerke, Kultfabrik, 75
Soul City, 24
The Stud, 59

the city with strict Catholic piety until the 20th century. Following Napoleon's defeat, Bavaria leapt into its Golden Age with an efficient state administration that promoted commerce and the arts. **Ludwig I** and **Maximilian I** contributed hugely to the evolution of the city, building splendid museums, while Bavaria's eccentric king **Ludwig II** constructed his famous "fairy-tale" castles (p. 464). In 1871, after Bismarck's wars solidified Prussian dominance, Bavaria was absorbed into the greater *Reich*. Munich became a cultural powerhouse, rivaling Berlin (to Munich's citizens, a glorified garrison town), as artists flocked to its blossoming scene.

Germany's defeat in WWI ended 700 years of Wittelsbach rule in Bavaria. Postwar depression and the reparations required by the Treaty of Versailles sent the economy into hyperinflation. The instability of Weimar Munich gave rise to reactionary anti-Semitic movements. **Adolf Hitler** found the city such a fertile recruiting ground for his Nazi party that he later called it "the capital of our movement." In 1923, Hitler unsuccessfully attempted to capture several municipal government officials in the **Beer Hall Putsch,** landing the future *Führer* in prison for a year. Echoes of the Nazi era still haunt Munich—the party's first concentration camp was constructed just outside the city at **Dachau** (p. 455). Despite Munich's location deep inside German air defenses, Allied bombs obliterated over 70% of the city center; much of it has since been rebuilt. The **1972 Olympics** (although marred by terrorism, as depicted in Steven Spielberg's recent film *Munich*) brought modernization to Munich. Large portions of the city center were pedestrianized and the subway system was extended, bringing a new era of glory to the city.

✶ INTERCITY TRANSPORTATION

Flights: Flughafen München (☎97 52 13 13). S1 and S8 trains run between the airport and the Hauptbahnhof (45min.; every 10min., €8.80, sit in the rear half of the S1 train). Group tickets cover 2-5 adults for €17 (see **Public Transportation,** p. 433). A **Lufthansa shuttle bus** (40min.) leaves from Arnulfstr. outside the Hauptbahnhof (every 20min. 5:10am-7:50pm). and returns from airport terminals 1 and 2 (every 20min. 6:20am-9:40pm; €9.50, round-trip €15). Also stops at "Nordfriedhof" U-Bahn station.

Trains: Munich's **Hauptbahnhof** is the transportation hub of southern Germany, with connections to: **Amsterdam, Netherlands** (7-9hr., every hr., €136); **Berlin** (6½hr., 2 per hr., €96); **Cologne** (6hr., 2 per hr., €112); **Frankfurt** (4hr., 2 per hr., €75); **Füssen** (2hr., every 2hr., €20); **Hamburg** (6hr., every hr., €115); **Innsbruck, Austria** (2hr., every 2hr., €28); **Paris, France** (8-10hr., 6 per day, €125); **Prague, Czech Republic** (6-7hr., 4 per day, €50); **Salzburg, Austria** (1¾hr., 2 per hr., €26); **Vienna, Austria** (5hr., 1 per hr., €68); **Zürich, Switzerland** (4½-5½hr., 4-5 per day, €60). For 24hr. schedules, fare information, and reservations (in German), call toll-free ☎01805 99 66 33 from outside of Germany or ☎11861 (€0.39 per min.) from within. The **Bayern-Ticket** (single €18, 2-5 people €25) is valid for all train transit from 9am until 3am the next day, and can take you all the way to Salzburg. **EurAide** (see **Tourist Offices,** p. 434) provides free information in English and books train tickets. The Hauptbahnhof's **Reisezentrum** (travel center) is open daily 7am-9:30pm, and **DER Reisebüro** (☎55 14 02 00; www.der.de) sells train tickets and railpasses M-F 9:30am-6pm, Sa 10am-1pm.

Ride Share: Mitfahrzentrale, Lämmerstr. 6 (☎194 40). Arranges intercity transportation with drivers going the same way. Around €30. Open M-Sa 8am-8pm.

Hitchhiking: *Let's Go* does not recommend hitchhiking as a safe mode of transportation. Those looking to share rides scan the bulletin boards in the **Mensa** (p. 442). Otherwise, hitchers try Autobahn on-ramps; those who stand beyond the blue and white Autobahn signs may be fined. Hitchers going to Salzburg take U1 or U2 to "Karl-Preis-Pl." Hitchers to Stuttgart take tram #17 to "Amalienburgstr." or S2 to "Obermenzing," then bus #162 to "Blutenburg." Those heading to Nuremberg and Berlin take U6 to "Studentenstadt"

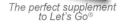

and walk 500m to the Frankfurter Ring. Those heading to the Bodensee and Switzerland take U4 or U5 to "Heimeranpl.," then bus #133 to "Siegenburger Str."

■ ORIENTATION

Munich rests on the banks of the Isar in the middle of south-central Bavaria, with King Ludwig's castles and the Alps only a short trip past its outskirts. **Marienplatz** is the center of Munich's sight-strewn **Altstadt**, or old town. To get there from the **Hauptbahnhof**, take any S-Bahn to "Marienpl.," or head out the main entrance and across Bahnhofpl. Continue east on Prielmayerstr. past the fountain at **Karlsplatz** (called **Stachus** by locals) and through the **Karlstor**; Marienpl. is straight ahead down the pedestrian mall. The huge **Deutsches Museum** lies on the well-named **Museumsinsel** (Museum Island) in the middle of the Isar river. North of the Altstadt is the **Residenz,** the former home of the Wittelsbach rulers; the **Hofgarten** beyond stretches to the corner of the **Englischer Garten**, which in turn sprawls toward the northeast reaches of the city. On the other side of town, the grand **Schloß Nymphenburg** rests beside the manicured **Botanischer Garten**. Sports fans head north of town to the **Olympiapark**, built for the 1972 Olympic Games. The **University of Munich** (a.k.a. **Ludwig-Maximilians Universität**) is north, next to **Schwabing**'s student-friendly restaurants and bookstores. The **Technical University** is also north of the city, near the museums of the Königspl. area. South of town is the **Glockenbachviertel**—filled with nightspots, including many gay bars. The area around the **Hauptbahnhof,** formerly dominated by sex shops, is improving and now houses many hotels. The large, open **Theresienwiese**, southeast of the Hauptbahnhof on the U4 and U5 lines, hosts **Oktoberfest**. Several publications help visitors navigate Munich; the most comprehensive (in English) is the monthly *Munich Found* (€3 at newsstands).

■ LOCAL TRANSPORTATION

Public Transportation: MVV, Munich's public transport system (☎41 42 43 44), runs M-Th and Su 5am-12:30am, F-Sa 5am-2am. S-Bahn to the airport starts running at 3:30am. Eurail, InterRail, and German railpasses are valid on the S-Bahn but *not* on the U-Bahn, trams, or buses. Buy tickets at the blue *MVV-Fahrausweise* vending machines and **validate them** in the blue boxes marked with an "E" **before entering the platform.** Disguised agents often check for tickets, levying a €40 fine on those who haven't validated them correctly. Always descend from the right-hand side of the S-Bahn. **Transit maps and maps of wheelchair-accessible stations** are at tourist offices and at MVV counters in U-Bahn and train stations. *Fahrpläne* (schedules) cost €1 at newsstands.

Prices: Single ride tickets €2.20 (valid for 2hr.). **Kurzstrecke** (short trip) tickets €1.10 (1hr. or 2 stops on the U- or S-Bahn, or 4 stops on a tram or bus). A **Streifenkarte** (10-strip ticket) costs €10 and can be used by more than 1 person. Cancel 2 strips per person for a normal ride, or 1 strip for a *Kurzstrecke*. Beyond the city center, cancel 2 strips per zone. A **Single-Tageskarte** (single-day ticket) is valid until 6am the day after purchase (€4.80). At €11, the **3-Day Pass** is a great deal. Alternatively, a **Partner-Tageskarte** (€8) can be used by up to 5 adults. The much-touted **Munich Welcome Card** (beginning at €7.50; p. 434) gives public transportation discounts. The **München XXL Ticket** offers day-long transit on all transportation in Munich and surroundings (€13 single; €22.50 for up to 5 individuals), and can be used to reach Dachau (p. 455).

Taxis: Taxi-München-Zentrale (☎216 10 or 194 10). Women can ask for female drivers.

Car Rental: Swing, Schellingstr. 139 (☎52 38 91 09). Upstairs at the are **Avis** (☎550 22 51; open M-F 7am-9pm, Sa-Su 8am-5pm); **Europecar** (☎549 02 40; open M-F 7am-9pm, Sa-Su 8am-7pm); **Hertz** (☎550 22 56; open M-F 7am-9pm, Sa-Su 9am-5pm); **Sixt** (☎0180 525 25 25; open M-F 6am-9pm, Sa-Su 8am-7pm).

Bike Rental: Radius Bikes (☎59 61 13), in the Hauptbahnhof opposite tracks 30-36. €3 per hr., €14 per day. Deposit €50, passport, or credit card. 10% discount for students and Eurail-holders, 20% with Munich Welcome Card (only one discount per person). Open daily May to mid-Oct. 10am-6pm. **Mike's Bike Tours** (☎25 54 39 87), across from the back entrance of the Hofbräuhaus, on Hochbreukenstr. All day €12, overnight €18. Half-off with a tour (p. 434). **DB CallBikes** (☎0700 05 22 55 22; www.callabike.de) is a Deutsche Bahn service, available by phone. Also located in front of the Hauptbahnhof. Rental €0.07 per min., max. €15 per day.

Bike Sale: Second Hand Sports, Nymphenburgerstr. 29 (☎59 70 74), U1 or U7 to "Stiglmaierpl." Used bikes €50+. Buyback for ½ price. English-speaking staff also services bikes. Open M 12:30-7pm, Tu-F 10:30am-7pm, Sa 10:30am-3:30pm. Cash only.

🛂 PRACTICAL INFORMATION

TOURIST OFFICES

🏛 **EurAide in English** (☎59 38 89; www.euraide.de), Room 2 adjacent to Track 11, Hauptbahnhof. Deutsche Bahn's English-speaking office books train tickets for all European destinations for free. The extensive website can be used to plan travel from abroad. Tickets for public transit (at standard prices), maps of Munich (€0.50), and tickets for English walking, bus, and bike tours are also available. Drop in for sound advice from the manager and pick up a free copy of his brochure *Inside Track*. Open daily June-Sept. 7:45am-12:45pm and 2-6pm (closed Su afternoon); Oct. 7:45am-12:45pm and 2-4pm; Nov.-Apr. 8am-noon and 1-4pm; May 7:45am-12:45pm and 2-4:30pm.

Main Office (☎23 39 65 00; www.muenchen.de/tourismus), next to the SB-Markt on Bahnhofpl. Although English is spoken, EurAide (see above) is a better resource for in-depth questions. The tourist office books rooms (for free with 10% deposit), dispenses English city maps (€0.30), and sells the **Munich Welcome Card,** which offers free public transportation and reduced prices at sights and museums (1-day ticket €7.50, 3-day ticket €17.50). The English guide *Young and About in Munich* (€0.50) lists beer gardens and gives tips on cycling and sightseeing. Open M-Sa 9am-8pm, Su 10am-6pm. **Branch** inside the entrance to the Neues Rathaus on Marienpl. also books rooms and sells city maps (€0.30). Open M-F 10am-8pm, Sa 10am-4pm.

TOURS

🏛 **Mike's Bike Tours** (☎25 54 39 88; www.mikesbiketours.com). Pedal, laugh, and down a few beers as you pick up some creative history from English-speaking guides. 4hr. tours (6.5km, €24) include bike rental and a *Biergarten* break. Tours daily mid-Apr. to Aug. 11:30am and 4pm; Sept. to mid-Nov. and Mar to mid-Apr. 2:30pm. Combo tickets available for castle and Dachau tours (p. 435). Meet at the Altes Rathaus in Marienpl.

Spurwechsel Bike Tours (☎692 46 99; www.spurwechsel.info). 2hr. German-language tours focusing on the secrets of Munich's landmarks, offered Apr. to Oct. F-Su and holidays at 11:15am. €14.50; bike rental included. English-language and theme tours available on request to groups of 8 or more; call for details. Meet at Marienpl.

The New Munich Free Tour (☎0176 233 02959; www.newmunich.com). Free 3hr. tour daily at 10:45am. Tips welcome. Also offers for-pay tours covering Dachau (p. 455) and the Third Reich (F-Sa at noon. €10, students €8). Meets at Marienpl.

Radius Tours (☎550 29 374; www.radiusmunich.com). Historical walking tours of the city in English, including a 2hr. tour of the *Altstadt* (Apr.-Oct. at 10am, €10, under 15 €5) and a Third Reich tour (Apr.-Oct. daily at 3pm; Nov.-Mar. Tu, F, Su at 11:30am. Same prices). Combo tickets available for both the walking tours and the guided tour of Dachau (p. 435). Walking tours meet opposite track 32 of the Hauptbahnhof.

Munich Walk Tours (☎207 07 2736; www.munichwalktours.de) leads 2hr. walks. €10, students €9. Beer- and Nazi-themed tours available. Tours offered daily mid-Oct. to Apr. at 10:45am (in Dec., Christmas market tours start at 2:45pm), and May to mid-Oct. at 10:45am and 2:45pm. Meet at the Neues Rathaus in Marienpl.

Panorama Tours, Arnulfstr. 8 (☎54 90 75 60; www.muenchenerstadtrundfahrten.de). 1hr. bilingual double-decker **bus tours** leave every hr. from the Hauptbahnhof daily Apr.-Oct. 10am-4pm, extra bus at 2:30pm. €11, children €6. 2½hr. tours leave daily at 10am and 2:30pm. Tours include admission and a guide at sites. €19-23, children €10-12. A 4½hr. Munich By Night tour runs Apr.-Nov. F-Sa 7:30pm. €60, including dinner. Hotel pickup available (day tours only). Office open M-F 9am-6pm, Sa 9am-1pm.

City Sightseeing Tours (www.city-sightseeing.com). **Bus tours** leave every hr. from the the Hertie department store across from the Hauptbahnhof 10am-4pm; F-Su also on the ½hr. €11, under 12 €6. Recorded information in 8 languages covers the city's highlights; tour includes a walk through the pedestrian historical center.

Castle Tours: There are many ways to be guided into the magical realm of mad King Ludwig II; see p. 464 for information on his castles.

Panorama Tours (above) offers a 10½hr. bus excursion (in English) to **Neuschwanstein** and **Linderhof** leaving Apr.-Oct. daily at 8:30am; Nov.-Mar. Tu-Su at 8:30am. €47, children €23; castle admission (€14.50) not included. Book ahead.

Mike's Bike Tours (above) offers guided daytrips in English that include a visit to **Neuschwanstein,** biking, swimming, and a stop at an alpine slide (€1.30). Tours leave most days during summer; check website for meeting times. By bus €49, by train €39; castle admission not included.

Dachau Tours: Always confirm that your guide is qualified by The Dachau Memorial.

The New Munich Free Tour (above) offers a daily guided tour of Dachau (Tu-Su at noon. €19, students €15, including transportation).

Radius Tours (above) gives a 5hr. English tour of Dachau. Tours daily May-Sept. at 9:15, 11:30am, 12:30pm; Oct. and Apr. at 9:15am, 12:30pm; Nov.-Dec. 23 and Jan. 3-Mar. at noon. €19, children under 14 €9.50. Meet 20min. before scheduled start time across from Track 32 of the Hauptbahnhof.

Mike's Bike Tours (above) provides transportation and a self-guided audio tour Apr. 15-Oct. 31 Tu-Su 9:45am. €7. Meet at the Hauptbahnhof's main tourist office.

 DO IT YOURSELF. Tour companies will get you to Dachau and Bavaria's castles for a price, but with a Bayern ticket (p. 32), five friends can save quite a bit. Hostels occasionally organize groups to take advantage of this opportunity; check the message board in your hostel lobby or inquire at the front desk.

CONSULATES

Canada: Tal 29 (☎219 95 70). S1-S8 to "Isartor." Open M-F 9am-noon; also from 2-4pm by appointment only. 24hr. emergency ☎00 800 2326 6831.

Ireland: Dennigerstr. 15 (☎20 80 59 90). Open M-F 9am-noon.

UK: Bürkleinstr. 10 (☎21 10 90; www.britishembassy.de). U4 or U5 to "Lehel." Phone open M-F 8:30am-noon and 1-5pm (F to 3:30pm), consul open M-F 8:45-11:30am and 1-3:15pm.

US: Königinstr. 5 (☎288 80; www.munich.usconsulate.gov). U3-U6 to Odeonspl. Open M-F 1-4pm. For visa info, call ☎090 01 85 00 55 M-F 7am-8pm (€1.86 per min.) or email ConsMunich@state.gov.

FINANCIAL SERVICES

Currency Exchange: ReiseBank (☎551 08 37; www.reisebank.de), at the front of the Hauptbahnhof, has decent rates. Open M-Sa 9:15am-12:30pm and 1-4:15pm.

BAYERN

American Express: Promenadepl. 6 (☎228 014 65; 24hr. hotline ☎08001 85 31 00), to the left of the Hotel Bayerischer Hof. Cashes travelers' checks. Open M-F 9am-1pm and 2-6pm, Sa 9:30am-12:30pm. **Branch** at Neuhauser Str. 47 (☎22 80 13 87). Open M-F 9:30am-6pm, Sa 10am-1pm.

LOCAL SERVICES

Luggage Storage: At the **airport** (☎97 52 13 75) 24hr. Staffed storage room in the main hall of the **Hauptbahnhof** (☎13 08 50 36). Lockers in main hall and opposite tracks 16, 24, and 28-36. €3-4 per 24hr. for up to 3 days. Open daily 4am-12:30am.

Lost Property: Fundbüro, Ötztaler Str. 17 (☎233 96045). U6 to "Partnachpl." Open Tu-Th 8am-noon and 2-6:30pm, F 7am-noon. **Hauptbahnhof** (☎13 08 66 64), by track 26. Open M-F 6:30am-11:30pm, Sa 7:45am-11pm, Su 7:45am-11:15pm.

Home Share:

Mitwohnzentrale Wolfgang Sigg GmbH/An der Uni, Fendstr. 6 (☎330 37 40; www.mwz-munich.de). U3 or U6 to "Munchener Freiheit." Walk south on Leopoldstr., make a left on Fendstr. At #6, buzz and go through the corridor to 2nd building. Apartments available by the month. Open M-F 9am-6pm.

City Mitwohnzentrale, Lämmerstr. 4 (☎194 20; www.mitwohnzentrale.de), by the Arnulfstr. exit of the Hauptbahnhof, also rents apartments. Open M-F 10am-1pm and 2-6pm.

Studentenwerk, Leopoldstr. 15 (☎38 19 60; www.studentenwerk.mhn.de), offers inexpensive housing for students. Thorough English-language website. Open M-F 8:30am-5pm.

Bookstores:

Words Worth, Schellingstr. 19 (☎280 91 41). U3 or U6 to "Universität." An orderly array of English titles in a quiet alcove off the main street. Open M-F 9am-8pm, Sa 10am-4pm.

Hugendubel, Marienpl. 22 (☎48 44 84; www.hugendubel.de). U3 or S1-S8 to "Marienpl." A 6-story bookstore and café offering hundreds of English titles. Enjoy books before purchase (rare in Germany) in cabbage-shaped alcoves. Open M-F 9:30am-8pm, Sa 9:30am-2pm.

The Munich Readery, Augustenstr. 104 (☎12 19 24 03; www.readery.de). U2 to "Theresienstr." A small secondhand bookshop with a good selection. Open M-Sa 11am-8pm.

Libraries: Bayerische Staatsbibliothek, Ludwigstr. 16 (☎28 63 80; www.bsb-muenchen.de), U6 to "Universität." A large library with over 8.3 million books, magazines, and newspapers. Reading room open until midnight. Open M-F 9am-9pm, Sa-Su 10am-5pm; closes earlier Aug.-Sept. **Bookshelf,** Blumenstr. 36 (☎61 62 27; www.the-bookshelf.de), U1 or U2 to "Sendlinger Tor." An English-language library. Open M, W, F 3-6pm, Sa 11am-3pm. 4-month trial membership €25; annually €42.

Visitor Publications: New In the City (www.new-in-the-city.com). Yearly publication in German and English (€6.50) available at newsstands. **SZ Woche,** the *Süddeutsche Zeitung*'s Th supplement with cultural listings (in German).

Gay and Lesbian Resources: Gay Services Information (☎260 30 56), open 7-10pm. Another point of reference is the 24hr. reception of **Hotel Deutsche Eiche,** Reichenbachstr. 13 (☎231 16 60). **Lesbian information** at the **LeTra Lesbentraum,** Angertorstr. 3 (☎725 42 72; letra@arcormail.de). Phone hotlines open M and W 2:30-5pm; Tu 11:30am-1pm; office open Th 7-9pm. Also see **Gay and Lesbian Munich,** p. 454.

Women's Resources: Kofra Kommunikationszentrum für Frauen, Baaderstr. 30 (☎201 04 50). Job advice, magazines, lesbian politics, books, and a small café. Open M-Th 4-10pm, F 2-6pm. **Frauentreffpunkt Neuperlach,** Oskar-Maria-Graf-Ring 20-22 (☎670 64 63; www.frauentreffpunkt-neuperlach.de). Services and venues for women, including an international coffeehouse. English conversation nights; check website or call for dates and times. **Lillemor's Frauenbuchladen,** Barer Str. 70 (☎272 12 05), is a women's bookstore. Open M-F 10am-6:30pm, Sa 10am-2pm.

Disabled Resources: Info Center für Behinderte, Schellingstr. 31 (☎211 70; www.vdk.de/bayern), lists Munich's resources for disabled persons. Open M-Th 9am-noon and 12:30-6pm, F 9am-3pm.

Ticket Agencies: To order event tickets by phone call **München Ticket** (☎548 18 18, €0.12 per min.; www.muenchenticket.de). Advance tickets are available at München Ticket's retail locations in the Rathaus in Marienpl. (open M-F 10am-8pm, Sa 10am-4pm) and at the Hauptbahnhof's information center. Open M-Sa 10am-6:30pm.

Laundromats: SB-Waschcenter, Lindwurmstr. 124. U1 to "Sendlinger Tor." Wash €3.50 (soap €0.30), dry €0.60 per 10min. Open daily 7am-11pm. **Branch,** Untersbergstr. 8. U2, U7 or U8 to "Untersbergstrasse." Free wireless Internet. Same prices and hours.

Swimming Pools: The city's 15 outdoor pools are open May to mid-Sept.; many feature adjacent indoor pools. Pick up *Münchener Bäder* at the tourist office for full listings (in German). Swim in the wake of the greats at the **Olympic Pool** (☎30 67 22 90) in Olympiapark. U3 to "Olympiazentrum." Open daily 7am-11pm.

EMERGENCY AND COMMUNICATIONS

Emergency: Police ☎110. **Ambulance** and **Fire** ☎112. **Emergency medical service** ☎192 22, home service 55 17 71. **Emergency road service** ☎0180 222 22 22.

Bahnhofsmission: The experienced staff at this 24hr. walk-in center help in non-medical emergencies ensuing at or near the Hauptbahnhof. Near track 11 at the Bayerstr. exit.

Rape Crisis Line: Frauennotruf München, Güllstr. 3 (☎76 37 37).

AIDS Hotline: ☎194 11 or 23 32 33 33. M-F 7-9pm.

Pharmacy: Bahnhofpl. 2 (☎59 41 19 or 59 81 19), on the corner outside the Hauptbahnhof. Open M-F 8am-8pm, Sa 8am-2pm.

Medical Services: Klinikum Rechts der Isar, across the river on Ismaninger Str. U4 or U5 to "Max-Weber-Pl." **Münchener AIDS-Hilfe,** Lindwurmstr. 71 (☎544 64 70). Free and anonymous STD/AIDS tests. Open M-Th 9:30am-6pm. F 9:30am-2pm. UK and US consulates carry lists of English-speaking doctors.

Internet Access: Wireless access is available for free at the Hauptbahnhof.

Easy Everything, on Bahnhofspl. Features over 500 computers; also offers printing and other computer-related services. €2.20 per hr. Unlimited passes for 24hr. (€5), 7 days (€15), or 30 days (€25). Open 24hr.

International Phone World, Schillerstr. 8. Internet €1.50 per hr. Phone cards available.

San Francisco Coffee Company, Im Tal 15 (☎995 29 73), near the Isartor (open M-Th 7am-10:30pm, F 7:30am-11pm, Sa 9am-11pm, Su 9am-10pm), or in Theatinerstr. 23/Odeonspl. (Open M-F 6:30am-11pm, Sa 7am-11pm, Su 8am-10pm.) Wireless access vouchers on sale at the counter, €2.90 per hr., €3.90 per day, €24.90 per month.

Post Office: (☎59 90 87 16). The yellow building opposite the Hauptbahnhof. Open M-F 7:30am-8pm, Sa 9am-4pm. **Postal Code:** 80335.

▚ ACCOMMODATIONS

The arrival of several new hostels and the wide availability of public transportation in Munich make it an easy place to stay as long as you plan ahead. During *Oktoberfest*, rooms are in short supply—begin your search for accommodations up to a year in advance. Be forewarned that **rates rise by 10-15% during Oktoberfest** for all types of accommodations. In summer, it's best to call before noon or book a few weeks in advance.

For extended stays, call the Mitwohnzentrale (p. 436) or try bargaining with a pension owner. Munich has a vibrant hostel scene and many recent additions, with options to suit all tastes and budgets. Many only admit guests under 26 or families with children. At most of Munich's hostels you can check-in all day, but start your search before 5pm. Don't plan on sleeping in a public area, including the Hauptbahnhof; police patrol all night long.

HOSTELS

NEAR THE HAUPTBAHNHOF

■ **Euro Youth Hotel,** Senefelderstr. 5 (☎59 90 88 11; www.euro-youth-hotel.de). Friendly, well-informed staff offers helpful information and spotless rooms. Fun and noisy travelers' bar serves *Augustinerbräu* (€2.80) daily 6pm-4am, lending the hostel a frat-house atmosphere. Breakfast €3.90. Internet access €1 per 20min, wireless €3 per 4hr. Wash €2.80. Dry €1.30. Reception 24hr. Large dorms €18.50; 3- to 5-person dorms €22. Singles €39; doubles €50, with shower, phone, and breakfast €60; quads €84. Rates vary; in winter, cheapest beds available online. MC/V. ❷

Wombat's, Senefelderstr. 1 (☎59 98 91 80; www.wombats.at/munich-hostel/index.php). Exceptionally clean with bathrooms in every room. Unusual touches include pleasant glass-enclosed "winter garden" and free welcome drink. Breakfast €4. Internet access €1 per 20min, wireless €3 per 4hr. Reception 24hr. Dorm beds €22; singles and doubles €62 per person. Cash only. ❷

Jaegers, Senefelderstr. 3 (☎55 52 81; www.jaegershotel.de). Modern, colorful hostel with a mellow lounge and welcoming English-speaking staff. Reception 24hr. Bed in 40-person dorm €19.50; smaller dorms €21-25; singles with bathroom €45; doubles with bathroom €78. Rates lower in winter. AmEx/MC/V. ❷

Jugendhotel "In Via" Marienherberge, Goethestr. 9 (☎55 58 05; invia-marienherberge@arcor.de). An unmarked yellow building with a big black door. **Open only to women.** Rooms are cheery and spotless. Kitchen, laundry, and TV facilities. Breakfast included. Wash €1.50, dry €1.50. Reception M-Th 8am-midnight, F 8am-4pm, Su 4pm-midnight. Check-out 9am. Lockout midnight-6am. Under 28 only. 4-bed dorms €22, €27; singles €30; doubles €50; triples €75. Cash only. ❷

CVJM Jugendgästehaus (YMCA), Landwehrstr. 13 (☎552 14 10; www.cvjm-muenchen.org/hotel). A quieter alternative to the area's rambunctious hostels. Co-ed rooms for married couples only. Breakfast and sheets included. Free Internet access. Max. stay 5 nights. Reception 8am-12:30am. Check-in 3pm. Check-out 10pm. Hostel closed Easter and Dec. 21-Jan. 10, 2007-08. Singles €35-41; doubles €59; triples €83. €2.50-3.50 extra for 27+. Reduced rates Dec.-Feb. MC/V. ❹

ELSEWHERE IN MUNICH

■ **Jugendlager Kapuzinerhölzl (The Tent),** In den Kirschen 30 (☎141 43 00; www.the-tent.de). Tram #17 (dir.: Amalienburgstr.) to "Botanischer Garten" (15min.). Follow the signs on Franz-Schrank-Str. and turn left on In den Kirschen. Night trams run every hr. all night. Join 250 international "campers" under a gigantic tent on a wooden floor. Evening campfires. Internet access €0.50 per 15min. Free city tours in German and English on W mornings. Free lockers. Kitchen facilities available. Wash €2. Dry €1.50. Passport or €25 required as key deposit. Reception 24hr. Open June-Aug. €9 gets you a foam pad, wool blankets, showering facilities, and breakfast. Beds €12. Camping €5.50 per campsite plus €5.50 per person. Cash only. ❶

■ **Jugendherberge Pullach Burg Schwaneck (HI),** Burgweg 4-6 (☎74 48 66 70; www.burgschwaneck.de), in a castle 12km outside the city center. S7 (dir.: Wolfrat-shausen) to "Pullach" (20min.). Follow signs down Margarethenstr. toward the huge soccer field (10min.). Caters largely to the under-18 crowd. Bowling €25. Pool €5 per hr. Breakfast and sheets included. Meals €4.80 (cold meal €4.30). Reception 7:30am-12:45pm and 1:30-5:30pm. Late arrivals call ahead. Curfew 11:30pm. 10-bed dorms €17; 4- to 6-bed dorms €19; singles €25; doubles €44. MC/V. ❷

Jugendherberge München Neuhausen (HI), Wendl-Dietrich-Str. 20. (☎13 11 56; jhmuenchen@djh-bayern.de). U1 (dir.: Westfriedhof) to "Rotkreuzpl." Go down Wendl-Dietrich-Str. past the Galeria Kaufhof; the entrance is 2 blocks ahead on the right. The most "central" of the HI hostels (3km from the city center). Free safes. Bike rental €10. Breakfast and sheets included. Sit-down dinner €5.40. Key deposit €15. Reception 24hr. Check-in 11:30am. Big co-ed dorm (33 beds) €20; 4- to 6-bed dorms €23, less after 1st night; doubles €46. MC/V. ❷

Jugendgästehaus Thalkirchen (HI), Miesingstr. 4 (☎723 65 50; www.jgh-muenchen.de). U3 (dir.: Fürstenried West) to "Thalkirchen." From Thalkirchnerpl., follow Schäftlarnstr. toward Innsbruck and bear right around the curve. Follow Frauenbergstr. and head left on Miesingstr. TV room, billiards, and washer/dryer (€3 each). Breakfast included. Reception 24hr. Check-in 2pm (call first after 6pm). 2- to 15-bed dorms €21; singles €23. Discounts for groups. Under 26 and families with children only. ❸

Haus International, Elisabethstr. 87 (☎12 00 60; www.haus-international.de). U2 (dir.: Feldmoching) to "Hohenzollernpl.," then tram #12 (dir.: Romanpl.) or bus #53 (dir.: Aidenbachstr.) to "Barbarastr." With billiards, ping pong, small *Biergarten*, TV room, cafeteria, and disco with bar. Reception 24hr. Singles €31, with bath €47; doubles €56, with shower €74; triples €81; quads €102; quints €120. AmEx/MC/V. ❸

CAMPING

Munich's campgrounds are open from mid-March to late October.

Campingplatz Thalkirchen, Zentralländstr. 49 (☎723 17 07; fax 724 31 77 for reservations). U3 (dir.: Fürstenried West) to "Thalkirchen," change to bus #135, and get off at the "Campingplatz" bus stop (20min.). 550 sites on the lush banks of the Isar. Jogging and bike paths nearby. TV lounge and restaurant. Wash €4. Dry €0.50. Reception open 7am-11pm. €4.50 per person, €1.50 per child under 14; €3-4 per tent; €4.30 per car. Showers €1. Caravans €11 per person. Cash only. ❶

Campingplatz Obermenzing, Lochhausener Str. 59 (☎811 22 35; fax 814 48 07). S3-S6 or S8 to "Pasing"; then bus #164 to "Lochhausener Str." Head up Lochhausener Str. from the bus stop; it's on the left (10min.). Friendly and well kept, but right next to the Autobahn. Reception daily July-Aug. 7:30am-7pm; Sept.-June 7:30am-noon and 3-7pm. Wash €4. Dry €1.50 per 7min. €4.50 per person, €2 per child under 14; €3.85 per tent, with car €6.50. Showers €1. No reservations. Cash only. ❶

HOTELS AND PENSIONS

Rooms fill quickly, so call ahead. Expect 10-20% rate increases during *Oktoberfest*.

NEAR THE HAUPTBAHNHOF

▨ **Creatif Hotel Elephant,** Lämmerstr. 6 (☎55 57 85; www.creatif-hotel-elephant.com). All newly renovated rooms with colorful decor, private bath, phone, and TV. Breakfast included. Free Internet access. Reception 24hr. Singles from €39; doubles from €59. Extra beds €15. Best rates through the website. AmEx/MC/V. ❹

Hotel Jedermann, Bayerstr. 95 (☎54 32 40; www.hotel-jedermann.de). Tram #18 or 19 (dir.: Freiham Süd) to "Hermann-Lingg-Str." Beautiful rooms, inviting common areas, and welcoming staff. Large breakfast buffet included. Free Internet access. Satellite TV and phones available. Singles from €34; doubles from €49. Extra bed €15. MC/V. ❸

Hotel Kurpfalz, Schwanthaler Str. 121 (☎540 98 60; www.kurpfalz-hotel.de). Tram #18 or 19 to "Holzapfelstr." Each colorfully decorated room includes phone, private bath, and satellite TV. Breakfast included. Laundry service available. Reception 24hr. Singles from €45; doubles from €59. Extra bed €15. Book early; prices increase steeply as availability decreases. Cash only. ❹

Pension Locarno, Bahnhofspl. 5 (☎55 51 64 or 55 51 65; www.pensionlocarno.de). Comfortable carpeted rooms with phone and cable TV. Breakfast €4. Reception 7:30am-5pm. Singles €40; doubles €50; triples €63. AmEx/DC/MC/V. ❹

Hotel-Pension Flora, Karlstr. 49 (☎59 70 67; www.hotel-flora.de). Breakfast included. Internet is €1 per 10min. Singles €45, with shower €60; doubles €56/80; triples €78/96; quads €88/104. MC/V. ❹

ELSEWHERE IN MUNICH

🏨 **Pension Theresia-Regina,** Luisenstr. 51 (☎52 12 50; www.hoteltheresia.de). U2 (dir.: Feldmoching) to "Theresienstr." Bright curtains enliven rooms. TV available upon request. Breakfast included. Reception (3rd fl.) 7am-9pm. Singles €30-33, with shower €50-60; doubles €46-52/68-72; triples €66-69/87-93; quads €80-88/96-100; quints €100-110. Cash only. ❸

Pension Isabella, Isabellastr. 35 (☎271 35 03; www.pensionisabella.de). U2 (dir.: Feldmoching) to "Hohenzollernpl." Walk west on Hohenzollernpl. and turn left on Isabellastr.; it's on the right. Spacious rooms and large, clean bathrooms. Breakfast included. Reception 8am-8pm. Singles €42, for 3+ nights €37; doubles €67/57; triples €86/71; quads €102/86. Cash only. ❹

Pension am Kaiserplatz, Kaiserpl. 12 (☎34 91 90). U3 or U6 to "Münchener Freiheit." With the Karstadt on your right, turn left on Herzogstr. and again on Viktoriastr.; it's on the right at the end of the street (10min). Close to bustling nightlife. Each elegant room is in its own period style, from Victorian to Modern. Breakfast (served in-room) included. Reception 8am-8pm. Singles €31, with shower €47; doubles €49-55/55-57; triples €66/69; quads €88-92; quints €105; 6-bed rooms €126. Cash only. ❸

Hotel-Pension am Markt, Heiliggeiststr. 6 (☎22 50 14; www.hotelinmunich.de). U3, U6, or S1-S8 to "Marienpl." Wheelchair-accessible. Breakfast included. Singles €43, with shower €69; doubles €78/95; triples €110/133; quads €118/145. MC/V. ❹

🍴 FOOD

The vibrant **Viktualienmarkt,** south of Marienpl., offers everything from basic to exotic, but prices can be steep. (Open M-Sa 7am-8pm, in summer Sa until 4pm.) Throughout the city, ubiquitous **Biergärten** (beer gardens) serve savory snacks and booze. For an authentic Bavarian lunch, spread some *Brez'n* (pretzels) with *Leberwurst* (liverwurst) or cheese. *Weißwürste* (white veal sausages) are another favorite, served with sweet mustard and a soft pretzel on the side; real *Müncheners* only eat them before 11am. Slice the skin open and devour their tender meat. *Leberkäse,* a local lunch, is a pinkish mix of ground beef and bacon which contains neither liver nor cheese. *Leberknödel* are liver dumplings served in soup or with *Kraut* (cabbage); *Kartoffelknödel* (potato dumplings) and *Semmelknödel* (bread and egg dumplings) should be eaten with a hearty chunk of German meat. Herbivorous travelers can enjoy *Käsespätzle* (egg noodles baked with cheese) or a plate of *Spargel* (asparagus), with a *Germknödel* (a sweet, jelly-filled dumpling topped with vanilla sauce) for dessert. The quarter of Munich's population born outside of Germany supplies the city with diverse ethnic offerings, including Turkish, Pakistani, Ethiopian, and Japanese. Many eateries change character as the day wears on, doubling as bars in the evening and sprouting extensive drink menus.

TRADITIONAL GERMAN

Weißes Bräuhaus, Tal 7 (☎290 13 80). Traditional restaurant founded in 1490. Brims with dishes like the "Münchener Voressen" (€7.90) made of calf and pig lungs. Choose from 40-50 options on the daily menu (€3-17) served by waitresses in classic Bavarian garb. Smaller portions on request (€4.50-10). Open daily 8am-midnight. MC/V. ❸

Augustiner Beerhall and Restaurant, Neuhauser Str. 27 (☎23 18 32 57). This restaurant, between Marienpl. and the Hauptbahnhof, offers Bavarian specialties and Augustiner brew (*Maß* €6). English menu. Entrées €4-13.50. Open daily 10am-midnight. ❸

Beim Sedlmayr, Westenriederstr. 14 (☎22 62 19), off the Viktualienmarkt. This renowned *Weißwurst* joint serves only Bavarian meat. Specials €4-14. Open M-F 9am-11pm, Sa 8am-4pm. Kitchen open M-F 9am-9:30pm, Sa 8am-3:30pm. Cash only. ❸

CAFÉS

▨ **Dukatz Kaffee im Literaturhaus,** Salvatorpl. 1 (☎291 96 00). The center of literary events in Munich since 1997. Gourmet food (€7-9) complements creative drink options (€2-4). Sip a cup of coffee and people-watch—you'll be observing the city's trendiest writers. Open M-Sa 10am-1am, Su 10am-7pm. Cash only. ❸

▨ **Schelling Salon,** Schellingstr. 54 (☎272 07 88), U3 or U6 to "Universität." Bavarian *Knödel* and billiards since 1872. Rack up at tables where Lenin, Rilke, and Hitler once played (€7 per hr.). Breakfast €3-5.10, German entrées €4-11. Open M and Th-Su 6:30am-1am; kitchen closes at midnight. A free **billiard museum** covers the history of pool dating back to the Pharaohs; open by advance request. Cash only. ❸

News Bar, Amalienstr. 55 (☎28 17 87), U3 or U6 to "Universität." Trendy café teeming with students. Large portions at reasonable prices. Breakfast €3-9. A wide assortment of salads, sandwiches, and pasta (€5-10). Open daily 7:30am-2am. AmEx/MC/V. ❸

Aran, Theatinerstr. 12 (☎25 54 69 82), is the most creative bakery in Munich, with inexpensive *panini;* pick a loaf and have it toasted with basil and mozzarella for €3.90. Also serves strong coffee. Open M-Sa 10am-8pm. Cash only. ❷

Türkenhof, Türkenstr. 78 (☎280 02 35), U3 or U6 to "Universität." Offers a wide selection of global cuisine, from Mexican to Thai. Popular among the low-key student crowd. Smoky and buzzing from noon until late. Variable daily menu with numerous veggie options. Entrées €5-8. Open M-Th and Su 11am-1am, F-Sa 11am-2am. Cash only. ❸

Café Reitschule, Königinstr. 34 (☎388 87 60). U3 or U6 to "Giselastr." Above a club, overlooking a horseback-riding school. *Weißbier* (wheat beer) €3.20. Breakfast served all day (€7-10). Entrées €7-15. Open daily 9am-1am. AmEx/MC/V. ❸

INTERNATIONAL

Shoya, Orlandostr. 5 (☎29 27 72), across from the Hofbräuhaus. The most reasonably priced Japanese restaurant in town. Fill up on rice dishes, teriyaki, and sushi (€4-10). Open daily 10:30am-midnight. Also at Frauenstr. 18 (☎24 20 89 89) at the Viktualienmarkt. Open Tu-Su 11am-midnight. MC/V. ❸

Papataki's, Leopoldstr. 42 (☎34 13 05). U3 or U6 to "Munchener Freiheit." Casual Greek restaurant and bar in the middle of Munich's late-night hotspot. Entrées €6-15; many vegetarian options. Open M-W and Su 11am-2am. Th-Sa 11am-5am. MC/V. ❸

Nage und Sauge, Mariennenstr. 2 (☎29 88 03; www.nageundsauge.de). S1-S8 to "Isartor." Known for their *focaccia* platters (€8.90-10.90), this artfully decorated Italian restaurant manages to be simultaneously hip and welcoming. Inventive mango soup with scampi €4.90. Open daily 5pm-1am. DJ music Sa. Cash only. ❸

La Fiorentina Trattoria Pizzeria Café, Goethestr. 41 (☎53 41 85), a few blocks from the Hauptbahnhof. This quiet haven from the bustle of the Hauptbahnhof neighborhood serves large pasta dishes (€6-8) off their daily menu. Main courses €5-17. Pizzas €4-8. Open M-F 11:30am-11pm, Sa 11:30am-3pm and 6-11pm. AmEx/MC/V. ❸

VEGETARIAN

▨ **Café Ignaz,** Georgenstr. 67 (☎271 60 93). U2 to "Josephspl.," take Adelheidstr. 1 block north and turn right on Georgenstr. Dinners range from crêpes to stir-fry dishes (€5-9) at this eco-friendly café. Breakfast buffet M and W-F 8-11:30am (€7); lunch buffet M-F noon-2pm (€6.50); brunch buffet Sa-Su 9am-1:30pm (€8). Open M and W-F 8am-10pm, Tu 11am-10pm, Sa-Su 9am-10pm. AmEx. ❷

BAYERN

Buxs, Frauenstr. 9 (☎291 95 50), on the Viktualienmarkt. Self-serve pastas, salads, and soups (€2 for 100g). Takeout available in glass (€3-6) or recyclable (€0.26) containers. Open M-F 11am-6:45pm, Sa 11am-3pm. Cash only. ❷

Prinz Myshkin, Hackenstr. 2 (☎26 55 96). U3 or U6, S1-S8 to "Marienpl." This internationally recognized restaurant is pricey but unique, with Asian-influenced cuisine featuring luscious paneers. Main courses €9.50-15. Open daily 11am-1am. AmEx/MC/V. ❹

OTHER

Poseidon, Westenriederstr. 13 (☎29 92 96), off the Viktualienmarkt. Bowls of *bouillabaisse* with bread (€10) in a bustling fish-market atmosphere. Other fish and seafood dishes €4-13. Join Müncheners in the know for the special sushi menu on Th (€20). Open M-W 8am-6:30pm, Th-F 8am-7pm, Sa 8am-4pm. Cash only. ❸

Mensa, Arcisstr. 17 (☎86 46 62 51; www.studentenwerk.mhn.de) to the left of the Pinakothek just below Gabelsbergstr. on Arcisstr. U2 or U8 to "Königspl." Students from the Technical University hit the cafeteria on the ground floor for light meals (€0.70-2). The Mensa upstairs serves large portions of cheap food (€2-4), with at least 1 vegetarian dish. To eat there, get a "Legic-Karte" in the library (€6 deposit and student ID required). Open M-Th 8am-4:30pm, F 8am-2:30pm; limited hours during vacations. 7 other cafeterias across the city; call or check online for hours and locations. ❶

DESSERT

▧ **Sarcletti's,** Nymphenburgerstr. 155 (☎15 53 14; www.sarcletti.de), U1 to "Rotkreuzpl." The best ice cream in town. Cones €0.80 per scoop. Mouthwatering specialties €5-12. Open M-F Apr.-Sept. 8am-11:30pm; Oct.-Mar. 8am-11pm. Cash only. ❸

LaPorte Confiseur, Heiliggeiststr. 1 (☎29 16 21 12), on the Viktualienmarkt. The La Portes have made delicious truffles and chocolates in the back of this boutique for over 15 years. Most items €5.20 per 100g. The French couple also makes crêpes (€1.60-2.15) and hot chocolate. Open M-F 10am-6:30pm, Sa 10am-5pm. Cash only. ❶

Café Hag/Confiserie Rottenhöfer, Residenzstr. 25-26 (☎22 29 15), across from the Residenz. Munich's oldest *Konditerei* specializes in an array of sweets (€2-4), served in an elegant interior. Open M-F 8:45am-7pm, Sa 8am-6pm. Cash only. ❶

◎ SIGHTS

▧ **RESIDENZ.** The richly decorated Residenz is the most visible presence of the Wittelsbach dynasty, whose state rooms now comprise the **Residenzmuseum.** The luxurious apartments reflect Renaissance, Baroque, Rococo, and Neoclassical styles. Also on display are collections of porcelain, gold and silverware, and a 17th-century court chapel. Highlights include the Rococo **Ahnengalerie,** hung with over 100 "family portraits" tracing the royal lineage, and the spectacular Renaissance **Antiquarium,** the oldest room in the palace. *(Max-Joseph-pl. 3. ☎29 06 71. U3-6 to "Odeonspl." Open daily Apr. to mid-Oct. 9am-6pm; in winter 10am-4pm. Last admission 30min. before closing. German language tours meet outside the museum entrance Su 11am. Admission €6, students €5, children €3.)* Behind the Residenz, the beautifully landscaped **Hofgarten** shelters a small temple. *(Free.)* The **Schatzkammer** (treasury) contains the most precious religious and secular symbols of Wittelsbach power: crowns, swords, crosses, and reliquaries collected during the Counter-Reformation to increase the dynasty's Catholic prestige. A comprehensive free audio tour of the Schatzkammer is available in 5 languages. *(Open same hours as Residenzmuseum. €6; students, seniors, and group members €5; under 18 free with adult. Combination ticket to Schatzkammer and Residenzmuseum €9; students and seniors €8.)* A collection of **Egyptian art** is also housed on the premises. *(☎28 92 76 30; open Tu-F 9am-5pm, Sa-Su 10am-5pm. Admission €4, students and seniors €3.)* Across Max-Joseph Pl. lies the golden-yellow Baroque

Theatinerkirche, completed by Ferdinand Maria in 1669 to commemorate his son's birth. The crypt houses the bronze coffins of the Wittelsbach clan. *(Church tours June-Sept. Th at 2pm, €3.50. Crypt open M-F 10am-1pm and 1:30-4:30pm, Sa 10am-3pm. €2)*

MARIENPLATZ. Sacred stone spires tower above the Marienpl., a major S- and U-Bahn junction and the social nexus of the city. The plaza, formerly known as *Marktplatz*, takes its name from the ornate 17th-century monument to the Virgin Mary at its center, the **Mariensäule**, built in 1638 to celebrate the city's near-miraculous survival of both the Swedish army and the plague. At the neo-Gothic **Neues Rathaus** (built in medieval style at the dawn of the 20th century), the **Glockenspiel** chimes with a display of a victorious Bavarian jouster. *(Daily at 11am and noon; summer also 5pm.)* At 9pm a mechanical watchman marches out and the Guardian Angel escorts the *Münchner Kindl* ("Munich Child," a symbol of the city) to bed. On the face of the **Altes Rathaus** tower, to the right of the Neues Rathaus, are all of Munich's coats of arms—with the notable exception of the Nazi swastika-bearing shield. Hitler commemorated his failed 1923 putsch in the ballroom, which is still used for official functions. *(Tower open daily 10am-7pm. €2, under 19 €1, under 6 free.)*

FRAUENKIRCHE. A vestige of the city's Catholic past and a symbol of Munich, the Frauenkirche towers were topped with their now-iconic domes in the mid-16th century. See the final resting place of Kaiser Ludwig der Bayer and take advantage of a German language tour (€3.50) Apr.-Oct. daily at 2pm, or ride the elevator to the top of the tower for a view of the old city. *(Frauenplatz 1. Church open daily 7am-7pm. Free. Towers open Apr.-Oct. M-Sa 10am-5pm. €3.50, students €1.50, under 6 free.)*

ASAMKIRCHE. This small Rococo masterpiece commemorates Prague's patron **St. John of Nepomuk**, who was thrown in the Moldau on the orders of the Emperor for allegedly refusing to violate the confidentiality of confession (in reality it was a political move). Ceiling frescoes narrate the story in detail. To either side of the church stand the residences of the two Asam brothers, Cosmas Damian and Egid Quirin, who financed its construction. Doors still connect their houses to the elevated church balcony. The church looks more expensive than it is; while the red marble is real, the blue-gray surface is just stucco. *(Sendlinger Str. 32; 4 blocks down Sendlinger Str. from the Marienpl. Open daily 9am-5:30pm.)*

PETERSKIRCHE. The golden interior of the 12th-century Peterskirche, which contains the skeleton of **Holy Munditia**, patron saint of single women, was "Baroquified" in the 18th century. Atop the tower, christened **Alter Peter** by locals, a spectacular view of Munich and (on clear days) the Alps awaits those who have what it takes to scale the 300 steps. *(Rindermarkt and Peterspl., across Marienpl. from the Neues Rathaus. Open M-Tu and Th-Su 7:30am-7pm. Tower open M-Sa 9am-7pm, Su 10am-7pm; in winter until 6pm. €1.50, students €1, children €0.30.)*

MICHAELSKIRCHE. Ludwig II of Bavaria rests peacefully with 40-odd other Wittelsbachs in the crypt of the 16th-century Jesuit Michaelskirche. Together with the later **Dreifaltigkeitskirche** and **Asamskirche,** it represents the pinnacle of the Bavarian Counter-Reformation, dubbed *Barockboom* by art historians. The construction of the church, intended by Wilhelm V "the Pious" to flaunt the city's Catholicism, almost bankrupted the state, and was marred by the immediate fall of the tower. Thinking that St. Michael had destroyed it for being too small, Wilhelm expanded construction, but the tower was never rebuilt for fear that St. Michael might see a new one as a challenge. Father Rupert Mayer, one of the few German clerics who spoke out against Hitler, preached here. *(Kaufingerstr. and Ettstr., 4 blocks from Marienplatz on Kaufingerstr. in direction of the Hauptbahnhof. Church open M-Sa 10am-7pm, Th until 8:45pm, Su 6:45am-10:15pm. German-language tours, May-Sept. W 2pm (€3.50), Sa noon (free). Concerts Su at 9am. Crypt open M-F 9:30am-4:30pm, Sa 9:30am-2:30pm. Free.)*

BAYERN

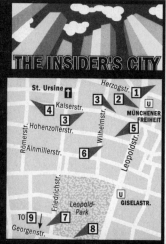

YOUNG SCHWABING: THE MUNICH BOHÈME

In 1900, the Schwabing quarter of Munich was home to the blossoming community of artists and writers who developed *Jugendstil*, Central Europe's version of Art Nouveau. Leaving ornate and classical styles behind, this revolutionary movement—headlined by Vassily Kandinsky and Paul Klee—was the first of the 20th century to break completely with tradition. Named after Munich's bohemian magazine *Die Jugend* (*The Youth*), the style celebrated curvilinear floral motifs and bright colors, and can still be spotted on Schwabing's facades.

1 **Erlöserkirche,** Ungererstr. 13. The first *Jugendstil* church, built 1899-1901, has green ceiling decorations, a baptismal font, *Jugendstil* columntops, and a cock on the roof. (*U3 or U6 to "Münchener Freiheit." Open M-Th and Sa 8am-5pm.*)

2 Check out the floral facade of **Leopoldstr. 77.**

3 **Bayrischer Revisionsverein,**

ENGLISCHER GARTEN. More expansive than New York's Central Park and London's Hyde Park, the Englischer Garten is the largest metropolitan public park in Europe. On sunny days, all of Munich turns out to fly kites, ride horses, and sunbathe. Nude sunbathing areas are designated **FKK** on signs and park maps. Several beer gardens are on the grounds, as is a Japanese tea house, a Chinese pagoda, and a Greek temple. Daring *Müncheners* surf the white-water rapids of the Eisbach, the artificial river that flows through the park. The bridge on Prinzregentenstr., close to the Haus der Kunst, is a great vantage point for these stunts.

SCHLOß NYMPHENBURG. Breathtaking Schloß Nymphenburg, modeled after Versailles, was built in 1662 and extended in the two centuries when France dominated Europe. The Rococo decorations and the Neoclassical themes in the grandiose two-story marble hall are reminiscent of Sun King Louis XIV's France, while the empire-style furniture in the electors' apartments is Napoleonic. The **Gallery of Beauties** is a fascinating collection of portraits of both noblewomen and commoners whom the king fancied or bedded. Particularly famous are **Helene Sedlmayer,** a market girl protected by the king, and **Lola Montez,** an English theatrical dancer with whom Ludwig had an affair well into his 70s, and who later led the 1848 revolution that caused his deposition. Situated in the landscaped gardens, the **Amalienburg,** the **Badenburg,** and the oriental **Pagodenburg**—all richly decorated, intimate manors—were once the locations of exclusive parties. The faux-ancient **Magdalen hermitage** was meant, with its fashionable grotto-style walls, to provoke penance in the courtiers. See how royalty rode and ate in style at the **Marstallmuseum** (Carriage Museum) and the **porcelain collection.** The gorgeous park was added in 1715 and rebuilt in the English style at the beginning of the 19th century. (*Tram #17 (dir.: Amalienburgstr.) to "Schloß Nymphenburg." ☎ 17 90 80. Complex open daily Apr.-Oct. 15 9am-6pm, Oct. 16-Mar. 10am-4pm. Badenburg, Pagodenburg, and Magdalen hermitage closed in winter. Schloß €5, students €4. Manors €2/1. Marstallmuseum €4/3. Entire complex €10/8; in winter €8/6; children under 18 free with adult. English audio guides free.*)

BOTANISCHER GARTEN. Next door to Schloß Nymphenburg, the immense Botanischer Garten sports rare and wonderful flora from around the world. Be sure not to miss the greenhouses bursting with palms and orchids, the alpine lake, and other exotic landscapes. (*Tram #17 (dir.: Amalienburgstr.) to "Botanischer Garten." ☎ 17 86 13 10; www.botmuc.de. Open daily May-Aug. 9am-7pm; Apr. and Sept. 9am-6pm; Feb.-Mar. and Oct. 9am-5pm; Nov.-Jan. 9am-4:30pm. €2, students €1.*)

NAZI-RELATED SIGHTS. Amid Munich's Baroque elegance are visible traces of Germany's Nazi past. Buildings erected by Hitler's regime stand as grim reminders of Munich's role as the ideological *Hauptstadt der Bewegung* (capital of the movement). The ceiling of the **Hofbräuhaus,** where the Nazi party held its first political rallies, still bears faint swastikas. The **Haus der Kunst,** built to enshrine Nazi principles of art, serves as a modern art museum (p. 447); swastika patterns have been left on its porch as reminders of its origins. The gloomy limestone building now housing the **Hauptschule für Musik und Theater** was built under Hitler's auspices and functioned as the **Führerbau,** his Munich headquarters. It was here that Chamberlain signed away the Sudetenland in 1938. At the **Königsplatz,** one block away from the Führerbau between the Antikensammlung and the Glyptothek Museums, thousands of books were burned on the night of May 10, 1933. Memorials dedicated to the **Weiße Rose** student movement, whose leaders were executed in Munich in 1943 for speaking out against the Third Reich, stand at the Ludwigs-Maximilians Universität and in the Hofgarten past the Staatskanzlei.

OLYMPIAPARK. Built for the 1972 Olympic Games, the lush and green Olympiapark contains the architecturally bold, tent-like **Olympia-Zentrum** and the 290m **Olympiaturm,** the tallest building in Munich. Three **tours** in English are available: the "Adventure Tour" of the entire park leaves Apr.-Oct. daily at 2pm from the Info-Pavilion, while a soccer stadium tour meets Mar.-Oct. daily at 11am. The **Roof Climb,** daily at 2:30pm, is a 2hr. exploration of the **Olympiastadion** with a rope and hook. *(Meet at the north box office of the Olympic Stadium. Architectural tour available upon request for groups of 10 or more. Adventure tours €7, students and ages 6-15 €5. Soccer Stadium tour €5/3.50. Roof climb €25/20, weekends €30/20.)* Tourists can marvel at the view from the top of the *Turm* or attend various outdoor events all summer, from flea markets to bungee jumps, in the park itself. *(Take U3 to "Olympiazentrum." Info pavilion ("Besucherservice") at skating rink ☎30 67 24 14. Open M-F 10am-6pm, Sa 10am-3pm. Tower open daily 9am-midnight. €4, students and ages 6-15 €2.50.)*

TIERPARK HELLABRUN. Animals roam (relatively) freely in Munich's zoo. There are no large fences to get in the way; creatures are kept in by a series of meandering streams. Eerie cave-dwellers surround visitors in the Hall of Bats. A brochure available at the entrance lists the feeding times of many animals, including penguins and tigers. *(Tierparkstr. 30. U3 (dir.: Furstenried West) to "Thalkirchen," then follow signs over the Isar to the Tierpark. Or bus #52 from Marienpl. to the "Fla-*

Kaiserstr. 14 and 29, display fruit and children, two typical elements of the style.

4 **Römerstr. 28** displays cherubs and water, other common motifs of *Jugendstil.*

5 Check out the pink **Hohenzollernstr. 10.**

6 Adam and Eve lie under a tree at **Ainmillerstr. 22,** the city's best-preserved *Jugendstil* building. Bourgeois contemporaries condemned the bright colors and threatening Medusas when it appeared in 1899.

7 The flowers on **Friedrichstr. 3** imitate nearby Leopoldpark.

8 **Georgenstr. 10,** brightly decorated with medallions depicting artists, sits on a street named for poet Stefan George, next door to the neo-Baroque **Pacelli-Palais** (Georgenstr. 8).

9 Finish up in Schwabing at the pub **Alter Simpl,** Türkenstr. 57 (☎272 30 83). Founded in 1903, it is named after *Simplizissimus,* a Munich satirical review, which (together with *Die Jugend*) was the Schwabing crowd's newspaper of choice. *Weißbier* €3.10. Open M-Th and Su 11am-3am, F-Sa 11am-4am. Cash only.

10 To cap off a Bohemian day, head out of Schwabing to the **Villa Stuck** museum (p. 447; not on map), a former *Jugenstil* mansion that now displays art of the movement.

mingo" entrance. ☎62 50 80; www.zoo-munich.de. *Open daily Apr.-Sept. 8am-6pm; Oct.-Mar. 9am-5pm. Wheelchairs can be borrowed from the front desk. €9, students €6.50, seniors €6, ages 4-14 €4.50, under 4 free.)*

🏛 MUSEUMS

Munich has been a superb museum city ever since Ludwig I decided to make it into an "Athens on the Isar" in the 19th century. The *Münchner Volkshochschule* (☎48 00 62 29) offers many museum tours for €6. State-run museums (including the three *Pinakotheken*) are €1 on Sunday.

MUSEUMSINSEL

DEUTSCHES MUSEUM. The Deutsches Museum is one of the world's most comprehensive science and technology museums. Exhibits include an early telephone, the work bench on which Otto Hahn first split an atom, and a recreated subterranean labyrinth of mining tunnels. A walk through the museum's 50+ departments covers over 17km. An English guidebook (€4) thoroughly explains all exhibits, though many signs are in English as well. The **planetarium** shows educational films during the day. *(4 shows daily; €2.)* Stroll through the fascinating sundial garden, located on the roof next to the planetarium, and savor its panoramic view of the city. *(Museumsinsel 1. S1-S8 to "Isartor" or tram #18 to "Deutsches Museum."* ☎217 91; *www.deutsches-museum.de. Open daily 9am-5pm. €8.50, students €3, under 6 free.)* The Deutsches Museum also maintains an impressive **flight museum** in a WWI hangar in Schleißheim and a **transportation museum.** *(Flight museum: Effnerstr. 18.* ☎315 71 40. *S-Bahn to "Oberschleißheim," then follow signs. Open daily 9am-5pm. Admission €3.50, students and seniors €2.50. Transportation museum: Theresienhöhe 14a.* ☎217 95 29. *U4-5 to "Schwanthalerhöhe." Open daily 9am-5pm, Th until 8pm. €2.50, students and seniors €1.50. Combined admission to flight, transportation, and science museums €10.)*

KÖNIGSPLATZ

The three *Pinakotheken* have free detailed audio guides available in English; be sure to pick one up by the entrance.

▓PINAKOTHEK DER MODERNE. A uniquely rich collection of 20th-century art is on display at this *Pinakothek*, which opened in 2000. The sleek museum, designed by Munich's own Stephan Braunfels, is particularly strong on "classical" modernism. Seminal works of expressionism, surrealism, futurism, and cubism share space with Jasper Johns, Gerhard Richter, Lucio Fontana, and exciting contemporary sculpture and video installations. The **design section** has something for everyone, from cars to jewelry. The museum's two other departments feature graphic art and architecture. *(Barerstr. 40. U2 to "Königspl." Take a right at Königspl., and a left after 1 block onto Meiserstr. Walk 1½ blocks to the museum.* ☎23 80 53 60. *Open Tu-W and Sa-Su 10am-5pm, Th-F 10am-8pm. €9.50, students €6.)*

▓ALTE PINAKOTHEK. Munich's finest 14th to 18th century, art is on display at this world-reknowned museum. Northern European artists are well represented, including Dürer, Cranach, Brueghel, Rembrandt, and Rubens. Look for Rubens' gigantic "The Last Judgment"—the museum's imposing galleries were sized for this canvas. Italian, French, and Spanish masterpieces are also on display. *(Barer Str. 27.* ☎23 80 52 16. *Open Tu 10am-8pm, W-Su 10am-5pm. €5.50, students €4.)*

▓NEUE PINAKOTHEK. The Neue Pinakothek houses the 19th century in art, from David to Klimt. Special attention given to German art and overlooked movements, with excellent impressionist holdings. Look for the iconic portrait of Goethe, by

Stiegler of Schönheitsgalerie fame. *(Barerstr. 29, next to the Alte Pinakothek. ☎23 80 51 95. Open M and Th-Su 10am-5pm, W 10am-8pm. Tour M noon. €5.50, students €4.)*

GLYPTOTHEK (SCULPTURE MUSEUM). Together with the Antikensammlung, the Glyptothek is a testament to the German love for all things Greek and Roman. The brightly painted plaster casts of Grecian statues will challenge your notions of classical art. *(Königspl. 3. U2 to "Königspl." Across Luisenstr. from the Lenbachhaus, opposite Antikensammlung. ☎28 61 00. Open W and F-Su 10am-5pm, Th 10am-8pm. Free tour Th at 6pm. €3.50, students €2.50. €5.50/3.50 together with admission to Antikensammlung.)*

ANTIKENSAMMLUNG (ANTIQUITIES MUSEUM). A collection of Greek and Etruscan vases and ceramic works of stunning quality; the artwork brings mythological and everyday subjects to life. *(Königspl. 1. U2 to "Königspl." Across Königspl. from Glyptothek. ☎59 98 88 30. Open Tu-Su 10am-5pm, W until 8pm. Free tour W at 6pm. €3.50, students €2.50. €5.50/3.50 together with admission to Glyptothek.)*

LENBACHHAUS. A rich assemblage of works chronicling Kandinsky's move to abstraction and the founding of the *Blaue Reiter* (Blue Rider) movement is housed in the opulent mansion of 19th-century painter **Franz von Lenbach.** His personal collection of masterpieces is on the upper levels. The museum also offers a collection of local landscapes and portraits. Together with the adjoining **Kunstbau,** the gallery shows modern exhibits of artists like Picasso and Klee. *(Luisenstr. 33. U2 to "Königspl." ☎23 33 20 00; www.lenbachhaus.de. Open Tu-Su 10am-6pm. Free tour Su 11am. €6, students €3; prices can vary with exhibit. Audio guide €3.)*

ELSEWHERE IN MUNICH

MÜNCHENER STADTMUSEUM (MUNICH MUNICIPAL MUSEUM). Exhibitions present aspects of Munich's city life and history: film, weapons, puppetry, posters, and more. **Classic films** (€4) every evening at 6 and 9pm, plus 11am and 3pm on Sundays. Foreign films in the original language with German subtitles; call ☎23 32 41 50 for a program. *(St.-Jakobs-Pl. 1. U3 or U6 or S1-S8 to "Marienpl." Walk down Rindermarkt Str. for 3 blocks; turn left on St.-Jakobs-Pl. ☎23 32 23 70; www.stadtmuseum-online.de. Open Tu-Su 10am-6pm. €4; students, seniors, and children €2; families €6; €1 admission Su.)*

BMW-MUSEUM. Bavaria's second-favorite export is on display at this architecturally daring, silver mushroom-shaped museum. Headphone stations (in English, French, German, and Spanish) guide you through the spiral path to the top of the building. The main building is closed for renovation until summer 2007; in the meantime, a temporary exhibition has been constructed at the foot of the **Olympiaturm** (p. 445). *(Main building at Petuelring 130. U3 to "Olympiazentrum," take the "Olympiaturm" exit and walk a block up Lerchenauer Str.; museum will be on your left. ☎38 22 56 52; www.bmw-museum.de. Open daily Mar. 28-Oct. 30 10am-10pm, Oct. 31-Mar. 26 8am-8pm. €2, students €1.50. Check website or call ahead for post-renovation prices and hours.)*

VILLA STUCK. This villa, designed by Munich artist **Franz von Stuck,** is the backdrop for paintings, design, and graphic art of the early 20th-century German *Jugendstil,* a movement that rejected tradition, celebrating nature, spring, the body, and youth. *(Prinzregentenstr. 60. U4 to "Prinzregentenplatz," then head down Prinzregentenstr. ☎455 55 10; www.villastuck.de. Open W-Su 11am-6pm. €6, students €3.)*

HAUS DER KUNST (HOUSE OF ART). Originally built by the Nazis as a "Hall of German Art" and a center for visual propaganda, this enormous building somehow survived the Allied bombing unscathed. Bucking the hyper-nationalism of its creators, the Haus der Kunst is now a major stop for traveling international exhibitions. The museum's yearly "Große Kunstausstellung" highlights contemporary German art. *(Prinzregentenstr. 1. U4 or U5 to "Lehel," then tram #17 one stop (dir.: Effnerpl.)*

☎ *211 27 11; www.hausderkunst.de. Open daily 10am-8pm, Th until 10pm. €5-9, depending on exhibit; students €3.50-7; ages 12-18 €2; under 12 free.)*

SPIELZEUGMUSEUM (TOY MUSEUM). Housed in the Altes Rathaus, this tiny toy-themed museum plays host to rotating exhibits like "100 Years of Teddy Bears." Check website for latest exhibition. *(Marienpl. 15. In the Altes Rathaus.* ☎ *29 40 01. www.toymuseum.de. Open daily 10am-5:30pm. €3, under 15 €1, families €6.)*

🎭 ENTERTAINMENT

THEATER AND OPERA

Munich's cultural cachet rivals the world's best. Sixty theaters are scattered throughout the city. Styles range from dramatic classics at the **Residenztheater** and **Volkstheater** to comic opera at the **Staatstheater am Gärtnerplatz** and experimental works at the **Theater im Marstall** in Nymphenburg. Standing room tickets run about €8. The **Hochschule für Music** on Arcisstr. also offers an unconventional assortment of free performances by the future masters of German music. Munich's **opera festival** (June 30-July 31, 2007) is held in the **Bayerische Staatsoper** (see below) and is accompanied by a concert series in the Nymphenburg and Schließheim palaces. *Monatsprogramm* (German, €1.50) and *Munich Found* (English, €3) list schedules for Munich's stages, museums, and festivals. In **Schwabing**, Munich shows its bohemian face with scores of small fringe theaters, cabaret stages, and art cinemas. On summer nights, the crowds milling about **Leopoldstraße**'s terrace-cafés create an exciting swarm. At the turn of the century this area was a center of European intellectual life, home to luminaries kike Brecht, Mann, Klee, Georgi, Kandinsky, Spengler, and Trotsky (see **Young Schwabing**, p. 444).

🎭 **Bayerische Staatsoper,** Max-Joseph-Pl. 2 (tickets ☎ 21 85 01, recorded information 21 85 19 20; www.bayerische.staatsoper.de). U3-U6 to "Odeonspl." or tram #19 to "Nationaltheater." Built by Max Joseph to bring opera to the people. Student tickets (€8) sold 1hr. before shows at the entrance on Maximilianstr. Bring student ID and another form of ID—they do not accept ISIC. Box office open M-Sa 10am-7pm and 1hr. before shows. Tickets can also be bought online. No performances Aug. to mid-Sept.

Gasteig Kulturzentrum, Rosenheimer Str. 5 (☎ 48 09 80; www.gasteig.de). S1-S8 to "Rosenheimerpl." or tram #18 to "Am Gasteig." The hall rests on the former site of the Bürgerbräukeller—where Adolf Hitler launched his failed Beer Hall Putsch—and houses a conservatory, music school, and the **Munich Philharmonic.** Buy tickets online or in the Glass Hall of the Gasteig (Open M-F 10am-8pm, Sa 10am-4pm).

Staatstheater am Gärtnerplatz, Gärtnerpl. 3 (☎ 20 24 11, box office 21 85 19 60; www.staatstheater-am-gaertnerplatz.de). U1 or U2 to "Fraunhoferstr.," then follow Reichenbachstr. to Gärtnerpl. Stages comic opera and musicals. €7 student tickets must be bought 2wk. in advance. Standing room tickets also available. Box office open M-F 10am-6pm, Sa 10am-1pm, and 1hr. before performances.

Drehleier, Rosenheimer Str. 123 (☎ 48 27 42; www.theater-drehleier.de). S1-S8 to "Rosenheimerpl." One of the Munich's best cabaret scenes, with food (€3-9) and drink. Tickets €18, students €15. Reservations required. Shows W-Sa 8:30pm, Su 8pm. Opening times vary; call or check website.

FILM

English films are usually dubbed; look for "OV" (original language) or "OmU" (subtitled) on the poster or in the listings. Munich's **Internationales Dokumentarfilmfestival** (www.dokfest-muenchen.de) will run from May 2-10, 2007. The broader **Filmfest München** (☎ 381 90 40; www.filmfest-muenchen.de) will take place from June 23-July 1, 2007. *In München* and other publications list movie screenings.

Museum Lichtspiele, Lilienstr. 2 (Tickets ☎0180 58 67 077 747, Programs 0180 58 67 077 647; www.museum-lichtspiele.de). Shows many English-language films, both the latest Hollywood fare and arthouse productions. Rocky Horror Picture Show screenings F-Su at 11pm. Admission €6.50, students €5.50.

Cinema München, Nymphenburgerstr. 31 (☎55 52 55; www.cinema-muenchen.com). U1 to "Stiglmaierpl.," then 2 blocks west on Nymphenburgerstr. Plays English-language films almost exclusively; most are current and American. So as not to forget you are in Munich, sip a beer (€2.50) while the movie shows. Reserve tickets early online as movies do sell out. €8-9, students €7. M-Tu and before 5pm W-Th €5.

MUSIC

Big-name pop stars perform at the **Olympiahalle** and the **Olympia-Stadion.** Follow the rest of the city to the Olympiapark on concert nights; you can relax on the grass and enjoy major artists for free (see **Priceless Entertainment,** at right).

Tollwood Festival (☎0700 38 38 50 24; www.tollwood.de). June 14-July 8 and Nov. 28-Dec. 12, 2007; June 19-July 13 and Nov. 26-Dec. 31, 2008. Munich's alternative culture festival attracts a large, mainly German, young audience. Featuring *Oktoberfest*-style beer tents, Tollwood offers all forms of performing art, from mime, theater, and dance to music, with international acts such as Air, Alice Cooper, and James Brown. *Tollwood* magazine, available from the tourist office, lists performances, which can be booked by phone. U3 to "Olympiazentrum." Special buses also depart from Westfriedhof (U1) and Scheidplatz (U2 or U3). Open M-F 2pm-1am, Sa-Su 11am-1am.

Feierwerk, Hansastr. 39-41 (☎769 36 00). U4, U5, or S7 to "Heimeranpl." and left down Hansastr. (10min.) The center of Munich's alternative concert scene, with seven stages and huge tents. Lots of independent rock, reggae, hip-hop, and electronica. Beer gardens open at 6pm, doors usually open at 8:30pm for 9pm concerts.

⬛ NIGHTLIFE

Munich's nightlife is a curious collision of Bavarian *Gemütlichkeit* and trendy cliquishness. Those of the latter persuasion are often called *Schicki-Mickis*—expensively dressed, coiffed, and beautiful specimens of both sexes. The city's streets bustle with raucous beer halls, loud discos, and exclusive cafés every night of the week. Most locals begin their benders at a *Biergarten*, which generally close before midnight and are most crowded in the early evening.

PRICELESS ENTERTAINMENT

The Olympia Stadium (p. 445), just 3km north of Munich's city center, hosts dozens of concerts every summer. While most charge admission, savvy *Müncheners* are unlikely pay for two hours in a cramped stadium seat; they know that the sounds of big-name bands carry freely to the surrounding park, where 850,000 square meters of beautifully manicured lawns encompass a swan-filled lake. On a typical concert night, half the city fills this sprawling park to listen in for free and relax under a summer sky.

The beer and *Bratwurst* are plentiful and the nearby fairground has games and some shockingly delicious chocolate covered-bananas. In 2006 alone, the Olympiazentrum played host to classic acts like the Rolling Stones, James Blunt, Eric Clapton, and B.B. King, along with pop stars Pink and Robbie Williams. If you're not comfortable with catching the sound waves without the eye candy behind the guitar (or the flute, as it may be), occasional free concerts occur here too, including classical concerts most nights in August. Check www.theatron.de for more info.

(Take U3 to "Olympiazentrum" and follow the crowds toward the stadium. ☎306 724 14; www.olympiapark-muenchen.de. Concerts usually start around 8pm.)

Alcohol keeps flowing at cafés and bars, which, except for Friday and Saturday nights, close their taps at 1am. Then it's off to the bump and grind of the clubs and discos. **Münchener Freiheit** (on the U3 and U6 lines) is the city's most famous (and most touristed) bar and café district. The bars, cafés, cabarets, and discos along **Leopoldstraße** in **Schwabing** attract tourists from all over Europe. The southwestern section of Schwabing, behind the university on **Amalienstraße** and **Türkenstraße,** is more low-key. High-end venues dot the **Maximilianstraße** and the old town center; more alternative vibes are in the **Glockenbachviertel.** Many of these venues require you to at least try the hipster look (leave the shorts and T-shirts at home). Otherwise, more laid-back fun is to be had at large, less central venues such as **Kultfabrik** (p. 453), **Muffathalle** (p. 454), and **Backstage** (p. 454). Pick up *Munich Found, In München,* or *Prinz* at newsstands to help you sort out the scene.

BEER HALLS AND GARDENS

When Bavaria agreed to become a part of a larger Germany, it insisted on one stipulation: that it be allowed to maintain its beer purity laws. Since then, Munich has remained loyal to six great labels: *Augustiner, Hacker-Pschorr, Hofbräu, Löwenbräu, Paulaner,* and *Spaten-Franziskaner.* Four main types of beer are served in Munich: *Helles* and *Dunkles* (standard light and dark beers); *Weißbier* (cloudy blond beer made from wheat instead of barley); and *Radler* ("shandy" or "cyclist's brew": half beer and half lemon soda). Munich's beer is typically 5% alcohol, though in *Starkbierzeit* (the first two weeks of Lent), Müncheners traditionally drink *starkbier,* a dark beer that is 8-10% alcohol. To find beer gardens, look for leaf symbols on tourist maps. *"Ein Bier, bitte"* will get you a liter, known as a *Maß* (€5-6). Specify if you want a *halb-Maß* (half liter, €3-4), though many places serve only *Weißbier* in 0.5L sizes. While some beer gardens offer veggie dishes, vegetarians may wish to eat elsewhere before a post-meal swig. In general it's acceptable to bring your own food; drinks, however, must be bought at the *Biergarten.* Bare tables usually mean *Selbstbedienung* (self service).

■ **Augustinerkeller,** Arnulfstr. 52 (☎59 43 93), at Zirkus-Krone-Str. S1-S8 to "Hackerbrücke." From the Haputbahnhof make a right on Arnulfstr. Founded in 1824, Augustiner is viewed by many as the finest *Biergarten* in town, with enormous *Brez'n* and dim lighting beneath 100-year-old chestnut trees. The real attraction is the delicious, sharp *Augustiner* beer (*Maß* €6.50). Food €3-15. Open daily 10am-1am; hot food until 10:30pm. Open daily 10:30am-midnight. AmEx/MC/V.

■ **Hirschgarten,** Hirschgarten 1 (☎17 25 91). Tram #17 (dir.: Amalienburgstr.) to "Romanpl." Walk south to the end of Guntherstr. The largest *Biergarten* in Europe (seating 9000) is boisterous and always crowded. Families come for the grassy park and carousel, and to see the deer that are still kept on the premises. Entrées €5-15. *Maß* €5.50. Open daily 9am-midnight; kitchen open until 10pm. Cash only.

■ **Zum Flaucher,** Isarauen 8 (☎723 26 77). U3 to "Brudermühlstr." Gorgeous 2000-seat *Biergarten* on the banks of the Isar. Lift a *Maß* (€2.60-3.40) with locals relaxing near the water, or join one of the frequent pickup soccer games. The perfect destination for a cycling excursion along the Isar, easy to reach from the bike trails along the river. Open May-Oct. daily 10am-midnight, Nov.-Apr. Sa-Su 10am-9pm. Cash only.

Hofbräuhaus, Platzl 9 (☎290 13 60). In 1589, Bavarian Duke Wilhelm the Pious earned his name by founding this monument to Germany's most revered beverage. 15-30,000L of beer are sold per day. Many tables are reserved, and hundreds of locals keep personal steins in the beer hall's safe. Go in the early afternoon to avoid tourists, or in the evening to see the true bustle of the beer hall. *Maß* €6.40. *Weißwürste* €3.50. Open daily 9am-midnight with live Bavarian music in the large hall below. AmEx/MC/V.

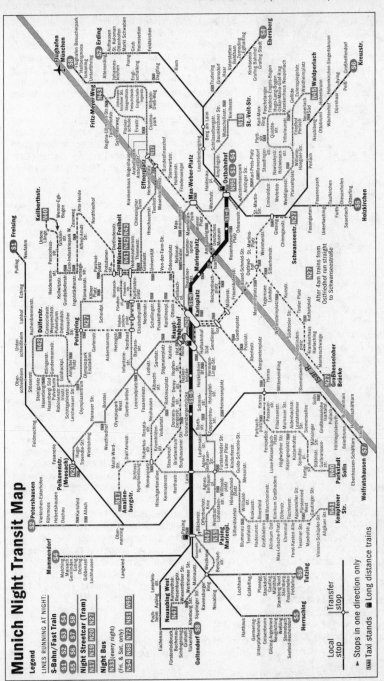

Munich Night Transit Map

Legend

LINES RUNNING AT NIGHT:

S-Bahn/Fast Train
S1 S2 S3 S4 S6 S7 S8

Night Streetcar (Tram)
N17 N19 N20 N27

Night Bus
N33 (every night)
(Fri. & Sat. only)
N54 N68 N72 N81 N95

Local stop
Transfer stop
➤ Stops in one direction only
TAXI Taxi stands
◉ Long distance trains

After 4am trains from Ostfriedhof run straight to Schwanseestraße

BAYERN

THE PROPER *PROST!*

It is a universally acknowledged truth that a European traveler in possession of a dry throat must be in want of a German *Bier*. Careless drinkers be warned: German drinking protocol is simple, but strictly enforced.

Bavarian custom requires each drinker to wait until everyone has received his or her beverage before any glass is touched. Once the whole party has been served, everyone greets each other with a hearty "*Prost*" (cheers). Failure to make eye contact with the person whose glass you're clinking is rude at best, and at worst is supposed to result in seven years of bad sex. (*Let's Go*, however, believes that readers are responsible for the quality of their own sex life.) After glasses have been tapped all the away around the group, everyone hits his or her *stein* to the table before taking the first sip.

This final tap is said to date back to King Ludwig I, who sent the political and social pressures of ruling Munich and Bavaria straight to his belly, growing quite fat in his old age. When he would *Prost* his companions at the dinner table, he would be so exhausted from holding up his *Maß* that he had to set down his beer again before he could muster up the energy to drink.

So channel the spirit of Ludwig, get ready for some eye-contact, and *Prost* with heartfelt drunken pride. And enjoy sex for the next seven years of your life.

Seehaus, Kleinhesselohe 3 (☎381 61 30). U6 to "Dietlindenstr.," then bus #144 (dir.: Giesing) to "Osterwaldstr." Directly on the Kleinhesseloher See in the Englischer Garten. In the evening, watch the sun set over the water as you enjoy a *Maß* (€6.60) and a pretzel (€3.20), or another delicacy from the cafeteria-style eatery. Open daily 10am-midnight; kitchen closes at 10:30pm. Cash only.

Taxisgarten, Taxisstr. 12 (☎15 68 27). U1 to "Gern," then 1 block east on Tizianstr. This small (1500 chairs) *Biergarten* is a local gem. Serves a scrumptious green variety of the normally orange Bavarian specialty *Obazda* (a mix of cheeses; €2.30). *Maß* €6.10. *Weißbier* €3.30. Open daily 11am-11pm, last call for drinks 10:30pm. Cash only.

Chinesischer Turm (☎38 38 73 19), in the Englischer Garten right next to the pagoda. U3 or U6 to "Giselastr." or bus #54 from Südbahnhof to "Chinesischer Turm." A fair-weather tourist favorite. Live, cheesy brass band music drifts from the pagoda. *Maß* €6.30. Open daily in balmy weather 10am-midnight. Below €20 cash only.

Löwenbräukeller, Nymphenburgerstr. 2 (☎52 60 21). U1 or U7 to "Stiglmaierpl." Castle-like entrance to a festive, enormous indoor beer hall and a shady garden tucked next to the massive Löwenbräu brewery. Come here to taste the real *Löwenbräu*, a bitter brew with a core of loyal middle-aged followers. *Maß* €7.20, €2 deposit for your glass. Open daily 10am-midnight, kitchen closes at 11pm. AmEx/MC/V.

Augustiner Bräustuben, Landsberger Str. 19 (☎50 70 47). S1-S8 to "Hackerbrücke." Walk down the bridge to Landsberger Str. and take a right. In the Augustiner brewery's former horse stalls. Devoted carnivores should try the *Bräustüberl* (duck, two cuts of pork, *Kraut*, and two types of dumplings; €9.90). Heaps of Bavarian food come at excellent prices (€5-9), although true to tradition, you will get no *Weißwurst* after noon. Open daily 10am-midnight; kitchen open daily 11am-11pm. MC/V.

Bavaria Bräu, Theresienhohe 7 (☎02 02 82). U4 or 5 to "Theresienwiese." At the original *Oktoberfest*, Prince Ludwig had a *Weißwurst* breakfast here. The rest is history. Raise a glass of the interesting, fruity brew in the company of locals at this outpost of the Hacker-Pschorr brewery (along with the Hackerkeller down the street), right next to the *Oktoberfest* grounds. Entrées €6-12. *Maß* €5.20. Open daily 10am-1am. MC/V.

BARS

Many of the cafés in Munich double as night spots, often serving drinks after dark.

■ **Tractenvogl,** Reichenbachstr. 47 (☎201 51 60). U1-U2 and U7-U8 to "Frauenhofer." Enjoy one of their 32 types of hot chocolate (some with alcohol, of course) in a cozy living room with chic lamps. Live bands F. Chocolate fondue Su (reservations required). Astra beer €1.50 daily 6-7pm; order a drink and Jäger is ½ price, 9-10pm. Open M-Th and Su 10am-1am, F-Sa 10am-3am. Cash only.

Café Am Hochhaus, Blumenstr. 29 (☎890 58 152). U1-U3 or U6 to "Sendlinger Tor." Sometimes a dance party, sometimes a relaxed café, the mood at the popular Café Am Hochhaus changes with the nightly crowd. Open M-Sa 8pm-3am or later. Cash only.

Sausalitos, Im Tal 16 (☎24 29 54 94). U3 or S1-S8 to "Marienpl." Mexican bar and restaurant jumping with crowds of local 20-somethings. Hearty entrées (including vegetarian options) €9-13. Drinks €6-9. Mixed drinks ½ price daily 5-8pm. Margaritas ½ price after 11pm. Open M-Th and Su 11am-1am, F-Sa 11am-2:30am. MC/V.

Killian's Irish Pub and **Ned Kelly's Australian Bar,** Frauenpl. 11 (☎24 21 98 99 and 24 21 99 10). U3 or S1-S8 to "Marienpl."; behind the Frauenkirche. Two venues in one, with live music, Irish and Australian beer and food, live sports coverage, and an outdoor *Biergarten.* Open M-Sa 11am-late, Su noon-late. AmEx/DC/MC/V.

Schwabinger 7, Feilitzschstr. 9 (☎33 24 27). U3 or U6 to "Giselastr." Look carefully for the sign on the street (at #7); the entrance is 2m on the right in the alley with a dark wooden door. This hole in the wall has no special nights and no special drinks, yet it's always busy. Open 8pm-late. Cash only.

K & K Klub, Reichenbachstr. 22 (☎20 20 74 63). U1-U2 or U7-U8 to "Frauenhofer." Grungy basement feel, with video games (€0.50) and a graffitied sliding door. An excellent launching point for a night of clubbing. Local DJs play house and electronic Th-Sa. Open M-W and Su 8pm-2am, Th-Sa 8pm-5am. Cash only.

Holy Home, Reichenbachstr. 21 (☎201 45 46), U1-U3 or U6-7 to "Sendlinger Tor." Red and orange color scheme ironically evokes a less-than-holy realm. Easygoing crowds of 20- and 30-somethings come for beer (€3), mixed drinks (€4-5), and the daily DJ. Open M-W and Su 7pm-1am, Th-Sa 7pm-3am. Cash only.

Feder und Kirsch, Reichenbachstr. 37 (☎59 97 89 90). U1-U2, or U7-U8 to "Frauenhofer." Enjoy Italian and Finnish cuisine at one of the black lacquer tables, or join a mixed crowd at the bar. Specials €3-15. Beer €2.60 (0.4L). Open Tu-W and Su 6pm-1am, Th-Sa 6pm-3am; kitchen closes at 11pm. Cash only.

Shamrock, Trautenwolfstr. 6 (☎33 10 81). U3 or U6 to "Giselastr." Nightly live music runs the gamut from blues to fiddling to rock in this Irish pub. Live soccer. Guinness €4 (0.5L). Open M-F 7pm-3am, Sa-Su 2pm-3am. MC.

CLUBS

In adjacent lots lie ■**Kultfabrik** (☎49 00 90 70; www.kultfabrik.info), Grafinger Str. 6, and ■**Optimolwerke** (☎450 69 20; www.optimolwerke.de), Friedenstr. 10, two massive complexes that provide dozens of nocturnal venues of all kinds. Take U5 or S1-S8 to "Ostbahnhof," then follow the constant stream of people onto Friedenstr. and Grafingerstr. Hours, covers, and themes vary among individual venues. All clubs have relaxed door policies, particularly in the summer. **Optimolwerke,** with 15 clubs, is smaller and caters to a slightly older crowd (mid-twenties to early thirties). **K41** (☎638 92 90; www.k41.de) is one of the most established and hippest venues, playing 70s disco music and house. Th is 80s night. (Open M-Sa.) The unconventional **Salon Erna** (☎63 89 29 11; www.salon-erna.de) is open all week. On Sunday night, Erna becomes Germany's rock 'n' roll capital, with lessons for dancers of all ages. If it's your birthday, enjoy free entry on Th and a complimentary bottle of champagne. Also popular with a swankier crowd is the **Milch und Bar** (☎44 21 88 21; www.milchundbar.de); check out Soul Sonic Funk Boutique on W. (Open M and W-Sa.) **Kultfabrik** features 21 clubs and attracts a crowd in its late teens and mid-twenties. Party the Russian way at **Kalinka** (☎40 90 72 60; www.clubkalinka.tk), recognizable by its 7-foot Lenin bust. Choose from 100 types of vodka and dance to techno under the hammer and sickle. (Open F-Sa.)

Muffathalle, Zellstr. 4 (☎45 87 50 10; www.muffathalle.de), in Haidhausen. Tram #18 (dir.: St. Emmeram) to "Deutsches Museum." This former power plant generates techno, hip-hop, spoken word, jazz, and dance performances. Open M-Sa 7pm-4am, Su 4pm-1am. Cover from €5. Buy tickets online or through München Ticket.

Atomic Café, Neuturmstr. 5 (☎ 228 30 52). The Bavarian take on late-60s mod glory. Sticks to 60s and 70s beats, avoiding a mainstream disco sound. Young audiences come for the live Britpop, R&B, ska, reggae. Cover €3-7. Beer €3.70 for 0.5L. Happy hour (9-10pm) mixed drinks €6. Open Tu-Th 10pm-3am, F-Sa 10pm-5am. Cash only.

Backstage, Wilhelm-Hale Str. 16 (☎126 61 00; www.backstage-online.com). Tram #16 or 17 to "Steubenpl." or #18 or 19 to "Lautensackstr" or bus #132 to Wilhelm-Hale Str. Underground scene, playing hardcore, rock, and electronica. Local crowd is a reflection of that night's act. *Maß* €2 from 7-11pm; *Biergarten* also shows movies and soccer games. Check online for concert listings. Open M-Th and Su 7pm-3am, F-Sa 7pm-5am.

Nachtgalerie, Arnulfstr. 17 (☎32 45 55 95; www.nachtgalerie.de). S1-S8 to "Hacker-brücke." At the end of the bridge, turn right and go down the stairs. Popular with young, drunken crowds. Two dance halls play party music and hip-hop. Steep €10 cover buys access to very cheap drinks; "porno vodka" (with pop rocks) €2. Open F-Sa 10pm-5am, and some Th; check website for dates. No cover first Th of every month. Cash only.

◩ GAY AND LESBIAN MUNICH

Although Bavaria has a reputation for traditionalism, gay nightlife thrives in Munich, centering around Müllerstr. in the **Glockenbachviertel,** and stretching from south of Sendlinger Tor through the Viktualienmarkt/Gärtnerpl. area to the Isartor. The crowd is mostly late-20s to 40s. Pick up *Sergej*, Munich's "scene magazine," at **Max&Milian Bookstore,** Ickstattstr. 2 (☎260 33 20; open M-Tu and Th-F 10:30am-8pm, W 10:30am-2pm and 3:30-8pm, Sa 11am-4pm), for listings of gay hotspots (also try *Our Munich*, available at the tourist office). **Sub: Schwules Kommunikations- und Kulturzentrum,** Müllerstr. 43 (www.subonline.org), offers an array of services and a café for gay men. (Information ☎260 30 56, staffed daily 7-11pm; violence hotline ☎192 28, daily 10am-7pm. Some English spoken. Center open M-Th and Su 7-11pm, F-Sa 7pm-midnight.) For lesbian information, call **Lesbentelefon.** (☎725 42 72. Open M and W 2:30-5pm, Tu 10:30am-1pm, Th 7-9pm.)

▧ **Café Selig,** Hans-Sachs Str. 3 (☎23 88 88 78. www.einfachselig.de). U1 or U2 to "Frauenhofer Str." Join the diverse crowd (mixed by day, mostly gay Sa-Su and at night) at this unpretentious café and bar, with international coffees, homemade cakes, and strudel (€5-7). M and W 9pm-1am, F 9am-3am, Sa-Su 9am-late. AmEx/MC/V.

▧ **Bei Carla,** Buttermelcherstr. 9 (☎22 79 01). Take S1-S8 to "Isartor," then walk south on Zweibrückenstr., take a right on Rumfordstr., a left on Klenzestr., and a left on Buttermelcherstr. Women in their 20s and 30s flock to this warm and inviting lesbian bar for conversation amid drinks and darts. Limited menu. Open M-Sa 4pm-1am, Su 6pm-1am. Cash only.

Morizz, Klenzestr. 43 (☎201 67 76). U1 or U2 to "Frauenhofer Str." Settle into low chairs for a mixed drink (€5-8.50) at this mixed café and bar. European and Thai dishes available until 12:30am. Open M-Th and Su 7pm-2am, F-Sa 7pm-3am. MC/V.

Inges Karotte, Baaderstr. 13 (☎201 06 69). U1 or U2 to "Frauenhoferstr." or S1-S8 to "Isartor." This unique lesbian pub has quirky decor and lively music. Serves diverse drinks to its mixed clientele. Open M-Sa 6pm-1am, Su 4pm-1am. Cash only.

Bau, Müllerstr. 41 (☎26 92 08. www.bau-munich.de). U1 or U2 to "Fraunhofer Str." Gay club with a construction theme. No mixed drinks—only beer (€2.70) and liquor (€2.50). Buy 1 get 1 free M 8-10pm; "beer bus" (every beer is €1 less than the one before) from 8-10pm and 1-3am. Open daily 8pm-3am. Cash only.

Kr@ftakt, Thalkirchenstr. 4 (☎21 58 88 81). Munich's only gay Internet café features a bar and a street café, popular for breakfast (€3.90) and brunch. The clientele is here more to socialize than for the Internet connection. Happy hour W 7-9pm (beer €1). Open M-Th and Su 10am-1am, F-Sa 10am-3am. MC/V.

N.Y. Club, Sonnenstr. 25 (☎62 23 21 52; www.nyclub.de). U1-U3 or U6 to "Sendlinger Tor." Fashionable gay men dance the night away. Cover from €5. Open F-Sa, and holidays from 11pm.

Café Nil, Hans-Sachs-Str. 2 (☎26 55 45; www.cafenil.de). U1 or U2 to "Fraunhofer Str." Take a right out of the U-Bahn down Klenzestr., a right on Ickstattstr., and a right on Hans-Sachs-Str. Sleek café and meeting place for gay men in their 20s and 30s. Mobbed on weekends. Beer €3 (0.4L). Open daily 3pm-3am. MC/V.

Soul City, Maximilianspl. 5 (☎59 52 72), U4 or U5 to "Karlspl." The biggest gay disco in Bavaria, with music from Latin to techno. Straight clubbers always welcome. Beer €4 (0.3L). Cover €6. Call for info about live concerts. Open Th-Sa 10pm-5am.

▒ OKTOBERFEST

Every fall, hordes of tourists make an unholy pilgrimage to Munich to drink and be merry in true Bavarian style. From noon on the penultimate Saturday of September through early October, it's all about consuming beer. The numbers for this festival have become truly mindboggling: participants chug five million liters of beer, but only on a full stomach of 200,000 *Würste. Oktoberfest* is the world's largest folk festival—in fact, the festival has gotten so large (and sometimes out of hand) that the city of Munich has stopped advertising it.

Oktoberfest began on October 12, 1810 to celebrate the wedding of the future king Ludwig I of Bavaria. Representatives from all over Bavaria met outside the city gates, celebrating with a week of horse racing on fields they named **Theresienwiese** in honor of the bride (U4 or U5 to "Theresienwiese"). The bash was such fun that Munich's citizens have repeated the revelry (minus the horses) ever since. An agricultural show, inaugurated in 1811, is still held every three years, and fair fare, from carousels to touristy kitsch, remains to amuse beer-guzzling participants.

The festivities begin with the "Grand Entry of the *Oktoberfest* Landlords and Breweries," a parade that ends around noon with the ceremonial drinking of the first keg, to the cry of *O'zapft is!*, or "it's tapped," by the Lord Mayor of Munich. Other special events include international folklore presentations, a costume and rifleman's parade, and an open-air concert. Each of Munich's breweries set up tents in the Theresienwiese. The touristy *Hofbräu* tent is the rowdiest. Arrive early (by 4:30pm) to get a table; you must have a seat to be served alcohol. Drinking hours are relatively short, about 9am to 10:30pm, depending on the day; fairground attractions and sideshows are open slightly later. Those who share a love of alcohol with their kin will appreciate the reduced prices of family days.

▶ DAYTRIPS FROM MUNICH

DACHAU

From Munich, take S2 (dir.: Petershausen) to "Dachau" (20min., €4 or 4 stripes on the Streifenkarte; included in Munich XXL ticket), then bus #724 (dir.: Krautgarten) or #726 (dir.: Kopernikusstr.) from in front of the station to "KZ-Gedenkstätte" (10min., €1 or 1 stripe on the

Streifenkarte). Camp open Tu-Su 9am-5pm. Informative 2½hr. English tours of the camp leave from the museum May-Sept. daily 1:30pm; Sa-Su and holidays additional tours at noon; Oct.-Apr. Th, Sa-Su, and holidays at 1:30pm (€3). 30min. introduction daily at 12:30pm, Sa-Su also at 11am; Oct.-Apr. only on Th, Sa-Su, and holidays (€1.50). Audio headsets in English, French, German, Hebrew, Italian, and Spanish are available inside the entrance to the camp for self-guided tours (€3, large group members €2). Museum guides available in Dutch, English, French, German, Hebrew, Hungarian, Polish, Russian, and Spanish €0.50; call ☎ 08131 66 99 70 for more information. Commercial tours also available (p. 435).

TIP | **BRING WATER.** Food and beverages are not available at Dachau; to prevent dehydration and stay energized, pack water and a snack.

The first thing prisoners saw as they entered Dachau was the inscription *Arbeit Macht Frei* (work will set you free) on the iron gate of the **Jourhaus,** the only entry to the camp. Dachau was the Third Reich's first concentration camp, opened in 1933 to house political prisoners on the former grounds of a WWI munitions factory. After Hitler visited the camp in 1937, it became a model for the construction of the 3000 other camps throughout Nazi-occupied Europe and a training-ground for the SS officers who would work at them. Dachau was primarily a work camp, as opposed to extermination camps like Auschwitz; during the war, prisoners made armaments and were hired out to work sites in the area. Many prisoners were worked to death. Those who volunteered for medical experiments in hopes of release were frozen to death or infected with malaria in the name of science. Although Dachau had a gas chamber, for unknown reasons it was tested but never put into full use. The tightly-packed **barracks,** designed for 6000 prisoners, once held 30,000 men; two have been reconstructed for purposes of remembrance, but the rest have been destroyed. Walls, gates, and a crematorium have also been restored in a chillingly sparse memorial to the camp's victims. On the site of the memorial are Jewish, Catholic, Lutheran, and Russian orthodox prayer spaces.

The museum, in the former administrative buildings, examines pre-1930s anti-Semitism, the rise of Nazism, the establishment of the concentration camp system, and the lives of prisoners through photographs, documents, and artifacts. Exhibits have captions in English. A short **film** (22min.) shows in English at 11:30am, 2, and 3:30pm. An additional display in the **bunker** chronicles the lives and experiences of the camp's prominent prisoners, including Georg Elser, the SS officer who attempted to assassinate Hitler in 1938.

ANDECHS MONASTERY AND BREWERY

From Munich, take S5 (dir.: Herrsching) to "Herrsching" (45min., use a €9.60 Tageskarte). Once in Herrsching, you have a number of options: take a bus to Andechs (10min.), either the MVV which runs only a few times a day, or a private bus which runs every 30min. (€2.10). You can also bike the 3.5km to Andechs, or walk there, following the brown signs through the town along the stream. Keep following the stream along Kienbachstr., then Andechstr., at the end of which, opposite a golden Madonna on a column, you can turn left onto the Kientalstr., a path which follows the river Kien through a wooded valley, or turn right and follow the (harder to find) scenic route. Each walk about 1hr.

Andechs, atop Heiligenberg hill on the Ammersee, has been a pilgrimage destination since the Middle Ages, due in part to its valuable collection of reliquaries. Its first cloister dates to 1392, but it gained notoriety in 1455, when **Albrecht III** founded a Benedictine monastery here. Albrecht is buried at Andechs, along with a number of 20th-century Wittelsbachs. Shut down during the 1803 secularization of all church property, Andechs was bought back by **Ludwig I** for an outrageous sum and reopened in 1843. Twenty-three monks are current members of the monastery; seven of them live on the hill. The **Andechs monastery** can be visited M-F at

2pm on an hour-long German tour. (€3; students and seniors €1.50. Group tours in English (min. 10 people) available by advance request; €4.50 per person).

If you don't visit the pink-and-white **Andechs Church**—with its sundial and typically Bavarian onion dome—*before* you hit up the brewery, you probably never will. The church was built after a fire in the 17th century had destroyed its predecessor and refurbished in full-blown Rococo for the 1755 tercentenary. Above the altar is a noteworthy fresco by **Johann Baptist Zimmermann**. (Free. Tower with panoramic view open M-Sa 9am-5pm, Su 12:15-5pm. €1.)

Modern-day pilgrims are motivated by the monks' famous Andechs brew, whose sale has financed the Benedictines' good works since 1455. German-language tours of the brewery, which produces 100,000 hectoliters of beer a year, take place Tu-W at noon (€3). Andechs beer is delicious but uniquely strong: the *Helles* has an alcoholic content of 11.5%, and *Doppelbock Dunkles* reaches a dizzy 18.5%. Join the imbibing crowds of locals at the panoramic **Bräustüberl ❷**, featuring both a terrace and a *Biergarten*. The beer (*Maß* €4.80) is cheaper than in Munich and the fresh-baked pretzels with butter from the monks' dairy are delicious. (☎081 52 37 62 61. Pretzels €2.60, butter €0.70. Open daily 10am-8pm; hot dishes 11am-6:30pm. AmEx/MC/V.) If you prefer seated service, the **Klostergasthof ❹** offers entrées for €7.50-18.50 or a *Maß* for €6. (☎08152 930 90. Open 10am-11pm; kitchen open until 10pm. MC/V.) The monks also make their own spirits, in four varieties (herbs, apples and pears, berries, and honey; €11.50 each). They're available at the **Klosterladen,** open Feb.-Dec. M-F 10am-5:30pm, Sa-Su 10am-6:30pm. Be careful on your way back down; many a drunken walker has come to an unhappy end in the Kien river. If you are still on your feet, gaze at the Ammersee from one of the ferries departing from Herrsching or take the bus to the Starnberger See, home to the highest per capita income in the whole Federal Republic.

ALLGÄU

Stretching from the shores of the Bodensee (Lake Constance) to the snow-capped peaks on the Austrian border, the Allgäu region boasts winsome villages in an alpine landscape. Largely ignored by international tourists, the area is known among Germans as a haven for hiking and skiing. For coverage of Lindau and the Bodensee, across the lake, see Baden-Württemberg, p. 426.

IMMENSTADT AND BÜHL AM ALPSEE ☎08323

Despite its 1360 name change from Immendorf, Immenstadt (pop. 14,000) is still no city, but a largely untouristed village near the tiny lakeside hamlet of Bühl am Alpsee (pop. 8000). Immenstadt provides a convenient base for excursions into the Allgäu mountains south of Kempten, while Bühl am Alpsee—the perfect hideaway for a lazy afternoon—is a decentralized collection of guesthouses, restaurants, and residential homes a world away from the lakeside resorts of the south. The **Kleiner Alpsee,** a 20min. walk from the center of Immenstadt, offers an extensive park frequented by a younger local crowd. Check out swimming action at **Freibad am Kleinen Alpsee,** Am Kleinen Alpsee on the other side of the lake, which has a heated pool. From the train station, walk left on Bahnhofstr. past the rotary, then take a right onto Badeweg and go straight for 15min. (☎87 20. Open daily late May to early Sept. 9am-7/8pm. €3, ages 6-18 and students €2.) Larger waters and a calmer clientele can be found at the Großer Alpsee, along the Badeweg from the Kleiner Alpsee. There, a small harbor sits just around the corner from a public beach. Check out the bronze swan statue along the pier, and don't be surprised if you're fighting for space with dappled pigs tanning in the sun. **Boat** rents paddleboats, rowboats, and sailboats. (☎21 03. €4.50-7.50 per hr.) (☎522 00. €13 per hr.;

€35 per day.) Two **skiing** areas are also close: **Alpsee Skizirkus** is in Ratholz, a
10min. ride on bus #(97)39 (dir.: Oberstaufen). (☎832 52 52. Open June-Nov. weekends; July to mid-Sept. daily 9am-4:30pm.) **Mittag Ski-Rodel Center** is on the south
edge of Immenstadt. (☎61 49. Open daily 8am-5pm. Day pass €4-12, under 18
€3.50-11, families €14-25.) The ski season runs roughly December to March. Try
your hand at ice skating in the winter at **Viehmarktplatz** off Badeweg near the train
station (☎521 90. Open daily 9am-5pm). Dozens of **hiking trails** dot the countryside.
The exquisite **Hornweg** trail begins at the cemetery trailhead. To get there walk
through the underpass along the river from the town center, and follow signs for
"Friedhof." The trail leads along the steep mountainside to the south (1½hr.). Or,
take the left fork (Untere Steig) from the trail head and follow along picturesque
waterfalls; a wooden chapel awaits at the top (20min.). For a rambling route, follow
signs for **Ruine Rothenfels und Hugofels** from the northern bank of the Ach river (1-
2hr.). The **Naturlehrpfad**, near Knottenried, a 2hr. walk north of town, is a family
favorite. Several trails link Immenstadt and Bühl, of which the flat and easy
Badeweg is the quickest (30min.).

    Goldener Adler ❸, Marienpl. 14, has spacious rooms with bath and TV. (☎85 49.
Breakfast included. €30 per person. Cash only.) Camp on the Großer Alpsee at
Allgäu Camping Am Alpsee ❶, Seestr. 25, 5min. from the bus stop. (☎77 26;
www.camping-allgaeu.de. Reception 7am-noon and 1:30-9pm. €4-4.70 per person,
€3.10-3.80 per child, €3.30-4.30 per tent, €1.25 per car, €5.30-6.10 per RV. Cash
only.) Accommodations charge a €1 per day *Kurtaxe*, children €0.50. A plentiful
market of fruits, meats, and more pops up Saturday (8am-noon) on **Marienplatz;** a
few fruit stalls may be there as well. For a sit-down meal, **Bistro Relax ❷**, on Bräuhausstr., serves Italian and German dishes in a dark wood interior. (☎77 87. Lunch
menu €4.50, 11am-2pm. Open M-F 10am-2am, F-Sa 10am-3am.)

    Immenstadt can be reached by **train** from Memmingen (45min., every hr.,
€11.70) and Füssen (2hr., every hr., €10). The friendly **tourist office,** Marienpl. 3,
finds rooms, gives out free area maps, and sells hiking maps (€5-6.60). They also
offer seven-day transportation passes (€10) with a *Kurkarte*, which are given to
hotel guests. (☎91 41 76; www.immenstadt.de. Open M-F 9am-noon and 2-
5:30pm.) From the station, turn right on Bahnhofstr. and follow it through to
Marienpl. Bühl's tourist office, Seestr. 5, at Großer Alpsee, has many of the same
maps and brochures as its Immenstadt cousin. Walk or take bus #(97)39, (dir.:
Oberstaufen) to "Gästeamt" (5min., 1 per hr., €1.45); the office is right next to the
bus stop. (☎91 41 78; fax 89 96. Open mid-June to mid-Sept. M-F 9am-noon and 2-
5:30pm; mid-Sept. to mid-June M-F 9am-noon and 2-5pm, Sa 10am-noon.) **Internet**
access is available at **Internet Café,** Hofgartenstr. 8. (€4 per hr. Open M-F 3-10pm,
Sa-Su 2-9pm.) The **post office,** Bahnhofstr. 38, is across from the station. (Open M-
F 9am-noon and 1:30-5pm, Sa 9am-noon.) **Postal Code:** 87509.

OBERSTDORF   ☎08322

Surrounded by the snow-covered Allgäu Alps and green-velvet foothills, Oberstdorf (pop. 8000) is a popular and convenient destination for lovers of the outdoors.
Intrepid climbers scale the nearby mountain peaks, while rambling forest paths
lead more level-headed hikers to secluded alpine lakes and solitary hillsides. The
early-to-bed, early-to-rise town is packed with guesthouses, restaurants, and
quaint stores, but the calm of the countryside is always just minutes away.

▐▋ **TRANSPORTATION AND PRACTICAL INFORMATION. Trains** link Oberst-
dorf to Immenstadt (30min., 1-2 per hr., €4.60). Rent a **bike** at **Zweirad Center Has-
selberger,** Hauptstr. 7, for €6-16 per day. (☎44 67. Open M-F 9am-noon and 2:30-

6pm, Sa 9am-noon.) The bustling Oberstdorf **tourist office** at Marktpl. 7, hands out brochures; walk straight down Hauptstr. from the station. (☎70 00; www.oberstdorf.de. Open 8:30am-noon and 2-6pm, Sa 9:30am-noon; mid-July to mid-Oct. and Dec.-Jan. M-F 8:30am-6pm, Sa 9:30am-noon.) The **branch** office at Bahnhofpl. 3, across from the station, is more convenient to book rooms. (☎70 02 17; fax 70 02 36. Open July-Sept. and Dec.-Jan. M-F 8:30am-8pm, Sa 9am-8pm, Su 9am-6pm; Oct.-Nov. and Feb.-June M 8:30am-6pm, Tu-F 8:30am-1pm and 2-6pm, Sa-Su 9:30am-noon and 2-6pm.) The **post office** is across from the station. (Open M-F 9am-noon and 1:30-5pm, Sa 9am-noon.) **Postal Code:** 87561.

⌨☼ ACCOMMODATIONS AND FOOD. All accommodations charge a nightly *Kurtaxe* of €1.65, ages 6-15 €1.30. Close to Oberstdorf, **Kornau** is home to the excellent **Jugendherberge Oberstdorf (HI) ❶**, Kornau Haus 8, tucked amid rolling hills over which Julie Andrews herself might come running and singing at any moment. Its spacious facilities, though often hijacked by school groups in the summer, include laundry (€0.50) and a rudimentary bar. Take the bus from Oberstdorf (dir.: Baad) to "Reute" (5min., 2-4 per hr., €1.50), continue in the direction of the bus, and take the first right. Be warned: the last bus leaves town before 9pm, weekends and winter before 8pm. (☎22 25; www.oberstdorf.jugendherberge.de. Cross-country ski rental €4 for first day, then €3 per day. Breakfast and sheets included. Reception 7am-noon and 2-11pm. Under 27 given preference; visitors older than 27 should call ahead. Dorms from €15.45, less for longer stays. Cash only.) **Paulanerbräu ❸**, Kirchstr. 1, is near Oberstdorf's idyllic church and just off its busiest streets. Rooms are large and white, with carpeted floors and firm beds. (☎967 60. Singles €23.50 with water, €29 with shower and toilet, €33 with bath and toilet; doubles twice as much. MC/V.) The tourist office will help you pick from their list of 1000 rooms in the area, starting at €13.

Upscale, but still affordable, cuisine can be found at **Café Mozart ❸**, cleverly located at Bachstr. 10. Enjoy simple but delicious daily strudel and *wurst* specials (most for €5-7) just down the street from the church. (☎80 07 62. Open daily 9:30am-6pm. Cash only.) There is a **grocery store** at Weststr. 3. (Open M-F 8am-6:30pm, Sa 7:30am-4pm.) **Vinzenz Murr ❶**, on Hauptstr. at Bahnhofpl., has meaty *Imbiß* dishes (€2-5) and a salad bar. (Open M-F 8am-6pm, Sa 8am-1pm.) For Asian food with lots of veggies (€2-6.50), visit **Asia Schnellimbiss Samson ❷**, Weststr. 7. (☎80 01 70. M-W 11:30am-2:30pm and 5-10pm, F-Su 5:30-11pm. Cash only.)

SOCIALIZE AND SAVE

Two strangers meet in front of a train station. With determination, the two stride toward one another. An awkward greeting is exchanged. This scene is not the beginning of a film noir flick, but a common occurrence in Germany. Since Deutsche Bahn introduced its group ticket (€25, offering unlimited one-day travel within a single *Land* for groups of 2-5 people) Germans have been breaking social boundaries, approaching strangers without introduction in attempts to form a group of five.

The travelers who eye each other furtively around the ticket machines are simply trying to figure out who is going their way. This practice is frowned upon by the Deutsche Bahn. It is becoming more common, however, and it's a convenient, if esoteric, way to commune with Germans who are sharing the price of their ride with you. For €5 each (cheaper than the *Maß* the night before), five travelers can head from Bayreuth, in the northernmost part of Bavaria, all the way down to Austria (the Bayern ticket considers Salzburg to be a border station). The Internet-savvy can even run an online search for the many message boards where travelers advertise their travel plans and agree on meeting points.

When choosing a travel partner, use common sense and trust your instincts. If you'd prefer to travel solo, you can still save by purchasing a single-person regional ticket for €18 (p. 32).

⚙ 🝗 **SIGHTS AND HIKING.** Three **Bergbahnen** (cable cars) whisk hikers to the heady alpine heights. The closest one, in town, delivers acrophiliacs to the top of **Nebelhorn**, the highest accessible mountain in the Allgäu Alps at 2224m. The path along the ridge to Großer Daumen via Westlicher Wengenkopf is difficult but popular with experienced hikers; an easier trail winds through the meadow below. (☎960 00; www.nebelhorn.de. **Weather info** ☎55 53 36 66. Runs May-Oct. daily 8:30am-4:30pm. Round-trip €24, children €18; round-trip to lowest station €14/ 11.) The **Fellhornbahn** climbs 2037m for an equally thrilling view. (☎960 00; www.fellhorn.de. Runs daily mid-May to June and Aug.-Oct. 9am-4:15pm; July 8:30am-4:45pm. Round-trip €16.50, children €12.50.) The less ambitious **Söllereckbahn** carries hikers up 1358m to mountainous hiking paths. (☎57 57; www.soellereckbahn.de. Round-trip €12, children €10; families pay only for the 1st child.) In winter, the Bergbahnen transport skiers and snowboarders (winter day pass €29, children €22.50). To reach the Nebelhornbahn station, walk down Nebelhornstr. from Hauptstr. To reach the Fellhornbahn, ride the "Fellhorn" bus from the train station. **Söllereck** is accessible by the bus marked "Baad." To swim against a mountain backdrop, splash around in the **Moorbad.** From the Marktpl., turn onto Oststr. and walk to the end. Follow the sign to the trail that leads to the Moorbad (15min. ☎48 63. Open in warm weather July-Aug. 10am-8pm; May-June and Sept. 10am-6pm. €3, students €2.50, children €2; after 5pm €2/1.50/1.35.) Three inconspicuous chapels in St. Loretto, south of town in an idyllic valley, conceal delicate altars and frescoes. Follow signs for Loretto from the Moorbad (15min.) or take Prinzenstr. and then Lorettostr. from the Marktpl. (20min.). One popular hiking route leads to the **Breitachklamm,** a chasm carved into the rock face by a frothy river; in winter, it's covered in fantastic ice formations. (☎08322 48 87. Trail open in summer 8am-5pm; in winter 9am-4pm.) The chasm is most easily approachable from Kornau, a sub-village of Oberstdorf. From the train station, take the bus (dir.: Baad) to "Kornau" (5min., every 15min., €1.80). Walk up the hill and hang a right after house #22. The road becomes a hiking trail over the Breitach river (1hr. to the Klamm). Or, from the train station, take the bus (dir.: Obermaiselstein/Bolsterlang) to "Breitachklamm."

MEMMINGEN   ☎08331

Memmingen is a city to be experienced on foot, with many of its main attractions visible from its cobbled streets and fish-filled canals. The Rococo buildings and 13th-century fortifications of the Altstadt provide the perfect backdrop for a quiet evening meal, while the nearby village Ottobeuren provides a popular diversion from the town by day. The white **Rathaus** in the Marktpl. hides behind a 16th-century facade, spruced up in 1765 with some Rococo additions. Off the Marktpl. on Zangmeisterstr., the 15th-century Gothic **St. Martinskirche** has well-preserved frescoes depicting the Passion of Christ. (Church open daily May-Sept. 10am-5pm; Oct. 1-Oct. 15 10am-4pm; Apr. 11am-2pm, Free. Tower tours May-Oct. daily 3pm; €1.50, ages 14-17 €1, under 14 €0.50. Early July-Aug. 30min. organ concert and 30min. tour free Sa 11am.) Walking down Kramerstr. through the pedestrian zone and left onto Lindentorstr., you'll find Gerberpl. and the **Siebendächerhaus** (Filter Roof House), a half-timbered house with seven roofs. The house was designed in 1601 by tanners looking to maximize airflow over drying skins; it now houses a **pharmacy.** (☎31 48. Open M-F 8:30am-12:30 and 2-6pm, Sa 8:30am-12:30pm.) In early June, *Memmingeners* drink tourists under the table during the annual *Bier*, *Wurst*, and *Musik* **Stadtfest** (Municipal Celebration). The **Fischertag Heimatfest** (Fisherman Day Homeland Celebration) takes place at the end of every school year in late July. Men empty the stream of fish in a race to earn the title of "Fishermen's King." The real festivities take place on Saturday, when residents parade in period dress, with lots of beer, marching bands, and boisterous singing.

Gasthof Lindenbad ❷, Lindenbadstr. 18, offers plain but comfortable rooms. Turn right down Bahnhofstr. and turn right through the second underpass to Linden-badstr. (☎32 78; fax 92 74 54. Breakfast included. Singles €23-30; doubles €50-58. MC/V.) Those hunting for food in the Altstadt needn't look far—the streets off of Maximilianstr. are covered with *Imbiße* (snack bars) and *Bäckerei* (bakeries).

Trains run to: Munich (1½hr., every hr., €18); Oberstdorf (1½hr., every hr., €12); Ulm (30-60min., every hr., €9.10). To get to the Altstadt, cross Bahnhofstr. and follow Maximilianstr. away from the station, then take a right on pedestrian Kramer-str. to **Marktpl.** (5min.). Rent **bikes** from **Matthäus Fickler,** Lindauerstr. 14. (☎22 58. €5 per day. Open M and F 9am-6pm; Tu-Th 9am-12:30pm and 2-6pm, Sa 9am-1pm.) The **tourist office,** Marktpl. 3, by the Rathaus, finds rooms and sells maps of nearby bike trails for €6-11. (☎85 01 72; www.memmingen.de. Open M-F 9am-5pm, Sa 9:30am-12:30pm.) An **ATM** can be found at the **Deutschbank** in Markpl. Take a right on Bahnhofstr. from the station and a left on Kalchstr. to reach **Bülent Özer,** Kalch-str. 35, for **Internet** access. (☎985 41 64. €4 per hr. Open M-Sa 10am-10pm.) The **post office,** Lindentorstr. 22, is near the Siebendächerhaus. (Open M-F 8:30am-5:30pm, Sa 9am-noon.) **Postal Code:** 87700.

DAYTRIP FROM MEMMINGEN: OTTOBEUREN   ☎08332

From Memmingen, take bus #955 to "Ottobeuren," from bus platform #2. (20min., €2.55, last return bus generally 6:50pm, but check to be sure), schedule available in the Memmingen tourist office or station ticket counter.

Ottobeuren is renowned for its towering basilica and **Benedictine Abbey,** representing the architectural height of the German Baroque. Since its founding in AD 764, Ottobeuren's abbey has morphed several times, finally in the 18th-century. An easily missed 13th-century statue of Christ on the first altar is the abbey's most venerated piece of art. (Church open daily 7am-8pm. Free.) The monastery is still inhabited by 23 monks. Visitors are allowed to see the grandiose **library,** the impressive **Emperor's Hall,** adorned with statues of the Kaisers, and a **museum** of old church artifacts. (☎79 80. Open mid-Mar. to Dec. daily 10am-noon and 2-5pm; Jan. M-F 10am-noon and 2-5pm; Feb. to mid-Mar. Sa-Su 10am-noon and 2-4pm, last entry 20min. before closing. €2.50, students €1.50, families €4.50, under 10 free.) Behind the abbey and next to its former brewery, **Klosterbräustüble ❸**, Luitpoldstr. 42, serves traditional German meals (€3.10-7.50) in a 750-year-old tavern and in the *Biergarten* outside. (☎92 50 02. Open M-Sa 11am-1am, Su 10am-1am. Cash only.)

BAYERISCHE ALPEN (BAVARIAN ALPS)

On a clear Munich day you can see a series of snow-covered peaks and forested slopes, a rugged terrain spanning from southeast Germany across Austria and into Italy. Ludwig II of Bavaria, the mysterious "Fairy-Tale King," built his idyllic palaces here, among mountain villages, glacial lakes, icy waterfalls, and world-class ski slopes. Castles, cows, and Christianity are some of the major players in the region—you'll see crucifixes high on mountaintops and hear the rattling of cowbells from across the valley. People still wear *Lederhosen,* and everyone, young or old, seems to be on the way to a hike. Rail lines are sparse, but buses cover the gaps. For travel information, contact **Fremdenverkehrsverband Oberbayern,** Bodensestr. 113, in Munich. (☎089 829 21 80. Open M-Th 9am-4pm, F 9am-12:30pm.)

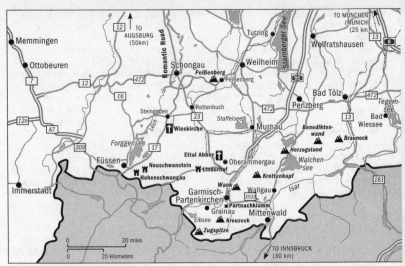

FÜSSEN   ☎ 08362

The word *Füssen* means "feet," an apt name for this little town (pop. 14,000) at the base of the Romantic Road, nestled in the foothills of the towering Bavarian Alps. Tourists are drawn year-round to the town's hiking routes and proximity to Ludwig's famed **Königsschlößer** (p. 464). Füssen's own castle, the **Hohes Schloß**, overlooking a sea of red-tiled roofs and the Lech River; each night, it its ghostly illumination is visible from the outdoor cafés of the Altstadt.

TRANSPORTATION AND PRACTICAL INFORMATION. Trains travel to: Augsburg (2hr., every 2hr., €15.70) and Munich (2hr., every hr., €19.80). **Bus** #9606 runs to Oberammergau (1½hr.; M-F 5-8 per day, Sa-Su 3-6 per day; €7.60 with *Tagesticket*) and Garmisch-Partenkirchen (2¼hr., €7.60 with *Tagesticket*). For a **taxi** call ☎ 77 00, 62 22, or 507 40. Rent **bikes** at **Preissschranke**, to the left of the station. (☎ 017 8374 02 19. €6-8. Open May.-Oct. M-F 9am-6:30pm, Sa 9am-2pm.)

The **tourist office** is at Kaiser-Maximilian-Pl. 1. From the station, turn left and walk the length of Bahnhofstr., then head across the roundabout to the big yellow building on your left. The staff finds rooms for free, sells hiking maps (€3-7), and organizes **guided hikes** of the area (Sa mornings, only with *Kurkarte*). (☎ 938 50; www.fuessen.de. Kiosk out front contains a hotel reservations line. Tours, some museum fees, and hikes free with *Kurkarte*, a €1.60 fee tacked onto overnight stays. Open July-Aug. M-F 8:30am-6:30pm; Sept.-Oct. and Apr.-June M-F 8:30am-6pm; Apr.-Sept. also Sa 10am-1pm; Oct.-Mar. M-F 9am-5pm, Sa 10am-noon.) The **police** station is at Herkomerstr. 17 (☎ 110), around the corner from the hostel. The **Bahnhof-Apotheke,** Bahnhofstr. 8, has a bell for night **pharmacy** service. (☎ 918 10. Open M-F 8:30am-1pm and 2-6:30pm, Sa 8:30am-12:30pm.) Access the **Internet** and drink free coffee at **Videoland@Internet,** Luitpoldstr. 11. (€2 per 30min., €3 per hr. Open M-Sa 4-10pm, Su 4-8pm.) The **post office** is at the corner of Bahnhofstr. and Rupprechtstr. (Open M-F 8:30am-5:15pm, Sa 8:30am-noon.) **Postal Code:** 87629.

ACCOMMODATIONS AND FOOD. Füssen's **Jugendherberge (HI) ❷**, Mariahilfer Str. 5, shares a neighborhood with local homes, vacation condos, and some intrepid sheep and goats unaffected by the passing trains. Turn right from the sta-

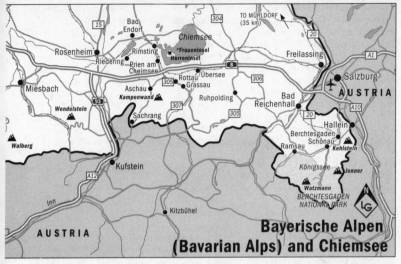

Bayerische Alpen (Bavarian Alps) and Chiemsee

tion and follow the railroad tracks for 15min. (☎77 54. Laundry €3.60. Reception daily Mar.-Sept. 7am-noon and 5-10pm; Oct.-Apr. 5-10pm. Closed Nov. Lock-out 11pm-6:30am, access code available. Lockers require €1-2 deposit. €17.75, 2nd and 3rd nights €17.15, additional nights €16.60. MC/V.) **Pension Haslach ❷**, Mariahilfer Str. 1b, is only a few doors down from the youth hostel. Give the bell a ring and Grandma Haslach will poke her head out of the second-floor chalet window to say whether her rooms—with sinks and quaintly quilted beds—are *frei* (free) or *belegt* (occupied). (☎24 26. Singles €25; doubles €45. Cash only.)

Reasonably priced bakeries, butcher shops, and *Imbiße* (snack bars) stand among the pricier cafés on **Reichenstr.**, particularly off the **Luitpold Passage.** If you're trail-bound, head to the **Plus** supermarket, on the right toward the rotary from the station. (Open M-Sa 8am-8pm.) **Gasthaus zum Schwanen ❸**, Brotmarkt 4, is tucked at the back of the Altstadt behind cut-glass windows and outdoor seating. (☎61 74. Open Tu-Sa 11:30am-2:30pm and 5:30-9:30pm. MC/V.) **Zum Hechten ❸**, Ritterstr. 6, has a more expensive sit-down restaurant upstairs, but has a vegetable- and pasta-oriented buffet below (€1.30 per 100g). (☎91 60 20. Open M-Sa 10:30am-5pm. MC/V.) **Pizza Pasta Americano ❶**, 23 Ritterstr., serves slices from €1.50 and whole pies from €5. (☎50 53 28. Open daily 11am-10pm. Cash only.)

◼ SIGHTS. Reminders of the local prince-bishop's medieval power linger in Füssen's architecture. The inner walls and towers of the **Hohes Schloß** courtyard display surreal *trompe l'oeil*—relics of a time when optical illusions of gold and marble were almost as valuable as the real thing. The late-medieval chambers and cloisters of the **Staatsgalerie** (Municipal Gallery), inside the castle walls, contain a large collection of ink drawings and paintings from the late Gothic period to the present. (☎90 31 64. Open Tu-Su Apr.-Oct. 11am-4pm; Nov.-Mar. 2-4pm. €2.50, students and seniors €2, under 14 free. Tours in German W 2:30pm.) Just below the castle is the Baroque **Mangkirche**, dating from the 9th century. An ancient fresco discovered during renovations in 1950 lights up the church's 10th century subterranean crypt. The abbey hosts an 18th-century Baroque library. (☎48 44. Tours year-round after Su services; Jan.-Oct. also Sat 10:30am; May-Oct. also Tu 4pm; July and Aug. also Tu and Th 4pm. Tours on demand Nov.-Dec.) Inside the **Anna-**

kapelle, commemorating victims of the bubonic plague, 20 macabre skeleton-decked panels depict everyone from the Pope and Emperor to the smallest child engaged in the *Totentanz* (dance of death) with the inscription: *Sagt ja, Sagt nein, Getanzt Müß Seyn* (say yes, say no, on the dance must go). The **Museum der Stadt** (City Museum) in the monastery details Füssen's history as a manufacturing center struck by flood, plague, and war. Attention is given to Füssen's lutemakers guild, Europe's oldest (est. 1562). Recreated workshops showcase the Renaissance lute and its many-stringed cousins, from double-gutted violins to the miniscule Pochette favored by Mozart's father. (☎ 90 31 46. Open Tu-Su Apr.-Oct. 10am-5pm; Nov.-Mar. 1-4pm. €2.50, students and children €2. Tours in German Tu and Th 2:30pm.) A combined ticket to the Stadtmuseum and the Staatsgalerie (€3) can be purchased at either museum, except during summer special exhibitions.

DAYTRIP FROM FÜSSEN: WIESKIRCHE

Bus #73 leaves from the station daily 11:05am (M-Sa only), 2:05 (M-F only), 12:35, 1:05, 3:30, 4:05, and 4:35pm and returns at 11:21am, 2:50, and 3:50pm. (Always check the bus schedule. Last return bus 3:50pm.) 1hr. €2.80, round-trip €5.60. The 2hr. bike ride from Füssen is pleasant. Follow the signs for Munich until you see Wieskirche signs. ☎ 08862 93 29 30; www.wieskirche.de. Open daily 8am-7pm.

Count yourself lucky if your bus ride from Füssen or Oberammergau to the Ammergau Alps includes a brief stop at the Wieskirche (Church in the Meadows), a small gem set in the midst of yellow wildflowers. The Rococo pilgrimage church houses a relic from the Miracle of Wies in 1738, when the wood-and-cloth likeness of the Scourged Savior began to cry. The interior of the church is breathtaking, with an optical-illusion ceiling that is actually flat. The painter and sculptor collaborated to blend the gold-gilded ornaments into the frescoed walls and ceiling, eliminating the boundary between the two- and three-dimensional worlds—see if you can spot the mischievous cherub poking his foot through the ceiling. Dominikus Zimmermann, the architect who built the church from 1746 to 1754, was so devoted to the building that he lived in the adjacent house until he died. In the small Abbot's Lodge (open only occasionally) on the east side of the church, the balustrade's monogram records the words of the church's founder, Abbot Marianus II Mayer, who supposedly scratched them into a window pane in the Prelate Hall with his diamond ring: *Hoc loco habit fortuna, hic quiescit cor* (Here in this place abides happiness; here the heart rests). On the way down to the bus stop, pop into the tiny Wieskapelle ("Old Chapel of God in the Meadow"), built in 1738, to view the illustrated celebration of the opening of the Wieskirche.

KÖNIGSSCHLÖßER (ROYAL CASTLES)

Perhaps it was to his credit that Maximilian II neglected to educate his sons in the mundane affairs of government, allowing them to cultivate a taste for literature and the arts instead. With Max's untimely death, the royal line was left in the hands of his naïve 18-year-old son Ludwig II, an existentially tragic figure often dismissed as a whimsical, but insane, boy-child. In truth, Ludwig was incurably isolated from those around him, burying his despair of modernity in castle plans and reading Schiller until the day before his death. A frenzied visionary and fervent Wagner fan, Ludwig created fantastic castles soaring into the alpine skies, a veritable fantasia inspired by scenes from the opera *Lohengrin*. Whether the king was actually crazy has never been determined—some claim that his detractors fabricated medical evidence—but in 1886 a band of upstart nobles and bureaucrats deposed Ludwig in a coup d'état, had him declared insane, and imprisoned him in Schloß Berg on the Starnberger See. Three days later, the king and his psychiatrist were discovered dead in the lake under mysterious circumstances—murder, suicide or a failed escape attempt, perhaps. Thousands of tourists flock to his castles daily to explore the captivating enigma of Ludwig's life, death, and self-fashioned dream-world.

◼ HOHENSCHWANGAU AND NEUSCHWANSTEIN CASTLES

From the Füssen train station, bus #73 or 78 to "Königsschlößer" (10min.; 2 per hr.; €1.60, round-trip €3.10) stops in front of the information booth. (☎ 81 97 65. Open daily 9am-6pm.) The Ticket-Service Center, Alpseestr. 12, is a short walk uphill on Alpseestr. A less-touristed path to Hohenschwangau starts from the left side of the information booth and meanders through the forest (10min.). Horse-drawn carriages run to Car Park D and Hotel Müller (uphill €3.50, downhill €1.50), and to Neuschwanstein (€5/2.50). To Neuschwanstein from Car Park D is the shortest but steepest trail to the top (20-40min.). After exiting Neuschwanstein, continue past the castle for Pöllat gorge and the Marienbrücke. The trail on the other side of the bridge winds through the gorge and back to the base of the hill (20min.; only in summer). Private buses run from Hotel Lisl to a point 5min. below Marienbrücke and 600m above Neuschwanstein (round-trip €2.60). A Tagesticket (€7.60) entitles castle-hoppers to unlimited regional bus use (not including the bus to Bleckenau); buy it on the bus. (☎ 08362 93 08 30; www.ticket-center-hohenschwangau.de.) Both castles open daily Apr.-Sept. 9am-6pm; Oct.-Mar. 10am-4pm. Required tours, available in 10 languages, included in entrance fee. Apr.-Sept. German and English tours of each castle every 20min.; Oct.-Mar. every 30min. Ticket sales for Neuschwanstein Apr.-Sept. 8am-5pm; Oct.-Mar. 9am-3pm. Hohenschwangau ticket sales close 30min. later. Tickets for both may be purchased at the Ticket-Service Center. Arrive early in the morning, or you may wait many hours for your ticket and tour. Tickets can be reserved in advance for a €1.60 fee per ticket; call ☎ 08362 93 08 30. Each castle €9, under 18 free with an adult; students and seniors €8. Combination ticket €17/15.

Ludwig II spent childhood summers at **Schloß Hohenschwangau,** the bright yellow neo-Gothic castle rebuilt by his father on the site of a crumbling medieval fortress. It was no doubt within these frescoed walls that he acquired a taste for the romantic German mythology of the Middle Ages. After Maximilian II died, nocturnal Ludwig ordered servants to paint a night sky upon the royal bedroom ceiling. The vast constellations were inlaid with crystals so that the "stars" would twinkle when lit from above with oil lamps. The castle also houses the piano and bed that Richard Wagner used during his visits.

Ludwig's desperate building spree across Bavaria peaked with the construction of glitzy **Schloß Neuschwanstein,** begun in 1869 to create jobs in a period of rising unemployment. Germany's most clichéd tourist attraction and the inspiration for Disney's Cinderella's Castle is as mysterious and paradoxical as Ludwig himself. The first sketches of the *Schloß* were reportedly drawn by a set designer, not an architect, and young Ludwig II lived to spend a mere 173 days in the extravagant edifice before he was betrayed by a servant and imprisoned. The palace mirrors Ludwig's untimely death; 63 rooms are unfinished, and the platform in the lavish throne room is eerily lacking a throne. Completed chambers include a neo-Gothic Tristan-and-Isolde bedroom, an artificial grotto, and an immense **Sängersaal** (Singers' Hall), an acoustic masterpiece built expressly for Wagnerian opera performances. Though the hall was never used in Ludwig's lifetime, concerts have taken place here since 1969, always in September (for more info, contact the Schwangau tourist office, ☎ 08362 819 80; www.schwangau.de). Almost all the castle walls are painted with scenes from Wagnerian operas; the king and composer were united in affection for Teutonic myth and tragic heroes, and Wagner acted as a confidante during the king's spells of uncertainty and abdication.

For the fairy godmother of all views, hike up to the **Marienbrücke,** spanning the **Pöllat gorge** behind Neuschwanstein (10min.). Though some may flinch at crossing the circa-1860 bridge over a 149 ft. waterfall, those with stout hearts and legs can continue uphill from here for a view of the castle and nearby lake (1hr.). In the opposite direction, descend the mountain from Schloß Hohenschwangau to the lilypad-topped **Schwansee.** Follow the Schwansee-Bundweg path through fields of flowers to a beach and secluded swimming hole. The **Alpseebad,** the famous lake adorning the background of most Neuschwanstein publicity shots, is closer and more crowded, but still picturesque. Hang-gliders preparing for a jump and sane people alike ride the **Tegelbergbahn** cable car 1720m up to the top of the Tegelberg. The valley station is to the left of the castles as you face the mountain; some buses continue on from the castle stop. (☎983 60. Open daily in summer 9am-5:30pm; in winter 9am-4:30pm. €9, students €8.50, children €4.50; round-trip €15/14/7.50.)

SCHLOß LINDERHOF

Bus #9622 runs between Oberammergau (p. 467) and the park (9:50am-4:55pm). The last bus leaves Linderhof at 6:40pm (20min., every hr., €5.40 round-trip), but check the schedule. Hikers and cyclists can follow the path along the Ammer river to Linderhof (10km). From the Oberammergau tourist office head left on Eugen-Papst-Str.; when the road forks at the bridge, select the gravel bike path and follow signs to Linderhof. ☎08822 920 30. Open daily Apr.-Sept. 9am-6pm; Oct.-Mar. 10am-4pm. Apr.-Oct. 12. Obligatory castle tours €7, students and seniors €6; Oct. 13.-Mar. only the palace is open. €6/5; under 18 free with an adult. Park open all day Apr.-Sept. Free. Lockers available to the left of the ticket office (€1).

Halfway between Füssen and Oberammergau is the exquisite **Schloß Linderhof,** Ludwig II's compact hunting palace, surrounded by a meticulously manicured park. In the design of the *Schloß*, Ludwig paid homage to the French Bourbon kings, in particular Louis XIV, just as he did with his *Herrenchiemsee* palace (p. 487). Though it lacks Neuschwanstein's pristine exterior, the decadent interior is a filled with royal goodies like Meißen porcelain (see **White Gold: A New Alchemy,** p. 612) and Gobelin chairs. The entire castle is slathered in 5kg of 24-carat gold leaf, except for the servants' room—they had to settle for silver. Across the ceiling in the entrance stretches the French Bourbon affirmation *Nec pluribus impar,* which loosely translates to "I'm too sexy for democracy." Living up to this motto, the royal bedchamber is unbelievably lush, with gold leaf and a crystal chandelier that weighs half a ton. Dark blue (the king's favorite color) velvet encases the bed, specially made to fit the 6'4" king. The "Dream King" was almost entirely nocturnal, waking at dusk and returning to bed after his breakfast, because he strongly disliked sunlight. He was also known for sequestering himself, fueling the myth that he had his dining table raised and lowered on a lift from the servants' quarters. The malachite tables were gifts from Russian Tsarina Marie Alexandrovna, who tried to match Ludwig (a "confirmed bachelor" to his death) with one of her daughters. Ludwig kept the tables and rejected the girls. The final room of the tour is the irregularly shaped *Spiegelsaal*. Mirrors cover the walls, making the elaborate ivory-chandeliered room appear to stretch into infinity.

More impressive than the palace itself is the magnificent **park** surrounding it. The force of water cascading down steps behind the palace powers the fountain in front. Once an hour, the dam is opened, and water shoots higher than the top of the building. To the right of the palace is an artificial **grotto;** red and blue floodlights illuminate trellises and stalagmites. A subterranean lake and floating lettuce-leaf boat complete Ludwig's personal 19th-century Disney ride. There are brilliant red-and-blue stained-glass windows on the **Maurischer Kiosk,** an elaborate, mosque-inspired building and the only sight on the grounds not built expressly for Ludwig. He saw it at the 1867 World Exposition in Paris and liked it so much that he had it brought home. Within these walls, Ludwig would sit on the peacock throne, smoke his water pipe, and order his servants to dress up in costumes and read him tales from *1,001 Nights*. Under the right moon, Ludwig the Sultan would even throw midnight Turkish orgies. Following the path down the hill to the left (20min.) is the reconstructed **Hunding-Hütte,** modeled after a scene in Wagner's *Die Walküre* from *Der Ring des Nibelungen*. In another of Ludwig's flights of fancy, bearskin-covered log benches surround a tree that is—surprise—artificial.

OBERAMMERGAU ☎08822

In a wide valley surrounded by mountains, meadows, and forests, the tiny alpine village of Oberammergau (pop. 8000) straddles the shallow Ammer River in the shadow of a crucifix-crowned cliff that hints at the town's widespread Christian sentiment. The village itself is a serene haven for visiting hikers and local wood-carvers, but the nearby Ettal Abbey and Schloß Linderhof provide entertainment for at least a few days.

⊟♂ TRANSPORTATION AND PRACTICAL INFORMATION. Oberammergau can be reached by **train** from Munich (1¾hr., every hr., €14.20) and Augsburg (2½hr., €16-21). It's also connected by **bus** to Garmisch-Partenkirchen (#9606; 40min., every hr., €3.60) and Füssen (#9606; 1¾hr., 8 per day, €7.60). The **tourist office** is at Eugen-Papst-Str. 9a. The staff has info on accommodations and hiking, and cycling maps for the area. Turn left from the station and right at the town center onto Eugen-Papst-Str. For late arrivals, there is a reservation line and hotel information out front. (☎923 10; www.oberammergau.de. Open M-F 8:30am-6pm, Sa 9am-noon; June-Sept. also Su 10am-noon.) The **police** are at Feldingg. 17 (☎110). The **post office**, 82487 Oberammergau, is across from the station. (☎920 70. Open M-F 8:30am-noon and 2-5pm, Sa 9am-noon.) **Postal Code:** 82487.

▐▌ ACCOMMODATIONS AND FOOD. The wood-paneled walls of **Gästehaus Gerda ❷**, Longinusg. 5, enclose knick-knack-filled, spacious rooms in a quiet residential part of the town near the Altstadt. Most rooms have bathroom and shower. (☎63 56. Singles €15.50-23; doubles €33.50-41. Cash only.) Oberammergau's **Jugendherberge (HI) ❶**, Malensteinweg 10, sits just beside the mild Ammer River 7min. upstream from the train station. Go left from the station up Bahnhofstr. and take a right on the gravel path just before the bridge; follow the path, keep the river on your left; the hostel is on the right. The four- to six-bed rooms are simple and spotless. (☎41 14; www.oberammergau.jugendherberge.de. Reception 8-11am and 4-10pm. Curfew 10pm. Closed mid-Nov. to Dec. Under 26 and families only. €14.90 plus €1.30 *Kurtaxe*.) Pick up groceries at **A&P Tengelmann**, Bahnhofstr. 9. (Open M-F 8am-8pm, Sa 7:30am-8pm.) Although most of the restaurants in town aren't well suited for budget travelers, **Gasthof Bayerische Löwe ❸**, Dedelerstr. 2, serves hearty Bavarian and vegetarian entrées for reasonable prices. Soups and salads run €2.80-5.20, while entrées are €6-12.

◙ SIGHTS. The richly painted ceiling frescoes of the 18th-century Rococo **St. Peter and Paul Church**, Herkulan-Schweigerg. 5, depict the martyrdoms of its two namesakes. The church's unique marble columns and its intricate stucco work add to the beautiful interior. From the tourist office, walk north on Eugen-Papst-Str., turn right on Verlegerg., and make another right onto Dorfstr. (Open dawn to dusk.) On your way, stop to admire the famous *Lüftlmalerei* (house fresco) on **Pilatushaus** (on Verlegerg.) from the small garden out back. Painted in 1784 by Franz Zwinck, it illustrates Christ's condemnation by Pilate and the events that followed. Watch local wood carvers and artists at work inside. (Tu-Sa 1-6pm. Free.) A short walk around the town will take you past a number of other elaborately frescoed stucco houses, usually bearing religious or folk-themed images.

In 1330, Ludwig I of Bavaria—not the Ludwig II of Neuschwanstein fame—founded the enormous **abbey** in the tiny village of **Ettal**, 4km south of Oberammergau. Since then, the abbey has conducted a brisk business of tourism, supplemented by a healthy dose of house-fermented beer and spirits. The **Klosterladen,** to the right as you face the church, sells divine bottles of Kloster-brewed beer

(€1.50) and stronger liquors, including a particularly delicious strawberry brew (€3.50). Vendors along the street peddle bottled beers of questionably appropriateness, but the smiling face of Pope Benedict XVI on the *Papst* (Papal) *Bier* is ever reassuring. Stuccoed and ornamented with gold and precious stones, the double-domed **sanctuary**, built in the 14th century, assumed its Baroque form after 18th-century renovations. (www.kloster-ettal.de. Open Apr.-Sept. M-Tu and Th-F 7:45am-7:45pm, W 8am-6pm, Su 8am-7:45pm; Oct.-Mar. 7:45am-noon. English tour €2.) The Schaukäserei, Mandlweg 1, is one of the most famous cheese-making houses in the area. Buy gastronomically daring amounts of cheese for €15 per kg, or enjoy a wide array of smaller milk-related snacks, from ice-cream to cheese wedges and bread, for less than €7.20. Walk with the graveyard on your left from the monastery and turn left on Mandlweg. (Tours Tu-Sa 11am, €2, under 16 free. Open Tu-Sa 10am-6pm, Su noon-5pm.) **Buses** #9622 and 9606 to Ettal from Oberammergau leave about every hr. from the train station (€1.90). Get off at "Ettal Klostergasthof." To **hike** to the abbey from the Oberammergau tourist office, turn left on Eugen-Papst-Str. When the road forks at the bridge, take the gravel path straight ahead to Ettal (1-2½hr.). The Ettal **tourist office,** Ammergauer Str. 9, lists rooms and has a map of hiking trails. (☎35 34; fax 63 99. Open M-F 8am-noon.)

GARMISCH-PARTENKIRCHEN   ☎08821

Once upon a time, the 1100-year-old hamlets of Garmisch and Partenkirchen were beautiful, unassuming Bavarian villages whose location at the foot of the Zugspitze—Germany's tallest peak—ensured their tranquil isolation. Once the 19th-century nature movement discovered the mountains, however, the two towns quickly became known for their magnificent ski slopes, trails, and climbing routes. Hitler persuaded the mayors of Garmisch and Partenkirchen to combine the two villages (pop. 8000) in 1935 in anticipation of the 1936 Winter Olympic Games. The towns are still united and casually known as Garmisch, much to the dismay of Partenkircheners. Though the fresco-filled town centers may look identical, Garmisch, in the west, is slightly more modern, while Partenkirchen, in the east, is more traditional. The crumbling and abandoned shepherd huts outside of town galvanize the suspicion that many elements remain unmolested by modernity.

█▐ **TRANSPORTATION AND PRACTICAL INFORMATION. Trains** to Munich (1½hr., every hr., €15) and international service to Innsbruck, Austria (1½hr., every hr., €12). **Bus** # 9606 arrives from Füssen (2hr., 6-7 per day, €7 with *Tagesticket*) and **Oberammergau** (40min., €3.60). **Public transportation** within the city costs €1, but it's free with a *Kurkarte* (issued at lodgings when you pay the mandatory *Kurtaxe*, €2). For a **taxi,** call ☎161. Rent **bikes** at **Sport Total,** Marienpl. 18. (☎14 25. €15 per day. Open M-F 9am-10pm, or call for an appointment. Also arranges base jumps, hot air balloon rides, rafting, and other outdoor activities for around €100.) The **tourist office,** Richard-Strauss-Pl. 2, distributes English hiking brochures and finds rooms for free. From the station, turn left on Bahnhofstr. and left again on Von-Brug-Str. about 200m up the road (10min.), then enter the pink building on the square. (☎18 07 00; fax 18 07 55. Open M-Sa 8am-6pm, Su and holidays 10am-noon.) For alpine **weather reports,** call ☎79 79 79 or the tourist office. Do **laundry** at **Waschsalon,** Zugspitzstr. 17. (Wash €4.90, soap included. Dry €1.80 per 15min. Open June to mid-Sept. M-F 9:30am-6pm, Sa 9am-noon; mid-Sept. to May M-F 10am-6pm.) The **police** station is at Münchenerstr. 80 (☎110, non-emergency 9170). Have your pharmaceutical fill at **Bahnhof-Apotheke,** Bahnhofstr. 36, to the right as you face the station. (☎24 50. Open M-F 8:30am-12:30pm and 2-6pm, Sa 8:30am-noon.) **Computerhaus,** Ludwigstr. 69, provides **Internet** access. (€1 per 15min. Open M-F 10am-6pm, Sa 10am-1pm.) The **post office** is across the street from the station. (Open M-F 8:30am-5:30pm, Sa 9am-noon.) **Postal Code:** 82467.

♠☐ ACCOMMODATIONS AND FOOD. Many *Gästehäuser* (Guest Houses) in town offer rooms with WC, shower, and breakfast for under €40, but they fill up quickly. The tourist office is an invaluable resource for finding such private rooms. The ▩**Naturfreundehaus ❶**, Schalmeiweg 21, is a hostel on the edge of the forest by a brook at the east end of Partenkirchen. From the station, walk straight on Bahnhofstr. as it becomes Ludwigstr., follow Ludwigstr. as it bends right, and turn left on Sonnenbergstr. Continue as it becomes Prof.-Michael-Sachs-Str. and then Schalmeiweg (25min.). Sleep in packed lofts with up to 16 fellow backpackers. (☎43 22. Breakfast €4. Use of kitchen €0.50. Reception 6-8pm. 10-bed dorms €8; 2- to 3-bed €10. Cash only.) For a positively Bavarian experience, spend a night at **Gasthof Werdenfelser Hof ❸**, Ludwigstr. 58, in Partenkirchen's historic district. Cozy wood-paneled singles and doubles ooze ambience. Amenities include a sink in every room. (☎36 21; fax 796 14. Breakfast included. Singles €35; doubles €70. AmEx/MC/V.) The restaurant-and-bar downstairs serves a broad menu for Bavaria (e.g. includes vegetarian dishes). Enjoy dinner (€6-12) with a side of live Bavarian music. (Open Tu-Su 11am-10pm. AmEx/MC/V.) **Campingplatz Zugspitze ❶**, Griesener Str. 4, is on highway B24 at the base of the Zugspitze; take the Eibsee bus from the station to "Schmölzabzweigung." (☎31 80; fax 94 75 94. Office open 8am-noon and 3-6pm. €5 per person plus €1.50 *Kurtaxe*, €3 per child; €3-5 per tent.)

Garmisch's restaurants are typically meat-centric and overpriced, but there are establishments that cater to a wider range of tastes and budgets. Get a big meal at **Saigon City Express ❷**, Am Kurpark 17a. Gung Po (€7) makes for a tasty break from *Wurst;* most dishes are €3-10. (☎96 93 15. Open Tu-Su 11am-2:30pm and 5-10:30pm. Delivery Tu-Sa 5-10pm, Su 11am-2:30pm and 5-10pm. Cash only.) Cheerful owners at **Taverne Thessaloniki ❷**, Ludwigstr. 76, serve huge platters of perfectly seasoned *souvlaki* (€6.50) to the strains of soulful Greek ballads. (☎90 97 40. Greek specialities €1.50-6.50. M-Sa 11am-10pm. Cash only.) More traditional Bavarian fare can be found at **Hofbräustüberl ❷**, Chamonixstr. 2. Enjoy a wide variety of soups (from €2.80) and meat dishes (from €4.50) outside in a veritable forest of red flowers, or sit inside surrounded by dark, seasoned wood. (☎717 16. Open daily 11am-11pm. MC/V.) The *Imbiße* (snack bars) on Von-Brug-Str. also offer cheap choices, and even cheaper groceries are available at **MiniMal**, Son-Brug-Str. 13. (Open M-F 8am-8pm, Sa 7:30am-8pm.)

◨▨ SIGHTS AND HIKING. Locals maintain that Garmisch-Partenkirchen survived both the bubonic plague and the Thirty Years' War due to its piety, and today Christianity still plays a central role in the life of the town. The gilded interior of **Pfarrkirche Garmisch St. Martin,** between Marienpl. and Mühlbach, provides a glimpse into the local religious establishment and its long history. The **St. Sebastian Kapelle** on the corner of Hindenburgstr. and Ludwigstr. was constructed over the mass graves of the nameless victims of the plague; today, its charm and peaceful gardens belie its sordid past.

The mountains are the main attraction in town, offering glacial views in the summer and snowy alpine antics in the winter. There are three ways to conquer the **Zugspitze,** the highest peak in Germany, though they should be attempted only in fair weather. **Option 1:** Take the cog train Zugspitzbahn from the Zugspitzbahnhof (50m behind the Garmisch main station) to "Eibsee." (☎79 70; www.zugspitze.de. Departs every hr. 8:15am-2:15pm. 1¼hr.) Continue with the **Gletscherbahn** cable car to the top at the 2950m high Zugspitzgipfel. (Round-trip, including train and cable car, €45; ages 16-17 €31.50; under 16 €26.50.) **Option 2:** Get off the train at Eibsee as in Option 1, but take the dramatically steep **Eibsee Seilbahn** to the top. (☎86 27. 10min. Departs every hr. from 8am; July-Aug. last return at 5:45pm, May-June and Sept.-Oct. 4:45pm. Closed for maintenance 2- to 6-week periods per year.)

Same prices as Option 1.) **Option 3:** Climb for about 10hr., usually as part of a two-day trip. **Do not attempt this ascent unless you are an experienced climber.** Get a map and check weather at either ☎ 79 79 79 or www.zugspitze.de.

For other views, take the new **Kreuzeckbahn** to Kreuzeck peak and sample the mild hikes. (1651m. Departures begin 8:30am; July-Oct. last return at 5pm, May-June 4:30pm. Round-trip €17, students €12, children €10.) Or, try the **Alpspitzbahn** cable car from the station southwest of town to Osterfelderkopf peak. (2050m. 9min.; July-Oct. departures begin at 8am, May-June 8:30am, last return at 5pm. Round-trip €19, ages 16-17 €14, children €12.) The three-day **Holiday Erlebnispass** is good for cable cars, buses, and trains (except to the Zugspitze), and includes admission to the **Olympic Eissport Zentrum.** (€4, ages 16-17 €3, under 16 €2.)

Biking to the **Eibsee**, 10km from Garmisch, can be a great daytrip. The soaring, snow-capped weight of the Zugspitze is reflected in the calm, crystal waters of a mountain lake. To avoid pedaling up the fairly steep uphill grade of the last 300m, take the Eibsee bus from Garmisch (one-way €4), or the Zugspitzbahn from the Zugspitzbahnhof to "Eibsee." On the other side of town, one of the most popular trails leads to the dramatic, 100m deep ▨**Partnachklamm** gorge. Take Bus #1 or 2 to the Olympic Ski Stadium, then follow the signs up to the gorge (35min.). Dark tunnels wind through the gorge, breaking out into tiny ledges separated from the water only by steel railing. Expect to get slightly wet. Other trails lead to the top of the gorge, where a small bridge affords spectacular, if somewhat disconcerting, views of the foaming water beneath. (Gorge open dawn-dusk, €2.) Other trails from the gorge area lead to the Ferchenbach Valley and the Rheintal. **WN Alpin,** Zugspitzstr. 51, specializes in mountaineering gear and rents **hiking and climbing equipment.** (☎ 503 40; www.wn-alpin.de. Open M-F 9am-12:30pm and 2-6pm, Sa 9am-12:30pm) For information about hiking trails and rock climbing, contact the **German Alpine Association** in Munich (☎ 089 29 49 40). There is also a **Mountain Guide Office** in Garmisch. (☎ 18 07 44. Open M and Th 4-6pm.)

BERCHTESGADEN NATIONAL PARK

The paintings of Romantic Caspar David Friedrich have impressed the iconic image of the Watzmann peak upon every German's mind. For centuries, the mountain—and the sparkling blue lakes and deep forests surrounding it—was dominated by herdsmen and shepherds. Soon artists, then tourists, flocked to these mountains, and the herdsmen became pension owners and guides. In 1978 the government realized that the plant protection area it had set up was not enough to preserve the ecosystem from the invading hordes of visitors, so it created the current national park. Today, trails guide hikers through high alpine pasture. Biking, bobsledding, paragliding, rafting, rowing, and skiing are also popular in the park. Due to their ecological impact, these activities are strictly regulated.

✱ ORIENTATION

Berchtesgaden National Park is a German peninsula jutting into a sea of Austrian Alps. To the north, it encompasses the towns of Berchtesgaden, Ramsau, and Schönau. The park and its environs extend along three valleys. The fjord-like **Königssee** valley holds the ski-friendly Jenner and the notoriously challenging Kehlstein to the east. The mighty **Watzmann**, the highest peak in the park and second-highest in the country (2713m), sits along the valley's western edge. According to legend, the cruel King Watzmann was turned into stone, and now looks down on Berchtesgaden with his wife and seven children—the Kleiner Watzmann and Watzmann Kinder peaks—by his side. On the far side of the Watzmann is the **Wimbach** valley, overlooked by the **Hochkalter** on the west. The third valley con-

BERCHTESGADEN NATIONAL PARK AT A GLANCE

AREA: 210sq. km. Lowest point 603m at the Königssee, highest point 2713m at the summit of Mt. Watzmann.

CLIMATE: Snowy winters, rainy springs, mild (16°C/60°F) summers. Cold at higher elevations, temperate at lower.

FEATURES: Extensive forest, steep rock faces, sparkling glacial lakes.

GATEWAYS: Berchtesgaden (p. 476), Ramsau (p. 480), and Schönau (p. 482).

CAMPING: Strictly forbidden. A system of alpine huts accommodates outdoor enthusiasts within the park.

FEES AND RESERVATIONS: There are no entrance or trail fees. Parking runs from €2.50 per day. Reservations not usually needed for huts, though they are a good idea in summer.

HIGHLIGHTS: Hiking through the Magic Forest, breathtaking views of the Königssee, the summit of the Watzmann.

tains the picture-perfect **Hintersee**, starting at Ramsau and continuing as the Klausbach valley, where the only public bus in the park circulates. At the convergence of the three valleys in the south lie the **Steinernes Meer** massif and a number of Austrian peaks, with the Austrian town of Maria Alm in the valley on the far side. The park's major rivers, perfect for rafting, are the **Königsseer Ache** and the **Ramsauer Ache,** which combine downstream to form the **Berchtesgadener Ache.**

TRANSPORTATION

Cars are not allowed into the park, with the exception of those bringing supplies to the many **Alpinehütte** (huts) scattered throughout; several roads on the park's outskirts lead to trailheads and nearby villages. The boat across the Königssee (p. 479) or the bus along the Klausbachtal (p. 476) are your best bet to penetrate the depths of the park. Good bases outside the park include **Berchtesgaden, Ramsau,** and **Schönau.** Berchtesgaden can be reached by bus and train, and offers bus connections to both Ramsau and Schönau (p. 476). Once within the park, there are 230km of well-marked **hiking trails,** six of which are navigable by **mountain bike** in the summer, and others by **touring skis** in the winter. You can start a hike from just about anywhere—trails run from every town, crisscrossing each other. If arriving by car, park in the parking lot at the end of Königsseerstr. in Schönau (€3 per day, €2 with *Kurkarte;* p. 477) or at one of the many smaller trailhead parking lots (€1-2 per day) and head into the park on foot.

PRACTICAL INFORMATION

Emergency: Fire or **ambulance** ☎112; **police** ☎110. For a hiking accident, you can also call ☎08652 192 22. If you have hiked into Austria, call ☎144. To send a distress signal, repeat a loud noise or visual signal 6 times in 1min., followed by a 1min. pause, then repeat. The response is a signal given 3 times per min. Official visual signals include flashing a red scarf or raising both arms above your head. Standing with 1 arm raised and the other at your side signifies that you do not need assistance.

National Park Information Centers: In addition to the main Nationalpark-Haus, there are 5 centers in the park located near most trail bases. Each houses an exhibit based around a certain theme and showers travelers with free brochures, posters, maps, and advice. Hikers will appreciate the green *Berchtesgadener Alpen für Wanderer und Bergsteiger* map (€6.50), which labels all hiking routes with numbers corresponding to signposts throughout the park, and shows the location of all of the *Alpenhütte* (alpine huts; see **Accommodations**) and *Gaststätte* (restaurants). The free *A National Park for Everyone,* in English, French, German, and Italian, includes a map and scenic hike info.

BAYERN

Wimbachbrücke, Wimbachweg 2, in the Wimbachbrücke lot below Ramsau. Houses an exhibit on the formation and geological past and present of the Wimbach gorge. Open daily 9am-5pm.

Hintersee, Hirschbichlstr. 26 (☎08657 14 31), at the foot of the Klausbach valley. Features a display on woodpeckers and eagles in the park, and another on rustic gardening and natural experiences. Open daily 9am-5pm; closed Nov.-Dec.

St. Bartholomä, at the St. Bartholomä ferry stop. Houses an exhibit on change and continuity in the wilderness. Open daily mid-May to mid-Oct. 9am-5pm.

Engert-Holzstube, Hirschbichlstr., halfway up the Klausbachtal. Accessible from the Klausbachtal trail. Exhibit explores the transition from economic activity to environmental preservation on the park lands. Open daily mid-May to mid-Oct. 9am-5pm.

Kuhroint, Watzmannkar, 2hr. from Königssee, just by the guesthouse. New. Open daily mid-May to mid-Oct. 9am-5pm.

🖾 **Nationalpark-Haus,** Franziskanerpl. 7, Berchtesgaden (☎08652 643 43; www.national-park-berchtesgaden.de). From the main train station, follow the "Zum Markt" signs and bear right on Maximilianstr., which runs through Franziskanerpl. The info center is attached to the church on the right. A must for anyone interested in outdoor activities—the staff are hiking geniuses. Check out the extensive rotating and permanent exhibits, including a 3D map of the national park and its hiking routes, a kid's playroom, and an exhibit on peasant life. Open daily 9am-5pm.

Tours: The park service leads free *Wanderführungen* (guided nature hikes) in German throughout the year. Check the "Wandern" brochure at the Nationalpark-Haus for days, times, and meeting points. Tours in English sometimes available for groups of 7 or more for a fee; advance notice required.

Fees and Reservations: Entrance to the park and all hikes are free. **Camping** within the park is forbidden, along with all forms of fire, including campfires and camp stoves.

Parking is available in the lot at the end of Königsseerstr. in Schönau (€3 per day) and at trailheads throughout the park (around €2.50 per day; check map for locations).

Gear: Sport M+R Brandner in Berchtesgaden or Ramsau. Both rent **bikes** and stock **hiking boots** and other **equipment.** Rent **skis** at the **M+R Brandner,** the **Ski School Berchtesgaden-Jenner** (☎086 52 66 710), or the **Jenner base lodge** in Schönau. A listing of 15+ additional rental locations servicing all of the major ski areas is also available at the Berchtesgaden, Ramsau, or Schönau tourist offices (ask for the "Winter" brochure).

Climate and Seasonality: During winter, the park sleeps under many feet of snow. In early summer it rains almost every day. Summer brings the warmest weather; average July temperature is around 16°C (60°F) and about 4°C warmer in valleys. Autumn is also beautiful, with forests ablaze in color. For current **weather information,** call ☎08652 96 72 97 or check www.dwd.de.

🏠 ACCOMMODATIONS

The National Park is an easy day trip from the bordering towns. If you want to try longer routes or stay up in the high country, 26 **Alpenhütte** ❷—simple huts offering food and a bed for €15-20—are scattered throughout and just outside of the park. These are the only authorized accommodations and are usually open from the end of May until October. Bring your own sheets for hygiene; mattresses and two blankets are standard issue for the huts. Don't expect many comforts; you'll be squished in next to others on mattresses on the floor, or in a bed for more money. The food is standard *Gaststätte* (tavern) fare with plenty of choices. Reservations are typically not necessary, although weekends in June, July, and September do get busy, and members of the German Alpine Society have priority over humble tourists. Camping is strictly forbidden.

Overnight accommodations are symbolized by a red hut on the *Berchtesgadener Alpen Wanderer* map. There are also houses that offer food but no

Berchtesgaden National Park

○ TRAILS
Jenner/Königssbachweg, **4**
Klansbachtaler/Blaneis, **8**
Maleminkl-Rundweg, **1**
Obersee, **7**
St. Bartholomä, **5**
Watzmann, **2**
Wimbachtal, **6**
Zauberwald (Magic Forest), **3**

accommodation; on the map these are represented by white huts outlined in red. On the free *National Park for Everyone* map, red numbered huts show both where food is available and where you can spend the night.

Alpeltalhütte, 1100m (☎08652 630 77). Obersalzburg ski region. 1½hr. hike from Vorderbrandstr. 39 beds, 22 mattresses. Open Dec. 25-Oct.

Blaueishütte, 1685m (☎08657 271 or 546). On Mt. Hochkalter. 2½-3hr. from Ramsau/Hintersee. 20 beds, 63 mattresses. Open mid-May to mid-Oct.

Carl-von-Stahl-Haus, 1736m (☎08652 27 52). Just below the Jenner on the border; ski tour region. 2hr. from Hintersee parking lot. 24 beds, 70 mattresses. Open year-round.

Gotzenalm, 1685m (☎08652 69 09 00). On Gotzenberg, 4hr. from Jenner Mittelstatoin. 15 beds, 65 mattresses. Open mid-May to mid-Oct.

Kärlingerhaus am Funtensee, 1633m (☎08652 29 95). Steinernes Meer ski tour region, 4hr. from St. Bartholomä. 48 beds, 182 mattresses. Open June to mid-Oct. Reserve in summer.

Kühroint-Hütte, 1420m (☎08652 73 39). On Watzmannkar. 2hr. from Königssee or 2hr. from Ramsau Wimbachbrüke. 22 mattresses. Open June-Sept.

Neue Traunsteiner-Hütte, 1570m (☎0171 437 89 19). On Reiteralm, 6hr. from Hintersee/Böselsteig. 40 beds, 100 mattresses. Open April to mid-Oct.

Purtschellerhaus, 1629m (☎08652 24 20). On Hoher Göll, 1hr. from Ofneralm bus stop. 10 beds, 50 mattresses. Open mid-May to Oct.

Schneibsteinhaus, 1670m (☎08652 25 96 or 637 15). On Torrenerjoch, just below the Jenner. 2hr. from Hinterband parking lot or 30min. from Bergstation Jennerbahn. 80 mattresses. Open May-Oct.

Störhaus, 1894m (☎08652 72 33). On Untersberg. 3½hr. from Bischofswiesen. 15 beds, 54 mattresses. Open June-Sept., with shelter available in winter.

Watzmannhaus, 1928m (☎08652 96 42 22). Way up the Watzmann, 3-4hr. from Wimbachbrücke. 56 beds, 148 mattresses. Open June to mid-Oct. (reservations required), shelter available in winter.

Wimbachgrieshütte, 1327m (☎08657 344). 2½hr. from Wimbachbrücke. 16 beds, 58 mattresses. Open May to mid-Oct.

◪ HIKING

Literally thousands of hikes can be put together from the network of marked trails that snake through the park. Most trail signs give the length and an estimated time for each section. The dotted lines are routes for experienced hikers only. Those planning a substantial hike should consider renting poles, available at **Bergsport Geistaller,** Griesstätterstr. 8 (☎08652 31 86) in Berchtesgaden. Poles are free for the first day, €2 per subsequent day. A few of the more popular, scenic hikes include:

Obersee (3½hr. round-trip not including ferry). Take the ferry (1hr.) to Salet (see **Königssee,** p. 479). Follow signs for the 15min. walk to the Obersee. From here, a counterclockwise route leads, in under 1hr., along the shimmering lake to the **Fischunkelalm,** which dispenses milk and butter in summer. Another 30min. of hiking leads to the stunning **Röthbach waterfall.** On the return trip, overheated hikers splash in the refreshing Obersee. If you don't check the time of the last ferry on your way out, you might spend the night at the wrong end of the lake.

Watzmann (12km, full day). The Watzmann was first conquered in 1799, although the last 200 years have done little to soften the strenuous hike. Only start it if you know what you are doing; the National Park helicopter has to fly out daily to this route to rescue hikers who overestimated their ability. From Berchtesgaden, take bus #846 to "Wimbachbrücke" (15min., every hr. 7:30am-7:15pm; limited weekend service; €2.30; round-trip €4.10), where there is an Information Center. Then follow signs through the parking lot and onto **trail 441.** Most hikers take 3-3½hr. to reach Watzmannhaus—when you pass the cow pasture, you're halfway there. The steep 785m vertical to the Hocheck summit (only worthwhile on clear days) is **for experienced hikers only.** The 2nd summit, Mittelspitze, can only be reached across a ridge with cables for support, and is a project **for experienced mountaineers only.** Pack a jacket and food.

Wimbachtal (18km; 6-8hr. round-trip). Long but rewarding. Take bus #846 (see Watzmann, above) to "Wimbachbrücke" and follow the signs to **Wimbachklamm** gorge to see the rock formations. Stroll along the Wimbach stream's striking valley to **Wimbachschloß,** built in 1784, which serves refreshments in the summer. You can turn around at this point, or continue to the **Wimbachgrieshütte** for phenomenal views of the Hochkalter opposite.

St. Bartholomä and Eiskapelle (6km; 2-3hr. round-trip not including ferry). This short but challenging Königssee hike starts from the beautiful St. Bartholomä church, now a restaurant (p. 479). After a visit to the National Park Information Center, follow signs past the St. Johann and Paul Chapel to the **Eiskapelle** (Ice Chapel), a dome formed at the front edge of the glacier by the river of melted snow running underneath.

Klausbachtaler Blaueis (6km, 5hr. round-trip). Start from the "Pfeiffensmacherbrücke" parking lot in Ramsau, where there will be signs for the Blaueishütte. Then, turn left 20min. into the hike. This strenuous hike heads up the side of Mt. Hochkalter to the Blaueishütte, 1680m over Ramsau. The incline steepens but the view of the valley is rewarding. The same valley also offers a great hike to the **Bindalm** (12km, 6-8hr.). Head past the Engert-Holzstube information point up to the **Bindalm,** from which you can hike into Austria or take the bus back from Weißbach to Hintersee.

Jenner/Königsbachweg (6.5km, 2hr. from summit to midstation). The hulking Jenner, a skiers' paradise located just outside of the park, can be hiked beginning with **trail 494** (trailhead at the Kessel stop on the Königssee) or **trail 493** (reachable by following Jennerbahnstr.). The less ambitious can take the **Jennerbahn** lift (p. 479) to the top, then hike part of the way back down. To get there, take bus #841 (dir.: Königssee) from the train station to the Königssee parking lot (€3). From the top, follow the signs to the Stahlhaus and then down over Königsbachalm to the Jennerbahn midstation, where you can ride the lift back down. Check out the Salzburg and Bayern signs outside the Stahlhaus, on the Austrian border.

Malerwinkel-Rundweg (4km, 1hr. round-trip). A short loop to "Painter's Outlook," one of the best scenic points on the Königssee, then back through a wooded area. From the Königssee parking lot, follow Jennerbahnstr. to the lift station, and bear right onto the gravel path after the gondola statue, coming out by the Königssee Schifffahrt docks; return by following the main shopping street.

🚲 BIKING

Mountain bikes are permitted on a limited number of routes around the edges of the national park, although the rest of the Berchtesgaden area there contains plenty to keep cyclists busy. Thoroughfares outside the park such as the **Mozart Route** are always buzzing with bikers. Cycling maps and trail guides are available from the Berchtesgaden tourist office (p. 477). Many routes involve steep climbs.

Klausbachtal. The whole Hirschbichl road from the Hintersee to the border with Austria is open only to the local bus, cyclists and hikers. From Ramsau you can also ride up to Klausköpfel for a panoramic view of the Ramsauer Tal.

Wimbachtal. One track goes across the lower northern face of the Hochkalter, while another leads along a valley to Eckau (hiking route #486). Another heads from the Wimbachbrücke up in an easterly direction, then south along the Watzmann massif past the Kühroint-Alm to the panoramic Archenkanzel, right by the information point.

Gotzenalm. Starts in Berchtesgaden and winds a semi-circle around Jenner's peak, then heads into the park along a valley parallel to the Königssee all the way to the Gotzenalm. Or continue around the Jenner all the way past the Carl-v.-Stahl hut into Austria. Routes run on the Kehlstein (but bikes are not permitted on the bus route) all the way to the Eagle's Nest, and into a small section of the park. Experienced cyclists only.

🧗 ⛷ OTHER OUTDOOR ACTIVITIES

Treff Aktiv, Jennerbahnstr. 19 (☎08652 667 10; www.treffaktiv.de), on the way to the Jennerbahn base station, offers various outdoor adventure trips, including **rafting** (€26, children €19), **paragliding** (from €109), mountain bike tours (from €31), and **canyoning** (€45, beginners' route €29). They also offer **ski weekends, climbing,**

bobsledding, rapelling, and **guided hikes.** To try out everything from ice climbing to paragliding to hot air ballooning, contact the **Berchtesgaden Outdoor Club** (☎086 52 977 60; www.outdoor-club.de), with 13 locations in the area.

The Jenner is the largest **ski** slope around, serviced by the Jennerbahn. (☎08652 958 10. Day pass €24, ages 6-15 €13.50.) The Berchtesgaden tourist office and most ticket counters also sell a five-day pass good for all 20 ski areas in the region (with *Kurkarte* €105, ages 6-14 €55). For the **Ski School Berchtesgaden-Jenner,** call ☎08652 66 710. Ask at the tourist office in Berchtesgaden for a list of ski and snowboard schools in the area, most of which also rent equipment. You can also get a trip down the Kunsteisbahn **bobsledding** track with **Rennbob-Taxi** from mid-October to February for €80, including all insurance and a "Bobsled Diploma." (☎08652 97 60 69; www.rennbob-taxi.de.)

BERCHTESGADEN   ☎08652

Nestled in the southeast Bavarian Alps, Berchtesgaden (pop. 7800) wins the affection of many world travelers for the natural beauty of its surroundings. Once part of the Archbishopric of Salzburg, the region was annexed by Bavaria in 1809 for its salt deposits. Encircling this town are the alpine peaks of Hoher Göll, Watzmann (the highest, at 2713m) and Hochkalter; the Königssee and Hintersee's shimmering waters; and the Zauberwald's pristine forests. Berchtesgaden is also well known for a more notorious attraction: Hitler's Kehlsteinhaus—the mountaintop retreat christened the "Eagle's Nest" by American troops who occupied it after WWII.

⌐ TRANSPORTATION

Trains: Every hr. to: **Bad Reichenhall** (30min., €3.40); **Mühldorf** (2hr., €14.70); **Munich** (3hr., €25.20); and **Salzburg, Austria** (1hr., €7.60).

Buses (RVO): The main terminal is just outside the train station. Tickets can be purchased on the bus (☎94 48 20). The *Urlaubsticket,* sold at the bus station and all tourist offices, provides unlimited bus travel for your choice of 6 days out of the next 7 (€18, under 13 €9; requires a *Kurkarte* for purchase). Buses run within Berchtesgaden until 7pm (€1). They also head to: **Bad Reichenhall** (€4.10); **Königssee** (€2.30); **Ramsau** (€2.60); **Salzburg** (€4).

Taxis: ☎40 41.

Bike Rental: Available at the **train station** ticket counter. €6-7 per day; €36 per wk. Deposit required. For a nicer bike, head to **Sport M+R Brandner,** Bergwerkstr. 52 (☎14 34). From the tourist office, cross the bridge and turn right onto Bahnhofstr., which turns into Bergwerkstr., or take bus #848 (dir.: Oberau) to "Watzmann Therme." €10 per day. Open M-F 8:30am-noon and 2-6pm, Sa 8:30am-1pm.

⬛▮ ORIENTATION AND PRACTICAL INFORMATION

Berchtesgaden is a lone German outpost among Austrian mountains. The train station lies along the clear and swiftly-flowing **Berchtesgadener Ache;** the main **Marktplatz** is on the hill above. From the train station, turn right immediately and look for the alcove labeled "Zum Markt" on the right before the post office. Go up the steep stairs, over the footbridge, and follow the "Zum Markt" and "Ortsmitte" signs through the woods to the pedestrian zone. At night, travelers may prefer to take a better-lit route, turning left from the train station and following Bahnhofstr. as it branches off up the hill to the left. The manicured **Kurgarten** is on the right just before the Marktpl. Turn right at the Marktpl. and you will be in the relative quiet of the **Schloßplatz** (castle courtyard) beneath the matronly spires of the church.

Tourist Office: Königsseer Str. 2 (☎96 70; www.berchtesgadener-land.com), opposite the train station in the yellow building. The free **Wanderpass** brochure includes tips (in German) on trails and hikes in the Berchtesgaden National Park. They also offer a list of daily guided tours, most of which are free. Visitors need a €1.80 *Kurkarte*, included with an overnight stay. Open mid-June to Oct. M-F 8:30am-6pm, Sa 9am-5pm, Su 9am-3pm; Nov. to mid-June M-F 8:30am-5pm, Sa 9am-noon. **Kur und Kongresshaus,** Maximilianstr. 9 (☎944 53 00; www.berchtesgaden.de) is another visitor's bureau, with a café-restaurant, garden, movie theater, and reading room with daily newspapers in German. From the station, follow the "Zum Markt" signs and bear right along Maximilianstr.—it's on the right before the parking garage. The staff helps find rooms. Open May to mid Oct. M-Sa 9am-6pm, Su 10am-1pm and 2-6pm. Dec.-May M-F 9am-6pm, Sa-Su 10am-1pm and 2-6pm. Mid Oct. to Nov. M-F 9am-6pm only.

Tours: Short, English-language tours of the **Kehlsteinhaus** depart daily at 10:35 and 11:45am. (Meet at the tunnel entrance to the elevator. Tours meet the buses; to catch the 10:35am tour, take the 9:45am bus #849 from Berchtesgaden; for the 11:45am tour, take the 10:45am bus. Bus to "Dokumentation Obersalzburg" €4.10 round-trip from Berchtesgaden. *Kurkarte* discount €1. Tours 35min. €5, under 12 free.) A 4hr. tour (in English) of the Kehlsteinhaus and the documentation center with the Nazi bunker system in Obersalzberg should be reserved at least 1 day in advance from **Berchtesgaden Mini Bus Tours** in the tourist office or online. (☎649 71; www.eagles-nest-tours.com. Tours meet at the tourist office mid-May to Oct. daily 1:15pm. €40, under 13 €30, under 6 not permitted.) The Bavarian hills are alive with the sound of mini-buses—the same company also runs **Sound of Music Tours** around Salzburg. (4hr. tours leave from the Berchtesgaden tourist office M-Sa 8:30am. Reservations required. €30, under 13 €20, under 6 free.)

Currency Exchange: Raiffeisen Bank, Metzgerstr. 3 (☎96 62 10), in the Marktpl. 24hr. **ATM.** Open M-F 8:30am-12:30pm and 2-4:30pm.

Laundromat: Waschsalon im Wittelsbach, Maximilianstr. 16. Nice and centrally located. Wash €3. Dry €2. Open daily 7:30am-9pm.

Police: Bayerstr. 7 (☎110, non-emergency ☎946 70). Follow "Zum Markt" signs from the station. Follow Hanielstr. to Bayerstr. and take a right.

Pharmacy: Bahnhof Apotheke, Bahnhofspl. 2 (☎32 37), in the front of the train station, to the left of the main exit. Open M-F 8am-7pm, Sa 8am-2pm.

Internet Access: Radio Denk, Maximilanstr. 13. €2.50 per hr. Open M-F 9am-6pm, Sa 9am-1pm. Also at **Computer Stadl,** Maximilianstr. 20 and Königsseer Str. 17. €1.50 per 15min. Both locations open M-Tu and Th-F 9am-1pm and 2-7pm, W 2:30-7pm, and Sa 9am-1pm. Access also available at the tourist information office (€4 per hr.)

Post Office: Franziskanerpl. 2½. Open M-F 9am-12:30pm and 2-5:30pm, Sa 9am-12:30pm. **Postal Code:** 83471.

🏠🏠 ACCOMMODATIONS AND CAMPING

Although most private rooms and pensions in Berchtesgaden run €30-80 per night, there are a few more budget-oriented options. If everything cheap is booked, as is often the case from mid-July to the end of August, try the neighboring town of **Ramsau** (p. 480). Take bus #846 from Berchtesgaden (30min., every hr., €2.60).

Jugendherberge (HI), Gebirgsjägerstr. 52 (☎943 70; jhberchtesgaden@djh-bayern.de), 25min. uphill from the station. Turn right from the station and follow Ramsauer Str. on the left for 15min., then take the first right on Gmundbrücke and follow the signs up the steep gravel path on the left. Or, take bus #839 (dir.: Strub Kaserne) to "Jugendherberge/Gmundbrücke" (every hr., €2). Modern facility overlooking the mountains. Breakfast and sheets included. Reception 7-9am and 5-7pm. Check-in until midnight. Curfew midnight. Closed Nov. 1-Dec. 26. 10-bed dorm €15.55. *Kurtaxe* €1.80, ages 6-16 €.80. Over 26 €4 extra. Private rooms for families €3 extra. MC/V. ❷

Haus Gürtler, Weinfeldweg 7 (☎39 11). Head down Maximilianstr. to the Schloßpl., turn left when you can see the pink belltower, and head up the steps as the sidewalk rises high above the street. Take the path leading up to join Weinfeldweg; the pension is the 3rd house on the left. The climb is steep but this pension rewards the intrepid with balconies overlooking a flower-filled garden. Breakfast included. Singles €21, doubles €42, less for stays of 3+ nights. Cash only. ❷

Villa Lockstein, Locksteinstr. 18 (☎614 96; fax 94 85 33). From the train station, take Bus #837 (dir. Maria Gern) to "Krankenhaus." Alternatively, walk up through town (follow "Zum Markt" signs), across the castle courtyard, and along Nonntal. Make the left up the steep hill and continue as it curves left (30min.). Rooms have mountain views and bathrooms. Breakfast included. €24 per night, after 3 nights €21. Cash only. ❷

Hotel Watzmann, Franziskanerpl. 4 (☎20 55; fax 51 74). From the station, take a right and follow the "Zum Markt" signs. Bear right onto Maximilianstr. The hotel is on the left. Hallways filled with Bavarian artifacts in a great location. Breakfast included. Singles €27-42, depending on season. AmEx/MC/V. ❸

Haus Achental, Ramsauer Str. 4 (☎45 49; fax 632 70). From the train station, take a right and walk 5min. down Ramsauer Str. Tidy rooms with private bathrooms right on the main road and train line; a convenient base for exploring the national park. Breakfast included. Singles €29, doubles €54, after 3 nights €26/47. Cash only. ❸

Campingplatz Allweglehen, (☎23 96; www.allweglehen.de), Allwegg. 4, at Untersalzburg, more than 1hr. walk upstream from the station. Take a right on Ramsauer Str. and keep on. €5.40 per person, €3.70 per child (4-16), €8.50 per tent and car. Cash only. ❶

▣ FOOD

Berchtesgaden is rife with expensive restaurants. Pick up a *Wurst* from a vendor, or score some groceries at the **Edeka Markt,** Königsseer Str. 20 (open M-Sa 7:30am-7pm) and fresh bread and pastries at the **Bäckerei-Konditorei Ernst,** Königsseer Str. 10. (Open M-F 6:30am-6pm, Sa 6:30am-noon, Su 7-10am. Cash only.)

Gasthof Goldener Bär, Weinachtsschützenpl. 4 (☎25 90). Bavarian entrées and every kind of sausage you could ever want. *Weißwurst* €1.90. Other entrées (including vegetarian options) €6-13. Open daily 9am-10pm. Cash only. ❸

Express-Grill Hendl, Maximilianstr. 8 (☎97 64 74). Hamburgers with fries juxtapose traditional Bavarian dishes like *bratwurst* with *sauerkraut* (€4) and *bayerische Schweinhax'n* (pork steak with crunchy skin; €1.20 per 100g). Limited seating. Open daily 10am-8:30pm. Cash only. ❶

Dalmacija, Marktpl. 5 (☎97 60 27), has typical bistro fare and simple pastas in small (€2.60-4.60) and large (€4.60-6.60) portions. Open daily 9am-midnight. Cash only. ❷

Café Spiesberger, Maximilianstr. 11 (☎25 24), serves homemade everything right in the center of town. Sandwiches €5-7. Open M-Sa 9am-6pm. Cash only. ❷

Gasthof Bier Adam, Marktpl. 22, ☎23 90. Upscale restaurant serving snacks (€5-8.40), fancy venison steak (€18), and other Bavarian entrées. Friendly staff and menu in 4 languages. Open daily 8:30am-midnight. AmEx/MC/V. ❹

▣ SIGHTS

KEHLSTEINHAUS. The Kehlsteinhaus, called the Eagle's Nest by invading American soldiers, was built for Hitler's 50th birthday as a place to entertain ambassadors. Though the *Führer* only visited the mountaintop "teahouse" 14 times (he was, ironically, afraid of heights and extremely claustrophobic, particularly in elevators), today it is a tourist must-see. A restaurant now fills the granite resort house, which survived the war intact. But the best reason for visiting—apart from the spectacular view from the 1834m mountain peak—is the trip up. The 6.3km road is an engineering marvel hewn from solid rock in less than two years by an army of 3000 men excused from conscription for health reasons. If you're making a day out of it, it's possible to hike all the way to the top from the "Kehlstein" bus stop. Reserve your spot on a return bus at the booth when you get off. Or, from the parking lot, go through the tunnel and take the elevator through the mountain to the summit. An hour should give you enough time to explore the mountaintop. A 5min. climb brings you to a cross memorializing the 10 men who died during the rapid construction of the Kehlsteinhaus. Beyond the cross, there's a beautiful 45min. hike to the summit which is only sensible in clear weather. Legend holds that the house's original brass mirrored walls were installed to quell Hitler's claustrophobia. *(Bus #849 (dir.: Hinterband, Dokumentation) to "Kehlstein Busabfahrt;" every 30min. 6:45am-6:15pm. Buses return to Hintereck and Berchtesgaden every 30min. (fewer on weekends), last one at 6:30pm. Buy an elevator ticket to the top of the mountain from the cashier's desk at the bus stop. Open May-Oct. daily except on days of heavy snow. €13.50, children €7.50; round-trip €16.10/8.)*

DOKUMENTATION OBERSALZBERG (DOCUMENTATION CENTER). This permanent exhibition is located where Hitler and his inner circle once made their homes (bombed in 1945), which, along with SS barracks, rounded off the Nazi Obersalzberg village. You can still explore the former "Türken" Gasthof, where the regime leaders met for beer, as well as the canteen of the Platterhof, the hotel which functioned as a vacation resort for the American army stationed in Germany until 1996. The museum offers an in-depth look at the history of Obersalzberg and the Nazi dictatorship. Pick up an audio guide (in English and German) to lead you through the hundreds of photographs and down to the cold bunkers reserved for party members in the event of an attack. *(Bus #838 (dir.: Hinterband) to "Kehlstein Busabfahrt." €4.10 round-trip. ☎ 94 79 60. www.obersalzberg.de. Open Apr.-Oct. daily 9am-5pm, last entry 4pm; Nov.-Mar. Tu-Su 10am-3pm. Audio guides €2. €2.50; military, teachers, students, and children free with ID.)*

KÖNIGLICHES SCHLOß. This castle belonged to an Augustinian prior who was also secular ruler of the area until 1803. A branch of the Wittelsbachs lived here in the 1930s. On display is fabulous furniture, antique weapons, a strong gallery of Gothic art (including two early Riemenschneider pieces) and the largest hunting trophy in Germany, a pair of 18.3kg antlers. The 50min. obligatory tour is in German, but English translations are available. *(From Maximilianstr., veer right at the parking garage. Turn left by Gasthof Triembacher and follow the signs to the Schloß. ☎ 94 79 80; www.haus-bayern.com. Open mid-May to mid-Oct. M-F and Su 10am-1pm and 2-5pm, last entry 1hr. before closing; mid-Oct. to Easter M-F 11am-2pm. €7, with Kurkarte €6, students €3.50, under 16 €3. Antler museum alone €3, children free.)*

KÖNIGSSEE. Wedged between extraordinary alpine cliffs, the blue-green Königssee is literally clean enough to drink. The *Fußgängerweg* (footpath) from Berchtesgaden winds through fields and over brooks, and is also bike-accessible. *(From the train station, cross the street; continue as the sidewalk curves to the left; look for the "Achenweg" sign at the small parking lot. Turn right and continue walking with your back to the train station and follow the "Königssee" signs for 5.5km. Or, take bus #839, 841, or 843 (dir.: Königssee) from the bus station (2 per hr. 9am-4pm, round-trip €4.10). Follow touristy Seestr. to reach the lake.)* At the end of Seestr. is the Königssee dock and the **Bayerische Seen Schifffahrt** counter, with cruises to other points on the lake, including the famous **Echo Wall** and **St. Bartholomä** church. **Salet** is beautiful, and the 45min. walk around the Obersee (see **Hiking,** p. 474) is well worth it. *(☎96 36 18; www.bayerische-seenschifffahrt.de. Boats operate every 30min. 8am-5:30pm. Round-trip €11 to St. Bartholomä, to Salet €14; under 14 €5.50/7. 10% discount before 9am.)* Schifffahrt's Ruderboote house to the left of the docks rents **rowboats.** *(Open mid-June to mid-Sept. 10am-6pm; May to mid-June and mid-Sept. to Oct. 11am-5pm. 2-person boat €5 per hr., 4-person €8. ID or €50 deposit required.)* The gorgeous **Malerwinkel** (Painter's Outlook) sits to the left of the lake; start the 1hr. loop to the left of the base of the **Jennerbahn** gondola. *(Round-trip €19.10; ascent only €14.20, ages 6-14 €11/8.)* The best aerial view is from the 1170m peak serviced by the Jennerbahn. If you're planning to do both the Königssee ferry and Jennerbahn gondola, buy a **See-Gipfel-Ticket** at either ticket booth for €26.50 (available May-Oct.).

SALZBERGWERK (SALT MINES). Visitors dress in old miner's outfits, toboggan down snaking passages in the dark, and raft on a saltwater lake in mines that have been operating since 1517. Allow 2hr. for dressing up and taking the tour. Audio recordings available in 13 languages. *(From the station, take bus #837, 840, or 848 to "Salzbergwerk" (1 per hr. 7:20am-7:20pm, €1). Or, trek 30min. left out of the train station down Begwerkstr., following the "Salzbergwerk" signs. ☎600 20. Open May to mid-Oct. daily 9am-5pm, last tour 4pm; mid-Oct. to Apr. daily 11:30-3pm. €13.50, ages 4-16 €7.90.)*

OBERSALZBERGBAHN. This cable car runs 1000m up the face of the Kehlstein. From there, choose one of the many hiking trails leading around the mountain. *(Take a left out of the train station and walk along Bahnstr. for 5min. The station will be on your right at the junction of Hwy. 319. Open 9am-5:50pm. Round-trip €9, €8 with Kurkarte; ages 6-15 €4.50/4.)* For an adrenaline rush, slide down the 600m **Sommerrodelbahn,** a metal slide built into the side of the mountain, at speeds of up to 40km per hr. *(Open May-Sept. daily 10am-8pm, closed on rainy days. €2, children €1.50).*

◼ NIGHTLIFE

Berchtesgaden has a modest nightlife scene, concentrated on Bahnhofweg and the adjoining section of Maximilianstr.

Kuckucksnest, Bahnhofsweg 2 (☎614 73). From the train station, follow the "Zum Markt" signs up the gravel path; the bar is across the bridge on the path up to town. Make new friends among a welcoming crowd of climbers and hikers. Beer €2.50 (0.5L). Mixed drinks €3.50. Cover for live events. Open M-Th and Su 8pm-2am, F-Sa 8pm-3am. Cash only.

Stehplatz, Maximilianstr. 16½ (☎629 67). Join a mixed crowd for a drink in the extremely friendly and laid-back atmosphere of this popular *Pils* pub. Beer €2.50 (0.5L). Shots €1.80-2.30. Open M-Sa 8pm-1am. Cash only.

Upstairs, Maximilianstr. 16½. (☎649 63), above Stehplatz. This rooftop terrace is the perfect place for a nightcap under a starry alpine sky. Beer €2.70 (0.5L). Mixed drinks €7-8. Food €3-5. Open daily 4pm-3am. Cash only.

Chill Out, Bahnhofsweg 1, next to Kuckucksnest (☎0171 99 74 877). Lounge bar with soft couches and cushy outdoor seating. Enjoy a mixed drink (€5-7) or glass of wine at the granite countertop. Hot food until 11pm. Open Th-Sa 7pm-1am. Cash only.

Kaserbar, Seestr. 2, under the McDonald's. (☎37 55). This bar draws a teenage crowd to (mostly) American music on a crowded floor. Pool and foosball tables. Drinks €2.50-4. Infrequent night buses run the 6km back to the Bahnhof through the wee hours, but make sure to check the timetable. Open Th-Sa 10pm-3am. Cash only.

NEAR BERCHTESGADEN: RAMSAU   ☎08657

Perched in the Alps 10km southwest of Berchtesgaden, and dominated by the magnificent, snow-capped Waltzmann and Hochkalter mountains, Ramsau (pop.

1800) is nirvana for hikers, cyclists, and skiers. In winter, knicker-clad tourists take advantage of cross-country ski trails, sled runs, and ice skating on the Hintersee. The 16th-century **Pfarrkirche** (Parish Church), Im Tal 82 (☎988 60), rises magnificently from the Ramsauer Ache river uphill from the tourist office. Check out the figurines of the saints on the balcony balustrade behind you. To clear your sinuses, head to the **Kleingradierwerk Ramsau,** a small "outdoor brine inhalatorium." Follow the white gravel path across the stream from the church to the left, and turn right at Wirsthaus Waldquelle. The wind blows the healing fumes to those sitting on the surrounding benches. Past the inhalatorium, the pebbly path leads to the **Kneipp-Gesundheitsanlage,** a mountain stream wading pool built by a local doctor to improve his patients' circulation. Cool your weary feet in the pool, or just dunk them in the Ramsauer Ache itself. A rewarding yet low-impact hike, the **Zauberwald** (Enchanted Forest) trail follows the Ache upstream through a forest to the sparkling Hintersee. From the "Marxenbrücke" bus stop, cross the bridge and take the first trail immediately on your right. Follow the path past the Wirsthaus im Zauberwald to the first sign for the Naturpfad; from then on, follow the arrows labeled "Zauberwald-Hintersee." Bus #846 returns to Ramsau from Hintersee's bus station (15min., every hr., €2). For more information on the network of well-marked hiking trails radiating from Ramsau, see p. 474.

Ramsau sports a wide selection of fairly inexpensive pensions. **Gästehaus Marxen ❷,** Hinterseer Str. 22, is a quiet, friendly cottage just up the road from the bus #846 "Marxenbrücke" stop and very close to the Zauberwald trail head. (☎213. Breakfast included. €18 per person, after 4 nights €13-15 per person. Cash only.) **Haus Freiblick ❷,** Riesenbichl 38, is slightly more expensive but centrally located by the "Neuhausenbrücke" bus stop. Cross the street and bear right on Riesenbichl, following it up the hill. (☎436. Breakfast included. €18 per person. Longer stays preferred. Cash only.) **Campingplatz Simonhof ❷,** Am Taubensee 19, basks on the Lattenbach river 5min. from the "Taubensee" bus stop (Bus #845; 3 per day). (☎284. €4.60 per person, €2.50 per child, plus *Kurtaxe* €1.80/0.80. Sites €5.50. Showers €0.50. Electricity €0.50 per kwh.) To get to **Gletscherquellenhütte ❸,** cross the stream before the Pfarrkirche. On the other side, follow the white gravel path to the right; signs will guide you into the woods for a 15min. stroll to the *Hütte.* Here, beer (from €2.50 per 0.5L) and fresh buttermilk (€2 per 0.33L) quench hikers' thirst. (☎14 14. Open daily Apr.-Oct. and Dec. 26-Jan. 6 11am-9pm. Cash only.) The colorful **Wirsthaus Waldquelle ❸,** Riesenbichl 25, offers seating on an outdoor patio with a view of the water-powered *Zwergspiele* (model dwarfs) in the garden, or indoors among the fauna of Bavaria. (☎291. Most meals €5-10. Open M-W and F-Su 11am-9pm. Cash only.) At **Gasthof Oberwirt ❷,** Im Tal 86, enjoy hot strudel and other specialties (entrées €7-11) as you gaze at the Hochkalter. (☎225. Open daily 11:30am-8:30pm. Cash only.) The cheerful **Bäckerei-Konditorei ❶,** Im Tal 1, offers a wide selection of bread and pastries. (☎12 51. Open M-F 6am-noon and 2-6pm, Sa 6am-noon, Su 6:30-9:30am. Cash only.) **Edeka,** Im Tal 58, sells groceries. (Open M-Sa 7:30am-12:30pm and 2:30-6pm. Cash only.)

Ramsau can be reached from Berchtesgaden by bus, bike, or foot. Bus #846 runs every hr. from the Berchtesgaden bus station, to your right as you leave the train station (15min., 6:10am-7:30pm, €2.60). Get off at "Neuhausenbrücke" to reach the center of town. Rent **mountain bikes** (€10 per day) or buy hiking boots at **Sport M+R Brandner,** Im Tal 64. M+R also rents winter sports equipment. (☎790. Open M-F 9am-noon and 2-6pm, Sa 9am-noon.) The **tourist office,** Im Tal 2, books rooms for free and offers self-service booking after hours. (☎98 89 20; www.ramsau.de. Open Oct.-June M-F 8am-noon and 1:15-5pm; July-Sept. M-Sa 8am-noon and 1:15-5pm, Su 9am-noon and 2-5pm.) **Exchange money** and traveler's checks at **Volks-Raiffeisenbank,** Im Tal 89. (☎390. 24hr. **ATM.** Open M-Tu and Th-F 8:30am-12:30pm and 2-4:30pm, W 8:30am-12:30pm.) **Postal Code:** 83486.

BAYERN

NEAR BERCHTESGADEN: SCHÖNAU ☎ 08652

Though not as serene as Ramsau, Schönau (pop. 2500) is a perfect starting point for hiking in the Königssee area of the park. The village lies on a plateau above Berchtesgaden, adjoins the bustling outdoor shopping street of Seestr. in nearby Königssee. For private rooms (€18-100), check with the tourist office. To get to **Gästehaus Germania ❷**, Im Maltermoos 7, from the tourist office, head up Untersteinerstr. and turn right at Waldhauserstr. Head up the incline and take a left on Im Maltermoos, which curves to the right again; the building is on the left. (☎ 42 09; www.pension-germania.de. July-Sept. doubles €22-25; Oct.-June doubles €19-22, double-as-single €25-30, all per person. Cash only.) Close to the Königssee is **Campingplatz Grafenlehen ❶**, Königssee Fußweg 71, about a 5min. walk to the lake. From Berchtesgaden, take bus #841 (dir.: Königssee) to "Königssee Tankstelle" by the gas station. Take a right on Schornstr. and another right onto Königsser Fußweg, following blue signs to the campground. (☎ 41 40. Shower included, warm water 6am-10pm. Reception 8am-8pm. €5.20 per person, €3.70 per child, €6 per car and tent. *Kurtaxe* €1.80/0.80. Cash only.) Grab some *Wurst*, or a *Germknödel mit Vanillesoße* (dumpling with vanilla sauce; €4.75) at the self-serve **Brotzeitstüberl ❶**, Seestr. 29., in Königssee. (☎ 44 06. Entrées €3.50-4.50. Open daily 10am-6pm.) Locals head to the **Jolly Pizzeria ❷**, Waldhauserstr. 18, for their generous pizzas in 60 (that's right, 60!) varieties. (☎ 645 00. Small €6-9, large €9-12. Open daily 5-11pm. Cash only.) **Edeka**, Untersteinerstr. 1, sells groceries. (Open M-F 7:30am-noon and 2-6pm, Sa 7:30am-1pm.) Schönau is a 30min. walk from Berchtesgaden. Follow the footpath to the Königssee and bear right when you cross Graf-Arco-Str.; it bridges the Königsseer Ache, leading to Untersteinerstr. **Buses** #839 and 843 runs from the Berchtesgaden train station to "Unterstein" (every 45min. 5:55am-7:15pm, €1.90), which puts you 300m uphill from the **tourist office**, Rathauspl. 1. (☎ 17 60; www.koenigssee.com. Open May-Oct. M-F 9am-6pm, Sa-Su 9am-4pm; Nov.-Apr. M-F 8am-5pm, Sa 9am-noon.) Machines in the Königssee parking lot also sell helpful pamphlets in several languages (€1). The **post office** is at Rathauspl. 1. (Open M-Tu and Th 9:30am-noon and 1-3:30pm, W 9:30am-noon, F 10:30am-1pm and 2-5pm, Sa 10-noon.) **Postal Code:** 83471.

BAD REICHENHALL ☎ 08651

For centuries, the fortunes of this alpine town have depended on "white gold," the natural salt water that flows from underground. The salt, once an important trading commodity, now draws pilgrims attracted by its purported healing powers; older Germans flock to Bad Reichenhall's baths and springs to breathe, drink, wade, and bathe in the city's briny symbol. A wide array of adventure sports also beckons, and the Bad Reichenhall-Salzburg bike trail connects Austria and Germany.

⌐🔢 TRANSPORTATION AND PRACTICAL INFORMATION. Trains run every hour to Munich (2hr., €23.50) and Salzburg (30min., €7.60). The new S-Bahn gets you to Salzburg in 20min. (€10.) Both trains and **buses** connect to Berchtesgaden (35min., every hr., €3.40). Most trains stop in Freilassing. Rent a **bike** at **Sigis Radllodn**, Frühlingstr. 4. (☎ 76 62 69. Cruisers €6 per day; mountain bikes €12. Open M-F 8:30am-6pm, Sa 8:30am-noon. Passport or ID deposit required. Cash only.) The 🖪**tourist office**, Wittelsbacherstr. 15, is on the same road as the station, across from the bank. The staff provides maps and free guides for hiking, climbing, canoeing, and nordic walking. (☎ 60 63 03; www.bad-reichenhall.de. Open May-Nov. M-F 8:30am-5:30pm, Sa 9am-noon; Dec.-Apr. M-F 9:30am-5pm, Sa 9am-noon. Internet access available at kiosk just outside door, or inside for €2.50 per hr., free with *Gastekarte*.) **Club Aktiv**, Frühlingstr. 61, offers **rafting, canyoning, mountain biking,** and **paragliding** packages. (☎ 672 38; www.rafting-fun.com. ½-day trips from

€35.) Do laundry at **Moni's,** Getriedeg. 3. (☎78 811. Wash €3, soap €0.50. Dry €4 per 32min. Open M-Sa 8am-8pm.) The **police station** is at Poststr. 19 (☎110, non-emergency 97 00). For **Internet** access, go to the tourist office or the popular **Café Amadeo,** Poststr. 29, where surfing costs €3.60 per hr. (☎640 41. Open M-F 8am-1am, Sa-Su 9:30am-1am.) The post office, Bahnhofstr. 35, is to the right as you exit the train station. (Open M-F 8am-6pm, Sa 8am-12:30pm.) **Postal Code:** 83435.

⌦ ACCOMMODATIONS AND FOOD. Bad Reichenhall has no hostel, but private rooms abound—the Bad Reichenhall tourist office keeps an extensive list. After one night at any accommodation you will have to pay the mandatory *Kurtaxe* (€2.50 or €1.90 depending on your location). In return you receive a *Gastekarte*, which gets you **discounts** and **free admission** at many area sites. **Gästehaus Villa Fischer ❷,** Adolf-Schmidt-Str. 4, is a small, pleasant pension a short walk from the Kurgarten. Take a right out of the train station on Bahnhofstr., a left on Rinckstr., a right on Salzburger Str., and a left on Adolph-Schmidt. (☎57 64. Breakfast included. Giant singles €23.50. Cash only.) A 20min. walk from the train station, **Landhaus Kirchholz ❷,** Salzburger Str. 44c, offers comfortable rooms (some with balconies overlooking the Alps). Take a left on Bahnhofstr., a right on Zenostr., and a left on Salzburger Str. (☎55 82. Singles €17. Doubles with private bath €43. Cash only.) Camping is available at **Campingplatz Staufeneck ❶,** 2km away in Piding. (☎21 34. Reception April-Oct. 7:30-11am and 5-10pm. €5.50 per person, €2.50 per tent. Showers €0.50. Electricity and laundry available.) Campers can park for 36hr. for a small fee in the parking lot opposite the **Rupertus Therme;** contact the tourist office for updated prices and amenities. A **grocery** store, **Aldi,** is directly to the left of the train station in the parking lot. (Open M-Sa 8am-8pm. Cash only.) Cafés and shops alternate with flowers and fountains along the pedestrian zones of Salzburgerstr. and Ludwigstr.; follow Bahnhofstr. to the right out of the station, take a left on Kurstr., and a right on Salzburgerstr. Try the world-famous, delectable *Mozartkugeln* (marzipan and chocolate balls; €0.50) at the fabulously gaudy **▧Café Reber ❸,** 10 Ludwigstr. (☎60 03 133. Open M-Sa 9am-6pm, Su 1-8pm. Cash only.) A quartet of bewigged Mozart impersonators perform free concerts Sa 11am-1pm. Just past the Alte Saline, the **Harlekin Café/Bistro ❷,** Anton-Winkler-Str. 3a, in the yellow building, offers a simple daily menu beneath a hat-covered ceiling (soup of the day €2.30, pasta €4). The café is also a non-profit social project, employing workers who are reentering the work force or need a protective environment. (☎98 43 04. Open M-F 10:30am-5pm. Cash only.) At local favorite **Murat's ❶,** Poststr. 24, the friendly owner will enhance your *Döner Kebap* with delicious fried eggplant, zucchini, and peppers (€4). The veggie variety is €3, and the "Big Döner," served on a plate, is €6. (☎76 72 76. Open M-Sa 8am-10pm. Cash only.) At **Gasthof Bürgerbräu ❸,** Am Rathauspl., throw back local beer direct from the in-house brewery (from €2.30 for 0.5L) to complement grilled meats in hefty quantities (€7-12) or vegetarian dishes and soups (€4-8). Bürgerbräu is Bad Reichenhall's local brew—don't even try ordering another beer. (☎60 89. Open M-W and Su 9am-11:30pm, F-Sa 9am-midnight. DC/MC/V.) The new **Sushi Bar and Wokman ❸,** Poststr. 44, serves delicious vegetarian noodle dishes (€5.60-6.20), sushi (platters from €7.50), and sashimi (€8.50-14.50) from their extensive pan-Asian menu. (☎76 61 92. Open daily 10:30am-10:30pm. Cash only.)

◰ SIGHTS. The **Salzmuseum** (Salt Museum), Alte Saline, is peppered with exhibits on the history of salt-making in the area. Obligatory 45 minute tours in German pass through briny underground passageways, past massive 15-ton wheels that have been turning uninterrupted for 150 years. (☎700 21 46. Tours May-Oct. daily at 10, 11am, 2, 3, and 4pm; Nov.-Apr. Tu-F, and first Su of the month 2, 3 and 4pm. English tours by request; call a week in advance. €5.90, with *Kurkarte* €5; ages 4-

16 €3.90. Combo ticket with the Berchtesgaden Salzwerk, p. 480, €16/9.50.) The **Städtisches Heimatmuseum** (Local History Museum), Getreidg. 4, offers a gigantic collection of everything from prehistoric jewelry to Nazi paraphernalia celebrating local military "heroes." (☎ 668 21. Open May-Oct. Tu-F 2-6pm and Su 2-6pm. €2, students €1, children €0.50.) At the museum or the tourist office, pick up a €3 guide (in German) to the **Reichenhaller Burgenweg,** an extensive 50km. circuit that covers the ancient watchtowers and castle ruins of the Reichenhall valley and is suitable for hiking, biking, and diving. The city's oldest church, **Münsterkirche St. Zeno,** was founded in the early 9th century. Barbarossa rebuilt it in Romanesque style in the 11th century, although a 16th-century fire destroyed nearly all of the original building. The church and much of its artwork, therefore, date to the Renaissance, but the impressive portal and the bas-reliefs in the adjoining cloister (one of which portrays Barbarossa himself) are striking reminders of the beauty of the more archaic building style. (Church open daily sunrise-sunset; cloister open by appointment, call ☎ 976 10.) The center of the town's "water cure" circuit is the palatial **Kurgarten.** From the train station, turn right down Bahnhofstr., then left onto Kurstr. and walk until you see the garden on the left. (Open daily Apr.-Oct. 7am-10pm; Nov.-Mar. 7am-6pm. Free. Summer concerts €5, children €2.50, with *Gästekarte* free.) The **Altes Kurhaus** hosts events, and across the park the Wandelhalle has a music pavilion, a giant chess set, and the *Trinksole* (a salt spring fountain) sells drinks from hot and cold springs. (Open M-F 8am-12:30pm and 2-5pm, Sa-Su 9am-3pm. Small cup €0.10, glass €2.) The 170m **Gradierwerk** out front is a bizarre wall known as an "open air inhalatorium." Built in 1912, it's covered with 250,000 *Dornbündel* (bundles of branches, briars, and thorns) through which saltwater mist trickles. For intense results, stroll around the downwind side and inhale for 30min. daily (open Apr.-Oct.). The **Predigtstuhlbahn,** Südtirolerpl. 1, the oldest twin-cable car in the world (1928), ascends 1614m of skiers' paradise to a lookout point and restaurant across the river. From the top, you can hike to Berchtesgaden and other valleys. (☎ 21 27 or 98 650. 1 trip every 30min. May-Sept. 9am-9pm, last uphill trip at 8pm. Oct.-Apr. 9am-6pm, last uphill trip at 5pm. One way €9, ages 6-14 €5. Round-trip €15, with *Kurkarte* €14, ages 6-14 €7.)

CHIEMSEE

Artists, architects, and musicians have chosen the Chiemsee region, situated between Munich and Salzburg, as the setting for their masterpieces for hundreds of years. The original inhabitants of these picturesque islands, meadows, forests, and marshlands surrounded by dramatic crescent-like mountains built its famed 9th-century island monasteries. Later, King Ludwig II chose the Herreninsel island for his last and most extravagant fairy-tale château. Modern visitors to the "Bavarian Ocean" are artists of leisure; the area has been overrun by resorts and rising prices. Much of the lake itself is now a *Naturschutzgebiet* (Nature Preserve) and its waters remain pristine despite droves of visitors. Even though it is prime real estate for the German elite, the Chiemsee area attracts a younger, more active audience as well, thanks to the variety of sports on tap, from wind-surfing and sailing to hiking and mountain biking. Prien, the largest lake town, functions as a hub for the other towns around the lake, including Aschau, resort paradise Bad Endorf, Sachrang, and the ski areas of Kampenwand.

PRIEN AM CHIEMSEE ☎ 08051

Tranquil Prien's best qualities are its proximity to the Chiemsee and its hub train station. This pleasant town surrounded by sheep pastures and *wanderwegs* (hiking trails) serves as a base for adventures on the lake and in the mountains.

🖪🗗 TRANSPORTATION AND PRACTICAL INFORMATION. On the southwestern corner of the Chiemsee, Prien has **train** connections to Munich (1hr., every hr., €13.40) and Salzburg (50min., every hr., €10). **Buses** to nearby towns leave from the parking lot to the left as you exit the train station (every 1-2hr., €1.50-6). Rent **bikes** at **Radsport Reischenböck,** Bahnhofpl. 6, 200m to your left after you exit the train station. (☎46 31. €8 per day. Open M-F 8am-noon and 2-6pm, Sa 8am-noon. Passport deposit required.) The **train station** is a few blocks from the city center and a 20min. walk north of the lake. To reach the Altstadt, turn right on Hochriesstr. from the station and then, at the end of the road, turn left on Seestr., which becomes Alte Rathausstr. The modern **tourist office,** 5min. away on the left at Alte Rathausstr. 11, gives out free maps, keeps a list of private rooms, and offers free **Internet** access. (☎690 50; www.tourismus.prien.de. Open May-Oct. M-F 8:30am-6pm, Sa 8:30am-4pm, Nov.-Apr. M-F 8:30am-5pm.) The Prien **police** station is nearby at Altes Rathausstr. 13 (☎110, non-emergencies 905 70). There is a 24hr. **ATM** at **Sparkasse,** 100m left of the Hauptbahnhof (☎90 78). **Internet** access is available at **Oscom Computer,** Seestr. 56. (€.10 per min. Open M-F 9am-noon and 1-5pm.) The **post office** is 400m to the left of the train station at Hochriesstr. 21. (Open M-F 8am-12:30pm and 2-5:30pm, Sa 9am-12:30pm.) **Postal Code:** 83209.

🖪 ACCOMMODATIONS AND CAMPING. Visitors with cars get the best deals in Prien, because outlying rooms, which offer better prices, are not well serviced by public transport. The best bet for an inexpensive room in Prien is a *privatzimmer* (private room) booked through the tourist office. The cheapest bed in town is at the **Jugendherberge (HI) ❷,** Carl-Braun-Str. 66, 20min. from the station and 10min. from the lake. From the station, turn right, then right on Seestr., and continue under the train overpass. After two blocks, go left on Staudenstr., which curves right and turns into Carl-Braun-Str. (☎687 70; fax 68 77 15. Breakfast included. Locker €2 deposit. Reception 8-9am, 5-7pm, and 9:30-10pm. Curfew 10pm; door code available. Open early Feb. to Nov. 4- to 6-bed dorms €17.45, less for longer stays. MC/V.) Although remote, **Schmiedhof ❷,** Ludwigstr. 119, often has room when everything else is full. Take bus #9494 from the first platform at the bus stop (1 every 2-4hr., €1.50) to "Bachham"; Schmiedhof is two houses down on the right. Many rooms have balconies and alpine views. (☎18 41. Breakfast and afternoon coffee and cake included. Singles €25; doubles €40; less for longer stays. Cash only.) **Campingplatz Hofbauer ❶,** Bernauer Str. 110, is a 25min. stroll from the center of town. From the station, turn left at Seestr., left again at the next intersection, and follow Bernauer Str. out of town past three gas stations and a McDonald's. (☎41 36; fax 626 57. Reception 7:30-11am and 2-8pm. Open Apr.-Oct. €6 per adult, €3 per child, €5.20 per site. Free showers. MC/V.)

🖪🖪 FOOD AND NIGHTLIFE. Prien has several grocery stores. **Lidl,** at the corner of Seestr. and Franziska-Hager Str. is open daily 8am-8pm. Or join a crowd of locals at the **farmer's market** behind the church. (Open F 9am-1pm.) Descend into the bustling beer cellar of **Wieninger Bräu ❸,** Bernauer Str. 13b, for *Schwabische Käsespätzle* (Bavarian cheese noodles; €9) and Lederhosen-clad waitstaff. (☎610 90. Entrées from €9. Open M and W-F 10am-midnight, Su 9am-midnight.) The inexpensive and conveniently located **Kur-Café Heider ❷,** Marktpl. 6, is in the pedestrian zone behind the church. (☎15 34. Sandwiches from €3.50. Open Tu-Sa 8am-6pm, Su 9am-6pm. Cash only.) Next door, the **Bäckerei Muller ❶,** Marktpl. 8, has a wide assortment of baked goods. (☎1543. Open Tu-Sa 8am-6pm, Su 8:30am-6pm. Cash only.) At the end of the lakefront promenade, **Café Neuer am See ❸,** Seestr. 104, serves interesting dishes such as ostrich and turkey in a curry sauce (€11.50) or *Hirschgulasch* (€9.80), a dish of red deer served with flour dumplings. (☎60 99 60. Open W-M 8am-11pm. MC/V.) Get your Asian vegetable fix at **Wok ❷,** Postweg

1, through the pedestrian walkway across from the train station. (☎96 30 797. Entrées €5-8. Open M-F 11am-9pm. Cash only.) **Mesner-stub'n ❸**, Urschalling 4, next to Kirche St. Jakobus, is a pleasant *Gaststätte* (tavern) serving upper Bavarian dishes (€4-13) and delicious beer. (☎39 71; www.mesnerstubn.de. Open M and W-Sa 3pm-1am, Su 10am-1am. Cash only.) **La Piazza ❸**, Seestr. 7., serves savory pasta dishes (€12-18) and large, thin-crust pizzas (€6-8) in a faux-Italian atmosphere. (☎56 52. Open Tu-Su 11am-2:30pm and 5-11pm. DC/MC/V.) A source of late-night entertainment in an otherwise sleepy town, **Café del Sol**, Seestr. 7, is a cozy bar with Asian-themed decor, a Spanish name, and Italian owners. (☎18 28; www.cafe-sol.net. Open Tu-Su noon-4am. Cash only.)

◨ ♫ **SIGHTS AND ENTERTAINMENT.** Prien's most exciting cultural feature, the ◪**Kirche St. Jakobus**, is in Urschalling, a pleasant 30min. walk from the center of town. From the tourist office, head left along Alte Rathausstr., then left on Beilhackstr., which soon becomes Trautersdorfer Str. Continue through Trautersdorf on what is now Bauernbergstr., then follow signs to Kirche St. Jakobus. Or, take the *Chiemgau Bahn* train for a 5min. ride to "Urschalling" (the stop is on request; speak to the conductor before departure). The church has a complete fresco cycle from the end of the 14th century: it was considered crude by followers and covered over, but restoration has revealed the striking, archaic figures. (☎58 86. Open daily 9am-6pm.) Prien's *Kneipp* water cure at the **Kleiner Kursaal** gardens behind the tourist office soothes sore feet. Nearby, the red-and-blue marble interior of the **Himmelfahrt Kirche** boasts beautiful 18th-century chandeliers, paintings, statues, and ceiling frescoes by **Johann Baptist Zimmermann**, of Wieskirche fame. On the square behind the church the small **Heimatmuseum** (Local History Museum) tells the story of distinctive local Bavarian culture through exhibits of clocks, fishing rods, coins, ceramics, and stuffed local fowl. (☎927 10. Open Apr.-Oct. W-Sa 10am-noon and 2-5pm. €2, students and seniors €1.50.) **Galerie im Alten Rathaus,** Alte Rathausstr. 22, shows international art and photography. (☎929 28. Open M and Th-F 2-5pm, Sa-Su 11am-1pm and 2-5pm.) **Bootsverleih Stöffl** rents the cheapest **boats** in town. From the train station, turn left and walk to the end of Seestr. Turn left before the ferry dock. (☎16 16. Open Apr.-Oct. daily 9am-dusk. Pedal boats €4.50-6 per hr.; rowing boats €5 per hr.; electric €9-19. Cash only.) **Prienavera Erlebnisbad,** Seestr. 120, just along the lakefront from the ferry wharf, has a sauna, fun pool, 25m pool, 70m slide, and an outdoor heated pool with view of the Chiemsee. (☎60 95 70; www.prienavera.de. Open M-F 10am-9pm, Sa-Su 9am-9pm. Beach pool open in summer 9am-8pm. Full-day admission €12, children under 15 €6.50. Sauna €3. Cash only.) The 3hr. **Chiemsee Tanzschiff** (dance ship) lake cruises leave select Fridays in summer from the Prien dock. (☎60 90 for dates, or ask at the tourist office. Departs Prien at 7:30pm. €15.) Chiemgau Biking offers a variety of **guided mountain bike tours** in the area (☎96 17 613; www.chiemgau-biking.de). Ask about the German-language **Naturerlebnistouren** (nature tours), at the tourist office. Experts lead visitors to the delta of the **Tiroler Achen**, around remote areas of the lake, and along the Alz river for dawn and sunset trips on a wooden raft. (All tours take place regularly in summer; €8-20.) For information on whitewater rafting, contact **Sport Lukas,** Schleching (☎086 49 243).

ISLANDS ON THE CHIEMSEE

Chiemsee Schifffahrt ferries float across the waters of the Chiemsee from Prien to **Herreninsel** (Gentlemen's Island), **Fraueninsel** (Ladies' Island), and towns on the other side of the lake. Both islands are extremely popular with German tourists and school groups, so take a ferry before 10am to avoid crowds. (Departs from the Prien dock roughly every 20min. in summer and every hr. in winter, 7:15am-7:30pm. Last ferry from the islands to Prien leaves Fraueninsel 7:00pm, Herreninsel 7:10pm. Round-trip to Herreninsel €5.90, under 15 €2.90; to Fraueninsel or both islands €7/5.) An Augustinian monastery on Herreninsel once complemented the still-extant Benedictine nunnery on Fraueninsel in religious isolation. Supposedly, mischievous members of the cloth met up on **Krautinsel** (Herb Island) and engaged in a scandalous practice: gardening. Today, the island is uninhabited and without ferry service. For more information on getting to the islands, call **Chiemsee-Schifffahrt** (☎60 90). To get to the dock, hang a right from the Prien train station and follow Seestr. for 15min. Or, take the **Chiemseebahn**, a slow, green 19th-century steam train, from the train station to the dock. (Every hr., 10am-6pm. €2, round-trip €3; under 15 €1/1.50. Tickets available from the booth next to the tracks or on the train. Combination train/ferry ticket available at the train station.)

HERRENINSEL. Frustrated by his powerlessness and already descending into the depression and delusion of his final days, King Ludwig II made one last stab at earthly perfection with the construction of the **Schloß Herrenchiemsee.** A monument to the "Sun King," Louis XIV of France, the ornate folly is a temple to Ludwig's admiration for his omnipotent 17th-century namesake (Ludwig is the German equivalent of Louis). Unfortunately, Ludwig's death in 1886 left the dream incomplete and the family coffers empty; the combination of overdone chambers and barren, uncompleted rooms in the palace betrays the sudden halt in construction. To get to the palace from the ferry landing, walk along the paved footpath (20min.) or ride in true kingly fashion in a horse-drawn carriage. (Apr.-Oct. every 15min.; €3, ages 6-17 €1.) The entire palace is an unparalleled extravagance, shamelessly copying Versailles, with a **Hall of Mirrors**, replicas of furnishings and artwork, and a lavish golden bed chamber dedicated to Louis's tradition of receiving his first and last appointments of the day while in bed. Ludwig II's private chambers include the most expensive chandelier ever produced by the famed Meißen porcelain factory (Ludwig had the blueprint destroyed to ensure the piece's uniqueness) and a dining room table that rose up through the floor on a specially designed dumbwaiter. Despite the lavish accommodations, Ludwig spent only 10 days total in the palace. A 12-room **museum** documenting his life through original garments and portraits is just inside the castle entrance and is included in the price of admission. (☎688 70. Open daily Apr. to mid-Oct. 9am-6pm, last tour 5pm; mid-Oct. to mid-Dec. and Jan.-Mar. 9:40am-4:15pm, last tour 3:40pm. German tours every 5min.; English tours every hr. 10:15am-4:15pm. Admission and obligatory tour €7; seniors, students, and disabled persons €6; under 18 free with adult.) Halfway down the path back to the dock is the former monastery, known as **Altes Schloß** since the days when Ludwig stayed there during the construction of his new palace. Herreninsel came to the fore in the 1940s, when the Federal Republic's constitution was drafted here; an exhibit explains the event. Also on view are remnants of the original building and artwork, as well as a large collection of works by Chiemsee landscapist **Julius Exter.** In summer, the Hall of Mirrors hosts concerts; call the Prien tourist office for more information. (Open daily Apr.-Sept. 9am-6pm; Oct. 10am-5:45pm. €3, students €2; free with admission to the castle.) On select summer days (May-Sept.), two local storytelling grandmothers lead an evocative **fairy-tale walk** around the Herreninsel. (☎086 67 71 99; www.maerchen-wanderung.de. May-Sept. €9, children €6. In German; check website for dates.)

FRAUENINSEL. Despite daily swarms of tourists, the Fraueninsel manages to maintain its rural island charm. Only footpaths wind through this restrained village realm of hard-working nuns and fishermen. From the dock, a path curls toward the **Klosterkirche** (Cloister Church), passing its medicinal herb garden. The nuns make their own marzipan, beeswax candles, and five kinds of *Klosterlikör* (cloister liquor; €4-8 for 0.2L), for sale in the **Klosterladen** convent shop. (Open M-Sa

10am-5:45pm; Su 1-5pm.) The abbey, which dates back to at least AD 766, memorializes **St. Irmengard,** the great-granddaughter of Charlemagne and earliest known abbess of the cloister. Her corpse was exhumed in the 17th century and encased in glass in 1928, though she's not much to look at after 1000 years. Facing the altar are countless messages written to Irmengard in thanks for deliverance after prayer. (Open daily 7:30am-6pm.) The **Torhalle** (Gatehouse) is the oldest surviving part of the cloister as well as the oldest completely preserved structure in southern Germany; its **Michaelskapelle** (St. Michael's Chapel) displays some archaic 11th-century frescoes and a few local artifacts with careful copies of prestigious medieval artwork, whose originals are everywhere from Italy to the Germanic Museum in Nuremberg. (Open June to mid-Oct. daily 11am-5pm. €2, students and seniors €1.50.) The gatehouse also exhibits paintings of the lake by the 19th-century painters' colony that flourished on the island. The entire Fraueninsel can be circumnavigated on foot in 45min. Eat on the mainland; restaurant prices on the island are higher than elsewhere since owners know they have tourists trapped. On select weekends in November and December, the Fraueninsel hosts a charming *Christkindlmarkt* (Christmas market; ask at Prien tourist office for dates).

ELSEWHERE NEAR THE CHIEMSEE

While Prien may be the "metropolis of the Bavarian sea," untold other towns melt into the landscape, offering idyllic resorts, nature hikes, and historical attractions.

ÜBERSEE. On the shore of the Chiemsee, Übersee has the best and longest beachfront of the region. The **Julius Exter Haus,** now a museum dedicated to the local artist, still features a lush garden. (Open May-Sept. Tu-Su 5-7pm. Free.) The tourist office offers weekly guided hikes, but everyone can hike from town up the Westerbuchberg hill to the medieval **St. Peter- und Pauls-Kirchlein.** The **Natur-Pavillon,** Hochfellnweg 1, educates visitors and school groups about the Chiemsee ecosystem. (☎08642 15 51. In German. Open May-Oct. W-Su 2-5:30pm.) Camp at the beachside **Chiemsee Camping Rödlgries ❶,** Rödlgries 1. (☎08642 470; www.chiemsee-camping.de. Late July to late Aug. €6-9 per car and per tent; €7 per adult, ages 7-17 €4.50, under 7 €3; rates lower at other times of year. Includes *Kurtaxe.* Free beach access and showers. Cash only.) Übersee has many traditional restaurants but not much else. Between the town and the beach, try **Chiemseestuben ❷,** Feldweisstr. 104, where spare ribs with french fries go for €7.50. (☎08642 389. Open M, Tu, Th-Sa 5pm-1am, Su 5pm-midnight. Hot food until 11:30pm. Cash only.) **Joe's American Bar/Café/Bistro ❷,** Feldweisstr. 4, just across the train tracks, serves cheap American food and occasional Thai dishes. Sandwiches, hamburgers, and sloppy joes (of course) all cost €4. (☎086 42 51 36. Open Tu-Sa 6pm-1am, Su 7pm-1am.) **Edeka,** Feldweisstr. 56, sells groceries. (☎08642 59 71 80. Open M-F 7:30am-7pm, Sa 7:30am-4pm. Cash only.) Übersee lies just past Prien on the Munich-Salzburg **train** line (€2.80 from Prien). In summer, it is also serviced by the **ferry.** Contact their **tourist office,** Feldwieserstr. 27. (☎08642 295; www.uebersee.com. Open M-F 8am-noon and 2-6pm, Sa 9am-noon. **Internet** access €0.50 per 30min.)

ASCHAU. A beautiful mountain town southwest of the Chiemsee, Aschau is positioned on the 410km Bodensee-to-Chiemsee bike route, offering everything from horseback riding to mountain gondola rides, along with tobogganing, skiing, and sailing. Across from the tourist office is the **Kurpark,** where weekly summer concerts are held. Walk 20min. farther down Kampenwandstr. and take a right onto Schloßbergstr. to reach the base of **Schloß Hohenaschau,** built by the Lords Konrad and Arnold von Hirnsberg as an outlook and protection point for the Prien valley in the 12th century. The Renaissance courtyard now hosts summer concerts, and the Holy Trinity Chapel features side altars by **Johann Baptist Zimmermann,** prime artist of Bavarian Rococo. (Obligatory tours May-Sept. Tu-F at 9:30, 10:30, and 11:30am; Apr. and Oct. Th only. Call well in advance for tours in English. €3, children €2.) A museum devoted to the history of the valley is also on the premises; entrance is included in the price of the tour. Just outside Aschau, the **Hochseilgarten,** Am Beerweiher 4, is a wooden **climbing park.** (☎08052 54 60; www.chiemgauerhochseilgarten.de. 3-4hr. with a trainer €48 per person. Call ahead.) The same company offers **rafting** and **canyoning** packages (www.rafting-canyoning.de). To **paraglide,** contact **Flugschule Chiemsee,** Drelindenweg 7, whose intro session is €100. (☎08052 94 94; www.flugschule-chiemsee.de. Call ahead.)

For rooms, your best bet is to get in touch with the helpful tourist office, or try **Gästehaus Kiesmüller ❸,** Burgweg 7. Walk from the castle or Kampenwand Bahn, or take bus #9502. From Kampenwandstr., it's ¼-mile away. Some rooms with alpine views, all with large private bath. (☎08052 21 16. Breakfast included. Open Christmas day-Oct. Singles €30; doubles €52. Reception 7am-7pm. Discounts for more than 3 nights. Cash only.) Most restaurants in Aschau are expensive, though plenty of *gastehaus*-style cottages offer traditional Bavarian food. **Memolino ❷,** Scheibenwandstr. 1, serves delicious Italian food. From train station make a left at sign and walk into the alcove. (☎95 69 43. Thin-crust pizzas €5-12. Open daily 11:30-2:30pm and 5-11pm. Cash only.) The self-service **Angermann SB ❶** cafeteria, Schulstr. 2, has inexpensive food (€4-6) and an attached deli with cheeses and meats. (☎08052 24 55. Open M-F 8am-6pm, Sa deli only from 7:30-noon. Cash only.) **Edeka,** Bahnhofstr. 6, 300 m left of the train station, sells groceries. (Open M-F 8am-8pm, Sa 7:30am-6pm. Cash only.)

From the Munich-Salzburg **train** line, get off at Prien and take the special **Chiemgau Bahn** (15 min.; every hr.; €1.80) from Platform 1a. Buses also run daily from the main street to Grassau and Rosenheim. The **Kampenwand Bahn** gondola takes visitors on a picturesque ride up and down the mountain. You can also ski or make the 2hr. hike down. (☎08052 44 11. Runs daily July-Aug. 9am-6pm €17, ages 5-15 €9; ascent only €12/6.50. May-June and Sept.-Nov. 9am-5pm €14.50/8; Dec.-Apr. 9am-4:30pm €10/5. Discounts before 9:30am or with *Kurkarte.*) Head first to the **tourist office,** Kampenwandstr. 38, 500m from the station. From the train station, take a left on Bahnhofstr., which turns into Kampenwandstr. (☎08052 90 49 37; www.aschau.de. Open mid-May to mid-Oct. M-F 8am-6pm, Sa 9am-noon, Su 10am-noon; mid-Oct. to mid-May M-F 8am-noon and 1:30-5pm.) The **post office** is at Kampenwandstr. 37. (Open M-Sa 9am-noon, M-Tu and Th-F 1:30-4:30pm.)

OTHER TOWNS. Just northwest of the Chiemsee, **Bad Endorf** is famed for its thermal baths; call the **tourist office,** Bahnhofstr. 6., for more information. (☎08053 30 08 22; www.bad-endorf.de. Open M-F 8am-5pm.) **Grassau,** a mountain village known as a health resort, is on the other side of the Kampenwand mountain from Aschau; contact its **tourist office,** Kirchpl. 3, for information. (☎08641 69 79 60; www.grassau.info. Open mid-June to mid-Sept. M-F 8am-noon and 1:30-6pm, Sa 9am-noon; May to mid-June and Oct. M-F 8am-noon and 1:30-5pm, Sa 9am-noon; Nov.-Apr. M-F 8am-noon and 1:30-5pm.) **Rimsting** is a 30min. walk north of Prien, and a great location for exploring the Eggstätter Seeplatte moors. Its **tourist office,** Schulstr. 4, will help you plan your visit. (☎08051 68 76 21; www.rimsting.de. Open June-Sept. daily 8:30am-noon and 1:30-6pm; in Aug. also Sa 10am-noon; Oct.-May M-Th 8:30am-noon and 1:30-4:30pm, F 8:30am-noon.) To reach the tiny town of **Sachrang,** an exquisite alpine village on the Austrian border, take bus #9502 (runs infrequently; consult a bus schedule) from the stop in front of Aschau's train station (free with *Kurkarte*). For more information on excellent skiing, mountain climbing, and walking tours, stop by the **tourist office,** Dorfstr. 20. (☎08057 378; www.sachrang.de. Open May-Oct. M-F 8am-noon and 3-5pm, Sa 10am-noon; Nov.-Apr. M-Tu and Th-F 8am-noon and 3-5pm, W 8am-noon.)

BURGHAUSEN
☎ 08677

The contrast between tiny Burghausen's bland and commercialized Neustadt, where most shops and services are, and the charming medieval Altstadt is only heightened by the imposing castle-fortress, the longest such complex in Europe, that presides over the city. Just across the Salzach River from Austria, Burghausen (pop. 19,000) was a residence of the Wittelsbachs from 1255 to 1503. On the 30min. walk between the ultra-modern train station and the fortress in the Altstadt, you'll become convinced that not a day has passed since the Middle Ages.

📧🛄 TRANSPORTATION AND PRACTICAL INFORMATION. Burghausen is most easily reached by **train** from: Mühldorf (30min., every hr., €6.20); Munich (2hr., every hr., €17.20); Passau (3hr., every 2hr., €22.10). The *Sudost Bayern Ticket* (€11) allows for a day of unlimited travel within southeastern Bavaria after 9am. From the front of the train station, follow Marktlerstr. to the right; it's a 30min. trek to the Altstadt. Or take city bus #1 from the bus station to "Stadtpl." (Every 30min. 6:35am-6:35pm; fewer Sa-Su. €1.) For a **taxi**, call ☎914 20. Rent **bikes** at **Sport Radauer**, Marktlerstr. 5-7. (☎88 13 35. €7 per day. Open M-Sa 8am-noon, 2-6pm.) The **tourist office,** Stadtpl. 112, in the peppermint-green Rathaus at the far end of the Stadtpl., books rooms for free. (☎88 71 40; www.burghausen.de. Open M-F 9am-5pm, Sa 10am-1pm.) To explore the Burghausen area by **boat,** join **Plätten-fahrten** on a 1½hr. tour down the Salzach River on a reconstruction of the medieval wooden boats that transported salt from Bad Reichenhall. Tours leave from the dock at Tittmoning, 18km south of Burghausen, and land at the Salzach dock in Burghausen. A **shuttle bus** (€3.60) runs to Tittmoning from the Stadtpl. stop at 1:05pm, or from the Bahnhof 5min. later. (☎88 71 40. Mid-May to mid-Sept. every Su; Aug. and Sept. occasional weekdays at 2pm. Check the tourist office for scheduled dates. €12, children and disabled persons €6.) Another popular excursion from Burghausen is the **Helmbrecht Pfad,** a 30km bike or walking loop that hits up all the medieval sights of the area and also features informational signs in both modern and medieval German. Ask at the tourist office for maps (in German) of this and other bike and walking routes in the Inn-Salzach area. Exchange your traveler's checks at the **Sparkasse,** Marktlerstr. 15, which has a 24hr. **ATM.** (Open M and Th 9am-noon and 2-5:30pm; Tu-W and F 9am-noon and 2-4:30pm.) The **police** station is located at Marketstr. 67 (☎110, non-emergency 969 10), and the **Stadt-Apotheke pharmacy** is Stadtpl. 40. (Open M-F 8:30am-12:30pm and 2-6pm, Sa 8:30am-noon.) In the Altstadt, **Stadtbibliothek** (library), Stadtpl. 109, just to the left of the tourist office, has **Internet** access for €2 per hr. (☎63 124. Open Tu-F 11am-6pm, Sa 10am-1pm.) Find **Internet** access near the Bahnhof at **Café Liquid,** just off Marktlerstr. 47 in the alcove next to the Edeka. (☎91 34 80. €3.80 per hr. Open M-F 11am-2am, Sa-Su 2pm-2am.) The **post office,** Marktlerstr. 17, is in the Neustadt, between Stadtpl. and the train station. (☎917 20. Open M-F 9am-5pm, Sa 9am-noon.) **Postal Code:** 84489.

📷🍴 ACCOMMODATIONS AND FOOD. The **Jugendherberge Burghausen (HI) ❷,** Kapuzinerg. 235, is close to the café-heavy In den Grüben area. Take city bus #1 from the train station to "Heilige-Geist-Spital." Walk straight and turn left on Kapuzinerg. (15min.). Or from Stadtpl., continue through the arch at the far side of the square on In den Grüben. At the end, cross the intersection to the left of the church onto Spitalg. and turn right on Kapuzinerg. (45min.). Most rooms have impressive views of the castle. (☎41 87; fax 91 13 18. Sheets and breakfast included. Reception 8-10am and 5-7pm. Reservations recommended. €18 per night. AmEx/MC/V.) Only four pensions exist within the city; your best bet is probably the welcoming **Salzburger Hof ❸,** In den Gruben 190. (☎91 10 00, fax 91 10 01.

Singles €35-45; doubles €45-65; triples €75. Cash only.) Private rooms (€20-25, some including breakfast), many on the outskirts of the city, can be found through the tourist office. On the banks of the Salzach, the **Alstadt Café ❷**, Stadtpl. 95, serves open-faced sandwiches (€4.10) and soups (€3) as well as breakfast items. Walk across Stadtpl. and through the tunnel. (☎44 13. Open daily 9am-5pm. Cash only.) For Bavarian dishes, **Hotel Post ❸**, Stadtpl. 39., knows its *Würstchen* after 450 years. (☎96 50. Most meals €7-10. Beer €2.70. Open daily 11:30am-11pm. AmEx/DC/MC/V.) Join local highschoolers at **Sandwich ❶**, Stadtpl. 53, for hamburgers (€1.60) or veggie burgers (€1.50). (☎91 46 34. Open M-Th 7am-2pm and 3pm-7pm, F 7am-2pm. Cash only.) Buy **groceries** at the huge **Edeka,** Marktlerstr. 45, near the Bahnhof. (☎87 57 27. Open M-F 8am-8pm, Sa 7:30am-8pm. Cash only.)

🅶 🅻 **SIGHTS AND ENTERTAINMENT.** The 900-year-old **Burg** extends over 1043m, making it the longest medieval fortress in Europe. Primarily expanded between 1255 and 1503, when the Wittelsbachs were divided into two competing clans, the Burg, together with **Burg Trausnitz** in Landshut, housed the rulers of eastern Bavaria. Considered impregnable, the fort was breached once—in 1742, lacking proper arms or reinforcements, Burghausen opened its gates without a fight to the Habsburg Empire. Days later, the brash 26-year-old *Hofkaminkehrermeister* (Master Chimney Sweep) **Karl Franz Cura** recruited 40 grenadiers, and freed the castle and the city in one fell swoop. These days, everyone can explore the **castle ramparts** after a 10min. scramble up the steep **Hofberg** footpath. The Hofweg starts to the right of **St. Jakobskirche,** a 12th-century church across from the Rathaus (look for the stairs). The grassy park area up the stairs offers a ravishing view of the town's red-tiled roofs and colorful gables. A long series of courtyards leads you to the central, residential fortification. Turn left to find the **Stadtmuseum** (Municipal Museum). Its four floors once comprised the ladies' chambers of the castle, and now display an eclectic mix of clothing, printing presses, and stuffed swans. (☎651 98. Open daily May-Sept. 9am-6:30pm; mid-Mar. to Apr. and Oct. 10am-4:30pm. €2, students and seniors €1.50, under 18 free.) Across the courtyard, the **Staatliche Sammlung** (Public Gallery) combines gigantic medieval artworks with the furniture of the former inhabitants of the Burg. The **St. Elisabeth** chapel, in the same building, has preserved its Gothic elegance. (☎46 59. Open daily Apr.-Sept. 9am-6pm, Th 9am-8pm; Oct.-Mar. 10am-4pm. €3, students €2, children free.) Atop the tower in the Sammlung, gain a wide view of the grassy banks of the **Wöhrsee**—a popular summer swimming spot—far below. The tower's panorama is well worth the 63 steps you'll have to climb to reach it. The eerie **Folterturm** (torture chamber), in the fourth courtyard, was in use until 1918. (Open daily June-Oct. 9am-6pm; Apr.-May daily 10am-5pm; Nov.-Mar. Sa-Su and holidays 11am-4pm. €2, children €0.80.) The **Hexenturm** across the way held accused witches until 1751. At the far end of **Stadtplatz** below stands the magnificent Baroque **Studienkirche St. Joseph,** a 1630 Jesuit convent. Pick up a building-by-building brochure at the tourist office to supplement the signage at the castle. On weekends 1½hr. **tours** are available. (Apr.-Oct. Sa-Su, and public holidays. Meet at 11am and 2pm at the northern entrance of the castle. Available in English, French, German, and Italian.) Every summer on the 2nd weekend in July, the Burg hosts **Burgfest Burghausen,** a medieval romp involving everything from men in leggings brandishing spears to circle dancing, madrigal choirs, and wild boars on spits.

Just upstream of the Stadtpl. is Burghausen's nightspot, In den Grüben, home to most of the town's cafés. Dance clubs center around the train station in the Neustadt. Most cafés, restaurants, and dance clubs open around 7 or 8pm and buzz until midnight. Every spring, In den Grüben hosts **B'Jazz Burghausen,** a jazz festival. Bronze plaques embedded in In den Grüben pay tribute to the masters who have played here. (☎14 11 or www.b-jazz.com for more information.)

BAYERN

LANDSHUT ☎ 0871

The House of Wittelsbach did not always call the Munich Residenz home—Landshut (pop. 60,800), less than an hour from Munich by train, was the main seat of government until 1255. In the 15th century, the Wittelsbach line split for three generations; half of Bavaria was ruled by the Landshut line, and this city on the Isar saw its golden age. The line died out in 1503, but the city is still the capital of Lower Bavaria. Its medieval castle and pastel stucco facades are an ideal setting for the Landshuter Hochzeit, a medieval three-week mid-summer festival with authentic jousting, dancing, and period plays. Celebrated every four years since 1903 (and next in 2009), it re-enacts the magnificent *Hochzeit* (wedding) that Duke Ludwig arranged for his son Georg in 1475.

◩ TRANSPORTATION

Trains run from Landshut to: Munich (1hr., 1-3 per hr., €11.70); Passau (1½hr., every 2hr., €17.60); Regensburg (45min., every hr., €10). To get to town from the station, take any local **bus;** all run to the town center. (€1.60, students €0.90; day pass €3.). Or follow Luitpoldstr. left and across the bridge. Go through the town gates and continue straight on Theaterstr.; turn left on Altstadtstr.; the Rathaus is ahead on the right (25min.). Call a taxi at ☎220 11. Rent **bikes** at **Fahrrad Geißler,** Ländg. 126, one block from the Altstadtstr., behind the Residenz. (☎225 19; €10 a day. Open M-F 8:30am-12:30pm and 1:45-6pm, Sa 9am-1pm.)

◪ PRACTICAL INFORMATION

The **tourist office,** Altstadtstr. 315, in the Rathaus, has free maps of the Altstadt and better ones of the entire city. The staff helps find hotel and private rooms but will not book them. (☎92 20 50; www.landshut.de. Open M-F 9am-5pm, Sa 9am-noon.) Pick up the free *Monatsprogramm* (in German), a monthly pamphlet listing concerts, art shows, dances, and films. **Rosen Apotheke,** Altstadtstr. 339, lists 24hr. **pharmacies.** (☎891 49. Open M-F 8:30am-6pm, Sa 8:30am-2pm.) Check email at the **Internet Café** on Altstadtstr. 362, about two blocks to the left when facing the Rathaus. (€2 per hr. Open daily 9am-1am.) The **post office** is left of the station as you exit. (Open M-F 8:30am-6pm, Sa 8:30am-noon.) **Postal Code:** 84032.

◪ ACCOMMODATIONS

The **Jugendherberge (HI) ❷** is at Richard-Schirrmann-Weg 6. From the tourist office, walk to the left up Altstadtstr., turn left on Alte Bergstr. at the "Burg Trausnitz" sign, and go right on Richard-Schirrmann-Weg. This modern hostel offers simple but comfortable two- to 14-bed dorms with private showers. (☎234 49. Breakfast included. Reception daily 8am-noon and 5-8pm. Closed Dec. 23-Jan. 8. €15.35, with shower €19.85. Multiple nights €14.20/18.40. Cash only.) **Hotel Garni Bergterrasse ❹**, Gerhart-Hauptmann-Str. 1, in the proximity of the Hofgarten (10min. from Altstadt), offers quiet rooms with TV. (☎891 90; www.hotel-bergterrasse.de. Singles €40; doubles €65.) Halfway between the train station and the Altstadt is **Hotel Park Café ❹**, Papiererstr. 36. From the station, walk straight on Luitpoldstr., turn left on Rennweg, and right on Nikolastr. which becomes Papiererstr. (15min.). The hotel has clean rooms with private bath, phone, and cable TV. (☎97 40 00; fax 974 00 40. Breakfast included. Singles €28, with bath €44; doubles €54/67. Cash only.) **Campingplatz Landshut-Mitterwöhr ❶**, Breslauer Str. 122, is on the Isar and has minigolf. From the Rathaus, walk right down Altstadtstr., straight ahead over Heilig-Geist-Brücke, then follow the sidewalk and gravel path directly to the right of the bridge along the river for 20min. At the second bridge, Adenauer-brücke, take stairs up to the street and walk left down Adenauerstr.; turn right onto Breslauer Str. at the camping sign. (☎533 66. Wheelchair accessible. Reception 8am-12:30pm and 3-8pm. Laundry €4.40. €4.50 per person, €2.50 per child, €3 per tent, €5.50 per site. Hot showers and electricity included. Cash only.)

▶ FOOD

Farmers sell produce in the **market** in front of the Rathaus (M-Th and Sa 7am-noon), and Friday on Am Alten Viehmarkt. **Café Cappuccino ❷**, Altstadtstr. 337, near the Rathaus, serves pizzas and pastas (€3-7), salads (€6.50-8), and breakfast. (☎270 92. Open M-Th 9am-midnight, F-Sa 9am-1am, Su 2-6pm. Cash only.) **Weißes Bräuhaus Krenkl ❸**, Altstadtstr. 107, has been serving Bavarian food since 1457. (☎248 01. Entrées €7-12. Beer €2.35. Open daily 9am-midnight. Cash only.) For Asian in the Altstadt, try **My Ly Wok & Sushi Bar ❷**, Ländg. 122. (☎430 42 42. Entrées €5-10. Open M-Sa 11:30am-3pm and 5:30-11pm, Su noon-3pm and 5:30-11pm. Cash only.) **Restaurant Pallas ❸**, Altstadtstr. 191, serves a Greek lunch buffet (M-Sa €6) and other Hellenic specialties. (☎233 33. English menu available. Open M-F 11:30am-2:30pm and 5pm-midnight, Sa-Su 11:30am-midnight. Cash only.)

◉ ♪ SIGHTS AND ENTERTAINMENT

Above the Altstadt sits **Burg Trausnitz,** a hefty brick and red-tiled fortress built in 1204 that can be reached by way of 350-odd steps. The seemingly impenetrable exterior conceals a pleasant courtyard with tiers of yellow arches. The castle was the luxurious abode of the Wittelsbach princes of Bavaria-Landshut until 1503, and its highlight is a tapestry series illustrating how Otto, founder of the Wittelsbach dynasty, gained his title of duke from Barbarossa by flashing his sword all over Italy. His fictional founding of Landshut is included for good measure. The castle interior can only be seen on a German-language tour, but rudimentary written Enligsh translations are available. (☎92 41 10. Open daily Apr.-Sept. 9am-6pm; Oct.-Mar. 10am-4pm. Tours given every 30-45min., last tour 1hr. before closing. €4, students and seniors €3, under 18 free with parent.) Also at the Burg is a new museum, the **Kunst und Wunderkammer** (Art and Wonder Chamber), with exhibits including exotic cartographic instruments. (Same hours, phone, and prices as Burg. Combination ticket €6, students and seniors €5.) The city **Hofgarten,** next to the Burg, offers beautiful views of the city. (Open dawn to dusk. Free.)

In the Altstadt, the world's highest brick church tower reaches a lofty 130m at the **St. Martinkirche.** Outside the church, the bust of architect Hans Burghausen defied the medieval custom of artistic anonymity. (☎922 17 80. Open daily Apr.-Sept. 7:30am-6:30pm; Oct.-Mar. 7:30am-5pm.) Across the street from the Rathaus, the unassuming facade of the **Stadtresidenz** (Town Residence) conceals the only Italian Renaissance-style palace north of the Alps. In the museum upstairs, a collection of regional arts and crafts spans the Bronze Age to the present. (☎922 38 90. Brisk 35min. obligatory German-language tours of the apartments every hr. Tu-Su Apr.-Sept. 9am-5pm; Oct.-Mar. 10am-4pm. English translations available €4, students €3, under 18 free.) At the edge of the Hofgarten park lies the **Skulpturen-museum im Hofberg** (Sculpture Museum), a collection of sculptures by German contemporary artist Fritz Koenig. His partially abstracted human figures are interspersed with an impressive international sculpture collection. (Am Prantlgarten 1. Walk down Kirchg. past St. Martinkirche, then continue on Binderg., turning right at the end. Brown signs lead the way. ☎890 21. Open Tu-Su 10:30am-1pm and 2-5pm. €3.50, students and children €2.)

BAYERISCHER WALD (BAVARIAN FOREST)

A national treasure, the Bavarian Forest is the largest range of wooded mountains in central Europe. The peaks (60 of which are over 1km high) cover 6000sq. km., and numerous creeks and rivers stretch from the Danube to the Austrian and Czech borders. In recent years, an insect known as the *Buchdrucker* (bark beetle) has attacked thousands of trees (be careful of falling branches), allowing new mountain spruce forest to regenerate. The remoteness of the towns discourages most non-German visitors from visiting this year-round paradise of hiking, camping, and cross-country skiing. A dozen **HI youth hostels** dot the forest; Regensburg's tourist office (p. 515) has a helpful brochure with addresses for all of them.

The Bavarian Forest is remarkable not only for its nature. Palaces, churches, and castle ruins hide tucked away in tiny villages. The region is famous for its crafts, particularly glass-blowing. The glass produced here is prized throughout the world, especially the dark green *Waldglas* (forest glass). Every forest town seems to have its own *Glashütte*, and Bavarian tourist officials have designated a 250km long route from Passau through the park as the *Glasstraße* (Glass Road).

BAYERISCHER WALD NATIONAL PARK

Founded in 1970, the **Bayerischer Wald National Park** was the first national park in Germany. Clearly-marked trails lace 59,900 acres of forest in this hiking mecca. The park strictly prohibits any activities that might alter the ecosystem, including camping and building fires, but there are many campsites at the park's edge. The newspaper *Informationsblatt Nationalpark Bayerischer Wald* gives the latest forest news, *Grenzenlose Waldwildnis* is a free park map, and *Ihre Gastgeber* lists accommodations in towns within the park and on its borders. All brochures are available in park centers and area tourist offices.

BAYERISCHER WALD NATIONAL PARK AT A GLANCE	
AREA: 240sq. km.	**FEATURES:** Lush forests, dramatic mountain peaks.
CLIMATE: Snowy winters; warm, sunny springs and autumns; cool summers. Precipitation year-round.	**GATEWAYS:** Grafenau (p. 498) and Zwiesel (p. 498).
HIGHLIGHTS: Extensive, well-kept hiking and biking trails; vivid fall foliage; excellent cross-country skiing.	**CAMPING:** Strictly forbidden within the park, although available nearby.
	FEES: None.

■ ■ TRANSPORTATION AND ORIENTATION

A series of open roadways run through the park, and many of the trailheads can be reached by car. Public transportation within the park is also very good. The environmentally friendly *Igelbusse* (hedgehog buses) of **RBO** *(Regionalbus Ostbayern)* run from Grafenau, Neuschönau, and Spiegelau to places in the park. The **Bayerwald Ticket** (€6) allows unlimited travel on **buses** and **trains** within the park for one day. Your best bet is to pick the trails you want to cover and have one of the tourist offices tell you the precise connections to take. The park is located in east-central Bavaria, bordering the Czech Republic's Bohemian Forest National Park on the east. It stretches from Mauth in the south to Bayerisch Eisenstein in the north. Zwiesel is outside the western border of the park in the north, while Grafenau lies to the southwest. Ninety-eight percent of the park is forested, and

Bayerischer Wald National Park (Bavarian Forest National Park)

○ HIKING TRAILS
Felswandergebiet, **13**
Kleiner und Großer
  Falkenstein, **3**
Racheltour, **6**
Rundweg Luchs-Lusen, **11**
Rundweg im Tier-Freigelände, **12**

Seelensteig, **8**
Waldspielgelände, **9**

● BIKING TRAILS
Großer Falkenstein, **2**
Nationalparkradweg, **5**
Regentalradweg, **4**

ACCOMMODATIONS
Bayerisch Eisenstein, **1**
Bischofsmais, **7**
Frauenau, **10**

the three most important (and hike-able) peaks within its borders are the **Lusen** (1373m), on the Czech border directly north of Neuschönau; the **Großer Rachel** (1453m), in the middle of the park; and the **Großer Falkenstein** (1315m), in the northernmost section of the park. The entire area is etched with extensive hiking trails, and biking is more common in the northern regions.

② PRACTICAL INFORMATION

Emergency: Police ☎ 110. **Ambulance** ☎ 192 22.

Information Offices: There are 4 within the park, in addition to the administrative offices located in Grafenau.

◪ **Informationszentrum Hans-Eisenmann-Haus,** Böhmstr. 35, 94556 Neuschönau (☎08558 961 50; www.nationalpark-bayerischer-wald.de). From Grafenau (p. 498), take Igelbus #7594 *(Lusen-Bus)* from stop 4 in front of the station to "Nationalpark Infozentrum" (approx. every hr. 8am-5pm). The Hans-Eisenmann-Haus is across the street. Exhibits, free pamphlets, a 20min. film (in English upon request), and *Wanderkarten* (hiking maps; €5.60). The *Südl Teil* (South Part) is for hiking in the area of the Haus, the *Nördl Teil* (North Part) for hikes to the north. Open mid-Jan. to mid-Mar. daily 9am-4pm, mid-Mar. to Oct. daily 9am-5pm. Buses run mid-May to Oct.

Erlebniszentrum Haus zur Wildnis, Ludwigsthal, 94227 Lindberg (☎09922 500 20). Open Jan.-Oct. daily 9am-5pm.

Infostelle Spiegelau, Konrad-Wilsdorf-Str. 1, 94518 Spiegelau (☎08553 960 017). Open Jan.-Oct. M-Th 8am-5pm, F 9am-3:30pm, Aug. to mid-Sept. also Sa 9-11am.

Infostelle Mauth, Mühlweg 2, 94151 Mauth (☎08557 97 38 38). Open Jan.-Oct. M-F 9am-5pm, Su 9am-noon.

Nationalparkverwaltung Bayerischer Wald, Freyunger Str. 2, 94481 Grafenau (☎08552 960 00; fax 08552 960 01 00). The park's administrative offices. Open M-Th 7:45am-noon and 1-4pm, F 7:45am-noon.

Tours: Guided hikes leave daily from the Hans-Eisenmann Haus (see above); contact them a day in advance to book a tour (€3 per person). The free seasonal *Führungen und Veranstaltungen* brochure, available at park info centers, lists tour times and themes. Most tours in German, with occasional offerings in English.

Gear: Rent bikes from **Radsport Leitl** (p. 498) in Zwiesel or from **Radsportshop de Graaf** (p. 498) in Grafenau. **Intersport Fuchs** (p. 498) in Grafenau rents skis.

Climate and Seasonality: The park is open and accessible year-round. Precipitation is heavy, and winter is very snowy, with only select trails cleared by the park service for cross-country skiing. Summer is relatively cool and moist, with frequent thunderstorms. Spring, which starts in May (snow remains until Apr.), and autumn (with its brilliant leaves) are warm and sunny. Sept. and Oct. are ideal times to visit. Vegetation is primarily coniferous forest at higher elevations, mixed forest at lower elevations.

◪ ACCOMMODATIONS

Camping is forbidden on park lands, but several designated camping areas cluster just beyond its borders. The single youth hostel in the park, located at Waldhäuser, is only open to school groups. Those wishing to stay in the park itself should stay at one of two privately-owned mountain huts, available to overnight hikers (call ahead for reservations). **Lusenschutzhaus** is near the 1373m peak of Mt. Lusen in the southern section of the park. (☎08553 12 12. Open May-Oct., Dec. 25-Jan. 6). **Falkensteinhaus** is 1315m up the Großer Falkenstein in the northern reaches of the park. (☎09925 90 33 66. Open May-Oct., Dec. 26-Jan. 6, weekends Jan.-May.) On free park maps, these huts are marked by a white house with a window and door. This is the same symbol given to huts where only food is available, so check beforehand. Most trails through the park pass a restaurant or *Gaststätte* (tavern) every hour or so. Other hostels at the fringes of the park are great starting points:

Frauenau, Haus St. Hermann, Hauptstr. 29 (☎0992 67 35). From Frauenau, hike around the beautiful *Trinkwassertalsperre*, a water reservoir in the middle of the park. Sheets €2.80. 12-bed rooms €9.10, with breakfast €12.25. Cash only. ❶

Bayerisch Eisenstein (HI), Brennesstr. 23 (☎0992 53 77). Germany's highest youth hostel (1330m) is convenient for hikes around the Arber mountains. Breakfast and sheets included. Reception 8am-1pm and 5-7pm. 4- to 6-bed rooms €14-16. MC/V. ❶

Bischofsmais, Oberbreitenau 1 (☎0992 02 55). Discover the busy (and touristy) streets of Bischofsmais, or take a 2hr. hike to *Teufelstisch* (Devil's Table). Breakfast and sheets included. Reception 10am-6pm. 3- to 4-bed rooms €15. Cash only. ❶

◪ HIKING

The hiking trails around the park are marked with a care that borders on obsession. All intersections are signposted and popular trails have inlaid wooden maps every 500m and color-coded signs every 100m. Trails with yellow signs are loops, and those with white markers lead from one trailhead to another. Guided hikes leave daily from the **Hans-Eisenmann-Haus** (p. 495). To explore the park on foot, pick up a *Wanderkarte* (hiking map).

Kleiner und Großer Falkenstein (10km, 4-5hr. round-trip). In the northern section; take the bus from Zwiesel or Ludwigsthal to "Zwieslerwaldhaus." From the Falkenstein parking lot, follow the white signs of a branch adorned with 2 bells for a 2½hr. climb past a lovely waterfall, then over Kleiner Falkenstein (with the hike's best view) and on to the top of its larger brother. Return either via same route or via another trail; buses also run from Ludwigsthal, Lindbergmühle, and Spiegelhütte. Steep in places.

Rundweg im Tier-Freigelände (7km. loop, 3-4hr.). A fun hike from the Hans-Eisenmann-Haus. Yellow signs mark this flat loop leading through a unique zoo: along the trail, animals such as brown bears, lynx, and wolves roam enclosures resembling their natural habitat. Carved wooden signs clarify strange German animal names. In the wild swine quarters, mama and baby pigs overrun the trail alongside the tourists.

Racheltour (4hr. round-trip). From Spiegelau, take the Rachel Bus to "Gfäll." Follow the marked bird symbols past the Liesl-fountain and the *Waldschmidthaus* (which serves beer). From there, it's a short final uphill trek to the highest peak in the entire park. Descent passes the *Rachelkapelle,* with views of the *Rachelsee* (with a 100m spur leading to the water's edge), and ends at the *Racheldiesthütte,* which offers food and a bus back down.

Felswandergebiet (2hr. round-trip). From the Hans-Eisenmann-Haus, take the Finsterau Bus to "Jugendwaldheim." Cross the street and follow the yellow signs depicting a bird with a spotted chest. Hike curves up through the rocky hilltops to outlook points on top of the Kanzel mountains from which, on a clear day, you may see the Alps, or be able to peer west over the former Iron Curtain into the Czech Republic. Can also be reached via a pleasant hike by following the white signs with 3 trees on them and arrows to "Felswandergebiet" from the Hans-Eisenmann-Haus parking lot.

Rundweg Luchs-Lusen (4km loop, 2½hr.). Lace up your boots and climb one of the highest peaks in the park. From Grafenau, take the bus past the Hans-Eisenmann-Haus to end of the line at the Lusen parking lot. From there, follow the yellow signs with the lynx (wildcat) picture. About 300m past the gorgeous view from granite outcroppings, the Lusenschutzhaus serves food to hungry hikers.

Waldspielgelände (1hr. round trip, plus playtime on the ziplines and see-saws). A non-looping trail with a series of playgrounds and physical challenges every 100m, starting in Spiegelau. Family-friendly.

◼ BIKING

Many trails are also accesible by **bike**; signs at the start indicate whether or not wheels are allowed. Pick the **Radwander- und Mountainbikekarte** in tourist offices in neighboring towns to check out bike trails in the park. Routes marked in purple are recommended only for fit folks with mountain bikes.

The Nationalparkradweg (100km) is the main trail through the forest, running southeast from Zwiesel and curving up to cross the Czech border. Accessible from Waldbahn-linked towns Bayerisch Eisenstein, Zwiesel, and Spiegelau, as well as towns on the Finsterau Igelbus line between Spiegelau and Finsterau.

The Regentalradweg, accessible from Bayerische Eisenstein, good for leisurely biking, follows the course from the Regen to Regensburg.

The Großer Falkenstein is circled by a 50km trail for fit bikers. Good beginning and/or endpoints are the train stations in Zwieselau, Zwiesel, or Ludwigsthal.

◢ WINTER ACTIVITIES

The park's main wintertime activity is cross-country skiing, which can be done on many of the hiking trails, making for a total of about 80km of skiing trails. The *Nationalparkgemeinde Neuschönau, Winter* map (free at the Hans-Eisenmann Haus) and the *Grafenau Winterland* maps show winter trails for both hiking and skiing. Ask at the Hans-Eisenmann-Haus for info on guided skiing tours.

GRAFENAU
☎ 08552

Just west of the national park, easily accessible Grafenau (pop. 83,000) is an ideal place to begin excursions on the web of hiking trails that laces the park's southern half. While there, visit the gorgeous Kurgarten behind the Rathaus.

To find the bright, friendly rooms of **Pension Tauscher ❷**, at Stifterstr. 22., take a right out of the tourist office, make another right on Freyungerstr., and a left when it forks onto Stifterstr. (☎ 626; www.pension-tauscher.de. Breakfast included. Singles €20; doubles €40, less after 3 nights. Cash only.) **Bäckerei Konditerei café Manzenberger ❶**, Am Stadtpl. 17, on the left side of the Stadtpl., is a typical bakery (Open M-F 6:30am-6pm, Sa 6:30am-noon. Cash only.) The **Edeka Activ Markt,** Spitalstr. 32, is a **grocery** store. Follow the Stadtpl. down the hill from Kröllstr. and take a left when it intersects with Spitalstr. Walk past the post office and through the underpass; it will be on your right. (Open M-F 8am-6:30pm, Sa 8am-2pm. Cash only.) After a long day in the woods, feast on salads, pizzas, meat and fish (€7-9) at **Café-Restaurant Fox ❸**, Stadtpl. 3. (☎ 92 03 77. Open daily M-F 8am-midnight, Sa 9am-midnight, Su 10am-midnight. Cash only.)

The village is the last stop on the special **Waldbahn** (forest train) line from Zwiesel (50min., every 2-3hr., €6 with the *Bayerwald* ticket) and can also be reached from Munich (€18 with the Bayern ticket) or Passau (3hr., €18). Within Grafenau, the **city bus** runs from the train station to town (€1, ages 5-15 €0.50). **Radsportshop de Graaf**, Rosenauerstr. 20, Grafenau, rents **bikes** 15min. from Stadtpl. (☎ 36 04 Open M-F 9am-12:30pm and 2-6pm, Sa 9am-1pm.) **Intersport Fuchs,** Hauptstr. 16, Grafenau, rents skis and snowshoes. (☎ 14 36. Open M-F 9am-6pm, Sa 9am-1pm.) Once in Grafenau, walk left out of the train station until you reach the **Stadtpl.** (200m). Walk across the square and take a left, then follow the signs to the right to reach the friendly **tourist office** in the back of the Rathaus, which books rooms for free and conducts free guided hikes every Tuesday at 11am. (☎ 96 23 43; www.grafenau.de. Open in summer M-Th 8:30am-4:30pm, F 8:30am-1pm, Sa 10-11:30am.) A computer outside lists available rooms and contacts prospective hosts for late arrivals. Other services include: **VR-Bank,** 100m to the left as you exit the train station, with a 24hr. **ATM.**; the **Marien-Apotheke pharmacy,** Stadtpl. 10 (☎ 35 38; open M-F 8am-6pm, Sa 8am-noon); and the **post office,** Spitalstr. 7. (☎ 97 43 81. Open M-F 8:30am-noon and 2-5pm, Sa 9-11:30am.) **Postal Code:** 94481.

ZWIESEL
☎ 09922

The abundance of its train connections and its proximity to the park makes Zwiesel (pop. 10,500) an excellent gateway to the Bavarian Forest. A skier's paradise in the winter, in summer the town highlights its 600-year history of glass-making. Summer nights heat up with the Grenzlandfest (Frontier Fest), held in mid-July.

🖪🚆 TRANSPORTATION AND PRACTICAL INFORMATION. Trains run every hour to **Munich** (3hr., €27) and **Plattling** (1hr., €9.10). City **buses** run 1 per hr. M-F 7:58am-5:58pm, Sa 7:58-11:58am. Tickets are €0.80 or free with a €1.30 *Kurkarte*, which should be given to you after a one-night stay. The Stadtlinie bus runs to the Stadtpl. from just outside the station. Rent **bikes** at **Radsport Leitl,** Theresienthaler-str. 25, Zwiesel, around the corner from the Bahnhof. (☎ 80 21 57. Touring bikes €5 per day, mountain bikes €10. Open M-F 8:30am-noon and 2-6pm, Sa 8:30am-noon.) The **tourist office,** Stadtpl. 27, in the Rathaus, is an ideal place to start a visit to the **forest** or the **Glas Park;** it provides maps and information on hiking and biking tours and finds private rooms for free. To get there from the train station, turn right and walk downhill on Dr.-Schott-Str. Bear left, cross the bridge, turn left after the Greek restaurant and head up through the Stadtpl.; the **Rathaus** is on the left.

(☎84 05 23; www.zwiesel-tourismus.de. Open M-F 8:30am-5:30pm, Sa 10am-noon, Nov.-Christmas M-F 9am-5pm.) Find **Internet** access at **Café Flair**, Dr.-Schott-Str. 18 (see **Food**). The **post office**, Stadtpl. 18-20, is across from the tourist office in the Edeka complex. (Open M-F 8am-6pm, Sa 8am-1pm). **Postal Code:** 94227.

🏠 **ACCOMMODATIONS.** Zwiesel has no youth hostel, but groups can opt for **Arbeiterwohlfahrt (AWO)** ❶, Karl-Herold-Str. 9, which offers fully furnished apartments and small houses 15min. from the town center. Walk left from the train station and make a left at the pedestrian walkway. Cross the tracks and continue straight on Waldesruhweg; where it curves left, go straight onto Karl-Herold-Str; AWO is on the left. (☎9175; www.awo-zwiesel.de. Reception daily 7am-5pm. 3- to 7-person dwellings €28-54 per night. *Kurtaxe* and additional cleaning charges not included. Cash only.) Located between the train station and Stadtpl., **Haus Lederer** ❷, Jägerg. 4, has three beautiful rooms with wood-paneled ceilings and a lovely veranda. Make a right out of the train station and a left on nearby Holzweberstr. Cross Fachschulstr. and cross the pedestrian bridge over the river. Continue onto Jagerg.; the pension is on the left. (☎92 46. Breakfast included. Singles €16. Doubles €32. Cash only.) Run by friendly English-speakers, the 35-bed **Pension Keilhofer** ❷, Hindenburgstr. 28, has exercise equipment, and TV in every room, From the Stadtpl., walk uphill and make a right on Frauenauerstr. Continue past the Busbahnhof and make a left on Hindenburgstr. The pension is on the right, just after Böhmerwaldstr. (☎30 37. Breakfast included. Singles €24. Doubles €44. Less for longer stays. Cash only.) Though large and commercial, **Azur-Camping Zwiesel** ❶, Waldesruhweg 34, is easily accessible from the train station, with mini-golf, volleyball, a playground, and a restaurant. (☎80 25 95; www.azur-camping.de/zwiesel. Reception M-Sa 8am-1pm and 3-6pm, Su 9am-1pm and 3-6pm. €5-7 per adult, €3.50-5.50 per child ages 2-12, €5.50-8.50 per campsite. Cash only.)

🍴 **FOOD.** A year-round **open-air market** convenes in the parking lot behind the Rathaus (Sa 7am-noon). **Edeka**, at Stadtpl. 18-20, sells **groceries.** (Open M-F 9am-7pm, Sa 8am-4pm. Cash only.) For Bavarian meals, try **Gasthaus zum Kirchenwirt** ❸, Bergstr. 1, which offers dishes like *Schweinbraten* (pig roast with *sauerkraut*) for €6-11, and free folk music Tu and Th at 8pm. (☎25 70. Open daily 11am-1am. Cash only.) Zwiesel's younger crowd heads to **Café Flair** ❷, Dr.-Schott-Str. 18, where every salad (€6-7) comes

THE LOCAL STORY

CAST IN GLASS

Glassmaking in Zwiesel dates to the 15th century. The region, also rich in potash, wood, and fuel glass ovens, continues to produce some of the world's finest glass. Ralph Hantich, a third-generation glassblower, reflects on the craft of glassblowing and the transformations reshaping his industry.

On being a glassmaker: I went to glass school and spent three years. I think the hardest job is the blowing, because you have to stay at a 1200°C oven. At the moment, it is very hard to get young people to do this job.

The material itself is fascinating—you'll never stop working with it if you get a special feeling for it.

On the future of glassblowing in Zwiesel: Now, location doesn't really matter. Factories are here because Zwiesel is known for glass, but it could easily be done in some other place. We have moved the 'hot' part of the production to Poland because of costs, and the clear glass comes here for decoration.

The biggest change in the past 30 years has been the development of automatic production, since before 30 years ago thin stems were not possible by machine. Now, China makes more quality work as the technical know-how arrives. The Chinese do the same work at one-tenth the price, which is a big problem for the business.

GIVING BACK

IT'S BAAAACK!

When it comes to meat, Germans know only one word: tradition. From *Wurst* to *Schnitzel*, the German meat lover's palate rarely extends beyond beef and pork.

But in the Altmühltal region of central Bavaria, a group of shepherds and environmentalists is bringing lamb into the mix. The Altmühltaler Lamm project, begun in 1997, encourages visitors to the Nature Park to eat lamb in order to keep shepherding economically viable and, by extension, to preserve the unique natural landscape that developed from human interaction with the existing forest.

When settlers came to the area in the Middle Ages, they cut down trees and brought in sheep, which ate all of the vegetation except juniper. As juniper grew dominant, a host of interesting animals and plants not usually found in Germany began to flourish here. Without the sheep, native plants would again overtake the juniper, driving some of these unusual flora and fauna from the area.

To keep local shepherds in business—and their sheep in the park—restaurants in the area prepare variety of dishes, from lamb gyros to filets. Their sheep are free range and organically fed, making the quality of their meat exceptional. Because the project's major selling point is the quality and social impact of the meat, it can be costly. Ask in any local tourist office for the local lamb specialist.

with its own flaming sparkler. Woven vinyl chairs mix well with leopard prints. (☎ 50 07 98. Internet access €3 per hr. 18+. Open daily 10am-1am. Cash only.) Above the Stadtpl., the **Stadt Café,** Stadtpl. 18-20, has an outdoor terrace, a sharp contrast to the elderly-diner feel inside. Salads and light meals €4-7. (☎ 29 72. Open M-Sa 9am-7pm, Su 10am-7pm.)

◪ **SIGHTS.** Just north of town is the **Glas Park Theresienthal,** with a museum of glass objects and several shops. The real reason to go is to peer behind-the-scenes into the factory. After getting a ticket at the museum, head down the gravel road to the big yellow house to see glass-blowers at work: no fences, no signs. (€2, children €1. Open M-F 10am-2pm. Buses shuttle to the Glas Park from the Stadtpl. M-F 11 per day from 8:30am; last return 6:30pm. €0.80.) The **Waldmuseum** (Forest Museum), Stadtpl. 27, behind the Rathaus, tells the tinkly tale of glass-making and teaches about everyday life in the forest. (☎ 608 88. Open mid-May to mid-Oct. M-F 9am-5pm, Sa-Su 10am-noon and 2-4pm; mid-Oct. to mid-May M-F 10am-noon and 2-5pm, Sa-Su 10am-noon; closed Nov. €2.50, students €1.)

ALTMÜHLTAL NATURE PARK

Spread over 3000 sq. km. of central Bavaria, the Altmühltal Nature Park follows the curve of the Altmühl river from the Altmühlsee through the river's merger with the Main-Donau-Kanal and on to Kelheim. Cyclists, hikers, kayakers, and climbers flock to this teeming rural valley, known for its impressive cliffs and fossil finds. Home to many adventure-friendly establishments, Eichstätt, the largest city, is the perfect jumping-off point for trips into the preserve.

◪ **PRACTICAL INFORMATION.** A car is not necessary to reach points on the Altmühl River, since a **railway** cuts across the park from Gunzenhausen to Ingolstadt, and the other part is covered by the **FreizeitBus** system, which connects Eichstätt and Riedenburg on weekdays and Riedenburg and Regensburg on weekends (day pass €6, with bike €9). The **Informationszentrum Naturpark Altmühltal,** Notre Dame 1, is cloistered in a former monastery downtown. To get there, walk through the Residenzpl. and take a right on Ostenstr. and then your first left; it's 200m up on the right. The center has exhibits on the natural and cultural history of the area, German-language **nature tours** (€2, children €0.50) on Thursdays in July and August, and other programming in the summer months; inquire for dates and times. (☎987 60; www.naturpark-altmuehltal.de. Open Easter to mid May and mid-Sept. to Oct. M-Sa 9am-5pm, Su 10am-5pm; mid-May to mid-Sept. daily until 6pm; Nov.-Easter M-Th 8am-noon and 2-4pm, F 8am-noon.) For information on everything from movie theaters to beach volleyball in the preserve, grab a copy of *Freizeit Tipps von A bis Z*. The information center will help English-speakers navigate the publications, many of which feature special English inlay sheets explaining common terms and symbols.

⌂ ACCOMMODATIONS. The Altmühltal Nature Park is strewn with little towns offering a wide range of establishments. While the area is rural, tourism is well established and private rooms are available for rent most everywhere. Be sure to pick up the *Gastgeberverzeichnis*, with about 600 accommodations listings, and the yellow camping brochure at the info center for a list of accommodations in the preserve. Most **camping ❶** is available right along the river for the convenience of boaters and bikers on the Altmühltal-Radweg; prices range €3.50-7.50 per person including tent. Boaters can also set up camp at various docks along the way for €3-5 per night per tent; look for signs along the river or pick up the yellow *Bootwandern* brochure for a list of locations.

⚠❄ OUTDOOR ACTIVITIES. Within the preserve, the primary activities of choice are biking and canoeing, and new hiking trails are currently being developed. Of the 800km of paved and well-maintained **bike paths**, the 160km **Altmühltal-Radweg**, which snakes along the river and runs straight through the middle of Eichstätt, is the most popular. The new 200km **Altmühltal-Panoramaweg** is a hillier, narrower trail for hikers and bikers along the river, passing the famous **12 Apostles** rock formation. **Bikes** can be rented all over the park. In Eichstätt, try **Fahrradgarage**, Herzogg. 3, in the alley between Marktpl. and the footbridge. (☎21 10; www.fahrradgarage.de. €8 per day. Open daily 9am-7pm.) The free *Bayernnetz für Radler* map and the yellow *Radwandern* brochure will help you navigate. Another good resource is the *Freizeit* map (€1), which gives trail information. Wide brown signs with a picture of a bike mark all trails except the Altmühltal-Radweg, marked by white signs and a cyclist logo. Fahrradgarage can also outfit you with **canoes** for a trip down the river (€26 per boat per day), and **Glas Booteverleih**, Industriestr. 18, rents canoes and **kayaks**. (☎30 55. M-F €10 per day, Sa-Su €12; under 16 20% off. Transport to the river €24-50. Call ahead. Open Apr.-Oct. daily 9am-6pm.) The tranquil Altmühl is generally very safe, especially if you stay to the right at the small rapids along the way. Inexperienced boaters should avoid Töging, where the river merges with the Main-Donau-Kanal and becomes more dangerous. Two major **tour** companies offer biking, hiking, canoeing, and kayaking excursions in the preserve, with guides, baggage transfer, bike rental and pick-up, and boat transport for longer trips. **San-aktiv-TOURS**, Bühringer Str. 11, in Gunzenhausen, offers six-day hiking trip on the Altmühltal-Panoramaweg for €299. (☎09831 49 36; www.san-aktiv-tours.de.) **NATOUR**, Gänswirtshaus 12, in Weißenburg, runs five-day cycling trips for €369. (☎09141 92 29 29; www.natour.de.) Altmühltal also offers extensive **hiking** and **rock-climbing** options. Pick up a Mittleres Altmühltal hiking map (€6.60) to help you navigate the trails around Eichstätt; paths are marked with yellow signs. Most good climbing is to the east of Eichstätt near the town of Dollnstein; consult the free yellow *Klettern* brochure (in German). For **horseback riding**, contact the Geyer family (☎994 64). The preserve is also a great place to try amateur **paleontology.** The Altmühl river valley was covered by a Jurassic tropical sea 150 million years ago and is now littered with fossil-rich limestone deposits. A prime location for digging is the open **Steinbruch** (Quarry) right outside of Eichstätt. To get there, take the bus from the Dompl. (in front of the Raiffeisenbank) to "Kinderdorf" (€2 round-trip, children €1.30). Beware—bus schedules vary greatly; you might want to bring a map along to navigate the 20min. walk back to town. At the quarry, you can visit a museum displaying striking fossils and minerals, or you can rent tools and look yourself. (Museum open year-round. Equipment €1.50. Tool rental kiosk ☎0160 72 53 309, open daily mid-Apr. to June and mid-Sept. to mid-Oct. 9:30am-5pm; June to mid-Sept. 9:30am-6pm.) The new 9km **Fossilienpfand** (Mineralogy Trail) departs from Eichstätt's train station and provides an overview of fossils and minerals in the area. Inquire at the park's information center or Eichstätt's tourist office.

EICHSTÄTT ☎ 08421

Pastel-colored 17th-century buildings, imposing churches, and a hilltop castle are the remnants of the once-mighty bishopric of Eichstätt (pop. 13,000), a gorgeous Baroque town that lies at the center of the massive Altmühltal Nature Park, on the margins of Franconia, Swabia, and Bavaria. The pilgrims who once flocked here have been replaced by droves of outdoorsy Germans who use Eichstätt as a home base for exploring the park on walks, hikes, and bike trails. The 160km Altmühltal Radweg is one of the most scenic bike routes in Germany. Home to the only Catholic university in the country, the 4000 students studying here help keep the old city running at a faster pace.

◪◪ TRANSPORTATION AND PRACTICAL INFORMATION. Eichstätt has two train stations. **Trains** run to Eichstätt-Bahnhof from Ingolstadt (20min., every hr., €4.60) and Nuremberg (1¼hr., every hr., €14.70). From Eichstätt-Bahnhof, another train takes you the last 5km to the Eichstätt-Stadt station closer to town (9min., 2 per hr., €1.30). The friendly **tourist office,** Dompl. 8, gives free **tours** of the old city (Sa 1:30pm), sells maps (€0.50) and event tickets, and books rooms for a €1.50 fee. Get off the train, walk through the station, turn right, and bear left across the Spitalbrücke; you'll see signs for the tourist office, which will be on the left. Ask about hiking opportunities. (☎600 14 00; www.eichstaett.de. Open Apr.-Oct. M-Sa 9am-6pm, Su 10am-1pm; Nov.-Mar. M-Th 10am-noon and 2-4pm, F 10am-noon.) Get money or exchange traveler's checks at **Sparkasse,** Gabrielistr. 5, just off Marktpl. (☎60 40. Open M-Th 8:30am-4:30pm; F 8am-3pm.) A convenient **pharmacy** is **Dom-Apotheke,** Dompl. 16. (☎15 20. Open M-F 8am-6pm, Sa 8am-noon.) Check email at **Internet-Café Mocca,** Westenstr. 32, off Marktpl. (☎90 75 40. €3 per hr. Open daily noon-11pm.) The **post office** is at Dompl. 7. (Open M-F 8:30am-6pm, Sa 9am-noon.) **Postal Code:** 85072.

◪◪ ACCOMMODATIONS AND FOOD. Well appointed rooms off marble hallways and a rose garden occupy a former monastery at the **Gästehaus der Benediktinerinnenabtei ❸,** Walburgiberg 6. From the train station, turn left on Freiwasserstr. and then make a right on Herzogsteg.; cross the bridge and make a left on Westenstr. Turn right after Internet-Café Mocca; follow the steep hill past the church; it's on the left. (☎98 870; www.bistum-eichstaett.de. Reception 8am-

8pm. Breakfast included. Kitchen facilities. Singles €34, doubles €56. Cash only.) Eichstätt's **Jugendherberge (HI)** ❷, Reichenaustr. 15, is modern and comfortable. Follow directions to Willibaldsburg (see **Sights,** p. 503), but turn right halfway up Burgstr. on Reichenaustr. The hostel is 200m down the street on your left. (☎98 04 10; www.eichstaett.jugendherberge.de. Breakfast included. Wash €1.50. Dry €1.50. Reception 8-9am and 5-7pm. Curfew 10pm, access code available for those over 18. Closed Dec.-Jan. 4- to 10-bed dorms €16.25, 2-3 nights €15.65, 4+ nights €15.10. MC/V.) **Haus Kirschner** ❷, Elias-Holl-Str. 27, is a small, welcoming pension 10min. farther down the street. Follow Reichenaustr. past the hostel; it becomes Elias-Holl-Str. (☎54 42; fax 90 22 07. Singles €17; doubles €30. Cash only.) The **Gasthof Ratskeller** ❸, Kardinal-Preysing-Pl. 8/10, a 5min. walk from the station, is slightly more expensive but has shower and TV in every room. Follow directions to the tourist office, but turn right after crossing the Spitalbrücke. Walk through the Residenzpl. and turn right on Leonrodpl. Turn left on Kardinal-Preysing-Pl.; the hotel is 20m ahead on your right in a white building with pink trim. (☎90 12 58; www.ratskeller-eichstaett.de. Reception until 10pm; enter through restaurant or ring the bell on the steps outside after hours or on W. Breakfast included. Singles €32; doubles €52. Cash only.) Campers head to the **Wohnmobil und Zeltplatz der Stadt Eichstätt** ❶, 20min. out of town on the city's Volksfestpl. by the river. Follow Ostenstr. and make a right at Wiesengäßchen just after the Schutzengelkirche. Walk on the pedestrian lane until it meets the bike trail; make a left and walk past the university gardens, staying along the river (10min.); it's on the left. (☎90 81 47. Staffed from Apr.-Oct., but open year-round. RV area closed the last week of Aug. and the 1st week of Sept. €6 per tent and RV, free Nov.-Mar. Electricity €2 per day. Free showers. Cash only.)

Netto Marken-Discount, Buchtal 30, has cheap **groceries.** (☎24 69. Open M-Sa 8am-8pm. Cash only.) **Manolo** ❷, Koplingerstr. 1, on top of the hill leading to the Burg, has nightly specials and tasty food served in a sleek interior or outdoor terrace. (☎90 93 53. Salads €5-7. Pastas €4.80-8. W casino night. Th ladies' night (free mixed drinks). F Happy hour 6-8pm and 11:30pm-1am. Open M-Th and Su 6pm-1am, F-Sa 6pm-2 or 3am. Cash only.) **La Grotta** ❷, in back of Marktpl. 13, offers pizzas and pasta (€4-7) on its patio. (☎72 80. Open daily 11am-2:30pm and 5-11pm; no lunch in winter. MC/V.) **Desperado** ❷, Marktg. 9, has Tex-Mex food in a tiny street off the Marktpl. Dig into a plate of nachos or a pizza (€4-5) at one of the large wooden tables. (Happy hour daily 7-8pm and 11:30pm-12:30am. Mixed drinks €3.50. Open M-Th and Su 7pm-1am, F-Sa 7pm-2am. Cash only.) **Walburgis Restaurant** ❸, on Westenstr. 29 off the Marktpl., serves Croatian cuisine from the grill for €8-12. Their lunch menu (M-F) has eight choices for around €7. (☎14 18. Open daily 11am-2:30pm and 5pm-midnight. Cash only.) To get to the **Mensa** ❶, in the Universität, which serves €2-4 meals, follow Ostenstr. past the Schutzengelkirche and continue for about 5min., turn right on Universitätsallee and look for a *Mensa* sign 100m ahead; the cafeteria is downstairs. (☎09131 800 20. Open M-Th 8:15am-7pm, F 8:15am-3pm; school holidays M-F 8:15am-2:45pm. Mensa cards require €10 upfront, including a €4.10 deposit.)

◙ SIGHTS. The **Willibaldsburg,** Burgstr. 19, the former residence of the local bishops, now hosts two museums. To reach the castle, walk out the back of the train station and over the tracks to Weißenburgerstr. Cross the street, bear right, and then take a quick left on Burgstr.; follow around the bend and continue on the pedestrian path, then through the tunnel. The 14th-century *Burg,* designed to dominate the city, was given its present look by the same architect who later built the famous Rathaus in Augsburg. Inside, the **Juramuseum** (Jurassic Museum) is filled with large tanks of rare tropical fish and coral, as well as Jurassic Period fossils from the Altmühltal Valley, which was once covered by a vast prehistoric sea.

Ten Archaeopteryx—primitive birds whose fossils were first discovered here—are on display. Be sure not to miss the Jutavenator Starki, a small carnivorous specimen and the most beautifully preserved dinosaur in Europe. At the entrance, climb up 98 winding steps to the top of the tower to see the city from above (closes daily at 5:45pm). The **Museum für Ur- und Frühgeschichte** (Early History Museum), also in the Willibaldsburg, starts with the emergence of *Homo sapiens* and runs through the Roman era, and has a near-complete mammoth skeleton. (Juramuseum ☎ 29 56. Free tours Su at 2pm. Museum für Ur- und Frühgeschichte ☎ 894 50. Box office for both museums ☎ 47 30. Both open Tu-Su Apr.-Sept. 9am-6pm; Oct.-Mar. 10am-4pm. Both museums €4, students €3, free for art history students. €0.50 English guide available for Juramuseum only.) The **Bastionsgarten**, near the entrance to the castle, offers an excellent view of the city and a 76m well—turn on the light on the right and look for where stone meets bedrock.

Across the river, Eichstätt proper centers on the extravagant **Residenzplatz**, where the bishops moved in the 17th century. 30min. German-language tours of the **Residenz** begin here for groups of at least five people. (☎ 702 20. Tours Easter-Oct. M-Th 11am and 3pm, F 11am, Sa-Su every 45min. 10:15-11:45am and 2-3:30pm. €1.) In a corner of Residenzpl., in the middle of a fountain, stands the **Mariensäule**, a sculpture of the Virgin Mary perched atop a slender column. Behind the Residenz is the 14th-century **Hoher Dom**, originally Gothic, although most of the interior is 19th-century neo-Gothic. (☎ 16 32. Open M and W-F 9:45am-4pm, Tu 9:45am-3:30pm, Sa 9:45am-3pm, Su 12:30-5pm.) The east apse features intricate stained glass and the striking late-Gothic figures of the **Hochaltar**, while the north aisle shelters the intricate 1492 stone **Pappenheim Altar**, a once-resplendent depiction of the crucifixion. To the right of the main altar is the **Mortuarium** cloister, the resting place of Eichstätt's bishops. At the far end, follow the stairs up to the **Domschatz und Diözesanmuseum** (Cathedral Treasury and Diocesan Museum), Residenzpl. 7, which house eighth-century religious pieces interspersed with modern art. (☎ 507 42. Open Apr.-Oct. W-F 10:30am-5pm, Sa-Su 10am-5pm. €2, students €1. Su and holidays free.) Two blocks farther on Leonrodpl. is the Baroque **Schutzengelkirche** (Guardian Angel Church), built during the Thirty Years' War. Its richly carved wooden pews, striking golden sunburst above the high altar, and sculpted soaring angels (567 in all) are the most visible signs of the Jesuits who used Eichstätt as a base to reconvert Bavaria to Catholicism.

INGOLSTADT   ☎ 0841

The old Danube town of Ingolstadt (pop. 121,000) was the site of the first Bavarian university in 1472 and a powerful Catholic center during the Counter-Reformation. Today, luxury car manufacturer Audi, based here since WWII, employs 25% of the town's population. Modern stores and services came in the company's wake, but the old town's charm has been carefully preserved. Neoclassical fortifications and churches are surrounded by greenery and the flow of the Danube. A lively place thanks to the university it shares with nearby Eichstätt, Ingolstadt celebrates each summer with the Festa del Vino (Italian wine festival), which culminates 1½ weeks later with the Bürgerfest (City Festival) on the first weekend in July.

⌐ TRANSPORTATION

Trains run to: Augsburg (1hr., every hr., €10); Munich (1hr., 2 per hr., €13.40); Regensburg (1hr., every hr., €11.70). **Bus** routes center on the Omnibusbahnhof in the middle of the city (single ride €1.60). Call a **taxi** at ☎ 194 10. **Rad Haus**, Kreuzstr. 2, rents **bikes**. (☎ 322 11; www.radhaus.de. €10 per day. Open in summer M-F 9:30am-12:30pm and 1:30-7pm, Sa 9am-4pm; in winter shorter hours.)

⁊ PRACTICAL INFORMATION

Ingolstadt's **tourist office,** Rathauspl. 4, in the Neues Rathaus, hands out maps and books rooms for free. To get there from the distant train station, take bus #10, 11, 15, or 16 to "Rathauspl." Or, for the 2.5km walk, make a right out of the station and follow Bahnhofstr. to Münchener Str. (to the right), which will turn into Brückenkopf. Head straight over the bridge down Donaustr. to Rathauspl. (☎305 30 30; www.ingolstadt-tourismus.de. Open Apr.-Oct. M-F 8:30am-5:30pm, Sa 9:30am-2pm; Nov.-Mar. M-F 9am-5pm, Sa 10am-2pm.) Free **tours** of the old city (in German) depart from the office. (May-Oct. Sa 2pm. €4.) Cash traveler's checks at **Volksbank,** Theresienstr. 32. (24hr. **ATM.** Open M-W 8:30am-12:30pm and 1:30-4:45pm, Th 8:30am-12:30pm and 1:30-5:45pm, F 8:30am-12:30pm and 1-1:45pm.) Do **laundry** at **Wasch-Center,** Hindenburgstr. 101. (☎414 95. Wash €3 per 6kg, dry €1.50. Open M-Sa 7am-10pm, Su 10am-8pm.) **Untere Apotheke pharmacy,** Moritzstr. 19, is near the Rathauspl., and posts 24hr. pharmacy information. (☎173 80. Open M, Tu, Th 8:30am-6:30pm; W and F 8:30am-6pm; Sa 8:30am-1pm.) Find **Internet** access at the @ **Café,** Sauerstr. 2, at Rathauspl. (☎881 33 50. €2 per hr., students €1.50. Open daily 10am-10pm.) The **post office** is in front of the train station. (Open M-F 8:30am-6pm, Sa 9am-12:30pm.) **Postal Code:** 85024.

⌂ ACCOMMODATIONS

Ingolstadt's **Jugendherberge (HI) ❶,** Friedhofstr. 4½, is in a renovated section of the town's old fortifications. From the tourist office, take Moritzstr. north and turn left on Theresienstr. to the Kreuztor. Walk through the gate and cross Auf der Schanz; the hostel is on the right (10min.). Large rooms with sinks. (☎305 12 80; fax 305 12 89. Breakfast included. Reception 8am-11:30pm. Curfew 11:30pm. Dorms €15.60; 2-3 nights €15, 4+ nights €14.45. Cash only.) **Gästehof Huber ❷,** Dorfstr. 12, offers simple rooms 15min. from the train station in the opposite direction of town. Take bus #15 or 16 to "Unserherr Schule." (☎723 35; www.gasthof-huber.de. Breakfast included. Reception M-Th and Sa 8am-11pm, Su 8am-2pm. Singles €21, with shower €30; doubles €36/52. MC/V.) Campers can go to **Campingplatz am Auwaldsee ❶,** 5km from town off the E45/Autobahn A9. Take a right from the station and follow Bahnhofstr. to Münchener Str. Before the bridge, look for the "Brückenkopf" bus stop on the right side of the street; catch bus #50 (dir.: Kälberschüttstr.; every hr. M-Sa 6am-8pm, Su and holidays 9am-8pm) or the infrequent #N9 night bus to "Am Auwaldsee." (☎961 16 16; ingolstadt@azur-camping.de. Reception 7am-1pm and 3-10pm. €5.50-7.50 per person. €6-9 per tent and car. Cash only.)

◖◗ FOOD AND NIGHTLIFE

Edeka, Ludwigstr. 29 in the basement of Galeria Kaufhof, sells groceries. (☎354 11. Open M-F 9am-7pm, Sa 9am-6pm. Cash only.) **Restaurant Mykonos ❸,** Ludwigstr. 9, dishes up Greek delights in a mini-Athens. Omelettes (€5.10) and Mediterranean specialties (€6-17) come with a free shot of *ouzo.* (☎33 765. Open daily 11am-3pm and 5pm-midnight. AmEx/DC/MC/V.) **Sigi's ❷,** Kreuzstr. 6, is a small and chic café with outdoor seating and a daily menu that hovers around €6. (☎329 52. Beer €2.50. Open M-Th 9am-2am, F-Sa 9am-3am, Su 2pm-2am. Cash only.) The university **Mensa ❶,** Konviktstr.1, near the Maria-de-Victoria church, charges students €3-4.20 for entrées. (Open M-F 11am-2:30pm.) The **Kreuztor** (Cross Gate) is the symbol of the Altstadt, and also the center of local nightlife, which clusters on **Kreuzstr.** and **Theresienstr. Neue Welt,** Griesbadg. 7, off Kreuzstr., with its own stage, is home to the local art and music crowd. Try the chili (€4.60), stuffed pitas (€3.80) or homemade *Tsatsiki* (€3.50). (☎324 70. Beer €2.60. M-Tu and Th Sept.-

July cabarets, alternative and R&B concerts 8:30pm, doors open at 7pm. Cover €10-20. Open M-Sa 7pm-1am. Cash only.) Local students hang out at the outdoor tables of **Mohrenkopf Café**, Donaustr. 8, one block from the river, as well as the adjacent Bar Centrale. (Breakfast until 2pm, Sa-Su until 4pm. Happy hour daily 6-8pm and 11pm-midnight. Beer €2.70. Open M-F 7:30am-1am, Sa 8am-1am, Su 9:30am-1am. Cash only.) For the latest entertainment, check out the German-language publications *Megazin* and *Espresso*, available at the tourist office.

👁 SIGHTS

The old city wall is magnificently represented by the turreted **Kreuztor** (built in 1385), topped by dainty stone ornaments. Just beyond the gate, the **Stadtmuseum** (Municipal Museum), Auf der Schanz 45, charts Ingolstadt's history and displays odd artifacts, like the embalmed horse of Swedish king **Gustavus Adolphus**, captured when he unsuccessfully attempted to lay siege to the town. (☎305 18 85. Open Tu-F 9am-5pm, Sa-Su 10am-5pm. €3, students and seniors €1.50.) Two blocks east is the late Gothic **Liebfrauenmünster,** full of ornate altars and immense columns. Counter-Reformation leader **Johann Eck** preached here, in front of a depiction of the early martyr **St. Catherine.** A few blocks south on the aptly named Anatomiestr., the ▓**Deutsches Medizinhistorisches Museum** (Medical History Museum), Anatomiestr. 18-20, occupies the former medical laboratory that inspired Mary Shelley to use Ingolstadt as the setting for *Frankenstein.* The museum houses a collection of medical oddities, from a "do-it-yourself" enema stool to gruesome amputation saws. (☎305 18 60. Open Tu-Su 10am-noon and 2-5pm. English translations available. €4.50, students and seniors €2.25.) At the corner of Jesuitenstr. and Neubaustr. is the **Maria-de-Victoria-Kirche.** This once sparse chapel was "Rococoed" with a vengeance in 1732, with an awe-inspiring fresco by **Cosmas Asam,** of Munich fame. (☎175 18. Open Tu-Su Mar.-Oct. 9am-noon and 1-5pm, May-Sept. also open M; Nov.-Feb. 1-4pm. €2, students and children €1.50, children free. Free organ concerts May-Sept. Su noon.) At the **Audi Forum** on Ettingerstr. the moving *Museum mobile* displays a fabulous array of past Audis as well as imaginative prototypes. The name of this luxury car company was originally *Horch* (hark), after auto innovator and entrepreneur **August Horch.** The Latin *Audi* (listen) was chosen in 1910 to help exports in an international market resistant to German-sounding products. Screens throughout display the names of Audi owners as they are called to pick up their cars; the constant stream of new vehicles shooting out of the garage is also visible from the souvenir shop, restaurant, and movie theater. (☎080 02 83 44 44. Take bus #11 to "Audi Forum" or walk the 2.5km from downtown. Open daily 9am-6pm. Museum tours €1. Factory and workshop tours M-F 10:30am, 12:30, and 2:30pm; €4, students €3, under 18 €2. Admission €2/1.50/1. English tours daily 11:30am. Films daily 5:30 and 8pm, Su 11am. Children's films Sa 3pm, Su 1 and 3pm. €6, children €4; Tu €3.) More of streamlined Ingolstadt is on show at the **Museum für Konkrete Kunst** (Museum for Concrete Art), Tränktorstr. 6-8, off Donaustr. near Konrad-Adenauer-Brücke, which displays wildly colorful pieces by international contemporary artists. (☎305 18 75. Open Tu-Su 10am-5pm. €3, students €1.50, under 15 free.) Across town is the 15th-century **Neues Schloß,** Paradepl. 4, a red-tiled castle now home to the **Bay-erisches Armeemuseum** (Bavarian Army Museum), a detailed exhibit of weapons and armor. (☎937 71 13. Open Tu-Su 8:45am-4:30pm. €3.50, students €3.)

PASSAU ☎ 0851

Baroque arches cast long shadows across the cobblestone alleys of Passau (pop. 50,700), a 2000-year-old city situated at the confluence of the Danube, Inn, and Ilz rivers. The splendor of the peninsular Altstadt recalls the era when Passau controlled lands in Austria, Bavaria, and the Czech Republic. The heavily-fortified castle, glorious cathedral, and several patricians' palaces stand alongside modern shops, cafés, and museums. This *Dreiflüssestadt* (three-river city) and university town, inspiration of the 12th-century epic poem *Nibelungenlied*, celebrates its culture with the **European Festival,** a summer-long art, music, theater, and film festival held every year since 1952 in support of a peaceful and unified Europe.

▐ TRANSPORTATION

Trains: Every 2hr. to: **Frankfurt** (4½hr., €67); **Munich** (2hr., €26); **Nuremberg** (2hr., €36). Every hr. to: **Regensburg** (1-2hr., €18) and **Vienna, Austria** (3½hr., €38). The **Hauptbahnhof** is west of the center on Bahnhofstr. **Ticket counter** open M-F 5:50am-6:30pm, Sa 6am-5:25pm, Su 8:50am-7:25pm. **Lockers** €1.50-€3.

Buses: **Regionalbus Ostbayern** (☎ 75 63 70) provides service from the train station to cities throughout eastern Bavaria. **SWP Passau** buses make a number of stops within the city and in neighboring towns. Single ticket €1.50.

Ferries: **Donau Schifffahrt** (☎ 92 92 92), ticket booth across from main tourist office. Sails to **Linz, Austria** (5hr.; May-Sept. Tu-Su 9am and 2pm, returns 8:40am and 2:20pm; €21, round-trip €24). The 45min. **"Three Rivers" tour** of the city leaves daily from docks 7 and 8, Mar.-Oct. every 30min. 10am-5pm and Nov.-Dec. at 11am, noon, 1 and 2pm (€6.50, under 15 €3.75).

Taxis: Call ☎ 194 10 or catch a cab at Ludwigspl.

Bike Rental: Rent a Bike (☎ 0800 460 24 60), in the Bahnhof at the window farthest to the left in the Reisezentrum. €12 per day, €9.50 with a DB rail ticket. Open Sa-Su 9-11:30am and 3-5:30pm, weekdays by phone appointment. **Fahrrad Klinik,** Braug. 10 (☎ 334 11; www.fahrradklinik-passau.de) charges €11 per day. Open M-F 9-noon and 1-6pm, Sa 9-noon. The stunning **Donau Radweg** bike path begins in Donaueschingen and continues through Passau into Austria—ask for a map at the tourist office.

▟ ▐ ORIENTATION AND PRACTICAL INFORMATION

To reach the city center from the train station, follow Bahnhofstr. to the right until you reach **Ludwigspl.** Bear left across Ludwigspl. to Ludwigstr., the start of the pedestrian zone, which becomes Rindermarkt, Steinweg, and Große Messerg. Continue straight onto Schusterg. when the street ends, and you'll soon be in the **Altstadt;** hang a left on Schrottg. and end up at the **Rathauspl.** (30min.). Uphill lies the **Veste Oberhaus** fortress. Farther east, the three rivers converge. The **Inn** is on the right; to the left is the (not-so-blue) **Danube,** and the third and smallest river, the **Ilz.** East of the Altstadt, Innstr. runs along the Inn to the university. Bridges span the Danube towards nightlife hotspot **Innstadt,** a German enclave on the Austrian side of the rivers.

Tourist Office: Rathauspl. 3 (☎ 95 59 80; www.passau.de), on the Danube next to the Rathaus. Free brochures, schedules, tour information, cycling maps, and guides. The staff books rooms (€3 deposit) and provides info on cheaper hotels and pensions (€18-67) in the area. *WasWannWo,* a free monthly German-language pamphlet, chronicles everything going on in Passau. Office open Easter to mid-Oct. M-F 8:30am-6pm, Sa-Su 9am-4pm; mid-Oct. to Easter M-Th 8:30am-5pm, F 8:30am-4pm. **Branch** at Bahnhofstr. 36, across from the train station and to the left (☎ 95 59 80; fax 572 98). Free maps and brochures outside after hours. Open Easter-Sept. M-F 9am-noon and 12:30-5pm, Oct.-Easter M-Th 9am-noon and 12:30-5pm, F 9am-noon and 12:30-4pm.

Tours: German-language walking tours (1hr.) May-Oct. M-Sa 10:30am and 2:30pm, Su 2:30pm. €3, children €1.50. Meet at the front entrance of the Stephansdom. English group tours available with advanced request.

Currency Exchange: Go right out of the train station down Bahnhofstr. to reach **Volks-bank-Raiffeisenbank,** Ludwigspl. 1 (☎33 50). 24hr. **ATM.** €1 fee per traveler's check cashed. Open M-W and F 8:30am-12:30pm and 1:15-4:15pm, Th 1:15-5pm.

Laundromat: Rent-Wash, Neuburger Str. 19. From Ludwigspl., walk up Dr.-Hans-Kapfin-ger-Str., follow it to the end as it curves right and becomes Neuburger Str., then bear left. Wash €2.50, soap €0.50. Dry €1.50. Open daily 7am-11pm.

Emergency: Police, Nibelungenstr. 17 (☎110, non-emergency 50 30). **Fire** ☎112. **Ambulance** ☎ 192 22.

Pharmacy: Bahnhofstr. 17 (☎513 01). Open M-Sa 8am-6pm.

Hospital: Klinikum Passau, Bischof-Pilgrim-Str. 1 (☎530 00).

Internet Access: Screenpark Media Services, Kl. Exerzierpl. 14 (☎75 67 611). €2 per hr. Open M-Sa 10am-8pm. Free at **Café Unterhaus,** Höllg. 12 (☎989 04 64), a trendy art gallery, bookshop, and café, a few blocks from the Rathaus. Open Apr.-Sept. M and W-Su 10am-1pm, Tu 10am-7pm; Oct.-Mar. M and W-Su noon-1am, Tu noon-7pm.

Post Office: Bahnhofstr. 27, to the right as you exit the station. Open M-F 8am-6pm, Sa 9am-12:30pm. **Postal Code:** 94032.

ACCOMMODATIONS AND CAMPING

Most pensions in downtown Passau start at €30, while those in the surrounding area run €11-35. The only hostel in town is usually swarming with German school-children, especially during June and July.

Fahrrad Pension, Bahnhofstr. 33. (☎34 784; www.fahrrad-pension.com). Exit the train station and walk 100m to the left; look for the "Bäckerei" sign. Cheap beds (4 per room, no bunks) in clean rooms over an aromatic bakery. €10. Cash only. ❶

Jugendherberge (HI), Veste Oberhaus 125 (☎49 37 80, fax 493 78 20). Perched high above the Danube, in the former quarters of the Veste Oberhaus sentinels. Cross the suspension bridge downstream from the Rathaus and follow the signs pointing up the steps and toward the museum (30-45min. uphill). Or, hop on the *Pendelbus* (shuttle) from Rathauspl. bound for the museum adjacent to the hostel (Easter to mid.-Oct. every 30min. M-F 10:30am-5pm, Sa-Su 11:30am-6pm; €2, same-day round-trip €2.50). Breakfast included. Reception 7:30am-11am, 5-10pm. Curfew 10pm, access code available. Dorms €18.35, slightly lower in winter. AmEx/MC/V. ❷

Pension Rößner, Bräug. 19 (☎93 13 50, www.pension-roessner.de). To get there from the Rathaus, walk downstream along the Danube. Directly on the river, these pleasant rooms are low-priced for the Altstadt. Call upstairs if no one is at the reception. All rooms with bath and radio, some with TV. Breakfast included. Singles €35; doubles €50-60. MC/V. ❸

Rotel Inn, Hauptbahnhof/Donauufer (☎951 60; www.rotel-inn.de). From the train station, walk straight ahead down the steps, down Haisseng., and through the tunnel to this outlandish hotel right on the river. Built in 1993 in the shape of a sleeping man to protest Europe's decade-long economic slumber, this self-proclaimed "Hotel of the Future" packs travelers into closet-sized rooms bedecked with primary-color plastics. Radio in every room. Breakfast €5. Reception 24hr. Open May-Sept. Rooms €25 for 1 person, €30 for 2. Cash only. ❷

Hotel Garni Herdegen, Bahnhofstr. 5 (☎95 51 60, www.hotel-herdegen.de). Located in the heart of the Neustadt. Offers large rooms with private bath, cable TV, radio, and phone. Breakfast included. Singles €36-45; doubles €68-79. AmEx/MC/V. ❹

Zeltplatz Ilzstadt, Halser Str. 34 (☎414 57). Follow directions to the hostel but turn right before the steps and walk along Angerstr. until Halser Str. Follow Halser Str. to the riverbank and go right when it becomes Grafenleite. Or take bus #1-4 from "Exerzierpl."

to "Ilzbrücke" at the start of Halser Str. Open May-Oct. Breakfast €3-4. Reception 8-10am and 5-9pm, but you can pitch your tent any time. €6, ages 7-17 €5, under 6 free. Phone and hot showers included. Cash only. ❶

🖸 FOOD

The student district centers on **Inn Str.** near the university. From Ludwigspl., head down Nikolastr. and turn right on Inn Str., which runs parallel to the Inn River; the street is dotted with good, relatively inexpensive places to eat. **Norma** is a supermarket at Bahnhofstr. 16b. (Open M-F 8:30am-7pm, Sa 8am-4pm. Cash only.) Find fresher but pricier food (produce, baked goods, cheese and meats, prepared foods) at **Schmankerl Passage,** Ludwigstr. 6. (Open M-F 7am-6pm, Sa 7am-4pm. Cash only.) There is an **open air market** in **Domplatz** Tuesday and Friday mornings.

▨ **Café Innsteg,** Innstr. 15 (☎512 57), 1 block from Nikolastr. This busy restaurant offers students and locals balcony seating and loud American music outside and a sleek sports bar inside. Sandwiches €2.60-5.40. Pastas €6-7. Daily menu (€4.50) 11:30am 2pm. Beer (0.5L) €2.40. Open M-Sa 8:30am-1am (hot food 11:30am-midnight), Su 8:30am-7pm (hot food 11:30am-6pm). Cash only. ❷

Café Kowalski, Oberer Sand 1 (☎24 87). From Ludwigspl., walk down Nikolastr. toward the Inn river; take a left on Gottfried-Schäffer-Str. and walk almost 2 blocks until you see the terrace on the left. Home to the largest *Schnitzel* in Passau. Hordes of college students chill with ice cream specialties (€3-5), mixed drinks (€2-5), fresh salads, and pastas (€3-8). Tu is students' night: *Studentenbier* (small beers) or tequila €1. W mixed drink specials from 8pm. Open daily 10am-1am. AmEx/DC/MC/V. ❷

Sensasian, Heuwinkel 9 (☎98 90 152). In the pedestrian zone. Delicious pan-Asian specialties (sushi, pad thai) with plenty of vegetarian options in a sleek, soft interior. Weekly menu €6.80. Open daily 10am-11pm. Cash only. ❷

Altes Bräuhaus, Bräug. 5 (☎490 52 52). Classic Bavarian and Austrian specialties in the Altstadt, on the Platz opposite the suspension bridge over the Donau. Main courses, such as *Bayerwald Schnitzel*, €6-10. Open daily 11am-1am. Cash only. ❸

🖸 SIGHTS

STEPHANSDOM. When fire devastated Passau, Italian artists were brought in to rebuild the city. This cathedral, the largest Baroque structure north of the Alps, is their centerpiece, despite its few Gothic remnants. The world's largest church organ stands above the choir loft. Its 17,774 pipes and multiple keyboards can hold five organists at once. *(Open daily in summer 6:30am-7pm; in winter 6:30am-6pm. No entrance during concerts. Organ concerts May-Oct. and Christmas week M-F at noon, €3, students and children €1; Th 7:30pm, €5, students, seniors, and children €3. Daily German-language tours May-Oct. and Christmas week M-F 12:30pm, meet in front of the side aisle; Nov.-Apr. M-F noon, meet underneath the main organ. €1.50, children €0.75.)*

VESTE OBERHAUS. Over the Luitpoldbrücke and up the footpath is the former palace of the bishop. Once a prison for the bishops' enemies and a fortress with control over the city and the rivers below, the complex now houses the **Kulturhistorisches Museum** (Cultural History Museum), with interactive rotating exhibits and 54 rooms of art and artifacts chronicling 2000 years of Passau's history, thorough written commentary in English, and great views of the city below from the **tower.** *(Shuttle bus from the Rathaus stops here every 30min. Last bus back leaves Oberhaus at 5:15pm. ☎49 33 50; www.oberhausmuseum.de. Open early Apr. to early Nov. M-F 9am-5pm, Sa-Su 10am-6pm; Nov.-Mar. Tu-Su 9am-5pm. €5, students €4. Tower €1, under 16 €0.50.)*

GLASMUSEUM. This huge collection of fancy glass work celebrates Bohemian production from the Baroque era to the present, and includes an elaborate glass birdcage, a copy of da Vinci's *Last Supper* engraved on a chalice, and various psychedelic *Jugendstil* experiments. Two of the rooms in which Austrian Empress Elisabeth once stayed have been preserved, complete with her gloves, socks, and toiletries. *(Am Rathauspl. ☎350 71. Open daily 1-5pm. €5, students €4, under 12 free with parents. Get a 20% discount by showing your Passau boat tour ticket.)*

ALTSTADT. Behind the cathedral is the **Residenzplatz,** lined with former patrician dwellings, and the **Residenz,** past home of Passau's bishops. The **Domschatz** (cathedral treasury) within the Residenz has an extravagant collection of the bishops' most precious items in its old library. Contemporary art exhibits are interspersed throughout the permanent collection. *(Enter through the back of the Stephansdom, to the right of the altar. Open Easter-Oct. M-Sa 10am-4pm. €1.50, students and children €1, families €2.50.)* The less opulent 13th-century Gothic **Rathaus** was appropriated from a wealthy merchant in 1298 to house the city government. The impressive high water marks from past floods (the last big one was in 2002) are marked on the outside wall beneath the clock. Inside, the **Prunksaal** (Great Hall) is a masterpiece of rich wooden paneling and dark marble. *(Open daily Apr.-Dec. 10am-4pm. €1.50, children €1.)* Across Rathauspl. and down Braug., just past the Altes Brauhaus stands the **Museum Moderner Kunst** (Museum of Modern Art), a small collection of paintings, sculpture, photography, and video installations. *(Bräug. 17. ☎383 87 90; www.mmk-passau.de. Open Tu-Su 10am-6pm. €5, students and children €3.)*

🎵 🎭 ENTERTAINMENT AND NIGHTLIFE

Passau's theater scene is centered on the **Theater-Opernhaus Passau,** Gottfried Schäfferstr. 2-4 (☎929 19 13; www.sudostbayerisches-staedtetheater.de). From Ludwigspl. walk down Nikolastr. to the river and take a left; the theater is just before the bridge. The theater produces operas and more modern plays. (Box office open Tu-F 10am-12:30pm and 4-5:30pm. Tickets from €7.50, reduced rates available 1hr. before showtime (usually 7:30pm). Closed early July to mid-Sept.).

Passau's students and young professionals party at the many bars and clubs on **Innstr.** by the university, or across the footbridge in the **Innstadt.** Although all beer gardens close at 11pm, the city still manages to stay out late. The best way to keep abreast of the nightlife scene is to get hold of *Pasta*, a free monthly magazine available at most bars, clubs, and cafés. *Innside*, available at the tourist office, focuses on events in the *Innstadt*. Both publications are in German.

▨ **Bluenotes,** Ledererg. 50 (☎343 77). Cross the Fünferteg footbridge, make a left on Severinstor, and hang another left on Ledererg. Enjoy your beer or mixed drink outside in the *Biergarten,* next to the live events of the *Scheune* (inquire for details). Happy hour every night 8-9pm and midnight-1am and all night W (mixed drinks €4.30). Bring your own grill items May-Sept. Open daily 6pm-1am. Cash only.

Camera, Am Ludwigspl. (☎343 20), around the corner from the McDonald's. Stark black exterior foreshadows an underground cavern of student angst and inebriation. Plays everything from alternative to pop. Live shows Tu in spring, early summer, and fall. Beer €2.20 (0.3L). Open daily 10pm-3am, weekends and holidays until 5am. Cover €4 for drink coupons (drink €4 worth of booze and you'll have earned it back). Cash only.

Prince/Sausito's, Heuwinkel 6 (☎36 238). In the pedestrian zone. A student-heavy international party scene. Open daily 8am-5am. W "Tequila Party" (tequila shots €1), F "Dirty Disco," Sa "Puti Club" (you'll have to figure this one out for yourself). Cash only.

Colors, Mariahilfstr. 8 (☎322 20). Right across the Innbrücke in Innstadt, past the Kirchenpl. Gulp down a *Helles* (€2.20) as you throw darts, shoot pool, or relax in the *Biergar-*

ten. Tu night Happy hour, mixed drinks €3-5. DJs spin everything from reggae to easy listening. Open daily 7pm-1:30am. Cash only.

GO, Kl. Klingergasse 7 (www.go-danceclub.de). A young crowd packs the dancefloor 3 nights a week for rap, R&B, and house. Beer €2.80. Mixed drinks €6.80-8. Open W and F-Sa 10pm-4am. Cover F-Sa €3. Cash only.

Café Aquarium, Unterer Sand 2 (☎25 90). On most nights, people come here to chill out with a mixed drink (€4.60-6.80) or ice cream, and to take advantage of free wireless Internet access. Beer €2.50. W karaoke nights (from 8:30pm). Cash only.

Selly's, Bratfischwinkel 5 (☎7 11 30). The place to go for gay and lesbian nightlife. Small, Italian-themed bar with nude faux-marble sculptures and potted plants. Open M, W-Th 7pm-1am. F-Sa 8pm-2am, Su 7pm-midnight. Cash only.

STRAUBING ☎09421

"They govern in Landshut, they pray in Passau, but you can really live in Straubing," said painter Carl Spitzweg of this historic Danube town—and live they do. Each summer, Straubing (pop. 44,500) hosts the 10-day Gäubodenvolksfest (Aug. 10-20, 2007; Aug. 9-19, 2008). Started as an agricultural fair in 1812, the festival has since evolved into a tribute to inebriation second in size only to Oktoberfest. Accompanying the Volksfest is the Ostbayernschau (East Bavaria Show), a regional trade and industry exhibition (i.e., more beer; Aug. 11-19, 2007; Aug. 11-18, 2008). Both are held in the Fest area "Am Hagen," 5min. north of the Markt.

◪ TRANSPORTATION

Trains run every hr. to: Landshut (1hr., €9.10); Munich (2hr., €18); Passau (1hr., €11.70); Regensburg (30min., €7.60). **Stadt-BUS-Verkehr Straubing** runs buses (€1.50, day pass €3); the tourist office has schedules. For **taxis,** call ☎98 98 60.

◪◪ ORIENTATION AND PRACTICAL INFORMATION

The Altstadt is 5min. northwest of the train station by foot. From the station, cross the street and make a left, walking past the traffic circle and bearing right on Bahnhofstr. Cross over Stadtgraben into the pedestrian zone and continue straight to the clock tower passage on Theresienpl. and Ludwigspl., which is lined with shops and eateries. Most sights lie between the mall and the Danube. The **tourist office,** Theresienpl. 20, is to the left after you walk through the clock tower passage. The office has free maps and brochures on Straubing and will find private rooms (from €20) for free. (☎94 43 07; www.straubing.de. Open M-W and F 9am-5pm, Th 9am-6pm, Sa 9am-noon.) German 1½hr. **tours** of the Altstadt are offered mid-May to mid-October; call ahead for English group tours. (W and Sa 2pm. €3, students and seniors €2, family ticket €6.) The **Neue Löwen-Apotheke pharmacy** is at Ludwigspl. 11. (☎106 65. Open M-F 8am-6pm, Sa 8:30am-1:30pm.) **Terminal,** Bahnhofstr. 13, has **Internet** access. (18+. €3 per hr. Open daily 8am-1am.) The **post office** is at Landshuter Str. 21. (Open M-F 8:30am-6pm, Sa 8:30am-noon.) **Postal Code:** 94315.

⌂ ACCOMMODATIONS

Your best bet for a cheap stay in Straubing is to book a private room at the tourist office. The **Gästehaus des Jugendwohnhaus Don Bosco ❷,** Pettenkoferstr. 16, is another budget option. Take Bus #4 to "Pettenkoferstr." or walk the 20min. from the train station. Make a left out of the station and another left at the traffic circle on Landshuterstr. Walk for about 15min. and turn left at the gas station on Oskar-von-Miller-Str. and then right on Pettenkoferstr.; it's on the right. Friendly hostel-like accommodations without the droves of German schoolkids. (☎329 69; fax 427 91. Breakfast included. Dorms €18; singles €19, with bathroom €22; doubles with bathroom €40. Cash only.) More central but closer, the **Gabelsberger Hof ❸**, Gabelsbergerstr. 21, has standard rooms above a Balkan restaurant. Make a left out of the station and another left at the Jahnpl. circle on Landshuterstr. By the post office, make a right on Dr.-Otto-Höchtl-Str. and then a right on Gabelsberger-str. (☎18 21 13; www.gabelsberger-hof.de. Breakfast included. Reception 11am-2:30pm and 5-11pm during restaurant operation. Singles €28; doubles €50. Cash only.) The **Jugendherberge (HI) ❶**, Friedhofstr. 12, is 15min. from the train station. Turn right from the front entrance and follow the curve of Bahnhofspl. left. Turn immediately right on Schildhauerstr. and take a second right on Äußere-Passauer-Str. Take a quick left on Friedhofstr.; the Jugendherberge is on your right. (☎804 36; fax 120 94. Breakfast included. Sheets €2. Reception 7-9am and 5-10pm. New arrivals after 5pm only. Curfew 10pm, until 11:30pm with €5 deposit. Open Apr.-Oct. 4-, 6-, or 8-bed dorms €9.10, over 27 €13.20. Cash only.) A **Campingplatz ❶** is at Wundermühlweg 9. From the tourist office, head left down Ludwigspl., turn left on Stadtgrabenstr., and go over the bridge. Walk for about 10min., then go left on Chamer Str. by the "Ruderclub" sign; the campground is on the left. (☎897 94. Open daily May to mid-Oct. Reception 7am-1pm and 3-10pm. €8 for 1 person with tent. €15 for 2 people with car and tent. €3 per additional adult, €2 per additional child. Showers, water, and electricity included. Cash only.)

❏ FOOD

A **farmer's market** is held Saturdays on Theresienpl. (Open 8am-2pm.) You can also find food, clothing, and more for next to nothing at the **Flohmarkt** (flea market) on Am Hagen (1st Sa of the month from 6am; closed Aug.). **Cantina La Cueva ❸**, Rot-Kreuz-Pl. 3, is a fun Mexican option, also with a small beer garden. From Lud-wigpl., go towards the river on Frauenhoferstr. until you reach Rot-Kreuz-Pl. Steer past the Caribbean-themed bar and head down the stairs for starters and entrées (€4-11). (☎853 34. M night wings and ribs buffet, €5.90. Happy hour all drinks €3.60 daily 6-8pm and 10pm-midnight. Open M-Sa 5pm-1am, Su 11am-2pm. Cash only.) Just opposite is the friendly **La Conchiglia ❷**, Rot-Kreuz-Pl. 5, where pizzas and pastas are €6-9. (☎815 05. Beer €2.20. Open M-Tu and Th-Su 11:30am-2:30pm and 5:30pm-midnight.) Cure your craving for cheap Sino-Japanese dishes (€6-9) at **Asian-Bistro-Dai ❷**, Ludwigspl. 16, inside the alleyway. (☎108 14. Lunch buffet M-Sa 11am-3pm, Su 11am-4pm. €5.50, under 10 €3. Open M 11am-3pm, Tu-Su 11am-3pm and 5-10:30pm. Cash only.) Find quality Bavarian food at **Weißbeierhaus ❷**, Theresienpl. 32. Their specialty, *Schweinshaxn* (pig thigh), is €6.90. (☎128 58. Beer €2.55. Open daily 9am-11pm. Cash only.) **Edeka Neukauf** is a **supermarket** on Ludwigpl. 29. (Open M-F 8am-7pm, Sa 8am-4pm. Cash only.)

◉ ♫ SIGHTS AND ENTERTAINMENT

The teal-green symbol of the city, the five-turreted Gothic **Stadtturm** (watch-tower), stands at the heart of the Marktpl. (Obligatory tours in German mid-Mar. to mid-Oct. Th and Su 2pm, Sa 10:30am. €3, students and children €2, under 6 free. Meet at the tourist office.) Just north of Theresienpl., a patchwork of well-preserved stained glass—including the *Moses Fenster* (window) by Dürer—gives the late-Gothic **Basilika St. Jakob**, Pfarrpl. 1a, a dim elegance. The **Gäubodenmu-seum**, Frauenhoferstr. 9, traces the history of the Gäuboden region of Lower Bavaria as far back as the Neolithic era and houses the world's most comprehen-sive collection of Roman equestrian armor. (☎974 10. Open Tu-Su 10am-4pm.

€2.50, students €1.50, children €1.) From the Gäubodenmuseum, walk one block on Zollerg. to the late-Gothic **Karmelitenkirche,** Albrechtsg. 21, built in the Middle Ages by the *Herzog* (duke) to support Carmelite monks, Shockingly jazzed up during the Baroque period, the church hardly reflects monkish austerity. One block down on Burgg., the small but striking **Ursulinenkirche** hides behind a simple white facade. This was the last feat of the renowned Asam brothers, whose masterpiece was the church of St. John Nepomuk near the Sendlinger Tor in Munich. The overflowing Rococo opulence includes excessive gold stucco and pink marble columns twirling up to the ceiling frescoes. (Accessible only by guided tour through the tourist office.) Down Fürstenstr. on the banks of the Danube, the irregular complex of the **Herzogsschloß,** begun in 1556, once housed the Wittelsbach branch that ruled Straubing. The castle is best seen from the exterior; most of the building is now used for office space. Lower Bavaria's only **synagogue,** Wittelsbacherstr. 2, dates to 1907, even though Jews were officially expelled from Straubing in 1442 by Duke Albrecht III. (☎13 87. Visits on request; call M-F 9am-12:30pm.) The **Basilika St. Peter,** built in the 1180s, is the oldest church in town; it stands on the remains of Roman fortifications. From the Stadtturm, walk east on Ludwigspl., turn left onto Stadtgrabenstr., and turn right just before the bridge onto Donaug. Bear right when the road splits; St. Peter's is a 10min. walk. The Romanesque basilica is surrounded by a medieval graveyard with wrought-iron crosses, ancient gravestones, and three Gothic chapels, which can only be viewed on the tourist office's guided walk. Particularly noteworthy is the 18th-century **All Souls Chapel,** with a fresco cycle of the *Totentanz* (Dance of Death). The **Agnes Bernauer Chapel** is dedicated to the famous Augsburg commoner who secretly married a Wittelsbach duke, but was drowned in the Danube by his father, who only approved of aristocratic girls. (Open daily dawn to dusk.)

⬛ NIGHTLIFE

The ⬛**Roxy,** Aprilg. 3, is easily Straubing's hippest nghtspot, featuring foosball, a dancefloor packed with a mix of teens and 30-somethings, and a DJ spinning classic rock. From the tourist office, turn right on Theresienpl. and left on Aprilg. (☎121 57. Cover €3. Beer (0.5L) €3. Open W and F 10pm-3am, Sa 10pm-5am. Cash only.) **Freiraum,** Flurlg. 8, is a delectable bar on a tiny street off Ludwigspl. Come here for the ice-cream and nightly specials or drinks. (☎96 09 62. Beer €2.40. Mixed drinks €4-6. Open M-Th 7:30am-1am, F 7:30am-2am, Sa 9am-2am, Su 10am-1am. Cash only.) **Peaches,** Steinerg. 14, just south of the Stadtturm, is a mellow cocktail bar that offers ½-price drinks on Tuesday nights. (☎105 92; www.peaches-straubing.de. Mixed drinks €4.60-7. Open Tu-Su 7pm-1am, Sa until 2am. Cash only.)

REGENSBURG   ☎0941

When Goethe first visited Regensburg (pop. 130,000), he wrote: "Regensburg is beautifully situated; the area couldn't help but attract a city." Nearly two millennia ago in AD 179, Roman emperor Marcus Aurelius laid the city's foundations by building the Castra Regina fortress where the Naab and Regen Rivers flow into the Danube. It was the first capital of Bavaria, the seat of the Perpetual Imperial Diet, and the site of the first German parliament. One of the few Bavarian cities to escape major bombing in WWII, Regensburg's historic sites—including the Steinerne Brücke, built in the 12th century—are remarkably intact. Today the city is alive with young people and everything needed to satisfy them. Indeed, Regensburg is said by many to have more cafés and bars by area than any other city on the entire European continent.

BAYERN

Regensburg

★ **ENTERTAINMENT &**
♦ **ACCOMMODATIONS**

NIGHTLIFE
Alte Filmbühne, **12**
Alte Mälzerei/
Cartoon, **23**
Apo. Theke, **13**
Banane, **3**
Cinemaxx, **22**
Karma, **18**
Jazzclub, **14**
Neue Filmbühne, **15**
Orange Bar, **4**

♠ **ACCOMMODATIONS**
Alte Mälzerei, **24**
Azur-Camping, **1**
Brook Lane Hostel, **17**
Hotel Am Peterstor, **20**
Jugendherberge, **7**
Spitalgarten, **2**

♥ **FOOD & DRINK**
Alloral, **9**
BaanThai, **16**
Café Felix, **19**
Café Galeria, **11**
Mensa, **21**
Picasso, **10**

♣ **BEER GARDENS**
Alte Linde, **6**
Goldene Ente, **5**
Historische Wurstküche, **8**

TO WALHALLA (9km)

Nibelungenbrücke

Regen

UNTERER WÖRD

Villapark

Adolf-Schmetzer-Str.

Werftstr.
Wöhrdstr.
Am Gries
BUSPARK-PL.
Grieser Steg
Eiserne Brücke

Andreasstr.
Ferry
Thundorfer Str.
DONAUMARKT
Laundry
Osteng.

DACHAU-PL.
Historisches Museum
Neues Rathaus
Minoriten weg
Von-der-Tann-Str.
Ostenallee
Landshuter Str.
Luitpoldstr.
Hemauerstr.
ERNST-REUTER-PL.

Galgenbergbrücke

Diözesanmuseum
St. Ulrich
Alte Kapelle
SCHWANEN-PL.
Bertoldstr.
Martin-Luther-Str.
Maximilianstr.

TO & (200m)

Pfaffensteiner Weg
Pfaffensteiner Steg
Steinerne Brücke
Porta Praetoria
Böök's
Brandelei
Gesandtenstr.
ALTER KORN-MARKT
St. Peter
Am Römling
Pröm
NEUPFARR-PL.
Edeka
Maierei
KRAUT-
Königs
Grasg.
St. Petersweg
Fröschgang
Fröschlein
Viereimers
Weinmarkt
Untere Bach
Obere Bach
Obermünsterstr.
Pflugerl

Hauptbahnhof
Bahnhofstr.

Liebistr.
Badstr.
Eiserner Steg
Gold-Bären-Str.
Kepler
Gedächtnishaus
Altes Rathaus
RATHAUS-PL.
HAIDPL.
Am Olberg
Silb-Fisch-G.
Emmerams-PL.
Fürst Thurn und Taxis Schloß
Albertstr.
Fürst-Anselm-Allee

Donau (Danube)

Holzländstr.
Weltlohstr.
Stahlzwingerweg
Dr. Johann-Maier-Str.

Keplerstr.
Engelburgerg.
Weißgerbergraben
ARNULFS-PL.
Winklerg.
Wollwirkg.
Jakobstr.
BISMARCK-PL.
Bismarck
PL. DER EINHEIT
Am Judenstein
AGIDIEN-PL.
Marschalstr.
Schottenstr.
Helenenstr.
Kumpfmühler Str.
Margaretenstr.

Wittelsbacherstr.
Dörnbergpark
Augustenstr.
Kumpfmühler Brücke
Kirchmeierstr.

Herzogs-park
Gumpelzhaimerstr.
Prebrunnstr.
Hochweg
Hans-Sachs Str.
Altdorfer Str.
Prüfeninger Str.
Dechbetterner Str.
Taxisstr.
Hoppestr.
Stadtpark
Liskircherstr.
Ladehofstr.

TO UNIVERSITY, ♦ (1.5km)
Friedenstr.
Bike Haus

TO ♦ (4km)

250 yards
250 meters

N

TRANSPORTATION

Trains: Every hr. to: **Munich** (1½hr., €21); **Nuremberg** (1hr., €15.50-21); **Passau** (1-1½hr., €18-22).

Ferries: Regensburger Personenschifffahrt (☎553 59; www.schifffahrtklinger.de), on Thunerdorfstr. next to the Steinerne Brücke. Ferries tourists to **Walhalla** (p. 517) with commentary in German and English (45min.; Apr.-Oct. daily 10:30am and 2pm; round-trip €10, students €6.50, children €4.50, families €23). Also offers a city tour in German (50min.; Apr.-Oct. daily every hr. 10am-4pm; €7.50/4.50/3/16).

Public Transportation: Routes, schedules, and fares for Regensburg's **bus** system are available at the Presse & Buch store in the Hauptbahnhof, or at the tourist office. Bus map (no fares or times) free. City info €0.50, area bus schedule €1.50. The transport hub is "Bustreff Albertstr.," 1 block straight and then to the right from the train station. Single ride within zone 1 €1.70; day ticket for zones 1 and 2 €3.50 (after 9am, good for 2 people, Sa-Su and holidays up to 5 people zones 1-3). Buy tickets at the *Automaten* in bus shelters or from the driver (sometimes more expensive) and **validate your ticket on the bus.** Buses run until midnight.

Taxis: Taxi Funk Vermittlung Regensburg ☎194 10, 570 00, or 520 52.

Bike Rental: Bike Haus, Bahnhofstr. 17 (☎599 88 08; www.bikeproject.de), near the Hauptbahnhof. Also provides maps and route suggestions. €9.50 per day, children €6. Open M-Sa 10am-1pm and 2-7pm; Oct.-Mar. also Su 10am-2pm and 3-7pm.

ORIENTATION AND PRACTICAL INFORMATION

Surrounded by parks, the concentrated Altstadt sits on the southern bank of the Danube, opposite its confluence with the Regen. To the south of the Altstadt are the train station and Bahnhofstr., and 1.5km farther south is the university. The modern Maximilianstr. leads from the Hauptbahnhof into the city.

Tourist Office: Rathauspl. (☎507 44 10; www.regensburg.de), in the Altes Rathaus. From the station, cross the street, follow the red "Altes Rathaus" signs down Maximilianstr. to Grasg., and take a left. Follow the street as it turns into Obermünsterstr., turn right at the end on Obere Bachg. and follow it 5 blocks on Rathauspl. The office, to the left across the square, provides free maps, sells tickets (M-Sa) and English-language guide books (€6-6.50), and books rooms for free, although online booking is recommended for foreign visitors. Open M-F 9:15am-6pm, Sa 9:15am-4pm, Su 9:30am-2:30pm. Apr.-Oct. also open Su until 4pm.

Tours: 1½hr. English-language walking tours of the city leave from the tourist office May-Oct. and Dec. on W and Sa 1:30pm. €6, students €4. Also at the tourist office are self-guided English **audio guides.** 3hr. rental €8. The "City Tour" bus leaves from the Dom Apr.-Oct. on the hr. 10am-4pm; June-Oct. also 5pm, no 1pm tour. 1hr. recorded information in English, French, and Italian. €7, students €5.50, families €15.

Banks: Volksbank, Pfaueng. 1 (☎584 70), 1 block from the Dompl. 24hr. **ATM.** Open M-W 8:30am-4pm, Th 8:30am-5:30pm, F 8:30am-3:30pm.

Lost and Found: In the Neues Rathaus (☎507 21 05; fundamt@regensburg.de). Open M-W 8am-noon and 12:30-4pm, Th 8am-1pm and 1:30-5:30pm, F 8am-noon.

Bookstore: Books in a Box, Goldene-Bären-Str. 12 (☎56 70 14). Entrance on Brückstr. 2nd-fl. shelf of English paperbacks. Open M-Sa 9am 8pm.

Laundromat: Wasch-Salon, Osteng. 4a. Wash €3. Dry €1.50. Open M-Sa 6am-10pm.

Emergency: Police ☎110. **Ambulance** ☎192 22. **Fire** ☎112.

Crisis Hotline: Caritas (☎502 10) counsels victims of rape or other trauma.

BAYERN

Pharmacy: Engel-Apotheke, Tändlerg. 24. (☎567 48 50), at Neupfarrpl. Open M-Th 8:30am-6:30pm, F 8:30am-6pm, Sa 9am-2pm.

Hospital: Evangelisches Krankenhaus, Emmeramspl. 10 (☎504 00), near the Thurn und Taxis Schloß, is the most centrally located.

Internet Access: In the Altstadt, at **City Point,** Wahlenstr. 6 (☎584 30 91). €3 per hr., €2 after 7pm and on Su. Wireless available. Open daily 9am-10:30pm. In the Hauptbahnhof, at **Lok.in.** €4 per hr. Open daily 6am-11:30pm.

Post Office: Next to the Hauptbahnhof. Open M-F 8am-6:30pm, Sa 8am-12:30pm. Dompl. **branch** open M-F 9am-6pm, Sa 9am-12:30pm. **Postal Code:** 93047.

🏠🏕 ACCOMMODATIONS AND CAMPING

Central Regensburg is short on cheap lodgings; reserve well in advance or expect to stay outside the city. If the hotels and pensions are full, the tourist office has a list of private rooms (a few are in the €22-30 range; most are €35-65). Otherwise, the hotels in outlying parts of town are cheaper and accessible by bus.

Brook Lane Hostel, Obere Bachg. 21 (☎690 09 66; www.herberge-regensburg.de), Clean rooms are the cheapest you'll find in the Altstadt. Great location with common room and access to kitchen and TV. Sheets €2.50. Check-in at supermarket or call number for service. Reserve in advance, especially on weekends. Check-out noon. Dorms €15-17.50, singles €25, doubles €35. Cash only. ❶

Alte Mälzerei's "Rent A Bed," Galgenbergstr. 20 (☎78 88 115; www.alte-maelzerei.de). This converted malt processing plant features a bar (see **Bars and Clubs**) and inexpensive accommodations. Expect noise. Check-in M-F 10am-noon and 1-4pm. 4- to 6-bed dorms €12.50, students €10. Cash only. ❶

Jugendherberge (HI), Wöhrdstr. 60 (☎574 02; fax 524 11), is a 25min. walk from the Hauptbahnhof on an island in the Danube. Bus #3, 8, or 9 from the station to "Wöhrdstr." (€1.70). Standard, clean rooms overrun by school groups. Breakfast included. Key deposit €10. Reception 7-10am and 3pm-midnight. Doors lock at midnight, access code available. Dorms €18.85, less for longer stays. AmEx/MC/V. ❷

Spitalgarten, St.-Katharinen-Pl. 1 (☎847 74; www.spitalgarten.de), inside a 13th-century hospital with a river view. Bus #17 from the station to "Stadtamhof." Enter by the pink *Biergarten.* Breakfast included. Reception until 6pm, midnight if you call ahead. Reserve well in advance. Singles €23; doubles €46. Cash only. ❷

Hotel Am Peterstor, Fröhliche-Türken-Str. 12 (☎545 45; fax 545 42), 5min. from the station. Rooms are neat and simple, with bath and TV. Breakfast €5. Reception 7-11am and 4-11pm. Singles €35; doubles €40. DC/MC/V. ❸

Azur-Camping, Am Weinweg 40 (☎27 00 25; www.azur-camping.de). Bus #6 (dir.: Wernerwerkstr.) to "Westheim." Reception 8am-1pm and 3-10pm. €5.50-7 per person, €4-6 per child, €6-9 per site. Small tent site without car €4.50-6. Prices higher in summer, lower Sept. to mid-Dec. and mid-Jan. to Mar. Cash only. ❶

🍴 FOOD

The 17th-century English dramatist Sir George Etherege noted that Regensburg's "noble, serene air makes us hungry as hawks." To satisfy that hunger, every other doorway is a café. Breakfast is an institution. You can't walk two blocks without seeing a **supermarket;** there's an **Edeka** in the basement of **Galeria Kaufhof,** Neupfarrpl. 8. (☎533 61. Open M-Sa 9am-8pm. Cash only.) The **Viktualienmarkt,** on Neupfarrpl., has fresh veggies and other basics. (Open daily 9am-4pm. Cash only.)

Café Felix, Fröhliche-Türken-Str. 6 (☎ 590 59; www.cafefelix.de). This crowded and lively café specializes in gigantic salads with ingredients from pineapple to prawns (€8-10). Beer €2.50 (0.5L). Nightly Happy hour (drinks €3.50) and special offers. Open M-Sa 9am-1am, Su 10am-1pm. Kitchen open until midnight. Cash only. ❸

Café Galeria, Kohlenmarkt 6 (☎ 56 14 08), near the Rathaus. The "small" breakfast of *Müsli* with yogurt, fresh fruit, and a huge basket of rolls and croissants is just €4.50. Fills with a hip, young crowd at night. Open daily 9am-2am. AmEx/DC/MC/V. ❸

BaanThai Restaurant, Dechbettenerstr. 6 (☎ 218 77), near the Dönberg park. Large meals served by the family owners outdoors among fragrant trees and elephant statues. Pad thai €9. Seafood specialties €10-14. English menu available. Open Tu-Sa 5pm-midnight, Su noon-2:30pm and 5pm-midnight. Cash only. ❸

Allora!, Engelburgerg. 18 (☎ 5 84 07 83), near Arnulfspl. in the alleyway between Engelburgerg. and Weißgerbergraben. Intimate atmosphere and rotating menu with vegetarian bent. Great homemade soup €2.80. Pastas and *gnocchi* €6.80-7.80. Fish €7.80. Open Tu-Su 10am-2pm and 6pm-1am. Kitchen open until midnight. Cash only. ❷

Picasso, Unter den Schwibbögen 1 (☎ 536 57), down Goliathstr. from the Altes Rathaus. Former Gothic chapel now features pasta instead of prayers under its lofty vaulted ceiling. Almost 20 varieties of pasta €4. Mixed drinks €3.50-4.50. Open M-Th and Su 10am-2am, F-Sa 10am-3am. Cash only. ❷

Mensa, on Albertus-Magnus-Str., in the park on the university campus. Bus #6 (dir.: Klinikum) or #11 (dir.: Burgweinting) to "Universität Mensa." Like eating in a college cafeteria (because it is one). Mensa card available from office downstairs, open M-F 8:30am-10:45am and 11:45am-2pm; student ID and €10 deposit required. Meals €2-4. Open M-Th 11:15am-1:45pm and 5-7pm, F 11:15am-1:45pm; Nov.-Feb. and May-July also open Sa 11:30am-1:30pm. No evening meals mid-Aug. to mid-Sept. ❶

⬛ SIGHTS

DOM ST. PETER. The soaring high-Gothic Dom St. Peter and the adjacent **Diözesanmuseum St. Ulrich** (St. Ulrich Diocesan Museum) are situated, unsurprisingly, on the city's Dompl. Begun in 1276, the cathedral was completed in 1486, but the delicately carved 105m twin spires were finished under King Ludwig I in the 19th century. *(☎ 516 88. Open Apr.-Nov. Tu-Su 10am-4:45pm. €2, students €1, families €4.)* The rich stained glass windows date from the 13th and 14th centuries. Inside the cathedral is the **Domschatz,** an impressive collection of gold and jewels. Underneath the Dom is the resting place for many of Regensburg's bishops and recently-unearthed Roman ruins. *(Dom Information ☎ 29 86 278. Open daily Apr.-Oct. 6:30am-6pm; Nov.-Mar. 6:30am-5pm. 1¼hr. German-language tours May-Oct. M-Sa 10, 11am and 2pm, Su 1 and 2pm; Nov.-Apr. M-Sa 11am, Su 1pm. Meet at Dompl. 5 info center. €2.50, students and children €1.50. English group tours available on advance request. Church choir sings for Solemn Mass, Su at 10am. Dom entry free. Domschatz ☎ 576 45. Open Apr.-Oct. Tu-Sa 10am-5pm, Su noon-5pm; Nov.-Mar. F-Sa 10am-4pm, Su noon-4pm. €2, students €1, families €4. Combination ticket for the Domschatz and Diözesanmuseum €3. Wheelchair access via the Eselturm.)*

WALHALLA. Down the river from Regensburg, Walhalla, a faux Greek temple modeled after the Parthenon and named for the mythic resting place of Norse heroes, is poised dramatically on the northern bank of the Danube. **Ludwig I** built the monument of ancient Germanic *Nibelungen* lore between 1830 and 1842 to honor everyone from German kings and generals to poets and scientists (see **Treasure and Trysts,** p. 368). The plaques above the busts honor those whose faces are unknown, such as the author of the *Nibelungenlied*. Albert Einstein is just one of the new members added since Ludwig's time: the Bavarian ministry of culture

BUSINESS FÜRST

Gloria, the *Fürstin* of Schloß Thurn und Taxis, blurs the line between history and celebrity gossip. She grew up in Africa, spent her teenage years rebelling, and joined the Young Socialists—perhaps because they threw the best parties. Between protests and partying, Gloria caught the eye of the playboy who was the last *Fürst* of Thurn und Taxis (once related to the Hohenzollerns and the Hapsburgs). In 1980 their wedding enthralled every housewife in Germany. She was 20, he was 54. Within three years, Gloria had given birth to three children, including the much-hoped-for male heir, and found her place as the doting matriarch of Regensburg's enormous *Schloß*.

When the *Fürst* died in 1990, the 30-year-old widow buried him according to family tradition—by having his organs removed and then embalming him. To save the decaying family property, Gloria paid the hefty inheritance tax by selling the family's jewelry to the government, and opened up the *Schloß* the public. Some rooms are now available for business functions (the ballroom costs €17,500, the palm garden €12,000). Gloria then told all in a 2004 autobiography.

If you see the family banner flying above the *Schloß*, keep your eyes peeled: you might spot the last representative of the Thurn und Taxis dynasty puttering about under dark hair and oversized sunglasses.

adds a bust every five or six years. Most recently, they chose **Sophie Scholl**, a young Munich student who was executed for leading the **Weiße Rose** resistance against Hitler in 1942 (p. 56). Even with the addition of Scholl, the number of females remains a paltry 5 of 191 busts. In summer, students gather on the hallowed steps for picnics and guitar-playing. *(Take the ferry from Regensburg (p. 515) or bus #5 from the Albertspl. bus station to "Donaustauf Walhallastr." for €2.70, then continue walking on Wörtherstr. to the gravel path leading up the hill. By bike, take the Donau Radweg. ☎96 16 80. Open Apr.-Sept. daily 9am-5:45pm; Oct. 9am-4:45pm; Nov.-Mar. 10-11:45am and 1-3:45pm. €3, students €2.50, children under 15 free with parent. Guide books and audio guides €4.)*

ALTES RATHAUS. A few blocks away from the cathedral is the yellow Gothic town hall, which served as the capitol building of the Holy Roman Empire from 1663-1803. The town council had to move to the adjacent "Neues Rathaus." The permanent meeting of the **Imperial Diet** made Regensburg home to a German parliament of sorts. This brought little wealth to the city, given that the Imperial delegation did not pay taxes on their imports. The town hall also houses a **Reichstagsmuseum** (Diet Museum). Chair heights reflect the legislators' political ranks: four steps high for the emperor, two for the electors (among them the Wittelsbachs), one for the 100 *Fürsten* (princes). The 50-odd free city representatives sat on ground level. *(45min. obligatory German tours Apr.-Oct. every 30min. M-Sa 9:30am-noon and 2-4pm, Su 10am-noon and 2-4pm; Nov.-Mar. every hr. English tours May-Sept. M-Sa 3pm. €6, students €3. Buy tickets at the tourist office next door.)*

KEPLERGEDÄCHTNISHAUS. The iconoclastic astronomer Johannes Kepler died here of meningitis in 1630. Period furniture, portraits, and facsimiles of his work are on display. *(Keplerstr. 5. ☎507 34 42. Open Sa-Su 10am-4pm. 45min. German-language tours at 10 and 11am, 2 and 3pm. €2.20, students €1.10, families €4.40.)* Up the street at Keplerstr. 2 is **Keplers Wohnhaus,** a colorful house where Kepler spent time away from his gold-nosed taskmaster, Tycho Brahe. It now houses a tanning salon.

DOKUMENT NEUPFARRPLATZ. Archaeological excavations from 1995-1998 revealed that under Regensburg's first Lutheran church (founded 1542) lie buried the remains of a Gothic synagogue destroyed in 1519. Regenburg's Jews were expelled in the 16th century from the last surviving Jewish community in a German city. Until then, it had been an integral part of the city. The 624 gold coins from the 14th century that were found at the Neupfarrpl.

dig bear witness to its wealth. Beneath the Jewish quarter are vestiges of ancient Roman constructions. A circular Nazi-era bunker is also on display. (☎941 507. *Obligatory German-language tour Th-Sa 2:30pm; July-Aug. also M and Su. Includes film presentation. Buy tickets at Tabak Götz, Neupfarrpl. 3. €5, students and seniors €2.50.)*

PORTA PRAETORIA. A Roman gateway, the Porta Praetoria is one of only two standing Roman ruins in Germany (the other is the Porta Nigra in Trier, p. 360). One of the earliest documents of Regensburg's past can be seen on the front wall of a house built into the ruins of an accompanying wall—a flat foundation stone from the fort of Castra Regina, inscribed with the date AD 179. *(Open 24hr. Free.)*

FÜRST THURN UND TAXIS SCHLOß. Across from the station, this 11th-century Benedictine cloister became the 500-room residence of the Prince of Thurn und Taxis in 1812. The originally Italian family—*Thurn und Taxis* is the Germanized version of *Torriani e Tassi* (which translates as "towers and badgers," symbols which feature prominently on their coat of arms)—earned its title in 1695, in recognition of the booming business it ran, the first Europe-wide postal service of the modern era. The Thurn clan ran the mail until it was taken over by Prussia in 1867. In 1991, when the latest *Fürst* died (see **Business Fürst,** at left) opened 25 rooms of the palace to public tours. *(Emeramspl. 5. ☎504 81 33. Open Apr.-Oct. M-F 10:30am-5pm, Sa-Su 9:30am-5pm; Nov.-Mar. Sa-Su 9:30am-4pm. 1½hr. tours Apr.-Oct. daily at 11am, 2, 3, and 4pm, Sa-Su additional tour at 10am; Nov.-Mar. Sa-Su at 10am, 11am, 2pm, and 3pm. €11.50, students with ID €9. English audio headsets available and included in price.)*

HISTORISCHES MUSEUM (HISTORICAL MUSEUM). Set within a former Franciscan monastery are archaeological finds from Roman times. St. Salvator, the massive Franciscan church, is also open to the public. *(Dachaupl. 2-4. ☎507 24 48. Open Tu-W and F-Su 10am-4pm, Th 10am-8pm. €2.50, students €1.10, families €4.40. Audio guides in Czech, English, German, and Italian €2.)*

🎵 🍸 ENTERTAINMENT AND NIGHTLIFE

Many of the cafés and beer gardens listed under **Food** double as nighttime haunts. Ask at the tourist office for a free copy of *Logo* or *Filter*, or pick up *Stadtzeitung* at cafés—these three German-language publications list events at bars and cafés. Beyond the bar and club scene, Regensburg is a fabulous city for movie- and theatergoers. Stop by the central box office in the **Theater am Bismarckplatz,** Bismarckpl. 7 (☎507 24 24), to inquire about theater, ballet, and opera performances, or kick back to live jazz performances at the **Jazzclub** in Leerer Beutel, Bertoldstr. 9. (☎56 33 75; www.jazzclub-regensburg.de. Most performances 8:30pm. Call or check online for upcoming events.) Across the train tracks from the Hauptbahnhof, Regensburg's massive **Cinemaxx,** Friedenstr. 25, plays new movies and offers films in their original English version Monday nights. (☎780 21 21; www.cinemaxx.de. Tickets €6-7, M and W-Th students €5, Tu €4.50.)

BEER GARDENS

🏅 **Historische Wurstküche,** Thundorfer Str. 3, (☎46 62 10), next to the Steinerne Brücke with a view of the river. Having recently celebrated its 850th birthday, the Wurstküche is the oldest operating fast-food joint in Europe—12th-century workers who built the nearby bridge broke for lunch here. 6 *Würste* with *sauerkraut* and bread €5.70. Beer €2.60 (0.5L). Open Apr.-Oct. daily 8am-7pm; Nov.-Mar. Su 8am-3pm. Cash only.

Alte Linde, Müllerstr. 1, (☎880 80) just over the Steinerne Brücke from the Wurstküche, to the left on the island. Serves students and professors delicious food (entrées €4-7) and beer (€5.40, 1L). Veggie options. Open daily 11am-midnight. AmEx/DC/MC/V.

Goldene Ente, Badstr. 32 (☎854 55). Under chestnut trees on the banks of the Danube, just across the Eiserner Steg footbridge. During summer this *Biergarten,* part of the oldest inn in Regensburg, serves steaks, *Würstchen,* and *Schnitzel* (€3-7). Helles €4.90 (1L). Open daily 11am-1am. Cash only.

BARS AND CLUBS

Alte Mälzerei, Galgenbergstr. 20 (☎78 88 10). Regensburg's lively "Art and Culture Factory," an old malt processing plant, now hosts a beer garden (€1.90 per 0.5L) and a bar, **Cartoon** (☎757 38; beer €2.50 per 0.5L; small meals €4-6.50) playing pop, jazz, funk, reggae, and blues. Garden open M-F 11am-1am, Sa-Su 2pm-1am. Bar open daily 2pm-1am. Check website or with the tourist office for event dates and prices. Cash only.

Orange Bar, Bei der Steinernen Brücke (☎280 56 67; www.orange-bar-regensburg.de). The Brady Bunch comes to Germany at this orange, 70s-themed bar. Daily Happy hour 8-9pm. Drink specials €4. F-Sa 21+. Open M-W 8pm-2am, Th-Sa 8pm-3am. Cash only.

Alte Filmbühne, Hinter der Grieb 8 (☎579 26). Take the staircase down to the green gate. Regensburg's funkiest scene attracts a diverse crowd and lots of students. Film posters and disco balls scattered every which way. Beer €2.30. Mixed drinks €4.50, M €2.50. 18+. Open June-Sept. daily 9pm-2am; Oct.-May 8pm-1am. Cash only.

Neue Filmbühne, Bismarckpl. 9 (☎570 37). Colorful hangout serves breakfast until 6pm, though most come for the Franconian *Flammkuchen* (small baguettes with melted cheese and ham; €6-7.50). Mixed drinks €5-6. Open daily 9am-1am. Cash only.

Apo.Theke, Rote Hahneng. 8 (☎58 43 999). Candles on bare wood tables are the setting for a bohemian crowd sipping wine (€3-4) and beer (€2.30). Free peanuts in the bucket by the door; just leave the shells on the floor with all the others. DJ music M, F, Sa. Open M-Th 10am-1am, F-Sa 10am-2am, Su 6pm-1am. Cash only.

Banane, Bei der Steinernen Brücke (☎52 9 70), upstairs from the Orange Bar. A place for harder rock music. Sharks, plastic women, and other oddities hanging from the ceiling and off the walls. Beer €2.60. mixed drinks €3-5. Nightly specials. Open M-Th and Su 8pm-1am, F-Sa 8pm-3am. Cover in winter €0.50 Th, €1 F-Sa. Cash only.

ROMANTISCHE STRAßE (ROMANTIC ROAD) AND BURGEN STRAßE (CASTLE ROAD)

Vineyards, groomed fields of sunflowers and wheat, rolling hills, and dense forests checker the landscape between Würzburg and Füssen. Officially dubbed the **Romantic Road** in 1950, the area has become the most heavily touristed part of Germany. In 1954, Bavaria christened the **Castle Road,** which runs east-west through the same region. Both routes have breathed new life into the region, though some towns have preserved their authentic appeal more than others.

Every day, Deutsche Bahn's **Europabus** shuttles throngs of tourists from Frankfurt to Füssen and back on the **Romantic Road.** The **Castle Road** runs from Mannheim to Prague, although Europabus only services the route from Mannheim to Nuremberg. Europabus's Castle Road bus service is timed to allow a transfer to the Romantic Road bus at Rothenberg. Travelers then head on the Romantic Road bus in the direction of Füssen. The tables below detail the bus schedule, as of 2006, along the Romantic and Castle Roads. To figure approximate prices between intermediate cities, subtract the cost listed for your point of departure from the cost listed for your point of arrival. For more information or to book tickets, visit www.touring.de or uk.romantischestrasse.de.

ROMANTIC ROAD

CITY	SOUTHBOUND	PRICE	NORTHBOUND	PRICE
Frankfurt	dep. 8am from FRA	–	arr. 9pm	€99
Würzburg	arr. 9:30am, dep. 10am	€22	arr. 7:20pm, dep. 7:35pm	€78
Rothenburg	arr. 12:15pm, dep. 12:45pm	€34	arr. 5:10pm, dep. 5:40pm	€65
Dinkelsbühl	arr. 1:35pm, dep. 2:05pm	€42	arr. 4:05pm, dep. 4:25pm	€58
Nördlingen	arr. 2:45pm, dep. 3pm	€48	arr. 3:15pm, dep. 3:30pm	€52
Augsburg	arr. 4:25pm, dep. 4:45pm	€60	arr. 1:15pm, dep. 2pm	€40
Hohenschwangau	arr. 6:50pm, dep. 7:05pm	€79	arr. 10:15am, dep. 10:30am	€21
Füssen	arr. 7:10pm, dep. 7:15pm	€80	arr. 10am, dep. 10:05am	€20
Munich	arr. 8:50pm	€99	dep. 8:15am from MUN	–

CASTLE ROAD

CITY	EASTBOUND	PRICE	WESTBOUND	PRICE
Mannheim	dep. 7:50am from MAN	–	arr. 9:25pm	€48
Heidelberg	arr. 8:05am, dep. 8:25am	€4	arr. 8:55pm, dep. 9:05pm	€45
Neckarsteinach	arr./dep. 8:50am	€7	arr./dep. 8:30pm	€43
Rothenburg	arr. 11:30am, dep. 12:30pm	€35	arr. 4:45pm, dep. 5:45pm	€14
Nuremberg	arr. 2:30pm	€48	dep. 3pm from NUR	–

For those without the railpass discount—or those who prefer to travel on their own schedule without a disembodied voice describing the view from the bus win-dow—a more economical way to see both routes is (paradoxically) to use the faster and more frequent trains, which run to every town except Dinkelsbühl. If you plan to travel by train or local bus, take into account that both run less frequently (or sometimes not at all) on weekends. Those traveling by car may have to park in lots outside the old city walls of some towns, but will have easy access to many suburban budget hotels, private rooms, and campgrounds that lie outside the reach of bus or train. The Romantic Road is an excellent opportunity for a leisurely bike journey, with campgrounds 10-20km apart. Hardcore cyclists could finish the 350km route in a few days, but at a more modest pace you'll be on the road a week or two. Tourist offices offer excellent cycling maps and information on campgrounds along the road. For information or reservations, call **Deutsche Touring**, Am Römerhof 17, 60486 Frankfurt (☎069 790 30; www.touring.de). For more information on the Romantic Road, contact the **Romantische Straße Arbe-**

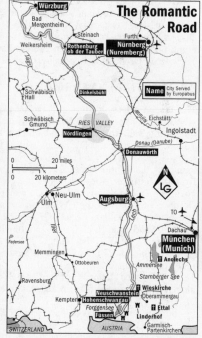

The Romantic Road

Würzburg
Bad Mergentheim
Steinach
Weikersheim
Rothenburg ob der Tauber
Fürth
Nürnberg (Nuremberg)

| Name | City Served by Europabus |

Schwäbisch Hall
Dinkelsbühl
Eichstätt
Schwäbisch Gmünd
RIES VALLEY
Nördlingen
Ingolstadt
Donau (Danube)
Donauwörth

0   20 miles
0   20 kilometers

Neu-Ulm
Ulm
Augsburg
TO
Dachau
München (Munich)
Andechs
Federsee
Memmingen
Ottobeuren
Ammersee
Starnberger See
Ravensburg
Wieskirche
Oberammergau
Neuschwanstein
Kempten
Hohenschwangau
Ettal
Forggensee
Linderhof
Füssen
SWITZERLAND
AUSTRIA
Garmisch-Partenkirchen

itsgemeinschaft, Waaggässlein 1, 91550 Dinkelsbühl (☎09851 55 13 87; www.romantischestrasse.de). For more info on the Castle Road, contact the **Burgen Straße Arbeitsgemeinschaft**, Rathaus, 74072 Heilbronn (☎07131 56 22 83). Even better, contact Munich's **Euraide** office (p. 434); they specialize in information and travel bookings for English-speaking tourists. All Euraide services are free.

AUGSBURG   ☎0821

Unlike the many eternally medieval and Baroque cities in Bavaria, Augsburg's peaked during the Renaissance. Founded in 15 BC by the Roman emperor Augustus, it's no wonder that this town (pop. 272,000) likes to consider itself the northernmost city of Italy. The second-oldest city in Germany, Augsburg was the financial center of the Holy Roman Empire and a major commercial hotspot by the end of the 15th century. The town owes its success in great part to the Fuggers, an Augsburg family that virtually monopolized the banking industry. After the Thirty Years' War, however, Munich eclipsed Augsburg as Bavaria's most important city. WWII destroyed most of the city, and while much of the Augsburg was built anew, major historical buildings have been carefully reconstructed.

▐ TRANSPORTATION

Augsburg is connected by **train** to: Berlin (6hr., 2 per hr., €91); Frankfurt (3hr., every hr., €64); Füssen (2hr., every hr., €15.70); Munich (45min., 3-5 per hr., €10-18); Nuremberg (1-2hr., 2 per hr., €20-30). Augsburg's **public transportation** hub is at Königspl., two blocks down Bahnhofstr. from the station (single ride €0.95, *Tageskarte* (daypass) €5.20); for transit information, head to the **VGA Info Center** there, which distributes free maps and schedules. (☎32 45 88 80. Open M-F 7am-6pm, Sa 9am-1pm.) For a **taxi**, call ☎350 25 or 363 33. Rent **bikes** at **EasyInternet**, Bahnhofstr. 29, across from the train station (☎508 18 78; open M-F 7am-midnight, Sa 8am-midnight, Su 10am-midnight) or at **Zweirad Baumi**, Jakoberstr. 70-72, just inside the Jakobertor. (☎336 21. €10 per day. Open M-F 10am-7pm, Sa 10am-4pm.)

▐ PRACTICAL INFORMATION

The **tourist office**, Rathauspl., (☎502 07 24 or 50 20 72 00 for reservations; www.regio-augsburg.de) offers free city maps and books rooms for a €2 fee. From the station, walk to the end of Bahnhofstr. and take a left at Königspl. on Annastr. Take the 3rd right and Rathauspl. will be on the left; the tourist office is on the right. (Open Apr.-Oct. M-F 9am-6pm, Sa 10am-4pm, Su 10am-2pm; Nov.-Mar. M-F 9am-5pm, until 6pm in Dec., Sa 10am-2pm.) **Bilingual walking tours** of the city leave from the Rathaus (Apr.-Oct. daily 2pm, Nov.-Mar. Sa 2pm; €7, students €5), and cover the Fuggerei and either the Goldener Saal or the Mozarthaus. From April to October, bus tours of the city in German and English leave from the same place and cover the Goldener Saal (Th-Su at 10am; €9, students €7). Other services include: **Sparkasse**, Halderstr. 3, two blocks east of the station, (open M and Th 8:30am-6pm; Tu-W 8:30am-4pm; F 8:30am-3pm); **Bücher Pustet**, Karolinenstr. 12 (☎50 22 40; open M-F 9am-7pm, Sa 9am-6pm.); **laundromat**, Heilig-Kreuz-Str. 32; enter on Klinkertorstr. (wash and dry €6-7; open M-Th 7:30am-5pm, F 7:30am-1pm). The **police station** is at Frolichstr. 2 (☎110, non-emergency 323 21 10). For a **pharmacy**, head to **Stern-Apotheke**, Maximilianstr. 27 on Moritzpl. (☎308 38. Open M-Tu and Th-F 8:30am-6:30pm, W 8:30am-6pm, Sa 8am-1pm.) **Internet** access can be found at **TeleCafé**, Jakoberstr. 1 (☎50 85 80. €1-2 per hr., min. €1. Open daily 10am-11pm.) Augsburg's **post office**, Halderstr. 29, is on the right as you exit the station. (Open M-F 8am-6:30pm, Sa 9am-1pm.) **Postal Code:** 86150.

▮▮ ACCOMMODATIONS AND FOOD

Augsburg's new **"Living Cube" Jugendherberge (HI) ❷**, Unterer Graben 6, has better-than-standard HI rooms behind its sleek reception. From Königspl., take bus #23 (dir: Firnhaberau) to "Pilgerhausstr." (M-Sa until 6pm), or tram #1 (dir: Neuer Ost-friedhof) to "Barfusserbrucke." (☎780 88 90; www.augsburg-jugendherberge.de. Internet €1-2 per hr. Breakfast included. Reception 3-10pm, call ahead for later check-in. 4-bed dorm €18; 2-bed €22.50; over 26 €4 extra. Single rooms with shower and toilet €40; doubles €53. Cash only.) The cheapest privacy you'll find in a central location is at **Jakober Hof ❸**, Jakoberstr. 39-41, 20min. from the station, across from the Fuggerei. Follow the directions to Rathauspl., then head downhill on Perlachberg, which becomes Barfüsserstr., and Jakoberstr. The rooms are spacious and modern with cable TV. (☎51 00 30; www.jakoberhof.de. Breakfast and parking included. Singles €28, with bath and TV €44; doubles €41, with shower €58, with bath €68. AmEx/MC/V.) The small **Pension Herrenhaüser ❸**, Georgenstr. 6, has a friendly owner and bright rooms with bathroom and TV. From the Haupt-bahnhof, take tram #2 to "Fischertor" and walk straight on Herrenhauserstr. and walk to Georgenstr. (☎346 31 73. www.pensionherrenhaeuser.online.de. Break-fast included. Singles €35; doubles €50-54. Cash only.) Pitch your tent at **Caravaning Park Augsburg ❶**, ABA Augsburg-Ost, Am Autobahnse. Take bus #23 (dir.: Firnhaberau) to "Hammerschmiede" and follow the signs 500m. (☎70 75 75; www.campingplatz-augusta.de. €18-20 flat rate per site. MC/V.)

Bahnhofstr., Annastr., Karolinenstr., and Maximilianstr. are lined with food stands in the summer; some of the *Imbiß* (snack bar) fare can be surprisingly pricey. A **Plus** supermarket is at the corner of Halderstr. and Hermannstr., at the southeast corner of the Königspl. park. (Open M-Sa 8am-8pm.) Try the **König von Flandern ❸**, Karolinenstr. 12, under the bookstore. Augsburg's first brewery, smell-ing of yeast and barley. Large portions of soup, salad, and meat entrées (€3-12) satisfy the most ravenous Bavarians. (☎15 80 50; www.koenigvonflandern.de. Beer €2 (0.3L), €1 daily 4-6pm. Open daily 11am-1am. Cash only.) The ever-popu-lar **Capitol Café ❷**, Maximilianstr. 25, serves breakfast until 5pm, large salads, and a wide variety of meat (€8-13) and vegetarian (€6-7) options. (☎349 72 82; www.capitol-augsburg.com. Beer €2.70 (0.5L). Mixed drinks from 6pm €6-7. Open M-Th and Su 10am-1am, F-Sa 10am-2am; food until 11pm. Cash only.)

◉ SIGHTS

Jakob Fugger "the Rich," once the world's wealthiest man, founded the **Fuggerei** quarter in 1521 as the first welfare housing project in the world. His motivation was not entirely selfless: in exchange for free housing, the poor had to pray for the Fugger family. Today, the narrow streets and 67 gabled houses are a haven for 150 low-income families, who even now must be Catholic and approved by the Fugger descendants. The **Fuggereimuseum,** Mittlerg. 13, within the Fuggerei, is arranged to portray a period home, and is one of the only apartment buildings in Augsburg to survive WWII. To reach the Fuggerei from the Rathaus, walk behind the **Perlacht-urm** tower on Perlachberg, which becomes Barfüsserstr., then Jakoberstr., and turn right under the archway. (Open daily Apr.-Oct. 8am-8pm, Nov.-Mar. 9am-6pm. €2, ages 8-18 €1. Includes entry to the Fuggerei quarter.) Fugger lived and tended to his business in the **Fugger Haus,** Maximilianstr. 36-38, where a dispute between Martin Luther and Cardinal Cajetan in October of 1518 precipitated the Reforma-tion. Mostly lost in the 1944 bombing, this palace's former beauty survives in the *Damenhof* courtyard, accessible through the bookstore (open M-F 8am-8pm, Sa 9:30am-4pm) or the restaurant. (Open daily 6pm-midnight.) The Lutheran **St. Anna**

Kirche, on Annastr. near the Königspl., is a strange mixture of Catholic and Protestant styles. Luther stayed here, pioneering the Reformation in Augsburg from this church. St. Anna is also the Fuggers' final resting place. (Open Tu-Sa 10am-12:30pm and 3-6pm, Su 10am-12:30pm and 3-5pm.)

Overlooking the broad Rathauspl. in the city center is the huge **Rathaus,** which encloses the impressive **Goldener Saal** (Gilded Hall), with reconstructed frescoes surrounded by gold centerpieces of the Augsburg Renaissance. (☎349 63 98. Open daily 10am-6pm. €2, students and children €1.) Those willing to climb 258 narrow steps can catch a view of Augsburg from the **Perlachturm,** next to the Rathaus; enter at Am Perlachberg and Karolinenstr. (Open May-Oct. daily 10am-6pm. €1, children €0.50.) Behind the Rathaus is the former **artisans' quarter,** a maze of small lanes laced with canals. Up Hoher Weg to the left is the **Hoher Dom,** the regional bishop's seat. Built in the 9th century, the cathedral was renovated in the 14th century in Gothic style, and later restored after WWII. The stained glass windows reportedly date from 1140, making them the oldest in the world. (Open daily in summer 6am-6:30pm, in winter 6am-5:30pm. German-language tours available M-Sa 10:15am-4pm.) The striking **Synagogue** is a testament to the 2000 Jews who lived in Augsburg until the 1930s. Turn right from the station on Halderstr.; the synagogue is on the left. Inside, the **Jewish Cultural Museum** has sophisticated exhibits displaying valuable ritual objects. (☎51 36 11. Open Tu-F 9am-4pm and Su 10am-5pm. €3.50, students and children €2. Guided visits in English, German, or Russian can be arranged.) **Bertolt Brecht's birthplace,** by a stream in a serene old neighborhood, was renovated in 1998 on the 100th anniversary of his birth. The museum chronicles the life of the influential 20th-century playwright and poet through photographs, letters, and poetry. From Rathauspl., head downhill on Perlachberg, and take the 3rd left onto Auf dem Rain 7. (Open Tu-Su 10am-5pm. €1.50, students and children €1.) The new **Maximilianmuseum,** Philippine-Welser-Str. 24, displays remarkable Renaissance sculptures and historical exhibits. Beyond the Fuggerhaus, walk through the garden of the Baroque **Schaezler Palace** to reach the **Staatsgalerie** (State Gallery), Maximilianstr. 46, a collection of religious art including works by Cranach, Holbein, and Dürer. (☎324 41 02. Both museums open Tu-Su 10am-5pm. Each €7, students and children €5.50.) The **Augsburg Puppenkiste** (Puppet Theater) Spitalg. 15, has a museum of the marionettes that still bring fame to the city. (Open Tu-Su 9am-7pm, ticket sales until 6pm. €4.20, ages 4-12 €2.70.)

ROTHENBURG OB DER TAUBER   ☎09861

As the crossroads of the Romantic and Castle Roads, Rothenburg ob der Tauber (pop. 12,000) caters to tourists seeking a one-day authentic medieval experience. But don't let the perpetual hordes of camera-wielding foreigners scare you away; this town, which originally blossomed around 1500, is full of side streets and small parks largely untouched by the tourist deluge. Carefully preserved, pastel-colored Rothenburg may seem more medieval than the Middle Ages themselves, but the town's charm—even if slightly affected—is undeniable nonetheless.

■ ☎ TRANSPORTATION AND PRACTICAL INFORMATION

Trains run to Steinach (15min., every hr., €1.80), where you can transfer to trains for Munich and Würzburg. **Buses** also serve the route, sometimes in place of the train in the evening. The **Europabus** (p. 521) leaves from the Busbahnhof, right next to the train station. For a **taxi,** call ☎20 00 or 72 27. Rent **bikes** at **Rad und Tat,** Bensenstr. 17. (☎879 84; www.mietraeder.de. Open M-F 9am-6pm, Sa 9am-1pm. €2.50 per hr., €10 per day. Reservations recommended in summer.) Rothenburg's **tourist office,** Marktpl. 2, books rooms and supplies free maps. You can also access the **Internet** for 15min. free of charge. Walk left from the station, bear right on Ansbacherstr., and follow it straight to the Marktpl. (15min.); the office is on your right, across the square in the pink building. (☎404 800; www.rothenburg.de. Open May-Oct. M-F 9am-noon and 1-6pm, Sa-Su 10am-3pm; Nov.-Apr. M-F 9am-noon and 1-5pm, Sa 10am-1pm.) **Tours** in German depart daily from the steps of the Rathaus (1½hr., Apr.-Oct. 11am and 2pm, €5), while English tours meet there daily at 2pm (€4). The night watchman leads a special tour with his lantern and iron spear; meet at the Rathaus. (Daily Easter-Christmas, in English 8pm. €6, students €4, under 13 free; in German 9:30pm, €5.) Local services include: **laundromat,** Johanniterg. 9 (☎27 75; wash and dry €5.50; open M-F 8am-6pm, Sa 8am-2pm.); **police,** Ansbacherstr. 72 (☎110, non-emergency ☎97 10); **Löwen-Apotheke,** Marktpl. 3., posting 24hr. **pharmacy** information (☎93 51 90; open M-F 8am-6pm, Sa 8:30am-12:30pm); **Internet** access at **Inter@Play,** Milchmarkt 3, two blocks from Marktpl. (☎93 55 99. €3 per hr. Open daily 8am-2am; closed holidays. €3 per hr.) The **post office** is at Bahnhofstr. 15, across from the station in the Zentro mall. (Open M-F 9:30am-5pm, Sa 9:30am-noon.) **Postal Code:** 91541.

ACCOMMODATIONS

An incredible number of private rooms (singles €15-30; doubles €28-45) not registered with the tourist office are available; look for *"Zimmer frei"* signs in the areas outside the city walls. Despite the abundance of rooms, reservations are recommended in the summer and around Christmas. There are also many pensions in town, some cheaper than others. The most charming budget one, **Pension Raidel ❷,** Wengg. 3, in the Altstadt, is a 500-year-old half-timbered house with rooms built and decorated by the owner. From Marktpl., head down Obere Schmiedg. and make a left on Wengg. (☎31 15; www.romanticroad.com/raidel. Breakfast included. Singles €19, with bath €39; doubles €39/49. Cash only.) The smaller, friendly **Pension Pöschel ❷,** Wengg. 22, across the street, has clean, standard rooms. (☎34 30; pension.poeschel@t-online.de. Breakfast included. Singles €20; doubles €35-45; triples €45-55. Cash only.) The family-run **Gasthof Goldene Rose ❸,** Spitalg. 28, on the main street, has cheery, spacious rooms with English-language books and magazines. Ask for a double (€46-50) in the blue house at the end of the garden. (☎46 38; www.zur-goldenen-rose.de. Breakfast included. Singles €18-22; doubles €38, with bath €48-62. AmEx/DC/MC/V.) In the Altstadt, **Pension Becker ❸,** Roseng. 23, offers conveniently located small rooms with private shower and toilet. (☎35 60; fax 35 40. Singles €31; doubles €48. MC/V.) Almost as expensive as neighboring pensions, the **Jugendherberge Rossmühle (HI) ❷,** Mühlacker 1, is a solid last resort. A horse-powered mill in the 16th century, it now sports ping-pong and pool tables, a TV room, Internet access (€2.40 per 30min.), and English-speaking staff. From the tourist office, take a left down Obere Schmiedg., and continue until you see the small, white *Jugendherberge* sign on the right. (☎941 60; jhrothenburg@djh-bayern.de. Breakfast included. Wash €2.50. Dry €2.50. Reception 7am-10:30pm. Curfew 10:30pm; door-code available. Dorms €19, doubles €44.)

FOOD

Rothenburg's festive *Schneeballen* (snowballs)—thin layers of fried dough rolled into large balls—are available all year. Their traditional powdered sugar coating is now often replaced by elaborate and messy guises involving chocolate, coconut, cointreau, marzipan, and amaretto. Buy them fresh at a *bäckerei*, such as **Café Freidel,** Markt 8 (☎78 18. Open M-Sa 6am-6pm, Su 10am-6pm. Cash only.) **Diller's** has six locations around town, including one at Obere Schmiedg. 7, and also offers these doughy concoctions for €1-3. (Open in summer M-Th and Su 9am-9pm, F-Sa

9am-10pm; in winter daily 11am-6pm. Cash only.) **Lidl**, Ehrlbacherstr. 48, is a cheap supermarket located just opposite Rad und Tat. (Open M-Sa 8am-8pm. Cash only.) The international tourist traffic supports scores of overpriced restaurants near the Marktpl., but it's not impossible to find good food at budget prices. Young people head outside the city walls to the **Malkerei ❸**, Schweinsdorfer Str. 25b. to have a beer (€2.40 for 0.5L), mixed drink (€5-7), or food from a rotating menu (€4-12). (www.malkerei.rothenburg.de. Su brunch 10am-2pm. Open Tu-Th 3pm-1am, F-Sa 3pm-2am, Su 10am-1am. Kitchen open Th-Su 6pm-11pm. Cash only.) Those looking for bygone days with their bread will enjoy dining in the oldest house (AD 980) in town at **Zur Höll** (To Hell) **❸**, Burgg. 8. Franconian food (€4-18) is served on scarred wooden tables in dim candlelight. (☎42 29. Open daily 5pm-1am. Cash only.) **Pizzeria Roma ❷**, Galgeng. 19, serves large portions of pasta, pizzas, and fresh salads (€4-7) at affordable prices. (☎45 40. Non-smoking section. Open Th-Tu 11:30am-midnight. MC/V.) **Gasthof Rödertor ❸**, Ansbacherstr. 7, by the Rödertor, has a *Biergarten* (Beer €2.60 for 0.4L) and potato-centric entrées (€4-11). (☎20 22. Open daily 11:30am-2pm and 5:30-10pm. AmEx/DC/MC/V.)

⊙ SIGHTS

The Renaissance **Rathaus** stands on the Marktpl. Climb the claustrophobia-inducing 60m tower and pay at the top to ascend the last few stairs for a panoramic view. (Open Apr.-Oct. daily 9:30am-12:30pm and 1:30-5pm; Nov. and Jan.-Mar. Sa-Su noon-3pm; Dec. daily noon-3pm. €1, children €0.50.) For a free view of the city and its surrounding countryside, climb atop the medieval **town wall**, accessible at points around the city's inner perimeter. According to local lore, during the Thirty Years' War, the conquering Catholic general Johann Tilly offered to spare the town from destruction if any local could chug a keg containing 3.25L (almost a gallon) of wine. Mayor Nusch successfully met the challenge, passed out for several days, then lived to a ripe old age. His saving *Meistertrunk* (Master Draught) is reenacted with great fanfare each year (May 25-28, Sept. 2, Oct. 6 and 10, 2007). Hang around with all the other tourists for an anti-climactic version of the episode acted out by the clock over the Marktpl. in the pink building (every hr. 11am-3pm and 8-10pm). Inside the courtyard behind the Rathaus are the **Historical Vaults**, once a medieval bakery and now a depiction of Rothenburg during the Thirty Years' War, the conflict that destroyed the wealth and prestige of both the city and the Holy Roman Empire. The first floor presents military and social history, while torture instruments lurk in the gloomy stone cells that form the dungeon. (☎867 51. Open Apr.-Oct. daily 9:30am-5:30pm; during Christmas market, 1-4pm. €2, students €1.50, ages 6-10 €0.50, under 6 free.)

The macabre exhibits in the ■**Medieval Crime Museum**, Burgg. 3-5, present the creative ways in which Europeans have punished one another. The rigidity of medieval law is evidenced in such grim instruments as chastity belts, iron maidens, gag bonnets, the stocks, and the pillory. Downstairs, exhibits detail ancient tortures; upstairs focuses on death and shaming devices. All displays explained in English. (☎53 59. Open daily Apr.-Oct. 9:30am-6pm; Dec. and Mar. 10am-4pm; Nov. and Jan.-Feb. 2-4pm. Last entry 45min. before closing. €3.50, students €2.30, children €1.70.) The **Jakobskirche**, Klosterg. 15, is famed for its Altar of the Holy Blood, a beautifully carved wooden *Last Supper* by Würzburg master Tilman Riemenschneider, who idiosyncratically placed Judas at the center. A former pilgrimage site, the church holds a famous reliquiary: three drops of Jesus' blood. The *Altar of the Twelve Apostles* is also a masterpiece, with paintings by Nördlingen artist Friedrich Herlin. (☎70 06 20. Open Apr.-Oct. M-Sa 9am-5:15pm, Su 10:30am-5:30pm; Dec. daily 10am-5pm; Nov. and Jan.-Mar. daily 10am-noon and 2-4pm. €2, students €0.50. Free German language tours May-Sept. and Dec. 11am and 2pm.

Free English tours Sa 3pm. Free 30min. organ concerts July-Aug. W 5pm.) A 13th-century Dominican convent now holds the **Reichsstadtmuseum** (Imperial City Museum), Klosterhof 5, with displays on local history and art. (☎93 90 43. Open daily Apr.-Oct. 10am-5pm; Nov.-Mar. 1-4pm. €3, students €2, children €1.50.)

DINKELSBÜHL ☎09851

Two centuries of economic depression following the Thirty Years' War left Din-kelsbühl (pop. 11,800)—once as prominent as Leipzig—entirely stagnant. Locals were too distracted by the violent civil strife between Catholics and Lutherans to attempt economic recovery. By the time they were ready to welcome modernity in, Ludwig I and his preservationist instinct got in the way, dictating in the early 19th century that no stone in Dinkelsbühl be touched. The presence of a large Catholic church at the center of a predominantly Lutheran town signals the con-tinuing relevance of the centuries-old religious conflict.

TRANSPORTATION AND PRACTICAL INFORMATION. Getting to Din-kelsbühl is not easy. From nearby Nördlingen, **bus** service runs to Dinkelsbühl. (M-F 7 per day, Sa-Su 2-4 per day, €4.40). Buses also go to and from Rothenburg ob der Tauber (M-F 9 per day, Sa-Su 1-3 per day; transfer at Dombühl or Feuchtwan-gen; €5.60.) The **tourist office,** on the Marktpl. across from the church, has maps (€0.30) and books rooms for free. The office also rents **bikes** (€3.60 per day). From the "Bahnhof" bus stop, turn right on Luitpoldstr. and then left onto Wörni-tzstr. and through the **Wörnitz Tor,** the oldest gate in the city, into the Altstadt. Veer right with the street to the Marktpl.; the tourist office is in the red building. (☎902 40; www.dinkelsbuehl.de. Open Apr.-Oct. M-F 9am-6pm, Sa 10am-1pm-and 1-4pm, Su 10am-noon; Nov.-Mar. M-F 10am-1pm and 2-5pm, Sa 10am-noon.) **Tours** of the town (in German) leave from St. Georgskirche. (Apr.-Oct. daily 2:30 and 8:30pm. €2.50, students €2. At 9pm the night watchman gives a free torchlight tour.) The **police** (☎110) are on Luitpoldstr. next to the post office. **Aesculap Apotheke,** Luit-poldstr. 27, to the left as you leave the bus station, is a **pharmacy.** (☎58 22 15. Open M-Sa 8am-8pm.) **Internet** access is available at **Fair Play,** Nördlingerstr. 9. (18+. €1 per 15min. Open M-Th and Su 9am-midnight, F-Sa 9am-1pm.) The **post office** is at Luitpoldstr. 13, is to the right of the "Bahnhof" bus stop. (Open M-F 9am-5pm, Sa 9am-noon.) **Postal Code:** 91550.

ACCOMMODATIONS AND FOOD. Built in 1508 as a grain store, the **Jugendherberge (HI) ❶,** Koppeng. 10, is one of the most beautiful buildings in the HI network. Leaving the tourist office, turn right down Segringer Str., and take a right on Bauhofstr. after passing the new Rathaus. At the first bus stop, swing left onto Koppeng. and up the uneven cobblestoned street; it's the large building at the top on the right. The ivy-draped fortress has a lush patio enclosed by stone walls; several forests worth of beams and paneling enclose the rooms. (☎95 09; www.dinkelsbuehl.jugendherberge.de. Breakfast included. Reception 5-7pm. Cur-few 11pm; key available. Open Mar.-Oct. 2- to 8-bed rooms €15.35, with private bath €18.35. Cash only.) Just outside the city walls in a cheerful neighborhood is **Privathaus Gockner ❷,** Veilchenweg 5, with bright rooms and a friendly English-speaking owner. From the tourist office, walk straight on Turmg. Continue through the park, cross over Südring, and walk past the fountain, turning right on Veilchenweg. (☎32 95; www.gockner.de. Breakfast included. Singles €20-23; dou-bles €40-46. Cash only.) If you are traveling in a group of four, ask for Room 31, an antique, country-style four-bed duplex, at the luxurious **Weißes Roß ❹,** Steing. 12. (☎57 98 90; Hotel-Weisses-Ross@t-online.de. Breakfast included. Doubles €68-90; triples €95; quads €110. AmEx/DC/MC/V.) Camp at **DCC Campingpark Romantische**

Str. ❶, north on Dürrwanger Str. (☎78 17; www.campingpark-dinkelsbuehl.de. €4 per person, ages 4-13 €2.50, €8.50 per tent and car. Electricity €1.80. V.)

The Italo-Turkish **Istanbul Imbiß** ❷, Nördlinger Str. 8, serves quality *Döner*, pizza, and salads (€3-7) amid colorful decorations. (☎55 36 15. Open M-Th and Su 10am-11pm, F-Sa 11am-midnight. Cash only.) **Weib's Brauhaus** ❸, Untere Schmiedg. 13, brews its own beer in house. Sit next to the brewing apparatus or in the intimate *Biergarten* and wash down traditional food (€5-12) with their Weißier (€2.20 for 0.5L). (☎57 94 90. Open daily 11am-2pm and 6-9:45pm, limited menu 9:45-10:30pm. Cash only.) **Gasthof Goldener Hirsch** ❹, Weinmarkt 6, has delicious Dinkelsbühl carp (fresh from Sept.-May; €8-12), classic Bavarian cuisine, and a few vegetarian dishes. (☎23 47. Open daily 8am-midnight. AmEx/DC/MC/V.)

🎫🎭 **SIGHTS AND ENTERTAINMENT.** The Romanesque tower of the **Münster St. Georg**, which dominates the Weinmarkt at the center of town, dates to the 13th century, though the late Gothic church was not begun until 1448. Inside the sandstone walls, an altar contains the fragmented skeleton of early martyr St. Aurelius, acquired in the 18th century. (Open Apr.-Oct. daily 9am-noon and 2-7 pm, Nov.-Mar. closes at 5pm. Free.) The lush **Parkring** promenade around the Altstadt separates the old and new parts of town and offers pleasant walks punctuated by clusters of ducks and willows. Dinkelsbühl miraculously survived Swedish occupation during the Thirty Years' War; this was later attributed to the tearful pleas of the town's children, led by the beautiful Lore Hirte. The event is reenacted every year in the **Kinderzeche Festival** (Children's Feast; July 13-22, 2007; July 18-27, 2008), with parades, fireworks, dances, and, of course, Lore and her flock of crying kids.

NÖRDLINGEN IM RIES ☎09081

The pleasant small town of Nördlingen (pop. 20,000), formerly a free city of the German *Reich*, sits proudly in a crater created by the impact of a meteor some 14.7 million years ago. The crater (known as the **Ries**, from *Raetia*, the name of the province under Roman rule), about 25km in diameter, was first an enormous lake. After the water drained naturally, the sediments it deposited gave the new town unusually fertile soil. As a result, Nördlingen grew into a trading center in the Middle Ages, with an important fair, the **Pfingstmesse**, which still takes place to this day (June 9-18, 2007). Nördlingen's almost perfectly circular wall, the only fully intact example in Germany, is built entirely from "Rieser Moonstones"— stones formed by the collision.

📧🚆 **TRANSPORTATION AND PRACTICAL INFORMATION. Trains** run to: Augsburg (1¼hr., every hr., €11.70); Munich (2-2½hr., every hr., €20-27); Nuremberg (2hr., every hr., €41); Ulm (2hr., 2 per hr., €16). **Bus** #501 also runs from Dinkelsbühl (45min.; M-F 7 per day, Sa-Su 2-4 per day; €4.40). The **tourist office**, Marktpl. 2, distributes free city maps and books rooms for free. (☎841 16; www.noerdlingen.de. Open Easter-Oct. M-Th 9am-6pm, F 9am-4:30pm, Sa 9:30am-1pm, Su 10am-1pm; Nov.-Easter M-Th 9am-5pm, F 9am-3:30pm.) It also offers 1hr. tours in German (Apr.-Oct. 2pm) from the Rathaus, or by torchlight (mid-May to mid Sept.) at 8:30pm (€3, under 13 free). The **police** can be found at Reimlingerstr. 7 (☎110). **Einhorn-Apotheke**, Polizeig. 7., is the oldest **pharmacy** in town, dating to 1387. (☎296 20. Open M-F 8am-6pm, Sa 8am-noon.) **Internet** access is at the **Stadtbücherei** on the Marktpl. on the opposite side of the Rathaus from St. Georg (€0.50 per 15min; open Tu and Sa 10am-1pm; W and F 10am-1pm and 2-6pm; Th 2-6:30pm), and at **Café Radlos** (p. 529). The **post office** is to the right of the train station as you exit. (Open M-F 8:30am-5pm, Sa 8:30am-11:30am.) **Postal Code:** 86720.

⚐☐ ACCOMMODATIONS AND FOOD. Nördlingen does not have a hostel, but there are numerous inexpensive guesthouses in town, clearly marked by *"Zimmer frei"* signs. You can also stop by the tourist office to find a room. **Gasthof Walfisch ❷**, Hallg. 15, is in the center of town near Marktpl. From the tourist office, head left onto Windg. and take a right on Hallg. The somber hallways and spacious rooms are complemented by the friendly service of the mother-son team that runs the house. (☎/fax 31 07. Breakfast included. Singles €20-30; doubles €40-60.) **Drei Mohren Gasthof ❸**, Reimlinger Str. 18, is just inside the town wall near the Reimlinger Tor. From Marktpl., follow Schäfflesmarkt to Reimlinger Str. (☎31 13; fax 287 59. Singles €20; doubles €40.) The **Hotel Braunes Ross ❸**, Marktpl. 12, is right on the Marktpl. (☎29 01 20; fax 290 12 28. Breakfast included. Singles €26-40; doubles €46-70. MC/V.) **◪Café Radlos ❸**, Löpsingerstr. 8, serves up everything from traditional Bavarian *Wurst* to Asian specialties. (☎50 40. Main courses €6-12. Internet access €2 per 30min. Open M-Tu and Th-Su 10am-1am. Kitchen open until 11pm. Cash only.) **Blaue Glocke ❷**, Herreng. 2, also attracts a younger crowd with its garden and hip artwork. Most Bavarian dishes €6-9. (☎99 65. Beer €2.20 (0.5L). Open M and W-F 11am-2pm and 5pm-1am, Sa-Su 5pm-1am. Cash only.)

◪ SIGHTS. Nördlingen's late Gothic **St. Georg Kirche,** which boasts a 90m bell-tower nicknamed "Daniel," was built entirely of meteoric rock, making it the only church in the world that is literally heaven-sent. Every night for the last 500 years, the town watchman has rung atonal bells from atop the tower and called out *"So G'sell so!"* ("You silly fool!") over the town's red rooftops every 30min. between 10pm and midnight. (Tower open daily Apr.-Oct. 9am-7pm; Nov.-Mar. 9am-5pm. €2, under 17 €1.50, family €4.10. Church open M-F 9:30am-12:30pm and 2-5pm, Sa 9:30am-5pm, Su 11am-5pm.) In a large, converted barn, the exhibitions and multimedia displays of **Rieskrater Museum,** Eugene-Shoemaker-Pl. 1, provide astronomical, geological, and historical information on the Ries meteorite. The museum also runs geology tours of the region, allowing visitors to join experts in field outings. Call for details and reserve at least four weeks in advance. (☎273 82 20. Open Tu-Su 10am-noon and 1:30-4:30pm. €4, students €2. English guide available; €3.30 plus €7 deposit. 2hr. Geology tour €40.) Look at dioramas and talk with Aksel Rinck, the enthusiastic man-of-the-tower, about the medieval town wall in Nördlingen's **Stadtmauermuseum** (City Wall Museum), inside the old watch-tower, Löpsinger Tor. (☎91 80. Open Apr.-Nov. daily 10am-4:30pm. €1.50, under 17 €1.) The city's **Stadtmuseum** (Municipal Museum), Vordere Gerberg. 1, located in the heart of the old cloth-dyeing quarters, explores the region's culture from the first farming settlements of 6000 BC to the present day. (☎273 82 30. Open Mar. to early Nov. Tu-Su 1:30-4:30pm. Free detailed English guide. €3, students €1.50.)

WÜRZBURG
☎0931

Sweeping vistas of the Main River, striking Baroque churches, and the 13th-century Marienburg fortress form the perfect setting to sample local white wines, a Würzburg (pop. 134,000) passion every bit as strong as any Bavarian fondness for *Bier*. The fortress and flamboyantly Rococo Residenz, now host to museums and festivals, are symbols of the past power of Würzburg's prince-bishops. These sovereigns, who governed this part of Franconia from 1168 until 1802, steered the region back to Catholicism even as its citizens longed to adhere to the principles of the Reformation. Today, the city is known for Julius-Maximilians-Universität, a hub for science which counts 13 Nobel Prize winners among its faculty. A large portion of the city was destroyed by bombings in the last days of WWII, but most of the historic buildings have been restored or rebuilt, making Würzburg a scenic gateway to the Romantic and Castle Roads.

BAYERN

⌐ TRANSPORTATION

Trains: To: **Bamberg** (1hr., every hr., €15.50); **Frankfurt** (2hr., 2 per hr., €20.80); **Munich** (3hr., every hr., €54); **Nuremberg** (1hr., every hr., €16-23); **Rothenburg ob der Tauber** (1hr., 1 per hr., €10).

Buses: Europabus (p. 521) traces the Romantic Road to **Füssen** and **Munich** daily starting at 10am. The bus station is to the right of the Hauptbahnhof.

Ferries: Personenschifffahrt (☎556 33; www.vpsherbert.de) ferries tourists to Veitschöchheim (one-way 40min.), leaving from **Alter Kranen** (near the Congress Center) at the white kiosk, every hr. 10am-4pm. €6, round-trip €9.

Public Transportation: Trams are the most efficient way around, but large sections outside the downtown are not covered. The **bus** network is comprehensive, but most routes do not run nights or weekends. Ask for **night bus** schedules at the **WSB kiosk** (open M-F 7:30am-6pm) in front of the Hauptbahnhof, or at the **WVV Center**, Juliuspromenade 64 (open M-F 8am-6pm, Sa 9am-1:30pm). Single fare €2. 6 trips €7.50. Day ticket €4, families €8.10. Sa-Su day ticket covers both days. For a **taxi**, call ☎194 10.

Bike Rental: Ludwig Korner, Bronnbacherg. 3 (☎53 340), just north of Marktpl. €8-10 per day, €45 per wk. Open M-F 9am-6pm, Sa 9am-2pm.

✦ 🛈 ORIENTATION AND PRACTICAL INFORMATION

To get to the city's center at **Marktplatz,** follow Kaiserstr. straight from the station for two blocks, then take a right on Juliuspromenade, and hang a left on **Schönbornstraße,** the main pedestrian and tram road; the Markt is a few blocks down and to the right. Trams #1, 3, and 5 run from the station to the Markt. The Main River separates the rest of the city from the steep surrounding hills.

Tourist Office: (☎37 23 98) in **Haus zum Falken,** a yellow Rococo building on the Marktpl. Provides free city maps, lists hotels, and books rooms for free. Open Apr.-Dec. M-F 10am-6pm, Sa 10am-2pm; May-Oct. also Su 10am-2pm; Jan.-Mar. M-F 10am-4pm, Sa 10am-1pm. The **main office,** Am Congress Centrum (☎37 23 35; www.wuerzburg.de), offers the same services. Near the Friedensbrücke, where Röntgenring intersects the Main, accessible by tram #2 or 4. Open M-Th 8:30am-5pm, F 8:30am-1pm. After hours, there's a map and hotel information on the board just outside the train station.

Tours: German-language tours of the city depart mid-Apr. to Oct. daily at 10:30am. (€5, students €3.50.) **English tours** daily 6:30pm; meet in front of Falkenhaus (€5). For nocturnal adventures, join the (German-speaking) **night watchman,** with lantern and spear, on his rounds of the Altstadt. W-Sa Apr.-Dec. 8 and 9pm; Jan.-Mar. 8pm only. Meet at the fountain across from the Rathaus. (€3, children free.) **Bus tours** (in German) leave the bus station and return 2hr. later. Mid-Apr. to Oct. M-Sa 2pm, Su 10:30am. (☎36 23 20. €8.90, students €7.90.) For a comprehensive list of tours (text in German), ask at the tourist office for the brochure *Führungen & Ausflüge.*

Budget Travel: STA, Zwinger 6. (☎521 76; wuerzburg@statravel.de). Open M-F 9:30am-6pm and Sa 9:30am-1pm.

Currency Exchange: Sparkasse, Barbarossapl. 2 (☎304 89 10). Open M-W and F 8:30am-4:30pm, Th 8:30am-6:30pm.

Bookstore: Hugendubel, Schmalzmarkt 12 (☎01801 48 44 84), will move to Krichenerhof in Oct. 2007. Open M-Sa 9:30am-8pm.

Laundromat: Waschhaus, Frankfurterstr. 13a. Wash €3. Dry €0.50 per 10min. Open M-Sa 7am-10pm.

Emergency: Police ☎110. **Fire** and **Ambulance** ☎112.

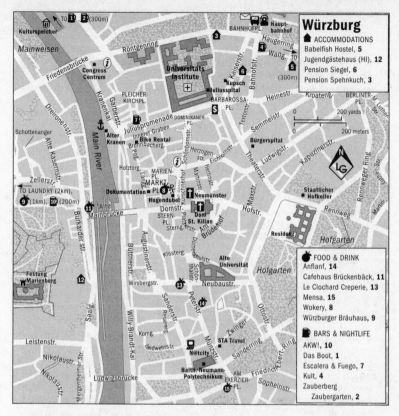

Würzburg

🏠 **ACCOMMODATIONS**
Babelfish Hostel, 5
Jugendgästehaus (HI), 12
Pension Siegel, 6
Pension Spehnkuch, 3

🍎 **FOOD & DRINK**
Anflanf, 14
Cafehaus Brückenbäck, 11
Le Clochard Creperie, 13
Mensa, 15
Wokery, 8
Würzburger Bräuhaus, 9

🍺 **BARS & NIGHTLIFE**
AKW!, 10
Das Boot, 1
Escalera & Fuego, 7
Kult, 4
Zauberberg
Zaubergarten, 2

Pharmacy: Engel Apotheke, Marktpl. 36 (☎32 13 40), posts 24hr. pharmacy information. Open M-F 8:30am-6:30pm, Sa 8:30am-4pm.

Hospital: Krankenhaus Juliusspital, Juliuspromenade 19 (☎39 30, emergency 19 84), between the train station and Marktpl.

Internet Access: N@tcity, Sanderstr. 27 (☎30 41 94 94; www.naetcity.de). €2.70 per hr., students €2.43. Open daily 10am-midnight.

Post Office: Bahnhofpl. 2. Open M-F 8am-6pm, Sa 9am-noon. **Postal Code:** 97070.

🔑 ACCOMMODATIONS

Würzburg's least expensive beds can be found near the Hauptbahnhof and around **Kaiserstr.** and **Bahnhofstr.**

🛏 **Babelfish Hostel,** Prymstr. 3 (☎304 0430; www.babelfish-hostel.de), 500m from the Hauptbahnhof. With your back to the station, turn left on Haugering and walk about 7min. to the grinning fish sign. New hostel with large kitchen and showers. Wheelchair-accessible. Sheets €2.50. Free Internet access. Wash and dry €3. Reception daily 7am-midnight. Check-out 11am. Key deposit €10. 10-bed dorms €16; 6- to 8-bed €17; 4-bed €18; 2-bed €22. Cash only. ❷

Jugendgästehaus (HI), Burkarderstr. 44 (☎425 90; fax 41 68 62), across the river. Tram #3 (dir.: Heidingsfeld) or #5 (dir.: Heuchelhof-Rottenbauer) to "Löwenbrücke," then backtrack 300m. Follow the Jugendherberge sign down the stairs, turn right, and walk through the tunnel; it's on the left. Enormous villa with great views. Wheelchair accessible. Breakfast included. Reception from 8am. Check-in 4:30-10pm. Curfew 1am; door code available. 4- to 8-bed dorms €19.80. Cash only. ❷

Pension Spehnkuch, Röntgenring 7 (☎547 52; fax 547 60). Turn right after leaving the station and walk 1min. down Röntgenring. Renovated rooms are simple, clean, and conveniently located. Breakfast included. Singles €31-33; doubles €56-62; triples €78-81. Call ahead Dec.-Feb. Cash only. ❸

Pension Siegel, Reisgrubeng. 7 (☎529 41; fax 529 67), features a neurotic mural in the stairwell and basic rooms situated just off Bahnhofstr. Breakfast included. No reception M-Sa 2-5pm, Su 12:30-6:30pm. Singles €33; doubles €62. Cash only. ❸

▮ FOOD

Würzburg's distinctive wines are sold in equally distinctive bottles, known as *Bocksbeutel* (goat bags; locals claim that they emulate the shape of goats' testicles). To sample the wine, **Juliusspital**, Juliuspromenade 19 (Apr. to mid-Nov. F-Sa 5pm), **Bürgerspital**, Semmelstr. 2 (Apr.-Oct. Sa 2pm), and **Staatlicher Hofkeller**, next to the Residenz (Mar.-Nov. Sa every hr. 10am-noon and 2-5pm; Su no 5pm tour), all offer 1hr. *Kellerführungen* (cellar tours; €5) including a glass of wine. Ask at the tourist office. For **groceries**, try **Kupsch**, Kaiserstr. 5, near Barbarossapl. (Open M-F 8am-8pm, Sa 8am-6pm. Cash only.) **Killian's Bäck**, Domstr. 7, is a bakery with seating, sandwiches, and ice cream in addition to a wide array of baked goods. (☎120 51. Open M-F 7am-7pm, Sa 7am-5pm, Oct.-May also Su 1-5pm. Cash only.)

Le Clochard Crêperie/Bistro, Neubaustr. 20 (☎129 07, www.leclochard.de). Crêpes, sandwiches, and vegetarian dishes (€4-8). Crêpe of the day and coffee €3.50, daily 3-5pm. Open M-Tu 5pm-1am, W-Su 10am-1am. MC/V. ❷

Auflauf, Peterpl 5 (☎57 13 43). *Auflauf* (casseroles) with ingredients ranging from shittake mushrooms to spicy shrimp and pineapple (€8-10). Lunch specials M-F noon-2:30pm €5.60. Open M-F noon-2:30pm and 5:30pm-midnight, Sa-Su noon-midnight. Kitchen open until 11:30pm. MC/V. ❸

Wokery, Schmalzmarkt 5 (☎404 19 22; www.wokery.de). Chinese buffet with vegetarian options. Pay by the size of your plate, not its weight. W-Sa from 7pm, all you can eat €6.66. Open Tu- 11am-8pm, W-Sa 11am-10pm. Cash only. ❷

Caféhaus Brückenbäck, Zellerstr. 2, by the Alte Mainbrücke (☎41 45 45). Large windows and a non-smoking section. Salads, sandwiches, and rice dishes €4-8.50. Open Tu-W and Su 8am-midnight, Th-Sa 8am-1am. Kitchen closes 11pm. Cash only. ❷

Würzburger Hofbraukeller, Höchbergerstr. 28 (☎429 70). *Biergarten* serving local brew (€3, 0.5L). Frankish specialties €6-11. Open M-Th 10am-midnight, F-Sa 10am-1am, Su 9am-midnight; garden closes daily at 11:30pm, food until 10pm. DC/MC/V. ❸

Mensa, Am Studentenhaus, 1 block from Sanderring, is a sparkling university dining hall serving international cuisine to local students and guests. Discount with student ID. Entrées €4-6. Open M-Th 7:30am-7pm, F 7:30am-2pm, Sa 11am-2pm. Breakfast from 7:30am. Lunch 11am-2pm, dinner (M-Th only) 4:30-7pm. ❷

◉ SIGHTS

▨**RESIDENZ.** Johannes Zick's ceiling fresco in the first-floor garden room epitomizes the extravagance of the 18th-century Residenz. The work is so bright that it has never needed to be restored; in fact, his use of such extravagant colors got him fired. The Italian painter Giovanni Tiepolo replaced him, creating the largest frescoed ceiling in the world, above the grand staircases. Now that restoration on Tiepolo's masterpiece is complete, his work in the *Kaisersaal,* which combines painting, sculpture and stucco for stunning depth, is undergoing repairs until 2009. Then-unknown architect Balthasar Neumann made the Residenz's shallow dome so well that it withstood Allied bombings. His glass room and gaudy pink marble Residenzhofkirche also deserve careful attention. The university's **Martin-von-Wagner-Museum,** in a wing of the Residenz, displays Greek antiques that belonged to the collector, whom Ludwig commissioned to create the Glyptothek and the Antikensammlung in Munich. A number of pieces, including early Italian and fleshy Baroque paintings, ended up in the intermediary's house. Behind the complex, the Hofgarten is trisected into an Italian amphitheater, a geometric Austrian garden with cone-shaped evergreens, and a faux-wild English garden (all the rage after 1780). *(From the station, walk down Kaiserstr., then Theaterstr. ☎ 35 51 70. Open daily Apr.-Oct. 9am-6pm; Nov.-Mar. 10am-4:30pm. Last entry 30min. before closing. Exceptionally informative tours in English depart daily at 11am and 3pm. €5, students and seniors €4. Martin-von-Wagner-Museum's painting gallery open Tu-Sa 9:30am-12:30pm. Greek collection open 2-5pm. The 2 galleries alternate being open Su 9:30am-12:30pm. Both free. Church open the same times as the Residenz. Free. Gardens open in summer dawn-8pm, in winter dawn-6pm. Free.)*

FESTUNG MARIENBERG (MARIENBERG FORTRESS). This striking fortress has been holding vigil over the Main since the 12th century, when the prince-bishops lived here before the Residenz was built. The *Fußweg* (footpath) to the fortress starts a short distance from the Medieval **Alte Mainbrücke,** lined with Baroque statues of saints and figures, and built to exalt the prince-bishops' prestige during the Counter-Reformation. The strenuous climb to the Festung reveals the strategic value of its lofty location. Within the fortress compound, you'll find the 11th-century **Marienkirche,** the 40m high 12th-century **Bergfried** watchtower under which lies the **Hole of Fear** (a dungeon), the **Fürstengarten** rose garden, and the 104m deep **Brunnentempel** well. *(Garden open M until 4pm, Tu-Su until 5:30pm. Well open M 9am-3:30pm, Tu-F 9am-5:30pm, Sa-Su only by guided tour.)* Artifacts from the lives of the prince-bishops, scale-models of Würzburg at both its ancient splendor and post-WWII deprivation, and *objets d'art* cluster in the **Fürstenbaumuseum** (Princes' Building Museum). *(☎ 355 17 53. Open Tu-Su Apr. to mid-Oct. 9am-6pm; mid-Oct. to Mar. 10am-4pm; last entry 30min. before closing. €4, students €3.)* Outside the walls of the main fortress, the long hallways of the **Mainfränkisches Museum** (Main-Frankish Museum), a former arsenal, are lined with religious statues featuring the expressive wooden sculptures of **Tilman Riemenschneider** (1460-1531), the "Master of Würzburg." Legend holds that Riemenschneider paid dearly for siding with the peasants in their 16th-century revolts: when the insurrection was suppressed, the bishop Julius Echter allegedly had the sculptor's fingers broken, preventing him from working again. Riemenschneider's house is now a restaurant on Franziskanerg., two blocks from Domstr. *(Take bus #9 from the Residenzpl. to "Festung," or a 30min. walk. Tours in German depart from the courtyard Apr.-Oct. Tu-F 11am, 2, and 3pm. Sa-Su every hr. 10am-4pm, no noon tour. €3, seniors and students €2. English guidebooks at museum shop or kiosks €2.60. Mainfränkisches Museum ☎ 20 59 40. Open Tu-Su Apr.-Oct. 10am-5pm; Nov.-Mar. 10am-4pm; last entry 30min. before closing. €3, students €1.50, under 14 free. Audio guide in English €3. Pass to both museums €5.)*

DOM ST. KILIAN. The 950-year-old Catholic cathedral was rebuilt in the 1960s after destruction in WWII. The interior's modern design represents the passage of time, from the menorah symbolizing the Old Testament to the white Christ emerging from a golden medallion at the altar. Outside, the rediscovered Rose Window is being restored through spring 2007. *(☎ 321 18 30; www.dom-wuerzburg.de. Open Easter-*

Oct. M-Sa 10am-5pm, Su 1-6pm; Oct.-Easter M-Sa 10am-noon and 2-5pm, Su 12:30-1:30pm and 2:30-6pm. Free. Tours M-Sa 12:20, Su 12:30 and include the otherwise inaccessible Schönbornkappelle. €2.50, students €1.50. Organ concerts M-Sa at 12:05pm.)

DOKUMENTATION ZENTRUM (DOCUMENTATION CENTER). On March 16, 1945, the Allies dropped 300,000 firebombs on Würzburg, obliterating the city. This small exhibit has photographs, a startling diorama of the city after the bombing, and names of the some of the victims on the ceiling. *(At the town hall by the Alte Mainbrücke, face the "Ratskeller" restaurant, and head into the small alley just to the left. The entrance is on the right just before the arch. Open daily 9am-11pm. Free.)*

♫ ⚑ ENTERTAINMENT AND NIGHTLIFE

In summer, Würzburg finds a reason to party almost every weekend, with the largest African festival in Europe (**Africa-Festival,** May 25-28, 2007), the lively **Kiliani-Volksfest** (July 7-23, 2007; take tram #4 to "Talavera")—dedicated to the patron saint Kilian, an Irish bishop who died a martyr's death in Würzburg—and the **Mozartfest** (June 1-July 1, 2007, www.mozartfest-wuerzburg.de), with many concerts in the beautiful Residenz gardens. Würzburg's young and beautiful party around **Sanderstraße,** a pedestrian street packed with bars and clubs, and the streets near the **Marktplatz** offer a number of outdoor cafés. For a list of concerts, events, and club parties, check out the free magazine *Frizz,* or pick up a copy of *Mein Würzburg* at the tourist office (€2.50).

AKW!, Frankfurterstr. 87 (☎417 800; www.akw-info.de). Take tram #2 or 4 to "Siebold Museum," walk 50m away from city and look for the small blue sign on the left. A bistro, beer garden, and club that attracts goth, indie, and reggae crowds on alternating nights. Cover €3-14; many events free. Beer €2.70 (0.5L). Bistro and beer garden open daily 3pm-2am. Food (€3-6) until midnight. Disco open F-Sa 10pm-5am. Cash only.

Das Boot, Veithöchheimerstr. 14 (☎593 53; www.das-boot.com). Large fishing ship anchored in the Main. Join wild students dancing to all genres of music. Cover Th €3, F €3-8, Sa €5. Beer €2.80 (0.5L). Th 2 beers €2.50, mixed drinks €4 (€4.50 all night F and until midnight Sa). Open Th 8pm-4am, F-Sa 9pm-5am. Cash only.

Kult, Landwehrstr. 10 (☎531 43), right off Sanderstr. toward the Ludwigsbrücke, is a mellow, alternative bar and café run as a co-op catering to students. Sa-Su create-your-own breakfast menu until 3pm. Entrées €4-8. Beer €2.50 (0.5L). Open M-F 9am-1am, Sa-Su 10am-1am or later. Cash only.

Zauberberg/Zaubergarten, Veithöchheimerstr 20 (☎329 36 80; www.zauberberg.info). Club, lounge, and cozy beer garden that becomes a hookah tent in winter. Beer €3.20 (0.5L). Th student night (drinks 2 for 1). 2nd F of the month gay night. Sa 30+. Cover Th €3, F-Sa €5, before 11pm €2.50; more for special events. Club open Th 9pm-4am, F-Sa 9pm-5am. Garden open M-Sa 4pm-1am, Su 1pm-1am. Cash only.

Escalera & Fuego, Juliuspromenade 7 (☎35 98 306). This restaurant and bar takes its Caribbean theme seriously, with a rainforest upstairs (check out the live baby shark) and a sandy beach outside. Mixed drinks €6-8, M-W €3.90. Happy hour daily 6-8pm and 1-2am. Open M-Th and Su 5pm-2am, F-Sa until 3am or later. Cash only.

NÜRNBERG (NUREMBERG)   ☎0911

Before the names Berlin or Munich meant anything, Nuremberg (pop. 500,000) was one of the most important cities in the German *Reich.* Albrecht Dürer, the foremost German Renaissance painter, worked here, part of a wider Nuremberg arts community that blossomed from the 14th-16th century. Although the Holy Roman Empire was a loose confederation and had no true capital, the free city of

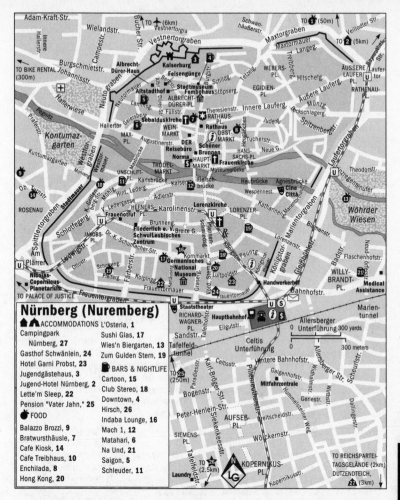

Nürnberg (Nuremberg)

♠♠ ACCOMMODATIONS
Campingpark
  Nürnberg, **27**
Gasthof Schwänlein, **24**
Hotel Garni Probst, **23**
Jugendgästehaus, **3**
Jugend-Hotel Nürnberg, **2**
Lette'm Sleep, **22**
Pension "Vater Jahn," **25**
🍴 FOOD
Balazzo Brozzi, **9**
Bratwursthäusle, **7**
Cafe Kiosk, **14**
Cafe Treibhaus, **10**
Enchilada, **8**
Hong Kong, **20**

L'Osteria, **1**
Sushi Glas, **17**
Wies'n Biergarten, **13**
Zum Gulden Stern, **19**

🍺 BARS & NIGHTLIFE
Cartoon, **15**
Club Stereo, **18**
Downtown, **4**
Hirsch, **26**
Indaba Lounge, **16**
Mach 1, **12**
Matahari, **6**
Na Und, **21**
Saigon, **5**
Schleuder, **11**

BAYERN

Nuremberg considered itself the unofficial one, holding Imperial Diets (councils) at the Kaiserburg. Drawing on this tradition, Hitler chose the city for his massive rallies, held each September from 1933 to 1938; it was from here that his 1935 Racial Purity Laws were proclaimed. Accordingly, the Allies took aim and by 1945 reduced 90% of the city's historical buildings to rubble. Because of Nuremberg's Nazi ties, the Allies also selected this city to host the war crimes tribunals of 1945.

Apart from the rally site and other Nazi relics, the city is famous for its toy fair and *Weihnachtsmarkt* (Nov. 30-Dec. 24, 2007), its sausages and gingerbread, and as the birthplace of composer Johann Pachelbel. Today, the city's Renaissance buildings are not the only things being reconstructed; every other year since the early nineties, the city has given a human rights award as part of the attempt by Nurembergers to refashion their city as the *Stadt der Menschenrechte* (City of Human Rights).

◧ TRANSPORTATION

Flights: The airport, Flughafenstr. 100 (☎937 00) is 7km north of Nuremberg. U2 connects the airport to the city (15min., €1.80).

Trains: To: **Berlin** (4½hr., every hr., €77); **Frankfurt** (2-3½hr., 2 per hr., €31.30); **Munich** (1½hr., 2 per hr., €27.30); **Prague, Czech Republic** (5-6hr., 2 per day, €41.80); **Regensburg** (1hr., 2 per hr., €15.50); **Stuttgart** (2-3hr., every hr., €27.30); **Würzburg** (1hr., 2 per hr., €15.70).

Public Transportation: U-Bahn, trams, buses, regional trains (R-Bahn), and S-Bahn. Single-ride within the city €1.80. *Kurzstrecke* (short distance) €1.40. 10-stripe *Streifenkarte* €8.30. Day or weekend card €3.60. The *Tagesticket Plus* day card covers 2 adults and 4 children for €6.30. The *Nürnberg* Card, available at the tourist office, covers 2 consecutive days of public transportation and entrance to almost all museums, as well as theater and store discounts, for €18.

Taxis: Taxizentrale ☎ 194 10 or **City Taxi** ☎27 27 70.

Bike Rental: Ride on a Rainbow, Adam-Kraft-Str. 55 (☎39 73 37; www.ride-on-a-rainbow.de), northwest of the Altstadt. Take Johannisstr. to Frauenholzstr. and turn right, then another right onto Adam-Kraft-Str. Bikes (not actually rainbow-colored) €8-10 per day. Open M-Tu and Th-F 10am-7pm, W 2:14-7:19pm, Sa 10am-3pm.

Ride Share: Mitfahrzentral, Hummelsteiner Weg 12 (☎194 40; www.citytocity.de). 100m from the southern exit of the Hauptbahnhof. Open M-F 9am-6pm, Sa 9am-1:30pm, Su 10am-1pm.

◧◪ ORIENTATION AND PRACTICAL INFORMATION

Nuremberg's lively central district lies within the old city wall. From the train station, the main shopping area is across Frauentorgraben down **Königstr.**, which leads through the city walls and down to the river Pegnitz. From the Hauptbahnhof, follow the "Ausgang City" signs down into the tunnel and the "Altstadt" signs out the other side; you'll end up on Königstr. **Lorenzpl.** and the **Hauptmarkt** are just beyond Königstr. and the river, in the Altstadt's pedestrian zone. The **Burg** sits on a hill overlooking the northernmost part of the Altstadt.

Tourist Offices: Königstr. 93 (☎233 61 31; www.nuernberg.de). Walk through the tunnel from the train station to the Altstadt and take a right; it will be on your left. The staff books rooms for free and offers English maps and city guides (€3-9), and event schedules. Open M-Sa 9am-7pm. **Branch** (☎233 61 35) on the Hauptmarkt near the fountain. Open May-Oct. M-Sa 9am-6pm, Su 10am-4pm; Nov.-Apr. M-Sa 9am-6pm; during the Christmas Market M-Sa 9am-7pm, Su 10am-7pm.

Tours: 2½hr. English tours depart from the Hauptmarkt tourist office May-Oct. and Dec. daily at 1pm. €8, under 14 free. A bilingual 2½hr. bus tour leaves from the Hallpl. (Mauthalle) May-Oct. and Dec. daily 9:30am. €11, students €9, under 12 €5.50 (☎20 22 910). The tourist office rents self-guided English-language audio tours. (www.cityaudiotours.de. €3 per hr., €9 per day.)

Budget Travel: DER Reisebüro, Hauptmarkt 29 (☎20 49 21; www.der.de), on the northwest corner of the Hauptmarkt. Deciphers timetables and gives travel information for a €3.50 fee. Train reservations €3. Open M-F 9:30am-6pm, Sa 10am-1pm.

Currency Exchange: Reisebank (☎22 67 78), in the central hall of the train station. 4.5% commission for currency exchange. Traveler's checks €6, AmEx free. Open M-Sa 7:30am-7:45pm, Su 8am-12:30pm and 1:15-4pm.

Luggage storage: In the Hauptbahnhof. Up to 72hr. €2-8.

Lost and Found: Fundbüro, Siebenkeesstr. 6 (☎431 76 24). Open M-W 9:30am-4pm, Th 9:30am-6pm, F 9:30am-12:30pm. For items lost on trains, go to **DB Fundstelle** (☎219 20 21) in the Hauptbahnhof. Open M-F 7:30am-7pm, Sa 8-11:30am and 12:15-6pm.

Gay and Lesbian Resources: Fliederlich e.V. SchwulLesbisches Zentrum, Breite G. 76 (☎423 45 70; www.fliederlich.de). Open M noon-2pm and W 11am-2pm. Additionally, gay men can call **Rosa Hilfe** (☎194 46; open W 7-9pm), and lesbian women can call **Lesben-Beratung** (☎42 34 57 25; open M 7-9pm).

Laundromat: SB Waschsalon, Tafelfeldstr. 42 (☎598 59 25). Wash €3.50. Dry €0.50 per 12min. Open M-Sa 7am-11pm.

Emergency: Police, Theresienstr. 3 (☎110). **Fire** ☎112. **Ambulance** ☎192 22.

Rape Crisis: Frauennotruf, Ludwigspl. 7 (☎28 44 00; www.frauennotruf.info).

Pharmacy: Königstr. 31 (☎22 45 51). Open M-F 8:30am-6:30pm, Sa 9am-4pm.

Hospital: Städtisches Klinikum Nord, Flurstr. 17 (☎39 80).

Medical Services: Bahnhofstr. 11a (€0.12 per min. ☎01805 19 12 12).

Internet Access: Tele Point, Königstorpassage 20, in the underground level of the train station. When you descend, at the city mosaic head left towards the U-Bahn. €1.50 per hr. Open daily 8am-midnight.

Post Office: Bahnhofpl. 1. Open M-F 8am-7pm, Sa 9am-2pm. **Postal Code:** 90402.

▚▞ ACCOMMODATIONS AND CAMPING

Nuremberg's budget options can fill quickly in summer; reserve in advance.

▨ **Jugendgästehaus (HI),** Burg 2 (☎230 93 60; fax 23 09 36 11). From the Hauptmarkt, head toward the golden fountain on the far left and bear right on Burgstr. Walk toward the castle and follow the sign to Burgenstr. (20min.). A 15th-century stable for the imperial castle, the hostel has Romanesque arches, a dizzying view of the city, and friendly multilingual staff. June and July define the phrase "overrun with schoolchildren;" reserve at least 3wk. in advance. Internet access €2 per 36min. Reception 7am-1am. Staffed 24hr. Curfew 1am, ask ahead for flexibility. 4- to 6-bed dorms €20.45, 2-3 nights €19.85, 4+ nights €19.30. MC/V. ❷

Lette'm Sleep, Frauentormauer 42 (☎99 28 128; www.backpackers.de). U2 to "Opernhaus." Incredibly friendly bilingual staff, social atmosphere, and colorful kitchen offset the dim lighting. Free Internet access. Sheets (optional) €3. Reception 24hr. Check-out noon. Reservations recommended. 8-bed women-only dorms and 12-bed dorms €16. 5- and 6-bed dorms €18, 3- and 4-bed dorms €20, doubles €48-52, apartments with private kitchen and bathroom from €65. MC/V. ❷

Pension "Vater Jahn," Jahnstr. 13 (☎44 45 07; fax 431 52 36). From the train station turn left onto Frauentorgraben, then left on Tafelfeldstr. through the underpass. Turn right on Bogenstr. and right again on Jahnstr. (10min.). Gleaming rooms, some with TV. Breakfast included. Reception 24hr. Singles €23, with bath €38; doubles €41, with shower €55. Extra bed €20. Cash only. ❸

Gasthof Schwänlein, Hintere Sterng. 11 (☎22 51 62; fax 241 90 08). From the station, take the underground passage to Königstr. and make an immediate left on Frauentormauerstr. Follow the town wall and bear right on Hintere Sterng.; the hotel is 200m down on the left. Quiet rooms above a restaurant. Breakfast included. Reservations by fax or mail only. Singles €28, with shower €32, with bathroom €38; doubles €44/52/58; triples €80. Cash only. ❸

Hotel Garni Probst, Luitpoldstr. 9 (☎20 34 33; fax 205 93 36). From the station, follow the underground passage to Königstor past Burger King; turn left on Luitpoldstr. The location is central, although nearby sex shops detract from the neighborhood's appeal. Generous breakfast included. Reception 24hr. Singles €21, with shower €35-40, with bath €41-51; doubles €43, with bath €57-67. Cash only. ❸

Jugend-Hotel Nürnberg, Rathsbergstr. 300 (☎521 60 92; fax 521 69 54). From the station, take U2 (dir.: Flughafen) to "Ziegelstein," then bus #21 (dir.: Buchenbühl) to "Zum Felsenkeller." Rustic and cheerful, but far from the action. All dorm rooms with bath. Breakfast €5. Reception M-F 8am-9pm, Sa-Su 8-11am and 7-9pm. Dorms €14.50; singles €24-28; doubles €36-46. €2.50 surcharge for 1-night stays. Cash only. ❶

Campingpark Nürnberg, Hans-Kalb-Str. 56 (☎981 27 17; www.knaus-campingplatz-nbg.de), in Volkspark Dutzendteich. S2 (dir.: Feucht/Altdorf) to "Frankenstadion." Tent rental available (5-person tent €16-71, depending on season). Reception 8am-1pm and 3-10pm. €6 per person, children €3, €3-5 per tent, €11 per site. Electricity and shower included. Cash only. ❶

🞖 FOOD

Nuremberg is famous for its *Rostbratwurst* (small, delectable grilled pork sausage), boiled *Sauere Zipfel* (sausage cooked in vinegar, salt, and spices), and *Lebkuchen*, a candied gingerbread traditionally devoured at Christmas. **Norma,** Hauptmarkt 11, across from the Frauenkirche, has cheap **groceries.** (Open M-F 8am-8pm, Sa 8am-6pm. Cash only.) The **Hauptmarkt** fills up with vendors selling fresh fruits and veggies in the mornings and afternoons (M-Sa).

Café Balazzo Brozzi, Hochstr. 2 (☎28 84 82), outside the Rosenau park. Airy café with private patio. Order at the counter. Breakfasts €3-8, Baguettes €2.40-4, Salads €1.80-10. Veggie options €4.50-8. Su Breakfast buffets and winter concerts (call for details). Open M-Sa 9am-11pm, Su 9am-9pm; closed first M of the month. Cash only. ❷

Wies'n Biergarten, Johann Sörgel Weg (☎240 66 88), in the Wöhrder Wiese. U2 to "Wöhrder Wiese." *Biergarten* popular with families and students playing pick-up soccer games. *Maß* €4.90. *Bratwürst* €5.40. Open May-Sept. daily 10am-10pm. Cash only. ❷

L'Osteria, Pirckheimerstr. 116 (☎55 82 83; www.losteria.info), northeast of the Altstadt just outside Maxtor. At this very busy local favorite, boisterous waiters serve up gigantic pizzas (€5.50-8.50). Open M-Sa 11am-midnight, Su 5pm-midnight. Cash only. ❷

Zum Gulden Stern, Zirkelschmiedg. 26 (☎205 92 88; www.bratwurstkueche.de), in the Altstadt. The oldest *Bratwurst* kitchen in the world roasts sausages over an open fire. 6 *Bratwürste* with *sauerkraut* €6.50. Open daily 11am-10pm. AmEx/DC/MC/V. ❸

Café Treibhaus, Karl-Grillenberger-Str. 28 (☎22 30 41), in the Altstadt south of Westtor. Serves snacks (€2-6), salads and pasta (€5-7), and breakfast (€3-9). Their large *Milchkaffee* (€3.10) raises foam to new heights. Open M-W 8am-1am, Th-F 8am-2am, Sa 9am-2am, Su 9:30am-1am. Kitchen open until 10:30pm. Cash only. ❷

Café Kiosk, Bleichstr. 5 (☎26 90 30). Join families and 20-somethings at this mellow Rosenau park café. Entrées €6-7.50. Beer €2.50. Open in good weather daily May-Sept. 10am-10pm, Apr. and Oct.-Nov. 10am-6pm. Cash only. ❷

Hong Kong Store, Vordere Sterng. 3 (☎24 30 28). *Imbiß*-style Thai-influenced food at deliciously cheap prices (€2.60-4.80). Standing room only. Grocery sells instant noodles and other Asian goodies. Open M-F 10am-7pm, Sa 10am-4pm. Cash only. ❶

Bratwursthäusle, Rathauspl. 1 (☎22 76 95), next to the Sebalduskirche. The most renowned *Bratwurst* in Nuremberg. *Rostbratwürste* €5.80. Bavarian dishes €2-6. Beer €2.90 (0.5L). Open M-Sa 10am-10:30pm (kitchen until 9:30pm). Cash only. ❷

Enchilada, Obstmarkt 10 (☎244 84 98; www.enchilada.de), behind the Frauenkirche. A popular Mexican restaurant with many vegetarian options and huge entrées (€8-16). Bar busy until midnight. Mixed drinks €7-9. Open daily 11am-1am. DC/MC/V. ❹

SIGHTS

After WWII, Nuremberg rose from the ashes of Allied bombing, rebuilding the **Handwerkerhof,** a tourist trap disguised as a history lesson, in faux-medieval style. The real sights lie farther up **Königstr.,** in the northwest corner of the Altstadt.

AROUND THE ALTSTADT AND KAISERBURG

KAISERBURG. Atop the hill, this symbolic structure offers the best vantage point for views of the city. The castle, originally erected in the 11th century and expanded significantly by Holy Roman Emperor **Friedrich Barbarossa,** is known as a *Pfalz* ("palatinate"), a hotel for the Emperor's frequent visits to the city. The original castle was almost completely destroyed in the 14th century, during a war with the **Hohenzollern** family, whose own *Burg* was next door. The aristocratic family left for Brandenburg, and the Kaiserburg was rebuilt in 15th- and 16th-century Gothic style. The spartan chambers (furniture, when needed, was borrowed from the homes of the Nuremberg elite) housed every Holy Roman Emperor after Konrad III—it was law that every German *Kaiser* spend at least his first day in office in Nuremberg, a testament to its prominence. Massive stone walls (13m tall and 7m thick) surround the castle and manicured gardens, and a 40m deep well once provided water during sieges. The castle can only be visited by tour, conducted in English through the tourist office and in German at the castle. (*☎244.65 90. Burg open daily Apr.-Sept. 9am-6pm; Oct.-Mar. 10am-4pm. Garden open daily in summer, 8am-8pm. Obligatory German tours every 30min.; last tour Apr.-Sept. 4:30pm; Oct.-Mar. 3:30pm. Admission to both Burg and museum €6, students €5.*)

LORENZKIRCHE. Destroyed in WWII, this 13th-century Gothic church has been carefully restored. Of particular interest is the 20m high **tabernacle,** built by Adam Kraft, whose self-portrait is one of the supports at the base of this stone masterpiece. Veit Stoß's 1517 wooden carving *Engelsgruß* (Annunciation) hangs in front of the altar. (*On Lorenzpl. ☎24 46 99 90. Open M-Sa 9am-5pm, Su noon-4pm. Free German language tours meet at the entrance in summer M-Sa 11am and 2pm, Su 2pm; in winter M-F 2pm; call ahead for English tours. Suggested donation €1, students €0.50.*)

HAUPTMARKTPLATZ. In 1349, during the Bubonic Plague, this square—the former Jewish quarter—was witness to a pogrom, fed by suspicions that Jews were responsible for the plague, that claimed hundreds of lives and destroyed the synagogue. In 1352, Karl IV commissioned the small Catholic **Frauenkirche,** whose ornate facade survived WWII, to occupy the place of the burnt synagogue. Crowds gather at noon to gape at the **Männleinlaufen,** the mechanical clock on the facade, whose seven electors pay homage to the seated Karl IV. The golden **Schöner Brunnen** (Beautiful Fountain) in the corner of the Platz resembles a Gothic steeple, composed of 40 carved figures, with Moses and the prophets up top. Hidden within the gate around the fountain is a golden "ring of the journey" (how it got there is a mystery); spinning it supposedly brings good luck. (*☎20 65 60. Church open M-Th and Sa 9am-6pm, F 9am-5pm, Su 12:30-6pm.*)

SEBALDUSKIRCHE. Across from the Rathaus, Nuremberg's oldest parish church (constructed 1230-1379) gained a Lutheran congregation in 1525. In the past, on the feast day of St. Sebaldus, the saint's remains were taken from their resting spot in the bronze tomb in front of the altar for a parade around town; now it is done every 30 years. Famous composer **Johann Pachelbel** (1651-1703), known for his *Canon in D,* was the principal organist here. (*☎21 42 500. Open daily June-Sept. 9:30am-8pm; Apr.-May and Oct.-Dec. 9:30am-6pm; Jan.-Mar. 9:30am-4pm.*)

RATHAUS. Built in 1340, the early Baroque Rathaus held the largest council chamber in central Europe before its destruction in 1945. The building's spooky **Loch-**

gefängnisse (dungeons) are filled with medieval torture instruments. (☎ *231 26 90. Open mid-Apr. to Oct. Tu-Su 10am-4:30pm, Feb. to mid-Apr. and Nov.-Dec. M-F 10am-4:30pm. Obligatory tours every 30min.; free English translation brochure available. €3, students €1.50.)*

FELSENGÄNGE (ROCK CELLAR). Constructed following a 1380 decree requiring all restaurants serving beer to brew and store it on location, this 25km web of tunnels and cellars below the Altstadt remains cool year-round. Converted to bomb shelters and sealed off as a precaution against gas bombs during WWII, the once well ventilated tunnels are now damp and deteriorating. *(Bergstr. 19, in the Altstadthof. ☎ 22 70 66. 1hr. tours in German descend daily from the statue in Albrecht-Dürer-Pl. 11am, 1, 3, and 5pm; English translation available. €4.50, students €3.50, children under 10 free.)*

RUINS OF THE THIRD REICH

REICHSPARTEITAGSGELÄNDE (NAZI RALLYING GROUNDS). The site of the Nazi Party Congress rallies of 1933 to 1938, which drew more than a half million people each year, now hosts a park, a storage area, and the **Nürnberg Symphony Orchestra.** The planned Nazi compound, which Hitler proudly declared "the largest building site in the world," was to become much larger than the city of Nuremberg. Here, tourists can explore still-extant parts of the grounds, witness the construction relics, and visit the thorough ▨**Dokumentationszentrum** (Documentation Center). The center explores the overwhelming emotional power of Nazi events—achieved by injecting strains of Wagnerian theater and Catholic ritual into fascist grandiosity—through exhibits covering the rise of Nazism, and the tribunals of 1946. The museum is in the **Kongresshalle** (Congress Hall), a prime example of Nazi architecture—massive, harsh, mixing Modernist straight lines with Neoclassical pretension, constructed with the intent to make the individual feel powerless. Intended to host the Nazi Party headquarters, the building was begun in 1935, but its construction was stalled by the onset of war. The 2km long **Große Str.,** leading across the **Volkspark,** was a symbolic link between Hitler and the German *Kaisers,* providing a view of Nazi headquarters at one end and the Kaiserburg at the other. The **Zeppelinwiese,** a field across the Großer Dutzendteich lake from the Kongresshalle where Hitler addressed more than 100,000 spectators at a time, was made infamous by Leni Riefenstahl's striking film **Triumph of the Will** (p. 75). Today, the Zeppelin field hosts rock concerts, and the Kongresshalle houses practice halls for the Nuremberg Symphony Orchestra. *(Take bus #36 or tram #9 to "Doku-Zentrum." For the Zeppelinwiese, walk around the lake from the Kongresshalle or take S2 (dir.: Feucht/Altdorf) to "Dutzendteich," then take the middle of 3 exits, head down the stairs, and turn left. Follow the paved path from the museum to reach other sections of the complex. ☎ 231 56 66; www.museen.nuernberg.de. Open M-F 9am-6pm, Sa-Su 10am-6pm. Last entry 5pm. €5, students €2.50. Free multilingual audio guides.)*

JUSTIZGEBÄUDE (COURTHOUSE). In Courtroom 600, Nazi leaders faced Allied judges during the infamous **Nuremberg war crimes trials.** Soon after the trials, in October 1946, 10 men were hanged for their crimes against humanity, the first ever to be punished for wartime human rights violations. The building is still a courthouse, but on weekends visitors can watch a short film in the room where the trials were held. *(Fürtherstr. 110. Take U1 (dir.: Fürth Klinikum) to "Bärenschanze" and continue away from the Altstadt on Fürtherstr. ☎ 231 54 21. Entry on the hr., with bilingual commentary and a video with English subtitles: Sa-Su 1-4pm. €2.50, students and children €1.25.)*

MUSEUMS

▨**GERMANISCHES NATIONALMUSEUM (NATIONAL GERMANIC MUSEUM).** This gleaming glass building chronicles Germanic art and culture from pre-history to the present. Highlights include Dürer's woodcuts, Rembrandt's etchings, and

Cranach's paintings, including his portrait of Martin Luther. Although the main galleries are closed for restoration until 2009, the exhibit *"Faszination Meisterwerk"* is on display until they reopen. Outside the museum's main entrance, the **Straße der Menschenrechte** (Avenue of Human Rights) has 27 white pillars engraved in 50 languages with the United Nations Universal Declaration of Human Rights. *(Kartäuserg. 1. U2 to "Opernhaus." ☎ 133 10. English tours every other Su at 2pm. Open Tu-Su 10am-6pm, W until 9pm. Upper floors of the museum close at 5pm. Audio guides €1.50. €5, students and seniors €4. Free W from 6-9pm, Tu, Th, F-Su from 5-6pm.)*

JÜDISCHES MUSEUM FRANKEN (JEWISH MUSEUM OF FRANCONIA). Housed in nearby Fürth, once the largest urban Jewish community in southern Germany, this museum chronicles the history and culture of Jews in Franconia, displaying everything from medieval religious manuscripts to everyday artifacts. Most notable are the *mikvah* (ritual bath) in the cellar, and the moveable roof that separates up to become a *sukkah*, a special open-roof structure for *Sukkot*, the Jewish harvest holiday. *(Königstr. 89, Fürth. U1 (dir.: Fürth Klinikum) to "Rathaus." ☎ 77 05 77. Open Tu 10am-8pm, W-Su 10am-5pm. €3, students and seniors €2.)*

ALBRECHT-DÜRER-HAUS. In his residence in Nuremberg from 1509 to 1528, Albrecht Dürer ran a successful production operation, sending prints across Europe with the help of his wife Agnes. Dürer is hailed as the first modern artist, due to his interest in self-portrait and his desire to paint naturalistically. Their lives are recreated vividly here, despite the lack of Dürer paintings (most are in Vienna, Munich, and Berlin). Guides dressed as Agnes Dürer lead tours. *(Albrecht-Dürer-Str. 39. Uphill from the Sebalduskirche. ☎ 231 25 68. Open Mar.-Oct. Tu-Su 10am-5pm, Th until 8pm; July-Sept. also M 10am-5pm; Nov.-Feb. Tu-F 1-5pm, Sa-Su 10am-5pm. English tours Sa at 2pm; German tours Th at 6 or 6:30pm, Sa at 3pm, and Su at 11am. €2. Audio guides in several languages also available. Haus €5, students €2.50. Ticket also valid for Stadtmuseum Fembohaus.)*

STADTMUSEUM FEMBOHAUS (FEMBO HOUSE MUNICIPIAL MUSEUM). Through lively audio guides and other exhibits, Fembohaus introduces you to Nuremberg's past and to the building's inhabitants, once Europe's most important cartographers. *(Burgstr. 15. Uphill from the Rathaus. ☎ 231 25 95. Open Tu-F 10am-5pm, Sa-Su 10am-6pm. €4, students €2. Ticket also valid for the Dürerhaus. Documentary €5/2.50.)*

NICOLAUS-COPERNICUS-PLANETARIUM. Sit back and watch the nighttime sky projected on a concrete dome above you. *(Am Plärrer 41. U1 or U2 to "Plärrer." ☎ 26 54 67; www.planetarium-nuernberg.de. Shows W 4pm and Th 7pm, 1st weekend of the month Sa-Su 4pm. During school holidays also Tu 2 and 4pm. Children's shows Th 4pm, 1st weekend of the month Sa-Su 2pm. €4.50, students €3, families €11.)*

🎵🎭 ENTERTAINMENT AND NIGHTLIFE

Nuremberg's Altstadt is packed with bars and clubs, the best of which can be found just down the hill from the Kaiserburg. Every July, Nuremberg holds the **Bardenfest** and **Klassik Open** music festivals, which combine all genres for an event-filled few weekends. Pick up the monthly *Plärrer* (€2) for musical and cultural events and the addresses of bars, discos, and cafés. Bars and discos also hand out the free guides *Doppelpunkt* (www.doppelpunkt.de) and *Curt* (www.curt.de). Visit www.rosawebworld.eu for up-to-date information on the city's gay scene.

The **Staatstheater Nürnberg** opera house and theater offers a 25% student discount (40% 1hr. before performances), and a 50% discount to **Nürnberg Card** holders. (Richard-Wagner-Pl. 2-10. ☎ 01801 34 42 76. Box office open M-F 9am-6pm, Sa 9am-1pm.) **Cine Città**, Gewerbemuseumspl. 3, is near the river on the eastern side of the Altstadt and has 17 German-language cinemas and the biggest IMAX theater in Europe. (U2 to "Wöhrder Wiese." ☎ 20 66 60; www.cinecitta.de. Tickets M-Th and Su 10am-noon and midnight-2am €6, noon-midnight €7, extra €1 for 3D IMAX; F-Sa 4:30pm-midnight €8.40. Open M-Th and Su until 2am, F-Sa until 3am.) **Roxy,** Julius-Loßman-Str. 116, shows mostly recent American releases. (Tram #8 (dir: "Worzeldorfer Str.) to "Nürnberg-Südfriedhof." ☎480 10 64; www.roxy-nuernberg.de. M-Tu €5, Th-Su €6.70. More for long films.)

Hirsch, Vogelweiherstr. 66 (☎42 94 14; www.der-hirsch.de). Night bus #65 to "Vogelweiherstr." Energetic crowds dance late into the night at this large club with disco F-Sa and concerts (110+ annually) M-Th. Multiple bars and *Biergarten* out front. Beer €3 (0.5L). Mixed drinks €5.50. Cover €3-15. Open F-Sa 10pm-5am, M-Th for frequent concerts (check online for schedule). Cash only.

Matahari, Weißgerberg. 31 (☎194 95 00; www.mataharibar.de). This small, crowded bar is one of the few without a contract with any particular brewery; each month they serve 2 different beers: 1 Franconian and 1 from Munich. Beer €2.50 (0.33L). Mixed drinks €7-8. Happy hour W-Th 8-9pm, with €2 beer and €4.50 mixed drinks. Th ladies' night. Open W-Th 9pm-2am, F-Sa 8pm-3am. Cash only.

Saigon, Lammsg. 8 (☎24 48 56 57; www.barnet.de). A classic late-night hangout, this intimate "bartender's bar" keeps to the basics—no special nights, no Happy hours, just innovative DJs and a crowd that changes with the hour. Free Internet access. Beer €2.80 (0.4L). Mixed drinks €6-8.50. Open daily 9pm-5am. Cash only.

Club Stereo, Kornmarkt 7 (www.club-stereo.net). Plays rock and indie music in its entirely black interior with large dance floor and alternative vibe. Busiest after 2am. Beer €2.90. Mixed drinks €6.50-7.50. Cover €5-8. Open June-Aug. Tu and F-Sa 11pm-5am, Sept.-May Tu and F-Sa 10pm-5am. Cash only.

Downtown, Obere Schmiedg. 5 (☎22 23 81). A young, casual crowd gathers in this intimate underground lair of multicolored lights, disco balls, tiger-print walls, and 70s and 80s music. Beer €3 (0.5L). Open W 9pm-3am, Th-Sa 9pm-5am. Cash only.

Indaba Lounge, Kornmarkt 7 (☎237 56 85; www.indaba-lounge.com). This tropical club attracts a snazzy young crowd. Plenty of relaxed lounging space, including a mellow patio. Small dancefloor. Mixed drinks €6.50-8. Wine €2. Cover €7-8, free if no special event. Open W 7pm-1am, Th 7pm-2am, F 7pm-3am, Sa 7pm-4am. Cash only.

Schleuder, Unsschlittpl. 9 (www.schleuder.de). A casual, accepting, and eclectic place with irregular events (check the website), a quirky crowd, and an offbeat owner who bartends with personality. Beer €3.60. Long drinks €6. Nightly DJ music. Open W-Sa 8:15pm-5am. 21+ F-Sa. Cash only.

Cartoon, An der Sparkasse 6 (☎22 71 70; www.cartoon-nbg.de). This popular gay bar's bright, modern interior attracts a hip 20-something crowd. Beer €3 (0.4L). Open M-Th 11am-2am, F-Sa 11am-3am, Su 2pm-1am. The bar downstairs, **CO2,** serves drinks in a pink leopard-print room. Mixed drinks €5-7.50. Happy hour 8-9pm; daily drink specials. Open W 6pm-3am, F-Sa 8pm-3am or later. Cash only.

Na Und, Marienstr. 25 (☎236 98 04; www.na-und-nuernberg.de). Friendly lesbian bar attracts a 25-40 crowd with German hits and oldies. Happy hour 7-9pm, every 3rd drink free. Beer €2.70 (0.5L). Mixed drinks €5-9. Open M-W and F-Su 6pm-3am. Cash only.

BAYREUTH ☎0921

Broad streets, resplendent 18th-century buildings, and a large English-style park give Bayreuth (buy-ROYT; pop. 74,000) an unexpectedly cosmopolitan flair. In the 18th century, the cultivated and ambitious Margravine Wilhelmine shaped Bayreuth according to her ideal of enlightened absolutism. In the 19th century, Richard Wagner, great *Meister* of opera, made it the center of his musical cult, and the city is an opera-lover's destination. Each year, it swells for the legendary

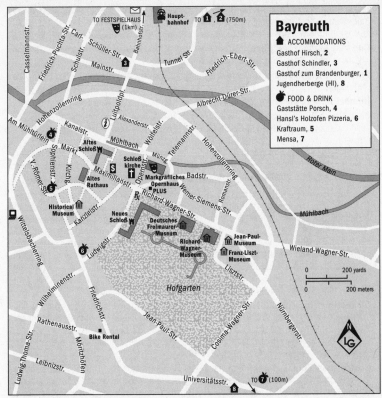

Bayreuth

🏠 ACCOMMODATIONS

Gasthof Hirsch, **2**
Gasthof Schindler, **3**
Gasthof zum Brandenburger, **1**
Jugendherberge (HI), **8**

🍎 FOOD & DRINK

Gaststätte Porsch, **4**
Hansl's Holzofen Pizzeria, **6**
Kraftraum, **5**
Mensa, **7**

Festspiele (annual operatic delirium from July 25 to August 28), and the wealth generated is evident in the array of international restaurants and carefully-groomed neighborhoods. Allied bombs obliterated the dark traces of Bayreuth's Nazi interlude, yet spared most of its Italianate architecture.

TRANSPORTATION AND PRACTICAL INFORMATION

The central **Altstadt** of Bayreuth is south of the train station, while the **Festspielhaus,** epicenter of all things Wagnerian, is just to the north. To get to the Altstadt, go left out of the train station and follow Bahnhofstr. until it becomes Luitpoldpl. and then ends at Kanalstr. One block ahead, a pedestrian zone, stretches from the Markt to Richard-Wagner-Str. The latter will lead you to the **Hofgarten,** a park flanked by most of the city's museums. South of the Altstadt is the university.

Trains: Train station is just north of the Altstadt. To: **Bamberg** (1½hr., every hr., €14.70); **Nuremberg** (1hr., 1-2 per hr., €14.70); **Regensburg** (2½hr., every hr., €22-32).

Bike Rental: Radgarten, Friderichstr. 40 (☎ 169 19 01; www.radgarten.de). €6 per day. Open M-Tu and Th 9am-1pm, W and F 9am-1pm and 4-8pm.

Tourist Office: Luitpoldpl. 9 (☎885 88; www.bayreuth-tourismus.de), 4 blocks to the left of the station in the "Reisebüro Bayreuth" building. Books rooms for free, and offers maps, a monthly calendar of events, and 2hr. **walking tours** in German. Tours May-Oct.

daily 10:30am; Nov.-Apr. Sa only (€5.50, students €3). Sells tickets to Bayreuth entertainment (except the Festspiele). Open M-F 9am-6pm, Sa 10am-2pm; May-Oct. also Su 10am-2pm. City maps and hotel lists are posted outside the door after hours.

Currency Exchange: Citibank, Maximilianstr. 46. Open M-Tu and Th 9am-1pm and 2-6pm, W and F 9am-1pm and 2-4pm.

Pharmacy: Hof Apotheke, Richard-Wagner-Str. 2 (☎652 10). Open M-F 8am-6pm, Sa 8am-2pm.

Internet Access: Zoom, Wittelsbacherring 2-6. 18+. €2 per hr. Open daily 6am-5am.

Post Office: Bürgerreutherstr. 1 (☎78 03 30). To the right and across the street as you exit the train station. Open M-F 8am-6:30pm, Sa 8:30am-1pm. **Postal Code:** 95444.

ACCOMMODATIONS

If you visit within a week of the **Festspiele,** be advised: *everybody* raises rates.

Jugendherberge (HI), Universitätsstr. 28 (☎76 43 80; fax 51 28 05). Bayreuth's hostel is outside the city center, past the Hofgarten near the university. On weekdays, take any bus from the station to "Marktpl.," then bus #6 (dir.: Campus) or #10 (dir: Kreuzsteinbad) to "Mensa" (€1.70). Or, walk down Ludwigstr. from the city center, take a left onto Friedrichstr., then veer left onto Jean-Paul-Str., which merges with Universitätsstr. (20min.). The hostel is large but friendly with snug dorms and tennis and volleyball courts. Breakfast included. Reception 7am-noon and 5-10pm. Check-in (strictly observed) 11am-noon, 5-7pm, and 9:30-10pm. Curfew 10pm; ask at desk for door code. Open Feb. to mid-Dec. Dorms €15.85; singles €18.85. MC/V. ❶

Gasthof Hirsch, St. Georgen 26 (☎267 14; fax 85 31 42). A 10min. walk from the station, on a corner building. Exit the back of the station, then turn left onto Brandenburger Str. Bear right when the street divides, and left on St. Georgen. During rehearsal time, the *Gasthof* becomes a hangout for opera workers. Breakfast included. Singles €20, 3+ nights €18; doubles €40/36. Cash only. ❷

Gasthof zum Brandenburger, St. Georgen 9 (☎78 90 60; fax 78 90 62 40). Across from Gasthof Hirsch. Sunny rooms with *Biergarten* out back. Breakfast included. Checkout 10am. Singles €24, with bath €35, 2 nights 21/31, 3+ nights 18/28; doubles €32-72; triples €47-94. ❷

Gasthof Schindler, Bahnhofstr. 9 (☎262 49). A block from the train station. Breakfast included. Reception M-Sa 8am-10pm, Su 9am-2pm. Singles €21-35; doubles €44-52; triples €55. Cash only. ❷

FOOD

Plus, Badstr. 10, sells cheap **groceries.** (Open M-Sa 8am-8pm.) **Bäckerei Görl,** Sophiestr. 32, serves sandwiches. (☎60 80 678. Open M-F 6am-6pm, Sa 6am-12:30pm.)

Kraftraum, Sophienstr. 16. (☎800 25 15). This organic café serves breakfast, noodles, salads, and sandwiches (€3-7) on its terrace. English menu available. Happy hour daily 5-7pm: mixed drinks €3.50-4. Open M-F 8am-1am, Sa-Su 9am-1am. Cash only. ❷

Gaststätte Porsch, Maximilianstr. 63 (☎646 49). Heaps of Franconian fare. *Schnitzel* €6-9. Beer €1.90 (0.5L). Open M-Sa 8:30am-10pm, Su 10am-8pm. Cash only. ❸

Hansl's Holzofen Pizzeria, Friedrichstr. 15 (☎543 44), at Jean-Paul-Pl. Pizzas €4-8. Salads €3-6. Open daily 10am-10:30pm. Cash only. ❷

Mensa, on the university campus. Take bus #4 (€1.70) from the Marktpl. to "Mensa," then walk past the buildings straight ahead; it's to the right up the steps. Trade the cashier your student ID and €4 for a card, then put money on the card at the *Auto-*

maten in the hall. Buy food and get your ID and €4, plus any remaining balance, back from the cashier. Hot entrées 11am-2pm and 4-8:30pm €2-4. Open Mar.-Apr. and Oct. daily 8am-6pm; May-July and Nov.-Feb. M-Th 8am-8:30pm, F 8am-2pm. ❶

👁 SIGHTS

MARKGRÄFLICHES OPERNHAUS. Commissioned in 1744 by Margravine Wilhelmine, sister of Frederick the Great, this pristine Baroque opera house and its gargantuan stage was the reason for Wagner's initial interest in Bayreuth. Amazingly, the ceiling fresco is painted in the wrong direction. About 80 shows still take place annually, but on off-days, the opera house offers a bombastic 25min. multimedia tour featuring the disembodied voice of the Margravine—a very Bayreuth (read: theatrical) experience. *(Opernpl. 14. ☎ 759 69 22. Open Apr.-Sept. 9:15am-6pm; Oct.-Mar. 10am-3:30pm. Shows every 45min. in German, English handout available. €5, students €4. Combination ticket with Neues Schloß €7/6. For opera tickets (€8-45) call ☎ 690 01.)*

RICHARD-WAGNER-MUSEUM. *Haus Wahnfried* (Delusional Peace) was once Wagner's custom-built home. It now exhaustively documents the composer's career and relationships with Ludwig II, father-in-law Franz Liszt, and Friedrich Nietzsche. Wagner music thunders throughout the exhibition, which winds chaotically up and down stairs. Exhibits are in German, but English guide booklets are available (€2.50). Behind the house are the graves of Wagner and his wife Cosima. *(Richard-Wagner-Str. 48. ☎ 757 28 16. Open Apr.-Oct. M, W, and F-Su 9am-5pm, Tu and Th 9am-8pm; Nov.-Mar. daily 10am-5pm. Music in the drawing room daily 10am, noon, and 2pm; videos 11am and 3pm. July-Aug. €4.50, students €2; Sept.-June €4/2.)*

NEUES SCHLOß. Margravine Wilhelmine, thought to be one of Europe's most cultured women, was forced to wed the Margrave of Bayreuth. To make the best of life in what must have seemed to her a provincial town, Wilhelmine built herself a gigantic palace. The walnut-panelled "palm room" and collection of Bayreuth porcelain are among the home's highlights. *(Ludwigstr. 21. Bus #2 to "Stadthalle." ☎ 759 69 21. Open Apr.-Sept. daily 9am-6pm; Oct.-Mar. Tu-Su 10am-4pm. €4, students €3.)*

FESTSPIELHAUS (FESTIVAL HOUSE). Wagner's 1872 construction is famed for its acoustics and classical aesthetic. Wagnerophile Ludwig II could only offer modest funds, resulting in a spartan structure—Wagner fans must endure rigid seats and limited leg room. Nonetheless, the Festspielhaus revolutionized European theatrics, with the first covered orchestra pit and forward-facing seats to keep the audience's attention squarely on the performers. *(Festspielhügel 2-3. From the train station, go right and up at the end of Siegfried-Wagner-Allee. ☎ 787 80. Tours Tu-Su Sept.-Oct. at 10, 11am, 2, and 3pm; Dec.-Apr. 10am and 2pm. €2.50.)*

HISTORISCHES MUSEUM (HISTORICAL MUSEUM). Documents the history of the city, including its Enlightenment heyday, its stint as Hitler's favorite city, and the fate of its Jewish population. Wagner's descendants were early adherents of Nazism, and Hitler had plans for lavish construction in Bayreuth, including a temple to himself. *(Kirchpl. 6. ☎ 76 40 10. Open July-Aug. daily 10am-5pm; Sept.-June closed M. €1.60, students, children, and seniors €0.50.)*

🎭 FESTIVALS

For Wagnerians, a visit to Bayreuth is a pilgrimage. Since 1876, every summer from July 25 to August 28, thousands have poured in for the **Wagner Festspiele,** held in the Festspielhaus that Wagner built for his "music of the future." All of his repertoire is performed annually, excepting his Ring Cycle operas, which show every four years (next in 2010). Tickets (€12-193, obstructed view €12, no view €6.50) go on sale mid-October and sell out immediately. Fanatics write to Bayreuther Festspiele, Postfach 100262, 95402 Bayreuth, well before September and hope for the best. Tickets are not available by phone or online.

BAMBERG ☎ 0951

Once known as the Rome of the north, windy Bamberg (pop. 71,000) straddles seven hills, covering the islands at the confluence of the Main-Donau canal and the two arms of the Regnitz river. Bamberg has been powerful and pious since 1007, when Heinrich II made it the center of the Holy Roman Empire in an attempt to push Christianity eastward. Crowned with a colossal cathedral and an imperial palace, Bamberg, which escaped WWII unscathed, is a thriving university town that once housed Hegel. Despite its location in wine-loving Franconia, this UNESCO World Heritage site has more breweries than Munich.

◧ TRANSPORTATION

Trains: The main station is on Ludwigstr. **Trains** run to: **Frankfurt** (3hr., every hr., €31-42); **Munich** (2½-4hr., 1-2 per hr., €18-48); **Nuremberg** (1hr., 3 per hr., €10); **Würzburg** (1hr., every hr., €15.50).

Public Transportation: An excellent transportation network centers on the **ZOB** (bus station) on Promenadestr. off Schönleinspl, where there is also an information center. To get there, walk down Luitpoldstr. from the train station and take the 2nd right after the bridge, or get on any bus with ZOB on the front. Single ride within the inner zone €1.10; 4-ride ticket €3.30. The 2-day *Touristenticket* (€6.60) offers unlimited travel within both zones. Family day cards €9.50.

Taxis: ☎ 194 10, 150 15, or 345 45.

Bike Rental: Fahrradhaus Griesmann, Kleberstr. 25 (☎ 229 67). €6.50 per day. Open M-F 9am-12:30pm and 2-6pm, Sa 9am-1pm.

◧◪ ORIENTATION AND PRACTICAL INFORMATION

The heart of Bamberg lies on an island between the **Main-Danube** canal and the **Regnitz River** (the Regen and Pegnitz Rivers combined). The winding streets of the **Altstadt** snake through the island (known as the *Sand*) and across the Regnitz away from the train station. To get to town from the station, walk down Luitpoldstr., cross the canal, and walk straight on Willy-Lessing-Str. until it empties into Schönleinspl. Turn right onto Lange Str. to reach the island section of the pedestrian zone; hang a left off Lange Str. up Obere Brückestr., through the archway of the Rathaus and across the Regnitz to reach the far section of the Altstadt (25-30min.). Or take any bus in front of the station to "ZOB." The **Bamberg Card,** available at the tourist office or the Deutsche Bahn Service point, is valid for 48hr., and is good for free public transportation, a tour of Bamberg, and admission to 5 museums (€8; children under 6 free with parent).

Tourist Office: Geyerswörthstr. 3 (☎ 297 62 00; www.bamberg.info), on an island in the Regnitz. Follow the directions to Lange Str., above, then follow signs over the footbridge and around the building. The staff books rooms for free and gives out good maps and the free pamphlet *Bamberger* (in German), which lists performances and exhibits. Open M-F 9:30am-6pm, Sa-Su 9:30am-2:30pm; closed Su Jan.-Mar. After-hours, a machine outside dispenses a map and hotel list (€1).

Tours: 2hr. city tours in German meet in front of the tourist office Apr.-Oct. M-Sa 10:30am and 2pm; Nov.-Mar. M-Sa 2pm (€5.50, students €4, under 10 free). English audio guides €5.50. Horse-drawn carriage tours of the Altstadt are offered Easter-Oct. Th-Su 1-6pm. Inquire at the tourist office (€8, ages 6-18 €5). Also ask about the 6hr. canoe tour (€25/15, min. 3 full-price participants) or the brewery tour, with a pamphlet and 5 beer vouchers (€20).

Budget Travel: Reisebüro Flugreise, Am Kranen 8 (☎986 42 33, www.deinurlaub.de). With STA services: books travel and prints ISICs.

Currency Exchange: Citibank, Hainstr. 2-4 (☎98 24 60), on Schönleinspl. Open M, Tu, Th 9am-1pm and 2-6pm, W and F 9am-1pm and 2-4pm.

Laundromat: Bamberger Waschsalon, Untere Königstr. 32 (☎215 17; www.bamberger-waschsalon.de), in the alleyway. Wash €4.60. Dry €3.60. Open M-Tu, W, F 8am-6pm, Th 8am-8pm, Sa 8am-2pm.

Emergency: Police, Schranne 2 (☎110, non-emergency 912 92 40). **Fire** and **Ambulance** ☎112. **Medical Assistance** ☎192 22.

Crisis Line: Caritas (☎299 95 70) counsels victims of rape and other crises.

Pharmacy: Martin Apotheke, Grüner Markt 21 (☎221 22). Open M-W and F 8:30am-6pm, Th 8:30am-7pm, Sa 9am-3pm.

Hospital: Klinikum Bamberg, Buger Str. 80 (☎50 30). Bus #18 to "Klinikum."

Internet Access: ND's Int@net Telecafé, Untere Königstr. 19. (☎297 57 17). €2.50 per hr. Happy hour noon-2pm and 8-9pm, €1.50 per hr. Open M-F 9am-10pm, Sa 10am-10pm, Su 12:30pm-10pm.

Post Office: Ludwigstr. 25, across from the train station. Open M-F 8am-6pm, Sa 8am-12:30pm. **Postal Code:** 96052.

▟ ACCOMMODATIONS AND CAMPING

Budget lodgings surround **Luitpoldstr.,** in front of the train station.

Jugendherberge Wolfsschlucht (HI), Oberer Leinritt 70 (☎560 02; jh-bamberg@stadt-bamberg.de). Bus #18 (dir.: Burg) from the ZOB to "Rodelbahn" (Until 8pm M-F every 20min., Sa-Su every hr.; €1). Walk downhill and turn left onto Oberer Leinritt just before the river. Next to a former boathouse and far from the city center, but with tidy rooms. Breakfast included. Reception 8am-1pm and 5-10pm. Curfew 10pm, key available. Reservations strongly recommended in summer. Closed mid-Dec. to mid-Jan. 4- or 6-bed dorms €16.85; doubles €40. MC/V. ❷

Bamberger Weissbierhaus, Obere Königstr. 38 (☎/fax 255 03), 10min. from the station. Walk straight from the station on Luitpoldstr. and turn left a block before the river. Spacious rooms with shared balcony overlooking a courtyard and *Biergarten*. Breakfast included. Dinner from €7. Reception 8am-2pm and 4:30-11pm. Singles €24; doubles €41-46; triples €63. Cash only. ❷

Hotel Central, Promenadestr. 3 (☎98 12 60; www.central-bamberg.com). Central location off Schönleinspl. Walk straight on Luitpoldstr. and double back and to your right when you get to Schönleinspl. Newly renovated, with phone and TV in every room. English-speaking staff. Breakfast included. Reception 7am-7pm. Check-out 10am. Singles €30-45; doubles €50-65; triples €80. Cash only. ❸

Fässla, Obere Königstr. 19-21 (☎265 16 or 22 998; fax 20 19 89). From the Hauptbahnhof, walk straight on Luitpoldstr. and turn right before the bridge. Above a popular beer hall. Rooms with TV, phone and, bath. Breakfast included. Singles €37; doubles €55-65; triples €70. Reservations recommended in summer. Cash only. ❹

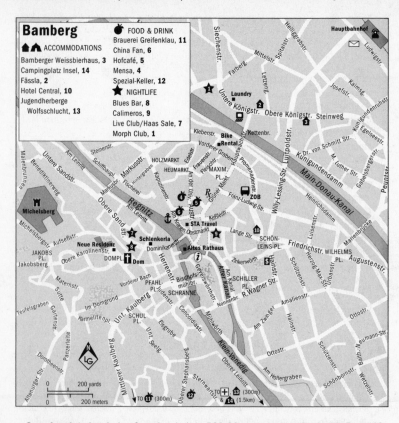

Bamberg

🍎 FOOD & DRINK
Brauerei Greifenklau, **11**
China Fan, **6**

🏠🏠⛺ ACCOMMODATIONS
Hofcafé, **5**
Bamberger Weissbierhaus, **3**
Mensa, **4**
Campingplatz Insel, **14**
Spezial-Keller, **12**
Fässla, **2**
Hotel Central, **10**
★ NIGHTLIFE
Jugendherberge
Wolfsschlucht, **13**
Blues Bar, **8**
Calimeros, **9**
Live Club/Haas Sale, **7**
Morph Club, **1**

Campingplatz Insel, Am Campingpl. 1 (☎563 20; campinginsel@web.de). Bus #18 (dir.: Burg) to "Campingpl." Prime riverside locale. Showers and toilets. Wash €2.50. Dry €3. Reception 7:30am-12:30pm and 1-11pm. €4.10 per adult, €3 per child, €7 per campsite. Electricity €0.50. Cash only. ●

🍴 FOOD

When looking for food, **Austr.** is a good place to start, although the surrounding hills conceal wonderful beer gardens. Bamberg and its countryside has the highest concentration of breweries in the world, its most unusual specialty being *Rauchbier* (smoked beer). The daring can try its sharp taste at **Schlenkerla,** Dominikanerstr. 6, *Rauchbier's* traditional home since 1678. (☎560 60. €2.15 for 0.5L. Open M and W-Su 9:30am-11:30pm.) **Norma,** 12 Promenadenstr., by the ZOB, has cheap groceries. (Open M-F 7am-8pm, Sa 7am-6pm.) **Bäckerei Postler,** Lange Str. 35, uses organic grains for their baked goods (☎219 36. Open M-F 6:30am-6pm, Sa 6:30am-1:30pm.) Grüner Markt hosts a **farmer's market** (M-F 8am-4pm, Sa 8am-2pm.)

🍴 **Spezial-Keller,** Oberer Stephansberg 47 (☎548 87). From Judenstr., head past the Stephanskirche up the Stephansberg. Turn left onto Sternwartstr., bear right past the *Gymasium* and turn in right at the gate. Walk all the way along the hedge, then turn left, and the Keller will soon be in view (20min.). This *Biergarten* is Bamberg's best-kept secret, offering a stunning hilltop view of the city, a playground, and *Rauchbier*. Entrées €4-9. Beer €2.20 (0.5L). Open Tu-Sa 3-11pm, Su 10am-11pm. Cash only. ❷

Hofcafé, Austr. 14, (☎254 47, www.hofcafe-bamberg.de). In a peaceful courtyard. Extensive menu with breakfast (€3-10) until 6pm. Vegetarian options (€6.80-7.20). Open M-W 8am-1am, Th-F 8am-2am, Sa 9am-2am, Su 9am-1am. Cash only. ❷

China Fan Imbiß, Fischstr. 9 (☎22 939), at Am Kranen. Cafeteria-style with seating available. Most entrées €3-5.50. Open daily 11am-9pm. Cash only. ❷

Brauerei Greifenklau, Laurenzipl. 20 (☎532 19), unbeknownst to tourists, has been serving its own brew at the top of the Kaulberg since 1719. Head up the Kaulberg road from the Schranne, following Laurenzistr. when it forks off to the right (15min.). Franconian pork roast with dumplings €7.40. Entrées €5-9. Beer €2.10 (0.5L). Open Tu-Sa 9am-11pm, Su 9:30am-2pm. Kitchen open 11:30am-9:30pm. Cash only. ❷

Mensa, Austr. 37, off Obstmarkt, serves cheap meals (under €3). Show any student ID as you pay. Open M-F 11:30am-2pm. Closed late July to mid-Oct. ❶

🄯 SIGHTS

DOM. Built by **Emperor Heinrich II,** the cathedral was consecrated in 1012, burned down twice, and rebuilt to its present-day form in 1237. The most famous object inside, the equestrian statue of the **Bamberger Reiter** (Bamberg Rider), dates to the 13th century. Just beneath the rider is the tomb of **Heinrich II** and **Queen Kunigunde,** with their life-size figures on top. Kunigunde walked over coals to prove her loyalty to her suspicious husband; both were later canonized. On the left side of the Dom is the **Diözesanmuseum** (Diocesan Museum), with the **Domschatz** (Cathedral Treasury) and beautiful ritual garments, including Heinrich's star-spangled cloak. *(Across the river and uphill from the Rathaus. Dom ☎50 23 30. Open daily Apr.-Oct. 9:30am-6pm, Nov.-Mar. 9:30am-5pm. Free. Museum ☎50 23 16. Open Tu-Su 10am-5pm. €3, students and seniors €2.50, under 15 free. 1½hr. tours in German of Dom and Domschatz gather Tu-Sa 10:30am at the ticket office in the cloisters. €3, students €2.50. Tours of the cathedral M-Th 10:30am and 2pm, F 10:30am, 2, 3pm, Sa 10:30am, 1, 2, 3pm, Su 1 and 3pm. €3, students €2.50. Tu-Su same meeting place; M meet at the Lady Portal. Organ concerts May-Oct. Sa noon.)*

NEUE RESIDENZ. The largest building in Bamberg was built between 1600 and 1703 to serve as the home of Bamberg's rulers. One wing is now a museum displaying medieval religious art, Cranach the Elder's famous *Lucretia*, and a comically inaccurate Noah's Ark. Admission includes a tour of the **parade rooms** and entry to the serene **rose garden.** *(Dompl. 8. Opposite the Dom. ☎51 93 90. Open daily Apr.-Sept. 9am-6pm; Oct.-Mar. 10am-4pm. Obligatory tours meet Apr.-Oct. daily every 15min., 1 fl. above the cashier's desk. English and French translations available. €4, students and seniors €3.)*

MICHAELSBERG. The former Benedictine monastery of St. Michael, founded in 1015 and rebuilt after a devastating fire in 1610, stands atop the hill behind the Dom. A guide to 578 medicinal flowers and herbs was painted on the ceiling by monks with an eye for detail, and the tomb of local **St. Otto** is located behind the altar. *(Open daily noon-6pm. Free.)* Outside in the courtyard, a **Bibelgarten** has 49 plants mentioned in the Bible, with accompanying verses. Also see the **Franconian Brewery Museum,** which teaches the fine art of turning hops into *Helles*. The terrace behind the church has a great view of Bamberg. *(Brewery Museum, Michaelsberg 10f. ☎530 16. Open Apr.-Oct. W-Su 1-5pm. €2, students €1.50.)*

ALTES RATHAUS. The old town hall guards the middle of the Regnitz. Built in the 15th century, the Rathaus was placed to display equal preference to church and state powers on either side of the river. Inside, the **Glanz des Barock** galleries contain the largest collection of porcelain in Europe. *(☎87 18 71. Gallery open Tu-Su 9:30am-4:30pm. €3.50, students and children €2.50.)*

PFAHLPLÄTZCHEN AND KLEIN VENEDIG. Streets between the Rathaus and the Dom are lined with 18th-century Baroque houses, many of which are not yet renovated. The pink house on the corner of Judenstr. is where Hegel edited proofs of *Phenomenology of Spirit.* At the time, unable to find a teaching position, the philosopher worked as editor of the Bamberg newspaper. Just downriver on Am Leinritt, catch the best glimpse of **Klein Venedig** (Little Venice.) The medieval buildings are former fishermen's houses. Little Venice is also the site of the *Sandkerwa* in August, an event which includes a fisherman's jousting contest.

❧ 🎭 FESTIVALS AND NIGHTLIFE

The third week of August is *Sandkerwa*. Originally a celebration of the *Sand* area churches, it is now a folk festival. The rest of the year, Bamberg's university and its famous beer make for a lively scene. **Sandstraße** is a well-known pub mile, but **Austraße** and **Lange Straße** also buzz with students.

> **Live Club,** Obere Sandstr. 7 (☎50 04 58; www.live-club.de), features live acts and a regular club night on M and Sa. The scene and music mix R&B, hip-hop, and hardcore. Cover (€4+) and hours depend on who's playing; check website for details. Open M and Sa. One floor up, **Haas Säle,** Obere Sandstr. 7 (☎51 93 53 29.), is a classy open-air terrace with golden stucco, tall palm trees, and swings. Beer €2.50 (0.5L). Open M-F 5pm-2am, Sa 2pm-2am, Su 10am-2am, later when busy. Cash only.

> **Morph Club,** Siechenstr. 7 (☎208 41 33; www.morphclub.org), at the intersection of Außere Löwenstr. and Untere Konigstr. Take bus #6 to "Löwenstr." Alternative scene with nightly techno, dance hall, reggae, and pop. Occassional concerts. Mixed drinks €5-7.50, beer €2.70 (0.5L). Cover €2.50-8. Open W-Sa 10pm-4am. Cash only.

> **Blues Bar,** Obere Sandstr. 18 (☎519 11 09.), is on the 2nd fl. of the building. Buying a beer (€2.40, 0.5L) gets you free live folk, blues, and rock among mellow students and other regulars. Open Tu-Th, Su 8pm-2am, F-Sa 8pm-3am. Cash only.

> **Calimeros,** Lange Str. 8 (☎20 11 72), undergoes a nightly transformation from Tex-Mex restaurant to raging club; you can tell it's a good night when everyone's dancing on the tables. M-W and Su Happy hour 5-7:30pm and 11pm-12:30am with caipirinha or margarita €3. Th Beer €1. Open M-Th 5pm-2am, F-Sa 5pm-3am. Cash only.

THÜRINGEN (THURINGIA)

 Thüringen has recovered spectacularly since reunification, and now this home of the *Bratwurst* boasts some of the most fascinating cities and towns in Germany. History buffs will find plenty of opportunities to walk, hike, eat, and even sleep in the footsteps of cultural luminaries like Luther, Goethe, Schiller, and Wagner. Outdoor enthusiasts will be delighted by the rewarding trails cutting through the hills, highlands, and idyllic Thüringer Wald.

HIGHLIGHTS OF THURINGIA

CLIMB THE TOWER of **Eisenach's Wartburg** (p. 570), which once sheltered Luther, and look over J.S. Bach's birthplace and the surrounding forest (p. 570).

LOSE YOURSELF among the ample trails of the gorgeous **Thüringer Wald** (p. 566), from the 6hr. **Goethewanderweg** to the 5-day **Rennsteig**.

CHANNEL THE SPIRITS of Goethe, Schiller, Hegel, and Novalis in the cultural center of **Weimar** (p. 551) and the university town of **Jena** (p. 558).

WEIMAR ☎ 03643

In its heyday, Weimar (pop. 64,000) attracted such cultural giants as Goethe, Schiller, and Johann Gottfried von Herder (grandfather of the Romantics), and the fame of these long-dead men still draws thousands to the city. Weimar residents are quick to point out that in 1999, their little city was declared the cultural capital of Europe. During the months leading up to the big celebration the city received a thorough face-lift, making it one of the most renovated cities in the former DDR. Although Goethe's presence is inescapable, Weimar's importance does not begin and end with the author. As the capital and namesake of the Weimar Republic, Germany's attempt at a democratic state after WWI, Weimar has a unique political significance in Germany's recent history. Hitler too was attracted by Weimar's rich culture, and founded the Hitler Youth movement here in 1926. The Bauhaus architectural movement also took root here, and students at the internationally-renowned conservatory and Bauhaus Universität bring cultural energy to the city.

◩ TRANSPORTATION

Trains: To: **Dresden** (2hr., every hr., €39); **Eisenach** (1hr., every hr., €11.70); **Erfurt** (15min., every hr., €4.40); **Frankfurt** (3hr., every hr., €49); **Jena** (20min., 2-3 per hr., €4.40); **Leipzig** (1hr., every hr., €22).

Public Transportation: Most of Weimar is easily walkable, but has an extensive **bus network.** Most buses run until midnight. Single tickets (€1.60) can be bought on board. Book of 4 tickets €4.80; day pass €3.80; weekly pass €8.50, students and seniors €6.50. Buy tickets at tourist offices, the main ticket office on Goethepl., or at newsstands with green and yellow "H" signs. Tickets must be validated on the buses.

Taxis: ☎ 90 36 00 or 90 39 00.

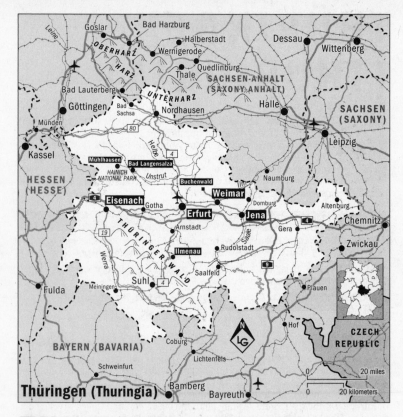

Thüringen (Thuringia)

✈ 🛈 ORIENTATION AND PRACTICAL INFORMATION

A series of open squares strung together by side-streets makes up Weimar's city center, which contains most of its sights. From the train station, Carl-August-Allee stretches downhill past the Neues Museum to Karl-Liebknecht-Str., which leads into Goethepl. (15min.). From there, Theaterpl. is down Wielandstr. to the left, and the Marktpl. is a short walk from Theaterpl. down Schillerstr.

The **Thuringen Card** (24hr. €13, 3-day €31) provides free or reduced entry to all of Weimar's major sights, excluding Goethe's Wohnhaus, as well as to sights in other Thuringen cities. The **WeimarCard** (€10) is valid for 72hr. of transportation, free or reduced entry to most sights, and 50% off tours. Purchase cards at tourist offices.

Tourist Offices: The modern and efficient **Weimar Information,** Markt 10 (☎74 50; www.weimar.de), is on the Markt across from the Rathaus. The staff sells maps (€0.20) and theater tickets, and books rooms for free. 2hr. **walking tours** (in German) leave the office daily at 10am and 2pm. €6, with Weimar Card €3, students €4, children under 11 free. The **Weimarer Wald** desk has info on outdoor activities in Thuringia. Open M-F 9:30am-6pm, Sa-Su 9:30am-3pm.

Currency Exchange: 4 banks are spread out on Schillerstr. and Frauentorstr. All have 24hr. **ATMs.**

Women's Resources: Frauenzentrum, Schopenhauerstr. 21 (☎871 16; www.frauenzen-trum-weimar.de), offers advice, has a basement *Frauenkulturcafé*, hosts cultural programs, and rents women rooms in a *Frauenpension*. Office open M 9am-4pm, Tu and Th 9am-6pm, W 9am-5pm, F 9am-noon. Check board outside for schedule.

Bookstore: Eckermann Buchhhandlung, Marktstr. 2 (☎415 90), sells English-language paperbacks. Open M-Sa 9:30am-8pm, Su 11am-6pm.

Library: Although non-residents can't check books out, the **Stadtbücherei,** Steubenstr. 1 (☎482 50), has many English-language books and Internet access (€5 per hr.). Open Tu-F 1-7pm, Sa 10am-1pm.

Laundromat: SB-Waschsalon, Graben 47, a few blocks from Goethepl. Wash €3.50. Dry €0.50 per 15min. Open M-Sa 8am-10pm; last wash at 8:30pm.

Pharmacy: Stadt Apotheke, Frauentorstr. 3 (☎20 20 93). Has a *Notdienst* (emergency service) buzzer. Open M-F 8am-7pm, Sa 9am-2pm.

Internet Access: Roxanne, on the Markt, is a bar, café, and record store. €2 per hr. Open M-Sa from 11:30am, Su from 3pm.

Post Office: Am Goethepl. 7-8. Open M-F 9am-6:30pm, Sa 9am-noon. **Postal Code:** 99421.

▓ ACCOMMODATIONS

Hababusch Hostel, Geleitstr. 4 (☎85 07 37; www.uni-weimar.de/yh). From Goethepl., follow Geleitstr.; after a sharp right, there's a statue on your left—the entrance is in the ivied corner behind it. Young Bohemians tired of sterile HI hostels will find an oasis of alternative travel here. Art students run the hostel—check out the creative bathroom lighting. Key deposit €10. Reserve singles and doubles ahead in summer. Reception 24hr. Dorms €10; singles €15; doubles €24. Cash only. ❶

Jugendherberge Germania (HI), Carl-August-Allee 13 (☎85 04 90; fax 85 04 91). To get there from the train station, walk directly straight downhill 2min. and it's on your right. This lovely yellow *Jugendstil* mansion offers clean, modern rooms often occupied by chatty schoolchildren. Breakfast included. Free Internet access. 24hr. reception. Check-in 3pm. Check-out 9:30am. 1st night €20.50, over 27 €23.50; each night thereafter €19/22. ❷

Jugendherberge Am Poseckschen Garten (HI), Humboldtstr. 17 (☎85 07 92; fax 85 07 93), is situated near the city center but fairly distant from the train station. Take bus #8 (dir.: Merketal) to "Am Poseckschen Garten." Turn right onto Am Poseckschen Garten, then left onto Humboldtstr.; the hostel is immediately on your left. A big turn-of-the-century brownstone a few blocks from the city center with 8- to 10-bed rooms. The hostel hosts many school groups, so book early. Internet access €0.10 per min. Breakfast and dinner included. 24hr. reception. 1st night €23, over 27 €26; subsequent nights €21.50/24.50. AmEx/DC/MC/V. ❷

▐ FOOD

For groceries try the **produce market** at the Marktpl. (open M-Sa 7am-5pm), or the **Rewe** supermarkets in the shopping mall on Theaterpl. and on the corner of Frauenplan and Steubenstr. (Open M-Sa 7am-8pm.)

THE REAL DEAL. If a restaurant in Weimar has any visible connection to Goethe—in its name, on its door, in its decor—it's probably overpriced. However, Weimar's restaurants don't have to drain your wallet; chances are there's a more reasonable, if less historic, option just down the street. *–Nicholas Commins*

▨ **Crêperie du Palais,** Am Palais 1 (☎40 15 81). French expats serve crêpes large enough to satisfy German appetites, in a plant-filled interior or on a tree-shaded terrace. Dinner and dessert crêpe combo €5-9. Open daily 9:30am-midnight. Cash only. ❷

ACC, Burgpl. 1-2 (☎85 11 61; www.acc-cafe.de). This café, cultural center, and gallery (upstairs, small donation requested) offers daily specials ranging from casseroles to curries for €5, with soup for €6.50. A variety of vegetarian options, salads, and classic *Abendbrote* (cheese and cold cuts) complete the menu, which changes every few weeks. Open daily May-Sept. 10am-1am; Oct.-Apr. 11am-1am. AmEx/MC/V. ❷

Maisel's Weisse, Rollplatz 2, (☎86 290), near St. Jakob's Kirche, serves generous Thuringian dishes for bargain prices (lunch specials €3.40, entrées €5-10). Open M-Sa 7am-midnight, Su 7am-10pm. AmEx/DC/MC/V. ❷

Residenz, Grüner Markt 4 (☎59 408; www.residenz-cafe.de). Weimar's oldest restaurant offers a taste of Thuringian cuisine at its best. Try the *Thüringer Grillplatte* (€11.20) for a taste of 3 local meats with sinus-clearing Thuringian mustard. Also serves vegetarian entrées. Open M-F 8am-1am, Sa-Su 9am-1am. MC/V min. €20. ❸

Mensa: Bauhaus-Universität, Marienstr. 13/15, just across the footpath in front of the Bauhaus building. Also accessible from Park an der Ilm. Join Weimar's artistic community on a terrace in warmer months, or for a snack in the **cafeteria** downstairs. A full meal in the **Mensa** upstairs runs €4-4.20 (€1.50-2 with student ID). Mensa open daily 11am-2pm. Cafeteria open Oct. to mid-July M-Th 7:30am-7pm, F 7:30am-3pm, Sa 11:30am-2pm; mid-July to Sept. M-F 7:30am-3pm. ❶

◉ 🏛 SIGHTS AND MUSEUMS

Weimar will always belong to its poets, whose plays, houses, and gravestones attract pilgrims from around the world. Goethe's hand has left indelible marks. Beyond the relics of Germany's lyrical titans, the **Neues Museum** and **Bauhaus Museum** house surprisingly fresh collections of art, and the **Stadtmuseum** sheds light on Weimar's fascinating and oft-neglected history. At all museums, the last entry is 15min. before closing.

GOETHEHAUS. While countless German towns leap at any excuse to build memorial *Goethehäuser* (Goethe slept here, Goethe tripped on this rock, Goethe stole my wife), this one is the real thing. The **Goethewohnhaus** elegantly presents the immaculate chambers where the genius entertained, wrote, studied, and ultimately died after 50 years in Weimar. The rooms are crammed with busts, paintings, and sculptures from his art collection, including over 18,000 rocks—not only could the man write, but he knew his geology. To preserve the exhibit's authenticity, no explanatory signs are posted in the Goethehaus, so be sure to pick up an English audio guide (€1). The rest of the **Goethe-Nationalmuseum** consists of an exhibit on Weimar's history. *(Frauenplan 1. Open Apr.-Sept. Tu-F and Su 9am-6pm, Sa 9am-7pm; Oct. Tu-Su 9am-6pm; Nov.-Mar. Tu-Su 9am-4pm. Expect to wait on summer weekends. €6.50, with Weimar Card €5.30, students €5. Tours in German Tu and F-Sa 1pm; Apr-Oct. also Sa 3pm; €2, students €1.50. Museum exhibit €2.50/2.)*

PARK AN DER ILM. Landscaped by Goethe, this sprawling park flanking the Ilm attests to the writer's artistic skill. Note the fake ruins built by the Weimar shooting club, the **Sphinx Grotto** from the late 18th century, and the **Kubus,** a gigantic black cube used as a theater and movie screen. On the park's far slopes is **Goethe's Gartenhaus,** the poet's first Weimar home and later his retreat from the city. A replica travels around Germany to abate the unquenchable national Goethe-thirst. *(Gartenhaus on Corona-Schöfer-Str. ☎543 375. Open daily Apr.-Oct. 10am-6pm; Nov.-Mar. 10am-4pm. €3.50, with Weimar Card €2.90, students €2.50.)* The watery **park caves** lie beneath the floor of a prehistoric sea—if you go on one of the hard hat cave tours

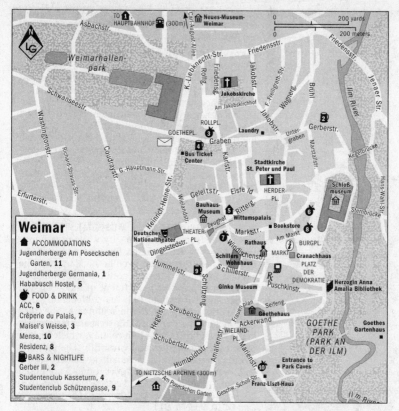

Weimar

🏠 **ACCOMMODATIONS**
Jugendherberge Am Poseckschen
  Garten, **11**
Jugendherberge Germania, **1**
Hababusch Hostel, **5**

🍎 **FOOD & DRINK**
ACC, **6**
Crêperie du Palais, **7**
Maisel's Weisse, **3**
Mensa, **10**
Residenz, **8**

🍷 **BARS & NIGHTLIFE**
Gerber III, **2**
Studentenclub Kasseturm, **4**
Studentenclub Schützengasse, **9**

(in German), you can nearly touch the Ice Age fossils dotting the low ceilings. Tours run every hour, but only if there are at least six people—2pm is the best time to try. An adjacent **museum** (signs in German) details the caves' history. *(Open Apr.-Oct. 10am-noon and 1-6pm. Tour and museum 3.50, with Weimar Card €2.90, students €2.50. Museum only €2.50/2.10/2.)* The **Herzogin Anna Amalia Bibliothek,** Goethe's old intellectual batting cage, is here as well. The impressive Rococo reading room will re-open in late 2007 after restoration. *(Pl. der Demokratie 1. Open daily 10am-5pm.)*

BAUHAUS-MUSEUM. In 1919, Walter Gropius assembled a prodigious group at Weimar's art school, dedicated to the principles of minimalism and functionalism; Their weavings, sculptures, prints, furniture, and even tea kettles—all displayed here—convey the breadth of the Bauhaus school's undertakings. *(Theaterpl., across from the Deutsches Nationaltheater. ☎ 54 59 61. Open daily 10am-6pm. €4.50, with Weimar Card €3.70, students and seniors €3.50. Museum tours Su 11am €2, students €1.50.)*

SCHILLERS WOHNHAUS. Sitting a neighborly distance from Goethe's residence, this yellow house was Schiller's home during the last three years of his life. As well as chronicling the poet's life, the museum exhibits the backgrounds to *The Maid of Orleans* and *William Tell*—both written here—and houses original drafts of his plays. One room displays over 600 medallions imprinted with Schiller's head.

BULBS AND BEER

When early October blows in each year, Weimar residents may look a tad unusual. Donning onion garlands by the dozens, one might mistake them for over-zealous vampire slayers preparing for Halloween. Thankfully, a different fest has these onion fans (literally) crying out for joy: the Onion Market Festival.

Once a small city-wide celebration, the onion festival has recently grown into one of little Weimar's biggest parties; over 200,000 visitors flood the town or the celebration. Merchants spend the preceding weeks stringing onions to make the aromatic, f not fashionable, garlands that deck Weimarians' necks during he festival weekend. Kegs are tapped, music from live bands ills Weimar's many squares, and ocals dance the night away.

Restaurants go onion-crazy for he weekend, as well, preparing all sorts of dishes in honor of the pungent bulbs. Whether you're here to eat, drink, dance, or simply venerate the veggie, the Onion Market Festival will surely keep you entertained. Just remember o pack a few tons of a breathmints.

The Onion Market Festival runs Friday to Sunday on the second weekend in October. Contact the Weimar ourist office (☎03643 74 50; www.weimar.de) for more information or to reserve rooms.)

(☎545 401. Schillerstr. 12. Open Apr.-Sept. M, W-F, Su 9am-6pm, Sa 9am-7pm; Oct. W-Su and M 9am-6pm; Nov.-Mar. M and W-Su 9am-4pm. €4, students €3. Audio guides €1.)

HISTORISCHER FRIEDHOF (HISTORIC CEMETERY). South of the town center, Goethe and Schiller rest side-by-side in the basement of the **Fürstengruft** (Ducal Vault) with a dozen or so Prussian nobles. Schiller died in an epidemic and was originally buried in a mass grave, but Goethe later combed through the remains until he found Schiller and had him interred here. Skeptics long argued that Goethe had chosen the wrong body, but Russian scientists confirmed the poet's identification in the 1960s. Goethe himself arranged to be buried in an airtight steel case. *(Open daily Mar.-Sept. 8am-9pm; Oct.-Feb. 8am-6pm. Free. Tomb open daily Apr.-Oct. 10am-6pm; Nov.-Mar. 10am-4pm. €2.50, with Weimar Card €2.10, students €2.)*

SCHLOßMUSEUM (CASTLE MUSEUM). The palace and tower from the former city walls now house three floors of art. The first floor is a major Lucas Cranach fest (the painter lived in the Marktpl.). The second is a minor-league collection of religious icons, an impressive assortment of medieval and Renaissance altars, and 19th- and 20th-century German works with some Rodin sculptures. The third floor includes a sampling of the **Weimarer Malerschule** of the second half of the 19th century, which focuses on simple landscapes and rural life. The palace's most impressive rooms, including the pastel banquet hall, reception rooms, and "poet rooms," are in the east wing. *(Burgpl. 4. To the left of the Marktpl. Open Tu-Su Apr.-Oct. 10am-6pm; Nov.-Mar. 10am-4pm. €5, with Weimar Card €4.10, students €4.)*

GINGKO MUSEUM. Sip free Gingko tea while you explore the history of the Gingko tree at this small but insightful museum above a store selling Gingko products galore. The one-room exhibit, which covers topics from the miraculous Hiroshima Gingko that sprouted only months after the atomic bombing to Goethe's fascination with the exotic plant. *(Windischenstr. 1, off the Markt. ☎80 54 52. Open M-F 10am-6pm, Sa-Su 10am-4pm. Free. English translations available.)*

NEUES MUSEUM WEIMAR (NEW MUSEUM). This museum exhibits modern art, with everything from squares of solid orange to splashy and frightening works of abstract art. *(Weimarpl. 5. ☎54 59 63. Open Tu-Su Apr.-Sept. 11am-6pm; Oct.-Mar. 11am-4pm. €3.50, students €2.50. Tours Su 11am; €2/1.50.)*

FRANZ-LISZT-HAUS. After an earlier stint in Weimar, the composer Franz Liszt spent his last years at this residence. The instruments and furnishings are supposedly original, but given Liszt's torrid love life, the single bed seems euphemistic. *(Marienstr. 17. Open Apr.-Oct. M and W-Su 10am-6pm. €4, with Weimar Card €3.20, students €2.)*

NIETZSCHE-ARCHIV. Nietzsche lived three years here, suffering from mental and physical illness, before his death in 1900. His sister, who returned from a struggling colony in Paraguay to care for him, archived the philosopher's work after his death, but distorted it during the process. Her totalitarian control over Nietzsche's papers contributed to the Nazis' misappropriation of parts of his philosophy to horrifying ends. On display is a history of the archive, many portraits of the man with his famous mustache, and a library designed by Henry van de Velde. *(Humboldtstr. 36. Open Apr.-Oct. Tu-Su 1-6pm. €2.50, with Weimar Card €2.10, students €2.)*

OTHER SIGHTS. The cobblestoned **Marktpl.** spreads out beneath the neo-Gothic **Rathaus,** which is closed to the public. Hitler addressed huge crowds here from the balcony of the **Hotel Elephant.** The **Stadtkirche St. Peter und Paul** features Cranach the Elder's last triptych altarpiece, which he started shortly before his death. Cranach the Younger finished the painting and inserted his father between John the Baptist and Martin Luther. The church is also called the "Herderkirche," in honor of philosopher and linguist **Johann Gottfried von Herder,** who preached here regularly in the 1780s. Amid all the gold and pink splendor is Cranach's original tomb covering. *(☎90 31 82. Down Jakobstr. Open Apr.-Oct. M-F 10am-5pm, Sa 10am-noon and 2-4pm, Su 11am-noon and 2-3pm; Nov.-Mar. daily 11am-noon and 2-3pm. Free.)* Climb the tower at **Jakobskirche** for a glimpse into the former bellringer's apartment. A ladder leads up into the church's steeple, where the tiny windows yield a surprisingly good view of the city below. *(Open May-Oct. daily 10am-4pm. Free.)*

🎵 📷 ENTERTAINMENT AND NIGHTLIFE

The best resource for theater and music in Weimar is the 🌟**Deutsches Nationaltheater,** Theaterpl. 2. The theater that inspired Goethe and Schiller still presents *Faust* regularly, along with Mozart and Verdi and classics from Shakespeare and his contemporaries. It's also the site where the **Weimar Constitution** was signed in 1919. (☎75 53 34. Box office open M 2-6pm, Tu-Sa 10am-6pm, Su 10am-1pm, and 1hr. before performances.) Tickets are also available at **Tourist Information,** the only ticket service open from early July to mid-Aug. (Tickets €8-55. 30% student and senior discount.) Weimar's nightlife consists of an eclectic collection of student clubs and cafés. The weekend scene is fueled by students who pack the few clubs in town. Pick up a copy of the German-language *Blitz*, or check the posters and bulletin boards at the Bauhaus-Universität Mensa (p. 554) for the latest goings-on.

Studentenclub Kasseturm, Goethepl. 10 (☎85 16 70; www.kasseturm.de). Serves up cheap drinks (shots €1-1.20) in an old medieval tower opposite the post office. The oldest student club in Germany, with dancing on the top 2 fl. and a relaxed beer cellar below. Disco W and F or Sa. Check board outside for weekly schedule. Cover €3-6, students €1-4, more for concerts. Open daily 2pm-late. Cash only.

Studentenclub Schützengasse, Schützeng. 2 (☎90 43 23), has regular live rock upstairs Tu and F-Sa and a DJ downstairs, with a (slightly) quieter *Biergarten* out back. Disco Tu and Sa. A variety of activities—from dance classes to jam sessions—other nights. Check the board outside for weekly schedule. 18+. Cover €1.50-2.50, students €1 off. Open M-Sa 8pm-3am. Cash only.

Gerber III, Gerberstr. 3, is a former squatters' house that now shelters an alternative, improvised bar. The topsy-turvy, graffiti-covered interior feels like something out of a distorted *Alice in Wonderland*. The building also hosts an occasional disco and a climbing wall. Bar open M-Sa 8pm-late. Cash only.

THÜRINGEN

🔖 DAYTRIP FROM WEIMAR

BUCHENWALD

Take bus #6 from Weimar's train station or Goethepl. (20min., M-Sa every hr., Su every 2hr.). Check the schedule; some #6 buses go to "Ettersburg" rather than "Gedenkstätte Buchenwald." Buses to Weimar stop at the KZ-Lager parking lot and the road by the Glockenturm.

A quarter-million Jews, Gypsies, homosexuals, communists, and political prisoners were incarcerated at the Buchenwald labor camp during WWII. Buchenwald was not explicitly an extermination camp, but over 50,000 prisoners died from malnutrition, mistreatment, or medical experimentation. The compound is now a vast gray expanse of gravel with the former location of the prison blocks marked by numbers and crumbling foundations. Some of the remaining buildings around the perimeter can still be visited, including the SS officers' quarters and the crematorium. The uncompromising starkness of the compound and the horror of its history stand in wrenching contrast to the Thuringian forests surrounding the site.

Buchenwald's first inmates were German political dissenters, but as the war drew on and the Red Army approached Polish camps, deportees from Poland, Denmark, Belgium, and Norway were transported to Buchenwald, along with many Jews originally deported to Auschwitz. At war's end, Buchenwald was the largest camp in existence, and 95 percent of its prisoners were non-Germans. But the end of the war did not signal the end of Buchenwald's dismal history. The Soviet Union incarcerated more than 28,000 Germans here, from suspected Nazis to anti-Communists. The graves of 10,000 of those prisoners, many of whom held guard at Buchenwald's Nazi camp, mingle with those of their victims.

The **Nationale Mahnmal und Gedenkstätte Buchenwald** (National Buchenwald Memorial) has two principal sights: the **KZ-Lager** and the **Mahnmal** (memorial). The former refers to the camp itself, while the latter is a solemn monument overlooking the surrounding countryside. The main exhibit of the camp, in the large storehouse building, documents the history of Buchenwald (1937-1945) and the general history of Nazism and German anti-Semitism. An exhibit about the Soviet internment camp is in the basement. Many tributes are scattered around the camp; the stones of the Jewish memorial at block #22 read: "So that the generation to come might know, the children, yet to be born, that they too may rise and declare to their children." The camp **archives** are open by appointment. (Archives ☎ 43 01 54, library 43 01 60. Exhibits open daily Apr.-Oct. 10am-6pm; Nov.-Mar. 10am-4pm. Last entry 45min. before closing. Outdoor camp area open daily until sundown.).

The DDR-designed **Mahnmal** and **Glockenturm** (bell tower) are 10min. from the camp on the other side of the hilltop. Either go straight up the main road that bisects the two parking lots, or take the footpath uphill from the old Buchenwald Bahnhof and continue on the main road. The actual memorial is a series of carved blocks depicting stylized scenes of violence. Behind the bell tower a commanding view of the region unfolds, overseen by the Plastikgruppe, a sculpture of ragged, stern-jawed socialist prisoners claiming their freedom. An information center near the Buchenwald bus stop shows a 30min. video with English subtitles on the hour, and has helpful English-language brochures (€0.25), a free walking tour, and audio guides (€3, students €2). Brochures and audio guides are available in nine languages, including English. (☎ 43 00. Same hours as above. A branch next to Weimar's Tourist Information on the Marktpl. has more information.)

JENA ☎ 03641

Jena's life is its university. Once undoubtedly the country's finest, the institution proudly displays its illustrious past, especially professor Friedrich Schiller, who lectured here in 1789 on the ideals of the French Revolution. His students, Novalis

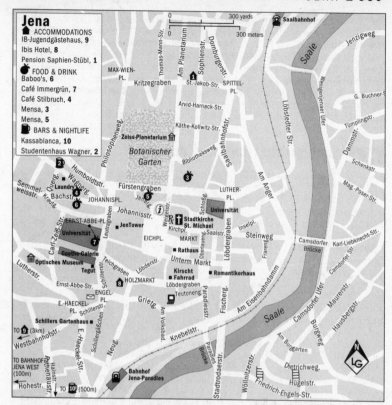

Jena

▲ **ACCOMMODATIONS**
IB-Jugendgästehaus, **9**
Ibis Hotel, **8**
Pension Saphien-Stübl, **1**

🍴 **FOOD & DRINK**
Baboo's, **6**
Café Immergrün, **7**
Café Stilbruch, **4**
Mensa, **3**
Mensa, **5**

🍷 **BARS & NIGHTLIFE**
Kassablanca, **10**
Studentenhaus Wagner, **2**

and Hölderlin, joined other literary greats such as Schlegel and Tieck to plant seeds of the German Romantic movement. The 19th century also saw Jena become a world leader in the field of optics: the microscope company Carl Zeiss founded then continues today as Jenoptik. In-depth museums celebrate Jena's tradition of intellectualism, and the students strolling through the city's streets at all hours keep this town a haven for bookish and fun-loving travelers alike.

📇 TRANSPORTATION AND PRACTICAL INFORMATION

Jena is in the Saale River Valley, 25km east of Weimar by **train** (20min., 2 per hr., €4.50). Three major train stations serve the town. Trains between Dresden and Erfurt stop at **Bahnhof Jena-West**, a 10min. walk from town, while trains on the Berlin-Munich and Saalfeld-Naumburg lines stop at **Jena Saalbahnhof**, 15min. north of the center. Most trains from the Saalbahnhof also stop at **Bahnhof Jena-Paradies**, only 5min. from town. Most of the city is connected by a bus and tram system centered on the "Zentrum" stop (single ride €1.50). To get to the town center from Bahnhof Jena-West, head downhill on Westbahnhofstr. until it becomes Schillerstr. Turn left up Schillerstr. to the towering university building. From Saalbahnhof, turn left down Saalbahnhofstr. and take a right on Saalstr., or take bus #15. From Jena-Paradies, turn right on the main road and then bear left up Neug., which leads to Holzmarkt and Löbderstr. Rent **bikes** at **Kirscht Fahrrad**, Löbdergraben 8, near

THÜRINGEN

the "Löbdergraben" bus stop. (☎ 44 15 39. €15 for the 1st day, €10 per additional day. Open M-F 9am-7pm, Sa 9am-4pm.) For a **taxi** call ☎ 55 66. **Jena Tourist-Information,** Johannisstr. 23 on Eichpl., hands out free maps, leads city **tours** in German (€4), and books private rooms (from €15) for free. (☎ 49 80 50; www.tourismus.jena.de. Open M-F 9:30am-7pm, Sa 9:30am-4pm, Su 11am-3pm. Tours M, W, Sa 2pm; Apr.-Oct. also Th 4pm.) The **Goethe-Apotheke** is on Weigelstr. 7, in front of the church. (☎ 45 45 45. Open M-F 8am-8pm, Sa 8am-4pm.) **C.net Computercafé,** Teutoneng. 2, has **Internet** access; enter from Grietg. (☎ 35 73 52. €3 per hr. Open M-F 1pm-midnight, Sa 11am-1am, Su 11am-midnight.) The **post office** is at Engelpl. 8 and has a 24hr. **ATM**. (Open M-F 9am-6:30pm, Sa 9am-1pm.) **Postal Code:** 07743.

ACCOMMODATIONS AND FOOD

The pension **Sophien-Stueb'l ❸**, St.-Jakob-Str. 15, though far from the train station, is close to the city center. From Paradies, turn right on Knebelstr., then left on Fischergr. and follow it as it becomes Loebdergraben. At Luther Pl., turn left on Fuerstengraben, then right on Am Planetarium. Make a right on St.-Jakob-Str.; the pension is on the next corner. (☎ 44 23 03. Breakfast included. Check-in 2pm. Check-out 10am. Singles €30, doubles €45. Cash only.) To get to the mammoth **IB-Jugendgästehaus ❷**, Am Herrenberge 3, take bus #10, 13, or 40 (dir.: Burgau) to "Zeiss-Werk." Go left as you get off the bus and then right on Mühlenstr. up the hill until it turns into Am Herrenberge (15min.). Or from Bahnhof Jena-West, turn left on Westbahnhofstr. and take a left on Tatzendpromenade. After it becomes Carl-Zeiss-Promenade, take a left on Mühlenstr. (35min.). (☎ 68 72 30. Breakfast and sheets included. Reception M-F 24hr., Sa-Su 7-11am and 5-10pm. 3- and 4-bed rooms €17, with shower €26. Cash only.) The pricey chain **Ibis Hotel ❺**, Teichgraben 1, is especially comfortable and in great location. From Jena-Paradies walk down Neug.; you'll see it on your left (5min.). All rooms have phone, TV, and bath. (☎ 81 30; fax 813 333. Breakfast €9. Reception 24hr. All rooms €53.)

A combination snack shop, café, and restaurant, **Baboo's Internationale Spezialitäten ❷**, Johannispl. 12, offers everything from chicken curry (€6.50) to pizza (€3). (☎ 42 66 66. Open daily 10am-2am. Cash only.) The fresh and friendly self-service **Café Immergrün ❷**, Jenerg. 6, just off Fürstengraben., is lined with comfortable couches and modern art. Daily vegetarian and meat specials run €2-4. (☎ 44 73 13. Open M-Sa 11am-1am, Su 10am-2:30pm and 3-10pm. Cash only.) **Café Stilbruch ❸**, Wagnerg. 1-2, offers a large selection of salads, baguettes, and piping hot *Pfannengerichte* (pan-cooked meals; €7-10). Later in the evening this café fills with cocktail patrons. (☎ 82 71 71. Open M-Th 8:30am-2am, F 8:30am-3am, Sa 9am-3am, Su 9am-2am. Cash only.) Jena's **Mensa ❶** is in a sparkling new location in Ernst-Abbe-Pl., across Leutragraben from the tower. (Full meals €4-4.50, with ISIC €1.40-1.60. Open M-F 8am-3pm. Cash only.) A **market,** on the Markt., sells fresh produce (Tu and Th-Sa 8am-noon), and there's a **Tegut** supermarket in the basement of the Goethe-Galerie. (Open M-Sa 8am-8pm.)

SIGHTS

The **Romantikerhaus** (Romantic House), Unterm Markt 12a, once bubbled with the raw creative energy of the Romantic period. Owned by philosopher and fiery democrat Johann Fichte from 1794-99, it hosted the poetic, philosophical, and musical get-togethers of the Romantics. Rather than reconstruct the house's furnishings, creative permanent and rotating exhibits teach visitors about the Romantic movement and its origins. (☎ 44 32 63; www.jena.de/kultur/romantik.htm. Signs in German. Open Tu-Su 10am-5pm. €4, students and seniors €2.50.) The **Optisches Museum** (Optical Museum), Carl-Zeiß-Pl. 12, presents the history of local optics

Wunderkind Carl Zeiss. A painstakingly detailed replication of Zeiss' laboratory, machines to test your own eyes, and amazing holograms are just some highlights of the collection. (☎ 44 31 65. Open Tu-F 10am-4:30pm, Sa 11am-5pm. €5, students and seniors €4. English audio guide €1.) Schiller's **Gartenhaus,** the poet's home at Schillergäßchen 2, just off Schillerstr, where the author used to chat with Goethe in the beautifully manicured garden, is now a museum. (☎ 93 11 88. Open Tu-Su 11am-5pm, Nov.-Mar. closed Su. English brochures available. €2.50, students and seniors €1.30.) The monolithic **JenTower,** across Leutragraben from the university, affords an excellent view of the city. (Open daily 11am-midnight. €3.) The **Stadt-kirche St. Michael,** off Eichpl., has three treasures: a 13th-century wooden St. Michael, a pulpit from which Luther twice preached, and Luther's tombstone, conspicuously not on his grave in Wittenberg. The folks at the Stadtkirche claim that a battle interrupted the stone's shipment from Jena to Wittenberg—a story that Wittenbergers find hard to swallow. (Open M-F 10am-5pm.) Nearby is the **Botanischer Garten,** an early treasure of Jena's medical faculty, renovated by Goethe. (Open daily May 15-Sept. 14 9am-6pm; Sept. 15-May 14 9am-5pm. Last entry 30min. before closing. €3, students €1.50.) The ◪**Zeiss-Planetarium,** Am Planetarium 5, the world's oldest, dazzles stargazers and classic rock fans alike with laser shows ranging from children's musicals to an English-language Queen extravaganza. (☎ 88 54 88; www.planetarium-jena.de. Check the poster on the gate for event times, usually 11am-7:30pm. Ticket office open Tu-W 10:30am-noon and 7-8pm, Th-F 10:30am-noon, Sa 1:30-6pm and 7-9pm, Su 10:30-11am and 1:30-5pm, and 30min. before all shows. Approx. €6, students €5.)

❄ ▨ FESTIVALS AND NIGHTLIFE

This university town has plenty going on. Pick up the *Tipps* guide at the tourist office, or start on **Wagnerg.,** an area popular with students and lined with bars and restaurants. At the end of the strip, set back in a garden, you'll find the **Studenten-haus Wagner,** Wagnerg. 26, headquarters for student culture. The chill, university-sponsored café doubles as a venue for plays, readings, live music, and movie screenings. (☎ 47 21 53. Open M-F 11am-1am, Sa-Su 7:30pm-1am. Café open M-Sa 6pm-late, Su 7:30pm-late. Cash only.) **Kassablanca,** Felsenkellerstr. 13a, sponsors an array of discos, concerts, and political discussions in a renovated, graffitied train depot. To get there from the center, turn left off Westbahnhofstr. onto Rathenaustr., take a left at the fork onto Hainstr., then turn right on Felsenkellerstr. Climb the hill—the neon-painted trains will be hard to miss on your right. (☎ 282 60; www.kassablanca.de. Cover €2-7. Usually open W-Sa from 8pm; check website for special events.) During **Kulturarena Jena,** a festival from early July to mid-August, the area in front of Jena's theater at Engelpl. becomes an open-air performance space. Two audiences gather for the concerts: the excited crowd in the arena itself, and the chill group lining the sidewalks and listening in for free. (☎ 49 26 85, ticket hotline 80 64 06; www.kulturarena.de. €9-17, students €7-14.)

ERFURT ☎ 0361

Street after street of ornate facades line this capital city, the *Thüringisches Rom* (Thuringian Rome). Erfurt (pop. 203,000) benefited from its strategic position on the trade route connecting medieval Europe with the Silk Road. The city's wealthy merchants funded 37 churches and several monasteries, one of which housed Martin Luther during his formative years as a monk. As a capital, Erfurt has a dynamic political history: Napoleon called a meeting of princes here and chatted with Goethe in what is now the Thüringer Staatskanzlei. More recently West German Chancellor Willy Brandt met here in 1970 with East German leader Willi Stoph, commencing *Ostpolitik*, the arduous process of East-West reconciliation (p. 61).

THÜRINGEN

▣ TRANSPORTATION

Flights: Flughafen Erfurt (☎ 656 22 22). Take bus #99 or tram #4 to "Hauptfriedhof," then bus #91 or 92 to the airport. Flights to major European airports.

Trains: To: **Berlin** (2½hr., every 2hr., €50); **Dresden** (2½hr., every hr., €42); **Frankfurt** (2½hr., every hr., €46); **Leipzig** (1hr., every hr., €25); **Weimar** (15min., 4 per hr., €7).

Public Transportation: Buses and **trams** run through the pedestrian zones and beyond. Single ticket €1.50, 4 tickets €5. *Tageskarte* (day ticket) €5. Buy tickets at *Automaten*, stores with *EVAG-Punkt* signs, or on board, then validate them on board. Night trams (numbered with an "N" prefix) cover most daytime routes, running every 15-30min. until 1am on weekdays and throughout the night on weekends, except 4-5am. The tourist office sells **Erfurt Cards** (€9.90, valid for 48hr. from time of purchase), good for unlimited transportation, city walking tours, and admission to the city's museums.

Taxis: ☎ 511 11. For those with bad memories, ☎ 555 55 or 66 66 66.

Bike Rental: Velo-Sport, Juri-Gagarin-Ring 72a (☎ 562 35 40). From the train station, take a right on Bahnhofstr. and a left on Juri-Gagarin-Ring. From €5 per day. Open Apr.-Sept. M-F 10am-7pm, Sa 9am-4pm.

▣ ☷ ORIENTATION AND PRACTICAL INFORMATION

Erfurt lies in the heart of Thuringia, only 15min. from Weimar. Its large train station and proximity to the **Thüringer Wald** make it a convenient gateway to the forest. The train station is south of the city center. Head straight down Bahnhofstr. to reach the **Anger**—the main drag—and then the Altstadt, which is bisected by the **Gera River.** Across the river lies the **Fischmarkt**, dominated by the **Rathaus.** From there, continue on Marktstr. to **Dompl.,** home of Erfurt's cathedral.

Tourist Office: Erfurt Tourismus Gesellschaft, Benediktspl. 1 (☎ 664 00; www.erfurt-tourismus.de), between the Rathaus and the Krämerbrücke. Pick up a copy of the free monthly *Erfurter Magazin* for event listings and *Takt* or *Fritz* for nightlife (all 3 are in German). Ask for a free map of Erfurt or the Thüringer Wald and a brochure in English or German to learn about Erfurt's most notable buildings (€1.30). The staff also reserves theater tickets and books rooms for free. Open M-F 10am-7pm (Jan.-Mar. closes 6pm), Sa 10am-6pm, Su 10am-4pm. 2hr. **tours** of the city in German depart from the office at 11am and 1pm Apr.-Dec. daily, Jan.-Mar. Sa-Su. €5.50, students €3. You can also rent a handheld **video guide** in English; €5.50 for 2hr., €7.50 for 4hr.

Currency Exchange: Deutsche Bank, from the station, take Bahnhofstr. to Juri-Gagarin-Ring; it's on the corner. 24hr. **ATM.** Open M, W, F 9am-4pm, Tu and Th 9am-6pm.

Gay and Lesbian Resources: At the **AIDS-Hilfe,** Windthorststr. 43a (☎ 346 22 97). Tram #3 (dir.: Windischholzhausen) or #6 (dir.: Wiesenhügel) to "Robert-Koch-Str.," then continue another block. On the edge of the Stadtpark behind the train station, a rainbow flag flies over a house that features a library (open W 7-9pm) and café. AIDS counseling available Tu 1-6pm, W 6-9pm. **Café Swiß** open Tu-Th 7pm-midnight. Women's **Frauencafé** on 1st and 3rd F 7pm-midnight, Su 3-8pm.

Women's Resources: Brennessel Frauenzentrum, Regierungsstr. 28 (☎ 565 65 10; www.frauenzentrum-brennessel.de). Specializing in support for abused women, the center offers information, counseling and emergency overnight stays, as well as a café, sauna, and cultural programs. Open M-F 9am-6pm, Th until 9pm.

Bookstore: Hugendubel, Am Anger 62 (☎ 48 44 84.), has many English-language books. Open M-Sa 9:30am-8pm.

Emergency: Police ☎ 110. **Fire and Ambulance** ☎ 112.

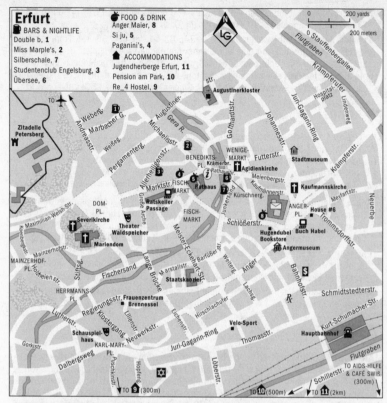

Erfurt

🍷 **BARS & NIGHTLIFE**
Double b, **1**
Miss Marple's, **2**
Silberschale, **7**
Studentenclub Engelsburg, **3**
Übersee, **6**

🍎 **FOOD & DRINK**
Anger Maier, **8**
Si ju, **5**
Paganini's, **4**

🏠 **ACCOMMODATIONS**
Jugendherberge Erfurt, **11**
Pension am Park, **10**
Re_4 Hostel, **9**

Pharmacy: Apollo-Apotheke, Juri-Gagarin-Ring 94 (☎24 11 66). Open M-F 7:30am-7pm, Sa 8am-4pm.

Internet Access: Internet Café (☎262 38 34) in the Ratskeller Passage across from the Rathaus. €1.50 per 30min. €5 back for every 5hr. you buy. Open M-F 10am-8pm, Sa 11am-7pm. **Buch Habel,** Anger 7 (☎59 85 80), on the 3rd fl. €1.50 per 30min. Open M-Sa 9:30am-8pm.

Post Office, Anger 66-73. Open M-F 9am-7pm, Sa 9am-1pm. **Postal Code:** 99084.

🏠 ACCOMMODATIONS

Re_4 Hostel, Puschkinstr. 21 (☎600 01 10). From the train station, turn left on Bahnhofstr., right on Schillerstr., and right on Puschkinstr. Housed in an old police station, this impeccable hostel makes the most of its past: in Room 13, formerly a prison cell, you can fall into bed behind bars. Breakfast €3.50. Sheets €1.50. Reception daily 8am-9pm. Check-in 2pm. Check-out noon. 4-bed dorms €12; 3-bed €15; singles €22.50, with shower €25; doubles €45/50. Cash only. ❶

Jugendherberge Erfurt (HI), Hochheimer Str. 12 (☎562 67 05). Take tram #5 to "Steigerstr." Backtrack and turn left onto Hochheimer Str.; the hostel is on the left corner at the 1st intersection. Breakfast included. Internet access €0.10 per min. Wheelchair accessible. Check-in 5pm, desk open from 3pm for reservations. Reservations recommended in summer. Singles, doubles, and dorms with bath €17 per person, over 27 €20. Nonmembers €3.10 extra per night. Cash only. ❷

Pension am Park, Löberwallgraben 22 (☎345 33 44; fax 654 56 31). From the train station, exit to the left and take a left under the bridge on Bahnhofstr. Turn right onto Schillerstr., and bear right onto Löberwallgraben (10min.). This fastidiously maintained old building features stylish rooms with phone and TV, and use of the kitchen. Breakfast included. Check-in 2pm. Check-out 11am. Singles €38; doubles €52. Cash only. ❹

◖ FOOD

The region's specialty, *Thüringer Bratwurst*, is sold at stands all over the city (€1.50-2). Check out the many outdoor *Eiscafés*, especially on the Fischmarkt. For **groceries**, try **Tegut,** Anger 74-75, next to the Kaufmannskirche. (Open M-Sa 7:30am-8pm.) There is also a fresh fruit and vegetable **market** on Dompl. (M-Sa 7am-2pm.) Many of Erfurt's *Biergarten* also serve inexpensive meals.

Anger Maier, Schlößerstr. 8 (☎566 10 58), at the edge of Angerpl. heading toward the Fischmarkt. One of the oldest bars in Erfurt, with an exceptional *Biergarten,* where guests enjoy shaded tables, a fountain, and an extensive menu. Specials €4-6, entrées €6-9. English menu upon request. Open M-Sa 9am-1am, Su 10am-6pm. MC/V. ❸

Paganini's, Fischmarkt 13-16 (☎643 06 92), slices its own spaghetti and stuffs its own tortellinis daily. Locals dine on pasta and pizza (€5-10) in the bustling interior or while serenaded by street musicians outside. Open daily 11:30am-midnight. AmEx/MC/V. ❸

Si ju, Fischmarkt 1 (☎655 22 95), in the Rathaus. This modern café serves reasonably-priced entrées (€5-8.50) in a prime location. Open daily 9am-1am. DC/MC/V. ❷

◉ SIGHTS

MARIENDOM. 800-year-old steps lead up to the heavenly cathedral that towers over the Dompl. Today, it is a Gothic extravaganza, though its 1154 foundation is Romanesque. Fifteen 14th-century stained-glass windows portray biblical stories and the lives of the saints, a life-size candelabra in the form of a saint is the oldest free-standing piece of bronze artwork in Germany, and a Romanesque sculpture of an enthroned Mary dates back to the 12th century. Opposite of the ornate altar is a gigantic baptismal font, connected to the ceiling to symbolize baptism's power to connect earth to heaven. Out of sight hangs the enormous **Gloriosa bell,** the biggest in medieval Europe, which only rings on important church holidays. Pause a moment by the gigantic **mural** of St. Christophorus, the patron of travelers, who is said to protect them from untimely death. *(Dompl. ☎646 12 65. Open May-Oct. M-F 9-11:30am and 12:30-5pm, Sa 9-11:30am and 12:30-4:30pm, Su 1-5pm; Nov.-Apr. M-Sa 10-11:30am and 12:30-4pm, Su 1-4pm. English translations available. Free.)*

SEVERIKIRCHE. The muted sandstone interior and the Gothic exterior of this church are similar to, and outshone by, the Mariendom, for which it served as a model with its unusual three towers. The enormous Baroque organ screams with flying golden angels, flames, and fake pastel marble, and the high altar is similarly impressive. The sandstone sarcophagus near the entrance supposedly holds the bones of St. Severus, for whom the church is named and who was made a Bishop in the year 284. The church is currently undergoing renovations; it will reopen in June 2007. *(Open May-Oct. M-F 9am-12:30pm and 1:30-5pm, Sa 9-11:30am and 12:30-4:30pm, Su 2-4pm; Nov.-Apr. M-F 10-11:30am and 12:30-4pm, Su 2-4pm. Free.)*

KRÄMERBRÜCKE. Funded in the 1400s by sales of awful-smelling Thuringian blue dye, the bridge—one of Erfurt's most interesting architectural attractions—still serves a commercial function, lined on both sides with shops that completely block the Gera from view. At the end of the bridge, the tower of the **Ägidienkirche** offers glimpses of Erfurt's red-roofed houses. *(☎373 33 01. Tower open Tu-Su 11am-5pm. €1.50, students €1.)*

ANGER. Erfurt's wide pedestrian promenade, the *Anger* (meadow), is one of the most attractive shopping areas in eastern Germany. Remarkable architecture, most of it 19th-century Neoclassical or *Jugendstil* (Art Nouveau), lines the street. Across from the post office is **House #6,** where Russian **Tsar Alexander I** stayed when he came to Erfurt to meet with Napoleon in 1808. The **Kaufmannskirche,** once the site of business transactions, sits at the end of the *Anger* behind the post office. The **Angermuseum,** Anger 18, housed in a yellow mansion, displays a small collection of medieval religious art from around Erfurt as well as rotating exhibitions of local contemporary art. The museum is closed until early 2008. *(☎562 33 11. Ask at the tourist office for hours and prices.)*

AUGUSTINERKLOSTER. Martin Luther spent 10 formative years as a Catholic priest and Augustine monk in this cloister, which has, over time, housed a hospital, an orphanage, and various schools. Today, it is home to a small community of nuns and is the meeting place for diverse church groups from around the world. Some of the cloister's original construction in 1277 still remains, and tours visit a cell that Luther once called home. *(From the tourist office, cross the Krämerbrücke, turn left on Gotthardstr., and cut left through Kirchg. Tours of the cloister every hr. except 1pm M-F 10am-5pm, Su 11am. €3.50, students €2.50. With the associated exhibit €5/4.)* The **library** has one of Germany's most extensive collections, including a number of early bibles with personal notations by Luther himself. When Allied bombs destroyed the library in February 1945, 268 people were killed, but the books (hidden elsewhere) were unscathed. *(☎576 60 22. Open M 2-6pm, Tu-W 8am-6pm, Th-F 10am-1pm.)*

RATHAUS. The stony neo-Gothic facade of Erfurt's Rathaus belies its more playful interior, which dates from the Romantic period. Along its staircases and hallways, murals depict fictional and factual events related to Erfurt including Dr. Faust conjuring up a vision of the cyclops Polyphemus before bewildered and skeptical Erfurt University students. *(Fischmarkt 1. ☎655 11 30. Signs in English. Open M-Tu and Th 8am-6pm, W 8am-4pm, F 8am-2pm, Sa-Su 10am-5pm. Free.)*

OTHER SIGHTS. At the end of the *Anger* is the red-and-white Baroque **Staatskanzlei** (State Chambers), location of a meeting between Goethe and Napoleon, who tried to lecture the poet for writing such gloomy tragedies. Goethe refrained from any retorts about pan-European conquest. Between the *Anger* and Dompl., the lively **Fischmarkt** is bordered by restored guild houses with wild facades. For a view of the city, climb the old walls of the **Zitadelle Petersberg** behind Dompl.

🎵 📷 ENTERTAINMENT AND NIGHTLIFE

Erfurt maintains an indulgent nightlife; the German-language monthly *Blitz* lists upcoming shows, concerts, parties, and special events. The **Theater Erfurt** puts on shows, ranging from operas and ballet to youth theater, at the **Schauspielhaus,** Dalbersweg 2. *(☎223 31 55. Box office, Schloesserstr. 4, open M-F 8am-7pm, Sa 9am-3pm. Tickets €10-22; student discounts available.)* Tickets to these and most other performances in Erfurt can also be purchased at the tourist office. Just off Dompl., the **Theater Waidspeicher** runs a marionette and puppet theater, and holds cabaret shows on weekends. (Box office Dompl. 18. ☎598 29 24; www.waidspeicher.de. Puppet shows €3-5, cabaret €8.50-12. Open Tu-F 3-5:30pm, Sa 10am-1pm.)

The area near Dompl. and the Krämerbrücke between **Michaelisstr., Marbacher G.,** and **Allerheiligenstr.** glows at night with cafés, candlelit restaurants, and bars;

Johannesstr. also has its share. The **Double b,** Marbacher G. 10, near Dompl., fuses Irish pub with German *Biergarten;* trendy Erfurters show up for the cordial atmosphere, good food, and cheap beers. (☎211 51 22. Entrées €4-8. Open M-F 8am-1am, Sa-Su 9am-1am. Cash only.) **Silberschale,** Kürschnerg. 3, off Rathausbrücke on the *Anger* side, has reasonably priced drinks and a back deck with seating right over the shallow Gera. (Open M-Sa 9am-1am or later, Su 9am-6pm. English menu available. Cash only.) **Uebersee,** Kürschnerg. 8, near Silberschale, hosts a boisterous crowd of locals. Check the board for daily drink specials. (☎644 76 07. Th beer (0.4L) €2. Open M-Sa from 8:30am, Su from 10:30am. MC/V.) The laid-back chain **Miss Marple's,** Michaelisstr. 42, features photos of Agatha Christie's humorous private eye on the walls and an entrance that is a dead ringer for a London phone booth. If you're looking for something to soak up that beer after a long night, check here—the kitchen serves great baguette sandwiches and Thüringer specialties (€3.50-10.50) until 2am. (☎540 33 99. Open M-Th and Su 6pm-2am, F-Sa 6pm-3am. Cash only.) The **Studentenclub Engelsburg,** Allerheiligenstr. 20-21, just off Marktstr., is an underground hotspot. On the ground floor, students devor cheap eats (€3.50-8) at the café/bar **Steinhaus.** Beer is €1.50 until 7pm and all night on Mondays. (Open M-F 3pm-3am, Sa-Su noon-3am). The cellar usually hosts live bands on Fridays and a two-floor **disco** from 10pm on Saturdays. (☎244 771 12; www.eburg.de. Concerts €5-12, students €2-10. Disco €4/2. Disco 18+; under 18 must leave concerts at midnight. MC.)

THÜRINGER WALD (THURINGIAN FOREST)

Extending from Eisenach in the northwest to the Saale river in the east, the vast Thüringen Wald is one of Germany's most magnificent landscapes. Because of the forest's proximity to Weimar and Jena, historical university cities that once sheltered many of Germany's foremost intellectuals, it enjoys the unmatched reputation that only poets can bestow. Following Goethe and Schiller's lead, droves of Romantic poets and philosophers found inspiration in the shadows of these trees.

Today, the romantic sensibility of the forest is more accessible than ever. One of the most popular routes through the region is the 168km long *Rennsteig.* Starting in Hörschel, cutting across southern Thuringia, and running south to Bavaria, the Rennsteig links the gorgeous scenery and villages scattered along its path. While history books date the trail to 1330, locals claim that it was first trod upon by prehistoric hunter-gatherers. In the middle of the route, Ilmenau is a good starting point in either direction: take Ilmenau's bus #300 (dir.: Suhl) to "Rennsteigkreuzung" (€2). The tourist offices in Erfurt (p. 561) or Eisenach (p. 568) sell guides and maps for an extended jaunt. If you're planning a multi-day hike, reserve trailside huts far in advance. For more info, contact **Fremdenverkehrsband Thüringer Wald,** Postfach 124, 98501 Suhl (☎03681 394 50; www.thueringer-wald.com) or **Gästeinformation Brotterode,** Bad-Vilbeler-Pl. 4, 98599 Brotterode (☎036840 33 33).

ILMENAU   ☎03677

The small town of Ilmenau (pop. 27,000) is very proud of its most famous visitor, Johann Wolfgang von Goethe. Residents constantly point out that Goethe came to their town a total of 28 times. The author first worked in Ilmenau as a mining minister under the Duke of Weimar, but came back later to seek inspiration from the stunning natural surroundings. The town uses Goethe to lure visitors, vaunting his in-town haunts as well as the *Goethewanderweg,* one of the many trails that leads from Ilmenau into the forest.

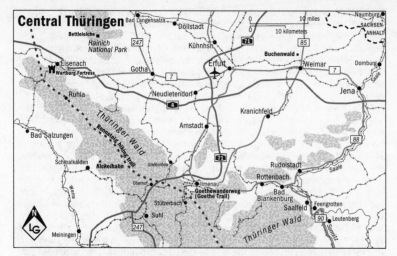

Central Thüringen

TRANSPORTATION AND PRACTICAL INFORMATION. Ilmenau can be reached by **bus** or **train** from Erfurt (1hr., every hr., €4.50). The **tourist office** is at Lindenstr. 12. From the station, cross the island and walk up Bahnhofstr. to Wetzlarer Pl. Follow the pedestrian zone until it becomes Lindenstr. (15min.). The staff leads city **tours** in German, provides hiking maps (€4.10) and books rooms (from €17) for free. (☎20 23 58; www.ilmenau.de. Open M-F 9am-6pm, Sa 9am-1pm. Tours W 10am, F 4pm; €3.) The pre-pay **City Cyber Café,** Kirchpl. 3, is one of the only places in town with **Internet** access. (☎89 64 00. €4.40 per hr. Open M-F 11am-11pm, Sa-Su 4-11pm.) The **post office,** Lindernstr. 1, is in the pedestrian zone near the tourist office. (Open M-F 9am-6pm, Sa 9am-noon.) **Postal Code:** 98693.

ACCOMMODATIONS AND FOOD. Jugendherberge Ilmenau (HI) ❶, Am Stollen 49, is in a drab area far from town, but convenient for hikers. Turn left out of the station and then left at August-Bebel-Str., crossing the tracks and veering right on the path along the tracks. After the sharp right curve, cross the bridge on your left and continue until the trail merges with Am Stollen (15min.). Or take bus A (dir.: TU Mensa; €1) to "Jugendherberge." (☎88 46 81; fax 88 46 82. Breakfast included. Internet access €0.10 per min. €10 key deposit. Reception 4-10pm. Check-out 9:30am. Curfew 10pm, but you can get a late-night key for an additional €10 deposit. €18, under 27 €15. Cash only.) The **Haus Neuschwander ❷,** Lindenstr. 37, is centrally located; to get there, walk down Lindenstr. from the tourist office, it will be on your left. All rooms have TV, refrigerator, and phone. (☎680 80. Reservations recommended in summer. Singles from €20; doubles from €36. Cash only.) For **groceries,** visit **Rewe,** in the basement of the City Kaufhaus on F.-Hoffmann-Str. in the pedestrian zone. (Open M-Sa 7am-8pm. If the Kaufhaus is closed, enter around back.) The **farmer's market** on the Markt sells fresh produce. (Tu 8am-6pm, F 8am-4pm.) **Zur Post ❷,** Mühltor 6, on Wetzlarer Pl., serves regional dishes like *Thüringer Rostbrätel* (pork roast with potatoes) for €5-8. (☎67 10 27. Open M-F 11am-2pm and 5-10pm, Sa-Su noon-10pm. MC.)

SIGHTS AND OUTDOOR ACTIVITIES. The 18.5km **Goethewanderweg** (Goethe Trail) begins in Ilmenau, up Marktstr. outside the town's **Goethemuseum,**

THÜRINGEN

Am Markt 1, a museum that focuses on Goethe's career in Ilmenau and the mining industry he oversaw. The museum will be closed for renovations for a year starting in 2007; inquire at the tourist office for details. (☎20 26 67. Open daily Tu-Su 9am-noon and 1-5pm. €1, students and seniors €0.50. English translations available.) The trail starts at the Markt by the museum, and is well marked by a looping G monogram; pay close attention to the signs, as other trails are denoted by similar schemes. The next of many Goethe landmarks is the grave of **Corona Schröter,** the first actress to portray the heroine of Goethe's classical play *Iphigenia in Tauris.* Following the signs out of the graveyard, turn left along Erfurterstr., follow the signs to Neue Marienstr., and head into the hills. Tall pines crowd both sides of the trail as it leads up to the **Schwalbenstein,** an outcropping overlooking the valley where Goethe wrote Act IV of *Iphigenia.* The middle section passes by the **Emmastein,** which Goethe drew as an example of the area's rock formations. The trail then leads down into the valley and through the tiny town of Manebach up to a reconstruction of the tiny **Goethehäuschen** (Goethe cottage), where the poet scratched his "Wanderer's Night Song" into the walls. A few meters before you come to **Hermannstein,** a huge rock that supported a castle during the Middle Ages, bear right to check out the tranquil cave Goethe loved to visit. Take a 200m detour off the trail to the **Kickelhahn,** a summit that provides a panoramic view of the Thuringian forest. Climb up the *Aussichtsturm* (look-out tower) for the view; on a clear day, you can see all the way to the Harz Mountains. One kilometer farther stands the **Jagdhaus Gabelbach,** the hunting house of Duke Karl August that Goethe frequented in the summer. The refurnished lodge features a display of some of the author's scientific experiments and drawings. (☎20 26 26. Open Apr.-Oct. Sa-Su 10am-5pm; Nov.-Mar. Sa-Su 11am-3pm. Last entry 15min. before closing. €2, students €1.50.) Head down the mountain along a creek and past a small pond to the Finsteres Loch, a picturesque green where Duke August's hunting parties, with Goethe in tow, once rested. At the end of the trail, **Stützerbach** is a tiny valley town where the local glass-works magnate often hosted the poet. His house is now the **Goethehaus** (☎036784 502 77.), but there are demonstrations of traditional glass-blowing as a nod to the patron. If you don't want to hike the 6hr. back to Ilmenau, you can take bus #300 (20min.). Go into Stützerbach, turn right onto Bahnhofstr., and then cut to your left through the parking lot next to the tourist office. Take a right onto Unterstr., which leads over a bridge and to the "Stützerbach, Erholung" bus stop on Schleusingerstr. (M-F every hr. until just before 9pm, Sa-Su until just before 8pm. €1.55.)

EISENACH ☎ 03691

Birthplace of Johann Sebastian Bach, residence-in-exile of Martin Luther, and site of the famous Wartburg castle, Eisenach (pop. 44,000) has garnered national and international attention for almost a millennium. Tourists started visiting the castle as early as the 16th century—mainly to see the black stain that Luther supposedly made on the wall of his small room while "fighting the devil with ink." By the 19th century, Wartburg, one of Goethe's favorite spots, had became a national symbol. Eisenach is also the perfect place to start a journey into the Thuringian Forest to the south or the Hainich National Park to the north. Buses run from Eisenach to the heads of various trails (the distance is also bikeable), and the national park, unlike Wartburg, is refreshingly undiscovered.

⊏♪ TRANSPORTATION AND PRACTICAL INFORMATION

Trains to: Erfurt (30-50min., 2 per hr., €9-17); Göttingen (1½-2½hr., every hr., €19-30); Kassel (1-1½hr., 1-2 per hr., €15-40); Weimar (1hr., 2 per hr., €12-20). Eisen-

Eisenach

⛺🏠 ACCOMMODATIONS
Campingplatz am Altenberger See, **6**
Jugendherberge Arthur Becker, **5**
Residenz Haus, **3**

🍴 FOOD & DRINK
BACH Cafe, **4**
Café Moritz, **2**
La Fontana, **1**

ach's **buses** (€1 per trip, €1.20 if bought on board) go to Wartburg. Buy tickets at the Busbahnhof (open M 6:30am-noon and 1-4pm, Tu and Th-F 7:45am-noon and 1-4pm, W 7:45am-noon and 1-3pm) or the tourist office. For a **taxi**, call ☎22 02 20. Rent **bikes** at **Fahrrad-Service Helm,** Katharinenstr. 139. (☎773 74. €7 per day. Open M-F 9am-6pm, Sa 9am-1pm.) Eisenach's **tourist office,** Markt 9, has information on Wartburg, hands out free maps, offers daily city **tours** (Apr.-Oct. daily 2pm, Nov.-Mar. Sa 2pm, 1½hr., €5), and books rooms for free. From the train station, walk on Bahnhofstr. through the arched tunnel and follow it left until you can turn right onto the pedestrian Karlstr. (☎792 30. Open M-F 10am-6pm, Sa 10am-4pm; Apr.-Oct. also Su 11am-1pm.) The **Georgen-Apotheke,** Georgenstr. 18-20, is a centrally located **pharmacy.** (☎74 24 74. Open M-F 7:30am-6:30pm, Sa 8:30am-12:30pm.) **Die Eule,** Karlstr. 3, in the pedestrian zone near the Markt, is a **bookstore** that offers **Internet** access. (☎85 03 88. €2 per 40min. Open M-F 9am-7pm, Sa 10am-6pm.) **Eisenacher Netc@fe,** Stickereig. 1, is open later. (☎73 19 41. €2 per hr. Open M-F 10am-11pm, Sa-Su 11am-11pm.) The **post office** is at Markt 16. (Open M-F 8:30am-6pm, Sa 8:30am-noon.) **Postal Code:** 99817.

🏠🍴 ACCOMMODATIONS AND FOOD

The **Residenz Haus ❸,** Auf der Esplanade, is next to the tourist office. Miniature witches and dolls decorate the spiraling staircase up to spacious rooms in this central 18th-century tower. (☎21 41 33. Breakfast €5. Singles and doubles €20 per person, students €15. Cash only.) **Jugendherberge Arthur Becker (HI) ❶,** Mariental 24, is a comfortable old villa far from town, but close to the *Schloß*. From the train station, take Bahnhofstr. to Wartburger Allee, which runs into Mariental. Pass the pond; it will be on your right (35min.). Or, take bus #3 (dir.: Mariental) to "Liliengrund Parkpl." Recently renovated, the hostel has an elegant dining room and terraces. (☎74 32 59; fax 74 32 60. Breakfast included. Reception M-F 7am-10pm, Sa-Su 7-10am and 3-10pm. Dorms €15, over 27 €18. MC/V.) The nearest camping is at **Am Altenberger See ❶** in Eckartshausen, with a sauna (€15 for up to 5 people) with a lake view. From the Eisenach bus station, take bus #31 to "Bad Liebenstein," or #135 to "Bad Salzungen" (Bus M-F every hr., Sa-Su 3 per day. ☎21 56 37. Reception 8am-1pm and 3-9pm. €5 per person, €3 per tent, €1.50 per car. MC/V.)

For **groceries** head to the **Edeka,** Johannispl. 2-4. The centrally located **La Fontana ❶**, Georgenstr. 22. serves delicious pizzas, pastas, and salads (all around €3). (☎74 35 39. Open M-Th and Su 11:30am-2:30pm and 5-11pm, F-Sa 11:30am-2:30pm and 5-11:30pm. Cash only.) **Café-Restaurant Moritz ❷**, Bahnhofstr. 7, is known for its Thüringian specialities (€3-9.50) and ice cream, served outside on nicer days. (☎74 65 75. Open M-F 8am-6:30pm, Sa-Su 10am-6:30pm. Cash only.) Bask in the classical climate of the Bachhaus at nearby **B-A-C-H Restaurant ❸**, Frauenplan 8. The elegant interior and unadulterated Thüringian menu (entrées €7.50-12) make it a fitting stop after the museum. (☎21 55 22. Open daily 11am-10pm. MC/V.)

👁 SIGHTS

▧ WARTBURG FORTRESS

Buses run between the train station and the castle parking lot (every hr. 9am-5pm, €1.20). Wartburgerallee leads to the foot of the hill, and a number of footpaths lead up the incline. If you weigh 50kg (132 lb.) or less, you can ride a donkey up the last stretch; €3. ☎770 73. Gates open daily Mar.-Oct. 8:30am-8pm, last tour 5pm; Nov.-Feb. 9am-5pm, last tour 3:30pm. To see the castle's interior, you must take a tour. Tours in English daily at 1:30pm. Tours in German leave every 10min. Due to a special exhibition, from early July to mid-Nov. 2007, there will be no tours, and the castle will be open to all visitors; pick up an English-language self-guided tour brochure (€3) at the ticket office. €6.50, students and children €3.50, seniors and the disabled €5.50. Museum and Luther study without tour €3.50, students €2. Photography permit €1.

The castle high above Eisenach's half-timbered streets lords over the northwestern slope of the rolling Thüringer Wald. It was founded in 1067 by the Franconian **Count Ludwig the Jumper,** who didn't own the land, but covered it with soil from his estate so as to build the castle "on his own land" with a clear conscience. By the turn of the 13th century, Wartburg's court was a famed cultural center. Six talented *Minnesänger* (medieval troubadours who established German choral music) competed here in the *Sängerkrieg* (singers' battles). These events, which inspired Wagner's opera *Tannhäuser*, are depicted in the castle's **Sängersaal** (Singers' Hall). Another important medieval resident was **St. Elizabeth,** whose legendary charitable deeds are represented in a 20th-century mosaic made from just under four million pieces of glass. From July 7-November 19, 2007, Wartburg will host a larger exhibit on St. Elizabeth to mark her 800th birthday. After its medieval heyday, Wartburg laid low for a few hundred years before receiving its most important guest, the refugee **Martin Luther,** in 1521. Disguised as a wanderer under the pseudonym Squire Jörg, Luther spent most of his time here translating the Bible and writing anti-Catholic treatises. The castle then stagnated for a few hundred years, but due in part to Goethe's efforts, Wartburg found new life in the 19th century. The castle's **Festsaal** (festival hall)—which is replicated in Ludwig II's famous Neuschwanstein (p. 464)—housed an 1817 meeting of 500 representatives of university fraternities, who formed Germany's first bourgeois opposition to the monarchy. A copy of the flag they toasted hangs in the room; its red, gold, and black colors were inspiration for Germany's present flag.

The renovated interior of the castle now matches the Romantic idea of the Middle Ages more closely than historical reality, but the structure itself has remained remarkably unchanged in the last 850 years. The view from the walls of the courtyard or atop the south tower is spectacular—if you look opposite Eisenach, you can see from the Thüringer Wald extend all the way to Hessen.

BACHHAUS. Next to an imposing Bach statue on Frauenplan are the recreated Bach family living quarters where Johann Sebastian is thought to have been born in 1685. Downstairs are period instruments like a clavichord, a spinet, and a well-preserved "house organ" from 1750, about the size of a telephone booth. Roughly every hour, one of the museum's guides plays Bach selections on these instruments and provides historical context in German. Restoration work on the building's exterior should end in June 2007, and the museum will open throughout the renovation period. *(Frauenplan 21. Turn off Wartburgallee down Grimmelg. to reach the house. ☎ 793 40. Open daily 10am-6pm. English translations available. €4, students €3.)*

OTHER SIGHTS. Town life centers on the pastel **Markt,** bounded by the tilting pink **Rathaus** and the **Georgenkirche,** an 800-year-old church where Bach family members were organists for 132 years and where J.S. Bach was baptized. The ornate diptych on the left side of the altar is where Martin Luther and **Jan Hus,** a Dutch minister and one of Luther's forerunners in the Reformation, once preached. *(Open daily 10am-noon and 2-5pm.)* Just up the street from the Markt is the latticed **Lutherhaus** museum, where Luther spent his school days. *(Lutherpl. 8. ☎ 298 30. Open daily 10am-5pm. €3, students and children €1.50. English translations available.)*

HAINICH NATIONAL PARK

Although Germans are no strangers to the well-worn paths of the Thüringer Wald, most are unfamiliar with the richly forested northwestern corner of the woods that is the Hainich National Park, which became Germany's 13th national park in 1997 and is still blazing new trails each year. The moment you venture inside, the rest of the world couldn't seem farther away. Towering beeches shelter wildcats, bats, and wild boars, and cast a rich green light over the forest floor.

HAINICH NATIONAL PARK AT A GLANCE	
AREA: 76 sq. km. **CLIMATE:** Temperate and moist. **FEATURES:** Mixed deciduous forest—the largest in Europe—swamps, and small ponds. **CAMPING:** Permitted only in designated campgrounds outside the park.	**HIGHLIGHTS:** Guided nature and wildlife walks, stunning hikes through the Thuringian forest. **GATEWAYS:** Eisenach (p. 568), Mühlhausen (p. 573), Bad Langensalza (p. 574). **FEES:** None.

ORIENTATION

Hainich is crescent-shaped, pointing south and east. It is accessible from three towns: the spa town **Bad Langensalza** at the eastern tip, **Mühlhausen** in the north, and **Eisenach** (p. 568), west of the southern tip. The quality of the trails around Bad Langensalza and Mühlhausen and their proximity to bus stops make them the best jumping-off points. The park is fairly flat (the highest "mountain," Alten Berg, tops out at 494m) and covered in beech forest mixed with ash and maple and draped with exotic orchids. The third of the park that extends west from **Craulaer Kreuz** is a protected zone where human intrusion beyond the hiking paths is prohibited. The eastern and southern areas were military training camps for Soviet and German armies from 1935 to 1997, but the forest is reclaiming the once ammunition-littered grounds. The north is scattered with swamps; the not-so-giant **Hünenteich** (Giant's Pond) in the northwest, is the largest body of water in the park.

TRANSPORTATION

Hainich is easy to navigate by car, and all trailheads have free parking. Biking is also a great option; Hainich is a beautiful ride from Bad Langensalza. Take Mühlhauserstr. out of the city and look for a white gravel path on the left as soon as you get out of the residential area. Follow it to the end, take a right, and ride straight to the park (20min.). From there you can bike well-marked trails or follow signs to the Thiemsburg trailhead to lock your bike.

Public transportation can be difficult to navigate and park buses don't run very often. **Trains** go to Bad Langensalza from Erfurt (1hr., 2 per hr., €6.20) and Weimar (1½hr., every hr., €9.10), and connect from Bad Langensalza to Mühlhausen (15min., every hr., €3.50), where buses run to the park's smaller towns. On weekdays, regular **buses** travel near the park from all three towns; a few also run on weekends. From the Bad Langensalza bus station, take bus #726 to "Thiemsburg" (15min.) and "Craula" (20min.) or #733 to "Weberstedt" (25min.). From the Mühlhausen bus and train stations, take bus #152 to "Kammerforst, Eichsf.-Str." (30min.). Bus #30 leaves from Eisenach's bus station to "Berka vor dem Hainich" (25min.) and "Lauterbach" (35min.) and goes on to Mühlhausen. (Buses run 4-12 per day 5am-7pm, until 5pm on weekends, €1.50-4.90). Check the schedule carefully—most buses run until around 6pm, but some stop as early as 3pm. On weekends, the **WanderBus** travels the perimeter of the park, stopping within walking distance of all trails. Buy your ticket on the bus (€2-4; bikes €1.80), which leave six times per day from the train and bus stations of Mühlhausen and Bad Langensalza. Bus information is available at tourist and park information centers.

▌ PRACTICAL INFORMATION

Emergency: Police ☎ 110. **Fire** ☎ 112. Any of the National Park Information Centers and tourist offices (see below) will arrange for emergency assistance in the park.

National Park Information Centers: Both centers—along with the tourist offices in Mühlhausen and Eisenach—offer trail maps and information on tours and transportation. The central office in Bad Langensalza is the most informative; the one in Kammerforst is at a trailhead bus stop. The national park **website** is www.nationalpark-hainich.de.

Bad Langensalza: Bei der Marktkirche 11 (☎03603 83 44 24). Open M-F 9am-6pm; May-Oct. Sa-Su 10am-4pm; Nov.-Apr. Sa only 10am-4pm.

Kammerforst: Str. der Einheit (☎036028 368 93). Open Apr.-Oct. M-F 10am-6pm, Sa-Su 10am-4pm; Nov.-Mar. daily 10am-4pm.

▧ **Tours and Events:** Throughout the year, the park organizes guided, German-language hikes and events, ranging from spying on wildcats and boars to celebrating Carnival in the winter forest. (2-8hr. Times and themes vary widely from week to week; information available at National Park Centers. Tours leave from trailheads around the park. Free; sometimes a small (typically €2.50) contribution is requested to cover costs.)

▐ ACCOMMODATIONS AND FOOD

Camping is prohibited within the park, although there are few facilities on the outskirts. Your best bet is to stay in a nearby town and take day trips—the park center in Bad Langensalza will refer you to rooms in the area. Eisenach (p. 568) and Mühlhausen (p. 573) have hostels; to reserve a private room, contact tourist offices. Craula, 20min. away from Bad Langensalza by bus #726 or the WanderBus, has the **Hainich-Herberge ❶**, Behringerstr. 81, with two- to six-bed rooms close to the park. The hostel, which occupies an old elementary school and has the finger-paint murals to prove it, is a 35min. walk to "Craulaer Kreuz," a head for three trails, and a 45min. walk to "Thiemsburg," the start of three others. (☎036254 815 56. Breakfast €3. Sheets €4. Dorms €13. Cash only.) There are two **snack shops** in the park: at the **Thiemsburg** trailhead (open daily Apr.-Oct. 10am-7pm; Nov.-Mar. daily 10am-4pm) and at the **Ihlefeld** trailhead. (Open Apr.-Oct. Sa-Su 10am-7pm.)

⚑ HIKING

Hainich has 10 trails that range from short jaunts to the 32km *Rennstieg*. Clear maps of the park and its trails, available at the park information centers, make mixing and matching trails easy; they are all well-marked with individual symbols and intersect frequently. All trails (except for the *Rennstieg* and *Waagebalken*) are loops easily accessible by car.

NORTH (NEAR MÜHLHAUSEN)

Betteleichenweg (11.2km). From the "Kammerforst, Eichsf.-Str." bus stop, continue in the same direction, take your 1st right, and continue straight until you see signs for the trail. Although much of the forest in this area is quite young, the highlight of the loop is the 1000-year-old *Betteleiche* (begging oak), with a time- and weather-worn hole large enough to walk through. The last section winds through the hills near Kammerforst and provides a sweeping view of Thuringia.

Saugraben (9.5km), via Betteleichenweg from Kammerforst (1.8km). Orchids bloom here in summer, and the end offers a view to the north as far as Mühlhausen.

EAST (NEAR BAD LANGENSALZA)

Baumkronenpfad (10km). From Bad Langensalza, walk, bike, or take the occasional Wanderbus to Hainich's newest attraction: a tree-top walkway straight out of Tarzan that ends at a futuristic observatory tower. (☎89 31 37. Walkway open daily 10am-7pm, last entry 6pm. Access to walkway €6, students €4.)

Rennstieg (32km). From Eigenrieden, west of Mühlhausen, to Behringen. Cuts straight through the national park and continues in forested areas outside the park's official borders. Not to be confused with Rennsteig, to the south.

Sperbersgrund (5.6km), Craula. Follow signs for "Craulaer Kreuz." The lovely Sperbersgrund is one of the few trails in the core zone of the park, a largely untouched area. At the end of the hike, the 400m detour provides a grand view of the Wartburg.

Thiemsburg (3.8km), Thiemsburg. The only trail starting from a bus stop features a wood telephone, a wood organ, and the largest tree in the park (5.45m circumference).

WEST (NEAR EISENACH)

Bummelkuppenweg (9km), Lauterbach. This trail along the "Hohe Straße," starts with a view of the Werra River, used in the 1800s to haul grain and salt to northern Germany.

Erlebnispfad Silberborn (2.5km), Berka vor dem Hainich. A short walk from the town brings visitors to this little trail full of gadgets—from crank organs that play animal sounds to boxes that emit forest smells—for a highly sensory trip into the woods.

MÜHLHAUSEN   ☎03601

Just north of Hainich National Park, the bustling town of Mühlhausen (pop. 38,000) began as a Franconian mill in the AD 8th century and grew into the walled city it still is today. Bach spent two years here as organist, and radical Reformationist **Thomas Müntzer** preached here. With a number of trailheads just short bus rides away, Mühlhausen is a great gateway to the park, while a perfectly preserved wall encircling the town and stunning churches and medieval architecture make the city a sight in its own right. In the Altstadt, the stunning 800-year-old **Marienkirche,** Bei der Marienkirche, the second largest church in Thuringia, towers over the town. The church now functions as a museum of religious relics and a monument to Thomas Müntzer, a Lutheran who instigated a 1525 peasant revolt so violent that even Luther disapproved. (☎87 00 23. Open Tu-Su 10am-

THÜRINGEN

5pm. English translations available. €3, students and seniors €2.) The **Divi-Blasii-Kirche,** Christianpl. 1, is also called the Bach Kirche in honor of its most famous organist, who played here from 1707 to 1708. The organ Bach used was removed in the 19th century, but a replica was built in the 20th century with the help of **Albert Schweitzer.** (☎44 65 16. Open M-Sa 10am-12:30pm and 1-5pm; May-Oct. also Su 1-5pm. Free.) A section of the *Stadtmauer* (city wall) at the **Rabenturm** at the end of Herrenstr. is climbable, and a small museum in a tower and along the wall has modern art exhibits and displays about city history. (☎81 60 20. Open Tu-Su 10am-5pm. €3, students and seniors €2.)

The **Jugendherberge Mühlhausen (HI) ❷,** Auf dem Tonberg 1, offers two-, four-, and six-bed rooms in a serene location removed from town. From the bus or train station take city line #5 or 6 to "Blobach" and follow the signs 500m farther to the Jugendherberge. By foot from the tourist office (20min.), walk up Ratsstr., turn left on Herrenstr., continue through the Frauentor opening in the city wall, and walk on Johannisstr. until you come to an alley on your right. Walk through the alley, then turn left onto Tonbergstr. and follow the signs. (☎81 33 18; fax 81 33 20. €12.50, over 27 €15.50. Cash only.) The bright and friendly **Pension Kuttelgasse ❸,** Kuttelg. 23, is located right in the Altstadt and has a **restaurant ❷** downstairs. (Entrées €1.60-5.60. Open M-Sa 11am-10pm, Su 11am-9pm.) From Steinweg, turn onto Linsenstr. Go two blocks and turn left on Kuttelg. (☎85 67 69. Breakfast €4. Singles €18. Cash only.) Around the Obermarkt, near Steinweg, are a variety of fresh produce stands, cheap cafés, and restaurants. The weekday lunch specials (€2.50-3) at the **Ratskeller ❷,** Ratsstr. 19, just down from the tourist office, are a bargain. (☎45 21 93. Open M-F 11am-2pm and 6pm-midnight, Sa 6pm-midnight, Su 7pm-midnight. Cash only.)

The **tourist office,** Ratsstr. 20, is a short walk from the bus and train stations. From the Busbahnhof, walk away from the parking lot up Stättestr., turn right on Steinweg, and take a left on the exceptionally narrow Ratsstr.; from the train station, walk straight up Karl-Marx-Str. to the city wall at Unter der Linde and follow the signs to Steinweg and then to the tourist office. The staff provides hiking maps, city maps (€0.50), leads city tours (Sa-Su 11am, €3.50, under 12 €2), and books rooms (from €13) for free. (☎40 47 70; www.muehlhausen.de. Open M-F 9am-5pm; Apr.-Oct. also Sa-Su 10am-4pm.) The **post office,** Untermarkt 31, is directly across from the Divi-Blasii-Kirche on Johann-Sebastian-Bach-Pl. and has a 24hr. **ATM.** (Open M-F 9am-6pm, Sa 9am-noon.) **Postal Code:** 99974.

BAD LANGENSALZA   ☎03603

Near the eastern tip of Hainich National Park, the city of Bad Langensalza (pop. 19,000) boasts a medieval Altstadt (dating from the 10th-century reign of Otto II), thermal baths and spas, and stunning Japanese gardens. The streets of the Altstadt are lined with churches, shops, fountains, and restored medieval houses. Just outside the *Stadtmauer* is the colorful **Rose Garden,** where dozens of rose varieties grow outside a small museum of scientific exhibits on the beautiful flowers. (Entrance on Vor dem Klagetor. Garden open daily May-Oct. 9am-8pm; Nov.-Apr. 9am-dusk. Museum open M-F 9am-6pm. Free.) Next door, the peaceful **Japanese Garden** combines a variety of gardens complete with stepping stones, a waterfall, a tunnel of bamboo, and the requisite bridge over a tranquil pond. (Entrance on Kurpromenade. Open daily May-Oct. 9am-8pm; Nov.-Apr. 9am-5pm. Free.)

Bad Langensalza is not a budget traveler's haven. The tourist office finds private rooms for free, however, and the town does sport several moderately priced pensions. **Pension Zur Lohgerberei ❸,** Löbersg. 2., offers comfy rooms with showers and balconies in the city center. From the train station, walk straight down Bahnhofstr. as it becomes Steinweg and bear left on Langestr. At Wiebeckpl. bear right on

Bergstr., take a quick right on Unter dem Berge, and veer left on Löbersg. (☎/fax 84 61 31. Breakfast included. Singles €30-35; doubles €40-45. Cash only.) Cafés and restaurants line Marktstr. and Jüdeng. and the Korn Markt. **Pico Bello ❷**, Wiebeckpl. 2, serves generous portions of saucy pastas and fresh pizzas (€2.50-7.50) just a few minutes away from the Markt. Inside, a column is plastered with posters advertising upcoming parties in the area. (☎84 61 78. Open Tu-F 11am-midnight, M and Sa-Su 5pm-midnight. Cash only.)

For a **taxi**, call ☎81 41 81. **Bikeshop Henning**, Langestr. 57, near the Sparkasse on Wiebeckpl., rents **bikes**. (☎84 62 67. Open M-F 9am-6pm, Sa 9am-noon. €6-8 per day.) The **tourist office**, Bei der Marktkirche 11, is across the Altstadt from the Bahnhof. From the train and bus station, walk down Bahnhofstr., turn right on Poststr., and follow the signs around the wall to the *Haus des Gastes*. The staff gives out maps of Hainich National Park (€3.95) and the city (€0.50, but there's a free one in the *Gastgeberverzeichnis* brochure), and leads city **tours** (check schedule and prices at tourist office; bus tours meet at tourist office June-Aug. Sa-Su 2pm; Sept. Su only. €5.50), and books rooms (from €15) for free. (☎83 44 24; www.bad-langensalza.de. Open M-F 9am-6pm; May-Oct. Sa-Su 10am-4pm; Nov.-Apr. Sa only.) The **post office**, Bei der Marktkirche 3-5, is next to the Marktkirche, and has a 24hr. **ATM**. (Open 8:30am-6pm, Sa 8:30am-noon.) **Postal Code:** 99947.

SACHSEN-ANHALT (SAXONY-ANHALT)

Saxony-Anhalt seems humble at first glance, but its tranquil grass plains encircle cities of international cultural significance. Although Wittenberg and Dessau draw thousands of tourists each year, they remain small enough to harbor traditional German character. The region suffers from the highest unemployment rate in Germany, but it is rapidly modernizing; ancient cathedral spires now share the skyline with scaffolding and cranes. Nature enthusiasts will delight in the Harz Mountains, a skiing and hiking paradise virtually undiscovered by English-speaking travelers.

HIGHLIGHTS OF SAXONY-ANHALT

RELIVE THE REFORMATION in **Wittenberg** (p. 576), the city where **Martin Luther** posted his **95 Theses.** The city still celebrates its native superstar and has recently been blessed with a **Hundertwasser**-designed high school.

SUBORDINATE FORM TO FUNCTION at the original **Bauhaus,** which imbues the city of **Dessau** (p. 579) with design-school hipness.

FOLLOW GOETHE to the top of the **Brocken** (p. 589), or visit the half-timbered towns of **Thale** (p. 593) and **Wernigerode** (p. 590) in the **Harz mountains** (p. 586).

WITTENBERG ☎ 03491

Wittenberg does its best to keep the memory of Martin Luther alive, and in 1938 it even went so far as to rename itself Lutherstadt Wittenberg. It was here that Luther nailed his 95 Theses to the Schloßkirche in 1517, initiating the Reformation that irrevocably changed Europe. His scandalous wedding—conducted despite his vows of celibacy as a final snub to Rome—was so perfectly dramatic that the town reenacts it every June in a three-day festival (see **A Protestant Proposal,** p. 578). Even in the officially atheistic DDR, many East Germans clung to the image of the maverick Luther as an emblem of courageous resistance. Since the fall of the DDR, religious pilgrims have returned in full force to Luther's city. Renaissance painter Cranach the Elder also makes his posthumous presence felt both in his paintings of Luther in the Lutherhalle and his world-renowned altar in the St. Marienkirche.

▐ TRANSPORTATION

Trains run to: Berlin (45min., every hr., €22); Dessau (40min., every hr., €6); Leipzig (1hr., every hr., €10); and Magdeburg (2hr., every hr., €15). To get to the pedestrian zone from the station, go toward the bus stop, turn left through the parking lot and down the street, and follow the curve right. Cross the street and walk straight until the **Lutherhalle** is on your left; the pedestrian zone begins at Collegienstr. Rent **bikes** at **Fahrradladen,** Coswiger Str. 21. (☎40 28 49. €7 per day. Open M-F 9am-6pm, Sa 10am-12:30pm.)

▐ PRACTICAL INFORMATION

The **Tourist Office,** Schloßpl. 2, at the western end of the pedestrian zone, provides maps in English (€0.50) and German (free), books rooms for free and gives **tours** in German. English tours are available at additional cost with advance arrange-

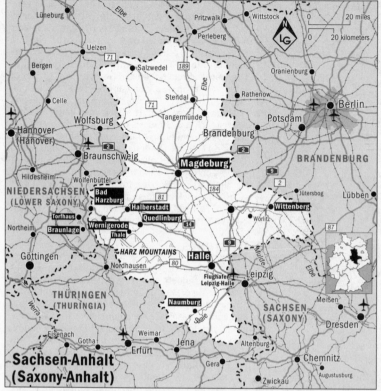

ments. (☎ 49 86 10; www.wittenberg.de. Open Mar.-Oct. M-F 9am-6pm, Sa 10am-3pm, Su 11am-4pm; Nov.-Feb. M-F 10am-4pm, Sa 10am-2pm, Su 11am-3pm. Tours leave May-Oct. M-F 2pm and Sa-Su 11am and 2pm from the Schloßkirche. €6. English audio guides €6.) One of many **banks** near the Rathaus, **Sparkasse,** Markt 20, has several 24hr. **ATMs.** (Open M-F 8:30am-6pm, Sa 9am-11:30am.) A **pharmacy, Löwen Apotheke,** is at Collegienstr. 62a. (Open M-Tu and Th-F 8am-6:30pm, W 8am-6pm, Sa 9am-noon.) **Internet** access is available at the **public library,** Schloßstr. 7. (☎ 40 21 60. €0.41 per 15min. Open M-Tu and Th-F 11am-6pm.) The **post office** is at Dessauer Str. 13. (Open M-F 9am-6pm, Sa 9am-noon.) **Postal Code:** 06886.

ACCOMMODATIONS AND FOOD

The **🛏Jugendherberge im Schloß (HI) ❷** is in the castle across from the tourist office. Medieval on the outside, modern on the inside, the hostel draws large school groups. (☎ 40 32 55; fax 40 94 22. Breakfast included. Internet €6 per hr. Reception 3-10pm. Lockout 10pm, keys €5 deposit. Dorms €16, over 27 €19.) Although far removed, homey **Gästehaus Wolter ❷,** Rheinsdorfer Weg 77, has sunny rooms with TV and spotless bathrooms. Take bus #302, 314, or 315 to "Elbedruck-erei," walk in the direction of the bus, take the first right, and veer right on Rheinsdorfer Weg. Or call Frau Wolter, who will happily pick you up from town. (☎ 41 25 78. Breakfast included. Reception 24hr. Singles €20; doubles €40. Cash only.)

A PROTESTANT PROPOSAL

ight years after he posted his heses on the doors of Witten-erg's Schloßkirche, Martin uther scandalously asked for the and of former nun Katherina von Bora. Despite the uproar caused y his advanced age (42 years) nd his breaking of clerical vows of celibacy, Luther and Katherina ved in 1525.

To past and present citizens of Wittenberg, this marriage repre-ented a courageous stance against the oppression of the Roman Catholic Church. In 1994, he city declared an annual festi-val in honor of the marriage, not-o-creatively titled *Luther's Hochzeit* (Luther's Wedding). Every year a large crowd floods he streets of Wittenberg to expe-ience German life as it was 500 ears ago. Polkas mingle with ounds of street musicians and ninstrels; guilds demonstrate the se of old tools; and *Bier* and *Wurst* are consumed in frighten-ng quantities. A modern Luther nd Katherina proudly parade hrough the town, trailed by revel-rs. As the sun sets, local bands lay in the streets and the crowds ance the night away.

This festival offers events in uthentic venues from the Refor-nation. Hotels fill up early, for although undiscovered by foreign ourists, the festival is becoming opular in Germany.

June 8-10, 2007. ☎03491 49 86 0; www.wittenberg.de.)

Budget eateries line Collegienstr. and Schloßstr. Enjoy stupendous starches at the **Wittenberger Kartof-felhaus ❷**, Schloßstr. 2, which serves savory spuds in a dining room presided over by a leafy tree. (☎41 12 00. Entrées €3.50-12. Open daily 11am-1am. V.) **Crê-perie Lorette ❷**, Collegienstr. 70, offers the best of two worlds: French food and German beer. Crêpes of every variety are available for €3-9. (☎40 40 45. Open M 9am-3pm and 5-8pm, Tu-F 9am-8pm, Sa noon-8pm. Cash only.) Next door, the lively **Irish Harp Pub**, Coll-egienstr. 71, has Guinness on tap and serves over 100 whiskeys, in addition to live rock or blues on Satur-day. (☎41 01 50. Open daily 4pm-3am. Cash only.) The artsy **Barrick**, Collegienstr. 81, draws people of all ages on the weekend to its secluded patio just off the main drive. Barrick features in-house cabaret (€13-20) on select dates; check the website for infor-mation. (☎40 32 60; www.barrik.de. Open M-Th and Su 6pm-1am, F-Sa 6pm-3am. Cash only.)

👁 SIGHTS

To the delight of some citizens and the chagrin of others, Wittenberg truly is an open-air museum, the living scene of Martin Luther. Plan your sightseeing around **Collegienstr.**, which is less than 1.5km long and encompasses all the major sights. The 🏛**Lutherh-alle**, Collegienstr. 54, once home to Luther's family, now chronicles the history of the Reformation through letters, texts, art, and artifacts (signs in English). Hundreds of early printed pamphlets, for and against Luther's ideas, show that the Reforma-tion was also a media revolution. Among these is a first-edition copy of Luther's ground-breaking trans-lation of the Bible. (☎420 30. Open Apr.-Oct. daily 9am-6pm; Nov.-Mar. Tu-Su 10am-5pm. €5, students €3, under 6 free.) Stroll down Lutherstr. from the Lutherhalle to see the oak tree under which Luther allegedly burned a papal bull. At the end of Mittelstr., on the Marktpl., is the 725-year-old **Hauptkirche St. Marien**, nicknamed "the Mother of the Reformation." In the church, known for its dazzling paintings by hometown prodigy **Lucas Cranach the Elder**, you can stand on the altar where Luther gave his famous "Invocavit" sermon. (☎40 44 15. From the Markt, face the Rathaus; the Kirchpl. on your right leads to the Hauptkirche. Open daily May-Oct. 10am-6pm; Nov.-Apr. 10am-4pm. Free information in English.) The **Cranachhof**, Markt 4, where Cranach lived most of his life, is now a museum about the artist; the courtyard hosts lively open-air performances. The **Galerie im Cranach-Haus** showcases modern art exhibitions. (☎420 19 20. Museum and gallery open daily 10am-5pm. €3, students €2.)

Wittenberg's elegant **Altes Rathaus**, Markt 26, dominates the Markt with its stately facade. Under renovation through the end of 2006, the building is home to an exhibit on modern biblical graphic art, with works by Beckmann, Picasso, and Chagal. (☎40 11 49. Open Tu-Su 10am-5pm. €3, students €2.) Statues of Luther and fellow reformer **Philip Melanchthon** share the plaza with one of Wittenberg's famous **Jungfernröhrwässer,** the 16th-century wells whose waters flow through original wooden pipes (the other is in the Cranachhof). The **Schloßkirche,** down Schloßstr., is crowned by a sumptuous Baroque cupola, and retains a copy of the complaints that Luther nailed to its doors. These doors are now nail-proof—the originals have been replaced by bronze ones inscribed with the 95 Theses in Latin. Luther is buried in the church, as are Melanchthon and Saxon Electors Johann the Steadfast and Friedrich the Wise. The **tower** offers a panoramic view of the area. (☎40 25 85. Church open daily 10am-6pm. Free. Tower open M-F noon-4pm, Sa-Su 10am-5pm. Last entry to tower 30min. before closing. Tower €2, students €1.)

In 1995, an art class at the local high school asked architect **Friedensreich Hundertwasser** to redesign their decrepit pre-fab school building in his whimsically eccentric style. Using both the students' drawings and his own ideas about nature and architecture as inspirations, he created the funkiest high school in Germany. Follow Sternstr. out of the city center (walking in the direction that the Lutherhalle faces) and turn right onto Schillerstr.; the **Hundertwasser-Schule,** Str. der Völkerfreundschaft 130, is the building on the left with the onion dome and trees growing out of it. (☎88 11 31. Open Apr.-Oct. M-F 1:30-5pm, Sa-Su 10am-5pm; Nov.-Mar. M-F 1:30pm-4pm, Sa-Su 10am-4pm. Tours €2, students €1.

DESSAU ☎0340

Founded as a medieval fortress in 1341, Dessau flourished under Princess Henrietta Katharina von Oranien in the 18th century. Famous residents include Moses Mendelssohn, a great German-Jewish philosophers and a fervent proponent of religious tolerance in the 19th century, and composer/playwright Kurt Weill, whose works encouraged artistic resistance against Nazism. Today, Dessau draws international visitors to its two UNESCO world treasures: the Bauhaus experiment in Modernist architecture, and the stunning gardens of Schloß Georgium.

▐■▐ TRANSPORTATION AND PRACTICAL INFORMATION

Trains run to: Berlin (1½hr., every hr., €18.30); Leipzig (40min., 2 per hr., €9.10); Wittenberg (40min., every hr., €6.20). Rent **bikes** at the **Mobilitätszentrale** kiosk, left of the train station's main exit. (☎21 33 66. €7 per day. Open daily 9am-5pm. Drop-off until 9pm.) The **tourist office,** Zerbster Str. 2c, finds private rooms and books hotel and pension rooms for free. Take tram #1, 3, or 4 from the train station's main exit to "Hauptpost." The office is behind the huge Rathaus-Center; walk toward the center and turn left into Ratsg. When you reach the end, the office will be on your right, across the street. The staff also sells the **Dessau Card** (€8), a three-day ticket that allows one adult and one child unlimited access to all buses and trams in Dessau, a number of local discounts, and entry to most sights and museums. (☎204 14 42; www.dessau.de. Open Apr.-Oct. M-F 9am-6pm, Sa 9am-1pm; Nov.-Mar. M-F 9am-5pm, Sa 10am-1pm.) **Tours** depart from the tourist office; English tours are available for groups if arranged in advance. (Apr.-Oct. daily at 11am, Sa at 10am. €5, students €4, children free.) For **Internet** access, try the **library,** Zerbstr. 10; alternatives are scarce. (☎204 23 47. €1 library use fee plus €1 per 30min. Open M-Tu and Th-F 10am-6pm, Sa 10am-1pm.) **Thalia,** a **bookstore** in the Rathaus Center, sells English-language paperbacks. (Open M-F 9:30am-8pm, Sa 8am-8pm.) The **post office,** is at the corner of Friedrichstr. and Kavalierstr. (Open M-F 8am-6:30pm, Sa 8am-12:30pm.) **Postal Code:** 06844.

ACCOMMODATIONS AND FOOD

Tourists in Dessau can spend a night in the ▨**Bauhaus** ❸, Gropiusallee 38, in aesthetically pleasing singles or doubles that feature in-room sinks and shared bathrooms. Contact Frau Kaatz in advance to make sure you can get a key. Otherwise, knock on the door of room 224 and specify that you want a room in the Bauhaus building. (☎650 83 18; kaatz@bauhaus-dessau.de. Reception M-F 9am-5pm. Flexible check-out 11am. €25-40 per person; 1-night stays €2 extra. Cash only.) The **Jugendherberge (HI)** ❶, Waldkaterweg 11, is a 25min. walk from the train station. From the station, make a left onto Rathenaustr., and follow it to the end; cross the intersection and follow Kühnauer Str. for two blocks until you cross Kiefernweg. About 50m farther, a small path on the right with red poles leads to the entrance. The hostel is moving in late 2006; call ahead for details. (☎61 94 52. Breakfast included. Sheets €3. Reception M-F 8am-3pm and 5-8pm, Sa-Su 4:30-7:30pm. Check-out 10am. Lockout 10pm, keys available. €15, over 27 €18.)

Affordable restaurants can be difficult to find in Dessau. The gleaming expanse of the newly built **Rathaus-Center** satisfies every craving for mall life; its bakeries and produce stands sell basic *Bratwurst und Brötchen* (€1.40), pizza, and Asian food. (Open M-F 9:30am-8pm, Sa 8am-8pm.) Also try the **street market** on Zerbstr., north of the Rathaus. (Open Tu and Th 7am-5pm.) The tragically hip **Klub im Bauhaus** ❷, in the Bauhaus school basement, is the ideal spot to indulge in angsty pretense over a light meal. The omelets (€4.30) and spaghetti (€6.20) won't disappoint. (☎650 84 44. Open daily 9am-midnight. AmEx/V, min. €15.) The **Ratskeller** ❸, Zerbster Str. 4a, located across the street from the Rathaus-Center, serves up the *Vegetarischer-Teller Dubarry* (€8), a tasty veggie and potato dish, as well as authentic Dessau *Milchreis* (rice pudding; €6). (☎221 52 83. www.Ratskeller-Dessau.de. Open daily 11am-midnight. MC/V.) The offbeat and artsy congregate for alternative *Kultur* at **Kiez Café** ❷, Bertolt-Brecht-Str. 29a, two blocks off Kurt-Weill-Str. The café features a theater (€1-3), art-film cinema (€4.50, students €3.50; Tu €4/3), and art studios. (☎21 20 32; www.kiez-ev.de. Café open M-Sa 8pm-2am, Su 8pm-1am. Cash only.)

SIGHTS

BAUHAUS. With its sheer sleek walls of glass and experimental approaches to lighting, the Bauhaus building—once a university, now the home of the Bauhaus public foundation—is as far ahead of its time today as it was when it opened in 1925. By bringing in experts from all fields of design, chief architect **Walter Gropius** made the Bauhaus not only a masterpiece of Modernism and a textbook example of the subordination of function to form, but a triumph of interdisciplinary cooperation as well. The building is open for self-guided tours and has rotating exhibits on current and past Bauhaus work throughout the complex. (*Gropiusallee 38. Follow directions to the Bauhaus building (p. 580). ☎650 82 51; www.bauhaus-dessau.de. Building and exhibition open daily 10am-6pm. 1hr. tour daily at 11am and 2pm; extra tours Sa-Su. Call ahead to arrange a tour of all Bauhaus sights in Dessau. €4, students €3.*)

BAUHAUS MEISTERHÄUSER. In a pine grove along the Ebertallee, the three famous Bauhaus "Master Houses" radiate white, boxy simplicity. Designed by Lyonel Feininger, the first houses the **Kurt-Weill-Zentrum.** Weill is celebrated extensively during the annual Kurt Weill Festival (Mar. 3-11, 2007). Restored and refurnished, the houses beautifully demonstrate the striking, no-frills principles of the Bauhaus movement. For the Bauhaus fanatic, it doesn't get much better than this. (*Ebertallee. ☎650 82 51. Kurt Weill Festival info ☎0180 55 64 564; www.kurt-weill-fest.de. Open Tu-Su Mar.-Oct. 10am-6pm; Nov.-Feb. 10am-5pm. €5, students €3. Combination ticket to the Bauhaus exhibition and the Meisterhäuser €8/5.*)

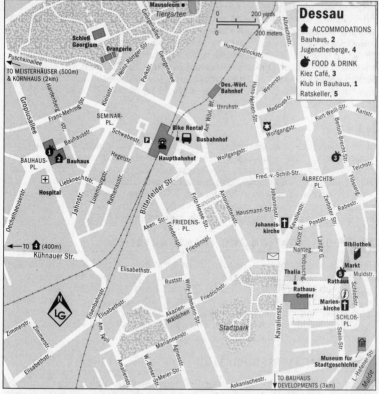

Dessau

⌂ ACCOMMODATIONS
Bauhaus, 2
Jugendherberge, 4

🍎 FOOD & DRINK
Kiez Café, 3
Klub in Bauhaus, 1
Ratskeller, 5

OTHER BAUHAUS BUILDINGS. To find the other spectacular Bauhaus buildings scattered around town, pick up a copy of the English-language brochures *Bauhaus Buildings in Dessau* (€1) and *Bauhaus* (€0.50) at the tourist office. Walk west along Ebertallee away from the Meisterhäuser; turn right on An der Kienheide, which becomes Elballee, and follow it to the end to reach Carl Fieger's **Kornhaus,** designed as the ultimate party house with a beer hall, café, dance floor, and two terraces. Today, the white tablecloths of the waterfront restaurant create a more refined atmosphere; the view of the Elbe from the circular glass dining room is worth the trip. (☎ 640 41 41. Open daily 11am-11pm.) To the south of the city and a bit farther out, two housing developments bear witness to the practical aspirations of the Bauhaus school. While the red brick **Laubenganghäuser** is hard to distinguish from neighboring DDR complexes, the nearby **Mittelring** stands out with its rigidly orthogonal houses. Only one house now displays its original facade: the city-owned **Moses-Mendelssohn-Zentrum,** Mittelring 38, which includes exhibits about the philosopher's life and work as a Jew in Dessau. (Tram #1 (dir.: Dessau-Süd) to "Damaschkestr." (15min.) ☎ 850 11 99. Open M-F 10am-5pm, Sa-Su 1-4pm. €2, students €1.)

NON-BAUHAUS ARCHITECTURE. Dessau also has its share of old-school architecture as ornate as Bauhaus is spare. In the 17th-century country estate **Schloß Georgium,** the **Anhaltische Gemäldegalerie** (Anhalt Picture Gallery) displays lesser-known paintings from the 16th-19th centuries along with modern German art. The

UNESCO-protected gardens surrounding the castle melt into lush forests that extend all the way to the Elbe. *(Puschkinallee 100. From the Bauhaus, turn right on Gropius-allee and right again on Puschkinallee. When you see Kleisstr. on your right, make a left into the park. Go behind the yellow buildings by the street and follow the path to the Schloß. ☎ 661 260 16. Schloß open Tu-Su 10am-5pm, W 10am-8pm. €3, students €2. Gardens open 24hr.)* With its off-beat exhibits on Dessau's history and contemporary concerns, the **Museum für Stadtgeschichte** (Municipal History Museum) in the Johannbau will satisfy all cravings for Dessau esoterica. *(Schloßpl. 3a. ☎ 220 96 12. Open Tu, Th, Sa-Su 10am-5pm, W 10am-8pm, F 1-5pm. €3, students €2.)*

HALLE ☎ 0345

Although unemployment is rampant in the former political and industrial capital of Saxony-Anhalt, Halle's university, art school, and first-rate art museum provide an exceptional cultural community. While nearby Leipzig boasts of Bach, Halle (pop. 240,000) has its own musical hero; Georg Friedrich Händel was born and raised here. The revival of interest in Händel after WWII rejuvenated Halle's artistic community; the music calendar culminates with the yearly Händel-Festspiele (May 31-June 10, 2007; see www.haendelfestspiele.halle.de for more info).

■ ■ ORIENTATION AND TRANSPORTATION

Halle is divided into several districts; most significant are the DDR-style **Neustadt** and the historic **Altstadt,** separated by the Saale River. The train station, major tram terminals, and all sights are in the Altstadt. **Trains** run to Leipzig (30min., 3 per hr., €5.70) and Naumburg (40min., every hr., €5.70). Though most of Halle is easily reached on foot, trams also cover the town. (Single ticket €1.50, €2.30 if bought on board; day pass €4.10). The main street is Große Ulrichstr., which becomes Geiststr. when it leaves the **Marktpl.**

■ PRACTICAL INFORMATION

The **tourist office** is in the StadtCenter Rolltreppe mall, Große Ulrichstr. 60. From the station, take the E.-Kamieth-Str. exit and walk through the pedestrian tunnel straight onto Leipzigerstr. Head past the **Leipziger Turm** to Marktpl. (15min.) Behind the large tower is Große Ulrichstr.; the tourist office is about 100m down the street. Or, from the station, take tram #2 (dir.: Eselmühle) or #5 (dir.: Heide) four stops to "Markt." The office hands out city maps, offers pamphlets on cultural events, and finds rooms for free. (☎ 47 23 30; www.halle-tourist.de. Open M-F 10am-6pm, Sa 10am-2pm.) Tours depart from the tourist office Mar.-Oct.; English tours are available with advance notice. (M-Sa 2pm, Su 10am. €4.50, students and children €2.50.) You can **exchange money** at the Reisebank in the train station. (Open M-Tu and Th-F 9:30am-12:30pm and 1:30-6pm, W 12:30-6pm.) The German-speaking **women's agency,** Robert-Franz-Ring 22, holds meetings and lectures, and also offers a hotline, gallery, library, café, and monthly parties. (☎ 202 43 31; www.weiberwirtschaft-halle.de. Open to women Tu noon-midnight, W-Th noon-4pm; women and men F noon-midnight.) **Telecafé,** Steinweg 38, has phones and computers with **Internet** access for €2 per hr. (☎ 678 74 58. Open M-Sa 9am-10pm, Su 11am-10pm.) The **post office** is at the corner of Hansering and Große Steinstr. (Open M-Th 9am-6:30pm, F 9am-6pm, Sa 9am-12:30pm.) **Postal Code:** 06108.

■ ■ ACCOMMODATIONS AND FOOD

Halle's **Jugendherberge (HI) ❶,** August-Bebel-Str. 48a, is located in a newly restored mansion (built in 1904) just north of the market. From the station's main entrance, turn left and walk through the tunnel onto Leipzigerstr. Then, take a right onto Hansering, pass through Joliot-Curie-Pl., and take August-Bebel-Str., to the right of the opera house. Or take tram #7 (dir.: Kröllwitz) to "Puschkinstr." Continue on Geiststr. one block, turn right onto Puschkinstr., and take a right onto August-Bebel-Str. This dignified, 70-bed hostel is in a pleasant student neighborhood a short walk from the city center. Ask for room #7—it has a balcony. (☎202 47 16; fax 202 51 72. Breakfast included. Sheets €3. Reception 7-10am and 5-11pm. Curfew midnight, but keys are available for €5 deposit. Dorms €16.70, under 27 €14. Cash only.) **Hotel Sonnenschein ❷**, Torstr. 19, is a great deal despite its location 15min. from the tourist office. To get there, follow Schmeerstr. and bear a slight left onto Rannischestr. Cross Franckepl. and walk five blocks down Steinweg; make a right onto Torstr. at Rannischer Pl. Well-furnished rooms complete with fantastic Hundertwasser paintings and private bathrooms. (☎678 44 45. Singles €25; doubles €39. Breakfast €5. MC/V.)

Cafés line Leipzigerstr. to the Marktpl., becoming livelier as they continue up Große Ulrichstr. toward Moritzburg. **Café Nöö ❷**, Große Klausstr. 11, just down Domstr. from the Dom, serves tasty pasta (€4.70-6.50), dramatic breakfasts, many vegetarian options, and the "Nöö salad": a tortilla bowl filled with turkey, chicken wings, shrimp, egg, and veggies for €6.60. (☎202 16 51. Open M-F 9am-3am, Sa-Su 10am-3am. Cash only.) At the **Café & Bar Unikum ❷**, Universitätsring 23, students and locals drink together amid smoke and modern art. Cheap salads, sandwiches, and daily specials (€2-7) make up the menu. (☎202 13 03. Open M-Th 9am-1am, F 9am-2am, Sa 6pm-2am, Su 6pm-2am. Cash only.) **Ökase ❷**, Kleine Ulrichstr. 2, is a hip vegetarian bistro serving up specials (€2-6) in a chill atmosphere. (Open M-F 10am-7pm. Cash only.) The Marktpl. hosts a **market** (M-F 10am-6pm, Sa 10am-2pm), and there's an **Edeka** supermarket on Leipzigerstr. near the train station (open M-F 8am-8pm, Sa 8am-4pm).

🄶 SIGHTS

Central Halle revolves around the **Marktpl.**, bustling with traffic, vegetable stands, and *Eiscafés* (ice cream shops). At its center is the **Roter Turm** (red tower). A number of popular myths surround the tower's name. According to one particularly gruesome legend, after the tower was completed in 1506, the blood of prisoners being executed on the adjoining gallows splattered onto the tower, giving it a grisly tint. Across from the tower is the intricate **Marktkirche Unsere Lieben Frauen** (Church of Our Loving Lady). The organ on which Händel began his musical studies is above the altar; after a century of silence, organists once again perform concerts on its keys. **Martin Luther's** eerie death mask, and the pulpit from which he supposedly preached in this church in the 16th century, are on display in a separate room. (Open M-Sa 10am-5pm, Su 3-5pm. Church free, Luther room €2. Free 30min. organ concerts Tu and Th 4pm.)

An 1859 centennial memorial to Händel sits in the Marktpl., but the most important Händel shrine is his family's mansion, the ◨**Händelhaus**, Große Nikolaistr. 5, a short walk from the market down Kleine Klausstr. Through hundreds of manuscripts and composition books and dozens of period instruments, the museum chronicles Händel's life from his 1685 birth in the house to his death in 1758 in London, where he lived for the last 50 years of his life. The museum also displays a beautiful collection of musical instruments from the 16th century onward. (☎50 09 00. Open daily 9:30am-5:30pm, Th until 7pm. Free. English audio guides free.) The **Dom** where Händel served as organist is a 5min. walk down Nikolaistr. from Händel's home. This ancient complex, once the favorite getaway of the Archbishops of Magdeburg, remains a significant repository of religious relics. Today, the church's most treasured offerings are the 17 life-size figures on its pillars dating from the 16th century. (☎202 13 79. Open June-Oct. M-Sa 2-4pm. Restoration in progress; call ahead to confirm hours.) Early summer brings the annual **Händel-Festspiele** (p. 582), a celebration of the composer's masterful Baroque music. Buy tickets at the Neues Theater (☎205 02 22. Open M-Sa 10am-8pm.)

To reach the whitewashed **Moritzburg fortress** from the Dom, head through Dompl. and downhill on Mühlg., then bear right and uphill on Schloßbergstr. The **Staatliche Galerie Moritzburg** (Moritzburg Municipal Gallery) occupies most of the 15th-century fortification, sometimes called "Gothicism's Swan Song." This art museum, the largest in Saxony-Anhalt, has three galleries that range from Renaissance to contemporary. Halle's once-extensive Expressionist collection offended Hitler, who drew heavily from this museum to furnish his infamous *Entartete Kunst* exhibit (Degenerate Art; see p. 69). Although much of the collection was burned or sold off by the Nazis, the salvaged works serve as a monument to artistic freedom. (☎21 25 90. Open Tu 11am-8:30pm, W-Su 10am-6pm; last entry 30min. before closing. €5, students €3. Last Su of the month free.)

🎵 🎭 ENTERTAINMENT AND NIGHTLIFE

The **Neues Theater** sells tickets to most shows in Halle's growing arts scene. (☎205 02 22. Open M-Sa 10am-8pm.) The free magazines *Fritz* and *Blitz* list shows, times, and locations. The elegant **Opernhaus Halle,** Universitätsring 24, shows everything from ballet to *Carmen*. (☎511 03 55; www.opernhaus-halle.de. Tickets €4-27, students €3-15.50. Box office open 1hr. before performances.) To hear the works of Händel and others, try the **Philharmonisches Staatsorchester Halle,** which plays at the Konzerthalle Ulrichkirche, Kleine Bräuhausstr. 26. (☎221 30 00. Tickets from €15, students 30% off. Box office open M-Tu and Th 10am-1pm and 3-6pm, W and F 10am-1pm, and 1hr. before shows.) Completed in 1990, the **Neues Theater,** Große Ulrichstr. 51, features Shakespeare, Molière, Brecht, and local playwrights. (☎20 500; www.nt-schauspiel-halle.de. €5-15.50, students €2.50-10. No performances mid-July to mid-Aug. Box office open M-Sa 10am-8pm and 1hr. before shows.) The **Kleines Thalia Theater,** on Thaliapassage off Geiststr., has avant-garde and children's shows. (☎20 40 50; www.thaliatheaterhalle.de. Box office open 1hr. before shows. €7, children and students €4. Some shows in the **Grosses Thalia Theater** on Kardinal-Albrecht-Str.)

Turm, Friedemann-Bach-Pl. 5., in the northeast tower of the Moritzburg fortress, hosts the city's *Studentenklub*. The music is a mix of disco, funk, blues, techno, and rock performed by local bands. Turm also hosts a jazz festival in July or August. A *Biergarten* and grill are outside. Student ID is required. (☎202 37 37; www.turm-net.de. Cover €3.50, students €2.50, concerts €8-20. Beer garden open daily by 10pm. Disco open W and F-Sa 10pm-late. 18+)

NAUMBURG   ☎03445

Home to Friedrich Nietzsche, Germany's most famous secular philosopher, walled Naumburg (pop. 30,000) has erased almost all traces of its former function as a Red Army post, and most construction sites have disappeared, leaving an energetic and sophisticated atmosphere in their wake. The green spires of Naumburg's famous cathedral, a 13th-century Gothic giant, are always in view.

🚆 TRANSPORTATION AND PRACTICAL INFORMATION. Trains to: Erfurt (50min., 1-2 per hr., €10); Halle (45min., 1-2 per hr., €7.60); Leipzig (35min., every 2hr., €16); Weimar (35min., every hr., €7.60). To reach town from the train station, bear right on Markgrafenweg and follow it until the end. Take the winding cobblestone road to your left uphill. At the top, a sign points to the Dom; follow it until you see the cathedral's huge towers above the rooftops. From the Dom, it's a short walk down Steinweg and then Herrenweg to the Naumburg Markt, the center of town. The **tourist office**, Markt 6, has free maps, leads city tours, and arranges stays in private rooms (from €16) for free. (☎27 31 12; www.naumburg.tourismus.de. Open Apr.-Oct. M-F 9am-6pm, Sa 9am-4pm, Su 10am-1pm; Nov.-Mar. M-F 9am-6pm, Sa 9am-2pm. Tours last 1½hr. and meet by the cathedral Sa at 10:30am and 2pm, Su at 10:30am, or by the tourist office W at 2pm and F at 8pm. €2.50, students €2.) For a **taxi** call ☎20 84 44. Head down Marienstr. from the Markt to reach the **post office**, Stephanpl. 6. (Open M-F 9am-6pm, Sa 9am-noon.) **Postal Code:** 06618.

▛▟ ACCOMMODATIONS AND FOOD. The private rooms listed with the tourist office are your best bet for budget accommodations in central Naumberg. The city also hosts several hostels and pensions. To reach Naumburg's **Jugendgästehaus (HI) ❶**, Am Tennispl. 9, follow Wenzelsstr. from the Marktpl. out of the old walled city to Bürgergartenstr., across and to the right, then follow the signs up the long hill to the hostel (30min.). The surprisingly large (204-bed) hostel is situated in Naumburg's residential outskirts. (☎/fax 70 34 22. Reception daily 7:30am-10pm. 3- to 5-bed dorms €15, over 27 €17.70; singles €18/20.70; doubles €34/39.40. Cash only.) For something closer to town, **Pension Hentschel ❷**, Lindenhof 16, has clean rooms with phones and baths. (☎20 12 30. Breakfast included. Singles €23; doubles €40. Cash only.) Cheap *kebaps* and other *Imbiß* (snack bar) fare can be found around the station or on streets off the Markt. For a cup of coffee or light meal, try **Zum Schrägen Engel ❷**, Engelsg. 3, (☎699 01 84). To get there, face the Rathaus from the Markt and walk all the way around the building. Built before 1517, this former bakery gained its Rococo facade in the 18th century. Now a café, it serves salads, omelets, and pastas (€5.60-9) amid modern art. (Open Tu-Su 10am-11pm. Cash only.) For a heartier meal, try the *Goulash* with mushrooms and *Knödel* (dumplings; €9.50) at the aromatic **Zillestube ❸**, Marieng. 2. (☎20 28 00. Most meals €6-10. Open W-Su noon-2pm and 5pm-midnight. Cash only.) Nighthawks head to the Markt, where bars like **Kanzlei** serves beer daily until 1am.

◪ SIGHTS. Beneath its ornate Gothic towers, the huge 13th-century **▨Naumburger Dom**, Dompl. 16-17, has captivating and unusual details at every corner, from the procession of animals up the railing in the east choir to the 12 statues inside the west choir. The most well known of these is **Uta**, who stands with her husband **Eckehard II** on the right side; they are widely considered to be the best example of Realism between classical times and the Renaissance. The artist, too humble to carve his name in the cathedral's stone, is remembered today simply as the *Naumburger Meister*. The musty **Domschatz** (Cathedral Treasury), across the courtyard, displays original medieval altars, books, and musical manuscripts. Ask for English pamphlets; English tours are available with prior arrangement. (☎23 01 10. Open Mar.-Oct. M-Sa 9am-6pm, Su noon-6pm. Nov.-Feb. M-Sa 10am-4pm, Su noon-4pm. Tour every hr. except noon. Last entry 30min. before closing. Dom and Domschatz €5.50, students and seniors €3.50. Dom only €4/3, Domschatz only €2/1.) The rest of Naumburg has glorified its pre-DDR history and recovered well in the wake of its 45 years as a Red Army post. Animated Marktpl. hosts a morning **market** (M, W, Sa 8am-3pm). Just off the market square is the **Stadtkirche St. Wenzel.** Its interior, with paintings by Cranach the Elder, boasts a Baroque organ tested and approved by Bach upon its completion in 1746. Climb the 72.5m tower, on the opposite side of the church from the entrance, for a stunning view of the city and surrounding countryside. (☎20 84 01. Open May-Oct. M-Sa 10am-noon and 2-5pm, Su only for services; Nov.-Apr. M-Sa 10am-4pm, Su noon-4pm. Free tours available with arrangement. Organ concerts May-Oct. W and Sa-Su at noon. €2.50. Other concerts 1st Sa of the month at 5pm, prices vary. Tower €1.50, under 18 €0.75.)

Those looking for something more secular should visit the **Nietzsche-Haus,** Weingarten 18, off Jakobstr., with a whole room devoted to the philosopher's escapades with the fairer sex. After living here as a child from 1850 to 1858, he returned in 1890 to live with his mother as his health declined. The second floor has a collection of Nietzsche literature for perusal. (☎20 16 38. Open Tu-F 2-5pm, Sa-Su 10am-4pm. €2, students €1.) The modern **Stadtmuseum Hohe Lilie** (Tall Lily Municipal Museum), Markt 18, next to the Rathaus, has exhibits on the history of the town, including a display on the region's beer and a room dedicated to the town's patron, St. Wenzel. Special exhibits are on the top floor. (☎20 06 48. Open daily 10am-5pm. €2, students €1.)

HARZ MOUNTAINS

Poet Heinrich Heine wrote that even Mephistopheles (the devil's liaison in Goethe's *Faust*) trembled when he approached the Harz, the devil's own mountains. It's easy to see why Heine—and a host of others, including Goethe and Bismarck—were fascinated by this mist-shrouded terrain. The region has practical appeal, too; the Harz were Germany's main mineral source until the 20th century. Since the region straddles the Iron Curtain, both East and West declared much of it off-limits for mining during Germany's 50-year division. The effects of that period's shaky economy can still be felt, although a recent surge in German tourism is bringing hope to this region still largely unknown to international visitors.

HARZ NATIONAL PARK

Hikers and spa-seekers populate the Harz National Park, which stretches from the northwestern **Oberharz** to the sheltered valleys of the south and **Wernigerode** in the east. Throughout the Harz, historic villages and dramatic mountains make for rewarding biking and hiking in summer and excellent skiing, skating, and tobogganing in winter.

HARZ NATIONAL PARK AT A GLANCE	
AREA: 247km².	**HIGHLIGHTS:** Hiking in Goethe's footsteps, skiing the Harz, enjoying the view from the Brockenbahn.
CLIMATE: Mild summers, snowy winters. Often foggy at high altitudes.	
FEATURES: Dense deciduous forests, mountainous terrain, bogs, and moors.	**GATEWAYS:** Bad Harzburg (p. 588), Goslar (p. 245), Wernigerode (p. 590), Halberstadt (p. 591), Quedlinburg (p. 592), Thale (p. 593).
CAMPING: Permitted only in designated campgrounds.	

▊ TRANSPORTATION

The **Harzer Schmalspurbahn** (narrow-gauge railway) consists of two railroads that serve the Harz. The **Brockenbahn** runs from **Nordhausen** to **Wernigerode,** passes through the unfortunately named towns of **Sorge** (Sorrow) and **Elend** (Misery), and chugs along to **Brocken.** The **Selketalbahn** cuts through the southeast valleys. **Trains** run every hr. in summer from 8:30am-8:30pm, although some routes only run until 4pm. Schedules are available at most tourist offices, at www.hsb-wr.de, and in the free monthly pamphlet *Wandern Tips.* The Harz regional **bus station** is located in Wernigerode (p. 590). A bus and rail schedule for the eastern Harz (€2), and another for the *Oberharz* (€1) are invaluable and available at both the **tourist office** (in Goslar, p. 245) and bus station. Schedules vary greatly between seasons

Harz Mountains

and some buses come only a few times per day. Although strenuous, hiking offers a more interesting way to experience this stunning landscape. Torfhaus, Braunlage, Gernrode, and most of the region's other towns are all within a day's hike of one another.

ORIENTATION AND PRACTICAL INFORMATION

The Harz National Park is located at the intersection of three *Länder:* Niedersachsen, Sachsen-Anhalt, and Thüringen. The park itself is nestled within the wider Harz region, which supports a population of nearly 900,000 and extends 100km from east to west and 40km from north to south. **Brocken,** the highest mountain in northern Germany (1142m), is situated near the center of the park's Sachsen-Anhalt half, while glacial lakes and valleys occupy the park's southern reaches.

Emergency: Police ☎110. **Fire** ☎112.

Park Administration: Wernigerode (☎03943 55 020; www.nationalpark-harz.de).

Nationalparkhäuser (Visitors' Centers): Located throughout the park, in **Torfaus** (☎05320 263; open daily Apr.-Oct. 9am-5pm; Nov.-Mar. 10am-4pm), **Sankt Andreasberg** (☎05582 92 30; open daily Apr.-Oct. 9am-5pm; Nov.-Mar. 10am-5pm), and **Brocken** (☎ 03945 55 00 06; open daily 9:30am-5pm).

CAMPING

In addition to hostels and pensions listed in the **Accommodations** sections of the Harz's gateway towns, visitors will find ample opportunity to camp near the park. The following campgrounds are located close to the park; check with local tourist offices or visit www.harz-urlaub.com for a more comprehensive listing.

Camping am See, Warmholzberg 70, 38820 Halberstadt (☎03941 57 07 91; info@camping-am-see.de).

Camping Prahljust, An den langen Brüchen 4, 38789 Clausthal-Zellerfeld (☎05323 78 393; camping@prahljust.de).

Harz Camp Bremer Teich, Familie Krause, 06507 Gernrode (☎03948 56 08 10; harz-camp-bremer-teich@web.de).

Komfort-Camping Panoramablick, Hinterdorf 79, 06493 Dankerode (☎03948 44 23 41; info@hotelcamping-ludwig.de).

⛰ HIKING

Three main **hiking** trails criss-cross the area surrounding the Brocken. You can follow in literary footsteps on the **Goetheweg** (p. 589), a relatively easy path (2½hr.) that begins near the Torfhaus bus stop and winds through moors, ancient forests, and high fields. Heine walked a longer but more scenic route from Ilsetal, accessible from Wernigerode by bus #288. The highlights of the **Heineweg** (8½hr.) are the surreal, natural rock formations high up along the path. Finally, a less-traveled (and very steep) unnamed path runs from Schierke. Plan a unique hiking experience with the *Wanderntips* hiking map (not to be confused with the monthly *Wandern Tips*), available at any regional tourist office.

The **Wurmberg Seilbahn** chairlift is an exhilarating way to approach the **hiking** paths around Braunlage, a small town on the park's southern fringe easily accessible by bus or train. Take the lift to the top (15min.) to reach the head of a 3hr. trail to Brocken. Or, get off at "Mittelstation" to reach the Schierke trail (2½hr.). Wurmburg (971m) itself is the second-tallest peak in the Harz, topped by a high-tech ski jump used for national competitions. The lift departs from the mountain base in the parking lot behind a winter-time ice rink. From the tourist office, turn left, then right on Kurpromenade along the river. (☎999 30. Open May-Oct. daily 9am-4:40pm. €5.50, round-trip €10. To "Mittelstation" €4.)

⚠ ❋ ACTIVITIES AND FESTIVALS

The Harz are famed for their **skiing,** sporting over 500km of cross-country and downhill trails. Skis can be rented in all of the Harz's gateway towns, many of which are trailheads for slopes and cross-country trails. Check www.harzwinter.de or www.skiharz.de to identify those most appropriate to your interests and abilities. **Ice skating** and **tobogganing** are also popular; the websites above list rinks and toboggan runs, and also detail winter festivals and special activities.

To see more of the Harz, consider renting a bike. The National Park features many trails suitable for **mountain biking.** For those less interested in strenuous activities, a day of rejuvenation may be a better bet. Relax just outside the park in Bad Harzburg's **Sole-Therme** (see below), or enjoy Braunlage's **Hallen- und Freizeitbad,** on Ramsenweg, which offers a pool and sauna. (☎27 88. Open Tu-W and Sa 10am-7pm, Th 10am-9pm, F 10am-5pm, Su 10am-2pm. Sauna €8. Pool €3.50 for 1½hr., €5 for 3hr. Last entrance 1½hr. before closing.)

Spring in the Harz brings the immense regional celebration of **Walpurgisnacht** (April 30; p. 594). The hedonistic festivities, immortalized by Goethe in his masterpiece *Faust*, center around legendary witches who sweep through the sky on broomsticks to alight on the peak of **Brocken.** *Wandern Tips* lists events and activities in Wernigerode, Goslar, and Quedlinburg. For more on cultural happenings, pick up a free copy of *Harz-Blick* at any Harz tourist office.

BAD HARZBURG   ☎05322

Perched on the edge of the Harz, just a few miles from Brocken, Bad Harzburg (pop. 24,000) is a popular jumping-off point for outdoor adventurers. The **Harzburger Sole-Therme,** Nordhauser Str. 3, provides all kinds of aquatic cures—hot and cold baths (€7.50 per 2½hr.), with saunas (€11.50)—and a variety of massage therapies. To get to the spa, continue down Herzog-Wilhelm-Str. past the tourist office and follow it as it becomes a pedestrian zone and a smaller path; the spa will be on your right. Bathing suits are mandatory, but rentals are available. (☎753 60. Men's trunks €1.50, women's suit €2.50. Open M-Sa 8am-9pm, Su 8am-7pm; saunarium men only W 8am-1pm, women only Th 8am-3pm.) To see the national park without the walk, the **Burgberg-Seilbahn** offers a short (6min.) lift to deep forests and a small castle ruin. (☎753 70. Runs May-Oct. 9am-5pm, Nov.-Apr. 10am-4pm. Up €2, down €1.60; round-trip €3.) Purchase a *Wanderntips* (€1) at the Seilbahn station to navigate the trails at the top. A number of trails also leave from Kurhausstr., behind the Kurhaus. Cross the highway by the Bergbahn to enter the national park (☎918 90; www.nationalpark-harz.de).

Hotels and pensions are in endless supply in Bad Harzburg, with guest houses starting at €10. A *Kurtaxe* applies (typically €3-5); in exchange, you get a *Kurkarte* good for free rides within town and discounts on sights. **Haus Königsmark ❷**, Am Schloßpark 15, is a pension in a quiet residential district. From the train station, turn right on Dr. Heinrich-Jasper Str. and left on Am Schloßpark. (☎502 06. Breakfast included. Singles €20; doubles €40. Cash only.) The **Bier-Bistro Cinema ❸**, Herzog-Wilhelm-Str. 97 (☎543 36), serves traditional German home-cooked meals (€4-10). Cake-and-coffee shops abound on Herzog-Wilhelm-Str., and a **supermarket** is located across the street from the train station.

Trains head to Brunswick (45min., every hr., €5); Goslar (10min., every 45min., €2); Göttingen (1½hr., every 1½hr., €14.70); Halle (2hr., every hr., €22.10); Hanover (1½hr., 2 per hr., €15.50); and Hildesheim (1hr., every hr., €10). **Buses** leave every hr. to Braunlage, Torfhaus, Wernigerode (each €2-4). For a **taxi**, call ☎90 00. **Brocken Bike,** Herzog-Wilhelm-Str. 6, rents bikes (€8-15 per day). The **tourist office,** Herzog-Wilhelm-Str. 86, just off the main drive, is in the Kurzentrum, the town's health center, with a smaller branch outside the Bahnhof. From the train station, walk straight down Herzog-Wilhelm-Str. (15min.). The staff recommends hikes, hands out maps, and books rooms for a €2.50 fee. (☎753 30; www.bad-harzburg.de. Open M-F 8am-8pm, Sa 9am-4pm.) On the second floor is the town **library,** where you can find **Internet** access for €1.50 per 30min. (☎90 15 15. Open M-Tu and Th-F 10am-1pm and 3-6pm, W 10am-1pm, Sa 10am-noon.) The **Sparkasse** bank, Herzog-Wilhelm-Str. 2, has a 24hr. **ATM.** The **police station** (☎91 11 10), Herzog-Wilhelm-Str. 47, is between the train station and the tourist office. The **post office,** Herzog-Wilhem-Str. 80, is across the fountain from the tourist office. (Open M-F 8:30am-12:30pm and 2:30-5:30pm, Sa 9am-noon.) **Postal Code:** 38667.

TORFHAUS   ☎05320

Although barely a town, tiny Torfhaus forces visitors to savor the view. Daytrippers park and hike up the most popular path to **Brocken.** Since Goethe's ascent in 1777, pilgrims have trekked the **Goetheweg,** the 16km round-trip trail to the summit. To get to the start, walk from the bus stop toward Braunlage and turn left at the yellow "Altenau-8km" sign. At the windy Brocken summit (2½hr. from Torfhaus), the **Brockenhaus Museum,** inside the former East German *Stasi* building, explains the peak's history, has a virtual flight over the Harz, and sells hiking maps. (Open daily June-Aug. 9:30am-5pm. €4, students €3.) From the top of the Brocken, trails head north toward Bad Harzburg. The **Brockenbahn** runs regularly, but the trip is long. (1hr. €14, round-trip €22.) Torfhaus lies midway between Bad Harzburg and Braunlage. The **Nationalparkhaus Torfhaus** (p. 587) hands out trail maps. **Ski-Verleih** (☎203), near the bus stop, rents downhill and cross-country skis (€12-15 per day). Walking away from Bad Harzburg, turn right at the "Altenau-8km" sign (15min.) for the **Jugendherberge (HI) ❶**, Torfhaus 3. (☎242; fax 254. Ski rentals from €5 per day. Check-in 4:30-7pm. Curfew 10pm, but house keys are available. €19.70, under 26 €16.70, including *Kurtaxe*.) **Postal Code:** 38667.

WERNIGERODE ☎ 03943

Wernigerode (pop. 35,500), crowned by one of Germany's most beautiful castles, was a hidden haunt of Goethe, but its central location between the western and eastern Harz make this secret too good to keep. Largely untouched by the 20th century, this town affords visitors the opportunity to retrace Goethe's steps.

⌐☐ TRANSPORTATION AND PRACTICAL INFORMATION. To get to Wernigerode from Magdeburg, change **trains** at Halberstadt (20min., every hr., €4.60); trains also run directly from Halle (1hr., every hr., €17.40), and Hanover (2hr., every 2hr., €20.20). A **bus** travels to and from Bad Harzburg (40min., every 2hr., €3.40). The town has two train stations: the central **Wernigerode-Westentor** and the more distant **Bahnhof Wernigerode.** "Westentor" is the next-to-last stop on the bus and the **Brockenbahn,** which connects the town to Brocken. To get there, cross the rail tracks and go straight, then turn right onto Ringstr., then left and up Western-str. to the Markt; continuing straight past the Markt onto Breite Str. will bring you to Nikolaipl. and the tourist office. The city bus stops at Bahnhof, but not at West-entor. Call ☎63 30 53 for a **taxi.** To get to the Marktpl. and the tourist office from Bahnhof, cross and turn right on Schreiberstr., which becomes Vor der Mauer, and then hang a left and walk down Albert-Bartels-Str.

The **tourist office,** Nicolaipl. 1, books private rooms (from €20) for free. Insist on a budget room, or ask for a directory and make calls yourself. The office also sells a town guide (€1.50) and gives out a less-extensive free one; both include maps. (☎63 30 35; www.wernigerode.de. Open May-Oct. M-F 9am-7pm, Sa 10am-4pm, Su 10am-3pm; Nov.-Apr. M-F 9am-6pm, Sa 10am-4pm, Su 10am-3pm.) **Tours** depart from the tourist office. (Daily 10:30am, also Sa 2pm.) There is a **Deutsche Bank** near the tourist office, at the corner of Kohlmarkt and Breite Str. (Open M-Tu 9am-1pm and 2-6pm, W 9am-1pm, F 9am-2pm.) The **police** station is on Nikolaipl. (☎65 30, emergency 110). **Rathaus-Apotheke,** a pharmacy, is on Nikolaipl. (☎63 24 39. Open M-F 8am-6:30pm, Sa 9am-1pm.) Exchange currency at the **post office,** Marktstr. 14. (Open M-F 9am-6pm, Sa 9am-noon.) **Postal Code:** 38855.

⌐☐ ACCOMMODATIONS AND FOOD. Wernigerode's **Jugendherberge (HI) ❶**; Am Eichberg 5, abounds in perks: music rooms, nightly events (including a Th night disco), ping-pong tables, and a sauna, all in a beautiful garden setting outside the city center. Take Bus #1, 4, or 5 to "Lutherstr." and follow the signs. (☎60 61 76; www.djh.de. Breakfast included. Sheets €3. Reception 7am-11pm. Check-in 2pm. €18.30, under 27 €15.50. Cash only.) For cheap food, visit the *Imbiße* (snack bars) that line Breit Str., the Markt, and Nikolaipl. or the **farmers' market** in the Marktpl. pedestrian zone (Tu and Th 10am-5pm). Tucked away at Steingruber Str. 19, the 300-year-old **Gasthaus zur Steingrube ❸** serves *Schnitzel* (€3.50) and other classics. Turn right off Breite Str. onto Ring Str., and then bear right onto Steingru-ber Str. (☎63 00 72. Open Tu-Su from 5pm. Cash only.) **Eurogrill ❶,** Westernstr. 6, offers salads and *Döner Kebap* (€2-3) just off the Markt. (☎60 55 65. Open daily 10am-11pm. Cash only.)

◉ SIGHTS. Schloß Wernigerode, originally built around 1110 in the wooded mountains above town, is a lavish monument to the German Empire. Count Otto zu Stolberg-Wernigerode undertook substantial renovations beginning in the 1860s, lending the castle a Romantic flair. The perfectly preserved **Königszimmer** guest suite, where Otto hosted the *Kaiser,* flaunts the Count's wealth with gold-plated wallpaper and other decadent adornments. The flower-trimmed terrace looks out on the Brocken. (☎55 30 30. Open May-Oct. daily 10am-6pm; Nov.-Apr. Tu-F 10am-4pm, Sa-Su 10am-6pm. Last entry 30min. before closing. Signs in

English and German. €4.50, students €4.) To get there, take the **Bimmelbahn** from the intersection of Teichdamm and Klingt. behind the Rathaus. (☎ 60 40 00. May-Oct. daily every 20min. 9:30am-5:50pm; Nov.-Apr. every 45min. 10:30am-5:50pm. €3, under 10 €1, round-trip €4.50.) Or, walk up the white brick Burgberg road and through the park to the castle (20min.). In the center of the Altstadt, the twin-horned **Rathaus** towers over the marketplace with strikingly sharp slopes and petite wooden figures of saints, virgins, and miners decorating the facade. The **Krummelsche Haus,** Breite Str. 72, is a private home covered with ornate carvings visible from the street. Several of Wernigerode's other residences tell a tale of superlatives. The **Älteste Haus** (Oldest House), Hinterstr. 48, has undergone surprisingly little renovation since an overhaul in 1438. The **Kleinste Haus** (Smallest House), Kochstr. 43, once home to a family of nine, is 2.95m wide, and its door is only 1.7m high. (Open daily 10am-4pm. €1.) The **Normalste Haus** (Normal-est House), Witzestr. 13, has no distinguishing traits.

HALBERSTADT   ☎ 03941

Founded in 804, Halberstadt (pop. 39,800) is the urban center of the Harz. Though 85% of the city was destroyed by Allied bombing and rebuilt in DDR style, many historical buildings have been restored.

☎❼ TRANSPORTATION AND PRACTICAL INFORMATION. Halberstadt sits in the northeast region of the Harz. **Trains** travel to Hanover (2hr., every 2hr., €23.10); Magdeburg (40min., every hr., €9.10); Thale and Wernigerode (40min. and 20min., respectively, 1 per hr., €4.60 daypass good for all Harz). Regular **buses** also service many Harz towns. **Trams** run through the city; #1 and #2 go from the Hauptbahnhof into the center (20min.; €0.90, daypass €2.50). The **tourist office,** Hinter dem Rathaus 6, is right off the main pedestrian way behind the Rathaus, next to which is the tram and bus stop "Holzmarkt." Free maps and room reservations await. (☎ 55 18 15; www.halberstadt.de. Open M-F 9am-6pm, Sa 10am-2pm.) The **post office,** Unter den Zwicken 1-3, is on the corner of Schmiedstr. (Open M-F 9am-6pm, Sa 9am-noon.) **Postal Code:** 38820.

❚❚ ACCOMMODATIONS AND FOOD. Halberstadt lacks a youth hostel, and most of the cheaper pensions are far from the center of town. **Altstadtpension Ratsmühle ❸,** Hoher Weg 1, is probably your best bet—from the tourist office, go right out the door, then right on the main street, and follow Hoher Weg until it becomes a pedestrian zone; it's on your left, next to the Gerberhaus restaurant sign. Plush rooms come complete with large bathrooms, TVs, and telephones. (☎ 57 37 90; www.ratsmuehle.de. Breakfast included. Singles €34; doubles €54.) Positioned just past the tourist office, the popular **Pappa La Pub ❸,** Martiniplan 6, serves traditional German food (€7-12) and good beer. (☎ 60 95 33. Open M-Th and Su 9am-11pm, F-Sa 9am-2am. Cash only.)

◪ SIGHTS. Most of Halberstadt's sights center on the Dompl., across from the Rathaus and home to the **Dom St. Stephanus,** built in the 13th and 14th centuries. Inside the impressive but well-worn Gothic cathedral, chains suspend a towering crucifix above the altar. To see the majority of the Dom, including the chapels and the altar area, you'll have to take a guided tour. The **Domschatz** boasts the largest collection of art from the Middle Ages held by a German church. (Dom open May-Oct. M-Sa 10am-5pm, Su 11am-5pm; Nov.-Apr. Tu-Su 11am-4pm. Domschatz same hours but closed M. Dom tours May-Oct. M 11:30am and 2:30pm; Tu-F 10, 11:30am, 2, and 3:30pm; Sa 11:30am, 2:30, and 4pm; Su 11:30am, 1, and 2:30pm. Nov.-Apr. M 11:30am and 2:30pm; Tu-Su 11:30am and 2:30pm. Dom free, Domschatz €2.) In front of the Dom are the jarring **Steine der Erinnerung** (Stones of Remembrance), a somber memorial to German Jews killed in the Holocaust and a reminder of Halberstadt's former status as a center of Judaism in Germany. During the 15th and 16th centuries, Christian purists periodically exiled the Jews from the town, but each time they recovered, to return in greater numbers, only to be driven out one final time on *Kristallnacht* in 1938.

The Dom is flanked by museums; the **Stadtisches Museum** (Municipal Museum), Dompl. 36, displays the city's history, starting with prehistoric bears, venturing into swords and Victorian dolls, and finishing with motorcycles and a machine gun. (☎55 14 74. Open Tu-F 9am-5pm, Sa-Su 10am-5pm.) The neighboring two-room **Museum Heineanum**, Dompl. 37, brings together dinosaur skeletons unearthed in Halberstadt with an array of preserved birds. (☎55 14 61. Open Tu-F 9am-5pm, Sa-Su 10am-5pm.) Books and letters at the **Gleimhaus**, Dompl. 31, reveal that **Johannes Wilhelm Ludwig Gleim** was not much of a writer, but a trusted friend of heavy-hitting authors of his day, including Goethe and Lessing. (☎687 10. Open May-Oct. Tu-F 9am-5pm, Sa-Su 10am-4pm; Nov.-Apr. Tu-F 9am-4pm, Sa-Su 10am-4pm.) Buy a combination ticket for all three museums at the Stadtisches Museum (€3, children €1.50). Across from the Dom, the 129 spiraling steps of the **Martinitürme** peak at a view of Halberstadt's church towers and distant Brocken. (☎55 19 95. Open May-Aug. Tu-F 9am-5pm, Sa-Su 10am-6pm. €0.75.)

QUEDLINBURG ☎03946

Quedlinburg's narrow, winding streets are crowded with pastel half-timbered houses, towering churches, and a charming castle on a hill. Untouched by Allied bombers during WWII, the city (pop. 23,000) is a UNESCO world cultural treasure. Quedlinburg retains the medieval charm that once made it the region's cultural and political center, and now attracts tourists from across the world.

🖪🖫 TRANSPORTATION AND PRACTICAL INFORMATION. Trains run every hr. to Magdeburg (1hr., €11.70) and Thale (10min., €1.80). **Buses** depart every hr. from the train station to most towns in the Harz range. **2 Rad Pavillon**, Bahnhofstr. 1b, rents **bikes**. (☎70 95 07. €6 per day. Open M-F 9am-6pm, Sa 9am-12:30pm.) Quedlinburg's **tourist office**, Markt 2, books rooms (from €13) and dispenses maps for free. From the station, head down Bahnhofstr. At the end of the street, turn left onto Heiligestr. and follow it as it curves right, becoming Steinbrücke and leading on directly to the Markt. (☎90 56 24 or 90 56 25; www.quedlinburg.de. Open May-Sept. M-F 9am-7pm, Sa 10am-4pm, Su 10am-3pm; Oct.-Apr. M-F 9:30am-6pm, Sa 10am-2pm.) **Tours** (€5) leave from the tourist office daily at 10am and 2pm; English-language tours are on Tuesday and Saturday at 2pm. **Exchange money** or use the 24hr. **ATM** in the **Commerzbank**, Am Markt 6. (Open M and W 9am-1pm and 2-4pm, Tu and Th 9am-1pm and 2-6pm, F 9am-1pm.) The **post office** is at the intersection of Bahnhofstr. and Turnstr. (Open M-F 9am-6pm, Sa 9am-noon.) **Postal Code:** 06484.

🖪🖫 ACCOMMODATIONS AND FOOD. For a room, look for "Zimmer frei" signs, inquire at the tourist office, or try **Pension Biehl ❸**, Blankenburger Str. 39. Head up Marktstr. from the Markt, turn left onto Marschlingerhof, which becomes Blankenburger Str., and continue on Blankenburger Str. as it wraps around a corner. This guesthouse offers rooms with sofa, TV, stereo, and bath in a quiet neighborhood. (☎/fax 70 35 38. Breakfast included. Singles €23; doubles €46. Cash only.) Quedlinburg's half-timbered **Jugendherberge ❷**, Neuendorf 28, offers inexpensive rooms in the heart of town. (☎81 17 03; www.djh-sachsen-anhalt.de. Breakfast included. Sheets €3. Dorms €18.70, under 26 €15. Cash only.)

Most restaurants in town cater to the tourist crowd at tourist prices. Twice a week, local farmers sell their harvest on the **Marktpl.** (W and Sa 8am-4pm.) On the way to the castle, grab a local brew in the backyard *Biergarten* of the **Brauhaus Lüdde ❷**, Blasistr. 14. just off the Markt. The circular brewing hall and bar are high-ceilinged and filled with shiny copper brewing kettles. Try the light *Pilsner* (€2) or the nutty *Schwarzbier Knuttenforz* (€2). Snacks (like sausages) run €3.50-8.50 and large meals are €10-14. (☎70 52 06. Open M-Sa 11am-midnight, Su 11am-10pm. MC/V.) **Wispel Bier-Pub ❶**, on the corner of Weberstr. and Steinweg, offers traditional food at rock-bottom prices (€1-4), but it's mainly a pub. (☎70 22 54. Open M-F 10am-11pm, Sa-Su 11am-11pm. Kitchen closes at 8pm. Cash only.) Housed in seven conjoined half-timbered houses, the pricey **Café Zum Roland ❸**, Breite Str. 2, serves local specialties (€6.50-14) along with a few vegetarian options. (Behind the Rathaus. ☎45 32. Open daily 10am-10pm. MC/V.)

G **SIGHTS.** The 17th-century **Rathaus** overlooks the Markt. A stone statue of **Roland** once again guards the stately building, after spending nearly four centuries buried underground as a punishment to the people of Quedlinburg for an attempted insurrection in the mid-14th century. Tucked behind the Rathaus, the **Benediktikirche** houses an altar decorated with delicate gilded angels and rich oil paintings. (Open M-F 11am-4pm.) The winding roads of **Schloßberg** insulate the **Schloß** complex within a narrow ring of half-timbered cottages. The 16th-century Renaissance castle overlooks the labyrinthine town below and the Harz Mountains beyond. The **Schloßmuseum** (Castle Museum) depicts city history from the Paleolithic era to the present and includes the chilling medieval prison box to which criminals were once confined. (☎90 56 81. Open Apr.-Oct. daily 10am-6pm; Nov.-Oct. M-Th and Sa-Su 10am-4pm. Last entry 30min. before closing. €3.50, students €2.) Nearby **Stiftskirche St. Servatius** houses the **Domschatz**—a treasure trove of gilded relics—and a **crypt.** (☎70 99 00. Open May-Oct. Tu-F 10am-6pm, Sa 10am-4pm, Su noon-6pm; Nov.-Mar. Tu-Sa 10am-4pm, Su noon-4pm; Apr. Tu-F 10am-5pm, Sa 10am-4pm, Su noon-5pm. Dom and Domschatz €4, students €3; with Schloßmuseum €6/4.) In the fragrant **Castle Gardens**, an English-language audio box (€1) narrates Quedlinburg's distinguished history as it guides untrained eyes across the city-wide view. (Open daily May-Oct. 6am-10pm; Nov.-Apr. 6am-8pm.)

Below the entrance to the *Schloß*, the vine-covered **Lyonel Feininger Galerie,** Finkenherd 5a, displays the watercolors, woodcuts, oil paintings, and comic strips of the influential Modernist painter. (☎23 84. Open Tu-Su Apr.-Oct. 10am-6pm; Nov.-Mar. 10am-5pm. €6, students €3.) The **Klopstockhaus,** next door at Schloßberg 12, displays a number of artifacts from the life of Enlightenment writer **Friedrich Gottlieb Klopstock,** including his personal letters. (☎26 10. Open W-Su Apr.-Oct. 10am-5pm; Nov.-Mar. 10am-4pm. €3, students €2.50.)

THALE   ☎03947

Thale's mountain scenery may seem pristine, but the town's beauty obscures its darker side: Thale's mountains are a den of myth and lore, the alleged haunt of witches, devils, and unicorns. With beautiful parks and ancient buildings interspersed among graffiti-covered walls, a devilish witches' convention every April, and surprisingly few tourists, Thale (pop. 15,100) is an undiscovered gem.

E∄ **TRANSPORTATION AND PRACTICAL INFORMATION. Trains** run 1 per hr. to: Halberstadt (45min., €4.60); Magdeburg (1½hr., €13.40); Quedlinburg (15min., €1.80). **Buses** depart to many Harz towns from the adjacent bus station. (Most every hr., €2-4.) **Taxis** can be requested by calling ☎25 35. Across from the train station, the **tourist office,** Bahnhofstr. 3, books rooms (€15-30) for free. Pick up a free copy of the German-language magazine *Thale*, which includes a town map. (☎25 97; www.thale.de. Open May-Oct. M-F 9am-5pm, Sa-Su 9am-3pm; Nov.-Apr. M-F 9am-5pm.) A **Sparkasse bank** on Bahnhofstr. **exchanges money** and has a 24hr. **ATM.** (Open M 8:30-12:30pm and 1:30-4pm, Tu 8:30am-12:30pm and 1:30-3pm, W 2-5:30pm, Th 8:30am-12:30pm, F 8:30am-12:30pm and 1:30-3:30pm.) The **police** station is located on Rudolf-Breitscheidstr. 10. (☎460. Turn left out of the train station, then take a right on Poststr., which becomes Rudolf-Breitscheidstr.) The **post office,** Karl-Marx-Str. 16-18, is a block away from the Sparkasse. (Open M-F 9am-6:30pm, Sa 9am-1pm.) **Postal Code:** 06502.

⌂▢ ACCOMMODATIONS AND FOOD. Thale's **Jugendherberge (HI) ❷**, Bodetal-Waldkater, is situated on Bodetal's pleasant brook. Turn right out of the station, make a left on Parkstr, take the first right, and keep walking along the river on Hubertusstr. The path is not well-lit at night. The spacious two- to six-bed rooms have river views. (☎28 81; www.djh.de/jugendherbergen/thale. Breakfast included. Sheets €3. Reception 3-6pm and 8-10pm. Dorm beds €16.20, under 26 €13.50. Cash only.) **Pension Kleiner Waldkater ❸**, next door on Bodetal, is in a 165-year-old brick house. (☎/fax 28 26. Single €35; doubles €54. Cash only.) **Hotel Wilder Jäger ❷**, Poststr. 18, is an inexpensive pension barely 200m to the left of the train station. (☎77 97 66; fax 77 90 78. Singles €25; doubles €50.) Thale's restaurant offerings are a bit limited; many food stands on Hexentanzpl. offer cheap eats. Beyond the Sparkasse, Karl-Marx-Str. has shops, restaurants, and bakeries. The free map from the tourist office also indicates cafés, restaurants, and supermarkets. If you're going into the woods for or returning after a day of hiking, look for the family-run **Rodelhaus ❶**, insulated by the surrounding forest at Rodelhaus 1. The restaurant serves German specialties (€2-5) at bargain prices. (☎22 65. Open May-Sept. Tu-Su noon-10pm; Oct.-Apr. W-F 6-10pm, Sa-Su 2-10pm. Cash only.)

▨ SIGHTS. Legend dates Thale's cultic history back to prehistoric times, when the sorceress **Watelinde** led pagan rituals that lured impressionable youths down the destructive fast-lane to witchery. This heritage is celebrated in the mountain-top tourist zone called **Hexentanzpl.**, which hosts the **Walpurgisnacht,** a yearly international witch conference. Every April 30, the entire town of Thale embarks on several days of black magic festivities. Don't be disappointed, though, if you find more souvenir vendors than supernatural women. To get to the Hexentanzpl., ride the **Kabinebahn** (a wire-suspension chairlift) up the side of the mountain. The Kabinebahn departs across the river from the hostel and provides stunning views of the valley below. (☎25 00. Daily May-Oct. 9:30am-6pm; Nov.-Apr. 10am-4:30pm. €3, round-trip €4.50, children €3.) Enthusiastic hikers can also attempt the climb on foot; to do so follow Hubertusstr. past the Jugendherberge and take a left onto the trail by the stone bridge. The **Roßtrappe,** a rocky peak across the valley from the Hexentanzpl., can be reached by hiking up Präsidentenweg and Esselsteig; the trail starts upriver from the chairlift station in the valley. Or take the **Sessellift** (another chairlift), which departs from the same place as the Kabinenbahn. (☎25 00. Lift open June-Aug. daily 9:30am-6pm; Sept.-May Sa-Su 10am-5:30pm. Round-trip €3.50, children €2.) Once at the Hexentanzpl., follow the signs to the **Walpurgishalle,** a museum commemorating the Harz's history of witchcraft. Stained-glass eyes stare down from the ceiling in the two-room building depicting Faustian pacts and witch hunts. (Open daily May-Oct. 10am-5pm. €2, children €0.50.) Next to the museum is the impressive **Harzer Bergtheater Thale,** a huge outdoor amphitheater, with performances oscillating between the sublime (Goethe's *Faust*) and the infernal (performances by German pop stars). Shows run May-September; schedules are available at the tourist office and posted along the path into the theater. (☎23 24. Tickets €8-20; 30% student discount.)

MAGDEBURG ☎ 0391

In ever-modernizing Magdeburg (pop. 228,000), ancient cathedrals square off against vibrant, unorthodox architectural trends. Even though the scars of two devastating wars are still visible among the concrete apartments erected by the socialist government, the capital of Sachsen-Anhalt has largely escaped post-DDR stagnation. With an illustrious history, tourist-friendly Magdeburg can't help but revel in its past as it moves ahead as a self-proclaimed "city with a future."

▐ TRANSPORTATION

Trains leave approximately every hr. to: Berlin (1½hr., €14.10); Hanover (1½hr., €16.20); Quedlinburg (1hr., €10.70). **Trams** and **buses** run across town. (Single ride €1.70; day ticket €3.50.) For a **taxi,** call ☎ 73 73 73 or 56 56 56.

✴ ▐ ORIENTATION AND PRACTICAL INFORMATION

Cutting through the shopping mall in front of the train station will bring you to **Ernst-Reuter-Allee,** which leads directly to **Breiter Weg,** the backbone of Magdeburg and the main pedestrian route. Most of the museums and sights are within a block or two of Breiter Weg, mainly between Ernst-Reuter-Allee and Häckelstr. The **tourist office,** Ernest-Reuter-Allee 12 (☎ 194 33; www.magdeburg-tourist.de), at Breiter Weg, hands out maps, books rooms for free, and sells event tickets. Pick up a free copy of the *Dates* magazine (in German) for a schedule of cultural events and nightlife. (☎ 540 49 04. Office open May-Sept. M-F 10am-7pm, Sa 10am-4pm; Oct.-Apr. M-F 10am-6:30pm, Sa 10am-3pm.) **Tours** (€3) in German leave from the office daily at 11am. **Courage,** Porsestr. 14, one block from the "Warschauer" stop on tram #8 (dir.: Buckau), is the local **women's center.** (☎/fax 404 80 89. Open 3rd M of the month 6-11pm). **Internet** access is available at **Netz-Welt,** Heidestr. 9. Take tram #10 (dir.: Sudenburg) to "Eiskellerpl." Follow Halberstädterstr. and take a left on Heidestr. (☎ 620 17 55. €1 per 30min. Open daily noon-2am.) The **post office** is on Breiter Weg. (Open M-F 9am-7pm, Sa 9am-noon.) **Postal Code:** 39104.

▐ ACCOMMODATIONS

Many homeowners run small pensions on Magdeburg's outskirts; call the tourist office to arrange a room. The ▐**Jugendherberge Magdeburger Hof (HI) ❷,** Leiterstr. 10, tucks away a colorful, futuristic interior and excellent rooms in a square dominated by nondescript apartment buildings. (☎ 532 10 10; www.jugendherberge.de/dh/magdeburg. Breakfast included. Internet €6 per hr. Reception 3pm-2am. Singles €18, over 27 €22.70; doubles €36/45.40.) **Campingplatz Barleber See ❶** is 45min. outside the city center. Take tram #10 on Breiter Weg (dir.: Barleber See) to the end (about 30min.), and continue down the main street (August-Bebel-Damm) about 1km. (☎ 50 32 44. Reception 7am-9pm. Open May-Sept. €7.50 per tent.)

▐ FOOD

Many inexpensive restaurants crowd the streets around the intersection of **Breiter Weg** and **Einsteinstraße** in **Hasselbachplatz,** the only part of downtown to survive the bombings of WWII. Back up Breiter Weg, the **Alter Markt** offers a bounty of cheap food like roasted chicken (€2) and fresh fruit. (Open M-F 8am-5pm, Sa 7am-noon.) **Ratskeller ❷,** Alter Markt 6, under the Rathaus, sports 18th-century decor and great deals. Excellent weekday lunch specials (€5) are offered from 11am-3pm. From 3-5pm daily all dishes are available for half-price plus €1. (☎ 568 23 23. Open M-Sa

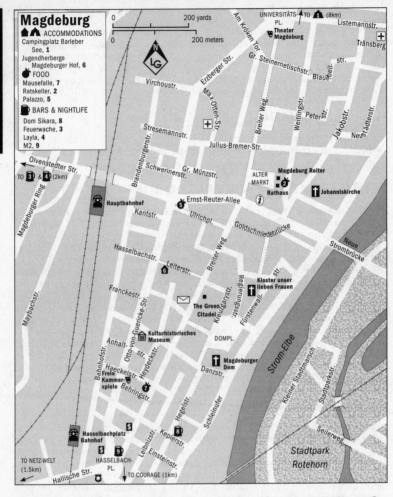

Magdeburg

⌂⌂ ACCOMMODATIONS
Campingplatz Barleber
  See, **1**
Jugendherberge
  Magdeburger Hof, **6**

🍴 FOOD
Mausefalle, **7**
Ratskeller, **2**
Palazzo, **5**

🍺 BARS & NIGHTLIFE
Dom Sikara, **8**
Feuerwache, **3**
Layla, **4**
M2, **9**

11am-11pm, Su 11am-9pm. AmEx/MC/V.) The lively marble-tiled **Palazzo ❷**, Ulrichpl. 1, serves Italian bistro fare; locals praise the delicious baguette sandwiches (€3-5). (☎531 32 33. Pastas €4.50-8. Salads €3-7.50. Pizza €4-8. Open M-Th and Su 9am-1am. Take out available. Reservations recommended. AmEx.) The giant piece of Swiss cheese crowning the bar at **Mausfalle** (Mouse Trap) ❸, Breiter Weg 224, exemplifies this restaurant's sense of humor. (☎543 01 35. Pastas €6-8.50. Salads €5-8. Mixed drinks €4.50-6.50, €3 Tu after 6pm. Th free salsa lessons 9pm. Open M-Th 9am-1am, F-Su 9am-3am.)

🅖 SIGHTS

Magdeburg's few dazzling medieval sights seem out of place in the rapidly-modernizing urban center. The main landmark and city symbol is the monumental

▧**Magdeburger Dom,** on Domstr., was the first Gothic church in Germany and the biggest cathedral in the former DDR. The hauntingly beautiful towers and cavernous interior house an amazing collection of religious sculptures from the 11th to 13th centuries. Otto I, the Holy Roman Emperor responsible for the first church on this site (built in AD 937), lies buried near the cathedral's front. (☎543 24 14. Open in summer M-Sa 10am-6pm, Su 11:30am-6pm; in winter M-Sa 10am-4pm, Su 11:30am-4pm. Free. Tours M-Sa 2pm, Su 11:30am and 2pm. €3, students €1.50.)

The ancient **Kloster unser lieben Frauen** (Cloister of our Loving Lady), Regierungstr. 4/6, Magdeburg's oldest surviving building, is near the Dom. This Romantic cloister now houses an art exhibition space, concert hall, and café. The shift in purpose hasn't compromised the monastic atmosphere—the grounds around the cloister are sheltered and tranquil, as is the nearby sculpture garden. (☎56 50 20. Exhibition hall and café open Tu-Su 10am-6pm. Free.) As you head away from the Dom and cross Breiter Weg on Danzstr., you'll pass the **Kulturhistorisches Museum** (Cultural History Museum), Otto-von-Güricke-Str. 68-73, on your left. The museum is a collage of history, science, and modern art, displaying items from Magdeburg's long history. (☎540 35 01. Open Tu-Su 10am-5pm. Free.) Among the uninspiring buildings of Breiter Weg, architect Friederich Hundertwasser's **Green Citadel,** a pink building where no two walls, columns, or windows are the same, looks to be straight out of Dr. Seuss's imagination. Home to a pricey hotel, kindegarten, and numerous businesses, the environmentally friendly Citadel appears a few centuries ahead of its time. Obligatory hour-long tours in German (€5), while informative, only enter the building for about 10min. (Breiter Weg 8-10. ☎544 66 67. Tours M-F 11am, 3, 5pm; Sa-Su every hr. 10am-5pm.) The **Johanniskirche,** by the Elbe behind the Alter Markt, once stood as a memorial to the 1945 bombing, which nearly destroyed it. The church has since been rebuilt to its pre-war glory. (☎53 65 00. Open Tu-Su 10am-5pm. €1, exhibitions €2.) Across the street rises the clock tower of the 17th-century **Rathaus,** in front of which stands a replica of the regally anonymous **Magdeburger Reiter** (built in 1240), the oldest free-standing equestrian figure in northern Europe. (The original is in the Kulturhistorisches Museum.)

♫ ▣ ENTERTAINMENT AND NIGHTLIFE

Magdeburg has a strong cultural scene. *Dates* and *Stadtpass* magazines list events at theaters, concert halls, clubs, and bars. The **Theater Magdeburg,** Universitätspl. 9, at the corner of Breiter Weg and Erzberger Str., hosts big-name operas, ballets, and experimental plays. (☎540 64 44. Box office open Tu-F 10am-7:30pm, Sa 9:30am-6:30pm, and 1hr. before performances.) The **Freie Kammerspiele,** in front of the Dom, puts a modern twist on the classics. (☎540 63 63. Box office open M-Th 4-6pm, F 2-6pm, and 1hr. before performances. Closed mid-July to early Sept.)

For nightlife, check out **Hasselbachplatz** or **Sudenburg** along Halberstädterstr. (S1 or S10 or bus #53 or 54 to "Eiskellerpl." or "Ambrosiuspl."). Though far from the city center (30min. by foot), **Kurt-Schmidt-Straße** and **Schönebecker Straße** also offer many clubs. Statues of Krishna watch the incense burn at the funky, irresistibly cool ▧**Dom Sikara,** Keplerstr. 9, a friendly, well-stocked bar attracting locals and foreigners alike. (☎563 91 38. Drinks €2-3. W all mixed drinks €3.33. Open daily 7pm-late.) Inside an old fire station, **Feuerwache,** Halberstädterstr. 140, hosts plays, art exhibits, and concerts, and serves as a winter café and a summer beer garden. (☎60 28 09. Drinks €1.50-3. Open daily 7pm-midnight.) Located south of Diesdorfstr., the candlelit **Layla,** Lessingstr. 86, serves German and Irish beer (and classic rock) to a crowd of easygoing regulars. (☎731 70 28. Open daily 10am-2am.)

SACHSEN (SAXONY)

Freed from the stagnation of the DDR and bent on revitalization, Saxony has embarked on some of Europe's most ambitious reconstruction projects. While older Saxons—most of whom were taught Russian in school—pass on the region's history, a hopeful new generation keeps its cities lively forward-looking. Though student-driven Leipzig, resurgent Dresden, and the legendary castles of August the Strong draw crowds from across the world, some of Saxony's greatest treasures, like the Saxon Switzerland National Park, have yet to be discovered by international tourists. Home to Germany's only native ethnic minority, the Sorbs, Saxony is marked by the verve and diversity of a region rebuilding itself in grand design.

HIGHLIGHTS OF SAXONY

CHILL OUT in the University of **Leipzig** (p. 629), which harbors an active **student culture** and a relaxed **café scene.**

CLIMB, HIKE, OR SKI the cliffs and mountains of the **Sächsische Schweiz** (p. 613).

ENLIGHTEN YOURSELF amid the world-class **museums** and grand **Baroque architecture** of **Dresden** (p. 598), before losing your head in the throes of its feverish **nightlife.**

DRESDEN ☎ 0351

Over the course of two nights in February 1945, Allied firebombs incinerated over three quarters of Dresden, killing between 25,000 and 50,000 civilians. With most of the Altstadt in ruins, the surviving 19th-century Neustadt became Dresden's nerve center: today, it is still an energetic nexus of nightlife and alternative culture. Modern buildings like the amazing Volkswagen *Gläserne Manufaktur* (Transparent Factory) share space with restored Baroque masterpieces by Pöppelmann and Bährs, creating an atmosphere conducive to revelry and reflection. In short, the capital of Saxony is always in motion, a city of vibrance and intensity that backpackers on the road from Berlin to Prague won't want to ignore.

▐ TRANSPORTATION

Flights: Dresden's **airport** (☎881 33 60; www.dresden-airport.de) is 9km from the city. S2 runs there from both main train stations. (25min., 2 per hr. 4am-11:30pm, €1.70.)

Trains: Dresden has 2 main train stations: the **Hauptbahnhof** in the Altstadt and **Bahnhof Dresden Neustadt** across the Elbe. Most trains stop at both stations. A 3rd station, **Dresden Mitte,** lies between the two but is rarely used because of its out-of-the-way location. The Hauptbahnhof is currently undergoing major renovation expected to last through 2006. In the meantime, many stores and services will change locations; ask at the **Reisezentrum** or in new service centers for information. Yellow *Abfahrt* posters list departures. Buy tickets from the machines in the main halls of the stations or at the **Reisezentrum** desks. Trains to: **Bautzen** (1hr., 1 per hr., €9.10); **Berlin** (3hr., 1 per hr., €32); **Budapest, Hungary** (11hr., 2 per day, €81); **Frankfurt am Main** (4½hr., 1

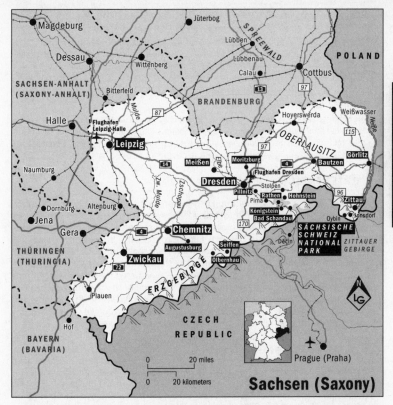

Sachsen (Saxony)

per hr., €76); **Görlitz** (1½hr., 1 per hr., €16.10); **Leipzig** (1½hr., 1-2 per hr., €18.30); **Munich** (7hr., 1-2 per hr., €108; **Prague, Czech Republic** (2½hr., 7 per day, €25.80); **Warsaw, Poland** (8½hr., 2 per day, €71); **Zittau** (2hr., 1 per 2hr., €15.90).

Ferries: Sächsische Dampfschifffahrt. (☎86 60 90, schedule information ☎866 09 40. Office and info desk open M-Th and Su 8am-6pm, F-Sa 8am-7:30pm.) Ships leave from the Elbe between Augustusbrücke and Carolabrücke in the **Altstadt** for **Seußlitz** in the north and through the **Sächsische Schweiz** to the Czech border town **Děčín** in the south. Ferries to: **Meißen** (2hr., €7.40, round-trip €13.70) and **Pillnitz** (1½hr., €9.20, round-trip €14.30). Day pass €20, children €10.

Ride Share: Mitfahrzentrale, Dr.-Friedrich-Wolf-Str. 2 (☎194 40). On Slesischen Pl., across from Bahnhof Neustadt. Open M-F 9am-8pm, Sa-Su 10am-4pm.

Public Transportation: Most of Dresden is manageable on foot, but **buses** and **trams** cover the whole city. Single ride €1.70, children €1.20. Day pass €4.50/3.50; weekly pass €16.50/10. Tickets are available from *Fahrkarten* dispensers at major stops, and on the trams. For information and maps, go to one of the **Service Punkt** stands in front of the Hauptbahnhof or at Postpl. Most major lines run every hr. after midnight—look for the moon sign marked "*Gute-Nacht-Linie.*" Dresden's **S-Bahn** network reaches from Meißen to the Czech border. Buy S-Bahn tickets from the *Automaten* or at the **Reisezentrum** and validate them in the red machines at the bottom of the stairwells to each track. On buses and trams, punch your ticket as you board.

Taxis: ☎21 12 11 or 888 88 88.

Car Rental: Sixt-Budget, An der Frauenkirche 5 (☎08 10 525 25 25), in the Hilton Hotel (open M-F 7am-7pm, Sa-Su 8am-noon), or the Hauptbahnhof (open M-F 7am-8pm). **Europcar,** Strehlener Str. 5 (☎87 73 20), at the Bayerische Str. exit of the Hauptbahnhof (open 24hr.), or at Bahnhof Neustadt, out the Slesischen Pl. exit and up the stairs, then left. Open M-F 7am-6pm, Sa 9am-noon, Su 9-11am.

Bike Rental: In the Hauptbahnhof near luggage storage (☎461 32 62). €7 per day. Open M-F 6am-8pm, Sa-Su 8am-8pm.

Hitchhiking: *Let's Go* does not recommend hitchhiking as a safe mode of transportation. Hitchers say they stand in front of the Autobahn signs at on-ramps. To get to **Berlin,** take tram #3 or 13 to "Liststr.," then bus #81 to "Am Olter." To **Prague, Eisenach,** or **Frankfurt am Main,** take bus #72 or 88 to "Luga," or #76, 85, or 96 to "Lockwitz."

✈ ORIENTATION

With a population of a half-million, Dresden crowds the banks of the Elbe river 60km northwest of the Czech border and 200km south of Berlin. The **Elbe** bisects Dresden, with the **Hauptbahnhof** south of the river, alongside the **Altstadt.** The **Neumarkt,** encompassing many of Dresden's major tourist attractions, lies between the **Altmarkt** and the Elbe. The area between the Hauptbahnhof and the Altmarkt is packed with strip malls and chain shops. The **Neustadt** north of the Elbe is, ironically, one of the oldest parts of the city, since it weathered the devastating bombings of WWII almost completely unscathed. The neighborhoods off of **Albertplatz** pulse with the lively energy of Dresden's young alternative scene. Five impressive bridges—**Marienbrücke, Augustbrücke, Carolabrücke, Albertbrücke,** and the "Blue Marvel" **Loschwitzbrücke** (p. 605)—connect the city's two halves.

⁊ PRACTICAL INFORMATION

Tourist Office: 2 locations: **Prager Str. 2a,** near the Hauptbahnhof (open Apr.-Oct. M-F 9:30am-6:30pm, Sa 10am-6pm; Nov.-Mar. M-F 10am-6pm, Sa 10am-4pm), and **Theaterpl.** in the Schinkelwache, a small building in front of the Semper Oper. (☎49 19 20; fax 49 19 21 16. Open Apr.-Oct. M-Th 10am-6pm, F 10am-7pm, Sa-Su 10am-5pm; Nov.-Mar. M-F 10am-6pm, Sa-Su 10am-4pm.) The staffs of both offices book rooms (€3 fee, rooms €20+) and sell city maps. The offices sell 2 cards that provide discounts on transportation and museums: the **Dresden City-Card** is valid for 48hr. of transport in the city-zone (€19) and the **Dresden Regio-Card** is good for 72hr. in the entire *Oberelbe* region, including Meißen and Sächsische Schweiz (€29). Call special city hotlines for general information (☎49 19 21 00), room reservations (☎49 19 22 22), city tours (☎49 19 21 40), and advance ticket purchases (☎49 19 22 33).

Currency Exchange: ReiseBank (☎471 21 77), in the Hauptbahnhof. €5 commission; no commission for American Express Travelers Cheques. Western Union money transfer service open M-F 8am-7:30pm, Sa 9am-noon and 12:30-4pm, Su 9am-1pm. After hours, self-service exchange machine in the Hauptbahnhof exchanges at less favorable rates. The **Deutsche Bank** at the corner of Konigsbrueckerstr. and Stetzscherstr. has a 24hr. **ATM,** as do many Neustadt and Altstadt banks.

Luggage Storage: Lockers at all train stations. €1-2 per 24hr.

Bookstore: Haus des Buches, Altmarkt 24 (☎65 64 60), in the arcade near Kreuzkirche. English books on 2nd fl. Open M-F 9:30am-8pm, Sa 9:30am-6pm.

Library: Haupt- und Musikbibliothek, Freiberger Str. 35 (☎864 82 33), in the World Trade Center. Lots of info about Saxony and Dresden. Small section of English books on the 1st fl. Open M-F 11am-7pm, Sa 10am-2pm.

Home Share: Mitwohnzentrale, Dr.-Friedrich-Wolf-Str. 2 (☎194 30). On Slesischen Pl., same building as Mitfahrzentrale. Open M-F 9am-7pm.

Gay and Lesbian Resources: Gerede-Dresdner Lesben, Schwule, und alle Anderen, Prießnitzstr. 18 (☎802 22 51, 24hr. hotline 802 22 50). Open M-F 10am-5pm.

Women's Resources: Frauenzentrum "sowieso," Angelikastr. 1 (☎804 14 70). *Frauenkneipe* (women's bar) Th-F from 7pm. Open M, W, F 9-11am, Th 3-6pm.

Laundromat: Eco-Express, 2 Königsbrückestr., on Albertpl. Wash €1.50 6-11am, €2 11am-11pm. Dry €0.50 per 10min. Open M-Sa 6am-11pm. Also try **"Crazy" Waschsalon,** 6 Louisenstr. Wash €2.50. Dry €0.50 per 10min. Open M-Sa 7am-11pm.

Emergency: Police ☎110. **Ambulance and Fire:** ☎112.

Pharmacy: Apotheke Prager Straße, Prager Str. 3 (☎490 30 14). Open M-F 8:30am-7pm, Sa 8:30am-4pm. The *Notdienst* sign outside lists rotating 24hr. pharmacies.

Internet Access: In the bar at **Hostel Mondpalast,** Louisenstr. 77 (☎563 40 50). €3 per hr. Open daily 8am-1am. **Groove Station,** Katharinenstr. 11-13. €3 per hr. Open M-Sa from 7pm, Su from 4pm.

Post Office: Königsbrückerstr. 21/29 (☎819 13 73), in the Neustadt. Open M-F 9am-7pm, Sa 10am-1pm. **Branches** in the Altstadt are on Weberg. at the Altmarkt Galerie. (open daily 9:30am-8pm) and near the appropriately named Postpl. Open M-F 9am-12:30pm and 1:30pm-6pm, Sa 9:30am-noon. **Postal Code:** 01099.

🏠🏕 ACCOMMODATIONS AND CAMPING

The Neustadt is home to a number of hostels close to Dresden's best nightlife. Quieter hostels and pricier hotels can be found closer to the sights around the Altstadt. Reservations are strongly recommended between April and October.

🔲 Hostel Mondpalast, Louisenstr. 77 (☎563 40 50; www.mondpalast.de). With a guestbook full of rave reviews, this stellar hostel provides all a backpacker could desire: good prices, comfortable beds in spacious rooms, a large kitchen and social dining room, and a bar downstairs. Breakfast €5. Sheets €2. Internet access €3 per hr. Key deposit €10. Reception 24hr. 10-bed dorms €13.50; 4- to 6-bed dorms €15-16; 3- to 4-bed dorms €16; singles €29, with shower €39; doubles €37/€50. MC/V. ❶

Hostel "Louise 20," Louisenstr. 20 (☎889 48 94; www.louise20.de). A ladder leads to a dorm attic in Dresden's newest hostel. Breakfast €4.50. Sheets €2.50. Key deposit €5. Reception 7am-11pm. Check-out noon. Dorms €10. 5-bed room €15, 3- to 4-bed rooms €16, singles €26, doubles €37. AmEx/MC/V. ❶

Kangaroo-Stop, Erna-Berger-Str. 8-10 (☎314 34 55; www.kangaroo-stop.de). Newly built Outback-themed backpackers' hostel on a quiet street close to Neustadt. Breakfast €4.50. Sheets €2.20. Free Internet access. Reception 7am-11:30pm. Check-in 2pm. Check-out 11am. 10-bed dorms €12.50; 5- to 6-bed dorms €14; 4-bed dorms €15; 3-bed dorms €16; singles €27; doubles €34. 10% ISIC discount. Cash only. ❶

Lollis Homestay, Goerlitzerstr. 34. (☎81 08 45 58; www.lollishome.de). Dresden's smallest, this hostel recreates the relaxed feel of a student flat with a kitchen and comfortable common room. Some rooms with bathtub cactus gardens. Internet access €2.50 per hr. Breakfast €3. Sheets €2. Laundry €3. Check-in 2pm. Check-out noon. 8-bed dorms €13; 6-bed dorms €15; singles €30; doubles €40; triples €54. F-Sa €1 extra. Weekly and monthly rates in winter. Cash only. ❶

Hostel Die Boofe, Hechtstr. 10 (☎801 33 61; www.boofe.de). This funky hostel has tie-dyed sheets and a basement sauna (€4.50 per hr.). Internet access €1 per hr. Breakfast €5. Reception 7am-midnight. Check-in 2pm. Check-out 10am. Book ahead. 4-bed dorm €15, with shower €17; singles €26/31; doubles €38/46. ❷

Pension Raskolnikoff, Böhmische Str. 34 (☎804 57 06; www.raskolnikoff.de). This 6-room pension shares a building with the eponymous restaurant and gallery (p. 603). The bohemian atmosphere, with fold-out couches and plywood furniture, is an escape from the standard hostel scene. Singles €30-40; doubles €40-50. AmEx/MC/V. ❸

Guest House Mezcalero, Königsbrückerstr. 64 (☎81 07 70; www.mezcalero.de). A spacious Mexican-themed guest house in a quiet courtyard. Breakfast €5. Singles from €33; doubles from €54. MC/V. ❸

City-Herberge, Lingnerallee 3 (☎485 99 00; www.city-herberge.de). Housed in an architecturally monstrous apartment complex, this centrally located, welcoming hostel has modern rooms and a bar downstairs. Breakfast included. 24hr. reception. Check-in 2pm. Check-out 10am. Jan.-Mar., July-Aug., and Nov. singles €31.50; doubles €46. Apr.-June, Sept.-Oct., and Dec. €36.50/52. AmEx/MC/V. ❸

Jugendherberge Dresden Rudi Arndt (HI), Hübnerstr. 11 (☎471 06 67, fax 472 89 59). Tram #3 (dir.: Coschütz) or #8 (dir.: Südvorstadt) to "Nürnberger Pl." Take Nürnbergerstr. and turn right onto Hübnerstr.; the hostel is at the 1st corner on the right. Small rooms with a friendly atmosphere, located in a quiet residential neighborhood. Breakfast included. Laundry €1.50. Check-in 3pm-1am. Curfew 1am. Reservations recommended. Dorms €19.90, under 27 €16.90. Cash only. ❷

Jugendherberge Dresden (HI), Maternistr. 22 (☎49 26 20; fax 492 62 99). Newly renovated, Saxony's largest hostel houses many school groups in sleek, bunk-free rooms. Breakfast included. Wheelchair accessible. Reception 24hr. Check-in 4pm. Check-out 9:30am. Mid-Mar. to Dec. 2- to 4-bed rooms €18, with shower €22; Jan. to mid-Mar. €17/21. Over 27 €3 per night extra. €1.50 surcharge for 1-night stays. Cash only. ❷

Campingplatz Mockritz, Boderitzerstr. 30 (☎471 52 50; www.camping-dresden.de). Bus #76 (dir.: Mockritz) from the Hauptbahnhof to "Campingpl. Mockritz." 10min. from Dresden, this family-run spot is surprisingly serene. Reception 8-11am and 4-8pm. €4.50 per person, €1.50 per tent, €1 per car. 3- or 4-person bungalows €45. MC/V. ❶

◪ FOOD

Dresden's increasing tourist population has pushed up food prices. In the Altstadt, almost all of the restaurants target tourists and price gouge accordingly, especially around **Muenzg.** and the **Frauenkirche.** The cheapest eats are at the *Imbiße* (snack bars) along **Prager Str.** and the **Postpl.** The Neustadt area between **Albertpl.** and **Alaunpl.** seems to spawn a new bar every few weeks and is home to most of Dresden's quirky, ethnic, vegetarian, and student-friendly restaurants. The free monthly *Spot*, available at the tourist office, details culinary options.

▩ **Café Aha,** Kreuzstr. 7 (☎496 06 73, www.ladencafe.de). This maverick restaurant celebrates ecologically sound foods. Each dish (€4-11) promotes fair trade; the café introduces food from a different developing country each month. Store downstairs sells international goods at fair trade prices. Store open M-F 10am-7pm, Sa 10am-6pm. Café open daily 10am-midnight; kitchen closes at 10:30pm. Cash only. ❷

▩ **Planwirtschaft,** Louisenstr. 20 (☎801 31 87). Offers traditional and neo-German cuisine made with ingredients direct from local farms. Inventive soups, fresh salads (€3.50-7), and entrées (€7-13). "Poor Student" meal (salad, mixed nuts, bread, and coffee or juice; €5.90) served amid dried grass and antique typewriters. English menu available. Open M-Th and Su 9am-1am, F-Sa 9am-2am. MC/V. ❸

Café Europa, Königsbrückerstr. 68 (☎804 48 10; www.cafe-europa-dresden.de). Open 24hr., this self-consciously hip café draws a crowd of students and 20-somethings with 120 different drinks. Huge pancakes (€3.90-4.60), great soups (around €3) and traditional entrées (€5-9.50) complement free Internet access. AmEx/DC/MC/V. ❷

Rauschenbach, Weisseg. 2, (☎821 27 60; www.rauschenbach-deli.de). Chandelier crystals dangle from soft red lights. Serves tapas and sandwiches (€2.50-4.20) to hoards of young locals. Reservations recommended F-Sa nights. Open M-Th and Su 9am-1am, F-Sa 9am-3am. AmEx/DC/MC/V. ❷

Blumenau, Louisenstr. 67 (☎802 65 02). One of the most popular and cheapest restaurants in the Neustadt. Friendly environment perfect for a morning *Milchkaffee* or evening drink. Entire front open to the street. Most dishes €3-6.70. Breakfast until 4pm. Extensive mixed drink menu. Open M-Th 8am-2am, F 8am-3am, Sa 9am-3pm, Su 9am-2am. AmEx/MC/V for purchases over €10. ❷

El Perro Borracho, Alaunstr. 70 (☎803 67 23), through the passageway and into the courtyard. Free-flowing Spanish wine and bright decor evoke a Mallorican beach vacation. Tasty tapas, from calamari to potato torillas, and other Spanish specialties. Main courses €8-13. Buffet breakfast 10am-3pm on weekends (€8). Open M-F 11:30am-2am, tapas from 6pm; Sa-Su 10am-3am, tapas from 3pm. Cash only. ❸

Raskolnikoff, Böhmischestr. 34 (☎804 57 06; www.raskolnikoff.de). A dim Dostoevskian haunt in a pre-war brownstone. Savory fare from all four hemispheres (€3.50-12). Locals slide onto wooden benches next to the tiki-ringed fountain in back. Open daily 10am-2am. AmEx/MC/V. ❸

 SIGHTS

ALTSTADT (OLD TOWN)

Destroyed during WWII and partially rebuilt during Communist times, Dresden's Altstadt is one of Europe's undisputed cultural centers. A gigantic restoration effort, slated for completion in 2007, further cements this reputation with each successful project. Most of Dresden's celebrated sights are near the **Theaterplatz.**

DRESDENER SCHLOß. Saxony's Wettin dynasty of electors, whose portraits adorn the northern wall of the **Fürstenzug** (a block-long mural that depicts over 900 years of Saxon kings), built their grand residential palace here. Like most of the Altstadt, it was ruined in the Allied firebombing, but restoration is approaching completion. Today, the *Schloß* houses the █**Grünes Gewölbe** (Green Vault), a remarkably intimate display of the Saxon electors' precious stones, many designed by jeweler **Johann Melchior Dinglinger.** Highlights of the collection include rare medieval chalices and cherry stones inscribed with over 100 pinhead-sized faces. *(☎491 420 00. Open M and W-Su 10am-6pm. €6, students €3.50. Audio guides (€2) available in English.)* The 100m tall █**Hausmannsturm** has a collection of sobering photographs of the Altstadt after the February 1945 bombings that, combined with the 360° view of the city from the top, impress upon visitors the enormity of the reconstruction project. *(Across from the Zwinger on Schloßpl. Open M and W-Su 10am-6pm. Captions in German. €2.50, students and seniors €1.50.)* The beautiful exterior sculptures of the **Katholische Hofkirche** (Catholic Court Church) hint at the building's striking white interior fit for the kings of Saxony who used to frequent it. The church was destroyed in WWII, but restoration has quickly returned it to near-perfect condition. The organ in the balcony miraculously survived the bombing and is the last and largest work of the world-famous organ-builder **Gottfried Silbermann.** *(Open May-Oct. M-Th 9am-5pm, F 1-5pm, Sa 10:30am-4pm, Su noon-4pm; Nov.-Apr. M-Sa until 5pm, Su noon-4pm. Free. Check the board outside the main entrance for tour times, usually M-Th 2pm, F-Sa 1pm.)*

ZWINGER. The extravagant collection of **Friedrich August I,** a.k.a. August the Strong, Prince Elector of Saxony and King of Poland, is housed in this elaborate palace, designed by August's senior state architect, **Matthäus Daniel Pöppelmann.** Championed as one of the most successful examples of Baroque design, the pal-

Dresden Altstadt

🏕🏠 ACCOMMODATIONS
Campingplatz Mockritz, **9**
City-Herberge, **6**
Ibis Hotel, **7**
Jugendgästehaus Dresden (HI), **3**
Jugendherberge Dresden
  Rudi Arndt (HI), **8**
🍴 FOOD & DRINK
Café Aha, **4**
Rauschenbach, **5**
Vis a Vis, **1**
⭐ NIGHTLIFE
Studentenklub Bärenzwinger, **2**

ace narrowly escaped destruction in the 1945 bombings. Some of the statues lining the grounds are still charred, but workers continually sandblast everything back to aesthetic perfection. **Gottfried Semper,** revolutionary activist and master architect, designed the northern wing, a later addition. The palace is now home to some of Dresden's finest museums (p. 607). *(North of Postpl., next to the Semper-Oper. Courtyard free. Palace open to Museum visitors only.)*

SEMPER-OPER. Dresden's famed opera house, on the Elbe by Augustusbrücke, displays the same opulence as the northern wing of the Zwinger. Painstaking restoration has returned the building to its original state, making it one of Dresden's most prominent attractions. *(Theaterpl. 2. ☎491 14 96; fax 491 14 58. The main entrance lists tour times, usually M-F every 30min. 11am-3pm. €5, students €3.)*

BRÜHLSCHE TERRASSE. Running along the river, the romantic Brühlsche Terrasse, a raised pedestrian walkway, offers a stunning view of the Elbe and the Katholische Hofkirche. Alchemist **Johann Friedrich Böttger** was imprisoned in the adjoining palace (the former seat of Saxony's government) by August the Strong until he developed the secret formula for porcelain in 1707. Dresden royalty used to stroll down this grand lane, still the classiest way to get from to the *Schloß.*

KREUZKIRCHE (CHURCH OF THE CROSS). In the Altmarkt, the former Church of St. Nicholas became the Church of the Cross when it received a splinter of the

Holy Cross. A second, more transient, name change came when the first Protestant communion in Dresden was celebrated here. Harder transitions followed: the church was leveled three times: by fire in 1669; in 1760 during the *Seven Years' War*; and again in 1897. Thanks to the modern steel supports used to rebuild the church after the last demolition, the Kreuzkirche survived WWII, despite severe fires that ruined the interior. The current rough plaster coating the sanctuary, originally intended to be temporary, has become a permanent reminder of war's destructive power. The tower offers a bird's-eye view of Neumarkt and Altmarkt. *(An der Kreuzkirche 6. ☎439 39 20. Church open Apr.-Oct. M-F 10am-5:30pm, Sa 10am-4:30pm, Su noon-5:30pm; Nov.-Mar. M-Sa 10am-3:30pm, Su noon-4:30pm. Free. Tower closes 30min. before church. Tower €1.50, €0.75 with Dresden Card.)* Although Richard Wagner went to school here, he did not sing in the **Kreuzchor,** a world-class boys' choir founded in the 13th century. *(Concerts Sa 6pm. €4-38, students €2.50-28.50.)*

FRAUENKIRCHE. Dresden's most famous silhouette was reduced to rubble by the 1945 bombings. The most complex and expensive project of its kind in Germany, reconstruction of the Frauenkirche began in 1994, and ended on Oct. 31, 2005. The cathedral's completion has brought floods of German tourists into Dresden to gaze at the circular ascending balconies, golden altar, and magnificent cupola. To avoid the largest crowds, come between 2-4pm on a weekday. *(Neumarkt. ☎498 11 31. Open M-F 10am-12pm and 1-6pm. Sa-Su hours vary, check the information center on Neumarkt for details or pick up a free copy of the German-language Leben in der Frauenkirche schedule at the tourist office and look for "Offene Kirche." Audio guides (€2.50) available in English.)*

NEUSTADT (NEW TOWN)

Across the Elbe, the some of Germany's best-preserved turn-of-the-century neighborhoods and a handful of Baroque holdouts are home to Dresden's busy cultural scene. A walk down the pedestrian Hauptstr. hits most of the sights and brings you to **Albertplatz,** with its magnificent twin fountains.

GOLDENER REITER (GILDED HORSEMAN). A gold-plated statue of August the Strong stands just across the Augustusbrücke on Haupstr. August's nickname has two sources: his physical strength, supposedly proved by an indented thumbprint on the Brühlsche Terrasse (more miraculous still since it was imprinted after his death), and his remarkable virility—legend has it he fathered 365 children, though the official tally is 15. Day and night, August shines with all his cocky gallantry.

DREIKÖNIGSKIRCHE (CHURCH OF THE MAGI). This church, designed in 1730 by Matthäus Pöppelmann, was destroyed in 1945. Now the original crumbling altar still stands tall amid the stark white halls of the newly rebuilt (1991) church. Inside, check out the *Dresden Danse Macabre,* a 12.5m Renaissance fresco, or climb the tower for a panoramic view. *(Hauptstr. 23. ☎812 41 00. Tower open M-Sa 10am-6pm, Su 11:30am-6pm. €1.50, students €1.)*

ELSEWHERE IN DRESDEN

Virtually untouched by the bombings, Dresden's outskirts are rife with spontaneity and local tradition. The banks of the Elbe are perfect for a scenic stroll, and the architecture of the mansions and villas is also well worth a look.

BLAUES WUNDER (BLUE MARVEL). A 19th-century suspension bridge connecting Blasewitz and Loschwitz, the Blue Marvel was the only bridge the Nazis didn't destroy to impede the Soviets at the end of WWII. The bridge is a great starting point for romantic summertime walks along the Elbe—the sunny **Körnerpl.,** on the Loschwitz side, is one of Dresden's prettiest squares. North of the square on Schillerstr. 19 is the tiny yellow **Schillerhäuschen,** where Beethoven first heard Schiller's poem *An die Freude* ("Ode to Joy"). He later adapted the poem for the final move-

Dresden Neustadt

▲ ACCOMMODATIONS		
Guest House Mezcalero, 4		
Hostel Die Boofe, 1		
Hostel "Louise 20," 9		
Hostel Mondpalast, 15		
Kangaroo Stop, 16		
Lollis Homestay, 8		
Pension Raskolnikoff, 17		
♦ FOOD & DRINK		
Blumenau, 14		
Cafe Europa, 2		
El Perro Borracho, 7		
Planwirtschaft, 10		
Raskolnikoff, 18		

▮ BARS		
Die 100, 5		
Brauhaus am Wald-		
schlösschen, 19		
★ NIGHTLIFE		
BOY's, 6		
DownTown &		
Groove Station, 11		
Flowerpower, 3		
Katy's Garage, 12		
Scheune, 13		

ment of his *Ninth Symphony*, now the official anthem of the EU. Down Körnerpl. is the ◪**Schwebebahn** (overhead railway). The vintage construction is the oldest of its kind in the world and offers stunning views of Dresden and the Elbe. (☎857 24 10. Tram #12 (dir.: Striesen) or #6 (dir.: Niedersedlitz) to "Schillerpl." Departs every 10min. Open daily Apr.-Oct. 10am-8pm; Nov.-Mar. 10am-6pm. €3, round-trip €4.)

DIE GLÄSERNE MANUFAKTUR. This nearly transparent €180 million Volkswagen factory was built to manufacture the company's new €90,000 luxury car, the Phaeton. The architecture is bold, with steel cones and glass walls. Phaetons in various stages of construction are stacked in plain view. Take the arched pathway that bridges the moat for a closer look, or call ahead for a tour that includes an amazingly realistic virtual test drive. (Lennestr. 1. ☎0180 589 62 68; www.glaesernemanufaktur.de. Tours M-F every 2hr. 8am-8pm by appointment.)

MESSE DRESDEN (CONVENTION CENTER). This industrial-looking convention center housed the famous "Slaughterhouse Circle" POW camp during WWI. Kurt Vonnegut was held here during the bombing of Dresden, inspiring his masterpiece *Slaughterhouse-Five*. Although there is little to see at the Messe, the curious travelers who take bus #82 (dir.: Dresden Messe) to the "Ostragehege" stop will be rewarded by of one of Dresden's architectural oddities: the former cigarette factory Yenidze. Built in 1907, it was modeled after a similar factory in Turkey, and boasts a jewelled, stained-glass dome and candy-striped pink-and-white facade.

🏛 MUSEUMS

After several years of renovations, Dresden's museums are once again ready to stand with the best in Europe. If you are planning on visiting more than one museum in a day, consider investing in a **Tageskarte** (€10, students and seniors €6), which covers one-day admission to the Albertinum museums, the *Schloß*, most of the **Zwinger** museums, and a number of other sights. Both **Dresden Cards** (p. 600) also include free or reduced entrance to many of the major museums.

ZWINGER COMPLEX

A €5 pass entitles you to take photos (without flash) at any Zwinger museum. All Zwinger museums are free with either **Dresden Card**.

■ GEMÄLDEGALERIE ALTE MEISTER (GALLERY OF THE OLD MASTERS). This
museum displays a world-class collection of paintings from 1400 to 1800, predominantly Italian and Dutch. Thanks to a particularly prudent museum director, these masterpieces were kept hidden during WWII. Raphael's *Sistine Madonna* tops the collection, which also includes such treasures as Cranach the Elder's luminous Adam and Eve paintings, and Rubens' *Leda and the Swan*. Designed explicitly to house the collections of August the Strong, these rooms have displayed some of the same paintings for over 200 years. *(From the Semper-Oper side, walk through the archway, and the gallery entry is on the right. ☎ 491 46 78. Open daily 10am-6pm. Gallery tours F-Su at 4pm. €2. Audio guides in English and German €2. €6, students and seniors €3.50.)*

PORZELLANSAMMLUNG (PORCELAIN COLLECTION). With over 20,000 pieces,
this museum boasts the largest collection of porcelain in Europe, with a spectacular selection of Meißen china. Exhibits of Asian porcelain from the 15-18th centuries are also exceptional. August the Strong invested in intricate religious icons, beautiful centerpieces, and a whole menagerie of life-size animals. *(Entry in the archway on Sophienstr. ☎ 491 46 22. Open Tu-Su 10am-6pm. €5, students and seniors €3.)*

RÜSTKAMMER (ARMORY). Rekindle dreams of chivalric valor with this collection of shiny but deadly toys from the court of the Wettin princes (16th-18th centuries). Highlights include stately silver- and gold-plated armor for man and steed, chain mail, and ivory-inlaid guns. The collection of diminutive armor belonged to Wettin toddlers. *(In the archway across from the Alte Meister. ☎ 491 46 82. Open Tu-Su 10am-6pm. €3, students and seniors €2, included in Gemäldegalerie Alte Meister admission fee.)*

MATHEMATISCH-PHYSIKALISCHER SALON. Europe's oldest "science museum," these two large rooms host an impressive collection of 16th- to 19th-century scientific instruments, far more stylish than their modern equivalents. Also serving as a science laboratory, this salon once set the official time for all of Saxony. *(In the northwest corner of the Zwinger courtyard. ☎ 94 01 46 66. Open Tu-Su 10am-6pm. €3, students €2. Audio guides in English €1.50 with a €10 deposit.)*

ALBERTINUM

Yet another construction project of August the Strong, this Baroque museum along the Elbe was designed by the inexhaustible Pöppelmann. Destroyed during WWII, it was quickly rebuilt, and now houses several renowned museums.

GEMÄLDEGALERIE NEUE MEISTER (GALLERY OF THE NEW MASTERS). This
gallery picks up in the 19th century where the Alte Meister leaves off, with a solid ensemble of German and French Impressionists, including Renoir, Degas, and Monet, and landscapes by hometown hero Caspar David Friedrich. Otto Dix's renowned *War* triptych is here, along with other *Neue Sachlichkeit* (Expressionist) works. *(☎ 491 47 14. Open M and W-Su 10am-6pm. €6, students and seniors €3.50; includes admission to Skulpturensammlung.)*

SKULPTURENSAMMLUNG (SCULPTURE COLLECTION). This immense collection of classical sculpture was rescued from a basement depot during the floods that struck Eastern Europe in 2002. Although several regular exhibition rooms upstairs are filled with the finest pieces, the majority of the collection is piled up for visitors to view in the Albertinum's vaulted cellar. Roman copies are displayed with Baroque plaster and marble completions of Greek fragments. The most prized possession of the museum is an extensive set of sculptured wall sections from a 2000-year-old Assyrian temple. *(Included in admission to the Gemäldegalerie.)*

ELSEWHERE IN DRESDEN

DEUTSCHES HYGIENEMUSEUM (GERMAN HEALTH MUSEUM). Famous for its "Glass Man," a transparent human model with illuminated organs, the world's first public health museum enlightens visitors with exhibits like "Life and Death," "Food and Drink," and "Sexuality." The museum also hosts rotating exhibits. English translations are available. *(Lingnerpl. 1, enter from Blüherstr.* ☎ *48 46 670; www.dhmd.de. Open Tu-Su 10am-6pm, last entry 5:30pm. €6, students and seniors €3.)*

VERKEHRSMUSEUM (TRANSPORTATION MUSEUM). Dresden's transport museum rolls through the history of German transportation, from carriages to bullet trains and BMWs. *(Augustusstr. 1, beside the Frauenkirche; enter on Jüdenhof.* ☎ *864 40, www.verkehrsmuseum.sachsen.de. Open Tu-Su 10am-5pm. €3, students and seniors €1.50.)*

STADTMUSEUM (MUNICIPAL MUSEUM). Inside the 18th-century *Landhaus* (State Capitol), this museum tells the story of the city since its birth in the 13th century. Early history of the *Deutsche Reich* can't compete with the colorful collection of 20th-century memorabilia, including the *Volksgasmask* (People's Gas Mask) and a model 1902 firefighter with a sprinkler helmet. The museum is currently undergoing extensive renovation slated for completion in late 2006. Check at the tourist office for more details. *(Wilsdruffer Str. 2, near Pirnaischer Pl.* ☎ *656 486 13. Open Tu-Th and Sa-Su 10am-6pm, F noon-8pm. €3, students €2. F free after 2pm.)*

♫ ENTERTAINMENT

Dresden has been a leader in the realms of theater, opera, and music for centuries. The **Semper-Oper** is the city's crown jewel, but there are enough smaller theaters to suit any taste. The tourist office by the Semper-Oper is a great resource for performances, but individual box offices offer better deals. Although most theaters take a *Pause* (summer break) from mid-July to early-September, open-air festivals fill the gap. The **Filmnächte am Elbufer** (Film Nights on the Elbe) festival in July and August offers an enormous movie screen and stage against the illuminated Altstadt. Most shows start at 9 or 9:30pm and cost around €6. (Office at Alaunstr. 62. ☎ 89 93 20; complete schedule at www.filmnaechte-am-elbufer.de, or in brochures available at the tourist office.) Like many palaces in the area the **Zwinger** hosts classical concerts on summer evenings (shows at 6:30pm, tickets at tourist office).

Sächsische Staatsoper (Semper-Oper), Theaterpl. 2 (☎ 491 10; www.semperoper.de). See opera's finest in this stately opera house. Box office at Schinkelwache open M-F 10am-6pm, Sa 10am-1pm, and 1hr. before shows.

Kulturpalast, Schloßstr. 2, am Altmarkt (☎ 486 66 66; www.kulturpalast-dresden.de). This civic center is home to the **Dresdner Philharmonie** (☎ 486 63 06; www.dresdnerphilharmonie.de) and hosts a wide variety of performances. Box office, Schloßstr. 2, open M-F 10am-7pm, Sa 10am-2pm.

Staatsoperette Dresden, Pirnär Landstr. 131 (☎ 20 79 90; www.staatsoperette-dresden.de). Musical theater and operetta from Lerner and Löwe to Sondheim. €4-19. Discounted shows Tu-Th. Box office open M 11am-4pm, Tu-Th 10am-7pm, F 11am-7pm, Sa 4-7pm, Su 1hr. before shows.

Staatsschauspiel (☎49 13 50; www.staatsschauspiel-dresden.de) puts on classic plays at the **Schauspielhaus,** Theaterstr. 2 and contemporary shows at the **Kleines Haus,** Glacisstr. 28. Schauspielhaus tickets €10-20, students €5-10; Kleines Haus tickets €12-17/6-10. Discounts M. Box office (Theaterstr. 2, ☎491 35 55) open M-F 10am-6:30pm, Sa 10am-2pm, and 1hr. before performances.

Theater Junge Generation, Meißner Landstr. 4 (☎429 12 20; www.tjg-dresden.de). Performs opera and summer theater in the Dresdner Schloß. Tickets €6-10. 50% Student discount. Box office, Rundkino Prager Str., open Tu-F 2-6pm, and 1hr. before shows.

projekttheater dresden, Louisenstr. 47 (☎810 76 10 or 810 76 11; www.projekttheater.de). Cutting-edge, international experimental theater in the heart of the Neustadt. Tickets €11, students €7. €1 off each ticket if you call to book in advance. Shows 8 or 9pm. Box office open 1hr. before shows.

Die Herkuleskeule, Sternpl. 1 (☎492 55 55; www.herkuleskeule.de). This bitingly political cabaret revels in blasting US culture. Tickets €9-19. On M-Th and Su, €5.50 student tickets available 30min. before shows if empty seats remain. Box office open M-F 1:30-6pm, Sa 10am-noon, and 1hr. before performances.

Die Bühne, Teplitzer Str. 26 in the University (☎46 33 63 51, www.die-buehne.net). Tram #11 or Bus #72 or 76 to "Strehlener Pl." Student theater showing contemporary plays, occasionally in English. Tickets around €4; call ahead to reserve.

◐ NIGHTLIFE

The entire Neustadt seems to spend the day anticipating 10pm. Ten years ago, the area north of Albertpl. was a maze of gray streets and crumbling buildings. Now a fast-paced, alternative community has sprung up among the 50 bars and clubs crammed into the square kilometer roughly bounded by **Königsbrückerstr., Bischofsweg, Kamenzerstr.,** and **Albertpl.** *Kneipen Surfer* (free at Neustadt hostels and restaurants) provides descriptions of every bar. Peruse the back of *SAX* (€3 at the tourist office, or ask to see one at any bar) or check www.dresden-nightlife.de for upcoming concerts and dances. The free German-language monthlies *Dresdner* and *Frizz,* available in many pubs, also list nighttime entertainment. For gay and lesbian nightlife, pick up the free *gegenpol* at the tourist office.

▧ Brauhaus am Waldschlößchen, am Brauhaus 8b (☎81 19 90; www.waldschloesschen.de). Tram #11 to "Waldschlößchen" or walk 25min. up Baunitzerstr. With views of Dresden's skyline, this brewery proves that Bavaria doesn't have a monopoly on *Bier.* Shaded terrace attracts chill Dresdeners of all ages who drink beer by the liter (€4.80). A cafeteria and restaurant offer guests the choice between cheap (*Wurst,* noodles, salad; €3.30) and classy (entrées €5-13.50). Open daily 11am-1am. AmEx/MC/V.

DownTown, Katharinenstr. 11-13 (☎801 39 23). Constantly packed, DownTown caters to those who want more than conversation. The music is loud, seating rare, and the crowd enthusiastic. Evenings begin upstairs at the bar, billiard hall, and tattoo parlor **Groove Station** (☎802 95 94). Expect pop, rock, and electronic music. Cover €3.50, students €2.50. Open daily 7pm-5am. Club open Th-Sa 10pm-5am. Cash only.

Wash Room, Hermann-Mende-Str. 1 (☎441 57 08). Take tram #7 or 8 to "Industriegelaende." Indoor waterfalls, films of crashing waves, and an indoor beach volleyball court fill this club, pulsating with electronica and frenetically colorful lights. Open F-Sa 10:22pm-5am. Cover F €5, Sa €4-8; 50% off 9:22-10:23pm. Cash only.

Flowerpower, Eschenstr. 11 (☎804 98 14). From Albertpl., walk up Königsbrückerstr. and take a left on Eschenstr.; it's on the left. Feels like a warehouse-turned-dorm room, with tapestries, couches, blacklights, and curtained booths. Lively until 5am with a dedicated crowd of 20-somethings. Beer €2.30. M student nights feature discounted beer and wine, and F is "Friday Night Fever" club night. Open daily 8pm-5am. Cash only.

Die 100, Alaunstr. 100 (☎801 39 57; www.cafe100.de). With over 250 wines (from €3 per glass) on the menu, this *Weinkeller* caters to the thrifty connoisseur. Unpolished, relaxed atmosphere in candlelit interior and intimate stone courtyard. Salads and sandwiches €3-4.20. Open daily 5pm-3am. Cash only.

Katy's Garage, Alaunstr. 42. Guarded by a gigantic stone armadillo, Katy's is one of the area's more energetic venues. A young, edgy crowd fills this small, smoky, crimson-colored club for dancing and drinking. M student night, Tu hip-hop, W parents night, Th reggae, F Brit and Indie pop. Cover up to €4. Open daily 8pm-5am. Cash only.

Scheune, Alaunstr. 36-40 (☎802 66 19). The granddaddy of the Neustadt scene, this bar serves as a starting point for many nights out. Performance space upstairs and Indian café downstairs (€4.50-10). Hosts the fantastic *Schaubudensommer* festival in July and the *Schaubudenwinter* in December. Cover €5-15. Café open M-F 5pm-2am, Sa-Su 10am-2am. Club opens at 8pm. Cash only.

Studentenklub Bärenzwinger, Brühlischer Garten 1 (☎495 14 09; www.baerenzwinger.de), under the garden between the Elbe and the Albertinum. This subterranean student lair attracts a diverse crowd with cheap drinks and a friendly staff. Beer €1.90. Summer theater July-Aug. €12, students €9. 18+. Concerts €7-10. Opens Tu and F-Sa 9pm for live shows and dancing. Cash only.

BOY's, Alaunstr. 80 (☎796 88 24; www.boysdresden.de), just beyond the Kunsthof Passage. A half-naked devil mannequin guards this popular gay-friendly bars, with a small but cozy dance floor. Drinks €2.70-6. Open Tu-Th 8pm-3am, F-Su 8pm-5am. MC/V.

◪ DAYTRIPS FROM DRESDEN

MORITZBURG

Take bus #326, 457, or 458 from Bahnhof-Neustadt to "Moritzburg, Schloß" (25min., €3.20). Return trip from "Moritzburg Markt" on Marktstr., parallel to Schloßallee. The more scenic (and slower and bumpier) route is the S-Bahn from Dresden to "Radebeul-Ost" (15min., €3.40), and then the 110-year-old Schmalspurbahn (narrow-gauge railway) from Radebeul-Ost to "Moritzburg" (30min., €5.30). From the Schmalspurbahn, follow the crowds up the hill to Schloßallee and take a right. Moritzburg's tourist office is at Schloßallee 3b. ☎035207 85 40; fax 854 20. Open daily Apr.-Oct. 10am-6pm; Nov.-Mar. M-Sa 9am-5pm.

Never one to be bashful about leaving his mark on the Saxon landscape, August the Strong tore down a little palace in 1723 and replaced it with ◪**Schloß Moritzburg,** a titanic Baroque hunting lodge. The immense yellow *Schloß* stands at the end of Moritzburg's main street, *Schloßallee,* on a pleasantly overgrown island in an artificial lake. Original, imaginatively decorated leather hides still plaster the palace's walls, on which countless reindeer antlers hang as a testament to August's hunting prowess (though most of them were gifts from visitors.) One popular exhibit is devoted entirely to reconstructed feather tapestries. (☎035 20 78 730; www.schloss-moritzburg.de. Open daily Apr.-Oct. 10am-5:30pm; Nov.-Mar. admission only for hourly guided tours; Feb.-Mar. and Nov.-Dec. Tu-Su 10am-4pm; Jan. Sa-Su 10am-4pm. Tours €2 Apr.-Oct., free Nov.-Mar.) A 40min. walk from the *Schloß,* the smaller pink hunting lodge, **Fasanenschlößchen,** was built by the great-grandson of August, Friedrich August III. Facing Schloß Moritzburg, follow Meißner Str. to the end of the lake on your right, then turn right and follow the path for about 15min. The Fasanenschlößchen will be closed for repairs at least until the end of 2007. On a small, idyllic jetty into the lake, the **Leuchtturm** (lighthouse) once served as a backdrop to the mock sea battles of bored, rich princes. Moritzburg is surrounded by extensive parks and forests criss-crossed by scenic paths, a huge gaming reserve, and the **Sächsisches Langestüt** (Saxon Studfarm), where August the Strong's prolific legacy is honored.

As the meeting place of *Brücke* artists from 1909 to 1911, Moritzburg developed a rich art tradition. After Käthe Kollwitz's home in Berlin was bombed near the end of WWII, Prince Ernst Heinrich offered the artist a place of retreat here. The **Käthe-Kollwitz-Gedenkstätte,** Meißner Str. 7., honors Kollwitz, one of Germany's most notable 20th-century artists, whose art depicts struggling workers, mourning parents, and impoverished children. The museum features a selection of her works, pictures, and excerpts from her diary. (☎035 20 78 28 18. Open daily Apr.-Oct. 11am-5pm; Nov.-Mar. noon-4pm. €3, students €2.)

PILLNITZ

Take tram #1 (dir.: Kleinzschachwitz) or #2 (dir.: Prohlis) to "Comeniuspl.," then bus #83 to "Pillnitz" (35min., €1.70). Or, the Sächsische Dampfschifffahrt (p. 599) can get you there by boat. (1½hr., €8.50, round-trip €13, children half-price.) Head straight through the main garden to the Alte Wache tourist office for maps, information, and tours.

A standout among August the Strong's many castles (which are almost as numerous as his mistresses), the gardens of **Schloß Pillnitz** are the perfect destination for an afternoon picnic or a contemplative stroll. The virile ruler inherited the nearly 300-year-old castle in 1694 and generously passed it on to his mistress the Countess Cosel a few years later. When the Countess got too uppity, August kicked her out and ordered the renovations that gave Schloß Pillnitz its distinctively foreign look. August's taste for Chinese style went beyond porcelain—the colorful turrets of the **Bergpalais** and **Wasserpalais,** as well as the castle's banquet hall, imitate Chinese architecture and art. Bordered on one side by the Elbe, the palace sits amid splendid gardens. In addition to a Baroque courtyard and labyrinth, Pillnitz is home to a diverse arboretum that includes rare and delicate Asian species. English and Chinese pavilions complete the regal effect. Inside the palace, the **Schloßmuseum** celebrates the lives of August the Strong and his Saxon successors. A short walk through the museum reveals that the *Schloß* hasn't yet been completely restored; its fading frescoes and cracking columns possess an authenticity rarely found in touristed palaces. Along with concise biographies of Saxon rulers, the museum features a terrific exhibit on court games and pastimes—some trifling, others deadly. The residences also house Dresden's **Kunstgewerbemuseum** (Museum of Decorative Arts), which displays numerous treasures of the Saxon-Polish dynasty. Beautiful furniture, textiles, and porcelain attest to the artistic prowess of Saxon craftsmen from the 15th-17th centuries. Most visitors, however, spend their time roaming the gardens. Concerts also take place in the garden during the summer; call for info. (☎261 32 01. Museums open May-Oct. daily 10am-6pm. Bergpalais open Tu-Su, Wasserpalais open M and W-Su. €4, students €2.50.)

MEIßEN ☎03521

For anyone who takes the 30km trip from Dresden, it is easy to understand why Saxon electors chose to build their home *Schloß* here. The current castle, built on the 1000-year-old foundations of Meißen's first fortress, has occupied the same spot for 500 years. The view from the hilltop onto Meißen, the Elbe, and the surrounding vineyards is magnificent. But the castle has not always served as a residence: in 1710, August the Strong turned it into a factory to mass-produce Meißen's "white gold"—**porcelain**, developed for the first time in Europe (see **White Gold: A New Alchemy,** p. 612). Today, visitors from around the world flock to this mecca of delicate dishware and the castle where it was once produced.

■■ **TRANSPORTATION AND PRACTICAL INFORMATION.** Meißen is easily reached from Dresden by **train** (40 min., €5.10) or **Sächsische Dampfschifffart ferry**

THE LOCAL STORY

WHITE GOLD: A NEW ALCHEMY

When King August II of Poland (August the Strong) heard in 1701 that famous alchemist Friedrich Böttger had moved to Dresden, the virile king imprisoned him until he could produce gold from cheaper metals. While in jail, Böttger—unable to meet August's impossible demand for alchemical gold—was teamed with Ehrenfried Walther von Tschirnhaus, who had been working on white porcelain for years. Böttger's reluctantly cooperated, announcing his success in 1708, one year after von Tschirnhaus' death. To rush the new invention into production, August ordered the Albrechtsburg castle in Meißen emptied to house his new porcelain factory. The king also stationed guards around the castle to keep the technique a secret, and kept Böttger captive for four more years until he had sworn not to reveal the discovery. Meißen quickly blossomed into a city of porcelain, with church bells and cathedral crucifixes made of the precious "white gold."

The factory remained in Albrechtsburg until 1864, when the development of new production techniques required a new building for continued production. The new factory still produces world-famous porcelain, no longer an intensely guarded secret: now all who travel to Meißen can watch the intricate art that once so fascinated the powerful August the Strong.

(p. 599). The **tourist office,** Markt 3, is across the Markt from the Frauenkirche. It distributes English-language maps and books private rooms (€17-26) for free. (☎419 40; fax 41 94 19. Open Apr.-Oct. M-F 10am-6pm, Sa-Su 10am-4pm; Nov.-Mar. M-F 10am-5pm, Sa 10am-3pm.) City **tours** depart from the tourist office daily at 1pm (€4, students €3), and every Wednesday at 7pm a costumed tour guide leads a "Romantic Evening Stroll" through the city (1½hr., €5, students and seniors €4). The **post office,** Poststr. 26, 01662 Meißen, is just across the Elbe from the train station. (Open M-F 9am-noon, 2-6pm and Sa 9am-noon.)

⚄ ACCOMODATIONS AND FOOD. The **Jugend-gästehaus Meißen ❶,** Wilsdrufferstr. 28, is often full. From the station, cross the railroad bridge and follow Oberg. until it meets Plosenweg. Turn left and continue uphill; the hostel is on the left across from the small market (15min.). Or, bus D (2 per hr.) runs from the train station up the steep hill. You'll be in a crowded 5-bed room, but the incredible price is worth it. Besides a great view of the city and a beautiful garden, the hostel offers a full kitchen and common room with TV and billiard table. (☎45 30 65. Breakfast €3. Sheets included. Reception M-F 5am-noon 4-8pm, Sa-Su 4-8pm. €12.) Another option, up the steps across from the Porzellan Manufaktur, is **Schweizerhaus ❸,** Rauhentalstr. 1. The great location and restaurant downstairs ooze convenience. (☎45 71 62. All rooms with shower. Reception daily until midnight. Singles €28-39; doubles €36-57.) For food, check out **Zum Goldenen Anker ❷,** Uferstr. 9. From the Markt, take Elbstr. to Heinrichspl., then Martinstr. Make a left onto Fahrmannstr., and another right onto Uferstr. Locals flock to this river-front restaurant serving excellent Saxon cuisine. Entrées €5-14. For German-speakers, the phonetic "Alte Schmiede" menu is hilarious. (☎45 78 72; fax 40 26 97. Cash only.) At **Schönitz ❷,** Neug. 22, between the Markt and Porcelin museum, try the bruschetta (€2.90) or the rosemary potatoes with bacon (€4.90). Entrées €5-11.50. (☎45 25 61. Open M-Sa noon-11pm. Cash only.) The **Café am Dom ❶,** next to the cathedral, has great cakes (€1-2), snacks, and an unbeatable view from a terrace graced with pear trees. (☎140 44 86. Open daily 10am-6pm. AmEx/DC/MC/V.) The farmer's market is on the Markt. (Open Tu-Sa 8am-5pm.) During the last weekend of September, Meißen revels in its annual wine festival.

◙ SIGHTS. The narrow, romantic alleyways of the Altstadt climb up to the **◪Albrechtsburg,** a castle and cathedral overlooking the city, originally the site of

Meißen's porcelain factory. From the train station, walk straight onto Bahnhofstr. and follow it over the Elbbrücke. Cross the bridge, continue straight to the Markt and turn right onto Burgstr. ascending till you reach the castle stairs. Or, board the green and white City Bus at the Markt or the station (€2.55, round-trip €3.60). The castle foundations were first built in 929 to protect the area's minority Sorb population (see **The Absorbing Sorbs,** p. 620). Master architect **Arnold von Westfalen** built the current castle in the 15th century for the ruling brothers Elector Ernst and Duke Albrecht of Wettin. Uninhabited for its first two centuries because of a falling out between the brothers, the castle was thoroughly restored when it became a porcelin factory in the 18th century, and lavish floor-to-vaulted-ceiling murals were added in the 19th century. Special exhibitions arrive every few months. Revolutionary during its time, the castle is considered to have given birth to German *Schloß* design. (☎470 70. Open Mar.-Oct. daily 10am-6pm; Nov.-Feb. 10am-5pm. Last entry 30min. before closing. €3.50, students €2.50. English audio guide €2.) Next door is the **Meißener Dom,** an early Gothic cathedral that gives visitors their money's worth with four priceless 13th-century statues by the anonymous *Naumburger Meister*, a triptych by Cranach the Elder, a porcelin crucifix, and the metal grave coverings of the Wettins. Construction on the cathedral began in 1250, and, amazingly, the stained glass window above the altar dates from the original construction. Tours ascend the open towers of the church and provide an unparalleled view of the town, the Elbe and the countryside. (Open Apr.-Oct. daily 9am-6pm; Nov.-Mar. 10am-4pm. €2.50, students €1.50. 30min. organ concerts May-Oct. M-Sa at noon (€0.50 after admission), Sa 6pm (€3.50-11.50 per person).Tower tours daily Apr.-Oct. every hr. 1-4pm. €1.50 after admission. Combination Dom and *Schloß* tickets €5.50/€3.50.) Europeans discovered the secret to making porcelain (previously known only in China) at Meißen in 1707. Once more tightly guarded than *Stasi* headquarters, today the delightful **Staatliche Porzellan-Manufaktur,** Talstr. 9, can be toured by anyone. From the Markt, turn left on Fleischerg., then right on Neug., which becomes Talstr. At the **Schauhalle,** visitors can peruse finished products including a 12 ft. centerpiece made in 1749 for August III. The real fun is the high-tech tour of the **Schauwerkstatt** (show workshop), in which deft porcelain artists paint perfectly detailed flowers before visitors' incredulous eyes. (☎46 82 08. Open daily May-Oct. 9am-6pm; Nov.-Apr. 9am-5pm. Without workshop, €6, students €3; with workshop, €8/4. Last entrance to workshop 45 minutes before closing. English headsets available €3.) Meißen's Gothic **Rathaus** stands directly across the way from the **Frauenkirche;** its 37 porcelain bells are the oldest such carillon in the entire, world and peal a different hymn every 3hr. (☎45 38 32. Church open May-Oct. daily 10am-noon and 2-4pm. Call ahead to confirm hours. Free.)

SÄCHSISCHE SCHWEIZ (SAXON SWITZERLAND) NATIONAL PARK

Sheer sandstone cliffs and mountains draped with lush forests distinguish the national park Germany has claimed as its own "Switzerland." Although archaeologists can trace settlements in the area back to the Bronze Age, the region truly flourished under the auspices of the Saxon electors of the Holy Roman Empire, for whom it served as the perfect destination for such activities as hunting expeditions and various court festivals. Over the past century, it has become one of the most popular national vacation destinations, but it's virtually unknown outside of Germany. Transportation within the park is very thorough and affordable, and hiking, biking, kayaking, and canoeing opportunities abound in this exceptional corner of Germany.

SACHSEN

SÄCHSISCHE SCHWEIZ NATIONAL PARK AT A GLANCE	
AREA: 368sq. km.	**GATEWAYS:** Bad Schandau (p. 618), Hohnstein (p. 617), Königstein (p. 617), and Rathen (p. 616).
CLIMATE: Temperate. Summers 20-30°C (68-86°F).	
FEATURES: Sandstone cliffs, table mountains, and river gorges interspersed with forested areas.	**HIGHLIGHTS:** Dramatic cliffs and valleys seen from atop the numerous rock formations, particularly stunning from the Bastei lookout point or the Königstein Festung.
CAMPING: Only in designated areas. Most campgrounds close Nov.-Mar.	**FEES:** No entrance or trail fees.

▐ TRANSPORTATION

The park is easily accessible by Dresden's S1, which starts in Meißen and runs from the Dresden Hauptbahnhof along the Elbe River. A regular **ferry** service, the **Sächsische Dampfschifffahrt,** also connects the towns along this section of the Elbe. If you plan to explore more than one town in a day, buy a *Tageskarte* (daypass; €5.10) from any *Fahrausweis* machine, located at most train stops. These work for the S-Bahn, buses, and many ferries in the area. The **Kirnitzschtalbahn,** an antique trolley, travels from Bad Schandau to **Lichtenhainer Wasserfall** (30min.; Apr.-Oct. 2 per hr. 9:30am-7pm, less frequently during winter). *Wanderwege* (footpaths) follow hills into the heart of the park, connecting towns in a spidery web.

▐▐ ORIENTATION AND PRACTICAL INFORMATION

The national park is divided into the *vorderer Teil* (front section) and the *hinterer Teil* (back sections). The Elbe River, along which most of the region's towns lie, runs from the Czech Republic in the southeast toward Dresden in the northwest, cutting the park in half. The best source of park information is the **Nationalparkhaus,** Dresdner Str. 2b, 01814 Bad Schandau. In addition to the knowledgeable, English-speaking staff, the house has an exhibit on the park's history and wildlife. (☎035022 502 40; www.lanu.de. Open Apr.-Oct. daily 9am-6pm, Nov.-Mar. Tu-Su 9am-5pm, closed for most of Jan.) Visitors can also obtain information from the **Tourismusverband Sächsische Schweiz,** Am Bahnhof 6, Bad Schandau (☎035022 495 00), the **Nationalpark-Verwaltung,** An der Elbe 4, Bad Schandau (☎035022 90 06 00), or by visiting www.saechsische-schweiz.de, which has extensive information on opportunities for **disabled visitors** to the park. For **emergencies** dial ☎110 for police, ☎112 for fire, or ☎115 for medical emergencies. In case of a mountain emergency, call the **Bergrettungsstationen** (mountain rescue stations; ☎035033 710 71).

▐ CAMPING

The entire region can be seen on a daytrip from Dresden, but vacationers looking for an extended stay can choose from many sorts of accommodations. Private rooms can be booked through tourist offices. For hostels and pensions, see individual town listings. The following campgrounds vary widely in services offered and space available, so calling ahead is recommended. Whatever the type of accommodation, reservations are a good idea between April and October.

Campingplatz Ostrauer Mühle, im Kirnitzschtal, Bad Schandau (☎035022 427 42; www.ostrauer-muehle.de). Open year-round.

Campingplatz Thorwaldblick, Schandauer Str. 37, Hinterhermsdorf (☎035974 506 48; www.thorwaldblick.de). Open year-round.

Campingplatz Königstein, Schandauer Str. 25e, Königstein (☎035021 682 24; www.camping-koenigstein.de). Open Apr.-Oct.

Waldcamping Pirna-Copitz, Äußere Pillnitzer Str., Pirna (☎03501 52 37 73; www.wald-camping-pirna.de). Open Apr.-Oct. Handicapped facilities available.

📖 HIKING

Hikes of all lengths and difficulty levels are available; only a few are listed here. Trails are well marked, but a map (€5.80), available at the Nationalparkhaus or any tourist office, is recommended. Be sure to wear proper hiking shoes or boots (improper shoes can slip on rocky cliffs), and bring your passport if you want to cross over to the nearby Czech Republic.

■ **Basteiaussicht** (2½hr.). Starting in Rathen, this easy hike with lots of stairs passes the startling outcrops and dramatic plunges of the **Bastei** cliffs in all their splendor. The lookout point offers a dizzying view of the forested Elbe valley. Rent boats at the *Amselsee* (Blackbird Lake), a section of river in the middle of the hike (€2.60 per 30min.).

■ **Schrammsteinaussicht** (4½hr.). This hike begins in Bad Schandau and includes the **Kipphorn** lookout point (480m), a stone ridge next to the Elbe valley. Among the highest spots in the park, this is the perfect vantage point from which to watch the sun rise or set. On a clear day, you can see all the way to Dresden. A relatively easy hike, excepting the 30min. ascent to the top of the ridge.

Kuhstall und Raubschloß (3hr.). Begins at the **Lichtenhainer Wasserfall.** Includes the cavernous **Kuhstall** rock formation and the site of the **Raubschloß** (Robbers' Castle) ruins. (Bus #241 from Bad Schandau or Königstein, every 2hr., 8am-6:30pm. Or, Kirnitzschtalbahn from Bad Schandau. Every 30min. 9:30am-8:30pm.)

Großer Zschirnstein (4hr.). Begins in Schöna (S1, every 30min., 5:30am-10:30pm). Leads to the **Kohlbornstein** (Cabbage Spring Stone) lookout point (372m), with a view of sandstone rock formations and the neighboring **Böhmische Schweiz** (Bohemian Switzerland) to the east.

Pfaffenstein (2hr.). Begins in Königstein. A moderately difficult hike among the park's many "stone needles," with stairs to the **Pfaffenstein** (Priest Stone) rock formation.

Unterer Affensteinweg (4½hr.). Begins in Bad Schandau. A narrow mountain path with many branches. Includes the **Frienstein** lookout point.

Am Brand (2hr.). Begins in Hohnstein. Includes the **Brand** (Fire) lookout point and the **Waitzdorfer Walls** rock formation. A relatively easy hike except for the 30min. climb up the stairs to the lookout point.

🚲 BIKING

The park website (www.saechsische-schweiz.de) suggests bike tours with lengths ranging from 20-70km. The Nationalparkhaus in Bad Schandau (p. 614) can give you information on paths. For bike rental, see Bad Schandau (p. 618), check the park website, or pick up a map at the Dresden Hauptbahnhof (p. 600). Biking in the park is only allowed from 7am-8pm.

Dresden to Schöna (3½hr.). A paved, bike-only path follows the Elbe from Dresden to Schöna. Pick up the path by the docks on the southern side of the Elbe. To avoid riding on streets with car traffic, cross the river with the ferry at **Königstein** and then again at Bad Schandau. Offers fantastic views of the Elbe and the park's rock formations.

Bad Schandau to Hinterhermsdorf (3hr.). The Elberadweg (Elbe bike path) heads off to the right as soon as you get off the ferry in Bad Schandau. Follow the marked bike paths through the back part of the park to Hinterhermsdorf. Includes the **Lindigtblick** ("pleasing view") lookout point and the **Lichtenhainer Wasserfall.**

⚠ OTHER ACTIVITIES

CLIMBING. The rock formations and sheer cliff faces of the Sächsische Schweiz make it a natural attraction for rock climbers. Although experienced climbers are permitted to brave the challenging cliffs on their own, *Let's Go* recommends that *all* visitors first stop by the Nationalparkhaus, which can inform climbers about park rules and direct the less experienced toward guides and climbing courses. In the interest of preserving the rock, metal safety devices like "friends" are forbidden, as are chemical climbing aids such as Magnesia. Some of the most popular climbing regions include Bielatal (239m), Rathener Gebiet (145m), Schmilkaer Gebiet (124m), Affensteine (115m), Großer Zschand (87m), Schrammsteingebiet (80m), and Brandgebiet (80m).

WATER SPORTS. Canoeing on the Elbe offers impressive views of the park from below. Some companies will take you upriver in a motorboat and let you canoe back. **Kanu-Aktiv-Tours,** Elbpromenade Schadauer Str. 17-19, Königstein, rents canoes and rubber dinghies for up to 10 people and offers guided water tours. (☎ 035022 507 04; www.kanu-aktiv-tours.de. Boats €30-90 per day. Tours €30-38.) **Spaß Tours,** Mennicke Str. 29, Stadt Wehlen, rents charter boats for trips anywhere between Bad Schandau and Meißen, and combination rentals that allow you to bike from Wehlen to Bad Schandau and paddle back. (☎ 035024 710 84. Canoes from €35 per day; family rafts (6 people) €50; large rafts (10 people) €75.)

RATHEN ☎ 035024

Situated on the Elbe just beyond the magnificent sandstone cliffs of the Bastei, the tiny vacation town of Rathen is distinguished by its **Felsenbühne,** one of the most beautiful open-air theaters in Europe. Each summer, Dresdeners make the trip to Rathen for innovative productions of operas, musicals, and theater classics. Tickets and schedules are available from the **Theaterkasse,** on the way to the theater. (From Rathen, take the second left uphill, and follow the signs. ☎ 77 70; www.dresden-theater.de. Tickets €8-21, students €6-19. Open May-Sept. 9am-5pm or until 30min. after the latest show begins. Tickets can also be purchased at the Bad Schandau tourist offices.) One good option for accommodations is on the **Burg Altrathen,** a steep hill above the town that provides panoramic views of the Bastei. To get to the **Gästehaus ❷,** in a castle perched above the Elbe, take a right up the narrow path to the left after the ferry landing, just past the Hotel Erbgericht. (☎76 00; www.burg-altrathen.de. Singles from €25; doubles from €50. Cash only.) **Pension Panorama ❷** serves as both a restaurant (entrées €3-11) and guest house. All the well-furnished rooms have TV and shower. Follow the road from the ferry straight into Rathen and turn right up the slope. (☎706 69; fax 797 08. Open M-W and F 5-11pm, Sa-Su noon-11pm. Singles €30-35; doubles €55. MC.) Rathen is easily accessible by **train** (Dresden's S1); take the ferry from the train station. (Runs daily 5:30am-midnight; €0.70, round-trip €1.30.) Or, take the S1 to nearby Stadt Wahlen and enjoy the plesant hike across the Bastei. A **tourist office** gives hiking advice and finds rooms (from €15) for free. From the landing, follow Zum Grünbar for 5min. and look on the left. (☎704 22; www.kurort-rathen.de. Open daily Apr. to mid-Oct. 8am-6pm, mid-Oct. to Mar. 10am-4pm.) **Postal Code:** 01824.

HOHNSTEIN
☎035975

Set back in the forest, away from the Elbe, the small village of Hohnstein ("high stone" in Old Saxon) surveys the valley and forests below it from a tall, stony ridge, and is linked to Rathen by hikes through one of the national park's most stunning valleys. To get here from Rathen, follow the shorter path through the hills (2hr., trail starts beyond the Amselsee), or the longer but easier path through the Polenz valley (3hr.). Be sure to stop at the ▓**Hockstein,** an isolated outcropping that provides a spectacular view of the valley below and of Hohnstein across the valley. Follow the signs from Hockstein through the **Wolfsslucht,** a steep, narrow passage between huge rocks. Afterward, you'll come to **Gauschgrotte,** a valley filled with green moss and rock formations. The **Museum der Geschichte des Burg Hohnstein** (History Museum of Burg Hohnstein), housed in the Naturfreundehaus, covers the 900-year history of the Burg with exhibits ranging from medieval armor and weapons to anti-fascist resistance in Dresden and the Sächsische Schweiz. An exhibit commemorates **Konrad Hahnewald,** the beloved father of the Naturfreundehaus and later the first non-Jewish prisoner of the Hohnstein concentration camp. The Burg's tower provides a panorama of the valley below and the Hockstein. (☎812 02. Open daily Apr.-Oct. 10am-5pm. €1.50, ages 6-16 €0.50, under 6 and Naturfreundehaus patrons free.) The fortress **Naturfreundehaus Burg Hohnstein ❷,** Am Markt 1, doubles as a hostel with dorms and smaller rooms. (☎812 02; fax 812 03. Breakfast included. Reception open 7:30am-8pm. Check-in 3pm. Check-out 10am. €22, children €13. Cash only.) To get to Hohnstein, take the S1 to "Pirna" (45min.) and then bus #236 or 237 to Hohnstein "Eiche" or "Markt" (40min., €4.10). Because buses run infrequently, hiking from Rathen to Hohnstein can be the fastest route to the town. The **tourist office,** Rathausstr. 10, across from the Rathaus, doles out information on the Burg and surrounding trails and finds rooms (from €16) for free. (☎194 33; fax 868 10. Open M-F 9am-5pm, Sa 9am-3pm.) **Postal Code:** 01848.

KÖNIGSTEIN
☎035021

The next stop on the Dresden S-Bahn's journey into the hills and dales of the Sächsische Schweiz is Königstein (pop. 3200). Above the town sits the monumental fortress **Festung Königstein,** its huge walls built right into stone cliffs. Complete with drawbridges and nearly impenetrable defenses (it was only captured once, in 1402 during a feud over the German throne), this is the castle you dreamed about

SACHSEN

as a kid. The oldest buildings that can be seen today date from the 16th century. Then a popular retreat for the kings of Saxony, it was later converted into a notorious state prison and used by the Nazis to stash stolen art. Between 1949 and 1955 it served as a juvenile correction center, but today the complex houses a variety of museums. From the city, it's a 40min. uphill struggle, but the view from atop the fortress's towering walls is worth the sweat. Follow the signs to the well-worn path. (☎646 07; www.festung-koenigstein.de. Captions in German. English pamphlets at the information office inside the castle. Open daily Apr.-Sept. 9am-8pm, exhibitions 10am-6pm; Oct. 9am-6pm, exhibitions 9am-5pm; Nov.-Mar. 9am-5pm. Last entry 30min. before closing. €5, students and seniors €3. English audio guides €2.50.) The double-decker **Festungs Express** buses also run to the fortress. Rides leave from Reißigerpl., just to the right down Bahnhofstr. from the S-Bahn station. (Apr.-Oct. 2 per hr. 9am-5pm. €3, children €1; round-trip €4/1.50. Buy tickets on board.) Paths also lead from the town up to the challenging 415m **Lilienstein,** hiked by August the Strong in 1708. To get there, take the **ferry** (€0.90) and make the first right after getting off. Stay on this paved road until you see a sign for "Lilienstein" marked with a blue stripe. The steep 2km hike takes 1½hr. and the summit has, in addition to a view of the Festung fortress opposite, a panorama of the fields and towns along the Elbe from Stadt Wehlen to Bad Schandau.

Naturfreundehaus Königstein ❸, Halbestadt 13, has clean and comfortable rooms and a dining area that overlooks the Elbe. All rooms have showers, and there's an enormous chess board out back. To get there, take the ferry across the Elbe and turn right. The hostel will be on your right after about 10min. (☎035022 994 80; www.nfhw.de. Breakfast and dinner included. Reception daily 8am-8:30pm. Check-in 2-6pm. Check-out 10am. Rooms €26-31. Cash only.) Fresh fruits and vegetables are sold at an open market on Tuesdays and Thursdays (8am-5pm) in the town's streets. Eat more heartily among antlers and paintings of the Elbe at **Schräger's Gasthaus ❷,** on Kirchg. 1, straight up Hainstr. from Reißigerpl. (Entrées €4.30-8.80. Open daily 11am-3pm and 5-11pm. Cash only.) Those who make it up the first part of the path to Lillienstein will be rewarded by the expansive view and Saxon specialties at the **Panoramahotel Lillienstein ❸,** Ebenheit 7. (☎35022 530. Open daily 11am-9:30pm. AmEx/MC/V.)

Housed in the **post office,** Schreiberberg 2, the **tourist office** books rooms (from €25) and posts a list of vacancies. From Reißigerpl., take Hainstr., then turn left on Pirnärstr. and right on Schreiberberg. (☎682 61; fax 688 87. Open M-F 9am-6pm, Sa 9am-noon. May-Oct. also Su 10am-1pm.) **Postal Code:** 01824.

BAD SCHANDAU   ☎035022

The most bustling town in the Sächsische Schweiz, Bad Schandau (pop. 3000) offers plenty of outdoor opportunities. Take the *Kirnitzschtalbahn* trolley car (from the Markt, take Marktstr. straight, turn right on Poststr., and then left on Kirnitzschtalstr.) to the modest but pleasant **Lichtenhain waterfall,** a favorite starting point for 3 and 4hr. hikes on the **Schrammsteine.** (Trolly runs Mar.-Oct. 2 per hr. 9:30am-7pm. €3, round-trip €4.)

Bad Schandau's hotels fill up quickly when the weather is pleasant. The **Jugendherberge Bad Schandau (HI) ❷,** Dorfstr. 14, is a 30min. walk down Rudolf-Sendig-Str. (turn right after Poststr.), then a trip up the elevator (€1.25, operates daily May-Sept. 9am-7pm, Oct. 9am-6pm, Nov.-Apr. 9am-5pm.) in the huge metal tower on your left, or a walk up the path alongside it. At the top take the paved path up to the right and then follow the signs. Heavy pack? Take bus #255 from "Bad Schandau Markt" to "Ostauer Scheibe." (Buses run 10am-6pm, every hr. €1.70.) Although far from the center of town, the hostel, which has singles, doubles, and some dorms, is near several trailheads. (☎424 08; www.djh-sachsen.de. Breakfast included. All rooms €16.90, over 27 €19.90.) In a town that closes down before 11pm, **Sigl's ❸**, Kirnitzschtalstr. 17, a relaxed bar and bistro, offers food and a wide selection of beers daily from 5pm until 2am. The restaurant doubles as a **hotel ❸** that's cheaper than those by the ferry dock. (☎407 02; fax 407 87. Apr.-Oct. singles €35; doubles €60-66. Nov.-Mar. €30/44-50. MC/V.)

Bad Schandau is connected to the rest of Saxony; the **S-Bahn** runs to Dresden (1hr., 2 per hr., €5.10). To get to town from the Bad Schandau train station, take the **ferry** (every 30min. 7:50am-9:20pm, €0.90) and walk uphill to the Markt, where you'll find the **tourist office**, Markt 12. The staff finds rooms (from €18), suggests hikes, and offers German-language **tours**. (☎900 30; www.bad-schandau.de. Open Apr.-Oct. daily 9am-9pm; Nov.-Apr. M-F 9am-6pm, Sa 9am-1pm. Tours M at 9:30am.) For a **taxi**, call ☎428 85 or 43 545. Rent a **bike** at **Rund Um's Fahrradverleih**, Sebnitzer Str. 5. (☎428 83. €7.50-9 per day. Open M-F 9am-noon and 2-6pm, Sa 9am-noon.) **Spieltreff**, Kirnitzschtalstr. 2, is one of the few **Internet** access points in the region. (☎430 20. €3 per hr. Open M-F 10am-11pm, Sa-Su noon-11pm.) The **post office**, Basteiplatz 5, is at the intersection of Kirnitzschtalstr. and Rudolf-Sendig-Str. (Open M-F 9am-noon and 2-6pm, Sa 9am-noon.) **Postal Code:** 01814.

OBERLAUSITZ (UPPER LUSATIA)

Bordering two of Germany's former Warsaw Pact neighbors (Poland and the Czech Republic), Oberlausitz has worked hard to overcome the of economic stagnation it experienced prior to reunification, and has had remarkable success. Many building projects in the area have been devoted to breathing new life into long-neglected architecture and removing overbearing Socialist structures. The area around Bautzen exemplifies the successful rejuvenation of this pleasantly rural region on the edge of eastern Germany.

BUDYŠIN (BAUTZEN)   ☎03591

Millennium-old Bautzen (pop. 42,000) displays its history on every corner. Above the Spree river, the city's ancient towers guard architectural treasures, be they Gothic, Baroque, or from the *Gründerzeit*—a prosperous period of industrial expansion in the late 19th century. Ruins dating back hundreds of years attest to the ravages of war and time. Before German invasions and fortifications came to Oberlausitz in the 10th century, however, the region was settled by Slavic Sorbs (see **The Absorbing Sorbs**, p. 620), who continue to live in and around Bautzen, still speaking Sorbian and now on good terms with the former German invaders.

◪ ▇ TRANSPORTATION AND PRACTICAL INFORMATION

The **S-Bahn** runs from Dresden (1hr., 2 per hr., €9.10). To catch a **taxi**, call ☎422 22 or 451 51. The **Avis** office at the train station **rents cars**. (☎406 40. Open M-F 8am-6pm, Sa 9am-noon.) To get to the **tourist office**, Hauptmarkt 1, walk from the train station straight through Rathenaupl. and bear left onto Bahnhofstr. Pass the post office on your right and cross the street, bearing left on Karl-Marx-Str. Turn left on Reichenstr., marked by a tall white tower. Follow Reichenstr. to the Hauptmarkt, the center of Bautzen's Altstadt. The tourist office is on the right of the big yellow Rathaus. The office has accommodations listings and finds rooms in hotels, pensions, and private homes (from €20) for free. The staff also offers **city tours** (€4, call ahead for English) and free city maps. (☎420 16; www.bautzen.de. Open M-F 9am-6pm, Sa-Su 9am-3pm. Tours M-F 2 and 7pm, Sa-Su 11am and 7pm.) To learn more about the Sorbs, visit the **Sorbische Kulturinformation** office, Postpl. 2. The staff has information on cultural events and homestays with local Sorbs. (☎421 05;

IE ABSORBING SORBS

he Sorbs, Germany's only indige-
nous ethnic minority, are descendants of Slavic tribes that settled
he Spreewald and Lusatian
mountains during the 6th and 7th
centuries. Since the formation of
he Sorb nationalist movement in
.848, small Sorbish-speaking
communities have maintained
distinct identities, holding fast to
ime-honored dialects and Sorbish traditions.

The Sorbs are famous for intri-
.ately dyed Easter eggs and
Osterreited, horseback process-
sions that take place every Eas-
.er. January 25 marks the
Vogelhochzeit (Birds' Wedding),
during which costumed children
act as birds grateful for seeds left
over from a marriage celebration.

Early industrialization dealt a
blow to Sorbish communities, as
Sorbs moved into German cities
or higher-paying jobs. The Nazis
nearly wiped out Sorbish culture
by forbidding traditional practices
and terrorizing communities. Now
well integrated into German society, the Sorbs once again face the
challenge of assimilation. Despite
post-war laws protecting Sorbish
culture and language, both are in
decline: only about 60,000 people still live in Sorbish communi-
ies. Younger generations of Sorbs
are moving to big cities in vast
numbers, but many communities
organize festivals and teach Sorbish in public schools to ensure
hat Sorbish culture remains
vibrant.

www.sorben.com. Open M-F 10am-6pm.) **Zum Korn-markt**, Kornmarkt 3, offers **Internet access.** (☎27 92 52. €1-2 per hr.) The **post office** is on Postpl. (Open M-F 8:30am-6:30pm, Sa 9am-noon.) **Postal Code:** 02625.

🏠🍴 ACCOMMODATIONS AND FOOD

Built into an ancient tower, Bautzen's **Jugendherberge (HI) ❷**, Am Zwinger 1, has spacious 1- to 6- bed rooms and a terrace. From the Hauptmarkt, go up Kornstr. (right of the tourist office) and stick with it as it bends right and turns into Schulerstr.; take a left after you go through the Schülertor. (☎403 47. Break-fast included. Reception M-F 7am-8pm, Sa-Su 6-8pm. Reservations recommended. €16.40, over 27 €19.40. Cash only.) Alternatively, treat yourself to **Stephan's Wirtshaus und Pension ❸**, Schloßstr. 1. From the Hauptmarkt, head uphill with the Rathaus on your right, past Dom St. Petri, and turn left. Stephan's is a block ahead on the left. This family-run pension is centrally located and has immaculate rooms, all with phone, TV, and shower; many have bath. (☎475 90; fax 475 91. Breakfast included. Reception daily 11am-2pm and 4-9:30pm. Check-out 11am. Rooms €40, 2 or more people €20 per person. MC.)

The Fleischmarkt, behind the Rathaus, hosts a **mar-ket** (Tu and Sa 9am-1pm, Th 9am-6pm). **Grocery stores** line Karl-Marx-Str. (Most open M-F 8am-6pm, Sa 8am-noon), and the **Kornmarkt-Center** south of the Kornmarkt has many produce shops and bakeries. (☎529 80. Open M-F 9:30am-8pm, Sa 9:30am-6pm.) Immerse yourself in Sorbian tradition at **Wjelbik ❸**, Kornstr. 7. Try the traditional *Stulle* (pork sandwich; €8) or *Hochzeitsuppe* (wedding soup; €3.50), and pick up a few words of Sorbish along the way. (☎420 60. Open M-F 11am-3pm and 5-11pm, Sa-Su 11am-11pm. MC/V.) Over 400-year-old recipes (including roasted stag) and a monastic ambiance make the medieval **Mönchshof ❸**, Burglehn 1, worth a visit. (☎49 01 41. Entrées €6.70-13.50. Reservations recommended. Open M-Th 11:30am-midnight, F-Sa 11:30am-1am, Su 11:30am-11pm. AmEx/DC/MC/V.) To experience a culinary approach to natural healing, visit **Zur Apotheke ❸**, Schloßstr. 21. The restaurant prepares a wide range of meals rich in herbs (€7-11) and much tastier than the offerings of actual pharmacies. (☎48 00 35. Open daily 11am-2pm and 5pm-midnight; Nov.-Mar. daily from 11:30am, closed on M. Cash only.)

📷 SIGHTS

SORBISCHES MUSEUM. The museum details the intriguing history and culture of the Sorbs. The displays include everything from handwritten Bible translations to model houses, Easter eggs, modern Sorbian art, *Dudelsacks* (bagpipes), and Sorbish violins. *(Ortenburg 3. On Schloßstr., through the Matthiasturm. ☎424 03. Open Apr.-Oct. M-F 10am-5pm, Sa-Su 10am-6pm; Nov.-Mar. M-F 10am-4pm, Sa-Su 10am-5pm. €2.50, students and children €1.50.)*

HAUPTMARKT. This square contains the grand yellow 13th-century **Rathaus**, backed up by the **Fleischmarkt** and the Gothic **Dom St. Petri**. First consecrated in 1221, the elegant Dom became eastern Germany's only *Simultankirche* (simultaneous church) in 1524. Two sets of pews in the church look up at two altars, one Catholic and one Protestant. Each week the church switches not only religions, but also entrances: Catholic week uses a door on the southeast side and during Protestant week a door on the west side opens. Until 1952 this division was made more clear by a 4m high screen down the middle of the church. The 83m tower provides a beautiful view of the city and of the Spree. Restoration work on the Dom should be completed by Jan. 2007. *(Left from the Reichenturm and down Reichenstr. Open June-Sept. M-Sa 10am-4pm, Su 1-4pm; May and Oct. M-Sa 10am-3pm, Su 1-3pm; Nov.-Apr. M-F 11am-noon. Tower open Sa 11am-6pm, Su 1-5pm. Free.)* The **Domstift**, the flashy red-and-gold structure behind the cathedral, houses the **Domschatz** (Cathedral Treasury), a collection of jewel-studded gowns, icons, and gold regalia. Ring the bell and ask to see the *Domschatzkammer*. *(Open M-F 10am-noon and 1-4pm. Free.)*

TOWERS. Bautzen has an unusual number of towers, some offering excellent views of the city and countryside. The white **Reichenturm** (Realm Tower) is the leaning tower of Bautzen. Built in 1490, it is now a full 1.44m from perpendicular. *(At the intersection of Kornmarkt and Reichenstr. Open daily Apr.-Oct. 10am-5pm. Last entrance 4:30pm. Tours €6. Admission €1.20, students €0.90, under 14 €0.60.)* A block away you'll find the stone **Wendischer Turm**, a tower built in 1566 that once served as the city's prison. Locals claim that the ghostly face above the gate of the **Nikolaiturm**, down An der Petrikirche from the Dom and to the right on Nikolaipforte, is a likeness of a former mayor who was bricked into the tower alive for opening the city to 16th-century Hussite attackers. Next door are the eerie columns and empty window-arches of the ruined **Nikolaikirche**, destroyed in 1634 during the Thirty Years' War. To the left of the Sorbisches Museum, follow the scenic **Osterweg** and **Reymannweg** paths around the city walls above the Spree, taking in the views of the 1480 **Mühlbastei** (Mill Tower), the spire of the 1429 **Michaelskirche**, and the 1558 **Alte Wasserkunst** (Old Water Works), now a technical museum. *(Museum open daily Feb.-Dec. 10am-5pm; Jan. Sa-Su only 10am-5pm. €1.50, students €1.)*

ZITTAUER GEBIRGE (ZITTAU MOUNTAINS)

The rocky cliffs of the Zittau Mountains rise in a sliver of Germany wedged between the Czech Republic and Poland. Once a favorite spot of medieval monks, these beehive-shaped mountains are now the conquests of choice for skiers, hikers, and landscape lovers. In 1491, the region was the scene of the vicious Bierkrieg (Beer War), when incensed citizens of nearby Görlitz protested Zittau's success as a beer-brewing town by destroying barrels of the brew. Despite unemployment rates of 20%, towns like Zittau keep the area vibrant and optimistic.

ZITTAU ☎03583

At the crossroads of three nations, Zittau (pop. 26,000) has served as a trading and cultural center for many centuries. Under the rule of the Bohemian kings, Zittau took on a dominant role in Oberlausitz and was as culturally prominent as Leipzig. Home to a Lenten Veil—one of eighteen remaining in the world—Zittau proudly displays its history as it recovers from its post-DDR depression.

⚏⚐ TRANSPORTATION AND PRACTICAL INFORMATION. Trains to Dresden (1½hr., every hr., €15.90) and Görlitz (1hr., every hr., €5.60). For a **taxi** call ☎51 25 00 or hail one at Marktpl. The **tourist office**, Markt 1, on the first floor of the Rathaus near the left side entrance, finds rooms (from €15) for free, provides free city maps and runs tours. From the train station, take Bahnhof Str. down the hill; continue straight on Bautzen Str. until you reach the Hauptmarkt and the yellow Rathaus on your left. (☎75 21 378; www.zittau.de. Open M-F 8am-6pm, Sa 9am-1pm; June-Sept. also Su 1-4pm.) Zittau is a starting point for the 115km **Upper Lusatian Mountain Path;** ask at the tourist office where to pick up the trail. A **pharmacy, Johannis Apotheke,** is at Johannisstr. 2, across the Marktpl. from the tourist office. (☎51 21 64. Open M-F 8am-6pm, Sa 8am-noon.) **Computer-Nutzer Laden,** Rosa-Luxembourg-Str. 34, offers **Internet** access. Turn left off Bahnhofstr. onto the Theaterring and follow it until Rosa-Luxembourg-Str. leads off to the left. (€3 per hr. Open Tu-Su 3pm-midnight, later F-Su.) A **post office** is at Haberkornpl. 1 and has a 24hr. **ATM.** (Open M-F 9am-6:30pm, Sa 9am-noon.) **Postal Code:** 02763.

⚏⚐ ACCOMMODATIONS AND FOOD. There are no HI hostels in Zittau, but the tourist office books rooms (from €15) for free. Book at least a week in advance in summer. A good option is **Pension Zwahr ❷,** Theodor-Korselt-Str. 10. From the station take Bahnhofstr. and make a left onto Theodor-Korselt-Str. All the rooms have bathrooms with showers. (☎51 12 50. Singles €26; doubles €38. Cash only.) The homey **Zimmervermietung Francke ❷,** Suedstr. 3, is in a quiet residential neighborhood 20min. from the Markt. From the train station, walk down Bahnhofstr. until you hit Toepferberg, then turn right and walk around the ring surrounding the city until you come to Aeussere Oybiner Str. Make a right, and then another right onto Haelterg. Bear left around a bend in the road, and then turn right onto Suedstr. Large rooms decorated with hearts and banners help make up for the clean—but barely curtained—street-level bathroom. (☎70 69 18. Reception 7am-8pm daily. Singles €25; doubles €40. Cash only.) For German cuisine amid hundreds of old clocks, head to **Seeger Schänke ❸,** Innere Weberstr. 38. (☎51 09 80. Entrées €5.40-12.50. Open daily 11am-2pm and from 6pm. Cash only.) The **Savi Café and Bar ❷,** Bautzner Str. 10, serves salads, pasta, traditional dishes (€3.50-7), and hearty breakfasts and offers Internet access. (☎70 82 97. Internet €2.40 per hr. Open M-F 9am-midnight, Sa noon-midnight, Su 2:30pm-midnight. Cash only.) **Filmsiß ❷,** Markt 8, decorated with movie posters and film reels, is a café that offers small entrées and cakes (€1.20-2.90) by day and an extensive drink list by night. (☎79 47 51. Open Tu-Th noon-11pm, F-Sa noon-1am, Su 2-6pm. Cash only.) Zittau also has a **Mensa ❶** at the intersection of Hochwaldstr. and Theodor-Koerner-Allee. Deposit €7 to get your own card, and then load it up with money for meals (€1.50-3). (Open M-Th 11am-2:15pm, F 11am-2pm.)

◪ SIGHTS. The **▨Museum der Kirche zum heiligen Kreuz** (Museum of the Church of the Holy Cross), Frauenstr. 23, at the corner of Theatterring and Frauenstr., houses an extremely rare **Lenten Veil** dating from 1472. With 90 panels displaying scenes from the Old and New Testaments, the gigantic painted curtain was used to shield the clergy and altar from the "unworthy" fasting churchgoers during Lent. The third largest Lenten Veil in Europe, the tapestry is marred by a huge steam stain from just after WWII, when some oblivious Russian soldiers used it as the roof of their open-air sauna. (Open Apr.-Oct. daily 10am-6pm, Nov.-Mar. Tu-Su 10am-5pm. German tours every hr. 10am-4pm. Last entry 30min. before closing.

€4, students and seniors €2.) Most of the other interesting sights are in **Altstadt**, around Marktpl. and Johannispl. **Johanniskirche,** originally built in 1255, was destroyed in 1757 by Prussian bombs and rebuilt in Baroque style. (☎51 09 33. Open M-F 10am-6pm, Sa-Su 10am-4pm.) Climb up its **Aussichtsturm** (lookout) for a view of the Zittauer Gebirge. (Open to visitors in pairs or groups M-F noon-6pm, Sa-Su 10am-4pm. €1.50, children €1.) From the church, walk directly down Bautzner Str. to reach the grand **Marktpl.** The yellow **Rathaus** was designed by Prussian architect Friedrich Schinkel in 1843. From the Rathaus, walk up Johannisstr., and follow it as it curves right, ending in Klosterpl. There you'll find the late Gothic **Klosterkirche** and the adjoining **Stadtmuseum** (Municipal Museum), housed in a former 13th-century Franciscan monastery stocked with medieval torture devices. (☎55 47 90. Open daily 10am-6pm. €2, students €1.50.) In a small park along Karl-Liebknecht ring is the **Blumenuhr**, a clock made entirely of flowers.

⚡ OUTDOOR ACTIVITIES. The dramatic Zittau Mountains offer travelers vast opportunities for exploration amid volcanic peaks and densely forested valleys. Over 300km of hiking trails traverse the mountains. A number of them can be can be reached from Zittau. Otherwise take the ZOJE steam train to the resort towns of Oybin or Jonsdorf. Ask at the Zittau tourist office for times and prices. To find accommodations in these towns call the tourist offices: Oybin ☎035844 733 11; Jonsdorf ☎035844 706 16. Bikers have no shortage of options in the Zittau Mountains. You can rent a bike in Zittau at Fahrrad Rother, Ottokarpl. 10 (☎70 23 27) or in Jonsdorf at Fahrrad Donath, Zittauer Str. 46 (☎035844 701 71).

Nießtal-Kloster St. Marienthal (38km). Begins in Zittau at Martin-Wehnert-Pl. and runs parallel to the Nisa river along the Polish border to Ostritz, then around to Schlegel, south to Hirschfelde, and back to Zittau. Includes the beautiful Kloster St. Marienthal.

Schloß Lemberk (26km). Begins in Jonsdorf and heads to the Czech border, then to Krompach, Hermanice, and the Schloß Lemberk; finally around to Petrovice, and back to Jonsdorf by way of the Oybin castle ruins.

CHEMNITZ ☎0371

For those interested in the history of the East German *Deutsche Demokratische Republik* (DDR), a visit to Chemnitz is a must. As the DDR's center of industry, Chemnitz was taken over by massive new developments on the *Str. der Nationen* (Street of Nations), and was even renamed Karl-Marx Stadt in 1952. As a result, the *Wende* (the "turn" of reunification) has been particularly challenging for Chemnitz, which struggles to rebuild its industry on capitalist terms.

▟ 🛈 TRANSPORTATION AND PRACTICAL INFORMATION

Trains run to: Dresden (1½hr., every hr., €11.70); Görlitz (3½hr., every hr., €25.80); Leipzig (1hr., every hr., €13.40); Prague (4½hr., 5 per day, €36). For a **taxi,** call ☎330 03 33. Chemnitz is connected by a system of trams and buses, almost all of which stop at "Zentralhalestelle" in the city center. The **bus station** is just a short walk down Georgstr. from the train station. Tickets are available at major stops and on every bus or tram. A *Kurzstrecke* ticket (€1) covers up to four stops, an *Einzelfahrt* ticket (€1.60) covers all rides within 1hr., and a *Tageskarte* (day pass; €2.90) is valid until 6am the next morning. To get from the train station to the city center, head straight down Georgstr. or Carolastr. After a block, you'll come to Str. der Nationen, the city's north-south axis. Turn left to get to the **tourist office,** Markt 1, in the Rathaus, which finds private rooms (from €13) for free, leads city **tours** (€5), and has free maps. (☎ 69 06 80; fax 690 68 30. Open M-F 10am-8pm, Sa 10am-3pm.) Check email at **Café Soleil**, Hainstr. 106. (☎ 651 38 99. €3.60 per hr. Open M-F noon-11pm, Sa-Su 3-11pm.) The **post office** is at Str. der Nationen 2-4. (Open M-F 9am-7pm, Sa 9am-2pm.) **Postal Code:** 09009.

🏠🍴 ACCOMMODATIONS AND FOOD

Pension Art Nouveau ❸, Hainstr. 130, is a 15min. walk from the station. Take an immediate right from Georgstr. onto Mauerstr. and go under the tunnel at the end on the right; turn left out of the tunnel and right immediately on Lessingstr., then left on Hainstr. You'll find clean, pleasant, uniformly furnished rooms with TV. Most have private baths, some have kitchens. (☎ 402 50 72; fax 402 50 73. Breakfast included. Check-in after 10am. Check-out 11am. Singles from €35; doubles €45. MC.) There's always a room at the massive **Hotel Europark ❷,** Schulstr. 38, which has both dorms and lavish hotel accommodations. From the station take tram #6 (dir.: Altchemnitz) 20min. to "Altchemnitz Center." Facing in the opposite direction of the train, turn left on Zöblitzerstr. The hotel is at the end of the street. (☎ 522 83 41. Reception 7am-3pm; information center open 24hr. Hostel: singles €16-21; doubles €28-31. Hotel: singles €33-38; doubles €40-44. AmEx/MC/V.) The **Jugendherberge (HI) ❷,** Augustusburgerstr. 369, is inexpensive but far-flung. Tram #5 (dir.: Gablenz) runs from "Brückenstr." to "Pappelhain." Follow the well-marked path for 30min., and take a left on Augustusburgerstr. During the week, bus #704 runs to "Walter-Kippel-Str.," right next to the hostel. (45min., every 2hr. M-F 8am-5pm, €1.60.) Many rooms have views of the surrounding farmland. (☎ 713 31. Reception daily 7am-9pm. Breakfast included. Check-in noon. Check-out 10am. €15.90, over 27 €17.80. MC.)

For a quick bite, *Imbiße* (snack bars) and a fresh market (Th-Sa mornings) surround the **Rathaus** at the end of Str. der Nationen. Larger appetites can be satisfied at the restaurants on the *Brühl*, a quiet pedestrian zone off Georgstr., or along Str. der Nationen near the Rathaus. **Turm Brauhaus ❷,** Neumarkt 2, serves heaping portions of German food (entrées €4-10). Try the house brews: the light Pils-like *Hellen*, or the sweeter *Kupfer* (both €1.40); or, treat yourself to a €15 brewery tour, including 0.5L to take home. (☎ 909 50 95. Open M-Th and Su 9am-1am, F-Sa 9am-3am. Cash only.) **Pizzeria Dolomiti ❷,** Str. der Nationen 12, sits between a McDonald's and a Marx statue. Enjoy a personal pizza for €3.40, or pasta for €4.70-6.90. (☎ 444 77 96. Open daily 11am-midnight. Cash only.) **Heck-Art ❷,** Mühlenstr. 2, is a hybrid gallery, chic bar, and bohemian café with a delicious lunch menu (€3.50-9.50) and an exhibition space upstairs. (☎ 694 68 18. Open daily 11am-1am. Kitchen closes at midnight. AmEx/MC/V.)

👁 SIGHTS

Chemnitz's former identity as **Karl-Marx-Stadt** is embodied in the politically charged works of art along the **Straße der Nationen.** Statues of frolicking children or happily scrubbed workers are everywhere, inscribed with cautionary messages like "the Party has a thousand eyes." No statue outshines the **head of Karl Marx,** an enormous, angular concrete chunk that's especially intimidating when lit at night. Also along the Str. der Nationen is the quiet **Theaterplatz,** bordered on three sides by large, serene buildings. Straight ahead is the 1992 **opera house,** a product of the early 90s push to build a new Chemnitz. To the right is the **Petrikirche,** first opened in 1888 and continually, painstakingly refurbished since 1992. On the left stands the **Kunstsammlungen Chemnitz,** an art museum that features a sampling of 19th- and 20th-century German art, and a huge collection of paintings and woodcuts by local Expressionist Karl Schmidt-Rotluff. (☎ 488 44 10; www.chemnitz.de/kunstsammlungen. Open Tu-Su noon-7pm. €5, students €2.50.) In a reconstructed castle that was destroyed in the Thirty Years' War, the **Schloßbergmuseum** includes an impressive collection of medieval art and a historical exhibit on the 800-year-old city. (☎488 45 01. Open Tu-F 1-8pm, Sa noon-11pm, Su 10am-6pm.) For a breath of fresh air, walk back to town through **Schloßteich**, a park centered on a lake across from the *Schloß*, or paddle around the lake itself (boats €3.70-6.40 per hr.). The **Museum für Naturkunde Chemnitz** (Natural History Museum), housed in the TIETZ shopping complex, shows what Chemnitz was like before the industrial invasion. Be sure to check out the petrified forest, discovered on location. (☎48 84 551. Open Th-Tu 10am-8pm. €4, students €2.50.)

ENTERTAINMENT AND NIGHTLIFE

The **Theater Chemnitz** dominates Chemnitz's high culture scene with opera, ballet, music, theater, puppet shows, and its annual production of Wagner's "Ring" opera. Tickets are available at the Theater-Service, Käthe-Kollwitz-Str. 7, behind the Theaterpl. museums. (☎696 96 96. Open M-F 9am-4:30pm. Tickets €9-48, 50% student discount if there are tickets left right before the show.) Though not known for nightlife, Chemnitz offers more dance venues than any neighboring towns, including **Fuchsbau**, Carolastr. 8. (☎67 17 17; www.fuchsbau.de. Open W, F and Sa 10pm-late.) **Heck-Art** (see **Accommodations and Food,** p. 624), which functions as a bar as the night progresses, is a little more refined.

DAYTRIP FROM CHEMNITZ: AUGUSTUSBURG

A day at the **Schloß** in Augustusburg will help you recover from post-industrial, post-Marx, monochromatic Chemnitz. At 516m above the town, this Renaissance **hunting lodge** of the Saxon electors gives a mesmerizing 360° panorama of the surrounding **Erzgebirge** (Ore Range) mountains—the Czech Republic is even visible on the horizon. At the castle, wander through the spacious courtyards or, to see inside, take a guided tour of the royal playhouse, which leads through the **Brunnenhaus** (well house) and the intimate **Schloßkapelle** (chapel), the only Renaissance chapel left in Saxony. The altar was painted by Cranach the Younger. (Tours €3, students €2.20.) Also here is a **Motorradmuseum** (Motorcycle Museum), which documents the history of the motorcycle since its invention in the late 19th century, with everything from early models to shiny BMWs from the 1980s, and racing video games at the end. If you prefer to travel in style, check out the **Kutschenmuseum** (Carriage Museum); the 1790 carriage is a palace on wheels. The **Museum für Jagdtier- und Vogelkunde des Erzgebirges** (Hunting and Game Museum) features dioramas of local game and ornate weapons. You can also visit the low-ceilinged **castle dungeon** to cringe at medieval torture apparati. (*Schloß* open daily Apr.-Oct. 9:30am-6pm; Nov.-Mar. 10am-5pm. Last entry 30min. before closing. Each museum €1.60-3.20, students €1.20-2.40. Day pass for all 4 €6.60, students €5.) The eagles and falcons that live at the *Schloß* swoop and dive in falconry exhibitions. (45min. Tu-Su 11am and 3pm. €5, students €4.50.)

The real treat of a visit to Augustusburg is the ◙**Jugendherberge (HI) ❷**, inside the castle. Thanks to recent renovations, you'll find immaculate woodwork and spotless washrooms. Best of all, the serene castle grounds are just out the door. Most rooms have 10-14 beds; singles and 2- and 4-bed rooms are also available. Call in advance as rooms are in high demand. (☎202 56. Breakfast included. Reception 7am-11pm. Check-in after 3pm. Check-out 10am. Curfew 10pm, but keys are available. Mid-Mar. to Oct.: 4- to 14-bed rooms €14.90; singles €25; doubles €44; over 27 €17.90/28/50. Nov. to mid-Mar. all prices €2 less per person. 1 night stays €1.50 extra. Cash only.) Get dinner and a drink in the candlelit **Augustuskeller ❹**, an original castle cellar. (☎207 40. Entrées from €7.90. Open Tu-Sa 11am-9pm, Su 11am-6pm. AmEx/DC/MC/V.)

Augustusburg hamlet can be reached by **bus** #704 (dir.: Augustusburg) or #705 (dir.: Eppendorf) from the Chemnitz *Busbahnhof*. (40min., 6:20am-5:10pm, €4.50.) The bus stops at the foot of the path to the castle. **Trains** also travel to Erdmannsdorf, located just down the mountain from Augustusburg (20min., 6am-10pm, €2.40). The castle is a beautiful 3km walk uphill. On weekends and holidays, a bus also runs from Chemnitz right up to the entrance of the *Schloß* itself. (30min., every 2hr. 8:30am-4:30pm, €1.60.) **Phone Code:** ☎037291.

OLBERNHAU ☎037360

Known as the "Stadt der sieben Täler" (City of Seven Valleys), Olbernhau rests on the banks of the river Flöha in the middle of the Erzgebirge (Ore Mountains). When large deposits of precious metals were discovered here in the 15th century, Olbernhau became an outpost on the Silver Trail, a road connecting the area's mining towns from Dresden to Zwickau. Although most of the profits from local mines financed the projects of kings like August the Strong, Olbernhau developed as a thriving trade city, known for its wood and metal handicrafts. Visitors can gawk at machinery once used to hammer raw ore into metal, or watch locals carve their wares. Olbernhau's location on the Flöha also makes it a great starting place for hikes through the wooded landscape of the Erzgebirge mountains or daytrips to nearby Seiffen.

■ TRANSPORTATION AND PRACTICAL INFORMATION. Olbernhau can be reached by **bus** from Chemnitz (1½hr.; M-F every hr. 5am-8pm, Sa-Su every 2hr. 6:30am-8pm; €5.20). Rent **bikes** from **Zweirad Sport,** Am Gessingpl. 4, just to the left of the bus station. (☎725 73. €5-7 per day. Open M-F 9am-6pm, Sa 9am-noon.) The **tourist office,** Grünthalerstr. 28, is located in the Rathaus. From the bus station, turn right on August-Bebel-Str.; it's on your right just before the river. The staff finds rooms (from €11) for free, hands out city maps, and sells a hiking map of the region (€1) marked with trail recommendations. (☎151 35; www.olbernhau.de. Open M-W and F 9am-5pm, Th 9am-6pm, Sa 9am-noon.) Just down the street is a **pharmacy, Herz-Apotheke,** Grünthalerstr. 16. (☎725 22; fax 723 03. Open M-F 8am-6pm, Sa 8am-noon.) **Fair Play,** Grünthalerstr. 107, offers **Internet** access. (☎272 74. €2 per hr. Open daily 10am-11pm.) **Sparkasse,** in the bus station, has 24hr. **ATMs.** The **post office,** Bahnhofstr. 1, is down the street from the bus station. (Open M-F 9am-6pm, Sa 9am-11:30pm.) **Postal Code:** 09526.

■ ACCOMMODATIONS AND FOOD. Although there are no hostels in Olbernhau, a number of pensions and private rooms provide budget accommodations. **Pension Weick ❷,** Töpferg. 18, has comfortable beds in rooms overlooking a garden terrace. From the bus station, turn right onto August-Bebel-Str. and follow it until it ends just after you cross the river. Turn left on Gerber-G. and bear right onto Töpferg.; the pension is on the right. Rooms have telephone, TV, and shower, but be sure to call early—there are only four rooms. (☎752 15. Breakfast included. Singles €20; doubles €38. Cash only.) Although more expensive, **Pension Berggasse ❸,** Bergg. 2, offers spacious rooms with phone, TV, and shower near the town center. From the bus station, turn right on August-Bebel-Str. Cross the bridge, turn left, and then immediately turn right on Bergg. (☎66 01 12; fax 66 01 13. Breakfast included. Reception daily 7am-10pm. Check-in 2pm. Checkout 10am. Singles €27; doubles €50. MC/V.) In between the town center and Saigerhuette, the ivy-decorated **Philipp's Pizzeria ❷,** Grünthalerstr. 45, serves pizzas and pastas for €3.40-7.70. (☎72 419. Open daily 11am-2pm and 5-11pm. MC.)

For an elegant meal in a historic location, try **Restaurant Hüttenschänke ❸**, In der Hütte, in the Saigerhütte museum. Tuxedo-clad waiters serve both traditional German fare and inventive dishes. (☎78 70. Entrées €7-15. Open daily 11am-10pm. AmEx/DC/MC/V.)

◪ SIGHTS. The 500-year-old **Saigerhütte**, once the center of the copper industry in Saxony, is now a museum and demonstration space for the crafts that make the Erzgebirge famous. In the **Althammer**, huge hammers, each weighing over half a ton, once pounded sheets of metal to a thickness of 0.03mm. The complex also houses an open workshop in the foundations of one of the original buildings, a series of old huts where visitors can watch workers spin wool or carve intricate wooden figurines by hand, and a **museum** on the history of the Saigerhütte. (☎733 67. Open Mar.-Oct. Tu-Su 9:30-11:30am and 1-4pm. Ask for an English audio guide to the Althammer; free with entry. Tours of the Althammer every hr. Last tour 4pm. €2, students and seniors €1. Other sections of the complex free.) **Haus der Heimat** (Local History Museum), Markt 7, documents the region's history and has a small but entertaining collection of mechanically animated miniature ferris wheels and town squares. (☎721 80. Open Tu-F 10:30am-4:30pm, Sa-Su noon-4:30pm. Last entry 4pm. Call tourist office for prices and information on special exhibits.) Many Olbernhau shops sell the town's characteristic wooden handicrafts. Watch townspeople carve the products they sell at **Schauwerkstatt**, Neuestr. 19, or peruse shelves of miniatures, nutcrackers, and the region's famous *Räuchermänner* (smoking-men) in the **Kunstgewerbe-Werkstätten**, Sandweg 3.

SEIFFEN   ☎ 037362

Situated in the heart of the Erzgebirge mountains and world-famous for the toys it has produced since 1750, Seiffen draws thousands of tourists every year to its workshops. Once a mining town, Seiffen's inhabitants turned to wood-working after its mineral resources dwindled in the 17th century. Over the years the imagination of Seiffen's toymakers have allowed this small village to flourish, and its toy museum enthralls both young and old with the beautiful, intricate, and sometimes gargantuan toys the town has produced.

⚏🚍 TRANSPORTATION AND PRACTICAL INFORMATION. Seiffen is accessible by **bus** #453 from Olbernhau, which stops at both the toy museum and "Seiffen Mitte," just a block away from the tour-

THE HIDDEN DEAL

IN ROYAL FOOTSTEPS

In the 18th century, Saxon Elector and King of Poland August the Strong toured the small villages in the Erzgebirge to watch the locals produce the handicrafts and mining the silver that made the region famous (and made August wealthy).

Today, anyone can follow August's footsteps during the seven-day *Kultur Wandern ohne Gepäck* (Cultural Hike Without Luggage). The week begins in Pobershau, passes through Olbernhau, and ends in Seiffen, catching all the important sights in each town. Best of all, hikers never have to carry their luggage; the organizers transport it separately.

The whole week costs €153 for six nights of lodging in private rooms, admission to the sights in every town, and a guide to regale you every step of the way. The hike is a great way to see the towns of the Erzgebirge and the stunning (but often overlooked) landscapes along the way, but be sure to plan ahead; you have to reserve your spot at least six weeks before departure.

(For more information, contact the Seiffen Tourist Office (☎037362 84 38; www.seiffen.de; open M-F 9am-5pm, Sa 9am-1pm). Booking service Apr.-Oct. Min. 5 travelers per hike.)

ist office (30min.; M-F every hr. 6:30am-8pm, Sa every 2hr. 9:50am-8pm, Su 9:50am, 2:50 and 4:25pm; €2.60). Rent **bikes** from **Sportwelt Preußler,** Hauptstr. 199. (☎888 50; www.sportwelt-preussler.de. €7-9 per day. Open M-F 9am-6pm, Sa 9am-noon.) The **tourist office,** Hauptstr. 95, hands out maps, recommends hikes, and finds rooms for free. From the Seiffen Mitte bus stop, walk downhill about 100m, and the office will be on your left. (☎84 38; www.seiffen.de. Open M-F 9am-5pm, Sa 9am-1pm.) **Sparkasse,** just down the street from the tourist office, has 24hr. **ATMs. Geschenkstube,** Bahnhofstr. 8, a handicrafts shop, houses the **post office** and offers **Internet** access. (1st 30min. €2.50, €2 per 30min. thereafter. Open M-F 9am-6pm, Sa 9am-1pm.) **Postal Code:** 09548.

◪◪ ACCOMMODATIONS AND FOOD. Due to the large tourist population, inexpensive accommodations are difficult to find in Seiffen. The tourist office finds private rooms (€12-20) for free. **Pension Diana ❸,** Steinhübel 21, is located on the edge of town but offers a spectacular view from 700m. From the "Seiffen Mitte" bus stop, walk down Hauptstr. and turn right up Bahnhofstr. At the post office, take a right up Glashüttenweg and walk 20min., then turn left on Steinhübelstr. Every room has a TV and shower. (☎82 86; www.diana-pension.de. Breakfast included. Singles €27; doubles €52. Cash only.) Although expensive, **Hotel Erbgericht ❹,** Hauptstr. 94, is situated in the middle of town. From "Seiffen Mitte" head downhill on Hauptstr.; it will be on your right after 100m. Miniature wooden figures greet you in the hotel's red-carpeted hallways. All rooms have TV, phone, shower or bath, and sauna access. (☎77 60; www.erzgebirgshotels.de. Breakfast included. Reception 24hr. Check-in 2pm. Check-out 11am. Jan.-Aug. singles €45, doubles €69; Sept.-Nov. €50/79; Dec. €57.50/94.) To reach the **Campingpark Ahornberg Seiffen ❶,** Deutschneudorferstr. 57, from "Seiffen Mitte," head left and downhill on Hauptstr. Turn left on Deutschneudorferstr. Although far from town, the campsite has a sauna, volleyball courts, and minigolf. (☎150; www.ahornberg-seiffen.de. €5 per person, €5 per plot; tent rental €8-10. AmEx/DC/MC/V.)

Cafés and restaurants line the entire length of Hauptstr. as it winds through town. **Backerei-Konditorei-Café Barthel ❶,** Hauptstr. 85, just down the street from the tourist office, offers delicious pastries (€0.70-1.50) and small dishes (€2-6). (☎761 16. Open M-Sa 6am-6pm, Su 1-6pm. Cash only.) **Café Buntes Haus ❸,** Hauptstr. 94, by Hotel Erbgericht, serves delicious regional specialties. (☎82 23. Entrées €4-13.50. Open daily 10am-10pm. AmEx/DC/MC/V.)

◪ SIGHTS. Seiffen's ◪**Spielzeug Museum** (Toy Museum), Hauptstr. 73, is without question the biggest attraction in the town. Three floors of toys and exhibitions detail the history of toy production in Seiffen and of the skillful toymakers who made it all possible. See over 5000 miniatures, nutcrackers, pyramids, chandeliers, and *Räuchermänner* (smoking men) from the past few centuries, including the 4m pyramid on the first floor; you can even play with some of them as you go. (☎82 39; www.spielzeugmuseum-seiffen.de. Open daily 9am-5pm. €3, students and seniors €2.50, under 13 €1.50. English guide €1.) To see how the Spielzeug Museum's wares are made, visit the ◪**Schauwerkstatt** (Demonstration Workshop), Hauptstr. 80. Stand inches away from the cutting, carving, drilling, gluing, and meticulous painting that goes into creating Seiffen's world-famous toys. (☎180. Open M-Sa 10am-12:30pm and 1-4pm. €1.30, students €0.65.) At the **Freilicht Museum** (Open-Air Museum), Hauptstr. 203, workers demonstrate traditional carving techniques. The museum also sells everything from scraps of wood to painted dioramas of the *Fall of Eden.* (☎83 88. Open daily 9am-5pm. €2.50, students €2.) Those not included to walking can take the **Bimmelbahn** train on a tour through the village and the surrounding areas. Beginning at the Spielzeug Museum, the 35min. tram ride highlights the important sights in town and drives to the surrounding villages for a view of the town from above. Hop off at the Freilicht Museum, then catch the next tram back to town. (☎86 87; www.bimmelbahn.net. Runs daily approx. every 45min. 10:30am-3:45pm. €2.50, children €1.50.) On the tour, you'll also drive by Seiffen's **Rundkirche**, Am Reicheltberg, an octagonal church built in the mid-18th century. Boasting a beautiful blue-and-white interior, the building contains the altar and chandeliers of its 16th-century predecessor. (Open daily 1-3pm. Tours daily at noon.)

WORTH THE WALK. Seiffen is filled with shops selling wooden handicrafts and toys. Although the stores lining Hauptstr. are the largest and most convenient, shops sequestered on the twisting side roads have cheaper prices.

LEIPZIG   ☎0341

Leipzig is the perfect German university city: large enough to have a life beyond academia, yet not so big that the influence of its students is diluted. Surrounded by a ring road, Leipzig might appear small on the map, but it's bursting at the seams with activity: music lovers, art critics, club fanatics, and adventure seekers meet here to satisfy their passions. Once home to Bach, Mendelssohn, Wagner, Nietzsche, Goethe, and Leibniz, the city enjoys an exceptionally rich cultural tradition and boasts world-class museums, churches, and restaurants.

█ TRANSPORTATION

Flights: Flughafen Leipzig-Halle (☎22 40), on Schkeuditzg., is 20km from Leipzig with international service throughout Europe. Outbound trains stop at the airport. (From the Hauptbahnhof, 15min., 2 per hr. 4am-11:50pm, €3.40.)

Trains: To: **Berlin** (1-2½hr., every hr., €26-36); **Dresden** (1-1½hr., 2 per hr., €18-26); **Frankfurt** (3½hr., every hr., €61); **Munich** (5hr., every 2hr., €74). Information counter near track 15, or in the Reisezentrum (travel center) at the entrance of the station.

Public Transportation: Information ☎194 49. Trams and buses cover the city; the hub is in front of the Hauptbahnhof. A *Kurzstrecke* ticket covers up to 4 stops (€1.50); a regular ticket covers all rides within 1hr. (€1.70). A *Tageskarte* (day card) is valid until 4am the day after purchase (€4.90). Weekly (€14.30) and monthly (€42.50) cards are valid until midnight of the last day. Tickets available from the tourist office, kiosks, the vending machines at major stops, and on some trams. Night buses (every hr.; look for the "N" prefix) take over after midnight. All night buses leave from the Hauptbahnhof.

Taxis: ☎48 84, 710 00, or 42 33. Toll-free ☎0800 800 42 33.

Car Rental: Avis, Europcar, Hertz, and **Sixt-Budget** have counters at the Hauptbahnhof's *Reisezentrum*. More offices at the airport.

Ride Share: Mitfahrzentrale, Goethestr. 7-10 (☎194 40), past the tourist office. To: **Berlin** (€13); **Dresden** (€8); **Frankfurt** (€23); **Munich** (€24). Open daily 8am-8pm.

Hitchhiking: *Let's Go* does not recommend hitchhiking as a safe mode of transportation. Hitchers going to Dresden and Prague report taking tram #3 (dir.: Taucha) to "Portitzer Allee" and continuing on Torgauerstr. to the Autobahn interchange. Those going to Berlin take tram #8 or 15 (dir.: Miltitz) to "Lindenauer Markt," switch to bus #131, get out at "Dölzig, Holl. Mühle," and walk to the Autobahn.

█ █ ORIENTATION AND PRACTICAL INFORMATION

Leipzig's **Innenstadt** lies within a ring of about a kilometer in diameter, which encloses most of the sights and nightlife as well as the university. On the Innen-

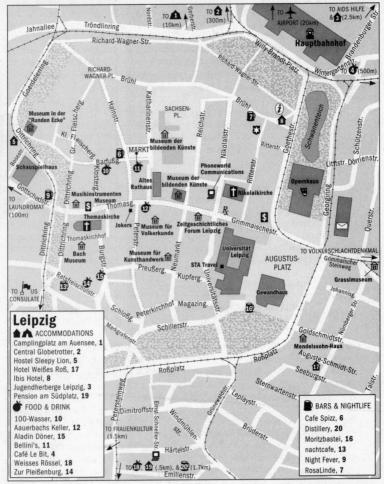

Leipzig

▲ ⌂ ACCOMMODATIONS

Camplingplatz am Auensee, **1**
Central Globetrotter, **2**
Hostel Sleepy Lion, **5**
Hotel Weißes Roß, **17**
Ibis Hotel, **8**
Jugendherberge Leipzig, **3**
Pension am Südplatz, **19**

🍴 FOOD & DRINK

100-Wasser, **10**
Aauerbachs Keller, **12**
Aladin Döner, **15**
Bellini's, **11**
Café Le Bit, **4**
Weisses Rössel, **18**
Zur Pleißenburg, **14**

🍸 BARS & NIGHTLIFE

Cafe Spizz, **6**
Distillery, **20**
Moritzbastei, **16**
nachtcafe, **13**
Night Fever, **9**
RosaLinde, **7**

stadt's north edge (a 10min. walk from the center of the Markt), the cavernous **Hauptbahnhof,** with three underground stories of shopping (most stores open M-Sa 9:30am-10pm), was Europe's largest train station before Berlin's Lehrter Bahnhof opened in 2006. **Augustuspl.** and the university are to the east of the Markt, and the striking **Thomaskirche** lies to the west.

Tourist Office: Richard-Wagner-Str. 1 (☎ 710 42 60; www.leipzig.de). From the Haupt-bahnhof, walk across Willy-Brandt-Pl., continue across the landscaped area, and turn left at Richard-Wagner-Str. Books rooms, distributes free maps, sells theater tickets and the **Leipzig Card,** good for free public transport and discounted museums (1-day, until 4am, €7.90; 3-day €16.50). Open M-F 10am-7pm, Sa 10am-4pm, Su 10am-2pm.

Tours: The tourist office leads German and English bus tours daily at 10:30am (2hr.; €12) and 1:30pm (2½hr.; €15, seniors and students €11). Themed walking tours daily, some in English (2hr., €6-8). For information call ☎ 710 42 80.

Budget Travel: STA Travel (☎211 42 20), in the corner of the university courtyard nearest Universitätsstr. Open M-F 10am-7pm, Sa 10am-2pm.

Consulate: US, Wilhelm-Seyferth-Str. 4 (☎213 84 18). Cross the Innenstadt ring behind the Neues Rathaus and follow Tauchnitzstr. until Wilhelm-Seyferth comes up on the left. The entrance is through Grassistr., the next street to the left.

Currency Exchange: Commerzbank, Thomaskirche 22, across the street from the church. Open M and W 9am-4pm, Tu and Th 9am-6pm, F 9am-1pm. Also has **ATMs.**

Women's Resources: Frauenkultur, Windscheidstr. 51 (☎213 00 30; www.frauenkultur.leipzig.w4w.net), is a center for art, meetings, and leisure. Take tram #9, 10, or 11 to "Connewitz, Kreuz," then make a right onto Selneckerstr. and turn right again onto Windscheidstr.; the building is located in 1st alley on the right. Office open M-F 9am-2pm, later for afternoon events. Runs evening women's café; call ahead for schedule.

Gay and Lesbian Resources: AIDS-Hilfe, Ossietzkystr. 18 (☎232 31 27; info@leipzig.aidshilfe.de). Take tram #1 (dir.: Schönefeld/Stannebeinpl.) to "Ossietzkystr./Gorkistr." The complex features a popular café (open Tu and Th 5-10pm), and distributes the magazine *gegenpol,* which has gay information for all of Saxony. Office open M and W 10am-6pm, Tu and Th 10am-10pm, F 10am-2pm. **Rosalinde** (p. 636) offers a variety of activities and support groups for GLBT individuals.

Home Share: Mitwohnzentrale, ☎194 30, in the same office as the **Mitfahrzentrale** (p. 629). Arranges long-term accommodations. Open daily 9am-7pm.

Bookstore: Jokers, in the Marktgalerie at Markt 12 (☎268 94 77), sells many English-language books. (Open M-Sa 10am-8pm.)

Laundromat: Maga Pon, Gottschedstr. 11 (☎337 37 82). Sip espresso (€1.50) while you wash your clothes at this hip café. Breakfast 10am-3pm (€3.50-8). Wash €3.50. Dry €1.50 per hr. Open daily 10am-midnight or later.

Emergency: Police ☎110. **Fire and Ambulance** ☎112.

Pharmacy: Löwen-Apotheke, Grimmaischestr. 19 (☎960 50 27). Open M-F 8am-8pm, Sa 9am-4pm.

Internet Access: Phoneworld Communications, Nikolaistr. 40 (☎230 82 68). €1 per 40min., €1.50 per hr. Open daily 9am-midnight.

Post Office: Augustuspl. 1-4, across from the Opernhaus on Grimmaische Steinweg. Open M-F 9am-8pm, Sa 9am-3pm. **Postal Code:** 04109.

ACCOMMODATIONS AND CAMPING

Hostel Sleepy Lion, Käthe-Kollwitz-Str. 3 (☎993 94 80; www.hostel-leipzig.de). A 10min. walk from the station; cross the street and turn right onto Richard-Wagner-Str. At its end, cross the overpass directly ahead and turn left. Follow Gördelerring until Käthe-Kollwitz-Str. branches off to the right. Or, take tram #1 (dir.: Lausen) or #14 (dir.: S-Bahnhof Plagwitz) to "Gottschedstr." Operated by young locals and close to nightlife, the Sleepy Lion draws an international crowd. Spacious rooms have personal lockers and shower. Sheets €2. Breakfast €3. Internet access €2 per hr. Bike rental €5 per day. Reception 24hr. 6- to 8-bed dorms €14-15; singles €28; doubles €40; quads €64. AmEx/MC/V. ❶

Central Globetrotter, Kurt-Schumacher-Str. 41 (☎149 89 60; www.globetrotter-leipzig.de). From the train station, take the west exit and turn right onto Kurt-Schumacher-Str. Wild spray-paint designs cover the walls of this clean hostel, run by the same people as the Sleepy Lion. Shared bathrooms and kitchen for guests. Breakfast €4. Internet access €2 per hr. Sheets €2. Reception 24hr. 6- to 8-bed dorms €13-14; singles €24; doubles €36; quads €60. AmEx/MC/V. ❶

Hotel Weißes Roß, Auguste-Schmidt-Str. 20 (☎960 59 51). From the station take tram #11 (dir.: Markkleeberg-Ost), #8 (dir.: Wilhelm-Leuschnerpl.) or #10 or #16 (dir.:

Lößnig) to "Augustuspl.," and walk down Augustuspl. When it becomes Roßpl., take the pedestrian walkway. Go through the archway opposite the curving skyscraper; the hotel is 100m straight ahead. Comfortable rooms in sepia tones; the attached restaurant serves relaxed locals. Breakfast included. Reception during café hours (M-F 5-10pm); call ahead at other times. Singles €31, with shower €35; doubles €46/55. Lower rates when less busy, longer stays negotiable. Cash only. ❸

Ibis Hotel, Brühl 69 (☎218 60; www.ibishotel.com). From the Hauptbahnhof, cross the street and head a block down Goethestr. Take a right onto the Brühl. If you run out of budget options, the classy Ibis (part of a large chain) is a 2min. walk from the train station. Impeccably clean with reliable service and no surprises. Reception 24hr. Rooms from €59. AmEx/DC/MC/V. ❺

Jugendherberge Leipzig (HI), Volksgartenstr. 24 (☎245 70 11; fax 245 70 12). Take tram #1 (dir.: Schönefeld/Stannebeinpl.) to "Löbauer Str." Continue walking in the direction of the tram, then bear right onto Löbauer Str. Take a right onto Volksgartenstr. After 3 blocks, cut across the parking lot of the bright orange apartment buildings; the hostel is on your right. 2- to 6-bed rooms fill this quiet high-rise. Breakfast and sheets included. Reception 2:30-11pm. Curfew 1am, but later return possible. Mar.-Oct. €21.90, over 27 €24.90; Nov.-Feb. €19.40/22.40. Cash only. ❷

Pension am Südplatz, Kochstr. 4 (☎301 96 06). Take tram #10 (dir.: Lößnig) or #11 (dir.: Markkleeberg-Ost) to "Südpl." Kochstr. curves off to the right. Clean and cheery rooms in the middle of hip Südpl. Breakfast included. Singles €29; doubles €45. ❷

Camping & Motel Am Auensee, Gustav-Esche-Str. 5 (☎465 16 00), by a lake in the nearby suburb of Wahren. From the station, take tram #10 (dir.: Wahren) or #11 (dir: Schkeuditz) to "Wahren." Turn left before the Rathaus onto Linkelstr. and follow the twisting main road (10min.); it will be on your right. Reception daily 7:30am-1pm and 2-9:30pm. €4 per person, €3-5 per tent, €2-6 per car. 1-bed bungalows €29; 2-bed €39, with shower €59; 3-bed €55. Public showers €0.75. MC/V. ❶

⬛ FOOD

Leipzig's Innenstadt, especially **Grimmaischestr.**, is well supplied with *Imbiße* (snack bars), bistros, and bakeries, and has a **market** on Richard-Wagner-Pl., at the end of the Brühl (Tu and F 9am-5pm). Escape downtown crowds with a jaunt to **Karl-Liebknecht-Str.**, packed with well-priced cafés and bars. To get there from the Markt, take Peterstr. to Petersteinweg (15min.), or hop on tram #11 (dir.: Markkleeberg-Ost) or 10 (dir.: Lößnig) to "Südpl." Most cafés offer Sunday brunch.

⬛ Bellini's, Markt 3-5. In the middle of the bustling Markt, this café and bar is crowded in the evening, with every chair turned toward the beautiful Altes Rathaus. Baguettes (€3.50-4) make filling snacks, and colorful salads and pastas (€7-9) satisfy cravings for something larger. Open daily 10am-1am, sometimes later. MC/V. ❷

100-Wasser Café, Barfussg. 15 (☎215 79 27). The tile designs are crazy, the wall decorations eccentric, and the English-speaking staff friendly. Pastas €5.50-7. Other entrées €5.50-13. Open M-Sa 8am-2am, Su 9am-2am. AmEx. ❷

Aauerbachs Keller, Grimmaischestr. 2-4 (☎21 61 00), across from the Altes Rathaus, inside the Mädlerpassage. In Goethe's *Faust,* Mephistopheles tricks some drunkards in this 16th-century tavern before carrying Faust away on an enchanted beer barrel. Check out *Faust* scenes on the walls over a long meal in this elegant but unpretentious restaurant. Entrées €9-35. Open daily 11:30am-midnight. ❸

Aladin Döner, Burgstr. 12 (☎976 67 07), just south of the Thomaskirche. Making the best *Döner* in town is hard when you've got so much competition. Free cup of tea at the end of your meal. *Döner kebap* with fries €3.50. Open daily 9am-2am. Cash only. ❶

Zur Pleißenburg, Ratsfreischulstr. 2 (☎960 26 53), located just down Burgstr. from the Thomaskirche. Head here to load up on pasta (€5.20) or to try a delicious *Bauernfrüh-stück* (omelet with ham and potatoes; €4.80) at this relaxed hangout. Open daily 9am-5am. Cash only. ❷

Weisses Rössel, Karl-Liebknecht Str. 64 (☎30 10 92), offers tasty, varied cuisine: pasta dishes and pizza (€7-9) fill out a menu with specialties, including a true veal *Wiener Schnitzel* (€10). Open M-Sa 6pm-2am, Su 10am-2am. AmEx/MC. ❸

Café Le Bit, Rosa-Luxemburg-Str. 36 (☎998 20 20), on the right corner at Friedrich-List-Pl. With your back to the station, turn left across Georgring onto Wintergartenstr., which becomes Rosa-Luxemburg-Str. and leads straight there (10min.). Bilingual staff serves exquisite crêpes (€1.80-3.50) in this quirky Internet café. Internet access €1.25 per 30min. Open M-F 9am-3am, Sa-Su 10am-3am. Cash only. ❷

◉ SIGHTS

Leipzig's Innenstadt is startlingly heterogeneous: on any one street you'll find elegant old townhouses, institutional DDR relics, and gleaming new shopping malls—the product of Leipzig's post-1991 building spree. Marktpl., at the heart of the city, is currently a construction site for a new bus station. Most of Leipzig's museums and sights are a short walk from Marktpl.

▓ VÖLKERSCHLACHTDENKMAL (MONUMENT OF THE BATTLE OF NATIONS). Outside the city ring, this massive pyramid, built in 1913 to look like a Mesopotamian ziggurat, memorializes the 120,000 soldiers who died in the 1813 Battle of Nations—a six-day struggle that turned the tide against Napoleon and determined many of Europe's national boundaries as they stand today. The inside bears witness to the extreme nationalism of the era in which it was built: gigantic stone soldiers lean sadly over their swords as war horses spiral up to the dome. If you brave the climb up the 364 steps to the top, you'll be rewarded with a fabulous view. *(Tram #15 from the Hauptbahnhof (dir.: Meusdorf or Probtheida) to "Völkerschlachtdenkmal" (15min.), then turn right. ☎961 85 38; www.voelkerschlachtdenkmal.de. Museum and memorial open daily Apr.-Oct. 10am-6pm; Nov.-Mar. 10am-4pm. €5, students €3. Free tour Sa 11am. English-language audio guides €1. Signs in English.)*

THOMASKIRCHE. Down Thomasg. from the Altes Rathaus is the church where the famed composer Bach spent the last 27 years of his career, serving as as cantor. Elegantly decorated in the neo-Gothic style, the church pays simple and fitting homage to the composer. His body was moved in 1950 to a grave beneath the floor in front of the altar. Highlights of the church include a crucifix from Bach's time, an astonishingly beautiful triptych from an anonymous master of the 15th century, and a historical musical instrument collection. The **Thomanerchor,** once directed by Bach, is one of Europe's most prestigious boys' choirs. *(☎960 28 55; www.thomaskirche.org. Church open daily 9am-6pm. Free. Thomanerchor performances F 6pm, €1. Also during Sunday services.)*

NIKOLAIKIRCHE. The 800-year-old Nikolaikirche witnessed the birth of Bach's *St. John Passion* as well as the DDR's peaceful revolution. In 1989, what began as simple weekly meetings at the Nikolaikirche, the only place where the *Stasi* (state police) could not interfere, turned into massive *Montagdemos* (Monday demonstrations) against the DDR. The sandstone facade hides an exceptional interior, including alabaster reliefs and towering green columns carved like palm fronds, a nod to a time when the church stood at the intersection of two major trade routes. *(Down Grimmaischestr. from the Altes Rathaus. Church open M-Sa 10am-6pm, Su 9:30am-6pm. Free. Free tours Tu and Th-F at 5pm, Sa at 11am.)*

🏛 MUSEUMS

Leipzig is rebuilding its museums in grand style. Almost all construction on the **Grassimuseum** has ceased, and it will be fully open by 2007. Some exhibits are temporarily closed; call the tourist office for updated information.

📷 MUSEUM IN DER "RUNDEN ECKE" (MUSEUM IN THE "ROUND CORNER").

The East German *Staatssicherheit*, or *Stasi*, was the largest per capita secret police force in world history. Over 91,000 official employees produced literally miles of paper and mountains of cassettes and photographs in their attempts to keep tabs on suspected "enemies of the state." Because Leipzig citizens occupied the building until December 4, 1989, most of the tools that the *Stasi* used to torment opponents are preserved and on display, including machines that helped them secretly open and reseal up to 2000 letters per day. The archive, including everything from handwriting samples to reports and samples of human scents, is the largest of its kind in Germany. The museum staff also gives tours of a bunker nearby that contains an exhibit detailing the unrealized plans of the *Stasi*. *(Dittrichring 24. ☎961 24 43; www.runde-ecke-leipzig.de. Open daily 10am-6pm. Free. Tours in German 3pm (€3, students €2), in English for groups by appointment. Ask for an English handout in the office. Bunker tours (€3) are at 1-4pm on the last Sa and Su of the month.)*

MUSEUM DER BILDENDEN KÜNSTE LEIPZIG (LEIPZIG FINE ARTS MUSEUM).

Leizpig's art collection includes works by Rubens, Boticelli, Cranach the Elder and the Younger, and an excellent collection of 19th-century German paintings. *(Katharinestr. 10, just behind the Altes Rathaus. ☎21 69 90; www.mdbk.de. Open Tu and Th-Su 10am-6pm, W noon-8pm. €7, students €5. Special exhibits €8.50/6. Both €11/8.)*

JOHANN-SEBASTIAN-BACH-MUSEUM.

The Bach Museum's informative exhibits emphasize his role as choir director, teacher, and city musician, focusing on the composer's life and work in Leipzig, where he wrote his *Mass in B minor* and both the *St. John* and *St. Matthew Passions*. In total he composed over 300 cantatas here. The museum plays host to concerts during the fall. In addition, Leipzig holds an annual Bach festival every June (June 7-17, 2007). *(Thomaskirchhof 16. ☎913 72 00. Open daily 10am-5pm. €4, students and seniors €2. Concerts €10/7.50. Free English audio guides. Public tours F 3pm, Sa 2pm, Su 11am and 3pm. €1.50.)*

MENDELSSOHN-HAUS.

This gorgeous house was the residence of composer Felix Mendelssohn-Bartholdy for two of the years that he lived in Leipzig. Mendelssohn led a revival of interest in Bach, conducting many concerts at the Gewandhaus. It was through his urging that the Bach statue outside the Thomaskirche was erected in 1843. Some rooms have been furnished to appear as Mendelssohn knew them, while others hold exhibits on his life and work. Ask for an English translation of exhibit text. *(Goldschmidtstr. 12. Take Augustuspl. away from the Opernhaus toward Roßpl., then a left down Goldschmidtstr. ☎127 02 94. Open daily 10am-6pm. €3. Concerts Su at 11am. €12, students €8.)*

GRASSIMUSEUM.

Consisting of three distinct museums, the Grassimuseum has just completed a major renovation, and its museums are reopening gradually through 2007. The **Museum für Völkerkunde** (Ethnology Museum) displays the dress and customs of peoples from all over the globe. *(Johannispl. 5-11. ☎973 19 00. Open Tu-Su 10am-6pm, Th 10am-8pm. €3, students €2, families €7. Special exhibitions €5/3.50/10.)* The **Musikinstrumenten Museum** holds the world's oldest clavichord and other fragile Renaissance instruments. Most fun of all is the *Klanglabor* ("noise laboratory"), where you can work out your aggressions on the gongs, steel drums, xylophones, and a pipe organ. *(Thomaskirchhof 20. ☎973 07 50. Open Tu-Su 11am-6pm. €3, students €2. Public tours Su 10:30am. Signs in English.)* The **Museum für Angewandte**

Kunst (Arts and Crafts Museum), slated to reopen in Dec. 2007, displays changing exhibits of artists' work in different media—programs indicate what's currently on display. *(Check www.grassimuseum.de for hours and prices.)*

ZEITGESCHICHTLICHES FORUM LEIPZIG (FORUM FOR CONTEMPORARY HISTORY). The forum provides a comprehensive and thoughtful look at Germany's history since WWII. Especially powerful are videos of the Berlin Wall's construction and of demonstrators in the angry protests of June 17, 1953 and the more peaceful ones of 1989. Exhibit descriptions are available in English. Special exhibits on the third floor cover contemporary issues in German society. *(Grimmaischestr. 6. ☎ 222 00; www.hdg.de. Open Tu-F 9am-6pm, Sa-Su 10am-6pm. Free.)*

STADTGESCHICHTLICHES MUSEUM (CITY HISTORY MUSEUM). Leipzig's city museum, housed in the Altes Rathaus since 1906, chronicles the city's history through the centuries. During the DDR days, the museum was directly controlled by the government, as were its exhibits. Now, permanent displays highlight the lives of Bach and Luther. Some captions are in English. *(Markt 1. ☎ 965 13 20. Open Tu-Su 10am-6pm. €4, students €3. Special exhibitions in the Neubau annex €3/2.)*

🎵 ENTERTAINMENT

The patrons who frequent the eclectic cafés scattered around Leipzig also support a world-class theater and music scene. Leipzig offers a variety of world-famous musical groups. The first is the **Gewandhaus-Orchester,** a major international orchestra that has been performing since 1843. Some concerts are free, but usually only when a guest orchestra is playing; otherwise, tickets must be purchased at the Gewandhaus box office, Augustuspl. 8. (☎ 127 02 80; www.gewandhaus.de. €43-50, Th concerts and some others 20% off for students. Open M-F 10am-6pm, Sa 10am-2pm, and 1hr. before performances.) Leipzig's acclaimed **Opera,** Augustuspl. 12, gives Dresden's Semperoper a run for its money. Last-minute tickets cost €6 for those under 27. (☎ 126 12 61; www.oper-leipzig.de. Phone reservations M-F noon-7pm. Counter open M-F 10am-8pm, Sa 10am-6pm, and 1½hr. before performances. Tickets €14-42, students 30% off.) The opera house is also an entry point to Leipzig's diverse **theater** scene, hosting the experimental **Kellertheater** (☎ 126 12 61) in its basement. The **Schauspielhaus,** Bosestr. 1 just off Dittrichring, produces the classics, and occasionally presents visually astounding pieces of outdoor vertical theater, in which the theater's side becomes the stage, and actors "walk" by climbing up the walls. (☎ 126 81 68; www.schauspiel-leipzig.de. Tickets €7-23, students €7-16.50. Box office open M-F 10am-7pm, Sa 10am-1pm, and 1½hr. before performance.) The **cabaret** scene, which features political satire almost exclusively, is centered around the understated **academixer,** Kupferg. 3-5, run by the Leipzig student body. This theater is one of the few without summer closings. (☎ 21 78 78 78; www.academixer.com. Box office open daily 10am-8pm. Tickets €11-18, students €6-18.) Also, check out the **Leipziger Pfeffermühle,** Thomaskirchhof 16, in the courtyard of the Bach Museum. (☎ 960 31 96; kabarett.pfeffermuehle@t-online.de. Open M-F 3-8pm. Tickets €15-18, students €10-18.) The **UT Connewitz,** Wolfgang-Heinze-Str. 12, presents films and live music to an audience of students and jovial locals in an old theater with a uniquely run-down ambience. (☎ 462 67 76. Call or check www.utconnewitz.de for upcoming events and prices.) **naTo,** Karl-Liebknecht-Str. 46 (☎ 30 39 133; www.nato-leipzig.de), shows indie films in original languages with German subtitles, as does the **Prager Frühling** cinema, in the Haus der Demokratie, Bernhard-Goering-Str. 152 (☎ 306 53 33). October brings Leipzig's renowned **film festival.** (Oct. 29-Nov. 4, 2007. Call ☎ 980 39 21 for information, or ask at the tourist office.)

NIGHTLIFE

Free German-language magazines *Fritz* and *Blitz* will fill you in on nightlife, but *Kreuzer* (sold at newsstands, €1.50) puts these to shame with information on concerts, films, and nightlife listings (make sure you get the monthly version). **Barfußgäßchen,** a street just off the Markt, serves as the see-and-be-seen bar venue for everyone from students to *Schicki-Mickis* (yuppies). In the summer there's only a narrow path to walk between the packed parasol-covered café tables. **Café Baum,** the oldest in the city, and **Markt Neun, Zigarre,** and **Varadero** all fill by 10pm. Though crowds dwindle by midnight, the most popular bars stay packed until 3am on a good night. Just across Dittrichring on **Gottschedstr.** and **Bosestr.,** a similar scene takes place in bars such as **Neue Szene** and the **Milchbar,** but with a slightly younger and more boisterous crowd. **Karl-Liebknecht-Str.** hosts Leipzig's alternative *Szene.* The bars are more spread out, but also more distinctive. Take tram #11 (dir.: Markkleeburg-Ost) or 10 (dir.: Lößnig) to "Südpl." The Irish pub **Killiwilly** at Karl-Liebknecht Str. 44 offers good cheer, while farther south, **Weißes Rössel** (p. 633) is more chill. Early on, the café scene dominates, but Leipzigers are just beginning; local dance clubs are packed throughout the student weekend (which begins, of course, on Wednesday).

Moritzbastei, Universitätsstr. 9 (☎ 70 25 90; www.moritzbastei.de), behind the university tower. University students spent 8 years excavating a series of medieval tunnels to create this energetic subterranean dance club. The result: a huge complex housing a café, hammock-filled *Biergarten,* movie theater, multilevel dance floor, and relaxed bars. **Café Barbakan,** at the entrance to one of the tunnels, opens daily after 10am. An **open-air movie theater** (screenings June-Aug. daily at 10pm, weather permitting) is next to the outdoor terrace and *Biergarten* (open in nice weather M-F 11:30am-midnight, Sa-Su 2pm-midnight.) The W and Sa ▧**All You Can Dance** disco blasts pounding music in cavernous vaulted brick rooms, producing reverberations you won't find anywhere else in Leipzig. Cover €4, students with ID €2.50; slightly more for concerts (some require advance ticket purchase; office open M-F 10am-6pm). Cash only.

Night Fever, Gottschedstr. 4 (☎ 149 99 90). Dance your way back to the time of the moonwalk in this super-fly disco. Crowds of 20- and 30-somethings relish the bright, colorful lights, plentiful drinks, and free cover. €1 coat/bag check. Tu all drinks at least €1 cheaper. 21+. Open Tu-Sa 9am-5am.

nachtcafé limited, Markgrafenstr. 10 (☎ 221 00 00; www.nachtcafe.com). Young crowd parties the night away to rap, techno, and hip-hop on 2 busy dancefloors. Cover €5. Open W and F-Sa from 10pm.

Distillery, at the end of Kurt-Eisner-Str. (☎ 35 59 74 00), near the corner of Lößinger Str. Take tram #9 (dir.: Markkleeberg-West) to the "K.-Eisner/A.-Hoffman-Str." stop and turn left. A little out of the way, this edgy industrial-yard-turned-club plays house, techno, and rock. Cover €5 before midnight, €8 after midnight; W no cover. Opens at 11pm, although things don't heat up until around 1am. Closed late July to early Sept.

RosaLinde, Brühl 64-66 (☎ 149 93 60; www.rosalinde.de). Described by some as the epicenter of Leipzig's gay and lesbian scene, RosaLinde is usually a laid-back bar staffed by friendly volunteers. Also holds a *Frauendisco* for women the 1st F of the month at 10pm (€2.50), a "Last Night" party the last Sa of the month at 10pm, and various other events. Drop by early evening to pick up a card listing support groups and special events. Open Tu-Th 5pm-midnight, F-Sa 7pm-late, Su 7pm-11pm. Cash only.

Café Spizz, Markt 9 (☎ 960 80 43; www.SPIZZ.org). Big jazz names show up occasionally for weekend concerts, while W "Boogie Nights" jam sessions attract an almost cult-like following. Weekend club nights entertain a slightly older crowd. Club cover €3, W free; concerts €20-80. Open W and F-Sa 10pm-5am. Cash only.

GATEWAY CITY: PRAGUE

During the Cold War, foreigners imposed the name "Eastern Europe" on the Soviet satellites east of the Berlin Wall, but the term has always expressed a political rather than geographical reality. From the nobility of Prague Castle to the darkly ethereal back alleys of Josefov, Prague (in Czech, "Praha"; pop. 1,200,000) is a city on the cusp of the divine. Holy Roman Emperor Charles IV filled Prague with soaring cathedrals and lavish palaces worthy of his rank. Since the lifting of the Iron Curtain, hordes of outsiders have flooded the capital; in summer, the tourist-to-resident ratio can soar above nine-to-one. Walk a few blocks from any of the major sights, however, and you'll be nearly alone in a maze of cobblestone alleys. Even in the hyper-touristed Staré Město (Old Town), Prague's majesty gleams: the Charles Bridge—packed so tightly in summer that the fastest way off is to jump—is still breathtaking at sunrise, eerie in a fog, and stunning after snowfall.

ESSENTIALS

KORUNY (Kč)		
AUS$1 = 16.81Kč		10Kč = AUS$0.60
CDN$1 = 20.44Kč		10Kč = CDN$0.49
EUR€1 = 28.33Kč		10Kč = EUR€0.35
NZ$1 = 14.16Kč		10Kč = NZ$0.71
UK£1 = 41.46Kč		10Kč = UK£0.24
US$1 = 22.50Kč		10Kč = US$0.44

DOCUMENTS AND FORMALITIES

VISA AND ENTRY INFORMATION. US citizens may stay in the Czech Republic for up to 90 days without a visa. Citizens of over 50 other countries may also travel in the country for varying numbers of days. Visas are not available at the border.

EMBASSIES AND CONSULATES. Foreign embassies are located in Prague. Czech embassies and consulates abroad include: **Australia,** 8 Culgoa Circuit, O'Malley, Canberra, ACT 2606 (☎612 6290 1386; www.mfa.cz/canberra); **Canada,** 251 Cooper St., Ottawa, ON K2P OG2 (☎613-562-3875; www.mfa.cz/ottawa); **Ireland,** 57 Northumberland Rd., Ballsbridge, Dublin (☎00 35-31 668 1135; www.mzv.cz/dublin); **New Zealand,** see Australia; **UK,** 26 Kensington Palace Gardens, London W8 4QY (☎20 7243 7913; czechembassy.org.uk); **US,** 3900 Spring of Freedom St. NW, Washington, D.C. 20008 (☎202-274-9123; www.mzv.cz/washington).

CZECH REPUBLIC	❶	❷	❸	❹	❺
ACCOMMODATIONS	under 320Kč	320-500Kč	500-800Kč	800-1200Kč	over 1200Kč
FOOD	under 80Kč	80-110Kč	110-150Kč	150-200Kč	over 200Kč

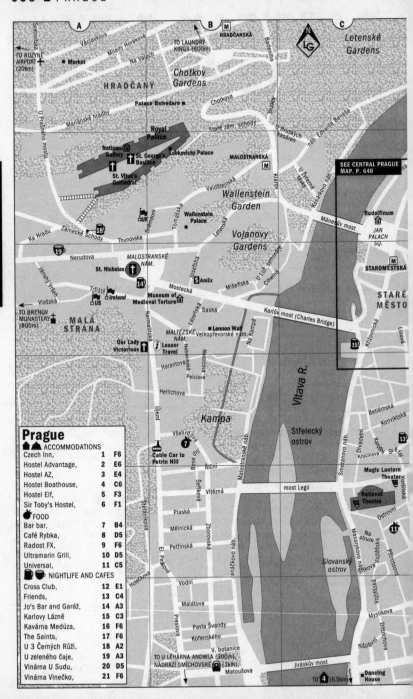

Prague

🏠🏠🏠 ACCOMMODATIONS

Czech Inn,	**1**	F6
Hostel Advantage,	**2**	E6
Hostel AZ,	**3**	E4
Hostel Boathouse,	**4**	C6
Hostel Elf,	**5**	F3
Sir Toby's Hostel,	**6**	F1

🍎 FOOD

Bar bar,	**7**	B4
Café Rybka,	**8**	D5
Radost FX,	**9**	F6
Ultramarin Grill,	**10**	D5
Universal,	**11**	C5

🌙📖 NIGHTLIFE AND CAFES

Cross Club,	**12**	E1
Friends,	**13**	C4
Jo's Bar and Garáž,	**14**	A3
Karlovy Lázně,	**15**	C3
Kavárna Medúza,	**16**	F6
The Saints,	**17**	F6
U 3 Černých Růží,	**18**	A2
U zeleného čaje,	**19**	A3
Vinárna U Sudu,	**20**	D5
Vinárna Vinečko,	**21**	F6

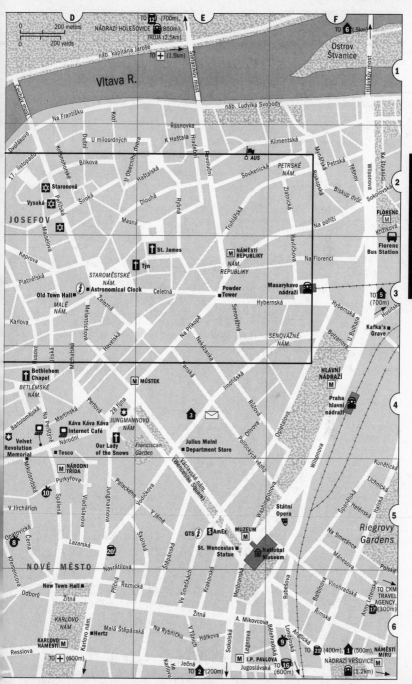

PRAGUE

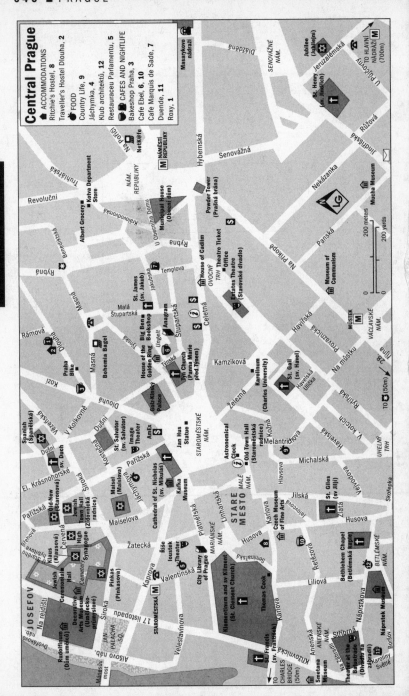

Central Prague

▲ ACCOMMODATIONS
Ritchie's Hostel, 8
Traveller's Hostel Dlouha, 2

◆ FOOD
Country Life, 9
Jáchymka, 4
Klub architektů, 12
Restauraceu Parlamentu, 5

☕ CAFES AND NIGHTLIFE
Bakeshop Praha, 3
Cafe Ebel, 6, 10
Cafe Marquis de Sade, 7
Duende, 11
Roxy, 1

▣ TRANSPORTATION

Flights: Ruzyně Airport (☎220 113 313), 20km northwest of the city. Take bus #119 to Metro A: Dejvická (daily 5am-midnight; 14Kč, luggage 10Kč per bag); buy tickets from kiosks or machines. **Airport buses** run by **Cedaz** (☎220 114 296) collect travelers from nám. Republiky and Dejvická Metro stops (2 per hr. 5:30am-9:30pm, 90Kč). **Taxis** to the airport are expensive (500-800Kč); try to settle on a price before departing.

Trains: Domestic ☎221 111 122, international 840 112 113; www.vlak.cz. Prague has 4 main terminals. **Hlavní nádraží** (☎224 615 249; Metro C: Hlavní nádraží) and **Nádraží Holešovice** (☎224 806 793; Metro C: Nádraží Holešovice) are the largest and cover most international service. Domestic trains leave **Masarykovo nádraží** (☎840 112 113; Metro B: nám. Republiky), on the corner of Hybernská and Havlíčkova, and from **Smíchovské nádraží** (☎972 226 150; Metro B: Smíchovské nádraží). International trains run to: **Berlin** (4½hr., 7 per day, 1400Kč, students 820Kč); **Dresden** (2½hr., 7 per day, 708/538Kč); **Munich** (6hr., 4 per day, 1980/1400Kč). If you're having trouble finding a competitive fare, consider booking a ticket to the border transportation hub, **Děčín** (from Dresden, 280Kč-425), and buying a seperate ticket from there to Prague (141Kč). If you have a railpass, purchasing a supplementary **Prague Excursion Pass** (p. 32) may be the most economical option.

Buses: Info ☎900 144 444; www.vlak-bus.cz. Open daily 6am-9pm. State-run **ČSAD** (Česká státní automobilová doprava; Czech National Bus Transport; ☎257 319 016) has several terminals. The biggest is **Florenc**, Křížikova 4 (☎224 219 680; Metro B or C: Florenc). Info office open daily 6am-9pm. Buy tickets in advance. To: **Berlin** (7hr., 4 per day, 481-990Kč). The **Tourbus** office (☎224 218 680; www.eurolines.cz), at the terminal, sells **Euroline** and airport bus tickets. Open M-F 7am-7pm, Sa 8am-7pm, Su 9am-7pm. Private bus services crop up frequently; for service from Germany to Prague, and vice versa, inquire at the local tourist office.

Ride Share: Mitfahrzentrale. Inquire German agencies several days before departing. For general info, see p. 36. Find local Mitfahrzentrale listings in Germany coverage.

◪ ORIENTATION

Spanning the **Vltava** River, greater Prague is a labyrinthine mess of suburbs; pick up an essential *plán města* (map) to detangle it. The Vltava runs south-northeast through the center, separating **Staré Město** (Old Town) and **Nové Město** (New Town) from **Malá Strana** (Lesser Town). On the right bank is **Staroměstské náměstí** (Old Town Square), the heart of Prague. From the square, the elegant **Pařížká ulice** (Paris Street) leads north to **Josefov**, the old Jewish quarter. South of Staré Město, Nové Město houses **Václavské náměstí** (Wenceslas Square), Prague's commercial core. To the west of Staroměstské nám., the **Charles Bridge** (Karlův Most) spans the Vltava, connecting Staré Město with **Malostranské náměstí** (Lesser Town Square). **Prague Castle** (Pražský Hrad) overlooks Malostranské nám. from **Hradčany** hill. The Hlavní nádraží train station and Florenc bus station lie northeast of Václavské nám, and are on the excellent Metro. To reach Staroměstské nám., take the Metro A line to Staroměstská and follow Kaprova away from the river.

▣ LOCAL TRANSPORTATION

Public Transportation: Buy tickets for the **Metro, tram,** and **bus** at newsstands, *tabák* kiosks, machines in stations, or DP (Dopravní podnik; transport authority) kiosks. Validate tickets in machines above escalators to avoid fines issued by plainclothes inspectors. 3 **Metro** lines run daily 5am-midnight: A is green on maps, B yellow, C red. **Night trams** #51-58 and **buses** #502-514 and 601 run every 30min. midnight-5am and cover the same areas as day trams and buses; look for dark blue signs with white letters at bus stops. 14Kč tickets are good for 20min. or 4 stops. 20Kč tickets are valid for 75min., with transfers, for travel in one direction. Large bags and bikes 10Kč. The DP office (☎296 191 817; www.dpp.cz; open daily 7am-9pm), in the Muzeum stop on Metro A and C lines, sells **multi-day passes** (1-day 80Kč, 3-day 220Kč, 1-wk. 270Kč).

Taxis: Radiotaxi (☎272 731 848) and **AAA** (☎140 14) are particularly reliable. 34Kč flat rate plus 25Kč per km and 5Kč per min. waiting.

TIP **GOING THE DISTANCE.** To avoid taxi scams, always ask in advance for a receipt ("Prosím, dejte mi paragon") with distance traveled and price paid.

PRACTICAL INFORMATION

TOURIST AND FINANCIAL SERVICES

Tourist Offices: Green "i"s mark tourist agencies, which book rooms and sell maps. **Pražská Informační Služba** (PIS; Prague Information Service; ☎12 444, from outside Prague 224 223 613; www.pis.cz) is in the *Staroměstské radnice* (Old Town Hall). Open Apr.-Oct. M-F 9am-7pm, Sa-Su 9am-6pm; Nov.-Mar. M-F 9am-6pm, Sa-Su 9am-5pm. Branches at Na příkopě 20 and Hlavní nádraží. Open in summer M-F 9am-7pm, Sa-Su 9am-6pm; otherwise M-F 9am-6pm, Sa-Su 9am-5pm. Branch in the tower by the Malá Strana side of the Charles Bridge. Open Apr.-Oct. daily 9am-7pm.

Budget Travel: Arctic, Václavské nám. 56 (☎222 721 595). Metro A: Můstek. Offers discounted airfare. Open M-Th 10am-6pm, F 10am-4pm. **BIJ Wasteels** (☎224 641 954; www.wasteels.cz), on the 2nd fl. of Hlavní nádraží, sells discounted international train tickets. Open M-F 8am-6pm, Sa 9am-4pm. Both serve those under 26 only.

Passport Office: Foreigner Police Headquarters, Olšanská 2 (☎974 841 356). Metro A: Flora. From the Metro, turn right on Jičínská and right again on Olšanská. Or, take tram #9 from Václavské nám. toward Spojovací and get off at Olšanská. To get a **visa extension,** get a 90Kč stamp inside, line up at doors #2-12, and prepare to wait up to 2hr. Limited English spoken. Open M-Th 7:30-11:30am, noon-4:30pm and 5-7pm.

Embassies and Consulates: Canada, Muchova 6 (☎272 101 800; www.canada.cz). Metro A: Hradčanská. Open M-F 8:30am-12:30pm and 1:30-4:30pm. **Ireland,** Tržiště 13 (☎257 530 061). Metro A: Malostranská. Open M-F 9:30am-12:30pm and 2:30-4:30pm. **UK,** Thunovská 14 (☎257 402 111). Metro A: Malostranská. Open M-Th 8:30am-5pm, F 8:30am-4pm. **US,** Tržiště 15 (☎257 022 000). Metro A: Malostranská. Open M-F 8am-4:30pm. **Australia,** Klimentská 10, 6th fl. (☎296 578 350). Open M-Th 8:30am-5pm, F 8:30am-2pm.

Currency Exchange: Exchange counters are everywhere; rates vary wildly, and are typically higher in train stations. Never change money on the street. **Chequepoints** are convenient and open late, but usually charge a large commission or fee. **Komerční banka,** Na příkopě 33 (☎222 411 111), buys notes and checks for a 2% commission. 24hr. **ATMs** *(Bankomats)* abound and can offer the best rates, but often charge large fees.

American Express/Interchange: Václavské nám. 56 (☎222 211 089). Metro A or C: Muzeum. AmEx **ATM** outside. Grants MC/V cash advances for a 3% commission. Western Union services available. Open daily 9am-10pm.

LOCAL SERVICES

Luggage Storage: Lockers in all train and bus stations (10Kč) have a 24hr limit. Luggage offices are in the basement of **Hlavní nádraží** (15-30Kč per day; open 24hr.) and halfway up the stairs at **Florenc** (30Kč per day; open daily 5am-11pm).

English-Language Bookstore: ◪**The Globe Bookstore,** Pštrossova 6 (☎224 934 203; www.globebookstore.cz). Metro B: Národní třída. Wide variety of new and used books and periodicals. Internet 1.50Kč per min. Open daily 10am-midnight.

EMERGENCY AND COMMUNICATIONS

Emergency: Police: ☎158. **Ambulance:** ☎0155. **Fire:** ☎150.

Medical Services: Na Homolce (Hospital for Foreigners), Roentgenova 2 (☎257 272 146, after hours 257 211 111; www.homolka.cz). Bus #167. Open M-F 7am-5pm. Emergency services 24hr. **Canadian Medical Center,** Velesavínská 1 (☎235 360 133, after hours 724 300 301; www.cmc.praha.cz). Open M-F 8am-6pm.

24hr. Pharmacy: U Lékárna Anděla, Štefánikova 6 (☎257 320 918, after hours 224 431 112). Metro B: Anděl. With your back to the train station, turn left and follow Nádražní until it becomes Štefánikova.

Telephones: Phone cards cost 200Kč per 50 units at kiosks and post offices. Don't let kiosks rip you off. Pay phones also take coins (local calls from 10Kč per min.).

Internet Access: ◪**Bohemia Bagel,** Masná 2 (www.bohemiabagel.cz) has a friendly atmosphere and delicious food. Metro A: Staroměstská. 2Kč per min. Open M-F 7am-midnight, Sa-Su 8am-midnight. Branch at Újezd 16. Open daily 9am-midnight.

Post Office: Jindřišská 14 (☎221 131 445). Metro A: Můstek. Airmail to the US takes 7-10 days. For *Poste Restante,* address mail as follows: First name LAST NAME, Poste Restante, Jindřišská 14, Praha 1 110 00, CZECH REPUBLIC. Open daily 2am-midnight. Tellers close 8pm. **Postal Code:** 1 110 00.

◪ ◪ ACCOMMODATIONS AND CAMPING

Reservations are a must at hotels, and a good idea at hostels. If you tote a backpack in Hlavní nádraží or Holešovice stations, you may be approached by hostel runners offering beds, often in university dorms empty for the summer. They may provide free transport, convenient for those arriving at night. Note that you may be pressured to commit before you can gauge the establishment's quality.

STARÉ MĚSTO

Travellers' Hostel, Dlouhá 33 (☎224 826 662; www.travellers.cz). Metro B: nám. Republiky. Seasonal branches at Husova 3 (☎222 220 078), Josefská (☎257 534 577), Střelecký Ostrov (☎224 932 991), U Lanové Dráhy 3 (☎257 312 403). Social atmosphere and unbeatable location in a building with the Roxy Club (p. 650). Breakfast included. Laundry 150Kč. Internet 1Kč per min. Reserve ahead. Dorms 380-550Kč; singles 1120Kč, with bath 1300Kč; doubles 1200/1300Kč. ISIC discount. ❷

Ritchie's Hostel, Karlova 9 (☎222 221 229; www.ritchieshostel.cz). Metro A: Staroměstská. From the Charles Bridge, head down Karlova past the small square. Basic, clean accommodations in the thick of the tourist district. Breakfast 25Kč. Dorms 390-500Kč, low season 350-500Kč; doubles 1890-2000Kč. MC/V. ❷

NOVÉ MĚSTO AND VINOHRADY

◪ **Czech Inn,** Francouzská 76 (☎267 267 600; www.czech-inn.com). Metro A: Náměsti Miru. From the Metro, take tram #4, 22, or 23 to Krymská and walk uphill. This ultra-modern hostel sets sky-high standards for budget accommodations. Breakfast 120Kč. Internet 50Kč per hr. Reserve far ahead. Dorms 390-450Kč; singles 1200Kč; doubles 1400Kč. Private room prices increase 200Kč on weekends. AmEx/DC/MC/V. ❷

Hostel Advantage (HI), Sokolská 11-13 (☎224 914 062; www.advantagehostel.cz). Metro C: I.P. Pavlova. Take the stairs on the left leading to Ječná and turn left on Sokolská. This well-kept hostel has comfortable rooms. Breakfast included. Free Internet access. Dorms 400Kč; singles 600Kč; doubles 1000Kč. ISIC discount %10. MC/V. ❷

Hostel Elf, Husitská 11 (☎222 540 963; www.hostelelf.com). Metro B: Florenc. From the Metro, take bus #207 to U Památníku; the hostel is up the stairs. Despite noisy train tracks nearby and temperamental showers, this graffiti-covered hostel is always packed with raucous backpackers. Breakfast included. Free Internet access. Dorms 320Kč; singles 800Kč, with bath 1000Kč; doubles 900/1200Kč. ❷

Hostel AZ, Jindřišská 5 (☎224 241 664; www.hostel-az.com). Metro A: Můstek. Across from the post office. Superb location; bright geometric murals add pizzazz to tidy, plain rooms. Dorms 400-450Kč; singles 1000Kč; doubles 1260Kč. MC/V. ❷

OUTSIDE THE CENTER

▨ **Sir Toby's,** Dělnická 24 (☎283 870 635; www.sirtobys.com). Metro C: Nádraží Holešovice. From the Metro, take the tram to "Dělnická," walk to the corner of Dělnická, and turn left. Classy hostel with a huge kitchen. Refurbished chapel serves as cellar bar. Free wireless Internet. Dorms 340-400Kč; singles 1000Kč; doubles 1350Kč. MC/V. ❷

▨ **Hostel Boathouse,** Lodnická 1 (☎241 770 051; www.hostelboathouse.com). Take tram #14 from Nářodni třída south toward Sídliště. Get off at Černý Kůň (20min.), go down the ramp to the left, and follow the yellow signs. Social atmosphere, caring staff, and home-cooked meals. Breakfast included. Dorms from 350Kč. ❷

◗ FOOD

Away from the city center, a feast of pork, dumplings, and beer costs about 90Kč. You'll be charged for everything the waiter brings to the table; check your bill carefully. **Tesco,** Národní třída 26 (Metro B: Národní třída) has groceries, (open M-F 7am-10pm, Sa 8am-8pm, Su 9am-8pm) and there's a **daily market** in Staré Město.

RESTAURANTS

STARÉ MĚSTO

▨ **Klub architektů,** Betlémské nám. 169/5A (☎224 401 214). Metro B: Národní třída. A 12th-century cellar with 21st-century ambience. Veggie options 70-150Kč. Meat entrees 160-320Kč. Open daily 11:30am-midnight. AmEx/MC/V. ❸

Jáchymka, Jáchymova 4 (☎224 819 621). Metro A: Staroměstská. A local favorite, Jáchymka serves gigantic, affordable cuts of meat. Salads from 30Kč. Entrees 150-335Kč. Open daily 11am-11pm. MC/V. ❸

Country Life, Melantrichova 15 (☎224 213 366; www.countrylife.cz). Metro A: Staroměstská. 3 fresh vegetarian buffets—hot, cold, and salad bar—are a welcome respite from meat-heavy Czech cuisine. Buffet 20-50Kč per 100g. Soup 20Kč. Juices from 20Kč. Open M-Th 9am-8:30pm, F 8:30am-5pm, Su 11am-8:30pm. Cash only. ❷

Restaurace u Parlamentu, Valentinská 8 (☎721 415 74). Metro A: Staroměstská. Serves Czech specialties (60-118Kč) and cold glasses of Pilsner Urquell. Popular with local business-lunchers. Open M-F 9:30am-11pm, Sa-Su 11am-11pm. MC/V. ❷

Café Bambus, Benediktská 12 (☎224 828 110; www.cafebambus.com). Metro B: nám. Republiky. Patrons nosh on Thai and Indian dishes (pad thai and curry each 130Kč) and Czech *palančinky* (crepes; 55-75Kč). Beer from 42Kč. Open M-F 9am-2am, Sa 11am-2am, Su 11am-midnight. AmEx/MC/V. ❷

NOVÉ MĚSTO

▨ **Radost FX,** Bělehradská 120 (☎224 254 776; www.radostfx.cz). Metro C: I.P. Pavlova. Stylish dance club and imaginative café with great vegetarian food. Entrées 120-195Kč. Brunch Sa-Su 95-140Kč. Open daily 9am-late. See also **Clubs,** p. 650. ❸

Universal, V jirchářích 6 (☎224 934 416). Metro B: Národní třída. Asian, French, and Mediterranean cuisines served in a dining room reminiscent of a Parisian café. Huge, fresh salads 131-195Kč. Entrees 149-299Kč. Su brunch buffet 185-205Kč. Open M-Sa 11:30am-1am, Su 11am-midnight. MC/V; 500Kč min. charge. ❹

Ultramarin Grill, Ostrovni 32 (☎224 932 249; www.ultramarin.cz). Metro B: Národní třída. International clientele, but the menu is purely American. Steak, duck, and lamb entrées 130-350Kč. Salads 100-180Kč. Open daily 10am-4am. AmEx/MC/V. ❸

MALÁ STRANA

Bar bar, Všehrdova 17 (☎257 313 246; www.barbar.cz). Metro A: Malostranská. Reggae-inspired basement café with affordable menu. Lunch noon-2pm 100Kč. Entrees 98-175Kč. Beer from 28Kč. Open Su-Th noon-midnight, F-Sa noon-2am. MC/V. ❷

U Tři Černých Ruží, Zámecká 5 (☎257 530 019; www.u3cr.com). Metro A: Malostranská. At the foot of the New Castle steps. A small, quirky restaurant serving up large portions and endless pints. Entrees 80-200Kč. Beer 18Kč. Open daily 11am-midnight. ❷

CAFÉS AND TEAHOUSES

▧ **Café Rybka**, Opatovická 7. Metro B: Národní třída. Congenial café with great coffee and a tiny bookstore. Espresso 25Kč. Tea 22Kč. Open daily 9:15am-10pm. Cash only.

▧ **Café Ebel**, Řetězová 9 (☎603 441 434; www.ebelcoffee.cz). Metro A or B: Staroměstská. Espresso (40-50Kč) expertly blended in-house. English spoken. Branch at Týn 2. Both open M-F 8am-8pm, Sa-Su 8:30am-8pm. AmEx/MC/V.

Kavárna Medúza, Belgická 17. Metro A: nám. Míru. Walk down Rumunská and turn left at Belgická. Local clientele by day, hipsters by night. Coffee 19-30Kč. Crêpes 52-70Kč. Open M-F 10am-1am, Sa-Su noon-1am. MC/V.

U zeleného čaje, Nerudova 19 (☎225 730 027). Metro A: Malostranská. This adorable shop at the foot of Prague Castle takes tea to new heights. Tea 35-75Kč. Open daily 11am-10pm. Cash only.

Bakeshop Praha, Kozí 1. Metro A: Staroměstská. Mouthwatering pastries, salads, sandwiches, and quiches. Branch at Lázenska 19. Eat-in 10% extra. Open daily 7am-7pm.

◉ SIGHTS

Escape crowds by venturing away from **Staroměstské náměstí**, the **Charles Bridge**, and **Václavské náměstí**. There are plenty of attractions hidden in the Jewish quarter of **Josefov**, the hills of **Vyšehrad**, and the streets of **Malá Strana**.

STARÉ MĚSTO (OLD TOWN)

Getting lost among the narrow roads and cobblestone alleys of Staré Město is probably the best way to appreciate the 1000-year-old neighborhood's charm.

CHARLES BRIDGE. Thronged with tourists and hawkers, the Charles Bridge (Karlův Most) is Prague's most recognizable landmark. On each side of the bridge, defense towers offer views of the city and the river. Five stars and a cross mark the spot where, according to legend, St. Jan Nepomucký was tossed over the side of the bridge for guarding the queen's extramarital secrets from a suspicious King Wenceslas IV in the 14th century. *(Metro A: Malostranská or Staroměstská.)*

OLD TOWN SQUARE. Staroměstské náměstí (Old Town Square) is the heart of Staré Město, surrounded by eight magnificent towers. *(Metro A: Staroměstská; Metro A or B: Můstek.)* Next to the grassy knoll stands the **Staroměstské Radnice** (Old Town Hall). The building has been missing a piece of its facade since the Nazis partially demolished it in the final days of WWII. Crowds gather on the hour to watch the **astronomical clock** chime as the skeletal Death empties his hourglass and a procession of apostles marches by. *(Open M 11am-6pm, Tu-Su 9am-7pm. Clock tower open M-F 2-*

7pm, Sa-Su 10am-7pm; enter through 3rd fl. Exhibition hall 20Kč, students 10Kč. Clock tower 50/40Kč.) Opposite the Staroměstské Radnice, the spires of **Týn Church** (Chrám Matka Boží před Týnem) rise above a mass of medieval homes. Buried inside is famous astronomer Tycho Brahe, whose overindulgence at Emperor Rudolf's lavish dinner party in 1601 may have cost him his life. Since it was deemed improper to leave the table unless the emperor himself did so, Tycho had to remain in his chair until his bladder burst. He died 11 days later, though scholars believe mercury poisoning may have been the culprit. (Open M-F 9am-noon and 1-2pm. Mass W-F 6pm, Sa 8am, Su 11am and 9pm. Free.) The bronze statue of 15th-century theologian **Jan Hus**, the country's most famous martyr, stands in the middle of the square. The **Golz-Kinský Palace,** in front of the statue, is the finest of Prague's Rococo buildings. (Open Tu-F 10am-6pm; closes early in summer for concerts.)

ST. NICHOLAS'S CATHEDRAL. While less impressive than its counterpart on the other side of the Vltava, this church houses a stunning crystal chandelier and has rich ceiling frescoes. (Metro A: Staroměstská. Open daily 8am-5pm. Free.)

NOVÉ MĚSTO (NEW TOWN)

Established in 1348 by Charles IV, Nové Město has become the commercial center of Prague, complete with American chain stores. The Franciscan Gardens offer visitors an oasis of natural calm amid the bustle of business.

WENCESLAS SQUARE. More a boulevard than a square, Wenceslas Square (Václavské náměstí) owes its name to the equestrian statue of Czech ruler and patron **St. Wenceslas** (Václav) that stands in front of the National Museum. Wenceslas has presided over a century of momentous events from his pedestal: the 1918 declaration of the new Czechoslovak state, the 1939 invasion by Hitler, the 1968 arrival of Soviet tanks, the 1969 immolation of Jan Palach in protest of the Soviet invasion, and the 1989 Velvet Revolution. The square stretches from the statue past department stores, discos, hotels, and glitzy casinos. **Radio Free Europe,** which provides global news updates and advocates peace, has been headquartered in a glass building behind the National Museum since 1995. (Metro A or C: Muzeum.)

FRANCISCAN GARDEN AND VELVET REVOLUTION MEMORIAL. Monks somehow manage to preserve this serene **rose garden** in the heart of Prague's commercial district. (Metro A or B: Můstek. Enter through the arch to the left of Jungmannova and Národní, behind the statue. Open daily mid-Apr. to mid-Sept. 7am-10pm; mid-Sept. to mid-Oct. 7am-8pm; mid-Oct. to mid-Apr. 8am-7pm. Free.) Down the street on Národní, a **plaque** under the arcades and across from the Black Theatre memorializes the hundreds of citizens beaten by police on November 17, 1989. A subsequent wave of protests led to the collapse of communism in Czechoslovakia during the Velvet Revolution.

DANCING HOUSE. Architect Frank Gehry (of Guggenheim-Bilbao fame) built the swaying Dancing House (Tančící dům) on Resslova at Rašínovo nábřeží. Since its 1996 unveiling, it has been called an eyesore by some and a shining example of postmodern design by others. (Metro B: Karlovo nám.)

JOSEFOV

Central Europe's oldest Jewish settlement lies north of Staroměstské nám., along Maiselova. In 1180, Prague's citizens built a 4m wall around the area. The closed neighborhood bred exotic tales, many of which centered around Rabbi Loew ben Bezalel and his legendary golem—a mud creature that supposedly came to life to protect Prague's Jews. Josefov thrived until WWII, when the Nazis sent its residents to death camps. Ironically, Hitler's wish to create a "museum of an extinct race" sparked the preservation of Josefov's cemetery and synagogues.

SYNAGOGUES. The **Maisel Synagogue** (Maiselova synagoga) displays artifacts from the Jewish Museum's collections, only returned to the Jewish community in 1994. *(On Maiselova, between Široká and Jáchymova.)* Turn left on Široká to reach the **Pinkas Synagogue** (Pinkasova). Drawings by children interred at the Terezín camp are displayed upstairs. Some 80,000 names line the walls downstairs, a sobering requiem for Czech Jews persecuted during the Holocaust. Backtrack along Široká and go left on Maiselova to visit the oldest operating synagogue in Europe, the 700-year-old **Old-New Synagogue** (Staronová), still the nexus of Prague's Jewish community. Farther up Široká on Dušní, the **Spanish Synagogue** (Španĕlská) has an ornate Moorish interior modeled after Granada's Alhambra. *(Metro A: Staroměstská. Synagogues open Apr.-Oct. M-F and Su 9am-6pm; Nov.-Mar. M-F and Su 9am-4:30pm. Closed Jewish holidays. Admission to all 6 of the area's synagogues except Staronová 300Kč, students 200Kč. Staronová 200/140Kč. Men must cover their heads; kippot 5Kč.)*

OLD JEWISH CEMETERY. The Old Jewish Cemetery (Starý židovský hřbitov) is Josefov's most visited sight. Between the 14th and 18th centuries, 20,000 graves were laid in 12 layers. The clusters of tombstones visible today were formed as older stones rose from the lower layers. *(At the corner of Široká and Žatecká. Open Apr.-Oct. M-F and Su 9am-6pm; Nov.-Mar. M-F and Su 9am-4:30pm. Closed Jewish holidays.)*

MALÁ STRANA

A seedy hangout for criminals and counter-revolutionaries for nearly a century, the cobblestone streets of Malá Strana have become prized real estate. In the main square, **Malostranské Náměstí**, the towering dome of the Baroque **St. Nicholas's Cathedral** (Chrám sv. Mikuláše) is one of Prague's most prominent landmarks. Mozart played the organ here when he visited Prague, and the cathedral now hosts nightly classical music concerts. *(Metro A: Malostranská. Follow Letenská to Malostranské nám. Open daily 9am-4:30pm. 50Kč, students 25Kč.)* Along Letenská, a wooden gate opens into the **Wallenstein Garden** (Valdštejnská zahrada). With a beautifully tended stretch of green and a bronze Venus fountain, this is one of the city's best-kept secrets. *(Letenská 10. Open Apr.-Oct. daily 10am-6pm. Free.)* The **Church of Our Lady Victorious** (Kostel Panna Marie Vítězné) is known for its famous wax statue of the **Infant Jesus of Prague**, said to bestow miracles on the faithful. *(Follow Letecká through Malostranské nám. and continue onto Karmelitská. Church open M-Sa 8:30am-6pm, Su 9:30am-8pm. Museum open M-Sa 9:40am-5:30pm, Su 1-6pm. Free.)* ■ **Petřín Gardens and View Tower,** on the hill beside Malá Strana, provides a tranquil retreat with spectacular views of the city. Climb the steep, serene footpath, or take the funicular from just above the intersection of Vítězná and Újezd. *(Look for Lanovka Dráha signs. Funicular daily 9am-11:20pm, 4-6 per hr., 20Kč. Tower open May-Aug. daily 10am-10pm.)*

PRAGUE CASTLE (PRAŽSKÝ HRAD)

Prague Castle, one of the biggest castles in the world, has been the seat of Czech government for over 1000 years. The first Bohemian royal family established their residence here in the 9th century; since then, the castle has housed Holy Roman Emperors, the communist Czechoslovak government, and now the Czech Republic's president. The main entrance is at the end of the lush **Royal Gardens** (Královská zahrada), where the Singing Fountain spouts its watery, harp-like tune in front of the **Royal Summer Palace.** Past the main gate, the **Šternberg Palace** houses art from the National Gallery. *(From Metro A: Malostranská, take trams #22 or 23 to Pražský Hrad and go down U Prašného Mostu. Open daily Apr.-Oct. 9am-5pm; Nov.-Mar. 9am-4pm. Royal Gardens open Apr.-Sept. 10am-6pm. Buy tickets opposite St. Vitus's Cathedral inside the castle walls. Tickets valid for 2 days at Royal Crypt, Cathedral and Powder Tower, Old Royal Palace, and the Basilica. 350Kč, students 175Kč.)*

ST. VITUS'S CATHEDRAL. Inside the castle walls stands the beautiful Gothic St. Vitus's Cathedral (Katedrála sv. Víta), which was not completed until 1929, 600 years after construction began. To the right of the high altar stands the silver **Tomb of St. Jan Nepomucký.** In the main church, the walls of **St. Wenceslas's Chapel** (Svatováclavská kaple) are lined with a painting cycle depicting the legend of Wenceslas. Climb the 287 steps of the **Great South Tower** for an excellent view, or descend underground to the **Royal Crypt,** which holds the tomb of Charles IV.

OLD ROYAL PALACE. The Old Royal Palace (Starý Královský Palác) is to the right of the cathedral, behind the Old Provost's House and the statue of St. George. The lengthy **Vladislav Hall** once hosted jousting competitions. Upstairs is the **Chancellery of Bohemia,** where the Second Defenestration of Prague took place in 1618. A Protestant assembly found two Catholic governors guilty of religious persecution and threw them out the window. They landed in a pile of manure and survived, but the event contributed to the beginning of the Thirty Years' War.

ST. GEORGE'S BASILICA AND ENVIRONS. Across the courtyard from the Old Royal Palace stands St. George's Basilica (Bazilika sv. Jiří), where the skeleton of St. Ludmila is on display. The St. Agnes convent next door houses the **National Gallery of Bohemian Art,** which displays pieces ranging from Gothic to Baroque. *(Open Tu-Su 10am-6pm. 100Kč, students 50Kč.)* To the right of the Basilica, follow Jiřská halfway down and take a right on tiny **Golden Lane** (Zlatá ulička). Alchemists once worked here attempting to create gold, and Kafka later lived at #22.

OUTER PRAGUE

The city's outskirts offer respite from the hordes of tourists. In the beautiful neighborhood of Troja, French architect J. B. Mathey's **château** overlooks the Vltava. The building has a terraced garden, oval staircase, and magnificent collection of 19th-century Czech artwork. *(From Metro C: Nádraží Holešovice, take bus #112 to Zoologická Zahrada. Open Apr.-Oct. Tu-Su 10am-6pm; Nov.-Mar. Sa-Su 10am-5pm. 100Kč, students 50Kč.)* **Břevnov Monastery,** the oldest monastery in Bohemia, was founded in AD 993 by King Boleslav II and St. Adalbert, who were guided by a divine dream to build a monastery atop a stream. *(From Metro A: Malostranská, take tram #22 uphill to Břevnovský klášter. Church open for mass, M-Sa 7am and 6pm, Su 7:30, 9am, 6pm. Tours Sa-Su 10am, 2, 4pm. 50Kč, students 30Kč.)* The **Prague Market** (Pražskátrznice) has acres of stalls selling all kinds of wares. *(Take tram #3 or 14 from nám. Republiky to Vozovna Kobylisy and get off at Pražskátrznice. Open M-F 7am-5pm, Sa 7am-2pm.)* Giant bronze babies, fixed in mid-crawl, climb up and down the **Prague Radio/TV Tower,** creating one of the most bizarre outdoor art installations in Europe. Get the most out of the strange spectacle by scheduling a nighttime visit, when the babies are silhouetted against the brightly-lit tower. *(Metro A: Jiřího z Poděbrad. Turn right on Slavikova, then right on Ondříčkova. The tower is in the park at the intersection with ul. Fibichova.)*

🏛 MUSEUMS

The city's museums often have striking facades but mediocre collections. Still, a few quirky exceptions are worth a visit.

MUCHA MUSEUM. The museum is devoted to the work of Alfons Mucha, the Czech Republic's most celebrated artist. Mucha, the pioneer of the Art Nouveau movement, gained fame for his poster series of "la divine" Sarah Bernhardt. *(Panská 7. Metro A or B: Můstek. Walk up Václavské nám. toward the St. Wenceslas statue. Go left on Jindřišská and left again on Panská. Open daily 10am-6pm. 140Kč, students 70Kč.)*

■ FRANZ KAFKA MUSEUM. This fantastic, newly opened multimedia exhibit of Kafka memorabilia uses photographs and original scribbles to bring visitors back to 19th-century Prague, as experienced by the renowned author. *(Cihelná 2. Metro A: Staroměstská. Head west on Kaprova, cross Mánesýv bridge, and turn left on Klarov, which becomes Cihelná. www.kafkamuseum.cz. Open daily 10am-6pm. 120Kč, students 60Kč.)*

NATIONAL GALLERY. The collection of the National Gallery (Národní Galerie) is spread among nine locations throughout Prague; the notable Šternberg Palace and Klášter sv. Jiří are in **Prague Castle** (p. 647). The **Trade Fair Palace and the Gallery of Modern Art** (Veletržní palác a Galerie moderního umwní) exhibit an impressive collection of 20th-century Czech and European art. *(Dukelských hrdinů 47. Metro C: Nádraží.Holešovice. All locations open Tu-Su 10am-6pm. 150Kč, students 70Kč.)*

MUSEUM OF COMMUNISM. This gallery is committed to exposing the flaws of the Communist system that oppressed the Czech people from 1948 to 1989. A model factory and interrogation office send visitors behind the Iron Curtain. *(Na Příkopě 10. Metro A: Můstek. Open daily 8am-9pm. 170Kč, students 150Kč.)*

MUSEUM OF MEDIEVAL TORTURE INSTRUMENTS. The collection and highly detailed explanations are sure to nauseate. In the same building, the **Exhibition of Spiders and Scorpions** shows live venomous creatures in their natural habitats. *(Mostécka 21. Metro A: Malostranská. Follow Letenská from the Metro and turn left. Open daily 10am-10pm. Torture museum 140Kč. Spiders exhibition 100Kč, children 80Kč.)*

SEX MACHINES MUSEUM. Three prurient floors house over 200 mechanical sexual appliances, ranging from antique lingerie to fetishist whips, chains, and leather. Erotic cinema plays vintage Spanish pornographic films. This museum is a favorite among groups of giggling teenagers. *(Melantrichova 18. Metro A: Staroměstská. www.sexmachinesmuseum.com. Open daily 10am-11pm. Students 150Kč.)*

♫ ENTERTAINMENT

To find info on Prague's performances, consult *Threshold*, *Do města-Downtown*, *The Pill* (all free at many cafés and restaurants), or *The Prague Post*. Between mid-May and early June, the **Prague Spring Festival** draws musicians from around the world. June brings all things avant-garde with the **Prague Fringe Festival** (☎ 224 935 183), featuring comedians, performance artists, and—wait for it—mimes. For tickets to the city's shows, try **Bohemia Ticket International,** Malé nám. 13. (☎ 224 227 832; www.ticketsbti.cz. Open M-F 9am-5pm, Sa 9am-1pm.)

The majority of Prague's theaters close in July and August, but the selection is extensive during the rest of the year. Get gussied up for the **National Theater** (Národní divadlo), Národní 2/4, which stages drama, opera, and ballet. (☎ 224 901 487; www.narodni-divadlo.cz. Metro B: Národní třída. Box office open Sept.-June daily 10am-8pm and 45min. before performances. Tickets 30-1000Kč.) Every performance at the **Black Light Theatre,** Pařížská 4, is silent, conveying the message through dance, pantomime, and creative use of black light. (☎ 222 314 448. Performances daily 8pm. Box office open daily 9am-8pm.)

 HIGH CULTURE, LOW BUDGET. Prague's state-run theaters will often hold a group of seats in the higher balconies until the day of the performance before selling them off at reduced prices. By visiting your venue of choice the morning of a performance, you can often score tickets for as little as 50Kč.

PRAGUE

▤ NIGHTLIFE

With some of the world's best beer on tap, it's no surprise that pubs and beer halls are Prague's popular nighttime haunts. Outside of Václavské náměstí, where the nightlife is always raging, Prague's pubs and clubs are scattered throughout the neighborhoods rather than clustered in specific areas. Tourists overrun the city center, so authentic pub experiences are largely restricted to outlying Metro stops. Many gay clubs distribute *Amigo* (90Kč; www.amigo.cz), a thorough English-language guide to gay life. Check www.praguegayguide.net or www.praguesaints.cz for a list of attractions and resources.

BARS

▨ **Vinárna U Sudu,** Vodičkova 10 (☎222 237 207). Metro A or B: Můstek. Cross Václavské nám. to Vodičkova and follow the curve left. An infinite labyrinth of cavernous cellars. Red wine 125Kč per 1L. Open M-Th 8am-3am, F-Sa 8am-4am, Su 8am-2am. MC/V.

▨ **Duende,** Karolíny Světlé 30. (☎775 186 077), right off the Charles Bridge. A diverse, laid-back crowd packs in even on those rare nights when Staroměstské nám. is dead. Beer from 19Kč. Shots 75Kč. Open daily 11am-1am.

Vinárna Vinečko, Lodynská 135/2 (☎222 511 035). Metro A: Nám. Miru. Head west on Rumunská and turn left on Lodynská. A wine bar in the heart of the Vinohrady district brimming with thirsty locals and expats. Wine 26-34Kč per 0.2L, 64-92Kč per bottle. Open M-F 11am-midnight, Sa-Su 2pm-midnight. MC/V.

Café Marquis de Sade, Templova 5. Metro B: nám. Republiky. Roomy microbrewery and bar decorated in red velvet. Beer from 35Kč. Shots 80Kč. Open daily 2pm-2am.

Jo's Bar and Garáž, Malostranské nám. 7. Metro A: Malostranská. For those homesick for Anybar, USA. Foosball, darts, card games, and a dance floor downstairs. American bar food—nachos, burgers, burritos, and steaks (60-295Kč). Beer from 31Kč. Long Island Iced Tea 115Kč. Open M-Th 11am-8pm, Sa-Su 11am-2am. AmEx/MC/V.

CLUBS

Karlovy Lázně, Novotného lávka 1, next to the Charles Bridge. Popularly known as "Five Floors," this tourist magnet boasts 5 levels of themed dancefloors. Cover 120Kč, 50Kč before 10pm and after 4am. Open daily 9pm-5am.

Palác Akropolis, Kubelíkova 27 (☎296 330 911). Metro A: Jiřího z Poděbrad. Head down Slavíkova and turn right onto Kubelíkova. 2 music rooms with separate DJs; live Czech bands several times a week. Beer from 25Kč. Open daily 8pm-5am.

Cross Club, Plynámi 23 (www.crossclub.cz). Metro C: Nádraží Holešovice. Plastered with mechanical oddities, including cogs, springs, and black lights, the rooms in this underground maze are mesmerizing. Beer 28Kč. Open M-Th and Su 2pm-late, F-Sa 4pm-late.

Radost FX, Bělehradská 120 (☎224 254 776; www.radostfx.cz). Metro C: I.P. Pavlova. This basement club has an industrial metallic bar, a small dancefloor, and couches. Beer from 30Kč. Cover 100-200Kč. Open Th-Sa 10pm-5am.

Roxy, Dlouhá 33. Metro B: nám. Republiky. Same building as the Traveller's Hostel (p. 643). Artsy studio and club with experimental DJs and theme nights. Beer 35Kč. Cover Tu and Th-Sa 100-350Kč. Open daily 10pm-late.

The Saints, Polská 32 (☎332 250 326; www.praguesaints.cz). Metro A: Jiřího z Poděbrad. Much more than a club, The Saints introduces GLBT visitors to Prague and organizes the local GLBT community. Small, comfy club with a mixed crowd and free wireless Internet access. Beer from 22Kč. Open daily 7pm-4am.

Friends, Bartolomejská 11 (☎224 236 272; www.friends-prague.cz). Metro B: Národní třída. The only GLBT club in Staré Město. Rotating schedule features parties and theme nights. Women and straight men welcome. Beer from 30Kč. Open daily 6pm-5am.

APPENDIX

CLIMATE

Germany's climate is temperate. Rain is common year-round, though it is especially prevalent in summer, when the weather can change with surprising rapidity.

TEMP. (LO/HI), PRECIPITATION	JANUARY			APRIL			JULY			OCTOBER		
	°C	°F	mm	°C	°F	mm	°C	°F	mm	°C	°F	mm
Berlin	-3-1	27-34	43	2-12	36-54	41	13-22	55-72	71	5-13	41-55	44
Frankfurt	-1-3	30-37	47	3-13	37-55	41	13-23	55-74	69	6-13	43-55	53
Hamburg	-1-3	30-37	61	2-11	36-52	46	12-21	54-70	81	6-12	43-54	62
München (Munich)	-4-2	25-36	46	3-13	37-55	56	12-22	54-72	127	4-12	39-54	60

To convert from °C to °F, multiply by 1.8 and add 32. To convert from °F to °C, subtract 32 and multiply by 0.55.

°CELSIUS	-5	0	5	10	15	20	25	30	35	40
°FAHRENHEIT	23	32	41	50	59	68	77	86	95	104

TELEPHONE CODES

COUNTRY CODES

In Germany, dial 00 to get an international line, then dial the code:

Australia	61		Italy	39
Austria	43		Netherlands	31
Belgium	32		New Zealand	64
Czech Republic	420		Poland	48
Denmark	45		South Africa	27
France	33		Switzerland	41
Hungary	36		United Kingdom	44
Ireland	353		US and Canada	1

CITY CODES

To call between cities in Germany, enter the city code of the town you're calling, followed by the local number. City codes can be found next to city names throughout the book. When calling from abroad, drop the first zero of the city code:

Aachen	0241		Kiel	0431
Bayreuth	0921		Köln (Cologne)	0221
Berlin	030		Leipzig	0341
Bonn	0228		Lübeck	0451
Braunschweig (Brunswick)	0531		Regensburg	0941
Bremen	0421		München (Munich)	089
Dresden	0351		Münster	0251
Düsseldorf	0211		Nürnberg (Nuremburg)	0911

Erfurt	0361
Frankfurt	069
Freiburg	0761
Göttingen	0551
Hamburg	040
Hannover (Hanover)	0511
Heidelberg	06221
Kassel	0561

Rostock	0381
Schwerin	0385
Stuttgart	0711
Trier	0651
Tübingen	07071
Weimar	03643
Wittenberg	03491
Würzburg	0931

MEASUREMENTS

Like the rest of the rational world, Germany uses the metric system. Keep this in mind when you see a road sign or any other distance indicator—those are kilometers, not miles, so whatever distance is being described is not as far away as Americans might think. German recipe books use metric measurements (and usually measure ingredients by weight rather than volume). And, unfortunately, gasoline isn't as cheap as it looks to those used to gallons: prices are *per liter*.

MEASUREMENT CONVERSIONS

1 inch (in.) = 2.54cm
1 foot (ft.) = 0.30m
1 yard (yd.) = 0.914m
1 mile (mi.) = 1.61km
1 ounce (oz.) = 28.35g
1 pound (lb.) = 0.454kg
1 fluid ounce (fl. oz.) = 29.57ml
1 gallon (gal.) = 3.785L
1 acre (ac.) = 0.405ha
1 square mile (sq. mi.) = 2.59km^2

1 centimeter (cm) = 0.39 in.
1 meter (m) = 3.28 ft.
1 meter (m) = 1.09 yd.
1 kilometer (km) = 0.62 mi.
1 gram (g) = 0.035 oz.
1 kilogram (kg) = 2.202 lb.
1 milliliter (ml) = 0.034 fl. oz.
1 liter (L) = 0.264 gal.
1 hectare (ha) = 2.47 ac.
1 square kilometer (km^2) = 0.386 sq. mi.

LANGUAGE

"Life is too short to learn German."
—Thomas Love Peacock

Most Germans speak at least rudimentary English, but you will encounter many who do not, especially in parts of Eastern Germany. Before asking someone a question in English, preface your query with a polite *Sprechen Sie Englisch?* (Do you speak English?). Even if your command of German is shaky, most Germans will be pleased when you try to speak to them in their native tongue.

PRONUNCIATION

With only a little bit of effort, you can make yourself easily understood in German. Unlike English, German pronunciation is for the most part consistent with spelling; there are no silent letters, and all nouns are capitalized.

German vowels and diphthongs also differ from their English counterparts: **A:** as in "father." **O:** as in "oh." **U:** as in "fondue." **Y:** as in "cool." **AU:** as in "wow." **IE:** as in "thief." **EI:** as in "wine." **EU:** like the OI in "boil." An **umlaut** over a letter (e.g., ü) makes the pronunciation longer and more rounded. An umlaut is sometimes replaced by an E following the vowel, so that "schön" becomes "schoen." An **Ä** sounds a lot like the short "e" in "effort," while an **Ö** is pronounced like the "e" in "perm." To make the **Ü** sound, round your lips to say "ooh," keep them in this position, and then try to say "ee" instead. Germans are very forgiving toward foreigners who butcher their mother tongue. There is, however, one important exception—place names. If you learn nothing else in German, learn to pronounce the names of cities properly. Berlin is "bare-LEEN," Hamburg is "HAHM-boorg," Munich (München) is "MEUWN-shen," and Bayreuth is "BUY-royt."

Adhere to the English pronunciation of consonants with the following exceptions: **J**: always pronounced as a Y. **K**: always pronounced, even before an N. **QU**: pronounced KV. **Single S**: pronounced as Z. **V**: pronounced as F. **W**: pronounced as V. **Z**: pronounced as TS. The hissing, aspirant **CH** sound, found in such basic words as *Ich* (I), *nicht* (not), and *sprechen* (to speak), is tricky for untrained English-speaking vocal cords. After A, O, U, or AU, it is pronounced as in Scottish, "loch"; otherwise it sounds like a soft CH, as in "chivalry." If you can't hack it, use an SH sound instead. **TH** is pronounced T. The consonant combination **SCH**, found at the beginning of many German words, is pronounced SH, as in "shut," while **ST** and **SP** are pronounced "SHT" and "SHP," respectively. **R** after a vowel is pronounced as in English; after a consonant or the beginning of the word, it's a uvular guttural—think a harsher version of the "r" in "rip," pronounced from the back of the throat.

German has one consonant that does not exist in English, **the "ß,"** which is alternately referred to as the *scharfes S* (sharp S) or the *Ess-tset*. It is a shorthand symbol for a **double-S,** and is pronounced just like an English "ss." The letter appears only in lower case and shows up in two of the most important German words for travelers: *Straße*, "street," which is pronounced "SHTRAH-sseh" and abbreviated "Str."; and *Schloß*, "castle," pronounced "SHLOSS." Note that the "ß" is being phased out and replaced with "ss" in an effort to standardize spelling.

NUMBERS, DATES, AND TIMES

A space or period rather than a comma is used to indicate thousands, so 10,000 is written 10 000 or 10.000. Instead of a decimal point, Germans use a comma, e.g., 3.1415 is written 3,1415. Months and days are written in the reverse of the American manner, e.g., 10.11.92 is November 10. Note that the number in the ones place is pronounced before the number in the tens place; thus "fünfundsiebzig" (FUHNF-oont-ZEEB-tsish; literally "five and seventy") is 75, *not* 57.

Germany uses the 24-hour clock for all official purposes; thus, *fünfzehn Uhr* (15.00) is 3pm and 20.00 is 8pm.

MONTHS					
January	February	March	April	May	June
Januar	Februar	März	April	Mai	Juni
July	August	September	October	November	December
Juli	August	September	Oktober	November	Dezember

DAYS OF THE WEEK						
Monday	Tuesday	Wednesday	Thursday	Friday	Saturday	Sunday
Montag	Dienstag	Mittwoch	Donnerstag	Freitag	Samstag/ Sonnabend	Sonntag

GERMAN PHRASEBOOK

The following phrasebook is meant to provide only the very rudimentary phrases you will need in your travels. Nothing can replace a full-fledged phrasebook or a pocket-sized English-German dictionary. German features both an informal and formal form of address; in the tables below, the polite form follows the familiar form in parentheses. Note that in German, nouns can take any one of three genders; masculine (taking the article **der;** pronounced DARE), feminine (**die;** pronounced DEE) and neuter (**das;** pronounced DAHSS). All plural nouns also take the **die** article, regardless of their gender in the singular.

GLOSSARY

das Abendessen: dinner
ab/fahren: to depart
die Abfahrt: departure
das Abteil: train compartment
Achtung!: beware!
die Altstadt: old town, historic center
das Amt: bureau, office
an/kommen: to arrive
die Ankunft: arrival
die Apotheke: pharmacy
die Arbeit: work
auf/steigen: to get on
aus/steigen: to get off
der Ausgang: exit
die Auskunft: information
die Ausstellung: exhibit
die Ausweis: ID
das Auto: car
die Autobahn: highway
der Autobus: bus
das Bad: bath, spa
das Bahn: railway
der Bahnhof: train station
der Bahnsteig: train platform
der Berg: mountain, hill
das Bett: bed
die Bibliothek: library
die Bundesrepublik Deutschland (BRD): Federal Republic of Germany (FRG)
das Brot: bread
die Brücke: bridge
der Brunnen: fountain, well
der Bundestag: parliament
die Burg: fortress, castle
der Busbahnhof: bus station
die Damen: ladies (restroom)
das Denkmal: memorial
die Dusche: shower
der Dom: cathedral
das Dorf: village
ekelig: disgusting
die Ehefrau: wife
der Ehemann: husband
die Einbahnstraße: one-way street
der Eingang: entrance
ein/steigen: board
der Eintritt: admission
das Essen: food
die Fähre: ferry
der Fahrplan: timetable
das Fahrrad: bicycle

der Fahrschein: train/bus ticket
der Familienname: last name
der Feiertag: holiday
die Festung: fortress
der Flohmarkt: flea market
der Flughafen: airport
das Flugzeug: airplane
der Fluß: river
das Fremdenverkehrsamt: tourist office
das Frühstück: breakfast
die Fußgängerzone: pedestrian zone
das Gasthaus: guest house
die Gaststätte: local bar with restaurant
die Gedenkstätte: memorial
geil: cool OR horny
das Gleis: track
der Hafen: harbor
der Hauptbahnhof: main train station
das Hauptpostamt: main post office
der Hof: court, courtyard
der Imbiß: fast-food stand
die Innenstadt: city center
die Insel: island
das Jugendgästehaus: youth hotel
die Jugendherberge: youth hostel
die Karte: ticket
das Kino: cinema
der Kiosk: newsstand
die Kirche: church
die Kneipe: bar
das Krankenhaus: hospital
das Kreuz: cross, crucifix
die Kunst: art
der Kurort: spa/resort
die Kurtaxe: overnight resort tax
die Kurverwaltung: resort tourist office
das Land: German state/province
die Lesbe: lesbian (n.)
der Markt: market
der Marktplatz: market square
das Meer: sea
die Mensa: university cafeteria
die Mitfahrzentrale: rideshare service office

die Mitwohnzentrale: long-term accommodation service
das Münster: cathedral
das Museum: museum
der Notausgang: emergency exit
der Notfall: emergency
der Notruf: emergency hotline
der Paß: passport
die Pension: cheap hotel
der Platz: square, plaza
die Polizei: police
das Postamt: post office
das Privatzimmer: room in a private home
die Quittung: receipt
das Rathaus: town hall
die Rechnung: bill, cheque
das Reisebüro: travel agency
das Reisezentrum: travel office in train stations
die S-Bahn: commuter rail
das Schiff: ship
das Schloß: castle
die Schule: school
schwul: gay (adj.)
der See: lake
die Speisekarte: menu
die Stadt: city
der Strand: beach
die Straße: street
die Straßenbahn: streetcar
die Tankstelle: gas/petrol station
das Tor: gate
die Toilette: bathroom
die U-Bahn: subway
umsteigen: to make a transit connection
die Universität: university
der Veganer/in: vegan
der Vegetarier/in: vegetarian
das Viertel: quarter, district, neighborhood
der Vorname: first name
die Vorsicht: caution
der Wald: forest
das WC: bathroom
wandern: to hike
der Wanderweg: hiking trail
der Weg: road, way
die Wurst: sausage
die Zeitung: newspaper
das Zimmer: room
der Zug: train

GREETINGS

ENGLISH	GERMAN
Hello	Hallo; Grüss Gott (in Bavaria)
Excuse me/Sorry	Entschuldigung/ Verzeihung
Could you please help me?	Kannst du (Könnten Sie) mir helfen bitte?
How old are you?	Wie alt bist du (sind Sie)?
Good morning	Guten Morgen
Good afternoon	Guten Tag
Good evening	Guten Abend
Good night	Gute Nacht

ENGLISH	GERMAN
Goodbye	Tschüß! (informal); Auf Wiedersehen! (formal)
My name is...	Ich heiße...
What is your name?	Wie heißt du (heißen Sie)?
Where are you from?	Woher kommst du (kommen Sie)?
How are you?	Wie geht's (geht es Ihnen)?
I'm fine.	Es geht mir gut.
Do you speak English?	Sprichst du (Sprechen Sie) Englisch?
I don't speak German.	Ich spreche kein Deutsch.

USEFUL PHRASES

Thank you (very much).	Danke (schön).
What?	Was?
When (what time)?	Wann?
Why?	Warum?
Where is...?	Wo ist...?
I'm from...	Ich komme aus...
America/USA	Amerika/den USA
Australia	Australien
Canada	Kanada
Great Britain	Großbritannien
Ireland	Irland
New Zealand	Neuseeland
My (xxx) is broken.	Meine (xxx) ist kaputt!
I'm not feeling well.	Mir ist schlecht.
I have a headache.	Ich habe Kopfweh.
I need a doctor.	Ich brauche einen Arzt.
Leave me alone!	Laß mich in Ruhe!
I'll call the police.	Ich rufe die Polizei.
Help!	Hilfe!
Yes/No	Ja/nein
Okay	Alles klar
Maybe	Vielleicht

English	German
Please.	Bitte.
No, thanks.	Nein, danke.
I don't care.	Es ist mir egal.
No problem.	Kein Problem.
I don't understand.	Ich verstehe nicht.
Please speak slowly.	Sprechen Sie bitte langsam.
Please repeat.	Bitte wiederholen Sie.
Pardon? What was that?	Wie, bitte?
How do you say that in German?	Wie sagt man das auf Deutsch?
What does that mean?	Was bedeutet das?
I want...	Ich möchte...
I'm looking for...	Ich suche...
I need...	Ich brauche...
How much does that cost?	Wieviel kostet das?
Where is the phone?	Wo ist das Telefon?
I don't know.	Ich weiß nicht.
Where is the toilet?	Wo ist die Toilette?
I have potato salad in my Lederhosen.	Ich habe Kartoffelsalat in meinen Lederhosen.
I am a university student (male/female).	Ich bin Student (m)/ Studentin (f).
Are there student discounts?	Gibt es Studentenermäßigungen?
How's the weather today?	Wie ist das Wetter heute?
Too bad.	Schade.

APPENDIX

CARDINAL NUMBERS

0	1	2	3	4	5	6	7	8	9	10
null	eins	zwei	drei	vier	fünf	sechs	sieben	acht	neun	zehn

CARDINAL NUMBERS										
11	12	20	30	40	50	60	70	80	90	100
elf	zwölf	zwanzig	dreißig	vierzig	fünfzig	sechzig	siebzig	achtzig	neunzig	hundert

ORDINAL NUMBERS					
1st	erste	5th	fünfte	9th	neunte
2nd	zweite	6th	sechste	10th	zehnte
3rd	dritte	7th	siebte	20th	zwanzigste
4th	vierte	8th	achte	100th	hunderte

DIRECTIONS AND TRANSPORTATION

(to the) right	rechts		(to the) left	links
straight ahead	geradeaus		Where is...?	Wo ist...?
next to	neben		opposite	gegenüber
How do I find...?	Wie finde ich...?		It's nearby.	Es ist in der Nähe.
How do I get to...?	Wie komme ich nach...?		Is that far from here?	Ist es weit weg?
one-way trip	einfache Fahrt		round-trip	hin und zurück
Where is this train going?	Wohin fährt der Zug?		When does the train leave?	Wann fährt der Zug ab?

ACCOMMODATIONS

Rooms available	Zimmer frei		I would like a room...	Ich möchte ein Zimmer...
No vacancies	besetzt		...with sink.	...mit Waschbecken.
Are there any vacancies?	Gibt es ein Zimmer frei?		...with shower.	...mit Dusche.
Single room	Einzelzimmer		...with a toilet.	...mit WC.
Double room	Doppelzimmer		...with a bathtub.	...mit Badewanne.
Dormitory-style room	Mehrbettzimmer/ Schlafsaal		nonsmoker	Nichtraucher
Do you have anything cheaper?	Haben Sie etwas billiger?		check out	abmelden

TIMES AND HOURS

open	geöffnet		closed	geschlossen
morning	Morgen		opening hours	Öffnungszeiten
afternoon	Nachmittag		today	heute
night	Nacht		yesterday	gestern
evening	Abend		tomorrow	morgen
What time is it?	Wie spät ist es?		break time, rest day	Ruhepause, Ruhetag
It's (seven) o'clock.	Es ist (sieben) Uhr.		At what time?	Um wieviel Uhr?

FOOD AND RESTAURANT TERMS

bread	Brot		water	Wasser
roll	Brötchen		tap water	Leitungswasser
jelly	Marmelade		juice	Saft
meat	Fleisch		beer	Bier
beef	Rindfleisch		wine	Wein
pork	Schweinefleisch		coffee	Kaffee
chicken	Huhn		tea	Tee
sausage	Wurst		soup	Suppe
cheese	Käse		potatoes	Kartoffeln

fruit	Obst		milk	Milch
vegetables	Gemüse		sauce	Soße
cabbage	Kohl		french fries	Pommes frites
I would like to order...	Ich hätte gern...		Another beer, please.	Noch ein Bier, bitte.
It tastes good.	Es schmeckt gut.		It tastes awful.	Es schmeckt widerlich.
I'm a vegetarian.	Ich bin Vegetarier (m)/ Vegetarierin (f).		I'm a vegan.	Ich bin Veganer (m)/ Veganerin (f).
Service included	Bedienung Inklusiv		Daily special	Tageskarte
Check, please.	Rechnung, bitte.		Give me a nutella sandwich.	Gib (Geben Sie) mir ein Nutellabrötchen.

OPPOSITES ATTRACT

together	zusammen		alone	allein/e
good	gut		bad	schlecht
happy	glücklich		sad	traurig
big	groß		small	klein
young	jung		old	alt
full	voll		empty	leer
warm	warm		cool	kühl
safe	sicher, ungefährlich		dangerous	gefährlich
alive	lebendig		dead	tot
special	besonders		simple	einfach
more	mehr		less	weniger
before	vor		after	nach
pretty	schön		ugly	häßlich

RIDICULOUS(LY) USEFUL PHRASES

Here's looking at you, kid.	Schau mich in die Augen, Kleines.		Many thanks for the pleasure ride in your patrol car.	Vielen Dank für den Ausritt in Ihrem Streifenwagen.
May I buy you a drink, darling?	Darf ich dir ein Getränk kaufen, Liebling?		I'm hung over.	Ich habe einen Kater.
Cheers!	Prost!		There is a disturbance in the force.	Es gibt eine Störung in der Kraft.
You're delicious.	Du bist lecker.		Inconceivable!	Quatsch!
That's cool. [coll.]	Das ist ja geil/crass.		Hasta la vista, baby.	Bis später, Baby.

APPENDIX

DISTANCES (KM) AND TRAVEL TIMES BY TRAIN

	Aachen	Berlin	Bonn	Bremen	Dresden	D-Dorf	Frankfurt	Hamburg	Hannover	Kassel	Köln	Leipzig	München	Nürnberg	Prague	Rostock	Stuttgart
Aachen		642	90	387	649	80	263	484	351	307	68	576	650	503	777	638	450
Berlin	6hr.		608	390	214	565	564	285	285	388	583	192	587	431	336	219	652
Bonn	1½hr.	5hr.		349	570	78	181	450	317	273	26	497	588	399	693	604	357
Bremen	4hr.	4hr.	3½hr.		488	298	467	119	133	281	324	370	745	573	609	297	657
Dresden.	8½hr.	3hr.	7hr.	6hr.		568	471	485	371	337	578	124	494	346	148	474	572
Düssel-dorf	1½hr.	4hr.	1hr..	3hr.	7hr.		231	423	272	228	41	493	618	449	764	577	414
Frankfurt	3½hr.	4hr.	2hr.	4hr.	6hr.	3hr.		497	362	194	192	398	399	223	528	651	216
Hamburg	5hr.	2½hr.	4½hr.	1hr.	5hr.	3hr.	3½hr.		163	311	425	377	775	607	640	184	679
Hannover	4hr.	2hr.	3hr.	1hr.	4½hr.	3hr.	2½hr.	1½hr.		176	292	263	640	478	507	338	565
Kassel	5hr.	3hr.	4hr.	2½hr.	5½hr.	4hr.	2hr.	2½hr.	1hr.		248	276	479	304	441	465	397
Köln	1hr.	4½hr.	30min.	3hr.	7½hr.	30min.	2½hr.	4hr.	3hr.	4hr.		505	579	432	709	579	379
Leipzig	7hr.	2hr.	6hr.	4hr.	1½hr.	6hr.	3¾hr.	4½hr.	3hr.	3½hr.	6hr.		422	274	254	366	499
München	7½hr.	7hr.	5hr.	6hr.	7hr.	6hr.	3½hr.	6hr.	4½hr.	4hr.	5½hr.	6hr.		162	413	761	221
Nürnberg	6hr.	5hr.	4hr.	4hr.	5hr.	5hr.	2hr.	4½hr.	3hr.	2½hr.	4½hr.	4hr.	2hr.		309	618	247
Prague	10hr.	4½hr.	9hr.	8hr.	2½hr.	9½hr.	8hr.	6½hr.	7hr.	8hr.	8½hr.	3½hr.	7hr.	6½hr.		8hr.	9hr.
Rostock	8hr.	3hr.	8hr.	4hr.	6hr.	7hr.	6hr.	2hr.	4hr.	5hr.	7hr.	5½hr.	9hr.	7½hr.	565		833
Stuttgart	4½hr.	5½hr.	3hr.	5hr.	7hr.	4hr.	1½hr.	5½hr.	4hr.	3hr.	3hr.	6hr.	2½hr.	2½hr.	500	8hr.	

INDEX

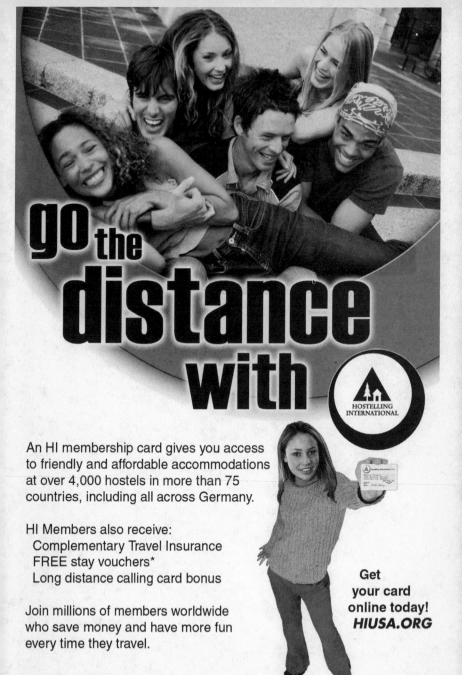

MAP INDEX

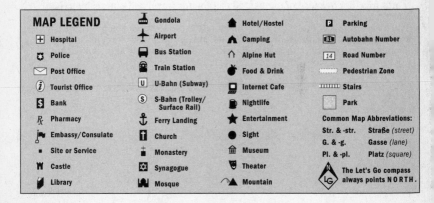

MAP LEGEND

⊞ Hospital	⛲ Gondola	♦ Hotel/Hostel	🅿 Parking
✪ Police	✈ Airport	▲ Camping	Ⓐ1 Autobahn Number
✉ Post Office	🚌 Bus Station	⛺ Alpine Hut	14 Road Number
ⓘ Tourist Office	🚆 Train Station	🍎 Food & Drink	Pedestrian Zone
🅂 Bank	Ⓤ U-Bahn (Subway)	💻 Internet Cafe	Stairs
℞ Pharmacy	Ⓢ S-Bahn (Trolley/ Surface Rail)	🍸 Nightlife	Park
⚑ Embassy/Consulate	⚓ Ferry Landing	★ Entertainment	**Common Map Abbreviations:**
▪ Site or Service	✝ Church	☀ Sight	Str. & -str. **Straße** (street)
♜ Castle	✚ Monastery	🏛 Museum	G. & -g. **Gasse** (lane)
📖 Library	✡ Synagogue	🎭 Theater	Pl. & -pl. **Platz** (square)
	☪ Mosque	⛰ Mountain	The Let's Go compass always points **NORTH**.

ABOUT LET'S GO

NOT YOUR PARENTS' TRAVEL GUIDE

At Let's Go, we see every trip as the chance of a lifetime. If your dream is to grab a machete and forge through the jungles of Brazil, we can take you there. If you'd rather bask in the Riviera sun at a beachside cafe, we'll set you a table. We write for readers who know that there's more to travel than sharing double deckers with tourists and who believe that travel can change both themselves and the world—whether they plan to spend six days in London or six months in Latin America. We'll show you just how far your money can go, and prove that the greatest limitation on your adventures is not your wallet, but your imagination.

BEYOND THE TOURIST EXPERIENCE

To help you gain a deeper connection with the places you travel, our fearless researchers scour the globe to give you the heads-up on both world-renowned and off-the-beaten-track attractions, sights, and destinations. They engage with the local culture, only to emerge with the freshest insights on everything from local festivals to regional cuisine. We've also opened our pages to respected writers and scholars to hear their takes on the countries and regions we cover, and asked travelers who have worked, studied, or volunteered abroad to contribute first-person accounts of their experiences. In addition, we've increased our coverage of responsible travel and expanded each guide's Beyond Tourism chapter to share more ideas about how to give back while on the road.

FORTY-SEVEN YEARS OF WISDOM

Let's Go got its start in 1960, when a group of creative and well-traveled students compiled their experience and advice into a 20-page mimeographed pamphlet, which they gave to travelers on charter flights to Europe. Four and a half decades later, we've expanded to cover six continents and all kinds of travel—while retaining our founders' adventurous attitude toward the world. Laced with witty prose and total candor, our guides are still researched and written entirely by students on shoestring budgets, experienced travelers who know that train strikes, stolen luggage, food poisoning, and marriage proposals are all part of a day's work.

THE LET'S GO COMMUNITY

More than just a travel guide company, Let's Go is a community. Our small staff comes together because of our shared passion for travel and our desire to help other travelers see the world the way it was meant to be seen. We love it when our readers become part of the Let's Go community as well—when you travel, drop us a postcard (67 Mt. Auburn St., Cambridge, MA 02138, USA), send us an e-mail (feedback@letsgo.com), or post on our forum (http://www.letsgo.com/connect/forum) to tell us about your adventures and discoveries.

For more information, visit us online: www.letsgo.com.